World of Warcraft® Programming

World of Warcraft® Programming

A Guide and Reference for Creating WoW Addons

Second Edition

James Whitehead II
Rick Roe

WILEY
Wiley Publishing, Inc.

World of Warcraft® Programming: A Guide and Reference for Creating WoW Addons, Second Edition

Published by
Wiley Publishing, Inc.
10475 Crosspoint Boulevard
Indianapolis, IN 46256
www.wiley.com

Copyright © 2010 by Wiley Publishing, Inc., Indianapolis, Indiana

Published simultaneously in Canada

ISBN: 978-0-470-48128-8

Manufactured in the United States of America

10 9 8 7 6 5 4 3 2 1

For general information on our other products and services please contact our Customer Care Department within the United States at (877) 762-2974, outside the United States at (317) 572-3993 or fax (317) 572-4002.

Wiley also publishes its books in a variety of electronic formats. Some content that appears in print may not be available in electronic books.

Library of Congress Control Number: 2009933378

About the Authors

James Whitehead II is the author of a number of popular addons for World of Warcraft, including LightHeaded, TomTom, Clique, PerfectRaid, and many other small but useful addons. He has been an active member of both the WoW UI and Lua communities since the World of Warcraft Beta began and has been writing addons ever since. When he actually has time to play the game, you can find him playing one of his many characters on the Emerald Dream (EU) server.

Jim currently resides in Oxford, England where he is pursuing his DPhil (PhD) in Computer Science at the Computing Laboratory. In his spare time he enjoys all things rowing, hacking on his Android phone, knitting, crocheting, and spending time with his friends.

Rick Roe—known in the WoW UI community as the zany goblin tinker Gazmik Fizzwidget—is the author of several popular addons including Feed-O-Matic and FactionFriend, as well as TrackMenu and a couple of others so useful that Blizzard made them obsolete by rolling their functionality into the default UI. When not slaving away for their goblin master, Rick's alter egos can often be found adventuring on Cenarius US.

Rick currently resides in Vancouver, Washington, with his wife and cats. His time outside of Azeroth is split between working to finish a computer science degree at Washington State University and building Mac and iPhone applications as an independent software developer.

About the Technical Editors

Daniel Stephens—more widely known in the WoW addon community as Iriel—was the Blizzard WoW UI Forum's first MVP. He has been helping others develop addons for several years, creating a few of his own along the way. His addons include DevTools (recently rolled into the base WoW UI) and he has made significant contributions to secure handlers and a number of other utilities. As somewhat of an altaholic, he has characters spread all over the realms, but considers Silver Hand (US) his original WoW home.

Daniel lives in the San Francisco bay area with his wife, cats, and camera. He spends his "not free" time doing systems design, architecture, and occasionally development work.

Esteban Santana Santana, known online as MentalPower, is both Lead Developer for the Auctioneer AddOns Package and one of the Administrators of Norganna's AddOns. He's been part of the WoW UI community since mid-2005 and has helped many people via the IRC channels and the various game and UI-related forums. When he logs into World of Warcraft, you can find him on the US-Alleria realm trying to level his various characters on the Emerald Dream guild.

Esteban currently resides in Carolina, Puerto Rico, and is a jack-of-all-trades IT person for Liberty Cablevision. In his spare time, he enjoys thrashing his buddies in a good game of Rock Band on the XBox 360.

Credits

Acquisitions Editor
Scott Meyers

Contributing Author
Nevin Flanagan

Project Editor
Maryann Steinhart

Technical Editors
Daniel Stephens
Rick Roe
Esteban Santana Santana

Production Editor
Rebecca Anderson

Copy Editor
Kim Cofer

Editorial Director
Robyn B. Siesky

Editorial Manager
Mary Beth Wakefield

Associate Director of Marketing
David Mayhew

Production Manager
Tim Tate

Vice President and Executive Group Publisher
Richard Swadley

Vice President and Executive Publisher
Barry Pruett

Associate Publisher
Jim Minatel

Project Coordinator, Cover
Lynsey Stanford

Proofreaders
Josh Chase and Nelson Kim, Word One

Indexer
J & J Indexing

Cover Image
Scott Johnson, FrogPants Studios LLC

Cover Designer
Michael E. Trent

Acknowledgments

James and Lee Whitehead, thank you for walking alongside your children as we journey down the winding road of life; we're blessed to have the two of you in our lives. Michelle Hastings, thank you for being such a role model of strength and determination for your little brother.

Robert Whitehead, thank you for always being yourself and making sure I don't stray far from who I am. Gregory Whitehead, thank you for being there for me whenever I need to "geek" out, I don't know many people that can get as excited as I do about silly things. Tom Harper, thank you for what you give me every single day. Everything about you makes me feel like the luckiest person alive.

Jamie Anderson, Edward Wilman, Amelia Earl, Rhianedd Jewell, Erika Nitsch, Daniel Jordan, and all my other friends at Oxford, thank you for keeping me busy, for helping me make excuses, and for being such a bad influence.

To Karen Hobson and everyone at WowInterface who have put up with me for five years now, thank you for all of your efforts in organizing all three books. To Mike, Kevin, Tom, Jacob, Sam, and everyone at Blizzard, thank you for creating such an amazing game and supporting us in our documentation efforts. To everyone at Wiley who helped bring these books into existence, thank you for your efforts to provide resources for the WoW user interface community. To Rick, thank you for stepping in when we needed you the most; your work has been instrumental in making this book what it is today. To Daniel, Nevin, and Esteban, thank you for all of your help in shaping the edges of this edition.

Finally, thank you to the World of Warcraft user interface community for everything you do.

— Jim

I'd first like to thank my coauthor, Jim, for offering me the opportunity to "graduate" from tech editing on the first edition to authoring on this second version. Crazy as the schedules and deadlines may have been, I'm still happier having been able to write my part instead of worrying about mucking with someone else's work in order to satisfy my nitpicky tendencies. Thanks also for all your infrastructure work—without your website and database I'd have been a scribe without paper.

To Daniel and Esteban fell the unenviable task of performing the role I did on the first edition—catching all the silly code errors and obtuse explanations we dumb authors make—and with it my sympathy and gratitude. I can but hope I haven't made your work too hard.

Thanks to Karen for playing den mother to the rowdy WoW UI community and giving us all a place to hook up; if it weren't for your efforts I'd never have found my way into this project. Thanks as well to Scott, Maryann, and everyone at Wiley for making the project happen!

Thanks (again) to Daniel and Jim not just for your work on the book but for providing development tools without which my tasks would've been a whole lot harder. And of course, thanks to my family, Karen, Doug, and Brad, for putting up with me for a couple decades and making me the person I am, and to my wonderful wife Anne: I can't imagine life without you, much less without the loving support you give for whatever crazy ideas I set myself to.

Finally, a very special thank you to Mike, Jacob, Sam, and Tom at Blizzard, without whose patience and willingness to answer oblique questions outside a normal work schedule we wouldn't have been able to figure out several important chunks of the API we're documenting. Next time I'm in SoCal, your drinks are on my tab.

— Rick

Contents at a Glance

Contents

Introduction

Since World of Warcraft (WoW) was released on November 23, 2004, it has been one of the most popular video games ever created. The game currently boasts more than eleven million subscribers; it seems that everyone knows *someone* who plays. World of Warcraft is an extremely immersive environment that allows you to customize your character, explore new worlds, and group with friends without requiring an enormous time commitment. Some players spend four to six hours a night raiding with their guilds trying to defeat the latest and greatest monster. Others prefer player-to-player combat, spending time in the Arena or Battlegrounds trying to improve their standing. Some players just enjoy playing the game with a group of friends when they have spare time. World of Warcraft has something to offer each of these players, and that's probably one of the primary reasons for its success.

One aspect of the game that reaches each of these play styles is user interface customization in the form of *addons*. For those players who are technically inclined or simply can't accept things being anything less than perfect, Blizzard has opened up its user interface to allow players to customize and change its overall functionality. Addons can be as simple as changing the colors of health bars or adding a new slash command to do random emotes, or as complicated as providing complex statistical analysis of a server's economy. Beyond opening up this world of customization, Blizzard continues to provide enhancements and support for the user interface community in a way that no other game developer has done.

The user interface community has grown immensely over the past few years, and shows no signs of stopping. This book was written to give the reader the tools necessary to create custom modifications to the World of Warcraft user interface, including an introduction to the languages, terminology, and structure of addon creation. There are thousands of addons out there waiting to be written, and this book provides you with the skills necessary to realize them.

Who This Book Is For

This book is designed to be useful to novice addon users who want to learn how to tweak existing addons, to budding addon authors looking to add more exciting features to their repertoire, and to advanced addon developers as a reference to the extremely complex WoW UI system. The only assumptions made throughout the book are that you are familiar with World of Warcraft and have an interest in programming. Readers who have had exposure to programming languages in any form will find many of the concepts presented to be familiar.

The reader with little to no prior programming experience should initially focus on the first section of the book, which teaches Lua, the programming language that is used to write addons. Although readers with no programming experience will learn enough to create and modify addons, they may want to pursue more general programming lessons from another source to supplement the material presented.

For readers with prior programming experience, the first few chapters will be very easy. The examples can be used to pick up the basic rules of the Lua programming language rather quickly. If you are already familiar with high-level scripting languages such as Python or JavaScript, you can easily skim the first few chapters and move right into the second section, which covers the basics of addon creation itself. These chapters detail how the WoW addon system works for the author, and lead you through writing your first addon.

Addon authors may want to skip directly to the third section of the book. Its chapters introduce specific concepts and walk through the creation of working example addons that use the concepts. Some of the more obscure difficult systems (such as secure snippets, dropdown menus, and state headers) are explored in depth.

In addition, the fourth section of the book contains an extremely comprehensive reference to the WoW API, including events and widgets.

How This Book Is Organized

This book is divided into four parts that introduce increasingly complex topics.

Part I is an introduction to Lua and XML, bringing you up to speed with the languages needed to create addons.

Part II discusses the way addons are built and the basics behind the frame system in World of Warcraft. In this part you create your first addon and become familiar with the WoW API.

Part III of the book guides you through some of the more advanced topics by creating a number of addons from start to finish.

Finally, Part IV is a comprehensive reference to the entire API, including functions, widgets, events, and secure templates.

What's on the Website

Every few months, Blizzard releases a new patch for World of Warcraft that may introduce new content, fix existing bugs, or even drastically change game mechanics. As a result, the material covered in this book will change from time to time. To help combat this problem, the authors have created a companion website for the book at `http://wowprogramming.com`. While we do not expect sweeping changes to the core concepts, the details of any specific changes will be listed on the website, including information about how those changes affect the material in this book. Besides serving as a glorified errata repository, the website also has online versions of all the references included in the book.

From Here

The World of Warcraft user interface community is a very exciting place with endless possibilities for customization and realization of ideas. World of Warcraft is a fun game in its own right; the capability to use it as a development platform for addons that can help users and enhance their game experience is an extra bonus that each of us can enjoy. So Enjoy!

Learning to Program

In This Part

Programming for World of Warcraft

World of Warcraft (WoW) was released Nov. 23, 2004, and very quickly became *the* model for Massively Multiplayer Online Role Playing Games (MMORPG). Providing an intuitive user interface and a low barrier to success the game is currently played by more than 11 million users, including their friends, co-workers, and families. WoW has something enjoyable for those players who spend six hours a night raiding with their guilds, the cubicle warriors who play for half an hour a day on their lunch breaks, and a large range of individuals in between.

Beyond killing monsters and questing for glory, there is another side to World of Warcraft, a game within a game. Blizzard has provided an extremely powerful system for creating third-party addons and writing macros, and users have been taking advantage of the open system since the beta test for the game. This book is designed to introduce you to the world of customizing World of Warcraft and show you how to create custom addons.

Customizing the User Interface

The World of Warcraft game client consists of two major parts: the game world and the user interface. The game world is the three-dimensional space in which your character resides. This includes the buildings and terrain, other players and enemies, and interactive objects such as herbs, mining veins, mailboxes, and signposts. The game world also includes some non–three-dimensional objects, namely the character names and titles, and the numbers that show the damage your character has done. These elements are not accessible through the scripting interface and cannot be modified.

The user interface comprises the other elements in the client, including the action buttons, unit frames, maps, and options windows. Addons can be written to add or modify existing elements to add functionality or to show information in a different way.

What Is an Addon?

An *addon* is a collection of files inside a named directory within the World of Warcraft directory. These files are loaded by the game's scripting system and executed within the client to make some modification to the user interface. This definition of addons does not include any third-party executables that are run outside the game (those sorts of programs are normally prohibited by WoW's terms of service).

The average addon consists of individual components that work together to create a final product, possibly including:

- A table of contents file that identifies the addon and the files to be loaded
- Media files, such as graphics and sounds
- Lua scripts that define the behavior of the addon
- XML files that define the visual elements of the addon

The first part of this book is designed to introduce you to the Lua programming language and the XML markup that is specific to World of Warcraft. These skills are an important part of writing addons effectively. If you are already proficient in Lua and XML, you can skip ahead to Part II of the book, which covers the use of the World of Warcraft API in creating addons; however, you will likely find the material in Part I worthwhile.

What Can Addons Do?

Addons typically fall into one or more of the following categories:

- Displaying additional information, such as the sale price of quest rewards (Figure 1-1), or approximately how many more of a given spell you can cast without running out of power (Figure 1-2).
- Changing the display of interface elements, such as the combat text information (Figure 1-3), or making the auction house interface easier to navigate (Figure 1-4).
- Providing new ways for the player to take action (targeting units, casting spells) within the game, such as replacement unit frames (Figure 1-5) or alternate action buttons (Figure 1-6).

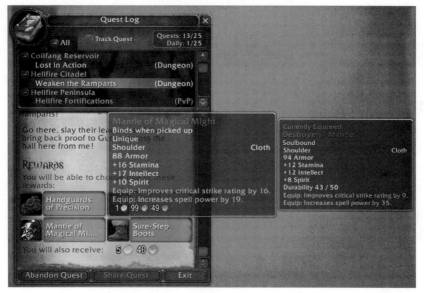

Figure 1-1: Valuation showing sell price for items

Figure 1-2: Dr. Damage displaying number of possible casts

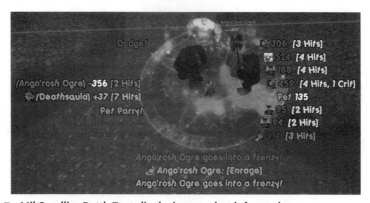

Figure 1-3: MikScrollingBattleText displaying combat information

Figure 1-4: Auctioneer displaying auction listings in a compact form

Figure 1-5: Grid unit frames showing the status of a raid

Figure 1-6: Bartender4 with ButtonFacade_Serenity providing alternate action buttons

Prior to the release of the Burning Crusade expansion pack to World of Warcraft, there were several addons that Blizzard deemed against the spirit and intention of the game. These addons were later disabled and changes were made to the scripting system to prevent their use. As a result the following actions are unavailable to addons:

- Automatic character movement
- Automatic target selection
- Automatic selection and use of spells or items
- Real-time communication with external programs

In the past, Blizzard has been asked about the limits of the scripting/macro system. Its response has been that it is interested in "smart players," not "smart buttons." In other words, addons and macros can work to display information to the users or allow them to access functionality in an easier way, but should not be used to make automatic decisions.

In addition, addons are forbidden from doing anything that would otherwise be against the World of Warcraft "Terms of Use," which you can find at http://worldofwarcraft.com/legal/termsofuse.html.

Exploring Your AddOns Directory

As mentioned previously, all addons must exist within a subdirectory under your World of Warcraft directory. Depending on what operating system you are using and how you have installed the game, this directory may exist in one of a few places (see Table 1-1). If you happen to be running Windows Vista, the location of your installation will depend on how the computer has been configured and where the game was installed. During the installation of Wrath of the Lich King or patch 3.0.2 you should have been asked to move the game to option #3. If you agreed to this change, you may have two versions of World of Warcraft, with the old one not being used any more.

Table 1-1: Default World of Warcraft Installation Directory

OPERATING SYSTEM	DEFAULT INSTALLATION DIRECTORY
Microsoft Windows 98, 2000, or XP	C:\Program Files\World of Warcraft
Microsoft Windows Vista (option #1)	C:\Program Files\World of Warcraft
Microsoft Windows Vista (option #2)	C:\Users\<username>\AppData\Local\ VirtualStore\Program Files\World of Warcraft
Microsoft Windows Vista (option #3)	C:\Users\Public\Games\World of Warcraft
Mac OS X	/Applications/World of Warcraft

If you have launched World of Warcraft previously, there should be an Interface directory within and an `AddOns` directory below that. This is where all addons are stored.

Blizzard Addons

Much of the functionality in the default user interface is implemented via modular addons that are loaded only when needed by the user. When the player visits an auctioneer, for instance, the game loads the `Blizzard_AuctionUI` addon.

Having the addons in separate load-on-demand modules allows addon authors to easily override the default functionality (such as replacing the auction house interface rather than just changing it). In addition, the modularity speeds up load times when starting the game. Table 1-2 describes the existing Blizzard addons.

Table 1-2: Blizzard Load-on-Demand Addons

ADDON NAME	PURPOSE
`Blizzard_AchievementUI`	Explore the achievements your character can complete and those he has already completed.
`Blizzard_ArenaUI`	Display unit frames for enemy units in arena PVP.
`Blizzard_AuctionUI`	Search for items available for sale, as well as posting new items up for auction.
`Blizzard_BarbershopUI`	Customize the facial features and hair style/color for your character.
`Blizzard_BattlefieldMinimap`	Display a smaller version of the world map, including the PVP objectives.
`Blizzard_BindingUI`	Customize the keyboard bindings made available by the default and custom interfaces.
`Blizzard_Calendar`	Display a calendar that shows the various scheduled game events and allows players to create their own events.
`Blizzard_CombatLog`	Present combat information in a linear combat log that can be filtered and colored via options.

Continued

Table 1-2: (*continued*)

ADDON NAME	PURPOSE
Blizzard_CombatText	Show various combat events in moving text in the user interface, customizable via the options screens.
Blizzard_DebugTools	Provide slash commands and utility functions that are useful to addon developers.
Blizzard_GMChatUI	Provide a chat window for communication with game masters.
Blizzard_GMSurveyUI	Allow the user to fill out a survey that has been sent by Blizzard following a GM interaction.
Blizzard_GlyphUI	Inscribe glyphs into your spellbook in order to customize your spells.
Blizzard_GuildBankUI	Add and remove items and gold from your guild's bank.
Blizzard_InspectUI	Inspect another player to view his equipment, combat stats, and talents.
Blizzard_ItemSocketingUI	Socket gems into an item.
Blizzard_MacroUI	Edit global and character-specific macros.
Blizzard_RaidUI	Display unit frames for the members in your raid.
Blizzard_TalentUI	Assign talent points and explore the various talent trees.
Blizzard_TimeManager	Show a clock on the minimap and provide a simple in-game timer.
Blizzard_TokenUI	View the various currency tokens that your character has earned.
Blizzard_TradeSkillUI	Explore the various recipes that are associated with a given tradeskill.
Blizzard_TrainerUI	Purchase skills available from a trainer.

Each of these directories contains a single file that has the addon's name and a .pub extension. As far as we can tell, this is some sort of signature used by the game to verify the authenticity of the addon. Addons that are written by Blizzard are given a special "secure" flag that allows them to take protected actions, something that is covered in Chapter 8. The code for the addons is actually stored in the data files for the game and can't be directly replaced.

Custom Addons

If you have downloaded any custom addons they will sit alongside the Blizzard addons in your `Interface\AddOns` directory inside subdirectories. Unlike the official addons, these addon directories actually contain the files that are necessary to load and run the addon. The organization and contents of these files varies depending on the addon. Each author has his or her own preferences and style and these differences are reflected in the way the addon is packaged and the way the code is written. Although we provide some recommendations for writing and packaging your addons, you are free to develop a style that works best for you.

Creating Your First Addon: HeyThere

Before you delve into Lua and XML, take a look at a very simple addon example so you'll have an idea of how the system works. To complete the example you need to know how to create a new directory on your computer. You also need to be familiar with a text editor that saves files without special formatting. On Windows, for example, you could use Notepad to edit files; on Mac OS X, the built-in Text Editor program is sufficient.

Creating Files and Directories

First create a new directory that will contain the addon. Navigate to your `Interface\AddOns` directory and create a new directory inside called `HeyThere`.
Open your text editor and type the following into the file:

```
## Interface: 30300
## Title: Hey There!
## Notes: Provides slash commands to greet other players

HeyThere.lua
```

Save this file in the new directory as `HeyThere.toc`. Open a new file in the editor and add the following:

```
SLASH_HEYTHERE1 = "/hey"
SLASH_HEYTHERE2 = "/heythere"
SlashCmdList["HEYTHERE"] = function(self, txt)
  if UnitExists("target") then
```

```
      SendChatMessage("Hello " .. UnitName("target"), "SAY")
   else
      SendChatMessage("Hey there everybody!")
   end
end
```

Save this file as `HeyThere.lua` in the same directory and close the text editor. Don't worry right now about what any of this code does; it's just an example addon to get you familiar with creating files and directories. You'll learn what the code does later in the book.

Loading and Testing the Addon

If you have World of Warcraft open, you must close it so it can recognize the new addon. Once you've re-opened the game client, log in to your account and stop at the character selection screen. In the bottom left of the screen should be a button named AddOns. Click it and a window similar to one shown in Figure 1-7 opens. The window shows that WoW recognizes your addon and will try to load it if it is enabled.

TIP You may find it useful to create a character on a server that is different from your main server for addon development. This allows you to easily change which addons are enabled and disabled without affecting the characters with which you normally play.

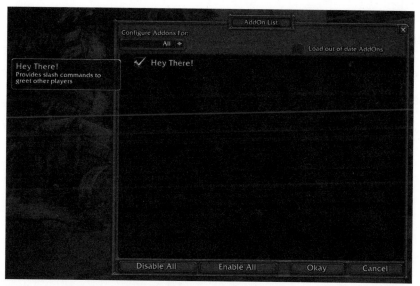

Figure 1-7: Addon selection screen showing your new addon

Ensure that the addon is enabled by checking the box to the left of the addon name. Click Okay to exit the addon selection screen and enter the game.

This addon adds two new slash commands that allow you to greet people in the world. You can type either **/heythere** or simply **/hey** and depending on whether you have something targeted your character will display one of two messages (see Figure 1-8).

Figure 1-8: HeyThere greeting with (left) and without (right) a target

If for some reason you do not see the addon in the addon selection list, ensure that you've created the files and directories correctly. The layout should be as follows:

- `Interface\AddOns\HeyThere`
- `Interface\AddOns\HeyThere\HeyThere.toc`
- `Interface\AddOns\HeyThere\HeyThere.lua`

If you get an error or have any other issues, double-check that you've typed everything correctly in each of the files. Alternatively, download the addon from this chapter's section of the website at `http://wowprogramming.com/chapters/01` and compare it to the version you have created.

Summary

This chapter introduced you to the addon system for World of Warcraft. The specific limitations and capabilities of the system were listed, along with a description of the addons that Blizzard has included with the game. You created your first addon and tested in-game to ensure it worked correctly.

Chapter 2 introduces you to the basics of the Lua programming language, used extensively when creating addons.

Exploring Lua Basics

Lua is a powerful, lightweight, embedded scripting language that is used in several large software projects, including WoW. Lua is a fairly small programming language, and you may find some similarities to other languages you already know. Lua is most often compared to Python because both are relatively easy for a non-programmer to use when compared to languages such as C or Java.

This chapter serves as a general introduction to the Lua programming language. If you have prior experience with Lua or have extensive experience using other programming languages, you may want to skim this chapter and run through some of the interactive exercises. Although these examples should be easy to understand without you needing to run them, we strongly encourage you to download a Lua interpreter so you can run through the examples on your own. In addition, an interpreter allows you to easily explore the language to increase your overall understanding of concepts.

ON THE WEB

You can read more about the Lua programming language at www.lua.org. The website contains a large amount of reference material, including an online version of *Programming in Lua*, a book entirely about the Lua programming language.

Downloading and Installing Lua

You have three easy ways to obtain a Lua interpreter:

1. Download WowLua, an addon the authors have written that gives you an interactive Lua interpreter within World of Warcraft.

2. Visit the book's website at `http://wowprogramming.com/utils/weblua` to use an interactive Lua interpreter in your web browser.

3. Download a Lua interpreter to your computer, so it can be run locally without access to the Internet or WoW.

The first option enables you to run a Lua interpreter directly within World of Warcraft. This is useful if you want to spend your time in the game watching things. The second allows you to run Lua without needing to download anything, so it will work even on computers where you can't install software. The third option allows you to work with Lua when you're not connected to the Internet, which also can be useful.

Any of these options will work for the examples in the first part of this book, so feel free to choose the ones that work best for you.

Downloading and Installing WowLua

We have created a version of the Lua interpreter that runs as an addon within World of Warcraft. This is the simplest way to install a Lua interpreter for anyone with experience using addons. It also has the advantage of letting you work within the game, allowing you to test your work on-the-fly, experiment with the default UI and other addons, and still be able to chat with your friends and guild.

Navigate to `http://wowprogramming.com/utils/wowlua-addon` and click the download link to get the latest version of the WowLua addon. This downloads a `.zip` file to your computer. Once you save the file, you can extract it using your favorite compression utility or by double-clicking it on a standard Windows XP or Mac OS X machine. A single folder called `WowLua` will be extracted. Place the folder in the `Interface\AddOns` folder underneath your World of Warcraft installation.

You can verify that the addon is installed properly by clicking the Addons button in the bottom-left corner of your character selection screen. You should see the addon listed in a fashion similar to that shown in Figure 2-1.

Figure 2-1: WowLua in the addon listing

Select a character and log in to the game. Type either **/lua** or **/wowlua** into the chat box to open the WowLua window (see Figure 2-2). You can close the window by clicking the X button in the top-right corner, or by pressing the Esc key.

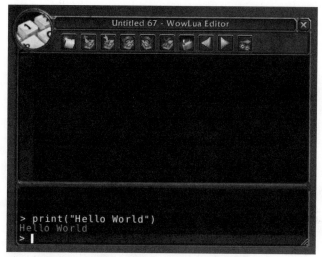

Figure 2-2: WowLua interactive interpreter

Using Lua on the Web

For those people who don't want to run these examples within WoW and have access to an Internet connection, we've created a simple webpage that serves as a Lua interpreter over the Web, called WebLua. Simply browse to `http://wowprogramming.com/utils/weblua` to begin.

The webpage requires JavaScript to function, so ensure you have it enabled in your web browser.

Downloading and Installing a Lua Interpreter

If you prefer to download an interpreter so you can work offline, packages are available for both Microsoft Windows and Mac OS X.

Microsoft Windows

You can download the interpreter for Microsoft Windows at `http://wowprogramming.com/utils/lua/windows`. The package doesn't require any installation; you can simply place it anywhere that is convenient for you. Extract the ZIP file to a new folder and place it where you can easily find it again.

To launch the Lua interpreter, go to the files you've extracted and double-click the icon for the interpreter. This opens a window that looks something like that shown in Figure 2-3. You can also create a shortcut to this file from which you can launch the interpreter.

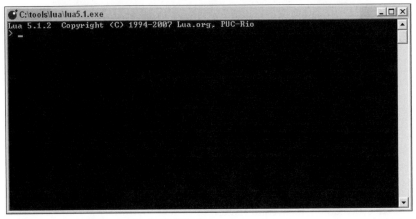

Figure 2-3: Lua running on Microsoft Windows

Mac OS X

You can find a package that can be used to install a Lua interpreter for Mac OS X at `http://wowprogramming.com/utils/lua/macosx`. The download is a standard disk image that can be mounted on your system. To mount it, navigate to the disk image and double-click it. The disk image contains a package (selected in Figure 2-4) that you can run to install Lua on your system. Double-click the package to install Lua on your system.

To launch the Lua interpreter, you need to open Terminal. This is an application normally located under Applications ➤ Utilities. A window appears, so you can type **lua** and press Enter to actually open the Lua interpreter. Figure 2-5 shows a terminal window with Lua running.

Figure 2-4: Lua for Mac OS X disk image

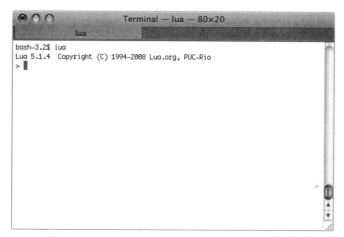

Figure 2-5: Lua running on Mac OS X

Using the Lua Interpreter

When you launch your interpreter for the first time, you are greeted with something similar to the following:

```
Lua 5.1.4  Copyright © 1994-2007 Lua.org, PUC-Rio
>
```

The first line contains the version string of the particular Lua interpreter you are using. As long as you are using a version that begins with 5.1 you should be okay. The second line of output is the prompt, where you can type commands to be run.

Running Commands

The Lua interpreter is interactive, enabling you to input commands and receive a response, like a conversation between two friends. You will receive instant feedback with any errors in your code, allowing you to tinker with the language to see how it works.

Type the following command at the prompt (you only need to type the part after the >, shown in bold):

```
> print("Hello Azeroth!")
```

You should see the following output:

```
Hello Azeroth!
>
```

This simple command takes the text string `Hello Azeroth!` and sends it to the function `print()`, which outputs the string to your window. You examine the nitty-gritty details of what this actually means later in this chapter.

> **NOTE** For the purposes of this chapter, consider a function to be a process that you can give information, and have it complete some task. In this case, you feed a string to the function, which prints it to the output window.

Understanding Error Messages

Inevitably, you will make a typo and get an error from Lua when running a command. The error messages are usually human-readable and will tell you where the problem occurred. Type the following command at the prompt (note that you're intentionally misspelling the word `print`):

```
> prnit("Hello Azeroth!")
```

The response, a typical error message in Lua, is similar to this:

```
stdin:1: attempt to call global 'prnit' (a nil value)
stack traceback:
        stdin:1: in main chunk
        [C]: ?
>
```

The first line gives you the error message and the line number on which the error occurred. In this case, Lua says that you tried to call a global `prnit`, which is a `nil` value. In layman's terms, it means you tried to call a function that doesn't exist.

The rest of the error message is called a stack traceback, which tells you where the error occurred. This will be useful when you begin calling functions from other functions.

Using History to Make Changes

Depending on the Lua interpreter you are using, you may be able to view the recent command-line history (the last few commands you've given the interpreter) by pressing the Up and Down arrow keys. Test this now by pressing the Up arrow key on your keyboard while in your Lua interpreter. (This always works in WowLua, but may not work correctly if you are using a standalone version of Lua.)

If it worked correctly, you should see the last line you typed (`prnit("Hello Azeroth!")`) and your cursor should be at the end of the line. If it didn't work, you may instead see something similar to the following:

```
> ^[[A
```

That simply means your specific interpreter doesn't handle history. Although you may find this inconvenient at times, it certainly shouldn't hamper your capability to run through the examples correctly.

Quitting the Interpreter

When you are done running code in the interpreter, in most cases, you can simply close the window. However, if you started the interpreter from a command line and want to return to it, you can use one of the following methods, depending on your operating system.

Microsoft Windows

On a Microsoft Windows system, Lua can be closed by pressing Ctrl+Z. This inserts the following into your interpreter:

```
> ^Z
```

In Windows this inserts a special character that means end-of-file, and it causes the interpreter to quit. You can also press Ctrl+C to outright kill your session.

Mac OS X

Mac OS X is a UNIX-based system, so the end-of-file character is different from that of the Windows systems. At your prompt, press Ctrl+D to insert the end-of-file character and end the session immediately. You can also use Ctrl+C to kill the session.

Working with Numbers

Almost every language has a way to calculate numeric values, and Lua is no different. Type the following into your interpreter:

```
> print(2 + 2)
```

As expected, you will see 4 as the response followed by another prompt. Although it may not be the most convenient calculator, the interpreter does enable you to perform calculations in your programs.

Basic Arithmetic Operations

Table 2-1 shows Lua's basic arithmetic operators. You can use any of them to compute a value.

Table 2-1: Lua Arithmetic Operators

OPERATION	IN LUA	EXAMPLE	RESULT
Addition	+	> print(4 + 4)	8
Subtraction	–	> print(6 - 10)	-4
Multiplication	*	> print(13 * 13)	169
Division	/	> print(10 / 2)	5
Exponentiation	^	> print(13 ^ 2)	169
Modulo	%	> print(8 % 3)	2
Unary Negation	–	> print(- (4 + 4))	-8

In addition to these operators, you can use parentheses to group expressions together to make more complex expressions. Consider the following example:

```
> print(2 * (1 + 2 + 3) ^ 3)
432
```

If you run this command with no parentheses in the expression itself, you get an entirely different answer:

```
> print(2 * 1 + 2 + 3 ^ 3)
31
```

Parentheses are used to make an expression explicit and ensure that it is evaluated properly. In the second case, the exponentiation operator is processed first, followed by the multiplication operator and then the addition operator, giving you the equivalent formula:

```
> print(2 + 2 + 27)
```

When in doubt, make your math explicit so it is easier to read when review is needed in the future.

Scientific Notation

Occasionally, you'll encounter an extremely large number such as 10,000,000,000,000,000 (10^15). Rather than type it out each time with zeros or use parentheses to make sure it's being calculated correctly inside another formula, you can use scientific notation. Lua may automatically display large numbers using scientific notation if printing them would be unwieldy. Run the following commands:

```
> print(10 ^ 15)
1e+015
> print(10 ^ -15)
1e-015
```

As you can see, Lua converts the numbers to scientific notation for the purpose of printing them. Conveniently, you can also write numbers in this fashion, which takes the first number and multiplies it by 10 raised to the second number (the e in between can be capitalized or lowercase). For example:

```
> print(1.23456e5)
123456
> print(1.23456 * (10 ^ 5))
123456
> print(1234e-4)
0.1234
> print(1234 * (10 ^ -4))
0.1234
```

You may not encounter numbers in scientific notation often, but understanding the output when Lua sends it back to you is important.

Hexadecimal Notation

Lua can natively convert a number in hexadecimal notation to the decimal value. You can use this as a quick hex-to-decimal conversion, or you may actually have a need to use hexadecimal notation in your systems. Lua expects a zero, followed by the letter x, followed by a string of valid hex digits (0–9, A–F, a–f).

```
> print(0x1)
1
> print(0xF)
15
> print(0x10)
16
> print(0x10a4)
4260
```

When writing code, you can refer to numbers in this format and Lua will convert them properly. As you can see from these examples, however, Lua only responds in decimal or scientific notation, regardless of how the numbers were input.

```
> print(2 * 0xF)
30
> print(0x10 ^ 2)
256
```

Understanding Floating Point

Every number in a standard Lua system is represented internally as a floating-point number. For average use this won't make a difference, but it can have some odd implications. Here's a simple (but confusing) example, which uses some concepts that you won't examine until later in this section of the book:

```
> pointTwo = 1.2 - 1.0
> print(pointTwo < 0.2)
true
> print(pointTwo)
0.2
```

The number 0.2 cannot be accurately represented as a floating-point number, so the programming language must do a bit of rounding when calculating the value, and then again when printing it. The floating-point numbers in Lua can accurately represent any integer from 10^{-37} through 10^{37}, so you shouldn't encounter many of these problems. This rounding can, however, serve as a source of calculation error when working with the real numbers.

ON THE WEB

Much information regarding floating-point numbers and the implications of the format exists out there on the Web. The following resources are all extremely helpful if you're interested in exploring the topic further:

(continued)

ON THE WEB *(continued)*

```
http://wikipedia.org/wiki/Floating_point
http://docs.sun.com/source/806-3568/ncg_goldberg.html
http://lua-users.org/wiki/FloatingPoint
```

Understanding Values and Variables

Like most other languages, Lua makes a distinction between values (such as the string `"Hello"` and the number `14`) and variables (or references). Understanding the underlying types of values and the distinction between a value and a variable can be helpful while programming.

Exploring Values and Their Types

A value is the actual thing that is used, such as the number `17`, or the string `"Hello"`. The number `14` is a different value from the number `27`, but they are both number values. The string `"Hello"` is a value, but it is a different type of value than the two numbers. (There's nothing tricky or complex that you need to understand about values, I promise!)

There are eight primitive types in the Lua programming language and every value you encounter will have one of them. You've already seen two different types, number and string. The line between a string and number can occasionally get blurry, such as drawing the distinction between the string `"4"` and the number `4`, but they remain discrete types.

Primitive Types

Table 2-2 describes Lua's primitive types. Every value ends up being one of these types, regardless of where it's encountered in the language.

You will encounter each of these types through the course of your work, so you should be aware of them.

Using the type() Function

Within Lua you can use the `type()` function to determine the type of a given value, which gives you flexibility when it comes to validation and verification in your programs. Type the following into your Lua interpreter:

```
> print(type(5))
number
```

Table 2-2: Lua's Primitive Types

TYPE	DESCRIPTION
number	All numbers (including hexadecimal numbers and those using scientific notation) have this type. Examples: 1, 7313, 1e5, 0xFFF1a
string	A sequence of characters. Examples: "Hello", "Test String".
boolean	The values true and false are of the boolean type.
function	A function is a collection of statements that can be called, and is introduced in Chapter 3.
table	A table is a mix between a traditional hash table (dictionary) and an array.
nil	The value nil is of the special type nil.
thread	A value of the thread type is a coroutine (limited lightweight thread) that can be used for asynchronous computation.
userdata	Userdata is traditionally a wrapper around some data structure defined in the host language (usually C).

What you've done here is call the type() function with a value of 5, and call the print() function with that result (you explore functions further in Chapter 3). The output shows that the type of the value 5 is number, as you'd expect. Here are some other examples:

```
> print(type("Hello Azeroth!"))
string
> print(type(2 * (1 + 2 + 3) ^ 3))
number
> print(prnit)
nil
```

In the third example note the misspelling of the variable prnit. As you saw earlier in this chapter, that is a nil value, so the type () function returns nil as expected. You can always use the type() function to find out which type your value is.

Using Variables

A *variable* can be seen as a temporary name for a specific Lua value, with the caveat that the same value may have multiple names. An example here will be more telling than words, so type the following into your interpreter (it may not have output after each line, so just move on to the next line):

```
> x = 4
> y = 2
```

```
> print(x + y)
6
```

In this example, you take the name x and bind it to the value 4; and bind the name y to the value 2. You then call the print function, and instead of using the numbers 4 and 2, you use the names x and y.

Valid Variable Names

A variable's name or *identifier* has to start with a letter or an underscore character. The name cannot contain anything other than letters, numbers, or the underscore character. In addition, it can't be any of the keywords that are reserved by Lua: and, break, do, else, elseif, false, for, function, if, in, local, nil, not, or, repeat, return, then, true, until, and while. A variable name is also case-sensitive, so the character a is different from the character A, meaning that the following are all different identifiers:

- MyVariable
- myVariable
- myvariable

Assigning Variables

Use the assignment operator = to bind a value to a variable name, with the variable name on the left and the value on the right. Try the following examples in your Lua interpreter:

```
> foo = 14
> print(foo)
14
> foo = "Hello!"
> print(foo)
Hello!
```

The first example binds the value 14 to the identifier foo, and you can print and use that variable instead of the value itself. The second binds the value "Hello" to the identifier, changing what the variable refers to.

Variables can be used on the right-hand side of an assignment operator as well, and what happens in those situations is different depending on the context. Try the following in your interpreter:

```
> x = 4
> y = x
> print(y)
4
> x = 3
> print(y)
4
```

The first line simply binds the value 4 to the identifier x. The second line, however, assigns the value bound to the identifier x to identifier y. This means quite literally that both x and y are names for the same value (the number 4). As a result, when you run x = 3, you simply change that binding, leaving y intact.

> **TIP** The distinction between values and variables can be confusing, especially when working through more advanced topics. Use the Lua interpreter as a tool to explore the rules and better understand what's happening.

Assigning Multiple Variables

On some occasions you will assign more than one variable at a time, and a convenient short form makes this easier. Run the following example:

```
> x, y = 3, 5
> print(x * y)
15
```

The assignment operator allows a list of variables on the left side and a list of values on the right side. That'll be a bit more useful when you get into functions and return values. If there are more variables on the left side than there are values on the right side, the remaining variables will be set to nil. If there are more values on the right side, they will just be thrown away.

Comparing Values

In many cases, you will need to compare different values to see how they are related. Several comparison operators (listed in Table 2-3) can be used.

Table 2-3: Comparison Operators

COMPARISON OPERATOR	EQUIVALENT LUA OPERATOR
equality	==
less than	<
greater than	>
less than, or equal	<=
greater than, or equal	>=
not equal	~=

These operate exactly as you'd expect, but you can play in the Lua interpreter to better understand them. When you print the result of a comparison, it will be of the boolean type (that is, true or false).

```
> print(1 == 1)
true
> print(1 < 3)
true
> print(1 > 3)
false
> print(2 <= 2)
true
> print(1 >= 3)
false
> print(1 ~= 3)
true
```

The equality operators (== and ~=) can be used to compare any two values, but the <, >, <=, and >= operators can only be used with values of the same type, such as when comparing number to number or string to string; otherwise you will get an error as follows:

```
> print(1 < "Hello")
stdin:1: attempt to compare number with string
stack traceback:
        stdin:1: in main chunk
        [C]: ?
```

In other words, whereas the == and ~= operators work for all values, the less than/greater than (< and >) family of operators is only defined for numbers and string values.

Working with Strings

You've already been introduced to the string type, and you've used it to print "Hello Azeroth!" in the interpreter. In this section you examine strings in a bit more detail.

Comparing Strings

The less than (<) and greater than (>) operators can be used on strings, but the result depends on the way your system internally sorts the different characters. For single character comparisons, the operator compares the two characters' order in the character set; for multiple character strings, it compares the order of the first two differing characters. For example:

```
> print("a" < "b")
true
> print("d" >= "c")
```

```
true
> print("abcd" < "abce")
true
> print("a" < "A")
false
> print("abcd" < "abcde")
true
> print("rests" < "test")
true
```

You may be surprised by the output from the fourth example. In the standard Lua character set, uppercase English letters precede lowercase letters, so the string `"a"` is actually greater than the string `"A"`. In the fifth example, the strings are identical until the first string runs out of characters. At this point, Lua sees that the second string still has the letter `"e"` and returns that the second is greater. However, in the final example, even though the first string is longer than the second one, the letter `"r"` is less than the letter `"t"`, so the whole string `"rests"` is less than `"test"`.

Concatenating Multiple Strings

Strings in Lua are immutable, which means they cannot be changed without creating an entirely new string. To add to a string, you use the special concatenation operator (`..`), which enables you to take two strings and fuse them together to make a new, larger string. Here are a couple of examples:

```
> x = "Hello"
> y = "Azeroth"
> print(x .. y)
HelloAzeroth
> foo = "a" .. "b" .. "c" .. "d" .. "e"
> print(foo)
abcde
```

Converting Numbers to Strings

As you can imagine, sometimes you will need to convert from numbers to strings and, in most cases, Lua handles this for you. Try the following:

```
> print("Number: " .. 4)
Number: 4
```

Lua automatically converts the number 4 to a string, and it's added to the string `"Number: "`. If you need to explicitly convert a number to a string, you can use the `tostring()` function, as in the following example:

```
> x = 17
> foo = tostring(x)
> print(type(foo))
string
```

The `tostring()` function takes whatever it is given (in this case a number) and turns it into a string value.

Converting Strings to Numbers

Conversely, you may have a string of digits that you'd like to convert to a number. Lua's built-in `tonumber()` function takes a value and turns it into a number. If the digits can't be converted (such as when the string doesn't contain a number), the function returns the value `nil`. Here are some examples:

```
> x = tonumber("1234")
> print(type(x))
number
> print(x)
1234

> x = tonumber("1e3")
> print(type(x))
number
> print(x)
1000
```

Here the strings are converted into numbers, and the results are printed to the screen. The `tonumber()` function has a few more tricks up its sleeve that you can explore in Chapter 7.

Quoting Strings

So far, you've used double quotes to create strings, but there are several ways to construct a string for use in Lua. When programming, it is considered proper style to use the same type of quote character (as described in the following sections) unless you have a specific reason for needing to use a different type. This helps other people read your code without confusion.

Single Quote (')

You can use the single quote mark (')—also called a tick or tick mark—to create a string, and this is standard convention. Nothing really special happens here unless you need to include a tick mark within your string. Look at the following examples:

```
> x = 'Hello'
> print(type(x))
string

> x = 'Isn't it nice?'
stdin:1: `=´ expected near `it´
```

The first example works correctly and creates a new string with the text `Hello` inside.

The second example throws an error that you should explore a bit more. What Lua sees here is an identifier (x), the assignment operator (=), and a string ('Isn'). Because Lua doesn't require any whitespace between most operations, it immediately starts the next part of the expression, which begins with the identifier t. The next thing the interpreter sees is another identifier called it, and doesn't know what to do with it. In this case, the interpreter infers that you meant to use the assignment operator and errors out with this suggestion.

You can get around this by *escaping* the tick mark that is inside the string to tell Lua that it's part of the string instead of the end of it. Here's an example:

```
> x = 'Isn\'t it nice?'
> print(type(x))
string
```

You tackle the details of string escaping shortly.

Double Quote (")

The double quote (") can be used the same way as the single quote, with the same caveat of needing to escape embedded quote characters. Here are some examples:

```
> x = "Hello"
> print(type(x))
string

> x = "Isn't it nice?"
> print(type(x))
string

> x = "I play the game "World of Warcraft""
stdin:1: '=' expected near 'of'
```

The second works because the tick mark isn't being used to delimit the quote, but the inner quote in the third example needs to be escaped with a backslash:

```
> x = "I play the game, \"World of Warcraft\""
> print(type(x))
string
```

Bracket Quote ([[ ]])

Lua has the concept of a long quote that enables you to include multiple lines and internal quote characters. These quotes begin with the open bracket character ([), have any number of equal signs (=), including 0, and then another open bracket (⌈). The string closes only when it finds the opposite combination (close brace, equal signs, close brace). Although this may seem overly complex, it enables you to tailor-make your quote start/end for the contents inside. Consider the following example:

```
> x = [[This is a long string, and I can include ' and "]]
> print(x)
This is a long string, and I can include ' and "
```

This includes no equal signs, which is the typical case. You could instead include any number of them, if you needed to use the string "]]" somewhere in your larger string, as in this example:

```
> x = [==[This is a long string, and I can include ]], ', and "]==]
> print(x)
This is a long string, and I can include ]], ', and "
```

You may not find yourself using the [[Some String]] syntax often, but it can be useful when the string spans multiple lines, or includes quote characters.

Escaping Special Characters

Beyond the ' and " characters, there are other characters that aren't necessarily type-able but need to be included in a string. Try to make a multiline string and see what happens:

```
> x = "First line
>> Second line"
stdin:1: unfinished string near '"First line'
```

Two things happen here: First, the prompt changes to two >> signs instead of the normal one. This means you have an unfinished block and the interpreter is waiting for you to finish the expression. Second, you get an error about an unfinished string. This is a peculiarity in the Lua interpreter, because nothing you can type on the second line will allow you to complete the expression.

You get around this by using \n, an escaped character that means newline. Type the following:

```
> x = "First line\nSecond line"
> print(x)
First line
Second line
```

When constructing a string, you can include any of the escape sequences listed in Table 2-4. Not all entries will have an effect when printed inside World of Warcraft, but you should be aware of what valid sequences exist because you may find them in preexisting strings.

Table 2-4: String Escape Sequences

SEQUENCE	DESCRIPTION
\a	audible bell
\b	backspace
\f	form feed
\n	newline
\r	carriage return
\t	horizontal tab
\v	vertical tab
\\	backslash
\"	double quote
\'	single quote
\xxx	ASCII character ddd

In World of Warcraft, you typically only encounter \n, \\, \", \', and \xxx, because the output widgets in World of Warcraft don't support the others.

NOTE More often than not, you will find escape codes used in localization strings for addons. Some locales contain characters that aren't type-able on all keyboards, so they are inserted using the \xxx syntax. In the deDE localization for World of Warcraft, the word Hunter is "J\195\164ger", which is typically displayed as Jäger. Localization is discussed further in Chapter 8.

Getting a String's Length

There are two ways to obtain the length of a specific string: using the # operator or using the string.len() function. The length of a string is often used when validating or parsing strings.

Using the # operator before a string value returns the length as a number, as shown in the following examples:

```
> print(#"Hello")
5

> foo = "This is a test string"
> print(#foo)
21
```

You can use the built-in function string.len() to accomplish the same feat. The period in between string and len means that this specific function is a part of the string namespace (which you learn more about in Chapter 4). Type the following into your interpreter:

```
> foo = "This is a test string"
> print(string.len(foo))
21
```

It returns the same value as the # operator because they both use the same underlying method to calculate the length.

Boolean Values and Operators

The boolean type is relatively simple and only has two possible values—true or false—but as with many things in programming, there's more than meets the eye. Three logical operators can be applied to Boolean values: and, or, and not.

Using the and Operator

The and operator is true when both of its arguments are true, and false when either of them is false or doesn't have a value. Examples help make this clearer:

```
> print(true and true)
true
> print(true and false)
false
> print(false and false)
false
> print(false and true)
false
```

This operator has one peculiarity that you might run into, illustrated by the following example:

```
> print(false and "Goodbye")
false
> print(true and "Hello")
Hello
> print(true and 4)
4
```

In the first example, Lua evaluates only as much of the expression as necessary. The and operator is being used, and it encounters a false value, so it simply returns false without evaluating the rest of the expression (referred to as short-circuit evaluation). In the last two examples, Lua does something similar: it encounters a true value, so it returns the second value as its result. That's because the expression true and value evaluates to true if and only if value itself would evaluate to true.

Using the or Operator

The `or` operator is true any time either of its arguments is true. Again, a simple set of examples should make this clear, because there are only two possible truth values:

```
> print(true or true)
true
> print(true or false)
true
> print(false or false)
false
> print(false or true)
true
```

This operator has a lower precedence than the `and` operator, so make sure you are using it correctly, and include parentheses when necessary. For example:

```
> print(false and false or true)
true
> print(true and false or false)
false
```

In the first example, even though `false and false` turns out to be `false`, it is part of a larger `or` statement, so the whole expression evaluates to `true`. This isn't Lua being confusing; it's the underlying Boolean logic at play.

TIP You can use the behavior of the `and` and `or` operators to shorten some of your expressions if you remember how they are evaluated. These operators allow you to make the equivalent of the a ? b : c statement in C, using Lua. You will encounter more useful examples of this later, but here's a small example:

```
> print(true and "Hello")
Hello
> print(false and "Hello" or "Azeroth!")
Azeroth!
```

Negation Using the not Operator

Simply enough, if you need to turn one Boolean value into the other, toggling it, you can use the `not` operator:

```
> print(not true)
false
> print(not false)
true
> print(not 4)
```

```
false
> print(not "Hello")
false
```

Again, because any value in Lua that is not `false` or `nil` evaluates to `true`, you can even negate those values.

Understanding the nil Value

Earlier in this chapter, you encountered the following error message:

```
stdin:1: attempt to call global 'prnit' (a nil value)
```

`nil` is a special thing that means lack of value in Lua. This is most often seen when working with variables and tables (which you learn about in Chapter 4). Type the following into your interpreter:

```
> print(SomeEmptyVariable)
nil
> print(type(SomeEmptyVariable))
nil
```

Because you have not bound the variable `SomeEmptyVariable` to anything yet, it holds the special value `nil`, which is of type `nil`. You can use this knowledge to check if a variable is currently unset, as in the following example:

```
> print(SomeEmptyVariable == nil)
true
> print(type(SomeEmptyVariable) == "nil"))
true
```

You can check to see if a value is equivalent to `nil`, using the `==` operator. You can also check the type of the value, to see if that is `nil`. Be sure to note the difference between the value `nil` and the string `"nil"`, because the `type()` function always returns a string.

Exploring Scope

So far, each and every variable you have declared has been a *global* variable, meaning it is accessible to all other parts of your program. There is another type of variable, which is called *local*, in that its visibility to the rest of the program is limited in some way. To fully understand the difference between global and local variables you need to understand the scope (or visibility rules) of blocks and chunks.

Blocks

The best way to illustrate a block is with an example, so type the following into your Lua interpreter:

```
> do
>> local i = 7
>> do
>> local i = 10
>> print("Inside: " .. i)
>> end
>> print("Outside: " .. i)
>> end
Inside: 10
Outside: 7
```

Apart from the new keywords do, end, and local, you're doing something fairly simple here. You assign the value 7 to the variable i, assign the value 10 to a new variable i, and then print each of them out as a string. In this case, the do keyword tells the interpreter to begin a block, and the end keyword shows where the block ends. It might make more sense when viewed indented:

```
do
  local i = 7

  do
    local i = 10
    print("Inside: " .. i)
  end

  print("Outside: " .. i)
end
```

By declaring the variable i as local, you've limited its scope to the current block, in this case, the code between within the same do and end keywords. You can access this variable as much as you like within those boundaries, but outside that it's as if the variable doesn't exist.

In addition to manually creating blocks using do and end, certain Lua constructs such as for loops, while loops, and function definitions implicitly begin a new block. You learn more about these constructs in Chapter 3.

> **NOTE** In World of Warcraft, your addons will be competing with any number of other addons that may use global variables. As a result, it is considered good practice to use local variables in many cases.

Chunks

Earlier in this chapter, you received a stack traceback with an error, and it may have referenced the main *chunk*. In Lua, a chunk is either the file being executed, or the string that is being run. Variables are also limited in scope to their specific chunk. This means a local variable declared at the top of one file won't be accessible in another file (they are different chunks).

In the Lua interpreter, each individual line you type is its own chunk, unless you wrap it in a block (such as the preceding do . . . end block). For this reason, the following code will not work:

```
> local i = 10
> print(i)
nil
```

This is just a peculiarity of the way the Lua interpreter works. To get around this, you can use do . . . end to wrap multiple lines of code:

```
> do
>> local i = 10
>> print(i)
> end
10
```

Scope and visibility will be more important when you start working with functions in Chapter 3, but it is important to understand the implication that almost all variables are global, unless specified otherwise.

Summary

This chapter gave you a very broad introduction to fundamental concepts central to the Lua programming language, including variables, values, types, operators, and scope. Chapters 3 through 6 give you a more in-depth introduction to specific aspects of the language, as it relates to World of Warcraft. The Lua programming language is used extensively outside WoW and a number of good reference books are available on the language as a whole.

Basic Functions and Control Structures

Chapter 2 showed you the basics of the Lua programming language using the `print()` and `type()` functions, without fully explaining what a function is. In addition, basic control structures such as loops and conditionals haven't been introduced yet.

The first part of this chapter explains the concept of functions and guides you through creating several of your own. The second half introduces the basic looping and conditional statements.

Using Functions

A function is a portion of a program that can be used to simplify repeated tasks or perform complex calculations. When a function is called it may be passed several *arguments*, that is, data that the function can use for the duration of its execution. When a function completes, it can return any number of values to the calling portion of the program.

Creating a Function

The `function` keyword is used to create a new function, which can then be stored in a variable or called directly. A basic function declaration looks like this (type this into your Lua interpreter):

```
> hello = function()
>> print("Hello World!")
>> end
```

The function constructor begins where you type `function()` and continues to the matching `end` keyword, with the code between these delimiters making up the body of the function. The Lua interpreter recognizes the new block of code and indents the prompt to show you're continuing the same section of code (until you type the final `end`). In this case, a function is created that takes no arguments (more on this in the next section) and prints the string `Hello World` before ending. The resulting function value is then assigned to the variable `hello`. Test this function by running the following:

```
> hello()
Hello World!
```

Now, instead of typing `print("Hello World")` every time you want to print that string, you can simply type `hello()` to call the new function. This is an extremely simple example, but you use the full power of functions as you move through the examples in this chapter.

Local Functions

The function constructor returns a new Lua value, so it can be assigned to a local variable the same as any other value. This can be useful when defining functions that are called within your addons, but need not be exposed for other addons to call. Local variables are difficult to explore in the Lua interpreter because each line of code is in its own scope, but you may find the technique of using local functions useful when working through the rest of this book.

SYNTACTIC SUGAR

Lua provides a different way to define functions that is more conventional and may be easier to read. Examine the following function definition:

```
function hello()
  print("Hello World!")
end
```

When the Lua interpreter encounters this definition, it is converted into the definition used in the previous section:

```
hello = function()
  print("Hello World!")
end
```

That is to say, the two definitions end up running the same code in the interpreter. Functions defined in this manner can be made local by adding the keyword `local` before the function constructor, such as:

```
local function hello()
  print("Hello World")
end
```

(continued)

Function Arguments and Returns

When a function is called, it can be passed any number of arguments to be used throughout the body of the function. In addition, a function may return any number of values when it completes. This allows for the creation of dynamic functions that can operate on values that are passed into the function, rather than some static formula or process.

Simple and repetitive tasks such as converting degrees Celsius to degrees Fahrenheit can easily be made into functions that use arguments and return values.

Converting Celsius to Fahrenheit

The conversion formula given for temperature conversion is "Multiply the temperature in degrees Celsius by 1.8 and add 32 to the result." Instead of performing this conversion with arithmetic each time, a function can be written that takes a number as an argument and returns the converted value as the answer. Type the following into your Lua interpreter:

```
convert_c2f = function(celsius)
  local converted = (celsius * 1.8) + 32
  return converted
end
```

Here, a function is created with a single argument, which is named `celsius`. The first line of the new function calculates the converted value and the second line returns it. To see how this works, type the following:

```
> print(convert_c2f(0))
32
> print(convert_c2f(-40))
-40
```

When the new function is called, the first argument passed to it (the number 0) is assigned to a local variable named `celsius` (corresponding to the name given in the function). This allows you to define the formula for conversion without needing to know the specific number you are converting.

Empty Arguments

Try the following in your interpreter:

```
> print(convert_c2f())
stdin:2: attempt to perform arithmetic on local 'celsius' (a nil value)
stack traceback:
        stdin:2: in function 'convert_c2f'
        stdin:1: in main chunk
        [C]: ?
```

When no value is passed as an argument, the argument gets the value of nil. The first line of the convert_c2f function tries to multiply celsius by 1.8 and errors out because nil can't be part of an arithmetic expression. A similar error will occur if you pass other non-number values into this function.

No Return Values

Not every function you encounter will have a return statement because not all functions need to return anything. The hello() function defined earlier in this chapter is one such example. In these cases any assignments or other expressions involving a call to the function will evaluate to nil. Here's an example:

```
> function hello() print("Hello World!") end
> test = hello()
Hello World!
> print(type(test))
nil
```

Functions as Lua Values

Each function in Lua is just a plain Lua value of the type function. These values can be compared (using == and ~=), bound to variable names, passed to functions, returned from functions, and used as keys in tables (tables are explored in Chapter 4). A Lua value that is treated this way is called a *first-class object*, and a language that supports functions in this way is said to have *first-class functions*.

Run the following in your interpreter:

```
> hello = function() print("Hello World!") end
```

This creates a new function called hello. This value can now be compared in the same way you'd compare any other Lua value.

```
> print(hello == hello)
true
> hello2 = hello
> print(hello2 == hello)
```

```
true
> hello2()
Hello World!
> hello2 = function() print("Hello World!") end
> print(hello2 == hello)
false
```

In the final lines of the preceding example, a new function is created and bound to `hello2`. Even though the new function has the exact same definition and body as `hello`, it is actually a distinct function.

Making Decisions with the if Statement

The `if` statement is the basis for decision making in Lua, and it supports simple conditionals as well as more complex statements. The syntax of the most basic `if` statement looks like this:

```
if <boolean expression> then
  -- do something
end
```

Simple Conditionals

An `if` statement can be used to execute a block of code conditionally when the Boolean expression evaluates to true. To better see this, type the following into your interpreter:

```
function conditional_test(num)
  print("You input: " .. num)
  if (num == 7) then
    print("You found the magic number!")
  end
end
```

This example function prints whatever number it gets passed, but if the number 7 is passed, it will print an additional special message. Input this function into your interpreter, and then test it with the following:

```
> conditional_test(3)
You input: 3
> conditional_test(7)
You input: 7
You found the magic number!
> conditional_test(13)
You input: 13
```

As with other arithmetic and Boolean expressions, the parentheses around the conditional are not strictly necessary, but they can certainly make code easier to read.

Complex Expressions

In addition to simple Boolean conditions, Lua supports more complex expressions so long as the expression evaluates to a Boolean value. That allows you to combine multiple conditions using the logical operators (and, or) into a single complex condition. The following are all valid conditions (where name and anonymous_flag are variables):

- name
- type(name) == "string"
- (not anonymous_flag) and (type(name) == "string")

The first example simply checks to see that the variable name is anything other than nil or false. The second example checks to verify that the variable name is a string, and the final example checks to see that the variable anonymous_flag is either false or nil, and the name variable is a string.

Extended Conditionals

An extended form of the if statement allows you to chain multiple conditions together, as well as provide a default for when no condition is matched. The full syntax for the if statement is:

```
if <boolean expression> then
    -- if part
elseif <boolean expression> then
    -- elseif part
elseif <boolean expression> then
    -- another elseif part
else
    -- else part
end
```

When the interpreter runs this expression, it checks each condition in order, stopping at the first expression that evaluates to true and running that portion of the code. If none of the expressions are true, the code in the else section is run. Not every if statement will include elseif or else options, but they are always available if you need them.

Using this form of if/elseif/else ensures that only one action in the entire if statement will be taken. If you were to write it using a series of simple if statements, more than one may be called, as in the following example.

```
if <first condition> then
  -- do something
end

if <second condition> then
  -- do something
end
```

Both types of constructs are useful but you should ensure you are using the correct one, so your program behaves correctly depending on whether you need to take one action based on a condition, or evaluate multiple conditions independently.

Displaying a Personalized Greeting

Conditionals can be used to verify the arguments to a function. For example, consider a function that takes a name (or nil) and prints out a personalized greeting. Define this function in your Lua interpreter:

```
function greeting(name)
  if (type(name) == "string") then
    print("Hello " .. name)
  elseif (type(name) == "nil") then
    print("Hello friend")
  else
    error("Invalid name was entered")
  end
end
```

The first condition checks to see if the name argument is a string, in which case it generates and prints a custom greeting. If the name argument is nil, meaning nothing was passed into the function, it will print the generic string Hello friend. Finally, if neither of the previous conditions match, the function triggers a custom error message using the error() function. Test this new function in your interpreter:

```
> greeting("Frank")
Hello Frank
> greeting()
Hello friend
> greeting(13)
stdin:7: Invalid name was entered
stack traceback:
        [C]: in function 'error'
        stdin:7: in function 'greeting'
        stdin:1: in main chunk
        [C]: ?
```

When the `error()` function is called, Lua provides the error message supplied along with a stack traceback. In this case, you can see that the error was triggered from the `greeting()` function, which was called from the *main chunk*.

The preceding `greeting()` function could have been written without using the `elseif` statement, by using nested `if` statements, as follows:

```lua
function greeting(name)
  if (type(name) == "string") then
    print("Hello " .. name)
  else
    if (type(name) == "nil") then
      print("Hello friend")
    else
      error("Invalid name was entered")
    end
  end
end
```

The nested style is useful in certain situations when you have multiple conditions but also need to have an `else` portion for each of them. In general, use whatever style you consider to be more readable and appropriate for the given situation.

Repeating Actions with the while Statement

Computers are often used to repeat tasks or simplify complex calculations that would otherwise require manual repetition. Lua provides the `while` statement, which will repeat a block of code as long as a specified condition is met. The `while` statement's syntax is:

```lua
while <boolean expression> do
  -- body
end
```

The Boolean expression is evaluated on each and every repetition of the loop, and the loop will continue as long as the condition evaluates to true.

Computing Factorials

The process of computing a number's factorial is a good example of something that is easily automated. The factorial of a number x is computed by multiplying all of the numbers from 1 to x together. Thus, 3 factorial is `1 * 2 * 3`. If a function `factorial()` is defined, you can simply type `print(factorial(9))` instead of `print (9 * 8 * 7 * 6 * 5 * 4 * 3 * 2 * 1)`. Define this function now by typing the following definition into your interpreter:

```
function factorial(num)
   local total = 1
   while (num > 1) do
     print("total: ".. total .. " num: " .. num)
     total = total * num
     num = num - 1
   end
   return total
end
```

This function includes a `print()` statement that will show you what the function does on each iteration of the loop. Before using this code in an addon, remove that line from the function, or simply comment it out. For now, test this in your Lua interpreter:

```
> print(factorial(5))
total: 1 num: 5
total: 5 num: 4
total: 20 num: 3
total: 60 num: 2
120
```

You can see each step of the loop and how the value is being calculated. Using debug statements like this can be really handy when writing code, but you have to remember to remove them before you release the code.

NOTE The condition of a `while` statement is checked prior to running the loop, and again on each subsequent run of the loop. This means if the condition is never met, the body of the `while` loop is never executed, and Lua just skips past it.

Differences Between while and repeat

The `repeat/until` loop is a variant of the `while` loop that has the following form:

```
repeat
   -- body
until <boolean expression>
```

The primary difference between the `while/do` loop and a `repeat/until` loop is that the condition of a `repeat` loop is checked at the *end* of the computation, so the loop of the body is always executed at least once. In other words, the condition in a `while` statement is checked in order to continue the loop, whereas the condition in a `repeat` loop is checked in order to exit the loop. Here's how you'd define a new factorial function using this construct:

```
function factorial2(num)
  local total = 1
  repeat
    total = total * num
    num = num - 1
  until (num < 1)
  return total
end
```

You can verify the results of this function by testing it with a few different values:

```
> print(factorial2(1))
1
> print(factorial2(2))
2
> print(factorial2(3))
6
> print(factorial2(5))
120
```

If you happened to test these two functions with some unexpected value, such as -3, you should see a difference between the results:

```
> print(factorial(-3))
1
> print(factorial2(-3))
-3
```

When running `factorial()`, the `num` variable is already less than 1, so the `while` body never runs; it simply returns the default value of 1. When `factorial2()` is called, the body of the loop happens once, which causes the different return value of -3.

Looping with the Numeric for Statement

As the preceding factorial function demonstrated, many loops begin at a simple integer value and then either increment or decrement to some predefined limit. In the case of `factorial(9)`, the loop starts at 9 and continues until it reaches 1. Rather than managing this sort of loop yourself, the `for` statement provides an easy way to write these loops:

```
for variablename = start_value, end_value, step_value do
  -- body
end
```

Table 3-1 explains the different arguments that must be supplied to the `for` statement.

Table 3-1: Arguments for Numeric for Loop

ARGUMENT	DESCRIPTION
variablename	A valid variable identifier, the counter variable
start_value	A number, the initial value of variablename
end_value	A number, the end value of the loop
step_value	The number by which to increment the counter after each loop

The following are examples of simple `for` loops:

```
> for i = 1, 3, 1 do
>> print(i)
>> end
1
2
3
> for i = 3, 1, -1 do
>> print(i)
>> end
3
2
1
```

These two loops translate (roughly) to the following code blocks using `while` loops:

```
do
  local i = 1
  while (i <= 3) do
    print(i)
    i = i + 1
  end
end
```

and

```
do
  local i = 3
  while (i >= 1) do
    print(i)
    i = i - 1
  end
end
```

When the step value in a `for` loop is not provided, Lua assumes a value of 1 for the loop. The earlier 1, 2, 3 example can thus be written as follows:

```
for i = 1, 3 do
  print(i)
end
```

Computing Factorials

The `for` loop can be used to make the `factorial()` function even more clear. Type the following definition into your interpreter:

```
function factorial3(num)
  local total = 1
  for i = 1, num do
    total = total * i
  end
  return total
end
```

Rather than manually writing the terminal condition for the `while` or `repeat` loop, you can just provide the `for` statement with a start value, and an upper bound. This example uses the variable `num`, which is evaluated to a number when the function is run.

Evaluation of Loop Conditions

In a `for` loop, the `end_value` and `step_value` are both calculated once, at the start of the loop. As a result, variables and expressions can be used for these values. These values cannot be changed mid-loop; they will have already been calculated. Consider the following example:

```
> upper = 3
> for i = 1, upper do
>> print(i)
>> upper = upper + 1
>> end
1
2
3
```

This example doesn't loop forever because loop conditions are only evaluated at the start of the loop.

Variable Scope in for Loops

When writing a `for` loop, remember that the counter variable name you supply will automatically be made local to that block and won't be accessible outside that level:

```
> i = 15
> for i = 1, 3 do print(i) end
```

```
1
2
3
> print(i)
15
```

In addition, changes made to the counter variable inside the loop do not affect the iteration. For example, the assignment to i in the following loop doesn't actually advance the loop counter:

```
> for i = 1, 10 do
>> print("Loop iteration: " .. i)
>> i = i + 1
>> end
Loop iteration: 1
Loop iteration: 2
Loop iteration: 3
Loop iteration: 4
Loop iteration: 5
Loop iteration: 6
Loop iteration: 7
Loop iteration: 8
Loop iteration: 9
Loop iteration: 10
```

If, for some reason, you need to save the control variable's value, you can declare a local variable just prior to the for loop, where you can save the number you need, as in the following example:

```
upper = 10
do
   local max
   for i = 1, upper do
     max = i
   end
   print(max)
end
```

When the loop terminates, max will be 10, which was the last value of the control variable.

Summary

This chapter introduced you to functions and showed you two different methods to create functions, using two different syntaxes. Conditionals and control structures were introduced, enabling you to easily perform repeated computations. The next chapter explores advanced techniques using functions and control structures.

## CHAPTER 4

Working with Tables

Keeping data in variables is handy when working on simple programs, but larger projects require an easier way to store data. Consider a simple address book program that enables you to electronically store contact information. Using variables, that might look something like this:

```
alice_name = "Alice Applebaum"
alice_phone = "+1-212-555-1434"
alice_address1 = "114 Auburn Street"
alice_address2 = "Apt 14"
alice_city = "Atlanta"
alice_state = "GA"
```

As you can see, using this method for more than a few simple entries would be unwieldy. Adding a new entry requires you to create a new variable name and enter each of the details in a new variable. Computers are all about automating processes, so there has to be a better way to deal with this.

Storing Data Using Tables

You may be familiar with tables or some analogous object from other programming languages (arrays, records, dictionaries, hash tables). In Lua, tables are objects that can be used to store other (usually related) values.

To understand how to use tables, it's important to grasp the concept of an associative table; which is how tables in Lua are implemented. An *associative table* is a collection of values that are each associated with a key. Code can then request a given key from a table and receive the value that is paired with that key, if such a pair exists.

Creating and Indexing Tables

Create a new table for Alice by running this code:

```
> alice = {}
```

In Lua, the table constructor {} creates a new table, in this case an empty one. Here, the new table has been assigned to the variable `alice`. You can index this table using square brackets and a key. Run the following:

```
> alice["name"] = "Alice Applebaum"
> alice["phone"] = "+1-212-555-1434"
> alice["address1"] = "114 Auburn Street"
> alice["address2"] = "Apt 14"
> alice["city"] = "Atlanta"
> alice["state"] = "Georgia"
```

Each line here tells Lua to look in the table `alice` using the provided key, and set that value to whatever is on the right side of the assignment operator. These elements can then be accessed later:

```
> print(alice["name"])
Alice Applebaum
> print(alice["address2"])
Apt 14
```

In each case, a key is matched up with a specific value and stored within the table. Each of these examples uses a string as the key, but Lua actually allows any value (except `nil`) to be used as a key. See this in the following example:

```
> alice[1] = "Test value"
> alice[2] = 14
> print(alice[1])
Test value
> print(alice[2])
14
```

Clearing an Element from a Table

When a table is indexed with a key that has not been set, the table will return the special value `nil`. Run the following:

```
> print(alice["fax"])
nil
```

This means, quite literally, that there is nothing stored in the table for the given key. In order to clear a key/value pair from a table, you just assign that key the value `nil`. Do this now to clear the two test values set previously:

```
> alice[1] = nil
> alice[2] = nil
```

Shortcuts for String Keys

Lua provides an easier way to index a table by string keys when those strings are a single identifier. This is extremely useful when working with data tables. Instead of typing this:

```
alice["address1"] = "114 Auburn Street"
```

you can type the following:

```
alice.address1 = "114 Auburn Street"
```

This shortcut method only works when the key begins with a letter or underscore character and consists of only letters, digits, and underscore characters. In addition, the key cannot be a reserved Lua keyword (such as end). All of the following identifiers are considered valid:

- myTable.someKey
- myTable.someKey12
- myTable.some_Key
- myTable._someKey
- myTable.start

But these will cause an error:

- myTable.12someKey
- myTable.some-key
- myTable.end
- myTable.or

This method of indexing a table is only provided as a convenience, and only works when your keys are in a specific format. You can still access the "invalid" keys using the full bracket notation.

Creating Populated Tables

In addition to using {} to create new empty tables, you can also use it to create an already populated table. This is accomplished by providing a set of key/value pairs within the constructor itself, using the following syntax:

```
myTable = {
  [key1] = value1,
  [key2] = value2,
  ...
}
```

Running the following can thus create an equivalent record for Alice:

```
alice = {
  ["name"] = "Alice Applebaum",
  ["phone"] = "+1-212-555-1434",
  ["address1"] = "114 Auburn Street",
  ["address2"] = "Apt 14",
  ["city"] = "Atlanta",
  ["state"] = "Georgia",
}
```

You can take advantage of shortcuts for string keys in the constructor too, by typing *someKey* instead of `["someKey"]`. This shortcut follows the same rules as dot notation for table indexing. This shortens the example record to:

```
alice = {
  name = "Alice Applebaum",
  phone = "+1-212-555-1434",
  address1 = "114 Auburn Street",
  address2 = "Apt 14",
  city = "Atlanta",
  state = "Georgia",
}
```

TRAILING COMMAS IN TABLE CONSTRUCTORS

The last line of each of these table examples has a trailing comma before the closing brace. The syntax of Lua allows this within tables so it is easier to add new key/value pairs to the end of the definition. If Lua didn't allow this and you forget to add a comma before adding a new line, you would get a compilation error.

When creating new tables in this format, having the trailing comma makes adding new entries easier, so it is a common practice to include them on every row.

Using Tables as Arrays

Lua tables have another unique property when they are used with consecutive integer keys starting at 1. These tables can be used as lists of values and include library functions for inserting values, removing values, and sorting the list. Tables used in this manner are typically referred to as *arrays*, due to some similarities they share with arrays in other programming languages. More specifically, the part of a table that has integer keys starting at 1 is referred to as the *array part* of the table.

Creating an Array

You can create a new array using the table constructor in one of the two following ways (they are equivalent):

```
tbl = {
  value1,
  value2,
  value3,
  ...
}

tbl = {
  [1] = value1,
  [2] = value2,
  [3] = value3,
  ...
}
```

In the first case you can omit the key names entirely, and just provide a comma-separated list of values. As you can see, arrays are just a special case of tables. Each of the functions covered in this section is only reliable when dealing with *consecutive* integer keys starting at 1. Although nil can be used as a value in a table, it indicates that a value is missing, so care must be taken to ensure that nil values don't appear in the array part of a table.

The two types of table constructors can be mixed, so you can define a table with an array part and key/value pairs at the same time. For example, the following is a valid table definition that combines the use of all three definition methods:

```
class_list = {
  "Alice",
  "Bob",
  "Carol",
  class_name = "Foundations of Engineering and Computer Science",
  ["class_code"] = "ECS101",
}
```

Getting the Length of an Array

The same length operator (#) that was introduced in Chapter 2 for use on strings is also used to get the length of the array part of a table. Test this now with these quick examples:

```
> tbl = {"alpha", "beta", "gamma", "delta"}
> print(#tbl)
4
```

```
> tbl = {}
> print(#tbl)
0
> tbl = {
>> "alpha",
>> "beta",
>> ["one"] = "uno",
>> ["two"] = "dos",
>> "gamma",
>> }
> print(#tbl)
3
```

You can see that # only counts the elements in the array part. This operator can be used to print the table's elements without your needing to hardcode the upper limit. For example:

```
> for i = 1, #tbl do
>> print(tbl[i])
>> end
alpha
beta
gamma
```

Adding Elements to an Array

Adding an element to an array is as simple as associating the value to the next integer key in sequence. More generally:

```
> tbl[#tbl + 1] = "new element"
```

This is a really tedious and error-prone way to do something relatively simple. Lua provides a `table.insert()` library function that makes adding elements a bit easier. The syntax for `table.insert()` is:

```
table.insert(tbl, [pos,] value)
```

The arguments are as follows:

- `tbl`—The table to alter
- `pos` (optional)—The position at which to add the new element
- `value`—The value to insert

The second parameter being enclosed in brackets indicates that it is optional and does not need to be included. If the position isn't included, the new value will be added to the end of the table.

Run the following in your interpreter to create a sample table and a function that will allow you to easily print the contents of the array part of a table that is passed in as an argument:

```
tmp = {"alpha", "beta", "gamma"}
function print_array(tbl)
  for i = 1, #tbl do
    print(i, tbl[i])
  end
end
```

To print the current list, use the following command:

```
> print_array(tmp)
1       alpha
2       beta
3       gamma
```

To add a new element to the end of the list, call `table.insert()` with the table you'd like to alter and the value you'd like to add:

```
> table.insert(tmp, "delta")
> table.insert(tmp, "epsilon")
> print_array(tmp)
1       alpha
2       beta
3       gamma
4       delta
5       epsilon
```

To insert a new value at a given position, call `table.insert()` with the optional second parameter `pos`, a number that indicates at what position you'd like to add the element. When you insert a value in this way, all elements after the given position will be renumbered and moved up.

```
> table.insert(tmp, 3, "zeta")
> print_array(tmp)
1       alpha
2       beta
3       zeta
4       gamma
5       delta
6       epsilon
```

When using the position argument, it's important to make sure you're supplying a valid number. The position should always be between `1`, which inserts the value at the front of the list, and `#tmp + 1`, which inserts it after the current last element. If you supply a value outside this range, the results are unpredictable.

Removing Elements from an Array

Lua includes a function to remove elements from a table, and the syntax is similar to its companion `table.insert()`:

```
value = table.remove(tbl [, pos])
```

This function takes up to two parameters:

■ `tbl`—The table to alter

■ `pos` (optional)—The element to remove from the table

The function signature is written as if it was an assignment. This is shorthand notation to show that the function also returns something:

■ `value`—The value removed from the table

Again, the brackets around `pos` show that it is an optional parameter. When a position isn't included, Lua will remove the last element in the table (that is, the element at the `#tbl` position).

To remove the last element of a table, use the following command:

```
> removed = table.remove(tmp)
> print_array(tmp)
1     alpha
2     beta
3     zeta
4     gamma
5     delta
> print(removed)
epsilon
```

By simply calling `table.remove()` with only a table argument, the last element has been removed and we're left with the rest of the table.

Here's how to remove a specific element in a table:

```
> removed = table.remove(tmp, 3)
> print_array(tmp)
1     alpha
2     beta
3     gamma
4     delta
> print(removed)
zeta
```

When an element is removed from the middle of the table (including the first element), all other elements are renumbered and shifted down. This ensures that the elements of the array are always numbered properly so the array part functions all work properly.

Just because a function has return values doesn't mean you have to do anything with them. You could just as easily call `table.remove()`, ignoring the return value entirely.

Sorting the Elements of an Array

When an array contains basic elements such as strings and numbers that can be easily compared, there is a standard library function to sort the list. The syntax of the `table.sort()` function follows:

```
table.sort(tbl [, comp])
```

The second argument to `table.sort()` is covered in detail in Chapter 5, but the first argument is the table that you would like to sort. You can call this function and pass it a table to be sorted as the first argument:

```
> print_array(tmp)
1     alpha
2     beta
3     gamma
4     delta
> table.sort(tmp)
> print_array(tmp)
1     alpha
2     beta
3     delta
4     gamma
```

Because the values in this table are strings, they are sorted alphabetically, in ascending order (this is the default). If the table contained numbers, they would be sorted in the same way.

A simple sort like this won't be effective for more complex values (such as tables), or when the values in an array are mixed (such as strings and numbers). Chapter 5 will show you how to use the second argument to `table.sort()` to custom tailor the `sort` function for these situations.

Using Tables as Namespaces

You've already been introduced to a few functions that are grouped together:

- `table.insert()`
- `table.remove()`
- `table.sort()`

When functions are grouped together in this manner, they are said to be part of a *namespace*, in this case, the `table` namespace. Namespaces provide a logical grouping of functions that are related, collected in a Lua table. Because tables can hold function values, the preceding functions are also accessible using:

- `table["insert"]()`
- `table["remove"]()`
- `table["sort"]()`

Creating a new namespace is a matter of writing your new functions, creating a new table, and setting the appropriate key/value pairs in your table.

Creating a Namespace of Utility Functions

You've already written a few utility functions that might be handy to keep around, such as `convert_c2f()`. You can create a new namespace to start storing these functions by defining a new table:

```
> util = {}
```

Adding Functions to a Namespace

You have two different ways to add functions to a namespace: by indexing the table and storing the value of an existing function, or by defining the function directly as part of the namespace.

Storing an Existing Function

If you've closed your previous Lua session, redefine your Celsius to Fahrenheit conversion function:

```
function convert_c2f(celsius)
   return (celsius * 1.8) + 32
end
```

Now that you have a function to which you can refer, run the following code to store it in the `util` table:

```
> util.celsius2fahrenheit = convert_c2f
```

This function can then be accessed directly from the `util` table:

```
> print(util.celsius2fahrenheit(0))
32
> print(util.celsius2fahrenheit(-40))
-40
```

Defining a New Function

Rather than define a function with a name and then set it as part of the namespace, you can define the function directly as part of the namespace. Run the following code:

```
function util.factorial(num)
  local total = 1
  for i = 1, num do
    total = total * i
  end
  return total
end
```

You may recall from Chapter 3 that this method of function definition is *syntactic sugar* and is translated by Lua into the following:

```
util.factorial = function(num)
  local total = 1
  for i = 1, num do
    total = total * i
  end
  return total
end
```

Using the first form is often the most convenient way to define functions, and it makes the code easier to read compared to the alternative methods. More often than not, when you read a namespace definition, you will see it in this form; however, as always, feel free to develop your own style.

Object-Oriented Programming with Tables

Tables can also be used for a different type of programming called *object-oriented programming*. In this type of programming, data is described as objects, which contain *methods*, special functions that act directly on or through that object. Lua provides some simple mechanisms to enable object-oriented programming, but does not strictly enforce any particular style of programming.

Creating a Non-Object-Oriented Counter

To illustrate some of the benefits this type of programming provides, run the following in your interpreter:

```
-- Create a new scope for local variables
do
```

```
-- Create a counter that cannot be accessed outside this scope
local counter = 0

-- Global functions to interact with counter
function counter_get()
  return counter
end

function counter_inc()
  counter = counter + 1
end
end
```

This block of code makes a simple, one-way counter that can't be decremented, but can be retrieved and incremented via the `counter_get()` and `counter_inc()` functions. Explore this by running the following in your interpreter:

```
> print(counter_get())
0
> counter_inc()
> counter_inc()
> print(counter_get())
2
> counter = counter - 1
stdin:1: attempt to perform arithmetic on global 'counter' (a nil value)
stack traceback:
        stdin:1: in main chunk
        [C]: ?
```

You can see that the counter variable is not accessible outside of the created scope and thus can't be altered without calling the provided functions. This code implements a single counter when, in fact, you might need more than one. Because these functions are tied to a specific counter variable, they are very limited.

Using Tables as Simple Objects

The following is a different implementation for the simple counter, making the counter an object with two methods, `get` and `inc`. Unlike the first example, the counter *can* be altered directly without calling the functions. Run the following code in your interpreter:

```
counter = {
  count = 0
}

function counter.get(self)
```

```
    return self.count
end

function counter.inc(self)
    self.count = self.count + 1
end
```

This program allows you to do the following:

```
> print(counter.get(counter))
0
> counter.inc(counter)
> print(counter.get(counter))
1
```

In this implementation, the actual counter variable is stored in a table (which serves as the object). Each of the functions that interact with this value has an argument named self, which is expected to be a counter object. You could make a new counter by running the following:

```
> counter2 = {
>> count = 15,
>> get = counter.get,
>> inc = counter.inc,
>> }
> print(counter2.get(counter2))
15
```

Because the functions are just Lua values and they are designed to work on an argument rather than some magical hidden variable, you can copy them into your counter. As a matter of fact, the functions will work correctly even if you call counter.get() but pass it the counter2 object:

```
> print(counter.get(counter2))
15
> print(counter.get == counter2.get)
true
```

This should be no surprise because you're just moving and copying references to the same functions around. Although this implementation is definitely more convenient than the first attempt, it can be made even easier. Right now, you have to call the function and pass in the counter object, causing you to type the object's name twice. Lua provides a bit of syntactic sugar that helps you.

Using : to Call Object Methods

In the preceding example you can refer to get and inc as object methods because they are written to be called within the context of an object. Lua provides a bit of syntactic sugar that makes calling an objects methods easier. Instead of typing `counter.get(counter)`, you can call `counter:get()`.

Lua translates `counter:get()` into `counter.get(counter)`, saving you a bit of typing and making code easier to read. This all happens behind the scenes and prevents from you having to pass the object in every time you make a method call.

Defining Functions Using :

You can use the `:` operator to define functions, making this type of programming even more natural. When this happens, Lua includes an implicit first argument called `self`. That's why you used the variable name `self` in the previous example.

Redefine the earlier functions by typing the following into your interpreter:

```
counter = {
  count = 0
}

function counter:get()
  return self.count
end

function counter:inc()
  self.count = self.count + 1
end
```

This code is roughly equivalent to the following definition:

```
counter = {
  count = 0
}

function counter.get(self)
  return self.count
end

function counter.inc(self)
  self.count = self.count + 1
end
```

Test this new version with the following code:

```
> print(counter:get())
0
> counter:inc()
> counter:inc()
> print(counter:get())
2
```

COMMON ERRORS

If you attempt to call a method that expects the `self` argument with a period instead of a colon, you might get an error similar to this:

```
stdin:2: attempt to index local 'self' (a nil value)
```

Most of the time, when you get this error, it means you are accidentally calling a method without passing a first argument, or you used a period where you meant to use a colon.

Making a Better Counter

The counter program still has room for improvement because the way new counters are created is relatively clunky. Run the following to define a more robust counter system:

```lua
-- Create a new scope for local variables
do
  local function get(self)
    return self.count
  end

  local function inc(self)
    self.count = self.count + 1
  end

  function new_counter(value)
    if type(value) ~= "number" then
      value = 0
    end

    local obj = {
      count = value,
      get = get,
      inc = inc,
    }

    return obj
  end
end
```

This example provides a single global function called `new_counter`, which takes the initial value of the counter as an argument. It returns a new object containing two methods and the counter value itself. This type of function is typically called a *factory function* because it just returns new objects each time you call it. Run a few tests to ensure the system works properly:

```
> counter = new_counter()
> print(counter:get())
```

```
0
> counter2 = new_counter(15)
> print(counter2:get())
15
> counter:inc()
> print(counter:get())
1
> print(counter2:get())
15
```

Although the implementation may seem a bit more complex than the previous attempts, creating and manipulating new counters is extremely easy. Choose whichever implementation makes the most sense in your code.

Extending Tables with Metatables

Each table in Lua is capable of having a *metatable* attached to it. A metatable is a secondary table that gives Lua extra information about how that table should be treated when it is used. For example, by default, when you try to print a table you are given a string that looks something like `table: 0x30d470`, which isn't extremely readable. Lua provides a way to change this behavior using metatables and metamethods.

Adding a Metatable

A metatable is nothing more than a table used to store extra information about the tables to which it is attached. They can be passed around, attached to multiple tables, and altered at any time. To begin redefining the behavior of a table, you must create a metatable and attach it to a table object, using the `setmetatable()` function. This function takes two arguments:

- `tbl`—The table to alter
- `mt`—The table to attach to `tbl`

In addition, `setmetatable()` returns a single argument, the table you passed in as the first argument. This can be helpful when creating new tables to pass directly to `setmetatable()`. Run the following code to create some tables to play with, and attach the same metatable to each of them:

```
tbl1 = {"alpha", "beta", "gamma"}
tbl2 = {"delta", "epsilon", "zeta"}
tbl3 = {}
mt = {}
setmetatable(tbl1, mt)
setmetatable(tbl2, mt)
setmetatable(tbl3, mt)
```

You can verify the metatable has been set correctly by using the `getmetatable()` function. This function simply takes a table as the first argument and returns the metatable, or `nil` if no metatable is attached.

```
> print(getmetatable(tbl1) == mt)
true
```

Now that you have an object with a metatable, you can begin redefining the behavior of the table.

Defining Metamethods

A *metamethod* is nothing more than a function stored with a specific key in a metatable. There are several possible metamethods, and they take a varying number of arguments. Each metamethod begins with two underscore characters. You can find a full list in the *Lua Reference Manual* (available online at `http://www.lua.org`), but the most frequently used ones are shown in Table 4-1.

Table 4-1: Relevant Metamethods

METAMETHOD	ARGUMENTS	DESCRIPTION
___add	2	Defines the behavior when used in addition operations.
___mul	2	Defines the behavior when used in multiplication operations.
___div	2	Defines the behavior when used in division operations.
___sub	2	Defines the behavior when used in subtraction operations.
___unm	1	Defines the behavior when negated (unary minus).
___tostring	1	Defines the behavior when the table is an argument to `tostring()`. This also affects the `print()` function, which calls `tostring()` directly.
___concat	2	Defines the behavior when used with the concatenation operator (..)
___index	2	Defines the behavior when the table is indexed with a key that doesn't exist in that table.
___newindex	3	Defines the behavior when a previously unset key in the table is being set.

Defining Basic Arithmetic Using ___add, ___sub, ___mul, and ___div

Each of the arithmetic metamethods ___add, ___sub, ___mul, and ___div takes two arguments and can (in theory) return anything you'd like. However, keep the following in mind:

- The result of one operation may be part of a larger arithmetic expression.

- If you return a non-number from your metamethod, you should ensure it is capable of handling further arithmetic.

- If you return nil, it will break any arithmetic expression it is a part of, so it's best to avoid that.

The following function defines addition between two tables as a new table with the elements of the first table's array part, followed by the elements of the second's array part. Add the following function to your Lua interpreter:

```
function mt.___add(a,b)
  local result = setmetatable({}, mt)

  -- Copy table a in first
  for i = 1, #a do
    table.insert(result, a[i])
  end

  -- Copy table b in second
  for i = 1, #b do
    table.insert(result, b[i])
  end

  return result
end
```

To simplify the function, the arguments have been named a and b. The first line creates a new results table and makes sure to set the metatable correctly; without this the result might not work in a larger arithmetic expression. The rest of the function is straightforward, copying the elements of each table to the new resulting table. Here is a simple test:

```
> add_test = tbl1 + tbl2
> print(#add_test)
6
> for i = 1, #add_test do print(i, add_test[i]) end
1    alpha
2    beta
3    gamma
4    delta
5    epsilon
6    zeta
```

The metamethod correctly handles the addition and creates a new table with the results of the addition. The other basic arithmetic operations could be defined in the same way. Instead of returning a table, these functions could return some meaningful number that can be used as part of a larger formula.

Defining Negation Using ___unm

The unary minus (negation) operator, __unm, expects exactly one argument, and should return the result of the argument being negated. In these examples, this will mean reversing the array part of the given table. Run the following code:

```
function mt.___unm(a)
  local result = setmetatable({}, mt)

  -- Reverse through the elements of the array
  for i = #a, 1,-1 do
    table.insert(result, a[i])
  end

  return result
end
```

Test table negation with a few examples:

```
> unm_test = -tbl1
> for i = 1, #unm_test do print(i, unm_test[i]) end
1    gamma
2    beta
3    alpha
> unm_test = -tbl1 + tbl2
> for i = 1, #unm_test do print(i, unm_test[i]) end
1    gamma
2    beta
3    alpha
4    delta
5    epsilon
6    zeta
```

Creating Meaningful Output with ___tostring

In the current example, it would be useful to print the table and have it display the elements rather than the unique string Lua provides. You can accomplish that using the ___tostring metamethod, which takes a single argument (the table) and should return a string.

Run the following code:

```
function mt.___tostring(tbl)
  local result = "{"

  for i = 1, #tbl do
```

```
    if i > 1 then
       result = result .. ", "
    end

    result = result .. tostring(tbl[i])
  end

  result = result .. "}"

  return result
end
```

Because you know the input will be a table, you start the string with the {
character. This function then loops through each element of the array. If the
loop is beyond the first element, a comma is added to the string to separate
each value. This is done so you don't have an extra comma at the end of the
output. Then the value itself is concatenated onto the result string. Finally,
when the loop is complete, you close the brace and return the string:

```
> print(tbl1)
{alpha, beta, gamma}
> print(tbl2)
{delta, epsilon, zeta}
> print(tbl3)
{}
```

When working with more complex objects, it can be very useful to provide a
meaningful text representation of your data, so the ___tostring metamethod
can be extremely handy.

Concatenating Tables Using ___concat

For these tables, concatenation will end up being the same thing as addition, so
you can simply use that function for the ___concat metamethod, as well. Both
metamethods take in two arguments and return a single result. In addition,
both are typically chained together, so you'll need to ensure the resulting
object is also capable of concatenation. Run the following test:

```
> mt.___concat = mt.___add
> print(tbl1 .. tbl2)
{alpha, beta, gamma, delta, epsilon, zeta}
```

Because the ___tostring metamethod is still active, the resulting table is
converted to string representation, even when printed like this.

Exploring Fallback Tables with ___index

Normally, when a table does not have a value associated with a given key, nil
is returned. That makes sense for run-of-the-mill tables, but at times it is more

appropriate to take other action instead. The ___index metamethod allows that to happen, following this procedure:

1. Code tries to access an unassociated key in a table.

2. If the table has an ___index metatable entry that is another table, look up the same key in that table and return it (or nil if it doesn't exist). This may possibly trigger the ___index metamethod of the second table, making a chain.

3. If the table has an ___index metatable entry that is a function, call the function with the table and the key as arguments, and return the result.

Example Using Tables

Let's expand on the previous example by creating a table with an ___index metamethod that allows for the translation of English phrases into German. Run the following code:

```
tbl4 = {["Night elf"] = "Nachtelf"}
setmetatable(tbl4, mt)

enUS_defaults = {
  ["Human"] = "Human",
  ["Night elf"] = "Night elf",
}

mt.___index = enUS_defaults
```

This example creates a new table that contains the German localization of the English phrase Night elf. In addition, there is a default table that contains the English phrases Human and Night elf. If the answer isn't found when tbl4 is indexed, Lua will look in the metatable's ___index entry and return that result. See this in action yourself:

```
> print(tbl4["Night elf"])
Nachtelf
> print(tbl4["Human"])
Human
> print(tbl3["Night elf"])
Night elf
```

Because the metatable is shared between the four tables being used in this exercise, if you access the Night elf or Human key in the table, you will get the English version of the phrase back. The ___index metatable entry here allows you to provide partial localization for the German language by displaying the English words by default when a translation isn't found.

Example Using Functions

Instead of using a table for the ___index entry, you can specify a function that takes two arguments: the table itself and the key being requested. This function enables you to add logic to the indexing of tables. Run the following code, which allows you to avoid having a long table of defaults where the keys and the values are the same:

```
defaults_mt = {
   ___index = function(tbl, key)
      if type(key) == "string" then
        print("Return default value of '" .. key .. "' for key: " .. key)
        return key
      else
        return nil
      end
   end,
}
setmetatable(enUS_defaults, defaults_mt)
```

Then test it with the following examples:

```
> print(tbl4["Night elf"])
Nachtelf
> print(tbl4["Human"])
Human
> print(tbl4["Gnome"])
Return default value of 'Gnome' for key: Gnome
Gnome
> print(tbl4[1])
nil
```

Note that the second to last example prints a message in addition to returning the value. In fact, a metamethod that is a function can do any number of things.

Catching Creation of Keys with ___newindex

Unlike the ___index metamethod, which is designed to handle keys being requested from a table, the ___newindex metamethod can be used when a new key has been set in the table. Specifically, it is called whenever an assignment is made to a non-existing key in a table.

___newindex takes three arguments:

- tbl—The table being indexed
- key—The key being used to index the table
- value—The value to assign to table[key]

When this metamethod is set, it is responsible for actually making the assignment happen. This can be used to stop a value from ever being set in the first place. Run the following code in your interpreter:

```
function mt.___newindex(tbl, key, value)
  if key == "banana" then
    error("Cannot set a protected key")
  else
    rawset(tbl, key, value)
  end
end
```

The `rawset()` function here allows you to bypass the metatable (covered in the next section), to prevent your metamethod from being called again. As long as this metatable is set, you will be unable to (through conventional means) set the key `["banana"]` in any of the example tables, as shown in the following:

```
> tbl1.apple = "red"
> print(tbl1.apple)
red
> tbl1.banana = "yellow"
stdin:3: Cannot set a protected key
stack traceback:
        [C]: in function 'error'
        stdin:3: in function <stdin:1>
        stdin:1: in main chunk
        [C]: ?
> print(tbl1.banana)
Return default value of 'banana' for key: banana
banana
```

Because the metamethod errors instead of setting the new entry, you have a pseudo-"protected" key in your tables.

Bypassing Metatables

When writing functions for the ___index and ___newindex metamethods, it may be necessary to bypass the metatable when getting or setting a value. This is accomplished using the `rawget()` and `rawset()` functions.

value = rawget(tbl, key)

The `rawget()` function takes the table to query and the key to look up, and returns the value of that key in the table without using the metatable for lookups. When you are writing a function that serves as a metamethod for a table, it is typically best to use `rawget()` to access values in that table.

rawset(tbl, key, value)

To set a value in a table without hitting the metatable, you can use the `rawset()` function. It takes in the table to be altered, the key to use, and the value to be placed in the table. You will encounter tables with ___newindex metamethods less frequently than those with ___index metamethods, but it's good to understand what tools are available, in case you need them.

Summary

In this chapter you learned how to use Lua tables to store data that can be easily read and indexed. Arrays were introduced as a special subset of tables with helper functions to insert/remove and sort array tables. Namespaces of functions were introduced along with basic object-oriented programming. Finally, you learned how to extend tables using metatables.

The next chapter introduces you to more advanced features of functions and control structures.

## CHAPTER 5

Advanced Functions and Control Structures

The functions and control structures introduced in Chapter 3 were relatively simple but gave you the capability to create nontrivial programs. This chapter introduces more advanced versions of functions and loops that allow you to accomplish the following:

- Create functions with a variable number of arguments
- Return multiple values from a function
- Loop through the key/value pairs in the hash part of a table
- Sort an array with table data

Multiple Return Values

In Lua, functions are able to return more than one value in a `return` statement, which makes accomplishing some tasks more natural. For example, colors in World of Warcraft are represented as both hexadecimal values (such as 99CCFF) as well as numeric percentages of red, green, and blue (such as 0.6, 0.8, 1.0). As a result, it can be useful to convert the hexadecimal values (which are widely used on the web) to the decimal equivalents.

Converting Hex to RGB

An example of a hexadecimal string is FFCC99, where the first two characters represent the value of the color red as a number between 0 and 255 in hexadecimal. The second set of characters is the value of green, followed by blue. The `string.sub()` function can be used to split the string into its three component color strings, whereas the `tonumber()` function can convert the string into a number. If the `tonumber()` function is called with the red part of the string `"FF"`, it won't return a meaningful result:

```
> print(tonumber("FF"))
nil
```

By default, the `tonumber()` function expects the number to be a decimal number (that is, in base-10), so it can't convert this base-16 number. The second argument of `tonumber()` specifies the base of the string that is being converted. In this case:

```
> print(tonumber("FF", 16))
255
```

Because the output needs to be a number between 0.0 and 1.0, this value can be divided by 255 to obtain the percentage value. Add a definition for `ConvertHexToRGB()` as follows:

```
function ConvertHexToRGB(hex)
  local red = string.sub(hex, 1, 2)
  local green = string.sub(hex, 3, 4)
  local blue = string.sub(hex, 5, 6)

  red = tonumber(red, 16) / 255
  green = tonumber(green, 16) / 255
  blue = tonumber(blue, 16) / 255

  return red, green, blue
end
```

Test this function with a few sample values:

```
> print(ConvertHexToRGB("FFCC99"))
1, 0.8, 0.6
> print(ConvertHexToRGB("FFFFFF"))
1, 1, 1
> print(ConvertHexToRGB("000000"))
0, 0, 0
```

Assigning Multiple Values

To get the results of a function with multiple return values such as `ConvertHexToRGB()`, you can use the following syntax:

```
var1, var2, var3, var4 = someFunction()
```

This calls `someFunction()` and assigns the first return to `var1`, the second return to `var2`, and so on. If there are more returns than variables, the extra returns are just discarded. In the case that there are more variables than returns, the remaining variables are set to `nil`.

Missing Return Values?

When you are working with multiple return values, a few odd things can happen. Look at the following example:

```
> print(ConvertHexToRGB("FFFFFF"))
1, 1, 1
> print(ConvertHexToRGB("FFFFFF"), "SomeOtherArgument")
1, SomeOtherArgument
```

Where did the other returns go? They were eaten by the following rule:

When a function call with multiple return values is the last argument to another function, or the last argument in a multiple assignment expression, all of the return values are passed or used. Otherwise, only the first return value is used or assigned.

You can see this behavior with the assignment operator in the following example:

```
> a, b, c, d = ConvertHexToRGB("FFFFFF"), "some", "more", "arguments"
> print(a, b, c, d)
1, some, more, arguments
```

Because the call to ConvertHexToRGB() is followed by additional values, Lua only uses the first return from the function call. There are a few technical reasons for this limitation, but it should not affect you very often. The exception to the rule can be seen in the following example:

```
> a, b, c, d = "first argument", ConvertHexToRGB("FFFFFF")
> print(a, b, c, d)
first argument, 1, 1, 1
```

TIP When working with multiple return values, you can always wrap the function call in parentheses to limit it to a single return value, as follows:

```
> print((ConvertHexToRGB("FFFFFF")))
1
```

Multiple Return Values in World of Warcraft

Several World of Warcraft API functions return multiple values. For example, the function GetRaidRosterInfo() takes a character's raid index (a number) and returns the following information:

- The name of the character
- The character's rank in the raid (leader, assistant, and so on)
- What subgroup the character is in

- The character's level
- The character's class (localized)
- The character's class (capitalized, in English)
- The name of the zone the character is currently in
- Whether the character is online
- Whether the character is dead
- If the character is a main tank or main assist
- Whether the character is master looter

This function provides a ton of information, but, typically, when you need one of the items, you need more than one. In this case, it's more efficient for the game client to return each of these items every time the function is queried, rather than having 11 different API functions.

SELECTING SPECIFIC VALUES

Functions with multiple return values provide a unique set of challenges, such as how to get at values that aren't at the start of the return list. There are two easy ways to do this: using dummy variables and using the `select()` statement.

Taking the `ConvertHexToRGB()` example, how could you extract just the green value?

Using a Dummy Variable

The function is going to return three results regardless of how you call it, but you can use dummy variables to *throw away* the results that aren't interesting. For example, you may see something that looks like this:

```
local _, g = ConvertHexToRGB("FFFFFF")
```

Because the underscore character is a valid identifier, it can be used to store values, but most sane programs choose more valid variable names. The underscore identifier has become somewhat of a de facto standard when you need to throw away the result of a function call simply because it's easy to type, and most likely not already in use, but its use is still considered bad practice.

Instead of using the underscore as a dummy variable, it's better to give each variable a meaningful name, and only use those that are necessary. That way if you ever need to look at that code in the future, you have a hint of what other information is available. Some situations can't be handled using this method, but Lua provides a utility function to compensate.

(continued)

SELECTING SPECIFIC VALUES *(continued)*

Using the select() Function

The `select()` function was designed to help solve this problem, by allowing you to choose a specific argument from a given list. This function takes any number of arguments, the first of which tells the function what to do. When `select()` is passed the `"#"` string as the first argument, it simply returns the number of arguments in the second part of the function. If `select()` is passed a number value, it returns that argument from the list, followed by anything after it. After this initial argument, `select()` takes any number of arguments, comma separated.

Confused yet? Look at a few examples:

```
> print(select("#", "alpha", "beta", "gamma"))
3
> print(select(1, "alpha", "beta", "gamma"))
alpha, beta, gamma
> print(select(2, "alpha", "beta", "gamma"))
beta, gamma
> print(select(3, "alpha", "beta", "gamma"))
gamma
> third = select(3, "alpha", "beta", "gamma")
> print(third)
gamma
```

If you just need to get a single value from the list, you can assign it directly to the variable, or wrap the `select()` call in parentheses so the extra values are thrown away.

You may find this function useful when working with some of the longer World of Warcraft API functions, such as `GetRaidRosterInfo()`. If you only need a single return, you can isolate it using a call to `select()`.

Accepting a Variable Number of Arguments

Many functions are designed to take a specific number of arguments, such as the `tonumber()` function, which takes a string, and optionally, a number base for the conversion. Other functions make more sense when they accept a variable number of arguments. Consider a function that calculates the arithmetic mean of a set of numbers. A simple version of this function that works with two arguments might look something like this:

```
function mean(num1, num2)
  return (num1 + num2) / 2
end
```

Unfortunately, if you need to compute the mean of three numbers, you would need to do it manually, call the function twice, or write a new function that takes three arguments instead. As you can imagine, this is highly inefficient, and Lua provides an easier way to write these types of functions so they can accept a variable number of arguments.

Declaring a Vararg Function

Functions with a variable number of arguments are called *vararg functions* for short, and they use an ellipsis (three periods) in their function declaration to indicate they take any number of arguments.

In Lua, the ellipsis can only appear as the last argument in a function declaration. Whenever the ellipsis is then used in the body of the function, the arguments that were supplied in the vararg slot are substituted. Take the print() function, which already accepts a variable number of arguments, and extend it by running the following code:

```
function test_print(...)
   print("testing", ...)
end
```

This function takes in any number of arguments and then passes them to the print() function, adding its own text to the start of the list. The output from running this function looks like this:

```
> test_print("alpha", "beta", 13, "gamma")
testing, alpha, beta, 13, gamma
```

When the function is run and Lua encounters the ... symbol, it replaces it with the list of arguments that were passed to the function. As a result, it can be used in the following ways:

```
-- Pass the arguments to another function
print(...)

-- Assign the arguments to variables
local var1, var2, var3 = ...

-- Construct a new table with the arguments
local tbl = {...}
```

The preceding example could be used to make a new function called newtable(), which takes in a set of arguments and makes a new table with those arguments in the array part of the table:

```
function newtable(...)
   return {...}
end
```

Test this function now:

```
> tbl = newtable("alpha", "beta", "gamma")
> for i=1, #tbl do
>> print(i, tbl[i])
>> end
1, alpha
2, beta
3, gamma
```

Using select() with ...

The `select()` function makes working with vararg functions very easy, because it can provide the number of arguments passed, as well as allow you to easily iterate through them without needing to assign them to variables. Consider the following function that takes a list of arguments and prints a line for each argument including the index and the argument itself:

```
function printargs(...)
  local num_args = select("#", ...)
  for i=1, num_args do
    local arg = select(i, ...)
    print(i, arg)
  end
end
```

Sample output:

```
> printargs("alpha", "beta", 13, "gamma")
1, alpha
2, beta
3, 13
4, gamma
```

This method lets you avoid creating a new table every single time, and allows the value `nil` to be passed as an argument. Remember that the length operator and the table library functions are only reliable when the array table does not contain any "holes" in the form of `nil` values. Run the following function definitions in your interpreter:

```
function test1(...)
  local tbl = {...}
  for i = 1, #tbl do
    print(i, tbl[i])
  end
end

function test2(...)
  for i = 1, select("#", ...) do
```

```
        print(i, (select(i, ...)))
    end
end
```

You can see an example of this issue by running the following:

```
> test1("alpha", "beta", "gamma", nil)
1, alpha
2, beta
3, gamma
> test2("alpha", "beta", "gamma", nil)
1, alpha
2, beta
3, gamma
4, nil
```

The first example stuffs the arguments into a table and then tries to get the length of the table. Because there is a nil value in the middle of the table, getting the length could return either two or four. This sort of unpredictability is specifically why you should use the second example.

In addition the first function needs to create a new table on each call, which will allocate and use more memory in the long run. The version using `select()` has no such hidden cost.

Generic for Loops and Iterators

Chapter 3 introduced the `for` statement, which allows you to repeat a computation over a series of numbers by supplying a start value, end value, and a value by which to increment the counter after each loop. Chapter 4 introduced storing data in both the array part and the hash part of Lua tables. Until this point there has been no way to *loop* through the elements of the hash part of the table, but Lua provides a more generic form of the `for` statement that, when combined with an iterator function, allows just that.

Wikipedia defines an *iterator* as "an object which allows a programmer to traverse through all elements of a collection, regardless of its specific implementation." In Lua specifically, you use an iterator function along with some extra information to loop through a collection.

Syntax of Generic for

The generic `for` loop syntax is a bit different than the numeric `for` loop:

```
for val1, val2, val3, ... in <expression> do
  -- body of for loop
end
```

A generic `for` loop can return many variables on each iteration (as many as defined by the iterator function, actually). Immediately after the `for` keyword, you supply a list of variable names that are used to store the returns on each iteration of the loop. The generic loop then determines what to traverse by evaluating `<expression>`, which should return the following three values:

- An iterator function that can be called on each iteration of the loop
- state, used by the iterator function on each subsequent call
- An initial value for the iterator value

Luckily, unless you plan to write your own iterator functions, you won't have to deal with any of this directly. A number of prewritten functions will create your iterators for you.

Traversing the Array Part of a Table

`ipairs()` is one such function that allows you to traverse the array part of a table without using the numeric `for` loop. Some programmers prefer this syntax to that of the numeric `for` loop. Run the following example:

```
> tbl = {"alpha", "beta", "gamma"}
> for idx, value in ipairs(tbl) do
>> print(idx, value)
>> end
1, alpha
2, beta
3, gamma
```

The `ipairs()` function takes a table and returns all the information the `for` loop requires to traverse the array part of the table, including the iterator function itself. Each call to the iterator function returns the numeric index of the element, and the element itself. These variables can be named whatever you'd like and, as always, are local to the scope of the `for` loop (meaning they cannot be accessed outside of that scope).

You can explore the `ipairs()` function a bit more by running the following in your interpreter:

```
> print(ipairs(tbl))
function: 0x300980, table: 0x3072c0, 0
> print(tbl)
table: 0x3072c0
```

It appears the `ipairs()` function returns an iterator function, the state (in this case it's just the table you passed in), and the initial value for the iterator (0). There's no real magic going on here, just a useful function allowing you to loop through array tables.

Traversing an Entire Table

Another function, called `pairs()`, allows you to traverse a table in its entirety, including both the array part and the hash table part. The usage is the same as `ipairs()`; just pass it the table and use it as part of a generic `for` loop:

```
> tbl = {"alpha", "beta", ["one"] = "uno", ["two"] = "dos"}
> for key, value in pairs(tbl) do
>> print(key, value)
>> end
1, alpha
2, beta
one, uno
two, dos
```

TRAVERSING USING PAIRS()

In the preceding example, the `pairs()` function seemed to traverse the table in the order the elements were added to the table, but this is just a coincidence. The specific order in which elements will be visited is unspecified by this function, even for numeric keys. If you specifically need to traverse the table's numeric elements in order, you should instead use the `ipairs()` function, which can guarantee this. The lack of order when using `pairs()` is due to the way hash tables are implemented, as a collection of associated key/value pairs with no internal order.

When using the `pairs()` function, you must ensure you don't add any elements to the table. This is because `pairs()` calls the `next()` function, which carries the following warning in the Lua 5.1 Reference Manual:

"The behavior of `next` is *undefined* if, during the traversal, you assign any value to a nonexistent field in the table. You may, however, modify existing fields. In particular, you may clear existing fields."

If you add an element to the table during the traversal, the iteration may simply not work, it may terminate early, or it may throw an error. It's important to keep this in mind when working with an iteration using `pairs()`.

In addition, you may encounter an error if you try to clear a key that was not previously set by assigning `nil` to it. This is due to the way tables are implemented. In general you should ensure you only ever assign to keys that existed prior to the iteration.

Clearing a Table

As stated in the Lua 5.1 Reference Manual for `next()`, you can clear the elements of a table while traversing it using `pairs()`. The following code will clear a table of all set elements:

```
for key, value in pairs(tbl) do
```

```
    tbl[key] = nil
end
```

Because `pairs()` works for all keys of a table, this is a quick way to ensure you've cleared all elements (in the event you need to re-use a table, for example). Note that this is different than just running `tbl = {}`, which would create a new table entirely, rather than clearing the existing table. You can see this by printing the value of the table before and after, and verifying that they are different:

```
> tbl = {"alpha", "beta", "gamma"}
> print(tbl)
table: 0x131800
> tbl = {}
table: 0x131ac0
```

Using Other Iterators

A number of other functions in Lua can be used to generate iterators that are extremely useful. The `string.gmatch()` function can be used with Lua pattern matching to create iterators over strings, and specific matches within that string. You learn more about this function and Lua pattern matching in Chapter 6, but here are some examples:

```
> for word in string.gmatch("These are some words", "%S+") do
>> print(word)
>> end
These
are
some
words
> for char in string.gmatch("Hello!", ".") do
>> print(char)
>> end
H
e
l
l
o
!
```

Sorting an Array of Table Data

The built-in `table.sort()` function only allows you to sort number and string data by default. Fortunately, `table.sort()` enables you to pass in a function to do the actual comparisons between elements, with the library function doing the overall sort based on the results of your function. This means you can write your own function to determine which of two tables is *bigger* when it comes to sorting.

Define Example Data

For the examples in this section you need some sample data to sort. Define the following in your Lua interpreter:

```
guild = {}

table.insert(guild, {
  name = "Cladhaire",
  class = "Rogue",
  level = 80,
})

table.insert(guild, {
  name = "Draoi",
  class = "Druid",
  level = 80,
})

table.insert(guild, {
  name = "Deathsquid",
  class = "Deathknight",
  level = 68,
})
```

Default Sort Order

By default, this list is sorted in the order it was inserted, because it's using the array part of the table. Run the following to verify this:

```
> for idx, value in ipairs(guild) do
>> print(idx, value.name)
>> end
1, Cladhaire
2, Draoi
3, Deathsquid
```

Rather than print `value` itself, which would show `table: 0x3003a0` instead of something meaningful, this code indexes the table and prints the value associated with the key `name`. This code segment could be altered to print the class, or the level if so desired.

Creating a Comparison Function

If you try to sort this data using `table.sort()`, you will get an error because Lua doesn't know how to compare table values (to determine what makes one table less than another).

```
> table.sort(guild)
attempt to compare two table values
```

```
stack traceback:
        [C]: in function 'sort'
        stdin:1: in main chunk
        [C]: ?
```

The `table.sort()` function takes a second argument specifically for this purpose, to allow the programmer to define how values should be compared. This function takes two arguments, and returns `true` if the first argument is less than the second argument, and false if the second argument is less than or equal to the first argument. That means you can sort two tables based on their member fields, or some other criteria you specify. Write the following function, which will compare two of the elements based on name:

```
function sortNameFunction(a, b)
  return a.name < b.name
end
```

Although the function is extremely short, that's all that is required to sort the array by name. Pass this function in as the second argument to `table.sort()`:

```
> table.sort(guild, sortNameFunction)
> for idx, value in ipairs(guild) do
>> print(idx, value.name)
>> end
1, Cladhaire
2, Deathsquid
3, Draoi
```

To reverse the sort order, just reverse the order of the comparison (note that the position of `b.name` and `a.name` in the comparison have changed):

```
function sortNameFunctionDesc(a, b)
  return b.name < a.name
end
```

Sort with this new function:

```
> table.sort(guild, sortNameFunctionDesc)
> for idx, value in ipairs(guild) do print(idx, value.name) end
1, Draoi
2, Deathsquid
3, Cladhaire
```

Creating a More Complex Sort Function

Assume you'd like to sort the preceding data by level and then by character name. You can write a function to sort by level, but there's no way to tell in what order it will put the two level 80 characters. The following comparison function accomplishes this more complex sort:

```
function sortLevelNameAsc(a, b)
  if a.level == b.level then
    return a.name < b.name
  end
  return a.level < b.level
end
```

All that is required is a simple check to see if the two levels are the same, and if they are, to compare the names of the characters. A sort function can be as complex as you need, as long as it returns true when the first argument should be sorted *less* than the second argument:

```
> table.sort(guild, sortLevelNameAsc)
> for idx,value in ipairs(guild) do print(idx, value.name, value.level) end
1, Deathsquid, 68
2, Cladhaire, 80
3, Draoi, 80
```

Summary

This chapter introduced the concepts of *vararg* functions, generic for loops, iterators, and sorting complex data in arrays. These concepts are relatively advanced, but come up often when designing and writing a new addon.

Lua Standard Libraries

Throughout the first part of this book, a number of Lua standard library functions have been introduced and used in code examples. Although this book does not cover every single Lua function included in the World of Warcraft implementation of Lua, this chapter introduces you to the some of the most prevalent functions that you will need when developing addons.

In addition to the Lua standard libraries, this chapter covers some functions specific to WoW that aren't really part of the game API itself. These functions are grouped at the end of the chapter.

NOTE The details in this chapter cover the parts of the Lua API that are most relevant to WoW. You can find a full reference for Lua online at `http://lua.org/manual/5.1`. This manual is also available in print: *Lua 5.1 Reference Manual* by R. Ierusalimschy, L. H. de Figueiredo, and W. Celes, Lua.org, August 2006 (ISBN 85-903798-3-3).

In addition, the chief architect of Lua has written an easy-to-read book about the Lua programming language that covers these (and more) functions in depth. You can find a version of this book written for an older version of Lua at `http://lua.org/pil`. If reading the older version is confusing, you can find the second edition at many online bookstores: *Programming in Lua* (second edition) by Roberto Ierusalimschy, Lua.org, March 2006 (ISBN 85-903798-2-5).

Each function is this chapter is presented with what is called the function's signature. A *function signature* describes what values are returned by the function, as well as what arguments are taken by the function. For example, consider the fictional function `foo()`:

```
someReturn = foo(arg1, arg2)
```

In this example, the function `foo()` takes two arguments (`arg1` and `arg2`) and returns a single value `someReturn`. These signatures can also indicate optional arguments, by enclosing them in square brackets:

```
somereturn = foo(arg1 [, arg2])
```

This notation indicates that the second argument to `foo()` is optional. When you see this, you should consult the description of the function and arguments to determine the behavior of the function because it varies.

Table Library

The table library provides several functions that allow you to easily add elements, remove elements, and sort array tables. In addition, a utility function is provided that works outside of the array part of the table, returning the maximum numeric index used in the table. The former functions all operate exclusively on the array part of the table, whereas the latter can be used on any type of table.

str = table.concat (table [, sep [, i [, j]]])

The `table.concat()` function concatenates all entries of the array part of a table, with an optional separator string sep. Given an array where all elements are strings or numbers, it returns `table[i]..sep..table[i+1] ...  sep..table[j]`. The default value for sep is the empty string, the default for i is 1, and the default for j is the length of the table. If i is greater than j, it returns the empty string.

```
> tbl = {"alpha", "beta", "gamma"}
> print(table.concat(tbl, ":"))
alpha:beta:gamma
> print(table.concat(tbl, nil, 1, 2))
alphabeta
> print(table.concat(tbl, "\n", 2, 3))
beta
gamma
```

This function is an easy way to print the elements of the array part of a table. As you can see, sep can be any string (including the newline character) because it's just concatenated with the entries in the table.

table.insert (table, [pos,] value)

The `table.insert()` function inserts a new element into the array, optionally at position pos, shifting other elements up to make space, if necessary. The default value for pos is n+1, where n is the length of the table. Therefore, a call of `table.insert(t,x)` inserts x at the end of table t.

```
> tbl = {"alpha", "beta", "gamma"}
> table.insert(tbl, "delta")
> table.insert(tbl, "epsilon")
> print(table.concat(tbl, ", "))
alpha, beta, gamma, delta, epsilon
> table.insert(tbl, 3, "zeta")
> print(table.concat(tbl, ", "))
alpha, beta, zeta, gamma, delta, epsilon
```

max = table.maxn (table)

The `table.maxn()` function returns the largest positive numerical index of the given table, or zero if the table has no positive numerical indices. To do its job, this function does a linear traversal of the entire table. Unlike most table functions, `table.maxn()` considers numerical keys instead of integer keys, so numerical constants and rational numbers are counted as well.

```
> tbl = {[1] = "a", [2] = "b", [3] = "c", [26] = "z"}
> print(#tbl)
3
> print(table.maxn(tbl))
26
> tbl[91.32] = true
> print(table.maxn(tbl))
91.32
```

value = table.remove (table [, pos])

The `table.remove()` function removes an element from the given table, shifting down other elements to close the space, if necessary. It returns the value of the removed element. The default value for `pos` is n, where n is the length of the table, so a call `table.remove(t)` removes the last element of table t.

```
> tbl = {"alpha", "beta", "gamma", "delta"}
> print(table.remove(tbl))
delta
> print(table.concat(tbl, ", "))
alpha, beta, gamma
```

table.sort (table [, comp])

The `table.sort()` function sorts the array part of a table by reordering the elements within the same table. If `comp` is given, it must be a function that receives two table elements and returns `true` when the first is less than the second (so that `not comp(a[i+1],a[i])` will be `true` after the sort for all `i`). If `comp` is not given, the standard Lua operator < is used instead.

This sort algorithm is not stable, which means that elements considered equal by the given comparison function may have their order changed by the sort.

```
> tbl = {"alpha", "beta", "gamma", "delta"}
> table.sort(tbl)
> print(table.concat(tbl, ", "))
alpha, beta, delta, gamma
> sortFunc = function(a,b) return b < a end
> table.sort(tbl, sortFunc)
> print(table.concat(tbl, ", "))
gamma, delta, beta, alpha
```

String Utility Functions

Lua provides several utility functions for working with and manipulating strings. Each of these functions is available as object-oriented method calls, as well as the library calls themselves. For example, the following two calls accomplish the same thing:

```
> str = "This is a string"
> print(string.len(str))
16
> print(str:len())
16
```

Table 6-1 describes the various utility functions and illustrates their use.

Table 6-1: String Utility Functions

FUNCTION	DESCRIPTION	EXAMPLE(S)
string.len(s)	Receives a string and returns its length. The empty string " " has length 0. Embedded zeros are counted, so "a\000bc\000" has length 5.	```> print(string.len("Monkey"))``` 5

string.lower(s)	Returns the input string with all uppercase letters changed to lowercase. All other characters are left unchanged. The definition of what an uppercase letter is depends on the current locale.	```> test = "Hello World!"```
		```> print(string.lower(test))```
		hello world!
		```> printtest:lower()```
		hello world!

FUNCTION	DESCRIPTION	EXAMPLE(S)

string.rep(s, n)	Returns a string that is the concatenation of n copies of the string s.	`> print(string.rep("Hello", 3))`
		`HelloHelloHello`
		`> test = "foo"`
		`> print(test:rep(3))`
		`foofoofoo`

string.reverse(s)	Returns a string that is the string s reversed.	`> print(string.reverse("Test"))`
		`tseT`
		`> test = "Hello World!"`
		`> print(test:reverse())`
		`!dlroW olleH`

string.sub(s, i [, j])	Returns the substring of s that starts at i and continues until j; i and j may be negative. If j is absent, it is assumed to be equal to -1 (which is the same as the string length). In particular, the call `string.sub(s,1,j)` returns a prefix of s with length j, and `string.sub(s, -i)` returns a suffix of s with length i.	`> test = "Hello World"`
		`> print(string.sub(test, 1, 3))`
		`Hel`
		`> print(test:sub(1, -1))`
		`Hello World`
		`> print(test:sub(-3, -1))`
		`rld`

string.upper(s)	Receives a string and returns a copy of this string with all lowercase letters changed to uppercase. All other characters are left unchanged. The definition of what a lowercase letter is depends on the current locale.	`> test = "Hello World!"`
		`> print(string.upper(test))`
		`HELLO WORLD!`
		`> print(test:upper())`
		`HELLO WORLD!`

Formatting New Strings

Throughout the book, you've used the concatenation operator to make new strings and format longer messages. This code to generate longer strings ends up being extremely difficult to read, and difficult to maintain. Lua provides a utility function called `string.format(formatstring, ...)` that will format a list of arguments according to a defined format.

A format string can contain literal characters and special conversion codes that are used along with the arguments to create the final result. Conversion codes begin with a percent sign (%) and contain one of the following specifiers that indicate what type of data the argument should be treated as:

- %c—Takes a number argument and formats it as the ASCII character that corresponds to the number.
- %d, %i—Takes a number argument and formats it as a signed integer.
- %o—Takes a number argument and formats it as an octal number.
- %u—Takes a number argument and formats it as an unsigned integer.
- %x—Takes a number argument and formats it as a hexadecimal number, using lowercase letters.
- %X—Takes a number argument and formats it as a hexadecimal number, using capital letters.
- %e—Takes a number argument and formats it as scientific notation, with a lowercase e.
- %E—Takes a number argument and formats it as scientific notation, with an uppercase E.
- %f—Takes a number argument and formats it as a floating-point number.
- %g and %G—Takes a number and formats it according to either %e (or %E if %G is specified) or %f, depending on which is shortest.
- %q—Formats a string so it can safely be read back into a Lua interpreter.
- %s—Takes a string and formats it according to the supplied options.

Several options can be used in a conversion specification between the percent sign and the type specifier. The following options can be included, in this specific order:

1. Sign specification (either a + or a −) that causes a sign to be printed with any number. By default, the sign is only printed with negative numbers.

2. A padding character (either a space, or a 0) that will be used when padding the result to the correct string width. By default, any results will be padded with spaces to meet the correct width, if specified.

3. An alignment specification that causes the result to be left-justified or right-justified. The default is right-justification, whereas a − character will make the result left-justified.

4. A width specification that specifies the minimum width of the resulting string.

5. A precision specification that dictates how many decimal digits should be displayed when formatting a floating-point number. When specified for strings, the resulting string will be cut off at this number of characters.

Confused yet? More often than not, you'll only use a very small subset of these options, but it's good to understand the abilities and limitations of the string formatting system. The examples in Table 6-2 should help clarify the basics of string formatting.

Table 6-2: Example Format Strings

COMMAND	RESULT
`string.format("%%c: %c", 83)`	`%c: S`
`string.format("%+d", 17.0)`	`+17`
`string.format("%05d", 17)`	`00017`
`string.format("%o", 17)`	`21`
`string.format("%u", 3.14)`	`3`
`string.format("%x", 13)`	`D`
`string.format("%X", 13)`	`D`
`string.format("%e", 1000)`	`1.000000e+03`
`string.format("%E", 1000)`	`1.000000E+03`
`string.format("%6.3f", 13)`	`13.000`
`string.format("%q", [["One", "Two"]])`	`"\"One\", \"Two\""`
`string.format("%s", "monkey")`	`monkey`
`string.format("%10s", "monkey")`	`monkey`
`string.format("%5.3s", "monkey")`	`mon`

IN WORLD OF WARCRAFT

WoW includes an extra option for `string.format()` **that allows you to choose a specific argument from the argument list, rather than having them in consecutive order. This option is not included in standard Lua 5.1, so you will need to use one of the interpreters provided on the book's website (**`http://wowprogramming.com/utils`**) to test this. If you are using the WoWLua addon, it should work correctly.**

To select a specific argument, include the number of the argument, followed by the dollar sign ($), immediately after the percent sign (%). For example:

```
> print(string.format("%2$d, %1$d, %d", 13, 17))
17, 13, 17
```

The first type identifier is modified to request the second argument, and the second identifier consumes the second argument to the format string. When selecting parameters in this way, you can't skip any and leave them unused.

(continued)

IN WORLD OF WARCRAFT *(continued)*

If you use parameters 1 and 3, you must also use parameter 2. You can mix parameter selection and normal type identifiers in the same format string without any issues.

WoW specifically includes this functionality to provide support for multiple languages. For example, the following string appears in English:

```
Cladhaire's Shadow Word: Pain is removed.
```

In German, the phrase used in this same situation is:

```
'Shadow Word: Pain' von Cladhaire wurde entfernt.
```

As you can see, the order of the arguments is swapped based on the way the phrase is constructed for German clients. Without parameter selection, WoW would have to handle each of these cases specifically, which would get very messy. Instead, the client uses string.format() along with parameter selection to craft these messages.

The English format string is `"%s's %s is removed."`, and the German format string is `"'%2$s' von %1$s wurde entfernt."`. Rather than maintain a long list of special messages, format strings are used to make the client consistent.

Pattern Matching

A common theme you will find when writing addons is the need to match and parse text supplied by the game against a given pattern. Lua provides a number of utility functions to accomplish these tasks. These functions can use patterns to describe what to search for when matching against a given string.

Character Classes

Patterns can use any of the character classes described in Table 6-3. Each class is designed to match a subset of all characters in a specific way. For example, the character class `%s` can be used to match any whitespace character, and `%a` can be used to represent any letter.

In addition, with any of the character classes that have a percent sign followed by a letter, the letter can be changed to uppercase to serve as a shortcut for the complement to the character class. In other words, `%s` will match any character that is not a space, and `%A` will match any character that is not a letter.

Take a look at some examples. Given the test string `"abc ABC 123 !@# \n \000 %"`, Table 6-4 shows what will be matched by a given pattern.

Table 6-3: Character Classes

CLASS	MATCHES
x (where x is not one of the magic characters ^ $()%.[]*+-?)	The character x itself.
. (period, or full stop)	Any character.
%a	Any letter.
%c	Any control character.
%d	Any digit.
%l	Any lowercase letter.
%p	Any punctuation character.
%s	Any space character.
%u	Any uppercase letter.
%w	Any alphanumeric character.
%x	Any hexadecimal digit.
%z	The character with representation 0 (for example,\000).
%x (where x is any non-alphanumeric character)	Represents the character x. This is the standard way to escape the magic characters. Any punctuation character (even the non-magic ones) can be preceded by a % when used to represent itself in a pattern. For example, to include a percent sign in the resulting string you would include %% in the format string.
[set]	Any characters included in set, which can be specified as a range of characters by listing the range with a hyphen (such as A-Z). All classes defined in this table may also be used as a part of set, including the other characters, which just represent themselves. For example, [%w_] matches all alphanumeric characters plus the underscore character, and [0-9%l%-] matches all digits plus the lowercase letters and the - character.
[^set]	The complement of any set (as previously defined). Therefore, [^%s] matches any non-space character.

Table 6-4: Example Patterns

PATTERN	STRING MATCHED
"a"	a
"."	a
"%a"	a
"%c"	\n
"%d"	1
%l"	a
%p	!
%s	space
%u	A
%w	a
%x	a
%z	\000
%%	%

Pattern Items

Each of the character classes previously defined can be used in the pattern items described in Table 6-5.

Table 6-5: Using Pattern Items

PATTERN	MATCHES
A single character class followed by a -	Zero or more repetitions of characters in the class. Unlike *, these repetition items always match the shortest possible sequence.
A single character class	Any single character in the class.
A single character class followed by an *	Zero or more repetitions of a character in the class. These repetition items always match the longest possible sequence.
A single character class followed by a +	One or more repetitions of characters in the class. These repetition items always match the longest possible sequence.
A single character class followed by a ?	Zero or one occurrence of a character in the class. This will always match one occurrence if it is possible to do so.

PATTERN	MATCHES
%n	For n between 1 and 9; matches a substring equal to the nth captured string (see the section later in this chapter on captures).
%bxy, where x and y are two distinct characters	Strings that start with x, end with y, and where the x and y are balanced. This means that if you read the string from left to right, counting +1 for an x and -1 for a y, the ending y is the first y where the count reaches 0. For instance, the item %b() matches expressions with balanced parentheses.

These pattern items can be very simple to use when you need to match a specific part of a string in a very general way. Table 6-6 gives a number of example patterns and the corresponding matches when run against the string `"abc ABC 123 !@# \n \000 %"`.

Table 6-6: Example Patterns

PATTERN	STRING MATCHED
%a	a
%a*	abc
%a+	abc
%a-	no string matched
%a-%s	abc
%a?	a
%ba3	abc ABC 123

Pattern Captures

A pattern can contain sub-patterns enclosed in parentheses, called *captures*. When a match succeeds, the part of the pattern enclosed in parentheses is stored (captured) for future use. Captures are numbered according to the order of their left parenthesis because they can be nested. For instance, in the pattern `"(a*(.)%w(%s*))"`, the part of the string matching `"a*(.)%w(%s*)"` is stored as the first capture (with number 1); the character matching `"."` is captured as number 2, and the part matching `"%s*"` has number 3.

Additionally, the empty capture `()` captures the current string position (a number). For instance, if you apply the pattern `"()aa()"` on the string `"flaaap"`, there will be two captures, the number 3 and the number 5.

Pattern Anchors

A pattern is quite literally a sequence of characters to be matched. Using ^ at the beginning of a pattern can match the beginning of a string, whereas using $ at the end of a pattern can match the end of a string. When used anywhere else in the pattern, these strings will match their literal equivalent. Anchors can be used to make a pattern more explicit.

Pattern Examples

Table 6-7 illustrates a number of common requirements for pattern matching and shows what that pattern might look like. These are general examples and may only work in specific cases.

Table 6-7: Example Patterns

REQUIREMENT	PATTERN
Match a non-space token in a string.	`"%S+"`
Match a string beginning with the text MYADDON: followed by at least one character, capturing the rest of the string.	`"^MYADDON:(.+)"`
Match a number, optionally with a fractional part after a decimal point, capturing the entire number. The number can be positive or negative.	`"(%-?%d+%.?%d*)"`
Match an assignment in the form xxxx=yyyy, where xxxx is alphanumeric and yyyy contains no spaces, and capture each individually.	`"(%w+)=(%S+)"`
Match a single quoted string, such as `'foo'` and `'bar'`.	`"%b''"`
Match the last nonspace token in a string.	`"%S+$"`

Pattern Matching Functions

Lua provides four functions that accept pattern strings:

- `string.gmatch(s, pattern)`
- `string.gsub(s, pattern, repl [, n])`
- `string.match(s, pattern [, init])`
- `string.find(s, pattern [, init [, plain]])`

These functions are also available as object-oriented method calls on the string itself, as with the utility functions discussed earlier. Each of them accomplishes a different task for strings, as you'll see.

string.gmatch(s, pattern)

The `string.gmatch(s, pattern)` function returns an iterator function that, each time it is called, returns the next set of captures from `pattern` over string `s`. If `pattern` specifies no captures, the entire match is produced in each call.

For example, the following loop iterates over all the words from string `s`, printing one per line:

```
> s = "hello world from Lua"
> for word in string.gmatch(s, "%a+") do
>> print(word)
>> end
hello
world
from
Lua
```

And here's an example that collects all sets of key=value pairs from the given string into a table:

```
> t = {}
> s = "from=world, to=Lua"
> for k, v in string.gmatch(s, "(%w+)=(%w+)") do
>> t[k] = v
>> end
> for k,v in pairs(t) do
>> print(k, v)
>> end
to, Lua
from, world
```

When working with `string.gmatch()`, remember that the pattern is designed to potentially match more than one occurrence, so the pattern shouldn't be anchored too heavily (in particular, using the ˆ and $ anchors would make the preceding example work incorrectly).

string.gsub(s, pattern, repl [, n])

The `string.gsub(s, pattern, repl [, n])` function returns a copy of `s` in which all (or the first `n`, if given) occurrences of the pattern have been replaced by a replacement string specified by `repl`, which may be a string, a table, or a function. `string.gsub()` also returns as its second value the total number of matches that occurred.

If `repl` is a string, its value is used for replacement. The character `%` works as an escape character: any sequence in `repl` of the form `%n`, with `n` between 1 and 9, stands for the value of the nth captured substring (see the following example). The sequence `%0` stands for the whole match. The sequence `%%` stands for a single %.

If `repl` is a table, the table is queried for every match, using the first capture as the key; if the pattern specifies no captures, the whole match is used as the key.

If `repl` is a function, this function is called every time a match occurs, with all captured substrings passed as arguments, in order. If the pattern specifies no captures, the whole match is passed as the argument.

If the value returned by the table query or by the function call is a string or a number, it is used as the replacement string; otherwise, if it is `false` or `nil`, there is no replacement (that is, the original match is kept in the string).

Here are some examples:

```
> print(string.gsub("hello world", "(%w+)", "%1 %1"))
hello hello world world, 2
> print(string.gsub("hello world", "%w+", "%0 %0", 1))
hello hello world, 1
> print(string.gsub("hello Lua", "(%w+)%s*(%w+)", "%2 %1"))
Lua hello, 1
> lookupTable = {["hello"] = "hola", ["world"] = "mundo"}
> function lookupFunc(pattern)
>> return lookupTable[pattern]
>> end
> print(string.gsub("hello world", "(%w+)", lookupTable))
hola mundo, 2
> print(string.gsub("hello world", "(%w+)", lookupFunc))
hola mundo, 2
```

string.match(s, pattern [, init])

The `string.match(s, pattern [, init])` function looks for the first match of `pattern` in the string `s`. If it finds one, the match returns the captures from the pattern; otherwise, it returns `nil`. If `pattern` specifies no captures, the whole match is returned. A third, optional numerical argument—`init`—specifies where to start the search; its default value is `1` and may be negative.

string.find(s, pattern [, init [, plain]])

The `string.find(s, pattern [, init [, plain]])` function looks for the first match of `pattern` in the string `s`. If it finds a match, find returns the indices of `s` where this occurrence starts and ends; otherwise, it returns `nil`. A third, optional numerical argument—init—specifies where to start the search; its default value is 1 and may be negative. A value of `true` as a fourth, optional argument, `plain`, turns off the pattern matching facilities, so the function does a plain "find substring" operation, with no characters in pattern being considered "magic." Note that if `plain` is given, `init` must also be given.

If the pattern has captures, then in a successful match the captured values are also returned, after the two indices.

Math Library

The math library provides an interface to several standard math functions and constants. Table 6-8 describes some of the more common functions in the math library. (It is not a full listing of the library; for that, please consult a proper Lua reference, which includes a full set of trigonometric functions such as math.cos, math.sin, math.tan, and so on.)

Table 6-8: Math Functions

FUNCTION	DESCRIPTION	EXAMPLE

`math.abs(x)`	Returns the absolute value of x.	`> print(math.abs(13))`
		`13`
		`> print(math.abs(-13))`
		`13`

`math.ceil(x)`	Returns the smallest integer larger than or equal to x.	`> print(math.ceil(1.03))`
		`2`
		`> print(math.cell(13))`
		`13`
		`> print(math.cell(17.99))`
		`18`

`math.deg(x)`	Returns the angle x (given in radians) in degrees.	`> print(math.deg(math.pi))`
		`180`
		`> print(math.deg(math.pi * 2.5))`
		`450`

`math.exp(x)`	Returns the value of the mathematical constant e raised to the x power.	`> print(math.exp(27))` `532048240601.8`

`math.floor(x)`	Returns the largest integer smaller than or equal to x.	`> print(math.floor(1.03))`
		`1`
		`> print(math.floor(13.0))`
		`13`
		`> print(math.floor(17.99))`
		`17`

Continued

Table 6-8: (*continued*)

FUNCTION	DESCRIPTION	EXAMPLE

`math.fmod(x, y)`	Returns the remainder of the division of x by y, rounding the quotient toward zero.	`> print(math.fmod(14, 3))`
		`2`
		`> (print(math.fmod(14, 2))`
		`0`

`math.log(x)`	Returns the natural logarithm of x.	`> print(math.log(532048240601.8))` `27`
`math.log10(x)`	Returns the base-10 logarithm of x.	`> print(math.log10(10^2))` `2`
`math.max(x, y, z, ...)`	Returns the maximum value among its arguments.	`> print(math.max(-13, 7, 32))` `32`
`math.min(x, y, z, ...)`	Returns the minimum value among its arguments.	`> print(math.min(-13, 7, 32, 17))` `-13`

`math.modf(x)`	Returns two numbers, the integral part of x and the fractional part of x.	`> print(math.modf(10.23))`
		`10, 0.23`
		`> print(math.modf(7/22))`
		`0, 0.31818181818182)`

`math.pi`	The value of the mathematical constant pi.	`> print(math.pi)` `3.1415926535898`

`math.pow(x, y)`	Returns x raised to the y power. (You can also use the expression x^y to compute this value.)	`> print(math.pow(2, 10))`
		`1024`
		`> print(math.pow(2, -10))`
		`0.0009765625`

`math.rad(x)`	Returns the angle x (given in degrees) in radians.	`> print(math.rad(180))`
		`3.1415926535898`
		`> print(math.rad(180) == math.pi)`
		`true`
		`> print(math.rad(450))`
		`7.8539816339745`

`math.random([m [, n]])`	Generates pseudo-random numbers. The numbers generated may not be sufficient for statistical analysis but provide an easy way to create pseudo-randomness in	`> print(math.random())`
		`7.8263692594256e-06`
		`> print(math.random(100))`
		`14`
		`> print(math.random(10, 20))`
		`18`

FUNCTION	DESCRIPTION	EXAMPLE
	a program. For example, this function can be used along with the `SendChatMessage()` World of Warcraft API function to allow your character to make random sayings based on certain events. When called without arguments, returns a pseudo-random real number between 0 and 1 (not including 1). When called with a number `m`, returns a pseudo-random integer between and including 1 and `m`. When called with two numbers `m` and `n`, returns a pseudo-random integer between and including `m` and `n`.	

`math.randomseed (x)`	The pseudo-random number generator used by Lua takes an initial seed and generates a sequence of numbers based on that seed. As a result, the same initial seed will always produce the same sequence. This function has been removed from the Lua implementation in World of Warcraft, but is listed here for completeness.	```> math.randomseed(1000)```
		 ```> print(math.random(100))```
		 ```1```
		 ```> print(math.random(100))```
		 ```54```
		 ```> print(math.random(100))```
		 ```61```
		 ```> -- reset the seed```
		 ```> math.randomseed(1000)```
		 ```> print(math.random(100))```
		 ```1```
		 ```> print(math.random(100))```
		 ```54```
		 ```> print(math.random(100))```
		 ```61```

`math.sqrt(x)`	Returns the square root of `x`. (You can also use the expression $x \wedge 0.5$ to compute this value.)	```> print(math.sqrt(169)```
		 ```13```
		 ```> print(math.sqrt(2))```
		 ```1.4142135623731```
		 ```> print(2 ^ 0.5)```
		 ```1.4142135623731```

NOTE Lua doesn't include a `math.round()` function because there are so many possible variations on what it means to "round" a number. `http://lua-users.org/wiki/SimpleRound` shows how to implement the following function, which rounds a number to a given decimal place:

```
function round(num, idp)
  local mult = 10^(idp or 0)
  return math.floor(num * mult + 0.5) / mult
end
```

World of Warcraft Additions to Lua

Several functions have been added to the Lua implementation in WoW as utility functions for developers:

- `strsplit(sep, str)`
- `strjoin(sep, ...)`
- `strconcat(...)`
- `getglobal(name)`
- `setglobal(name, value)`
- `debugstack([start[, count1[, count2]]])`

These functions are available in the WowLua addon, on the WebLua webpage, and in the interpreters that are available for download via the book's companion website. They may not be available in Lua distributions obtained elsewhere.

`strsplit(sep, str)` takes a given string `str` and splits it into separate strings on each occurrence of any character in the separator string `sep`. This function returns each individual string (with separator characters removed) to the caller.

```
> print(strsplit(":", "foo:bar:blah"))
foo, bar, blah
> print(strsplit(" ", "This is a string"))
This, is, a, string
```

The `strjoin(sep, ...)` function takes a list of strings and concatenates them together with the separator string `sep`, returning the result.

```
> print(strjoin(" ", "This", "is", "a", "test", "string"))
This is a test string
> print(strjoin(", ", "alpha", "beta", "gamma"))
alpha, beta, gamma
```

The `strconcat(...)` function takes a list of strings and concatenates them together into one long string, which is returned.

```
> print(strconcat("This", "is", "a", "test"))
Thisisatest
```

```
> print(strconcat("alpha:", "beta:", "gamma"))
alpha:beta:gamma
```

getglobal(name) takes a variable name as a string and returns the so-named global variable, if it exists. This function is deprecated in World of Warcraft, meaning it should no longer be used but has not yet been removed. It is included, along with setglobal, in case you see it in code from older addons.

```
> greek1, greek2, greek3 = "alpha", "beta", "gamma"
> for i=1,3 do
>> print(getglobal("greek" .. i))
>> end
alpha
beta
gamma
```

The setglobal(name, value) function takes a variable name as a string, along with a corresponding value, and sets the so-named global variable to the new value.

```
> print(myVariable)
nil
> setglobal("myVariable", 17)
> print(myVariable)
17
```

The debugstack([start[, count1[, count2]]]) function returns the current calling stack according to three inputs, as described in Table 6-9.

Table 6-9: debugstack Inputs

INPUT	TYPE	DESCRIPTION
start	Number	The stack depth at which to start the stack trace (defaults to 1, the function calling debugstack)
count1	Number	The number of functions to output at the top of the stack (default 12)
count2	Number	The number of functions to output at the bottom of the stack (default 10)

This function only operates correctly in WoW. The standalone Lua interpreter has its own method of providing stack traces.

Function Aliases

In World of Warcraft, many of the library functions have been given shorter aliases so they are easier to access and type. Table 6-10 contains a full listing of these aliases.

Table 6-10: Global Aliases

ALIAS	ORIGINAL FUNCTION	ALIAS	ORIGINAL FUNCTION
abs	math.abs	gsub	string.gsub
ceil	math.ceil	strbyte	string.byte
cos	math.cos	strchar	string.char
deg	math.deg	strfind	string.find
exp	math.exp	strlen	string.len
floor	math.floor	strlower	string.lower
frexp	math.frexp	strmatch	string.match
ldexp	math.ldexp	strrep	string.rep
log	math.log	strrev	string.reverse
max	math.max	strsub	string.sub
min	math.min	strupper	string.upper
mod	math.fmod	foreach	table.foreach
rad	math.rad	foreachi	table.foreachi
random	math.random	getn	table.getn
randomseed	math.randomseed	sort	table.sort
sqrt	math.sqrt	tinsert	table.insert
format	string.format	tremove	table.remove
gmatch	string.gmatch		

Summary

Lua has three major libraries that contain utility functions. The table library provides ways to insert, remove, and sort array tables; the string library has a number of useful utilities for tasks such as turning a string into all lowercase, uppercase, or even reversing the string. In addition to these utility functions, this chapter introduced the basics of Lua pattern matching and string formatting using `string.format()`, `string.match()`, and `string.find()`.

Learning XML

As mentioned in Chapter 1, you use two languages to build user interfaces for World of Warcraft. You have already been introduced to Lua, the programming language that defines the behavior of the interface, but you haven't yet tackled eXtensible Markup Language (XML), used to create the graphical frames that comprise WoW's user interface. That's what this chapter is all about.

XML as a Markup Language

A markup language takes text content and adds extra information to the document, mixing it in with the text itself. The markup typically describes something about the text itself, such as the structure of the document or how the text should be displayed on screen. Following are examples of two notable markup languages, HTML and LaTeX:

HTML

```
<html>
  <head>
    <title>My Document</title>
  </head>
  <body>
    <h1>Heading One</h1>
      <p>
        This text is <strong>bold</strong>.
      </p>
  </body>
</html>
```

LaTeX

```
\documentclass{article}
\title{My Document}
\begin{document}
\maketitle
\section{Heading One}
This text is \textbf{bold}.
\end{document}
```

Each of these examples provides basic information about the structure of the content by creating new headings and sections, and delimiting the actual body of the document. In addition, the `<strong>` and `\textbf{}` tags are intermixed with the text to indicate that a specific word should be displayed in a bold face font.

XML's Relationship to HTML

Whereas HTML is a markup language describing presentation with a minimal amount of structural information, XML is entirely a structural language, describing the relationship between elements but providing no cues about how they should be presented. Consider this example XML document:

```
<addressbook name="Personal">
  <entry>
    <firstname>Alice</firstname>
    <lastname>Applebaum</lastname>
    <phone>+1-212-555-1434</phone>
    <address>
       114 Auburn Street
       Apt 14
       Atlanta, GA
    </address>
  </entry>
</addressbook>
```

Unlike the earlier HTML example, this has no presentation cues, and most applications wouldn't know how to display this information. An XML document typically structures information according to some set of rules (such as a schema definition, which you will explore later this chapter). In short, XML is a cousin of the HTML standard that is generalized for multiple uses, and is stricter in its syntax and structure.

Components of XML

XML is designed to be both human-readable and computer-readable, so it has a strict required structure. An XML document includes tags, elements, attributes, and entities, each of which is discussed in the following sections.

XML Tags

An XML tag is an identifier that begins and ends with angle brackets, such as `<tag>`. The tags are case-sensitive, so `<Tag>` is a different tag name than `<tag>`. A closing tag is the same as an opening tag, but has a forward slash immediately after the open bracket, such as `</tag>`. The XML standard doesn't define any specific tags, only the rules defining how and when tags should appear.

XML Elements

Elements are the lowest level of structure and content in an XML document, taking some content and enclosing it in a set of open/close tags. A basic element from the earlier XML example is the `<entry></entry>` section, which defines an XML element with the name `entry`. An XML element can contain any type of content, including more markup. Elements are governed by the following rules:

- A nonempty element must begin with an opening tag and end with a closing tag.
- An element with no content can either be delimited with start/end tags or be a self-closing tag. A self-closing tag has a forward slash immediately before the closing angle bracket, such as `<tag />` or `<tag/>`.

Again, the XML standard doesn't really define any element types or tags, but merely describes how the document should be structured so it conforms to the standard.

XML Attributes

In addition to containing generic content, each XML element can have any number of attributes, which are named values belonging to that element. An attribute is declared in the start tag (or the self-closing tag, if used) like this:

```
<tag attribute="value"></tag>
```

Attributes can have any name, but the XML standard requires that all values be quoted using either balanced single quotes or balanced double quotes. This ensures that any program conforming to the XML standards can parse the document.

Unlike an element's content, which describes more of a parent/child relationship, attributes describe something specific about the element, such as the name of the element. The `addressbook` element has the name `Personal`, so it can be distinguished easily from any other `addressbook` that has been defined. The distinction isn't made through the XML standard but is extremely useful when parsing and validating an XML document.

XML Entities

The XML specification forbids the ampersand (&) and the less-than sign (<) from appearing within an element. In addition it might be confusing to see single quotes (') , double quotes (") and the greater than sign (>) in a document. To compensate for this, XML provides a number of escaped entities that can be included in the place of these characters. Table 7-1 shows a list of the most common XML entities:

Table 7-1: XML Entities

CHARACTER	EQUIVALENT ENTITY
&	&
<	<
>	>
"	"
'	'

Creating Well-Formed XML

A well-formed XML document is one that is valid and parsable from a syntactic point of view; that is, it follows all the required rules defined by the standard. Before jumping into the rules for a well-formed document, look at the definitions of root and non-root elements:

- **Root element:** A root element is an element that is not nested within another element. The first element in an XML file is the only root element.

- **Non-root element:** An element that is nested within another element.

For a document to be well formed, it must comply with the following:

- Any non-empty elements begin with a start tag and end with an end tag.

- Empty elements may either be delimited with start and end tags or be marked as a self-closing element.

- All attribute values are quoted with balanced single or double quotes.

- Tags may be nested, but must not overlap. In particular, each non-root element must be contained entirely within another element. This disallows something like `<b>Some <i>Text</b></i>`, because the `<i>` element is not contained entirely within another element.

Checking the syntax of an XML document can be as simple as opening it in your favorite web browser, although more specialized tools are available. Most modern browsers are XML-capable and can tell you which line of the document failed. In addition, you can use the XMLValidate utility on the book's web page (`http://wowprogramming.com/utils/xmlvalidate.`) to see whether your document is well formed.

Validating an XML Document

The XML format itself describes the syntax of the language—that is, the rules that make an XML document well-formed—but doesn't delve into the semantics, such as what attributes can belong to a given element, and what relationships can exist between given elements.

One method of describing the semantics of a given XML document is a schema definition. These definitions can come in a few forms, such as:

- Document Type Definition (DTD), a format native to XML.
- XML Schema, a W3C standard for declaring a schema.
- RELAX NG, a simple schema language available in XML formats as well as a shorter version.

World of Warcraft defines its schema using the XML Schema standard. The following section of the chapter focuses on this standard, and how to read it and use it for validating your files.

Example Schema Definition

The following is a simple XML Schema definition for an address book:

```
<xs:schema
  xmlns:xs="http://www.w3.org/2001/XMLSchema">
  <xs:element name="addressbook" type="AddressBook"/>
  <xs:complexType name="AddressBook">
    <xs:sequence>
      <xs:element name="name" type="xs:string"/>
      <xs:element name="phone" type="xs:string"/>
      <xs:element name="address" type="xs:string"/>
    </xs:sequence>
  </xs:complexType>
</xs:schema>
```

The initial line is standard for declaring a schema; it simply points to the standard document for the W3C definition of the XML Schema definition. The second tag defines a new element named `addressbook`, creating a new `<addressbook>` tag, and associating it with the named type `AddressBook`. The rest of the sequence defines what it means to be of type `AddressBook`, namely a sequence of four different named elements that is simply string content.

Example XML Document

The following is a file that declares its schema to exist in the file `addressbook.xsd`. Assuming both files are in the same directory, this file can be validated against the schema directly:

```
<addressbook
   xmlns:xsi="http://www.w3.org/2001/XMLSchema-instance"
   xsi:noNamespaceSchemaLocation="addressbook.xsd">
   <name>Alice Applebaum</name>
   <phone>+1-212-555-1434</phone>
   <address>
      114 Auburn Street
      Apt 14.
      Atlanta, GA
   </address>
</addressbook>
```

You can use a number of utilities to validate an XML schema on different platforms:

- XMLNanny (MacOSX), `www.xmlnanny.com`
- Microsoft Visual Studio (Windows), `www.microsoft.com/express`
- XMLSpy, `www.altova.com/xml-editor`
- Decision Soft's Online XML Validator, `http://tools.decisionsoft.com/ schemaValidate`

Figure 7-1 shows this XML document being validated against the given schema using XMLNanny. In addition to these downloadable tools there is a very simple web-based validator that you can use at `http:// wowprogramming.com/utils/xmlvalidate`.

The document passes the validation step because it's been structured correctly and the schema has been followed exactly. As a matter of fact, the example schema requires the elements of `<addressbook>` to appear in the exact order shown. If you were to swap the order of `<name>` and `<phone>`, the document would no longer validate. To add the elements in any order, as long as you include them all, you can change the `<xs:sequence>` and its matching close tag to read `<xs:all>`.

Exploring the Schema

One advantage of a strict markup like XML being used for layout is that all the information necessary to write complex layouts is contained within the schema itself. The schema reveals to you all of the valid options for any given tag or attribute. In addition, a number of tools are available to make it easier for you to edit XML files.

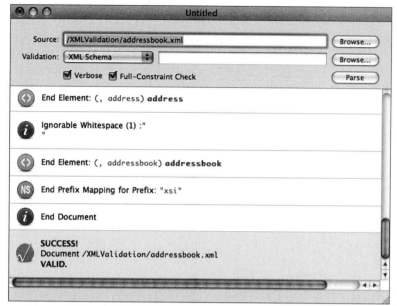

Figure 7-1: Validating with XMLNanny

For example, XMLSpy, Visual Studio, and other XML editors can provide auto-complete when you're creating a new file, so attribute names are automatically completed, and some editors even give you dropdowns to select the values when they are defined.

XML in World of Warcraft

The WoW user interface has an incredibly detailed XML schema that dictates exactly what tags, attributes, and values are valid when defining frames. To better understand how everything is structured, you can unpack the latest XML schema following the directions given in Chapter 8. It will extract to the `Blizzard Interface Data (enUS)/FrameXML/UI.xsd` file under your WoW installation, where `enUS` is your locale. Here's an excerpt from the file:

```
<xs:simpleType name="ORIENTATION">
  <xs:restriction base="xs:NMTOKEN">
    <xs:enumeration value="HORIZONTAL"/>
    <xs:enumeration value="VERTICAL"/>
  </xs:restriction>
</xs:simpleType>

<xs:simpleType name="ColorFloat">
  <xs:restriction base="xs:float">
    <xs:minInclusive value="0.0"/>
```

```
      <xs:maxInclusive value="1.0"/>
    </xs:restriction>
</xs:simpleType>

<xs:complexType name="ColorType">
  <xs:attribute name="r" type="ColorFloat" use="required"/>
  <xs:attribute name="g" type="ColorFloat" use="required"/>
  <xs:attribute name="b" type="ColorFloat" use="required"/>
  <xs:attribute name="a" type="ColorFloat" default="1.0"/>
</xs:complexType>

<xs:complexType name="GradientType">
  <xs:sequence>
    <xs:element name="MinColor" type="ColorType"/>
    <xs:element name="MaxColor" type="ColorType"/>
  </xs:sequence>
  <xs:attribute name="orientation" type="ORIENTATION" default="HORIZONTAL"/>
</xs:complexType>
```

This excerpt from the WoW XML schema defines a series of types that are used later in the schema, along with attributes and valid values. The first block defines a new type called ORIENTATION. This value is an enumeration, which means it must be one of the listed values, specifically HORIZONTAL or VERTICAL.

The second block defines a new type called ColorFloat, which must be a floating-point number. In this case, it must be between the values 0.0 and 1.0 inclusive. Next, a complex type called ColorType is defined; it has three required attributes and one optional attribute. Any element of this type must supply values for r, g, and b (which must conform to the rules for ColorFloat), and may optionally provide a value for a. These correspond to the red, green, blue, and alpha values of a given color.

Finally, a complex type GradientType is defined; it takes exactly two items in sequence, a <MinColor> tag and a <MaxColor> tag, both of type ColorType. Additionally, this tag can take an orientation attribute, described earlier.

Using a GradientType

Assuming there is a <Gradient> tag with the type GradientType defined somewhere, the following would be a valid usage of this schema:

```
<Gradient orientation="VERTICAL">
  <MinColor r="1.0" g="0.0" b="0.3" a="1.0"/>
  <MaxColor r="0.0" g="0.0" b="0.0" a="1.0">
</Gradient>
```

When used as part of a texture in the game, this appears as a gradient from red to black, with the gradient traveling vertically. This is exactly how the `<Gradient>` tag should be used.

Exploring Blizzard's XML User Interface Customization Tool

Blizzard has provided us with a tool to extract the XML files that comprise the default user interface. To extract it, you must download the User Interface Customization tool from `http://www.worldofwarcraft.com/ui`. This website contains versions for Microsoft Windows as well as for Mac OS X. Once you've downloaded the file, extract the program and run it. On loading, you'll see the screen shown in Figure 7-2.

You have two options:

- Install Interface Data—Extracts all of the code that defines the default user interface, the XML schema that defines the markup, as well as two tutorial addons with step-by-step descriptions.
- Install Interface Art—Extracts all the graphics files that are used in the default interface, such as icons, border textures, and so on.

If you choose to extract the interface data, the following two subdirectories will be created in your World of Warcraft directory:

- Blizzard Interface Data (enUS)
- Blizzard Interface Tutorial

If you extract the interface art, the following subdirectory is created:

- Blizzard Interface Art (enUS)

You may find that your directories extract with a different directory name. The enUS in the example stands for U.S. English, the language that the interface files use. If you use a German WoW client, you may instead see deDE, for example. You learn more about localization a little later in the book.

The Blizzard Interface Data directory contains two subdirectories, FrameXML and AddOns. The files contained in FrameXML are loaded each time the client starts, whereas the files in the AddOns directory are loaded under certain circumstances (see the listing in Chapter 1 for more information).

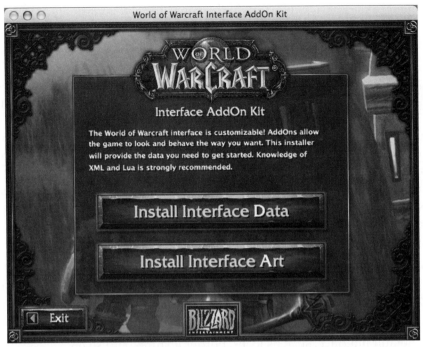

Figure 7-2: User Interface Customization tool

BLIZZARD INTERFACE ART

Although Blizzard provides a way to extract the art that is used throughout the game, the graphics files are in a proprietary format called BLP2. Blizzard uses that format for its graphics and, unfortunately, no official tools have been released to support it.

Foxlit, an enterprising member of the user interface community, has written a web page that can convert these files on demand, and we have the opportunity to host a version of it on the book's companion website: http://wowprogramming.com/utils/blp2png.

Simply upload a BLP file that you'd like converted, and the web page will return a PNG image that can be saved and edited. Remember, however, that World of Warcraft only loads BLP and TGA files, so you'll have to convert it to TGA after making any changes.

Alternatively, you can browse the contents of the interface art directories online at http://wowprogramming.com/utils/artbrowser. Each of the images are hosted in PNG format for you to view and download.

Summary

XML is a broad specification that allows virtually endless combinations of schemas and structure, but when dealing with World of Warcraft, you focus on a very particular subset defined by the schema. The default user interface uses XML for all of its frame layout and creation, and you can take advantage of this by using Blizzard's own code to learn more about the system.

Programming in World of Warcraft

In This Part

Anatomy of an Addon

As discussed in Chapter 1, an addon for World of Warcraft is a collection of text and media files packaged together and loaded to extend the core functionality of the game client. At the more virtual level an addon is also a collection of functions, tables, frames, textures, and font strings.

This chapter explains the contents of an addon's files, and introduces you to the widgets system and the event-based programming system used in WoW.

Exploring an Addon's Files and Folders

An addon consists of a table of contents file that defines certain metadata about an addon (such as name, author, version, and a list of files to be loaded), along with XML frame definitions, Lua scripts, and other media files. This section details the actual contents of these files.

Table of Contents (.toc) File

The one file that must be included in every addon is the table of contents (TOC) file, which must have the same name as the addon's directory. For example, if an addon's directory name is MyAddon, it must contain a file called `MyAddon.toc`. The TOC file provides vital information about the addon (such as title, description, author, and so on) along with a list of files to be loaded by the game client. A sample `.toc` file might look like this:

```
## Interface: 30300
## Title: My Addon Name
```

```
## Author: My Name Here
## Notes: This is my sample addon

MyAddon.xml
MyAddon.lua
```

Each line beginning with ## contains a definition of some sort of metadata. For example, the ## Title metadata is displayed on the addon selection screen, and ## Notes contains a longer description that is displayed when you mouse over the addon in that list. The lines after the directives are simply a list of files to be loaded by the addon.

Interface:

```
## Interface: 30300
```

The interface version directive (## Interface: 30300 in this example) provides a basic versioning mechanism that the client uses for the addon selection screen. The game client uses this number to verify that an addon is compatible with the current game version. If the version is not compatible, the game will label it with one of two states:

- Out of date—This state indicates that there has been a patch to the game client since the addon was written. This is strictly just a warning; the addons may work just fine if you check "Load out of date AddOns" at the top of the screen. The version number typically only changes when there is an actual change to the API, so this warning should be heeded.

- Incompatible—When a major change happens to the game client (such as an expansion pack), the addon selection screen will display this status and will refuse to load the addon. A new version of the addon should be downloaded to ensure it operates correctly in the new API.

Figure 8-1 shows two addons, one flagged as out of date and the other as incompatible. TinyPad could be loaded by checking the Load out of date AddOns checkbox, but nothing can force the incompatible addon to load.

Figure 8-1: Addon selection screen

Just because an addon is listed as out of date doesn't mean there's anything particularly wrong with it, only that the game client has been patched since the

.toc file was last updated. When that happens, it's a good reminder to update your addons and make sure you're using the latest versions. This helps you get the latest bug fixes and features, and also makes it easier for the author of the addon to support you.

The interface number is generally built from the version number of the WoW client. For example, the interface number for the 3.3.0 client is 30300. However, this does not necessarily change each time there is a patch. If after a WoW patch you're not sure what interface number to use in building your own addons, you can extract the latest FrameXML files using the User Interface Customization Tool introduced in Chapter 7 and consult the FrameXML.toc file.

ADDON SELECTION SCREEN

You can access the addon selection screen by clicking the AddOns button at the bottom-left of the character selection screen. This button appears when you have downloaded and installed an addon in the appropriate place.

From the selection screen, addons can be enabled and disabled on a per-character or global basis. The global settings work only for a single server, so if your characters are on different servers, you will need to configure them independently. The addon selection screen can be used to browse the addons that are available on a given system, as well as any dependencies they may have.

When things go wrong with an addon, checking the addon selection screen to ensure the addon isn't flagged as "Out of date" or "Incompatible" is a good place to start to ensure the addon is actually being loaded.

Title:

```
## Title: Hello Friend
```

When addons are listed in the addon selection screen, they are sorted and shown by their ## Title directive, rather than by the name of the addon's TOC file or directory. This can be somewhat confusing as you try to determine which directory corresponds to which addon title in game, but these problems are relatively infrequent and easy to resolve. The default value for this option is the name of the addon's directory.

The ## Title directive can be localized, meaning it can display different text depending on which language the user's client is set to display. To localize it for Spanish language users, for instance, you'd add a hyphen followed by a locale code, such as ## Title-esES: Hola Amigo. When your addon is loaded on a WoW client with that locale, the custom name will be displayed instead of the generic one supplied in the ## Title directive. Localization of addons is covered in more depth later in this chapter.

Notes:

```
## Notes: Greet other players
```

The `## Notes` directive gives you the capability to provide a longer description of your addon. This field can also be localized to provide a different description depending on client locale in the same way as `## Title`, and may also contain color codes to highlight portions of the text. Figure 8-2 shows the tooltip displayed by the WoWLua addon `.toc` file.

Figure 8-2: WowLua tooltip, generated from ## Title and ## Notes directives

Dependencies:, ## RequiredDeps:

```
## Dependencies: Juggernaut, Alpha
## RequiredDeps: Juggernaut, Alpha
```

Occasionally, one addon requires another to be loaded in order to function. For example, certain addons are organized into individual addon plugins, all requiring one central addon. To express this, you give the `## Dependencies` or `## RequiredDeps` directive a list of comma-separated addon names. The game client will load all required dependencies of an addon before trying to load the addon itself.

When an addon is missing a required dependency, or the dependency addon has been disabled, an error message is displayed, as shown in Figures 8-3 and 8-4. You can move your mouse over the addon name to view a list of dependencies and see which ones are missing.

Figure 8-3: Addon with dependency disabled

Figure 8-4: Addon with dependency missing

Dependencies also ensure addons are loaded in the proper order, so if `Beta` relies on `Alpha`, the client will load `Alpha` before it loads `Beta`. This is even true for a long chain of dependencies. `## Dependencies` and `## RequiredDeps` both work the same for this directive. Addons should obviously try to avoid circular dependencies, because no addon will ever be loaded in that case.

OptionalDeps:

```
## OptionalDeps: Juggernaut, Alpha
```

When an addon can interact with another addon, but doesn't strictly require it to function, it can be listed as an optional dependency using the `## OptionalDeps` directive. All this directive does is ensure that the optional dependencies are loaded before this addon, if they are available. This directive takes a comma-separated list of addon names. The names listed must match the `.toc` file and the directory names of the given addons.

LoadOnDemand:

```
## LoadOnDemand: 1
```

As mentioned in Chapter 1, each of the Blizzard addons is configured to load on demand, meaning that the client will load and initialize the addon in response to some game event. This saves memory and load time by not loading all of the addons each time the player logs in to the game, but only when he needs them. Because not all addons may be written in a way that supports load on demand (LoD), there is a directive that flags an addon as LoD capable.

An LoD addon can still use the other directives, and still appears in the addon list, but will not be loaded until explicitly requested by another addon. Many addons use this functionality for their configuration systems, only loading them when the user tries to make a configuration change.

This option takes either a `1` or a `0`, where `1` means the addon is LoD capable, and `0` means it is not. If this value isn't supplied in the TOC, it defaults to `0`.

LoadsWith:

```
## LoadsWith: Blizzard_RaidUI
```

The `## LoadsWith` directive can be combined with `## LoadOnDemand` to load an addon as soon as another is being loaded. For example, an addon that alters the default Blizzard Raid UI could include `## LoadsWith: Blizzard_RaidUI` to be loaded along with the default raid interface. This directive has rather limited use but expands the usefulness of LoD components quite a bit. If multiple addons are listed, the addon will be loaded as soon as any of those listed finishes loading.

DefaultState:

```
## DefaultState: disabled
```

Not all addons are meant to be loaded on each and every character, so this directive enables you to set the default state of an addon. The flag tells the client whether an addon should be checked (enabled) in the addon selection screen by default. As soon as a user overrides this setting by checking or unchecking the addon, the user preference is respected. If not supplied, this value defaults to enabled.

LoadManager:

```
## LoadManager: AddonLoader
```

Adding to the complexity (and versatility) of the LoD system is the ## LoadManager directive, which indicates that some other addon will take responsibility for loading this addon. The addon is flagged as LoD as long as the load manager addon is installed and enabled.

The most prevalent load manager is called AddonLoader and is available from a few different locations, including:

- http://wowace.com/projects/addon-loader
- http://wowinterface.com/downloads/info11476-r77-release.html

AddonLoader is used by several addons as a LoadManager. The developer can provide conditions in the TOC that AddonLoader then uses to decide when the addon should be loaded. For example, an addon that is specific to Rogues can be flagged with ## X-LoadOn-Class: Rogue, and it will be loaded for any rogue characters but not for any others.

This method requires the developer to add these flags to the TOC file and the user to download AddonLoader, but it provides major benefits when used correctly. You can find documentation about using AddonLoader online at http://www.wowwiki.com/AddonLoader.

SavedVariables:

```
## SavedVariables: JuggernautDB
```

The only way an addon can save information between sessions is to define a Lua variable and list the name of the variable in the ## SavedVariables directive in its TOC file. This tells the game to save the contents of that variable out to a file when the game is closed, and read it back in when the game is started up again. The variable can be a string, number, Boolean, or table.

SavedVariablesPerCharacter:

```
## SavedVariablesPerCharacter: JuggernautDB
```

The ## SavedVariablesPerCharacter: VariableName directive operates in the same way as ## SavedVariables:, except a different file is saved and loaded for each character you log in with. If you log in to character Alice, her settings will be saved separately from those for Bob. Nothing special needs to happen in the addon; it's all handled automatically by the client.

NONSTANDARD METADATA DIRECTIVES

Beyond the officially supported metadata tags, you may see any number of other tags included in the .toc file of custom addons. One customary directive is ## Author. This information isn't displayed by default client, but can be accessed by other addons in-game.

```
## Author: ArgyleSocks
```

X-Label Directives

In addition, custom directives can be defined with an X, followed by a hyphen and then some label. These directives can contain any string of data, limited to roughly 1,000 characters. For example, an addon could include a web address using an ## X-Website directive.

Each of the X label directives is localized by the game client, so you can include all of the following and only the correct version will be available through the GetAddOnMetadata() API function:

```
## X-FAQ-Website: http://www.myaddon.com/faq/
## X-FAQ-Website-esES: http://www.myaddon.com/faq/esES
## X-FAQ-Website-deDE: http://www.myaddon.com/faq/deDE
```

Addon Categories

The addon community has developed a standard set of addon categories that can be included in the metadata for an addon, making it easier to group similar types of addons together when listing or displaying them. Here's the list of categories:

Action Bars	Frame Modification	Priest
Auction	Guild	Quest
Audio	Healer	Raid
Battlegrounds/PvP	Hunter	Rogue

(continued)

NONSTANDARD METADATA DIRECTIVES *(continued)*

Buffs	Interface Enhancements	Shaman
Caster	Inventory	Tank
Chat/Communication	Library	Tradeskill
Combat	Mage	UnitFrame
Compilations	Mail	Warlock
Data Export	Map	Warrior
Development Tools	Miscellaneous	
Druid	Paladin	

You could use one of these categories or define your own set — that's the beauty of addon metadata. To supply your category, simply use the `##` `X-Category:` `CategoryName` **directive.**

XML Files

`HelloFriend.xml`

A table of contents file can list any number of XML files to be loaded. Markup in these files will be validated against the WoW UI XML schema file as it's parsed and loaded. XML files can also load Lua scripts using the `<Script file="SomeFile.lua"/>` tag. Each XML file should contain a top-level `<Ui>` element.

To validate your XML document, you will also need to include the schema information in the `<Ui>` element. Here's an example:

```
<Ui xmlns="http://www.blizzard.com/wow/ui/"
    xmlns:xsi="http://www.w3.org/2001/XMLSchema-instance"
    xsi:schemaLocation="http://www.blizzard.com/wow/ui/
    http://wowprogramming.com/FrameXML/UI.xsd">
```

This may need a bit of explanation. The `xlmns` attribute defines the namespace that the document is hoping to conform to. It must match the namespace declared in the given schema. In this case, it is a value defined by Blizzard. The `xmlns:xsi` attribute tells the validating program to which schema instance the schema will conform. Finally, `xsi:schemaLocation` is a pair of strings, the first being the name of a namespace and the second being the location where that schema can be found.

The example specifies that the `http://www.blizzard.com/wow/ui/` schema can be found in the online document `http://wowprogramming.com/FrameXML/ UI.xsd`. This is a file that is kept updated on the website for validation purposes. Instead of using the online version, you could specify the path to the `UI.xsd` file on your local machine. The location of this file depends on your specific installation, but it will be unpacked when you use the User Interface Customization Tool.

As your XML files are loaded, any errors will appear in the `Logs\FrameXML.log` file in your base World of Warcraft installation. If your addons aren't behaving properly, it's a good idea to check this file to ensure there wasn't an error in validating or parsing your code.

Lua Script Files

```
HelloFriend.lua
```

The TOC file can list any number of Lua files that exist somewhere underneath the addons directory. Each of these files is loaded, parsed, and then executed by the game client in the order listed in the TOC file. Because each file is run independently, local variables defined in one file will not be available in another file; if you need to share data between different files you should ensure that you use global variables of some sort.

Media Files

Addons can include custom graphics, sounds, and fonts to be displayed (or played) within the game client, providing a different visual style or audio cues. These files are included within the addon directories themselves, and are addressed by full pathname from the WoW directory.

Music

Assume you have a file called `CreepySound.mp3` included as part of an addon called `Goober` that resides in the following location:

```
World of Warcraft\Interface\Addons\Goober\CreepySound.mp3
```

It can then be played by running the following command in-game (remember to escape the backslash character because Lua uses it as the escape character):

```
/run PlaySoundFile("Interface\\Goober\\CreepySound.mp3")
```

The WoW client can natively play MP3 files as well as WAV files. Converting files to these formats can be accomplished through a number of tools freely available on the Internet.

Graphics

WoW accepts two graphics formats when loading textures for frames. In addition to being in the right format, each graphic must meet the following basic requirements to be loaded:

1. The file's width and height must be greater than or equal to 2, and smaller than 1024 pixels.

2. The height and width of the file must be a power of two, although they need not be the same.

For example, a file that is 32 x 64 is acceptable, whereas a file that is 512 x 400 is not (because the height is not a power of two). In addition, the file can, and should, contain an alpha channel, something that is particular to the specific graphics editing software you are using.

More information on creating and editing custom graphics for addons is available in Chapter 20.

Following is a look at the two primary graphics formats used in WoW: BLP2 and TGA.

BLP2 Format

If you have extracted the Blizzard Interface Art using the User Interface Customization Tool (as shown in Chapter 7), you may have noticed that all the files that were created have a `.blp` extension. That file format was created by Blizzard, and has been used in both Warcraft III and World of Warcraft. Even though Blizzard provides a way to extract the files, there is still no official tool that can convert these files. The companion website for the book provides a way to convert these graphics to the PNG format, which is easier to view and edit; see Chapter 7 for more information.

The only time this book deals with `.blp` files is if any original game art is altered, in which case the texture is provided in the `.tga` format instead.

TGA Format

Wikipedia defines a `.tga` file as a Truevision Advanced Raster Graphics Adapter (TARGA) file. This is a simple graphics file format that can be used to store color images, including transparency information. TGA files never use lossless compression, which means the image is not degraded as a result of saving the image, as happens with JPG files. Most modern graphics editors can save to this file format natively, and Chapter 20 provides an extensive tutorial on creating files to be used in the game.

Localizing Your Addons

Localization as it relates to addon development is the process of converting the text and icons used in the application to a format that is meaningful for users from other regions of the world, who may speak different languages. WoW boasts more than 10 million subscribers, many of them coming from regions in Europe and Asia. You may see the word "localization" abbreviated to L10n, which stands for "L" followed by 10 other letters, followed by an "n." Similarly, you may see I18n as an abbreviation for "Internationalization." However you call it, localization makes your addons more accessible.

Valid Locales

Blizzard provides a number of game locales with World of Warcraft. Table 8-1 shows a list of the current valid game locale codes. For each of these languages, Blizzard has translated each in-game message and string so they are meaningful to users from that region.

Table 8-1: Valid Client Locales

LOCALE CODE	CORRESPONDING LANGUAGE
deDE	German
enUS	American English
enGB	British English
esES	Spanish
esMX	Spanish (Mexico)
frFR	French
koKR	Korean
ruRU	Russian
zhCN	Simplified Chinese
zhTW	Traditional Chinese

Although there is technically an enGB locale, the game will never display that locale anywhere (in particular, GetLocale() will not return it).

Reasons for Providing Localization

When users play the game in their native language, it's often easier for them to make split-second decisions if they aren't trying to read an entirely different language as part of a custom addon. Imagine if you were a native Spanish speaker who played the game in Spanish, but had addons that displayed your information in English. Even if you're a fluent reader of both languages, your brain may find difficulty in switching between the two quickly.

From a purely practical standpoint, why not provide support for localization in your addon? Most users are willing and able to help authors with the addon localization, and if the addon is organized well, it can be a very easy task to keep localizations up to date.

Encouraging Users to Contribute

More often than not, users will approach authors with localization files, but the author can take some steps to ensure the addon is easy to localize. This typically means the following:

1. Include a dedicated localization file with no other addon logic, including a set of constants of a lookup table to be used instead of string constants.

2. Provide information in the `readme.txt` file for your addon and the addon's website on how users can contact you to help with localization.

3. Provide comments about what a specific message means so it can easily be translated. Although the word "speed" means only one thing in English, it may translate to different words depending on the language.

Implementing Localization

Because localization implementations are simply different means of structuring Lua programs, there are countless ways to do it. This section describes one particular way to implement localization.

When working with non-English locales, you should ensure that your editors work properly with UTF-8 markup. Most modern text editors work just fine, but older, less-featured editors may show garbage instead of the correct markup.

Add a File for Each Locale

Begin by adding a new localization file for each locale for which you have translations. If you don't have any translations to begin with, simply create a file for the "base" locale in which you've developed the addon. For my addons, this means adding a `Localization.enUS.lua` file to my directory structure. Add the file to the top of the `.toc` file to ensure that it's loaded first.

Create a Global Table Containing the Base Strings

Create a new global table called *MyAddon*`Localization` in the `Localization.enUS.lua` file, replacing *MyAddon* with the name of your addon. For instance, if your addon is named BurgerDoodle, your global table would be called `BurgerDoodleLocalization`.

You can use full strings or tokens to add the base translations to this file.

Using Full Strings

The following is a set of table definitions that takes the entire string to be translated and uses it as both the key and the value. The reason for this will become apparent later.

```
MyAddonLocalization = {}
MyAddonLocalization["Frames have been locked"] = "Frames have ↵
been locked"
MyAddonLocalization["Frames have been unlocked"] = "Frames have ↵
been unlocked"
```

This tends to work for smaller strings but, as you can see, can be quite verbose for longer string keys.

Using Tokens

Instead of using the entire string as the table key, you can use a smaller string or "token." The same localization file might look like this:

```
MyAddonLocalization = {}
MyAddonLocalization["FRAMES_LOCKED"] = "Frames have been locked"
MyAddonLocalization["FRAMES_UNLOCKED"] = "Frames have been unlocked"
```

Using the Localization Table

The reason for loading the localization file first is to ensure that the tables are available when the rest of the addon files are loading. For example, you can display the "locked" message using the following:

```
print(MyAddonLocalization["Frames have been locked"])
```

or

```
print(MyAddonLocalization["FRAMES_LOCKED"])
```

If that appears too verbose for you, you could make a shortcut to the global table. This is typically done with the variable L, which is used in other software realms for localization:

```
local L = MyAddonLocalization
print(L["Frames have been locked"])
```

If you've opted for the token method, you can even use syntactic sugar to make it easier to type:

```
print(L.FRAMES_LOCKED)
```

Adding New Locales

New languages can be added by defining new files and following the standard you've already established. The new files should be listed *after* the base locale in the .toc file, but *before* the main addon. For example, create a localization file for German by creating Localization.deDE.lua with the following contents:

```
if  GetLocale() == "deDE" then
   if not MyAddonLocalization then
```

```
        MyAddonLocalization = {}
    end
    MyAddonLocalization["FRAMES_LOCKED"] = "Frames wurden gesperrt"
    MyAddonLocalization["FRAMES_UNLOCKED"] = "Frames wurden entsperrt"
end
```

The first line checks to ensure that the user's locale is deDE; otherwise, the translation file is skipped. The second line creates the global table if it doesn't already exist, and the rest is the same as the base locale file, with the values of the table being the translated strings.

Now the message printed on a German client will be displayed in the native language rather than in English.

Handling Partial Translations

What happens if some strings have been translated into German but not others? Currently, because the main English table is created first, and the German table is loaded after it, any English strings that haven't been translated to German will be displayed in English. This gives you a mix of the two rather than an error message.

Introducing Frames, Widget Scripts, and Events

Although the previous section explained the different components of addons, it only covered the details of the files stored on your computer. There's quite a bit more to getting an addon up and running. This section introduces you to the different components that make up an addon within the game.

Frames, FontStrings, and Textures

Every visual component in an addon begins with a frame, which serves as the container for font strings and textures. A number of *types* of frames serve different purposes. For example, the following is a short list of some of the different frame types (a full listing is given in Chapter 10):

- StatusBar—Used to display a numerical value in a given range, such as health, mana, or a progress bar.

- CheckButton—Used for any button that has an on and an off state, such as checkboxes or radio buttons.

- EditBox—Allows the user to supply input via the keyboard.

- ScrollingMessageFrame—Can display a series of text messages in a scrolling frame.

The main differences between the different types are the functions that they provide to customize them. For example a StatusBar allows you to set the minimum and maximum values for the bar, and the `ScrollingMessageFrame` enables you to add and clear messages from the frame.

Most frames by themselves have no actual visible components, but `FontStrings` and `Textures` can be used to add text and graphics to frames.

Displaying Text with FontStrings

A `FontString` is a special type of object that is dedicated to displaying text. The following attributes — and a number of others — can be customized via XML or Lua:

- Font, size, color, outline, and shadow
- Justification (both vertical and horizontal)
- Whether the text should wrap in the middle of a word

Almost all text that is visible within the UI is a `FontString` customized in a specific way, set to display certain text.

Showing Graphics and Colors with Textures

Textures in World of Warcraft serve a similar purpose to font strings, except for graphics, colors, and gradients, which can be used to display a graphic file stored on disk, a solid color, or a gradient from one color to another.

Anchoring Objects On-Screen

All object placement in World of Warcraft is accomplished through a series of *anchors* that attach one point on an object to one point on another object. The concepts of anchoring are covered in-depth in Chapter 9.

Responding to Interaction with Widget Scripts

World of Warcraft allows you to respond to user interaction (such as clicking a button) via widget scripts. These scripts are numerous and varied, depending on the type of widget being used. Table 8-2 shows a few widget scripts and their purpose.

Setting these scripts is relatively simple, just a matter of providing a Lua function to handle the event. Widget scripts are covered in depth in Chapter 12.

Responding to Game Events

Most of the benefit of using addons is being able to respond to certain game events (such as entering combat or requesting a duel) and displaying something to the user. All handling of game events happens through frames.

Table 8-2: Widget Scripts

WIDGET TYPE	SCRIPT	DESCRIPTION
Button	OnClick	Fires when the user clicks the button, or when other code calls the button's `Click()` method.
EditBox	OnEscapePressed	Fires when the escape key is pressed while the focus is in the edit box.
ScrollFrame	OnVerticalScroll	Fires when the scroll frame is scrolled vertically.
Frame	OnEnter	Fires when the mouse enters the boundaries of the frame.
Frame	OnShow	Fires each time the frame is shown (from a hidden state).
Frame	OnEvent	Fires when the frame has registered for a game event, and the event occurs.

To register for a game event, you can call the `Frame:RegisterEvent()` method, which accepts the name of the event as a string. Once registered, you can set the `OnEvent` widget script to run code when the event fires.

The following code creates a frame (with no display) that prints a message to your chat frame when you enter and leave combat. (Don't worry about the names of the events; you'll find some of them can be pretty peculiar.) In this case the event to indicate you are entering combat is `PLAYER_REGEN_DISABLED`, because that is when you stop regenerating health.

```
if not MyCombatFrame then
  CreateFrame("Frame", "MyCombatFrame", UIParent)
end
MyCombatFrame:RegisterEvent("PLAYER_REGEN_ENABLED")
MyCombatFrame:RegisterEvent("PLAYER_REGEN_DISABLED")

function MyCombatFrame_OnEvent(self, event, ...)
  if event == "PLAYER_REGEN_ENABLED" then
    print("Leaving combat...")
  elseif event == "PLAYER_REGEN_DISABLED" then
    print("Entering combat!")
  end
end

MyCombatFrame:SetScript("OnEvent", MyCombatFrame_OnEvent)
```

That may be confusing right now, but this is just meant to be an introduction to game events.

Loading of an Addon

The loading of an addon can also be somewhat confusing, so this section shows you the different stages of the loading process.

1. When World of Warcraft is opened, the AddOns directory is scanned to build a list of addons the user has installed, including their metadata (metadata will not be reloaded again until you completely close the WoW client).

2. Player logs in to World of Warcraft and is shown the character selection screen for a given server.

3. At this point the player can enable and disable addons for either the currently selected character or for all of the characters on the server.

4. Player selects a character and begins entering the game world.

5. Default user interface XML and Lua files are loaded in the order specified in `FrameXML.toc`. This may cause Blizzard addons to load on demand, depending on the situation.

6. Enabled, non-load-on-demand addons that do not have errors on the AddOns page are loaded:

    a. If this addon is dependent on any other addons and they are not currently loaded, load them first, in an order that is dependent on the operating system (some are alphabetic, others are by date created).

    b. The addon's Table of Contents file is read to create a list of files to be loaded.

    c. Each file is processed in order, and any `LoadAddon()` commands are processed immediately. Any `script` elements in XML files are processed immediately upon encountering them.

    d. The saved variables for this addon are loaded (if present from a previous game session).

    e. The `ADDON_LOADED` event is fired with the first argument set to the name of the addon that has completed loading. Depending on the load structure of your addons, the first event you see may not be for your addon.

7. Blizzard's saved variables, key binding, and macros begin loading and synchronizing (this continues in the background).

8. The `SPELLS_CHANGED` event fires, indicating that the player's spellbook has loaded and is available to the user interface.

9. The PLAYER_LOGIN event fires indicating that most information about the game world should be available to the user, and sizing and positioning of frames should have been completed.

10. The PLAYER_ENTERING_WORLD event fires, indicating that the player has entered the game world.

At some point after this sequence the VARIABLES_LOADED event should fire, indicating that Blizzard's saved variables, macros, and key bindings have been loaded or synchronized.

Summary

This chapter introduced you to the different components of an addon, both on your computer and within the game world. You learned about the various directives that can be included in a table of contents file. The frame and event system was introduced briefly.

Learning about concepts is well enough, but you're reading this book to learn how to actually create addons. The next five chapters will lead you through creating an addon called BagBuddy for World of Warcraft. Each chapter introduces you to the details of a specific section of the user interface, and then you will use those skills to implement a portion of the addon.

Each chapter will build on the code from the previous chapter, so try to work through the chapters in order. If you do choose to work out of order, there will be full code listings at the end of each chapter to prevent confusion.

## CHAPTER 9

Working with Frames, Widgets, and Other Graphical Elements

Chapter 8 introduced the concepts of frames, textures, and font strings. This chapter builds on that introduction, showing you how to create the foundations for an addon called BagBuddy.

Although the frame definitions in this chapter are written using XML, you also see how the same effect could be achieved using purely Lua code. XML is used for this addon because it is helpful to validate against the WoW XML schema, and it helps separate the frame definitions from the behavioral code of an addon.

Introducing BagBuddy

Each of the different race and class combinations has its own sets of problems. One area in which they all have issues is inventory. Items you loot go into the first free slot in your bags, so while playing your bags can become an unsorted mess. Countless addons help you sort your inventory, or display it in a more meaningful way.

The addon you create in this chapter takes a different approach and is meant to work alongside your inventory. BagBuddy is an extra panel in the user interface that can filter your inventory by name or rarity, and always displays results with most-recently-looted first. That way if you need to find something that you've just looted, you can open BagBuddy and it should be displayed at the top of the list.

Creating an Addon Skeleton

BagBuddy consists of an XML definition of the frames, and a Lua script that defines the behavior and logic of the addon. Start by creating a new directory within your `Interface\AddOns` folder called `BagBuddy`. Inside this new directory create a file called `BagBuddy.toc` and add the following content:

```
## Interface: 30200
## Title: BagBuddy
## Notes: A handy helper that allows you to filter your inventory

BagBuddy.lua
BagBuddy.xml
```

Now create `BagBuddy.xml`, adding just the basic definition of the `<Ui>` element that you have seen before:

```
<Ui xmlns="http://www.blizzard.com/wow/ui/"
  xmlns:xsi="http://www.w3.org/2001/XMLSchema-instance"
  xsi:schemaLocation="http://www.blizzard.com/wow/ui/
  http://wowprogramming.com/FrameXML/UI.xsd">
</Ui>
```

Finally, create an empty file called `BagBuddy.lua`. You won't be adding any code to it for the next few chapters, but creating it now ensures that the WoW client will recognize the file without needing to be restarted.

Creating a Frame

The World of Warcraft user interface is based around the central concept of frames. All textures and font strings must belong to a parent frame. Frames can register for events and receive notification of game events. In addition, the user can interact with frames, for example by clicking them. As a result, most addons begin with a definition of a frame. BagBuddy is no different.

In `BagBuddy.xml`, add the following code inside the `<Ui>` element:

```
<Frame name="BagBuddy" parent="UIParent">
  <Size x="384" y="512"/>
  <Anchors>
    <Anchor point="CENTER" relativePoint="CENTER" ↵
relativeTo="UIParent"/>
  </Anchors>
</Frame>
```

This code creates a new frame called *BagBuddy* that is a child of `UIParent`. The frame is given a width of 384 and a height of 512, and is anchored to the center of `UIParent`, making it appear in the middle of the player's screen.

Parenting

Every frame, texture, and font string can have at most one parent, and in fact textures and font strings are required to have a parent. In addition, a frame may have any number of child frames. Having an explicit mechanism for parenting helps define a hierarchy for the user interface:

1. When a parent is hidden, all child frames cease to be visible. If this weren't the case, you'd have to manually hide all the other elements that might be attached to a frame.

2. A frame's effective scale is defined by multiplying the frame's scale by its parent's effective scale. If the parent is scaled to be larger or smaller, then all of the children are grown or shrunk by the same amount.

3. A frame's effective transparency (alpha) value is defined by multiplying the frame's alpha by its parent's effective alpha. This enables you to make not only a button transparent, but to "dim out" a frame and all of its children at the same time.

Most of the Blizzard default frames are parented to `UIParent`. This is a special frame that is used to hide the user interface when the player presses Alt+Z. In addition, having a single common parent allows the interface to be scaled consistently, making everything smaller or larger. When creating new frames, most times you should parent the frames to `UIParent` at some point to ensure they work the same as the other frames to which the user may be accustomed.

When creating frames using XML, parenting also provides you with an easy to way to name your frames consistently. Any name can include the string `$parent`, which is expanded to the name of the parent frame when actually being loaded.

You have three different ways to set the parent/child relationship between objects: specifying a parent explicitly using XML attributes, using the hierarchy of XML elements to define the relationship, or calling the `SetParent()` method on an object directly:

- **Attributes**—Use the `parent` XML attribute to define a parent/child relationship in an XML frame. This attribute's value should be the name of a frame that is to be set as the parent. In the preceding example, this is used to parent `BagBuddy` to `UIParent`. You cannot use this attribute to set the parent of a texture or font string.

- **XML hierarchy**—Each object is by default given a parent simply through its nested location within the XML file. Although creating sub-frames, font strings, and textures is covered later in this chapter, you should know that when defined in XML, a parent/child relationship is automatically established.

■ **The** `SetParent()` **method**—Once an object has been created, you can call the `SetParent()` method to change the parent. This function takes a single argument: the frame object of the new parent (not its name).

Giving Objects Sizes

Naturally, before the user interface can know what to do with your objects, it needs to know how large or small they are. The size of an object can be given using the `<Size>` XML element, using either absolute or relative dimensions.

Absolute Dimensions

Absolute dimensions are specific pixel values that define how large an object will be. In the earlier XML definition for BagBuddy, the frame is set to be 384 units wide by 512 units tall using the size tag:

```
<Size x="384" y="512"/>
```

Most of Blizzard's own XML code uses the following format instead:

```
<Frame name="MyFrame">
  <Size>
    <AbsDimension x="384" y="512"/>
  </Size>
</Frame>
```

Either method declares the size in the same way. The more compact notation is generally considered more readable and easier to type.

Relative Dimensions

Instead of using absolute values, a frame can express its height and width as a percentage of its parent. Consider the following XML snippet that creates two new frames:

```
<Frame name="RelativeExample">
  <Size x="100" y="50"/>
</Frame>
<Frame name="RelativeExampleChild" parent="RelativeExample">
  <Size>
    <RelDimension x="0.5" y="0.5"/>
  </Size>
</Frame>
```

The first frame, `RelativeExample`, has a size in absolute dimensions (100 units wide by 50 units high), but the second is defined using relative dimensions. As a result, `RelativeExampleChild` will be 50 units wide by 25 units high. You won't see this method of sizing used very often (as a matter of fact it's not currently used in the default interface), but it is still available as an option.

Anchoring Objects

All object placement in World of Warcraft is done through a series of anchors that attach one point on a frame to some other point on another frame. Figure 9-1 shows the nine different anchor points on the frame.

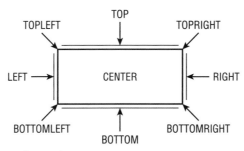

Figure 9-1: Available anchor points

In XML, anchors are placed within the `<Anchors>` element. A frame can have any number of anchors, each defined using the `<Anchor>` element with the following attributes:

- `point`—The point being anchored. The next section explains what each of the anchor points is and how it works.

- `relativeTo`—The frame to which the point is being anchored. This attribute is optional; if omitted, the default is the frame's parent.

- `relativePoint`—The point to attach to on the `relativeTo` frame. This attribute is optional; if omitted, the default is the point being anchored.

In addition to these attributes, the `<Anchor>` element can contain an `<Offset>` element, with which you can specify an offset in absolute or relative dimensions (this element is used in the same way as the `<Size>` element, allowing `x` and `y` attributes, or an absolute or relative dimension definition). The code for BagBuddy anchors the center point of the new frame to the center of `UIParent`, which spans the full game screen.

Along the same lines, the following example creates a new frame called `MyFrame1` and another frame called `MyFrame2`. The first frame sits in the center of the user interface, and the second frame sits directly to the right of `MyFrame1`. This is accomplished by anchoring the top-left point of `MyFrame2` to the top-right point of `MyFrame1`. In this way the top edges are aligned with each other, and the frames sit side by side.

```
<Frame name="MyFrame1" parent="UIParent">
  <Size x="50" y="50"/>
  <Anchor>
    <Anchor point="CENTER" relativePoint="CENTER"/>
  </Anchors>
</Frame>
<Frame name="MyFrame2" parent="UIParent">
  <Size x="50" y="50"/>
  <Anchor>
    <Anchor point="TOPLEFT" relativePoint="TOPRIGHT" ↵
relativeTo="MyFrame"/>
  </Anchors>
</Frame>
```

In this example, the top-left corner of `MyFrame2` is attached to the top-right corner of `MyFrame1`, aligning their top edges and placing them side-by-side. When there is no offset, the `<Offset>` tag can be left out entirely, and the `<Anchor>` tag can be made self-closing. The frames could be aligned using the left point of `MyFrame2` and the right point of `MyFrame1`, but if the frames are different sizes, the top edges would not align.

Sticky Anchors

Anchoring a frame is not a one-time placement used to position the frame, but rather a sticky attachment between two objects. In the preceding example, if you later move `Frame1`, `Frame2` will follow it to obey the defined anchor points.

SetAllPoints

If you want an object to have the same placement and size as another frame, you can use the `setAllPoints` XML attribute, or the `SetAllPoints()` method. This sets all of the anchor points on the second frame to the same points on the parent frame. You'll see this attribute in use later in this chapter.

Anchor Examples

The easiest way to visualize anchoring is to look at examples and determine how the objects might be anchored together. Table 9-1 contains a number of anchor examples, along with the anchor points that were used. Each of these examples attaches FrameA to FrameB.

Table 9-1: Anchoring Examples

DESCRIPTION	EXAMPLE
FrameB's TOPLEFT anchored to FrameA's TOPRIGHT	
FrameB's TOPLEFT anchored to FrameA's RIGHT	
FrameB's TOPLEFT anchored to FrameA's BOTTOMRIGHT	
FrameB's TOP anchored to FrameA's BOTTOM	
FrameB's RIGHT anchored to FrameA's LEFT with an x-offset of −5 and a y-offset of −5	

Using Lua to Create Frames

```
<Frame name="BagBuddy" parent="UIParent">
  <Size x="384" y="512"/>
  <Anchors>
    <Anchor point="CENTER" relativePoint="CENTER" ↵
relativeTo="UIParent"/>
  </Anchors>
</Frame>
```

The equivalent definition in Lua looks like the following:

```
CreateFrame("Frame", "BagBuddy", UIParent)
BagBuddy:SetWidth(384)
BagBuddy:SetHeight(512)
BagBuddy:SetPoint("CENTER", UIParent, "CENTER")
```

The `CreateFrame` function takes several arguments. The first argument is a string that tells WoW what type of frame to create. This is the same string as the XML tag you are using (in this case `Frame`). If you were creating a status bar instead of a frame, you would specify `StatusBar`. The second argument is the name of the frame (this is optional, because you can create frames that have no names). The third argument is the parent frame object, not the name of the parent.

You can find more information on the frame methods used in this code in the Widget reference.

Adding Layers of Textures and Font Strings

If you tried to re-create any of the prior frame definitions (or loaded the BagBuddy addon), you might have been confused as to why you couldn't see any of the frames. Although the frames were created and placed on screen, they did not have any visual components for you to see. This section introduces textures and font strings:

- Texture—A texture is used to display some sort of graphic, color, or color gradient within the game. Textures are created using the <Texture> XML element.

- FontString—A font string is used to display text in a specific font, size, and color. Font strings can be further customized to display outlines, drop shadows, and other standard effects. Font strings are created using the <FontString> XML element.

Layering Frames and Graphics

To understand how to layer graphics and frames to display correctly, you must first know a bit about the different layering techniques and how the user interface is rendered.

Frame Strata

The most basic level of frame layering is the frame strata. Simply, all the frames in a given frame strata are rendered later than frames in a lower strata, and before those in a higher strata. Overlapping frames will be displayed layered from lowest to highest. Table 9-2 describes the available frame strata.

Table 9-2: Possible Frame Strata Values from Lowest to Highest

FRAME STRATA	DESCRIPTION
BACKGROUND	For frames that don't interact with the mouse. Any frame in this strata is blocked from receiving mouse events unless the frame level is higher than 1.
LOW	Used by the default user interface for the buff frame, durability frame, party interface, and pet frame.

FRAME STRATA	DESCRIPTION
MEDIUM	Default frame level for UIParent, and all children of UIParent, unless overwritten.
HIGH	Used by the default user interface for the action buttons and tutorial frames, as well as the interface error and warning frames.
DIALOG	Used for any dialog-type frame that pops up and expects user interaction.
FULLSCREEN	Any full-screen frame such as the World Map or the User Interface options should reside in this frame strata.
FULLSCREEN_DIALOG	A dialog strata that exists above the FULLSCREEN strata, for dialogs and dropdown menus.
TOOLTIP	Highest frame strata available. Used for mouseover tooltips so they are displayed regardless of the strata.
PARENT	Inherit the frame strata of the parent frame.

Setting a frame to be drawn on a specific strata is easy; you simply include the frameStrata attribute in the XML definition or use the SetFrameStrata() method. For example:

```
<Frame name="MyFrame" frameStrata="HIGH">
</Frame>
```

or

```
MyFrame:SetFrameStrata("HIGH")
```

This is the technique used by the default user interface to allow pop-up windows such as the confirmation dialog to appear over any other frames that might be displayed on screen.

Frame Levels

Within a frame strata, each frame has a frame level, which determines the order in which it is rendered (from lowest to highest). Frame levels can be messy to set, but sometimes they are the only way to accomplish a specific type of layering. When FrameA contains a child, FrameB, the frame level of FrameB will automatically be one higher than that of FrameA. This means that any child frames will (by default) be rendered on top of their parent, if they are overlapping elements. The frame level can be set using the frameLevel attribute, which should be a number, or using the SetFrameLevel() method.

In addition, a frame can be marked as a top-level frame using the `toplevel` attribute or the `SetTopLevel()` method. A top-level frame is automatically promoted to the highest frame level on a given strata when it is clicked, so it is shown on top. This is useful when frames are movable to bring the frame that is being moved to the front. The following is an example frame with `frameStrata`, `frameLevel`, and `toplevel` all set:

```
<Frame name="MyFrame" frameStrata="HIGH" frameLevel="5" toplevel="true">
</Frame>
```

or in Lua:

```
MyFrame = CreateFrame("Frame", "MyFrame")
MyFrame:SetFrameStrata("HIGH")
MyFrame:SetFrameLevel(5)
MyFrame:SetToplevel(true)
```

Graphical Layers

All textures and font strings within a frame are grouped into graphical layers. When creating a new texture or font string you must specify on which layer the graphics should be drawn. The various layer levels are listed in Table 9-3 in order from the backmost layer, to the frontmost layer.

Table 9-3: Graphical Layers

LAYER	DESCRIPTION
BACKGROUND	The background of your frame should be placed here.
BORDER	Holds any graphical borders or artwork that need to appear above the BACKGROUND layer but below any other layer.
ARTWORK	For your frame's artwork. This is typically any nonfunctional decorative or separating artwork that needs to appear above the background and border but below the functional portions of the frame.
OVERLAY	The highest standard layer; any elements that need to appear above all other layers should be placed here.
HIGHLIGHT	This special layer is displayed only when the mouse is moved over the frame that is parent to the textures and font strings on the layer. For this layer to function properly, the frame must have mouse events enabled.

Figure 9-2 shows the first four layers using colored textures and different font strings. These images are then placed on top of each other and layered by the user interface.

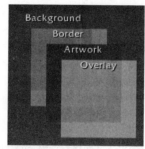

Figure 9-2: Graphics layers rendered in-game

Figure 9-3 shows the highlight layer being displayed by moving the mouse over the containing frame.

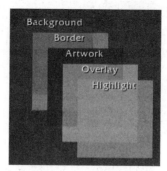

Figure 9-3: Highlight layer being shown on mouseover

For graphical elements that exist within the same draw layer of the same frame, the rendering order is random. Font strings are always rendered on top of textures within the same graphical layer, to ensure the text is displayed over the graphic. As a result, there is no need to put your text on a separate higher graphical layer to be visible.

BagBuddy Frame Design

Now that you have all the terminology straight, you can start building the BagBuddy frame. Normally when creating a new addon, I hand sketch what I would like the frame to look like, and how I would like it to operate. This gives me something to work from when writing my code. Rather than subjecting you to my horrible drawing skills, you can see the finished addon in Figure 9-4.

You may notice that the frame looks a little bit like the bank frame. That's because the artwork is actually old artwork for the bank! The designers left the graphics in the game files, so you're able to use them. This allows you to create a frame that fits within the Blizzard style, while not requiring you to be a graphic artist.

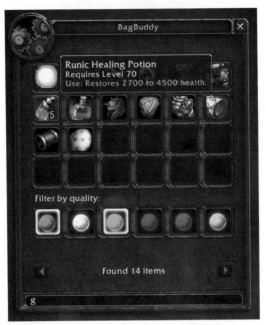

Figure 9-4: BagBuddy frame

In the top-left corner there is a circular graphic showing gears. This is an item icon, shaped to fit the circle in the correct way. In the top-right corner you can see a close button. When the user clicks this button, the frame closes. At the top of the frame, a text string is displayed, telling the user the name of the addon.

In the middle of the frame you can see a list of items. Moving your mouse over the items displays the tooltip, as you might expect. Where the bank bags might normally be are a series of colored orbs. These orbs allow you to filter the item list by item quality (note that the colors match the item rarity colors in-game).

At the bottom of the frame is a line of status text that shows how many items were found. Next to that are two buttons that allow you to page through the results. The button on the left moves you to the previous page, and the button on the right moves you to the next page. Finally, there is a small edit box at the very bottom of the frame that allows you to search for items by name. In this case we've set the filter to the letter "g" and have found 14 results that contain that letter.

Over the course of this chapter, you create the frame background, portrait icon, title text, and status text.

Finding Graphics

You may be wondering how you might browse through the game files, looking for a graphic to add to your frames. In Chapter 7 you were shown how to extract the interface art, but the files that are extracted cannot be natively viewed on most computers.

Luckily, you have two easy ways to browse those pictures. The first is an addon that you can run in the game, and the second is a website that makes it easy to browse the images.

TexBrowser AddOn

The author of Omen2 and other popular addons, Antiarc, has written an in-game browser for the textures included in the game files. The addon is called TexBrowser and you can find it at `http://wow.curse.com/downloads/wow-addons/details/texbrowser.aspx`.

Because this addon contains a large list of the available textures, it does not load automatically (this helps prevent slowing down your login and normal gameplay). You can use AddonLoader (discussed in Chapter 8) or run the commands listed on the addon's webpage:

```
/run LoadAddOn("TexBrowser")
/tex
```

Figure 9-5 shows the TexBrowser window, viewing different available textures. One neat feature of TexBrowser is that it's not limited to the interface textures, but actually lists some textures that are used in the game environment, such as spell textures.

ArtBrowser on Wowprogramming.com

To allow you to view the available graphics without having access to World of Warcraft, we created a web application that allows you to browse the textures. Just load `http://wowprogramming.com/utils/artbrowser` in your web browser, and you'll have access to all of the interface images in easy-to-view PNG format.

Adding Textures

Textures are two-dimensional graphics that are rendered by the game client for the user interface. A texture can consist of a graphics file loaded from disk, a solid color, or a gradient from one color to another. The following is a very basic texture definition:

```
<Layers>
  <Layer level="BACKGROUND">
```

```
      <Texture name="$parent_Icon" ↵
file="Interface\Icons\Ability_Rogue_Sprint">
          <Size x="50" y="50"/>
          <Anchors>
            <Anchor point="CENTER"/>
          </Anchors>
        </Texture>
      </Layer>
  </Layers>
```

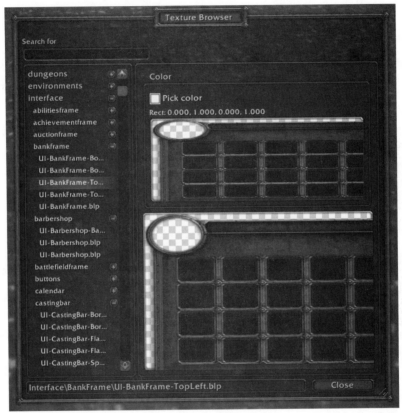

Figure 9-5: TexBrowser viewing the available textures

Remember that all texture definitions must happen inside a frame definition, so first you indicate that you're going to define the details of the graphical layers. Next you create a layer on the correct level, and inside you define the new texture.

A texture definition is very similar to the frame definitions you have already seen. Textures are both sized and anchored the same way as frames. A new attribute, `file`, is introduced here, used to specify a texture file to be loaded and displayed. If you were to include this definition in your BagBuddy addon you would see an icon in the very center of your screen.

Defining BagBuddy's Background Textures

Open `BagBuddy.xml` and add the following code after the `</Anchors>` tag:

```
<Layers>
  <Layer level="BORDER">
    <Texture file="Interface\BankFrame\UI-BankFrame-TopLeft">
      <Anchors>
        <Anchor point="TOPLEFT"/>
      </Anchors>
    </Texture>
    <Texture file="Interface\BankFrame\UI-BankFrame-TopRight">
      <Anchors>
        <Anchor point="TOPRIGHT"/>
      </Anchors>
    </Texture>
    <Texture file="Interface\BankFrame\UI-BankFrame-BotLeft">
      <Anchors>
        <Anchor point="BOTTOMLEFT"/>
      </Anchors>
    </Texture>
    <Texture file="Interface\BankFrame\UI-BankFrame-BotRight">
      <Anchors>
        <Anchor point="BOTTOMRIGHT"/>
      </Anchors>
    </Texture>
  </Layer>
</Layers>
```

For now, ignore the fact that you're putting the *background* on the BORDER layer. This code simply creates four new textures, one anchored to each corner of the frame. Figure 9-6 shows the four different textures. These graphics, when put together, create the frame shown in Figure 9-7.

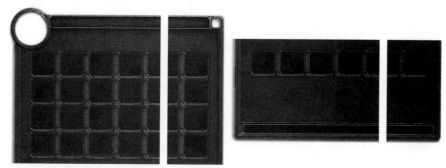

Figure 9-6: From left to right: top left corner, top right corner, bottom left corner, and bottom right corner textures.

Figure 9-7: BagBuddy frame with BORDER textures

Coloring Textures

Most textures used in addons for World of Warcraft are made up of graphic images that are placed on screen. However, the user interface also supports the use of color to enhance a texture, display a solid color, or create a gradient from one color to another.

Using Solid Colors

If you want to color a graphic image included with the `file` attribute, or just display a solid color, you include the `<Color>` element in the texture definition. This element accepts four attributes (`r`, `g`, `b`, `a`) as the three color components red, green, and blue, and the alpha (opacity) value. Each should be a number between 0.0 and 1.0. The following example shows a sample frame definition that creates a red square in the center of the screen with 50% transparency:

```
<Frame name="RedSquareTest" parent="UIParent">
  <Size x="50" y="50"/>
  <Anchors>
    <Anchor point="CENTER"/>
  </Anchors>
  <Layers>
    <Layer level="BACKGROUND" setAllPoints="true">
      <Color r="1.0" g="0.0" b="0.0" a="0.5"/>
    </Layer>
  </Layers>
</Frame>
```

Creating a Gradient

In addition to solid colors, a texture can also display a gradient between two different colors. To do this, you define a minimum color and a maximum color, using the `<Gradient>` tag. Figure 9-8 shows two example gradients.

Figure 9-8: Horizontal gradient (top) and vertical gradient (bottom)

The `<Gradient>` element takes a single, optional attribute, `orientation`, which can be either `HORIZONTAL` or `VERTICAL`. The default is a horizontal gradient. The tag must contain two elements, `<MinColor>` and `<MaxColor>`, each of which takes the standard color attributes `r`, `g`, `b`, and `a`.

A `<Gradient>` tag alone won't create a gradient; it must be combined with a `<Color>` tag. At each step in the gradient, the color values from the `<Color>` tag are multiplied by the current gradient value to determine what color is displayed on screen. The easiest way to handle this is to create a white color and then apply the gradient:

```
<Color r="1.0" g="1.0" b="1.0" a="1.0"/>
```

This ensures that your gradient begins at your `<MinColor>` and ends at your `<MaxColor>` because the base color value for each component is 1.0, which doesn't change the value it's multiplied against. Here's the XML used to create the gradients shown in Figure 9-8:

```
<Ui xmlns="http://www.blizzard.com/wow/ui/"
  xmlns:xsi="http://www.w3.org/2001/XMLSchema-instance"
  xsi:schemaLocation="http://www.blizzard.com/wow/ui/
  http://wowprogramming.com/FrameXML/UI.xsd">
  <Frame name="GradientTest" parent="UIParent">
    <Size x="200" y="200"/>
    <Anchors>
      <Anchor point="CENTER" relativePoint="CENTER" ↵
relativeTo="UIParent"/>
    </Anchors>
    <Layers>
      <Layer level="BACKGROUND">
```

```
<Texture name="$parentHorizontal">
  <Size x="200" y="100"/>
  <Anchors>
    <Anchor point="TOPLEFT" relativePoint="TOPLEFT"/>
  </Anchors>
  <Color r="1.0" g="0.0" b="0.0" a="1.0"/>
  <Gradient orientation="HORIZONTAL">
    <MinColor r="1.0" g="0.0" b="0.0" a="1.0"/>
    <MaxColor r="0.0" g="0.0" b="0.0" a="1.0"/>
  </Gradient>
</Texture>
<Texture name="$parentVertical">
  <Size x="200" y="100"/>
  <Anchors>
    <Anchor point="BOTTOMLEFT" relativePoint="BOTTOMLEFT"/>
  </Anchors>
  <Color r="1.0" g="1.0" b="1.0" a="1.0"/>
  <Gradient orientation="VERTICAL">
    <MinColor r="0.0" g="0.0" b="0.0" a="1.0"/>
    <MaxColor r="1.0" g="1.0" b="0.0" a="1.0"/>
  </Gradient>
</Texture>
    </Layer>
  </Layers>
  </Frame>
</Ui>
```

Adding the Portrait Texture

The reason the previous section placed the seemingly background textures on the BORDER layer was to make the portrait graphic that will appear in the circle at the top-left fit correctly. Trying to match the artwork perfectly would be very difficult, so instead an image is created that is just slightly larger than the opening, and layered so the excess is covered. This layering makes the images appear to go together better than we could have achieved by editing them.

Add this layer definition *before* the BORDER layer, but within the `<Layers>` element:

```
<Layer level="BACKGROUND">
  <Texture name="$parent_Portrait" parentKey="portrait" ↵
file="Interface\Icons\INV_Misc_EngGizmos_30">
    <Size x="60" y="60"/>
    <Anchors>
      <Anchor point="TOPLEFT">
        <Offset x="7" y="-6"/>
      </Anchor>
    </Anchors>
  </Texture>
</Layer>
```

The sizing and placement of this texture should be familiar to you by now, but a new attribute called `parentKey` is included. To understand how it works, you must know that a frame in Lua is just a special kind of Lua table. When this attribute is set, WoW sets the named key in the parent frame's table to be the texture. In this case, you will be able to access the portrait texture in the following ways:

- `BagBuddy_Portrait`
- `BagBuddy.portrait`
- `BagBuddy["portrait"]`

The first is possible because the texture is named using the name attribute. The second uses the table access shortcut notation to access the `portrait` key in the BagBuddy table. The third example just uses the full notation for the same.

You can access the portrait using the first option because it has a distinct name. The second two are a result of setting the `parentKey` attribute. This may not seem useful right now, but it becomes incredibly helpful when working with lots of subframes and textures.

Unfortunately, the graphic we are using is a square (shown in Figure 9-9) and Figure 9-10 shows how everything appears when it is used. The major problem is that the edges of the image stick out from behind the background of the frame.

Figure 9-9: Texture being used for BagBuddy portrait circle

Thankfully, because this same problem crops up in a number of places in the default user interface (such as the bag frames), Blizzard provides you with a function that crops the image to appear as a circle, so it works correctly with these types of frames. The function is called `SetPortraitToTexture` and it takes the texture object as the first argument, followed by the filename to use.

To call this function, set an `OnLoad` script for this frame. You learn more about frame scripts in Chapter 12, but essentially you are telling WoW to run a specific script when this frame is being loaded. Add the following XML after the `</Layers>` tag, and before the `</Frame>` tag:

```
<Scripts>
  <OnLoad function="BagBuddy_OnLoad"/>
</Scripts>
```

Figure 9-10: BagBuddy with a square portrait image

Now you need to define the corresponding function in `BagBuddy.lua`:

```
function BagBuddy_OnLoad(self)
    SetPortraitToTexture(self.portrait, ↵
"Interface\\Icons\\INV_Misc_EngGizmos_30")
end
```

An `OnLoad` script is always passed a single argument, the frame itself. Just call `SetPortraitToTexture`, passing in the portrait texture and the name of the texture file to be displayed. Figure 9-11 shows the new version of the frame, without the edges sticking out at the corner.

Creating Textures in Lua

In addition to creating frames, you can also create textures using Lua. Take the definition of the portrait texture for BagBuddy:

```
<Layer level="BACKGROUND">
  <Texture name="$parent_Portrait" parentKey="portrait">
    <Size x="60" y="60"/>
    <Anchors>
      <Anchor point="TOPLEFT">
        <Offset x="7" y="-6"/>
      </Anchor>
```

```
        </Anchors>
      </Texture>
    </Layer>
```

Figure 9-11: BagBuddy after using SetPortraitToTexture to crop the image

Assuming that you've already created the BagBuddy frame using Lua previously, you could create this texture like this:

```
BagBuddy.portrait = BagBuddy:CreateTexture("BagBuddy_Portrait", ↵
"BACKGROUND")
BagBuddy.portrait:SetWidth(60)
BagBuddy.portrait:SetHeight(60)
BagBuddy:SetPoint("TOPLEFT", 7, -6)
```

Because each texture and font string need to belong to a parent, there is simply a method you call on the frame itself to create a new texture. The first argument to `CreateTexture` is the name of the new texture and the second is the layer on which to place the texture. There is a third argument that you learn more about in Chapter 10.

If you then wanted to set a graphics file to be loaded, you could accomplish this with the `SetTexture` method:

```
BagBuddy.portrait:SetTexture("Interface\\Icons\\INV_Misc_EngGizmos_30")
```

Indeed, you can specify a solid color using the same method; for example, the following code sets the texture to be solid blue with 50% transparency:

```
BagBuddy.portrait:SetTexture(0.0, 0.0, 1.0, 0.5)
```

Similarly, methods exist that allow you to set the gradient min and max colors. In general, if there is a way to accomplish something in XML, there is a way to accomplish it in Lua as well.

Creating Text using FontStrings

Adding text to your frames is very similar to adding textures. Inside a `<Layer>` element, you define a `<FontString>` element and then customize it. Font strings have many different XML attributes that can be used to change the style of the displayed text, shown in Table 9-4.

Table 9-4: Attributes Available to FontString Elements

ATTRIBUTE	DESCRIPTION
font	The path to a font file to be used when displaying the text. This can be a file included with WoW, or a true type font supplied by a custom addon.
bytes	A positive number expressing a limit on the number of characters to be displayed in the FontString.
text	The text to be displayed.
spacing	Sets the spacing, in pixels, between lines if the FontString has multiple lines.
outline	Specifies the outline type of the FontString. Should be one of the following values: NONE, NORMAL, THICK.
monochrome	A Boolean value specifying whether the font should be monochromatic (grayscale).
nonspacewrap	A Boolean value that specifies whether long strings without spaces are wrapped or truncated. When this is true, the string is wrapped.
justifyV	Specifies the vertical justification of the text using one of the following values: TOP, MIDDLE, BOTTOM.
justifyH	Specifies the horizontal justification of the text as one of the following values: LEFT, CENTER, RIGHT.
maxLines	Specifies the maximum number of lines to be displayed in a FontString.
indented	Specifies whether or not lines after the first line in the FontString are indented, if the FontString has multiple lines.
inherits	Specifies a font definition from which attributes and elements should be inherited.

Further Customization

In addition to the XML attributes, the following elements can be added to a `FontString` to customize the display:

- `<FontHeight>`—Can be specified using the `val` attribute, or using `<AbsValue>` or `<RelValue>`. Specifies the height of the font string in pixels or a relative value.

- `<Color>`—Changes the color of the font string; specified using the `r`, `g`, `b`, and `a` attributes.

- `<Shadow>`—Adds a drop shadow to the font. The color and placement of the shadow is specified by the `<Color>` and `<Offset>` elements, which are required.

Using Font Definitions

Although having the flexibility to specify so many different attributes for each font string is a good thing, it can become quite cumbersome when writing addons and actually creating them regularly. You can delineate font (or font string) definitions that can be used to inherit settings. Fonts and font strings are a bit of an exception to the template system, which is covered in Chapter 10. For now, use the predefined template `GameFontNormal` for the title string in the BagBuddy window by adding the following code to the BagBuddy definition in the `<Layers>` element, after the definition of the BACKGROUND layer:

```
<Layer level="OVERLAY">
    <FontString name="$parent_Title" parentKey="title" inherits= ↵
"GameFontNormal" text="BagBuggy">
        <Anchors>
            <Anchor point="TOP">
                <Offset x="0" y="-18"/>
            </Anchor>
        </Anchors>
    </FontString>
</Layer>
```

Here you create a new font string on the OVERLAY layer, anchored to the top of the frame. You place the text on the OVERLAY layer to ensure that it is always displayed on top of the textures you have already defined, which exist in the BACKGROUND and BORDER layer. You inherit the settings from the `GameFontNormal` definition, which defines the gold-colored text that you see through the user interface. Font definitions and templates are shown in Chapter 10, along with further explanation about how to create your own templates.

Creating FontStrings in Lua

The `CreateFontString()` method can be used to create new font strings. It takes three arguments, the name of the new font string, the layer on which to draw the font string, and an optional font definition or template from which to inherit. You could create the font string from the previous section with the following code:

```
BagBuddy.title =
BagBuddy:CreateFontString("BagBuddy_Title", "OVERLAY", ↵
"GameFontNormal")
BagBuddy.title:SetPoint("TOP", 0, -18)
BagBuddy.title:SetText("BagBuddy")
```

Understanding Object Visibility

A somewhat confusing topic when dealing with UI objects is the concept of visibility. For an object to be actually drawn on screen, it must fulfill the following requirements:

1. The object must have some visual component, such as text, graphics, background color, or border. A frame with none of these is not visible, and a texture or font string without any contents is equally invisible.

2. The object must have a positive height and width. Although this may seem obvious, it's easy to forget one or the other.

3. The object must be placed somewhere within the bounds of the screen. If it's anchored outside the viewable window, it can't be displayed.

4. The object and each of its parents must be shown.

In this case, the word "shown" means that the object is not hidden. An object can be hidden in two ways:

- It can start out hidden by setting the `hidden` attribute in the XML definition to true.

- It can be made hidden by calling the object's `:Hide()` method.

There are two API functions that can be used to troubleshoot an object's visibility:

- `IsShown()` —Returns 1 if the frame is shown, a state that can be toggled using the `Show()` and `Hide()` methods.

- `IsVisible()` —Returns 1 if the frame and all of its parents are shown.

Finding Existing Frames

Frequently when placing your own frames on the screen, you will want to anchor them to an existing frame. If you know the name of the frame you can easily accomplish this, but as you've seen, sometimes the frame structure is a bit convoluted. In the World of Warcraft 3.2 patch, a new utility was added that allows you to see information about the frames at a given point on the screen. You can invoke this utility with the `/framestack` slash command, which is used to toggle it on and off. Figure 9-12 shows how the information is displayed in-game.

Figure 9-12: /framestack tooltip showing the frames under the mouse cursor

The tooltip provides quite a bit of information. It lists the frames within a given frame strata from highest to lowest. Within each strata, it lists the frame along with the frame level in that strata (again from highest to lowest). That enables you to see the way in which the current location on the screen is being rendered, and also makes it easier to see how frames that you didn't create might be constructed.

Summary

This chapter introduced the basics of creating frames in both XML and Lua. You learned about the sizing mechanisms, and the anchoring system that is used to position frames on the screen. In addition you developed the base look for the BagBuddy addon using layers to ensure the graphics appear correctly.

Chapter 10 shows how you can use frame templates to ease the burden of creating lots of very similar frames.

The Code

BagBuddy.toc

```
## Interface: 30200
## Title: BagBuddy
## Notes: A handy helper that allows you to filter your inventory

BagBuddy.lua
BagBuddy.xml
```

BagBuddy.lua

```
function BagBuddy_OnLoad(self)
    SetPortraitToTexture(self.portrait, ↵
"Interface\\Icons\\INV_Misc_EngGizmos_30")
end
```

BagBuddy.xml

```xml
<Ui xmlns="http://www.blizzard.com/wow/ui/"
  xmlns:xsi="http://www.w3.org/2001/XMLSchema-instance"
  xsi:schemaLocation="http://www.blizzard.com/wow/ui/
  http://wowprogramming.com/FrameXML/UI.xsd">

  <Frame name="BagBuddy" parent="UIParent">
    <Size x="384" y="512"/>
    <Anchors>
      <Anchor point="CENTER" relativePoint="CENTER" ↵
relativeTo="UIParent"/>
    </Anchors>
    <Layers>
      <Layer level="BACKGROUND">
        <Texture name="$parent_Portrait" parentKey="portrait" ↵
file="Interface\Icons\INV_Misc_EngGizmos_30">
          <Size x="60" y="60"/>
          <Anchors>
            <Anchor point="TOPLEFT">
              <Offset x="7" y="-6"/>
            </Anchor>
          </Anchors>
        </Texture>
      </Layer>
      <Layer level="BORDER">
        <Texture file="Interface\BankFrame\UI-BankFrame-TopLeft">
          <Anchors>
            <Anchor point="TOPLEFT"/>
          </Anchors>
        </Texture>
```

```
            <Texture file="Interface\BankFrame\UI-BankFrame-TopRight">
              <Anchors>
                <Anchor point="TOPRIGHT"/>
              </Anchors>
            </Texture>
            <Texture file="Interface\BankFrame\UI-BankFrame-BotLeft">
              <Anchors>
                <Anchor point="BOTTOMLEFT"/>
              </Anchors>
            </Texture>
            <Texture file="Interface\BankFrame\UI-BankFrame-BotRight">
              <Anchors>
                <Anchor point="BOTTOMRIGHT"/>
              </Anchors>
            </Texture>
          </Layer>
        </Layers>
        <Scripts>
          <OnLoad function="BagBuddy_OnLoad"/>
        </Scripts>
      </Frame>
    </Ui>
```

Saving Time with Frame Templates

Chapter 9 introduced the concept of using frame templates to save time. Rather than specifying the same attributes and elements over and over again, you can create a single template and later inherit from it when creating new frames. In this chapter you'll create a frame template for the item slots in BagBuddy and then create frames dynamically from the template.

Understanding Templates

Templates provide developers with an easy way to define common sets of attributes and elements and then create multiple frames that utilize the template, inheriting all of that setup. Say, for example, that you need to create a row of three 16×16 buttons that contain a single texture. Without templates, the code might look something like this:

```
<Button name="Button1">
  <Size x="16" y="16"/>
  <Layers>
    <Layer level="BACKGROUND">
      <Texture name="$parentIcon" parentKey="icon">
        <Color r="1.0" g="1.0" b="1.0"/>
      </Texture>
    </Layer>
  </Layers>
</Button>
<Button name="Button2">
  <Size x="16" y="16"/>
  <Anchors>
    <Anchor point="TOPLEFT" relativePoint="TOPRIGHT" relativeTo="Button2"/>
```

```
   </Anchors>
   <Layers>
     <Layer level="BACKGROUND">
       <Texture name="$parentIcon" parentKey="icon">
         <Color r="1.0" g="1.0" b="1.0"/>
       </Texture>
     </Layer>
   </Layers>
</Button>
<Button name="Button3">
  <Size x="16" y="16"/>
  <Anchors>
    <Anchor point="TOPLEFT" relativePoint="TOPRIGHT" relativeTo="Button2"/>
  </Anchors>
  <Layers>
    <Layer level="BACKGROUND">
      <Texture name="$parentIcon" parentKey="icon">
        <Color r="1.0" g="1.0" b="1.0"/>
      </Texture>
    </Layer>
  </Layers>
</Button>
```

Using frame templates, you could instead write the following:

```
<Button name="MyButtonTemplate" virtual="true">
  <Size x="16" y="16"/>
  <Layers>
    <Layer level="BACKGROUND">
      <Texture name="$parentIcon" parentKey="icon">
        <Color r="1.0" g="1.0" b="1.0"/>
      </Texture>
    </Layer>
  </Layers>
</Button>

<Button name="Button1" inherits="MyButtonTemplate"/>
<Button name="Button2" inherits="MyButtonTemplate">
  <Anchors>
    <Anchor point="TOPLEFT" relativePoint="TOPRIGHT" relativeTo="Button2"/>
  </Anchors>
</Button>
<Button name="Button3" inherits="MyButtonTemplate">
  <Anchors>
    <Anchor point="TOPLEFT" relativePoint="TOPRIGHT" relativeTo="Button2"/>
  </Anchors>
</Button>
</Ui>
```

Using a template in this case only saves 13 lines, but imagine if you needed to create a row of eight buttons instead of three! You can use the `CreateFrame()` function to create new frames, saving yourself quite a bit of code.

Templates can be created and inherited for the following type of elements:

- Frames
- Font strings
- Textures
- Animations
- Animation groups

In addition, the template system is overloaded to work with font definitions and font strings. A font string can, of course, inherit from a font string template and inherit the attributes and elements, but may also inherit from a font definition. When this happens, the font string does not really inherit the attributes, but rather links itself to the font definition. If the font definition were to later change, the font string would change along with it.

Throughout this chapter, font definitions are referred to as a distinct concept from templates.

Advantages of Using Templates

The primary advantage of using templates is the capability to create complex elements repeatedly without needing to retype them for each instance. To accomplish this, templates take advantage of the means to automatically name elements using `$parent`, and make sub-elements accessible using the `parentKey` attribute.

Naming Elements Using $parent

Using the string `$parent` in an element's name in order to include the parent's name becomes very important when working with templates, to ensure that frames are consistently named. Prior to the 3.0 patch, this was the primary method used to name frames in the default user interface.

Many of the default templates, such as the dropdown menu template, require a frame to have a name for them to function properly. They make heavy use of parent-named textures and sub-frames in the code that manages them. In the future, these templates might be converted to use the `parentKey` attribute instead, so the naming required might be removed, but there have been no moves in that direction yet.

In the preceding example, the textures created in the template will be accessible as `Button1Icon`, `Button2Icon`, and `Button3Icon`. Programmatically, code might find the icon of such a button using the following code (assuming that the variable `self` is set to one of the three buttons):

```
_G[self:GetName() .. "Icon"]:SetTexture(1, 0, 0)
```

This code fetches the name of the frame, concatenates the string `Icon` on the end, and looks that key up in the global environment. It then calls the

`SetTexture` of the resulting texture, to color it red. Although accesses such as this are better handled using the `parentKey` attribute, naming frames is still very important. As shown at the end of Chapter 9, users and developers can use the `/framestack` command to determine what frames are on screen at a given point in time. If you make lots of unnamed frames, it is very difficult to distinguish among them. For that reason, you are encouraged to create named frames in addition to utilizing the `parentKey` attribute where appropriate.

Setting Keys Using the parentKey Attribute

In addition to being useful in normal frame definitions, the `parentKey` attribute can be used in template definitions to make textures, font strings, and sub-frames accessible. Rather than perform a name lookup, you could set the texture of a button's icon using the following code (assuming that the variable `self` is set to one of the three buttons):

```
self.icon:SetTexture(1, 0, 0)
```

In addition to being more efficient, this method is easier to read and doesn't require the code to know whether or not frames are named. Although the majority of the templates in the default user interface do not yet take advantage of this feature, it's a nice and easy way to define and access the elements of a frame.

Creating a Template for BagBuddy's Item Buttons

Each item slot in BagBuddy will show the item's icon and the number of items of a given type in your inventory. In addition, there will be a colored border around each item showing its rarity (that is, purple for epic, blue for rare, and so on). The default user interface already has a template that contains all of these elements, called `ItemButtonTemplate`.

In fact, you could inherit directly from `ItemButtonTemplate`, but that wouldn't be a very good example. In addition, if Blizzard makes any changes to its template, your addon might break. Instead you will copy the code from the FrameXML definition and adapt it to your own needs. Open `BagBuddy.xml` and add the following at the top of the file, inside the `<Ui>` element:

```
<Button name="BagBuddyItemTemplate" virtual="true">
  <Size>
    <AbsDimension x="37" y="37"/>
  </Size>
  <Layers>
    <Layer level="BORDER">
      <Texture name="$parentIconTexture" parentKey="icon"/>
```

```
            <FontString name="$parentCount" parentKey="count"
  inherits="NumberFontNormal" justifyH="RIGHT" hidden="true">
            <Anchors>
              <Anchor point="BOTTOMRIGHT">
                <Offset>
                  <AbsDimension x="-5" y="2"/>
                </Offset>
              </Anchor>
            </Anchors>
          </FontString>
        </Layer>
        <Layer level="OVERLAY">
          <Texture name="$parentGlow" parentKey="glow" alphaMode="ADD"
  file="Interface\Buttons\UI-ActionButton-Border">
            <Size x="70" y="70"/>
            <Anchors>
              <Anchor point="CENTER"/>
            </Anchors>
            <Color r="1.0" g="1.0" b="1.0" a="0.6"/>
          </Texture>
        </Layer>
      </Layers>
  </Button>
```

This template is named `BagBuddyItemTemplate`. Because the names of templates are global, you should ensure that your name won't conflict with another template. The easiest way to do this is to prefix it with some text and use a meaningful name. You give the frame a size, and define a single graphics layer on the BORDER level. Inside this group, you create an icon texture and a single font string to display the item count.

Setting Button Textures

Each button in World of Warcraft can have a few different types of textures that are displayed in different states. The `NormalTexture` is shown when the button is in a resting state. When the user clicks the button, the `PushedTexture` is displayed. Finally the `HighlightTexture` appears when the mouse is hovering over the button. Define these in `BagBuddyItemTemplate`, after the `</Layers>` tag but before the `</Button>` tag:

```
<NormalTexture name="$parentNormalTexture" file="Interface\Buttons\UI- ↵
Quickslot2">
  <Size>
    <AbsDimension x="64" y="64"/>
  </Size>
  <Anchors>
    <Anchor point="CENTER">
```

```
        <Offset>
          <AbsDimension x="0" y="-1"/>
        </Offset>
      </Anchor>
    </Anchors>
  </NormalTexture>
  <PushedTexture file="Interface\Buttons\UI-Quickslot-Depress"/>
  <HighlightTexture file="Interface\Buttons\ButtonHilight-Square"
  alphaMode="ADD"/>
```

The pushed and highlight textures inherit the size and the placement of the normal texture, because the game just changes the image file being displayed. You can see a new texture attribute that is used in the highlight texture, called alphaMode. This attribute has five different options:

- DISABLE—Ignores the alpha channel completely when rendering the texture.

- BLEND—Uses the alpha channel with a normal blending overlay.

- ALPHAKEY—Interprets the alpha with any black value being transparent, and any non-black value being opaque.

- ADD—Uses the alpha channel with an additive blending overlay.

- MOD—Ignores the alpha channel, multiplying the image against the background.

The template uses the ADD alpha mode to achieve its particular highlight effect.

Creating New Frames with Your Template

Now that you've defined the template, you need to actually create some frames using it. Although you could do this in XML, you would need to create 24 different frames and set anchors on each of them individually. Instead you will do it using Lua, which is much shorter. Open BagBuddy.lua and add the following inside the BagBuddy_OnLoad function:

```
-- Create the item slots
self.items = {}
for idx = 1, 24 do
  local item = CreateFrame("Button", "BagBuddy_Item" .. idx, self, ↵
"BagBuddyItemTemplate")
  self.items[idx] = item
  if idx == 1 then
    item:SetPoint("TOPLEFT", 40, -73)
  elseif idx == 7 or idx == 13 or idx == 19 then
```

```
    item:SetPoint("TOPLEFT", self.items[idx-6], "BOTTOMLEFT", 0, -7)
  else
    item:SetPoint("TOPLEFT", self.items[idx-1], "TOPRIGHT", 12, 0)
  end
end
```

You first create a table that will be used to store the individual buttons. This will make it easier to iterate over the buttons when displaying items. For each index you create a new button from the template you created. Then you programmatically set the anchors:

- If you're creating the first button, anchor it to the frame itself in the first button slot.

- When creating the first button in any subsequent row, anchor the new button to the first column of the prior row.

- For all other buttons, anchor the new button to the previous button on the row.

By contrast, accomplishing the same thing in XML would require 3 to 5 lines for each button for a total of somewhere between 70 and 250 lines. When creating just a few instances of a template, I tend to include them in the XML, but whenever I'm doing something very repetitive like this I prefer to create the frames in Lua.

As you move your mouse over the item buttons you can see the highlight texture appear. This allows you to easily see which button you are currently hovering over.

Exploring Font Definitions

Font definitions are a bit of an exception when it comes to the template system in World of Warcraft. Although they use the same inheritance mechanism, they work quite differently. This section looks at a specific font definition to provide an understanding of how they work. You can find the definition of GameFontNormalSmall in FontStyles.xml, which can be extracted using the Blizzard Interface Toolkit, introduced in Chapter 8. The code for the template is as follows:

```
<Font name="GameFontNormalSmall" inherits="SystemFont_Shadow_Small" ↵
virtual="true">
  <Color r="1.0" g="0.82" b="0"/>
</Font>
```

The font definition includes the virtual attribute, but it's essentially ignored. Remember, you are creating a font definition (which is an actual in-game object) rather than just creating a template. This particular definition inherits from another template called SystemFont_Shadow_Small, defined in Fonts.xml:

```
<Font name="SystemFont_Shadow_Small" font="Fonts\FRIZQT__.TTF"
virtual="true">
  <Shadow>
    <Offset>
      <AbsDimension x="1" y="-1"/>
    </Offset>
    <Color r="0" g="0" b="0"/>
  </Shadow>
  <FontHeight>
    <AbsValue val="10"/>
  </FontHeight>
</Font>
```

This template doesn't inherit from any other template, and actually defines the font file that is used to display text, along with a drop shadow and the height of the text. The font used is called Friz Quadrata and is included in the game files. The font template defines a drop shadow to the bottom right of the text with an offset of 1 pixel in each direction. The color of the shadow is set to black, and the height of the font is set to 10 pixels.

When the GameFontNormalSmall font definition inherits from SystemFont _Shadow_Small, it links itself to the original font. Any changes made to the parent font will be reflected in the inheriting font. The only change the new template makes is to set the color to gold, but any of the attributes or elements defined in a font definition can be overridden while inheriting.

Altering a Font Definition

The major difference between templates and font definitions is that font definitions can be altered once you are in-game, and the changes will trickle down the inheritance tree. For example, you can run the following code to change the height of SystemFont_Shadow_Small from 10 to 13:

```
/run SystemFont_Shadow_Small:SetFont("Fonts\\FRIZQT__.TTF", 13)
```

Figure 10-1 shows the player unit frame and the social panel at the default font size, and after running the code.

As you can see, only those elements that inherited from SystemFont_Shadow _Small (and by inheritance GameFontNormalSmall) are changed. The color and shadow definitions remain set, but the font size has been changed. In the same way, you could actually replace the font file that is being used to display some text, and it will immediately be reflected in-game throughout the font inheritance tree.

Figure 10-1: The player unit frame and social panel with default (left) and altered (right) font settings

Investigating UIPanelTemplates

There are a number of already defined templates that you may find useful when creating your own addons. Many of them are defined in `UIPanelTemplates.xml`, but there are templates defined throughout the default user interface. This section explores a few of the more commonly used templates with code to create an example and an image of each.

Run the following code to define a helper function that will enable you to move any of the frames you have created (this function is used in the example code):

```
function MakeMovable(frame)
   frame:SetMovable(true)
   frame:RegisterForDrag("LeftButton")
   frame:SetScript("OnDragStart", frame.StartMoving)
   frame:SetScript("OnDragStop", frame.StopMovingOrSizing)
end
```

For now, just ignore what the code is doing; you will learn more about interacting with widgets in Chapter 12.

UIPanelButtonTemplate

The `UIPanelButtonTemplate` template is used for the buttons on the main game menu and on many of the panels in the user interface. The button can be resized (in fact, you must supply a size because the template does not) and contains a gold label in the center. Figure 10-2 shows the frame created by the following code:

```
local frame = CreateFrame("Button", "UIPanelButtonTemplateTest",
UIParent, "UIPanelButtonTemplate")
frame:SetHeight(20)
frame:SetWidth(100)
frame:SetText("Test Button")
frame:ClearAllPoints()
frame:SetPoint("CENTER", 0, 0)
MakeMovable(frame)
```

Figure 10-2: Example frame created from UIPanelButtonTemplate

UIPanelCloseButton

The `UIPanelCloseButton` template (which lacks the word template in its name) is used for the close button that appears on most of the panels in the user interface. As a matter of fact, you should be careful if you click on the example button you create, because it will hide your entire user interface due to a script defined in the template. You can re-show your UI by pressing Alt+Z. Figure 10-3 shows the close button created by the following code:

```
local frame = CreateFrame("Button", "UIPanelCloseButtonTest",
UIParent, "UIPanelCloseButton")
frame:ClearAllPoints()
frame:SetPoint("CENTER", 0, 0)
MakeMovable(frame)
```

Figure 10-3: Close button created using UIPanelCloseButton

UIPanelScrollBarTemplate

Although the `UIPanelScrollBarTemplate` template is meant to be used with the built-in scroll frame templates, you could certainly instantiate it in other circumstances. The template defines a button that scrolls up, a button that scrolls down, and the scroll "knob" that can be dragged to set the scroll value. Figure 10-4 shows the scroll bar created with the following code:

```
local frame = CreateFrame("Slider", "UIPanelScrollBarTemplateTest", ↵
UIParent, "UIPanelScrollBarTemplate")
frame:ClearAllPoints()
frame:SetPoint("CENTER", 0, 0)
frame:SetHeight(100)
frame:SetWidth(20)
frame:SetScript("OnValueChanged", nil)
frame:SetMinMaxValues(0, 100)
frame:SetValue(70)
MakeMovable(frame)
```

Figure 10-4: Scroll bar frame created using UIPanelScrollBarTemplate

InputBoxTemplate

When creating a new input box, you can use the `InputBoxTemplate` template to create the background and border. It seems to have an issue when you create it dynamically in Lua (in particular, the middle portion of the background does not resize itself properly). Figure 10-5 shows the example created with the following Lua code, designed to work around this bug:

```
local frame = CreateFrame("EditBox", "InputBoxTemplateTest", ↵
UIParent, "InputBoxTemplate")
frame:SetWidth(250)
frame:SetHeight(20)
InputBoxTemplateTestMiddle:ClearAllPoints()
```

```
InputBoxTemplateTestMiddle:SetPoint("LEFT", InputBoxTemplateTestLeft, ↵
"RIGHT", 0, 0)
InputBoxTemplateTestMiddle:SetPoint("RIGHT", InputBoxTemplateTestRight, ↵
"LEFT", 0, 0)
frame:ClearAllPoints()
frame:SetPoint("CENTER", 0, 0)
frame:SetAutoFocus(false)
frame:SetText("This is an example input box")
MakeMovable(frame)
```

If you'd rather use XML you can create the frame in the following way to avoid the bug (which is a result of the frame being created initially without a size):

```
<EditBox name="InputBoxTemplateTest" parent="UIParent" inherits= ↵
"InputBoxTemplate">
  <Size x="250" y="20"/>
  <Anchors>
    <Anchor point="CENTER"/>
  </Anchors>
  <Scripts>
    <OnLoad>
      self:SetAutoFocus(false)
    </OnLoad>
  </Scripts>
</EditBox>
```

This is an example input box

Figure 10-5: Example input box using InputBoxTemplate

UICheckButtonTemplate

To create a toggleable checkbox, you can use `UICheckButtonTemplate`. This template contains the actual check button itself, with a text label on its right side. Figure 10-6 shows the example created with the following code:

```
local frame = CreateFrame("CheckButton", "UICheckButtonTemplateTest", ↵
UIParent, "UICheckButtonTemplate")
frame:ClearAllPoints()
frame:SetPoint("CENTER", 0, 0)
_G[frame:GetName() .. "Text"]:SetText("Example checkbutton")
MakeMovable(frame)
```

Figure 10-6: Example check button using UICheckButtonTemplate

TabButtonTemplate

The tabs at the bottom of the character and social panels are created using TabButtonTemplate. To work with them properly, you can use a number of utility functions defined in UIPanelTemplates.lua. One such function is PanelTemplates_TabResize, which is used in the following example. Figure 10-7 shows the tab button resulting from the code.

```
local frame = CreateFrame("Button", "TabButtonTemplateTest", UIParent, ↵
"TabButtonTemplate")
frame:ClearAllPoints()
frame:SetPoint("CENTER", 0, 0)
frame:SetText("Example Tab")
PanelTemplates_TabResize(frame)
MakeMovable(frame)
```

Figure 10-7: Panel tab created using TabButtonTemplate

UIRadioButtonTemplate

To create a radio button rather than a checkbox, you can create a frame using UIRadioButtonTemplate. To deselect any other radio buttons when one is selected, you would need to manage that logic on your own. Figure 10-8 shows the radio button created using the following example code:

```
local frame = CreateFrame("CheckButton", "UIRadioButtonTemplateTest", ↵
UIParent, "UIRadioButtonTemplate")
frame:SetHeight(20)
frame:SetWidth(20)
frame:ClearAllPoints()
frame:SetPoint("CENTER", 0, 0)
_G[frame:GetName() .. "Text"]:SetText("Example radio button")
MakeMovable(frame)
```

Figure 10-8: Radio button created using UIRadioButtonTemplate

Summary

This chapter showed how templates can be used to better organize frame, texture, and font string definitions. You created a template for BagBuddy and used it to dynamically create new item buttons in Lua. You also explored the various UIPanelTemplates already defined in the default user interface.

The Code

BagBuddy.lua

```lua
function BagBuddy_OnLoad(self)
  SetPortraitToTexture(self.portrait, ↵
"Interface\\Icons\\INV_Misc_EngGizmos_30")

  -- Create the item slots
  self.items = {}
  for idx = 1, 24 do
    local item = CreateFrame("Button", "BagBuddy_Item" .. idx, ↵
self, "BagBuddyItemTemplate")
    self.items[idx] = item
    if idx == 1 then
      item:SetPoint("TOPLEFT", 40, -73)
    elseif idx == 7 or idx == 13 or idx == 19 then
      item:SetPoint("TOPLEFT", self.items[idx-6], "BOTTOMLEFT", ↵
0, -7)
    else
      item:SetPoint("TOPLEFT", self.items[idx-1], "TOPRIGHT", ↵
12, 0)
    end
  end
end
```

BagBuddy.xml

```xml
<Ui xmlns="http://www.blizzard.com/wow/ui/"
  xmlns:xsi="http://www.w3.org/2001/XMLSchema-instance"
  xsi:schemaLocation="http://www.blizzard.com/wow/ui/
  http://wowprogramming.com/FrameXML/UI.xsd">

  <Button name="BagBuddyItemTemplate" virtual="true">
    <Size>
      <AbsDimension x="37" y="37"/>
    </Size>
    <Layers>
      <Layer level="BORDER">
        <Texture name="$parentIconTexture" parentKey="icon"/>
        <FontString name="$parentCount" parentKey="count" ↵
inherits="NumberFontNormal" justifyH="RIGHT" hidden="true">
          <Anchors>
            <Anchor point="BOTTOMRIGHT">
              <Offset>
                <AbsDimension x="-5" y="2"/>
              </Offset>
            </Anchor>
          </Anchors>
        </FontString>
```

```
        </Layer>
        <Layer level="OVERLAY">
          <Texture name="$parentGlow" parentKey="glow" ↵
alphaMode="ADD" file="Interface\Buttons\UI-ActionButton-Border">
            <Size x="70" y="70"/>
            <Anchors>
              <Anchor point="CENTER"/>
            </Anchors>
            <Color r="1.0" g="1.0" b="1.0" a="0.6"/>
          </Texture>
        </Layer>
      </Layers>
      <NormalTexture name="$parentNormalTexture" ↵
file="Interface\Buttons\UI-Quickslot2">
        <Size>
          <AbsDimension x="64" y="64"/>
        </Size>
        <Anchors>
          <Anchor point="CENTER">
            <Offset>
              <AbsDimension x="0" y="-1"/>
            </Offset>
          </Anchor>
        </Anchors>
      </NormalTexture>
      <PushedTexture file="Interface\Buttons\UI-Quickslot-Depress"/>
      <HighlightTexture ↵
file="Interface\Buttons\ButtonHilight-Square" alphaMode="ADD"/>
    </Button>

  <Frame name="BagBuddy" parent="UIParent">
    <Size x="384" y="512"/>
    <Anchors>
      <Anchor point="CENTER" relativePoint="CENTER" ↵
relativeTo="UIParent"/>
    </Anchors>
    <Layers>
      <Layer level="BACKGROUND">
        <Texture name="$parent_Portrait" parentKey="portrait" ↵
file="Interface\Icons\INV_Misc_EngGizmos_30">
          <Size x="60" y="60"/>
          <Anchors>
            <Anchor point="TOPLEFT">
              <Offset x="7" y="-6"/>
            </Anchor>
          </Anchors>
        </Texture>
      </Layer>
      <Layer level="OVERLAY">
        <FontString name="$parent_Title" parentKey="title" ↵
```

```
      inherits="GameFontNormal" text="BagBuggy">
            <Anchors>
              <Anchor point="TOP">
                <Offset x="0" y="-18"/>
              </Anchor>
            </Anchors>
          </FontString>
        </Layer>
        <Layer level="BORDER">
          <Texture file="Interface\BankFrame\UI-BankFrame-TopLeft">
            <Anchors>
              <Anchor point="TOPLEFT"/>
            </Anchors>
          </Texture>
          <Texture file="Interface\BankFrame\UI-BankFrame-TopRight">
            <Anchors>
              <Anchor point="TOPRIGHT"/>
            </Anchors>
          </Texture>
          <Texture file="Interface\BankFrame\UI-BankFrame-BotLeft">
            <Anchors>
              <Anchor point="BOTTOMLEFT"/>
            </Anchors>
          </Texture>
          <Texture file="Interface\BankFrame\UI-BankFrame-BotRight">
            <Anchors>
              <Anchor point="BOTTOMRIGHT"/>
            </Anchors>
          </Texture>
        </Layer>
      </Layers>
      <Scripts>
        <OnLoad function="BagBuddy_OnLoad"/>
      </Scripts>
    </Frame>
  </Ui>
```

## CHAPTER 11

Exploring the World of Warcraft API

World of Warcraft is an incredibly complex game. At any given moment—even with the default UI—there can be a massive amount of information on the screen: unit frames showing players' and mobs' health, mana, hostility, and PvP status; buffs and their durations; action buttons with various states such as cooldown, number of uses, and range indication; tracked quests; and so on. To get much of this information, you must query the *application programming interface*, or API.

> **NOTE** API is a generic term in the software field describing a set of functions and data structures that are used by a program to interact with its environment.
> Another example of an API is Win32, which allows Windows programs to read and create files, display controls such as buttons and checkboxes, communicate over a network, launch other applications, and so on.

Similar to the API that the Lua programming language provides, World of Warcraft provides a large set of functions that allow you to query information about the state of the game. Other functions allow you to change something about the client, such as selecting different quests in the quest log, or changing what map is displayed in the world map frame. This chapter introduces you to the API system provided by World of Warcraft.

Understanding the WoW API

The World of Warcraft API consists of several types of functions including C functions (functions defined in C and exposed to the Lua environment), Lua-defined functions (found in Blizzard's FrameXML files), and protected functions, which can only be used by Blizzard code because of security and automation concerns.

The functions cover quite a wide range of topics from changing game settings to posting auctions. Some operate like Lua library functions; others provide a specific interface to some aspect of gameplay.

As you progress through this chapter, you may want to flip to Chapter 27, "API Reference," to see the details of the various APIs presented. It will both help you to understand the content of this chapter and give you a glimpse into the kinds of functions available to you.

Normal APIs

Most of the built-in functions you'll use on a regular basis are defined in C, rather than in Lua. They interact with the various subsystems of the WoW client to gather information about the state of the game and to take action in several ways. One example is `UnitHealth`, which returns the health of a specified *unit* (a creature or player referenced by a unit ID). Run the following statement in-game, and it displays your current number of hit points:

```
/run print(UnitHealth("player"))
```

The unit ID in this case is `"player"`, which always refers to you, the player. Use `"target"` instead, and it prints the health of your target, or `nil` if you have no target.

This introduces a recurring theme in the WoW API. Many groups of functions operate on a certain type of data. In the preceding example, the data type is unit ID. Some of the many functions that use unit IDs are `UnitMana`, `UnitExists`, and `UnitLevel`.

Library-like APIs

The Lua standard libraries provide a wide range of functions for string manipulation, mathematic operations, and so on. However, not all functions that are exposed in a standard Lua installation are appropriate for inclusion in WoW. Because addons are not allowed to access any files directly, the `io` library obviously isn't included. The `debug` and `os` libraries also contain some more potentially hazardous functions, so they aren't included. However, some of the functions provided by these libraries are benign enough that their functionality has been exposed through new functions. Table 11-1 shows some of these library-API relationships.

NOTE Some of the parameters and returns may vary between the standard versions and those included in the WoW client. See Chapter 27, "API Reference," for documentation of each function.

Table 11-1: Library Functions and Their API Equivalents

STANDARD LIBRARY	EQUIVALENT WOW API
os.date	date
os.time	time
os.difftime	difftime
debug.traceback	debugstack

In addition to direct library translations, several functions specific to WoW play a support role in addon development but do not directly relate to anything in-game. These have semantics similar to library functions but are technically part of the WoW API. They are easily identifiable because their names are entirely lowercase—debugprofilestart and hooksecurefunc, for instance. Some of these functions are defined by the game client, but others are defined in the game's FrameXML code.

FrameXML Functions

The code for the default user interface includes definitions for a number of utility functions. Although they may not be considered APIs in the strictest sense, their usage is consistent enough with true API functions that they deserve documentation here. For example, consider the definition of the TakeScreenshot function:

```
function TakeScreenshot()
  if ( ActionStatus:IsShown() ) then
    ActionStatus:Hide();
  end
  Screenshot();
end
```

This function is designed to make it easier to take screenshots programmatically. Normally after you take a screenshot the "Screen Captured" message is displayed. This function hides that text so you can take multiple screenshots in quick succession.

The most unique characteristic of FrameXML-defined functions is that you can examine their inner workings. All of the APIs mentioned so far are hidden behind the Lua-C interface. You can call the functions from Lua and use the values they return, but in general there is no way to know exactly how they operate.

Protected Functions

Early in WoW's life, addons had free reign over all functions available in the API. Some of these functions included movement control, combat activities, and other features the designers have since deemed inappropriate for addons. That early leeway made it relatively trivial—especially with a bit of help from external programs—to write "grinding bots" that would completely control your character while you went to the movies. Set it up before work and by the time you got home you could have gained a few levels and received massive amounts of loot to sell.

A similar problem were "button masher" addons like Emergency Monitor and Decursive. A player could repeatedly press a single key or mouse button and the addon would do all the decision-making: who to target, what spell to cast, and so on.

Subsequent patches removed these capabilities by marking the offending functions as protected. Protected functions can be called only by built-in code. In addition there is another class of functions that are only protected during combat. WoW is able to tell when the running code is from an addon or macro versus a built-in file, so it can prevent the protected function from running in those cases. Table 11-2 describes a small sampling of protected functions to give you an idea of their nature.

Table 11-2: Sample of Protected Functions

FUNCTION	DESCRIPTION
Jump	Causes the character to jump
CastSpellByName	Attempts to cast the given spell
ToggleAutoRun	Controls the character's auto-run
TargetUnit	Targets the specified unit
PetAttack	Sends your pet to attack
RegisterUnitWatch	Registers a frame to be shown/hidden based on a unit

These are just examples. All movement, targeting, ability use, and action bar manipulation functions are completely protected. The API reference section in Chapter 27 shows which functions are protected, so you know whether or not you can call them.

NOTE You may be wondering how it is possible to write an action bar or unit frame addon at this point, considering that spell-casting and targeting functions are protected. This problem is resolved by using secure templates, which are covered in Chapter 15.

Unit Functions Up Close

The first logical grouping of APIs to examine is unit functions. As previously mentioned, these functions expose data about players, mobs, and NPCs. Most of the functions are quite simple; they take in one or two unit IDs and return some information to the calling code. Table 11-3 shows a few of the different unit functions.

Table 11-3: Example Unit Functions

UNIT FUNCTION	DESCRIPTION
exists = UnitExists(unit)	Returns 1 if the unit exists, nil otherwise. For example, UnitExists("target") returns 1 only if you have a target selected. Many of the other unit functions return nil if UnitExists is nil.
name, realm = UnitName(unit)	Returns the name of the specified unit. If the unit is a player in a cross-realm battleground, the second return is the server name, otherwise it is nil.
level = UnitLevel(unit)	Returns the level of the unit or −1 if you're not supposed to know the level (special bosses, enemy players more than 10 levels above you).
reaction = UnitReaction(unit, otherUnit)	Determines the reaction of unit to otherUnit. Returns a number from 1−7, where 1 is extremely hostile, 7 is as friendly as possible, and nil is returned if unknown.
health = UnitHealth(unit)	Returns the health of the unit. For the player, the player's pet, party/raid members, and their pets, health is the absolute number of hit points. All other units return a percentage from 0−100.
mana = UnitPower(unit[, powerType)	Same as UnitHealth but for mana, rage, energy, and focus (collectively referred to as mana throughout the API). By default this function returns the current power type that unit is using, but you can specify a second argument to query another power type (for example, the mana of a druid who is shapeshifted).
healthMax = UnitHealthMax(unit)	Returns the maximum health of the unit (actual number of hit points or 100 depending on the same criteria as UnitHealth).
manaMax = UnitManaMax(unit)	Same as UnitHealthMax but for mana.

Each of these functions takes in unit IDs that follow a very simple pattern. A unit ID can be one of the tokens listed in Table 11-4 with either pet added to the end, or possible target included an arbitrary number of times. For example, party1target shows the target of your first party member, and party2pettarget represents the target of your second party member's pet. Additionally, the WoW client will accept the name of a party or raid member as a unit ID. These unit ID tokens are not case-sensitive.

NOTE Not every function will work correctly on all unit IDs. The documentation in Chapter 27 explains those cases.

Table 11-4: Base Unit IDs

UNIT ID	REFERS TO...
player	The character controlled by the player.
pet	The player's pet.
Vehicle	The player's vehicle.
target	The player's target (equivalent to "playertarget").
focus	The player's focus target.
mouseover	The unit underneath the mouse cursor. Includes characters in the 3-D world and any frame with a set unit attribute.
partyN	The Nth party member where N is a number from 1–4. None of the party unit IDs refers to the player.
partypetN	The Nth party member's pet.
raidN	The Nth raid member where N is a number from 1 to however many members there are in the raid. The highest N always refers to the player, and the lowest N always refers to the raid leader. There is no correlation between the N for raid units and the N for party units.
raidpetN	The Nth raid member's pet.
arenaN	The Nth enemy in the arena.
npc	The currently selected NPC. UnitExists only returns true for this unit while you are interacting with an NPC (that is, when you are turning in a quest, using a vendor, and so on).
none	No unit. It was created to allow activation of the target selection cursor even when you are targeting something vulnerable to the spell you are casting.

In addition to these token-based unit IDs, most functions will accept the name of a party or raid member. For example, if you have a party member called "Healadin" you could query his health by running:

```
/run print(UnitHealth("Healadin"))
```

Querying Item Information for BagBuddy

To get the information you need for BagBuddy, you have to access three different (but related) API systems:

- **Container API**—Provides information about your bags, and the items in your bags.
- **Item API**—Provides various information about specific game items.
- **Inventory API**—Provides information about the items the player currently has equipped.

In this section, you implement a simple function that scans your bags for items, then sorts them and displays them in the BagBuddy frame. Later, you extend this update function to allow for filtering of items based on name and rarity.

Scanning Bags with the Container API

Start with an example function that can scan the player's bags for empty slots. Run the following code snippet in-game:

```
local freeSlots = 0
for bag = 0, NUM_BAG_SLOTS do
  for slot = 1, GetContainerNumSlots(bag) do
    local texture = GetContainerItemInfo(bag, slot)
    if not texture then
      freeSlots = freeSlots + 1
    end
  end
end
print("You have", freeSlots, "free slots in your containers.")
```

This container API uses bag IDs and slot IDs. A bag ID can be any of the following values:

- 0—The player's backpack
- 1—The player's first bag (from the right)
- 2—The player's second bag (from the right)
- 3—The player's third bag (from the right)
- 4—The player's fourth bag (from the right)

In the future, WoW may add more bag slots, so when you iterate over the bags in the preceding snippet, start at 0 and go through to NUM_BAG_SLOTS. Because each bag might have a different number of slots, you use the GetContainerNumSlots() function to query the max number of slots. This function takes in a bag ID and returns the number of slots in that bag.

The second (inner) loop goes through each slot in the bag and uses the GetContainerItemInfo() function to query information about the item in the given slot. In this case, the function returns the following information:

- texture—The path to the icon texture for the item.
- count—The number of items in the stack at the given container slot.
- locked—Indicates if the item is currently locked (such as when the item has been dragged to a mail slot, or the trade window).
- quality—A number representing the quality/rarity of the item.
- readable—Indicates if the item can be read; for example, a book or scroll.
- lootable—Indicates if the item can be looted; for example, a chest or clam that can be opened.
- link—A hyperlink for the item in a given slot that can be passed to the item functions for more information.

If the slot does not contain an item, texture (the first return) will be nil. You can check it to easily see if the slot contains an item. The preceding snippet checks to see if this value is missing, and counts it as a free slot if that's the case. Although there is an easier function to obtain this information, GetContainerNumFreeSlots(), you'll be using the same type of loop in BagBuddy.

Querying Detailed Item Information

You get quite a bit of information from the container API, but you can't get other basic information such as the item's name. For that, you need to utilize the item API. It enables you to get the following information about an item (among other details):

- The item's name.
- The item's rarity.
- The maximum stack size for the given item.
- The sale price of the item at a vendor.
- The level required to use the item.

Item Identifiers

To use the item API, you need some way to specify the item you'd like to query. You could simply specify the item name, but due to names not being completely unique, this only works when the item is in the player's inventory or containers. The more specific form allows you to specify the numeric item ID, or an item's hyperlink or item string.

Numeric Item ID

Each item in World of Warcraft is uniquely identified by a numeric ID. Table 11-5 shows a list of common items and their item IDs. Notice that some of the names are the same, whereas the IDs are distinct.

Table 11-5: Sample Mapping Between Items and Item IDs

ITEM NAME	ITEM ID
Hearthstone	6948
Insignia of the Alliance	18864
Insignia of the Alliance	29593
Militia Dagger	2224

The first Insignia of the Alliance item is the class-specific insignia for Paladins. The second is the Shaman-specific trinket. Although they no longer have different effects, they remain distinct items as far as WoW is concerned. Another advantage to utilizing item IDs instead of names is that the lookup will work correctly regardless of what locale client the player is using. If you try to look up an item with its English name on a French client, it will not work correctly.

In addition, the database sites for World of Warcraft (including WoW Armory) use these IDs. For example, the URL to access information about the Militia Dagger is `http://www.wowarmory.com/item-info.xml?i=2224`.

Item Strings

A problem with using just item IDs is that they don't include any information about a specific instance of an item. Say you have a pair of gloves that is enchanted with *Enchant Gloves - Gatherer*, an enchantment that gives you +5 skill in Mining, Herbalism, and Skinning. When you query the item by numeric ID, it will not include the enchantment. An item string combines the item ID with this information, and consists of the string `item:` followed by nine different numeric values, separated with colons. Table 11-6 shows the different values included in the string.

Table 11-6: Components of Item Strings

NAME	DESCRIPTION
itemID	The numeric item ID.
enchantID	A numeric identifier representing the permanent item enchantment.
jewellD1	A numeric identifier indicating a socketed gem in the given item.
jewellD2	See above.
jewellD3	See above.
jewellD4	See above.
suffixID	A numeric suffix identifier. This is how the game differentiates between an item that is "of the Monkey" and "of the Whale."
uniqueID	Information pertaining to a specific instance of an item, such as who crafted it or how many charges are left on a multi-charge item. The specific meaning of these numbers is unclear, and appears to be something generated and used by Blizzard on the server end of the game.
linkLevel	The level of the character supplying the link. This is used by the new Heirloom items to calculate the correct item tooltips.

Like most things in the WoW API, examples tend to make a bit more sense. The following is a list of example item strings, and the information they contain:

- `item:6948:0:0:0:0:0:0:0:0`—Hearthstone with no additional information about stats, creator, or level.

- `item:10042:0:0:0:0:0:614:0:0`—Cindercloth Robe with a suffix "of the Monkey" that adds +11 Agility and +11 Stamina.

- `item:42992:0:0:0:0:0:0:0:45`—Discerning Eye of the Beast, the heirloom mana trinket, shown scaled to level 40.

- `item:41319:3842:3642:3466:0:0:0:0:80`—Hateful Gladiator's Kodohide Helm with +30 Stamina +25 Resilience enchantment, and a gem that provides +32 Stamina and Stun Duration Reduced by 10 and a +9 Spell Power and +12 Stamina gem.

As you can see, any values not provided at the end default to 0. This means you can avoid specifying the item level or unique id if you don't have that information (or simply specify that they are 0).

Item Hyperlinks

Once you understand the format of an item string, creating an item hyperlink is very easy. A hyperlink, in general, consists of the following format:

```
|H<DATA>|h<DISPLAYTEXT>|h
```

The pipe (|) character is used in World of Warcraft as an escape character, much like Lua itself uses the backslash (\). The hyperlink begins with a |H, followed by the data for the hyperlink. In the case of item links, this is just the item string itself. The data ends with |h, followed by the text that is actually displayed in the hyperlink, including the left and right brackets. The hyperlink ends with a final |h. To color the link, you can wrap it using color codes.

For example, a script that can print a hyperlink for your Hearthstone might look like this:

```
print("|cffffffff|Hitem:6948:0:0:0:0:0:0:0:0|h[Hearthstone]|h|r")
```

The color code for white is specified, the hyperlink data is included, and the text of the link itself follows. You may encounter different types of hyperlinks in your exploration of the WoW API, but you won't find yourself creating them very often. More often than not, when you need a hyperlink you simply query the API and use whatever is returned.

Using the Item API

Once you have an item identifier, the item API is simple to use. In particular you are concerned with the GetItemInfo() function, which takes in such an identifier and returns the following:

- name—The name of the item.
- link—A hyperlink for the item.
- quality—Quality (rarity) level of the item.
- iLevel—Internal level of the item.
- reqLevel—Minimum character level required to use or equip the item.
- class—Localized name of the item's class/type.
- subclass—Localized name of the item's subclass/subtype.
- maxStack—Maximum stack size for the item (that is, largest number of items that can be held in a single bag slot).
- equipSlot—Non-localized token identifying the inventory type of the item.
- texture—Path to an icon texture for the item.
- vendorPrice—Price an NPC vendor will pay to buy the item from the player.

We are only concerned with the item's name, which is the first return from the function. You will use this to sort the items once you've finished scanning.

To prevent against item *scanning*, where someone tries to get information about items that aren't yet in the game, this function returns only information about those items that the player has seen. In particular, the item must exist in the player's local item cache.

Writing a Bag Scanner

You can put together the different APIs to update BagBuddy to actually display the player's inventory. Open `BagBuddy.lua` and add the following function definition at the end of the file:

```
function BagBuddy_Update()
  local items = {}

  -- Scan through the bag slots, looking for items
  for bag = 0, NUM_BAG_SLOTS do
    for slot = 0, GetContainerNumSlots(bag) do
      local texture, count, locked, quality, readable, lootable, link =
        GetContainerItemInfo(bag, slot)
      if texture then
        -- If found, grab the item number and store other data
        local itemNum = tonumber(link:match("|Hitem:(%d+):"))
        if not items[itemNum] then
          items[itemNum] = {
            texture = texture,
            count = count,
            quality = quality,
            name = GetItemInfo(link),
            link = link,
          }
        else
          -- The item already exists in our table, just update the count
          items[itemNum].count = items[itemNum].count + count
        end
      end
    end
  end
end
```

This function goes through all of the player's bag slots and checks to see if the slot is empty or not. For each item it finds, it parses the item link to get the item number and then stores the following information in a table:

- The path to the item's icon texture.
- The number of items in the stack.
- The quality number for the item.
- The item's name.
- The item's link.

You use the item number rather than the name because it enables you to differentiate between different items that share a name. You could use the item link, but the uniqueID component of the link may be different (for example, if the items were crafted by two different people). If you used the item link, the items would appear to be different.

If (during the loop) you encounter an item that you've already added to the table, you simply increment the item's count in the table entry that has already been stored.

Sorting the Player's Inventory

To ensure the inventory is displayed in a consistent order, you will sort them by name. Add the following function definition somewhere before the update function:

```
local function itemNameSort(a, b)
  return a.name < b.name
end
```

This function simply takes in two tables that are being compared, and compares the names of the items. Now you can use the function by adding the following to BagBuddy_Update(), at the end of the function:

```
local sortTbl = {}
for link, entry in pairs(items) do
  table.insert(sortTbl, entry)
end
table.sort(sortTbl, itemNameSort)
```

This code simply loops over all of the stored items, and adds each entry to a new temporary table. Then you call table.sort(), passing in your sorting function to do the heavy lifting.

Displaying the Inventory

Now that you have a sorted list of inventory items, you can write some code to display them in the BagBuddy frame. Add the following to BagBuddy_Update(), after the sorting and before the end of the function:

```
-- Now update the BagBuddyFrame with the listed items (in order)
for i = 1, 24 do
  local button = BagBuddy.items[i]
  local entry = sortTbl[i]

  if entry then
    -- There is an item in this slot

    button.icon:SetTexture(entry.texture)
    if entry.count > 1 then
      button.count:SetText(entry.count)
      button.count:Show()
    else
      button.count:Hide()
    end

    if entry.quality > 1 then
      button.glow:SetVertexColor(GetItemQualityColor(entry.quality))
```

```
        button.glow:Show()
    else
        button.glow:Hide()
    end
    button:Show()
  else
    button:Hide()
  end
end
```

Because you already know you have 24 buttons in the frame, simply loop over each of them. You also have a list of items that are sorted in order, so you know that the first item in the list should be displayed in the first button.

A lot happens on each iteration of the loop. First you check to see if there is a corresponding item in the list. If there isn't you just hide the button. Otherwise you first set the item's icon texture. If there are multiple items with the same item number, you update the item count font string. Finally, you check the quality of the item. If the quality is greater than one (that is, the item is green, blue, purple, or higher), you shade the glow texture to the appropriate color, obtained with the GetItemQualityColor() function.

This function takes in a quality index, and returns the red, green, and blue color components (between 0.0 and 1.0). These can then be passed into any of the functions that accept colors in that form, such as the texture method SetVertexColor(). The different quality indices are listed in Table 11-7.

Table 11-7: Item Quality Indices

INDEX	DESCRIPTION	COLOR	EXAMPLE ITEM
0	Poor	Grey	Broken I.W.I.N. Button
1	Common	White	Archmage Vargoth's Staff
2	Uncommon	Green	X-52 Rocket Helmet
3	Rare or Superior	Blue	Onyxia Scale Cloak
4	Epic	Purple	Talisman of Ephemeral Power
5	Legendary	Orange	Fragment of Val'anyr
6	Artifact or Heirloom	Light Yellow	Bloodied Arcanite Reaper

Testing the Update Function

You haven't set anything up to call the function, but you can call it manually by running the following code in-game:

```
/run BagBuddy_Update()
```

Figure 11-1 shows BagBuddy after running the update function. The items are all sorted by name, and multiple items are combined into a single virtual stack. Any item that is higher than common quality glows to show the familiar rarity colors (this will be hard to see in the figure). The frame shows only the first 24 items, or less if you don't have that many items in your inventory.

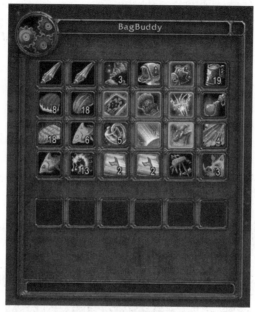

Figure 11-1: BagBuddy showing a sorted inventory

Finding the Right API Functions

The most difficult part when starting to work with the World of Warcraft API is finding the right function or event (which you'll learn about in Chapter 13). Although we would love to provide a simple guide that tells you what functions and events to use for any situation, the API consists of more than 1,900 functions and 530 events. Any guide would be incredibly large, and near impossible to write. Instead we hope to give you a set of guidelines that you can use to find the right functions.

Exploring the API Categories

This book contains a chapter that lists a number of different categories, and the functions that belong to the given group. This is a good place to start if you're looking to better understand a portion of the API. Be aware that many functions are listed in multiple categories. The same reference is available (and kept up-to-date) online at `http://wowprogramming.com/docs/api_categories`.

Although it does not always contain an updated list of available functions, the World of Warcraft API listing at WoWWiki (`http://wowwiki.com/World_of_Warcraft_API`) lists functions by various categories as well.

Examining the FrameXML Code

A useful question whenever you are trying to accomplish something in a custom addon is to ask:

"Does the default user interface do this?"

If so, then somewhere in the code for the default UI is the technique used to accomplish the task; it's just a matter of finding it. For example, you might want to display the player's haste rating and percentage effect somewhere in your addon. A quick look at the API categories doesn't reveal anything immediately so you instead look at the default user interface.

That information is displayed on the character panel in the stats section at the bottom. To find out where that panel is defined, you can do a bit of investigative work. Start by running the /framestack command that was introduced in Chapter 9. From the information you get there, it appears that PaperDollFrame and CharacterFrame are both good candidates. Conveniently enough, these frames are defined in files by the same name in the FrameXML code.

Opening CharacterFrame.xml shows you the definition of the different tabs, so it appears that that's the outmost frame that contains the sub-frames. The CharacterAttributesFrame in PaperDollFrame.xml, however, looks like a good candidate. Now that you've found the frame, you can open PaperDollFrame.lua to look around.

At the top of the file you see a number of global constants defined. Looking for one having to do with haste, you find the following constants:

```
CR_HASTE_MELEE = 18;
CR_HASTE_RANGED = 19;
CR_HASTE_SPELL = 20;
```

When haste was first introduced in the game, there were different versions for melee, ranged, and spell. In *Wrath of the Lich King* they were all combined into a single haste rating. Pick the melee version and search for that throughout the whole file.

The only instance in the file is in the following line of code, in the aptly named PaperDollFrame_SetAttackSpeed() function:

```
statFrame.tooltip2 = format(CR_HASTE_RATING_TOOLTIP, ↵
GetCombatRating(CR_HASTE_MELEE), GetCombatRatingBonus(CR_HASTE_MELEE));
```

Now you can test these two functions to see if they work for your needs. Run the following code in-game:

```
/run print(GetCombatRating(CR_HASTE_MELEE))
/run print(GetCombatRatingBonus(CT_HASTE_MELEE))
```

You will find that although the returns from GetCombatRating() are the same, you may have different results for the actual percent bonus. This bonus could depend on any number of factors, and you'll want to take that into consideration when using it in your addon.

Looking at Another Addon

If you can't find a place in the default user interface that does what you want, but know that other addons somehow accomplish it, you can always look at the other addon. When doing this, keep in mind that the code we write as authors is not completely open for copying. When in doubt, you may find it useful to contact the author to see how he's done something and ask if you can use a similar method in your own addon.

Of course, sometimes it's just a simple as finding the right function, which you can then just use directly in your own addon.

Asking for Help!

Each situation will be slightly unique, so it's always useful to ask for help when working on your own addon. A number of websites, forums, and chat rooms support addon development for World of Warcraft (see Appendix D for more information). When asking for help, we suggest the following:

- When initially presenting your problem, try to explain what you are trying to accomplish instead of how you are trying to accomplish it. This gives the people who are helping you a chance to understand the problem without getting caught up in a specific way of doing it. This can sometimes reveal a much nicer solution to the problem.

- Provide as much code as possible and indicate the areas that are having problems. Posting 10 lines of code out of a 300-line function makes it very difficult to see what is happening. You can post large bits of code on sites like `http://pastey.net` and `http://pastebin.com`.

- If you are getting an error, give the *specific* error text, and post the code involved in the error.

- Be patient! Not everyone is always waiting around to pounce on a new question. You should continue to explore in your own time, and hopefully someone will be able to help you.

Summary

This chapter introduced you to APIs in the general sense, and gave you a specific example of how to use the item and container API to access information about the player's containers and items. Understanding the way these functions interact with the game is essential to creating effective addons that accomplish a variety of goals.

The Code

BagBuddy.lua

```lua
function BagBuddy_OnLoad(self)
  SetPortraitToTexture(self.portrait, ↵
"Interface\\Icons\\INV_Misc_EngGizmos_30")

  -- Create the item slots
  self.items = {}
  for idx = 1, 24 do
    local item = CreateFrame("Button", "BagBuddy_Item" .. idx, ↵
self, "BagBuddyItemTemplate")
    self.items[idx] = item
    if idx == 1 then
      item:SetPoint("TOPLEFT", 40, -73)
    elseif idx == 7 or idx == 13 or idx == 19 then
      item:SetPoint("TOPLEFT", self.items[idx-6], ↵
"BOTTOMLEFT", 0, -7)
    else
      item:SetPoint("TOPLEFT", self.items[idx-1], ↵
"TOPRIGHT", 12, 0)
    end
  end
end

local function itemNameSort(a, b)
  return a.name < b.name
end

function BagBuddy_Update()
  local items = {}

  -- Scan through the bag slots, looking for items
  for bag = 0, NUM_BAG_SLOTS do
    for slot = 0, GetContainerNumSlots(bag) do
      local texture, count, locked, quality, readable, ↵
lootable, link = GetContainerItemInfo(bag, slot)
      if texture then
        -- If found, grab the item number and store other data
        local itemNum = tonumber(link:match("|Hitem:(%d+):"))
        if not items[itemNum] then
          items[itemNum] = {
            texture = texture,
            count = count,
            quality = quality,
            name = GetItemInfo(link),
            link = link,
          }
        else
```

```
              -- The item already exists in our table, update count
              items[itemNum].count = items[itemNum].count + count
          end
        end
      end
  end

  local sortTbl = {}
  for link, entry in pairs(items) do
    table.insert(sortTbl, entry)
  end
  table.sort(sortTbl, itemNameSort)

  -- Now update the BagBuddyFrame with the listed items (in order)
  for i = 1, 24 do
    local button = BagBuddy.items[i]
    local entry = sortTbl[i]

    if entry then
      -- There is an item in this slot

      button.icon:SetTexture(entry.texture)
      if entry.count > 1 then
        button.count:SetText(entry.count)
        button.count:Show()
      else
        button.count:Hide()
      end

      if entry.quality > 1 then
        button.glow:SetVertexColor( ↵
GetItemQualityColor(entry.quality))
        button.glow:Show()
      else
        button.glow:Hide()
      end
      button:Show()
    else
      button:Hide()
    end
  end
end
```

## CHAPTER 12

Interacting with Widgets

You've already created the base frame for BagBuddy, and added graphics, text, and item buttons created using templates. However, other than the highlight texture on the item buttons, the frames are entirely static and you can't really interact with them. In this chapter you learn about different types of frames, such as buttons, status bars, and edit boxes. Once you've created new frames, you learn how to add dynamic behavior to them.

Each different type of frame widget in World of Warcraft has certain scripts that can be set to respond to changes. For example, a button can set an OnClick script to run code when the button is clicked, or OnEnter to do something when the mouse moves over the button. Other more complex widgets, such as edit boxes, allow you to respond to different types of key presses.

This chapter is meant as an introduction to interacting with widgets; for a full listing of the available frame scripts and methods, please refer to the Widget Reference in Chapter 29.

Making BagBuddy's Buttons Interactive

The most often used widget (other than the basic frame type) is a Button. Buttons are used all over the default user interface to accomplish different types of tasks:

- Player, target, and other unit frames
- Action buttons
- Buff and debuff icons

- Dropdown (selection) menus
- Menu buttons

In BagBuddy you will use buttons for the rarity filters and the close button in the top-right corner of the frame, in addition to the already created item buttons. Let's start exploring interactive widgets by setting `OnEnter` and `OnLeave` scripts for the item buttons.

Setting Frame Scripts via XML

You can add a frame script to an XML definition by adding a `<Scripts>` tag with one or more script definitions inside. Add the following code to the definition of `BagBuddyItemTemplate`, after the `</Layers>` tag but before the `<NormalTexture>` tag:

```
<Scripts>
  <OnEnter>
    print("Mouse has entered", self:GetName())
  </OnEnter>
  <OnLeave>
    print("Mouse has left", self:GetName())
  </OnLeave>
</Scripts>
```

If you load up the game, you should be able to run your mouse over any of the item buttons, and the game will display a message for each of the different scripts. The output may look similar to the following:

```
Mouse has entered BagBuddy_Item6
Mouse has left BagBuddy_Item6
Mouse has entered BagBuddy_Item20
Mouse has left BagBuddy_Item20
```

This is one of two ways to set frame scripts using XML. For each type of script, you simply write code that is then compiled to a function and run in response to that widget event. Each different type of script handler is passed certain arguments; you can see that the variable `self` is used here, which isn't explicitly defined.

The `OnEnter` and `OnLeave` scripts are passed two different arguments:

- `self`—The button that the mouse has just entered.
- `motion`—A Boolean flag indicating if the event was caused by the mouse moving over the frame. When this value is false, the frame being shown while the mouse is already over its position may have caused the event.

Using the function Attribute

We prefer to avoid writing any code directly in XML files because keeping the frame definition code separate from any behavior code makes it easier to maintain addon code. To do this, you can create your functions in BagBuddy.lua and assign them directly in the XML using the function attribute. Replace the <Scripts> section you wrote in the last section with the following:

```
<Scripts>
  <OnEnter function="BagBuddy_Button_OnEnter"/>
  <OnLeave function="BagBuddy_Button_OnLeave"/>
</Scripts>
```

Now open BagBuddy.lua and add the following two functions somewhere in the file:

```
function BagBuddy_Button_OnEnter(self, motion)
  print("Mouse has entered", self:GetName())
end

function BagBuddy_Button_OnLeave(self, motion)
  print("Mouse has left", self:GetName())
end
```

Because you're writing your own functions, you need to specify the arguments to access them; other than that, the functions are the same.

Setting Frame Scripts Using Lua

As with most things dealing with the frame system in World of Warcraft, frame scripts can be set using Lua instead of XML. This is accomplished using the SetScript() method for frames. If you include the function definitions for BagBuddy_Button_OnEnter and BagBuddy_Button_OnLeave, you could just add the following to the end of the BagBuddy_OnLoad function:

```
for idx, button in ipairs(self.items) do
  button:SetScript("OnEnter", BagBuddy_Button_OnEnter)
  button:SetScript("OnLeave", BagBuddy_Button_OnLeave)
end
```

It doesn't make much sense to structure your code this way when you're using a frame template. With a different type of addon, though, you might need to set scripts in this way, so it's good to know the possibility exists.

Using the SetScript() method is the only way to clear an existing script from a frame. To accomplish this, you simply pass nil as the second argument.

Showing Item Tooltips Using OnEnter and OnLeave

Having the item buttons print something to the chat window is great, but it's not very useful; instead you can display the item's tooltip. You can accomplish this using the GameTooltip object provided by the default user interface. Figure 12-1 shows the tooltip for the Death Knight spell Blood Presence.

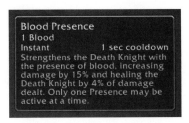

Figure 12-1: GameTooltip showing tooltip for Blood Presence

To show a tooltip, you typically use the following process:

1. Call the GameTooltip:SetOwner() method, passing in the frame object that will temporarily own the tooltip, a string that tells the system how to anchor the tooltip, and optionally a set of offsets.

2. Call one of the many Set methods to tell the tooltip what information to display. In this case, you'll use the SetHyperlink method, passing in the item hyperlink.

3. Show the tooltip by calling GameTooltip:Show().

But first you need to store the item link in a place where the script handler can access it. Open BagBuddy.lua and change the update loop at the end of BagBuddy_Update() to the following (the highlighted lines are the only changes):

```
for i = 1 , 24 do
    local button = BagBuddy.items[i]
    local entry = sortTbl[i]

    if entry then
        -- There is an item in this slot

        button.link = entry.link
        button.icon:SetTexture(entry.texture)
```

```
    if entry.count > 1 then
      button.count:SetText(entry.count)
      button.count:Show()
    else
      button.count:Hide()
    end

    if entry.quality > 1 then
      button.glow:SetVertexColor(GetItemQualityColor(entry.quality))
      button.glow:Show()
    else
      button.glow:Hide()
    end
    button:Show()
  else
    button.link = nil
    button:Hide()
  end
end
end
```

During the iteration of the loop, you just update the `link` key in the frame table using the link stored in the item entry. If there isn't an item to display the button, you clear the value from the frame table. Next, you need to update the script handler functions. Replace the definitions of the `OnEnter` and `OnLeave` handlers with the following:

```
function BagBuddy_Button_OnEnter(self, motion)
  if self.link then
    GameTooltip:SetOwner(self, "ANCHOR_TOPRIGHT")
    GameTooltip:SetHyperlink(self.link)
    GameTooltip:Show()
  end
end

function BagBuddy_Button_OnLeave(self, motion)
  GameTooltip:Hide()
end
```

In the `OnEnter` handler, you first check to see if the button is set to display an item. Then you tell the tooltip to anchor itself to the top right of the item button, and set it to display the item. The corresponding `OnLeave` script simply hides the tooltip.

If you load the addon and run the `BagBuddy_Update()` function, you should be able to mouse over the items in BagBuddy to display item tooltips. Figure 12-2 shows one such tooltip.

Figure 12-2: BagBuddy showing an item tooltip OnEnter

Adding Clickable Buttons to BagBuddy

Although you eventually will make the item buttons clickable to use, that is a protected action and is a bit more complicated than just setting a script handler. However, you don't need to do anything special to create a close button and a set of filter buttons.

Introducing the OnClick Handler

The `Button` frame type can register to receive mouse clicks. World of Warcraft recognizes several different mouse buttons, calling the default ones `LeftButton`, `RightButton`, `MiddleButton`, `Button4`, and `Button5`. There are some computer mice that have more than five buttons, and these continue as `Button6`, `Button7`, etc. Which physical button on your mouse corresponds to a given button name is between your operating system and the WoW client. In addition to different mouse buttons, you can register for either the click portion or the release portion of the click.

To register for mouse clicks, you must call the `RegisterForClicks()` method. This function accepts a list of strings, each indicating a type of click you would like to register for. By default, all buttons are registered for the `LeftButtonUp` click, which is the release portion of a left button click. The following are all valid:

- `LeftButtonUp`
- `MiddleButtonDown`
- `Button4Up`
- `AnyUp`
- `AnyDown`

The last two are special buttons that register automatically for all release button clicks and down button clicks, respectively.

Once you've registered for clicks, you can set an OnClick script on the frame to receive the click events. When the client calls an OnClick handler, it passes the following arguments:

- self—The frame object that the handler was called for.
- button—A string indicating which mouse button was used to click the frame.
- down—A Boolean flag indicating if the mouse click was triggered by a downward click, rather than the releasing of a click.

You can run the following code in-game to play with the different mouse buttons and the release/press portions of a click. Click the game button with multiple buttons on your mouse to see the differences between them. Also, click and hold the button so you can see the difference between the "up" and "down" portions of a click.

```
if not ClickFrame then
    ClickFrame = CreateFrame("Button", "ClickFrame", UIParent, ↵
"GameMenuButtonTemplate")
end

ClickFrame:ClearAllPoints()
ClickFrame:SetPoint("CENTER", 0, 0)
ClickFrame:SetText("Click Frame")

ClickFrame:RegisterForClicks("AnyUp", "AnyDown")

ClickFrame:SetScript("OnClick", function(self, button, down)
    local name = self:GetName()
    print(name, button, down)
end)
```

You should see a line of output added to your chat frame showing the name of the frame, ClickFrame, and the button that was clicked along with whether or not the click captured was on the release of the click.

Creating a Close Button Using Templates

Because almost every window in the default user interface has a close button, naturally there is a template you can use to save some time. After the </Layers> tag in the definition for BagBuddy, add the following definition:

```
<Frames>
    <Button name="$parent_Close" parentKey="close" ↵
```

```
    inherits="UIPanelCloseButton">
        <Anchors>
          <Anchor point="TOPRIGHT">
            <Offset x="-30" y="-8"/>
          </Anchor>
        </Anchors>
    </Button>
</Frames>
```

The template already includes the code that is used to actually hide the frame. The template is defined in `UIPanelTemplate.xml`:

```
<Button name="UIPanelCloseButton" virtual="true">
  <Size>
    <AbsDimension x="32" y="32"/>
  </Size>
  <Scripts>
    <OnClick>
      HideParentPanel(self);
    </OnClick>
  </Scripts>
  <NormalTexture file="Interface\Buttons\UI-Panel-MinimizeButton-Up"/>
  <PushedTexture file="Interface\Buttons\UI-Panel-MinimizeButton-Down"/>
  <HighlightTexture
     file="Interface\Buttons\UI-Panel-MinimizeButton-Highlight"
     alphaMode="ADD"/>
</Button>
```

When the button is clicked, the `HideParentPanel()` function is called with the frame passed as the first argument. This function is defined in `UIParent.lua` and is simply a short function that quickly looks up the parent frame, and then hides it.

Creating Clickable Filter Buttons

You are going to create seven different buttons that can be used to filter items by their rarity, shown in Figure 12-3. Because you already have a template that contains more than what you need, you can just inherit from `BagBuddyItemTemplate` and ignore the count text and glow texture, or you could define a new template. In this case, you'll choose to re-use the existing template, making your code much shorter. Add the following template definition following the item template definition, but before the code for the main BagBuddy frame:

```
<CheckButton name="BagBuddyFilterTemplate" ↵
inherits="BagBuddyItemTemplate" virtual="true">
  <Scripts>
```

```
    <OnEnter function="BagBuddy_Filter_OnEnter"/>
    <OnLeave function="BagBuddy_Filter_OnLeave"/>
    <OnClick function="BagBuddy_Filter_OnClick"/>
  </Scripts>
  <CheckedTexture file="Interface\Buttons\CheckButtonHilight" ↵
alphaMode="ADD"/>
</CheckButton>
```

Figure 12-3: Filter buttons with filtered inventory

You'd like to be able to display a tooltip when the mouse is over the frame, so you define new `OnEnter` and `OnLeave` scripts in the template. These scripts overwrite the original definitions from `BagBuddyItemTemplate`, which is very useful.

You may also have noticed that the `Button` tag is changed to a `CheckButton` tag. That gives you access to the `GetChecked()` method, which enables you to see if the button is currently selected. There is also `SetChecked()` method, but you won't need to use it in this addon. The state of the button changes automatically when the user clicks it, so all you need to do is check to see if it's actually set in your `OnClick` handler.

Finally, you set the `CheckedTexture` for the button. This is a special texture for check buttons that is shown when the button is selected, and is hidden otherwise. In this case it's just a highlight around the edge of the button that should indicate this state.

Creating the Filter Buttons Dynamically

Now you must create the filter buttons, and you'll do this dynamically in the OnLoad function where you're doing other initialization. At the bottom of the function, add the following code:

```
-- Create the filter buttons
self.filters = {}
for idx=0,5 do
  local button = CreateFrame("CheckButton", "BagBuddy_Filter" .. idx, ↵
self, "BagBuddyFilterTemplate")
  SetItemButtonTexture(button, ↵
"Interface\\ICONS\\INV_Misc_Gem_Pearl_03")
  self.filters[idx] = button
  if idx == 0 then
    button:SetPoint("BOTTOMLEFT", 40, 200)
  else
    button:SetPoint("TOPLEFT", self.filters[idx-1], "TOPRIGHT", 12, 0)
  end

  button.icon:SetVertexColor(GetItemQualityColor(idx))
  button:SetChecked(false)
  button.quality = idx
  button.glow:Hide()
end

self.filters[-1] = self.filters[0]
```

This code first creates a table to store the filter buttons, and then creates a series of buttons named BagBuddyFilterX, where X is a number between and including 0 and 5. Each button's icon is set to a pearl texture, because it's white and looks like an orb, so you can easily color it and it's recognizable. The first button is anchored specially, but the others are all anchored to the previous button.

For each button, you use the SetVertexColor() texture method to change the color of the item being displayed. You call the API function GetItem QualityColor() to obtain the correct quality color. This gives you six different glowing colored orbs that indicate the quality color. Next, you uncheck each filter button using the SetChecked() method, passing false in as an argument. Then you store the quality index in the button table itself. This allows you to later determine what quality index the button is meant to be filtering for. Next, you hide the glow texture because you won't be using it for these buttons. Finally, you set up a link between the -1 filter and the 0 filter. That's due to the API that occasionally returns -1 rarity for some items. Figure 12-4 shows the filter buttons after creation.

Figure 12-4: BagBuddy rarity filter buttons

Adding Custom Tooltips

You've already learned one way to display tooltips for the item buttons, using the GameTooltip:SetHyperlink method. However, the text you want to display for the filter buttons isn't something the game can associate to a game object (such as a player or an item). Instead, you can use the GameTooltip:SetText() method to add a line of text directly to the tooltip. Define the following functions at the bottom of BagBuddy.lua:

```
function BagBuddy_Filter_OnEnter(self, motion)
  GameTooltip:SetOwner(self, "ANCHOR_TOPRIGHT")
  GameTooltip:SetText(_G["ITEM_QUALITY" .. self.quality .. "_DESC"])
  GameTooltip:Show()
end

function BagBuddy_Filter_OnLeave(self, motion)
  GameTooltip:Hide()
end
```

Global variables are set on every client that can be used to access the name of the various quality levels. For example, on an English client, ITEM_QUALITY1_DESC is set to Poor.

Making the Filter Buttons Clickable

Making the buttons actually filter the item results involves two steps. The first is setting a click handler that triggers the update function. The second step is a bit more complex, and requires changes to the already written update function. The click handler is relatively simple, so add the following function to the bottom of BagBuddy.lua:

```
function BagBuddy_Filter_OnClick(self, button)
  BagBuddy.qualityFilter = false
  for idx = 0, 5 do
    local button = BagBuddy.filters[idx]
    if button:GetChecked() then
      BagBuddy.qualityFilter = true
    end
```

```
    end
    BagBuddy_Update()
 end
```

You'll use `BagBuddy.qualityFilter` as a Boolean flag that indicates whether *any* of the quality filters have been selected. The first thing you do in the `OnClick` handler is set this to `false`. Then you loop through each of the filter buttons and check if they are set. If any of them are selected, you change the value to `true`. Finally, you call the `BagBuddy_Update()` function to update the results.

Updating the Results

Rather than having you re-type the entire `BagBuddy_Update()` function, you can just edit the first main loop, which is responsible for scanning the player's bags. The sort and display loops don't need to change, because they'll do the same thing. Replace the scanning loop with the following code:

```
-- Scan through the bag slots, looking for items
for bag = 0, NUM_BAG_SLOTS do
  for slot = 0, GetContainerNumSlots(bag) do
    local texture, count, locked, quality, readable, lootable, link = ↵
GetContainerItemInfo(bag, slot)

    if texture then
        local shown = true

        if BagBuddy.qualityFilter then
          shown = shown and BagBuddy.filters[quality]:GetChecked()
        end

        if shown then
          -- If an item is found, grab the item number and store data
          local itemNum = tonumber(link:match("|Hitem:(%d+):"))
          if not items[itemNum] then
            items[itemNum] = {
               texture = texture,
               count = count,
               quality = quality,
               name = GetItemInfo(link),
               link = link,
            }
          else
            -- The item already exists in table, just update the count
            items[itemNum].count = items[itemNum].count + count
          end
        end
    end
  end
end
```

You've done a bit of restructuring here, adding a variable (`shown`) that is set on each iteration to indicate whether or not the item has passed all the given filters. This will be useful when you add name filters, but for now it helps you filter based on quality. The code checks to see if `BagBuddy.qualityFilter` is set, and if so checks the filter button to see if it's selected. If it is, the item "passes" and is added to the items table.

It's important to note that when no quality filters are selected, all items will automatically pass this check. Filters are additive, so you can select the Epic and Rare filters, as shown in Figure 12-5, and all items that match either quality level will be shown.

Figure 12-5: BagBuddy with the Rare and Epic filters selected

Navigating Multiple Pages

As it stands, BagBuddy displays only the first 24 filtered items in your bags. Although this might be useful if your bags are small, it doesn't really work well with a level 80 character with larger bags. It would be useful to be able to move between different "pages" of results to find what you need.

To add this feature to BagBuddy, you'll need to add two more buttons and a font string. The buttons will be placed in the bottom portion of the frame, allowing the user to click to go to the next (or previous) page. The font string will be used to display some status information, such as how many pages of items match the current filters.

Adding XML Definitions for Buttons and Status Text

Open `BagBuddy.xml` and add the following definitions after the `</Button>` tag for the close button, and before the `</Frames>` tag:

```
<Button name="BagBuddy_PrevButton" parentKey="prev">
  <Size x="32" y="32"/>
  <Anchors>
    <Anchor point="CENTER" relativeTo="BagBuddy" ↵
relativePoint="BOTTOMLEFT">
      <Offset>
        <AbsDimension x="50" y="150"/>
      </Offset>
    </Anchor>
  </Anchors>
  <Scripts>
    <OnClick function="BagBuddy_PrevPage"/>
  </Scripts>
  <NormalTexture file="Interface\Buttons\UI-SpellbookIcon-PrevPage-Up"/>
  <PushedTexture
    file="Interface\Buttons\UI-SpellbookIcon-PrevPage-Down"/>
  <DisabledTexture
    file="Interface\Buttons\UI-SpellbookIcon-PrevPage-Disabled"/>
  <HighlightTexture file="Interface\Buttons\UI-Common-MouseHilight"
alphaMode="ADD"/>
</Button>

<Button name="BagBuddy_NextButton" parentKey="next">
  <Size x="32" y="32"/>
  <Anchors>
    <Anchor point="CENTER" relativeTo="BagBuddy" ↵
relativePoint="BOTTOMRIGHT">
      <Offset>
        <AbsDimension x="-70" y="150"/>
      </Offset>
    </Anchor>
  </Anchors>
  <Scripts>
    <OnClick function="BagBuddy_NextPage"/>
  </Scripts>
  <NormalTexture file="Interface\Buttons\UI-SpellbookIcon-NextPage-Up"/>
  <PushedTexture
    file="Interface\Buttons\UI-SpellbookIcon-NextPage-Down"/>
  <DisabledTexture
    file="Interface\Buttons\UI-SpellbookIcon-NextPage-Disabled"/>
  <HighlightTexture file="Interface\Buttons\UI-Common-MouseHilight" ↵
alphaMode="ADD"/>
</Button>
```

There shouldn't be any unfamiliar concepts in these definitions. You use the previous page and next page buttons from the spellbook interface. Each button calls a different function when clicked, which is responsible for moving the page ahead or back. Before you leave the XML file, add the following to the OVERLAY layer in the XML file, after the definition of the title font string:

```
<FontString name="$parent_Status" parentKey="status" ↵
inherits="GameFontHighlight">
  <Anchors>
    <Anchor point="CENTER" relativePoint="BOTTOM">
      <Offset x="-10" y="150"/>
    </Anchor>
  </Anchors>
</FontString>
```

Writing OnClick Handlers for Navigation Buttons

The click handlers for the navigation buttons are quite simple, actually. You'll use the BagBuddy.page variable to indicate what page you are on. You'll make sure that the previous button is disabled when you're at the front of the listing, and the next button when you are at the end. That makes the logic pretty simple. Add this to the end of BagBuddy.lua:

```
function BagBuddy_NextPage(self)
  BagBuddy.page = BagBuddy.page + 1
  BagBuddy_Update(BagBuddy)
end

function BagBuddy_PrevPage(self)
  BagBuddy.page = BagBuddy.page - 1
  BagBuddy_Update(BagBuddy)
end
```

The font string and the button enable/disable states will be handled in the update function itself.

Altering the Update Function for Pages

Surprisingly, the changes you need to make to add page navigation to the update function are pretty simple. The scan remains the same; you just need to change the actual update loop. Again, the code is provided in-full, with the changed lines highlighted.

```
-- Now update the BagBuddyFrame with the listed items (in order)
local max = BagBuddy.page * 24
local min = max - 23
```

```
for idx = min, max do
  local button = BagBuddy.items[idx - min + 1]
  local entry = sortTbl[idx]

  if entry then
    -- There is an item in this slot

    button.link = entry.link
    button.icon:SetTexture(entry.texture)
    if entry.count > 1 then
      button.count:SetText(entry.count)
      button.count:Show()
    else
      button.count:Hide()
    end

    if entry.quality > 1 then
      button.glow:SetVertexColor(GetItemQualityColor(entry.quality))
      button.glow:Show()
    else
      button.glow:Hide()
    end
    button:Show()
  else
    button.link = nil
    button:Hide()
  end
end
```

Instead of looping through the first 24 items, you'll use `BagBuddy.page` to calculate the maximum item and the minimum item you'll need to display. So if you're on page 2, `max` is going to be 48 and `min` is going to be 25. Then you loop starting at `min` and working up through to `max`. To make sure you get the right button for a given item index, you need to subtract the minimum number from the current index and add one.

This is because, when on page 2, the fifth item being displayed has an index in `sortTbl` of 29. To get the right button number, you take 29, subtract 25 (which is the minimum item index being displayed), and add 1, giving you 5. There are no other changes to this function.

Enabling and Disabling Navigation Buttons

After you've filtered and displayed your items, you should enable and disable the navigation buttons to ensure they can't be clicked accidentally. This is accomplished using the `Button:Disable()` method, which disables clicking functionality and can change the display of the button. Add the following code after the update loop:

```
-- Update page buttons
if min > 1 then
  BagBuddy.prev:Enable()
else
  BagBuddy.prev:Disable()
end
if max < #sortTbl then
  BagBuddy.next:Enable()
else
  BagBuddy.next:Disable()
end
```

First you check to see if the minimum item being displayed is greater than one, and if so you enable the previous button. If the last item being displayed is less than the last item in the sorted list, then you enable that button. The buttons are then only disabled when you're at the start of the list (for previous) and at the end of the list (for next).

Creating and Updating Status Text

When paging filtered items, it helps to show how many items have been found so the user can see which page they are on. Add a new font string to BagBuddy.xml, after the definition of the title font string:

```
<FontString name="$parent_Status" parentKey="status" ↵
inherits="GameFontHighlight">
  <Anchors>
    <Anchor point="CENTER" relativePoint="BOTTOM">
      <Offset x="-10" y="150"/>
    </Anchor>
  </Anchors>
</FontString>
```

Now you can update the text after changing the button states. Add the following code right after the navigation button enable/disable block you've just added in BagBuddy.lua:

```
-- Update the status text
if #sortTbl > 24 then
  local max = math.min(max, #sortTbl)
  local msg = string.format("Showing items %d - %d of %d", min, max, ↵
#sortTbl)
  BagBuddy.status:SetText(msg)
```

```
else
   BagBuddy.status:SetText("Found " .. #sortTbl .. " items")
end
```

The code displays a different message depending on whether there is more than one page of items to display. If so, you create a temporary variable that is set to the smaller of either the max item being displayed, or the length of the sortTbl table. Because your message looks like "Showing items 49 - 56 of 56", you need this information to accurately display the last item being shown.

Final Changes to Support Navigation

You need to make two more changes to support navigation. The first is initializing BagBuddy to start on page 1. You can do this by adding the following to the end of the BagBuddy_OnLoad function:

```
-- Initialize to show the first page
self.page = 1
```

Secondly, you need to alter the filter buttons to set the page back to 1 every time a filter is clicked. This is to ensure that you don't get stuck on page 2 when there are less than 24 items to display. Change BagBuddy_Filter_OnClick to the following (changed lines are highlighted):

```
function BagBuddy_Filter_OnClick(self, button)
   BagBuddy.qualityFilter = false
   for idx = 0, 5 do
     local button = BagBuddy.filters[idx]
     if button:GetChecked() then
       BagBuddy.qualityFilter = true
     end
   end
   BagBuddy.page = 1
   BagBuddy_Update()
end
```

Adding a Name Filter to BagBuddy

At this point, you have a working inventory addon that allows you to filter by rarity to better find items. The addon won't update when your inventory changes; you learn how to do that in Chapter 13. The next feature you are going to add is the ability to filter your inventory by name. To accomplish this, you use an EditBox, a widget that is quite unlike the Button type you've been using so far this chapter.

Creating an EditBox

The most prevalent edit box in the default user interface is the one that appears when you press Enter: the chat edit box. Using it you can input commands, type messages to friends, or even run Lua code. The edit box you use for BagBuddy won't have all of these features because all it needs to do is accept text from the user.

You must exercise caution when working with an EditBox, whether you are creating it in Lua or XML. It has an odd property that causes it to automatically take the keyboard's focus when it is displayed and doesn't (by default) have a way to relinquish this control. As a result, if you don't pay attention you could wind up needing to restart your client to regain control of the keyboard.

You can, however, set a property (via an XML attribute or Lua) and a frame script to provide better behavior. Open BagBuddy.xml and add the following definition before the </Frames> tag in the BagBuddy definition, but after the code for the previous and next buttons:

```
<EditBox name="$parent_Input" parentKey="input" autoFocus="false">
  <Size x="400" y="20"/>
  <Anchors>
    <Anchor point="BOTTOMLEFT">
      <Offset x="32" y="100"/>
    </Anchor>
  </Anchors>
  <Scripts>
    <OnEscapePressed>
      self:ClearFocus()
    </OnEscapePressed>
    <OnTextChanged>
      BagBuddy_Update()
    </OnTextChanged>
  </Scripts>
  <FontString inherits="GameFontHighlight"/>
</EditBox>
```

The important part of this code is the autoFocus attribute being set to false. This ensures that the edit box won't automatically try to steal the keyboard whenever it is shown. It's not enough, however, to ensure that there is an easy way to get the keyboard's focus away from the EditBox. For this you set an OnEscapePressed script. This script handler fires anytime the edit box has focus and the player presses the escape key. Because most people are used to pressing escape to clear the focus from an input box, whether it be on the Web or in World of Warcraft, it's a good behavior to emulate. The handler body simply calls the self:ClearFocus() method. This method is specific to the EditBox type, and simply releases control of the keyboard so it can be used elsewhere.

> **TIP** If you happen to get stuck inside an `EditBox` there are a few things you can do to escape, all involving getting the chat frame edit box open:
>
> ■ Right-click your target frame or a party member's frame. Select the Whisper option, which should open the chat frame's edit box.
>
> ■ Click someone's name in your chat frame and select the Whisper option, which should open the chat frame's edit box.
>
> Once you've got a place where you can run code, you can reload your user interface, attach new scripts, or do something else that will stop the runaway edit box.

You may have noticed what appears to be a dangling `FontString` element at the end of the `EditBox` definition. Because an `EditBox` is always displaying text in some fashion, you need to indicate the font that should be used to accomplish this. In Lua you can set this using the `:SetFont()` and `:SetFontObject()` methods, but in XML you can just include it as shown in the preceding code.

The last thing you may have noticed is the `OnTextChanged` script handler. This handler is passed a single argument, the edit box itself. You can extract the text from the edit box using the `GetText()` method. Your handler simply calls BagBaddy's update function to handle any further work.

Filtering by Name

Now you have an edit box that the users can type in, but you need to actually do something with the text they type. For this, you'll need to make some minor changes to the `BagBuddy_Update` function. Right before the scan loop begins in that function, add the following:

```
local nameFilter = BagBuddy.input:GetText():lower()
```

This code just calls the `GetText()` method on the input box to retrieve the text and then converts it to lowercase. You'll do the same with the item name when you actually compare it to the user input, so it works properly even if the user types capital letters.

Now you add a check during the search loop that actually performs the check to see if the item's name matches the user input. Add the following code after the block that checks the item against the quality filters:

```
if #nameFilter > 0 then
  local lowerName = GetItemInfo(link):lower()
  shown = shown and string.find(lowerName, nameFilter, 1, true)
end
```

This is all you need to add to make filtering work properly. First you check to see if the text in the edit box is non-empty (that is, if the length of the string is more than 0). If so, you take the name of the item and make it lowercase and compare it to the name filter. As a result, only those items that match the name filter (if it is set) will make it into the item list. Figure 12-6 shows BagBuddy filtering to show only items whose names contain the word "potion."

Figure 12-6: BagBuddy filtering by item name

Exploring Widget Types

In this chapter you have worked with the normal `Frame` type, in addition to `Button` and `EditBox`. Quite a number of different widget types exist, all distinguished by the type of script handlers and methods that are available. This section details actual examples of the different types of frames to show how they are typically used. Full details about each of these types is available in Chapter 29, "Widget Reference."

When exploring these widget types, it's often useful to look at an existing example to see how they are used, and what other attributes and elements might exist in the XML definition.

Button

Buttons are used to allow user input by clicking a meaningful icon or visual button with text. Buttons can react to clicks and, in some cases, even cast spells and target units. Examples of buttons include the configuration buttons on the main menu, and the buttons on the player's action bars (shown in Figure 12-7). Buttons often show different textures when the mouse is moved over them, or when they are pressed or disabled. Most buttons display text or icons to convey more meaning.

Figure 12-7: Main menu buttons (left) and action bar buttons (right)

CheckButton

A CheckButton is a special kind of button that have only two states: checked and unchecked. They are used to convey toggleable options, and normally come with text labels to explain which options the checkbox alters. Check buttons are used primarily in custom configuration interfaces and the user interface options screen, as shown in Figure 12-8.

Figure 12-8: Checkboxes in the interface options screen

ColorSelect

The ColorSelect frame type (see Figure 12-9) is used by the chat interface to change output color for channels, along with the background of the chat windows. It pops up as a dialog box that enables you to select a color (possibly with alpha transparency) to use for a specific option.

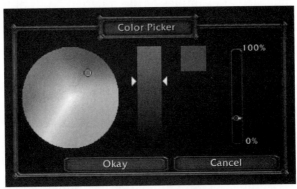

Figure 12-9: ColorSelect example frame as a dialog box

This widget type doesn't define any new scripts, but has a number of methods that allow you to set and get the value of the color wheel and other color selection elements.

EditBox

The `EditBox` type of frame is used to allow for text input, along with basic history and editing capabilities. The simplest example of an edit box is attached to the chat frame, enabling you to run commands and communicate with other players, as shown in Figure 12-10.

Figure 12-10: Chat frame's EditBox

GameTooltip

A GameTooltip is a frame that can display two columns of data that further describe the UI element you currently have your mouse over, including buttons, items, and even players in the 3-D world. Figure 12-11 shows an item tooltip.

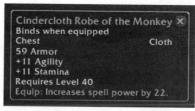

Figure 12-11: Item tooltip

MessageFrame

MessageFrames are used by the game to send a stream of errors, warnings, or messages to the user. This is most often seen with the `UIErrorsFrame`, which displays any issues with spellcasting, as shown in Figure 12-12.

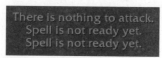

Figure 12-12: UIErrorsFrame showing spellcasting errors

Minimap

The Minimap frame type is special in that there can only ever be one of them. The minimap in the default user interface is used for navigation (see

Figure 12-13) and is normally the only one that exists. The portion of the minimap that is rendered using this widget type is only the map-specific part of the image, whereas the rest of the elements are attached graphics, buttons, and fontstrings.

Figure 12-13: Minimap used for navigation

Model

Models are used to display three-dimensional models in-game, potentially with the capability to pan and zoom in on the model. Models are used in the default UI within the character window, dressing room at the auction house, and the tabard planner in the major cities. Figure 12-14 shows the tabard vendor window, using models.

Figure 12-14: Tabard vendor showing player model

ScrollingMessageFrame

Being a Massively Multi-player Online Role-Playing Game, WoW has a fair amount of communication between its players, and these are typically displayed in scroll message frames, namely the ChatFrame, shown in Figure 12-15.

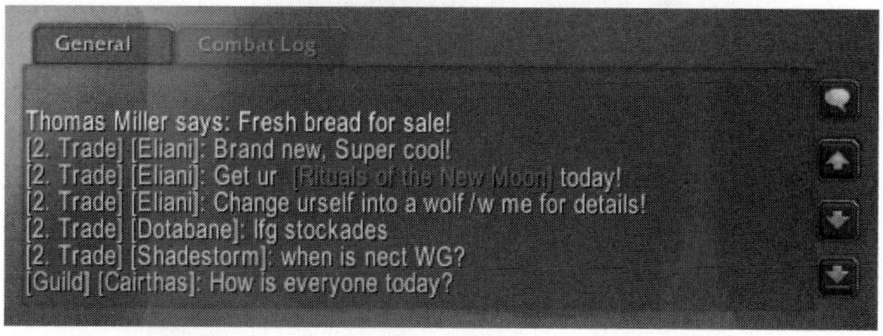

Figure 12-15: ChatFrame showing chat messages

ScrollFrame

When something is too large to be displayed in its native window, a scroll frame can be included to allow the user to scroll either vertically or horizontally. The `ScrollFrame` widget type is frequently used throughout the user interface, particularly within the friends window, the skills window, the auction house, and the quest log (see Figure 12-16).

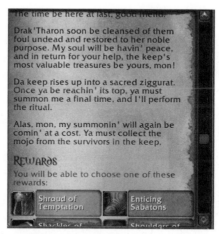

Figure 12-16: Scroll frame used in the quest log

SimpleHTML

For presenting data, scrolling message frames aren't always suitable, such as when reading a book or item in-game. In these situations, a special type of frame is used that allows for basic HTML-like markup. When combined with multiple pages or a scroll frame, data becomes easier to present. Figure 12-17 shows a plaque in Stormwind, which uses a SimpleHTML frame.

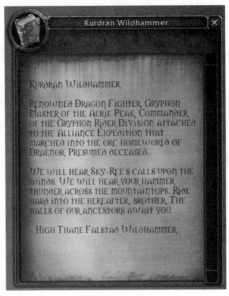

Figure 12-17: SimpleHTML frame displaying a plaque

Slider

Sliders are used when there is a range of numbers that can possibly be selected. They're used primarily in the default user interface options screen (see Figure 12-18). Sliders enable the developer to set a minimum value, a maximum value, and the default step that the slider will allow, so you can control precision.

Figure 12-18: Sliders in the default interface options

StatusBar

StatusBars are used throughout the default user interface to show progress or percentages, such as in the skills window (see Figure 12-19). To use a status bar, you must supply a texture to be shown, as well as minimum/maximum values for the bar. Then you can simply set the value of the bar to show the correct value.

Figure 12-19: StatusBars displayed in the skills window

Summary

This chapter introduced you to two different types of interactive widgets that can be used in custom addons. You created multiple buttons that showed tooltips when the mouse moved over them, and buttons that could be clicked to accomplish some task. In addition, you utilized an edit box to accept input from the user.

The Code

BagBuddy.lua

```
function BagBuddy_OnLoad(self)
  SetPortraitToTexture(self.portrait, ↵
"Interface\\Icons\\INV_Misc_EngGizmos_30")

  -- Create the item slots
  self.items = {}
  for idx = 1, 24 do
    local item = CreateFrame("Button", "BagBuddy_Item" .. idx, ↵
self, "BagBuddyItemTemplate")
    self.items[idx] = item
    if idx == 1 then
      item:SetPoint("TOPLEFT", 40, -73)
    elseif idx == 7 or idx == 13 or idx == 19 then
      item:SetPoint("TOPLEFT", self.items[idx-6], "BOTTOMLEFT", ↵
0, -7)
    else
      item:SetPoint("TOPLEFT", self.items[idx-1], "TOPRIGHT", ↵
12, 0)
    end
  end

  -- Create the filter buttons
  self.filters = {}
```

```
   for idx=0,5 do
      local button = CreateFrame("CheckButton", ↵
"BagBuddy_Filter" .. idx, self, "BagBuddyFilterTemplate")
      SetItemButtonTexture(button, ↵
"Interface\\ICONS\\INV_Misc_Gem_Pearl_03")
      self.filters[idx] = button
      if idx == 0 then
        button:SetPoint("BOTTOMLEFT", 40, 200)
      else
        button:SetPoint("TOPLEFT", self.filters[idx-1], ↵
"TOPRIGHT", 12, 0)
      end

      button.icon:SetVertexColor(GetItemQualityColor(idx))
      button:SetChecked(false)
      button.quality = idx
      button.glow:Hide()
   end

   self.filters[-1] = self.filters[0]

   -- Initialize to show the first page
   self.page = 1
end

local function itemNameSort(a, b)
   return a.name < b.name
end

function BagBuddy_Update()
   local items = {}

   local nameFilter = BagBuddy.input:GetText():lower()

   -- Scan through the bag slots, looking for items
   for bag = 0, NUM_BAG_SLOTS do
     for slot = 0, GetContainerNumSlots(bag) do
        local texture, count, locked, quality, readable, ↵
lootable, link = GetContainerItemInfo(bag, slot)

        if texture then
          local shown = true

          if BagBuddy.qualityFilter then
            shown = shown and BagBuddy.filters[quality]:GetChecked()
          end

          if #nameFilter > 0 then
            local lowerName = GetItemInfo(link):lower()
            shown = shown and string.find(lowerName, nameFilter, ↵
```

```
1, true)
        end

      if shown then
        -- If an item is found, grab the item number and ↵
store other data
        local itemNum = tonumber(link:match("|Hitem:(%d+):"))
        if not items[itemNum] then
          items[itemNum] = {
            texture = texture,
            count = count,
            quality = quality,
            name = GetItemInfo(link),
            link = link,
          }
        else
          -- The item already exists in our table, just ↵
update the count
          items[itemNum].count = items[itemNum].count + count
        end
      end
    end
  end
end


local sortTbl = {}
for link, entry in pairs(items) do
  table.insert(sortTbl, entry)
end
table.sort(sortTbl, itemNameSort)

-- Now update the BagBuddyFrame with the listed items (in order)
local max = BagBuddy.page * 24
local min = max - 23

for idx = min, max do
  local button = BagBuddy.items[idx - min + 1]
  local entry = sortTbl[idx]

  if entry then
    -- There is an item in this slot

    button.link = entry.link
    button.icon:SetTexture(entry.texture)
    if entry.count > 1 then
      button.count:SetText(entry.count)
      button.count:Show()
    else
      button.count:Hide()
```

```
          end

      if entry.quality > 1 then
         button.glow:SetVertexColor(↵
GetItemQualityColor(entry.quality))
         button.glow:Show()
      else
         button.glow:Hide()
      end
      button:Show()
    else
      button.link = nil
      button:Hide()
    end
  end

  -- Update page buttons
  if min > 1 then
    BagBuddy.prev:Enable()
  else
    BagBuddy.prev:Disable()
  end
  if max < #sortTbl then
    BagBuddy.next:Enable()
  else
    BagBuddy.next:Disable()
  end

  -- Update the status text
  if #sortTbl > 24 then
    local max = math.min(max, #sortTbl)
    local msg = string.format("Showing items %d - %d of %d", ↵
min, max, #sortTbl)
    BagBuddy.status:SetText(msg)
  else
    BagBuddy.status:SetText("Found " .. #sortTbl .. " items")
  end

end

function BagBuddy_Button_OnEnter(self, motion)
  if self.link then
    GameTooltip:SetOwner(self, "ANCHOR_TOPRIGHT")
    GameTooltip:SetHyperlink(self.link)
    GameTooltip:Show()
  end
end

function BagBuddy_Button_OnLeave(self, motion)
  GameTooltip:Hide()
```

```
end

function BagBuddy_Filter_OnEnter(self, motion)
  GameTooltip:SetOwner(self, "ANCHOR_TOPRIGHT")
  GameTooltip:SetText(_G["ITEM_QUALITY" .. ↵
self.quality .. "_DESC"])
  GameTooltip:Show()
end

function BagBuddy_Filter_OnLeave(self, motion)
  GameTooltip:Hide()
end

function BagBuddy_Filter_OnClick(self, button)
  BagBuddy.qualityFilter = false
  for idx = 0, 5 do
    local button = BagBuddy.filters[idx]
    if button:GetChecked() then
      BagBuddy.qualityFilter = true
    end
  end
  BagBuddy.page = 1
  BagBuddy_Update()
end

function BagBuddy_NextPage(self)
  BagBuddy.page = BagBuddy.page + 1
  BagBuddy_Update(BagBuddy)
end

function BagBuddy_PrevPage(self)
  BagBuddy.page = BagBuddy.page - 1
  BagBuddy_Update(BagBuddy)
end
```

BagBuddy.xml

```
<Ui xmlns="http://www.blizzard.com/wow/ui/"
  xmlns:xsi="http://www.w3.org/2001/XMLSchema-instance"
  xsi:schemaLocation="http://www.blizzard.com/wow/ui/
  http://wowprogramming.com/FrameXML/UI.xsd">

  <Button name="BagBuddyItemTemplate" virtual="true">
    <Size>
      <AbsDimension x="37" y="37"/>
    </Size>
    <Layers>
      <Layer level="BORDER">
        <Texture name="$parentIconTexture" parentKey="icon"/>
        <FontString name="$parentCount" parentKey="count"↵
```

```
          inherits="NumberFontNormal" justifyH="RIGHT" hidden="true">
                <Anchors>
                  <Anchor point="BOTTOMRIGHT">
                    <Offset>
                      <AbsDimension x="-5" y="2"/>
                    </Offset>
                  </Anchor>
                </Anchors>
              </FontString>
            </Layer>
            <Layer level="OVERLAY">
              <Texture name="$parentGlow" parentKey="glow" ↵
alphaMode="ADD" file="Interface\Buttons\UI-ActionButton-Border">
                <Size x="70" y="70"/>
                <Anchors>
                  <Anchor point="CENTER"/>
                </Anchors>
                <Color r="1.0" g="1.0" b="1.0" a="0.6"/>
              </Texture>
            </Layer>
          </Layers>
          <Scripts>
            <OnEnter function="BagBuddy_Button_OnEnter"/>
            <OnLeave function="BagBuddy_Button_OnLeave"/>
          </Scripts>
          <NormalTexture name="$parentNormalTexture" ↵
file="Interface\Buttons\UI-Quickslot2">
              <Size>
                <AbsDimension x="64" y="64"/>
              </Size>
              <Anchors>
                <Anchor point="CENTER">
                  <Offset>
                    <AbsDimension x="0" y="-1"/>
                  </Offset>
                </Anchor>
              </Anchors>
          </NormalTexture>
          <PushedTexture file="Interface\Buttons\UI-Quickslot-Depress"/>
          <HighlightTexture ↵
file="Interface\Buttons\ButtonHilight-Square" alphaMode="ADD"/>
        </Button>

      <CheckButton name="BagBuddyFilterTemplate" ↵
inherits="BagBuddyItemTemplate" virtual="true">
          <Scripts>
            <OnEnter function="BagBuddy_Filter_OnEnter"/>
            <OnLeave function="BagBuddy_Filter_OnLeave"/>
            <OnClick function="BagBuddy_Filter_OnClick"/>
          </Scripts>
```

```
      <CheckedTexture file="Interface\Buttons\CheckButtonHilight" ↵
alphaMode="ADD"/>
  </CheckButton>

  <Frame name="BagBuddy" parent="UIParent">
    <Size x="384" y="512"/>
    <Anchors>
      <Anchor point="CENTER" relativePoint="CENTER" ↵
relativeTo="UIParent"/>
    </Anchors>
    <Layers>
      <Layer level="BACKGROUND">
        <Texture name="$parent_Portrait" parentKey="portrait" ↵
file="Interface\Icons\INV_Misc_EngGizmos_30">
          <Size x="60" y="60"/>
          <Anchors>
            <Anchor point="TOPLEFT">
              <Offset x="7" y="-6"/>
            </Anchor>
          </Anchors>
        </Texture>
      </Layer>
      <Layer level="OVERLAY">
        <FontString name="$parent_Title" parentKey="title" ↵
inherits="GameFontNormal" text="BagBuggy">
          <Anchors>
            <Anchor point="TOP">
              <Offset x="0" y="-18"/>
            </Anchor>
          </Anchors>
        </FontString>
        <FontString name="$parent_Status" parentKey="status" ↵
inherits="GameFontHighlight">
          <Anchors>
            <Anchor point="CENTER" relativePoint="BOTTOM">
              <Offset x="-10" y="150"/>
            </Anchor>
          </Anchors>
        </FontString>

      </Layer>
      <Layer level="BORDER">
        <Texture file="Interface\BankFrame\UI-BankFrame-TopLeft">
          <Anchors>
            <Anchor point="TOPLEFT"/>
          </Anchors>
        </Texture>
        <Texture file="Interface\BankFrame\UI-BankFrame-TopRight">
          <Anchors>
            <Anchor point="TOPRIGHT"/>
```

```
          </Anchors>
        </Texture>
        <Texture file="Interface\BankFrame\UI-BankFrame-BotLeft">
          <Anchors>
            <Anchor point="BOTTOMLEFT"/>
          </Anchors>
        </Texture>
        <Texture file="Interface\BankFrame\UI-BankFrame-BotRight">
          <Anchors>
            <Anchor point="BOTTOMRIGHT"/>
          </Anchors>
        </Texture>
      </Layer>
    </Layers>
    <Frames>
      <Button name="$parent_Close" parentKey="close" ↵
inherits="UIPanelCloseButton">
        <Anchors>
          <Anchor point="TOPRIGHT">
            <Offset x="-30" y="-8"/>
          </Anchor>
        </Anchors>
      </Button>
      <Button name="BagBuddy_PrevButton" parentKey="prev">
        <Size x="32" y="32"/>
        <Anchors>
          <Anchor point="CENTER" relativeTo="BagBuddy" ↵
relativePoint="BOTTOMLEFT">
            <Offset>
              <AbsDimension x="50" y="150"/>
            </Offset>
          </Anchor>
        </Anchors>
        <Scripts>
          <OnClick function="BagBuddy_PrevPage"/>
        </Scripts>
        <NormalTexture ↵
file="Interface\Buttons\UI-SpellbookIcon-PrevPage-Up"/>
        <PushedTexture ↵
file="Interface\Buttons\UI-SpellbookIcon-PrevPage-Down"/>
        <DisabledTexture ↵
file="Interface\Buttons\UI-SpellbookIcon-PrevPage-Disabled"/>
        <HighlightTexture ↵
file="Interface\Buttons\UI-Common-MouseHilight" alphaMode="ADD"/>
      </Button>

      <Button name="BagBuddy_NextButton" parentKey="next">
        <Size x="32" y="32"/>
        <Anchors>
          <Anchor point="CENTER" relativeTo="BagBuddy" ↵
```

```
relativePoint="BOTTOMRIGHT">
            <Offset>
              <AbsDimension x="-70" y="150"/>
            </Offset>
          </Anchor>
        </Anchors>
        <Scripts>
          <OnClick function="BagBuddy_NextPage"/>
        </Scripts>
        <NormalTexture ↵
file="Interface\Buttons\UI-SpellbookIcon-NextPage-Up"/>
        <PushedTexture ↵
file="Interface\Buttons\UI-SpellbookIcon-NextPage-Down"/>
        <DisabledTexture ↵
file="Interface\Buttons\UI-SpellbookIcon-NextPage-Disabled"/>
        <HighlightTexture ↵
file="Interface\Buttons\UI-Common-MouseHilight" alphaMode="ADD"/>
      </Button>
      <EditBox name="$parent_Input" parentKey="input" ↵
autoFocus="false">
        <Size x="400" y="20"/>
        <Anchors>
          <Anchor point="BOTTOMLEFT">
            <Offset x="32" y="100"/>
          </Anchor>
        </Anchors>
        <Scripts>
          <OnEscapePressed>
            self:ClearFocus()
          </OnEscapePressed>
          <OnTextChanged>
            BagBuddy_Update()
          </OnTextChanged>
        </Scripts>
        <FontString inherits="GameFontHighlight"/>
      </EditBox>
    </Frames>
    <Scripts>
      <OnLoad function="BagBuddy_OnLoad"/>
    </Scripts>
  </Frame>
</Ui>
```

## CHAPTER 13

Responding to Game Events

By this point you should be fairly comfortable making new frames, textures, and font strings. You've defined several templates for use in your own addons, explored Blizzard's own FrameXML templates, and learned how to make your widgets more interactive by responding to widget scripts and user input. This chapter introduces the next aspect of user interface programming: responding to changes in the game client using the event system and event-based programming.

Understanding Events

Events are a way for the game client to notify addons of a change in the state of the game. For example, when the player's health changes, the user interface needs to be informed so it can update the status bar. If it weren't for events, the game client would need to continuously update the health bar, which would be very wasteful.

Events range from the extremely detailed to simple notifications that *something* has changed. A good example of the former is the UNIT_COMBAT event. This event is used for the combat notifications that appear on the player frame. It fires whenever a unit takes damage, is healed, or performs some other combat action (such as dodging, missing, or parrying). When the event is finally triggered, it provides the following information:

- The unit that was affected
- The action type that occurred (wound, dodge, heal, and so on)

- A modifier to the action, such as crushing or critical
- The amount of damage or healing that was received
- A number indicating the type of damage that was dealt

Registering for Events

To do anything meaningful with game events, you must first register for them. Like many other things in the user interface, you do this through frames. Every frame object has a `RegisterEvent()` method for this purpose. It expects a single string argument, the name of the event. Run the following code in-game to create a new frame, and register for the UNIT_COMBAT event:

```
MyEventFrame = CreateFrame("Frame", "MyEventFrame", UIParent)
MyEventFrame:RegisterEvent("UNIT_COMBAT")
```

You cannot register for more than one event at a time, but you can simply call `RegisterEvent()` multiple times, or write a helper function that can do multiple registrations for you.

Once a frame has been registered for an event, it will continue to receive event information until the event has been unregistered. The `Unregister Event()` event is provided for this purpose, taking the same argument as `RegisterEvent()`.

Responding to Events with OnEvent

To actually respond to events, you must set an `OnEvent` widget script for the frame that has registered for events. Each widget script can have at most one handler, so you will likely register for multiple events on the same frame, and your handler must be capable of differentiating between different events. This is done by examining the arguments that are passed to your handler:

- `self`—The frame that registered for the event
- `event`—The event that is being triggered
- `...`—A list of additional arguments to the event

Because the handler is given the name of the event as well as the frame itself, you can use basic conditional statements to differentiate between different events. For example, if you register for both UNIT_HEALTH and UNIT_MANA and need to distinguish between them, you could do the following:

```
if event == "UNIT_HEALTH" then
  -- do something with the unit health
elseif event == "UNIT_MANA" then
```

```
  -- do something different with mana
end
```

Add an `OnEvent` script to the `MyEventFrame` you created previously. Run the following code in-game:

```
function MyEventFrame_OnEvent(self, event, ...)
  print("Event handler", event, ...)
end

MyEventFrame:SetScript("OnEvent", MyEventFrame_OnEvent)
```

Alternatively, you could just create the new function inline:

```
MyEventFrame:SetScript("OnEvent", function(self, event, ...)
  print("Event handler", event, ...)
end)
```

An even shorter form (that doesn't allow you to add a custom message to the start) simply sets the print function as the script handler:

```
MyEventFrame:SetScript("OnEvent", print)
```

The result of any of these will be a message sent to the chat frame each time the event occurs. You can test this by fighting with something in-game. You should receive messages for both you and your enemy. Figure 13-1 shows some messages from combat.

Figure 13-1: Event messages for UNIT_COMBAT

In this case you can see that the event has five arguments that are passed to the handler. You'll work with the UNIT_COMBAT event more in Chapter 14 and learn what each of these arguments are.

This simple method of setting up event handlers to print debug information can be useful when working on an addon because it lets you see easily which arguments were sent with a given event. Alternatively, you could use the new /eventtrace command that was added to WoW in 3.2. It is discussed at the end of this chapter.

Query Events

There are certain API calls that require communication with the server, instead of getting their information locally from the game client. For example, when you want to update your guild roster, you call the `GuildRoster()` function. You might expect the information to be available immediately, but the information is all stored on the server so you must wait for the `GUILD_ROSTER_UPDATE` event, which signifies that the data has been received by the client and is available.

When working with an API system, always read the related documentation so you will understand how the information becomes available.

Tracking Changes to Inventory for BagBuddy

The event-based system used in World of Warcraft is conceptually simple, but in practice it can be a bit tricky to work this. In this section, you'll use the `BAG_UPDATE` event to add some functionality to BagBuddy. To sort the inventory with the most recently looted items first, you must monitor changes to the player's inventory. The `BAG_UPDATE` event fires whenever something changes in the player's bags, so it gives you just what you need.

Examining the BAG_UPDATE Event

`BAG_UPDATE` is a very interesting event because it can fire for a number of reasons, and doesn't really provide much information. In fact, there is only one argument to the event: the numeric index of the bag that was updated. The event fires whenever the state of the player's containers changes, such as when the player moves items from one bag to another, or loots a new item.

If you write a simple addon to monitor the event, you might see that it can fire multiple times back to back. For example, if you loot two items and one of them goes into an existing stack, and the other goes into a new slot elsewhere in your inventory, the event then fires for each of the bags that changed. In addition, the `BAG_UPDATE` event's first argument is sometimes a negative number due to the internal implementation of the player's inventory and equipment. As a result, you'll need to ignore any negative values, and run your handler only when a legitimate bag has been updated.

Tracking New Inventory Items

For the purposes of BagBuddy, you just want to watch to see new items enter the inventory so you can somehow tag them with the time they were looted. Then when you go through the display loop in `BagBuddy_Update`, you can sort according to that value.

You'll need a place to store the item counts for each bag, so add the following to the end of `BagBuddy_OnLoad` in `BagBuddy.lua`:

```
self.bagCounts = {}
```

Now add the following function definition somewhere in `BagBuddy.lua`:

```
function BagBuddy_ScanBag(bag, initial)
  if not BagBuddy.bagCounts[bag] then
    BagBuddy.bagCounts[bag] = {}
  end

  local itemCounts = {}
  for slot = 0, GetContainerNumSlots(bag) do
    local texture, count, locked, quality, readable, lootable, link = ↵
GetContainerItemInfo(bag, slot)

    if texture then
      local itemId = tonumber(link:match("|Hitem:(%d+):"))
      if not itemCounts[itemId] then
        itemCounts[itemId] = count
      else
        itemCounts[itemId] = itemCounts[itemId] + count
      end
    end
  end

  if initial then
    for itemId, count in pairs(itemCounts) do
      BagBuddy_ItemTimes[itemId] = BagBuddy_ItemTimes[itemId] or time()
    end
  else
    for itemId, count in pairs(itemCounts) do
      local oldCount = BagBuddy.bagCounts[bag][itemId] or 0
      if count > oldCount then
        BagBuddy_ItemTimes[itemId] = time()
      end
    end
  end

  BagBuddy.bagCounts[bag] = itemCounts
end
```

This function takes a numerical bag index, and a flag called `initial`. The flag will indicate whether the function is being called on the first scan of a session because there would be no prior count with which to compare.

Next, the function loops over all of the slots in the given bag and checks to see if there is an item in the slot. If so, it parses the item ID from the hyperlink and updates the local `itemCounts` table with the new count.

Item times are stored in the global `BagBuddy_ItemTimes` tables, which we will create in a later section. When the `initial` flag is set, the item times are set using the prior value, if possible, or the current time. At any other time, the item counts are compared to the previous item counts. If the count has gone up, then the item time is set to the current time. Finally, the new `itemCounts` table is stored in `BagBuddy.bagCounts` so it can be used on the next inventory change.

Note that you're using the item number here to store the loot time, otherwise items with different unique IDs would show up as distinct items. Ideally you would use the item string (excluding the unique ID portion) so you can differentiate between items that have different enchants or sockets. This version just lumps those types of items into a single stack for simplicity.

Writing a New Sorting Function

The previous version of this addon sorted items by name, but now you want to include item loot time as part of the sorting. Insert a new sorting function by adding the following definition before `BagBuddy_Update()`:

```
local function itemTimeNameSort(a, b)
  -- If the two items were looted at the same time
  local aTime = BagBuddy.itemTimes[a.num]
  local bTime = BagBuddy.itemTimes[b.num]
  if aTime == bTime then
    return a.name < b.name
  else
    return aTime >= bTime
  end
end
```

The function checks to see if the loot times are the same, in which case it sorts the items by name. If the times are different, then they are sorted in descending order (by using `>=` instead of `<`) in the comparison. To use this new sorting function, you need to make some small changes to the update.

Altering BagBuddy_Update

The changes to `BagBuddy_Update` are very simple; you just need to add the item number to the entry table and call the new sort function. In `BagBuddy_Update`, the new item table code should be changed to the following (changed line is highlighted):

```
if not items[itemNum] then
  items[itemNum] = {
    texture = texture,
```

```
        count = count,
        quality = quality,
        name = GetItemInfo(link),
        link = link,
            num = itemNum,
    }
else
```

Finally, change the call to `table.sort` from

```
table.sort(sortTbl, itemNameSort)
```

to

```
table.sort(sortTbl, itemTimeNameSort)
```

Adding an OnEvent Handler

To actually catch the BAG_UPDATE events, you need to add an event handler. Open BagBuddy.xml and add the following to the <Scripts> element in the definition of the BagBuddy frame:

```
<OnEvent function="BagBuddy_OnEvent"/>
```

Now open BagBuddy.lua and add this function definition somewhere toward the end of the file:

```
function BagBuddy_OnEvent(self, event, ...)
    if event == "ADDON_LOADED" and ... == "BagBuddy" then
        if not BagBuddy_ItemTimes then
            BagBuddy_ItemTimes = {}
        end
        for bag = 0, NUM_BAG_SLOTS do
            -- Use the optional flag to skip updating times
            BagBuddy_ScanBag(bag, true)
        end
        self:UnregisterEvent("ADDON_LOADED")
        self:RegisterEvent("BAG_UPDATE")
    elseif event == "BAG_UPDATE" then
        local bag = ...
        if bag >= 0 then
            BagBuddy_ScanBag(bag)
            if BagBuddy:IsVisible() then
                BagBuddy_Update()
            end
        end
    end
end
```

This handler is set to watch for two events: ADDON_LOADED and BAG_UPDATE. ADDON_LOADED is used as an initialization event because it indicates that an addon is fully loaded. However, addons can sometimes load out of order due to dependencies and other API calls, so you have to check the first argument to the function to see *which* addon has finished loading.

When BagBuddy's ADDON_LOADED event is encountered, the BagBuddy_ ItemTimes table is created and the initial scan is run for each of the player's bags. After that, the addon no longer cares about the ADDON_LOADED event, so it un-registers it. Finally, the handler registers for the BAG_UPDATE event, so it can detect changes to the player's inventory.

The BAG_UPDATE portion of the handler is very simple; it just checks to see if the bag index is greater than or equal to 0 (the player's backpack) and then runs the bag scan. If the frame is visible, it calls BagBuddy_Update() to update the frame. This ensures that the frame is always showing the latest information.

Finally, you need to register for the ADDON_LOADED event, so add the following to the end of BagBuddy_OnLoad():

```
self:RegisterEvent("ADDON_LOADED")
```

Now when you log into the game and loot some items, you should then see them sorted with the most recently looted items shown first. In addition you can still filter the items by rarity or name and have them sorted by loot time.

Cleaning Up

Right now the frame is visible when the game is loaded, and can't easily be re-opened once it's been closed. In addition, it would be nice if the frame would operate like the rest of the panels in the user interface. Luckily there's an easy system that allows you to do that.

At the top of BagBuddy_OnLoad() add the following code:

```
UIPanelWindows["BagBuddy"] = {
  area = "left",
  pushable = 1,
  whileDead = 1,
}
```

UIPanelWindows is a special global table that contains definitions of the various panels that are controlled by the user interface. The key is the name of the frame and the value is a table of options. In this case, you indicate that the window should appear on the left side of the screen, can be pushed toward the center by another panel, and should be visible while the player is dead. Additionally, by adding your frame to the UIPanelWindows table, it automatically gains the capability to be closed by pressing the Escape key rather than having to click the close button.

Unfortunately, by the time the `BagBuddy_OnLoad()` function is run, the frame will already have been shown, so it won't be treated as one of the special UI panels. Additionally, it doesn't seem to make much sense to have the frame shown every time the player logs in. Open `BagBuddy.xml` and change the opening tag for BagBuddy to the following (the addition has been highlighted):

```
<Frame name="BagBuddy" parent="UIParent" hidden="true">
```

Now when you'd like to see the frame, you can run the following command and BagBuddy will behave the same as the other UI panels:

```
/run ShowUIPanel(BagBuddy)
```

Adding a Slash Command

You can make it easier to open BagBuddy by adding the following slash command definition to the end of `BagBuddy.lua`:

```
SLASH_BAGBUDDY1 = "/bb"
SLASH_BAGBUDDY2 = "/bagbuddy"
SlashCmdList["BAGBUDDY"] = function(msg, editbox)
  BagBuddy.input:SetText(msg)
  ShowUIPanel(BagBuddy)
end
```

This provides two new slash commands (`/bb` and `/bagbuddy`) that both work in the same way. Any text typed after the slash command will be put into the edit box and used as a name filter, then the panel is shown. Now instead of running a script command, you can just type `/bb` to open the frame.

Slash commands are further discussed in Chapter 17.

Storing Data with SavedVariables

With this version of BagBuddy, the item times are reset every time the user interface is reloaded. If you reload your user interface in the middle of a questing session and then open BagBuddy, you will find that the items are again sorted by name rather than by loot time, making that feature a bit less useful. To fix this, you need some way to carry data from session to session.

World of Warcraft offers a system that allows addons to register certain global variables to be saved between game sessions. These are called *saved variables*, named after the table of contents directive that is used to specify them. There are two different types of saved variables:

- **SavedVariables**—Account-wide, accessible to any character on a given account.

- **SavedVariablesPerCharacter**—Separate for each individual character, so not even two characters on the same server can share them.

Although you could obviously take a normal saved variable and partition it so multiple users can use it without interfering with each other's data, each character truly has access to all of the data. On the other hand, there is no way to simulate a normal saved variable with a per-character saved variable because all saving and loading is handled directly by the game client.

Registering a New Saved Variable

Using saved variables is quite easy; you just need to add a directive to your addon's table of contents file, and restart the game client. When the game client is loaded, it loads any stored data and makes it available to your addon (more on this later). When the game client is closed, a character logs out, or the user interface is reloaded, the data is saved out to disk.

Start by adding a saved variable to `BagBuddy.toc`. Open the file and add the following after the `## Notes` directive:

```
## SavedVariablesPerCharacter: BagBuddy_ItemTimes
```

There's really no reason that users would need access to each other's times, so you can declare your saved variable to be per-character only. That way you don't have to be concerned about storing your data in any specific place; you can just leave it in the table itself.

For this change to take effect, you will need to quit your client and re-open it. Changes that are made to the metadata of an addon's table of contents file are refreshed only when the client is opened, not on user interface reload.

Saved Variables and ADDON_LOADED

When an addon is being loaded (that is, when the code is actually being parsed and run) any saved variables are not yet available. Once the addon has finished initializing, the client loads the saved variables and fires the ADDON_LOADED event. Although the reasons for this weren't discussed in the previous section, that is why initialization is delayed until ADDON_LOADED.

Using Items from BagBuddy

Finding items in your inventory is great, but it would be nicer to be able to click to use them once you've found them. This can be accomplished using *secure templates*, which are discussed in Chapter 15. For now, you can make the following changes to your code to enable that functionality.

In BagBuddy_OnLoad(), change the loop that creates item slots to register for right-clicks (change is highlighted):

```
-- Create the item slots
self.items = {}
for idx = 1, 24 do
    local item = CreateFrame("Button", "BagBuddy_Item" .. idx, self, ↵
"BagBuddyItemTemplate")
    item:RegisterForClicks("RightButtonUp")
    self.items[idx] = item
    if idx == 1 then
        item:SetPoint("TOPLEFT", 40, -73)
    elseif idx == 7 or idx == 13 or idx == 19 then
        item:SetPoint("TOPLEFT", self.items[idx-6], "BOTTOMLEFT", 0, -7)
    else
        item:SetPoint("TOPLEFT", self.items[idx-1], "TOPRIGHT", 12, 0)
    end
end
```

In BagBuddy_Update(), add the following highlighted line in the conditional that indicates there is an item in the slot. This sets the button up to use the named item when it is right-clicked.

```
if entry then
    -- There is an item in this slot

    button:SetAttribute("item2", entry.name)
    button.link = entry.link
    button.icon:SetTexture(entry.texture)
```

The last two changes must be made in BagBuddy.xml. First, change the opening tag for BagBuddyItemTemplate from

```
<Button name="BagBuddyItemTemplate" virtual="true">
```

to

```
<Button name="BagBuddyItemTemplate" ↵
inherits="SecureActionButtonTemplate" virtual="true">
```

Finally, add an attribute definition between the `</Layers>` tag and the `<Scripts>` tag for `BagBuddyItemTemplate`:

```
<Attributes>
  <Attribute name="type2" type="string" value="item"/>
</Attributes>
```

Now when you open BagBuddy, you should be able to use items (such as food, potions, bandages, and quest items) by right-clicking on them.

Finding the Right Event Using /eventtrace

One of the most challenging aspects of writing an addon for World of Warcraft is finding the right events to ensure your addon functions properly. Some applications are very simple, such as using UNIT_HEALTH to monitor the health of an in-game unit. Others, such as those dealing with the player's containers and inventory, can be a bit tricky to deal with at times.

The `Blizzard_DebugTools` addon included with the default user interface provides the slash command `/eventtrace` that makes tracking down event information a bit easier. The command has a few different forms:

- `/eventtrace start`—Start capturing events, whether or not the window is shown.

- `/eventtrace stop`—Stop capturing events.

- `/eventtrace`—Show the window if it is currently hidden, and start capturing events if the window hasn't been shown before. Otherwise, hide the window.

- `/eventtrace <num>`—If the addon is not currently capturing events, capture exactly <num> events and then stop capturing events.

The results are displayed for you in an easy-to-navigate window, shown in Figure 13-2.

You can scroll through the resulting events to view their arguments and the time at which they were called. In addition, the event trace will show you how much time elapsed between two events (if any) and how many times the screen was updated.

When you need to find out what events fires under a certain situation (such as when you cast a spell on an enemy), you can start an event trace and replicate the situation. Then you can stop the event trace and explore the events that fired to get the information you need.

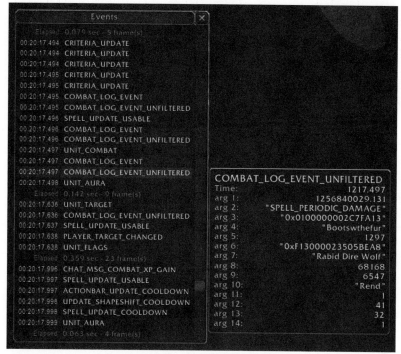

Figure 13-2: /eventtrace window showing event information

Summary

This chapter explored how the game client notifies addons of changes to the state of the game. You added event handling to BagBuddy to track changes to the player's inventory. The last few chapters have introduced you to all of the vital parts of creating an addon. The next chapter pulls everything together to create another fully-functional addon called CombatTracker.

The Code

BagBuddy.lua

```
function BagBuddy_OnLoad(self)
  UIPanelWindows["BagBuddy"] = {
    area = "left",
    pushable = 1,
    whileDead = 1,
  }

  SetPortraitToTexture(self.portrait, ↵
"Interface\\Icons\\INV_Misc_EngGizmos_30")

  -- Create the item slots
```

```
      self.items = {}
    for idx = 1, 24 do
      local item = CreateFrame("Button", "BagBuddy_Item" .. idx, ↵
  self, "BagBuddyItemTemplate")
      item:RegisterForClicks("RightButtonUp")
      self.items[idx] = item
      if idx == 1 then
        item:SetPoint("TOPLEFT", 40, -73)
      elseif idx == 7 or idx == 13 or idx == 19 then
        item:SetPoint("TOPLEFT", self.items[idx-6], "BOTTOMLEFT", 0, -7)
      else
        item:SetPoint("TOPLEFT", self.items[idx-1], "TOPRIGHT", 12, 0)
      end
    end

    -- Create the filter buttons
    self.filters = {}
    for idx=0,5 do
      local button = CreateFrame("CheckButton",
        "BagBuddy_Filter" .. idx, self, "BagBuddyFilterTemplate")
      SetItemButtonTexture(button, ↵
  "Interface\\ICONS\\INV_Misc_Gem_Pearl_03")
      self.filters[idx] = button
      if idx == 0 then
        button:SetPoint("BOTTOMLEFT", 40, 200)
      else
        button:SetPoint("TOPLEFT", self.filters[idx-1], "TOPRIGHT", 12, 0)
      end

      button.icon:SetVertexColor(GetItemQualityColor(idx))
      button:SetChecked(false)
      button.quality = idx
      button.glow:Hide()
    end

    self.filters[-1] = self.filters[0]

    -- Initialize to show the first page
    self.page = 1

    self.bagCounts = {}

    self:RegisterEvent("ADDON_LOADED")
  end

  local function itemNameSort(a, b)
    return a.name < b.name
  end

  local function itemTimeNameSort(a, b)
```

```
      -- If the two items were looted at the same time
   local aTime = BagBuddy_ItemTimes[a.num]
   local bTime = BagBuddy_ItemTimes[b.num]
   if aTime == bTime then
     return a.name < b.name
   else
     return aTime >= bTime
   end
end

function BagBuddy_Update()
  local items = {}

  local nameFilter = BagBuddy.input:GetText():lower()

  -- Scan through the bag slots, looking for items
  for bag = 0, NUM_BAG_SLOTS do
    for slot = 0, GetContainerNumSlots(bag) do
      local texture, count, locked, quality, readable, lootable, ↵
link = GetContainerItemInfo(bag, slot)

      if texture then
        local shown = true

        if BagBuddy.qualityFilter then
          shown = shown and BagBuddy.filters[quality]:GetChecked()
        end

        if #nameFilter > 0 then
          local lowerName = GetItemInfo(link):lower()
          shown = shown and string.find(lowerName, nameFilter, 1, true)
        end


        if shown then
          -- If an item is found, grab item number and store other data
          local itemNum = tonumber(link:match("|Hitem:(%d+):"))
          if not items[itemNum] then
            items[itemNum] = {
              texture = texture,
              count = count,
              quality = quality,
              name = GetItemInfo(link),
              link = link,
              num = itemNum,
            }
          else
            -- The item already exists, just update the count
            items[itemNum].count = items[itemNum].count + count
          end
```

```
        end
      end
    end
end

local sortTbl = {}
for link, entry in pairs(items) do
  table.insert(sortTbl, entry)
end
table.sort(sortTbl, itemTimeNameSort)

-- Now update the BagBuddyFrame with the listed items (in order)
local max = BagBuddy.page * 24
local min = max - 23

for idx = min, max do
  local button = BagBuddy.items[idx - min + 1]
  local entry = sortTbl[idx]

  if entry then
    -- There is an item in this slot

    button:SetAttribute("item2", entry.name)
    button.link = entry.link
    button.icon:SetTexture(entry.texture)
    if entry.count > 1 then
      button.count:SetText(entry.count)
      button.count:Show()
    else
      button.count:Hide()
    end

    if entry.quality > 1 then
      button.glow:SetVertexColor(GetItemQualityColor(entry.quality))
      button.glow:Show()
    else
      button.glow:Hide()
    end
    button:Show()
  else
    button.link = nil
    button:Hide()
  end
end

-- Update page buttons
if min > 1 then
  BagBuddy.prev:Enable()
else
  BagBuddy.prev:Disable()
```

```
    end
    if max < #sortTbl then
      BagBuddy.next:Enable()
    else
      BagBuddy.next:Disable()
    end

    -- Update the status text
    if #sortTbl > 24 then
      local max = math.min(max, #sortTbl)
      local msg = string.format("Showing items %d - %d of %d", min, ↵
max, #sortTbl)
      BagBuddy.status:SetText(msg)
    else
      BagBuddy.status:SetText("Found " .. #sortTbl .. " items")
    end

end

function BagBuddy_Button_OnEnter(self, motion)
  if self.link then
    GameTooltip:SetOwner(self, "ANCHOR_TOPRIGHT")
    GameTooltip:SetHyperlink(self.link)
    GameTooltip:Show()
  end
end

function BagBuddy_Button_OnLeave(self, motion)
  GameTooltip:Hide()
end

function BagBuddy_Filter_OnEnter(self, motion)
  GameTooltip:SetOwner(self, "ANCHOR_TOPRIGHT")
  GameTooltip:SetText(_G["ITEM_QUALITY" .. self.quality .. "_DESC"])
  GameTooltip:Show()
end

function BagBuddy_Filter_OnLeave(self, motion)
  GameTooltip:Hide()
end

function BagBuddy_Filter_OnClick(self, button)
  BagBuddy.qualityFilter = false
  for idx = 0, 5 do
    local button = BagBuddy.filters[idx]
    if button:GetChecked() then
      BagBuddy.qualityFilter = true
    end
  end
  BagBuddy.page = 1
```

```lua
    BagBuddy_Update()
end

function BagBuddy_NextPage(self)
  BagBuddy.page = BagBuddy.page + 1
  BagBuddy_Update(BagBuddy)
end

function BagBuddy_PrevPage(self)
  BagBuddy.page = BagBuddy.page - 1
  BagBuddy_Update(BagBuddy)
end

function BagBuddy_ScanBag(bag, initial)
  if not BagBuddy.bagCounts[bag] then
    BagBuddy.bagCounts[bag] = {}
  end

  local itemCounts = {}
  for slot = 0, GetContainerNumSlots(bag) do
    local texture, count, locked, quality, readable, lootable, ↵
link = GetContainerItemInfo(bag, slot)

    if texture then
      local itemId = tonumber(link:match("|Hitem:(%d+):"))
      if not itemCounts[itemId] then
        itemCounts[itemId] = count
      else
        itemCounts[itemId] = itemCounts[itemId] + count
      end
    end
  end

  if initial then
    for itemId, count in pairs(itemCounts) do
      BagBuddy_ItemTimes[itemId] = BagBuddy_ItemTimes[itemId] or time()
    end
  else
    for itemId, count in pairs(itemCounts) do
      local oldCount = BagBuddy.bagCounts[bag][itemId] or 0
      if count > oldCount then
        BagBuddy_ItemTimes[itemId] = time()
      end
    end
  end

  BagBuddy.bagCounts[bag] = itemCounts
end

function BagBuddy_OnEvent(self, event, ...)
```

```
    if event == "ADDON_LOADED" and ... == "BagBuddy" then
      if not BagBuddy_ItemTimes then
        BagBuddy_ItemTimes = {}
      end
      for bag = 0, NUM_BAG_SLOTS do
        -- Use the optional flag to skip updating times
        BagBuddy_ScanBag(bag, true)
      end
      self:UnregisterEvent("ADDON_LOADED")
      self:RegisterEvent("BAG_UPDATE")
    elseif event == "BAG_UPDATE" then
      local bag = ...
      if bag >= 0 then
        BagBuddy_ScanBag(bag)
        if BagBuddy:IsVisible() then
          BagBuddy_Update()
        end
      end
    end
end

SLASH_BAGBUDDY1 = "/bb"
SLASH_BAGBUDDY2 = "/bagbuddy"
SlashCmdList["BAGBUDDY"] = function(msg, editbox)
  BagBuddy.input:SetText(msg)
  ShowUIPanel(BagBuddy)
end
```

BagBuddy.xml

```
<Ui xmlns="http://www.blizzard.com/wow/ui/"
  xmlns:xsi="http://www.w3.org/2001/XMLSchema-instance"
  xsi:schemaLocation="http://www.blizzard.com/wow/ui/
  http://wowprogramming.com/FrameXML/UI.xsd">

  <Button name="BagBuddyItemTemplate" ↵
inherits="SecureActionButtonTemplate" virtual="true">
    <Size>
      <AbsDimension x="37" y="37"/>
    </Size>
    <Layers>
      <Layer level="BORDER">
        <Texture name="$parentIconTexture" parentKey="icon"/>
        <FontString name="$parentCount" parentKey="count" ↵
inherits="NumberFontNormal" justifyH="RIGHT" hidden="true">
          <Anchors>
            <Anchor point="BOTTOMRIGHT">
              <Offset>
                <AbsDimension x="-5" y="2"/>
              </Offset>
            </Anchor>
```

```
              </Anchor>
            </Anchors>
          </FontString>
        </Layer>
        <Layer level="OVERLAY">
          <Texture name="$parentGlow" parentKey="glow" alphaMode="ADD"
            file="Interface\Buttons\UI-ActionButton-Border">
            <Size x="70" y="70"/>
            <Anchors>
              <Anchor point="CENTER"/>
            </Anchors>
            <Color r="1.0" g="1.0" b="1.0" a="0.6"/>
          </Texture>
        </Layer>
      </Layers>
      <Attributes>
        <Attribute name="type2" type="string" value="item"/>
      </Attributes>
      <Scripts>
        <OnEnter function="BagBuddy_Button_OnEnter"/>
        <OnLeave function="BagBuddy_Button_OnLeave"/>
      </Scripts>
      <NormalTexture name="$parentNormalTexture" ↵
file="Interface\Buttons\UI-Quickslot2">
        <Size>
          <AbsDimension x="64" y="64"/>
        </Size>
        <Anchors>
          <Anchor point="CENTER">
            <Offset>
              <AbsDimension x="0" y="-1"/>
            </Offset>
          </Anchor>
        </Anchors>
      </NormalTexture>
      <PushedTexture file="Interface\Buttons\UI-Quickslot-Depress"/>
      <HighlightTexture file="Interface\Buttons\ButtonHilight-Square"
        alphaMode="ADD"/>
    </Button>

    <CheckButton name="BagBuddyFilterTemplate"
      inherits="BagBuddyItemTemplate" virtual="true">
      <Scripts>
        <OnEnter function="BagBuddy_Filter_OnEnter"/>
        <OnLeave function="BagBuddy_Filter_OnLeave"/>
        <OnClick function="BagBuddy_Filter_OnClick"/>
      </Scripts>
      <CheckedTexture file="Interface\Buttons\CheckButtonHilight"
        alphaMode="ADD"/>
    </CheckButton>
```

```
<Frame name="BagBuddy" parent="UIParent" hidden="true">
  <Size x="384" y="512"/>
  <Anchors>
    <Anchor point="CENTER" relativePoint="CENTER"
      relativeTo="UIParent"/>
  </Anchors>
  <Layers>
    <Layer level="BACKGROUND">
      <Texture name="$parent_Portrait" parentKey="portrait"
        file="Interface\Icons\INV_Misc_EngGizmos_30">
        <Size x="60" y="60"/>
        <Anchors>
          <Anchor point="TOPLEFT">
            <Offset x="7" y="-6"/>
          </Anchor>
        </Anchors>
      </Texture>
    </Layer>
    <Layer level="OVERLAY">
      <FontString name="$parent_Title" parentKey="title"
        inherits="GameFontNormal" text="BagBuggy">
        <Anchors>
          <Anchor point="TOP">
            <Offset x="0" y="-18"/>
          </Anchor>
        </Anchors>
      </FontString>
      <FontString name="$parent_Status" parentKey="status"
        inherits="GameFontHighlight">
        <Anchors>
          <Anchor point="CENTER" relativePoint="BOTTOM">
            <Offset x="-10" y="150"/>
          </Anchor>
        </Anchors>
      </FontString>

    </Layer>
    <Layer level="BORDER">
      <Texture file="Interface\BankFrame\UI-BankFrame-TopLeft">
        <Anchors>
          <Anchor point="TOPLEFT"/>
        </Anchors>
      </Texture>
      <Texture file="Interface\BankFrame\UI-BankFrame-TopRight">
        <Anchors>
          <Anchor point="TOPRIGHT"/>
        </Anchors>
      </Texture>
      <Texture file="Interface\BankFrame\UI-BankFrame-BotLeft">
        <Anchors>
```

```
            <Anchor point="BOTTOMLEFT"/>
          </Anchors>
        </Texture>
        <Texture file="Interface\BankFrame\UI-BankFrame-BotRight">
          <Anchors>
            <Anchor point="BOTTOMRIGHT"/>
          </Anchors>
        </Texture>
      </Layer>
    </Layers>
    <Frames>
      <Button name="$parent_Close" parentKey="close"
        inherits="UIPanelCloseButton">
        <Anchors>
          <Anchor point="TOPRIGHT">
            <Offset x="-30" y="-8"/>
          </Anchor>
        </Anchors>
      </Button>
      <Button name="BagBuddy_PrevButton" parentKey="prev">
        <Size x="32" y="32"/>
        <Anchors>
          <Anchor point="CENTER" relativeTo="BagBuddy"
            relativePoint="BOTTOMLEFT">
            <Offset>
              <AbsDimension x="50" y="150"/>
            </Offset>
          </Anchor>
        </Anchors>
        <Scripts>
          <OnClick function="BagBuddy_PrevPage"/>
        </Scripts>
        <NormalTexture
          file="Interface\Buttons\UI-SpellbookIcon-PrevPage-Up"/>
        <PushedTexture
          file="Interface\Buttons\UI-SpellbookIcon-PrevPage-Down"/>
        <DisabledTexture
          file="Interface\Buttons\UI-SpellbookIcon-PrevPage-Disabled"/>
        <HighlightTexture
          file="Interface\Buttons\UI-Common-MouseHilight"
          alphaMode="ADD"/>
      </Button>

      <Button name="BagBuddy_NextButton" parentKey="next">
        <Size x="32" y="32"/>
        <Anchors>
          <Anchor point="CENTER" relativeTo="BagBuddy"
            relativePoint="BOTTOMRIGHT">
            <Offset>
              <AbsDimension x="-70" y="150"/>
```

```xml
              </Offset>
            </Anchor>
          </Anchors>
          <Scripts>
            <OnClick function="BagBuddy_NextPage"/>
          </Scripts>
          <NormalTexture
            file="Interface\Buttons\UI-SpellbookIcon-NextPage-Up"/>
          <PushedTexture
            file="Interface\Buttons\UI-SpellbookIcon-NextPage-Down"/>
          <DisabledTexture
            file="Interface\Buttons\UI-SpellbookIcon-NextPage-Disabled"/>
          <HighlightTexture
            file="Interface\Buttons\UI-Common-MouseHilight"
            alphaMode="ADD"/>
        </Button>
        <EditBox name="$parent_Input" parentKey="input"
          autoFocus="false">
          <Size x="400" y="20"/>
          <Anchors>
            <Anchor point="BOTTOMLEFT">
              <Offset x="32" y="100"/>
            </Anchor>
          </Anchors>
          <Scripts>
            <OnEscapePressed>
              self:ClearFocus()
            </OnEscapePressed>
            <OnTextChanged>
              BagBuddy_Update()
            </OnTextChanged>
          </Scripts>
          <FontString inherits="GameFontHighlight"/>
        </EditBox>
      </Frames>

      <Scripts>
        <OnLoad function="BagBuddy_OnLoad"/>
        <OnEvent function="BagBuddy_OnEvent"/>
      </Scripts>
    </Frame>
</Ui>
```

## CHAPTER 14

Tracking Damage with CombatTracker

You've worked through all of the different aspects of writing an addon while creating the BagBuddy addon. You've learned how to use the WoW API to query information from the game client, registered for and responded to game events, and created widgets with which users can interact. In this chapter, you'll put all of these skills together to create an addon called CombatTracker.

Defining Specifications

Before sitting down to code, it's important to understand exactly what an addon will be expected to do and have a general idea of how it should operate from the user perspective. What isn't important at this stage is how you will implement the addon; the design needs to be decided first.

CombatTracker User Experience

The specification for CombatTracker covers the following details:

1. A frame that can be dragged and moved by the user will be created on screen.

2. When the player enters combat, the addon will store the current time and change the frame to display "In Combat."

3. Each time the player takes damage from an NPC, the frame's display will be updated to show the amount of time that has been spent in combat, the amount of damage that has been sustained, and the incoming damage per second.

4. When combat has ended, the frame will display final statistics.

5. The frame will be a button and, when clicked, will send the incoming damage-per-second summary to the player's party, if he is in one; otherwise, it will simply be displayed on the screen.

Finding the Right Game Events

First figure out the events for which you will need to register. In this case, you need to be notified of when the player enters or leaves combat. When in combat, you need to know when the player takes damage. This section details the three events that CombatTracker needs to function:

- `PLAYER_REGEN_DISABLED`

- `PLAYER_REGEN_ENABLED`

- `UNIT_COMBAT`

PLAYER_REGEN_DISABLED

Upon entering combat, a player no longer regenerates health over the course of time, with the exception of spells, talents, and equipment that provide specific amounts of health regeneration every five seconds. As a result, the `PLAYER_REGEN_DISABLED` event can be used to indicate when the player has engaged in combat, according to the game client. This event doesn't necessarily mean that the player has sustained any damage; it just indicates to the game client that the player is now considered to be in combat.

From a user interface perspective, this event also enables addon authors to do any last-minute setup for any addons that use secure templates. You learn more about secure templates in Chapter 15 but, in short, they allow for addons to cast spells and target units through a special system that cannot be altered while in combat. This event gives those addons one last chance to configure themselves.

`PLAYER_REGEN_DISABLED` has no arguments included when it fires.

PLAYER_REGEN_ENABLED

The `PLAYER_REGEN_ENABLED` event fires when the player begins normal health regeneration again. It means the player's normal health regeneration has started and is fired consistently when the player exits combat. As a result, it can be used by an addon to track the player exiting combat (even though the event isn't named `PLAYER_EXIT_COMBAT` or something similar). The event has no arguments included when it fires.

UNIT_COMBAT

Several events deal with the player sustaining damage, but you will be using the UNIT_COMBAT event. Anytime a unit the player is interested in (such as party members, raid members and their targets, and so on) has a change in hit points that relates to combat, this event fires with the following arguments describing the change:

- unit—The identifier for the unit that experienced the change.

- action—The type of combat action that happened. Some example values are the strings HEAL, DODGE, BLOCK, WOUND, MISS, PARRY, and RESIST.

- modifier—If the action was a combat attack, it could possibly be a glancing hit, critical hit, or crushing blow. Example values are the strings GLANCING, CRUSHING, and CRITICAL.

- damage—The amount of damage sustained, or the amount of health healed.

- damagetype—The type of damage that occurred, using one of the following number values:

    - 0—physical damage
    - 1—holy damage
    - 2—fire damage
    - 3—nature damage
    - 4—frost damage
    - 5—shadow damage
    - 6—arcane damage

Creating the Addon's Skeleton

Although the entire CombatTracker addon (and most addons, actually) could be written in just a single Lua file or a single XML file, this implementation will separate the design and layout of the frames from the code that defines the addon's behavior. Create your addon skeleton:

1. In your AddOns directory, create a new directory called CombatTracker.

2. In this new directory create a file called CombatTracker.toc, with the following content:

```
## Interface: 30200
## Title: CombatTracker
## Notes: Tracks incoming DPS, and how long you spend in combat

CombatTracker.lua
CombatTracker.xml
```

3. Create an empty file called `CombatTracker.xml`, which will be used to create the frames.

4. Create an empty file called `CombatTracker.lua`, which will be used to define the addon's behavior.

If you exit the game and open the WoW client backup, you should see CombatTracker listed in the AddOn List along with the description, as shown in Figure 14-1.

Figure 14-1: CombatTracker in the AddOn List

Defining CombatTracker's XML Frame

Begin by adding the `<Ui>` element to `CombatTracker.xml`. Remember, this should be the outermost element of every XML file:

```
<Ui xmlns="http://www.blizzard.com/wow/ui/"
  xmlns:xsi="http://www.w3.org/2001/XMLSchema-instance"
  xsi:schemaLocation="http://www.blizzard.com/wow/ui/
  http://wowprogramming.com/FrameXML/UI.xsd">
</Ui>
```

Next, add the definition for the main frame. Following the specifications, this frame needs to be clickable, so it will use the `Button` widget type. Add the following code inside the `<Ui>` element:

```
<Button name="CombatTrackerFrame" parent="UIParent" enableMouse="true" ↵
movable="true" frameStrata="LOW">
  <Size x="175" y="40"/>
  <Anchors>
    <Anchor point="TOP" relativePoint="BOTTOM" relativeTo="Minimap">
      <Offset x="0" y="-10"/>
    </Anchor>
  </Anchors>
</Button>
```

This code defines a new `Button` called `CombatTrackerFrame` and defines its size and placement along with some attributes:

- `name`—Declares a name for the frame. When the frame is created, the global variable with this name will be set to the created frame so it can be referred to in other code.

- `parent`—Defines the parent of a frame, used by the UI system to decide the scale, opacity, and visibility of a frame. Frame parents are discussed further in Chapter 10.

- `enableMouse`—Enables mouse input for the frame, allowing you to click it and register for drag events.

- `movable`—Tells the user's interface that this frame is movable. This is simply an on/off switch; you will have to write the code to actually accomplish the movement on your own.

- `frameStrata`—Frames in the user interface can be layered so some frames appear above or below others. The value of this attribute tells the UI what strata the frame should be drawn on.

The default placement of the frame will be just below the minimap, but the user can move it to a more desirable location.

Next give the frame some visible elements, so it can be seen on screen. For this, you will use a special type of texture called a *backdrop* to provide a background and border for the frame.

Defining a Backdrop

A backdrop is a special way to define a background for a frame. They consist of background files (which are, shockingly, used for the background of the frame) and edge files (which are used to place a border around the frame). Add the following backdrop definition within the `<Button>` element, but after the `</Anchors>` tag:

```
<Backdrop bgFile="Interface\DialogFrame\UI-DialogBox-Background" ↵
edgeFile="Interface\DialogFrame\UI-DialogBox-Border" tile="true">
  <BackgroundInsets>
    <AbsInset left="11" right="12" top="12" bottom="11"/>
  </BackgroundInsets>
  <TileSize>
    <AbsValue val="32"/>
  </TileSize>
  <EdgeSize>
    <AbsValue val="32"/>
  </EdgeSize>
</Backdrop>
```

This sets up the frame to use the same background and border textures as the default dialog box (the frame that pops up when you're looting a bind-on-pickup item). If you're setting the backdrop using Lua instead of XML, you'll need to call the `SetBackdrop()` method, passing in a table definition with the same information:

```
frame:SetBackdrop({
  bgFile = "Interface\\DialogFrame\\UI-DialogBox-Background",
  edgeFile = "Interface\\DialogFrame\\UI-DialogBox-Border",
  tile = true,
  tileSize = 32,
  edgeSize = 32,
  insets = {
    left = 11,
    right = 12,
    top = 12,
    bottom = 11,
  }
})
```

Adding a Font String

Now that your frame has a background and border, you need to add a line of text to display the combat information. Include the following code within the `<Button>` after the `</Backdrop>` tag:

```
<Layers>
  <Layer level="OVERLAY">
    <FontString name="$parentText" inherits="GameFontNormalSmall" ↵
justifyH="CENTER" setAllPoints="true" text="CombatTracker"/>
  </Layer>
</Layers>
```

The code snippet defines a new graphical layer (at the OVERLAY level) and creates a new `FontString`.

This completes the visual definition of the frame, so save the XML file and log in to the game to see how it looks.

Testing CombatTrackerFrame

Before getting much further into the addon, log in to World of Warcraft to verify that the XML definition is correct. You should see the minimap with the new `CombatTrackerFrame` directly below it, similar to Figure 14-2.

Figure 14-2: CombatTrackerFrame anchored below the minimap

At this point, nothing can be done with the frame because no scripts have been written to define its behavior. To make the addon fully functional, it needs scripts to handle clicking, dragging, and handlers for events.

If for some reason you do not see the frame, check the `Logs/FrameXML.log` file under your World of Warcraft directory. It may contain information about any errors you have made in creating the file. Alternatively, you can validate the file using one of the validation tools mentioned in Chapter 7.

Adding Script Handlers to CombatTrackerFrame

The behavior in this addon will be defined in `CombatTracker.lua`, but before you can write those functions you must refer to them in the frame definition in `CombatTracker.xml`. Open the `.xml` file and add the following section right after the `</Layers>` tag in the `<Button>` definition:

```
<Scripts>
  <OnLoad>
    CombatTracker_OnLoad(self)
  </OnLoad>
  <OnEvent>
    CombatTracker_OnEvent(self, event, ...)
  </OnEvent>
  <OnClick>
    CombatTracker_ReportDPS()
  </OnClick>
  <OnDragStart>
    self:StartMoving()
  </OnDragStart>
  <OnDragStop>
    self:StopMovingOrSizing()
  </OnDragStop>
</Scripts>
```

As mentioned in Chapter 8, each frame type has a number of widget scripts that can be set with a handler function. Table 14-1 describes the scripts you're using here (you can find more details about these scripts and the arguments they accept in Chapter 29, "Widget Reference").

Table 14-1: Script Handlers Used in CombatTracker

SCRIPT	USE
<OnLoad>	The basic initialization function for CombatTracker will be called CombatTracker_OnLoad(). It's called from the <OnLoad> handler on the frame when the frame has finished initializing. It works only for frames that are defined in XML.
<OnEvent>	The addon will respond to a number of events, so you must define an OnEvent script to handle them. The CombatTracker_OnEvent() function will be responsible for each of the events. The handling function will need to know which event it's being passed, so ensure you are passing the frame self, the event name event, and the variable set of arguments . . . to the function.
<OnClick>	When the player right-clicks CombatTrackerFrame, the OnClick script handler will call the CombatTracker_ReportDPS() function to print the current combat status. The status message will be sent to party chat if the player is in a party, otherwise it will be printed to the chat frame.
<OnDragStart>	The code for allowing a frame to be dragged and placed is very simple, so the code is written directly in the script handler rather than in a function defined in CombatTracker.lua. Later, if you wanted to add options to the addon, such as allowing the user to lock the frame in place, you could move this code into the Lua file to consolidate everything.
	Each frame that has the movable attribute set to true can call the self:StartMoving() method, which causes the frame to follow the mouse. As a result, all that's required to set up frame movement when dragged is to call this function.
<OnDragStop>	Stopping the frame from moving is a matter of calling self:StopMovingOrSizing(). This function also flags the frame as *user placed*, meaning the next time the addon loads, the frame will be put in the same place the user dropped it. This is quite a handy side effect.

Adding Functions to CombatTracker.lua

To properly calculate the incoming damage, the time spent in combat, and the average incoming DPS during combat, a few values need to be stored. These will be created as local variables at the top of `CombatTracker.lua`. Open that file and add the following lines:

```
-- Set up some local variables to track time and damage
local start_time = 0
local end_time = 0
local total_time = 0
local total_damage = 0
local average_dps = 0
```

Four more functions must be created to have a fully functional addon:

■ `CombatTracker_OnLoad(frame)`

■ `CombatTracker_OnEvent(self, event, ...)`

■ `CombatTracker_UpdateText()`

■ `CombatTracker_ReportDPS()`

These functions are discussed in the following sections.

CombatTracker_OnLoad(frame)

As you may recall from your work in Chapter 4, the variable name `self` has a bit of a special meaning in Lua. When a function inside a table is called using the colon syntax, the first argument that Lua passes is the table itself with the name `self`. In addition, when the World of Warcraft client calls a frame script, the first argument is called `self` and points to the frame itself. This can be confusing, so when you define functions that are called from XML, it is a good idea to make the variable names more meaningful. In the script handler for `OnLoad`, the script is given the frame object in the `self` variable, and will pass it on to the `CombatTracker_OnLoad()` function. The function definition, however, will name it *frame*. That way there's no question about what type of value it contains.

Add the following function definition to the bottom of `CombatTracker.lua`:

```
function CombatTracker_OnLoad(frame)
  frame:RegisterEvent("UNIT_COMBAT")
  frame:RegisterEvent("PLAYER_REGEN_ENABLED")
  frame:RegisterEvent("PLAYER_REGEN_DISABLED")
  frame:RegisterForClicks("RightButtonUp")
  frame:RegisterForDrag("LeftButton")
end
```

This function registers the combat tracker frame for the three events that need to be watched. It also registers to receive right-click events, along with drags with the left mouse button.

CombatTracker_OnEvent

The `CombatTracker_OnEvent()` function handles three different types of events, so it will be one large conditional with special code for each event name. Add the function as follows to the bottom of `CombatTracker.lua`:

```
function CombatTracker_OnEvent(frame, event, ...)
  if event == "PLAYER_REGEN_DISABLED" then
    -- This event is called when we enter combat
    -- Reset the damage total and start the timer
    CombatTrackerFrameText:SetText("In Combat")
    total_damage = 0
    start_time = GetTime()
  elseif event == "PLAYER_REGEN_ENABLED" then
    -- This event is called when the player exits combat
    end_time = GetTime()
    total_time = end_time - start_time
    average_dps = total_damage / total_time
    CombatTracker_UpdateText()
  elseif event == "UNIT_COMBAT" then
    if InCombatLockdown() then
      local unit, action, modifier, damage, damagetype = ...
      if unit == "player" and action ~= "HEAL" then
        total_damage = total_damage + damage
        end_time = GetTime()
        total_time = math.mind(end_time - start_time, 1)
        average_dps = total_damage / total_time
        CombatTracker_UpdateText()
      end
    end
  end
end
```

The following sections explore the events handled by this function as well as `CombatTracker_UpdateText()`, a function that's called at the end of `CombatTracker_OnEvent()`.

PLAYER_REGEN_ENABLED

The PLAYER_REGEN_ENABLED section of the conditional happens when the player exits combat, which means it's time to clean up and display the final results. The `GetTime()` function is used to set the `end_time` variable. It returns the current value of the in-game timer. The actual value doesn't matter because you're just going to subtract the start time from the end time to give you the difference (in seconds).

Finally, the `CombatTracker_UpdateText()` function is called to handle the update of the actual text on the frame. You could do the updating directly in this function, but the same code will be needed at a later point. Rather than having the same code in two places, it's cleaner to make a new function that does the common work.

PLAYER_REGEN_DISABLED

The `PLAYER_REGEN_DISABLED` event fires when the player enters combat, so it needs to set up the accounting variables to ensure the addon gets a clean slate for each combat. It simply calls `CombatTrackerFrameText:SetText()` to change the frame to say "In Combat." It also sets the `total_damage` variable back to 0 and initializes the `start_time` variable with the current time.

UNIT_COMBAT

Most of the addon's logic actually happens in the `UNIT_COMBAT` section, so it's a bit larger than the other two. First you check to see if the player is in combat (by checking the `InCombatLockdown()` function), so you can ignore any messages that arrive outside of combat. Because event arguments are passed to the function as a vararg, you assign them to named variables so they are more easily accessible.

You're interested only in those events that happen to the player and want to skip those events in which the player is being healed, so check the `unit` and `action` arguments. If both conditions pass, the current amount of damage is added to the total, the end time is updated, and the total time and average DPS are calculated. Because the time might be less than a second (and there is no way to divide by zero) you use the `math.min()` function to choose either the time difference, or 1, whichever is larger. Finally the `CombatTracker_UpdateText()` function is called to update the frame.

CombatTracker_UpdateText()

`CombatTracker_UpdateText()` is a simple function that updates the status on the `CombatTrackerFrame` using `string.format()`. Add the following function definition to the bottom of `CombatTracker.lua`:

```
function CombatTracker_UpdateText()
  local status = string.format("%ds / %d dmg / %.2f dps", ↵
total_time, total_damage, average_dps)
  CombatTrackerFrameText:SetText(status)
end
```

When run, this format string shows the number of seconds in combat, followed by the amount of damage taken, and the average incoming DPS for that combat period.

CombatTracker_ReportDPS()

The `CombatTracker_ReportDPS()` checks calls the `GetNumPartyMembers()` function to determine whether or not the player is in a party. If the number is greater than 0, the player is in a party. Add the following function to your `CombatTracker.lua`:

```
function CombatTracker_ReportDPS()
  local msgformat = "%d seconds spent in combat with %d incoming ↵
damage.  Average incoming DPS was %.2f"
  local msg = string.format(msgformat, total_time, total_damage, ↵
average_dps)
  if GetNumPartyMembers() > 0 then
    SendChatMessage(msg, "PARTY")
  else
    print(msg)
  end
end
```

This function uses a format string to craft the outgoing message, and then uses `GetNumPartyMembers()` to decide where to send it. If the player is in a party, the `SendChatMessage()` function is used to send the message to the party; otherwise, the `print()` function is used to send it to the chat frame so the player can see it.

Testing CombatTracker

You have completed all the code necessary for a fully functional Combat-Tracker addon. Load the game and select a character. You should be greeted with the CombatTracker frame right below your minimap.

Testing is a very important part of addon writing if you plan to release your addons to the public. When you write a set of features, it's prudent to test them yourself before you ship the addon to the public to ensure that users won't get error messages and be reporting them to you after the fact. That sort of troubleshooting is always more difficult than errors you encounter on your own. Systematically test each portion of the addon.

Frame Dragging

By clicking the frame, holding down the mouse button, and dragging your mouse to another part of the screen, you should be able to move the Combat-Tracker frame. Figure 14-3 shows it placed beneath the player frame.

Figure 14-3: CombatTracker anchored beneath the player frame

Just testing that the frame starts and stops dragging isn't enough. Make sure you can reload your UI and have the frame be restored to the new position by running **/console reloadui**. This is a slash command that reloads all of the Blizzard User Interface and all custom addon code. It's quite useful when making changes during development, or for testing purposes.

> **NOTE** Once you've moved the frame from its initial anchored position, you may need to adjust it any time you switch between windowed and full-screen mode, or when you change screen resolution. You can re-anchor the frame to the minimap with the following two slash commands:

```
/run CombatTrackerFrame:ClearAllPoints()
/run CombatTrackerFrame:SetPoint("TOP", Minimap, "BOTTOM", 0, -10)
```

The first command clears any anchors the frame already has, and the second command re-anchors the frame to the minimap, as was done originally in the XML file.

Right-Click Reporting: Part I

The addon is set to print a status report or send it to your party chat when CombatTracker is right-clicked. What happens if the user clicks the frame before CombatTracker has had a chance to track any data? You can't assume your users will wait until they've already gone through combat to click, so test that now.

Luckily, because of the way you initialized the local variables (with 0s), the game can print a meaningful message, like the one shown in Figure 14-4.

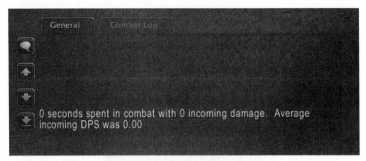

Figure 14-4: CombatTracker reporting before entering combat

Testing Combat Tracking

Log in to a character and go find something to fight. Hopefully, it's something you won't have much difficulty killing but whose level is close enough to yours that it can hurt you. Immediately upon entering combat, you should see the frame change, as shown in Figure 14-5.

Figure 14-5: CombatTracker showing "In Combat."

After each hit of incoming damage, the frame should be updated to show the current statistics. If you are fighting something from range, you won't see the frame update until the mob actually tries to hit you. Figure 14-6 shows CombatTracker working in combat.

Figure 14-6: CombatTracker showing running statistics

Right-Click Reporting: Part II

When combat has ended, your frame updates with the final statistics and remains there until you enter combat again or reload the user interface. There is one more test that needs to be run on the right-click reporting, and that's making sure it displays correct statistics at the end of combat, and that it properly sends a message to party chat when the player is in a party.

Figure 14-7 shows CombatTracker reporting before joining a party, as well as after joining forces with another player.

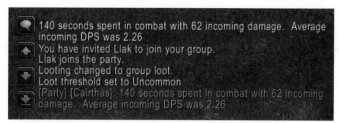

Figure 14-7: CombatTracker reporting both in and out of a party

Summary

Creating an addon involves making decisions about the user experience and scope of the addon, investigating what functions and events are required to make the addon functional, and writing the addon itself. The process of deciding how the user will experience your addon and what features make it into the final product is often the most difficult part of writing an addon.

The next chapter explains the intricacies of frames, widgets, and other graphics elements in depth.

Part

III

Advanced Addon Techniques

In This Part

Taking Action with Secure Templates

The design of World of Warcraft mandates that any meaningful action that can affect the game world, such as casting a spell, using an item, or attacking an enemy, be triggered by the player clicking a button or pressing a key bound to that action. This was originally only mentioned in the terms of use, which forbid any form of automation; but as the game developed, it became clear that the requirement needed to be enforced in the Lua scripting engine. This restriction is carried out by a system of trusted and untrusted code, which prevents addons from taking these actions for the player, as well as a mechanism called *secure templates* that allows addons to safely modify how the player interacts with the game, without enabling automation.

In this chapter, you learn how to create and customize your own buttons that the player can use to take in-game actions; you also learn what actions your addons can take directly and which you must assign to a button for the player. In addition you'll discover how to troubleshoot problems that can occur due to the differences between trusted (Blizzard) and untrusted (addon) code.

Why Are Secure Templates Necessary?

Although World of Warcraft offers an enormous variety of activities for its players to engage in, fighting with creatures or other players holds the most excitement and interest for most players. Combat is the most common activity in the game, and the most sensitive. Decisions made on a split-second basis determine whether you win a battleground, defeat a raid boss, or destroy a quest mob; or whether you lie broken on a lost battlefield, run out of mana while healing your tank, or spend time running back to your corpse for "just one more try."

While the initial version of WoW matured and addon authors became more experienced, many addons were created that took action for the players. Some addons were written to automatically decide what healing spell to cast on whom, to provide the most effective healing in a party or raid. Other addons were written that could run the player from one location to another (for example, running your ghost to its corpse or from city to city).

As these addons became more widespread, WoW designers and developers became concerned that they actually destroyed the fun of playing the game. They certainly made victory easier, but players no longer needed to even pay attention to the game they were playing. Over the course of several patches, the designers took steps to reduce addons' capability to make such decisions, culminating in the patch 2.0 security model.

Under this model, all code that is supplied with the game is considered *secure*, whereas code provided by addons is insecure or *tainted*. Only secure code can call certain API functions such as casting a spell or using an item. Moreover, if insecure code tries to interfere with secure code, its *taint* will spread to the secure code and prevent the spell, item, or other secured operation from working. This stops addons from exploiting the default user interface to bring back addon automation.

As you'll see, the security model is fairly complex. Needless to say, it would have been easier for Blizzard to simply eliminate the capability for users to write custom addons, but there is plenty to be gained by allowing for rich customization of the user experience. Instead, Blizzard introduced a very restrictive security model, but offers a number of *secure templates* that provide a system for addon authors to take certain approved action, with limits. These templates are pre-programmed, using *attributes* to determine what spell to cast or other action to take, whom to cast it on, and other similar information. Although addons can change the attribute values without tainting the secure script's capability to do its job, they can only do so under controlled conditions (typically outside of combat), because the secure frames are protected.

Protected Frames

A *protected frame* is one that is capable of taking restrictive action, as defined by the developers. During combat, only secure code can create, modify, or control these frames, preventing addon code from doing things such as placing the "right" action button or unit frame under your mouse so the player can just mindlessly click. However, unlike truly protected functions like `CastSpell()`, these restrictions are lifted outside of the combat, allowing addons to create new frames, move frames around, and reconfigure attributes.

If an addon (or the user) tries to make a restricted change on a frame during combat, the user interface will display a notification in the chat frame, rather than popping up a distracting notification. You will learn more about these "blocked addon" messages, and the taint log that can be used to troubleshoot them, later in this chapter.

When a frame is protected, any frame that it is parented or anchored to is also implicitly protected. This makes sense because otherwise you'd be able to move or hide the unprotected frame to defeat the restrictions. Luckily there is an widget method that allows you determine if a frame is protected (either implicitly or directly): `Frame:IsProtected()`. The function returns two values:

- `isProtected`—1 if the frame is protected and subject to the restrictions of protected frames; otherwise `nil`.
- `explicit`—1 if the frame is explicit; nil if the frame is only protected implicitly due to a relationship with another frame.

Frame methods that affect positioning, visibility, interactivity, or secure control are restricted from being called on protected frames during combat. Here's a list of those methods:

AllowAttributeChanges	Lower	SetHorizontalScroll
ClearAllPoints	Raise	SetParent
Disable	SetAllPoints	SetPoint
Enable	SetAttribute	SetScale
EnableKeyboard	SetFrameLevel	SetToplevel
EnableMouse	SetFrameStrata	SetVerticalScroll
EnableMouseWheel	SetHeight	SetWidth
Hide	SetHitRectInsets	Show

The protection itself is accomplished by defining an XML template with the `protected` attribute set to `true`. This feature is not exactly useful for our own purposes; the true power comes to us indirectly via secure templates.

> **NOTE** It is possible to create code that modifies protected frames in combat, under certain restrictions. WoW 3.0 introduced a system called secure handlers, which allows you to submit code for secure execution on frames, as long as it follows the designers' guidelines on what is permitted in combat; this system is covered in detail in Chapter 25.

Controlling Secure Frames Using Attributes

As mentioned in the last section, secure templates are pre-configured using named *attributes*. Unlike local or global variables, or keys set in frame tables, they cannot be tainted. This allows data to be passed from insecure code (addons) to secure code (secure templates) without compromising security. Setting attributes on a frame is a restricted action, and insecure code can't do it during combat, as we've already said.

Frame attribute can be set by using the `SetAttribute()` method, or by using the `<Attribute>` element in XML. For example:

```
frame:SetAttribute("spell", "Flash Heal")
```

or

```
<Attributes>
  <Attribute name="spell" type="string" value="Flash Heal"/>
</Attributes>
```

You can obtain the value of an attribute using the `GetAttribute()` method. The usage is fairly simple:

```
value = frame:GetAttribute("spell")
```

The value of an attribute can be any kind of Lua table, but the name is always a string. Unlike most Lua conventions, *name* is not case-sensitive; if you call `frame:SetAttribute("item", "5")`, `frame:GetAttribute("ITEM")` will return the string `"5"`.

Whenever a frame is set on a frame, the frame's `OnAttributeChanged` handler script is called, allowing code to react to attribute changes. Attributes don't carry taint, so the `OnAttributeChanged` script can be used to trigger secure code in response to an addon setting an attribute. The script is passed the frame object, the name of the attribute, and the value. Despite attribute names being case-insensitive, the name argument to an `OnAttributeChanged` script will always be lowercase.

WARNING The choice of the word "attribute" is appropriate, but potentially confusing, because in XML lingo, "attribute" is the term that describes the properties given to an element within the element's start tag (for example, `name="$parentButton"`, and so on). They are similar in that they associate a value with a name and a parent object. Where it is important, we will discriminate them with the terms *frame attribute* and *XML attribute*.

Using Secure Templates

Using secure templates doesn't magically make your code secure. Code that is created from your addon will always be considered tainted, and won't be able to defeat the secure restrictions. Secure templates are useful because they contain a number of pre-written widget scripts that are still secure, and thus can take restricted action based on attributes.

Although there are several secure templates defined in `FrameXML\Secure Templates.xml` and `FrameXML\SecureHandlers.xml`, this chapter focuses on one of the more widely used templates, `SecureActionButtonTemplate`. The template definition is very simple, just calling `SecureActionButton_OnClick` when the button is clicked.

Create your own frame or template that inherits from `SecureActionButton Template`, and it will securely call `SecureActionButton_OnClick` when clicked, as long as you do not assign your own `OnClick` handler. Each frame can have only one handler per widget script, so setting a new one would remove the secure version that actually does the work!

Defining Behaviors for Action Buttons

How are the secure templates programmed using frame attributes? The easiest way to show how they are used is with an example. Run the following code in game to create a new secure action button for you to work with:

```
SABTest = CreateFrame("Button", "SABTest", UIParent, ↵
"SecureActionButtonTemplate,UIPanelButtonTemplate2")
SABTest:SetWidth(80)
SABTest:SetHeight(20)
SABTest:SetText("SABTest")
SABTest:SetPoint("CENTER", 0, 0)
SABTest:SetAttribute("spell", "Attack")
SABTest:RegisterForClicks("AnyUp")
```

Because secure templates provide no visual appearance themselves, you'll normally need to add some elements to make the button visible. You can do this by adding layers and texture as per usual, but here you just inherit from a template that already has visual components.

Everything here should seem familiar, other than the `SetAttribute` call at the end. In this case, you're setting the `spell` attribute to the string `Attack`. That tells the secure action button's `OnClick` handler to cast the Attack spell, which starts or stops the player's auto-attack, when the button is programmed to cast a spell.

NOTE The `type` tag attribute has a default value of `string`, and an overwhelming portion of the frame attributes used by the secure templates are expected to contain strings, so in practice it is almost always omitted.

Casting a Spell

Once you've run the code, you should have a small, red button (see Figure 15-1) in the middle of your screen that does nothing when clicked. Although you've programmed the button to cast Attack when it's casting a spell, you haven't told it that it should be casting a spell.

Figure 15-1: A simple action button

Run the following command:

```
/run SABTest:SetAttribute("type", "spell")
```

This corrects the omission by telling the button that when it is clicked it should try to cast a spell. If you find an enemy and click the button, your auto-attack should be toggled on or off.

Casting a Beneficial Spell

If you have a character that can cast beneficial spells (healing, cleansing, or buffing), you can set your button up to cast that spell on yourself. Change the spell attribute to the beneficial spell (changing Renew to the name of the spell):

```
/run SABTest:SetAttribute("type", "spell")
/run SABTest:SetAttribute("spell", "Healing Wave")
```

This tells the button to cast a spell when clicked, and specifies that the Healing Wave spell should be cast. If you find and target a friendly target, you can click the button, and the spell should be cast on your targeted unit.

You can specify the unit to target with an action by using the unit attribute. Run the following:

```
/run SABTest:SetAttribute("unit", "player")
```

Now whenever you click the button, the spell will be cast on you. This illustrates just one of the many ways multiple attributes on the same frame can interact to bring varied results.

Casting a Harmful Spell

The same principle can be used to cast a harmful spell on a target. Run the following to change the attributes:

```
/run SABTest:SetAttribute("spell", "Lightning Bolt")
/run SABTest:SetAttribute("unit", "target")
```

Looking Under the Hood

So what is actually going on when you click your button? The code can be found in FrameXML\SecureTemplates.lua, in the SecureActionButton_OnClick()

function. It may be a bit difficult to follow along (the buttons are very powerful), but here are the basic steps:

1. The `type` attribute is checked to determine which type of action to take. In this case, your button is set to cast a spell by using the `spell` type.

2. The `spell` attribute is retrieved to determine what spell to cast.

3. The unit attribute is checked to see if you're specifying a particular unit on which to cast the spell.

4. The `CastSpellByName` is called securely with the name of the spell and, optionally, the unit.

This is where the nature of protected frames, protected functions, taint, and attributes finally come together. Only secure code is allowed to call `CastSpellByName`. Because the `SecureActionButton` template is defined in the FrameXML, it and all of its handlers are secure. The template has the `protected` attribute set to `true`, so any frame that inherits from this template will also be protected. The `SetAttribute` method is protected outside of combat, which means Blizzard can precisely control when and how the player is allowed to configure the buttons that take protected action.

Specifying Units to Affect

Many templates can act on units in various ways. For example, quite a few types of `SecureActionButtons` do their actions on the specified unit. You can control the unit directly via the `unit` attribute, which was shown in the previous example.

Alternatively, if you use a `"unitsuffix"` attribute, its value will be appended to the `"unit"` attribute of the button's parent. Chapter 26 shows you how to use this attribute to create child pet frames for a set of unit frames without having to manually specify the pet units.

You can also make the button respond to your self-cast modifier by setting its `"checkselfcast"` attribute to a true value.

Other Types and Their Uses

If you look at the source for the `SecureActionButton` template, you likely noticed the table `SECURE_ACTIONS` that is defined. Each entry in this table defines a new *type* that is recognized by the secure template, and defines a set of subordinate attributes that further control the button's behavior.

The following is a list of the type attributes that are accepted by the `SecureActionButton` template, and a list of the sub-attributes that further customize that secure action. Types marked with a (U) respond to the unit attribute and equivalents, if present.

actionbar—Used to manipulate your action bar page.

   action—Describes how to change the action bar page. A single number means change directly to that page. A string with two numbers separated by a comma (for example, `"1, 2"`) will swap between the two given pages. It will switch directly to the first number if you are on a page other than the two given. Finally, you can use either `"increment"` or `"decrement"` to go up one page or down one page, respectively. They will both wrap to the other end if you go too far.

action (U)—Activates an action slot. Subordinate attribute:

   action (optional)—The action slot number to use. If you omit this attribute, the action will be determined by the button's ID in the same manner as the default UI. In other words, if you have a button with an ID of 1, the actual action used would depend on your stance, action bar page, and so on, just like the first button on the main action bar. See `UseAction` (API) for more information.

pet (U)—Uses one of your pet's abilities. Subordinate attribute:

   action—The pet action index of the ability you wish to use. See `CastPetAction` (API) for more information.

multispell—Configures a multi-cast action slot to use a specific spell. Subordinate attributes:

   action—The multi-cast action slot you would like to configure.

   spell—The spell you would like to configure for the given action slot.

spell (U)—Casts the named spell. Subordinate attribute:

   spell—The name of the spell to cast. See `CastSpellByName` (API) for more information.

item (U)—Uses the given item. Subordinate attributes (two deprecated attributes you may notice in the FrameXML code are intentionally omitted):

   item—Specifies the item to use. This attribute can take a number of forms depending on how you want to access the item:

   - `"Name of Item"`—By name.
   - `"item:12345"`—By item ID.
   - `"13"`—By inventory slot number for equipped items.
   - `"3 12"`—By bag and slot number for items in your bags.

macro—Runs a macro. Subordinate attributes:

   macro—The macro to run. This can be the numerical index or the name of a macro to run.

macrotext—The text of a macro. Set this to a Lua string containing the macro you want to run. This text is limited to 1023 bytes (usually but not always single characters). A `"macro"` attribute will override a `"macrotext"` one.

cancelaura—Removes a buff from the player, including secured buffs such as druid forms. Subordinate attributes:

index—The number of the buff to remove from the player, in an arbitrary order.

spell—The name of the buff to be removed. Ignored if `index` is present.

rank—The rank of buff to remove. Ignored if `index` is present.

stop—Cancels the target selection cursor (glowing blue hand). No subordinate attributes are used.

target (U)—Manages unit targeting. If the unit attribute is set to none, the action will clear the player's target. If the player has a spell that is awaiting a target (showing the glowing hand), the action will choose the target for that spell. If the player's cursor is holding an item, this action will drop the item on that unit (initiate trade, equip, and so forth). Otherwise, this action just targets the specified unit.

focus (U)—Focuses on the given unit.

assist (U)—Assists the specified unit.

maintank (U)—Sets the unit as a main tank for the raid. Subordinate attribute:

action—A string indicating what assignment action should be taken:

- `set`—Sets the role on the given unit.
- `clear`—Clears the role from the given unit.
- `toggle`—Toggle the role for the given unit.

mainassist (U)—Sets the unit as a main assist for the raid.

action—A string indicating what assignment action should be taken:

- `set`—Sets the role on the given unit.
- `clear`—Clears the role from the given unit.
- `toggle`—Toggle the role for the given unit.

click—Securely simulates a click on another button. Subordinate attribute:

clickbutton—The button to click. This must be a direct reference, not the name of the button.

attribute—Securely sets an attribute on a frame, allowing one button to configure another. Useful in combination with state handlers (see Chapter 25). Subordinate attributes:

attribute-frame—A direct reference (*not* by frame name) to the frame on which an attribute will be set. If this is `nil`, it defaults to the button itself.

attribute-name—The name of the attribute to set.

attribute-value—The value to set the attribute to.

If the `type` attribute is set to something other than one of these predefined actions, such as "reveal", the button will check the following places:

- `self:GetAttribute("_reveal")`
- `self["reveal"]`

If the value stored is a function, it will call the function passing in the following arguments:

- The button object itself.
- The unit attribute, if set.
- The mouse click that triggered the click handler.

If the value is a string, the secure handler will dispatch the contents of the string as a secure handler `_onclick` call, covered in Chapter 25.

This method of function dispatch is used by the default user interface to display the popup menus for unit frames.

Item Targets

If an action you are taking can target an item instead of a unit—using a poison, for example—you can use the following attributes to specify what item to target:

- `target-slot`—An inventory slot number by itself, or a bag slot number along with `target-bag`.
- `target-bag`—Specifies a bag number (0–4, right to left on the default bag bar). You must also include a `target-slot` attribute.
- `target-item`—The name of the item.

Using an "item" Type Button

Using the `SABTest` button you created earlier, run the following commands in-game to set up some new behavior on your button. You'll want to run these tests on a character that has some bandages to spare so you can see the full effect. Wherever you see *Heavy Frostweave Bandage* in the following code samples, rename it to whatever bandages you have available.

```
/run SABTest:SetAttribute("type", "item")
/run SABTest:SetAttribute("item", "Heavy Frostweave Bandage")
/run SABTest:SetAttribute("unit", "player")
```

The first line tells the button to use an item when it's clicked. The second specifies the bandages you want to use. Finally, the `unit` attribute tells the button to use the item on the player. If your bandages were in the first slot of your backpack, you could use an `item` attribute of `"0 1"` instead of the name of the bandage, and it would always use whatever was in that slot.

Because bandages can only be used when you're missing some health, you'll want to head out into the wilderness and pick a fight with some easy mob. There are plenty of other creative ways to reduce your health percentage (such as un-equipping and re-equipping a piece of stamina gear). Whenever you feel like bandaging yourself, click the `SABTest` button and enjoy.

Using an Item with a "macro" Type Button

If you have spent any time in the UI customization community before diving into addon programming, you should be at least marginally familiar with macros. One very simple example is a self-use macro. On an action button this macro will behave exactly like the `SABTest` example from the preceding section.

```
/use [target=player] Heavy Frostweave Bandage
```

Attaching this macro to the `SABTest` button is fairly straightforward:

```
/run SABTest:SetAttribute("type", "macro")
/run SABTest:SetAttribute("macrotext", ↵
"/use [target=player] Heavy Frostweave Bandage")
```

Notice that even if you still have the `unit` attribute from the previous self-bandage configuration, it will be completely ignored. `"macro"` type action buttons leave that sort of decision entirely up to the macro itself.

> **NOTE** A thorough treatment of the macro system is beyond the scope of this book. However, you can find further information in several places. Blizzard provides an introductory macro guide at `http://worldofwarcraft.com/info/basics/macros.html`. Although it does not currently cover conditional macros, it has been updated with excellent basic information.
>
> Cogwheel, a member of the WoW UI community, also created Cogwheel's Complete Macro Guide, which currently resides at `www.wowwiki.com/Making_a_macro`. As far as we know, its creator no longer maintains the page but it remains one of the most comprehensive guides to WoW macros available, with detailed descriptions of all the common (and many obscure) slash commands and macro options.

Making Simple Choices

Writing addons that take protected actions is great, but what you've seen so far is not very flexible. Sure, you can configure a button any way you want—while you're out of combat. And that's the real trick: to make an addon behave even like the default UI, you have to be able to make certain changes during combat. A action bar addon needs to change pages when you switch forms. Unit frames that you can actually click to target need a way to show and hide themselves.

Covering all of the possible options in this chapter isn't very practical (the secure snippets system is covered in Chapter 25), but this section does introduce you to two of the most frequently used options for secure templates: modifier keys and mouse buttons.

Working with Modified Attributes

The attributes you've worked with so far are universal. That is, there can be only one unit attribute set on a given frame. The default user interface allows you to take different action depending on whether you've right-clicked or left-clicked a frame. Addons using secure templates can make a similar distinction, and also add the capability to use modifier keys (Alt, Ctrl, and Shift) to select the correct action.

Format of a Modified Attribute

If you call the attributes you've worked with so far *root* or *unmodified* attributes, then a *modified* attribute consists of a prefix, followed by the root, followed by a suffix.

- Prefix—Determines which modifier keys to check. The prefix doesn't have to be set, but should have a hyphen (dash) after it if it does.

- Root—The name of the root or unmodified attribute, the object that the prefix and suffix modify.

- Suffix—The mouse button that can be used to trigger this action. If this attribute isn't included, it will default to any mouse button. You can also specify this explicitly by using an asterisk (*) as a wildcard.

For example, set up your SABTest button with the following attributes (set up for a Level 2 Priest):

```
/run SABTest:SetAttribute("type", "spell")
/run SABTest:SetAttribute("spell", "Lesser Heal")
/run SABTest:SetAttribute("unit", "player")
/run SABTest:SetAttribute("shift-type1", "spell")
/run SABTest:SetAttribute("shift-spell1", "Power Word: Fortitude")
```

This configures the button to cast Lesser Heal on the player when clicked with the left button, but when Shift+left-clicked, it casts Power Word: Fortitude on the player instead. For the last attribute, the prefix is `shift`, the root attribute is `spell`, and the prefix is `1`.

The prefix can be any combination of `alt`, `ctrl`, and `shift`, chained together with hyphens. They must appear in alphabetical order, so the combination of Alt and Shift would be `alt-shift` and Alt, Ctrl, and Shift together would be `alt-ctrl-shift`. The mouse button is just a number that maps to a specific mouse button.

Inheritance of Attributes

Attributes have some default inheritance that can make it easier to set things up. For example if you were to right-click the `SABTest` button while holding your Ctrl and Alt keys, it will check for the following `"spell"` attributes in order:

1. `alt-ctrl-spell2`
2. `*spell2`
3. `alt-ctrl-spell*`
4. `*spell*`
5. `spell`

Remember that an asterisk (*) is used to match *any* prefix or suffix.

You can also map modifier keys to arbitrary names by using a `"modifiers"` attribute on the button. This attribute uses the following format, with items in brackets (`[ ]`) being optional:

```
MODIFIER[:name][,MODIFIER[:name]]...
```

`MODIFIER` can be a normal modifier (`ALT`, `CTRL`, or `SHIFT`) or a modifier variable, such as `SELFCAST`. See `IsModifiedClick` (API) for details. If no `name` is specified, the lowercase version of the modifier will be returned. For example:

```
SPLITSTACK:split,ALT
```

This value will give a prefix of `"split-"` if you are holding down the stack-splitting modifier or `"alt-"` if you are holding the Alt key.

Choosing an Action by Mouse Button

You have most likely guessed that to pick a spell based on a mouse button you need to specify a suffix. The most basic suffixes are the numbers 1 to 5, which indicate mouse buttons:

1. Left button
2. Right button
3. Middle button
4. Button 4
5. Button 5

WARNING The prefix/suffix system is a bit stricter than you might first assume. The five attribute variations mentioned earlier create some specific situations worth noting. For example, although you can use `"spell"` as a last resort fallback, `"spell12"` will match only if you're not holding any modifier keys.

When in doubt, decide whether it is more appropriate for you to use wildcards, or strict attributes.

Delegating Attribute Responsibility

If you have a number of secure action buttons that are closely related, perhaps an action bar, modified attributes provide a `"useparent"` facility to delegate an attribute to the button's parent, which makes it easier to apply configurations to multiple buttons. If `SecureButton_GetModifiedAttribute` does not find a match with one of the five variations, it will check for a `"useparent-`*`root`*`"` or `"useparent*"` attribute. If it finds one, it will get the modified attribute from the parent.

For example, the default UI's action buttons have a `"useparent-unit"` attribute. With one simple setting, you can make all of the buttons on the main bar cast normally with a left-click, or always on yourself with a right-click:

```
/run MainMenuBarArtFrame:SetAttribute("*unit2", "player")
```

Choosing an Action by Hostility

You can customize the "mouse button" in a way that is checked against the suffix.

Two new attributes allow you to change the nature of the button based on the nature of the specified unit: `"helpbutton"`, meaning you can cast beneficial spells on the unit, and `"harmbutton"`, meaning you can attack the unit. The value of these attributes is a string that will be used for the suffix in subsequent modified attribute checks. You can continue the previous example with Shadow Word: Pain and Power Word: Shield by making a single button that automatically picks between the two:

```
/run SABTest:SetAttribute("unit", "target")
/run SABTest:SetAttribute("harmbutton", "nuke")
/run SABTest:SetAttribute("helpbutton", "heal")
/run SABTest:SetAttribute("*spell-nuke", "Shadow Word: Pain")
/run SABTest:SetAttribute("*spell-heal", "Lesser Heal")
```

Some targets can be neither helped nor harmed (neutral NPCs, for instance). In cases like that, the preceding example will do nothing. You must explicitly set a unit attribute; otherwise `helpbutton` and `harmbutton` will be ignored.

It is worth noting that `"helpbutton"` and `"harmbutton"` themselves can also be modified. That way you can create different suffixes depending on which actual mouse button was used to click the button.

Applying Action Buttons in Practice

At this point, all the fundamentals of the secure template system have been covered. Now that you have a grasp of the various interactions among attributes, suffixes, protected frames, and taint, you can put it into practice by making changes to existing action buttons and creating new ones.

Modifying an Existing Frame

The standard behavior of a unit frame is to target its unit when left-clicked. The target frame also follows this convention, even though targeting your target is not normally a useful action. You can reclaim some of that "click-space" by typing the following into WoWLua (if you're over level 8 or so, substitute whatever sort of bandage you're currently using):

```
/run TargetFrame:SetAttribute('item', "Linen Bandage")
/run TargetFrame:SetAttribute('shift-type*', 'item')
/run TargetFrame:SetAttribute('ctrl-type*', 'item')
/run TargetFrame:SetAttribute('alt-type*', 'item')
```

The plain click is left as a `target` action because it is still useful to take action on your current target if you have, say, a beneficial spell ready to cast (your cursor shows the blue glow). But now, when you left-click your target's portrait with a modifier down, you'll bandage your target. Right-clicking your target still brings up his unit menu, with raid marker options and so on. That's because `TargetFrame` inherits from `SecureUnitButtonTemplate`, a special subspecies of `SecureActionButtonTemplate` designed for unit frames that sets the `*type2` attribute to a menu function.

> **NOTE** There is a slightly simpler, but less intuitive way to define bandaging as the behavior on any modified click, and that is to set the `'type'` or `'*type1'` attributes to `'item'` and the `'type*'` or `'type1'` attributes to `'target'`. That way, the target action is selected only when the click is actually unmodified.

If you have several changes to make to a frame, you may find it useful to add a `SetFrameAttributes` function like this one:

```
function SetFrameAttributes(self, attributes)
    for name, value in pairs(attributes) do
        if type(name) == 'string' then
            self:SetAttribute(name, value)
        end
    end
end
TargetFrame.SetAttributes = SetFrameAttributes
```

That enables you to set multiple attributes with an understandable list format:

```
TargetFrame:SetAttributes{
    unit = 'target', -- this was also preset by the frame definition
    type = 'target', -- so was this
    ['*type2'] = 'menu', -- and this
    item = 'Linen Bandage',
    ['shift-type*'] = 'item',
    ['ctrl-type*'] = 'item',
    ['alt-type*'] = 'item'
}
```

This approach generates a throw-away table; it's suitable for one-time or otherwise infrequent setup, but should be avoided for frequent changes.

A Complex Action Button

The last example for this chapter builds a single button from scratch that can cast one of three spells—depending on what modifier keys are held—on one of three friendly targets, depending on which mouse button was used and whether the target was friendly. The example uses priest abilities; feel free to adjust the attributes to your liking and experiment with different configurations.

This mini-addon adds an action button to the lower-left region of the screen. Click it to cast the spell Greater Heal; Shift+click for Power Word: Shield; and Ctrl+click for Renew. Moreover, it offers some more options on who to heal or protect: while it usually casts on your target, right-clicking casts on your focus, and clicking while you have an enemy targeted automatically casts on yourself, without changing your target.

Here's what to do:

1. Create a directory called QuickCasterButton in your Interface\AddOns directory.

2. Create a file inside this new directory named QuickCasterButton.toc, containing the following lines:

   ```
   ## Interface: 30300
   ## Title: QuickCasterButton
   ## Notes: Casts a variety of helpful spells on different targets
   QuickCasterButton.xml
   ```

3. Create another file in the same directory named QuickCasterButton.xml, and open it in a text editor.

4. Enter the beginning tags for the UI definition (required for any addon XML file) and the button frame:

```
<Ui xmlns="http://www.blizzard.com/wow/ui/"
 xmlns:xsi="http://www.w3.org/2001/XMLSchema-instance"
 xsi:schemaLocation="http://www.blizzard.com/wow/ui/
 http://wowprogramming.com/FrameXML/UI.xsd">
```

This example illustrates one of the most common uses of `SecureAction ButtonTemplate`, which is to marry it to `ActionButtonTemplate` via multiple inheritance; this creates a button that has the "look and feel" of the stock action buttons pre-built. The commonly used `ActionBarButtonTemplate` begins with these two templates, and then adds functions to keep the buttons' appearance up-to-date with what they do. In this case, using the templates directly keeps things simple.

5. Enter the anchor code to place the button in the lower left:

```
<Anchors>
 <Anchor point="BOTTOMLEFT" relativeTo="UIParent">
  <Offset x="180" y="280" />
 </Anchor>
</Anchors>
```

6. Open the `<Attributes>` tag and define the button as a spell button:

```
<Attributes>
 <Attribute name="type" value="spell" />
```

7. Define the default spell for the button, as well as spells for Shift+click and Ctrl+click:

```
<Attribute name="spell" value="Greater Heal" />
<Attribute name="shift-spell*" value="Power Word: Shield" />
<Attribute name="ctrl-spell*" value="Renew" />
```

8. Now define the units for the button to affect. `nil` is usually the same as `"target"`, but for `harmbutton` to work in the next step, an actual target needs to be defined:

```
<Attribute name="unit" value="target" />
<Attribute name="*unit2" value="focus" />
```

A very powerful technique is to vary one attribute according to the modifier and another one according to the button. In this example, the mouse button clicked specifies the unit to cast on, and the modifiers choose the spell to cast. In this way, a whole grid of unit-spell combinations can be created with comparatively few frame attributes.

9. Define the name of the button you want used when the target is an enemy, and then define the unit to use when that button is clicked:

```
<Attribute name="harmbutton" value="self" />
<Attribute name="*unit-self" value="player" />
```

10. Close the `Attributes` section and start a `Scripts` section so you can do needed setup on the button:

```
</Attributes>
<Scripts>
```

11. Buttons, by default, are only registered for left-clicks when they're created, so you need to fix that if you want to right-click the button:

```
<OnLoad>
  self:RegisterForClicks("AnyUp")
```

12. Because there is no action slot to which the button's icon will be updated, you need to set a static texture for its appearance:

```
    _G[self:GetName().."Icon"]:SetTexture(↵
[[Interface\Icons\Spell_Holy_ImprovedResistanceAuras]])
```

13. The last step is close out the open tags and save the file:

```
        </OnLoad>
      </Scripts>
    </Button>
  </Ui>
```

Figure 15-2 shows the fully functional QuickCasterButton that you can use to cast spells.

Figure 15-2: The functional QuickCasterButton

Understanding Taint and Working Safely Around Secure Code

The secure code system depends on its function being very thorough. Any attempt by insecure code to interfere with a secure action will cause the secure action to fail or further spread the taint. Addons that approach or manipulate secure buttons or other UI elements depend on a very close association of secure and contagiously insecure code, and it's easy to end up getting the influence of insecure code where it doesn't belong, causing familiar elements of the UI to break in new and inventive ways.

If you're getting error messages about actions only permitted to the Blizzard UI, or "Interface action failed because of an AddOn" messages are cropping up in your chat log, it's important to understand how taint works and spreads if you're going to try and fix these issues. If you're not familiar with the protection violation error message, you can reproduce it by running `CastSpellByName("Attack")` using WoWLua, producing the error shown in Figure 15-3.

Figure 15-3: Protected function error

Notice that the message references WowLua. When WoW loads a Lua file, every value created by the addon (functions and other globals) is marked as such. In this case, the code in WowLua that executes your commands is known to be tainted. When it tries to access `CastSpellByName`, the WoW game code refuses to comply. Instead, it throws an error with the name of the addon that caused the taint.

> **NOTE** The `CastSpellByName` function itself is not blocked for tainted code. Rather, it is the actual casting of spells that is blocked. For example, if you try to cast a spell that you do not have, `CastSpellByName` will fail silently. Additionally, you can safely use `CastSpellByName` to open tradeskills.

Enabling Taint Logging

Sometimes the way taint spreads can seem mysterious because of the various and complex interactions of different parts of the UI code (addons, macros, and built-in code). First, run the following command to turn on taint logging:

```
/console taintLog 1
```

The taint log shows you a time line of when taint occurs and how the taint blocks an action. Level 1 only shows taint events if they lead up to a blocked action. Level 2 records every single occurrence of taint including those that are completely innocuous (and indeed inevitable). To turn off taint logging, pass it a zero (0). The following is an example taint log attempting to run `CastSpellByName`:

```
5/28 15:01:43.302  An action was blocked because of taint from WowLua -
CastSpellByName()
5/28 15:01:43.302      WowLua:1
5/28 15:01:43.302      pcall()
5/28 15:01:43.302      Interface\AddOns\WowLua\WowLua.lua:217 RunScript()
5/28 15:01:43.302      Interface\AddOns\WowLua\WowLua.lua:600 Button_Run()
```

```
5/28 15:01:43.302      Interface\AddOns\WowLua\WowLua.lua:276 Button_OnClick()
5/28 15:01:43.302      WowLuaButton_Run:OnClick()
```

The first line shows the actual event, the call to `CastSpellByName` that generated the error message shown in Figure 15-3. The other indented lines show a stack trace leading up to the event to help you track down the source of any problems. Upcoming sections take a closer look at some other taint logs.

Taint logs are saved as `taint.log` in the `Logs` folder of your WoW installation. Like chat logs, they are only written to disk when the game exits or the UI is reloaded. To see the taint log for your current session, you must manually reload the UI and then open the file quickly because WoW sometimes likes to empty it during gameplay.

Execution Taint

There are two ways to spread taint. One is temporary and only exists when a particular chain of code is executing. The other is more persistent and the cause of many headaches. The first is what you experienced in the preceding example. The taint travels up the call stack from one function to another. For example, enter the following command in the chat box (not WowLua):

```
/run WowLua:ProcessLine("CastSpellByName('Attack')")
```

WowLua works by reading each line of text you enter and then running it as Lua code. With the preceding command, you are manually calling the function that does this, telling it to attempt to cast the `Attack` spell. The important point to note is that the game blames WowLua for the infraction, not the macro command. Figure 15-4 illustrates the taint path and the state of the blame.

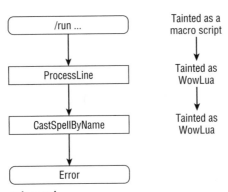

Figure 15-4: Execution taint path

The taint begins when the macro processes the `/run` command (remember that macros fall under the same restrictions as addons). At this point, the taint is attributed to the macro command. If you were to call `CastSpellByName` directly, the error would mention "A macro script." Instead, you call

WowLua:ProcessLine, which now receives blame for the taint. The function executes the code sent, which in turn tries to call CastSpellByName. You can also follow this path through the taint log.

```
5/27 22:06:26.890  An action was blocked because of taint from WowLua -
CastSpellByName()
5/27 22:06:26.890      CastSpellByName('Attack'):1
5/27 22:06:26.890      pcall()
5/27 22:06:26.890      Interface\AddOns\WowLua\WowLua.lua:177 ProcessLine()
5/27 22:06:26.890      WowLua:ProcessLine("CastSpellByName('Attack')"):1
5/27 22:06:26.890      RunScript()
5/27 22:06:26.890      Interface\FrameXML\ChatFrame.lua:1826 ?()
5/27 22:06:26.890      Interface\FrameXML\ChatFrame.lua:3332 ChatEdit_ParseText()
5/27 22:06:26.890      Interface\FrameXML\ChatFrame.lua:3052 ChatEdit_SendText()
5/27 22:06:26.890      Interface\FrameXML\ChatFrame.lua:3073 ↵
ChatEdit_OnEnterPressed()
5/27 22:06:26.890      ChatFrameEditBox:OnEnterPressed()
```

Working from bottom to top, the log begins when you press Enter in the chat box. Next, it works its way up to RunScript(), which applies the first taint in the sequence, blaming it on "A macro script." The macro script then calls WowLua:ProcessLine, which receives blame for the taint.

Execution taint is transient because none of the functions involved is permanently affected in any way. The default UI uses CastSpellByName for certain cases of spell casting. Even after erroneously calling, as shown here, WoW still behaves correctly. The taint itself goes away as soon as the original /run command finishes.

Variable Taint

Less forgiving than execution taint, variable taint can permanently (for the session) affect certain aspects of the built-in code. Variable taint is almost an extension of execution taint; they both play off of each other, and even overlap in some ways. Any tainted execution path has the potential to cause variable taint.

Recall from Part I the ideas of values and references. World of Warcraft has modified its Lua engine to store a taint flag with every value in the Lua environment that identifies if the value is tainted, and the addon that caused the taint. This is how the preceding example determined the blame. Variable taint is caused when a tainted code path creates a new value or reference. Any time your code makes a new global variable, function, table, and so on, that new value is now tainted. Where you begin to run into trouble is when you start modifying variables used by the default UI. Here's an example in action. Type the following line into WowLua:

```
/run NUM_ACTIONBAR_BUTTONS = NUM_ACTIONBAR_BUTTONS
```

Now try to use any ability on your action bar and you will see an addon blocked messages similar to the one you saw before. The function `ActionButton_CalculateAction` in `FrameXML\ActionButton.lua` uses this variable to determine which action slot to activate when you press the button. As soon as the code accesses the tainted value, the execution path becomes infected with execution taint. This causes an error when the code attempts to run the `UseAction` function. The only way to "cure" this condition is to reload the UI.

> **NOTE** The taint error from setting `NUM_ACTIONBAR_BUTTONS` will probably not appear if you are using a custom bar mod. The default UI's action buttons calculate which action slot to use based on `NUM_ACTIONBAR_BUTTONS`, the button's ID (set via the `id` XML attribute), and some other pieces of data. Addons' action buttons usually do not use IDs, so `ActionButton_CalculateAction` never runs into the tainted value.

`NUM_ACTIONBAR_BUTTONS` could be set to some number directly, but it is important to realize that the taint is caused simply by the act of assignment itself. The fact that the value came from a secure variable does not exempt you from taint.

Another chart is helpful to picture the interactions. Figure 15-5 shows the series of events that occurs when you click the action button after tainting `NUM_ACTIONBAR_BUTTONS`. Again, note that it's the simple action of reading the tainted variable that causes the execution path to be tainted.

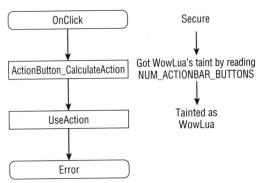

Figure 15-5: Code path tainted by a modified variable

Take a look at the resulting taint log:

```
5/28 15:27:23.454  Global variable NUM_ACTIONBAR_BUTTONS tainted by WowL
ua -
WowLua:1
5/28 15:27:23.454     pcall()
5/28 15:27:23.454        Interface\AddOns\WowLua\WowLua.lua:217 RunScript()
```

```
5/28 15:27:23.454        Interface\AddOns\WowLua\WowLua.lua:600 Button_Run()
5/28 15:27:23.454        Interface\AddOns\WowLua\WowLua.lua:276 Button_OnClick()
5/28 15:27:23.454        WowLuaButton_Run:OnClick()
5/28 15:27:23.454  Execution tainted by WowLua while reading ↵
NUM_ACTIONBAR_BUTTONS - Interface\FrameXML\ActionButton.lua:139 ↵
ActionButton_CalculateAction()
5/28 15:27:23.454        Interface\FrameXML\SecureTemplates.lua:253 handler()
5/28 15:27:23.454        Interface\FrameXML\SecureTemplates.lua:460
5/28 15:27:23.454  An action was blocked because of taint from WowLua -
UseAction()
5/28 15:27:23.454        Interface\FrameXML\SecureTemplates.lua:258 handler()
5/28 15:27:23.454        Interface\FrameXML\SecureTemplates.lua:460
```

The first "Global variable tainted" event shows the taint being applied to NUM_ACTIONBAR_BUTTONS. The next "Execution tainted" event, which was originally triggered by the button's OnClick handler, occurs during ActionButton_CalculateAction, as anticipated. Finally, UseAction is blocked from executing because the code path was tainted.

NOTE This particular taint log illustrates a particular distinction between taint log levels 1 and 2. Notice that all three events share the same time stamp. At level 1, WoW waits until taint actually causes a blocked action before reporting it. When the action blocked message is generated, WoW goes back through its taint history and retrieves the first two events, and all three events are then output to the log. If you were to click the action button a second time, all three events would be logged again, even though the first one happened some time ago.

On the other hand, level 2 records each event exactly as it happens. Every global variable set by an addon generates a tainted message. Every time Blizzard code reads an insecure variable, it generates an execution tainted message. This makes level 2 extremely verbose, but it can also be more telling for a given issue.

Creeping Taint

One of the problems you may come across when dealing with taint issues is the gradual spreading of variable taint. Say you have a tainted variable used by the default UI (such as the earlier NUM_ACTIONBAR_BUTTONS example). As explained, as soon as the built-in code accesses this variable, it becomes tainted. Well, what happens when the tainted execution path then modifies some other variable? That variable is now afflicted with the same taint that is affecting the current execution path.

This process can happen repeatedly, often unnoticed, with each new tainted variable potentially causing even more taint. In this way, your addon can taint entire subsystems of the UI without modifying more than a single variable. Not only can it spread far and wide, but the speed of the spreading can be misleading. Some code in the default UI runs based on events that are not exactly frequent. One piece of misplaced taint may not cause any problems until you join a raid group or travel to another continent, for example.

These situations are where the taint logs can really shine. When you receive an "action blocked" message during development, simply turn on taint logging and you can track down the problems. Level 2 is especially helpful in a case like this because it allows you to see exactly when each variable becomes tainted.

Summary

This chapter covered a lot of ground. By now, you should be acquainted with:

- The basic intent of the secure code system, which is to protect the game from automation while still enabling customization.

- The concept of protected frames and which of their characteristics are restricted from changes during combat.

- How frame attributes allow secure code to receive control messages safely from addon code.

- How taint can propagate from addon code to Blizzard code and cause the UI to fail, and how to identify and prevent this.

The secure template system uses a wide assortment of specific features—taint, protected functions and frames, attributes, and so on—to achieve a much larger goal. It needs to protect the game against too much automation and, at the same time, allow addons to alter the way you interact in combat. There is still a lot to cover, but once you understand the basics laid out here, the rest will flow much more freely.

## CHAPTER 16

Binding Keys and Clicks to Addon Code

Most of the user input discussed so far has revolved around the mouse and graphical interface elements. Chapter 12 gave you a taste of `OnClick`, `OnEnter`, and a few other handlers, as well as the `Button` and `EditBox` widgets. In Chapter 15, you learned how to change the behavior of action buttons depending on which mouse button was used and/or which modifier keys were pressed at the time. This chapter shows you how to interact with the keyboard and mouse directly, outside the context of UI widgets.

TIP The only forms of user input the WoW interface recognizes at the time of this writing are keyboard and mouse. If you want to use alternative means to control the game, say a gamepad or voice commands, you have to configure the hardware or software so that they imitate a keyboard or mouse. There is evidence of possible joystick or gamepad support in a future patch, but nothing is officially part of the UI yet.

The key binding system treats both types of input the same way. Each key or mouse button goes by a particular name. For basic letters, numbers, and symbols, the name is simply the result of hitting the key with Caps Lock on. Special keys and mouse buttons have descriptive names like LEFT, NUMPAD3, or BUTTON1. For the sake of simplicity, we'll refer to these as *keys*, which you can take to mean "key or mouse button name." You use the key-binding interface (accessible from the main game menu) as shown in Figure 16-1 to assign these various keys to specific actions.

Keys and commands have a *many-to-one relationship*—you can bind many keys to one command, but you can't bind one key to many commands. You can see this in the screenshot, which has two columns of key buttons for each command (behind the scenes, you're not limited to two).

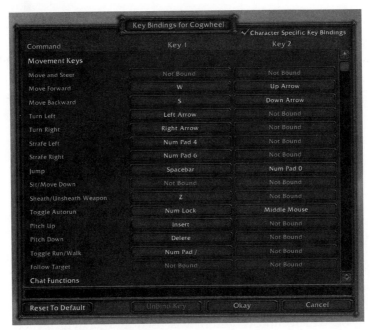

Figure 16-1: WoW key binding interface

The commands that appear in the default key binding interface are specified in `FrameXML\Bindings.xml`. You can also provide a `Bindings.xml` file in the root directory of your addon to add custom bindings to the list.

Defining Bindings in XML

The structure of `Bindings.xml` is very simple. The root element is `Bindings`, and each command is represented by a single `Binding` element. The key binding interface builds the list of bindings in the same order they appear in the file. When addons provide a `Bindings.xml`, their bindings appear at the end of the list in the order the addons are loaded. Take a look at an entry from the default user interface:

```
<Bindings>
  ...
  <Binding name="TOGGLESHEATH">
    ToggleSheath();
```

```
  </Binding>
   ...
</Bindings>
```

The name attribute, in this case TOGGLESHEATH, sets the name of this particular action. You use this name with the SetBinding() functions later in this chapter. The key binding interface looks for a global string variable called BINDING_NAME_*name* to label the binding in the list. For example, the value of BINDING_NAME_TOGGLESHEATH is Sheath/Unsheath Weapon in the English version of WoW (see Figure 16-1).

Once you bind a key to a command, the code inside the Binding tag is executed whenever you press the key. In this case, because z is bound to TOGGLESHEATH, pressing z calls the ToggleSheath function, which cycles through your equipped weapons.

NOTE There are certain situations in which key bindings might not appear to work correctly, such as when you try to use a keyboard binding while an EditBox widget has the keyboard focus. Similarly for mouse buttons, any time the cursor is over a mouse-enabled frame, the frame consumes button clicks for use with OnClick, OnMouseDown, and so on, whether or not the handlers have been defined for the frame.

Key bindings are consulted only if the keys or buttons aren't consumed by some other aspect of the user interface.

Here's another example from the built-in Bindings.xml that illustrates a couple more features:

```
<Binding name="MOVEANDSTEER" runOnUp="true" header="MOVEMENT">
  if ( keystate == "down" ) then
    MoveAndSteerStart();
  else
    MoveAndSteerStop();
  end
</Binding>
```

As with the previous example, this binding includes a name attribute and a Lua chunk. The new header attribute sets up a heading for the key binding interface. In this case WoW looks for BINDING_HEADER_<attribute> to determine the text of the header. You can see in Figure 16-1 that BINDING_HEADER_MOVEMENT is defined as Movement Keys in the English client.

Of particular note is the runOnUp attribute, which tells the game to execute the binding code twice: once when the key is pressed down, and again when the key is released. The code sample shows that WoW provides a keystate parameter of either `"down"` or `"up"`, allowing you to determine which condition triggered the execution.

Creating Your Own Binding Actions

Now that you have an idea of the structure of the bindings file, take a moment to experiment with some bindings of your own. For the next few sections, you'll work on an addon called BindingTest. Create a directory under your `AddOns` directory called `BindingTest`. Create `BindingTest.toc` and add the following to the file:

```
## Interface: 30200
## Title: Key Bindings Test
## Notes: Demonstrates the usage of Bindings.xml

BindingTest.lua
BindingTest.xml
```

Create empty `BindingTest.lua` and `BindingTest.xml` files; you'll add code to them later. Finally, create a file called `Bindings.xml` and input the following code:

```
<Bindings>
  <Binding name="BINDING_TEST1" header="BINDING_TEST">
    BindingTest_Test1()
  </Binding>
  <Binding name="BINDING_TEST2" runOnUp="true">
    BindingTest_Test2(keystate)
  </Binding>
</Bindings>
```

Notice that `Bindings.xml` is not listed in the table of contents file—WoW always loads `Bindings.xml` if present.

If you start up WoW and open the key bindings interface, you should see something like Figure 16-2.

Notice how there's an empty space where the header will go, and how your custom bindings are simply labeled with the action names from `Bindings.xml`. To remedy this, open your addon's Lua file and add the following global strings:

```
BINDING_HEADER_BINDING_TEST = "Test bindings for Chapter 16"
BINDING_NAME_BINDING_TEST1 = "Test binding #1"
BINDING_NAME_BINDING_TEST2 = "Test binding #2"
```

Save the file and reload the user interface using the `/reload` slash command. Now when you open the key bindings screen it should look like Figure 16-3.

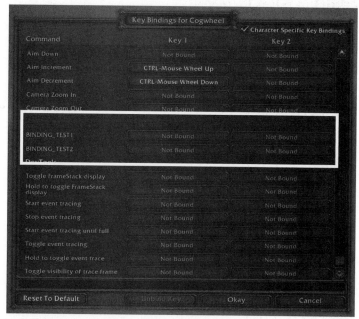

Figure 16-2: Key binding interface with blank test bindings

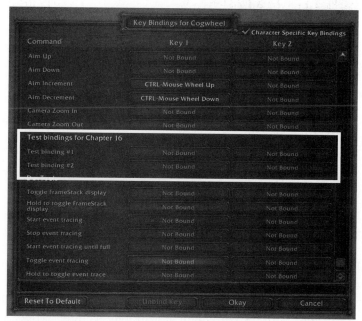

Figure 16-3: Key binding interface with named test bindings

At this point, you can go ahead and bind keys to these two test bindings. You'll probably want to use keys that aren't already bound to something important to save you a bit of trouble when you get back to actually *playing* the game. Because you haven't defined the functions yet, activating the key bindings triggers a Lua error. Add these functions to `BindingTest.lua` and give them basic behavior as follows:

```
function BindingTest_Test1()
  print("Test binding #1 activated")
end

function BindingTest_Test2(keystate)
  if keystate == "down" then
    print("Test binding #2 pressed")
  else
    print("Test binding #2 released")
  end
end
```

After reloading the UI, spend a few moments experimenting with the two keys you bound. You'll see results similar to Figure 16-4.

Figure 16-4: Sample output from key bindings

One point worth noting from this screenshot is that more than one binding can be "in progress" simultaneously. This is illustrated in the last four lines where Test #2 is pressed, then Test #1 is activated twice, and finally Test #2 is released. The number of separate keys that you can use at the same time varies depending on your keyboard hardware and operating system.

Binding Keys to Actions

The key binding interface works fairly well for basic binding control, but it does have a few limitations. First off, many users complain about the interface itself because it's rather difficult to navigate—especially when you start piling on more and more addons with their additional sections. There's also the problem mentioned earlier where only two keys are shown for a given action.

You may choose to bypass the default interface altogether for your addon, or perhaps you want to make an addon that replaces the key binding interface itself with something a bit more flexible. Either way, you'll need to set the key bindings programmatically.

Building a Simple Binding UI

To give you an overview of the various binding APIs, create a basic binding interface for the BindingTest addon. This interface will consist of two buttons, one for each binding action. You left-click the buttons to add a binding and right-click to remove a binding. Figure 16-5 shows an example of this interface in use.

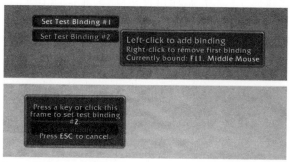

Figure 16-5: Basic key binding interface

To begin, open `BindingTest.xml` and add the following code:

```
<Ui xmlns="http://www.blizzard.com/wow/ui/"
  xmlns:xsi="http://www.w3.org/2001/XMLSchema-instance"
  xsi:schemaLocation="http://www.blizzard.com/wow/ui/
  http://wowprogramming.com/FrameXML/UI.xsd">

  <Button name="BindingTestButtonTemplate" inherits= ↵
"UIPanelButtonTemplate2" virtual="true">
    <Size x="150" y="24"/>
    <Scripts>
      <OnLoad function="BindingTestButton_OnLoad"/>
      <OnClick function="BindingTestButton_OnClick"/>
      <OnEnter function="BindingTestButton_OnEnter"/>
      <OnLeave function="BindingTestButton_OnLeave"/>
    </Scripts>
  </Button>
</Ui>
```

The two buttons will be identical in most respects, so you define a template from which the buttons will inherit. The `OnLoad` script will initialize the button with a label and associated binding information based on the button's ID. The `OnClick` script will display the bindings frame when clicked, and the `OnEnter`/`OnLeave` scripts will show and hide the tooltip.

Create a frame to hold the buttons and the buttons themselves by adding the following code immediately after the template definition, within the `Ui` tag.

```
<Frame name="BindingTestFrame">
  <Size x="1" y="1"/>
  <Anchors>
    <Anchor point="CENTER"/>
  </Anchors>
  <Frames>
    <Button name="BindingTestButton1" ↵
      inherits="BindingTestButtonTemplate" id="1">
      <Anchors>
        <Anchor point="BOTTOM" relativePoint="CENTER"/>
      </Anchors>
    </Button>
    <Button name="BindingTestButton2" ↵
      inherits="BindingTestButtonTemplate" id="2">
      <Anchors>
        <Anchor point="TOP" relativePoint="CENTER"/>
      </Anchors>
    </Button>
  </Frames>
</Frame>
```

The outer frame doesn't really provide any functionality of its own; it simply serves to encapsulate the two buttons. If you'd prefer not to have the buttons directly in the center of the screen, you can anchor `BindingTestFrame` elsewhere and the buttons will move with it.

The buttons themselves are anchored such that one sits directly above the position of `BindingTestFrame` and the other sits just below.

Finally, you need a frame that can capture keyboard and mouse input so you can assign the bindings as necessary. You'll use a button widget to take advantage of the `OnClick` handler. Start off by creating the basic appearance of the button as follows:

```
<Button name="BindingTestCaptureFrame" hidden="true" enableKeyboard= ↵
"true" frameStrata="DIALOG">
  <Size x="175" y="90"/>
  <Anchors>
    <Anchor point="CENTER"/>
  </Anchors>
  <Backdrop bgFile="Interface\Tooltips\UI-Tooltip-Background" edgeFile= ↵
"Interface\Tooltips\UI-Tooltip-Border" tile="true">
```

```
    <EdgeSize val="16"/>
    <TileSize val="16"/>
    <BackgroundInsets left="5" right="5" top="5" bottom="5"/>
    <Color r="0" g="0" b="0"/>
  </Backdrop>
</Button>
```

Because this frame pops up in response to clicking one of the two buttons, it starts off hidden. As soon as you show the frame it captures all key presses thanks to the `enableKeyboard` attribute. The backdrop section gives the frame an appearance similar to a tooltip. Next, add a font string immediately after the `</Backdrop>` tag, but before the `</Button>` tag. This font string will be used to display instructions to the user. Here's the code:

```
<Layers>
  <Layer level="ARTWORK">
    <FontString inherits="GameFontNormal" parentKey="text">
      <Anchors>
        <Anchor point="TOPLEFT">
          <Offset x="10" y="-10"/>
        </Anchor>
        <Anchor point="BOTTOMRIGHT">
          <Offset x="-10" y="10"/>
        </Anchor>
      </Anchors>
    </FontString>
  </Layer>
</Layers>
```

Finally, add the script definitions after the `</Layers>` tag:

```
<Scripts>
 <OnLoad function="BindingTestCapture_OnLoad"/>
 <OnShow function="BindingTestCapture_OnShow"/>
 <OnKeyDown function="BindingTestCapture_OnKeyDown"/>
 <OnClick function="BindingTestCapture_OnClick"/>
</Scripts>
```

The `OnLoad` script initializes the frame. The `OnShow` script changes the text of the frame to indicate which binding is being changed. The `OnKeyDown` and `OnClick` scripts are used to capture the keyboard and mouse input, respectively.

Load the game at this point and you'll see two blank buttons (see Figure 16-6) in the middle of the screen that don't do anything interesting when pressed.

Figure 16-6: Blank binding test buttons

Defining Basic Behaviors

Now it's time to add the behavior to your UI. Open the addon's Lua file if it's not already open. After the global binding labels at the top of the file, add the following strings:

```
local BUTTON_CAPTION = "Set Test Binding #%d"
local TOOLTIP_TEXT1 = "Left-click to add binding"
local TOOLTIP_TEXT2 = "Right-click to remove first binding"
local TOOLTIP_BINDING_LIST = "Currently bound: |cFFFFFFFF%s|r"
local LIST_SEPARATOR = "|r, |cFFFFFFFF"
local CAPTURE_TEXT = [[
Press a key or click this frame to set test binding #|cFFFFFFFF%d|r.

Press |cFFFFFFFFESC|r to cancel.]]
```

These strings are used as follows:

- `BUTTON_CAPTION`—This is the label for the two main buttons.
- `TOOLTIP_xxxx`—These are the text that appears in the tooltip.
- `LIST_SEPARATOR`—The "Currently bound" section of the tooltip lists each key bound to the button's associated action. This is the separator between items in the list. Note the use of color codes to make the key names stand out.
- `CAPTURE_TEXT`—This is the text for the capture frame.

So you'll be able to see the progress of your work at each step, create stubs for all of the scripts you defined in the XML by adding the following code to the end of the Lua file:

```
function BindingTestButton_OnLoad(self)
end

function BindingTestButton_OnClick(self, button)
end

function BindingTestButton_OnEnter(self)
end
```

```
function BindingTestButton_OnLeave(self)
end

function BindingTestCapture_OnLoad(self)
end

function BindingTestCapture_OnShow(self)
end

function BindingTestCapture_OnKeyDown(self, key)
end

function BindingTestCapture_OnClick(self, button)
end
```

Start off the addon's behavior by filling in the `Button_OnLoad` function as follows:

```
function BindingTestButton_OnLoad(self)
   local id = self:GetID()
   self:SetText(BUTTON_CAPTION:format(id))
   self.action = "BINDING_TEST"..id
   self:RegisterForClicks("LeftButtonUp", "RightButtonUp")
end
```

First the function sets the text of the button based on the button's ID. Next it stores the name of the associated binding action. Finally, it registers the button to receive left- and right-clicks. Reload your UI and the buttons should now look like Figure 16-7.

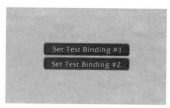

Figure 16-7: Binding test buttons with labels

Of course, the labels bear false witness because the buttons don't actually do anything yet. Fix that by filling in the `Button_OnClick` function:

```
function BindingTestButton_OnClick(self, button)
   if button == "LeftButton" then
      BindingTestCaptureFrame.button = self
```

```
      BindingTestCaptureFrame:Show()
   elseif button == "RightButton" then
      -- Binding removal code will go here
   end
end
```

As you can see, a left-click shows the capture frame after initializing it with the selected button. For now, the right-click behavior is empty. You'll fill that in later after working with some of the binding APIs.

Before reloading the UI, you'll want to make sure there's a way to close the capture frame. Because it captures all keyboard input, you won't be able to use any other key bindings until it's hidden. This means you won't be able to bring up the chat box to type `/run ReloadUI()` or `/run BindingTestCaptureFrame:Hide()`. At best, you can click the game menu button and log out. To prevent this difficulty, add a check for the Escape key to `Capture_OnKeyDown`:

```
function BindingTestCapture_OnKeyDown(self, key)
   if key == "ESCAPE" then
      self:Hide()
      return
   end
end
```

Reload the UI and your buttons will now bring up a blank capture frame as shown in Figure 16-8.

TIP If you ever find yourself stuck with a keyboard capturing frame and can't access the main menu or don't want to log out completely, you can use a few tricks to bring up the chat box.

First, check your chat log. If you have any messages from anyone in any channel, you can click their name to begin a whisper. Similarly, if there are any friendly characters nearby, you can target them and right-click their portrait to start a whisper. You can also find whisper targets by bringing up the Who window. Once you've initiated a whisper, you can use the edit box to type any slash command.

Figure 16-8: Blank binding test capture frame

You have just a couple more clerical matters to attend to before moving on to the binding functions. Fill in the `Capture_OnLoad` and `Capture_OnShow` functions as follows:

```
function BindingTestCapture_OnLoad(self)
   self:RegisterForClicks("AnyUp")
end

function BindingTestCapture_OnShow(self)
   self.text:SetText(CAPTURE_TEXT:format(self.button:GetID()))
end
```

Now the frame is prepared to respond to any mouse click and also displays instructions for setting the binding as shown in Figure 16-9.

Figure 16-9: Final binding test capture frame

Using SetBinding()

With the housekeeping tasks out of the way, you can now concentrate on the bindings themselves. The heart of the binding API is the `SetBinding()` function, which associates a key with a binding action:

```
success = SetBinding("key"[, "action"])
```

The `key` parameter is a string representing the desired key press (for example, `SHIFT-F5`) and the `action` parameter is the name of the binding action you want the key to trigger. If the action is omitted (or `nil` for clarity) the binding is removed from the key. `SetBinding()` returns `1` or `nil` depending on whether the binding was successfully set.

The capture frame knows what action to use by looking at its `button` field, which was set by `BindingTestButton_OnClick`. So the main job of `BindingTestCapture_OnKeyDown` is to build the `key` parameter and call `SetBinding()`. Now, `OnKeyDown` captures every key individually, even modifier keys. Because you can't bind modifier keys, you should ignore them by adding the following code to the end of the `OnKeyDown` function:

```
local modifier = key:sub(2)
if modifier == "SHIFT" or
```

```
      modifier == "CTRL" or
      modifier == "ALT" or
      key == "UNKNOWN" then
   return
end
```

When `OnKeyDown` receives a modifier key, it differentiates between keys on the left and right sides of the keyboard. For example, the left shift key is called `LSHIFT` and the right shift key is called `RSHIFT`. The first line in the preceding snippet eliminates a bit of redundancy in the `if` clause by stripping the first character off the key. You also check for `UNKNOWN`, which is triggered by keys that WoW doesn't recognize (like Scroll Lock and Pause on Windows).

You should also add special treatment for the key normally used to take screenshots. Otherwise there would be no way to take a screenshot of the binding. Add the following code immediately after the previous snippet:

```
if GetBindingFromClick(key) == "SCREENSHOT" then
   TakeScreenshot()
   return
end
```

The function `GetBindingFromClick`, defined in `FrameXML\UIParent.lua`, returns the action associated with the current key press, if any. If the action turns out to be `SCREENSHOT`, this code takes a screenshot and aborts the function.

Once you've eliminated the special cases, you can begin building the `key` argument. Although you ignored the modifier keys when they directly triggered `OnKeyDown`, you need to check their status to apply the appropriate prefixes to the key. Add this code following the screenshot check:

```
if IsShiftKeyDown() then
   key = "SHIFT-"..key
end
if IsControlKeyDown() then
   key = "CTRL-"..key
end
if IsAltKeyDown() then
   key = "ALT-"..key
end
```

Note that the order of these modifier checks is crucial; `SetBinding` only accepts modifier prefixes in the order `ALT-CTRL-SHIFT-`. In this snippet, you're adding them one at a time, as applicable, to the beginning of the key. If you pressed A with all the modifier keys held down, the `key` parameter would progress as follows:

```
      A
SHIFT-A
```

```
    CTRL-SHIFT-A
ALT-CTRL-SHIFT-A
```

Now that you have the key argument built, you can call `SetBinding()` and close the capture frame. Add these final two lines to the `OnKeyDown` function:

```
SetBinding(key, self.button.action)
self:Hide()
```

This code actually calls the binding API and then hides the binding UI.

At this point, the addon does most of what it advertises. If you press one of the buttons, it brings up the capture frame. Then when you press a key combination, it sets the binding and hides the capture frame. You should be able to see the new bindings in the WoW key binding UI, unless you already had two bindings in place. Even then your binding is still there but the UI isn't designed to show more than two. This addon won't be so limited. Later you add functionality to the tooltips that lists all keys bound to the given action.

> **NOTE** If you test out the addon, you may notice that the key bindings don't survive through a UI reload. `SetBinding` on its own doesn't commit any changes to the server. You can use this to your advantage because you don't have to be as careful about overwriting your existing bindings. However, if you open up the built-in key binding UI, clicking Okay saves the bindings you created with this addon. Be sure to hit Cancel instead if you don't want to save the changes (it will also revert the changes you did make). You learn more about binding storage in a later section.

Earlier we mentioned that the key binding API treats mouse clicks and button clicks in the same way. This means the `OnClick` handler can simply call `OnKeyDown` with the appropriate mouse button name. Unfortunately, the names used for mouse click handlers aren't the same as what the binding APIs expect, as shown in Table 16-1.

This translation is extremely simple thanks to Lua's tables. Immediately before the definition of `BindingTestCapture_OnClick`, add the following code:

```
local buttonKeys = {
  ["MiddleButton"] = "BUTTON3",
  ["Button4"] = "BUTTON4",
  ["Button5"] = "BUTTON5"
}
```

> **NOTE** You are omitting `LeftButton` and `RightButton` because those mouse buttons have such crucial roles in gameplay that it's usually a bad idea to remove their bindings. Otherwise you'd be unable to target units in the game world, turn the camera, or interact with objects such as doors, chests, NPCs, corpses, and so

on. It's possible to bind their actions (CAMERAORSELECTORMOVE and TURNORACTION, respectively) to other keys, but you still have to position the mouse cursor over the object with which you're trying to interact.

As an exercise, you might consider allowing re-binding of the left and right mouse buttons. After the binding is made, leave the capture window open and ask for a new key for the appropriate action.

Table 16-1: Mouse Clicks and Their Corresponding Binding Keys

MOUSE CLICK	BINDING KEY
LeftButton	BUTTON1
RightButton	BUTTON2
MiddleButton	BUTTON3
Button4	BUTTON4
Button5	BUTTON5

Now all you need to do is make sure the clicked button is in the table and pass it to OnKeyDown. Fill in BindingTestCapture_OnClick as follows:

```
function BindingTestCapture_OnClick(self, button)
  local key = buttonKeys[button]
  if not key then
    return
  end
  BindingTestCapture_OnKeyDown(self, key)
end
```

And with that, your test addon can now capture all the bindings it was designed to handle.

Working with Existing Bindings

Now that you can add all the bindings you want, it would be helpful to implement binding removal. We left a place for this code inside BindingTestButton_OnClick earlier in the chapter. Edit that function so it looks like this:

```
function BindingTestButton_OnClick(self, button)
  if button == "LeftButton" then
    BindingTestCaptureFrame.button = self
    BindingTestCaptureFrame:Show()
```

```
  elseif button == "RightButton" then
    local key = GetBindingKey(self.command)
    if key then
      SetBinding(key, nil)
    end
    BindingTestButton_OnEnter(self)
  end
end
```

The `GetBindingKey` API function accepts the name of a command and returns a list of all the keys bound to the action. For this simple interface, you're only interested in the first one. The code checks to see if there's a binding for the button's command and if so, clears it. The last line in the new code triggers `OnEnter` to refresh the tooltip, which you will implement next.

Displaying an Action's Bindings

As mentioned earlier, the tooltip explains how to use the binding buttons and shows a list of all keys currently bound to the button's action. Tooltips are covered in depth in Chapter 24, but the usage here should be simple enough to understand. To start, create and show the tooltip when the mouse enters the button. Add the following code to `BindingTestButton_OnEnter`:

```
GameTooltip:SetOwner(self, "ANCHOR_BOTTOMRIGHT")
GameTooltip:AddLine(TOOLTIP_TEXT1)
GameTooltip:AddLine(TOOLTIP_TEXT2)
```

The first line clears the tooltip and anchors it to the bottom-right corner of the button. The next two lines add the basic left- and right-click instructions. Next, build the list of keys with the following code:

```
local list = {GetBindingKey(self.command)}
for i, key in ipairs(list) do
  list[i] = GetBindingText(key, "KEY_")
end
```

Here you're using `GetBindingKey` again, but this time you store all the results in a table. Then you use `GetBindingText` (defined in `FrameXML\UIParent.lua`) to translate the key names into more human-readable forms. For instance, `BUTTON3` becomes `Middle Mouse`. Finish up this function as follows:

```
GameTooltip:AddLine(
  TOOLTIP_BINDING_LIST:format(table.concat(list, LIST_SEPARATOR)),
    NORMAL_FONT_COLOR.r,
    NORMAL_FONT_COLOR.g,
    NORMAL_FONT_COLOR.b,
```

```
      1
    )
```

```
GameTooltip:Show()
```

The first argument to `GameTooltip:AddLine` is built by joining all the key names together with `LIST_SEPARATOR` between them, and then formatting this into the `TOOLTIP_BINDING_LIST` string. Because the list can potentially grow pretty long, the last argument of `1` tells the tooltip to wrap the text of this line. `AddLine` has optional color parameters positioned before the wrap flag, so you need to provide arguments to avoid unintended effects.

> **TIP** You can find global constants for WoW's standard text colors in **FrameXML\FontStyles.xml**.

As I'm sure you've guessed, the last line of the preceding code shows the tooltip. Now fill in `BindingTestButton_OnLeave` as follows to hide the tooltip after the mouse leaves the button:

```
function BindingTestButton_OnLeave(self)
    GameTooltip:Hide()
end
```

This addon now has all of its promised functionality. If you test it now you should be able to see results similar to Figure 16-5.

Understanding Binding Storage

Manipulating bindings is all well and good, but it doesn't help much if the changes are only temporary. In this section you explore how to save the changes you make.

You can save bindings in two different ways: account-wide or character-specific. Normally the player will choose which one to use via the checkbox at the top of WoW's key binding interface. To find out which set is currently active you use the function `GetCurrentBindingSet`. This function returns 1 for account-wide and 2 for character-specific bindings. Once you've determined which set you want to save, you simply call `SaveBindings` and the deed is done.

To make the binding test addon save its changes, simply add the following line after each of the calls to `SetBinding` in `BindingTestButton_OnClick` and `BindingTestCapture_OnKeyDown`:

```
SaveBindings(GetCurrentBindingSet())
```

In a more comprehensive binding interface you would need a way to undo the changes you make with `SetBinding`. WoW's key binding interface does this when you hit Cancel. You could add a Save button that delays the saving of bindings until it's clicked, and then you can "restore" the saved bindings by simply loading them:

```
LoadBindings(GetCurrentBindingSet())
```

Binding Keys to Secure Actions

For addons, basic binding commands like you've dealt with so far are only useful for actions unrelated to combat. They're fine for things like displaying a configuration window, reloading the UI, opening a chat window, and so on. But as you learned in Chapter 15, your Lua code isn't allowed to directly trigger actions resulting in ability/item use or target selection. Because of this limitation, there is a set of APIs much like `SetBinding` that can trigger various secure actions:

- `success = SetBindingSpell("key"[, "spellname"])`—Binds the key directly to a spell. Be sure the name you provide conforms to the requirements of `CastSpellByName`.

- `success = SetBindingItem("key"[, "itemname" or "itemlink"])`—Binds the key to use the given item.

- `success = SetBindingMacro("key"[, macroid or "macroname"])`—Binds to the specified macro. The macro parameters should match the expectations of `RunMacro`.

- `success = SetBindingClick("key"[, "framename"[, "button"]])`—Click bindings act as if the key press were a mouse click on the specified frame. The `button` parameter is passed to the frame's various mouse handlers as the name of the mouse button. If you omit this parameter, it defaults to `LeftButton`.

As with `SetBinding`, if you provide a key argument but no others, the binding is removed from that key.

The first two are pretty self-explanatory. Although they're limited in scope, they prove useful in many situations. `SetBindingMacro` is a bit more flexible because macros can perform decision making, take multiple actions, and so on. However, because macros are highly user-specific and there's limited storage, you should use this only if the point of your addon is to interact with the user's own macros. If you need a binding to trigger your own complex behavior, you should implement that behavior in a secure button and use `SetBindingClick`.

Working with Click Bindings

To give you an idea of how click bindings work, run the following script in WowLua or put it into a new addon:

```
local testButton = CreateFrame("Button", "ClickBindingTestButton")
testButton:RegisterForClicks("AnyUp", "AnyDown")
testButton:SetScript("OnMouseDown", function(self, button)
  print("OnMouseDown:", button)
end)
testButton:SetScript("OnMouseUp", function(self, button)
  print("OnMouseUp:", button)
end)
testButton:SetScript("PreClick", function(self, button, down)
  print("PreClick:", button, (down and "Down" or "Up"))
end)
testButton:SetScript("OnClick", function(self, button, down)
  print("OnClick:", button, (down and "Down" or "Up"))
end)
testButton:SetScript("PostClick", function(self, button, down)
  print("PostClick:", button, (down and "Down" or "Up"))
end)
```

Using either WowLua or a /run command, bind some keys to the button like the following:

```
SetBindingClick("A", "ClickBindingTestButton")
SetBindingClick("B", "ClickBindingTestButton", "Zebra")
```

If you press and release B at this point, you should see the following output:

```
OnMouseDown: Zebra
PreClick: Zebra Down
OnClick: Zebra Down
PostClick: Zebra Down
OnMouseUp: Zebra
PreClick: Zebra Up
OnClick: Zebra Up
PostClick: Zebra Up
```

As you can see, the binding goes through all the motions that would normally be associated with a real mouse click. In fact, in an early Burning Crusade beta when these functions were first implemented, moving the mouse while holding down a key bound to an action button would drag the ability off the button!

Creating Secure Bindings in XML

One problem you may have noticed with these specialized binding functions is that there's no representation in the key binding UI. Luckily these four functions are simply conveniences. Each one is equivalent to calling `SetBinding` with a specially built action of one of these forms:

```
SPELL spellName
ITEM itemNameOrLink
MACRO macroNameOrID
CLICK frameName:mouseButton
```

For example, the earlier `SetBindingClick` examples would translate to:

```
SetBinding("A", "CLICK ClickBindingTestButton:LeftButton")
SetBinding("B", "CLICK ClickBindingTestButton:Zebra")
```

You can use these new actions in `Bindings.xml` so that they appear in WoW's UI. The two example bindings would look like the following:

```
<Binding name="CLICK ClickBindingTestButton:LeftButton" runOnUp="true"/>
<Binding name="CLICK ClickBindingTestButton:Zebra" runOnUp="true"/>
```

Creating the labels for these bindings takes a bit of trickery because variables can't have spaces in their names. However, these are global variables, so you can use any string as an index to the global environment. One way to do this by setting the key directly in the `_G` table:

```
_G["BINDING_NAME_CLICK ClickBindingTestButton:LeftButton"] = ↵
"ClickBindingTest LeftButton"

_G["BINDING_NAME_CLICK ClickBindingTestButton:Zebra"] = ↵
"ClickBindingTest Zebra"
```

These bindings would now appear in the key binding interface with their human-readable labels.

Summary

This chapter has provided you with all the tools you need for day-to-day key binding tasks, from integrating with the built-in binding UI to setting bindings programmatically. You have also seen some techniques useful for building your own binding UIs or perhaps even creating a dedicated addon to improve on WoW's binding interface.

The next chapter shows how to create slash commands for your addons, adding to the functionality you've already created.

The Code

BindingTest

BindingTest.toc

```
## Interface: 30200
## Title: Binding Test
## Notes: Demonstrates the usage of Bindings.xml

BindingTest.lua
BindingTest.xml
```

BindingTest.xml

```
<Ui xmlns="http://www.blizzard.com/wow/ui/"
  xmlns:xsi="http://www.w3.org/2001/XMLSchema-instance"
  xsi:schemaLocation="http://www.blizzard.com/wow/ui/
  http://wowprogramming.com/FrameXML/UI.xsd">

  <Button name="BindingTestButtonTemplate" inherits=
"UIPanelButtonTemplate2" virtual="true">
    <Size x="150" y="24"/>
    <Scripts>
      <OnLoad function="BindingTestButton_OnLoad"/>
      <OnClick function="BindingTestButton_OnClick"/>
      <OnEnter function="BindingTestButton_OnEnter"/>
      <OnLeave function="BindingTestButton_OnLeave"/>
    </Scripts>
  </Button>

  <Frame name="BindingTestFrame">
    <Size x="1" y="1"/>
    <Anchors>
      <Anchor point="CENTER"/>
    </Anchors>
    <Frames>
      <Button name="BindingTestButton1"
        inherits="BindingTestButtonTemplate"
        id="1">
```

```
          <Anchors>
            <Anchor point="BOTTOM" relativePoint="CENTER"/>
          </Anchors>
        </Button>
        <Button name="BindingTestButton2"
          inherits="BindingTestButtonTemplate"
          id="2">
          <Anchors>
            <Anchor point="TOP" relativePoint="CENTER"/>
          </Anchors>
        </Button>
      </Frames>
    </Frame>

  <Button name="BindingTestCaptureFrame" hidden="true" ↵
enableKeyboard="true" frameStrata="DIALOG">
      <Size x="175" y="90"/>
      <Anchors>
        <Anchor point="CENTER"/>
      </Anchors>
      <Backdrop bgFile="Interface\Tooltips\UI-Tooltip-Background" ↵
edgeFile="Interface\Tooltips\UI-Tooltip-Border" tile="true">
        <EdgeSize val="16"/>
        <TileSize val="16"/>
        <BackgroundInsets left="5" right="5" top="5" bottom="5"/>
        <Color r="0" g="0" b="0"/>
      </Backdrop>
      <Layers>
        <Layer level="ARTWORK">
          <FontString inherits="GameFontNormal" parentKey="text">
            <Anchors>
              <Anchor point="TOPLEFT">
                <Offset x="10" y="-10"/>
              </Anchor>
              <Anchor point="BOTTOMRIGHT">
                <Offset x="-10" y="10"/>
              </Anchor>
            </Anchors>
          </FontString>
        </Layer>
      </Layers>
      <Scripts>
        <OnLoad function="BindingTestCapture_OnLoad"/>
        <OnShow function="BindingTestCapture_OnShow"/>
        <OnKeyDown function="BindingTestCapture_OnKeyDown"/>
        <OnClick function="BindingTestCapture_OnClick"/>
      </Scripts>
    </Button>
</Ui>
```

BindingTest.lua

```lua
BINDING_HEADER_BINDING_TEST = "Test bindings for Chapter 16"
BINDING_NAME_BINDING_TEST1 = "Test binding #1"
BINDING_NAME_BINDING_TEST2 = "Test binding #2"

local BUTTON_CAPTION = "Set Test Binding #%d"
local TOOLTIP_TEXT1 = "Left-click to add binding"
local TOOLTIP_TEXT2 = "Right-click to remove first binding"
local TOOLTIP_BINDING_LIST = "Currently bound: |cFFFFFFFF%s|r"
local LIST_SEPARATOR = "|r, |cFFFFFFFF"
local CAPTURE_TEXT = [[
Press a key or click this frame to set test binding #|cFFFFFFFF%d|r.

Press |cFFFFFFFFESC|r to cancel.]]

function BindingTest_Test1()
  print("Test binding #1 activated")
end

function BindingTest_Test2(keystate)
  if keystate == "down" then
    print("Test binding #2 pressed")
  else
    print("Test binding #2 released")
  end
end

function BindingTestButton_OnLoad(self)
  local id = self:GetID()
  self:SetText(BUTTON_CAPTION:format(id))
  self.action = "BINDING_TEST"..id
  self:RegisterForClicks("LeftButtonUp", "RightButtonUp")
end
function BindingTestButton_OnClick(self, button)
  if button == "LeftButton" then
    BindingTestCaptureFrame.button = self
    BindingTestCaptureFrame:Show()
  elseif button == "RightButton" then
    local key = GetBindingKey(self.action)
    if key then
      SetBinding(key, nil)
      SaveBindings(GetCurrentBindingSet())
    end
    BindingTestButton_OnEnter(self)
  end
end

function BindingTestButton_OnEnter(self)
  GameTooltip:SetOwner(self, "ANCHOR_BOTTOMRIGHT")
```

```
  GameTooltip:AddLine(TOOLTIP_TEXT1)
  GameTooltip:AddLine(TOOLTIP_TEXT2)

  local list = {GetBindingKey(self.action)}
  for i, key in ipairs(list) do
    list[i] = GetBindingText(key, "KEY_")
  end

  GameTooltip:AddLine(
  TOOLTIP_BINDING_LIST:format(table.concat(list, LIST_SEPARATOR)),
  NORMAL_FONT_COLOR.r,
  NORMAL_FONT_COLOR.g,
  NORMAL_FONT_COLOR.b,
  1
  )

  GameTooltip:Show()
end

function BindingTestButton_OnLeave(self)
  GameTooltip:Hide()
end

function BindingTestCapture_OnLoad(self)
  self:RegisterForClicks("AnyUp")
end

function BindingTestCapture_OnShow(self)
  self.text:SetText(CAPTURE_TEXT:format(self.button:GetID()))
end

function BindingTestCapture_OnKeyDown(self, key)
  if key == "ESCAPE" then
    self:Hide()
    return
  end

  local modifier = key:sub(2)
  if  modifier == "SHIFT"
    or modifier == "CTRL"
    or modifier == "ALT"
    or key == "UNKNOWN" then
    return
  end

  if GetBindingFromClick(key) == "SCREENSHOT" then
    TakeScreenshot()
    return
  end
```

```
  if IsShiftKeyDown() then
    key = "SHIFT-"..key
  end
  if IsControlKeyDown() then
    key = "CTRL-"..key
  end
  if IsAltKeyDown() then
    key = "ALT-"..key
  end

  SetBinding(key, self.button.action)
  SaveBindings(GetCurrentBindingSet())
  self:Hide()
end

local buttonKeys = {
  ["MiddleButton"] = "BUTTON3",
  ["Button4"] = "BUTTON4",
  ["Button5"] = "BUTTON5"
}
function BindingTestCapture_OnClick(self, button)
  local key = buttonKeys[button]
  if not key then
    return
  end
  BindingTestCapture_OnKeyDown(self, key)
end
```

Bindings.xml

```xml
<Bindings>
  <Binding name="BINDING_TEST1" header="BINDING_TEST">
    BindingTest_Test1()
  </Binding>
  <Binding name="BINDING_TEST2" runOnUp="true">
    BindingTest_Test2(keystate)
  </Binding>
</Bindings>
```

ClickBindingTest

ClickBindingTest.toc

```
## Interface: 30200
## Title: Click Binding Test
## Notes: Demonstrates the use of click bindings

ClickBindingTest.lua
```

ClickBindingTest.lua

```lua
local testButton = CreateFrame("Button", "ClickBindingTestButton")
testButton:RegisterForClicks("AnyUp", "AnyDown")
testButton:SetScript("OnMouseDown", function(self, button)
  print("OnMouseDown:", button)
end)
testButton:SetScript("OnMouseUp", function(self, button)
  print("OnMouseUp:", button)
end)
testButton:SetScript("PreClick", function(self, button, down)
  print("PreClick:", button, (down and "Down" or "Up"))
end)
testButton:SetScript("OnClick", function(self, button, down)
  print("OnClick:", button, (down and "Down" or "Up"))
end)
testButton:SetScript("PostClick", function(self, button, down)
  print("PostClick:", button, (down and "Down" or "Up"))
end)
```

Creating Slash Commands

World of Warcraft players interact daily with slash commands. Whether it's `/ignore Ikeelyou` or a hasty `/gquit` after ninja looting Kael'thas on your guild's first takedown, you're using slash commands.

As an addon author, you'll often find it easier or just plain useful to have slash commands to either spur your addon to action or to enable configuration. Generally speaking, it's much quicker to write out a quick slash command system than to have a fully functioning graphical configuration screen.

Creating Basic Slash Commands

WoW provides a fairly straightforward way to implement slash commands. They require two basic components: a set of global variables for the commands and a handler function in a global table. Here is a quick example:

```
SLASH_FANCYPRINT1 = "/fancyprint"
SlashCmdList["FANCYPRINT"] = function(msg)
  print("|cff11ff11" .. Printed:|r " .. msg)
end
```

Once you've run that code, type the following in the chat frame's edit box:

```
/fancyprint This is my first slash command!
```

You should see a message printed to the chat frame that says, "This is my first slash command!", after a green heading that says "Printed".

Now take a look at the process that made this possible. WoW stores all the slash command handlers in a table called `SlashCmdList`. The table is indexed by arbitrary strings determined by the addon author. These indexes are used to construct global variable names of the following format:

```
SLASH_INDEXn
```

In the previous example, the index is FANCYPRINT and the global variable is SLASH_FANCYPRINT1. When you ran the slash command, WoW started looking through all the entries in SlashCmdList. For each entry in the list, the system started counting up from 1 and looked at the constructed global variables that might match. As soon as it looked at SLASH_MESSAGE1 and saw the match, it ran the associated function from SlashCmdList, passing all of the text provided to the command.

This arrangement allows for great flexibility. Type SLASH_FANCYPRINT2 = "/fp" in WowLua and then try using that slash command with /fp I created a slash command alias. Again you should see a message pop up with those words.

As you just saw, incrementing the number in the global variable allows for multiple slash commands to be aliased to the same handler. This also comes in handy for localization.

So just to recap, here's a checklist for creating slash commands:

- Create a handler function that takes a single string parameter.

- Pick a unique index name (ideally something that contains the addon's name, to avoid collisions) and add the function to SlashCmdList.

- Create one or more global variables named SLASH_INDEXn containing the slash commands.

As you can see, creating slash commands is the easy part. Getting them to do anything less trivial than the preceding example is another story. Remember that anything the user types in after the slash command is passed as a single string to the handler. To do anything useful with it, you'll have to do some basic string parsing. The rest of this chapter focuses on a few simple techniques.

> **WARNING** The slash command system keeps a cache of the commands you use during a session, which reduces the impact of macros on game performance. It also means that if you try to overwrite a SlashCmdList entry without reloading the UI you need to update the cache. For example, if you use the slash command you created in WowLua, then make a change to the code and execute the script, WoW will try to use the original function the next time you run the command.
>
> You can run the following code manually or add it to the end of your script:
>
> ```
> wipe(hash_SlashCmdList)
> ```

This is necessary only if you are making a change to a slash command handler that you have already defined. It is not necessary when you're first creating your new command.

The details of the cache are beyond the scope of this chapter, but the general technique is described in Appendix A. You can also see the command handling code for yourself in `FrameXML\ChatFrame.lua`.

Tokenizing Strings

Tokenization is the process of dividing a string into smaller pieces called *tokens* based on certain rules. One of the simplest ways to accomplish this is with the WoW-specific function `string.split` (or `strsplit`). This function splits a string at occurrences of given delimiters. For example:

```
string.split(" ", "1 + 3 * 5")
```

This splits the given string at every space (the delimiter), returning the tokens `"1"`, `"+"`, `"3"`, `"*"`, and `"5"`.

As the example hints, you can create a simple calculator using this technique. Create a new addon with just a Lua file or open up WowLua. To keep the calculator simple, it will recognize only four operators: addition (+), subtraction (−), multiplication (*), and division (/). Furthermore, there will be no order of precedence of operations. In other words, $1 + 3 * 5 = 20$, not 16.

The operations themselves are contained in a table indexed by the operator. Enter the following code into WowLua or the new addon you created:

```
local operators = {
  ["+"] = function(a, b)
    return a + b
  end,
  ["-"] = function(a, b)
    return a - b
  end,
  ["*"] = function(a, b)
    return a * b
  end,
  ["/"] = function(a, b)
    return a / b
  end
}
```

Each operator simply accepts two numbers and returns the result of the operation. Because all the operations proceed in order of occurrence, your main calculation function can simply iterate through the returns of `string.split` as follows:

```
local function calculate(number1, ...)
  for i = 1, select("#", ...), 2 do
    local operator, number2 = select(i, ...)
    number1 = operators[operator](number1, number2)
  end

  return number1
end
```

The first number is placed into the variable `number1`. The loop begins by retrieving the first operator and the second number. Then it calls the appropriate operator function with the two given numbers and assigns the new value to `number1`. Each time through the loop it picks a new operator and second number, and performs the calculation. Once it passes the last parameter, the function returns the final value of `number1`.

Now all that's left is to create the slash command to split the message and print the result of the calculation:

```
SLASH_SIMPLECALC1 = "/calculate"
SLASH_SIMPLECALC2 = "/calc"
SlashCmdList["SIMPLECALC"] = function(message)
  print(calculate(string.split(" ", message)))
end
```

Run the script or load the addon and you should be able to use the slash commands as expected. Here are some examples:

```
/calculate 1 + 3 * 5
20
/calc 3 * 2 + 4 / 5.5
1.8181818181818
/calc 4
4
```

Obviously this is functional, but it has a couple of pitfalls. Because the string is split at every occurrence of the space character, it's as if there is an empty string between any two consecutive spaces. For example:

```
/calculate 3  + 4
Error: attempt to call field '?' (a nil value)
```

With the extra space between the 3 and the +, the string is split into the tokens `"3"`, `""`, `"+"`, `"4"`. This means the `calculate` function tries to use `""` as an index to the `operators` table, which is obviously an error. A similar problem occurs if you omit a space:

```
/calc 3+4 * 5
Error: attempt to perform arithmetic on local 'a' (a string value)
```

Here the string is tokenized into `"3+4"`, `"*"`, and `"5"`. The `calculate` function tries to call the multiplication operator with `"3+4"` as one of the numbers, again an obvious error.

Although these drawbacks affect the usability of this calculator addon, splitting on spaces is still sufficient for many purposes. Later in this chapter you'll use this technique again but in a much more powerful way. For now, let's relax the syntax for the calculator addon.

Tokenizing with Patterns

Parsing strings is a topic that can fill a volume in its own right. Many different techniques exist depending on the complexity of your rules. Entire computer languages have been designed specifically to describe the syntax of other languages. Although a full treatment is obviously beyond the scope of this book, we can at least show you some of the tricks Lua brings to the table.

Chapter 6 provided a glimpse of Lua patterns that enable you to look for specific arrangements of characters within a string. Now you'll use them to identify individual components of the calculator commands.

Setting Up the Patterns

First you should put the syntax of the commands into more definite terms. The format for these commands is as follows:

```
number [ operator number [ operator number [ ... ] ]
```

This gives you the overall structure you need to follow when parsing the string. Later you design the parsing functions to follow this general pattern. Next you need to break down the format of each component. Operators are simply one of the four operator characters. Numbers are a bit more complex:

```
[sign][digits][decimal]digits
```

From here, you can easily construct the patterns for each component. To keep the code flexible, you won't use a specialized pattern for the operators.

Instead you'll simply match any single character and check whether it's in the list of operators. This means the pattern is simply a single period (.).

Table 17-1 shows the subpatterns that are used to create the final pattern of `"[+-]?%d*%.?%d+"` (see Chapter 6 for details).

Table 17-1: Number Subpatterns

COMPONENT	PATTERN
sign (optional)	`[+-]?`
digits (optional)	`%d*`
decimal (optional)	`%.?`
digits (required)	`%d+`

Now add the following code above any of the existing functions:

```
local NUMBER_PATTERN = "^%s*([+-]?%d*%.?%d+)"
local OPERATOR_PATTERN = "^%s*(.)"
local END_PATTERN = "^%s*$"
```

Because the calculator will allow any amount of whitespace between numbers and operators, you put the target pattern inside parentheses to make it a capture and precede it with a check for the optional whitespace: `%s*`. Notice that you specify the beginning of the string immediately before the whitespace (^). If this weren't in there, the pattern might skip over invalid syntax until it finds a piece of valid syntax. Consider the following example:

```
/calculate 5 + should error here 5
10
```

After processing the plus sign, your code would try to match the number pattern against the string " `should error here 5`". Without the start-of-string check, the pattern will find a match at the end of the string: " `5`", completely ignoring the extraneous words.

You'll also notice that we've added a pattern called END_PATTERN to handle any extra space at the end of the command.

Preparing for the Tokenization

One helpful side-effect of doing in-depth parsing is the ease with which you can check for errors. In this calculator addon two possible errors exist: missing/invalid number or unrecognized operator. Add the following error strings after the patterns you just created:

```
local NUMBER_ERROR = "No valid number at position %d"
local OPERATOR_ERROR = "Unrecognized operator at position %d: '%s'"
```

Errors are indicated by a flag called `errorState`, which is set by a custom `error` function. Add the following code immediately before the `calculate` function:

```
local errorState = false

local function reportError(message)
  print(message)
  errorState = true
end
```

Now edit the `calculate` function to look like the following:

```
local function calculate(number1, ...)
  if errorState then
    return
  end

  for i = 1, select("#", ...), 2 do
    local operatorFunction, number2 = select(i, ...)
    number1 = operatorFunction(number1, number2)
  end

  return number1
end
```

If you're already in an error state, then you just return and do nothing. The last change you need to make before diving into the heart of the string parsing is to clear the error state before calling the calculate function, and replace the `string.split` call with the new tokenize function you'll be creating:

```
SlashCmdList["SIMPLECALC"] = function(message)
  errorState = false
  print(calculate(tokenize(message)))
end
```

Parsing the Formula

The calculator formulas start off with a number and then are an optional repetition of operator/number pairs. Your main `tokenize` function will pick up the first number and then call a second recursive function, `getpairs`, to . . . well . . . get the subsequent pairs.

Add the `tokenize` function before the `SlashCmdList` entry with the following code:

```
local function tokenize(message)
  local _, finish, number = message:find(NUMBER_PATTERN)
  if not number then
    reportError(NUMBER_ERROR:format(1))
    return
  end
```

The first line runs `string.find` to look for the first number in the formula (remember every string has the `string` table as its metatable). If it doesn't find a number, it prints the error and returns. Finish the function with the following code:

```
    finish = finish + 1
    if message:match(END_PATTERN, finish) == "" then
      return number
    else
      return number, getpairs(message, finish)
    end
  end
```

The `finish` variable contains the position of the last character in the found number. In other words, if the formula is "102 + 5", `finish` would be 3, corresponding to the 2 in 102. The first line of this code increments `finish` by one to indicate the start of the rest of the message.

Next it looks for END_PATTERN in the message, starting at the new location. If it matches, `tokenize` returns the number it found. Otherwise it returns the number and calls `getpairs` to parse the rest of the message. Begin this function just above `tokenize`:

```
local function getpairs(message, start)
  local _, operatorFinish, operator = message:find(OPERATOR_PATTERN, ↵
start)
  local operatorFunction = operators[operator]
  if not operatorFunction then
    reportError(OPERATOR_ERROR:format(start, operator))
    return
  end
```

As you can see, this checks for a valid operator and triggers an error if it's not recognized. Next, search for a number from the position just past the operator:

```
  operatorFinish = operatorFinish + 1
  local _, numberFinish, number = message:find(NUMBER_PATTERN, ↵
operatorFinish)
  if not number then
    reportError(NUMBER_ERROR:format(operatorFinish))
    return
  end
```

And finally, finish the function just like `tokenize`:

```
  numberFinish = numberFinish + 1
  if message:match(END_PATTERN, numberFinish) then
    return operatorFunction, number
  else
```

```
        return operatorFunction, number, getpairs(message, numberFinish)
    end
end
```

After reloading, you can see the earlier errors are now fixed, and bona fide errors have sane messages:

/calculate 3 + 4
7
/calc 3+4 * 5
35
/calc 3+ 4 +
No valid number at position 7
/calc 3 + 4 & 9
Unrecognized operator at position 7: `&'

Using a Command Table

Some addons provide a single slash command with multiple, possibly nested subcommands. For example, to show the GUI for Omen, you would use the following command:

```
/omen gui show
```

You can easily create this kind of functionality with a relatively simple parsing system that uses a table to represent the command hierarchy. The parser you develop here uses a table indexed with the name of the commands.

Each entry in the table is a string, a function, or a table. If the command is a string value, it is printed as-is. If the command is a function, the parser calls the function with the rest of the slash command's message. If the command is a table, the parser treats it as another command table and processes the rest of the message against it. If the command isn't found, the parser looks for an entry called "help" and processes it as usual.

Go ahead and create a new addon with just a Lua file and enter the following example table:

```lua
local testCommandTable = {
  ["gui"] = {
    ["width"] = function(width)
      print("Setting width to", width)
    end,
    ["height"] = function(height)
      print("Setting height to", height)
    end,
    ["show"] = function()
      print("Showing")
```

```
      end,
      ["hide"] = function()
        print("Hiding")
      end,
      ["help"] = "GUI commands: width <width>, height <height>, show, ↵
 hide"
    },
    ["data"] = {
      ["load"] = function(profile)
        print("Loading profile:", profile)
      end,
      ["save"] = function(profile)
        print("Saving profile: ", profile)
      end,
      ["reset"] = function()
        print("Resetting to default")
      end,
      ["help"] = "Data commands: load <profile>, save <profile>, reset"
    },
    ["help"] = "CommandTable commands: gui, data"
  }
```

As you can see, this is a very concise way of defining a wide range of functionality. That is, once you get the engine out of the way. Begin the command processing function with the following code:

```
local function DispatchCommand(message, commandTable)
  local command, parameters = string.split(" ", message, 2)
  local entry = commandTable[command:lower()]
  local which = type(entry)
```

The first line of the function splits the message at the first space. Notice the extra argument of 2, which tells `string.split` to return a maximum of two strings, limiting the number of splits.

The next line retrieves the entry from the given command table, then the function determines what type of entry it is. The rest of the function is essentially a restatement in Lua of our earlier description:

```
if which == "function" then
  entry(parameters)
elseif which == "table" then
  DispatchCommand(parameters or "", entry)
elseif which == "string" then
  print(entry)
elseif message ~= "help" then
  DispatchCommand("help", commandTable)
end
end
```

Now all you need to do is tie it together with a slash command:

```
SLASH_COMMANDTABLE1 = "/commandtable"
SLASH_COMMANDTABLE2 = "/cmdtbl"
SlashCmdList["COMMANDTABLE"] = function(message)
  DispatchCommand(message, testCommandTable)
end
```

And voila! Twenty-one lines of code later and you have a powerful slash command handler that uses a simple table for configuration. Here is some sample output:

```
/cmdtbl gui show
Showing
/commandtable data
Data commands: load <profile>, save <profile>, reset
/cmdtbl GUI Width 13
Setting width to 13
```

Summary

In this chapter you learned the basics of slash commands and how to get a barebones command up and running. You also examined a set of tips and tricks you can use to make your code more flexible and cleaner. Slash commands aren't flashy, and in some circles they get a bad rap, but they're powerful, flexible, and, if implemented correctly, elegant. One very powerful aspect of slash commands versus graphical configuration interfaces is that slash commands can be used in macros, allowing users to change their settings on-the-fly using buttons on their action bars.

The Code

SlashCalc

```
local NUMBER_PATTERN = "^%s*([+-]?%d*%.?%d+)"
local OPERATOR_PATTERN = "^%s*(.)"
local END_PATTERN = "^%s*$"

local NUMBER_ERROR = "No valid number at position %d"
local OPERATOR_ERROR = "Unrecognized operator at position %d: '%s'"

local errorState = false
```

```lua
local function reportError(message)
  print(message)
  errorState = true
end


local operators = {
  ["+"] = function(a, b)
    return a + b
  end,
  ["-"] = function(a, b)
    return a - b
  end,
  ["*"] = function(a, b)
    return a * b
  end,
  ["/"] = function(a, b)
    return a / b
  end
}

local function calculate(number1, ...)
  if errorState then
    return
  end

  for i = 1, select("#", ...), 2 do
    local operatorFunc, number2 = select(i, ...)
    number1 = operatorFunc(number1, number2)
  end

  return number1
end

local function getpairs(message, start)
  local _, operatorFinish, operator = ↵
message:find(OPERATOR_PATTERN, start)
  local operatorFunction = operators[operator]
  if not operatorFunction then
    reportError(OPERATOR_ERROR:format(start, operator))
    return
  end

  operatorFinish = operatorFinish + 1
  local _, numberFinish, number = message:find(NUMBER_PATTERN, ↵
operatorFinish)
  if not number then
    reportError(NUMBER_ERROR:format(operatorFinish))
    return
  end
```

```
    numberFinish = numberFinish + 1
    if message:match(END_PATTERN, numberFinish) then
      return operatorFunction, number
    else
      return operatorFunction, number, getpairs(message, ↵
numberFinish)
    end
  end

  local function tokenize(message)
    local _, finish, number = message:find(NUMBER_PATTERN)
    if not number then
      reportError(NUMBER_ERROR:format(1))
      return
    end
    finish = finish + 1
    if message:match(END_PATTERN, finish) == "" then
      return number
    else
      return number, getpairs(message, finish)
    end
  end


  SLASH_SIMPLECALC1 = "/calculate"
  SLASH_SIMPLECALC2 = "/calc"
  SlashCmdList["SIMPLECALC"] = function(message)
    errorState = false
    print(calculate(tokenize(message)))
  end
```

## CHAPTER 18

Responding to Graphic Updates with OnUpdate

Although most code written in World of Warcraft is event-based, in certain situations code should be run more frequently (possibly based on time). Although there is no simple API method to accomplish this in World of Warcraft, you can use OnUpdate scripts to fill these needs.

For example you can use OnUpdate scripts to do the following:

- Delay code by a set amount of time.
- Group events that fire rapidly together into a single batch to process.
- Run code repeatedly, with time in between.

This chapter introduces the graphic update system that drives OnUpdate scripts, and leads you through creating simple addons to implement each of these scripts.

Understanding Graphic Updates

A standard measure for graphics performance in a game like World of Warcraft is your *framerate*, which is measured in frames per second (FPS). The graphics engine redraws the screen that many times to show changes to the interface and the game world. You can view your framerate (see Figure 18-1) by pressing Ctrl+R.

Every time the screen is redrawn, the OnUpdate script fires for any frame that is visible (even if it has no graphical components). In addition, the arguments to the script tell you how much time has passed since the last screen refresh. Together, these can be used to make a very primitive (but effective) timer.

Figure 18-1: Framerate being displayed in-game

Delaying Code Using OnUpdate

Say you have a function, such as one that says a random witty phrase, that you want to run in the future. You can write a helper function that uses an OnUpdate script to run code in the future. Run the following code in-game:

```
if not DelayFrame then
  DelayFrame = CreateFrame("Frame")
  DelayFrame:Hide()
end

function Delay(delay, func)
  DelayFrame.func = func
  DelayFrame.delay = delay
  DelayFrame:Show()
end

DelayFrame:SetScript("OnUpdate", function(self, elapsed)
  self.delay = self.delay - elapsed
  if self.delay <= 0 then
    self:Hide()
    self.func()
  end
end)
```

This code defines a new function called Delay() that takes a time in seconds, and a function to be run. It sets up the DelayFrame and when the correct amount of time has passed it calls the function. The following defines a little bit of code that uses this function to send taunting messages during combat:

```
if not TauntFrame then
  TauntFrame = CreateFrame("Frame")
end

local tauntMessages = {
  "Is that the best you can do?",
  "My grandmother can hit harder than that!",
  "Now you're making me angry!",
  "Was that supposed to hurt?",
  "Vancleef pay big for your head!",
  "You too slow! Me too strong!",
}
```

```
TauntFrame.CHANCE = 0.5      -- Chance that a message will happen
TauntFrame.DELAY = 3.0       -- Maximum delay before a message is sent

local isDelayed = false
local function sendTauntMessage()
  local msgId = math.random(#tauntMessages)
  SendChatMessage(tauntMessages[msgId], "SAY")
  isDelayed = false
end

TauntFrame:RegisterEvent("UNIT_COMBAT")
TauntFrame:SetScript("OnEvent", function(self, event, unit, action, ...)
  if unit == "player" and action ~= "HEAL" and not isDelayed then
    local chance = math.random(100)
    if chance <= (100 * self.CHANCE) then
      local delayTime = math.random() * self.DELAY
      Delay(delayTime, sendTauntMessage)
      isDelayed = true
    end
  end
end)
```

First this code creates a frame so it can register events, and then it defines a small table of taunting messages. Next, two simple configuration variables are created and stored within the new frame. A function is created to actually handle the choosing and sending of messages.

When the player is hit in combat and there isn't already a delayed message waiting to be sent, you generate a random number between 1 and 100. If this number is less than or equal to 100 times the configured chance, the sendTauntMessage() function is scheduled for a random time in the future. Figure 18-2 shows this addon in action.

Figure 18-2: Taunt messages being sent during combat

The chance for the message to trigger, as well as the delay, can be configured while the code is running by changing *TauntFrame.CHANCE* and *TauntFrame.DELAY* to new values. You can experiment to find a balance that is good for you.

Grouping Events to Avoid Over-Processing

The following simple bit of code watches the player's inventory and warns him when it falls below a certain threshold. You can use the BAG_UPDATE event to watch for changes to the player's bags.

```
if not BagWatchFrame then
    BagWatchFrame = CreateFrame("Frame")
end

BagWatchFrame.WARN_LEVEL = 0.2
BagWatchFrame.message = "You are running low on bag space!"
BagWatchFrame.fullMessage = "Your bags are full!"

local function bagWatch_OnEvent(self, event, bag, ...)
    local maxSlots, freeSlots = 0, 0

    for idx = 0, 4 do
        maxSlots = maxSlots + GetContainerNumSlots(idx)
        freeSlots = freeSlots + GetContainerNumFreeSlots(idx)
    end

    local percFree = freeSlots / maxSlots
    local msg

    if percFree == self.percFree then
        -- Don't warn the user at the same level more than once
    elseif percFree == 0 then
        msg = BagWatchFrame.fullMessage
    elseif percFree <= self.WARN_LEVEL then
        msg = BagWatchFrame.message
    end
    if msg then?
        RaidNotice_AddMessage(RaidWarningFrame, msg, ↵
ChatTypeInfo["RAID_WARNING"])
    end
    self.percFree = percFree
end

BagWatchFrame:RegisterEvent("BAG_UPDATE")
BagWatchFrame:SetScript("OnEvent", bagWatch_OnEvent)
```

This code is set to warn the player when he has less than 20% of his bag space free. It uses the GetContainerNumSlots() and GetContainerNumFreeSlots() functions to determine how much space each bag has, and how much is free. When the percentage of free slots is less than BagWatchFrame.WARN_LEVEL, the code calls RaidNotice_AddMessage() to add a message to the raid notice frame. Figure 18-3 shows the addon warning as the player fills his last two slots.

Figure 18-3: Free slot warning displayed in the RaidWarningFrame

There is a problem with this code that can be seen when using the Equipment Manager. The Equipment Manager is a system that allows you to save multiple gear sets, and switch them with a single button. That's accomplished by rapidly equipping (or un-equipping) items as necessary. The Equipment Manager is disabled by default, but can be enabled on the Controls menu under Interface Options.

Depending on your latency to the server, the number of items you are equipping or un-equipping, and the number of slots you have free in your bags, you may find this code warning you multiple times for the same equipment change. That is because the BAG_UPDATE event is firing more than once in a short period of time. You can use an OnUpdate to help fix this problem, as you see in the next section.

Grouping Multiple Events

The original code can be altered to not immediately trigger the bag scan, but instead to schedule it for some time in the future using an OnUpdate. Edit the code as follows, noting the highlighted differences from the previous version:

```
if not BagWatchFrame then
   BagWatchFrame = CreateFrame("Frame")
end


BagWatchFrame.THROTTLE = 0.5
BagWatchFrame.WARN_LEVEL = 0.2
BagWatchFrame.message = "You are running low on bag space!"
BagWatchFrame.fullMessage = "Your bags are full!"

local function bagWatch_ScanBags(frame)
   local maxSlots, freeSlots = 0, 0

   for idx = 0, 4 do
      maxSlots = maxSlots + GetContainerNumSlots(idx)
      freeSlots = freeSlots + GetContainerNumFreeSlots(idx)
   end

   local percFree = freeSlots / maxSlots
   local msg

   if percFree == frame.percFree then
```

```
            -- Don't warn the user at the same level more than once
        elseif percFree == 0 then
            msg = frame.fullMessage
        elseif percFree <= frame.WARN_LEVEL then
            msg = frame.message
        end
        if msg then
            RaidNotice_AddMessage(RaidWarningFrame, msg, ↵
ChatTypeInfo["RAID_WARNING"])
        end
        frame.percFree = percFree
    end

BagWatchFrame:RegisterEvent("BAG_UPDATE")
local counter = 0
BagWatchFrame:SetScript("OnUpdate", function(self, elapsed)
        counter = counter + elapsed
        if counter >= self.THROTTLE then
            bagWatch_ScanBags(self)
            counter = 0
            self:Hide()
        end
end)
BagWatchFrame:SetScript("OnEvent", function(self, event, ...)
        BagWatchFrame:Show()
end)
```

Rather than calling the bag scan function (which has been renamed) directly, the OnEvent handler just shows BagWatchFrame, causing the OnUpdate script to fire. Once the configured amount of time has passed (in this case 0.5 seconds), the bag scan will occur. This means that even if several BAG_UPDATE events fire within that half-second period, the scan will only be run once.

Repeating Code with OnUpdate

You can also use OnUpdate scripts to run code repeatedly in order to perform some periodic calculation. For example, you could alter the CombatTracker addon you created in Chapter 14 to update the frame every second or so during combat, giving you a running average instead of only displaying at the end.

Add the following function to the end of CombatTracker.lua:

```
local throttle = 1.0
local counter = 0
function CombatTracker_OnUpdate(self, elapsed)
    counter = counter + elapsed
    if counter >= throttle then
```

```
        CombatTracker_UpdateText()
        counter = 0
    end
end
```

Finally, you should set the OnUpdate script when the player enters combat, and clear it when the player leaves combat. Under the PLAYER_REGEN_ENABLED condition in CombatTracker_OnEvent(), add the following:

```
frame:SetScript("OnUpdate", nil)
```

Within the PLAYER_REGEN_DISABLED condition, add this line:

```
frame:SetScript("OnUpdate", CombatTracker_OnUpdate)
```

Now as long as you are in combat the calculation will be updated every second.

Considering Performance with OnUpdate Scripts

Remember that the code in your OnUpdate handler is called on every screen update. If the screen refreshes at 60 frames per second, then your script will be called 60 times per second. As a result you should be sure to consider performance when writing your functions. Don't over-scrutinize your code into some monster, but be aware that a poorly written OnUpdate script can affect the frame rate of the client. In particular you should consider the following:

- The game client runs code sequentially. As a result, all OnUpdate scripts are run before the client continues to process events or update the graphics.
- If your function does not need to run every screen refresh, you can use a throttle to introduce a delay.
- Local variables are faster than global variables, so you can squeeze out a bit of extra performance by using them.

Summary

This chapter discussed using OnUpdate scripts to introduce delays or run code periodically. You created a number of small addons that use OnUpdate scripts to perform various tasks.

The next chapter introduces you to function hooking, and using a combination of an OnUpdate timer and function hooking to alter the default user interface.

Altering Existing Behavior with Function Hooking

Most addons are designed as self-contained additions to the default user interface. These addons make use of the provided API and the frames and functionality in the default user interface. Sometimes, however, it makes sense to alter the existing behavior of the UI. One way that can be accomplished is known as *function hooking*. This chapter introduces the concept of function hooking, including specific rules to follow and pitfalls to avoid.

What Is Function Hooking?

"Hooking a function" is mostly just a fancy way of saying "changing the behavior of a function." Like any other Lua variable, you can overwrite a function value with a new one of your creation. Then, any time code tries to call the function, it will use yours instead. More specifically, though, function hooking means that the original function still runs, at least when a function hook behaves properly.

Function hooks are used to alter the behavior of an existing function in one of the following ways:

- Altering the arguments to or the return values from the original function.
- Preventing the original function from running.
- Taking extra action each time the function is called.

The following code, for example, adds a timestamp to any messages that are added to the default chat frame via the `ChatFrame1:AddMessage()` function:

```
local origAddMessage = ChatFrame1.AddMessage

function ChatFrame1.AddMessage(self, text, ...)
  local timestamp = date("%X")
  text = string.format("%s %s", timestamp, text)
  return origAddMessage(self, text, ...)
end
```

The first code line takes the function referenced by `ChatFrame1.AddMessage` and stores it in the local variable `origAddMessage`. Then, a new function is created in its place. The new function gets the current time of day and adds it to the text argument. Finally, it calls the original function `origAddMessage`, passing it the modified text.

There are a couple important points to note in the example. First, the new function takes a variable number of arguments. The purpose of this is twofold. Selfishly, it allows you to only pay attention to the first couple of parameters. More importantly, though, it prevents the function from breaking expected behavior. If the number or order of parameters ever changes in the default UI's `AddMessage` function, as long as the text remains in the same position, your hook will still operate as expected, and will play nicely with other code that uses it.

The other point to note is that the results of `origAddMessage` are returned as the last step. That may seem a bit redundant because at the time of this writing `AddMessage` does not return anything. However, like the use of vararg, this practice future-proofs your function in case the default UI begins expecting a return value. In general if you need to hook a function, someone else may also and you should be prepared to make your replacement act like the original function as much as possible.

Modifying Return Values

There are two basic types of function hooking. The preceding example is what's known as a *pre-hook*, indicating that the hook takes its primary action before triggering the original function. This is directly visible in the code with the call to (and return from) `origAddMessage` as the last step.

A *post-hook*, on the other hand, does its business after the original function returns. That can allow you to change return values from the function, altering the behavior of any code that calls it. You can, of course, combine the two techniques, although the differentiation will prove useful when you start dealing with secure hooks.

Post-hooks can be a bit trickier to get right using the preceding techniques. First you must call the original function and store the results so you can alter them before finally returning them. Your first inclination may be to store them in a table, but that is difficult to do properly when the function can return `nil` values.

The following sections show two different methods of getting around this limitation when creating a function hook. These examples both work as a simple "piggy bank" for World of Warcraft. The `GetMoney()` function is hooked and the result is altered. When you open your backpack, the amount of gold displayed will be different than the actual amount you have on hand. The amount of the adjustment will be controlled by the global variable `SAVED_MONEY`, which will be subtracted from the real amount of money you have.

These examples won't prevent you from spending the money in your invisible store; in fact, if your character has less than `SAVED_MONEY` money (1 gold in the preceding example), your backpack display may show a nonsense value because the money frames aren't designed to show negative values.

Using a Variable Argument Function

In reality you only care about the first return from the `GetMoney()` function because at the moment it only has one. You can create a pair of functions that allows easy access that value while still being able to return any others that may be added in the future.

```
SAVED_MONEY = 10000
local origGetMoney = GetMoney

local function newGetMoney(realMoney, ...)
  return realMoney - SAVED_MONEY, ...
end

function GetMoney(...)
  return newGetMoney(origGetMoney(...))
end
```

First you define the new variable `SAVED_MONEY`, and store a reference to the original `GetMoney()` function. Next you create a helper function that will take in the returns from the original function, altering the first one by subtracting `SAVED_MONEY` from it, and returning the rest. You then create the new global function `GetMoney()`, which calls the helper, passing in the results of calling the original.

Using Utility Functions capture() and release()

The following method could potentially use a bit more memory and be less efficient, but provides an easy way to handle storing the return values of a function so they can be examined and possibly altered. The trick is centered on replacing `nil` values with a special marker value so the normal table processing functions work. The `capture()` function is defined as follows:

```
function capture(...)
  return { select("#", ...), ...}
end
```

`capture()` captures the results in a table, but adds the number of arguments to the first slot in the table. That way, when the release function needs to return the results, it can consult that value to ensure it returns all of the arguments. The release function is defined as follows:

```
function release(tbl, index)
local size = tbl[1]
  index = index or 2
  if index <= size then
    return tbl[index], release(tbl, index + 1)
  end
end
```

Releasing the arguments is a bit more difficult, but still straightforward. First, the function takes a second argument that defaults to 2, ensuring that when the developer calls `release()`, he'll get everything starting with the second slot (remember that the number of arguments stored is in the first slot). You check to make sure the index is in the right range, and begin returning the results.

These functions can then be used as follows:

```
SAVED_MONEY = 10000
local origGetMoney = GetMoney

function GetMoney(...)
  local result = capture(origGetMoney(...))
  result[1] = result[1] - SAVED_MONEY
  return release(result)
end
```

Although both of these methods may seem overly complex, they will give you the most future-proof code. Function hooking is not something that is used regularly in writing addons, and care must be taken when it is being used.

Hooking Widget Scripts

Hooks are often used when dealing with frame scripts. For example, your addon may want to react to the click of some button in the default UI while still allowing the button to behave normally. Consider the Abandon Quest button in the Quest Log that enables you to drop a quest from your log. It currently pops up a confirmation dialog but doesn't give any specific warning when a quest is already complete.

The first step in a frame script hook is to use the `GetScript` method to retrieve the function currently used by the script handler:

```
local origOnClick = QuestLogFrameAbandonButton:GetScript("OnClick")
```

The `GetScript()` method returns either a reference to the function handler, or `nil` if no handler is currently set. This is equivalent to the first line of each of the last two examples.

WARNING Always check to see if a script is already set before replacing it, even if the frame you're hooking doesn't normally specify one. Another addon may be interested in the same button you are, and blindly replacing the script would break that other addon. If there is no original function, you can skip that step in your new function — but always check.

Next you need to create the replacement function:

```
local msg = "*** WARNING! YOU ARE ABOUT TO ABANDON A COMPLETED QUEST ***"

local function newOnClick(...)
  local questIndex = GetQuestLogSelection()
  local completed = select(7, GetQuestLogTitle(questIndex))
  if completed then
    RaidNotice_AddMessage(RaidWarningFrame, msg, ↵
ChatTypeInfo["RAID_WARNING"])
  end

  if origOnClick then
   return origOnClick(...)
  end
end
```

The code to check and warn in this situation is relatively simple. First, you use the `GetQuestLogSelection()` function to get the current selected quest index, and then use `GetQuestLogTitle()` to determine whether you have completed it yet. If so, it prints the warning and then dispatches the call to the original handler function.

Now that you have the replacement function, you need to set it as the new `OnClick` handler for the frame:

```
QuestLogFrameAbandonButton:SetScript("OnClick", newOnClick)
```

Hooking a Function Securely

As Chapter 15 showed, mucking around with variables that are used by the default UI can cause any number of problems due to taint. You may need to hook a (seemingly benign) function for your addon, but if it's used in any secure code paths, the taint can have far-reaching effects.

Most times, you can accomplish your task without changing its behavior. For this purpose, WoW provides a `hooksecurefunc` function that creates a taint-free post-hook. Because the hook runs after the original function, you cannot change the original function's behavior. Furthermore, any returns from your hook are discarded so you cannot change the behavior of code that calls the hook. The signature for `hooksecurefunc` is as follows:

```
hooksecurefunc([table,] functionName, hookFunction)
```

Note that you can only hook functions with global names or that are members of a table. For example, the following code prints a message every time you press an action button or otherwise trigger `UseAction`.

```
hooksecurefunc("UseAction", function(slot, unit)
  ChatFrame1:AddMessage(format(
    "You used action %d on %s",
    slot, unit or "<no unit>"
  ))
end)
```

To hook a table method securely, simply add the table as the first argument. For example, say you want to be notified when any code calls the `Show` method on a frame.

Hooking the `Show` method on a frame is a bit different from responding to the `OnShow` widget script. For example, if the frame is already shown and an addon calls the `Show` method, this hook will respond, whereas the `OnShow` script will not fire.

The following code prints a message any time you try to show `someFrame`:

```
hooksecurefunc(someFrame, "Show", function(self)
  ChatFrame1:AddMessage("Attempting to show someFrame")
end)
```

In both of these examples that you are much freer with regard to parameters and returns. Because the returns are discarded and changing any arguments has no effect on the rest of the code path, you can arrange your function in whatever way makes the most sense.

Hooking Scripts Securely

Reacting to a widget handler call without changing its behavior is actually simpler than the "normal" hook method you saw earlier. Analogous to `hooksecurefunc`, every widget has a `HookScript` method that achieves essentially the same result. Your new hook will be called with all the same arguments after the original script, and any returns will be discarded. For example, the following will safely hook the `OnClick` handler of your player frame, keeping track of each time the button is clicked:

```
clickCounter = 0
PlayerFrame:HookScript("OnClick", function()
  clickCounter = clickCounter + 1
  print(clickCounter, "clicks and counting...")
end)
```

This hook only applies to the specified button (to capture every secure button click, use `hooksecurefunc` on `SecureActionButton_OnClick` instead). You don't even need to worry about checking if a script is already set; `HookScript` will handle that for you!

Deciding When to Hook

Although function hooks are undoubtedly a useful tool, they do have a few important caveats. These range from performance issues to the potential breakage of elements in the default UI or other addons. In many cases, function hooking is unnecessary, and there are less obtrusive alternatives.

Understanding the Hook Chain

To fully appreciate some of the problems that can arise from sloppy hooking, think for a moment what would happen if two addons hooked the same function. Take the `GetMoney` example from earlier. When any piece of code calls `GetMoney`, it first activates the hook from your addon, and then your addon calls the original function. If another addon comes along and hooks it again, another link is added to the *hook chain*. The hook chain is simply a way to visualize the interaction between the two addons and the base function. In this example it looks like the following:

```
Other Addon → Your Addon → Built-in GetMoney
```

Secure hooks (via `hooksecurefunc` and `HookScript`) don't really follow the same chain analogy. Instead, they're more like a key ring where each hook is a key. After the function does its business, the secure hook system goes through each hook one by one, executing them independently. This does not make them immune to the following problems, though.

You Can't Rely on Order

Your addon has no way of knowing the order in which the hooks take place. If the other addon is loaded before yours, the hook chain would look like this instead:

```
Your Addon → Other Addon → Built-in GetMoney
```

Never rely on your addon being in a certain place in the chain. The order of addon loading is controlled entirely by the game engine. You can buy a little bit of leeway with dependencies and such, but that requires knowing in advance the name of every addon that might interfere. If you find yourself in a situation where the order matters, you should probably re-evaluate the overall design of your addon.

There Is No "Unhook"

Another issue the hook chain brings to the table is that it's dangerous to "unhook" a function. With the earlier hook chain, if you were to remove your hook by running `GetMoney = origGetMoney`, you would also be removing the hook from the other addon because your `origGetMoney` was stored before the other addon got a chance to hook it. More fundamentally, secure hooks are impossible to remove; the API simply does not have any facility for it.

If you do need to unhook a function, it's best to simply check a flag in your hook and change the flag whenever you need to apply or remove the hook. Of course, that leads to the next potential problem.

Hooking Hits Performance

Each hook on a given function adds a new layer of function calls. In pseudo-code, that looks like this:

```
LastHook(...)
  AnotherHook(...)
    SecondHook(...)
      FirstHook(...)
        OriginalFunction(...)
        return ...
      return ...
    return ...
  return ...
```

At each new level, Lua has to copy the arguments so that it can call the next function, and then copy the return values as they come back out. With secure hooks, the calls are not nested like that, but there's still just as much data copying going on. Most of the time, this doesn't cause any noticeable problems. However, if you hook a function that is called many times per frame, you may create a perceptible drop in the performance of the client.

Finding Alternatives

We don't want to scare you away from hooking completely; it definitely has its time and place. However, you should consider possible alternatives first to avoid these problems. Table 19-1 contains some common scenarios in which your first instinct might be to hook, along with possible alternatives. Don't hesitate to ask for help from the UI community either. With a wider experience base, you may end up with new ideas that help your entire addon function more efficiently.

Table 19-1: Hooking Alternatives

POTENTIAL HOOK	ALTERNATIVE
OnShow of a frame from the default UI or another addon	Create a new frame with its own OnShow handler as a child of the target frame. Any time the target frame is shown or hidden, yours will be, too. Removing your hook is as simple as re-parenting your frame.
MerchantFrame_OnShow to respond to opening a vendor window	Register for the MERCHANT_SHOW event and process the merchant data on your own. Unregister the event to unhook. This also prevents any conflicts if the user has a custom merchant frame.
SetAttribute to track attribute changes on a frame	Set or hook the OnAttributeChanged script instead. The nature of the widget handler fits the purpose of the hook better than the method.

Designing an Addon: MapZoomOut

MapZoomOut is a simple addon that, whenever the player changes the zoom of the minimap, starts a timer that returns the map to full zoom after 20 seconds. This ensures that the player can change the zoom temporarily, but that the map always reverts to the full size (to help with things like tracking and tradeskills).

Specifying the behavior:

- When the minimap zoom is changed via the SetZoom() method, a timer will begin.

■ When the timer reaches 20 seconds, the zoom will be changed until it is fully zoomed out again.

Implementation details:

■ The `Minimap:SetZoom(zoomLevel)` method is used to change the zoom of the minimap.

■ The minimum zoom level is 0, which is fully zoomed out.

■ The maximum zoom level can be obtained by calling `Minimap:GetZoomLevels()`.

■ The two minimap zoom buttons (the plus and minus) use the `SetZoom()` method to change the zoom level.

■ When the minimap zoom buttons are used, they include logic to enable or disable themselves (so the zoom-out button is disabled when you are at zoom level 0).

■ The current zoom level can be obtained using the `GetZoom()` method.

■ To start the timer, the `SetZoom()` method will need to be hooked.

MapZoomOut won't require an `.xml` file, so create the basic addon directory and then add `MapZoomOut.toc` using the following content:

```
## Interface: 30200
## Title: MapZoomOut
## Notes: Zooms the map out to the full level after a given time

MapZoomOut.lua
```

Creating a Timer Frame

Create a new file called **MapZoomOut.lua**, and add the following line to the top of the file:

```
local timerFrame = CreateFrame("Frame")
```

This creates a frame with no global name and assigns it to a local variable so it can be used later in the file. It will trigger the timer with `OnUpdate`.

Initial Setup

Add these lines to the bottom of the `MapZoomOut.lua` file, creating a variable to store the delay amount for the timer, a variable for the timer counter, and a reference to the original `Minimap:SetZoom()` function:

```
local DELAY = 20
local counter = 0
local origSetZoom = Minimap.SetZoom
```

These local variables will be used later in the file to check the timer, as well as to call the original `SetZoom` function.

Create the Function Hook

The new function is simple; it just calls `timerFrame:Show()` and changes the counter to `0` to reset the timer. It then calls the original `SetZoom` function to change the zoom level. Add this function definition to the bottom of `MapZoomOut.lua`:

```lua
function Minimap.SetZoom(...)
    -- Show the timer frame, starting the timer
    timerFrame:Show()
    counter = 0

    -- Call the original SetZoom function
    return origSetZoom(...)
end
```

The function parameters or returns are simply passed to the original function using `...`, and the results are returned to the calling function. This ensures that the function will operate well with whatever calls it, because it augments behavior rather than altering the original function.

Writing the Timer Code

The timer is a bit more complex than the earlier example simply for aesthetic reasons. The easy way to write this addon would be to call `origSetZoom(Minimap, 0)` when the timer expires, but this causes a pretty large change in the minimap and doesn't look all that pleasing. Instead, this function will zoom out step by step, producing a more gradual zoom.

Add the following code to the bottom of `MapZoomOut.lua`:

```lua
local function OnUpdate(self, elapsed)
    -- Increment the counter variable
    counter = counter + elapsed

    if counter >= DELAY then
        -- Check current zoom level
        local z = Minimap:GetZoom()
        if z > 0 then
            origSetZoom(Minimap, z - 1)
        else
            -- Enable/Disable the buttons
            MinimapZoomIn:Enable()
            MinimapZoomOut:Disable()
            self:Hide()
        end
    end
end
```

The beginning of the timer is the same, incrementing the counter and checking it against the delay. Inside the conditional, you store the current zoom level in local variable z so it can be referenced. If the minimap is currently zoomed in (z > 0), the map is zoomed out by one level, but the counter isn't reset. That ensures the timer's payload will run on the next frame update as well. This alone accomplishes the gradual zoom-out rather than the single frame change.

Finally, once the minimap is zoomed all the way out, the MinimapZoomIn button is enabled, and the MinimapZoomOut button is disabled. Then the timer frame hides itself so its OnUpdate won't be called again.

Final Setup

The last step is setting the OnUpdate script for timerFrame, and then deciding what to do when the addon first loads. Because the user may load the game with the minimap already zoomed in, the code will check to see if it should start the timer or hide it to begin with (so it doesn't run).

Add the following code to the bottom of your MapZoomOut.lua file:

```
timerFrame:SetScript("OnUpdate", OnUpdate)
if Minimap:GetZoom() == 0 then
  timerFrame:Hide()
end
```

Testing MapZoomOut

As with any addon you create, test the functionality to ensure it works properly with no side effects. In this case, test the following:

- Using the zoom-in button, zoom in to each level, and verify that the map is zoomed out after DELAY seconds each time.

- Manually call the Minimap:SetZoom() function by running /script Minimap:SetZoom(3). The addon should detect the change, and begin the timer even though the buttons weren't pushed.

Summary

Function hooking can be a useful tool in a programmer's box, but it comes with a hefty instruction booklet and set of warnings. In particular, follow these principles when creating function hooks:

- Use the same parameters and returns.

- Call the original function and maintain the hook chain.

- Don't alter the order or meaning of arguments or returns, because other functions may rely on them.

- Don't depend on your hook being in a certain place in the chain. This also means you should never unhook a function.

- Look for alternatives first. Hooking may not always be the best solution.

In addition, special care must be taken when hooking Blizzard scripts and functions because certain actions are restricted to the default user interface.

The Code

MapZoomOut

MapZoomOut.toc

```
## Interface: 30200
## Title: MapZoomOut
## Notes: Zooms the map out to the full level after a given time

MapZoomOut.lua
```

MapZoomOut.lua

```lua
local timerFrame = CreateFrame("Frame")
local DELAY = 20
local counter = 0
local origSetZoom = Minimap.SetZoom

function Minimap.SetZoom(...)
  -- Show the timer frame, starting the timer
  timerFrame:Show()
  counter = 0

  -- Call the original SetZoom function
  return origSetZoom(...)
end

local function OnUpdate(self, elapsed)
  -- Increment the counter variable
  counter = counter + elapsed

  if counter >= DELAY then
    -- Check current zoom level
    local z = Minimap:GetZoom()
    if z > 0 then
      origSetZoom(Minimap, z - 1)
    else
      -- Enable/Disable the buttons
```

```
        MinimapZoomIn:Enable()
        MinimapZoomOut:Disable()
        self:Hide()
      end
    end
  end
end

timerFrame:SetScript("OnUpdate", OnUpdate)
if Minimap:GetZoom() == 0 then
  timerFrame:Hide()
end
```

## CHAPTER 20

Creating Custom Graphics

When creating addons for World of Warcraft, you can often build your frames using only the default Blizzard artwork, icons, and buttons. However, if your addon requires something more specific, it can be created using any major graphics editor. This chapter details the major steps needed to create a custom texture for WoW in the GNU Image Manipulation Program (GIMP), Adobe Photoshop CS, and Corel Paint Shop Pro X.

Common Rules for Creating Graphics

Graphics (or textures) in WoW have a few specific requirements they must meet for them to be loaded and rendered in-game as part of a custom UI:

- The height and width of the texture must be a power of two, although they do not have to be the same power of two. This means 32x256 and 512x512 are both valid, but 50x128 is not. In addition, textures are limited to a maximum of 512 pixels in either dimension. If you have a larger graphic, you can break it into tiles and use multiple Texture objects to display it.

- The graphic must be saved in either BLP or TGA format. BLP is a proprietary format that Blizzard uses internally, and there are no official tools that allow these files to be easily created or edited. TGA files can be read and written in most major graphics editors.

▪ Textures should be saved with an 8-bit alpha channel along with the 24-bit color data. This allows for both partial and full transparency in textures.

▪ Graphics files must reside in an addon's directory to be accessible to the game client.

The GIMP

Creating a texture with transparency is relatively simple in the GIMP because of the way it handles the alpha channel. The trick is creating the image with a transparent background, and paying particular attention when creating the various elements of the image.

Create a New Image

To create a new image with the GIMP:

1. Select File ⇨ New in the main GIMP window.

2. In the window that appears (see Figure 20-1), enter the width and height of your image. Keep in mind that you don't need to fill the entire space, but both the height and width must be a power of two.

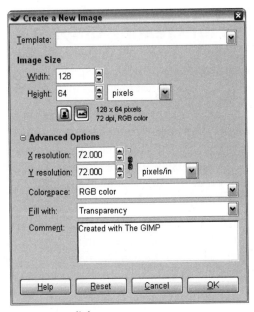

Figure 20-1: GIMP's New Image dialog

3. Expand the Advanced Options section of the New dialog.
4. Ensure RGB color is selected for the Colorspace.
5. Set Fill With to Transparency, so the new base image is fully transparent.
6. Click OK.

Adding Graphical Components

A new window opens showing the base transparent image (see Figure 20-2). You can add any graphical components to this image, including layers. Unfortunately, I'm just a simple programmer and lack any and all graphical manipulation skills, so I can't give you too many pointers. This example creates a very simple custom button.

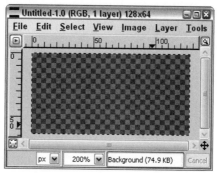

Figure 20-2: Editing window for new transparent image in the GIMP

Figure 20-3 shows a newly created custom icon, combining a simple border graphic and a picture of my dog Daisy. This image is 64x64 and has transparent edges (specifically for the rounded corners).

Figure 20-3: New custom icon created in the GIMP

Saving Textures

As long as the graphic was created with a transparent background, you should be able to save it without any issues. Save the new image using the following steps:

1. Merge all the layers before attempting to save because TGA does not support layers. This step isn't necessarily required but makes the subsequent steps easier.

2. Select File ➪ Save.

3. In the Save dialog, name your file with a .TGA extension and click the Save button.

4. An options dialog pops up (shown in Figure 20-4). Check both checkboxes and click OK. This compresses the image in a lossless way (so it loses no quality) but creates a smaller file size.

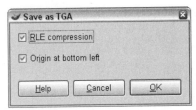

Figure 20-4: Save as TGA dialog in the GIMP

Personally, I find that creating images in the GIMP the easiest, because the only trick is ensuring the image is the right size with a transparent background.

Adobe Photoshop

Creating a texture in Photoshop is similar to creating one in the GIMP, but the interface is quite a bit different. The same basic steps apply, the image creation and saving being the most important.

Create a New Image

To create a new image with Photoshop:

1. Open Photoshop and select File ➪ New.

2. The New dialog opens (see Figure 20-5).

3. Change the height and width to your desired dimensions.

4. Ensure the Background Contents dropdown has Transparent selected.

5. Click OK to create the new image.

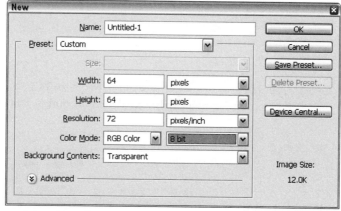

Figure 20-5: Adobe Photoshop file creation dialog

Adding Graphical Components

Create the graphic as required (you're the one familiar with Photoshop here), but take care to follow these rules:

■ Make sure there isn't a Background layer in your document when you are ready to save.

■ If you need to merge visible layers, use Merge All, but don't flatten the image. Flattening the image gives it a background, which loses the transparency information.

Transparency in Adobe Photoshop is different than in GIMP. In particular, you won't see an alpha channel created by default in the Channels window. The transparent background means nothing when the image is flattened and saved. To achieve transparency, you must create the alpha channel.

Creating an Alpha Channel

When your image is complete and ready to save, run the following steps to create an alpha channel:

1. Merge the visible layers so you have a single layer containing the nontransparent portions of your image.

2. Select the layer in the layers palette.

3. Open the Select menu and select Load Selection.

4. You will be prompted with a dialog box (see Figure 20-6), but the default options should be correct. Click OK. This selects each pixel in the current layer that isn't transparent.

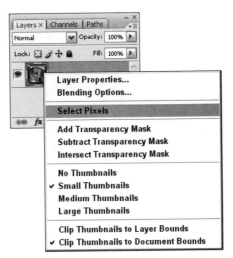

Figure 20-6: Load Selection dialog

5. In the Channels window, there is a small icon that will "Save Selection As Channel" (see Figure 20-7). Click it, creating an alpha channel based on the selection.

Figure 20-7: Save Selection As Channel button in the Channels window

The new 8-bit alpha channel gives you different levels of opacity for an image with more forgiving transparency. Now that the transparency information is stored in a channel, you can flatten the image if you'd like (although there is no compelling reason to do so).

Saving an Image

Once the alpha channel is created, saving the image is a matter of selecting File ➪ Save As. The Save As dialog provides several options (shown in Figure 20-8).

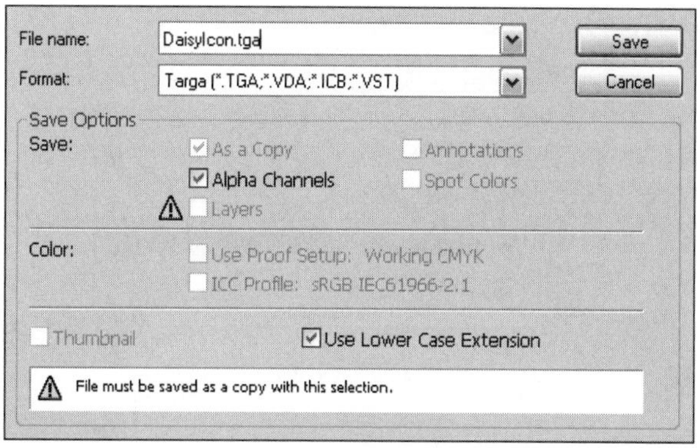

Figure 20-8: Options in Photoshop's Save As dialog

You can choose any name you'd like for the image, but ensure the file format is set to Targa (*.tga) and that the filename ends in the `.tga` extension. If your image has layers, the As A Copy option will be automatically selected, and the Layers option will be deselected with an error warning next to it. This simply means that TGA doesn't support layers, so the image will be flattened before saving. Ensure that Alpha Channels is selected. Click Save.

A final TGA options dialog (see Figure 20-9) opens to allow you to select the color resolution and add compression to the image. Select 32 bits/pixel, and check the box for Compress (RLE).

Figure 20-9: Targa Options dialog

Once the image is saved, it can be copied into your WoW installation and tested.

Paint Shop Pro

Paint Shop Pro is similar to Adobe Photoshop in most respects, particularly in the way it handles transparency. As a result, you'll need to take similar steps to ensure the transparent images you create are saved correctly.

Creating a New Image

To create a new image with Paint Shop Pro:

1. Select File ➪ New.

2. The New Image options dialog (see Figure 20-10) opens. Specify the dimensions of your image.

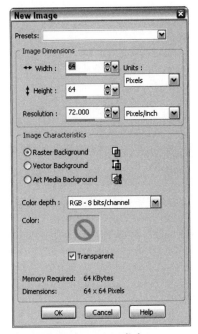

Figure 20-10: Corel Paint Shop Pro New Image dialog

3. Select a Raster Background with a color depth of RGB - 8 bits/channel.

4. Check the Transparent box to give your image a transparent background.

5. Click OK.

Adding Graphical Components

Create your image as you usually do in this application, ensuring that you don't use the Flatten Image option. You will need the transparent background to make certain the alpha channel is created correctly.

Creating an Alpha Channel

Once your image is created, use the following steps to create an alpha channel for transparency:

1. Select Layers ➪ New Mask Layer ➪ From Image (see Figure 20-11). This will create a new mask layer consisting only of the pixels in your image.

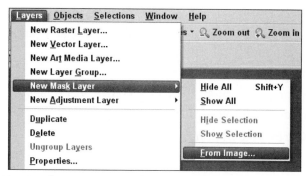

Figure 20-11: New Mask Layer menu option

2. In the Add Mask From Image dialog (see Figure 20-12), select Source Opacity in the Create Mask From section to ensure the new alpha channel is created using the transparency you defined when creating the image.

Figure 20-12: Add Mask From Image dialog box

3. Click OK. This adds a new layer mask to your image.
4. Select Layers ➪ Load Save Mask ➪ Save Mask to Alpha Channel.
5. A dialog box displays, allowing you to preview the image transparency and giving you an opportunity to name the new channel. Click OK.

Your image now has a proper alpha channel that can be used to save the image with transparency.

Saving an Image

Follow these steps to save an image in Paint Shop Pro:

1. Select File ➪ Save As.

2. In the dialog that appears, choose TGA Truevision targa (*.tga) as the image format, and name your image.

3. Click the Options button.

4. In the Save Options dialog box (see Figure 20-13), select a 24-bit image and compression for your image.

5. Click OK to exit the options dialog.

Figure 20-13: Targa options in Paint Shop Pro

6. Click Save.

7. If you still have layers in your image, you may get a warning dialog (see Figure 20-14) telling you that the image will be merged and then saved. Click Yes.

Figure 20-14: File format limitations dialog in Paint Shop Pro

Testing Your Texture

To test the new texture, you need to fully exit World of Warcraft and add a small custom addon to house the image. (You could instead add it to an existing addon, but that exercise is left to the reader, when appropriate.)

1. Create a folder `IconTest` underneath your `AddOns` directory.

2. Add a file `IconTest.toc` with the following contents:

   ```
   ## Interface: 30200
   ## Title: IconTest
   ## Notes: Simple icon test addon

   IconTest.xml
   ```

3. Add a file `IconTest.xml` with the following contents. Change `DaisyIcon` to the name of your icon filename.

   ```
   <Ui xmlns="http://www.blizzard.com/wow/ui/"
     xmlns:xsi="http://www.w3.org/2001/XMLSchema-instance"
     xsi:schemaLocation="http://www.blizzard.com/wow/ui/
     http://wowprogramming.com/FrameXML/UI.xsd">
     <Button name="IconTest" parent="UIParent">
       <Size x="64" y="64"/>
       <Anchors>
         <Anchor point="CENTER"/>
       </Anchors>
       <Layers>
         <Layer level="BACKGROUND">
           <Texture name="$parentIcon" ↵
   file="Interface\AddOns\IconTest\DaisyIcon" setAllPoints="true"/>
         </Layer>
       </Layers>
     </Button>
   </Ui>
   ```

4. WoW doesn't require you to specify extensions when loading textures; it will try to load both a `.BLP` and a `.TGA` automatically.

5. Copy your icon file to the `IconTest` directory.

6. Load up World of Warcraft and hope you don't have any errors in your XML.

If you have created the texture correctly, it should appear in the center of your screen (see Figure 20-15).

If you've made any errors, you might experience one of two symptoms: no button appears, or you see only a solid green box.

Figure 20-15: Custom texture being viewed in-game

No Button Appears

If you see no button at all, double-check your XML definition, and ensure you have no errors in your `FrameXML.log` file. You can also use a web browser to check that your XML document is well-formed. Ensure that your test addon appears in the AddOn listing. Did you make sure to exit WoW before you added the new files?

A Green Box Appears

When there is an issue loading a given texture in World of Warcraft, the texture will be colored solid green (see Figure 20-16). Typically, this is a result of a typo on the filename being used for the texture.

Figure 20-16: Solid green texture, indicating an error

Depending on how the texture was created (from an XML definition or through a Lua function call), a number of issues could result in a green texture being displayed.

XML Texture Definition

A texture created in XML may have one of the following issues:

- The file doesn't exist.
- The graphic was saved incorrectly.
- The filename was not specified correctly.
  - Filenames in XML should only have single backslashes between directories.

■ Filename path separators *must* be backslashes, even on a Mac OS X or UNIX system, because of the way the client loads and parses the filenames.

Lua Texture Definition

When troubleshooting texture errors in Lua, the following issues may exist:

■ The file doesn't exist.

■ The graphic was saved incorrectly.

■ The filename was not specified correctly.

   ■ Backslashes in filenames must be escaped (using a double backslash). Alternatively, you can use long string notation to specify the filename:

```
[[Interface\AddOns\YourAddOnName\Path\To\Texture]]
```

   ■ Filename path separators *must* be backslashes, even on a Mac OS X or UNIX system, because of the way the client loads and parses the filenames.

Summary

Every graphical editor has differences and settings that are necessary to create an image with partial transparency for use in World of Warcraft. The GIMP enables you to create your image and simply save it as a TGA file, whereas both Photoshop and Paint Shop Pro require you to create an alpha channel based on a mask or selection.

## CHAPTER 21

Responding to the Combat Log and Threat Information

Following the Burning Crusade expansion for World of Warcraft, a new system was introduced to allow addons to get detailed information about the combat events happening around the player. The system allows for very powerful addons that can record and display combat log information. This chapter introduces you to the complex combat log system through the creation of an addon called CombatStatus.

Understanding the Combat Log

The combat log is one of the most complex systems in World of Warcraft, which is understandable considering how much of the game is actually based around combat. An addon can use two events to get combat log information, COMBAT_LOG_EVENT and COMBAT_LOG_EVENT_UNFILTERED. The first event is used by the actual Blizzard_CombatLog addon to display filtered events, and the second will fire for any combat event regardless of whether or not it matches the currently set filters. Most addons will use the unfiltered event to ensure that players get an opportunity to see each event.

Event Arguments

Each combat event is guaranteed to have at least eight arguments that describe the different actors involved in the combat event. Not all events will have two actors (a source and a destination) because that information isn't necessarily available. The standard arguments to the event appear in the following order:

- `timestamp`—This is a server-based timestamp of when the event occurred, with millisecond precision. If you are logging events or comparing events between clients, this can help with matching different events up with each other.

- `combatEvent`—More than forty different combat events might be sent as a combat log event and this argument helps to distinguish between these different sub-events. Example sub-events are `UNIT_DIED`, `SPELL_STOLEN`, and `SWING_DAMAGE`. There's more information about the different combat events in the next section.

- `sourceGUID`—Each unit (or other entity) involved in a combat log event is distinguished by a GUID (Globally Unique IDentifier). These values exist for all entities—including those which cannot be referenced by unitID—and always specifically identify the entity to which they refer—even for cases where multiple units share the same name. This allows addons to keep track of individual actors in combat regardless of such factors. Further explanation of GUIDs is provided later in this chapter.

- `sourceName`—Because the combat log is most interested in displaying the name of the actor, it makes sense to include that in the event arguments. This is the name of the source actor for the given combat event.

- `sourceFlags`—This field contains information about the actor, such as whether it is a non-player character, a pet, or some other type of object. In addition the flags contain information about the relationship between the player and the actor, such as whether or not it was the player's target at the time the event occurred.

- `destGUID`—The same information as `sourceGUID` for the destination actor.

- `destName`—The same information as `sourceName` for the destination actor.

- `destFlags`—The same information as `sourceFlags` for the destination actor.

There are normally additional event arguments, but they change depending on the type of `combatEvent`.

Combat Sub-Events

To determine the particular arguments and information being passed in a combat log event, you must examine the `combatEvent` argument. Currently forty-eight different types of sub-events might occur, but even sub-events can be split further into a prefix and a suffix.

Combat Event Prefix

The event prefix indicates the *type* of the event, such as whether it involves physical damage like an auto-attack, a ranged attack, spell, or damage to a building or structure in-game. The additional arguments will be after the initial eight arguments that come with the COMBAT_LOG_EVENT_UNFILTERED.

- SWING—This prefix is encountered for any auto-attack damage. No additional arguments are sent for this type of event prefix.

- RANGE—Any ranged attacks, such as auto shot, shoot bow/gun/ crossbow/wand, and throwing, will use this prefix, which sends the spell information as additional arguments. The spell information is passed in additional arguments: spellId, spellName, and spellSchool.

- SPELL—This prefix is used for all spellcast events, as well as other types of non-periodic spell actions. The spell information is passed in additional arguments: spellId, spellName, and spellSchool.

- ENVIRONMENTAL—This prefix is used for damage caused by the environment, such as when a player touches a bonfire, is immersed in lava, falls from great height, or begins to drown. The type of environmental damage is passed as an additional argument: environmentType.

Bit Fields and Spell Schools

Throughout the combat log, bit fields are used for arguments where more than one *setting* might be set in a single argument. The term *bit field* comes from the binary representation of numbers, where a number is made up of a number of *bits*. Table 21-1 shows the basic spell schools with their numeric values and binary representation.

Table 21-1: Spell Schools and Numeric Representations

SPELL SCHOOL	NUMERIC VALUE	BINARY REPRESENTATION
Physical	1	00000001
Holy	2	00000010
Fire	4	00000100
Nature	8	00001000
Frost	16	00010000
Shadow	32	00100000
Arcane	64	01000000
Frostfire	20	00010100

You can see that the binary values are non-conflicting and as a result they can be combined. The spell school for Frostfire Bolt (20) combines the value for Frost (16) and Fire (4). More importantly, we can get the component values back out of the combined number using bitwise operations. Try the following within WoW:

```
> print(bit.band(20, 16))
16
> print(bit.band(20, 4))
4
> print(bit.band(20, 8))
0
```

As a matter of fact, there's only one way to build the number 20 by adding the basic spell schools together. Even if you were to add the physical, holy, fire, and nature schools together, you would only get to 15. You could try adding the physical holy and frost schools together but that only gets you to 19. This is a special feature of bit masks that are built in this way.

To compare bit fields, you can utilize the three major bitwise operations:

- and—The bitwise and of two numbers is a resulting number where each bit is set to 1 only if the same bit is set to 1 for the two input numbers. This function is available as the bit.band() function.

- or—The bitwise or of two numbers is a resulting number where each bit is set to 1 if either of the input bits is set to 1. This function is available as the bit.bor() function.

- xor—The bitwise xor of two numbers is a resulting number where each bit is set to 1 if exactly one of the two input bits is set to 1. This function is available as the bit.bxor() function.

In practice, you will very rarely use anything other than bitwise and because it allows you to see if a given bit flag is set for a given number. In the preceding examples, you take the number 20 (which is 00010100 in binary representation) and compare it to 16 (00010000), 4 (00000100), and 8 (0001000).

All you have to do is check the resulting number to see if it's greater than 0 (that is, if there are *any* bits set). You experiment more with bit masks later in this chapter.

Combat Event Suffix

The rest of the combat event following the prefix indicates the remaining arguments to the combat event. The arguments will start following any additional arguments from the prefix portion of the combat event. The particular order will make more sense when you look at complete events put together. The following is a list of valid suffix types:

- DAMAGE and BUILDING_DAMAGE—Used to indicate damage to the destination actor. If the damage was done to a building rather than a normal unit, the BUILDING_DAMAGE event will fire instead of DAMAGE. The following additional arguments are included:

  - amount—The amount of damage inflicted.

  - overkill—A number, zero or more, indicating how much overkill damage was inflicted (that is, how much extra damage was done beyond the amount required to kill/destroy the target).

  - school—The school of the inflicted damage, that is, whether the damage was physical, caused by fire, and so on.

  - resisted—A number, zero or more, indicating how much damage was resisted due to magical resistance attributes.

  - blocked—A number, zero or more, indicating how much damage was blocked due to a physical shield.

  - absorbed—A number indicating how much damage was absorbed by a spell or ability, or nil.

  - critical—1 if the damage inflicted was a critical hit, otherwise nil.

  - glancing—1 if the damage inflicted was a glancing blow, otherwise nil.

  - crushing—1 if the damage inflicted was a crushing blow, otherwise nil.

- MISSED and PERIODIC_MISSED—Used to indicate that an attack missed in some way. The following arguments are included:

  - missType—One of the following strings, indicating the type of miss that occurred: ABSORB, BLOCK, DEFLECT, DODGE, EVADE, IMMUNE, MISS, PARRY, REFLECT, and RESIST.

  - amountMissed—The amount of damage that missed.

- CAST_START—This combat event is only fired for the SPELL prefix, and indicates the start of a spell cast. This only fires for spells with a cast time. No additional arguments are included.

- CAST_SUCCESS—This combat event is fired for any type of spell cast including channeled and instant cast spells. It indicates that the spell was cast successfully. No additional arguments are included.

- CAST_FAILED—This combat event is fired whenever a spell cast has failed for some reason. The following additional argument is included:

  - failedType—A message indicating why the spell cast failed.

- HEAL, PERIODIC_HEAL, and BUILDING_HEAL—One of these combat events fires when a healing effect occurs. Depending on whether the spell is a periodic effect, a heal on a building, or a one-shot heal on a unit, one of these three events will fire. The following arguments are included:

  - amount—The amount of healing that occurred.

  - overhealing–A number, zero or greater, indicating the amount of healing that occurred beyond that required to bring the target to full health.

  - absorbed—A number indicating the amount of healing that was absorbed.

  - critical—1 if the heal was a critical heal, otherwise nil.

- ENERGIZE and PERIODIC_ENERGIZE—Energize events occur when an actor gains health, mana, or some other type of power through some ability or item. Depending on whether the spell is a periodic effect or a one-shot effect, one of these two events will fire. For example, the ENERGIZE event fires when the Death Knight "Butchery" effect is triggered, giving the player 20 extra runic power. The following arguments are included:

  - amount—The amount of power gained.

  - powerType—The type of power that was gained. It can be one of the following values:

    - -2—Health
    - 0—Mana
    - 1—Rage
    - 2—Focus (pets)
    - 3—Energy
    - 4—Pet happiness
    - 5—Runes
    - 6—Runic power

- LEECH and PERIODIC_LEECH—When one actor "steals" a resource from his target, such as when using the Viper Sting or Drain Mana spells, one of these events will occur. Depending on whether the spell is a periodic effect or a one-shot effect, one of these two events will fire. The following arguments are included:

- `amount`—The amount of power gained.

- `powerType`—The type of power that was gained. See the listing for the ENERGIZE suffix.

- `extraAmount`—The extra amount of power that was gained as a bonus of the spell. For example, Viper Sting awards 300% of the power leeched.

- `DRAIN` and `PERIODIC_DRAIN`—When one actor drains a resource from his target, one of these events will occur. Depending on whether the spell is a periodic effect or a one-shot effect, one of these two events will fire. The following arguments are included:

  - `amount`—The amount of power gained.

  - `powerType`—The type of power that was gained. See the listing for the ENERGIZE suffix.

  - `extraAmount`—The extra amount of power that was gained as a bonus of the spell. For example, Viper Sting awards 300% of the power leeched.

Spell-Only Suffixes

The following combat suffixes only fire for the SPELL prefix:

- `SUMMON`—Fires when an actor summons an NPC such as a totem or non-combat pet. No additional arguments are included.

- `RESURRECT`—Fires when a player is resurrected. No additional arguments are included.

- `CREATE`—Fires when a new object is created (as opposed to summoned NPCs), such as a hunter's pet or mage portal. No additional arguments are included.

- `INSTAKILL`—Fires when a spell instantly kills an actor. No additional arguments are included.

- `INTERRUPT`—Fires when a spell is interrupted. The first set of spell arguments (from the prefix) will be the ability that was responsible for the interruption. The following arguments are included:

  - `extraSpellID`—The numeric identifier for the spell that was interrupted.

  - `extraSpellName`—The name of the spell that was interrupted.

  - `extraSchool`—The school of the spell that was interrupted.

- EXTRA_ATTACKS—Fires when an actor does additional damage through extra attacks, such as those granted by Windfury Weapon or the Thrash Blade proc. The following argument is included:
  - amount—The number of extra attacks granted by the ability. The actual damage is listed as additional entries in the combat log.

- DURABILITY_DAMAGE—This event fires when a spell or ability causes damage to an actor's items. For example, Nefarion's hunter call in Blackwing Lair or Ragnaros' Melt Weapon ability, which reduce the durability of the player's items.

- DURABILITY_DAMAGE_ALL—This event fires when a spell or ability causes damage to all of an actor's items.

- AURA_APPLIED—Fires when an aura is applied to an actor. The following argument is included:
  - auraType—A string indicating the type of the aura. Observed values are BUFF and DEBUFF.

- AURA_APPLIED_DOSE—Fires when a stackable aura is applied to an actor, such as Lifebloom or Penance. The following arguments are included:
  - auraType—A string indicating the type of the aura. Observed values are BUFF and DEBUFF.
  - amount—The number of doses applied.

- AURA_REFRESH—Fires when an aura is refreshed with a new application. The following argument is included:
  - auraType—A string indicating the type of the aura. Observed values are BUFF and DEBUFF.

- AURA_REMOVED—Fires when an aura is removed from an actor. The following argument is included:
  - auraType—A string indicating the type of the aura. Observed values are BUFF and DEBUFF.

- AURA_REMOVED_DOSE—Fires when a dose is removed from a stackable aura, such as Lifebloom or Penance. The following arguments are included:
  - auraType—A string indicating the type of the aura. Observed values are BUFF and DEBUFF.
  - amount—The number of doses removed.

- AURA_BROKEN—Fires when an aura has been broken by damage. The following argument is included:
  - auraType—A string indicating the type of the aura. Observed values are BUFF and DEBUFF.

- AURA_BROKEN_SPELL—Fires when an aura has been broken by a spell. The following arguments are included:
  - extraSpellID—The numeric identifier for the spell that was broken.
  - extraSpellName—The name of the spell that was broken.
  - extraSchool—The school of the spell that was broken.
  - auraType—A string indicating the type of the aura. Observed values are BUFF and DEBUFF.
- DISPEL—Fires when an aura is dispelled. The following arguments are included:
  - extraSpellID—The numeric identifier for the spell that was dispelled.
  - extraSpellName—The name of the spell that was dispelled.
  - extraSchool—The school of the spell that was dispelled.
  - auraType—A string indicating the type of the aura. Observed values are BUFF and DEBUFF.
- DISPEL_FAILED—Fires when an aura fails to be dispelled. The following arguments are included:
  - extraSpellID—The numeric identifier for the spell that was dispelled.
  - extraSpellName—The name of the spell that was dispelled.
  - extraSchool—The school of the spell that was dispelled.
  - auraType—A string indicating the type of the aura. Observed values are BUFF and DEBUFF.
- STOLEN—Fires when an aura is stolen. The following arguments are included:
  - extraSpellID—The numeric identifier for the spell that was stolen.
  - extraSpellName—The name of the spell that was stolen.
  - extraSchool—The school of the spell that was stolen.
  - auraType—A string indicating the type of the aura. Observed values are BUFF and DEBUFF.

Special Combat Events

The following combat events do not follow the prefix/suffix conventions and therefore must be considered individually:

- DAMAGE_SHIELD—Fires when a shield causes damage to an actor. To process this event you can use the same arguments for the SPELL prefix, with the additional arguments from the DAMAGE suffix.

- DAMAGE_SPLIT—This occurs when damage is split among multiple targets. To process this event you can use the same arguments for the SPELL prefix, with the additional arguments from the DAMAGE suffix.

- DAMAGE_SHIELD_MISSED—Fires when a shield causes damage to an actor, but that damage misses in some way. To process this event you can use the same arguments for the SPELL prefix, with the additional arguments from the MISSED suffix.

- ENCHANT_APPLIED—Fires when an enchantment is applied to an item. The following arguments are passed:

  - spellName—The name of the enchantment.

  - itemID—The numeric identifier of the item.

  - itemName—The name of the item that was enchanted.

- ENCHANT_REMOVED—Fires when an enchantment is removed from an item. The following arguments are passed:

  - spellName—The name of the enchantment.

  - itemID—The numeric identifier of the item.

  - itemName—The name of the item that was enchanted.

- PARTY_KILL—Fires when a member of your party kills a unit.

- UNIT_DIED—Fires when a unit dies.

- UNIT_DESTROYED—Fires when a unit is destroyed.

Unit GUIDs

All units in World of Warcraft have a globally unique identifier. From the details posted by Blizzard on the WoW Forums:

- An NPC has a single GUID from spawn until death or despawn. When it respawns, it gets a new GUID.

- Pets and totems get a new GUID every time they are summoned.

- NPC and pet GUIDs can be recycled after server or instance restart.

- Player GUIDs are unique and persist as long as the player is on a given server.

The combat log automatically sends the GUID for the source and destination unit for each event. In addition, you can query the GUID for a specific unit using the UnitGUID() function. Recently a new function was added, allowing you to query class, race, and sex information about another player unit using his GUID. The `GetPlayerInfoByGUID()` function takes in a GUID argument, and returns the following:

- `localizedClass`—The name of the unit's class in the client's current locale.

- `classFilename`—A non-localized token identifying the unit's class (which can be used for looking up other class identifiers, such as color values in the `RAID_CLASS_COLORS` table).

- `localizedRace`—The name of the unit's race in the client's current locale.

- `raceFilename`—A non-localized token identifying the unit's race.

- `sex`—A number identifying the unit's gender: 1 for neuter or unknown, 2 for male, or 3 for female.

Format of GUIDs

Due to the large amount of items that require GUIDs, they are quite large numbers. In fact, the numbers are bigger than the numbers that Lua can hold in their number values. As a result, the GUIDs are stored and returned as strings. For example `"0x0100000002AB26D5"` is the GUID of one of my characters.

Internally, parts of the GUID are bit fields as well. For example, you can determine whether or not the entity behind a GUID is a player, NPC, or pet. To do this, you need to convert your GUID string to a number and take the mask of the upper portion:

```
function GUIDToType(guid)
  local typeMask = 0x00F
  local upper = tonumber(guid:sub(1, 5))
  local type = bit.band(upper, typeMask)
  if type == 0 then
    print("GUID " .. guid .. " is a player")
  elseif type == 3 then
    print("GUID " .. guid .. " is an NPC")
  elseif type == 4 then
    print("GUID " .. guid .. " is an NPC")
  end
end
GUIDToType(UnitGUID("player"))
```

Other information is embedded in the GUID for most units but isn't used for our purposes. GUIDs do provide you with a way to get information about entities in your combat log which cannot be identified by a unitID, but note that the format of such information may be subject to change.

Unit Flags

The final argument that is sent for the source and destination is a set of flags. These flags indicate the following information about each entity:

- The type of the entity as one of the following: object, guardian, pet, NPC, or player.

- Whether the entity is controlled by a player or is an NPC.

- The entity's reaction to the player (that is, friendly, hostile, or neutral).

- The relationship between the player and the entity's controller. This relationship can be the player, the player's party, the player's raid, or an outsider.

- If the entity is a raid target, main tank, main assist, or the player's focus or target unit at the time the message is received.

You use bitwise operations to get this information.

COMBATLOG_OBJECT_TYPE_MASK

To obtain the type of an object, you can use the global variable COMBATLOG_OBJECT_TYPE_MASK. You then compare the resulting value with one of the following global variables:

- COMBATLOG_OBJECT_TYPE_MASK

- COMBATLOG_OBJECT_TYPE_GUARDIAN

- COMBATLOG_OBJECT_TYPE_PET

- COMBATLOG_OBJECT_TYPE_NPC

- COMBATLOG_OBJECT_TYPE_PLAYER

For example, to check if the entity with given unit flags is a pet, you can use the following code:

```
local typeFlags = bit.band(unitFlags, COMBATLOG_OBJECT_TYPE_MASK)
local isPet = typeFlags == COMBATLOG_OBJECT_TYPE_PET
```

COMBATLOG_OBJECT_CONTROL_MASK

You can utilize this mask to determine if a player or an NPC currently controls an entity. These flags do properly update when entities are mind controlled, allowing you to distinguish between an ally of yours attacking the enemy and an ally of yours attacking you under duress. The valid results for these flags are:

- COMBATLOG_OBJECT_CONTROL_NPC

- COMBATLOG_OBJECT_CONTROL_PLAYER

COMBATLOG_OBJECT_REACTION_MASK

The reaction of an entity is a bit misleading—you might think that if an enemy is attacking you or one of your allies they would show up as hostile. Instead, the reaction indicates the predisposition of an entity toward the player. As a result, one of the *yellow*-colored mobs in the game that won't automatically attack you will show up as having a neutral reaction to you even if it's fighting you!

The valid results for these flags are:

- COMBATLOG_OBJECT_REACTION_HOSTILE
- COMBATLOG_OBJECT_REACTION_NEUTRAL
- COMBATLOG_OBJECT_REACTION_FRIENDLY

COMBATLOG_OBJECT_AFFILIATION_MASK

An object's affiliation indicates its relationship to the player. The possible results start with the closest to the player (that is, something that is owned by the player) and move out to outsiders (entities that are not part of the player's raid or party). Possible results are:

- COMBATLOG_OBJECT_AFFILIATION_OUTSIDER
- COMBATLOG_OBJECT_AFFILIATION_RAID
- COMBATLOG_OBJECT_AFFILIATION_PARTY
- COMBATLOG_OBJECT_AFFILIATION_MINE

The numeric values of the global variables starts with 1 for MINE and increases toward OUTSIDER with 8. Although we recommend against relying on the numeric values of these variables rather than using the global constants, the ordering of the values isn't likely to change in the future without notice. You could therefore check to see that something is either owned by you or someone in your party by checking that the result is less than or equal to COMBATLOG_OBJECT_AFFILIATION_PARTY.

COMBATLOG_OBJECT_SPECIAL_MASK

The special flags are used to indicate if the entity has some special way to be distinguished, from the player's perspective. An entity might have no special flags set, giving the result:

- COMBATLOG_OBJECT_NONE

The flags might indicate that the entity has one of the eight raid icons on it:

- COMBATLOG_OBJECT_RAIDTARGET8
- COMBATLOG_OBJECT_RAIDTARGET7

- ◼ COMBATLOG_OBJECT_RAIDTARGET6

- ◼ COMBATLOG_OBJECT_RAIDTARGET5

- ◼ COMBATLOG_OBJECT_RAIDTARGET4

- ◼ COMBATLOG_OBJECT_RAIDTARGET3

- ◼ COMBATLOG_OBJECT_RAIDTARGET2

- ◼ COMBATLOG_OBJECT_RAIDTARGET1

The entity might have been set as a *Main Tank* or *Main Assist*:

- ◼ COMBATLOG_OBJECT_MAINTANK

- ◼ COMBATLOG_OBJECT_MAINASSIST

In addition the flags could indicate that the entity was the player's target or focus at the time the event arrived (although it may have since changed):

- ◼ COMBATLOG_OBJECT_FOCUS

- ◼ COMBATLOG_OBJECT_TARGET

Using CombatLog_Object_IsA

There is a utility function that can make working with combat log flags a bit easier. It takes in a set of unit flags and a "filter" mask. If the unit matches the given mask, it returns 1; otherwise it returns nil. These predefined filters are as follows:

- ◼ COMBATLOG_FILTER_EVERYTHING—Any entity.

- ◼ COMBATLOG_FILTER_FRIENDLY_UNITS—Entity is a friendly unit.

- ◼ COMBATLOG_FILTER_HOSTILE_PLAYERS—Entity is a hostile player unit.

- ◼ COMBATLOG_FILTER_HOSTILE_UNITS—Entity is a hostile non-player unit.

- ◼ COMBATLOG_FILTER_ME—Entity is the player.

- ◼ COMBATLOG_FILTER_MINE—Entity is a non-unit object belonging to the player; for example, a totem.

- ◼ COMBATLOG_FILTER_MY_PET—Entity is the player's pet.

- ◼ COMBATLOG_FILTER_NEUTRAL_UNITS—Entity is a neutral unit.

- ◼ COMBATLOG_FILTER_UNKNOWN_UNITS—Entity is a unit currently unknown to the WoW client.

Writing CombatStatus

As an example of how the combat log can be used to get detailed information about combat in World of Warcraft, you will create an addon called CombatStatus. The initial version will show the damage per second and heals per second for your party, including pets.

The addon is structured with the following observations in mind:

- You can take advantage of unit flags to make capturing all of your party's events easier. In particular, you can check for COMBATLOG_OBJECT_ AFFILIATION_PARTY to get the relevant events.

- Because combat data arrives with GUID information rather than unitIDs, you'll need to make sure you store and index all data using GUIDs. This will ensure that you don't lose any information if the order of unitIDs change.

- A player might have more than one pet (for example, druids and their treant pets, or shaman elemental totems). Rather than trying to consider them individual pets, you can just collapse them into a single "pet" unit for each of your party members. You can use the SPELL_SUMMON combat log event to detect new units coming into play so we can track their GUIDs.

Creating the Basic Addon Structure

In your Addons folder, create a new directory called CombatStatus. Inside, create a new file called CombatStatus.toc with the following contents:

```
## Interface: 30300
## Notes: Provides a DPS meter for your party

CombatStatus.lua
CombatStatus.xml
```

Although you aren't using any XML templates in this addon currently, it's better to create the file now in case you choose to add some at a later time. Create a new CombatStatus.xml file and add the basic <Ui> element declaration:

```
<Ui xmlns="http://www.blizzard.com/wow/ui/"
    xmlns:xsi="http://www.w3.org/2001/XMLSchema-instance"
    xsi:schemaLocation="http://www.blizzard.com/wow/ui/
    http://wowprogramming.com/FrameXML/UI.xsd">
</Ui>
```

To add the frame declaration and a system for initialization that you'll expand on in later sections, create a new file `CombatStatus.lua` with the following contents:

```
local CombatStatus = CreateFrame("Frame", "CombatStatus", UIParent)

function CombatStatus:OnEvent(event, ...)
  if event == "PLAYER_LOGIN" then
    self:Initialize()
  end
end

-- Begin initialization section
-- Set the event handler so it can drive everything else
CombatStatus:SetScript("OnEvent", CombatStatus.OnEvent)

if IsLoggedIn() then
  CombatStatus:Initialize()
else
  CombatStatus:RegisterEvent("PLAYER_LOGIN")
end
```

The bulk of this code should seem familiar to you, but the section at the bottom might seem a bit odd. As you've seen throughout the book, a number of API functions don't operate properly before the PLAYER_LOGIN event. Normally you would just register for the PLAYER_LOGIN event, but when an addon is flagged as load-on-demand it might be loaded after that event has already fired. So you check the IsLoggedIn() API function to see if that event has already passed, and if so, you call the initialization function directly.

As you add new functions to this addon, make sure to add them before the initialization section at the bottom (beginning with the SetScript call), but after the frame creation on the first line. Due to the complexity of this addon, you will want to wait until the addon is finished before you test because some functions reference others that are not yet defined.

Initializing CombatStatus

The setup for your addon will occur in the Initialize() method. There you will set up the data tables, register for events, and create the display components of the addon. Add the following initialization function to `CombatStatus.lua`. It's not necessary to include the comments in your version of the code, but that is entirely up to you.

```
function CombatStatus:Initialize()
  self.combat_time = 0          -- The amount of time in combat
  self.party_damage = {}        -- Store the party's DPS
```

```
    self.party_heals = {}                    -- Store the party's heals
    self.pet_guids = {}                      -- Store GUID mappings for pets

    -- This is a metatable that returns 0 for any non-set values.  It will
    -- allow us to use table entries without having to check them first
    local zero_mt = {
      __index = function(tbl, key)
        return 0
      end,
    }

    setmetatable(self.party_damage, zero_mt)
    setmetatable(self.party_heals, zero_mt)

    -- This table will be used to store snapshots of the data every few
    -- seconds, allowing us to calculate DPS and HPS over a smaller
    -- period of time.  It will be indexed by unitid and each value will
    -- be a table that returns 0 for default and holds the damage in the
    -- damage field, and the heals in the heals field.
    self.snapshots = {}

    local emptytbl_mt = {
      __index = function(tbl, key)
        local new = setmetatable({}, zero_mt)
        rawset(tbl, key, new)
        return new
      end,
    }

    setmetatable(self.snapshots, emptytbl_mt)

    self.player_guid = UnitGUID("player")

    self:RegisterEvent("PARTY_MEMBERS_CHANGED")
    self:RegisterEvent("UNIT_PET")
    self:RegisterEvent("COMBAT_LOG_EVENT_UNFILTERED")
    self:RegisterEvent("PLAYER_REGEN_ENABLED")
    self:RegisterEvent("PLAYER_REGEN_DISABLED")

    self:CreateFrames()
    self:UpdateFrame()
  end
```

You define a number of entries in the frame's table to store the state of the addon. The first variable will allow you to track the amount of time the player has been in combat. This allows you to take the total amount of damage done, and divide it by the total amount of time spent in combat to get a unit's DPS. You store the damage and heals in separate tables (although you could certainly conceive of different ways of doing this). You also need a place to store a mapping from pet GUID to owner GUID to ensure you can properly handle pets.

You create a new metatable that returns 0 for any non-set values. This allows you to avoid having to check if a value in the table is set before you try to add anything to it. In the case of the damage tables, you can do the following:

```
self.party_damage[guid] = self.party_damage[guid] + damageAmount
```

instead of:

```
local oldValue = self.party_damage[guid] or 0
self.party_damage[guid] = oldValue + damageAmount
```

It may be a minimal gain, but it's also less prone to error. The snapshots table is used to store periodic snapshots of the damage so you can display a running average of everyone's DPS. The table will be indexed by GUID and the value is a table that contains two entries (health and heals) that both default to 0. You use a metatable to create these tables automatically in the same way you have the prior metatable default to 0.

Finally, you register for the following events:

- PARTY_MEMBERS_CHANGED—Use this event to see when the composition of the player's party changes. This enables you to re-scan the pet mappings and update the frame.

- UNIT_PET—This event fires when a unit's pet status changes, such as when a Warlock or Hunter summons or dismisses a pet. This won't cover the cases where temporary pets are summoned; you'll catch those in another way.

- COMBAT_LOG_EVENT_UNFILTERED—Because this addon is all about collecting information from the combat log, naturally you need to register for this event. This event is likely to fire very frequently so you will want to take precautions to ensure you don't do anything computationally intensive in response to it.

- PLAYER_REGEN_DISABLED—Likewise, this event fires when the player enters combat.

- PLAYER_REGEN_ENABLED—This event indicates that the player is no longer in combat, so you can use it to swap between your two different states.

Finally, you call the CreateFrame() method to create the status bars. Then you call the UpdateFrame() method to actually run the update function. For now, these methods don't exist, but they will be filled in later.

Updating Pet Mappings

The strategy you're going to take with pets is to map the pet GUID to the owner GUID, so multiple pets get collapsed into a single amount of damage. Add the following function that will take a unitID and update the GUID map for that unit's pets:

```
function CombatStatus:UpdatePets(unit)
  local petUnit

  if unit == "player" then
    petUnit = "pet"
  else
    petUnit = unit:gsub("(party)(%d)", "%1pet%2")
  end

  if petUnit and UnitExists(petUnit) then
    local guid = UnitGUID(unit)
    local petGUID = UnitGUID(petUnit)
    self.pet_guids[petGUID] = guid .. "pet"
  end
end
```

To look up information about pets you need to use the unitID for the pet, but you're only given the unitID for the owner. For party members these IDs are `partypet1`, `partypet2`, `partypet3`, and `partypet4`. You can use a simple substitution using patterns to transform `party1` into `partypet1`, as shown in the preceding code.

You need to cover the special case of the player's pet, which is just the unitID "pet." Once you have the correct unitID, you check to see if the unit exists and if so you get the GUID. Rather than doing a direct mapping from the pet GUID to the owner GUID, you do a mapping from the pet GUID to the owner GUID with the string "pet" added to the end.

If you didn't add this string you would need to store the pet's damage in another table (because the damage table is indexed by GUID). Otherwise, you would no longer be able to distinguish between the pets and the original unit itself.

Storing Damage and Healing Information

You're using the COMBAT_LOG_EVENT_UNFILTERED to get information about your party's damage and healing, so you need a function that extracts the right information from the various possible events. Create the following function in CombatStatus.lua:

```
local damageEvents = {
  SWING_DAMAGE = true,
```

```
        RANGE_DAMAGE = true,
        SPELL_DAMAGE = true,
        SPELL_PERIODIC_DAMAGE = true,
        DAMAGE_SHIELD = true,
        DAMAGE_SPLIT = true,
    }

    local healEvents = {
        SPELL_HEAL = true,
        SPELL_PERIODIC_HEAL = true,
    }

    function CombatStatus:ProcessEntry(timestamp, combatEvent, srcGUID, ↵
    srcName, srcFlags, destGUID, destName, destFlags, ...)
        if damageEvents[combatEvent] then
            local offset = combatEvent == "SWING_DAMAGE" and 1 or 4
            local amount, overkill, school, resisted, blocked, absorbed = ↵
    select(offset, ...)

            -- Check if this is a pet, and if so map the pet's GUID to the party
            -- member's GUID using the mapping table.
            if self.pet_guids[srcGUID] then
                srcGUID = self.pet_guids[srcGUID]
            end
            self.party_damage[srcGUID] = self.party_damage[srcGUID] + amount
        elseif healEvents[combatEvent] then
            local amount, overhealing, absorbed = select(4, ...)
            self.party_heals[srcGUID] = (self.party_heals[srcGUID] or 0) + ↵
    (amount - overhealing)
        elseif combatEvent == "SPELL_SUMMON" then
            -- A unit of ours has summoned a new pet/totem.  Here we map the
            -- new GUID to the party member's with the string "pet" added.
            -- This way we can use a single table to store damage for all units
            self.pet_guids[destGUID] = srcGUID .. "pet"
        end
    end
```

Because you are only concerned about events that are caused by damage or events that are caused by healing you can use a lookup table to know whether to continue processing. If the incoming event doesn't match one of the entries in the table, the function just returns.

If you look at the prefix/suffix information earlier in this chapter, you'll see that SWING_DAMAGE is the only damage event that doesn't contain information about the spell that caused the damage (because it's caused by auto-attacking). The first line of the damage event processing block sets a variable called offset that is used to select() the right arguments from the arguments that were passed in. If you're on a SWING_DAMAGE event the offset is set to 1, otherwise it's set to 3.

You then select the amount of damage and other relevant information from the arguments. You check the pet GUID mapping table to see if you need to convert the pet GUID to the owner's GUID. Then, you store the damage into the damage table.

Heals are even easier because you don't have to worry about pet's healing (for the purposes of this addon, we're choosing not to track pet heals). You don't want to count overhealing, however, which is what happens when, for example, a heal lands for 6000 healing but the target is only missing 3000 damage. In this case, the API will show 3000 overhealing, so you subtract this from the amount healed.

The SPELL_SUMMON event indicates that someone in your party has summoned a new pet (such as a totem or a druid's treants). When this happens and you don't have the unitID, you just update the GUID mapping table directly.

Taking "Snapshots" of Damage and Healing

Every few seconds you are going to take a snapshot of the current damage and healing, allowing you to calculate averages over every few seconds rather than only being able to display overall stats. Add the following function definition to CombatStatus.lua:

```
local units = {"player", "pet", "party1", "partypet1", "party2", "partypet2", ↵
"party3", "partypet3", "party4", "partypet4"}
function CombatStatus:TakeSnapshot()
  -- This function loops through all the valid unit ids and stores
  -- the current DPS or HPS so we can later subtract it.
  for idx, unit in ipairs(units) do
    local guid = UnitGUID(unit)

    if guid then
      if self.pet_guids[guid] then
        guid = self.pet_guids[guid]
      end

      self.snapshots[guid].damage = self.party_damage[guid]
      self.snapshots[guid].heals = self.party_heals[guid]
    end
  end
end
```

Because you need to loop over the unitIDs in both the update and the snapshot functions, you create a table that has each of the unitIDs you're concerned with. For each unit, you look up the GUID and if it's a known pet GUID you translate it using your mapping table. Then you update the entry in the snapshots table with the current damage and healing information.

Writing an OnUpdate Function

You need a simple timer to handle the periodic updates to the damage and healing information. Add the following function definition to `CombatStatus.lua`:

```lua
local counter = 0
local throttle = 5.0
function CombatStatus:OnUpdate(elapsed)
  counter = counter + elapsed
  if counter >= throttle then
    counter = 0
    self:UpdateFrame(throttle)
    self:TakeSnapshot()
  end
end
```

Every five seconds when the frame is shown, the frame will be updated and then a new snapshot will be taken. If you took the snapshot first, then everyone would always show 0 dps because it would have nothing to compare against. You pass the `throttle` argument to the update function, so it knows what time period to divide the damage by.

Responding to Events

You need to glue everything together by responding to the events you have registered for. Replace the `OnEvent` function with the following version:

```lua
function CombatStatus:OnEvent(event, ...)
  if event == "COMBAT_LOG_EVENT_UNFILTERED" then
    -- Check to see if the source of the event is someone within the
    -- circle of our party
    local srcFlags = select(5, ...)
    if bit.band(srcFlags, COMBATLOG_OBJECT_AFFILIATION_MASK) > ↵
COMBATLOG_OBJECT_AFFILIATION_PARTY then
      return
    end
    self:ProcessEntry(...)
  elseif event == "PARTY_MEMBERS_CHANGED" then
    for i = 1, GetNumPartyMembers() do
      local unit = "party" .. i
      self:UpdatePets(unit)
    end
    if not self.in_combat then
      self:UpdateFrame()
    end
  elseif event == "UNIT_PET" then
    local unit = ...
    self:UpdatePets(unit)
```

```
    elseif event == "PLAYER_REGEN_DISABLED" then
      self.in_combat = true
      self.combat_start = GetTime()
      counter = 0                             -- Reset the OnUpdate counter
      self:TakeSnapshot()
      self:SetScript("OnUpdate", self.OnUpdate)
    elseif event == "PLAYER_REGEN_ENABLED" then
      self.in_combat = false
      self.combat_time = self.combat_time + GetTime() - self.combat_start
      self:SetScript("OnUpdate", nil)
      self:UpdateFrame()
    elseif event == "PLAYER_LOGIN" then
      self:Initialize()
    end
  end
```

The different sections of this function are explained in the following section.

COMBAT_LOG_EVENT_UNFILTERED

The COMBAT_LOG_EVENT_UNFILTERED event will happen the most often, so you want to ensure that it can be processed quickly. You put it at the top of the event handler and only pass it to the processing function when the event originates from an entity in the player's party.

PARTY_MEMBERS_CHANGED

When the composition of the player's party changes, you need to scan and update the pet GUID mappings. Whenever the PARTY_MEMBERS_CHANGED event fires, you loop through each of the party units and call the UpdatePets() method, passing in the unit. Then, if the player isn't currently in combat, you update the frame. You don't force an update when the player is in combat just because you already know it'll update when the OnUpdate triggers.

UNIT_PET

When a unit summons a pet, the UNIT_PET event will fire, with the first argument being the unitID. As a result, you just call your UpdatePets() function, passing in the unitID.

PLAYER_REGEN_DISABLED

You'll need some way to track whether or not the player is in combat. You could use the InCombatLockdown() function, but instead this addon uses the PLAYER_REGEN_DISABLED event to set a flag on the frame. At the same time, you also store the current time in the combat_start variable (so you can later subtract it to get elapsed time). Then you take a snapshot to ensure you have a point for comparison, and set the OnUpdate script so it will start triggering.

PLAYER_REGEN_ENABLED

The PLAYER_REGEN_ENABLED event will fire when the player leaves combat, and as a result the logic in this section is much the reverse of entering combat. You turn the combat flag off, and update the total amount of combat time by subtracting the current time from the start time. Next you clear the OnUpdate function and update the frame, which will show the total stats instead of the rolling average.

Creating the Frame Display

As an initial example, the display for this addon will be series of text strings that contain the damage and healing information. Eventually, you'll want to expand it to use status bars instead of text strings. Create your CreateFrames() function:

```
function CombatStatus:CreateFrames()
  self:ClearAllPoints()
  self:SetPoint("TOP", MinimapCluster, "BOTTOM", 0, -15)
  self:SetWidth(300)
  self:SetHeight(150)

  self.rows = {}
  for i = 1, 10 do
    local row = self:CreateFontString(nil, "OVERLAY", ↵
"GameFontHighlight")
    row:SetText("Blah")
    self.rows[i] = row

    if i == 1 then
      row:SetPoint("TOPLEFT", 0 ,0)
    else
      row:SetPoint("TOPLEFT", self.rows[i-1], "BOTTOMLEFT", 0, 0)
    end
  end
end
```

The frame is anchored directly below the minimap cluster and consists of 10 different font strings.

Updating the Frame Display

The actual calculations are accomplished in the UpdateFrame() method. Add this method to your file anywhere below the TakeSnapshot() method, because it uses the units table defined just before that function.

```
function CombatStatus:UpdateFrame(elapsed)
  for idx, unit in ipairs(units) do
    local row = self.rows[idx]
```

```
      if UnitExists(unit) then
        local guid = UnitGUID(unit)
        if self.pet_guids[guid] then
          guid = self.pet_guids[guid]
        end

        local dps, hps
        if elapsed  and elapsed > 0 then
          -- We are being called from the OnUpdate so we compare
          -- against the snapshot rather than calculating the
          -- total DPS and HPS

          dps = (self.party_damage[guid] - self.snapshots[guid].damage) ↵
/ elapsed
          hps = (self.party_heals[guid] - self.snapshots[guid].heals) ↵
/ elapsed
        elseif self.combat_time > 0 then
          dps = self.party_damage[guid] / self.combat_time
          hps = self.party_heals[guid] / self.combat_time
        else
          dps = 0
          hps = 0
        end

        -- Actually update the frame with the new values here
        local name = UnitName(unit)
        local dpstext = self:ShortNum(dps)
        local hpstext = self:ShortNum(hps)
        row:SetFormattedText("[%s] DPS: %s, Heal %s", name, dpstext, ↵
hpstext)
        row:Show()
      else
        row:Hide()
      end
    end
  end
end
```

The overall strategy here is to loop over each of the unitIDs and check to
see if the unit exists. If so, you fetch the GUID, translating it to a pet GUID if
necessary. Then you have two different sets of calculations. If the elapsed value
it set, it indicates the amount of time that has passed since the last snapshot.
In this case, you divide the difference between the current damage and the
snapshot by the elapsed time. Otherwise, you take the total damage and divide
by the total time in combat.

You use a utility function you're going to write to convert the numeric DPS
into a shorter version. Finally, you set the text string to display the heal per
second and damage per second. Define the ShortNum() method:

```
function CombatStatus:ShortNum(num)
  local large = num > 1000
```

```
    return string.format("%.2f%s", large and (num / 1000) or num, ↵
large and "k" or "")
end
```

This function takes in a number and if it's greater than 1000, converts it to a shorter form. This function will turn the damage 3337 into 3.34k, making it much easier to read and compare.

Future Additions

In its current form, CombatStatus is very primitive. Instead of showing status bars (or some other, flashier way of displaying the data), it uses simple formatted font strings. There are blank spaces left when units don't exist and it's not customizable in any way. Think about a few enhancements you might want for this basic addon, and consider releasing your own updated version!

Summary

This chapter introduced the combat log event system, including how to distinguish between the different combat events. You learned the different prefixes and suffixes that make up different events, including the arguments that differ between them. You created an addon that can track the damage and healing of your party both as a running average and total average. The next chapter shows you how to create scroll frames for displaying your data.

## CHAPTER 22

Creating Scroll Frames

When creating a custom user interface, you may have a need to display data that is too large for a reasonably sized window. World of Warcraft allows you to create frames that can scroll both horizontally and vertically, giving you more flexibility in the display of your data. This chapter shows you how to create two different types of scroll frames that are used throughout the default user interface.

A `ScrollFrame` is used to allow horizontal and vertical smooth scrolling of data that is too large for the containing frame. In the default user interface, the Quest Log uses a scroll frame when the quest description is too long for the window (see Figure 22-1). This type of scroll frame allows for smooth pixel-by-pixel scrolling of the contents.

A faux scroll frame is, as the name suggests, a way to simulate a scroll frame without actually using one. The Auction House uses this technique to display a list of auctions, shown in Figure 22-2. Because each row of the listing has the same size, only enough rows are created to show a single page of the listing instead of creating one for every single item.

As the user scrolls through the listing, the rows are updated to display different elements of the list. For certain applications this method is more efficient than trying to create a set of frames for every single row of the listing.

The inner workings of a scroll frame are very complex, so suffice it to say that the user interface first has to render the contents, and then render the scroll frame to contain it. This can be very inefficient, and you should avoid using scroll frames in tense situations, such as combat.

This chapter first shows you how to create actual scroll frames, and then introduces the basics of creating `FauxScrollFrames`.

Scroll frame   Scroll bar

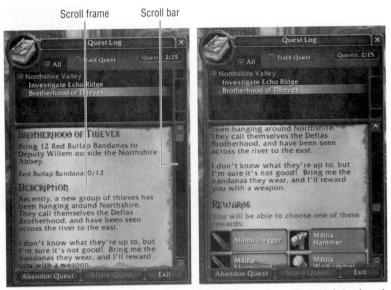

Figure 22-1: Quest Log scroll frame not scrolled (left) and scrolled (right), showing more of the quest text.

Figure 22-2: Auction House using a FauxScrollFrame

Using Scroll Frames

A scroll frame comprises the scrolling frame itself (the frame actually doing the visual clipping of its contents) and the scroll child (a frame that contains the contents). The scroll child can be a frame, a button or any other frame type. Although the scroll frame provides an API for scrolling horizontally and vertically, it does not provide any scroll bars on its own.

You can experiment with scroll frames by creating a new addon skeleton called ScrollFrameTest, so you have a place to put the test code for this chapter. Create ScrollFrameTest.toc with the following contents:

```
## Interface: 30300
## Title: ScrollFrameTest
## Notes: Test addon for scroll frames

ScrollFrameTest.xml
ScrollFrameTest.lua
```

Next, create the basic frame definition within ScrollFrameTest.xml:

```
<Ui xmlns="http://www.blizzard.com/wow/ui/"
  xmlns:xsi="http://www.w3.org/2001/XMLSchema-instance"
  xsi:schemaLocation="http://www.blizzard.com/wow/ui/
  http://wowprogramming.com/FrameXML/UI.xsd">
  <ScrollFrame name="ScrollFrameTest">
    <Size x="150" y="150"/>
    <Anchors>
      <Anchor point="CENTER"/>
    </Anchors>
    <Layers>
      <Layer level="BACKGROUND">
        <Texture setAllPoints="true">
          <Color r="0.0" g="0.0" b="0.0"/>
        </Texture>
      </Layer>
    </Layers>
  </ScrollFrame>
</Ui>
```

This definition creates a 150x150 frame in the center of the screen with a black background.

Adding a Scroll Child

The actual contents of the frame are defined within the <ScrollChild> element when using XML, or set with the SetScrollChild() method when using Lua. Add the following section to ScrollFrameTest.xml immediately after the </Layers> tag:

```
<ScrollChild>
  <Frame>
    <Size x="250" y="250"/>
    <Layers>
      <Layer level="ARTWORK">
        <Texture file="Interface\Icons\Spell_Shadow_DemonicFortitude">
```

```
        <Size x="100" y="100"/>
        <Anchors>
          <Anchor point="CENTER"/>
        </Anchors>
      </Texture>
    </Layer>
  </Layers>
 </Frame>
</ScrollChild>
```

The `<ScrollChild>` element should contain exactly one frame (or frame derivative) that contains the contents of the scroll frame. This child frame can be any size, but it will be visually clipped to the size of the `<ScrollFrame>` element. As a matter of fact, the horizontal and vertical scroll ranges are defined by the size of this child frame.

Load the game and you should see an image in the center of your screen similar to that shown in Figure 22-3.

Figure 22-3: ScrollFrameTest

Manipulating a ScrollFrame

Like any other specific type of frame, a `ScrollFrame` has different methods and handler scripts available. For example, the following methods can be used on scroll frames:

- `GetHorizontalScroll()`—Returns the current scroll value of the horizontal scroll component.

- `GetVerticalScroll()`—Returns the current scroll value of the vertical scroll component.

- `SetHorizontalScroll()`—Sets the scroll value of the horizontal scroll component.

- `SetVerticalScroll()`—Sets the scroll value of the vertical scroll component.

- `GetHorizontalScrollRange()`—Returns the maximum scroll range for the horizontal scroll component.

- `GetVerticalScrollRange()`—Returns the maximum scroll range for the vertical scroll component.

- `UpdateScrollChildRect()`—Updates the virtual size of the scroll child. This function should be called when the contents of the scroll frame are changed.

You can use these methods to center the image, using the following scripts in-game:

```
/run ScrollFrameTest:SetHorizontalScroll(-50)
/run ScrollFrameTest:SetVerticalScroll(50)
```

Note that the horizontal scroll requires a negative value to scroll the child to the right, whereas vertical scroll takes a positive number to scroll the child up. This is consistent with the way coordinates in the user interface work, where (0,0) is the bottom-left corner of the screen. Figure 22-4 shows the frame when adjusted using these commands.

Figure 22-4: ScrollFrameTest scrolled 50 pixels to the left and 50 pixels up.

Adding Scroll Bars

As you have seen, creating a scroll frame is simple, but isn't very helpful to your users if they have to use slash commands to scroll the frame. This section shows you an easy way to create a scroll bar using the `Slider` frame type.

Add the following to `ScrollFrameTest.xml`, after the `</Layers>` tag and before the `<ScrollChild>` tag. The particular order is important if you are validating your XML file, since the schema requires any sub-frames to be defined before the scroll child.

```
<Frames>
  <Slider name="ScrollFrameTest_HSlider" orientation="HORIZONTAL"
    minValue="0" maxValue="100" defaultValue="0" valueStep="1">
    <Size x="150" y="25"/>
    <Anchors>
        <Anchor point="TOP" relativePoint="BOTTOM" ↵
relativeTo="ScrollFrameTest"/>
    </Anchors>
```

```
      <Scripts>
        <OnValueChanged>
            ScrollFrameTest:SetHorizontalScroll(-1 * self:GetValue())
        </OnValueChanged>
      </Scripts>
      <ThumbTexture name="$parentThumbTexture"
        file="Interface\Buttons\UI-ScrollBar-Knob">
        <Size x="25" y="25"/>
      </ThumbTexture>
    </Slider>
    <Slider name="ScrollFrameTest_VSlider" orientation="VERTICAL"
      minValue="0" maxValue="100" defaultValue="0" valueStep="1">
      <Size x="25" y="150"/>
      <Anchors>
        <Anchor point="LEFT" relativePoint="RIGHT" ↵
  relativeTo="ScrollFrameTest"/>
      </Anchors>
      <Scripts>
        <OnValueChanged>
          ScrollFrameTest:SetVerticalScroll(self:GetValue())
        </OnValueChanged>
      </Scripts>
      <ThumbTexture name="$parentThumbTexture"
        file="Interface\Buttons\UI-ScrollBar-Knob">
        <Size x="25" y="25"/>
      </ThumbTexture>
    </Slider>
  </Frames>
```

These two XML definitions create two sliders with a range between 0 and 100, because the child frame is exactly 100 pixels larger than the scroll frame in either dimension. When the sliders are moved, the horizontal or vertical scroll is updated on the scroll frame. These simple scroll bars use the `UI-ScrollBar-Knob` graphic for the slider "thumb" graphic, and could be extended to use the border and backgrounds from those scroll bars, as well. Figure 22-5 shows the scroll frame operating in-game.

Figure 22-5: ScrollFrameTest scroll frame, with scroll bars.

Now the frame can also be adjusted via the sliders, using the `SetValue()` method, as in the following commands:

```
/run ScrollFrameTest_HSlider:SetValue(50)
/run ScrollFrameTest_VSlider:SetValue(50)
```

Creating Faux Scroll Frames

A faux scroll frame is a bit more complex to make because it must be tailored to the specific need. For example, you typically create a template and then a series of entries to make a single page. This section shows you how to create a line of icons onscreen that can be scrolled through in order to display all valid macro icons for selection. The API functions used here are the following:

- `GetNumMacroIcons()`—Returns the number of available macro icons.

- `GetMacroIconInfo(index)`—Returns the texture for the selected macro index.

This addon displays six icons side by side, and the slider is used to scroll between the available icons. Begin by creating an addon skeleton called `MacroIconTest`, and putting the following into `MacroIconTest.toc`:

```
## Interface: 30300
## Title: MacroIconTest
## Notes: Test addon for a faux scroll frame

MacroIconTest.lua
MacroIconTest.xml
```

Create `MacroIconTest.xml` with the following contents:

```
<Ui xmlns="http://www.blizzard.com/wow/ui/"
  xmlns:xsi="http://www.w3.org/2001/XMLSchema-instance"
  xsi:schemaLocation="http://www.blizzard.com/wow/ui/
  http://wowprogramming.com/FrameXML/UI.xsd">
  <Button name="MacroIconTest_IconTemplate" virtual="true">
    <Size x="32" y="32"/>
    <NormalTexture name="$parentIcon" setAllPoints="true"/>
      <HighlightTexture alphaMode="ADD"
          file="Interface\Buttons\ButtonHilight-Square"/>
  </Button>
</Ui>
```

This simple XML template is used to create each of the icon slots. It defines a default texture, as well as a highlight texture to give a bit more visual feedback. Insert the following XML before the `</Ui>` tag to create a set of icons:

```
<Frame name="MacroIconTest">
  <Size x="192" y="32"/>
  <Anchors>
```

```
                    <Anchor point="CENTER"/>
                  </Anchors>
                  <Frames>
                    <Button name="$parentIcon1" inherits="MacroIconTest_IconTemplate">
                      <Anchors>
                        <Anchor point="TOPLEFT"/>
                      </Anchors>
                    </Button>
                    <Button name="$parentIcon2" inherits="MacroIconTest_IconTemplate">
                      <Anchors>
                        <Anchor point="TOPLEFT" relativePoint="TOPRIGHT" ↵
           relativeTo="$parentIcon1"/>
                      </Anchors>
                    </Button>
                    <Button name="$parentIcon3" inherits="MacroIconTest_IconTemplate">
                      <Anchors>
                        <Anchor point="TOPLEFT" relativePoint="TOPRIGHT" ↵
           relativeTo="$parentIcon2"/>
                      </Anchors>
                    </Button>
                    <Button name="$parentIcon4" inherits="MacroIconTest_IconTemplate">
                      <Anchors>
                        <Anchor point="TOPLEFT" relativePoint="TOPRIGHT" ↵
           relativeTo="$parentIcon3"/>
                      </Anchors>
                    </Button>
                    <Button name="$parentIcon5" inherits="MacroIconTest_IconTemplate">
                      <Anchors>
                        <Anchor point="TOPLEFT" relativePoint="TOPRIGHT" ↵
           relativeTo="$parentIcon4"/>
                      </Anchors>
                    </Button>
                    <Button name="$parentIcon6" inherits="MacroIconTest_IconTemplate">
                      <Anchors>
                        <Anchor point="TOPLEFT" relativePoint="TOPRIGHT" ↵
           relativeTo="$parentIcon5"/>
                      </Anchors>
                    </Button>
                  </Frames>
                </Frame>
```

If you jump into the game at this point, you'll have an invisible set of boxes that can be moused over (the highlight texture will still show) but that don't actually display anything. Jump to `MacroIconTest.lua` and add the following function:

```
function MacroIconTest_UpdateIcons(startIcon)
  local name = "MacroIconTestIcon"

  for i=1,6 do
    local texture = GetMacroIconInfo(startIcon + (i - 1))
```

```
      local button = getglobal(name .. i)
      button:SetNormalTexture(texture)
    end
  end
```

This function accepts a single argument, namely the index of the icon that should be displayed first. It then loops through the six different icon buttons and changes their texture accordingly. The loop assumes the first icon is numbered 1, because the GetMacroIconInfo() function makes the same assumption.

TIP Not all data is available immediately within the game client. For example, the number of icons and the texture information about each macro icon isn't available until after the client has been partially initialized. Generally, this information is available after the PLAYER_LOGIN event, which is fired just before the client begins displaying the 3-D world. Some functions may need to be delayed until after this event to work properly.

Add the following behavior scripts to the MacroIconTest frame by putting the following section immediately after its </Frames> tag:

```
<Scripts>
  <OnLoad>
    self:RegisterEvent("PLAYER_LOGIN")
  </OnLoad>
  <OnEvent>
    if event == "PLAYER_LOGIN" then
      GetNumMacroIcons()
      MacroIconTest_UpdateIcons(1)
    end
  </OnEvent>
</Scripts>
```

Here you register for the PLAYER_LOGIN event, and when that event fires, the OnEvent script calls GetNumMacroIcons(), and then calls the MacroIconTest_UpdateIcons() function to update the icon display. When guild banks were introduced, the macro icon system was changed so icon information isn't available until the GetNumMacroIcons() function has been called at least once, hence the call here. Load the game client, and you should see something like that shown in Figure 22-6 in the center of your screen.

Figure 22-6: MacroIconTest frame

Test the update function by running some of the following macros:

- `/run MacroIconTest_UpdateIcons(15)`
- `/run MacroIconTest_UpdateIcons(180)`
- `/run MacroIconTest_UpdateIcons(-1)`

Notice that in the last example, rather than an error the first two icons are shown as blank.

Adding Scroll Bars

As in the previous example, a slider can be used to scroll through the list of icons. Add the following to your `MacroIconTest.xml` file after the `</Frame>` tag from the main frame:

```
<Slider name="MacroIconTest_HSlider" orientation="HORIZONTAL">
  <Size y="25"/>
  <Anchors>
    <Anchor point="TOPLEFT" relativePoint="BOTTOMLEFT" ↵
relativeTo="MacroIconTest"/>
    <Anchor point="TOPRIGHT" relativePoint="BOTTOMRIGHT"
           relativeTo="MacroIconTest"/>
  </Anchors>
  <Backdrop edgeFile="Interface\Buttons\UI-SliderBar-Border"
          bgFile="Interface\Buttons\UI-SliderBar-Background" tile="true">
    <EdgeSize>
      <AbsValue val="8"/>
    </EdgeSize>
    <TileSize>
      <AbsValue val="8"/>
    </TileSize>
    <BackgroundInsets>
      <AbsInset left="3" right="3" top="6" bottom="6"/>
    </BackgroundInsets>
  </Backdrop>
  <ThumbTexture name="$parentThumbTexture"
              file="Interface\Buttons\UI-ScrollBar-Knob">
    <Size x="25" y="25"/>
  </ThumbTexture>
</Slider>
```

This creates a slider bar with a backdrop and border to make it look a bit more like a scroll bar. Add the scripts section to the slider by putting the following after the `</Backdrop>` tag and before the definition of the thumb texture:

```
<Scripts>
  <OnLoad>
    local max = GetNumMacroIcons()
```

```
    self:SetMinMaxValues(1, max - 5)
    self:SetValueStep(1.0)
    self:SetValue(1)
  </OnLoad>
  <OnValueChanged>
    MacroIconTest_UpdateIcons(value)
  </OnValueChanged>
</Scripts>
```

The resulting addon is shown in Figure 22-7, including the scroll bar with border and background.

Figure 22-7: MacroIconTest addon showing various macro icons

Scrolling with the Mouse Wheel

As an extra method of scrolling the icons, you can add support for scrolling with the mouse wheel. This involves setting an OnMouseWheel script. Add the following to the <Scripts> section of the MacroIconTest frame (not the slider):

```
<OnMouseWheel>
  MacroIconTest_OnMouseWheel(self, delta)
</OnMouseWheel>
```

Then add this function to MacroIconTest.lua:

```
function MacroIconTest_OnMouseWheel(self, delta)
  local current = MacroIconTest_HSlider:GetValue()

  if (delta < 0) and (current < GetNumMacroIcons()) then
    MacroIconTest_HSlider:SetValue(current + 1)
  elseif (delta > 0) and (current > 1) then
    MacroIconTest_HSlider:SetValue(current - 1)
  end
end
```

This function definition just piggybacks onto the slider bar's min and max values to ensure it doesn't go outside those boundaries. You should now be able to scroll the frame using both the slider and the mouse wheel.

Problems with Slider Precision

You may notice that if you scroll using slash commands or the mouse wheel, you can scroll through the icons one-by-one. If you try to use the slider instead, you can't really tell how many icons are scrolling on each step. That's because there are more than a thousand icons to be displayed, and the slider widget only has so much precision when working with the mouse.

You could fix this by changing the *step* value for the slider. In this case, change it to 3, so the slider will move in steps of 3. Unfortunately, if you change the precision of the slider, the mouse wheel can no longer scroll icon-by-icon. You may never run into this issue, but here's the change you would make to allow this (altered lines are highlighted):

```
<OnLoad>
    local max = GetNumMacroIcons()
    self:SetMinMaxValues(1, max - 5)
    self:SetValueStep(3.0)
    self:SetValue(1)
</OnLoad>
```

Summary

A visual scroll frame is a smooth, pixel-by-pixel scroll frame that can be used to display contents that are too large for the parent window. Scroll frames of this nature are used in the default user interface in the Quest Log, and within the edit box in the macro window.

A faux scroll frame uses a set number of frames to display a list of rows or columns by changing offsets using the scroll bar. These scroll frames don't change visually when you scroll through them; rather, they redraw the rows with different information. These pseudo scroll frames are used in the Auction House, Friends list, and several other places in the default user interface.

The Code

ScrollFrameTest

ScrollFrameTest.toc

```
## Interface: 30300
## Title: ScrollFrameTest
## Notes: Test addon for scroll frames

ScrollFrameTest.xml
ScrollFrameTest.lua
```

ScrollFrameTest.xml

```
<Ui xmlns="http://www.blizzard.com/wow/ui/"
  xmlns:xsi="http://www.w3.org/2001/XMLSchema-instance"
  xsi:schemaLocation="http://www.blizzard.com/wow/ui/
```

```
    http://wowprogramming.com/FrameXML/UI.xsd">
    <ScrollFrame name="ScrollFrameTest">
      <Size x="150" y="150"/>
      <Anchors>
        <Anchor point="CENTER"/>
      </Anchors>
      <Layers>
        <Layer level="BACKGROUND">
          <Texture setAllPoints="true">
            <Color r="0.0" g="0.0" b="0.0"/>
          </Texture>
        </Layer>
      </Layers>
      <Frames>
        <Slider name="ScrollFrameTest_HSlider" ↵
orientation="HORIZONTAL"
          minValue="0" maxValue="100" defaultValue="0" valueStep="1">
          <Size x="150" y="25"/>
          <Anchors>
            <Anchor point="TOP" relativePoint="BOTTOM" ↵
relativeTo="ScrollFrameTest"/>
          </Anchors>
          <Scripts>
            <OnValueChanged>
              ScrollFrameTest:SetHorizontalScroll(-1 * ↵
self:GetValue())
            </OnValueChanged>
          </Scripts>
          <ThumbTexture name="$parentThumbTexture"
            file="Interface\Buttons\UI-ScrollBar-Knob">
            <Size x="25" y="25"/>
          </ThumbTexture>
        </Slider>
        <Slider name="ScrollFrameTest_VSlider" orientation="VERTICAL"
          minValue="0" maxValue="100" defaultValue="0" valueStep="1">
          <Size x="25" y="150"/>
          <Anchors>
            <Anchor point="LEFT" relativePoint="RIGHT" ↵
relativeTo="ScrollFrameTest"/>
          </Anchors>
          <Scripts>
            <OnValueChanged>
              ScrollFrameTest:SetVerticalScroll(self:GetValue())
            </OnValueChanged>
          </Scripts>
          <ThumbTexture name="$parentThumbTexture"
            file="Interface\Buttons\UI-ScrollBar-Knob">
            <Size x="25" y="25"/>
          </ThumbTexture>
        </Slider>
```

```
      </Frames>
      <ScrollChild>
        <Frame>
          <Size x="250" y="250"/>
          <Layers>
            <Layer level="ARTWORK">
              <Texture ↵
file="Interface\Icons\Spell_Shadow_DemonicFortitude">
                <Size x="100" y="100"/>
                <Anchors>
                  <Anchor point="CENTER"/>
                </Anchors>
              </Texture>
            </Layer>
          </Layers>
        </Frame>
      </ScrollChild>
    </ScrollFrame>
  </Ui>
```

MacroIconTest

MacroIconTest.toc

```
## Interface: 30200
## Title: MacroIconTest
## Notes: Test addon for a faux scroll frame

MacroIconTest.lua
MacroIconTest.xml
```

MacroIconTest.lua

```
function MacroIconTest_UpdateIcons(startIcon)
  local name = "MacroIconTestIcon"

  for i=1,6 do
    local texture = GetMacroIconInfo(startIcon + (i - 1))
    local button = getglobal(name .. i)
    button:SetNormalTexture(texture)
  end
end

function MacroIconTest_OnMouseWheel(self, delta)
  local current = MacroIconTest_HSlider:GetValue()

  if (delta < 0) and (current < GetNumMacroIcons()) then
    MacroIconTest_HSlider:SetValue(current + 1)
  elseif (delta > 0) and (current > 1) then
    MacroIconTest_HSlider:SetValue(current - 1)
  end
end
```

MacroIconTest.xml

```xml
<Ui xmlns="http://www.blizzard.com/wow/ui/"
  xmlns:xsi="http://www.w3.org/2001/XMLSchema-instance"
  xsi:schemaLocation="http://www.blizzard.com/wow/ui/
  http://wowprogramming.com/FrameXML/UI.xsd">
  <Button name="MacroIconTest_IconTemplate" virtual="true">
    <Size x="32" y="32"/>
    <NormalTexture name="$parentIcon" setAllPoints="true"/>
    <HighlightTexture alphaMode="ADD" ↵
      file="Interface\Buttons\ButtonHilight-Square"/>
  </Button>
  <Frame name="MacroIconTest">
    <Size x="192" y="32"/>
    <Anchors>
      <Anchor point="CENTER"/>
    </Anchors>
    <Frames>
      <Button name="$parentIcon1" ↵
inherits="MacroIconTest_IconTemplate">
        <Anchors>
          <Anchor point="TOPLEFT"/>
        </Anchors>
      </Button>
      <Button name="$parentIcon2" ↵
inherits="MacroIconTest_IconTemplate">
        <Anchors>
          <Anchor point="TOPLEFT" relativePoint="TOPRIGHT" ↵
relativeTo="$parentIcon1"/>
        </Anchors>
      </Button>
      <Button name="$parentIcon3"
inherits="MacroIconTest_IconTemplate">
        <Anchors>
          <Anchor point="TOPLEFT" relativePoint="TOPRIGHT" ↵
relativeTo="$parentIcon2"/>
        </Anchors>
      </Button>
      <Button name="$parentIcon4" ↵
inherits="MacroIconTest_IconTemplate">
        <Anchors>
          <Anchor point="TOPLEFT" relativePoint="TOPRIGHT" ↵
relativeTo="$parentIcon3"/>
        </Anchors>
      </Button>
      <Button name="$parentIcon5" ↵
inherits="MacroIconTest_IconTemplate">
        <Anchors>
          <Anchor point="TOPLEFT" relativePoint="TOPRIGHT" ↵
relativeTo="$parentIcon4"/>
```

```
          </Anchors>
        </Button>
        <Button name="$parentIcon6" ↵
inherits="MacroIconTest_IconTemplate">
          <Anchors>
            <Anchor point="TOPLEFT" relativePoint="TOPRIGHT" ↵
relativeTo="$parentIcon5"/>
          </Anchors>
        </Button>
      </Frames>
      <Scripts>
        <OnLoad>
          self:RegisterEvent("PLAYER_LOGIN")
        </OnLoad>
        <OnEvent>
          if event == "PLAYER_LOGIN" then
            GetNumMacroIcons()
            MacroIconTest_UpdateIcons(1)
          end
        </OnEvent>
        <OnMouseWheel>
          MacroIconTest_OnMouseWheel(self, delta)
        </OnMouseWheel>
      </Scripts>
    </Frame>
    <Slider name="MacroIconTest_HSlider" orientation="HORIZONTAL">
      <Size y="25"/>
      <Anchors>
        <Anchor point="TOPLEFT" relativePoint="BOTTOMLEFT" ↵
relativeTo="MacroIconTest"/>
        <Anchor point="TOPRIGHT" relativePoint="BOTTOMRIGHT" ↵
relativeTo="MacroIconTest"/>
      </Anchors>
      <Backdrop edgeFile="Interface\Buttons\UI-SliderBar-Border"
        bgFile="Interface\Buttons\UI-SliderBar-Background"
        tile="true">
        <EdgeSize>
          <AbsValue val="8"/>
        </EdgeSize>
        <TileSize>
          <AbsValue val="8"/>
        </TileSize>
        <BackgroundInsets>
          <AbsInset left="3" right="3" top="6" bottom="6"/>
        </BackgroundInsets>
      </Backdrop>
      <Scripts>
        <OnLoad>
          local max = GetNumMacroIcons()
          self:SetMinMaxValues(1, max - 5)
```

```
            self:SetValueStep(1.0)
            self:SetValue(1)
        </OnLoad>
        <OnValueChanged>
          MacroIconTest_UpdateIcons(value)
        </OnValueChanged>
      </Scripts>
      <ThumbTexture name="$parentThumbTexture"
        file="Interface\Buttons\UI-ScrollBar-Knob">
        <Size x="25" y="25"/>
      </ThumbTexture>
    </Slider>
</Ui>
```

## CHAPTER 23

Creating Dropdown Menus

Dropdown menus are used throughout the default user interface to provide the user with a list of selectable items. Some menus, such as the menu that appears when you right-click your player frame (shown in Figure 23-1), are used to provide a list of actions or configuration options based on context. Other menus have artwork that makes them appear as more standard dropdown-style menus, such as the dropdown used for the column selection in the Who list panel, shown in Figure 23-2.

At a first glance, the system to create these dropdowns may seem rather complex. This chapter helps to demystify the dropdown system in World of Warcraft, showing you how to create them and make them work for your addons.

Creating a Basic Dropdown

Creating a dropdown involves four major steps. Luckily, Blizzard provides a robust set of templates and functions that make creating them fairly easy. This section leads you through these steps:

1. Adding a button that can be clicked to show the dropdown menu. This may be a button that already exists in your addon or something entirely new.

2. Creating a new frame that inherits Blizzard's `UIDropDownMenuTemplate` template. It is not strictly necessary to create your own frame, but this method allows you to ensure no other addons will accidentally alter your dropdown.

Figure 23-1: Dropdown menu displayed when right-clicking on the player frame

Figure 23-2: Column dropdown in the Who list panel

3. Initializing the dropdown menu once it has been created.

4. Writing code that causes a click on the button to toggle the display of the dropdown menu.

For this example, you need to create a new addon called DropDownTest. Create the basic addon skeleton including `DropDownTest.toc`, `DropDownTest.lua`, and `DropDownTest.xml`.

Adding a Toggle Button

Using the Blizzard template `GameMenuButtonTemplate`, create a button by adding the following code to `DropDownTest.xml`:

```
<Ui xmlns="http://www.blizzard.com/wow/ui/"
  xmlns:xsi="http://www.w3.org/2001/XMLSchema-instance"
  xsi:schemaLocation="http://www.blizzard.com/wow/ui/
  http://wowprogramming.com/FrameXML/UI.xsd">
  <Button name="DropDownTest_Button" inherits="GameMenuButtonTemplate" ↵
parent="UIParent" text="DropDownTest">
    <Anchors>
      <Anchor point="CENTER"/>
    </Anchors>
    <Scripts>
      <OnClick>
        DropDownTest_ButtonOnClick(self, button, down)
      </OnClick>
```

```
      </Scripts>
    </Button>
  </Ui>
```

To make a quick and easy button, this code uses the `GameMenuButton Template`. The text is set using the XML attribute, and the new button is anchored to the center of the user interface. When the button is clicked, it calls the `DropDownTest_ButtonOnClick()` function and passes the proper arguments.

Creating a Dropdown Frame

The default Blizzard interface uses templates for its dropdown menus and, as a result, you can re-use the templates as a basis for your own menus. Add the following frame definition to `DropDownTest.xml`:

```
<Frame name="DropDownTest_DropDown" inherits="UIDropDownMenuTemplate"
frameStrata="FULLSCREEN_DIALOG">
  <Scripts>
    <OnLoad>
      DropDownTest_DropDownOnLoad(self)
    </OnLoad>
  </Scripts>
</Frame>
```

This frame simply inherits from the given template and sets the `frameStrata` to be `DIALOG_FULLSCREEN`. This allows the dropdown menu to be used on another frame that is already set to display on the full screen frame strata. When the frame is first created, `DropDownTest_DropDownOnLoad()` is called to handle the initialization of the dropdown menu.

Initializing the Dropdown

Two things need to happen when you are initializing a dropdown menu. First, you must define a function that will be responsible for describing the actual buttons and adding them to the menu. Second, you must call the global `UIDropDownMenu_Initialize()` function to do some setup and accounting on the frame.

Adding Buttons to the Dropdown

This initialization function is called by the default user interface to set up the actual buttons that appear within the dropdown menu. The function is passed the dropdown frame as the first argument, and a second argument, `level`, indicates what level of the dropdown is being displayed (for multilevel menus). This example does not use this argument because it will only contain three items on the same level; multilevel menus are covered later in this chapter.

Add the following function to your `DropDownTest.lua` file:

```
function DropDownTest_InitializeDropDown(self, level)
  -- Create a table to use for button information
  local info = UIDropDownMenu_CreateInfo()

  -- Create a title button
  info.text = "DropDown Test"
  info.isTitle = 1
  UIDropDownMenu_AddButton(info)

  -- Create a normal button
  info = UIDropDownMenu_CreateInfo()
  info.text = "Sample Item 1"
  UIDropDownMenu_AddButton(info)

  -- Create another normal button
  info = UIDropDownMenu_CreateInfo()
  info.text = "Sample Item 2"
  UIDropDownMenu_AddButton(info)
end
```

The `UIDropDownMenu_CreateInfo()` function here is used to get an empty *info* table to be filled with button attributes and eventually passed into `UIDropDownMenu_AddButton()`. Internally this function re-uses tables to prevent excessive memory usage for larger menus.

Calling UIDropDownMenu_Initialize()

To tell the user interface what initialization function should be called when the dropdown is shown, you must call `UIDropDownMenu_Initialize()`. This function takes in the dropdown frame as the first argument, and the initialization function as the second. Call this function by adding the following to `DropDownTest.lua`:

```
function DropDownTest_DropDownOnLoad(self)
  UIDropDownMenu_Initialize(self, DropDownTest_InitializeDropDown)
end
```

Your initialization function will now be called each time the menu is opened, and again every time the state of the menu changes (for example when you check an option, or open a submenu).

Toggling the Dropdown Menu

The final step is actually opening the dropdown menu when the user clicks the button you've created. The Blizzard template code defines a toggle function, called `ToggleDropDownMenu()`, that allows you do this, as well as specify some basic positioning information. The function takes eight possible arguments, but only the first six are typically used:

- `level` (number)—The initial level to display. This number is passed directly to the initialization function.
- `value`—A value used to set the global variable UIDROPDOWNMENU_MENU_ VALUE, which is used primarily in multilevel menus. This is discussed in detail later in this chapter.
- `dropDownFrame`—The actual dropdown frame to display.
- `anchorName` (string)—The name of the frame to which the dropdown should be anchored. This can also be the string cursor, in which case the dropdown is anchored to the cursor position at the moment this function is called.
- `xOffset` (number)—A horizontal offset in units for the dropdown menu.
- `yOffset` (number)—A vertical offset in units for the dropdown menu.

Add the following function to `DropDownTest.lua` to call `ToggleDropDown Menu()` when the test button is clicked:

```
function DropDownTest_ButtonOnClick(self, button, down)
  local name = self:GetName()
  ToggleDropDownMenu(1, nil, DropDownTest_DropDown, name, 0, 0)
end
```

Because this example displays only one level of the menu, the function passes 1 as the level and doesn't include a menu value. The dropdown will be anchored to the button itself, with no offset from the default location.

Testing the Dropdown

Log in to World of Warcraft with the DropDownTest addon enabled; a game button should display in the center of your screen. Click the button and you should see the dropdown menu shown in Figure 23-3.

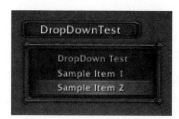

Figure 23-3: Dropdown menu created by the DropDownTest addon

The example menu won't do anything at the moment, but later in this chapter you learn how to make the menu elements functional so they can be used for configuration and other purposes. By default, the menu will timeout after a certain period of inactivity, and clicking the test button while the menu is open closes it outright.

Creating Multilevel Dropdowns

Creating a multilevel dropdown menu is straightforward once you understand how a dropdown menu is created and initialized. In particular, the first argument passed to the initialization function is a numeric value, the level of the dropdown being displayed.

Consider a dropdown with two submenus called Alpha and Beta. Assume each menu has distinct items that will be displayed. Because the root level of the menu is 1, the level for both Alpha and Beta is 2. If each of them had submenus, they would be level 3, and so on. To differentiate between Alpha and Beta, you will set a *value* element in the button table.

Rewrite the `DropDownTest_InitializeDropDown()` function in your test addon, as follows:

```
function DropDownTest_InitializeDropDown(self, level)
    if level == 1 then
        local info = UIDropDownMenu_CreateInfo()
        info.text = "DropDown Test"
        info.isTitle = true
        UIDropDownMenu_AddButton(info, level)

        info = UIDropDownMenu_CreateInfo()
        info.text = "Alpha Submenu"
        info.hasArrow = true
        info.value = "Alpha"
        UIDropDownMenu_AddButton(info, level)

        info = UIDropDownMenu_CreateInfo()
        info.text = "Beta Submenu"
        info.hasArrow = true
        info.value = "Beta"
        UIDropDownMenu_AddButton(info, level)
    elseif (level == 2) and (UIDROPDOWNMENU_MENU_VALUE == "Alpha") then
        local info = UIDropDownMenu_CreateInfo()
        info.text = "Alpha Sub-item 1"
        UIDropDownMenu_AddButton(info, level)
    elseif (level == 2) and (UIDROPDOWNMENU_MENU_VALUE == "Beta") then
        local info = UIDropDownMenu_CreateInfo()
        info.text = "Beta Sub-item 1"
```

```
            UIDropDownMenu_AddButton(info, level)
      end
end
```

You'll notice quite a few differences from the original function, namely the use of the `hasArrow` and `value` attributes in some of the button tables. `hasArrow` tells the template code to treat the button as a menu header and to display the arrow graphic. The `value` attribute is used to distinguish between different submenus.

In the initialization function, if the level is 2, the value of `UIDROPDOWNMENU_MENU_VALUE` is checked. This variable is set to the value attribute of the menu header. These values can be anything—tables, functions, numbers, and strings—as long as you can use them to distinguish between menus.

An optional second argument to the `UIDropDownMenu_AddButton()` function indicates the level at which the new button should be added. Without this, entering a submenu would only add buttons to the root menu instead of popping out an additional level, and that would be confusing.

The resulting menu can be seen in Figures 23-4 and 23-5.

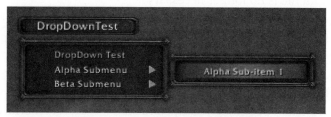

Figure 23-4: Example dropdown menu with Alpha expanded

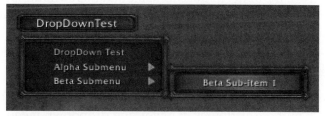

Figure 23-5: Example dropdown menu with Beta expanded

Adding Functionality to Dropdowns

In addition to displaying text, dropdowns may contain more interactive elements, such as checkboxes and color pickers. This section shows you how to make dropdowns more interactive using these elements, and how to add functionality to standard text buttons.

Customizing Text Elements

Each text element in a dropdown menu can be customized using the following attributes:

- `text` (string)—Text to be displayed on the menu item.
- `isTitle`—A boolean flag indicating if the button should be treated as a title button (not clickable and gold text).
- `disabled`—A boolean flag indicating if the button is disabled.
- `colorCode`—A string containing a color code to be applied to the text in the format |cAARRGGBB, including alpha, red, green, and blue. This attribute is valid only for buttons that are enabled.
- `notClickable`—A boolean flag indicating that the button should not be clickable. This forces the button's color to white, so you cannot color an un-clickable item.
- `notCheckable`—A boolean flag indicating that the button cannot be checked. This causes the button's width to shrink because the check button graphic is no longer necessary.
- `tooltipTitle` (string)—Title to be displayed in the tooltip that appears when hovering the mouse over the menu option. Tooltips are only displayed when Beginner Tooltips are enabled under Interface Options.
- `tooltiptext` (string)—Text to be displayed in the tooltip that appears when hovering the mouse over the menu option. Tooltips are only displayed when Beginner Tooltips are enabled under Interface Options.
- `textHeight` (number)—The height of the font used for the button text.
- `justifyH`—If the button is not checkable and this attribute is set to CENTER, the text on the button will be centered. No other text justification options are available.
- `fontObject`—A Font object to be used as a replacement for the normal and highlight fonts in the dropdown.

You can replace your `DropDownTest_Initialize()` function with the following to see each of these attributes in a working dropdown menu. Figure 23-6 shows the corresponding dropdown menu.

```
function DropDownTest_InitializeDropDown(self, level)
  -- Create a table to use for button information
  local info = UIDropDownMenu_CreateInfo()

  info.text = "Title Button"
  info.isTitle = true
  UIDropDownMenu_AddButton(info)

  info = UIDropDownMenu_CreateInfo()
```

```
    info.text = "Disabled Button"
    info.disabled = true
    UIDropDownMenu_AddButton(info)

    info = UIDropDownMenu_CreateInfo()
    info.text = "Colored Text"
    info.colorCode = "|cFF33FF22"
    UIDropDownMenu_AddButton(info)

    info = UIDropDownMenu_CreateInfo()
    info.text = "Not Clickable"
    info.notClickable = true
    UIDropDownMenu_AddButton(info)

    info = UIDropDownMenu_CreateInfo()
    info.text = "Not Checkable"
    info.notCheckable = true
    UIDropDownMenu_AddButton(info)

    info = UIDropDownMenu_CreateInfo()
    info.text = "Button with Tooltip"
    info.tooltipTitle = "Tooltip title"
    info.tooltipText = "Contents of the tooltip"
    UIDropDownMenu_AddButton(info)

    info = UIDropDownMenu_CreateInfo()
    info.text = "Centered Text"
    info.justifyH = "CENTER"
    info.notCheckable = true
    UIDropDownMenu_AddButton(info)

    info = UIDropDownMenu_CreateInfo()
    info.text = "Text with custom font"
    info.fontObject = SystemFont_Small
    UIDropDownMenu_AddButton(info)
end
```

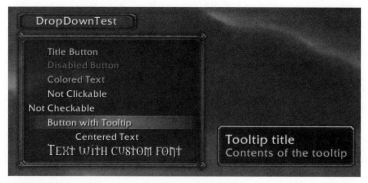

Figure 23-6: Dropdown menu showing various buttons

Function Menu Items

Any menu item can be set to call a function when it is clicked by using the following set of attributes:

- `func`—The function to be called when the button is clicked.
- `arg1`—An argument to be passed to the function when it is called.
- `arg2`—Another argument to be passed to the function when it is called.
- `keepShownOnClick`—A boolean flag indicating whether or not the drop-down menu should remain showing instead of disappearing when the button is clicked.

Although the attributes are called `arg1` and `arg2`, they are actually the second and third arguments that are passed to the function. The first argument is the button itself (which contains all of the valid attributes in the original info table).

Add a function-enabled button to your dropdown using the following code:

```
info = UIDropDownMenu_CreateInfo()
info.text = "Function Button"
function info.func(button, arg1, arg2)
  print("CALL: Arg1: " .. tostring(arg1) .. " Arg2: " .. tostring(arg2))
end
info.arg1 = "Foo"
info.arg2 = "Bar"
UIDropDownMenu_AddButton(info)
```

CheckButton Menu Items

Many dropdown menus are used for configuration, such as the "Player vs. Player" setting that can be accessed by right-clicking the player frame. These toggleable items make use of the checkbox included in each dropdown entry, and the `checked` attribute to signify that the item is checked.

```
info = UIDropDownMenu_CreateInfo()
info.text = "Toggleable setting"
info.checked = SOME_SETTING
function info.func(button, arg1, arg2)
  SOME_SETTING = not SOME_SETTING
  print("SOME_SETTING is " .. tostring(SOME_SETTING)
end
UIDropDownMenu_AddButton(info)
```

This code defines a new button that can be clicked to change the value of the global variable SOME_SETTING. Because it starts off with a value of `nil`, the button won't be checked to start. Every time the button is clicked it will toggle the setting and print a message to the chat frame. Figure 23-7 shows the button when the SOME_SETTING is true.

Figure 23-7: Dropdown Test showing the "Toggleable setting" option

If you don't want the menu to be hidden when someone clicks to toggle a setting, you can use the keepShownOnClick attribute. The handler function will still be called, and the checkbox will change without hiding the menu.

ColorPicker Menu Items

A dropdown menu can contain small color swatches that display a color, and can be clicked to show a color picker frame. These allow for easy customization of colors in a hierarchical dropdown menu. The color swatch can be customized with the following attributes:

- hasColorSwatch—A boolean flag indicating if the menu item should display a color swatch. This swatch can then be clicked to open the color picker frame.

- r—The red component of the color swatch (0–255).

- g—The green component of the color swatch (0–255).

- b—The blue component of the color swatch (0–255).

- swatchFunc—A function called by the color picker when the color has changed.

- hasOpacity—A flag (1, nil) that adds the opacity slider to the color picker frame.

- opacity—The percentage of opacity, as a value between 0.0 and 1.0, indicating the transparency of the selected color.

- opacityFunc—A function called by the color picker when the opacity changes.

- cancelFunc—A function called by the color picker when the user clicks the Cancel button. This function is passed the previous values to which the color picker is reverting.

The following example uses the color picker to change the color of the player's name on the player frame. The code accesses the font string PlayerName to get the current color values, as well as to set the new color.

```
info = UIDropDownMenu_CreateInfo()
info.text = "Button Text Color"
info.hasColorSwatch = true
local oldr, oldg, oldb, olda = DropDownTest_ButtonText:GetTextColor()
info.r = oldr
info.g = oldg
info.b = oldb
function info.swatchFunc()
   local r, g, b = ColorPickerFrame:GetColorRGB()
   DropDownTest_ButtonText:SetTextColor(r, g, b)
end
function info.cancelFunc(prev)
   DropDownTest_ButtonText:SetTextColor(prev.r, prev.g, prev.g)
end
UIDropDownMenu_AddButton(info)
```

When the dropdown is initialized, the function stores the current color of the text string using DropDownTest_ButtonText:GetTextColor(), storing the returns in the r, g, and b attributes of the new menu item. When the user changes the color on the picker, the swatch function fetches the selected color from the color picker frame and changes the color of the text.

When the cancel function is called, a table containing the previous color is passed, so the cancel function uses it to restore the original color. This definition creates the menu item shown in Figure 23-8. When the user clicks the color swatch, the color picker frame (see Figure 23-9) opens. The color of the text on the dropdown button is then changed to reflect the new choice.

Figure 23-8: Menu item to change the color of the button text

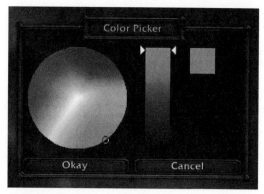

Figure 23-9: The ColorPicker frame that appears when the color swatch is selected

Using Dropdowns for Selection

The examples earlier in this chapter used dropdowns to create popup menus. Although these are used throughout the default user interface, dropdowns can also be used to provide a selection box.

Three utility functions are provided to facilitate the graphical setup of the frame:

- UIDropDownMenu_SetWidth(frame, width, padding)
  - frame—The dropdown frame to adjust.
  - width—The desired width of the frame.
  - padding—An amount of padding on either side of the text; defaults to 25.
- UIDropDownMenu_SetButtonWidth(frame, width)
  - frame—The dropdown frame to adjust.
  - width—The desired width of the button.
- UIDropDownMenu_JustifyText(frame, justify)
  - frame—The dropdown frame to adjust.
  - justify—The desired justification of the text, LEFT, RIGHT, CENTER.

Any dropdown that inherits from UIDropDownMenuTemplate is capable of being used as a selection dropdown. Run the following Lua script in-game to create a new sample menu:

```
if not DropDownMenuTest then
  CreateFrame("Frame", "DropDownMenuTest", UIParent,
```

```
"UIDropDownMenuTemplate")
end

DropDownMenuTest:ClearAllPoints()
DropDownMenuTest:SetPoint("CENTER", 0, 0)
DropDownMenuTest:Show()

local items = {
  "Alpha",
  "Beta",
  "Gamma",
  "Delta",
}

local function OnClick(self)
  UIDropDownMenu_SetSelectedID(DropDownMenuTest, self:GetID())
end

local function initialize(self, level)
  local info = UIDropDownMenu_CreateInfo()
  for k, v in pairs(items) do
    info = UIDropDownMenu_CreateInfo()
    info.text = v
    info.value = v
    info.func = OnClick
    UIDropDownMenu_AddButton(info, level)
  end
end


UIDropDownMenu_Initialize(DropDownMenuTest, initialize)
UIDropDownMenu_SetWidth(DropDownMenuTest, 100);
UIDropDownMenu_SetButtonWidth(DropDownMenuTest, 124)
UIDropDownMenu_SetSelectedID(DropDownMenuTest, 1)
UIDropDownMenu_JustifyText(DropDownMenuTest, "LEFT")
```

`UIDropDownMenu_SetWidth` is used to adjust the size of the text portion of the dropdown menu, in this case to a value of 100. You should ensure that the dropdown is wide enough to display any of the possible items. `UIDropDownMenu_SetButtonWidth` allows you to set the width of the clickable portion of the menu. Normally this is set to 24, which is the width of the actual button graphic. Here it's set to 124, making the entire selection box clickable.

`UIDropDownMenu_JustifyText` can be called to change the text justification (in this case, the text is left-justified). Finally, a call to `UIDropDownMenu_SetSelectedID` selects an item from the list to be displayed by its index in the list. Figure 23-10 shows the resulting selection menu.

Figure 23-10: Selection dropdown menu

Menu items can be selected by name, by value, or by numeric index using `UIDropDownMenu_SetSelectedName`, `UIDropDownMenu_SetSelectedID`, and `UIDropDownMenu_SetSelectedValue`. You should use whichever method makes the most sense for you.

Automating Menu Creation with EasyMenu

The process of creating dropdowns can be tedious, especially considering that the table definitions can be verbose. Blizzard provides a system called EasyMenu to ease the creation of menus, allowing you to define them in tables ahead of time. This reduces the amount of code you need to write and localizes all changes to the dropdown to a set of table definitions.

Create an addon skeleton called `EasyMenuTest` with the standard `EasyMenu.toc` and `EasyMenu.lua`. This menu will be created in Lua, without using XML. Add the following code to `EasyMenu.lua`:

```
if not EasyMenuTest then
  CreateFrame("Frame", "EasyMenuTest", UIParent, ↵
"UIDropDownMenuTemplate")
end

if not EasyMenuButton then
  CreateFrame("Button", "EasyMenuButton", UIParent, ↵
"GameMenuButtonTemplate")
end

menuTbl = {
  {
    text = "Alpha",
    hasArrow = true,
    menuList = {
```

```
          { text = "AlphaAlpha", },
          { text = "AlphaBeta", },
          { text = "AlphaGamma", },
      },
    },
    {
      text = "Beta",
      hasArrow = true,
      menuList = {
          { text = "BetaAlpha", },
          { text = "BetaBeta", },
          { text = "BetaGamma", },
      },
    },
    {
      text = "Some Setting",
      checked = function()
        return SOME_SETTING
      end,
      func = function()
        SOME_SETTING = not SOME_SETTING
      end,
    },
}

EasyMenuButton:SetText("EasyMenu Test")
EasyMenuButton:SetPoint("CENTER", 0, 0)
EasyMenuButton:SetScript("OnClick", function(self, button)
  EasyMenu(menuTbl, EasyMenuTest, "EasyMenuButton", 0, 0, nil, 10)
end)
```

This example creates new button and dropdown frames and sets the button to call the `EasyMenu()` function when it is clicked. Figure 23-11 shows the resulting menu from the table definition. You may have noticed that the `checked` attribute is set to a function here. This allows you to have dynamic settings for checked items, because otherwise the `true`/`false` value would be fixed when the table definition is created.

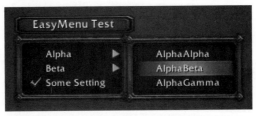

Figure 23-11: DropDown menu created using EasyMenu

EasyMenu is extremely useful when you are creating a menu of mostly static items, but falls short when working with more dynamic menus.

Creating Dynamic Menus

As you create more advanced addons, you may need to create a dropdown menu based on returns from an API function. Occasionally you can create the table ahead of time and use EasyMenu, but you can always use the more verbose method introduced at the start of the chapter.

Type and run the following code snippet to create a dropdown that shows the status of the "World Explorer" achievement; showing you which zones you have explored and what areas you have not:

```
if not ExplorerDropDown then
  CreateFrame("Frame", "ExplorerDropDown", UIParent, ↵
"UIDropDownMenuTemplate")
end

ExplorerDropDown:ClearAllPoints()
ExplorerDropDown:SetPoint("TOPLEFT", 50, -100)
ExplorerDropDown:Show()

local function initialize(self, level)
  local info, achievementId
  if UIDROPDOWNMENU_MENU_VALUE then
    achievementId = UIDROPDOWNMENU_MENU_VALUE
  else
    achievementId = 46      -- Set the achievement to "World Explorer"
  end
  local id, name, points, completed = GetAchievementInfo(achievementId)
  local numCriteria = GetAchievementNumCriteria(achievementId)
  for i = 1, numCriteria do

    local text, criType, completed, quantity, totalQuantity, name, ↵
flags, assetID, quantityString, criteriaID = ↵
GetAchievementCriteriaInfo(achievementId, i)
    info = UIDropDownMenu_CreateInfo()
    info.text = text
    info.checked = completed

    if (criType == CRITERIA_TYPE_ACHIEVEMENT) and assetID then
      if GetAchievementNumCriteria(assetID) > 0 then
        info.hasArrow = true
        info.value = assetID
      end
```

```
        end
        UIDropDownMenu_AddButton(info, level)
    end
  end
end

UIDropDownMenu_Initialize(ExplorerDropDown, initialize)
UIDropDownMenu_SetWidth(ExplorerDropDown, 125)
UIDropDownMenu_SetButtonWidth(ExplorerDropDown, 124)
UIDropDownMenu_SetText(ExplorerDropDown, "World Explorer!")
```

First you create the dropdown frame as in the previous examples, and then query the achievements API to get the criteria for the "World Explorer" achievement (which happens to be achievement ID 46). Each criteria of the selected achievement that is itself an achievement is tested to see if it too contains subitems, and if so shows the arrow and sets the value attribute. Figure 23-12 shows the dropdown menu in action.

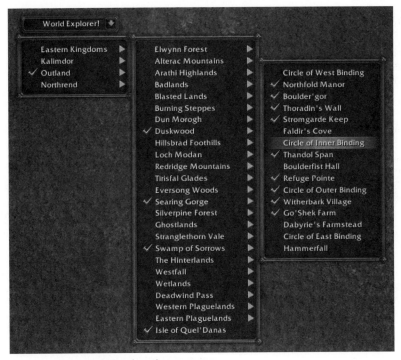

Figure 23-12: World Explorer dropdown menu

Summary

This chapter showed you how to create basic dropdown menus for your own buttons as well as how to create selection dropdowns. You used a manual method of initializing dropdowns, and used the EasyMenu system to automatically create them.

The next chapter shows you how to construct and scan tooltips for information.

Scanning and Constructing Tooltips

Tooltips are by far one of the most pervasive UI elements in World of Warcraft. Whenever you move your mouse over a player, item, spell, talent, or almost anything else in the game, you see a small tooltip in the bottom right of your screen. This chapter introduces you to the inner workings of tooltips, showing you how to create your own and how to get information that is available only via tooltips.

Understanding the Tooltip System

Tooltips are used in World of Warcraft to display detailed information about aspects of the game that might not be available through the game API. For example, Figure 24-1 shows a spell tooltip that displays the name of the spell, the resource cost for casting it, and the range along with the description of the spell.

Tooltips are also used to provide contextual help when the mouse is over a user interface element. For example, Figure 24-2 shows the tooltip displayed when the mouse is over the player's agility stat on the character frame, and Figure 24-3 shows the tooltip displayed when the mouse is over the player frame. This tooltip displays only if WoW's "Beginner tooltips" option is enabled. This option is enabled by default, but if you've turned it off you might not see the tooltip.

All tooltips in the default user interface are created using the `GameTooltip` frame type, which has methods to fill the tooltip with information about different types of game objects (quests, items, spells, and so on).

Figure 24-1: Spell tooltip for Obliterate

Figure 24-2: Agility tooltip on character frame

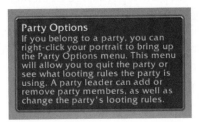

Figure 24-3: Tooltip for the player frame

Different Types of Tooltips

You may have encountered two different types of tooltips while playing the game. To prevent confusion between the two, let's call them *contextual tooltips* and *static tooltips*. Most of the material in this chapter applies to either type of tooltip, but you should be aware of the two types.

Contextual Tooltips

A contextual tooltip is used to give additional information about some other item of interest, such as an interface element or something in the three-dimensional game world. When the mouse moves over such an item the tooltip is displayed, and is hidden when the mouse leaves that element. In the default user interface, the most often used contextual tooltip is named `GameTooltip`.

Static Tooltips

A static tooltip can be used to display information on its own, without needing to be tied to a particular interface element. For example, any links that are sent to you on the guild/party/trade channels are opened in a static tooltip. This allows you to look at the information and move it around your screen rather than having to leave your mouse in one place. In the default user interface, the most often used static tooltip is named `ItemRefTooltip`.

Tooltip Contents

As a frame, a tooltip consists of a series of lines of font strings, in two columns. Figure 24-4 shows these columns and the names of the individual font strings. As you can see, the first line is slightly larger than the others. This allows the first line to be used as a title that stands out from the rest of the text.

Figure 24-4: GameTooltip with individual font string labels

When setting the contents of a tooltip, you normally won't address these font strings directly. Instead, you will make use of the GameTooltip API to either load a predefined tooltip or add your own text.

Run the following code to set up and show the static tooltip `ItemRefTooltip` on the screen. This allows you to use the various methods of setting/adding text to the tooltip without needing to constantly set it up.

```
ItemRefTooltip:SetOwner(UIParent, "ANCHOR_PRESERVE")
ItemRefTooltip:SetText("Hello World!")
ShowUIPanel(ItemRefTooltip)
```

This initial snippet shows the tooltip and displays the string `Hello World!`. The tooltip can be moved around, but if you close it you will need to run the snippet again to make the tooltip reappear.

Custom Text in a Tooltip

You have three different ways to manually add text to a tooltip. The `SetText` method lets you set the text of the first line only, the `AddLine` method allows you to add a line at a time (with an option to wrap strings that are too long), and the `AddDoubleLine` method lets you add text to both the left and right columns.

SetText("text" [, r [, g [, b [, a]]]])

If your tooltip text consists of a single string that can be displayed in the same size and color, you can use the `:SetText()` method to accomplish this. It accepts five arguments:

- `text`—The text to be displayed in the tooltip.
- `r`—The red component of the text color (optional).
- `g`—The green component of the text color (optional).
- `b`—The blue component of the text color (optional).
- `a`—The alpha value of the text (optional).

The text string can contain embedded color codes. For example, make sure the static tooltip is still shown, and then run the following code:

```
ItemRefTooltip:SetText("Tooltip Title\n" ..
  "|cffffffffThis is some text in a tooltip.\n" ..
  "It can contain multi-line strings.|r")
```

Figure 24-5 shows the resulting tooltip. Note that all of the text is the same size, and the second and third lines are a different color. The tooltip will be sized wide enough to fit the contents, so you must be responsible for any wrapping that is necessary.

Figure 24-5: Tooltip created using SetText

AddLine("text" [, r [, g [, b [, a [, wrap]]]]])

Rather than just destructively setting the text of a tooltip, the `AddLine` method allows you to incrementally add lines. This function takes six arguments:

- `text`—The text to be displayed on the tooltip.
- `r`—The red component of the text color (optional).
- `g`—The green component of the text color (optional).
- `b`—The blue component of the text color (optional).
- `a`—The alpha value of the text (optional).
- `wrap`—True to wrap a long string of text onto multiple lines if necessary, false or omitted otherwise.

Each call to this method adds another line to the tooltip. Run the following to add a line to the already open tooltip:

```
ItemRefTooltip:AddLine("This is a very long string that will be wrapped ↵
due to the fifth argument to this function", 1, 1, 1, true)
ItemRefTooltip:Show()
```

Figure 24-6 shows the tooltip with the additional line added. You should be able to see a slight size difference between the first line and the new line. In addition, the tooltip remains roughly the same size, but the new text has been wrapped to fit this width.

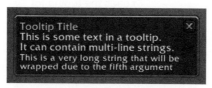

Figure 24-6: Result of adding a line to the previous tooltip

AddDoubleLine("text1", "text2" [, r1 [, g1 [, b1 [, r2 [, g2 [, b2]]]]]])

The `AddDoubleLine` function can be used to add text to both columns at once, coloring them independently. The first argument is the left string and the second argument is the right string. Run this code to add a two-column line to the tooltip, shown in Figure 24-7:

```
ItemRefTooltip:AddDoubleLine("Left", "Right", 0.2, 1, 0.2, 1, 0.2, 0.2)
ItemRefTooltip:Show()
```

Figure 24-7: Tooltip with a two-column line

Game Element Tooltips

The `GameTooltip` frame type provides several special methods that allow you to load the tooltip with the information for some game element. Table 24-1 shows a list of these methods and the game elements for which they can load tooltips. The usage for these methods vary and you should consult the API documentation for whichever function is required.

Table 24-1: GameTooltip Methods for Loading Information

METHOD NAME	DESCRIPTION
SetAuctionItem	Loads the tooltip for an item that is for sale in the auction house.
SetAuctionSellItem	Loads the tooltip for an item the player is currently placing for sale in the auction house.
SetBackpackToken	Loads the tooltip for a currency token being displayed in the backpack frame.
SetBagItem	Loads the tooltip for an item in a given bag/slot.
SetBuybackItem	Loads the tooltip for an item available for buyback at a merchant.
SetCurrencyToken	Loads the tooltip for a currency token.
SetEquipmentSet	Loads the tooltip for an equipment set, specified by name.
SetExistingSocketGem	Loads the tooltip for a gem already in the item currently open for socketing.
SetGlyph	Loads the tooltip for one of the player's glyphs.
SetGuildBankItem	Loads the tooltip for an item in the player's guild bank.
SetHyperlink	Loads the tooltip for a spell, enchant, item, or quest from a hyperlink.
SetHyperlinkCompareItem	Loads the tooltip for the item currently equipped in the slot used by an item (represented by a hyperlink).
SetInboxItem	Loads the tooltip with information about an item attachment in the player's mailbox.
SetInventoryItem	Loads the tooltip with information about an equipped item (on the player, or on a friendly player unit within inspect distance).
SetLootItem	Loads the tooltip with information about an item in the loot window.
SetLootRollItem	Loads the tooltip with information about an item being rolled on by the player.
SetMerchantCostItem	Loads the tooltip with information about a non-monetary item cost for an item a merchant is selling.
SetMerchantItem	Loads information about an item available from a merchant.

METHOD NAME	DESCRIPTION
SetPetAction	Loads the tooltip with information about an action on the pet action bar.
SetPossession	Loads the tooltip with information about the type of possession the player is currently engaged in.
SetQuestItem	Loads the tooltip with information about an item that is required to complete, or a reward for a quest.
SetQuestLogItem	Loads the tooltip with information about an item that is required to complete, or a reward for a quest in the player's quest log.
SetQuestLogRewardSpell	Loads the tooltip with information about the spell that is a reward for the currently selected quest in the quest log.
SetQuestLogSpecialItem	Loads information about any special items that must be used to complete the given quest in the quest log.
SetQuestRewardSpell	Loads the tooltip with information about the spell reward for the currently viewed quest at an NPC.
SetSendMailItem	Loads the tooltip with information about an item attached to the mail currently being sent.
SetShapeshift	Loads the tooltip with information about one of the player's shapeshifts.
SetSocketGem	Loads the tooltip with information about the gem being placed into the item currently open for socketing.
SetSocketItem	Loads the tooltip with information about the item currently open in the socketing UI.
SetSpell	Loads the tooltip with information about a spell in the player's (or pet's) spellbook.
SetTalent	Loads the tooltip with information about a talent.
SetTotem	Loads the tooltip with information about one of the player's active totems.
SetTracking	Loads the tooltip with information about the currently selected tracking type.

Continued

Table 24-1 (*continued*)

METHOD NAME	DESCRIPTION
SetTradePlayerItem	Loads the tooltip with information about an item being traded by the player.
SetTradeSkillItem	Loads the tooltip with information about a tradeskill item, or required reagent for the item.
SetTradeTargetItem	Loads the tooltip with information about an item being traded by the target.
SetTrainerService	Loads the tooltip with information about a service available from a trainer.
SetUnit	Loads the tooltip with information about a given unit.
SetUnitAura	Loads the tooltip with information about an aura on a given unit.
SetUnitBuff	Loads the tooltip with information about a buff on a given unit.
SetUnitDebuff	Loads the tooltip with information about a debuff on a given unit.

Adding Information to the Tooltip

To see how to add information to a tooltip, you'll write a very simple snippet that adds information to item tooltips. The 3.1 patch to World of Warcraft added an equipment manager system that allows you to organize weapons, armor, and other equipment into sets that can be quickly equipped together. Unfortunately, there is no tooltip indicator that shows if an item belongs to any sets.

Loading the Tooltip with Item Information

When you move your mouse over items in your containers, the default user interface uses the GameTooltip:SetBagItem() method to fill the tooltip with the item's information. Likewise, when moving the mouse over the player's inventory (the items you actually have equipped), the GameTooltip:SetInventoryItem() method is called.

The timing of tooltips is a bit odd, since you might expect them to be immediately loaded with the item information. What actually happens is that the client may request the item information from the server, and when the information is properly loaded and displayed, the OnTooltipSetItem widget handler is called. An addon or script can use this handler to trigger any scans of or additions to the information in the tooltip.

Run the following code in-game:

```
local numSets = GetNumEquipmentSets()
local inSet = {}

for i=1,numSets do
    local name, icon, setID = GetEquipmentSetInfo(i)
    local items = GetEquipmentSetItemIDs(name)
    for slot,item in pairs(items) do
        if inSet[item] then
            inSet[item] = inSet[item] .. ", " .. name
        else
            inSet[item] = name
        end
    end
end


local function OnTooltipSetItem(self)
local name, link = self:GetItem()
    if name then
        local equippable = IsEquippableItem(link)
        local item = link:match("Hitem:(%d+)")
        item = tonumber(item)
        if not equippable then
            -- Do nothing
        elseif inSet[item] then
            GameTooltip:AddLine("Equipment Set: " .. inSet[item], 0.2, 1, ↵
0.2)
        else
            GameTooltip:AddLine("Item not in an equipment set", 1, 0.2, ↵
0.2)
        end
        cleared = true
    end
end


GameTooltip:HookScript("OnTooltipSetItem", OnTooltipSetItem)
```

The first section of code loops through all of the equipment sets and creates a string for each item that lists the sets to which it belongs. The second section sets an `OnTooltipSetItem` widget script that will be run anytime an item is displayed in the tooltip. It checks to see which item is being shown, and then adds a line indicating which equipment sets the item is in, if any.

The last line hooks the `OnTooltipSetItem` script on the contextual tooltip `GameTooltip`. As a result, the script will run anytime you move your mouse over an item in-game—loot windows, trade windows, and the player inspect window, for instance. It will not run when you click on an item link in the chat window because that utilizes the `ItemRefTooltip`, which hasn't been hooked here.

Getting Information from Tooltips

The client API has technical limitations that make some information available only in the various game tooltips. For example, no API function currently exists that can indicate whether an item is soulbound to the player character—this information can only be found in the item's tooltip. This is one of the more difficult things to do because you have to deal with localized values and can't always be sure of the order in which information will appear. For instance, Figure 24-8 shows three different item tooltips.

Figure 24-8: Example item tooltips

You can see that the bound status of each tooltip appears in the second line of text in the left-hand column if the item is bound in some way. The difficulty is when working with items that aren't bound because other information will be in that place.

Accessing Individual Tooltip Lines

A tooltip is just a special sort of frame that contains a series of font strings. There are two columns in the tooltip and as many lines as needed to display the information. For the `GameTooltip` and `ItemRefTooltip` (and indeed, any tooltip that inherits from `GameTooltipTemplate`) frames, these font strings are regularly named:

- `GameTooltipTextLeft1`
- `GameTooltipTextLeft2`
- `GameTooltipTextRight1`
- `GameTooltipTextRight2`

You can get the contents of the second tooltip line in the left column by calling `GameTooltipTextLeft2:GetText()`.

Checking Soulbound Status

Here you write a simple snippet of code that changes the border color of the tooltips when an item is soulbound. To accomplish this, use the `OnTooltipSetItem` script to detect items being loaded. Then access the individual tooltip lines to see if the item is soulbound, and change the border color. Run the following code:

```
GameTooltip:SetScript("OnTooltipSetItem", function(self)
    local boundText = GameTooltipTextLeft2:GetText()
    if boundText == ITEM_SOULBOUND or
        boundText == ITEM_ACCOUNTBOUND then
        self:SetBackdropBorderColor(0, 0, 0)
    end
end)
```

Using Global Strings for Localization

You might be tempted to use the strings `Soulbound` and `Account Bound`, but then your addon will work only on English clients. Instead, this code uses the globally defined strings `ITEM_SOULBOUND` and `ITEM_ACCOUNTBOUND`. The strings are defined in `FrameXML/GlobalStrings.lua` as follows:

```
ITEM_SOULBOUND = "Soulbound";
ITEM_ACCOUNTBOUND = "Account Bound";
```

These localized strings are loaded by the default user interface, and differ depending on which locale the client is using. By comparing the tooltip against the global values, you can ensure the code works properly regardless of what language the user interface is displayed in.

The best place to look for the global strings for some part of the user interface is the `GlobalStrings.lua` file; search by the contents of the string used in your version of the client.

Replacing a Script Instead of Hooking a Script

In this example, the code uses the `SetScript` method to set the widget script handler on the frame directly, rather than using the `HookScript` method. Each frame can have only one handler for each widget script, so this will overwrite any script that is already set. It's generally better to use `HookScript()` for an addon released to to the public because `SetScript()` may destroy handlers placed by other addons, leading to runtime errors.

You could alter the snippet to use `HookScript()`, but if you want to tweak it and run it multiple times, you'll notice that every version of your script that you run is called every time the tooltip is loaded. If these versions conflict with each other, they might give you very confusing results. In development, using `SetScript()` is fine, but more often than not you will want to use `HookScript()`.

Summary

In this chapter you learned how tooltips are constructed and how to add your own information to them. In addition, you were introduced to a simple technique for scanning information from a game tooltip. In the next chapter, you learn how to use the secure snippets functionality of secure templates to take protected action in combat.

## CHAPTER 25

Taking Protected Action in Combat

In Chapter 15, you learned how the secure template system protects WoW game play from being automated through the user interface, by preventing protected frames from being moved, shown or hidden, created, or having their behavior changed during combat. However, several legitimate occasions exist when it might be desirable for these things to happen during combat; for instance, if someone's target dies or is deselected during combat, the target frame should be hidden, and shown again when the player picks a new target. The stock target frame can rely on the fact that Blizzard wrote it and its code is secure, but an addon that wants to provide a similar feature needs to use a different mechanism.

Just before the Wrath of the Lich King expansion was released, a new system was introduced to allow addons to load code of their own for secure execution, and for Blizzard to strictly control what information and actions are available to code that is being run securely. These chunks of controlled, authorized code are referred to as *snippets*.

Snippets: The Basis of Secure Action

Of course, the whole system of protected game actions is founded on the principle that addon code is "tainted," and that secure code becomes tainted as soon as addon code tries to interfere with it. Snippets solve part of this problem.

How Can Addon Code Be Secure?

A snippet is a string containing Lua source code, typically stored in a frame attribute. Because it is stored in a frame attribute, secure code can retrieve it without becoming tainted; and because that code can remain secure, it can compile the attribute contents into an executable function that is also secure. When it compiles this function, it can also restrict its access to specific functions and variables so that the secure function can't use information that the Blizzard designers don't want influencing sensitive decisions.

Writing a Snippet

A snippet is the body of a function, without the `function (args, ...)` and final `end` tags. These elements are provided by the secure code that compiles the snippet into a usable function. Because many snippets emulate frame script handlers (`OnClick`, `OnShow`, and so on), the argument list is generally the same as it would be in the equivalent XML script `<OnClick>`, `<OnShow>`, and so forth.

Snippets often contain code comprised of quotes, line breaks, and other characters that normally need to be escaped inside Lua string literals. Because of this, there is an emerging convention to enclose snippet literals in [[long brackets,]] which ignore all special characters (except the end of the bracket). This has the advantage of allowing you to format your code in a more natural fashion, as well as often making it easier for you to distinguish the secure and insecure parts of your addon code.

You can demo a very simple snippet with the following line:

```
/run SecureHandlerExecute(PlayerFrame, [[self:Hide()]])
```

By itself, this isn't terribly exciting. Insecure code can't use `SecureHandler Execute` during combat, and that code could always hide the player frame directly. `SecureHandlerExecute` is mostly used to perform setup on more complex secure handler frames. The real power of snippets and secure execution comes from the ability to attach snippets to frames that will run them securely in response to user input or selected state changes. Before we move on to that, though, put the player frame back by running the following code (snippets can be stored in variables as well as in string literals):

```
local showAction = [[self:Show()]]; ↵
SecureHandlerExecute(PlayerFrame, showAction)
```

Secure Handler Frames

To get WoW to compile and run your snippets, you have to store and attach them correctly. The most common mechanism for this is a set of protected templates called the secure handlers.

Much the same way as `SecureActionButtonTemplate` provides a secure function as its `OnClick` handler, these templates each provide one or two secure functions as various script handlers. Each of these functions looks for a snippet in a fixed relevant attribute and executes it when its corresponding handler is triggered; for example, when someone clicks a button inheriting from SecureHandlerClickTemplate, that button's OnClick function looks for a snippet in its _onclick frame attribute and tries to execute it. It also passes a reference to the button clicked and copies of the button and down arguments to the script as arguments to the snippet.

Secure handler templates are available for most scripts that represent a user interaction (OnClick, OnDoubleClick, OnMouseUp/OnMouseDown, OnMouseWheel, OnEnter/OnLeave, and OnDragStart/OnReceiveDrag), as well as scripts for responding to certain actions that can only be triggered by protected code (OnShow/OnHide and OnAttributeChanged), which are discussed in more detail later in the chapter.

As an example, you can create an addon that modifies the stock UI's extra action bars (the ones that can be turned on around the bottom and right edges of the UI), so that each one only appears when you're mousing over it. Because the frames you have to create will have no visual elements of their own, and you are primarily trying to interact with existing UI elements, this is easier to do from Lua. Run the following code in-game:

```
local mousein = [[
  self:GetFrameRef("subject"):Show()
]]
local mouseout = [[
  self:GetFrameRef("subject"):Hide()
]]
for i, bar in ipairs{MultiBarRight, MultiBarLeft, ↵
MultiBarBottomRight, MultiBarBottomLeft} do
  local watcher = CreateFrame("Frame", "ShyBarsWatcher"..i, ↵
bar:GetParent(), "SecureHandlerEnterLeaveTemplate")
  watcher:SetFrameLevel(bar:GetFrameLevel() - 1)
  watcher:SetAllPoints(bar)
  bar:SetParent(watcher)
  bar:Hide()
  watcher:SetAttribute("_onenter", mousein)
  watcher:SetAttribute("_onleave", mouseout)
  SecureHandlerSetFrameRef(watcher, "subject", bar)
end
```

This code loops over each of the supplemental action bars, and attaches a frame to each bar that will "watch" for mouseover events. The only really new part here is the use of the SecureHandlerEnterLeaveTemplate to create the new frames. This is the template that triggers certain snippets when someone mouses in or out of it. The rest of the code uses the SetAllPoints() method to make sure that the frame is watching the same area that the bar takes up when it's present and makes sure that the watcher frame will not cover its bar when shown (this could make the action bar difficult to click).

This isn't a perfect example of making the action bars hide (for instance, if your mouse leaves the area while being over one of the extra action bars, they might not hide), but it's a good first approximation that shows the basics of the snippets system.

> **WARNING** The game stores a character's preferred setting for which action bars should be shown on the server, and they aren't available to the client until the VARIABLES_LOADED event has fired. If you were loading this into an addon, you would want to delay hiding the bars until then, because the stock UI would reshow them.

Now, let's break down the two chunks of code that are less familiar. The `mousein` and `mouseout` local variables at the beginning of the file are chunks of code in string form; that is, snippets. `SetAttribute()` calls attach these snippets to the attributes that the template's `OnEnter` and `OnLeave` handlers will invoke. The other issue is that to make sure that secure snippets can't use disallowed information, they are run with a limited version of the global environment that only includes certain functions, and frames don't normally exist there. So, to make the action bar frame that will be shown and hidden available to the snippets, you have to store it in something called a frame reference; this is basically a sanitized version of the frame (called a frame handle, discussed more later), stored in the first frame's `frameref-subject` attribute (or whatever name you supplied when you set the frame reference). Because the `_onenter` and `_onleave` scripts will be called with `watcher` as `self`, the frame can then be retrieved with `self:GetFrameRef("subject")`.

Handler Template Reference

The simpler, and more common, secure templates respond directly to various sorts of user interaction; these are generally triggered with the mouse, but some can also be triggered from key binding actions by using `SetBindingClick`. Table 25-1 shows a list of the valid templates. Each template in the first column supplies a handler for the frame script that calls the snippet named in the second column, providing the arguments listed in the third column. For these templates, the arguments provided to the snippet are in the same order, and have the same names, as would be supplied to the equivalent script element contents in an XML frame definition; that is, an `_onclick` snippet receives the same set of implicit arguments as the code in an `<OnClick>...</OnClick>` element.

The last "interaction" template is slightly more complicated. Dragging a frame through the `StartMoving()` method call is not a protected operation (because it is inherently interactive), so `SecureHandlerDragTemplate` is primarily intended for buttons that you can drag things in or out of, such as customizable action buttons. The `button` argument is the button that was held down to initiate the drag action, but the other arguments are the same information returned by `GetCursorInfo()`—the kind of action or resource held on the cursor, the identifier or value of the cursor's contents (such as the amount of money or the ID of the spell or item), and possible supplemental information (such as whether a spell is a `"BOOK"` spell or a `"PET"` spell) passed in vararg argument(s).

Table 25-1: Secure Handler Templates and Their Snippets

TEMPLATE	SNIPPETS	ARGUMENTS
`SecureHandlerClickTemplate`	`_onclick`	`self, button, down`
`SecureHandlerDoubleClickTemplate`	`_ondoubleclick`	`self, button, down`
`SecureHandlerMouseUpDownTemplate`	`_onmouseup`	`self, button`
	`_onmousedown`	`self, button`
`SecureHandlerMouseWheelTemplate`	`_onmousewheel`	`self, delta`
`SecureHandlerEnterLeaveTemplate`	`_onenter`	`self`
	`_onleave`	`self`
`SecureHandlerDragTemplate`	`_ondragstart`	`self, button, kind, value, ...`
	`_onreceivedrag`	`self, button, kind, value, ...`
`SecureHandlerShowHideTemplate`	`_onshow`	`self`
	`_onhide`	`self`
`SecureHandlerAttributeTemplate`	`_onattributechanged`	`self, name, value`
`SecureHandlerStateTemplate`	`_onstate-*`	`self, stateid, newstate`

Moreover, the `_ondragstart` and `_onreceivedrag` snippets may use a `return` statement to have the game load the cursor with something new or exchange its current contents. For instance, if you want to write a button that uses the action slots to store its content much like the stock buttons do, you can have the button inherit from both `SecureActionButtonTemplate` and

SecureHandlerDragTemplate, and use the following snippet in the button's _ondragstart and _onreceivedrag attributes:

```
local pickupAction = [[return "action", self:GetAttribute("action")]]
button:SetAttribute("_ondragstart", pickupAction)
button:SetAttribute("_onreceivedrag", pickupAction)
```

Your drag handlers can return any of the following sequences:

```
return "action", actionSlot
return "bag", equippedBag
return "bagslot", bagID, slotNumber
return "inventory", inventorySlot
return "item", name or itemID
return "macro", name or macroIndex
return "petaction", petSlot
return "spell", index, "BOOK" or "PET"
return "spell", name or spellID
return "companion", "MOUNT" or "CRITTER", index
return "equipmentset", name
return "money", amount
return "merchant", slot
```

You can also add `"clear"` to the beginning of any of these lists to clear the cursor first, such as to pick up the contents of an action slot without dropping anything into it that was already on the cursor. For instance, you might change the drag-start handler to

```
button:SetAttribute("_ondragstart", [[return "clear", "action", ↵
self:GetAttribute("action")]])
```

The last group of templates are intended to react to changes in frame visibility or attribute values. These changes can be triggered by other snippets acting on frames securely, or by state drivers that you have registered for the frame (discussed in more detail later in the chapter).

Integrating a Click Handler with a Secure Action Button

One other facility offered by SecureActionButtonTemplate is the ability to run click snippets for undefined `"type"` attributes. If, for instance, button:GetAttribute("type") == "menu" and button:GetAttribute("_menu") contains a snippet, the secure action button will run it as a click handler, with self, button, and down arguments. This means that you can intermingle secure actions with other secure behaviors on a single button by using modifier and mouse button selection. For instance, you can easily create menus for

expanded click-casting, as in the following example addon for paladin characters, `BlessedMenus`. Start by creating a `BlessedMenus` folder in your `AddOns`
directory, then create the file `BlessedMenus.toc` and enter the following:

```
## Interface: 30300
## Title: BlessedMenus
## Notes: Creates menus on party frames to select spells to cast on them
BlessedMenus.xml
BlessedMenus.lua
```

Next, create the file `BlessedMenus.xml` in the same directory, and start by
entering the following:

```
<Ui xmlns="http://www.blizzard.com/wow/ui/"
    xmlns:xsi="http://www.w3.org/2001/XMLSchema-instance"
    xsi:schemaLocation="http://www.blizzard.com/wow/ui/
    http://wowprogramming.com/FrameXML/UI.xsd">
  <Button name="BlessedMenusSpellButtonTemplate" enableMouse="true" ↵
inherits="SecureActionButtonTemplate" virtual="true">
    <Size x="144" y="16" />
    <Layers>
      <Layer level="ARTWORK">
        <Texture parentKey="icon">
          <Size x="16" y="16" />
          <Anchors>
            <Anchor point="TOPLEFT" />
          </Anchors>
        </Texture>
      </Layer>
    </Layers>
    <ButtonText inherits="GameFontHighlight" justifyH="LEFT" />
    <HighlightTexture alphaMode="ADD">
      <Color r="0.75" g="0.75" b="0.6" a="0.5" />
    </HighlightTexture>
  </Button>
</Ui>
```

This is the beginning of a template that you can use for popup menu entries.
So far, it's basically a horizontal bar containing a text string, with a small
icon at the left side. It has a plain yellow highlight texture to indicate which
menu item is currently being pointed at. Add the basic action button attributes
between the `</Layers>` and `<ButtonText>` tags:

```
<Attributes>
  <Attribute name="type" value="spell" />
  <Attribute name="useparent-unit" value="true" type="boolean" />
</Attributes>
```

These define the consistent parts of the button behavior. All these menu items will be spell buttons, and they will cast on the unit whose frame was clicked to bring up the spell menu. Note that you use the `type` tag attribute here to set the frame attribute to a value with the Lua type `"boolean"`.

Add a `Scripts` section immediately after the `Attributes` block and before the `<ButtonText>` tag:

```
<Scripts>
  <OnLoad>
     self:GetFontString():SetPoint("LEFT", self.icon, "RIGHT", 2, 1)
     self:RegisterEvent("PLAYER_ENTERING_WORLD")
  </OnLoad>
</Scripts>
```

The first line ensures that the button's text is placed correctly in the button (because the icon texture is created using a key rather than a name, you can't currently refer to it from an XML `<Anchor>` tag's `relativeTo` attribute). The last line prepares the button to deal with the fact that its spell icon isn't available when your addon first loads, which is fully addressed in the next handler (add it right before the `</Scripts>` tag):

```
<OnEvent>
  self.icon:SetTexture(GetSpellTexture(self:GetAttribute("spell")))
</OnEvent>
```

This handler is run in response to the PLAYER_ENTERING_WORLD event, when the client has fully loaded spell icons. These icons are actually loaded by the earlier SPELLS_CHANGED event, but that event does not fire when you reload the UI, so the more reliable PLAYER_ENTERING_WORLD is used. Also, if you watch event traces, you will see that the SPELL_CHANGED event fires quite a number of times during logging in. Waiting until the PLAYER_ENTERING_WORLD event helps you avoid all of these.

Paladins use three major groups of beneficial spells, so you'll create three menus, one for each. To facilitate that, create a menu template in the same file, right before the `</Ui>` tag:

```
<Frame name="BlessedMenusMenuTemplate" hidden="true" ↵
protected="true" virtual="true">
   <Size x="160" y="18" />
   <Backdrop bgFile="Interface\Tooltips\UI-Tooltip-Background" ↵
edgeFile="Interface\Tooltips\UI-Tooltip-Border" tile="true">
      <EdgeSize val="16"/>
      <TileSize val="16"/>
      <BackgroundInsets left="4" right="4" top="4" bottom="4"/>
      <BorderColor r="1" g="1" b="1" />
      <Color r="0.09" g="0.09" b="0.19" a="1.0" />
   </Backdrop>
```

```
      <Attributes>
        <Attribute name="useparent-unit" value="true" type="boolean" />
      </Attributes>
    </Frame>
```

This creates a simple tooltip-type frame. Like the child buttons, the useparent-unit attribute is set so that unit requests on the buttons can pass all the way up to whatever unit button currently owns the menu. Now that the templates are ready, you can save and close the XML file; the rest of the heavy lifting is done dynamically at load time, so create the file BlessedMenus.lua in the BlessedMenus directory, if needed, and start it by entering the following:

```
local function BlessedMenu(name, ...)
  local self = CreateFrame("Frame", name, nil, ↵
"BlessedMenusMenuTemplate")
  self.buttons = {}
  for i=1, select('#', ...) do
    local spellName = select(i, ...)
    local button = CreateFrame("Button", nil, self, ↵
"BlessedMenusSpellButtonTemplate")
    self.buttons[i] = button
    button:SetAttribute("spell", spellName)
    button:SetText(spellName)
    if i == 1 then
      button:SetPoint("TOPLEFT", 8, -8)
    else
      button:SetPoint("TOPLEFT", self.buttons[i - 1], ↵
"BOTTOMLEFT", 0, -2)
    end
  end
  self:SetHeight(#self.buttons * 18 + 14)
  return self
end
```

This function does all the work of creating a menu frame, as well as creating and placing the choice buttons in the menu, which it does by name. Add the following code to create three menus using this function:

```
local heals = BlessedMenu("BlessedMenusHeals",
  "Holy Light",
  "Flash of Light",
  "Lay on Hands"
)

local hands = BlessedMenu("BlessedMenusHands",
  "Hand of Protection",
  "Hand of Freedom",
  "Hand of Salvation",
  "Hand of Sacrifice"
)
```

```
local blessings = BlessedMenu("BlessedMenusBlessings",
  "Blessing of Might",
  "Blessing of Kings",
  "Blessing of Wisdom"
)
```

Now that you've defined the menus, it's time to start preparing the code that will drive the secure behaviors. Add the following:

```
local openSpellList = [[
  local menu = IsAltKeyDown() and "blessings"
          or IsControlKeyDown() and "heals"
          or IsShiftKeyDown() and "hands"
  menu = menu and self:GetFrameRef(menu)
  if menu and menu:IsShown() and menu:GetParent() == self then
    menu:Hide()
    return
  end
  if menu then
    menu:Hide()
    menu:SetParent(self)
    menu:SetPoint("TOPLEFT", "$cursor")
    menu:SetFrameLevel(self:GetFrameLevel() + 2)
    menu:Show()
  end
]]
```

This is the snippet code that the party and player buttons will run when clicked with certain modifiers, which you add in a moment. It uses information about the current modifiers to determine which frame reference to retrieve and open. If that menu is already open on the unit frame in question, it hides it and takes no further action; if the menu is not open (hidden), or is open on another unit frame, it is re-parented to the frame that was clicked, making sure it appears above the frame clicked, and opened. It is also moved to appear by the point clicked, using an arguments to SetPoint(), $cursor, that places the point anchored by the mouse's current location (it will not automatically follow the mouse). But of course, the code will never run unless it is attached to some frames; add the load-time code to do so just after the snippet:

```
for i, frame in ipairs{PlayerFrame, PartyMemberFrame1, ↵
PartyMemberFrame2, PartyMemberFrame3, PartyMemberFrame4} do
  frame:SetAttribute("shift-type1", "spelllist")
  frame:SetAttribute("ctrl-type1", "spelllist")
  frame:SetAttribute("alt-type1", "spelllist")
  frame:SetAttribute("_spelllist", openSpellList)
  SecureHandlerSetFrameRef(frame, "blessings", BlessedMenusBlessings)
  SecureHandlerSetFrameRef(frame, "heals", BlessedMenusHeals)
  SecureHandlerSetFrameRef(frame, "hands", BlessedMenusHands)
end
```

This code starts by iterating over the player frame and the frames for all party members and making the same changes to each one:

First, it sets `"spelllist"` as the type for modified left-clicks. This type is not defined by the secure action button template, so it will look for a function in `self.menu` or a snippet in `self:GetAttribute("_spelllist")`. You should use the latter because setting a key on the frame would introduce taint. As you did with the `ShyBars` example given before (the one that auto-hides the extra action bars), you use `SecureHandlerSetFrameRef` to import references to the actual frames into the environment for the snippet to access when it runs. Figure 25-1 shows the BlessedMenus addon.

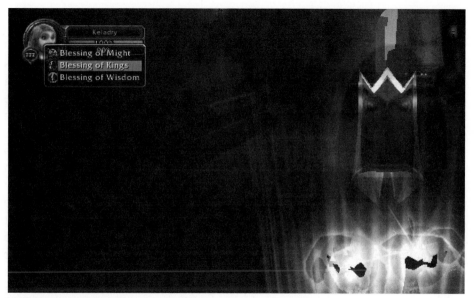

Figure 25-1: BlessedMenus in action

A couple issues still exist with `BlessedMenus`; if you show one menu while another one is open (such as by Shift+clicking, then Alt+clicking), they will overlap, instead of closing the first one. Also, the menu does not disappear when you choose an option from it. You learn how to address both these issues in the following sections.

Preserving State and Controlling Information

The secure frame management system in versions 2.0–2.4 of WoW used a single variable per header, called *state*, to summarize all the factors it used to control frames. It was possible to use multiple control factors, but if you had an addon like the original version of Goose that could show or hide frames based on three different factors (whether or not you were in stealth, in combat, or mounted), it needed eight different states (two possibilities for combat times two for stealth times two for mount equals eight) and it had to be able to handle all the possible combinations of which state to go to when any one of these factors changed.

Two things make the existing system generally easier to manage. First, snippets are capable of examining the game state, attributes on relevant frames, and similar factors, directly when triggered to determine the state they should set up. Second, the snippets associated with a frame can store as many distinct pieces of information as they need to keep track of, in private globals.

Private Global Environments

Each function has an environment, which is a table where it stores and seeks any global variable references made in its body. Because each new function is created with the same environment as the function that created it, all the functions created in the stock UI or addon files normally share the same environment unless they specify otherwise at some point.

The functions created when the secure handler infrastructure compiles snippets use their own environments, which is part of how their access to game information that's not supposed to be used for secure actions is strictly controlled (such as how low on health your target is, for example). Because functions are also normally found by calling global variables, functions that retrieve prohibited information simply aren't available from inside a secure environment. But snippets running in that environment can also store their own globals there, which persist from one call to another. Moreover, all the snippets associated with a frame typically share an environment, allowing them to share input into their frame's state.

As a simple example of how this can be used, you can fix one of the issues with BlessedMenus, namely, that when you open one menu on a frame and then another, the first one stays open behind the second one.

Open BlessedMenus.lua and look for your definition of the openSpellList snippet. Alter it to look like this (changed lines are highlighted):

```
local openSpellList = [[
    local menu = IsAltKeyDown() and "blessings"
             or IsControlKeyDown() and "heals"
             or IsShiftKeyDown() and "hands"
    menu = menu and self:GetFrameRef(menu)
    if lastMenu and lastMenu:IsShown() and ↵
lastMenu:GetParent() == self then
        lastMenu:Hide()
        if lastMenu == menu then
```

```
            return
        end
    end
    if menu then
      menu:Hide()
      menu:SetParent(self)
      menu:SetPoint("TOPLEFT", "$cursor")
      menu:SetFrameLevel(self:GetFrameLevel() + 2)
      menu:Show()
      lastMenu = menu
    end
]]
```

Every time you open a menu, you store it in the lastMenu variable. Then when you go to later open another menu, you can hide whatever was shown last. lastMenu is neither a local variable nor an argument to the function, so Lua will treat it as a global. However, you won't see any changes to it outside the snippet by looking in _G.lastMenuOpened; it's a private global in the frame's own personal environment. You can use it as a way to track which menu you last opened so that you can close it as needed before opening another one.

Secure API Functions

Private globals are usually used as a way for snippets to store internal state information, but because functions in Lua are actually variables that contain references to those functions, the private environment is also how snippets are restricted to secure portions of the API. The following standard Lua functions work similarly inside a snippet to the way they do in the normal World of Warcraft Lua environment: type, select, tonumber, tostring, print, pairs, ipairs, next, unpack, and the table, string, and math libraries, as well as their deprecated global forms such as tremove.

The following WoW API functions are available to snippets in basically the same form as they work in normal code:

```
SecureCmdOptionParse              GetMouseButtonClicked
GetShapeshiftForm                 GetActionBarPage
IsStealthed, UnitExists           GetBonusBarOffset
UnitIsDead, UnitIsGhost           IsMounted, IsSwimming
UnitPlayerOrPetInParty            IsFlying
UnitPlayerOrPetInRaid             IsFlyableArea
IsRightAltKeyDown                 IsIndoors
IsLeftAltKeyDown                  IsOutdoors
IsAltKeyDown                      GetBindingKey
IsRightControlKeyDown             HasAction
IsLeftControlKeyDown              IsHarmfulSpell
IsControlKeyDown                  IsHarmfulItem
```

```
IsLeftShiftKeyDown                 IsHelpfulSpell
IsRightShiftKeyDown                IsHelpfulItem
IsShiftKeyDown                     RegisterStateDriver
IsModifierKeyDown                  GetActionInfo
IsModifiedClick
```

The following player information functions behave basically the same as the equivalent unit information functions, but only allow you to inquire about the player:

```
PlayerCanAttack                    PlayerIsChanneling
PlayerCanAssist                    PlayerInCombat
```

UnitHasVehicleUI is available inside the secure environment, but only returns useful information for units that are friendly to the player: true for friendly units that have a vehicle interface, false for friendly units that don't, and nil for all non-friendly units.

Two new player information functions are also available to snippets: Player InGroup returns "raid" if the player is in a raid group, "party" if the player is in a party but not a raid group, and nil if the player is not in any group; Player PetSummary returns the name and creature family of the player's pet, if any.

The table module inside the secure environment includes one function that is not part of the normal table module. For security reasons, the snippet execution engine will not compile snippets that create tables directly using the table constructor {}. Instead, you can create tables for your snippets to store information using table.new(...). If arguments are supplied, they are added to the new table under consecutive integer keys, starting from 1. There is no way to initialize a table with non-integer keys using table.new(), but you can set them afterward using conventional table syntax.

The other action the secure environment has to prohibit to snippets is the creation of functions, but repetitive tasks can be executed in a similar way using the control object provided in each frame's environment.

The control Object

The secure environment provides something called a control object to serve two principal functions: The first is to be able to trigger insecure functions that have full access to presentational elements such as textures (but without secure privileges to affect protected execution), and the second is to isolate small chunks of repetitive code in snippets, so that they can be called like functions.

When you have to make cosmetic updates to a frame based on changes to its attributes or other triggers, you can assign a function to a key on that frame in advance. Then, when secure code running in that frame's environment wants to trigger that function, it can call control:CallMethod(keyName, ...). This will find originalFrame as the frame owning the secure environment, retrieve `originalFrame[keyName]`, and if it is a function, call it with `(originalFrame, ....)` as arguments. The call will be made insecurely, so the function will run without any special privileges, but with full access to the global environment. When the function returns, the snippet that called it remains secure, but any returns from the method function called are discarded and not available to the secure environment.

The `control` object can also run snippets, whether provided as string literals or stored in variables. The `control:Run(snippet, ...)` function will run the specified snippet with the owning frame as `self` and the remaining arguments passed as the vararg expression. The `control:RunFor(frameHandle, snippet, ...)` function will run the supplied snippet with `frameHandle` as `self`, with the rest of the arguments passed in the vararg expression, but still in the environment of the frame calling `control:RunFor`.

The `control:RunAttribute(name, ...)` function is very similar to `control:Run`, but instead of taking snippet code directly, it retrieves the snippet to run from `owningFrame:GetAttribute(name)`. This is presently about the only way to securely interact with any attribute on a frame that starts with an underscore.

The final method of the `control` object is largely obsolete, but can occasionally used as a timesaver. `control:ChildUpdate(snippetID, message)` checks each child of the calling frame for a `"_childupdate-"..snippetID` attribute or a `"_childupdate"` attribute in that order. It then calls that snippet on that child, with the child itself, `snippetID`, and `message` as arguments, in the child frame's environment.

Frame Handles

Because true tables can't exist in WoW's secure sandboxes (the objects manipulated by the `table` library are actually special proxy objects), frames can't be imported directly into snippet code. To allow secure code to manipulate frames, proxy objects called *frame handles* are created. The `self` argument received by most snippets is actually a frame handle, and `SecureHandlerSetFrameRef` stores a frame handle in an attribute on the target frame where it can be retrieved.

For the most part, frame handles act like frames. They have many of the same methods, but a few important distinctions exist:

- Frame handles are actually userdata objects, so you cannot set values on their keys as you can with frames.

- Most frame handle methods throw an error if used during combat for a frame handle that represents an unprotected frame.

- Frame handles also have some changed methods, as well as a few methods that don't normally exist on real frames.

To get a taste for using frame handles, press Esc to enable your right action bar, navigate to Interface Options, select ActionBars, and check the Right Bar checkbox. Then run the following script in-game:

```
local function ConstructButton(name, parent, baseTexture)
  local self = CreateFrame("Button", parent:GetName()..name, parent, ↵
"SecureHandlerClickTemplate")
  parent[name:lower()] = self
  self:SetHeight(32)
  self:SetWidth(32)
  self:SetNormalTexture(baseTexture.."-Up")
  self:SetPushedTexture(baseTexture.."-Down")
  self:SetHighlightTexture(baseTexture.."-Highlight", "ADD")
  return self
end

local advance = MultiBarRight.advance or ConstructButton("Advance", ↵
MultiBarRight, [[Interface\MainMenuBar\UI-MainMenu-ScrollUpButton]])
advance:SetPoint("BOTTOM", MultiBarRight, "TOP")
advance:SetAttribute("_onclick", [[
  bar = bar or self:GetParent()
  local page = tonumber(bar:GetAttribute('actionpage')) or 4
  if page <= 1 then
    page = 7
  end
  bar:SetAttribute("actionpage", page - 1)
  buttons = buttons or table.new(bar:GetChildren())
  for i, button in ipairs(buttons) do
    button:SetAttribute("touch")
  end ]]
)
local regress = MultiBarRight.regress or ConstructButton("Advance", ↵
MultiBarRight, [[Interface\MainMenuBar\UI-MainMenu-ScrollDownButton]])
regress:SetPoint("TOP", MultiBarRight, "BOTTOM")
regress:SetAttribute("_onclick", [[
  bar = bar or self:GetParent()
  local page = tonumber(bar:GetAttribute('actionpage')) or 2
  if page >= 6 then
    page = 0
  end
  bar:SetAttribute("actionpage", page + 1)
  buttons = buttons or table.new(bar:GetChildren())
  for i, button in ipairs(buttons) do
    button:SetAttribute("touch")
  end ]]
)
```

The first function creates a new button when called, and sets up certain cosmetic details. The next block uses this function to create a button, and attaches it to the rightmost extra action bar at the top end. Then it sets up a snippet to handle clicks on the button, decreasing the effective page number of the action bar. Finally, it does something similar to create another button, attached to the bottom of the action bar, which increases the bar's page number by one. You now can rotate the rightmost extra action bar through all six action pages independently of the main bar.

Take a particular look at a few parts of the snippet. The first line looks for a frame handle to the button's own parent (`MultiBarRight`) if necessary and caches it in a private global to save on future lookups (because these buttons will never change parents, this is fine; for a mod like `BlessedMenus`, avoid caching parents for frames whose parentage can change dynamically). The next part is the main logic; it uses `:GetAttribute()` on the parent frame handle to determine the bar's current page, and advances it to the next page, rotating back to the other end of the cycle if needed. It also uses `:SetAttribute()` to change the bar to the newly chosen page.

The last part uses `:GetChildren()` if needed to cache a list of the buttons on the bar, and iterates across them, setting the `touch` attribute to `nil`. This is done in order to trigger `ActionBarButtonTemplate`'s `<OnAttributeChanged>` handler and cause it to refresh the buttons.

Allowed Actions

Using frame handles is intended to be as much like using frames as possible. All of the following methods work on frame handles in basically the same way as they do on frames, except that they throw an error if used on an unprotected frame in combat (frames that are protected by virtue of having a protected child still count as protected for most purposes here):

```
GetID()                  IsShown()              IsVisible()
GetWidth()               GetHeight()            GetRect()
GetScale()               GetEffectiveScale()    GetFrameLevel()
GetAttribute(name)       GetChildren()          GetParent()
GetNumPoints()           GetPoint(i)            SetID(id)
SetWidth(width)          SetHeight(height)      SetScale(scale)
SetAlpha(alpha)          ClearAllPoints()       SetAttribute(name, value)
Raise()                  Lower()                SetFrameLevel(level)
Disable()                Enable()               GetName()
IsProtected()            GetObjectType()        IsObjectType(ot)
```

All of these function work even on unprotected frames in combat, and can be used to avoid errors caused by using disallowed frame handles.

Additional or Changed Actions

Several frame handle methods are exclusive to frame handles, or require special considerations when used on frame handles.

Show(skipAttr)

Hide(skipAttr)

By default, these methods of frame handles set or clear the `statehidden` attribute, which is used by a few other parts of the UI. You can pass `true` to these functions to prevent them from changing this attribute.

SetPoint(point, relframe, relpoint, xofs, yofs)

You can't omit the `relframe` argument to assume the frame parent when calling `SetPoint` from a snippet, although you can pass the `"$parent"` string instead of a frame handle. You also can't omit the `relpoint` argument if you want to pass any offset values.

`relframe` should be one of the following:

- A valid handle to an explicitly protected frame (effective protection is not sufficient)

- `nil` or the string `"$screen"` to anchor to the root window

- The string `"$parent"` to anchor to the frame's parent

- The string `"$cursor"`, which will place the frame offset from the cursor's position when the call is made. The frame will *not* automatically track the cursor.

SetAllPoints(relframe)

This is subject to most of the same changes as `SetPoint()`, but `"$cursor"` is not a valid target.

SetParent(handle)

Like `SetPoint()`, the handle passed as the new parent must be an explicitly protected frame.

GetFrameRef(label)

This method is only available to frame handles, because it's not very useful for normal frames. It returns the frame handle stored in `self:GetAttribute("frameref-"..label)`. It's generally used as a convenient way to retrieve frame references passed in using `SecureHandlerSetFrameRef`.

GetEffectiveAttribute(name, button, prefix, suffix)

This is used as an interface to `SecureButton_GetModifiedAttribute`, to retrieve attributes that vary based on modifier keys and mouse button the way `SecureActionButtonTemplate` does. You can omit some of the arguments to search attributes based on the current system status.

GetChildList(tbl)

This is used to conserve memory and performance when you frequently need to re-create a list of a frame's children. It appends the frame's children to the table passed in and returns it again for convenience. It does not purge the old contents automatically, but you can run the table through `table.wipe` to do so before passing it in if you need to.

GetMousePosition()

This returns the cursor's current position over the frame, normalized to the frame; that is, (0,0) is the frame's lower left and (1,1) is its upper right. If the mouse is not over the frame, this method returns `nil`.

IsUnderMouse(recursive)

This returns `true` if the frame is under the current mouse position. If you pass `true` for `recursive`, it will also return `true` if any of the frame's children are under the mouse.

SetBindingClick(priority, key, name, button)

SetBinding(priority, key, action)

SetBindingSpell(priority, key, spell)

SetBindingMacro(priority, key, macro)

SetBindingItem(priority, key, item)

ClearBinding(key)

ClearBindings()

These are analogous to the `SetOverrideBinding*` functions in the global environment, except that they are described as frame methods. The calling frame is considered the owner of the override binding so established.

An *override binding* is a temporary binding that does not affect your saved key binding settings. It lasts until cleared or until the client is closed or the UI reloaded. When a key is pressed, the client searches first for the most recent override binding set with the priority argument true, if any exist; if none are still assigned, it looks for the most recent override binding assigned without priority. If no override bindings are found for that key, the regular binding, if any, is triggered.

RegisterAutoHide(duration)

UnregisterAutoHide()

AddToAutoHide(handle)

These methods are usually used to support "hesitating menus," menus that automatically close after a brief time if a selection isn't made from them. `RegisterAutoHide(duration)` indicates that the frame should be hidden `duration` seconds after the mouse leaves it, unless the mouse reenters it during that time, in which case the timer starts again when the mouse leaves the area. `UnregisterAutoHide()` simply cancels any pending hide delay on the frame.

AddToAutoHide(handle) includes handle's screen area in the block that will be monitored to determine if the mouse focus is on the frame or its other points of interest, in order to determine if the timer will run down or not. For instance, it allows a frame to stay visible as long as the mouse is over it or any of its children.

Wrapping Frame Scripts

Suppose for a moment you're leveling a druid, and running a lot of dungeons like Razorfen Downs for gear and experience because you have a regular group. Before every trip into a dungeon, and every so often while you're inside, you recast Mark of the Wild or Thorns on the whole group. This task is repetitive and kind of mindless, so you might want to make an addon that will make it easier (if you don't have a druid, mages and priests also tend to go through the same thing until they're high enough to learn group buff spells). The foundation of this frame, BuffCycler, is very simple, based on what you learned in Chapter 15 about action buttons. Run the following lines in-game:

```
local BuffCycler = BuffCycler or CreateFrame("Button", "BuffCycler", ↵
UIParent, "ActionButtonTemplate,SecureActionButtonTemplate")
BuffCyclerIcon:SetTexture[[Interface\Icons\Spell_Nature_Regeneration]]
BuffCycler:SetAttribute("type", "spell")
BuffCycler:SetAttribute("spell", "Mark of the Wild")
BuffCycler:SetPoint("TOPRIGHT", BuffFrame, "TOPLEFT", -300, 0)
```

Of course, in its current form, this addon button only casts Mark of the Wild on your current target. Figure 25-2 shows the BuffCycler button in-game.

Figure 25-2: BuffCycler

A Simple Click Wrapper

If you're familiar with making macros, you may already have learned that cycling reliably through a set of targets isn't the sort of thing that macros can do easily or well. But programmatic logic doesn't have much of a problem with it, provided it's allowed to work in combat. You can add that behavior to the button with a function called SecureHandlerWrapScript:

```
SecureHandlerWrapScript(BuffCycler, "OnClick", BuffCycler, [[
  local unit = self:GetAttribute("unit")
  if unit == "player" then
    unit = "party1"
  elseif unit == "party1" then
    unit = "party2"
  elseif unit == "party2" then
    unit = "party3"
  elseif unit == "party3" then
    unit = "party4"
  elseif unit == "party4" then
    unit = "player"
  end
  if unit and UnitExists(unit) then
    self:SetAttribute("unit", unit)
  else
    self:SetAttribute("unit", "player")
  end
]])
```

What this code effectively does is "hook" BuffCycler's OnClick handler with the code in the long brackets, so that that code is called before SecureAction Button_OnClick. The secure handler mechanisms create the hook as secure code, so that it will not taint the call to SecureActionButton_OnClick. You can also supply a second string (not used in this case) to be called as a "post-hook," which is why it's referred to as "wrapping" the existing script. These hooks can be used in a number of ways:

- As used here, they can set up the button's functional attributes to prepare it for its click, as well as internally recording information about the "state" of the addon, such as where it is in a series of actions.

- A pre-hook snippet can use the return statement to modify the argument values passed to the original frame script. For instance, because a click handler takes button as an argument, a wrapper around OnClick can return changed values for button to be used by the original handler when it gets called.

- A pre-hook snippet can also return false to completely suppress the original handler from running. It can do this conditionally based on things like frame attributes or previously stored information, as well as current API checks of approved information, such as whether you have a target, or other legitimate macro conditions.

Notice that the `SecureHandlerWrapScript` call refers to `BuffCycler` twice. When you call `SecureHandlerWrapScript`, you have to give it two frames, which can be the same or different frames. The first one is the frame whose script handler you will actually wrap. The second one (the third argument) is the "owner" of the script; any private variable references (explained in more detail a little later in the chapter) are associated with that frame. All scripts owned by a frame have access to all private variables created by any script owned by that frame.

To prevent exploits, only an explicitly protected frame (one inheriting from a template with the `protected="true"` tag attribute) can be designated as a script owner. Moreover, snippets wrapping a frame script will not be run if the wrapped frame becomes unprotected, such as by having all its protected children re-parented to other frames. Its original script will be run without modification, and its wrappers will resume functioning if it becomes protected again.

WARNING At the time of this writing, implicit protection is not sufficient to allow script wrappers to run on a frame; any script wrappers on a frame that is not explicitly protected will be created successfully, but will be silently ignored. It is possible that a future version of the secure handlers will lift this restriction, but until such a change is made, you can make protected proxy frames with suitable scripts and have them manipulate references to the frames you want to control.

It is also possible to unwrap a script, so that it returns to its original behavior. `SecureHandlerUnwrapScript(wrappedFrame, scriptName)` will securely restore the original handler, and return the `prebody` snippet, owning header frame, and `postbody` snippet, allowing you to put the wrapper back on if needed.

Using a Post-Hook

If two strings are supplied to `SecureHandlerWrapScript`, the second one is a post-hook snippet called after the original handler completes. Most pre-hooks can include a message as an additional return value; if this message is non-nil, the post-hook is called and receives the message as an additional argument.

Post-hooks are commonly used to perform clean-up or change an addon's state information after an action completes, setting it up for the next action. You can use this to make the menu frames created by `BlessedMenus` act more like conventional popup menus, closing after a choice is made from them. Open up the `BlessedMenus.xml` file and find the first template, `BlessedMenusSpellButtonTemplate`. Locate its `OnLoad` handler and add the following statement at the end of the handler:

```
SecureHandlerWrapScript(self, "OnClick", self:GetParent(),
  [[return nil, "closeMenu"]],
  [[if message == "closeMenu" then owner:Hide() end]]
)
```

A pre-hook is always required, partly because a post-hook will never be called unless the pre-hook returns a message to call it with. In this case, returning `nil` as the button value means that the button argument will be passed unchanged to the original click script.

The post-hook snippet receives the same arguments as the pre-hook snippet (but with any changes returned by the pre-hook snippet), plus one more, `message`, which is largely irrelevant in this example. The other point worth noting is the global value, `owner`. Each secure environment stores a reference to the frame handle for the frame with which the environment is associated. Because the menu containing the button is the header frame for the wrapping snippets, `owner` always refers to it. This is the simplest way to allow the menu's buttons to close their containing menu.

Script Wrapper Reference

The scripts that can be wrapped are mostly the same ones found on `SecureHandler` templates; they deal specifically with user interaction or protected triggers. The following scripts support secure wrappers, with the following arguments to their pre-hook and post-hook snippets.

SCRIPT	PRE-HOOK	POST-HOOK
OnClick	button, message = preHook(self, button, down)	postHook(self, message, button, down)
OnDoubleClick	button, message = preHook(self, button, down)	postHook(self, message, button, down)
PreClick	button, message = preHook(self, button, down)	postHook(self, message, button, down)
PostClick	button, message = preHook(self, button, down)	postHook(self, message, button, down)
OnEnter	allow, message = preHook(self)	postHook(self, message)
OnLeave	allow, message = preHook(self)	postHook(self, message)
OnShow	allow, message = preHook(self)	postHook(self, message)
OnHide	allow, message = preHook(self)	postHook(self, message)

OnDragStart	varies	postHook(self, message, button)
OnReceiveDrag	varies	postHook(self, message, button)
OnMouseWheel	allow, message = preHook(self, offset)	postHook(self, message, offset)
OnAttribute Changed	allow, message = preHook(self, name, value)	postHook(self, message, name, value)

Pre-hook snippets wrapping OnDragStart and OnReceiveDrag are a little more complicated than others because their return values can be used to control the cursor contents. They can return false as other pre-hook snippets can to suppress the original script, or they can return type information in the same manner as the _ondragstart and _onreceivedrag snippets of SecureHandlerDragTemplate. They can also return "message" and a message value to prompt a postHook to execute.

Triggered Changes

Of course, sometimes you need to trigger a snippet in response to something other than user input; the situations in which you can do this are limited, to prevent automation, but they do exist, supported by a mechanism called *state drivers*.

State Drivers

A state driver is a set of commands to an internal manager that takes action on that frame when one or more elements of the game state change. It works similarly to a conditional clause in a macro, selecting an argument based on a set of authorized conditions, and passing that argument to a specified action on a frame, usually showing it, hiding it, or setting an attribute. They are established with the RegisterStateDriver or RegisterUnitWatch functions.

For instance, execute the following code in-game:

```
run RegisterStateDriver(PlayerFrame, "visibility", "[combat] show; hide")
```

The stock player frame should disappear from the upper left. Do something to enter combat—such as start a duel—and it should reappear, disappearing automatically once combat is over. This works even for protected frames, as you just saw; although, not surprisingly, you cannot register or change a state driver during combat from insecure code.

"visibility" is a special case. When you pass it as the second argument, the frame will be shown whenever your conditions statement (the third argument) evaluates to "show" and hidden whenever it evaluates to "hide". For any other string stateName you pass as the second argument, the state driver will set the attribute on the frame named "state-"..stateName to whatever string the conditions evaluate to, provided that value has actually changed since the last time (a full explanation of conditions is provided at the end of the section). You can then set that frame to react to that attribute change by having it inherit from SecureHandlerStateTemplate or SecureHandlerAttributeTemplate (in the next section). If you want to remove state triggers from a particular frame, you can use UnregisterStateDriver(frame, action) to remove a specific one or UnregisterStateDriver(frame) to remove all of them.

> **TIP** RegisterUnitWatch is a convenient, simplified interface to a common use case, wanting a unit frame to hide or show according to whether its unit currently exists, the way the stock target frame does. If you want the frame to be notified without changing its visibility, you can call RegisterUnitWatch(frame, true) and the driver will set the state-unitexists attribute on the frame to true or false instead.
>
> RegisterUnitWatch(frame, useState) is almost equivalent to being an alias for a preconfigured call to RegisterStateDriver, although there are two important distinctions; you cancel it with UnregisterUnitWatch, and if you track a frame with RegisterUnitWatch and change the frame's unit attribute, it will start dynamically tracking the new unit rather than requiring you to unregister and reregister the state driver.

State Responders

To perform other secure actions in response to changes in a frame's attributes or visibility, various templates are available:

- SecureHandlerShowHideTemplate
- SecureHandlerAttributeTemplate
- SecureHandlerStateTemplate

Responding to Show/Hide

SecureHandlerShowHideTemplate is the simplest, and useful because you can use it to respond to any change in visibility, not just ones triggered by state drivers. For instance, you can tweak BlessedMenus so that the menus close when the user presses the Esc key.

Open BlessedMenus.lua and find the definition of the BlessedMenu function. Change the first few lines as follows:

```
local function BlessedMenu(name, ...)
  local self = CreateFrame("Button", name, nil, ↵
"BlessedMenusMenuTemplate")
  self.buttons = {}
```

Next, open `BlessedMenus.xml` and find the frame definition for `BlessedMenusMenuTemplate`. First, find the `protected="true"` tag attribute on the `<Frame>` tag and change it to `inherits="SecureHandlerShowHideTemplate,` `SecureHandlerClickTemplate"`. Then change the `<Frame>` tag itself and its corresponding `</Frame>` tag to `<Button>` and `</Button>` tags. Finally, just before the `</Attributes>` tag, add three more attribute definitions:

```
<Attribute name="_onshow" value="self:SetBindingClick(false, ↵
'ESCAPE', self:GetName(), 'Escape')" />
    <Attribute name="_onhide" value="self:ClearBindings()" />
    <Attribute name="_onclick"
      value="if button == 'Escape' then self:Hide() end" />
```

XML doesn't support long brackets, so you should be careful when writing snippets to be stored in XML attributes—for example, by using single quotation marks around strings within the snippet, since a double quotation mark would be interpreted as the end of the XML attribute. If your code is more complicated, such that avoiding quotation marks becomes an issue, you can use `:SetAttribute()` calls in a frame's or template's `OnLoad` code instead of specifying snippets in XML attributes.

This code modifies the frames used as menus by making them clickable. It attaches secure code so that when the frame is shown, it will temporarily bind the Escape key to click the menu itself (rather than its buttons) with the virtual mouse button `"Escape"` (because mouse clicks are represented to the UI using strings, any string value can be used as a "button"). When that click (and only that click) happens on the menu, the menu will close itself. When the menu is closed for any reason, it will give up its hold on the Escape key and return it to its previous function.

Responding to Attribute and State Changes

`SecureHandlerAttributeTemplate` is a fairly straightforward template. It will fire the frame's `_onattributechanged` snippet whenever one of the frame's attributes (whose name does not start with an underscore) is changed, supplying the name and value of the changed attribute as arguments. `SecureHandlerStateTemplate` gives a little more structure to its use and is better integrated with the state drivers. It is only triggered by changes in attributes whose names start with `"state-"`. When one happens, it looks for a snippet in the frame attribute with the same name as the changed attribute, but prefixed with "_on"; that is, if triggered by a change to the state-unitexists attribute, it looks for a snippet to handle that attribute in the _onstate-unitexists attribute. Instead of the raw name and value arguments, it calls that snippet with the stateid argument, which is the name of the changed attribute minus the "state-" portion, and the newstate argument, which is the same as value. That is, if the state handler was triggered by a change in the state-unitexists attribute, the stateid argument will be "unitexists".

To see one rather remarkable way you can use SecureHandlerState Template, enter the following block into a fresh page in-game (if you don't have a priest to test this with, substitute spells or items appropriate to your character):

```
local self = AvatarCaster or CreateFrame("Button", "AvatarCaster", ↵
nil, "SecureActionButtonTemplate,SecureHandlerStateTemplate")
self:Hide()

self:SetAttribute("_onstate-mouseover", [[
  if newstate == "exists" then
    local name = self:GetName()
    self:SetBindingClick(false, "SHIFT-BUTTON1", name, "shift1")
    self:SetBindingClick(false, "CTRL-BUTTON1", name, "ctrl1")
    self:SetBindingClick(false, "SHIFT-BUTTON2", name, "shift2")
    self:SetBindingClick(false, "CTRL-BUTTON2", name, "ctrl2")
  else
    self:ClearBindings()
  end ]]
)
RegisterStateDriver(self, "mouseover", ↵
"[target=mouseover,exists] exists; noexists")

self:SetAttribute("unit", "mouseover")
self:SetAttribute("type", "spell")
self:SetAttribute("*spell-shift1", "Power Word: Fortitude")
self:SetAttribute("*spell-shift2", "Power Word: Shield")
self:SetAttribute("*spell-ctrl1", "Flash Heal")
self:SetAttribute("*spell-ctrl2", "Renew")
```

Run this script once you've finished it. Try holding down Shift or Control and clicking various character or monster avatars in the game-world display; observe how spells are cast on them directly without changing your target. Now, you can break down how it works.

The frame is created from a combination of SecureActionButtonTemplate (so that it can actually cast spells) and SecureHandlerStateTemplate (so that it can respond to changes in the game state). The AvatarCaster or portion simply prevents you from creating a new frame if you need to run the script more than once, such as by making an error in the script the first time. The frame is purely functional, and requires no visual presentation such as textures or font strings.

The _onstate-mouseover snippet will be called whenever the state-mouseover attribute is set, with "mouseover" as the stateid argument and the new value of the attribute as the newstate argument. Because this snippet is only being used for one state variable, it disregards the stateid argument. If state-mouseover is set to "exists", the button will rebind several mouse clicks so that they "click" this action button even though the mouse is no longer over it. These bindings do not replace any standard bindings associated with these button clicks; instead, they are "owned" by the frame whose handle sets them, and last until the frame releases them (as it does when the snippet is called with "noexists").

Rather than standard values such as "LeftButton", the button argument received by the button's OnClick handler will be a special value such as "shift1". This workaround is need to preserve information about which modifiers were down when the click was made, because when a binding that includes modifiers, such as SHIFT-F1, is pressed, the binding's actual code is resolved as if Shift (or whatever modifiers are included in the binding) were not being held down; this prevents the action button from finding traditional modified attributes such as shift-spell1.

The RegisterStateDriver call establishes a driver so that when your mouse cursor is pointing at a targetable player or creature, the button's state-mouseover attribute will be set to either "exists" or "noexists", accordingly. It will not actually set the frame's attribute value if the new value would be the same as the old value, so the frame's _onstate-mouseover snippet will only be called when it actually changes.

The last block of code sets up the spellcasting characteristics of the button, as explained in Chapter 15. Two points are worthy of note: the button's unit is "mouseover", so that spells will be cast on whatever player or mob is under the mouse in the world frame; and the attributes are phrased to key off of the custom button values supplied by the SetBindingClick calls in the previous code snippet.

State Conditionals

The key to registering state drivers that actually do what you want is understanding the conditional system. If you are familiar with writing macros, you have likely seen it already; macros that select a spell based on modifier keys or the nature of the target rely on the same system. When you give it a string, it returns a portion of that string based on the game state by calling a function called SecureCmdOptionParse.

This function starts at the beginning of the string and looks for the first matching pair of square brackets ([]) and anything they contain. If it does not find a pair of brackets, it goes to either the first semicolon it finds, if there is one, or the end of the string, if there isn't, and returns everything from where it is up to that point, trimming off any leading or trailing whitespace. If it does find such a pair, it separates the contents into a series of conditions wherever it finds commas, and determines the truth value of each condition. If all of them are true, it looks for either the next semicolon after the end bracket, or the end of the string, and returns anything before the point it finds, starting from the last closing square bracket before that point, again trimming off any leading or trailing whitespace. If any of the conditions are false, it repeats its search, starting from after the ending bracket of the set of conditions it just checked. Figure 25-3 shows the breakdown of parsing a secure command.

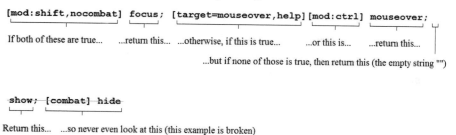

Figure 25-3: Breaking down conditionals

A comprehensive list (as of the time of this writing) of recognized conditions follows. The system is case-sensitive; conditions must be in lowercase to be recognized, except for the names of spells, units, or creature types, for which case is disregarded. If a condition is encountered that is not recognized, it is automatically treated as being false, and a system message appears in your chat window indicating that an unknown macro option was encountered and what it was. A recognized condition prefaced with no is also a valid condition, meaning the opposite of what the condition tests for; for instance, [nocombat] returns true if you are not in combat.

Target Specifiers and Unit Conditions

Although most conditions, such as [combat], are general inquiries about the player's game state, certain conditions apply to a specific unit, such as [dead]. By default, such conditions refer to the player's current target; but if you want to ask about the status of another unit, you can include a [target=unitID] clause in your conditions. By itself, a [target=unitID] specifier is always true; this is useful in many macros (because in a macro, such a specifier will also redirect a spell or item being cast to its unit), but not in state driver conditionals. However, they still have many uses in state drivers when combined with specific unit conditions, such as [target=mouseover,exists] in the AvatarCaster example earlier.

Any acceptable unitID can be supplied. Remember that names of pets or characters in your raid or party are also valid unitIDs, but names of mobs, totems, enemies, or allied players outside your group are not.

State Variables

Some conditions can have more than one value. For instance, [modifier] is true if any of the Ctrl, Shift, and Alt keys are held down, but [modifier:ctrl] is true only if the Control key, specifically, is down, whether or not other modifier keys are down.

A state variable can be checked for more than one possible value by stringing them together; for example, [modifier:shift/alt] is true if either the Shift or the Alt key is down. If you negate this condition, first the whole condition is evaluated, then the result is negated, so [nomodifier:shift/alt] is true if neither the Shift key nor the Alt key is down. This means that if you want to test if the Control key and only the Control key is being held, you can use the compound condition [modifier:ctrl, nomodifier:shift/alt].

Some condition variables can be checked meaningfully without checking them for a particular value; that is, [channeling] is true if you are presently channeling any spell, but [channeling:Blizzard] is only true if you are particularly channeling the Blizzard spell. However, some condition variables always have a value, so you must specify one or more values to get a meaningful result. [actionbar:3] is only true if your main action bar is set to page 3, but [actionbar] is always true, because you are always on some page or another.

Unit Conditions

The following conditions are tested against your target, unless you specify another target using a [target=unitID] phrase:

- [exists] —Indicates whether the unit exists, regardless of its condition. So [noexists] will be true if you have no target.

- [harm] —Indicates that the unit exists and that you are able to cast attack spells on it. So [target=focus,noharm] means that either you have no focus or that it is not attackable.

- [help] —Indicates that the unit exists and that you could target it with beneficial spells such as buffs or heals. It is possible, although very uncommon, for both [help] and [harm] to be true for a given unit; it is more common for both [noharm] and [nohelp] to be true for a unit, such as certain NPCs; and naturally, if [noexists] is true for a unit, then both [nohelp] and [noharm] will also be true.

- [dead] —True if the unit exists and is dead or a ghost. Currently, [nodead] is usually more functional, and usually needs to be in a [exists,nodead] clause to be useful.

- [party] and [raid] —True if the target is in the same party or raid with you, respectively. If [party] is true, [raid] will also be true, but not always the other way around. Be careful not to confuse these conditions with [group:party] and [group:raid], described later.

General Conditions

These conditions always apply to the condition of the player character or the client UI, regardless of which unit might be specified in the conditional clause. Several of the following conditions have abbreviations or synonyms that you can use if you need to make your code more concise:

- [actionbar:1/2/3/4/5/6], [bar:1/2/3/4/5/6]—These both return true if the given page (or one of the given pages) is currently the active page in the UI. In state drivers, this can be useful for synchronizing two or more action bars together so that one changes when another does.

- [bonusbar:1/2/3/4/5]—Used to handle special additional action bar pages such as those provided when a warrior switches stances or when a druid switches shapeshift forms. Assuming that the character has learned all appropriate stances, forms, or similar capabilities, they are numbered as shown in Table 25-2.

Table 25-2: Bonus Bar Values for Various Classes and Modes

BONUS BAR	WARRIOR	DRUID	ROGUE	PRIEST/WARLOCK
1	Battle Stance	Bear Form/ Dire Bear Form	Stealth	Shadowform or Metamorphosis
2	Defensive Stance	Cat Form	Shadow Dance	
3	Berserker Stance	Moonkin Form/Tree of Life Form		

There are two other numbers: 4, which is presently not used by the stock UI, and 5, a special case available to all players, used when you are possessing another unit or controlling a vehicle.

- [button:1/.../5/<virtual click>], [btn:1/.../5/<virtual click>]—Because it selects based on what mouse button was clicked on an action button to trigger the current action, this option is very useful in macros, but is almost totally purposeless for use in state drivers.

- [channeling], [channeling:<spell name>{/<spell name>}]—In its general form, this condition is true if the player is channeling any spell;

with a value or list of values, it is true while the player is channeling any of the listed spells.

■ [combat]—True whenever the player character or his pet is engaged in combat.

■ [equipped:<item type>], [worn:<item type>]—True if the player character has an item that is of the given type or subtype equipped and equipped in the given inventory slot.

■ It can check for any of the following item types or subtypes; it cannot check for a specific item by name:

Arrow	Leather	Shields
Bullet	Librams	Staves
Bows	Mail	Thrown
Cloth	Miscellaneous	Totems
Crossbows	One-Hand	Two-Hand
Daggers	One-Handed Axes	Two-Handed Axes
Guns	One-Handed Maces	Two-Handed Maces
Fishing Poles	One-Handed Swords	Two-Handed Swords
Fist Weapons	Plate	Wands
Idols	Polearms	

■ [flyable]—Returns true if the player is in an area where flying is allowed. This also returns true even if the player lacks a skill needed to fly in that area.

■ [flying]—True if the player is flying; that is, off the ground on a flying mount or in a flying form. It is not true when the character is in the air because he is jumping or falling, even with a slow fall effect.

■ [group], [group:party], [group:raid]—[group] is true when you are in any kind of group; [group:raid] is true whenever you are in any kind of raid group, including battlegrounds. [group:party] and [group:party/raid] are legal syntax, but are both effectively longer synonyms for [group].

■ [indoors]—True whenever the player is indoors.

■ [modifier:shift/ctrl/alt/<MODIFIEDCLICK>],   [mod:shift/ctrl/alt/<MODIFIEDCLICK>]—[modifier] and [mod] by themselves are true whenever the player is holding any of the Shift, Control, or Alt keys down. With a specified key or list of keys, they are true whenever any of the specified keys are down.

This condition also supports abstract, rebindable modifiers such as SELFCAST (which defaults to the Alt key). See the IsModifiedClick and SetModifiedClick functions (API) for more information.

- [mounted] —True whenever the player character is on any kind of mount, including automated flight path (taxi) mounts, but typically not when operating a vehicle.

- [outdoors] —True whenever the player character is outdoors. It uses a separate API from [indoors] (pertaining to the usability of certain spells and items, which does not necessarily correspond to whether a roof is over the player's head), so it is not always synonymous with [noindoors], although this will generally be the case.

- [pet], [pet:<pet name>], [pet:<pet type>] — [pet] is true whenever the player character is controlling a pet of any kind, including a vehicle or possessed unit. With an argument or list of arguments, it is true if the player character is controlling a pet whose name or type (such as owl or succubus) matches any of the listed arguments.

- [spec:n] —True if the player character's currently active talent specialization index is in the list of arguments. At the time of this writing, only the values 1 and 2 are possible, but this could be expanded at some point in the future.

- [stance], [form], [stance:0/1/2/.../n], [form:0/.../n] —By itself, [stance] or [form] returns true if the player character is in any stance or shapeshift form; this will always be true for warriors. With a list of numerical arguments, it is true when the player character's current stance or form index is in the argument list. Table 25-3 shows the possible indices, depending on class:

Table 25-3: Stance Values for Different Classes

INDEX	WARRIOR	DRUID	ROGUE	PRIEST	SHAMAN	WARLOCK
1	Battle Stance	Bear Form/Dire Bear Form	Stealth	Shadow form	Ghost Wolf	
2	Defensive Stance	Aquatic Form				Metamorphosis
3	Berserker Stance	Cat Form	Shadow Dance			
4		Travel Form				

Druid stance values are a bit more complicated because, due to talents, the player might have Tree of Life form or Moonkin Form. In that case, stance 5 will contain this form, and stance 6 will contain the player's flight form (either Flight Form or Swift Flight Form). If the player does not have either of those talented stances, the flight forms will be moved into stance 5.

This condition is closely related, but not identical, to [bonusbar].

- [stealth]—True if the player character is in any kind of stealth condition, including rogue stealth, druid prowl, night elf shadowmeld, or mage invisibility. There is presently no way to determine if a hunter pet is in stealth from the conditional system.

- [swimming]—True whenever your character is in the water.

Summary

This chapter addresses quite a lot of material, but fortunately most of it is based on a few common principles. By now, you should grasp how to:

- Write snippets that use implied arguments, private globals, frame handles, and a restricted environment.

- Attach these snippets to frames for secure execution by using SecureHandler templates or script wrappers.

- Register state drivers to take action on frames, and construct conditionals that will select the values you want to use based on game state.

The Code

BlessedMenus

BlessedMenus.toc

```
## Interface: 30300
## Title: BlessedMenus
## Notes: Creates menus on party frames to select spells to cast on them
BlessedMenus.xml
BlessedMenus.lua
```

BlessedMenus.xml

```
<Ui xmlns="http://www.blizzard.com/wow/ui/"
   xmlns:xsi="http://www.w3.org/2001/XMLSchema-instance"
   xsi:schemaLocation="http://www.blizzard.com/wow/ui/
   http://wowprogramming.com/FrameXML/UI.xsd">
   <Button name="BlessedMenusSpellButtonTemplate" enableMouse="true" ↵
inherits="SecureActionButtonTemplate" virtual="true">
    <Size x="144" y="16" />
    <Layers>
```

```
        <Layer level="ARTWORK">
          <Texture parentKey="icon">
            <Size x="16" y="16" />
            <Anchors>
              <Anchor point="TOPLEFT" />
            </Anchors>
          </Texture>
        </Layer>
      </Layers>
      <Attributes>
        <Attribute name="type" value="spell" />
        <Attribute name="useparent-unit" value="true" type="boolean" />
      </Attributes>
      <Scripts>
        <OnLoad>
          SecureHandlerWrapScript(self, "OnClick", self:GetParent(),
          [[return nil, "closeMenu"]],
          [[if message == "closeMenu" then owner:Hide() end]]
          )
          self:GetFontString():SetPoint("LEFT", self.icon, "RIGHT", 2, 1)
          self:RegisterEvent("PLAYER_ENTERING_WORLD")
        </OnLoad>
        <OnEvent>
          self.icon:SetTexture↵
(GetSpellTexture(self:GetAttribute("spell")))
        </OnEvent>
      </Scripts>
      <ButtonText inherits="GameFontHighlight" justifyH="LEFT" />
      <HighlightTexture alphaMode="ADD">
        <Color r="0.75" g="0.75" b="0.6" a="0.5" />
      </HighlightTexture>
  </Button>
  <Button name="BlessedMenusMenuTemplate" hidden="true" ↵
inherits="SecureHandlerShowHideTemplate,SecureHandlerClickTemplate" ↵
virtual="true">
    <Size x="160" y="18" />
    <Backdrop bgFile="Interface\Tooltips\UI-Tooltip-Background" ↵
edgeFile="Interface\Tooltips\UI-Tooltip-Border" tile="true">
      <EdgeSize val="16"/>
      <TileSize val="16"/>
      <BackgroundInsets left="4" right="4" top="4" bottom="4"/>
      <BorderColor r="1" g="1" b="1" />
      <Color r="0.09" g="0.09" b="0.19" />
    </Backdrop>
    <Attributes>
      <Attribute name="useparent-unit" value="true" type="boolean" />
      <Attribute name="_onshow" value="self:SetBindingClick(false, ↵
'ESCAPE', self:GetName(), 'Escape')" />
      <Attribute name="_onhide" value="self:ClearBindings()" />
      <Attribute name="_onclick"
```

```
                    value="if button == 'Escape' then self:Hide() end" />
        </Attributes>
      </Button>
</Ui>
```

BlessedMenus.lua

```lua
local function BlessedMenu(name, ...)
  local self = CreateFrame("Frame", name, nil, ↵
"BlessedMenusMenuTemplate")
  self.buttons = {}
  for i=1, select('#', ...) do
    local spellName = select(i, ...)
    local button = CreateFrame("Button", nil, self, ↵
"BlessedMenusSpellButtonTemplate")
    self.buttons[i] = button
    button:SetAttribute("spell", spellName)
    button:SetText(spellName)
    if i == 1 then
      button:SetPoint("TOPLEFT", 8, -8)
    else
      button:SetPoint("TOPLEFT", self.buttons[i - 1], "BOTTOMLEFT", ↵
0, -2)
    end
  end
  self:SetHeight(#self.buttons * 18 + 14)
  return self
end

local heals = BlessedMenu("BlessedMenusHeals",
  "Holy Light",
  "Flash of Light",
  "Lay on Hands"
)

local hands = BlessedMenu("BlessedMenusHands",
  "Hand of Protection",
  "Hand of Freedom",
  "Hand of Salvation",
  "Hand of Sacrifice"
)

local blessings = BlessedMenu("BlessedMenusBlessings",
  "Blessing of Might",
  "Blessing of Kings",
  "Blessing of Wisdom"
)

local openSpellList = [[
local menu = IsAltKeyDown() and "blessings"
```

```
      or IsControlKeyDown() and "heals"
      or IsShiftKeyDown() and "hands"
menu = menu and self:GetFrameRef(menu)
if lastMenu and lastMenu:IsShown() and ↵
lastMenu:GetParent() == self then
  lastMenu:Hide()
  if lastMenu == menu then
    return
  end
end
if menu then
  menu:Hide()
  menu:SetParent(self)
  menu:SetPoint("TOPLEFT", "$cursor")
  menu:SetFrameLevel(self:GetFrameLevel() + 2)
  menu:Show()
  lastMenu = menu
end
]]

for i, frame in ipairs{PlayerFrame, PartyMemberFrame1, ↵
PartyMemberFrame2, PartyMemberFrame3, PartyMemberFrame4} do
  frame:SetAttribute("shift-type1", "spelllist")
  frame:SetAttribute("ctrl-type1", "spelllist")
  frame:SetAttribute("alt-type1", "spelllist")
  frame:SetAttribute("_spelllist", openSpellList)
  SecureHandlerSetFrameRef(frame, "blessings", BlessedMenusBlessings)
  SecureHandlerSetFrameRef(frame, "heals", BlessedMenusHeals)
  SecureHandlerSetFrameRef(frame, "hands", BlessedMenusHands)
end
```

## CHAPTER 26

Creating Unit Frames with Group Templates

Earlier in this book you learned how to create a very simple unit frame, and then later extended it by making it clickable using secure templates. With some work, you could extend this addon to show your party or raid, but because each individual frames is a secure template, it cannot be created or configured while the player is in combat.

One way around this is to create all of the frames ahead of time and use the "unit watch" system to show them as needed. For something like party frames, this might even make the most sense, because you can create the frames before the player enters combat, and the secure template system will show and hide them as necessary. However, this method isn't well suited to displaying larger groups like raids.

What if you want to display your raid group and sort it by class or raid role? This would allow you to always have the tanks in one location and the unit frames of your healers in another. Unfortunately, there doesn't seem to be a way to do this in the default user interface. Luckily, Blizzard provides several templates that allow developers to create raid, party, and pet frames that update and configure themselves even while the player is in combat. The templates allow you to pre-program the type and configuration of the frames, as well as directions of how the frames should be placed and sorted.

In this chapter you use the `SecureGroupHeaderTemplate` to create a fully functional party/raid unit frame addon called SquareUnitFrames.

Configuring a SecureGroupHeader

The role of the secure group headers is actually pretty straightforward, managing only the parts that aren't possible in addon code. The header's primary responsibility is managing the creation and placement of frames. As players join your party or raid, the secure template handles the creation of new frames for each of them. If an addon were to try this while the player is in combat, the new frames would be locked down, unable to be modified. The group headers enable your addon to do last-minute configuration *before* the frame is ever locked down.

The process for creating a new group header is roughly as follows:

1. Create a new header frame that inherits from `SecureGroupHeader Template`. This may be a custom XML template that inherits from the Blizzard template and adds things such as artwork and labels, or just the raw template itself.

2. Set attributes on the new header for some of the following:

    ▪ What characters, classes, groups should be displayed in the header?

    ▪ Should the header be displayed when the player is in a party, raid, solo, or all of the above?

    ▪ When new frames are created, how should they be anchored to the existing frames?

    ▪ How should the frames be sorted?

    ▪ Should the frames be grouped, or displayed in columns and rows?

3. Supply an XML template (optionally) that the header will use to create new unit frames. Again, this could just be the standard `SecureUnitButton` or a custom template with artwork and other elements.

4. Provide a configuration function (optionally) that will be called when a new unit frame is created, allowing for last-minute customization by addons.

Of course, creating a fully functional raid addon is a bit more complicated than this, but once you've mastered the basics of using the template, other features can be added to your addon as necessary.

Configuration Options

A `SecureGroupHeader` has plenty of options that can be set using attributes. These options can be grouped into three major classes: filtering, grouping and sorting, and display. Tables 26-1, 26-2, and 26-3 describe these attributes.

When specifying a `groupBy` attribute, you must also supply a `groupingOrder` or the template will encounter an error, because `groupingOrder` doesn't have any default values.

Table 26-1: Filtering Attributes

ATTRIBUTE	TYPE	DESCRIPTION
showRaid	boolean	When `true`, the group header is shown when the player is in a raid.
showParty	boolean	When `true`, the group header is shown when the player is in a party. This attribute doesn't imply `showRaid` but can work alongside it.
showPlayer	boolean	When `true`, the header includes the player when not in a raid (normally, the player would not be visible in a party listing).
showSolo	boolean	When `true`, the header is shown when the player is not in any group. This option implies `showPlayer`.
nameList	string	A comma-separated list of player names to be included in the listing. This option is not used if `groupFilter` is specified.
groupFilter	string	A group number, or any combination of the following strings: ■ A comma-separated list of raid group numbers ■ A comma-separated list of uppercase class names in English (`WARRIOR`, `PRIEST`, and so on) ■ A comma-separated list of uppercase group roles (`MAINTANK`, `MAINASSIST`)
strictFiltering	boolean	When `true`, a character must match both a group and a class from the `groupFilter` list. This allows you to specify `"1,WARRIOR"`, which shows all warriors in group 1.

Table 26-2: Grouping and Sorting Attributes

ATTRIBUTE	TYPE	DESCRIPTION
groupBy	string	Specifies a grouping to apply before the list of players is sorted. Can be one of the following values: `"GROUP"`, `"CLASS"`, or `"ROLE"`. The sorting within these groups can be specified with the `groupingOrder` attribute.

Continued

Table 26-2 (*continued*)

ATTRIBUTE	TYPE	DESCRIPTION
groupingOrder	string	Specifies what order should be applied to the groups before they are sorted individually. This should be a comma-separated string of group numbers, uppercase class names, or uppercase role names (depending on what type of grouping was specified).
sortMethod	string	Specifies what sorting method should be used for ordering raid frames. Can be either `"NAME"` or `"INDEX"`, where index will sort the raid by the internal raid ID. This value defaults to `"INDEX"`.
sortDir	string	Specifies the sort order using `"ASC"` for ascending, and `"DESC"` for descending. This value defaults to `"ASC"`.

Table 26-3: Display Attributes

ATTRIBUTE	TYPE	DESCRIPTION
template	string	The name of an XML template to use when creating new frames. This can be a custom template, or the simple `SecureUnitButtonTemplate`.
templateType	string	The frame type of the XML template being used (`Button`, `StatusBar`, and so on).
point	string	A valid XML anchor point. This point will be used to anchor a new frame to an existing frame. The code will intelligently use the opposing anchor points, so if you specify `"TOP"`, it will anchor the `"TOP"` point of the new frame to the `"BOTTOM"` point of the previous frame.
xOffset	number	An x offset (in pixels) to be used when anchoring new frames.
yOffset	number	A y offset (in pixels) to be used when anchoring new frames.
maxColumns	number	The maximum number of columns that the header will create. The default for this attribute is a single column.

ATTRIBUTE	TYPE	DESCRIPTION
unitsPerColumn	number	The maximum number of units that will be displayed in a single column. When this value is nil, there is no limit.
startingIndex	number	The index in the final sorted list at which to start displaying units. This value defaults to 1.
columnSpacing	number	The amount of space (in pixels) between the columns. This value defaults to 0.
columnAnchorPoint	string	The anchor point for each new column. A value of "LEFT" causes the columns to grow to the right.
initial-anchor	string	The initial anchor point for new unit frames. This can be used to place the frame in a different starting location (such as growing from the bottom up instead of top down). This value should be a comma-separated list containing anchor point, relative anchor point, x offset, and y offset.
initial-width	number	The initial width of the unit frame in pixels.
initial-height	number	The initial height of the unit frame in pixels.
initial-scale	number	The initial scale of the unit frame.
Initial-unitwatch	boolean	Whether or not the frame should register for unit watch when initially created. If this attribute is set to the string state, the frame will be notified via the w attribute. If this attribute is set to any other true value, the frame will be shown or hidden depending on whether or not the unit exists.

In Table 26-3, a column means the initial level of grouping for the raid frames. Because you can specify a custom anchor point for the frames (using the point attribute), your columns could actually be horizontal, and your rows could be vertical. In addition, when using a multicolumn display, you must specify a columnAnchorPoint or the template will generate an error.

Initial Configuration Function

In addition to the predefined attributes, a group header can identify an initial configuration function that will be called after a frame has been created, but before it is fully locked down by the user interface. Setting the `initialConfigFunction` key in the header's table to a function enables this feature.

This function will be able to set attributes on the frame and do any other one-time configuration bits. This is a good chance to register events and click handlers, or set up any secure click actions. Although the frame is not completely locked down, you are still unable to move/hide/show the frame from within this function.

Creating SquareUnitFrames

As with all of your addons, start by creating an addon skeleton called **SquareUnitFrames**, containing both a Lua and an XML file. Create `SquareUnitFrames.toc` and add the following:

```
## Interface: 30300
## Title: SquareUnitFrames
## Notes: Square shaped party/raid frames

SquareUnitFrames.xml
SquareUnitFrames.lua
```

Constructing the Template

A normal `SecureUnitButton` won't have any visual elements and you know you want to display at least the unit's name, health, and power. Open up `SquareUnitFrames.xml` and include the following code to define the button template:

```xml
<Ui
  xmlns="http://www.blizzard.com/wow/ui/"
  xmlns:xsi="http://www.w3.org/2001/XMLSchema-instance"
  xsi:schemaLocation="http://www.blizzard.com/wow/ui/
  http://wowprogramming.com/FrameXML/UI.xsd">
  <Frame name="SquareUnitFrames_UnitTemplate" virtual="true">
    <Size x="36" y="36"/>
    <Layers>
      <Layer level="BACKGROUND">
        <Texture setAllPoints="true">
          <Color r="0.0" g="0.0" b="0.0"/>
        </Texture>
      </Layer>
    </Layers>
    <Scripts>
      <OnShow function="SquareUnitFrames_Frame_OnShow"/>
    </Scripts>
  </Frame>
</Ui>
```

This code creates a new template called SquareUnitFrames_UnitTemplate
that will be used by the group header to create new frames. The template
defines a solid black background texture, sized 36-by-36 pixels. The rest of the
sub-frames will be children of this main frame.

After the </Layers> tag and before the <Scripts> tag, add the following
frame definitions:

```
<Frames>
  <Button name="$parent_Unit" parentKey="unit" ↩
inherits="SecureUnitButtonTemplate">
    <Size x="34" y="34"/>
    <Anchors>
      <Anchor point="TOPLEFT">
        <Offset x="1" y="-1"/>
      </Anchor>
    </Anchors>
    <Layers>
      <Layer level="OVERLAY">
        <FontString name="$parent_Name" parentKey="name"
        inherits="GameFontHighlight" setAllPoints="true"/>
      </Layer>
    </Layers>
    <Frames>
      <StatusBar name="$parent_HealthBar" parentKey="healthBar">
        <Size x="34" y="30"/>
        <Anchors>
          <Anchor point="TOPLEFT"/>
        </Anchors>
        <BarTexture file="Interface\Buttons\UI-Listbox-Highlight2"/>
        <BarColor r="1.0" g="1.0" b="1.0"/>
      </StatusBar>
      <StatusBar name="$parent_PowerBar" parentKey="powerBar">
        <Size x="34" y="3"/>
        <Anchors>
          <Anchor point="TOPLEFT" relativeTo="$parent_HealthBar"
          relativePoint="BOTTOMLEFT">
            <Offset x="0" y="-1"/>
          </Anchor>
        </Anchors>
        <BarTexture file=↩
"Interface\TargetingFrame\UI-TargetingFrame-BarFill"/>
        <BarColor r="1.0" g="1.0" b="1.0"/>
      </StatusBar>
    </Frames>
  </Button>
</Frames>
```

This first sub-frame is the actual button that displays the unit's name, health,
and power (for example, mana, rage, or energy). The button is anchored and

sized in a way that causes the background to appear as a one-pixel border on all sides. The textures used here were chosen for a specific visual style, but you could use any texture for your status bars. The health bar dominates most of the frame, whereas the power bar is just 3 pixels high.

Creating a Header Template

Although you could create a header purely in Lua and set attributes on it in your main script, setting the attributes in XML may be preferable because it allows the frame to be validated as a whole (and remain alterable in Lua). After the template definition in SquareUnitFrames.xml but before the </Ui> tag, add the following code:

```
<Frame name="SquareUnitFrames_Header" parent="UIParent"
   inherits="SecureGroupHeaderTemplate" movable="true">
  <Anchors>
    <Anchor point="CENTER"/>
  </Anchors>
  <Attributes>
    <Attribute name="showParty" type="boolean" value="true"/>
    <Attribute name="showRaid" type="boolean" value="true"/>
    <Attribute name="showPlayer" type="boolean" value="true"/>
    <Attribute name="showSolo" type="boolean" value="true"/>
    <Attribute name="maxColumns" type="number" value="8"/>
    <Attribute name="unitsPerColumn" type="number" value="5"/>
    <Attribute name="columnAnchorPoint" type="string" value="TOP"/>
    <Attribute name="point" type="string" value="LEFT"/>
    <Attribute name="template" type="string"
    value="SquareUnitFrames_UnitTemplate"/>
    <Attribute name="templateType" type="string" value="Frame"/>
    <Attribute name="xOffset" type="number" value="-1"/>
    <Attribute name="yOffset" type="number" value="1"/>
  </Attributes>
</Frame>
```

This new frame template inherits from SecureGroupHeaderTemplate and begins anchored in the center of the screen. The attributes section programs how the header is to behave. You learn more about each of the possible attributes in the next section but for now, know that this frame will include the player in its display, and will be shown when the player is in a raid, in a party, or soloing. Frames are organized into columns of five, with eight columns total. The grid of frames groups from left to right and the template you've just defined is used to create the child frames.

Because each frame has a one-pixel black border, two frames stacked vertically would have two pixels in between, and a one-pixel border around. To prevent this and make the borders consistent, xOffset and yOffset are set to tell the header how to anchor new frames.

Additionally, the header is flagged as movable, because at some point in the future it may be useful for the player to be able to move the frames around the screen.

Setting Name and Status Bars

If you were to load the addon at this point, the frames wouldn't display anything; however, to update the name and health/power bars the frame needs to know when the unit it's supposed to be displaying has changed. When the group header reconfigures the frames, it hides each frame and then re-shows them. You can use this to update the frame by defining an OnShow script.

Open SquareUnitFrames.lua and add the following function:

```
function SquareUnitFrames_Frame_OnShow(button)
  local unit = button:GetAttribute("unit")

  if unit then
    local guid = UnitGUID(unit)
    if guid ~= button.guid then
      SquareUnitFrames_ResetUnitButton(button.unit, unit)
      button.guid = guid
    end
  end
end


-- Actually show the header frame
SquareUnitFrames_Header:Show()
```

In its current state, the group header has a tendency to show and hide the frames more often than is strictly necessary. Knowing this, you implement a small check to ensure you only reset the frame when the underlying unit actually changes. First you check to make sure that the frame actually has the unit attribute set, and then retrieve the GUID for that unit. You may recall from Chapter 21 that the GUID is a globally unique identifier for each unit so you can use this to track these changes.

You call an external function to actually update the button, and the reason for this will become apparent later in the chapter. Suffice it to say that the reset code is called from multiple places, so abstracting the code into a function enables you to avoid maintaining it in two different places. Define the following function after SquareUnitFrames_Frame_OnShow and before the call that actually shows the header frame:

```
function SquareUnitFrames_ResetUnitButton(button, unit)
  SquareUnitFrames_ResetHealthBar(button, unit)
  SquareUnitFrames_ResetPowerBar(button, unit)
```

```
        SquareUnitFrames_ResetName(button, unit)
    end
```

This function takes two arguments: the unit button sub-frame and the unit that is being displayed by the frame. It in turn calls three more functions, for the same reason. These implementations are extremely straightforward, so add them now:

```
function SquareUnitFrames_ResetName(button, unit)
    local name = UnitName(unit) or UNKNOWN
    button.name:SetText(name)
end

function SquareUnitFrames_ResetHealthBar(button, unit)
    local classColor = RAID_CLASS_COLORS[class]
    local class = select(2, UnitClass(unit)) or "WARRIOR"

    button.healthBar:SetStatusBarColor(classColor.r, ↵
classColor.g, classColor.b)
    button.healthBar:SetMinMaxValues(0, UnitHealthMax(unit))
    button.healthBar:SetValue(UnitHealth(unit))
end

function SquareUnitFrames_ResetPowerBar(button, unit)
    local powerType, powerToken = UnitPowerType(unit)
    local powerColor = PowerBarColor[powerToken]

    button.powerBar:SetStatusBarColor(powerColor.r, ↵
powerColor.g, powerColor.b)
    button.powerBar:SetMinMaxValues(0, UnitPowerMax(unit))
    button.powerBar:SetValue(UnitPower(unit))
end
```

In certain cases a unit's name might not be available, so you supply a default of `Unknown` just so your unit frame displays something reasonable in those cases. You use the global `RAID_CLASS_COLORS` table to look up the correct color for the unit, and `PowerBarColors` to find the correct color for the power bar. Figure 26-1 shows the resulting unit frame, if you load the addon in-game.

Figure 26-1: SquareUnitFrames showing a frame for the player

A frame is created for your character and anyone else in your party or raid, but the name doesn't appear to have been set. In fact, this is just a layering issue with the textures for the status bars. Even though the font string for the unit's name is on the OVERLAY layer, before graphical layers are checked, frame levels are used to layer the graphics. Because both of the status bars are children of the unit frame, they are at least one frame level higher than the button, causing the textures for the status bars to appear above the font string.

There is no *good* way to fix this, but one way is to manually lower the frame level of the status bars to match the main button. This may not work in all cases, but in these simple unit frames it works quite well.

Nudging Frame Levels

Because the status bar frame levels only need to be adjusted when the frame is first created, this is a great place to utilize `initialConfigFunction`. At the top of `SquareUnitFrames.lua`, add the following function definition:

```
function SquareUnitFrames_InitialConfig(frame)
  -- Nudge the status bar frame levels down
  frame.unit.healthBar:SetFrameLevel(frame.unit:GetFrameLevel())
  frame.unit.powerBar:SetFrameLevel(frame.unit:GetFrameLevel())
end
```

Then, right before the line that calls `SquareUnitFrames_Header:Show()`:

```
SquareUnitFrames_Header.initialConfigFunction = ↵
SquareUnitFrames_InitialConfig
```

Now whenever a frame is created, the initial configuration function is called and the frame levels are nudged so the frame displays correctly. Figure 26-2 shows `SquareUnitFrames` at this stage, with the names and colored status bars visible.

Figure 26-2: SquareUnitFrames showing the player frame, after nudging frame levels.

Responding to Events and Clicks

The names are a bit squished and the frames don't actually update when the player's health or power change, but if you have people leave and join your party you should see the frames reconfiguring during combat. This section makes the frames a bit more responsive by responding to events.

Targeting the Unit on Left-Click

Currently when you click the unit frames, they do nothing other than eat the mouse click. As you learned in Chapter 15, you can fix this by setting attributes on the secure frame. Add the following to the XML definition for the unit button, inside the main template. The code goes between the `</Frames>` tag and the `</Button>` tag:

```
<Attributes>
  <Attribute name="useparent-unit" type="boolean" value="true"/>
  <Attribute name="*type1" type="string" value="target"/>
</Attributes>
```

The first attribute directs the frame to use the unit attribute from its parent. Remember that the unit button isn't the one being created by the group header, so the attribute won't be set on it. Inheriting the parent's attribute in this way ensures that any changes during combat work correctly. The second attribute tells the frame to set all left-clicks to target the unit. In addition to this, you could actually bind spells, macros, and other types of actions supported by the `SecureUnitButton` template.

Moving the Header

As fun as creating unit frames is, having them stuck in the middle of your screen can seriously impact your playing! You've done this a few times already in this book, so add the following scripts to the unit button's definition inside the template (after the `</Frames>` tag and before the `<Attributes>` element):

```
<Scripts>
  <OnDragStart function="SquareUnitFrames_Button_OnDragStart"/>
  <OnDragStop function="SquareUnitFrames_Button_OnDragStop"/>
  <OnHide function="SquareUnitFrames_Button_OnDragStop"/>
</Scripts>
```

And add the corresponding functions to `SquareUnitFrames.lua` anywhere before the last three lines that show the header:

```
function SquareUnitFrames_Button_OnDragStart(self, button)
  SquareUnitFrames_Header:StartMoving()
  SquareUnitFrames_Header.isMoving = true
end

function SquareUnitFrames_Button_OnDragStop(self, button)
  if SquareUnitFrames_Header.isMoving then
    SquareUnitFrames_Header:StopMovingOrSizing()
  end
end
```

Note that these functions call `StartMoving()` and `StopMovingOrSizing()` on the header, rather than on the frame itself. This ensures that the entire set of unit frames moves together. Now add the final line to your initialization function `SquareUnitFrames_InitialConfig`, to register the button for drag events:

```
button.unit:RegisterForDrag("LeftButton")
```

Reload your user interface and you should be able to drag the frames around the screen, and click them to target the unit. If you are in the middle of dragging the frame when someone joins or leaves the party, the header will stop moving. This is because when the button you are dragging (the actual unit frame you click) is hidden, the game client will not fire an `OnMouseUp` event. If the `OnHide` script wasn't set that way, the header would get stuck to your mouse.

Health Update Events

Unit frames aren't very useful without an accurate depiction of the unit's health, so you should register for three events, by adding the following code to the bottom of your initial configuration function:

```
frame:RegisterEvent("UNIT_HEALTH")
frame:RegisterEvent("UNIT_MAXHEALTH")
frame:RegisterEvent("PLAYER_ENTERING_WORLD")
```

The first two events you should already be familiar with from your work earlier in this book, but `PLAYER_ENTERING_WORLD` is a bit peculiar. Without it, your unit frames would work in most situations, but in specific circumstances (such as when the player releases in Tempest Keep and is resurrected outside) the unit frames could get "stuck" on the wrong health display until another event occurred. To prevent this, all unit frames will reset themselves whenever this event occurs.

Add the `OnEvent` script to the definition of `SquareUnitFrames_UnitTemplate`, not the sub-button you've been working on previously, putting the following directly after the `OnShow` definition:

```
<OnEvent function="SquareUnitFrames_Frame_OnEvent"/>
```

Create the corresponding handler by defining a new function:

```
function SquareUnitFrames_Frame_OnEvent(self, event, arg1, ...)
  local unit = self:GetAttribute("unit")
  if not unit then
    return
  end

  -- Handle any events that don't accept a unit argument
  if event == "PLAYER_ENTERING_WORLD" then
    SquareUnitFrames_ResetUnitButton(self.unit, unit)
  elseif arg1 and UnitIsUnit(unit, arg1) then
```

```
        if event == "UNIT_MAXHEALTH" then
            self.unit.healthBar:SetMinMaxValues(0, UnitHealthMax(unit))
            self.unit.healthBar:SetValue(UnitHealth(unit))
        elseif event == "UNIT_HEALTH" then
            self.unit.healthBar:SetValue(UnitHealth(unit))
        end
    end
end
```

This function first checks to ensure that the frame's unit attribute is set; otherwise the frame is not displaying a unit. Then the handler responds to the PLAYER_ENTERING_WORLD event, because it doesn't matter *which* unit is being shown by the frame. Then you check that the unit being altered (passed in arg1) is the same as the unit the frame is displaying. Inside this condition, the unit health and maximum health events are handled, just changing the status bars as appropriate.

Power Update Events

Properly displaying and updating the power bar for a unit frame is inherently much more difficult, because a unit can have multiple types of power. Mana, Energy, Rage, Runic Power, and Focus can all be queried by the UnitPower() API function, but they all fire different types of events. Those sneaky Druids who are able to switch between Rage, Energy, and Mana when they shapeshift further complicate the issue.

Rather than registering for all of the events and then having to check that you're responding to the correct one, you'll only register each frame for the events that are actually relevant. Replace your existing SquareUnitFrames_ ResetPowerBar function with the following two functions (or add the first function and just make the appropriate changes to the second):

```
local function unregisterManyEvents(frame, ...)
    for i=1, select("#", ...) do
        local event = select(i, ...)
        frame:UnregisterEvent(event)
    end
end

function SquareUnitFrames_ResetPowerBar(button, unit)
    local powerType, powerToken = UnitPowerType(unit)
    local powerColor = PowerBarColor[powerToken]
    local alive = not UnitIsDeadOrGhost(unit)

    local parent = button:GetParent()
    unregisterManyEvents(parent, "UNIT_MANA", "UNIT_RAGE", ↵
"UNIT_FOCUS","UNIT_ENERGY", "UNIT_RUNIC_POWER")
    unregisterManyEvents(parent, "UNIT_MAXMANA", "UNIT_MAXRAGE", ↵
"UNIT_MAXFOCUS", "UNIT_MAXENERGY", "UNIT_MAXRUNIC_POWER")
```

```
    parent:RegisterEvent("UNIT_" .. powerToken)
    parent:RegisterEvent("UNIT_MAX" .. powerToken)

    button.powerBar:SetStatusBarColor(powerColor.r, ↵
powerColor.g, powerColor.b)
    button.powerBar:SetMinMaxValues(0, UnitPowerMax(unit))
    button.powerBar:SetValue(UnitPower(unit))
end
```

The `unregisterManyEvents` function is a simple utility that allows you to un-register multiple events from a frame without having to do each of them on a separate line. In the power bar reset function, you query the client to see what type of power the unit currently has, then look up the appropriate color in the constant table. The `powerToken` is the type of power in English uppercase (such as `RAGE`, `MANA`, or `RUNIC_POWER`).

The function then unregisters all of the possible events, of which there are ten—five for normal updates and five for when the maximum value changes. Next you use a simple trick to decide what events to register by adding the `powerToken` to `UNIT_` and `UNIT_MAX_`. This allows you to avoid having a large `if` statement handling each of the five cases. Finally, the color is set and the values on the status bar are updated.

Actually registering the events and handling them is the easy bit. Add the following to the initial configuration function, remembering that the actual power events will be registered when the reset power bar function is called:

```
frame:RegisterEvent("UNIT_DISPLAYPOWER")
```

The actual event handler can use the same trick that you used in the preceding code, but it needs to query the client in order to test. Add the following line to `SquareUnitFrames_Frame_OnEvent` immediately after the line that begins `elseif arg1 and`:

```
local powerType, powerToken = UnitPowerType(unit)
```

Then add the conditions inside the sub-conditional that ensures that the unit attribute is set, and the unit actually exists (the same block where you handle health and power updates):

```
elseif event == "UNIT_DISPLAYPOWER" then
    SquareUnitFrames_ResetPowerBar(self.unit, unit)
elseif event == "UNIT_" .. powerToken then
    self.unit.powerBar:SetValue(UnitPower(unit))
elseif event == "UNIT_MAX" .. powerToken then
    self.unit.powerBar:SetMinMaxValues(0, UnitPowerMax(unit))
    self.unit.powerBar:SetValue(UnitPower(unit))
```

When the unit's display power changes you reset the entire bar to ensure that it's re-colored and the min/max values are correct. To test the other two events, you just concatenate the `powerToken` again and update the status bars accordingly. Now the unit frame should properly show power gain and loss, and switch correctly when a unit's power type changes.

Responding to Name Changes

At times either the game client is unable to resolve a name immediately, or the name of a unit token might change. When this happens, the `UNIT_NAME_UPDATE` event fires, so you can update your frames accordingly.

Add the event registration to your initial configuration function:

```
frame:RegisterEvent("UNIT_NAME_UPDATE")
```

Now add the event to your `OnEvent` function, by adding the following in the same block as the health and power updates (because this event passes the unit argument):

```
elseif event == "UNIT_NAME_UPDATE" then
    SquareUnitFrames_ResetName(self.unit, unit)
```

That's the end of the compulsory portion of creating a normal unit frame. The next section shows you how to add a number of enhancements to your frames.

Enhancing SquareUnitFrames

This is the fun part of addon writing! Once you have something basic working, you're able to add features until you have the addon just right for your purposes. Here are the features you are going to add to make this addon a bit more useful:

- Highlight units on mouseover, so it's clear who the player is selecting
- Highlight the unit that is the player's current target
- Show the unit's threat level by coloring the unit name
- Show dead players more prominently
- Prevent WoW from truncating longer names with . . .
- Replace the mana bar with a pet frame when the unit has a pet

Highlighting Units on Mouseover

This is probably the simplest modification, because Blizzard's system already has so much support for it. Remember that any texture in the

HIGHLIGHT layer is displayed when the mouse is over that texture. Simply add the following at the bottom of the unit sub-button definition inside the template:

```
<HighlightTexture file=↵
"Interface\Buttons\ButtonHilight-Square" alphaMode="ADD"/>
```

Now each time you move your mouse over a unit in the grid, you'll see a border around the frame. Figure 26-3 shows this feature in action!

Figure 26-3: SquareUnitFrames highlighting units on mouseover

Showing the Targeted Unit

Showing the targeted unit is a bit more complex, because you need to watch for changes to the player's target and then update accordingly. First you should create a texture in the unit button inside the template that can be shown to indicate selection. Add the following in the OVERLAY layer of the unit sub-button definition:

```
<Texture name="$parent_Selected" parentKey="selected" ↵
setAllPoints="true"
   file="Interface\Buttons\CheckButtonHilight" alphaMode="ADD" ↵
hidden="true"/>
```

Next you need to register for the PLAYER_TARGET_CHANGED event so you can show the texture on the selected unit and ensure the texture is hidden on all others. Add the event registration to your initial config function:

```
frame:RegisterEvent("PLAYER_TARGET_CHANGED")
```

Now add the following condition to your event handler after PLAYER_ENTERING_WORLD; there is no need to check the unit argument for this event:

```
elseif event == "PLAYER_TARGET_CHANGED" then
  if UnitIsUnit(unit, "target") then
    self.unit.selected:Show()
  else
    self.unit.selected:Hide()
  end
```

Although this will work in most cases, you should probably add it to the reset button function as well; otherwise if your party members were to change while you keep the same target, your unit frames wouldn't properly show it. Add this code to SquareUnitFrames_ResetUnitButton:

```
if UnitIsUnit(unit, "target") then
  button.selected:Show()
else
  button.selected:Hide()
end
```

Figure 26-4 shows the difference between mouseover highlighting and the selection texture.

Figure 26-4: SquareUnitFrames showing both the selected unit and the unit the mouse is over.

Displaying Threat Levels

In the Wrath of the Lich King expansion, WoW introduced a threat system that can be queried by addons. Although the functions can be queried for specific mobs, you are only concerned with the global threat of each unit (that is, whether or not a mob is focusing on the unit). Fortunately, this is very easy to accomplish. Add the following code to the bottom of SquareUnitFrames_ResetName:

```
local status = UnitThreatSituation(unit)
if status and status > 0 then
  local r, g, b = GetThreatStatusColor(status)
  button.name:SetTextColor(r, g, b)
else
  button.name:SetTextColor(1, 1, 1)
end
```

This function queries the threat situation status for the given unit, and then retrieves the correct color and applies it to the font string. Now register for the event in your initial configuration function:

```
frame:RegisterEvent("UNIT_THREAT_SITUATION_UPDATE")
```

Finally, add the condition to the event handler as follows, in the sub-conditional that checks the unit argument, after the UNIT_NAME_UPDATE condition:

```
elseif event == "UNIT_THREAT_SITUATION_UPDATE" then
  local status = UnitThreatSituation(unit)
  if status and status > 0 then
    local r, g, b = GetThreatStatusColor(status)
```

```
      self.unit.name:SetTextColor(r, g, b)
   else
      self.unit.name:SetTextColor(1, 1, 1)
   end
```

Figure 26-5 shows a raid group with names colored to indicate threat level.

Figure 26-5: SquareUnitFrames showing threat levels for party members

Showing Dead Players

Right now if someone in your group were to die, it would be difficult to see if they were actually dead or just very low on health. You can fix this by changing the status bar's color to gray and filling it in. Change your implementation of SquareUnitFrames_ResetHealthBar to the following:

```
function SquareUnitFrames_ResetHealthBar(button, unit)
   local class = select(2, UnitClass(unit)) or "WARRIOR"
   local classColor = RAID_CLASS_COLORS[class]
   local alive = not UnitIsDeadOrGhost(unit)

   if alive then
      button.healthBar:SetStatusBarColor(classColor.r, ↵
classColor.g, classColor.b)
      button.healthBar:SetMinMaxValues(0, UnitHealthMax(unit))
      button.healthBar:SetValue(UnitHealth(unit))
      button.dead = false
   else
      button.healthBar:SetStatusBarColor(0.3, 0.3, 0.3)
      button.healthBar:SetMinMaxValues(0, 1)
      button.healthBar:SetValue(1)
      button.dead = true
   end
end
```

The first two lines are the same, but then you use the UnitIsDeadOrGhost function to (shockingly) check to see if the unit is either dead or a ghost. You then either color the status bar based on the class color, or change it to grey and fill it in. You also set a flag on the unit button that you'll use in the event handler to indicate whether the status bar is currently showing the player as dead or alive.

Change the UNIT_HEALTH and UNIT_MAXHEALTH portion of the event handler to the following:

```
if event == "UNIT_MAXHEALTH" then
   if self.unit.dead ~= UnitIsDeadOrGhost(unit) then
      SquareUnitFrames_ResetUnitButton(self.unit, unit)
```

```
    else
      self.unit.healthBar:SetMinMaxValues(0, UnitHealthMax(unit))
      self.unit.healthBar:SetValue(UnitHealth(unit))
    end
  elseif event == "UNIT_HEALTH" then
    if self.unit.dead ~= UnitIsDeadOrGhost(unit) then
      SquareUnitFrames_ResetUnitButton(self.unit, unit)
    else
      self.unit.healthBar:SetValue(UnitHealth(unit))
    end
```

Here you just check to see if your flag is different from the return of
`UnitIsDeadOrGhost` and then adjust the frame accordingly. When a unit dies
the API still shows it as having power, so color that grey as well. Open up
`SquareUnitFrames_ResetPowerBar` and replace the last three lines:

```
button.powerBar:SetStatusBarColor(powerColor.r, powerColor.g, ↵
powerColor.b)
button.powerBar:SetMinMaxValues(0, UnitPowerMax(unit))
button.powerBar:SetValue(UnitPower(unit))
```

with the following:

```
local alive = not UnitIsDeadOrGhost(unit)
if alive then
    button.powerBar:SetStatusBarColor(powerColor.r, ↵
powerColor.g, powerColor.b)
else
    button.powerBar:SetStatusBarColor(0.3, 0.3, 0.3)
end

button.powerBar:SetMinMaxValues(0, UnitPowerMax(unit))
button.powerBar:SetValue(UnitPower(unit))
```

Change the event handler by replacing the power event conditions with the
following code:

```
  elseif event == "UNIT_" .. powerToken then
    if self.unit.dead ~= UnitIsDeadOrGhost(unit) then
      SquareUnitFrames_ResetPowerBar(self.unit, unit)
    else
      self.unit.powerBar:SetValue(UnitPower(unit))
    end
  elseif event == "UNIT_MAX" .. powerToken then
    if self.unit.dead ~= UnitIsDeadOrGhost(unit) then
      SquareUnitFrames_ResetPowerBar(self.unit, unit)
    else
      self.unit.powerBar:SetMinMaxValues(0, UnitPowerMax(unit))
      self.unit.powerBar:SetValue(UnitPower(unit))
    end
```

Figure 26-6 shows the unit frames with a dead unit, which is much easier to see when it's shaded.

Figure 26-6: SquareUnitFrames showing a dead unit shaded out

Displaying Unit Names

Currently, whenever `SquareUnitFrames` displays a name that is longer than four characters (and some names that are shorter), it is truncated with an ellipsis (" … ") at the end. This isn't very desirable—an ellipsis takes up much of the unit button's width, space that could be better used to display more characters of the name—but WoW doesn't really provide an easy way to fit as much of a name as possible in a font string of limited width.

What you can do instead is try different substrings of the name in order to fit as many characters as you can in a 30-pixel-wide font string. This algorithm might look like this:

```
local substring(name, length)
for length=#name, 1, -1 do
    substring = string.sub(name, 1, length)
    button.name:SetText(substring)
    if button.name:GetStringWidth() <= 30 then
        button.shortname = substring
        return
    end
end
```

First you take the entire string and set a font string to display it. Then you check to see what the width of the resulting display is. You continue to take one less character and as soon as you have something that is less than or equal to 30 pixels in width, you accept it and store it in the button (so you can re-use it later instead of re-calculating it).

This process, however, will have a big problem with names that contain non-alphanumeric characters, such as letters with accents and other special symbols. These characters are encoded using a standard called UTF-8. Although UTF-8 is very far outside the scope of this book, you can read more information about it at `http://en.wikipedia.org/wiki/Utf8`. What you need to know is that although each of those special characters can be represented by multiple bytes, Lua's string library treats each byte as an individual character. The following is sample output from World of Warcraft:

```
> print(string.len("Grüber"))
7
```

Even though Grüber has only six *visible* characters, it's actually made up of seven different characters from the Lua string library's point of view. If you tried to examine the substring between character positions 1 and 3 you would only get half of the "ü" character. That's because Lua's built-in string processing functions aren't UTF-8 aware.

Luckily we've done the work so you don't have to, and have created a function that takes in a string, a start index, and a number of characters to retrieve. Define this function directly above your definition of SquareUnitFrames_ResetName (you can include the comments if you'd like):

```
-- This function can return a substring of a UTF-8 string, properly
-- handling UTF-8 codepoints.  Rather than taking a start index and
-- optionally an end index, it takes the string, the start index, and
-- the number of characters to select from the string.
--
-- UTF-8 Reference:
-- 0xxxxxx - ASCII character
-- 110yyyxx - 2 byte UTF codepoint
-- 1110yyyy - 3 byte UTF codepoint
-- 11110zzz - 4 byte UTF codepoint

local function utf8sub(str, start, numChars)
    local currentIndex = start
    while numChars > 0 and currentIndex <= #str do
        local char = string.byte(str, currentIndex)
        if char >= 240 then
            currentIndex = currentIndex + 4
        elseif char >= 225 then
            currentIndex = currentIndex + 3
        elseif char >= 192 then
            currentIndex = currentIndex + 2
        else
            currentIndex = currentIndex + 1
        end
        numChars = numChars - 1
    end
    return str:sub(start, currentIndex - 1)
end
```

Next, change the definition of SquareUnitFrames_ResetName to the following:

```
function SquareUnitFrames_ResetName(button, unit)
  local name = UnitName(unit) or "Unknown"

  local substring
  for length=#name, 1, -1 do
    substring = utf8sub(name, 1, length)
    button.name:SetText(substring)
```

```
      if button.name:GetStringWidth() <= 30 then
        return
      end
    end

    local status = UnitThreatSituation(unit)
    if status and status > 0 then
      local r, g, b = GetThreatStatusColor(status)
      button.name:SetTextColor(r, g, b)
    else
      button.name:SetTextColor(1, 1, 1)
    end
  end
end
```

Sure, it's a lot of code to accomplish something that should be relatively easy, but it makes the frames look so much neater. Figure 26-7 shows the difference between the old version and the new improved version.

Figure 26-7: SquareUnitFrames showing truncated names, and the version using the fitting algorithm

Adding Pets to SquareUnitFrames

The state handlers system makes it extremely easy to add a pet frame that is shown/hidden correctly, even when the player is in combat. The first thing you need to do is create the frame definition in the XML file. Add the following after the `</Button>` tag for the unit sub-button, but before the `</Frames>` tag for the XML template:

```xml
<Button name="$parent_Pet" parentKey="pet"
  inherits="SecureHandlerShowHideTemplate,SecureUnitButtonTemplate">
  <Size x="34" y="5"/>
  <Anchors>
    <Anchor point="BOTTOMLEFT">
      <Offset x="1" y="1"/>
    </Anchor>
  </Anchors>
  <Frames>
    <StatusBar name="$parent_HealthBar" parentKey="healthBar"
      setAllPoints="true">
      <BarTexture file="Interface\Buttons\UI-Listbox-Highlight2"/>
```

```
        <BarColor r="0.0" g="1.0" b="0.0"/>
      </StatusBar>
    </Frames>
    <Attributes>
      <Attribute name="useparent-unit" type="boolean" value="true"/>
      <Attribute name="unitsuffix" type="string" value="pet"/>
      <Attribute name="*type1" type="string" value="target"/>
    </Attributes>
    <HighlightTexture file="Interface\Buttons\UI-Listbox-Highlight2"
      alphaMode="ADD"/>
  </Button>
```

This definition inherits from SecureHandlerShowHideTemplate as well as
SecureUnitButtonTemplate. This enables you to run code when the frame
is shown or hidden, and allows you to enable left-click to target the unit.
The frame is hidden by default, and you'll register it to be shown whenever
the unit has a pet. The unitsuffix attribute here, when combined with
useparent-unit, ensures that the frame inherits the unit attribute from its
parent, and adds pet to the end, giving you the pet's unit identifier.

Add the following code to the end of SquareUnitFrames_InitialConfig:

```
    RegisterUnitWatch(frame.pet)
    frame.pet:SetFrameRef("unit", frame.unit)
    frame.pet:SetAttribute("_onshow", [[
    local unit = self:GetFrameRef("unit")
    unit:SetHeight(28)
    ]])
    frame.pet:SetAttribute("_onhide", [[
    local unit = self:GetFrameRef("unit")
    unit:SetHeight(34)
    ]])

    frame.pet.unit = frame.unit

    frame.pet:HookScript("OnShow", SquareUnitFrames_Pet_OnShow)
    frame.pet:HookScript("OnHide", SquareUnitFrames_Pet_OnHide)
```

The first line simply registers the pet frame to be shown/hidden based on
the existence of the unit it's set to display. Next two secure snippets are created
that will be run when the frame is shown and hidden. The first changes the
height of the unit frame to be 6 pixels smaller, and the second changes it back
to the original height.

Next, you set button.pet.unit to be equal to button.unit. This allows
you to easily access the unit button from within the pet button's handlers.
Finally, you hook the OnShow and OnHide widget scripts so you can run some
non-secure code. This is because non-secure frames cannot be altered from
secure snippets, and vice versa. You want to hide the power bar (which is not
secure), so this is the best way to accomplish this.

Define these two functions somewhere in your Lua file before the header show at the end:

```
function SquareUnitFrames_Pet_OnShow(self)
  self.unit.healthBar:SetHeight(28)
  self.unit.powerBar:Hide()
end

function SquareUnitFrames_Pet_OnHide(self)
  self.unit.healthBar:SetHeight(30)
  self.unit.powerBar:Show()
end
```

The height of the health bar is changed and the power bar is shown or hidden. What all of this will accomplish is making the unit frame a bit smaller, and removing the power bar. Then the pet health bar is placed below the unit frames (but big enough that it can still be easily seen and clicked).

Add a function that resets the pet button when requested, so it can be used elsewhere in the code:

```
function SquareUnitFrames_ResetPetButton(button, unit)
  if UnitExists(unit) then
    local health = UnitHealth(unit)
    local maxHealth = UnitHealth(unit)
    button.healthBar:SetMinMaxValues(0, maxHealth)
    button.healthBar:SetValue(health)
  end
end
```

Add a call to this function in the `SquareUnitFrames_Frame_OnShow` function, right after the call to `SquareUnitFrames_ResetUnitButton` (note that you append `pet` to the end of the unit token so it looks at the correct unit):

```
SquareUnitFrames_ResetPetButton(button.pet, unit .. "pet")
```

Finally, add event handlers for the unit's health by adding the following to the `OnEvent` script. This code should be added in the outermost `else` statement, after the first `UnitIsUnit` block (if you're confused, you can always skip to the end of the chapter and see where it lies in the context of the whole function):

```
elseif arg1 and UnitIsUnit(unit .. "pet", arg1) then
  if event == "UNIT_MAXHEALTH" then
    self.pet.healthBar:SetMinMaxValues(0, UnitHealthMax(arg1))
    self.pet.healthBar:SetValue(UnitHealth(arg1))
  elseif event == "UNIT_HEALTH" then
    self.pet.healthBar:SetValue(UnitHealth(arg1))
  end
end
```

It's a relatively small amount of code to write for such a big change to functionality. Figure 26-8 shows a warlock without a pet and with an imp summoned and fighting.

Figure 26-8: SquareUnitFrames for a warlock without a pet (left) and with a summoned pet (right).

Creating a SecureGroupPetHeaderTemplate

If instead of adding pets to an existing frame, you just want to have a header consisting solely of pets, Blizzard has provided a template just for this purpose. In addition to the attributes allowed by the `SecureGroupHeaderTemplate`, the following two attributes can be used to customize the display of party/raid pets:

- `useOwnerUnit` (boolean)—When `true`, the `unit` attribute on the created frames corresponds to the owner's unit instead of the pet's unit.
- `filterOnPet` (boolean)—When `true`, the pet's names are used when sorting and filtering.

In addition to these specific attributes, the pet header accepts the same attributes as the normal secure group header.

Summary

Although stringent limitations exist as to what can be accomplished in an addon, a number of powerful templates allow developers to make extremely functional addons. This chapter introduced you to the group header templates, and created an extensive party/raid addon.

The Code

SquareUnitFrames

SquareUnitFrames.toc

```
## Interface: 30300
## Title: SquareUnitFrames
## Notes: Square shaped party/raid frames

SquareUnitFrames.xml
SquareUnitFrames.lua
```

SquareUnitFrames.xml

```
<Ui
  xmlns="http://www.blizzard.com/wow/ui/"
  xmlns:xsi="http://www.w3.org/2001/XMLSchema-instance"
  xsi:schemaLocation="http://www.blizzard.com/wow/ui/
  http://wowprogramming.com/FrameXML/UI.xsd">

  <Frame name="SquareUnitFrames_UnitTemplate" virtual="true">
    <Size x="36" y="36"/>
    <Layers>
      <Layer level="BACKGROUND">
        <Texture setAllPoints="true">
          <Color r="0.0" g="0.0" b="0.0"/>
        </Texture>
      </Layer>
    </Layers>
    <Frames>
      <Button name="$parent_Unit" parentKey="unit"
        inherits="SecureUnitButtonTemplate">
        <Size x="34" y="34"/>
        <Anchors>
          <Anchor point="TOPLEFT">
            <Offset x="1" y="-1"/>
          </Anchor>
        </Anchors>
        <Layers>
          <Layer level="OVERLAY">
            <FontString name="$parent_Name" parentKey="name"
              inherits="GameFontHighlight" setAllPoints="true"/>
            <Texture name="$parent_Selected" parentKey="selected"
              setAllPoints="true"
              file="Interface\Buttons\CheckButtonHilight"
              alphaMode="ADD" hidden="true"/>
          </Layer>
        </Layers>
        <Frames>
          <StatusBar name="$parent_HealthBar"
            parentKey="healthBar">
            <Size x="34" y="30"/>
            <Anchors>
              <Anchor point="TOPLEFT"/>
            </Anchors>
            <BarTexture
              file="Interface\Buttons\UI-Listbox-Highlight2"/>
            <BarColor r="1.0" g="1.0" b="1.0"/>
          </StatusBar>
          <StatusBar name="$parent_PowerBar" parentKey="powerBar">
            <Size x="34" y="3"/>
            <Anchors>
              <Anchor point="TOPLEFT"
```

```
                            relativeTo="$parent_HealthBar"
                            relativePoint="BOTTOMLEFT">
                            <Offset x="0" y="-1"/>
                        </Anchor>
                    </Anchors>
                    <BarTexture
                        file="Interface\TargetingFrame\UI-TargetingFrame-↵
BarFill"/>
                    <BarColor r="1.0" g="1.0" b="1.0"/>
                </StatusBar>
            </Frames>
            <Scripts>
                <OnDragStart
                    function="SquareUnitFrames_Button_OnDragStart"/>
                <OnDragStop
                    function="SquareUnitFrames_Button_OnDragStop"/>
                <OnHide function="SquareUnitFrames_Button_OnDragStop"/>
            </Scripts>
            <Attributes>
                <Attribute name="useparent-unit" type="boolean"
                    value="true"/>
                <Attribute name="*type1" type="string" value="target"/>
            </Attributes>
            <HighlightTexture
                file="Interface\Buttons\ButtonHilight-Square"
                alphaMode="ADD"/>
        </Button>
        <Button name="$parent_Pet" parentKey="pet"
            inherits="SecureHandlerShowHideTemplate,↵
SecureUnitButtonTemplate">
            <Size x="34" y="5"/>
            <Anchors>
                <Anchor point="BOTTOMLEFT">
                    <Offset x="1" y="1"/>
                </Anchor>
            </Anchors>
            <Frames>
                <StatusBar name="$parent_HealthBar" parentKey="healthBar"
                    setAllPoints="true">
                    <BarTexture
                        file="Interface\Buttons\UI-Listbox-Highlight2"/>
                    <BarColor r="0.0" g="1.0" b="0.0"/>
                </StatusBar>
            </Frames>
            <Attributes>
                <Attribute name="useparent-unit" type="boolean"
                    value="true"/>
                <Attribute name="unitsuffix" type="string" value="pet"/>
                <Attribute name="*type1" type="string" value="target"/>
            </Attributes>
```

```
        <HighlightTexture
          file="Interface\Buttons\UI-Listbox-Highlight2"
          alphaMode="ADD"/>
      </Button>
    </Frames>
    <Scripts>
      <OnShow function="SquareUnitFrames_Frame_OnShow"/>
      <OnEvent function="SquareUnitFrames_Frame_OnEvent"/>
    </Scripts>
  </Frame>

  <Frame name="SquareUnitFrames_Header" parent="UIParent"
    inherits="SecureGroupHeaderTemplate" movable="true">
    <Anchors>
      <Anchor point="CENTER"/>
    </Anchors>
    <Attributes>
      <Attribute name="showParty" type="boolean" value="true"/>
      <Attribute name="showRaid" type="boolean" value="true"/>
      <Attribute name="showPlayer" type="boolean" value="true"/>
      <Attribute name="showSolo" type="boolean" value="true"/>
      <Attribute name="maxColumns" type="number" value="8"/>
      <Attribute name="unitsPerColumn" type="number" value="5"/>
      <Attribute name="columnAnchorPoint" type="string"
        value="TOP"/>
      <Attribute name="point" type="string" value="LEFT"/>
      <Attribute name="template" type="string"
        value="SquareUnitFrames_UnitTemplate"/>
      <Attribute name="templateType" type="string" value="Frame"/>
      <Attribute name="xOffset" type="number" value="-1"/>
      <Attribute name="yOffset" type="number" value="1"/>
    </Attributes>
  </Frame>
</Ui>
```

SquareUnitFrames.lua

```lua
function SquareUnitFrames_InitialConfig(frame)
  -- Nudge the status bar frame levels down
  frame.unit.healthBar:SetFrameLevel(frame.unit:GetFrameLevel())
  frame.unit.powerBar:SetFrameLevel(frame.unit:GetFrameLevel())
  frame.unit:RegisterForDrag("LeftButton")

  frame:RegisterEvent("UNIT_HEALTH")
  frame:RegisterEvent("UNIT_MAXHEALTH")
  frame:RegisterEvent("PLAYER_ENTERING_WORLD")
  frame:RegisterEvent("UNIT_DISPLAYPOWER")
  frame:RegisterEvent("UNIT_NAME_UPDATE")
  frame:RegisterEvent("PLAYER_TARGET_CHANGED")
  frame:RegisterEvent("UNIT_THREAT_SITUATION_UPDATE")
```

```
      RegisterUnitWatch(frame.pet)
      frame.pet:SetFrameRef("unit", frame.unit)
      frame.pet:SetAttribute("_onshow", [[
      local unit = self:GetFrameRef("unit")
      unit:SetHeight(28)
      ]])
      frame.pet:SetAttribute("_onhide", [[
      local unit = self:GetFrameRef("unit")
      unit:SetHeight(34)
      ]])

   frame.pet.unit = frame.unit

   frame.pet:HookScript("OnShow", SquareUnitFrames_Pet_OnShow)
   frame.pet:HookScript("OnHide", SquareUnitFrames_Pet_OnHide)
end

function SquareUnitFrames_Frame_OnShow(button)
  local unit = button:GetAttribute("unit")

  if unit then
    local guid = UnitGUID(unit)
    if guid ~= button.guid then
      SquareUnitFrames_ResetUnitButton(button.unit, unit)
      SquareUnitFrames_ResetPetButton(button.pet, unit .. "pet")
      button.guid = guid
    end
  end
end

function SquareUnitFrames_ResetUnitButton(button, unit)
  SquareUnitFrames_ResetHealthBar(button, unit)
  SquareUnitFrames_ResetPowerBar(button, unit)
  SquareUnitFrames_ResetName(button, unit)

  if UnitIsUnit(unit, "target") then
    button.selected:Show()
  else
    button.selected:Hide()
  end

  local status = UnitThreatSituation(unit)
  if status and status > 0 then
    local r, g, b = GetThreatStatusColor(status)
    button.name:SetTextColor(r, g, b)
  else
    button.name:SetTextColor(1, 1, 1)
  end
end
```

```
-- This function can return a substring of a UTF-8 string,
-- properly handling UTF-8 codepoints.  Rather than taking a start
-- index and optionally an end index, it takes the string, the
-- start index and the number of characters to select from the
-- string.
--
-- UTF-8 Reference:
-- 0xxxxxx - ASCII character
-- 110yyyxx - 2 byte UTF codepoint
-- 1110yyyy - 3 byte UTF codepoint
-- 11110zzz - 4 byte UTF codepoint

local function utf8sub(str, start, numChars)
  local currentIndex = start
  while numChars > 0 and currentIndex <= #str do
    local char = string.byte(str, currentIndex)
    if char >= 240 then
      currentIndex = currentIndex + 4
    elseif char >= 225 then
      currentIndex = currentIndex + 3
    elseif char >= 192 then
      currentIndex = currentIndex + 2
    else
      currentIndex = currentIndex + 1
    end
    numChars = numChars - 1
  end
  return str:sub(start, currentIndex - 1)
end

function SquareUnitFrames_ResetName(button, unit)
  local name = UnitName(unit) or "Unknown"

  local substring
  for length=#name, 1, -1 do
    substring = utf8sub(name, 1, length)
    button.name:SetText(substring)
    if button.name:GetStringWidth() <= 30 then
      return
    end
  end

  local status = UnitThreatSituation(unit)
  if status and status > 0 then
    local r, g, b = GetThreatStatusColor(status)
    button.name:SetTextColor(r, g, b)
  else
    button.name:SetTextColor(1, 1, 1)
  end
end
```

```lua
function SquareUnitFrames_ResetHealthBar(button, unit)
  local class = select(2, UnitClass(unit)) or "WARRIOR"
  local classColor = RAID_CLASS_COLORS[class]
  local alive = not UnitIsDeadOrGhost(unit)

  if alive then
    button.healthBar:SetStatusBarColor(classColor.r, ↵
classColor.g, classColor.b)
    button.healthBar:SetMinMaxValues(0, UnitHealthMax(unit))
    button.healthBar:SetValue(UnitHealth(unit))
    button.dead = false
  else
    button.healthBar:SetStatusBarColor(0.3, 0.3, 0.3)
    button.healthBar:SetMinMaxValues(0, 1)
    button.healthBar:SetValue(1)
    button.dead = true
  end
end

function SquareUnitFrames_ResetPowerBar(button, unit)
  local powerType, powerToken = UnitPowerType(unit)
  local powerColor = PowerBarColor[powerToken]

  local alive = not UnitIsDeadOrGhost(unit)
  if alive then
    button.powerBar:SetStatusBarColor(powerColor.r, ↵
powerColor.g, powerColor.b)
  else
    button.powerBar:SetStatusBarColor(0.3, 0.3, 0.3)
  end

  button.powerBar:SetMinMaxValues(0, UnitPowerMax(unit))
  button.powerBar:SetValue(UnitPower(unit))
end

function SquareUnitFrames_Button_OnDragStart(self, button)
  SquareUnitFrames_Header:StartMoving()
  SquareUnitFrames_Header.isMoving = true
end

function SquareUnitFrames_Button_OnDragStop(self, button)
  if SquareUnitFrames_Header.isMoving then
    SquareUnitFrames_Header:StopMovingOrSizing()
  end
end

function SquareUnitFrames_Frame_OnEvent(self, event, arg1, ...)
  local unit = self:GetAttribute("unit")
  if not unit then
    return
```

```
    end

-- Handle any events that don't accept a unit argument
if event == "PLAYER_ENTERING_WORLD" then
  SquareUnitFrames_ResetUnitButton(self.unit, unit)
elseif event == "PLAYER_TARGET_CHANGED" then
  if UnitIsUnit(unit, "target") then
    self.unit.selected:Show()
  else
    self.unit.selected:Hide()
  end
elseif arg1 and UnitIsUnit(unit, arg1) then
  local powerType, powerToken = UnitPowerType(unit)
  if event == "UNIT_MAXHEALTH" then
    if self.unit.dead ~= UnitIsDeadOrGhost(unit) then
      SquareUnitFrames_ResetUnitButton(self.unit, unit)
    else
      self.unit.healthBar:SetMinMaxValues(0, UnitHealthMax(unit))
      self.unit.healthBar:SetValue(UnitHealth(unit))
    end
  elseif event == "UNIT_HEALTH" then
    if self.unit.dead ~= UnitIsDeadOrGhost(unit) then
      SquareUnitFrames_ResetUnitButton(self.unit, unit)
    else
      self.unit.healthBar:SetValue(UnitHealth(unit))
    end
  elseif event == "UNIT_DISPLAYPOWER" then
    SquareUnitFrames_ResetPowerBar(self.unit, unit)
  elseif event == "UNIT_" .. powerToken then
    if self.unit.dead ~= UnitIsDeadOrGhost(unit) then
      SquareUnitFrames_ResetPowerBar(self.unit, unit)
    else
      self.unit.powerBar:SetValue(UnitPower(unit))
    end
  elseif event == "UNIT_MAX" .. powerToken then
    if self.unit.dead ~= UnitIsDeadOrGhost(unit) then
      SquareUnitFrames_ResetPowerBar(self.unit, unit)
    else
      self.unit.powerBar:SetMinMaxValues(0, UnitPowerMax(unit))
      self.unit.powerBar:SetValue(UnitPower(unit))
    end
  elseif event == "UNIT_NAME_UPDATE" then
    SquareUnitFrames_ResetName(self.unit, unit)
  elseif event == "UNIT_THREAT_SITUATION_UPDATE" then
    local status = UnitThreatSituation(unit)
    if status and status > 0 then
      local r, g, b = GetThreatStatusColor(status)
      self.unit.name:SetTextColor(r, g, b)
    else
      self.unit.name:SetTextColor(1, 1, 1)
```

```
          end
        end
      elseif arg1 and UnitIsUnit(unit .. "pet", arg1) then
        if event == "UNIT_MAXHEALTH" then
          self.pet.healthBar:SetMinMaxValues(0, UnitHealthMax(arg1))
          self.pet.healthBar:SetValue(UnitHealth(arg1))
        elseif event == "UNIT_HEALTH" then
          self.pet.healthBar:SetValue(UnitHealth(arg1))
        end
      end
    end
end

local function unregisterManyEvents(frame, ...)
  for i=1, select("#", ...) do
    local event = select(i, ...)
    frame:UnregisterEvent(event)
  end
end

function SquareUnitFrames_ResetPowerBar(button, unit)
  local powerType, powerToken = UnitPowerType(unit)
  local powerColor = PowerBarColor[powerToken]
  local alive = not UnitIsDeadOrGhost(unit)

  local parent = button:GetParent()
  unregisterManyEvents(parent, "UNIT_MANA", "UNIT_RAGE",
    "UNIT_FOCUS","UNIT_ENERGY", "UNIT_RUNIC_POWER")
  unregisterManyEvents(parent, "UNIT_MAXMANA", "UNIT_MAXRAGE",
    "UNIT_MAXFOCUS", "UNIT_MAXENERGY", "UNIT_MAXRUNIC_POWER")

  parent:RegisterEvent("UNIT_" .. powerToken)
  parent:RegisterEvent("UNIT_MAX" .. powerToken)

  button.powerBar:SetStatusBarColor(powerColor.r, ↵
powerColor.g, powerColor.b)
  button.powerBar:SetMinMaxValues(0, UnitPowerMax(unit))
  button.powerBar:SetValue(UnitPower(unit))
end

function SquareUnitFrames_Pet_OnShow(self)
  self.unit.healthBar:SetHeight(28)
  self.unit.powerBar:Hide()
end

function SquareUnitFrames_Pet_OnHide(self)
  self.unit.healthBar:SetHeight(30)
  self.unit.powerBar:Show()
end

function SquareUnitFrames_ResetPetButton(button, unit)
```

```
  if UnitExists(unit) then
    local health = UnitHealth(unit)
    local maxHealth = UnitHealth(unit)
    button.healthBar:SetMinMaxValues(0, maxHealth)
    button.healthBar:SetValue(health)
  end
end

-- Actually show the header frame
SquareUnitFrames_Header.initialConfigFunction = ↵
SquareUnitFrames_InitialConfig
SquareUnitFrames_Header:Show()
```

Reference

In This Part

API Reference

The World of Warcraft API contains more than a thousand functions that can be used to interact with the game client, and obtain information about the state of the game. This chapter includes an alphabetic listing of each of these functions with detailed descriptions of what each function does, what arguments it takes, and what values it returns to the caller.

Although all efforts were made to provide the most up-to-date listing of functions, the API is a constantly moving target, changing from patch to patch. For the most current listing of the API please visit the book's companion website at `http://wowprogramming.com/docs`. Information about upcoming changes to the API can be found on the official World of Warcraft UI & Macros Forums: `http://forums.worldofwarcraft.com/board.html?forumId=11114`.

API Reference Conventions

Following each function is a description of what the function does, along with the function signature, followed by any arguments, returns, or example snippets of code.

Function Signatures

A function signature is a short way to express the name of a function, the arguments that the function expects to be called with, and any values that the function may return. Consider the following signature for the `CalculateAuctionDeposit()` function:

```
deposit = CalculateAuctionDeposit(runTime)
```

This notation indicates that the function accepts a single argument called `runTime`, and returns a single value called `deposit`. These aren't requirements for names: they are simply names given to each of the arguments and returns, to make the signature easier to read and understand.

If a function signature is omitted, then the function takes no arguments, and returns no values. This is equivalent to the function signature `FunctionName()`, so these signatures are not listed.

Optional Arguments

When a signature contains an optional argument, it is wrapped in square brackets to indicate this. Here's the function signature for `BuyMerchantItem()`:

```
BuyMerchantItem(index [,quantity])
```

This signature shows that the function returns no arguments and takes an argument `index`, along with an optional argument `quantity`. The specific details of what the optional argument does are listed in the description for that argument, which is displayed below the signature.

Functions can have multiple nested optional arguments, like `SendChatMessage()`:

```
SendChatMessage("text" [,"chatType" [,"language" [,"channel"]]])
```

This function requires the first argument `text`, but can also take up to three more arguments. The optional arguments are nested in this way because to include the argument `language`, you must also include something for `chatType` (even if it's the value nil). Likewise, to supply a `channel` argument, you must also supply values for `chatType` and `language`.

Argument Choices

Certain functions, such as `IsAddOnLoaded()`, have alternative choices in their arguments:

```
loaded = IsAddOnLoaded(index) or IsAddOnLoaded("name")
```

This function can take either the index of addon in the addon listing, or the name of an addon. It then returns whether or not the addon is currently loaded by the game client. When there are distinct choices for the function signature, each signature is added to the end in this way.

Argument and Return Listings

Following a function signature is a detailed listing of the arguments and returns for the given function. The arguments and returns are both given in a similar format. Here is the listing for the `GetSocketTypes()` function:

Argument:

    `index`—The index of the socket to query. (`number`)

Return:

gemColor—The color of the given gem socket. (string)

- Blue
- Yellow
- Red
- Meta

Under each section is a list of named arguments, followed by a description of the argument. After the description is an indicator that tells you which type of Lua value to pass (or what type to expect from the function). In this case, the function accepts a numeric argument called index and returns a string that is the color of the socket. If the argument is optional, this will be indicated in the argument listing as well as in the function signature.

Common API Flags

Throughout the API, there are a number of common attributes that a given function might have, for example those functions that cannot be called by addons during combat. Table 27-1 shows a listing of the various API flags.

When a function is flagged with one of the API flags, you will see a margin icon indicating this. Although most flags are self explanatory, you can always refer back to Table 27-1 for more information.

Table 27-1: API Flags

FLAG	DESCRIPTION
blizzardui	This function is not a C API but a Lua function declared in Blizzard's default user interface. Its implementation can be viewed by extracting the addon data using the Addon Kit provided by Blizzard.
confirmation	This function does not prompt the user for confirmation before its results take effect -- that behavior is provided by the default UI, and this function is called from the confirmation dialog
hardware	This function requires a key or mouse press in order to be used, but may not be protected.
luaapi	This function is defined in the Lua standard libraries
maconly	This function is designed for the Mac OS X client only.
nocombat	This function cannot be called during combat.
protected	This function is protected and can only be called by the Blizzard user interface.

API Meta-Types

To clarify the documentation of API functions, we have created a number of meta-types that are used to describe what sort of values are accepted in an argument or returned from an API function. These are not actual Lua types, but a classification of accepted values in various API sub-systems. When a meta-type applies to an argument or return value, this is indicated after the Lua type in the argument listing. Meta-types enable you to consolidate the documentation for classes of API functions, rather than having to document the same list of values over and over again. This section describes these types.

1nil

Many API functions use values indicative of a binary state but do not utilize the Boolean `true` and `false` values in Lua. Due to the way the functions are limited, they use the number value 1 for `true`, and `nil` for `false`. Because Lua treats `nil` as a false value and any non-nil value as true in a conditional, these values can generally be used the same as Boolean values in conditional statements (such as `if IsInGuild() then ... end`). However, you should avoid making direct comparisons using this type of value: for example, the condition `if IsInGuild() == true then ... end` will never be triggered. These types of variables are called `1nil` values, to distinguish them from Boolean values.

actionID

The `actionID` meta-type is used to identify one of the player's action bar slots. In UI terms, action bar slots are a layer of abstraction between spells or items and the mechanisms available to the player for using them conveniently. For example, instead of the default UI internally using `SetBindingSpell()`, `SetBindingMacro()`, and so on whenever the player changes the contents of the visible action bars, it instead manages a set of key bindings corresponding to the action bar slots.

Every player has at least NUM_ACTIONBAR_PAGES * NUM_ACTIONBAR_BUTTONS (in the current client, 6 * 12, or 72) action slots corresponding to the six default action bar pages. In addition, players of certain classes (or with certain talents) may have additional actionIDs available corresponding to the "bonus" action bars that automatically become available when changing stances, stealthing, shapeshifting, etc.

ah-list-type

There are three different types of auction house listings, represented by string values. These ah-list-type values may be one of the following:

- list—The items that are currently for sale in the auction house.
- bidder—The items for which the player has placed a bid.
- owner—The items that the player has placed up for auction.

anchorPoint

Frames and graphical regions are anchored to each other using anchor points, represented by the anchorPoint meta-type. These points are simple strings that indicate a point on the region. The following are valid anchor point strings:

CENTER	LEFT	BOTTOMRIGHT
BOTTOM	RIGHT	TOPLEFT
TOP	BOTTOMLEFT	TOPRIGHT

arenaTeamID

The arenaTeamID API meta-type identifies one of the (up to three) arena teams to which a player can belong. These indices begin at 1 for the player's smallest team and increase with size. For example, if the player belongs to a 2v2 team and a 5v5 team then 1 will indicate the 2v2 team while 2 refers to the 5v5 team. However, if the player belongs to a 3v3 team and a 5v5 team but no 2v2 team, then 1 will indicate the 3v3 team, and 2 will again indicate the 5v5 team. If the player is on teams of all three sizes, then 1 indicates the 2v2 team, 2 indicates the 3v3 team and 3 indicates the 5v5 team.

The Blizzard UI's Lua function ArenaTeam_GetTeamSizeID can be used to translate a team size (2, 3, or 5) to the appropriate arenaTeamID for the player.

auraFilter

Buffs and debuffs can be filtered in the WoW API using strings that represent complex aura filters, indicated by the auraFilter meta-type. These strings can contain any number of filterers separated by either the pipe character (|) or a space. Possible filter values currently include:

- HELPFUL—Helpful spells (buffs).
- HARMFUL—Harmful spells (debuffs).
- PLAYER—Spells that can be cast by the player on themselves.

- RAID—Spells that can be cast by the player on their raid.
- CANCELABLE—Spells that can be cancelled.
- NOT_CANCELABLE—Spells that cannot be cancelled.

For example the string HELPFUL|RAID will filter to show only those helpful spells that the player can cast on their raid. You cannot use both the HARMFUL and the HELPFUL filters at the same time, as they cancel each other out. In addition, these two filters should not be used in the UnitBuff and UnitDebuff functions, as they are already implicitly included in their implementation and as such will be ignored.

backdrop

A backdrop definition is a Lua table with specific attributes that match directly with the elements in the <Backdrop> definition in an XML definition. It has the following structure:

```
{
  -- path to the background texture
  bgFile = "Interface\\DialogFrame\\UI-DialogBox-Gold-Background",
  -- path to the border texture
  edgeFile = "Interface\\DialogFrame\\UI-DialogBox-Gold-Border",
  -- true to repeat the background texture to fill the frame,
false to scale it
  tile = true,
  -- size (width or height) of the square repeating background
tiles (in pixels)
  tileSize = 32,
  -- thickness of edge segments and square size of edge corners
(in pixels)
  edgeSize = 32,
  -- distance from the edges of the frame to those of the background
texture (in pixels)
  insets = {
    left = 11,
    right = 12,
    top = 12,
    bottom = 11
  }
}
```

bitfield

A bitfield is a numeric value combining several binary flags into one number. The flags can be inspected individually using the bitwise functions in the bit library. For example (using GetItemFamily and related constants):

```
GetItemFamily("Crystallized Air")
-- returns 1224
bit.bor(0x0008,0x0040,0x0080,0x0400)
-- returns 1224
-- these are the masks for tradeskill bags.
```

```
bit.band(GetItemFamily("Crystallized Air"), 0x0040)
-- returns 64, or 0x0040: the item fits in an Enchanting Bag
bit.band(GetItemFamily("Crystallized Air"), 0x0020)
-- returns 0, or 0x0000: the item does not fit in an Herb Bag
```

binding

A `binding` is a string identifying one or more keyboard keys or mouse buttons, used with key binding and modified click API functions and the OnKeyDown/OnKeyUp script handlers. Most letter, number, and symbol keys are identified by their (uppercase) letter, number, or symbol.

Other keys are identified by a series of global variables with names prefaced by KEY_; for instance, the localized name for the binding NUMPAD0 can be found in _G["KEY_NUMPAD0"]. Some keys have platform-specific names; for example, the localized name for the binding PRINTSCREEN can be found in _G["KEY_PRINTSCREEN _MAC"] (revealing that it refers to the F13 key found on Mac extended keyboards).

Modifier keys are identified as follows:

- LSHIFT, RSHIFT, SHIFT—Left, right, or generic Shift key
- LCTRL, RCTRL, CTRL—Left, right, or generic Control key
- LALT, RALT, ALT—Left, right, or generic Alt (or Option) key
- STRG—German equivalent to CTRL key

Mouse buttons are identified by the token BUTTON followed by the button number—BUTTON1 for the primary (left) button, BUTTON2 for the right button, BUTTON3 for middle, and so on.

For use in key bindings, several key/button identifiers can be strung together with hyphens to indicate a key combination; e.g. CTRL-SHIFT-SPACE, RALT-F12, SHIFT-BUTTON1.

chatMsgType

The `chatMsgType` is a string identifying the common type of a set of chat window messages; used in chat window functions for determining which windows display which messages, and the colors for displaying each message type.

Each CHAT_MSG event has a corresponding chatMsgType identified by the part of the event name following the initial CHAT_MSG_; e.g. the chatMsgType for CHAT_MSG _COMBAT_FACTION_CHANGE is COMBAT_FACTION_CHANGE. A list of pre-configured chatMsgTypes can be found as keys in the global table ChatTypeInfo.

colorString

Formatting used to colorize sections of text when being displayed in a FontString. A `colorString` takes the form |c(colorvalue)(text)|r:

- colorvalue—A string of four hexadecimal formatted bytes describing component values of the color. Each byte can be a value from 00 (representing zero intensity of the component) to ff (representing full intensity of the component):

1. Alpha value, but currently unused: always `ff`
2. Red component of the color
3. Green component of the color
4. Blue component of the color

- `text`—The text to be colorized.

For example the string `|cffffff00Yellow Text|r` will display yellow text when sent to a font string or message frame. Color strings can be used for display anywhere in the UI, but can only be delivered in a chat message if included as part of a hyperlink.

containerID

A `containerID` is a numeric identifier for one of the player's bags or other containers. Possible values:

- `-2`—Keyring
- `-1`—Main storage area in the bank
- `0`—Backpack

In addition a number from 1 through `NUM_BAG_SLOTS` indicates a bag slot, numbered as presented in the default UI from right to left. Container identifiers from `NUM_BAG_SLOTS` + 1 through `NUM_BAG_SLOTS` + `NUM_BANKBAGSLOTS` represent the bank bag slots, numbered as presented in the default UI from left to right.

containerSlotID

A `containerSlotID` is a numeric index of an item slot within a container. Slots are numbered from left to right, top to bottom, as presented in the default UI.

frameStrata

A `frameStrata` value is a string identifying the general layering order of frames. Where frame level provides fine control over the layering of frames, frame strata provides a coarser level of layering control. Frames in a higher strata always appear "in front of" frames in lower strata regardless of frame level. Available frame strata are listed below in order from lowest to highest:

- `BACKGROUND`—Used by default for static UI elements such as the PlayerFrame and Minimap
- `LOW`—Used by default for lower-priority UI elements such as the party member and target frames
- `MEDIUM`—Default frame strata for general usage
- `HIGH`—Used by default for higher-priority UI elements such as the Calendar and Loot frames
- `DIALOG`—Used by default for alerts and other dialog boxes which should appear over nearly all other UI elements

- ▪ FULLSCREEN—Used by default for full-screen windows such as the World Map
- ▪ FULLSCREEN_DIALOG—Used by default for alerts or dialog boxes which should appear even when a full-screen window is visible
- ▪ TOOLTIP—Used for mouse cursor tooltips, ensuring they appear over all other UI elements

glyphIndex

A glyphIndex is a numeric glyph index, ordered by the level at which the glyphs are discovered. Specifically:

1. The major glyph at the top of the user interface (level 15)
2. The minor glyph at the bottom of the user interface (level 15)
3. The minor glyph at the top left of the user interface (level 30)
4. The major glyph at the bottom right of the user interface (level 50)
5. The minor glyph at the top right of the user interface (level 70)
6. The major glyph at the bottom left of the user interface (level 80)

GUID (Globally Unique IDentifier)

Each entity in World of Warcraft is identified by a globally unique identifier (GUID), a unique 64-bit number that is generally presented as a string containing a hexadecimal representation of the number (e.g. "0xF530007EAC083004"). (Note that Lua in WoW does not support 64-bit integers, so this value cannot be converted in a lossless way with tonumber.)

The type of unit represented by a GUID can be determined by using bit.band() to mask the first three digits with 0x00F:

- ▪ 0x000—A player
- ▪ 0x003—An NPC
- ▪ 0x004—A player's pet (i.e. hunter/warlock pets and similar; non-combat pets count as NPCs)
- ▪ 0x005—A vehicle

Further content of the GUID varies by unit type: player, NPC, pet, or vehicle.

Players

The remaining thirteen digits are unique to a player character at least within that character's battlegroup (that is, they remain unique and constant even in cross-server battlegrounds). This number is also semi-permanent—it persists from character creation until deletion, renaming, or server transfer.

NPCs

For NPCs, the remaining digits break down as follows:

- ▪ Digits 4-6—Unused.

- Digits 7-10—NPC creature ID: identifies the specific named NPC (e.g. Hogger, Loque'nahak) or type of NPC (e.g. Sunfury Nethermancer, Shattertusk Mammoth). Converting to decimal results in the ID found on database sites such as http://wowhead.com; can also be used with the PlayerModel widget API SetCreature to view the NPC's model.
- Digits 11-16—Spawn counter: identifies the individual NPC (i.e. differentiates between the Gamon you recently killed and the Gamon that respawned a few minutes later.

Pets

Hunter pets immediately after taming retain the GUID they had as a wild creature; after re-summoning or logout/login, their GUID changes to the pet format. Remaining digits can be broken down as follows:

- Digits 4-10—A constant value unique to the individual pet: like a player's unique ID it is constant across multiple sessions.
- Digits 11-16—Spawn counter: changes when the pet is dismissed and re-summoned.

Vehicles

Vehicles have the same format and content as NPCs.

GUID Example

For example, the GUID 0xF530007EAC083004 can be deconstructed as follows:

Digits 1-3 are "F53"; bit.band(0xF53, 0x00F) == 0x003, so this is an NPC.

Digits 7-10 are "7EAC"; 0x7EAC == 32428, which you can look up to find the NPC is an Underbelly Rat.

Digits 11-16 have no intrinsic meaning, but distinguish this Underbelly Rat from all others spawned since the last server reset.

The following code is an example of a function to decode GUIDs:

```
function ParseGUID(guid)
   local first3 = tonumber("0x"..strsub(guid, 3,5))
   local unitType = bit.band(first3,0x00f)

   if (unitType == 0x000) then
      print("Player, ID #", strsub(guid,6))
   elseif (unitType == 0x003) then
      local creatureID = tonumber("0x"..strsub(guid,9,12))
      local spawnCounter = tonumber("0x"..strsub(guid,13))
      print("NPC, ID #",creatureID,"spawn #",spawnCounter)
   elseif (unitType == 0x004) then
      local petID = tonumber("0x"..strsub(guid,6,12))
      local spawnCounter = tonumber("0x"..strsub(guid,13))
      print("Pet, ID #",petID,"spawn #",spawnCounter)
   elseif (unitType == 0x005) then
```

```
        local creatureID = tonumber("0x"..strsub(guid,9,12))
        local spawnCounter = tonumber("0x"..strsub(guid,13))
        print("Vehicle, ID #",creatureID,"spawn #",spawnCounter)
    end
end
```

Hyperlink

A hyperlink is a string containing markup allowing the client to present it as a link, which the player can click to view more information about or take action regarding the data it represents.

Hyperlinks take the form |H(linktype):(linkdata)|h(text)|h, where (linktype) determines the type of link, (linkdata) is a code referencing the linked information, and (text) is the text visible to the player. Some API functions which operate on links do not require a full hyperlink, only its linktype:linkdata portion.

Links are often encapsulated in a colorString. In such cases, the full color String-wrapped link is the only form of the link allowed to be used in chat; attempting to transmit an invalid link may cause the player to be disconnected from the server.

The WoW client recognizes several kinds of hyperlinks, identified by their linktype:

player	spell	talent	item
playerGM	enchant	achievement	
glyph	quest	trade	

They are described in the following sections. If linkdata elements noted as optional are omitted the client can still resolve the link.

player

Example: |Hplayer:Aerdrig|h[Aerdrig]|h

Represents a player character. Left-clicking a player link in the default UI opens the ChatFrameEditBox to send a whispered message to the character. Right-clicking opens a menu with options for inviting the character to the player's party/raid, adding the character to the ignore list, or reporting the chat message in which the link appears as spam. The linkdata for a player link consists solely of the player's name (or in cross-realm battlegrounds, the player's name and home realm separated by a hyphen, e.g. "Gundark-Broxigar").

playerGM

Example: |HplayerGM:Eyonix|h[Eyonix]|h

A variation on the player type used exclusively for Game Master chat.

glyph

Example: |cff66bbff|Hglyph:23:460|h[Glyph of Fortitude]|h|r

Represents a glyph inscribed in a character's spellbook. Clicking a glyph link in the default UI shows a tooltip with its description. The linkdata for a glyph link follows the format `socket:glyphID`:

- `socket` (optional)—The socket in which the glyph is placed; values 21 through 26 correspond to glyphIndex values 1 through 6.
- `glyphID`—A unique identifier for the glyph effect; not used elsewhere in the API.

spell

Example: `|cff71d5ff|Hspell:46584|h[Raise Dead]|h|r`
Represents a spell. Clicking a spell link in the default UI shows a tooltip with its description. The linkdata for a spell link consists solely of the spellID number uniquely identifying the spell, usable with APIs such as `GetSpellInfo()`.

enchant

Example: `|cffffd000|Henchant:59387|h[Certificate of Ownership]|h|r`
Represents a trade skill recipe (originally used only for Enchanting, but now applies to all trade skills). Clicking a spell link in the default UI shows a tooltip with its description (and that of the item it creates, if applicable). The linkdata for a spell link consists solely of the spellID number uniquely identifying the trade skill recipe, usable with APIs such as `GetSpellInfo()`.

quest

Example: `|cffffff00|Hquest:982:17|h[Deep Ocean, Vast Sea]|h|r`
Represents a quest from a character's quest log. Clicking a quest link in the default UI shows a tooltip with a brief description of the quest and its objectives. When the client displays a quest link sent by another character, it automatically alters the enclosing `colorString` to reflect the difficulty of the quest relative to the player's level. The linkdata for a quest link follows the format `questID:level`:

- `questID`—A unique numeric identifier for the quest. This number corresponds with the numbers found on data sites such as `http://wowhead.com`.
- `level` (optional)—Recommended character level for attempting the quest. (A level of -1 means the quest is appropriate for any level; used for holiday quests.)

talent

Example: `|cff4e96f7|Htalent:1396:4|h[Unleashed Fury]|h|r`
Represents a talent. Clicking a talent link in the default UI shows a tooltip with its description. The linkdata for a talent link follows the format `talentID:points`:

- `talentID`—A unique identifier for the talent; not used elsewhere in the API.
- `rank` (optional)—Number of points spent in the talent, minus one: if this value is omitted or -1, the tooltip shows the talent as it appears in the Talents UI when zero points have been spent; if this value is 0, the tooltip shows the talent as it appears when one point has been spent on it. Values greater than the number of available ranks for a talent are interpreted as -1.

achievement

Example: |cfffff00|Hachievement:2336:060000000279E425:1:10:14:8:429
4967295:4294967295:4294967295:4294967295|h[Insane in the Membrane]
|h|r

Represents an achievement earned or in progress by a player. Clicking an achievement link in the default UI shows a tooltip with a summary of the achievement and (if applicable) its criteria. The linkdata for an achievement link follows the format achievementID:playerGUID:completed:month:day:year:bits1:bits2:bits3:bits4. If only the first element achievementID is specified, the client resolving the link will show the player's progress or completion of the achievement; otherwise, all elements are required:

- achievementID—A unique identifier for the achievements; usable with various Achievement API functions.
- playerGUID (optional)—GUID of a player character whose progress or completion of the achievement is linked (return value of UnitGUID() without the "0x" prefix).
- completed (optional)—1 if the character has completed the achievement; otherwise 0.
- month (optional)—Index of the month (1 = January) in which the character completed the achievement, or 0 if the achievement is incomplete.
- day (optional)—Day of the month on which the character completed the achievement, or 0 if the achievement is incomplete.
- year (optional)—Year (two-digit year) in which the character completed the achievement, or -1 if the achievement is incomplete.
- bits1, bits2, bits3, bits4 (optional)—Encoded data fields interpreted by the client to show completion of achievement criteria.

trade

Example: |cffffd000|Htrade:45361:339:375:60000000279E425:Q/nPf6nprU3
/n/fA8/Bw/PA+/B+/Aw/HA+/Bw/HA+5nfg////////P////HAAAQAA+DAAAAAAA|
h[Inscription]|h|r

Represents the entire list of recipes for a character's trade skill or profession. The linkdata for an achievement link follows the format spellID:skill:maxSkill:playerGUID:data. All elements are required:

- spellID—The spellID number uniquely identifying the trade skill and its rank (e.g. Apprentice Tailoring vs. Journeyman Tailoring), usable with APIs such as GetSpellInfo().
- skill—The character's current skill in the profession
- maxSkill—The maximum skill for the character's current rank in the profession (e.g. 375 for Master rank).
- playerGUID—GUID of the character whose profession is linked (return value of UnitGUID() without the "0x" prefix).

■ `data` —Encoded data field interpreted by the client to show the character's list of known trade skill recipes.

item

Examples: `|cffa335ee|Hitem:45457:3828:3395:3395:0:0:0:0:80|h[Staff of Endless Winter]|h|r`, `|cff1eff00|Hitem:36360:0:0:0:0:0:-37:16338 78093:80|h[Frostpaw Legguards]|h|r`

Represents an item. Clicking an item link in the default UI shows a tooltip with information about the item. Control-clicking an equippable item opens the DressUpFrame to preview how the item would look on the player character if equipped. The linkdata for an item link follows the format `itemID:enchant: gem1:gem2:gem3:gem4:suffixID:uniqueID:level:`

■ `itemID`—The item's `itemID`.

■ `enchant` (optional)—Unique identifier of the enchantment applied to the item; not used elsewhere in the API.

■ `gem1`, `gem2`, `gem3`, `gem4` (optional)—Unique identifiers of the enchantments provided by gems socketed in the item (not the itemIDs of the gems themselves); not used elsewhere in the API.

■ `suffixID` (optional)—Identifies the specific variation represented for random-property items (e.g. "... of the Monkey", "... of Frost Protection", etc.). A positive number indicates a variation with specific stat values (e.g. `1200` = "of the Bear", 8 stamina 8 strength; `1220` = "of the Bear", 14 stamina 15 strength); a negative number indicates a type of variation, with actual stat values to be determined by decoding the `uniqueID`.

■ `uniqueID` (optional)—A number used internally by the WoW client/server architecture to track a specific occurrence of an item: used for crafted items which display "<Made by Name>" in their tooltips and for random-property items. For items with a negative `suffixID`, using `bit.band(uniqueID, 0xFFFF)` reveals the factor used to calculate the item's stats.

■ `level`—Level of the character linking the item; used for "Heirloom" items whose stats change based on the level of the character equipping them.

inventoryID

An `inventoryID` identifies an inventory slot used (mostly) for the equipping of items. Inventory ID numbers exist not only for the armor and weapon slots seen in the default UI's character window, but also for bag slots, bank bag slots, the contents of the bank's main storage area, and the contents of the keyring. Inventory slots are not defined as constants in the default UI; to obtain the `inventoryID` for a slot, use one of the following functions:

■ `GetInventorySlotInfo`

■ `BankButtonIDToInvSlotID`

■ `ContainerIDToInventoryID`

■ `KeyRingButtonIDToInvSlotID`

itemID

The `itemID` uniquely identifies an item; usable with APIs such as `GetItemInfo()`. These identifiers match those utilized on database sites such as `http://wowhead.com`.

itemLocation

The `itemLocation` is a bitfield describing the location of an item owned by the player. The following example code illustrates masks that can be compared with an `itemLocation` to determine the exact location described:

```
local ITEM_INVENTORY_PLAYER = 0x00100000
local ITEM_INVENTORY_BACKPACK = 0x00200000
local ITEM_INVENTORY_BAGS = 0x00400000
local ITEM_INVENTORY_BANK = 0x00800000
local MASK_BAG = 0xf00
local MASK_SLOT = 0x3f
local bagMap = {
    [0x100] = 1,
    [0x200] = 2,
    [0x400] = 3,
    [0x800] = 4,
}
local function ItemInBag(itemLocation)
    if bit.band(itemLocation, ITEM_INVENTORY_BAGS) > 0 then
        local bag = bagMap[bit.band(itemLocation, MASK_BAG)]
        local slot = bit.band(itemLocation, MASK_SLOT)
        return bag, slot
    elseif bit.band(itemLocation, ITEM_INVENTORY_BACKPACK) > 0 then
        local slot = bit.band(itemLocation, MASK_SLOT)
        return 0, slot
    end
end

local function ItemEquipped(itemLocation)
    if bit.band(itemLocation, ITEM_INVENTORY_PLAYER) > 0 then
        local slot = bit.band(itemLocation, MASK_SLOT)
        return slot
    end
end
```

itemQuality

`itemQuality`, unsurprisingly, indicates the quality (or rarity) of an item. Possible values and examples:

1. Poor (gray): Broken I.W.I.N. Button
2. Common (white): Archmage Vargoth's Staff
3. Uncommon (green): X-52 Rocket Helmet
4. Rare / Superior (blue): Onyxia Scale Cloak

5. Epic (purple): Talisman of Ephemeral Power

6. Legendary (orange): Fragment of Val'anyr

7. Artifact / Heirloom (light yellow): Bloodied Arcanite Reaper

itemString

An `itemString` refers to the `linktype:linkdata` portion of an item link (the part containing the `itemID`, e.g. `item:19019`); see the hyperlink meta-type for more details.

justifyH

`justifyH` is a string describing the horizontal justification of text within a widget. Possible values: `LEFT`, `CENTER`, `RIGHT`.

justifyV

`justifyV` is a string describing the vertical justification of text within a widget. Possible values: `TOP`, `MIDDLE`, `BOTTOM`.

layer

`layer` is a string identifying the layer in which a region's graphics are drawn relative to those of other regions in the same frame; graphics in higher layers (as listed below) are drawn "on top of" those in lower layers.

- `BACKGROUND`—First (lowest) layer
- `BORDER`—Second layer
- `ARTWORK`—Third layer; default for regions for which layer is not specified
- `OVERLAY`—Fourth layer
- `HIGHLIGHT`—Fifth (highest) layer; regions in this layer are automatically shown when the mouse is over the containing Frame (if the Frame's `enableMouse` property is `true`).

macroID

The `macroID` is an index of one of the player's saved macros. Macros shared by all characters on player's account are indexed from `1` to `MAX_ACCOUNT_MACROS`; macros specific to the current character are indexed from `MAX_ACCOUNT_MACROS + 1` to `MAX_ACCOUNT_MACROS + MAX_CHARACTER_MACROS`.

powerType

The `powerType` meta-type is used to indicate one of the different power types that characters can have. Possible values are:

0. Mana
1. Rage
2. Focus
3. Energy
4. Happiness
5. Runes
6. Runic Power

rollID

The default user interface assigns a unique numeric identifier for all items that are able to be rolled on by the party. This identifier can be obtained by checking the `rollID` member of the specific group loot frame. For example: `/run print(Group LootFrame1.rollID)`.

spellbookID

`spellbookID` is an index of a spell in the player's (or pet's) spellbook; usable with APIs such as `GetSpellInfo()`.

spellID

`spellID` is a globally unique number that identifies a spell (and its rank). It is usable with APIs such as `GetSpellInfo()`, and is also useful with database sites.

standingID

The `standingID` identifies a level of reputation:

1. Hated
2. Hostile
3. Unfriendly
4. Neutral
5. Friendly
6. Honored
7. Revered
8. Exalted

The default UI provides constants which can be helpful in displaying standing information.

The localized name for the standing N can be found in the global variable `FACTION_STANDING_LABELN` or `FACTION_STANDING_LABELN_FEMALE`; e.g. `FACTION_STANDING_LABEL4 == "Neutral"`.

NOTE Although the male (unlabeled) and female forms are the same in the enUS client, the same is not true for other languages. Be sure to use the appropriate form for the character's gender.

Color values for each standing (as seen in reputation status bars in the default UI) can be found in the table `FACTION_BAR_COLORS`.

unitID

You see `unitID` used throughout the API to identify units of interest. Possible values:

- `player`—The player him/herself
- `pet`—The player's pet
- `vehicle`—The vehicle currently controlled by the player
- `target`—The player's current target
- `focus`—The player's focused unit (as can be set by typing **/focus name**)

- mouseover—The unit currently under the mouse cursor (applies to both unit frames and units in the 3D world)
- npc—The unit the player is currently interacting with (via the Merchant, Trainer, Bank, or similar UI); not necessarily an NPC (e.g. also used in the Trade UI)
- party1 to party4—Another member of the player's party. Indices match the order party member frames are displayed in the default UI (party1 is at the top, party4 at the bottom), but are not consistent among party members (i.e. if Thrall and Cairne are in the same party, the player Thrall sees as party2 may not be the same player Cairne sees as party2).
- partypet1 to partypet4—A pet belonging to another member of the player's party
- raid1 to raid40—A member of the player's raid group. Unlike with the party tokens, one of the raid unit IDs will belong to the player. Indices have no relation to the arrangement of units in the default UI.
- raidpet1 to raidpet40—A pet belonging to a member of the player's raid group
- arena1 to arena5—A member of the opposing team in an Arena match

A unitID can also be formed by appending "target" to an existing unitID, referring to that unit's target. This can be done repeatedly. For example, consider a raid situation where the token raid13 refers to a priest: raid13target might be a rogue the priest is healing, raid13targettarget might be the boss monster the rogue is attacking, and raid13targettargettarget might be the warrior tanking the boss.

Many (but not all) API functions that accept a unitID also accept the name of a unit (assuming that unit is in the player's party or raid). For example, UnitHealth ("Cladhaire") will return the same value as UnitHealth ("party1") if the unit party1 is the player named Cladhaire. In such situations, a unit's target can still be accessed by appending -target; for example, UnitHealth ("Cladhaire-target").

API Reference

 AbandonQuest

> Confirms abandoning a quest.
>
> Use SetAbandonQuest() first to select the quest to abandon.

 AbandonSkill

> Unlearns a skill (used only for professions).
>
> AbandonSkill(index)
>
> **Arguments:**
>
> index—Index of an entry in the skills list (between 1 and GetNumSkill Lines()) (number)

AcceptAreaSpiritHeal

> Accepts the next upcoming periodic resurrection from a battleground spirit healer.

Automatically called in the default UI in response to the `AREA_SPIRIT`
`_HEALER_IN_RANGE` event which fires when the player's ghost is near a
battleground spirit healer.

AcceptArenaTeam

Accepts an invitation to join an arena team.

| Hardware |

AcceptBattlefieldPort

Accepts the offered teleport to a battleground/arena or leaves the
battleground/arena or queue.

```
AcceptBattlefieldPort(index, accept)
```

This function requires a hardware event when used to accept a teleport; it can
be called without a hardware event for leaving a battleground/arena or its
queue.

Arguments:

`index`—Index of a battleground or arena type for which the player is queued
(`number`)

`accept`—1 to accept the offered teleport; `nil` to exit the queue
or leave the battleground/arena match in progress (`1nil`)

AcceptDuel

Accepts a proposed duel.

AcceptGroup

Accepts an invitation to join a party or raid.

Usable in response to the `PARTY_INVITE_REQUEST` event which fires when the
player is invited to join a group. This function does not automatically hide
the default UI's group invite dialog; doing such requires calling `StaticPopup`
`_Hide("PARTY_INVITE")`, but only after the `PARTY_MEMBERS_CHANGED` event
fires indicating the player has successfully joined the group.

AcceptGuild

Accepts an invitation to join a guild.

Usable in response to the `GUILD_INVITE_REQUEST` event, which fires when
the player is invited to join a guild.

AcceptLFGMatch

Accepts a proposed LFG match.

Usable after a group match has been proposed to the player via the
`LFG_MATCH_REQUEST` event.

AcceptLevelGrant

Accepts a level offered by the player's Recruit-a-Friend partner.

AcceptQuest

Accepts the quest offered by a questgiver.

Usable following the `QUEST_DETAIL` event in which the questgiver presents
the player with the details of a quest and the option to accept or decline.

AcceptResurrect

Accepts an offered resurrection spell.

Not used for self-resurrection; see UseSoulstone() for such cases.

Confirmation   **AcceptSockets**

Accepts changes made in the Item Socketing UI.

Any gems added are permanently socketed into the item, and any existing gems replaced by new gems are destroyed. This function only has effect while the Item Socketing UI is open (i.e. between the SOCKET_INFO_UPDATE and SOCKET_INFO_CLOSE events).

AcceptTrade

Accepts a proposed trade.

Once both players have accepted, the trade process completes and the actual exchange of items/money/enchants takes place.

Confirmation   **AcceptXPLoss**

Resurrects the player at a spirit healer, accepting possible consequences.

Resurrecting at a spirit healer generally results in a loss of durability (both equipped items and those in the player's bags) and may also result in the Resurrection Sickness debuff.

Early in the development of World of Warcraft, resurrecting at a spirit healer caused a loss of experience points. The change to a loss of item durability was made before the initial public release of World of Warcraft, but the name of this function was never changed.

ActionHasRange

Returns whether an action has a range restriction.

hasRange = ActionHasRange(slot)

Arguments:

slot—An action bar slot (number, actionID)

Returns:

hasRange—1 if the action has a range restriction; otherwise nil (1nil)

AddChatWindowChannel

Adds a chat channel to the saved list of those displayed in a chat window.

zoneChannel = AddChatWindowChannel(index, channel)

Used by the default UI's function ChatFrame_AddChannel() which manages the set of channel messages shown in a displayed ChatFrame.

Arguments:

index—Index of a chat frame (between 1 and NUM_CHAT_WINDOWS) (number)

channel—Name of a chat channel (number)

Returns:

zoneChannel—0 for non-zone channels, otherwise a numeric index specific to that channel (number)

AddChatWindowMessages

Adds a message type to the saved list of those displayed in a chat window.

```
AddChatWindowMessages(index, "messageGroup")
```

Used by the default UI's function `ChatFrame_AddMessageGroup()`, which manages the set of message types shown in a displayed ChatFrame.

Arguments:

`index`—Index of a chat frame (between 1 and `NUM_CHAT_WINDOWS`) (number)

`messageGroup`—Token identifying a message type (string, chatMsgType)

AddFriend

Adds a character to the friends list.

```
AddFriend("name")
```

Arguments:

`name`—Name of a character to add to the friends list (string)

AddIgnore

Adds a character to the ignore list.

```
AddIgnore("name")
```

Arguments:

`name`—Name of a character to add to the ignore list (string)

AddMute

Adds a character to the muted list for voice chat.

```
AddMute("name")
```

The Muted list acts for voice chat as the Ignore list does for text chat: muted characters will never be heard regardless of which voice channels they join the player in.

Arguments:

`name`—Name of a character to add to the mute list (string)

AddOrDelIgnore

Adds the named character to the ignore list, or removes the character if already in the ignore list.

```
AddOrDelIgnore("fullname")
```

Arguments:

`fullname`—Name of a character to add to or remove from the ignore list (string)

AddOrDelMute

Adds or removes a character from the voice mute list.

```
AddOrDelMute("unit") or AddOrDelMute("name")
```

Adds the character to the list if he/she is not already on it; removes the character if already on the list.

The Muted list acts for voice chat as the Ignore list does for text chat: muted characters will never be heard regardless of which voice channels they join the player in.

Arguments:

unit—A unit to mute (string, unitID)

name—Name of a character to mute (string)

AddOrRemoveFriend

Adds the named character to the friends list, or removes the character if already in the friends list.

```
AddOrRemoveFriend("name", "note")
```

Arguments:

name—Name of a character to add to or remove from the friends list (string)

note—Note text to be associated with the friends list entry created (string)

AddPreviewTalentPoints

Spends (or unspends) talent points in the Talent UI's preview mode.

```
AddPreviewTalentPoints(tabIndex, talentIndex, points, isPet, ↵
talentGroup)
```

Arguments:

tabIndex—Index of a talent tab (between 1 and GetNumTalentTabs()) (number)

talentIndex—Index of a talent option (between 1 and GetNumTalents()) (number)

points—Number of points to spend on the talent, or a negative number to unspend points. Values larger than allowed for the talent will be clipped to the maximum value (e.g. attempting to spend ten points on a talent that has five ranks will only spend up to five points). (number)

isPet—True to edit talents for the player's pet, false to edit talents for the player (boolean)

talentGroup—Which set of talents to edit, if the player has Dual Talent Specialization enabled (number)

- 1—Primary Talents
- 2—Secondary Talents
- nil—Currently active talents

AddQuestWatch

Adds a quest to the objectives tracker.

```
AddQuestWatch(questIndex)
```

Arguments:

questIndex—Index of a quest in the quest log (between 1 and GetNumQuestLogEntries()) (number)

AddTrackedAchievement

Adds an achievement to the objectives tracker UI.

```
AddTrackedAchievement(id)
```

Arguments:

id—The numeric ID of an achievement (number)

AddTradeMoney

Adds the money currently on the cursor to the trade window.

ApplyBarberShopStyle

Purchases the selected barber shop style changes.

Does not exit the barber shop session, so further changes are still allowed.

The BARBER_SHOP_SUCCESS and BARBER_SHOP_APPEARANCE_APPLIED events fire once the style change takes effect.

ArenaTeamDisband

Disbands an arena team.

```
ArenaTeamDisband(team)
```

Only has effect if the player is captain of the given team.

Arguments:

team—Index of one of the player's arena teams (number, arenaTeamID)

ArenaTeamInviteByName

Invites a character to one of the player's arena teams.

```
ArenaTeamInviteByName(team, "name")
```

Arguments:

team—Index of one of the player's arena teams (number, arenaTeamID)

name—Name of a character to invite (string)

`Confirmation` ### ArenaTeamLeave

Leaves an arena team.

```
ArenaTeamLeave(team)
```

Arguments:

team—Index of one of the player's arena teams (number, arenaTeamID)

ArenaTeamRoster

Requests arena team roster information from the server.

```
ArenaTeamRoster(team)
```

Does not return information directly: the ARENA_TEAM_ROSTER_UPDATE event fires when information from the server becomes available, which can then be retrieved using GetNumArenaTeamMembers() and GetArenaTeamRosterInfo().

Roster update requests are limited to once every 10 seconds *per team*. For example, calling ArenaTeamRoster(1) twice within ten seconds will not result in a second ARENA_TEAM_ROSTER_UPDATE event, but calling ArenaTeamRoster(1) and ArenaTeamRoster(2) within ten seconds will result in two ARENA_TEAM_ROSTER_UPDATE events (one for each team).

Arguments:

team—Index of one of the player's arena teams (number, arenaTeamID)

Confirmation	**ArenaTeamSetLeaderByName**

Promotes an arena team member to team captain.

```
ArenaTeamSetLeaderByName(team, "name")
```

Only has effect if the player is captain of the given team.

Arguments:

`team`—Index of one of the player's arena teams (`number`, arenaTeamID)

`name`—Name of a team member to promote (`string`)

Confirmation	**ArenaTeamUninviteByName**

Removes a member from an arena team.

```
ArenaTeamUninviteByName(team, "name")
```

Arguments:

`team`—Index of one of the player's arena teams (`number`, arenaTeamID)

`name`—Name of a team member to remove (`string`)

ArenaTeam_GetTeamSizeID

Converts an arena team size to the appropriate numeric arena team identifier.

```
teamID = ArenaTeam_GetTeamSizeID(teamSize)
```

Arguments:

`teamSize`—The size of the arena team (i.e. 2 for 2v2, 3 for 3v3, etc.) (`number`)

Returns:

`teamID`—The numeric identifier for the arena team of the given size (`number`, arenaTeamID)

Protected	**AscendStop**

Stops movement initiated by `JumpOrAscendStart`.

Used by the `JUMP` binding, which also controls ascent when swimming or flying. Has no meaningful effect if called while jumping (in which case movement is generally stopped by hitting the ground).

Protected	**AssistUnit**

Targets the unit targeted by another unit.

```
AssistUnit("unit") or AssistUnit("name")
```

Arguments:

`unit`—A unit to assist (`string`, unitID)

`name`—The name of a unit to assist (`string`)

Protected	**AttackTarget**

Begins auto-attack against the player's current target.

(If the "Auto Attack/Auto Shot" option is turned on, also begins Auto Shot for hunters.)

AutoEquipCursorItem

Equips the item on the cursor.

The item is automatically equipped in the first available slot in which it fits. To equip an item in a specific slot, see `EquipCursorItem()`.

Causes an error message (UI_ERROR_MESSAGE) if the item on the cursor cannot be equipped. Does nothing if the cursor does not contain an item.

AutoLootMailItem

Automatically takes any attached items and money from a mail message.

```
AutoLootMailItem(mailID)
```

If the message does not have body text (which can be saved as a permanent copy), also deletes the message.

Arguments:

mailID—Index of a message in the player's inbox (between 1 and GetInboxNumItems()) (number)

AutoStoreGuildBankItem

Withdraws the item(s) from a slot in the guild bank, automatically adding to the player's bags.

```
AutoStoreGuildBankItem(tab, slot)
```

Arguments:

tab—Index of a guild bank tab (between 1 and GetNumGuildBankTabs()) (number)

slot—Index of an item slot in the guild bank tab (between 1 and MAX_GUILDBANK_SLOTS_PER_TAB) (number)

BankButtonIDToInvSlotID

Returns the inventoryID corresponding to a bank item or bag slot.

```
inventoryID = BankButtonIDToInvSlotID(buttonID [, isBag])
```

Arguments:

buttonID—Numeric ID of an item or bag slot in the bank UI (number)

isBag (optional)—1 if the given ID corresponds to a bank bag slot; nil if the ID corresponds to an item slot (1nil)

Returns:

inventoryID—An inventory slot ID usable with various Inventory API functions (number, inventoryID)

Example:

```
-- While mousing over a button in the bank
local button = GetMouseFocus()
print("Inventory Slot:", BankButtonIDToInvSlotID(button:GetID(), ↵
button.isBag))
```

BarberShopReset

Resets barber shop options to the currently worn styles.

Changes the underlying data (and thus the character's appearance) only; the default barbershop UI does not update.

`Confirmation` ### BindEnchant

Confirms enchanting an item (when the item will become soulbound as a result).

Usable following the BIND_ENCHANT event which fires upon attempting to perform an enchantment that would cause the target item to become soulbound.

 Confirmation

BuyGuildBankTab

Purchases the next available guild bank tab.

BuyGuildCharter

Purchases a guild charter.

```
BuyGuildCharter("guildName")
```

Usable if the player is interacting with a guild registrar (i.e. between the GUILD_REGISTRAR_SHOW and GUILD_REGISTRAR_CLOSED events).

Arguments:

guildName—Name of the guild to be created (string)

Confirmation

BuyMerchantItem

Purchases an item available from a vendor.

```
BuyMerchantItem(index, quantity)
```

Arguments:

index—Index of an item in the vendor's listing (between 1 and GetMerchantNumItems()) (number)

quantity—Number of items to purchase (between 1 and GetMerchantItemMaxStack(index)) (number)

BuyPetition

Purchases an arena team charter.

```
BuyPetition(team, "name")
```

Arguments:

team—Index of the size of team to create (number, arenaTeamID)

name—Name of the team to create (string)

Confirmation

BuyStableSlot

Purchases the next available stable slot, without confirmation.

Only available while interacting with a Stable Master NPC (between the PET_STABLE_SHOW and PET_STABLE_CLOSED events and only if IsAtStable Master() returns true).

BuyTrainerService

Purchases an ability or recipe available from a trainer.

```
BuyTrainerService(index)
```

Arguments:

index—Index of an entry in the trainer service listing (between 1 and GetNum TrainerServices()) (number)

BuybackItem

Repurchases an item recently sold to a vendor.

```
BuybackItem(index)
```

Arguments:

index—Index of an item in the buyback listing (between 1 and GetNumBuybackItems()) (number)

CalculateAuctionDeposit

Returns the deposit amount for the item currently being set up for auction.

deposit = CalculateAuctionDeposit(runTime)

Only returns useful information once an item has been placed in the Create Auction UI's "auction item" slot (see ClickAuctionSellItemButton()). Deposit amount for an auction varies based on the item being auction, the auction's proposed run time, and the auction house being used (i.e. faction or neutral).

Arguments:

runTime—Run time of the proposed auction (number)

- 720—12 hours
- 1440—24 hours
- 2880—48 hours

Returns:

deposit—Amount of the deposit (in copper) (number)

CalendarAddEvent

Saves the event recently created (and selected for editing) to the calendar.

Until this function is called, an event created with CalendarNewEvent(), CalendarNewGuildEvent(), or CalendarNewGuildAnnouncement() will not exist on the calendar—that is, guild members or invitees will not see it, and it will not persist if the player closes the calendar, reloads the UI, or goes to view or edit another event.

CalendarCanAddEvent

Returns whether the player can add an event to the calendar.

canAdd = CalendarCanAddEvent()

Returns:

canAdd—True if the player can add an event to the calendar; otherwise false (boolean)

CalendarCanSendInvite

Returns whether the player can invite others to a calendar event.

canInvite = CalendarCanSendInvite()

Returns:

canInvite—True if the player can invite others to a calendar event; otherwise false (boolean)

CalendarCloseEvent

Deselects (ends viewing/editing on) an event.

After calling this function, results of attempting to query or change event information are not guaranteed until a new event is created or another existing event is opened.

CalendarContextDeselectEvent

Clears the event selection used only for `CalendarContext` functions.

The selection state cleared is used only by other `CalendarContext` functions; other calendar event functions use a selection state (if needed) set by `CalendarOpenEvent`, `CalendarNewEvent`, `CalendarNewGuildEvent`, or `CalendarNewGuildAnnouncement`.

CalendarContextEventCanComplain

Returns whether the player can report an event invitation as spam.

```
canReport = CalendarContextEventCanComplain([monthOffset,] day, index)
```

If all arguments are omitted, uses the event selected by `CalendarContextSelectEvent`.

Arguments:

`monthOffset` (optional)—Month containing an event relative to the calendar's currently displayed month (number)

- `-1`—Month preceding the calendar's current month
- `0`—Current month (i.e. same month as `CalendarGetMonth()`)
- `1`—Month after the calendar's current month
- `nil`—Use the event selected by `CalendarContextSelectEvent` and ignore further arguments

`day`—Day of the month containing an event (number)

`index`—Index of an event on the given day (from 1 to `CalendarGetNumDayEvents()`) (number)

Returns:

`canReport`—`true` if the player can report the event as spam; otherwise `false` (boolean)

CalendarContextEventCanEdit

Returns whether the player can edit an event.

```
canEdit = CalendarContextEventCanEdit([monthOffset,] day, index)
```

Arguments:

`monthOffset` (optional)—Month containing an event relative to the calendar's currently displayed month (number)

- `-1`—Month preceding the calendar's current month
- `0`—The calendar's current month (i.e. same month as CalendarGetMonth())
- `1`—Month after the calendar's current month
- `nil`—Use the event selected by `CalendarContextSelectEvent` and ignore further arguments

`day`—Day of the month containing an event (number)

index—Index of an event on the given day (from 1 to `CalendarGetNumDay Events()`) (number)

Returns:

`canEdit`—True if the player can edit the event (`boolean`)

CalendarContextEventClipboard

Returns whether the player can paste an event.

`canPaste = CalendarContextEventClipboard()`

Returns:

`canPaste`—`true` if an event has been copied via `CalendarContextEventCopy`; otherwise `false` (`boolean`)

CalendarContextEventComplain

Reports an event invitation as spam.

`CalendarContextEventComplain([monthOffset,] day, index)`

Arguments:

`monthOffset` (optional)—Month containing an event relative to the calendar's currently displayed month (`number`)

- `-1`—Month preceding the calendar's current month
- `0`—Current month (i.e. same month as `CalendarGetMonth()`)
- `1`—Month after the calendar's current month
- `nil`—Use the event selected by `CalendarContextSelectEvent` and ignore further arguments

`day`—Day of the month containing an event (`number`)

`index`—Index of an event on the given day (from 1 to `CalendarGetNumDay Events()`) (`number`)

CalendarContextEventCopy

Copies an event for later pasting.

`CalendarContextEventCopy([monthOffset,] day, index)`

Arguments:

`monthOffset` (optional)—Month containing an event relative to the calendar's currently displayed month (`number`)

- `-1`—Month preceding the calendar's current month
- `0`—Current month (i.e. same month as `CalendarGetMonth()`)
- `1`—Month after the calendar's current month
- `nil`—Use the event selected by `CalendarContextSelectEvent` and ignore further arguments

`day`—Day of the month containing an event (`number`)

`index`—Index of an event on the given day (from 1 to `CalendarGetNumDay Events()`) (`number`)

CalendarContextEventGetCalendarType

Returns the type of a calendar event.

```
calendarType = CalendarContextEventGetCalendarType([monthOffset,] ↵
day, index)
```

If all arguments are omitted, uses the event selected by
`CalendarContextSelectEvent`.

Arguments:

`monthOffset` (optional)—Month containing an event relative to the calendar's
currently displayed month (number)

- `-1`—Month preceding the calendar's current month
- `0`—Current month (i.e. same month as `CalendarGetMonth()`)
- `1`—Month after the calendar's current month
- `nil`—Use the event selected by `CalendarContextSelectEvent` and ignore
  further arguments

`day`—Day of the month containing an event (number)

`index`—Index of an event on the given day (from 1 to `CalendarGetNumDay`
`Events()`) (number)

Returns:

`calendarType`—Token identifying the type of event (string)

- `GUILD_ANNOUNCEMENT`—Guild announcement (does not allow players to
  sign up)
- `GUILD_EVENT`—Guild event (allows players to sign up)
- `HOLIDAY`—World event (e.g. Lunar Festival, Darkmoon Faire,
  Stranglethorn Fishing Tournament, Call to Arms: Arathi Basin)
- `PLAYER`—Player-created event or invitation
- `RAID_LOCKOUT`—Indicates when one of the player's saved instances resets
- `RAID_RESET`—Indicates scheduled reset times for major raid instances
- `SYSTEM`—Other server-provided event

CalendarContextEventPaste

Pastes a copied event into a given date.

```
CalendarContextEventPaste(monthOffset, day)
```

Does nothing if no event has been copied via `CalendarContextEventCopy`.

Arguments:

`monthOffset`—Month containing an event relative to the calendar's currently
displayed month (number)

- `-1`—Month preceding the calendar's current month
- `0`—Current month (i.e. same month as `CalendarGetMonth()`)
- `1`—Month after the calendar's current month

`day`—Day of the month (number)

> **Confirmation**

CalendarContextEventRemove

Deletes an event from the calendar.

```
CalendarContextEventRemove([monthOffset,] day, index)
```

Arguments:

monthOffset (optional)—Month containing an event relative to the calendar's currently displayed month (number)

- ▪ -1—Month preceding the calendar's current month
- ▪ 0—Current month (i.e. same month as CalendarGetMonth())
- ▪ 1—Month after the calendar's current month
- ▪ nil—Use the event selected by CalendarContextSelectEvent and ignore further arguments

day—Day of the month containing an event (number)

index—Index of an event on the given day (from 1 to CalendarGetNumDay Events()) (number)

CalendarContextEventSignUp

Signs the player up for a guild event.

```
CalendarContextEventSignUp([monthOffset,] day, index)
```

Arguments:

monthOffset (optional)—Month containing an event relative to the calendar's currently displayed month (number)

- ▪ -1—Month preceding the calendar's current month
- ▪ 0—Current month (i.e. same month as CalendarGetMonth())
- ▪ 1—Month after the calendar's current month
- ▪ nil—Use the event selected by CalendarContextSelectEvent and ignore further arguments

day—Day of the month containing an event (number)

index—Index of an event on the given day (from 1 to CalendarGetNum-DayEvents()) (number)

CalendarContextGetEventIndex

Returns the month, day, and index of the event selection used only for CalendarContext functions.

```
monthOffset, day, index = CalendarContextGetEventIndex()
```

The selection state referenced by this function is used only by other CalendarContext functions; other calendar event functions use the selection state set by CalendarOpenEvent, CalendarNewEvent, CalendarNew GuildEvent, or CalendarNewGuildAnnouncement (if they use a selection state at all).

Used in the default UI to implement the calendar's context menu (on right-click).

Returns:

monthOffset—Month relative to the calendar's currently displayed month
(number)

- -1—Month preceding the calendar's current month
- 0—Current month (i.e. same month as CalendarGetMonth())
- 1—Month after the calendar's current month

day—Day of the month (number)

index—Index of the event on the given day (from 1 to
CalendarGetNumDayEvents()) (number)

CalendarContextInviteAvailable

Accepts an event invitation.

```
CalendarContextInviteAvailable([monthOffset,] day, index)
```

Arguments:

monthOffset (optional)—Month containing an event relative to the calendar's
currently displayed month (number)

- -1—Month preceding the calendar's current month
- 0—Current month (i.e. same month as CalendarGetMonth())
- 1—Month after the calendar's current month
- nil—Use the event selected by CalendarContextSelectEvent and ignore
  further arguments

day—Day of the month containing an event (number)

index—Index of an event on the given day (from 1 to
CalendarGetNumDayEvents()) (number)

CalendarContextInviteDecline

Declines an event invitation.

```
CalendarContextInviteDecline([monthOffset,] day, index)
```

Arguments:

monthOffset (optional)—Month containing an event relative to the calendar's
currently displayed month (number)

- -1—Month preceding the calendar's current month
- 0—Current month (i.e. same month as CalendarGetMonth())
- 1—Month after the calendar's current month
- nil—Use the event selected by CalendarContextSelectEvent and ignore
  further arguments

day—Day of the month containing an event (number)

index—Index of an event on the given day (from 1 to
CalendarGetNumDayEvents()) (number)

CalendarContextInviteIsPending

Returns whether the player has been invited to an event and not yet responded.

```
pendingInvite = CalendarContextInviteIsPending([monthOffset,] ↵
day, index)
```

Arguments:

`monthOffset` (optional)—Month containing an event relative to the calendar's currently displayed month (`number`)

- `-1`—Month preceding the calendar's current month
- `0`—Current month (i.e. same month as `CalendarGetMonth()`)
- `1`—Month after the calendar's current month
- `nil`—Use the event selected by `CalendarContextSelectEvent` and ignore further arguments

`day`—Day of the month containing an event (`number`)

`index`—Index of an event on the given day (from `1` to CalendarGetNum DayEvents()) (`number`)

Returns:

`pendingInvite`—`True` if the player is invited to the event and has yet to respond; otherwise `false` (`boolean`)

CalendarContextInviteModeratorStatus

Returns the player's moderator status for an event.

```
modStatus = CalendarContextInviteModeratorStatus([monthOffset,] ↵
day, index)
```

Arguments:

`monthOffset` (optional)—Month containing an event relative to the calendar's currently displayed month (`number`)

- `-1`—Month preceding the calendar's current month
- `0`—Current month (i.e. same month as `CalendarGetMonth()`)
- `1`—Month after the calendar's current month
- `nil`—Use the event selected by `CalendarContextSelectEvent` and ignore further arguments

`day`—Day of the month containing an event (`number`)

`index`—Index of an event on the given day (from `1` to CalendarGet NumDayEvents()) (`number`)

Returns:

`modStatus`—The player's level of authority for the event, or "" if not applicable (`number`)

- `CREATOR`—The player is the original creator of the event
- `MODERATOR`—The player has been granted moderator status for the event

CalendarContextInviteRemove

Removes an invitation from the player's calendar or removes the player from a guild event's signup list.

```
CalendarContextInviteRemove([monthOffset,] day, index)
```

Arguments:

monthOffset (optional)—Month containing an event relative to the calendar's currently displayed month (number)

- -1—Month preceding the calendar's current month
- 0—Current month (i.e. same month as CalendarGetMonth())
- 1—Month after the calendar's current month
- nil—Use the event selected by CalendarContextSelectEvent and ignore further arguments

day—Day of the month containing an event (number)

index—Index of an event on the given day (from 1 to CalendarGetNum DayEvents()) (number)

CalendarContextInviteStatus

Returns the player's invite status for an event.

```
inviteStatus = CalendarContextInviteStatus([monthOffset,] day, index)
```

Arguments:

monthOffset (optional)—Month containing an event relative to the calendar's currently displayed month (number)

- -1—Month preceding the calendar's current month
- 0—Current month (i.e. same month as CalendarGetMonth())
- 1—Month after the calendar's current month
- nil—Use the event selected by CalendarContextSelectEvent and ignore further arguments

day—Day of the month containing an event (number)

index—Index of an event on the given day (from 1 to CalendarGetNum DayEvents()) (number)

Returns:

inviteStatus—The player's status regarding the event (number)

1—Invited	5—Out
2—Accepted	6—Standby
3—Declined	7—Signed up
4—Confirmed	8—Not signed up

1 is also used for non-invitation/non-signup events.

CalendarContextInviteType

Returns the invite type for an event.

```
inviteType = CalendarContextInviteType([monthOffset,] day, index)
```

Arguments:

`monthOffset` (optional)—Month containing an event relative to the calendar's currently displayed month (`number`)

- ▪ `-1`—Month preceding the calendar's current month
- ▪ `0`—Current month (i.e. same month as `CalendarGetMonth()`)
- ▪ `1`—Month after the calendar's current month
- ▪ `nil`—Use the event selected by `CalendarContextSelectEvent` and ignore further arguments

`day`—Day of the month containing an event (`number`)

`index`—Index of an event on the given day (from `1` to CalendarGetNum DayEvents()) (`number`)

Returns:

`inviteType`—Invitation/announcement type for the event (`number`)

- ▪ `1`—Characters can only be explicitly invited to the event (or event is a non-invite/non-signup event)
- ▪ `2`—Event is visible to the player's entire guild; guild members can sign up and other characters can be explicitly invited

CalendarContextSelectEvent

Selects an event for use only with other `CalendarContext` functions.

```
CalendarContextSelectEvent([monthOffset,] day, index)
```

The selection state set by this function is used only by other `CalendarContext` functions; other calendar event functions use the selection state set by `CalendarOpenEvent`, `CalendarNewEvent`, `CalendarNewGuildEvent`, or `CalendarNewGuildAnnouncement` (if they use a selection state at all).

Used in the default UI to implement the calendar's context menu (on right-click).

Arguments:

`monthOffset` (optional)—Month containing an event relative to the calendar's currently displayed month (`number`)

- ▪ `-1`—Month preceding the calendar's current month
- ▪ `0`—Current month (i.e. same month as `CalendarGetMonth()`)
- ▪ `1`—Month after the calendar's current month
- ▪ `nil`—Use the event selected by `CalendarContextSelectEvent` and ignore further arguments

`day`—Day of the month containing an event (`number`)

`index`—Index of an event on the given day (from `1` to CalendarGetNum DayEvents()) (`number`)

CalendarDefaultGuildFilter

Returns default options for the guild member Mass Invite filter.

`minLevel, maxLevel, rank = CalendarDefaultGuildFilter()`

Returns:

`minLevel`—Lowest level of characters to invite (number)

`maxLevel`—Highest level of characters to invite (number)

`rank`—Lowest guild rank of characters to invite (number)

CalendarEventAvailable

Accepts invitation to the selected calendar event.

Only applies to player-created events and invitations sent by other players; has no effect if the current calendar event is of another type.

CalendarEventCanEdit

Returns whether the player can edit the selected calendar event.

`canEdit = CalendarEventCanEdit()`

Returns:

`canEdit`—True if the player can edit the current event; otherwise `false` (`boolean`)

CalendarEventCanModerate

Returns whether an event invitee can be granted moderator authority.

`canModerate = CalendarEventCanModerate(index)`

Arguments:

`index`—Index of a character on the event's invite list (between 1 and `CalendarEventGetNumInvites()`) (number)

Returns:

`canModerate`—True if the given character can be given moderator authority for the event; otherwise `false` (`boolean`)

CalendarEventClearAutoApprove

Disables the auto-approve feature (currently unused) for the selected calendar event.

CalendarEventClearLocked

Unlocks the selected calendar event.

Locked events do not allow invitees to respond or guild members to sign up, but can still be edited.

CalendarEventClearModerator

Removes moderator status from a character on the selected event's invite/signup list.

`CalendarEventClearModerator(index)`

Moderators can change the status of characters on the invite/signup list and invite more characters, but cannot otherwise edit the event.

Arguments:

`index`—Index of a character on the event's invite list (between `1` and CalendarEventGetNumInvites()) (`number`)

CalendarEventDecline

Declines invitation to the selected calendar event.

Only applies to player-created events and invitations sent by other players; has no effect if the current calendar event is of another type.

CalendarEventGetCalendarType

Returns the type of the selected calendar event.

`calendarType = CalendarEventGetCalendarType()`

Returns:

`calendarType`—Token identifying the type of event (`string`)

▪ `GUILD_ANNOUNCEMENT`—Guild announcement (does not allow players to sign up)

▪ `GUILD_EVENT`—Guild event (allows players to sign up)

▪ `PLAYER`—Player-created event or invitation

CalendarEventGetInvite

Returns information about an entry in the selected event's invite/signup list.

`name, level, className, classFileName, inviteStatus, modStatus, ↵`
`inviteIsMine, inviteType = CalendarEventGetInvite(index)`

Arguments:

`index`—Index of a character on the event's invite list (between `1` and `CalendarEventGetNumInvites()`) (`number`)

Returns:

`name`—Name of the character (`string`)

`level`—The character's current level (`number`)

`className`—Localized name of the character's class (`string`)

`classFileName`—Non-localized token representing the character's class (`string`)

`inviteStatus`—The character's status regarding the event (`number`)

`1`—Invited	`5`—Out
`2`—Accepted	`6`—Standby
`3`—Declined	`7`—Signed up
`4`—Confirmed	

`modStatus`—The character's level of authority for the event, or "" if not applicable (`number`)

▪ `CREATOR`—The character is the original creator of the event

▪ `MODERATOR`—The character has been granted moderator status for the event

`inviteIsMine`—True if this list entry represents the player; otherwise `false` (`boolean`) inviteType—Invitation/announcement type for the event (number)

- 1—Characters can only be explicitly invited to the event
- 2—Event is visible to the player's entire guild; guild members can sign up and other characters can be explicitly invited

CalendarEventGetInviteResponseTime

Returns the time at which a character on the selected event's invite/signup list responded.

```
weekday, month, day, year, hour, minute = ↵
CalendarEventGetInviteResponseTime()
```

Returns all zeros if the character has not yet responded or is the event's creator.

Returns:

weekday—Index of the day of the week (starting at 1 = Sunday) (number)

month—Index of the month (starting at 1 = January) (number)

day—Day of the month (number)

year—Year (full four-digit year) (number)

hour—Hour part of the time (on a 24-hour clock) (number)

minute—Minute part of the time (number)

CalendarEventGetInviteSortCriterion

Returns the current sort mode for the event invite/signup list.

```
criterion, reverse = CalendarEventGetInviteSortCriterion()
```

Returns:

criterion—Token identifying the attribute used for sorting the list (string)

- class—Sorted by character class (according to the global table CLASS_SORT_ORDER)
- name—Sorted by character name
- status—Sorted by invite status

reverse—True if the list is sorted in reverse order; otherwise false (boolean)

CalendarEventGetNumInvites

Returns the number of characters on the selected calendar event's invite/signup list.

```
numInvites = CalendarEventGetNumInvites()
```

Returns:

numInvites—Number of characters on the event's invite/signup list (number)

CalendarEventGetRepeatOptions

Returns a list of localized event repetition option labels (currently unused).

```
... = CalendarEventGetRepeatOptions()
```

Returns:

...—List of localized event repetition option labels (list)

CalendarEventGetSelectedInvite

Returns the index of the selected entry on the selected event's invite/signup list.

```
index = CalendarEventGetSelectedInvite()
```

In the current default UI, selection behavior in the invite list is implemented but disabled; selecting an invite list entry has no effect on the behavior of other APIs.

Returns:

`index`—Index of a character on the event's invite list (between 1 and Calendar EventGetNumInvites()), or 0 if no selection has been made (`number`)

CalendarEventGetStatusOptions

Returns a list of localized invite status labels.

```
... = CalendarEventGetStatusOptions()
```

Returns:

`...`—List of localized invite status labels (`list`)

CalendarEventGetTextures

Returns a list of instance names and icons for dungeon or raid events.

```
name, icon, expansion = CalendarEventGetTextures(eventType)
```

Arguments:

`eventType`—Type (display style) of event to query (`number`)

- ▪ 1—Raid dungeon
- ▪ 2—Five-player dungeon

Returns:

`name`—Name of an instance (may include heroic designation) (`string`)

`icon`—Unique part of the path to the instance's icon texture; for the full path, prepend with `"Interface\LFGFrame\LFGIcon-"` (`string`)

`expansion`—Expansion to which the instance belongs; localized names can be found in the constants `EXPANSION_NAME0`, `EXPANSION_NAME1`, etc. (`number`)

CalendarEventGetTypes

Returns a list of event display style labels.

```
... = CalendarEventGetTypes()
```

Returns:

`...`—A list of localized event display style labels (`list`)

CalendarEventHasPendingInvite

Returns whether the player has been invited to the selected event and not yet responded.

```
pendingInvite = CalendarEventHasPendingInvite()
```

Returns:

`pendingInvite`—True if the player has been invited to the event and not yet responded; otherwise `false` (`boolean`)

CalendarEventHaveSettingsChanged

Returns whether the selected event has unsaved changes.

```
settingsChanged = CalendarEventHaveSettingsChanged()
```

Returns:

`settingsChanged`—`True` if any of the event's attributes have been changed since the event was last saved; otherwise `false` (`boolean`)

CalendarEventInvite

Attempts to invite a character to the selected event.

```
CalendarEventInvite("name")
```

If successful, the `CALENDAR_UPDATE_INVITE_LIST` event fires indicating the character has been added to the invite list; otherwise the `CALENDAR_UPDATE _ERROR` event fires containing a localized error message.

Arguments:

`name`—Name of a character to invite (`string`)

CalendarEventIsModerator

Returns whether the player has moderator status for the selected calendar event.

```
isModerator = CalendarEventIsModerator()
```

Also returns true if the player is the event's creator.

Returns:

`isModerator`—`True` if the player has moderator status for the event; otherwise `false` (`boolean`)

CalendarEventRemoveInvite

Removes a character from the selected event's invite/signup list.

```
CalendarEventRemoveInvite(index)
```

Cannot be used to remove the event's creator (fires a `CALENDAR_UPDATE_ERROR` event with nil error message if such is attempted).

Arguments:

`index`—Index of a character on the event's invite list (between 1 and Calendar EventGetNumInvites()) (`number`)

CalendarEventSelectInvite

Selects an entry in the selected event's invite/signup list.

```
CalendarEventSelectInvite(index)
```

In the current default UI, selection behavior in the invite list is implemented but disabled; selecting an invite list entry has no effect on the behavior of other APIs.

Arguments:

`index`—Index of a character on the event's invite list (between 1 and Calen-darEventGetNumInvites()) (`number`)

CalendarEventSetAutoApprove

Enables the auto-approve feature (currently unused) for the selected calendar event.

CalendarEventSetDate

Changes the scheduled date of the selected calendar event.

```
CalendarEventSetDate(month, day, year)
```

Arguments:

month—Index of the month (starting at 1 = January) (number)

day—Day of the month (number)

year—Year (full four-digit year) (number)

CalendarEventSetDescription

Changes the descriptive text for the selected event.

```
CalendarEventSetDescription("description")
```

Arguments:

description—Descriptive text to be displayed for the event (string)

CalendarEventSetLocked

Locks the selected calendar event.

Locked events do not allow invitees to respond or guild members to sign up, but can still be edited.

CalendarEventSetLockoutDate

Changes the lockout date associated with the selected event (currently unused).

```
CalendarEventSetLockoutDate(month, day, year)
```

This feature is not enabled in the current version of World of Warcraft; saving an event in which the lockout date has been changed will revert it to its default of 1, 1, 1, 2000 (January 1, 2000).

Arguments:

month—Index of the month (starting at 1 = January) (number)

day—Day of the month (number)

year—Year (full four-digit year) (number)

CalendarEventSetLockoutTime

Changes the lockout time associated with the selected event (currently unused).

```
CalendarEventSetLockoutTime(hour, minute)
```

This feature is not enabled in the current version of World of Warcraft; saving an event in which the lockout time has been changed will revert it to its default of 0, 0 (midnight).

Arguments:

hour—Hour part of the time (on a 24-hour clock) (number)

minute—Minute part of the time (number)

CalendarEventSetModerator

Grants moderator status to a character on the selected event's invite/signup list.

```
CalendarEventSetModerator(index)
```

Moderators can change the status of characters on the invite/signup list and invite more characters, but cannot otherwise edit the event.

Arguments:

index—Index of a character on the event's invite list (between 1 and Calendar EventGetNumInvites()) (number)

CalendarEventSetRepeatOption

Changes the repetition option for the selected event (currently unused).

```
CalendarEventSetRepeatOption(title)
```

This feature is not enabled in the current version of World of Warcraft; saving an event in which the repeat option has been changed will revert it to its default of 1 (Never).

Arguments:

title—Index of a repeating event option; see CalendarEventGetRepeat Options() (number)

CalendarEventSetSize

Changes the maximum number of invites/signups for the selected event (currently unused).

```
CalendarEventSetSize(size)
```

This feature is not enabled in the current version of World of Warcraft; saving an event in which the max size has been changed will revert it to its default of 100.

Arguments:

size—Maximum number of invites/signups for the event (number)

CalendarEventSetStatus

Sets the status of a character on the selected event's invite/signup list.

```
CalendarEventSetStatus(index, inviteStatus)
```

Arguments:

index—Index of a character on the event's invite list (between 1 and Calendar EventGetNumInvites()) (number)

inviteStatus—The player's status regarding the event (number)

1—Invited	5—Out
2—Accepted	6—Standby
3—Declined	7—Signed up
4—Confirmed	8—Not signed up (displays as "")

1 is also used for non-invitation/non-signup events.

CalendarEventSetTextureID

Changes the raid or dungeon instance for the selected event.

```
CalendarEventSetTextureID(index)
```

Only applicable if the event's `eventType` is set to 1 or 2 (see `CalendarEventSetType`).

A list of dungeon or raid instances can be found by calling `CalendarEventGetTextures` with the current `eventType`. That function returns three values (`name`, `icon`, and `expansion`) for each instance in the list; e.g. to get the `index` for use with this function, find the index of the instance's name in that list and divide by 3.

Arguments:

`index`—Index of a dungeon or raid instance (`number`)

CalendarEventSetTime

Changes the scheduled time of the selected event.

```
CalendarEventSetTime(hour, minute)
```

Arguments:

`hour`—Hour part of the time (on a 24-hour clock) (`number`)

`minute`—Minute part of the time (`number`)

CalendarEventSetTitle

Changes the title for the selected event.

```
CalendarEventSetTitle("title")
```

Arguments:

`title`—A title to be displayed for the event (`string`)

CalendarEventSetType

Changes the display type of the selected event.

```
CalendarEventSetType(eventType)
```

Arguments:

`eventType`—Display type for the event; used in the default UI to determine which icon to show (`number`)

1—Raid dungeon   4—Meeting

2—Five-player dungeon   5—Other event

3—PvP event

CalendarEventSignUp

Signs the player up for the selected calendar event.

Only applies to guild events; has no effect if called when the current calendar event is not a guild event.

CalendarEventSortInvites

Sorts the event invite/signup list.

```
CalendarEventSortInvites("criterion", reverse)
```

Does not cause the list to automatically remain sorted; e.g. if sorted by status and a character's status is changed, the list will not be resorted until this function is called again.

Arguments:

criterion—Token identifying the attribute to use for sorting the list (string)

- ▪ class—Sort by character class (according to the global table CLASS_SORT_ORDER)
- ▪ name—Sort by character name
- ▪ status—Sort by invite status

reverse—True to sort the list in reverse order; otherwise false (boolean)

CalendarGetAbsMonth

Returns date information for a given month and year.

```
month, year, numDays, firstWeekday = CalendarGetAbsMonth(month, year)
```

Arguments:

month—Index of a month (starting at 1 = January) (number)

year—Year (full four-digit year) (number)

Returns:

month—Index of the month (starting at 1 = January) (number)

year—Year (full four-digit year) (number)

numDays—Number of days in the month (number)

firstWeekday—Index of the weekday (starting at 1 = Sunday) for the first day of the month (number)

CalendarGetDate

Returns the current date (in the server's time zone).

```
weekday, month, day, year = CalendarGetDate()
```

Only returns valid information after the PLAYER_ENTERING_WORLD event has fired.

Returns:

weekday—Index of the day of the week (starting at 1 = Sunday) (number)

month—Index of the month (starting at 1 = January) (number)

day—Day of the month (number)

year—Year (full four-digit year) (number)

CalendarGetDayEvent

Returns information about a calendar event on a given day.

```
title, hour, minute, calendarType, sequenceType, eventType, texture, ↵
modStatus, inviteStatus, invitedBy, difficulty, inviteType = ↵
CalendarGetDayEvent(monthOffset, day, index)
```

Information can only be retrieved for events which might be visible in the calendar's current month—i.e. those in the current month as well as those in (roughly) the last week of the previous month and (roughly) the first two weeks of the following month. To reliably retrieve information for events outside the calendar's current month, first change the calendar's month with `CalendarSetMonth`.

Arguments:

`monthOffset`—Month containing an event relative to the calendar's currently displayed month (`number`)

- `-1`—Month preceding the calendar's current month
- `0`—The calendar's current month (i.e. same month as CalendarGetMonth())
- `1`—Month after the calendar's current month

`day`—Day of the month containing an event (`number`)

`index`—Index of an event on the given day (from `1` to CalendarGetNum-DayEvents()) (`number`)

Returns:

`title`—Title displayed for the event (`string`)

`hour`—Hour part of the event's start time (on a 24-hour clock) (`number`)

`minute`—Minute part of the event's start time (`number`)

`calendarType`—Token identifying the type of event (`string`)

- `GUILD_ANNOUNCEMENT`—Guild announcement (does not allow players to sign up)
- `GUILD_EVENT`—Guild event (allows players to sign up)
- `HOLIDAY`—World event (e.g. Lunar Festival, Darkmoon Faire, Stranglethorn Fishing Tournament, Call to Arms: Arathi Basin)
- `PLAYER`—Player-created event or invitation
- `RAID_LOCKOUT`—Indicates when one of the player's saved instances resets
- `RAID_RESET`—Indicates scheduled reset times for major raid instances
- `SYSTEM`—Other server-provided event

`sequenceType`—Display cue for multi-day events, or `""` if not applicable (`string`)

- `END`—Last day of the event
- `INFO`—An additional specially-labeled day related the event
- `ONGOING`—Continuation of the event
- `START`—First day of the event

`eventType`—Display type for the event; used in the default UI to determine which icon to show (`number`)

`0`—Holiday or other server-provided event

`1`—Raid dungeon

`2`—Five-player dungeon

`3`—PvP event

`4`—Meeting

`5`—Other event

texture—Unique portion of the path to a texture for the event (e.g. "Calendar_ChildrensWeek"). The mechanism by which a full texture path can be generated is not public API, but can be found in Addons/Blizzard_Calendar /Blizzard_Calendar.lua after extracting default UI files with the AddOn Kit. (string)

modStatus—The player's level of authority for the event, or "" if not applicable (number)

- CREATOR—The player is the original creator of the event
- MODERATOR—The player has been granted moderator status for the event

inviteStatus—The player's status regarding the event (number)

1—Invited	5—Out
2—Accepted	6—Standby
3—Declined	7—Signed up
4—Confirmed	8—Not signed up

1 is also used for non-invitation/non-signup events.

invitedBy—Name of the character who created (or invited the player to) the event (string)

difficulty—Difficulty of the dungeon or raid instance associated with the event (used only for RAID_LOCKOUT and RAID_RESET events, not player-created raid/dungeon events) (number)

- 1—Normal
- 2—Heroic

inviteType—Invitation/announcement type for the event (number)

- 1—Characters can only be explicitly invited to the event (or event is a non-invite/non-signup event)
- 2—Event is visible to the player's entire guild; guild members can sign up and other characters can be explicitly invited

CalendarGetEventIndex

Returns the month, day, and index of the selected calendar event.

```
monthOffset, day, index = CalendarGetEventIndex()
```

Returns:

monthOffset—Month relative to the calendar's currently displayed month (number)

- -1—Month preceding the calendar's current month
- 0—Current month (i.e. same month as CalendarGetMonth())
- 1—Month after the calendar's current month

day—Day of the month (number)

index—Index of the event on the given day (from 1 to CalendarGetNum DayEvents()) (number)

CalendarGetEventInfo

Returns information about the selected calendar event (for player/guild events).

```
title, description, creator, eventType, repeatOption, maxSize, ↵
textureIndex, weekday, month, day, year, hour, minute, ↵
lockoutWeekday, lockoutMonth, lockoutDay, lockoutYear, lockoutHour, ↵
lockoutMinute, locked, autoApprove, pendingInvite, inviteStatus, ↵
inviteType, calendarType = CalendarGetEventInfo()
```

Returns:

`title`—Title displayed for the event (`string`)

`description`—Descriptive text about the event (`string`)

`creator`—Name of the character who created the event (`string`)

`eventType`—Display style for the event; used in the default UI to determine which icon to show (`number`)

1—Raid dungeon	4—Meeting
2—Five-player dungeon	5—Other event
3—PvP event	

`repeatOption`—Index of an event repetition option (see CalendarEventGetRepeatOptions); currently unused (always 1) (`number`)

`maxSize`—Maximum number of invites/signups; currently unused (always 100) (`number`)

`textureIndex`—Index of the dungeon or raid instance (between 1 and `select("#", CalendarEventGetTextures(eventType))` / 3 (`number`)

`weekday`—Index of the day of the week on which the event starts (starting at 1 = Sunday) (`number`)

`month`—Index of the month in which the event starts (starting at 1 = January) (`number`)

`day`—Day of the month on which the event starts (`number`)

`year`—Year in which the event starts (full four-digit year) (`number`)

`hour`—Hour part of the event's start time (on a 24-hour clock) (`number`)

`minute`—Minute part of the event's start time (`number`)

`lockoutWeekday`—Currently unused (`number`)

`lockoutMonth`—Currently unused (`number`)

`lockoutDay`—Currently unused (`number`)

`lockoutYear`—Currently unused (`number`)

`lockoutHour`—Currently unused (`number`)

`lockoutMinute`—Currently unused (`number`)

`locked`—1 if the event is locked (preventing invitees from responding); otherwise `nil` (`1nil`)

`autoApprove`—1 if signups to the event should be automatically approved (currently unused); otherwise `nil` (`1nil`) `pendingInvite`—1 if the player has been invited to this event and has not yet responded; otherwise `nil` (1nil)

`inviteStatus`—The player's status regarding the event (`number`)

1—Invited	4—Confirmed	7—Signed up
2—Accepted	5—Out	8—Not signed up
3—Declined	6—Standby	

`inviteType`—Invitation/announcement type for the event (`number`)

- 1—Player has been explicitly invited to the event and can accept or decline
- 2—Event is visible to the player's entire guild; player can sign up if desired

`calendarType`—Token identifying the type of event (`string`)

- `GUILD_ANNOUNCEMENT`—Guild announcement (does not allow players to sign up)
- `GUILD_EVENT`—Guild event (allows players to sign up)
- `PLAYER`—Player-created event or invitation
- `SYSTEM`—Other server-provided event

CalendarGetFirstPendingInvite

Returns the index of the first invitation on a given day to which the player has not responded.

`index = CalendarGetFirstPendingInvite(monthOffset, day)`

Arguments:

`monthOffset`—Month to query relative to the calendar's currently displayed month (i.e. 0 for current month, 1 for next month, -1 for previous month) (`number`)

`day`—Day of the month to query (`number`)

Returns:

`index`—Index of the event on the given day (from 1 to CalendarGetNum-DayEvents()) (`number`)

CalendarGetHolidayInfo

Returns additional information about a holiday event.

```
name, description, texture = ↵
CalendarGetHolidayInfo(monthOffset, day, index)
```

Information can only be retrieved for events which might be visible in the calendar's current month—i.e. those in the current month as well as those in (roughly) the last week of the previous month and (roughly) the first two weeks of the following month. To reliably retrieve information for events outside the calendar's current month, first change the calendar's month with `CalendarSetMonth`.

Arguments:

`monthOffset`—Month to query relative to the calendar's currently displayed month (i.e. 0 for current month, 1 for next month, -1 for previous month) (`number`) day—Day of the month to query (`number`)

index—Index of an event on the given day (from 1 to CalendarGetNum
DayEvents()) (`number`)

Returns:

name—Localized name of the event (`string`)

description—Localized text describing the event (`string`)

texture—Unique portion of the path to a texture for the event (e.g. "Cal-
endar_ChildrensWeek"). The mechanism by which a full texture path can be
generated is not public API, but can be found in Addons/Blizzard_Calendar
/Blizzard_Calendar.lua after extracting default UI files with the AddOn Kit.
(`string`)

CalendarGetMaxCreateDate

Returns the latest date for which events may be scheduled.

```
weekday, month, day, year = CalendarGetMaxCreateDate()
```

Currently, events can only be created up to one year from the last day of the
current month (e.g. if the current date is May 19, 2009, the player is not allowed
to create events scheduled for later than May 31, 2010). The default Calendar
UI also does not allow viewing months beyond this date.

Returns:

weekday—Index of the day of the week (starting at 1 = Sunday) (`number`)

month—Index of the month (starting at 1 = January) (`number`)

day—Day of the month (`number`)

year—Year (full four-digit year) (`number`)

CalendarGetMaxDate

Returns the latest date usable in the calendar system.

```
weekday, month, day, year = CalendarGetMaxDate()
```

This function currently always returns December 31st, 2030 as the max date.

Returns:

weekday—Index of the day of the week (starting at 1 = Sunday) (`number`)

month—Index of the month (starting at 1 = January) (`number`)

day—Day of the month (`number`)

year—Year (full four-digit year) (`number`)

CalendarGetMinDate

Returns the earliest date usable in the calendar system.

```
weekday, month, day, year = CalendarGetMinDate()
```

This function currently returns November 24th, 2004 as the minimum date.
This is the date that World of Warcraft was launched in the U.S.

Returns:

weekday—Index of the day of the week (starting at 1 = Sunday) (`number`)

month—Index of the month (starting at 1 = January) (`number`) day—Day of the month (number)

year—Year (full four-digit year) (number)

CalendarGetMinHistoryDate

Returns the earliest date for which information about past player events is available.

```
weekday, month, day, year = CalendarGetMinHistoryDate()
```

Applies to events created by the player, invites the player accepted, and guild events or announcements. Currently, the default UI only shows past events from up to two weeks before the current date.

Returns:

weekday—Index of the day of the week (starting at 1 = Sunday) (number)

month—Index of the month (starting at 1 = January) (number)

day—Day of the month (number)

year—Year (full four-digit year) (number)

CalendarGetMonth

Returns information about a calendar month.

```
month, year, numDays, firstWeekday = CalendarGetMonth([monthOffset])
```

Arguments:

monthOffset (optional)—Month to query relative to the calendar's currently displayed month (i.e. 0 for current month, 1 for next month, -1 for previous month). Defaults to the calendar's current month if omitted. (number)

Returns:

month—Index of the month (starting at 1 = January) (number)

year—Year (full four-digit year) (number)

numDays—Number of days in the month (number)

firstWeekday—Index of the weekday (starting at 1 = Sunday) for the first day of the month (number)

CalendarGetMonthNames

Returns a list of localized month names.

```
... = CalendarGetMonthNames()
```

Returns:

...—A list of localized month names in calendar order (i.e. 1 = January) (list)

CalendarGetNumDayEvents

Returns the number of calendar events on a given day.

```
numEvents = CalendarGetNumDayEvents(monthOffset, day)
```

Arguments:

monthOffset—Month to query relative to the calendar's currently displayed month (i.e. 0 for current month, 1 for next month, -1 for previous month) (number)

day—Day of the month to query (number)

Returns:

numEvents—Number of events on the given day (number)

CalendarGetNumPendingInvites

Returns the number of calendar invitations to which the player has yet to respond.

```
numInvites = CalendarGetNumPendingInvites()
```

Returns:

numInvites—Number of pending calendar invitations (number)

CalendarGetRaidInfo

Returns information about a raid lockout or scheduled raid reset event.

```
title, calendarType, raidID, hour, minute, difficulty = ↵
CalendarGetRaidInfo(monthOffset, day, index)
```

Information can only be retrieved for events which might be visible in the calendar's current month—i.e. those in the current month as well as those in (roughly) the last week of the previous month and (roughly) the first two weeks of the following month. To reliably retrieve information for events outside the calendar's current month, first change the calendar's month with CalendarSetMonth.

Arguments:

monthOffset—Month to query relative to the calendar's currently displayed month (i.e. 0 for current month, 1 for next month, -1 for previous month) (number)

day—Day of the month to query (number)

index—Index of an event on the given day (from 1 to CalendarGetNum DayEvents()) (number)

Returns:

title—Title displayed for the event (number)

calendarType—Token identifying the type of event (string)

■ RAID_LOCKOUT—Indicates when one of the player's saved instances resets

■ RAID_RESET—Indicates scheduled reset times for major raid instances

raidID—ID number of the instance to which the player is saved, or 0 if not applicable (number)

hour—Hour part of the time at which the instance resets (on a 24-hour clock) (number)

minute—Minute part of the time at which the instance resets (number)

difficulty—Difficulty of the dungeon or raid instance associated with the event (number)

■ 1—Normal

■ 2—Heroic

CalendarGetWeekdayNames

Returns a list of localized weekday names.

```
... = CalendarGetWeekdayNames()
```

Returns:

. . . —A list of localized weekday names in calendar order (i.e. 1 = Sunday)
(list)

CalendarIsActionPending

Returns whether an update to calendar information is in progress.

```
isPending = CalendarIsActionPending()
```

Returns true while the client is synchronizing its calendar information from the
server; e.g. after calling CalendarOpenEvent, CalendarAddEvent, or Calendar
UpdateEvent. During such periods, using other calendar API functions to
query or change event information may not have valid or expected results.

Returns:

isPending—True if an update to calendar information is in progress; otherwise
false (boolean)

CalendarMassInviteArenaTeam

Repopulates the current event's invite list with members of one of the player's
arena teams.

```
CalendarMassInviteArenaTeam(index)
```

Clears any invites already listed. Can only be used for events not yet created
(i.e. saved to the calendar).

Arguments:

index—Index of an arena team type (number)

- 1—2v2 team
- 2—3v3 team
- 3—5v5 team

CalendarMassInviteGuild

Repopulates the selected event's invite list with members of the player's guild.

```
CalendarMassInviteGuild(minLevel, maxLevel, rank)
```

Clears any invites already listed. Can only be used for events not yet created
(i.e. saved to the calendar).

Arguments:

minLevel—Lowest level of characters to invite (number)

maxLevel—Highest level of characters to invite (number)

rank—Lowest guild rank of characters to invite (number)

CalendarNewEvent

Creates a new event and selects it for viewing/editing.

CalendarNewGuildAnnouncement

Creates a new guild announcement and selects it for viewing/editing.

Guild announcements are visible to all guild members but do not allow
signups or invitations.

CalendarNewGuildEvent

Creates a new guild event and selects it for viewing/editing.

Guild events are visible to all guild members and allow members to sign up (or non-members to be invited).

CalendarOpenEvent

Selects a calendar event for viewing/editing.

`CalendarOpenEvent(monthOffset, day, index)`

Arguments:

`monthOffset`—Month to query relative to the calendar's currently displayed month (i.e. 0 for current month, 1 for next month, -1 for previous month) (`number`)

`day`—Day of the month to query (`number`)

`index`—Index of an event on the given day (from 1 to CalendarGetNum DayEvents()) (`number`)

CalendarRemoveEvent

Removes the selected event invitation from the player's calendar or removes the player from the selected guild event's signup list.

NOTE: May disconnect the player if called when the selected calendar event is not a received invitation or a guild event.

CalendarSetAbsMonth

Set's the calendar's month to an absolute date.

`CalendarSetAbsMonth(month [, year])`

Arguments:

`month`—Index of the month (starting at 1 = January) (`number`)

`year` (optional)—Year (full four-digit year); uses current year if omitted (`number`)

CalendarSetMonth

Sets the calendar's month relative to its current month.

`CalendarSetMonth(monthOffset)`

Arguments:

`monthOffset`—Month containing an event relative to the calendar's currently displayed month (`number`)

- `-1`—Month preceding the calendar's current month
- `0`—The calendar's current month (i.e. same month as CalendarGetMonth())
- `1`—Month after the calendar's current month

CalendarUpdateEvent

Saves changes made to the selected event.

Until this function is called, changes made to an event will not be saved—they will not propagate to guild members or invitees, and the event will revert to its previous state if the player closes the calendar, reloads the UI, or goes to view or edit another event.

Only applies to existing events; for newly created events use `CalendarAdd Event()` once the event's attributes and initial invite list are set.

CallCompanion

Summons a non-combat pet or mount.

```
CallCompanion("type", index)
```

If called referencing the current non-combat pet, dismisses it. Does nothing if given an index greater than `GetNumCompanions(type)`.

Arguments:

`type`—Type of companion (string)

- `CRITTER`—A non-combat pet
- `MOUNT`—A mount

`index`—Index of a companion (between 1 and `GetNumCompanions(type)`) (number)

| Protected | CameraOrSelectOrMoveStart

Begins camera movement or selection (equivalent to left-clicking in the 3-D world).

After calling this function (i.e. while the left mouse button is held), cursor movement rotates the camera. Final results vary by context and are determined when calling `CameraOrSelectOrMoveStop()` (i.e. releasing the left mouse button).

Used by the `CAMERAORSELECTORMOVE` binding (not customizable in the default UI), which is bound to the left mouse button by default.

| Protected | CameraOrSelectOrMoveStop

Ends action initiated by `CameraOrSelectOrMoveStart`.

```
CameraOrSelectOrMoveStop(isSticky)
```

After calling this function (i.e. releasing the left mouse button), camera movement stops and normal cursor movement resumes. If the cursor has not moved significantly since calling `CameraOrSelectOrMoveStart()` (i.e. pressing the left mouse button) and is over a unit, that unit becomes the player's target; if the cursor has not moved significantly and is not over a unit, clears the player's target unless the "Sticky Targeting" option is enabled (i.e. the "deselectOnClick" CVar is 0).

Used by the `CAMERAORSELECTORMOVE` binding (not customizable in the default UI), which is bound to the left mouse button by default.

Arguments:

`isSticky`—If 1, the camera will remain static until cancelled. Otherwise, the camera will pan back to be directly behind the character (1nil)

CameraZoomIn

Zooms the camera in by a specified distance.

```
CameraZoomIn(distance)
```

The max distance of the camera is set in the Interface Options screen, and the maximum distance allowed is enforced by this setting, and the game client. Depending on the setting, this is between 15.0 and 24.0 in the current version of the client.

Arguments:

distance—The distance to zoom in (number)

CameraZoomOut

Zooms the camera out by a specified distance.

```
CameraZoomOut(distance)
```

This function is used to zoom the camera out. The max distance of the camera is set in the Interface Options screen, and the maximum distance allowed is enforced by this setting, and the game client. Depending on the setting, this is between 15.0 and 24.0 in the current version of the client.

Arguments:

distance—The distance to zoom out (number)

CanAlterSkin

Lets you check if the player can change their skin color.

```
canAlter = CanAlterSkin()
```

Returns true if the player can change their skin color while using the barbershop.

Returns:

canAlter—Can the player change skin color (boolean)

CanCancelAuction

Returns whether one of the player's auctions can be canceled.

```
canCancel = CanCancelAuction(index)
```

Generally, non-cancelable auctions are those which have completed but for which payment has not yet been delivered.

Arguments:

index—Index of an auction in the "owner" listing (number)

Returns:

canCancel—1 if the auction can be canceled; otherwise nil (1nil)

CanComplainChat

Returns whether a chat message can be reported as spam.

```
canComplain = CanComplainChat(lineID)
```

Arguments:

lineID—Unique identifier of a chat message (11th argument received with the corresponding CHAT_MSG event) (number)

Returns:

canComplain—1 if the player can report the given chat message as spam; otherwise nil (1nil)

CanComplainInboxItem

Returns whether a mail message can be reported as spam.

```
complain = CanComplainInboxItem(mailID)
```

Returns nil for messages from Game Masters or friends, as well as for messages generated by the game itself (Auction House mail, quest messages from NPCs, etc).

As with most mail functions, only provides valid information if used while the mail UI is open (between the MAIL_SHOW and MAIL_CLOSE events).

Arguments:

mailID—Index of a message in the player's inbox (between 1 and GetInboxNumItems()) (number)

Returns:

complain—1 if the inbox item can be reported as spam; otherwise nil (1nil)

CanEditGuildEvent

Returns whether the player is allowed to edit guild-wide calendar events.

```
canEdit = CanEditGuildEvent()
```

Returns:

canEdit—1 if the player can create or edit guild calendar events, otherwise nil (1nil)

CanEditGuildInfo

Returns whether the player is allowed to edit the guild information text.

```
canEdit = CanEditGuildInfo()
```

This text appears when clicking the "Guild Information" button in the default UI's Guild window.

Returns:

canEdit—1 if the player can edit the guild information; otherwise nil (1nil)

CanEditGuildTabInfo

Returns whether the player is allowed to edit a guild bank tab's iinformation.

```
canEdit = CanEditGuildTabInfo(tab)
```

Arguments:

tab—Index of a guild bank tab (between 1 and GetNumGuildBankTabs()) (number)

Returns:

canEdit—1 if the player can edit the guild bank tab; otherwise nil (1nil)

CanEditMOTD

Returns whether the player is allowed to edit the guild Message of the Day.

```
canEdit = CanEditMOTD()
```

Returns:

canEdit—1 if the player can edit the guild MOTD, otherwise nil (1nil)

CanEditOfficerNote

Returns whether the player is allowed to edit guild officer notes.

```
canEdit = CanEditOfficerNote()
```
Returns:

canEdit—1 if the player can edit officer notes; otherwise nil (1nil)

CanEditPublicNote

Returns whether the player is allowed to edit guild public notes.

```
canEdit = CanEditPublicNote()
```
Returns:

canEdit—1 if the player can edit public notes, otherwise nil (1nil)

CanEjectPassengerFromSeat

Returns whether the player can eject the occupant of a seat in the player's vehicle.

```
canEject = CanEjectPassengerFromSeat(seat)
```
Arguments:

seat—Index of a seat in the player's vehicle (number)

Returns:

canEject—True if the player can eject the seat's occupant; false if the player cannot eject the occupant or if the seat is empty (boolean)

CanExitVehicle

Returns whether the player is in a vehicle.

```
canExit = CanExitVehicle()
```

Used in the default UI to determine whether to show the "Leave Vehicle" button while controlling siege vehicles, turrets, and certain special mounts and quest entities.

Returns:

canExit—1 if the player is in a vehicle and can exit; otherwise nil (1nil)

CanGrantLevel

Returns whether the player can give levels to a Recruit-a-Friend partner.

```
canGrant = CanGrantLevel("unit")
```
Arguments:

unit—Unit to gift a level (string, unitID)

Returns:

canGrant—1 if the player can grant a level to the unit; otherwise nil (1nil)

CanGuildBankRepair

Returns whether the player is allowed to pay for repairs using guild bank funds.

```
canRepair = CanGuildBankRepair()
```
Returns:

canRepair—1 if the player can use guild bank funds for repair; otherwise nil (1nil)

CanGuildDemote

Returns whether the player is allowed to demote lower ranked guild members.

```
canDemote = CanGuildDemote()
```

Returns:

canDemote—1 if the player can demote lower ranked guild members; otherwise nil (1nil)

CanGuildInvite

Returns whether the player is allowed to invite new members to his or her guild.

```
canInvite = CanGuildInvite()
```

Returns:

canInvite—1 if the player can invite members to their guild, otherwise nil (1nil)

CanGuildPromote

Returns whether the player is allowed to promote other guild members.

```
canPromote = CanGuildPromote()
```

The player may promote other members only up to the rank below his or her own.

Returns:

canPromote—1 if the player can promote other guild members; otherwise nil (1nil)

CanGuildRemove

Returns whether the player is allowed to remove members from his or her guild.

```
canRemove = CanGuildRemove()
```

The player may only remove lower ranked members from the guild.

Returns:

canRemove—1 if the player can remove a member from their guild, otherwise nil (1nil)

CanHearthAndResurrectFromArea

Returns whether the player is in a world PvP zone offering an exit option.

```
status = CanHearthAndResurrectFromArea()
```

Used by the default UI to show the MiniMapBattlefieldFrame and provide a menu option for leaving if the player is in a world PvP combat zone (i.e. Wintergrasp).

Returns:

status—1 if in a world PvP zone with an exit option; otherwise nil (1nil)

CanInspect

Returns whether a unit can be inspected.

```
canInspect = CanInspect("unit", showError)
```

Returns `nil` if the unit is out of inspect range, if the unit is an NPC, or if the unit is flagged for PvP combat and hostile to the player.

Arguments:

unit—A unit to inspect (`string`, unitID)

showError—`True` to fire a `UI_ERROR_MESSAGE` event (causing the default UI to display an error message) if the unit cannot be inspected; otherwise `false` (`boolean`)

Returns:

canInspect—1 if the unit can be inspected; otherwise `nil` (`1nil`)

CanJoinBattlefieldAsGroup

Returns whether the battleground for which the player is queueing supports joining as a group.

```
canGroupJoin = CanJoinBattlefieldAsGroup()
```

Returns:

canGroupJoin—1 if the currently displayed battlefield supports joining as a group (`1nil`)

CanMerchantRepair

Returns whether the vendor with whom the player is currently interacting can repair equipment.

```
canRepair = CanMerchantRepair()
```

Returns:

canRepair—1 if the vendor can repair equipment; otherwise `nil` (`1nil`)

CanQueueForWintergrasp

Returns whether the player can queue for Wintergrasp.

```
canQueue = CanQueueForWintergrasp()
```

Returns:

canQueue—Can the player queue for Wintergrasp (`boolean`)

CanSendAuctionQuery

Returns whether the player can perform an auction house query.

```
canQuery, canMassQuery = CanSendAuctionQuery("list")
```

All auction query types are throttled, preventing abuse of the server by clients sending too many queries in short succession. Normal queries can be sent once every few seconds; mass queries return all results in the auction house instead of one "page" at a time, and can only be sent once every several minutes.

Arguments:

list—Type of auction listing (`string`)

- bidder—Auctions the player has bid on
- list—Auctions the player can browse and bid on or buy out
- owner—Auctions the player placed

Returns:

canQuery—1 if the player can submit an auction query; otherwise nil (1nil)

canMassQuery—1 if the player can submit a mass auction query; otherwise nil (1nil)

CanSendLFGQuery

Returns whether the player can perform a given LFM query.

canSend = CanSendLFGQuery(type, index)

LFM requests are throttled, preventing abuse of the server by clients sending too many queries in short succession. The server may block repeat requests for the same query parameters while allowing requests with different parameters—checking this function before calling LFGQuery() verifies whether the specific query parameters are currently allowed.

Arguments:

type—Index of an LFG query type (in the list returned by GetLFGTypes()) (number)

index—Index of an LFG entry (in the list returned by GetLFGTypeEntries (type)) (number)

Returns:

canSend—true if the player can submit a LFG query for the given type/index, otherwise false (boolean)

CanShowAchievementUI

Returns whether the Achievements UI should be enabled.

canShow = CanShowAchievementUI()

Used by the default UI to determine whether to show or hide the menu button for Achievements (as it also does for Talents); currently always returns true.

Returns:

canShow—true if the Achievements UI should be enabled, otherwise false (boolean)

CanShowResetInstances

Returns whether the player can reset instances.

canResetInstances = CanShowResetInstances()

Used to determine whether to display the "Reset Instance" option in the unit popup menu for the player.

Only instances to which the player is not saved may be reset (i.e. normal 5-man dungeons, not heroic dungeons or raids), and only by a solo player or group leader.

Returns:

canResetInstances—1 if the player can currently reset instances; otherwise nil (1nil)

CanSignPetition

Returns whether the player can sign the currently offered petition.

```
canSign = CanSignPetition()
```

Petitions can only be signed once per account, rather than once per character.

Returns:

canSign—1 if the player can sign the offered petition; otherwise nil (1nil)

CanSummonFriend

Returns whether a unit can be summoned via Recruit-a-Friend.

```
canSummon = CanSummonFriend("name") or CanSummonFriend("unit")
```

Indicates whether the target unit is currently summonable, not just whether that unit's account is linked to the player's via the Recruit-A-Friend program.

Arguments:

name—Exact name of a player to summon (string)

unit—A unit to summon (string, unitID)

Returns:

canSummon—1 if the unit can be summoned, otherwise nil (1nil)

CanSwitchVehicleSeat

Returns whether the player can change vehicle seats.

```
canSwitch = CanSwitchVehicleSeat()
```

Tells you if the player can switch seats in general, whereas UnitVehicleSeatInfo() tells you if the player can switch into a specific seat.

Returns:

canSwitch—Can the player change vehicle seats (boolean)

Example:

```
local controlType, occupantName, occupantRealm, canEject, ↵
canSwitchSeats = UnitVehicleSeatInfo("player", 1)
if( CanSwitchVehicleSeat() and canSwitchSeats ) then
  print("You can switch to seat #1!")
end
```

CanSwitchVehicleSeats

Returns whether the player is in a vehicle with multiple seats.

```
canSwitch = CanSwitchVehicleSeats()
```

Returns:

canSwitch—1 if the player can switch seats; otherwise nil (1nil)

CanUseEquipmentSets

Returns whether the player has enabled the equipment manager.

```
enabled = CanUseEquipmentSets()
```

Despite the name, this returns true when the player has enabled the use of the equipment manager through the interface or CVars.

Returns:

enabled—Has the player enable the equipment manager (boolean)

CanViewOfficerNote

Returns whether the player is allowed to view guild officer notes.

canView = CanViewOfficerNote()

Returns:

canView—1 if the player can view officer notes, otherwise nil (1nil)

CanWithdrawGuildBankMoney

Returns whether the player is allowed to withdraw money from the guild bank.

canWithdraw = CanWithdrawGuildBankMoney()

Returns:

canWithdraw—1 if the player can withdraw money from the guild bank; otherwise nil (1nil)

CancelAreaSpiritHeal

Declines the next upcoming periodic resurrection from a battleground spirit healer.

Usable in response to the AREA_SPIRIT_HEALER_IN_RANGE event which fires when the player's ghost is near a battleground spirit healer.

> Confirmation

CancelAuction

Cancels an auction created by the player.

CancelAuction(index)

When canceling an auction, the deposit amount is not refunded.

Arguments:

index—Index of an auction in the "owner" listing (number)

CancelBarberShop

Exits a barber shop session.

Causes the player character to stand up, returning to the normal world, and fires the BARBER_SHOP_CLOSE event. Any style changes already paid for (with ApplyBarberShopStyle()) are kept; any changes since are discarded.

CancelDuel

Cancels a proposed duel, or declines an offered duel.

CancelItemTempEnchantment

Cancels a temporary weapon enchant.

CancelItemTempEnchantment(slot)

Examples of temporary enchants include mana oils, sharpening stones, and Shaman weapon enhancements.

Arguments:

slot—1 to cancel the mainhand item enchant, 2 to cancel the offhand item enchant (number)

CancelLogout

Cancels a pending logout or quit.

Only has effect if logout or quit is pending (following the `PLAYER_CAMPING` or `PLAYER_QUITING` event).

CancelPendingEquip

Cancels equipping a bind-on-equip item.

```
CancelPendingEquip(index)
```

When the player attempts to equip a bind-on-equip item, the default UI displays a dialog warning that equipping the item will cause it to become soulbound; this function is called when canceling that dialog.

Arguments:

index—Index of a pending equip warning; currently always 0 as only one equip warning will be given at a time (number)

CancelPendingLFG

Cancels active LFG searches, removing the player from the LFG queue and declining any automatic group invitations.

CancelShapeshiftForm

Cancels the current shapeshift form.

Unlike other Shapeshift APIs, this function refers specifically to shapeshifting; therefore including some abilities not found on the default UI's ShapeshiftBar and excluding some which are. For example, cancels shaman Ghost Wolf form and druid shapeshifts but not warrior stances, paladin auras, or rogue stealth.

CancelSummon

Declines an offered summons.

Usable between when the `CONFIRM_SUMMON` event fires (due to a summoning spell cast by another player) and when the value returned by `GetSummonConfirmTimeLeft()` reaches zero.

CancelTrade

Cancels a trade in progress.

Can be used if either party has accepted the trade, but not once both have.

CancelTradeAccept

Cancels the player's acceptance of a trade.

If the player has accepted the trade but the target has not, reverts the player to the pre-acceptance state but does not end the trade.

CancelUnitBuff

Cancels a buff on the player.

```
CancelUnitBuff("unit", index [, "filter"]) or ↵
CancelUnitBuff("unit", "name" [, "rank" [, "filter"]])
```

Arguments:

unit—A unit to query (only valid for 'player') (string, unitID)

index—Index of an aura to query (number)

name—Name of an aura to query (string)

rank (optional)—Secondary text of an aura to query (often a rank; e.g. "Rank 7") (string)

filter (optional)—A list of filters to use separated by the pipe '|' character; e.g. "RAID|PLAYER" will query group buffs cast by the player (string)

- CANCELABLE—Query auras that can be cancelled
- HARMFUL—Query debuffs only
- HELPFUL—Query buffs only
- NOT_CANCELABLE—Query auras that cannot be cancelled
- PLAYER—Query auras the player has cast
- RAID—Query auras the player can cast on party/raid members (as opposed to self buffs)

| Protected | **CastPetAction** |

Casts a pet action on a specific target.

```
CastPetAction(index [, "unit"])
```

Arguments:

index—Index of a pet action button (between 1 and NUM_PET_ACTION_SLOTS) (number)

unit (optional)—A unit to be used as target for the action (string, unitID)

| Protected | **CastShapeshiftForm** |

Casts an ability on the stance/shapeshift bar.

```
CastShapeshiftForm(index)
```

Arguments:

index—Index of an ability on the stance/shapeshift bar (between 1 and GetNumShapeshiftForms()) (number)

| Protected | **CastSpell** |

Casts a spell from the spellbook.

```
CastSpell(id, "bookType")
```

Only protected (i.e. usable only by the Blizzard UI) if the given id corresponds to a spell which can be cast (not a passive spell) and is not a trade skill; can be used by addons to cast the "spells" that open trade skill windows.

Arguments:

id—Index of a spell in the spellbook (number, spellbookID)

bookType—Type of spellbook (string)

- pet—The pet's spellbook
- spell—The player's spellbook

| Protected | **CastSpellByID** |

Casts a spell specified by id (optionally on a specified unit).

```
CastSpellByID(spellID [, "target"])
```

Only protected (i.e. usable only by the Blizzard UI) if the given spell is castable (not passive) and is not a trade skill; can be used by addons to cast the "spells" that open trade skill windows.

Arguments:

spellID—ID of the spell to cast (number, spellID)

target (optional)—A unit to target with the spell (string, unitID)

| Protected |

CastSpellByName

Casts a spell specified by name (optionally on a specified unit).

```
CastSpellByName("name" [, "target"])
```

Only protected (i.e. usable only by the Blizzard UI) if the given spell is castable (not passive) and is not a trade skill; can be used by addons to cast the "spells" that open trade skill windows.

Arguments:

name—Name of a spell to cast (string)

target (optional)—A unit to target with the spell (string, unitID)

| No Combat |

ChangeActionBarPage

Changes the current action bar page.

```
ChangeActionBarPage(page)
```

Arguments:

page—The action bar page to change to (number)

ChangeChatColor

Changes the color associated with a chat message type.

```
ChangeChatColor("messageGroup", red, green, blue)
```

Arguments:

messageGroup—Token identifying a message type (string, chatMsgType)

red—Red component of the color value (0.0 - 1.0) (number)

green—Red component of the color value (0.0 - 1.0) (number)

blue—Red component of the color value (0.0 - 1.0) (number)

ChannelBan

Bans a character from a chat channel.

```
ChannelBan("channel", "fullname")
```

Has no effect unless the player is a moderator of the given channel

Arguments:

channel—Name of the channel (string)

fullname—Name of the character to be banned (string)

ChannelInvite

Invites a character to join a chat channel.

```
ChannelInvite("channel", "name")
```

Arguments:

channel—Name of a channel (string)

name—Name of a character to invite (string)

ChannelKick

Removes a player from the channel.

```
ChannelKick("channel", "fullname")
```

Has no effect unless the player is a moderator of the given channel

Arguments:

channel—Name of the channel (string)

fullname—Name of the character to kick (string)

ChannelModerator

Grants a character moderator status in a chat channel.

```
ChannelModerator("channel", "fullname")
```

Has no effect unless the player is the owner of the given channel

Arguments:

channel—Name of the channel (string)

fullname—Name of the character to promote to moderator (string)

ChannelMute

Grants a character ability to speak in a moderated chat channel.

```
ChannelMute("channelName", "name") or ChannelMute(channelId, "name")
```

Arguments:

channelName—Name of a channel (string)

channelId—Index of a channel (number)

name—Name of a character to mute (string)

ChannelSilenceAll

Silences a character for chat and voice on a channel.

```
ChannelSilenceAll("channelName", ["unit"] or ["name"]) or
ChannelSilenceAll(channelId, ["unit"] or ["name"]) or
ChannelSilenceAll(["channelName"] or [channelId], "unit") or
ChannelSilenceAll(["channelName"] or [channelId], "name")
```

Arguments:

channelName—Name of a channel (string)

channelId—Index of a channel (number)

unit—Unit to silence (string, unitID)

name—Name of a character to silence (string)

ChannelSilenceVoice

Silences the given character for voice chat on the channel.

```
ChannelSilenceVoice("channelName", ["unit"] or ["name"]) or
ChannelSilenceVoice(channelId, ["unit"] or ["name"]) or
```

```
ChannelSilenceVoice(["channelName"] or [channelId], "unit") or
ChannelSilenceVoice(["channelName"] or [channelId], "name")
```

Only a raid/party/battleground leader or assistant can silence a player.

Arguments:

channelName—Name of a channel (string)

channelId—Index of a channel (number)

unit—Unit to silence (string, unitID)

name—Name of a character to silence (string)

ChannelToggleAnnouncements

Enables or disables printing of join/leave announcements for a channel.

```
ChannelToggleAnnouncements("channel")
```

Arguments:

channel—Name of the channel for which to enable or disable announcements (string)

ChannelUnSilenceAll

Unsilences a character for chat and voice on a channel.

```
ChannelUnSilenceAll("channelName", ["unit"] or ["name"]) or
ChannelUnSilenceAll(channelId, ["unit"] or ["name"]) or
ChannelUnSilenceAll(["channelName"] or [channelId], "unit") or
ChannelUnSilenceAll(["channelName"] or [channelId], "name")
```

Arguments:

channelName—Name of a channel (string)

channelId—Index of a channel (number)

unit—Unit to unsilence (string, unitID)

name—Name of a character to unsilence (string)

ChannelUnSilenceVoice

Unsilences a character on a chat channel.

```
ChannelUnSilenceVoice("channelName", ["unit"] or ["name"]) or
ChannelUnSilenceVoice(channelId, ["unit"] or ["name"]) or
ChannelUnSilenceVoice(["channelName"] or [channelId], "unit") or
ChannelUnSilenceVoice(["channelName"] or [channelId], "name")
```

Arguments:

channelName—Name of a channel (string)

channelId—Index of a channel (number)

unit—Unit to unsilence (string, unitID)

name—Name of a character to unsilence (string)

ChannelUnban

Lifts the ban preventing a character from joining a chat channel.

```
ChannelUnban("channel", "fullname")
```

Has no effect unless the player is a moderator of the given channel

Arguments:

channel—Name of the channel (string)

fullname—Name of the character to for which to lift the ban (string)

ChannelUnmoderator

Revokes moderator status from a character on a chat channel.

```
ChannelUnmoderator("channel", "fullname")
```

Has no effect unless the player is the owner of the given channel

Arguments:

channel—Name of the channel (string)

fullname—Name of the character to demote from moderator (string)

ChannelUnmute

Removes a character's ability to speak in a moderated chat channel.

```
ChannelUnmute("channelName", "name") or ChannelUnmute(channelId, "name")
```

Arguments:

channelName—Name of a channel (string)

channelId—Index of a channel (number)

name—Name of a character to unmute (string)

ChannelVoiceOff

Disables voice chat in a channel.

```
ChannelVoiceOff("channel") or ChannelVoiceOff(channelIndex)
```

Arguments:

channel—Name of a channel (string)

channelIndex—Index of a channel (number)

ChannelVoiceOn

Enables voice chat in a channel.

```
ChannelVoiceOn("channel") or ChannelVoiceOn(channelIndex)
```

Arguments:

channel—Name of a channel (string)

channelIndex—Index of a channel (number)

Blizzard UI | **ChatFrame_AddMessageEventFilter**

Adds a function to filter or alter messages to the chat display system.

```
ChatFrame_AddMessageEventFilter("event", filter)
```

The filter function will be called each time a message is sent to one of the default chat frames (ChatFrame1, ChatFrame2, ..., ChatFrame7). The function will be passed the chat frame object that the message is being added to, along with the event that caused the messages to be added, and the arguments to that event.

A filter function may return `true` if the message should be filtered, or `false` if the message should be displayed. Following this boolean flag, the message can return a list of (possibly) altered arguments to be passed to the next filter function.

See examples for details.

Arguments:

`event`—A `CHAT_MSG_` Event for which the filter should be used (`string`)

`filter`—A function to filter incoming messages (`function`)

Examples:

```
-- Example #1
-- a filter to hide all yelled messaged containing certain text
function noGoldSpam(self,event,msg)
 local badWords = {"gold","%$","www","%.com","%.net","%.org"}
 local matchCount = 0;
 for _, word in ipairs(badWords) do
  if (string.match(msg, word)) then
   matchCount = matchCount + 1;
  end
 end
 if (matchCount > 1) then
  return true;
 else
  return false;
 end
end
ChatFrame_AddMessageEventFilter("CHAT_MSG_YELL",noGoldSpam)

-- Example #2
-- a filter to display icons next to item links in loot messages
function addLootIcons(self, event, msg, ...)
 local _, fontSize = GetChatWindowInfo(self:GetID())
 local function iconForLink(link)
  local texture = GetItemIcon(link)
  return "\124T"..texture..":"..fontSize.."\124t"..link
 end
 msg = string.gsub(msg, "(\124c%x+\124Hitem:.-\124h\124r)", iconForLink)
 return false, msg, ...
end
ChatFrame_AddMessageEventFilter("CHAT_MSG_LOOT", addLootIcons)
```

Blizzard UI

ChatFrame_GetMessageEventFilters

Returns the list of filters registered for a chat event.

`filterTable = ChatFrame_GetMessageEventFilters("event")`

See `ChatFrame_AddMessageEventFilter()` for details about chat message filters.

Arguments:

`event`—A `CHAT_MSG_` Event (`string`)

Returns:

filterTable—A table containing any filters set for the given event, with numeric keys corresponding to the order in which filters were registered (table)

Blizzard UI **ChatFrame_RemoveMessageEventFilter**

Removes a previously set chat message filter.

ChatFrame_RemoveMessageEventFilter("event", filter)

See ChatFrame_AddMessageEventFilter() for details about chat message filters.

Arguments:

event—CHAT_MSG_ Event from which to remove a filter (string)

filter—A filter function registered for the event (function)

CheckBinderDist

Returns whether the player is in range of an NPC that can set the Hearthstone location.

inRange = CheckBinderDist()

Usable following the CONFIRM_BINDER event which fires when the player speaks to an Innkeeper (or similar) NPC and chooses to set his or her Hearthstone location. Used in the default UI to hide the confirmation window for such if the player moves too far away from the NPC.

Returns:

inRange—1 if the player is in range of an NPC that can set the Hearthstone location; otherwise nil (1nil)

CheckInbox

Requests information on the player's mailbox contents from the server.

Information is not returned immediately; the MAIL_INBOX_UPDATE event fires when data becomes available for use by other Mail/Inbox API functions.

CheckInteractDistance

Returns whether the player is close enough to a unit for certain types of interaction.

canInteract = CheckInteractDistance("unit", distIndex)

Arguments:

unit—A unit to query (string, unitID)

distIndex—Number identifying one of the following action types (number)

1—Inspect   3—Duel

2—Trade   4—Follow

Returns:

canInteract—1 if the player is close enough to the other unit to perform the action; otherwise nil (1nil)

CheckReadyCheckTime

Finishes a ready check initiated by the player.

Causes the READY_CHECK_FINISHED event to fire. Only has an effect 30 seconds after starting a ready check.

CheckSpiritHealerDist

Returns whether the player is in range of a spirit healer.

inRange = CheckSpiritHealerDist()

Usable following the CONFIRM_XP_LOSS event which fires upon speaking to a spirit healer while dead and choosing the option to immediately resurrect. Used in the default UI to hide the confirmation window for such if the player moves too far away from the spirit healer.

Returns:

inRange—1 if the player is in range of a spirit healer; otherwise nil (1nil)

CheckTalentMasterDist

Returns whether the player is in range of an NPC that can reset talents.

inRange = CheckTalentMasterDist()

Usable following the CONFIRM_TALENT_WIPE event which fires when the player speaks to a trainer NPC and chooses to reset his or her talents. Used in the default UI to hide the confirmation window for such if the player moves too far away from the NPC.

Returns:

inRange—1 if the player is in range of a talent trainer; otherwise nil (1nil)

ClearAchievementComparisonUnit

Disables comparing achievements/statistics with another player.

ClearCursor

Clears any contents attached to the cursor.

If the cursor contains an item picked up from inventory (equipment slots) or a container, the item returns to its point of origin and the inventory or container slot is unlocked. (To destroy an item, see DeleteCursorItem()).

If the cursor contains an action, that action is deleted (but not the spell, item, macro, etc that it represents).

If the cursor contains any other data type, nothing happens other than the cursor being reverted to its default state; picking up such objects has no effect on their points of origin.

`Protected` **ClearFocus**

Clears the player's focus unit.

ClearInspectPlayer

Ends inspection of another character.

After this function is called, data about the inspected unit may not be available or valid.

Used in the default UI when the InspectFrame is hidden.

ClearLFGAutojoin

Disables the option to automatically join a group matching current LFG criteria.

ClearLFMAutofill

Disables the option to automatically fill the player's group when Looking for More.

ClearLookingForGroup

Cancels active LFG searches, removing the player from the LFG queue.

ClearLookingForMore

Cancels active LFM searches, removing the player from the LFG queue.

ClearOverrideBindings

Clears any registered override bindings for a given owner.

```
ClearOverrideBindings(owner)
```

An override binding is a temporary key or click binding that can be used to override the default bindings. The bound key will revert to its normal setting once the override has been removed.

Arguments:

owner—A Frame (or other widget) object for which override bindings are registered (table)

Protected **ClearPartyAssignment**

Removes a group role assignment from a member of the player's party or raid.

```
ClearPartyAssignment("assignment" [, "unit"]) or
ClearPartyAssignment("assignment" [, "name" [, exactMatch]])
```

If no unit (or name) is given, removes the role assignment from all members of the party or raid.

Arguments:

assignment—A group role to assign to the unit (string)

■ MAINASSIST—Remove the main assist role

■ MAINTANK—Remove the main tank role

unit (optional)—A unit in the player's party or raid (string, unitID)

name (optional)—Name of a unit in the player's party or raid (string)

exactMatch (optional)—True to check only units whose name exactly matches the name given; false to allow partial matches (boolean)

ClearSendMail

Clears any text, items, or money from the mail message to be sent.

Protected **ClearTarget**

Clears the player's current target.

ClearTutorials

Disables contextual tutorial display.

ClickAuctionSellItemButton

Picks up an item from or puts an item into the "Create Auction" slot.

If the cursor is empty and the slot contains an item, that item is put onto the cursor. If the cursor contains an item and the slot is empty, the item is placed into the slot. If both the cursor and the slot contain items, the contents of the cursor and the slot are exchanged.

Only has effect if the player is interacting with an auctioneer (i.e. between the AUCTION_HOUSE_SHOW and AUCTION_HOUSE_CLOSED events). Causes an error message (UI_ERROR_MESSAGE) if the item on the cursor cannot be put up for auction (e.g. if the item is soulbound).

Example:

```
-- Places the first item in your backpack in the auction house item slot
PickupContainerItem(0, 1)
ClickAuctionSellItemButton()
```

ClickLandmark

Processes a hyperlink associated with a map landmark.

```
ClickLandmark(mapLinkID)
```

Possible landmarks include PvP objectives (both in battlegrounds and in world PvP areas), town and city markers on continent maps, and special markers such as those used during the Scourge Invasion world event. Some landmarks (such as those for towns on a zone map) exist but are not visible in the default UI.

Hyperlinks are not used for any of the landmarks currently in the game; this function does nothing when called with a landmark which does not have a hyperlink.

Arguments:

mapLinkID—Hyperlink ID associated with a map landmark, as retrieved from GetMapLandmarkInfo() (number)

ClickSendMailItemButton

Picks up an item from or puts an item into an attachment slot for sending mail.

```
ClickSendMailItemButton(index, autoReturn)
```

If the cursor is empty and the mail attachment slot contains an item, that item is put onto the cursor. If the cursor contains an item and the slot is empty, the item is placed into the slot. If both the cursor and the slot contain items, the contents of the cursor and the mail attachment slot are exchanged.

Only has effect if the player is interacting with a mailbox (i.e. between the MAIL_SHOW and MAIL_CLOSED events). Causes an error message (UI_ERROR_MESSAGE) if an invalid mail attachment slot is specified or if the item on the cursor cannot be mailed (e.g. if the item is soulbound).

Arguments:

index—Index of a mail attachment slot (between 1 and ATTACHMENTS_MAX _SEND) (number) autoReturn—True to automatically return the item in the given attachment slot to the player's bags; false or omitted to put the item on the cursor (boolean)

Example:

```
-- Places the first item in your backpack in the auction house item slot
PickupContainerItem(0, 1)
ClickSendMailItemButton()
```

ClickSocketButton

Picks up or places a gem in the Item Socketing UI.

```
ClickSocketButton(index)
```

If the Item Socketing UI is open and the cursor contains a socketable gem, places the gem into socket index. If the cursor does not hold an item and socket index is not locked, picks up the gem in that socket.

Only has an effect while the Item Socketing UI is open (i.e. between the SOCKET_INFO_UPDATE and SOCKET_INFO_CLOSE events).

Arguments:

index—Index of a gem socket (between 1 and GetNumSockets()) (number)

Example:

```
-- Put the item in the top left slot of the backpack into the
-- first gem socket
PickupContainerItem(0,1)
ClickSocketButton(1)
```

ClickStablePet

Inspects or moves a pet in the Pet Stable UI.

```
selected = ClickStablePet(index)
```

Action taken depends on cursor contents as well as the index passed:

- If the cursor does not contain a pet, selects the given pet slot.
- If the cursor contains the active pet and index is a stable slot, places the pet into the stable (but not necessarily into the given slot).
- If the cursor contains a stabled pet, and index is 0, makes the stabled pet the active pet (and puts the active pet into the stable).

Arguments:

index—Index of a stable slot (number)

- 0—Active pet
- 1 to NUM_PET_STABLE_SLOTS—A stable slot

Returns:

selected—1 if the function selected a stabled pet, rather than placed a pet in the stable slot (1nil)

ClickTargetTradeButton

Interacts with an item in a slot offered for trade by the target.

```
ClickTargetTradeButton(index)
```

Only meaningful when used with the last (7th) trade slot: if an enchantment-type spell is currently awaiting a target (i.e. the glowing hand cursor is showing), targets the item in the given trade slot for the enchantment. (The enchantment to be applied then shows for both parties in the trade, but is not actually performed until both parties accept the trade.)

Arguments:

index—Index of an item slot on the target's side of the trade window (between 1 and MAX_TRADE_ITEMS) (number)

ClickTradeButton

Picks up an item from or puts an item in a slot offered for trade by the player.

```
ClickTradeButton(index)
```

Results vary by context:

- If an item is on the cursor and no item is in the trade slot, the item is put into the trade slot and the cursor becomes empty
- If no item is on the cursor and an item is in the trade slot, the item is put on the cursor and removed from the trade slot
- If an item is on the cursor and an item is in the trade slot, the item from the cursor is put into the trade slot and the item from the trade slot is put on the cursor
- If both cursor and trade slot are empty, nothing happens

Arguments:

index—Index of an item slot on the player's side of the trade window (between 1 and MAX_TRADE_ITEMS) (number)

Example:

```
-- with the Trade UI already open, puts the item in the first
-- backpack slot into the first trade slot
PickupContainerItem(0,1)
ClickTradeButton(1)
```

CloseArenaTeamRoster

Ends interaction with the Arena Team Roster.

Called in the default UI when closing the Arena Team Roster frame. After this function is called, roster information functions may no longer return valid data.

CloseAuctionHouse

Ends interaction with the Auction House UI.

Causes the AUCTION_HOUSE_CLOSED event to fire, indicating that Auction-related APIs may be unavailable or no longer return valid data.

CloseBankFrame

Ends interaction with the bank.

Causes the BANKFRAME_CLOSED event to fire, indicating that APIs querying bank contents may no longer return valid results.

CloseBattlefield

Ends interaction with the battleground queueing UI.

Causes the BATTLEFIELDS_CLOSED event to fire, indicating that Battlefield queueing-related APIs may no longer have effects or return valid data.

CloseGossip

Ends an NPC "gossip" interaction.

Causes the GOSSIP_CLOSED event to fire, indicating that Gossip APIs may no longer have effects or return valid data.

CloseGuildBankFrame

Ends interaction with the guild bank vault.

Fires the GUILDBANKFRAME_CLOSED event, indicating that APIs related to the Guild Bank vault may no longer have effects or return valid data. (APIs related to guild bank permissions are still usable.)

CloseGuildRegistrar

Ends interaction with a guild registrar.

Fires the GUILD_REGISTRAR_CLOSED event, indicating that guild registrar APIs may no longer have effects or return valid data.

CloseItemText

Ends interaction with a text object or item.

Causes the ITEM_TEXT_CLOSED event to fire, indicating that ItemText APIs are no longer valid.

Called by the default UI when closing the ItemTextFrame, which is used for both readable world objects (books, plaques, gravestones, etc) and readable items (looted books, various quest-related scrolls and parchments, saved mail messages, etc).

CloseLoot

Ends interaction with a lootable corpse or object.

Causes the LOOT_CLOSED event to fire, indicating that Loot APIs may no longer have effects or return valid data.

If the corpse was designated as the player's loot (via the Round Robin, Group Loot, or Need Before Greed loot methods), the corpse's loot becomes available to the rest of the group. If (and only if) the loot was generated from Disenchanting, Prospecting, Milling or similar, all loot items are automatically picked up.

CloseMail

Ends interaction with a mailbox.

Fires the MAIL_CLOSED event, indicating that Mail/Inbox APIs may no longer have effects or return valid data.

CloseMerchant

Ends interaction with a vendor.

Causes the MERCHANT_CLOSED event to fire, indicating that Merchant APIs may no longer have effects or return valid data.

ClosePetStables

Ends use of the Pet Stables UI/API.

Causes the PET_STABLE_CLOSED event to fire, indicating that stables-related APIs are no longer valid.

ClosePetition

Ends interaction with a petition.

Fires the PETITION_CLOSED event, indicating that Petition APIs may no longer have effects or return valid data.

ClosePetitionVendor

Ends interaction with an arena registrar.

Fires the PETITION_VENDOR_CLOSED event, indicating that arena registrar APIs may no longer have effects or return valid data.

CloseQuest

Ends interaction with a questgiver.

Fires the QUEST_FINISHED event, indicating that questgiver-related APIs may no longer have effects or return valid data.

CloseSocketInfo

Ends interaction with the Item Socketing UI, discarding any changes made.

Causes the SOCKET_INFO_CLOSE event to fire, indicating that Socket API functions may no longer have effects or return valid data.

CloseTabardCreation

Ends interaction with the guild tabard creator.

Fires the CLOSE_TABARD_FRAME event, indicating that tabard creation APIs may no longer have effects or return valid data.

CloseTaxiMap

Ends interaction with the Taxi (flight master) UI.

Causes the TAXIMAP_CLOSED event to fire, indicating that Taxi APIs may no longer have effects or return valid data.

CloseTrade

Ends interaction with the Trade UI, canceling any trade in progress.

Causes the TRADE_CLOSED event to fire, indicating that Trade APIs may no longer have effects or return valid data.

CloseTradeSkill

Ends interaction with the Trade Skill UI.

Fires the TRADE_SKILL_CLOSE event, indicating that TradeSkill APIs may no longer have effects or return valid data.

CloseTrainer

Ends interaction with a trainer.

Fires the TRAINER_CLOSED event, indicating that Trainer APIs may no longer have effects or return valid data.

CollapseAllFactionHeaders

Collapses all headers and sub-headers in the Reputation UI.

This function works for both major groups (Classic, Burning Crusade, Wrath of the Lich King, Inactive, etc.) and the sub-groups within them (Alliance Forces, Steamwheedle Cartel, Horde Expedition, Shattrath City, etc.).

CollapseChannelHeader

Collapses a group header in the chat channel listing.

```
CollapseChannelHeader(index)
```

Arguments:

index—Index of a header in the display channel list (between 1 and GetNumDisplayChannels()) (number)

CollapseFactionHeader

Collapses a given faction header or sub-header in the Reputation UI.

```
CollapseFactionHeader(index)
```

Faction headers include both major groups (Classic, Burning Crusade, Wrath of the Lich King, Inactive, etc.) and the sub-groups within them (Alliance Forces, Steamwheedle Cartel, Horde Expedition, Shattrath City, etc.).

Arguments:

index—Index of an entry in the faction list; between 1 and GetNumFactions() (number)

CollapseQuestHeader

Collapses a header in the quest log.

```
CollapseQuestHeader(questIndex)
```

Arguments:

questIndex—Index of a header in the quest log (between 1 and GetNumQuestLogEntries()), or 0 to collapse all headers (number)

CollapseSkillHeader

Collapses a group header in the Skills UI.

```
CollapseSkillHeader(index)
```

If index specifies a group header in the list, the group is collapsed; if it specifies a skill, the header containing the skill is collapsed.

Arguments:

index—Index of an entry in the skills list (between 1 and GetNumSkill Lines()) (number)

CollapseTradeSkillSubClass

Collapses a group header in the trade skill listing.

```
CollapseTradeSkillSubClass(index)
```

Causes an error if index does not refer to a header.

Arguments:

index—Index of a header in the trade skill list (between 1 and
GetNumTradeSkills()) (number)

CollapseTrainerSkillLine

Collapses a group header in the trainer service listing.

```
CollapseTrainerSkillLine(index)
```

Causes a Lua error if the entry is not a header (see
GetTrainerServiceInfo()).

Arguments:

index—Index of a header in the trainer service listing (between 1 and
GetNumTrainerServices()), or 0 to collapse all headers (number)

CombatLogAddFilter

Adds a filter to the combat log system.

```
CombatLogAddFilter("events", "srcGUID", ["destGUID"] or [destMask]) or
CombatLogAddFilter("events", srcMask, ["destGUID"] or [destMask]) or
CombatLogAddFilter("events", ["srcGUID"] or [srcMask], "destGUID") or
CombatLogAddFilter("events", ["srcGUID"] or [srcMask], destMask)
```

Each time this function is called a new filter is added to the combat log system.
Any combat log entry that passes the filter will be fired as a
COMBAT_LOG_EVENT event in order from oldest to newest.

Arguments:

events—Name of a combat log event type to include in the filtered
list, or a comma-separated list of multiple names (string)

srcGUID—GUID of the source unit (string, guid)

srcMask—Bit mask of the source unit (number, bitfield)

destGUID—GUID of the destination unit (string, guid)

destMask—Bit mask of the destination unit (number, bitfield)

CombatLogAdvanceEntry

Advances the "cursor" position used by other CombatLog functions.

```
hasEntry = CombatLogAdvanceEntry(count, ignoreFilter)
```

Information about the entry at the "cursor" position can be retrieved with
CombatLogGetCurrentEntry(). That function then advances the cursor to
the next entry, so calling it repeatedly returns all information in the combat log;
this function can be used to "rewind" the combat log to retrieve information
about earlier events or skip entries without retrieving their information.

Arguments:

count—Number of entries by which to advance the "cursor"; can be negative to
move to a previous entry (number)

ignoreFilter—True to use the entire saved combat log history; false
or omitted to use only events matching the current filter (boolean)

Returns:

hasEntry—1 if an entry exists at the new cursor position; otherwise nil (1nil)

CombatLogClearEntries

Removes all entries from the combat log.

CombatLogGetCurrentEntry

Returns the combat log event information for the current entry and advances to the next entry.

```
timestamp, event, srcGUID, srcName, srcFlags, destGUID, destName, ↵
destFlags, ... = CombatLogGetCurrentEntry([ignoreFilter])
```

See `COMBAT_LOG_EVENT` for details of the event information.

The combat log maintains a "cursor" in the list of entries; this function returns information about the event at the cursor position and advances the cursor to the next entry. Since this function is used by the default UI's combat log display, the cursor position is usually at the end of the log; calling it thus returns nothing. The function `CombatLogSetCurrentEntry()` can be used to "rewind" the combat log cursor, enabling retrieval of information about earlier events.

Arguments:

`ignoreFilter` (optional)—`True` to use the entire saved combat log history; `false` or omitted to use only events matching the current filter (`boolean`)

Returns:

`timestamp`—Time at which the event occurred (same format as `time()` and `date()`, but with millisecond precision) (`number`)

`event`—Type of combat log event (`string`)

`srcGUID`—GUID of the unit that initiated the event (`string`, guid)

`srcName`—Name of the unit that initiated the event (`string`)

`srcFlags`—Flags indicating the nature of the source unit (`number`, bitfield)

`destGUID`—GUID of the unit that was the target of the event (`string`, guid)

`destName`—Name of the unit that was the target of the event (`string`)

`destFlags`—Flags indicating the nature of the target unit (`number`, bitfield)

`...`—Additional arguments specific to the event type (`list`)

CombatLogGetNumEntries

Returns the number of available combat log events.

```
CombatLogGetNumEntries(ignoreFilter)
```

Arguments:

`ignoreFilter`—`True` to use the entire saved combat log history; `false` or omitted to use only events matching the current filter (`boolean`)

CombatLogGetRetentionTime

Returns the amount of time combat log entries are stored.

```
seconds = CombatLogGetRetentionTime()
```

Returns:

`seconds`—Amount of time entries remain available (`number`)

CombatLogResetFilter

Removes any filters applied to the combat log.

CombatLogSetCurrentEntry

Sets the "cursor" position used by other CombatLog functions.

```
CombatLogSetCurrentEntry(index [, ignoreFilter])
```

Information about the entry at the "cursor" position can be retrieved with
`CombatLogGetCurrentEntry()`. That function then advances the cursor to
the next entry, so calling it repeatedly returns all information in the combat log;
this function can be used to "rewind" the combat log to retrieve information
about earlier events.

The argument `index` can be positive or negative: positive indices start at the
beginning of the combat log (oldest events) and count up to the end (newest
events); negative indices start at -1 for the newest event and count backwards
to `-CombatLogGetNumEntries(ignoreFilter)` for the oldest.

Arguments:

`index`—Index of a combat log event (between 1 and `CombatLogGetNum`
`Entries(ignoreFilter)`, or between -1 and `-CombatLogGetNumEntries`
`(ignoreFilter)`) (number)

`ignoreFilter` (optional)—`True` to use the entire saved combat log history;
`false` or omitted to use only events matching the current filter (boolean)

CombatLogSetRetentionTime

Sets the amount of time combat log entries will be stored.

```
CombatLogSetRetentionTime(seconds)
```

Arguments:

`seconds`—The desired time (number)

CombatLog_Object_IsA

Returns whether an entity from the combat log matches a given filter.

```
isMatch = CombatLog_Object_IsA(unitFlags, mask)
```

Arguments:

`unitFlags`—Source or destination unit flags from a combat log entry (number,
bitfield)

`mask`—One of the following global constants: (number, bitfield)

- `COMBATLOG_FILTER_EVERYTHING`—Any entity
- `COMBATLOG_FILTER_FRIENDLY_UNITS`—Entity is a friendly unit
- `COMBATLOG_FILTER_HOSTILE_PLAYERS`—Entity is a hostile player unit
- `COMBATLOG_FILTER_HOSTILE_UNITS`—Entity is a hostile non-player unit
- `COMBATLOG_FILTER_ME`—Entity is the player
- `COMBATLOG_FILTER_MINE`—Entity is a non-unit object belonging to the
  player; e.g. a totem
- `COMBATLOG_FILTER_MY_PET`—Entity is the player's pet
- `COMBATLOG_FILTER_NEUTRAL_UNITS`—Entity is a neutral unit

- `COMBATLOG_FILTER_UNKNOWN_UNITS`—Entity is a unit currently unknown to the WoW client

Returns:

`isMatch`—1 if the entity flags match the given mask (1nil)

CombatTextSetActiveUnit

Sets the main unit for display of floating combat text.

`CombatTextSetActiveUnit(unit)`

Certain types of floating combat text are only displayed for the "active" unit (normally the player): incoming damage, incoming heals, mana/energy /power gains, low health/mana warnings, etc. This function is used by the default UI to allow the player's vehicle to "stand in" for the player for purposes of combat text; using this function with units other than "player" or "vehicle" has no effect.

Arguments:

`unit`—Unit to show main combat text for (`unitid`)

ComplainChat

Reports a chat message as spam.

`ComplainChat(lineID)` or `ComplainChat("name" [, "text"])`

Used in the default UI when right-clicking the name of a player in a chat message and choosing "Report Spam" from the menu.

Arguments:

`lineID`—Unique identifier of a chat message (11th argument received with the corresponding `CHAT_MSG` event) (`number`)

`name`—Name of a player to complain about (`string`)

`text` (optional)—Specific text to complain about (`string`)

ComplainInboxItem

Reports a mail message as spam.

`ComplainInboxItem(mailID)`

Arguments:

`mailID`—Index of a message in the player's inbox (between 1 and `GetInboxNumItems()`) (`number`)

CompleteQuest

Begins turning in a quest to a questgiver.

Usable following the `QUEST_PROGRESS` event in which it is determined whether the player can complete the quest.

Does not complete the quest turn-in process; after calling this function, the `QUEST_COMPLETE` event fires as the questgiver presents rewards (or sometimes only closure to the quest narrative); following that event, the `GetQuest Reward()` function finishes the turn-in.

ConfirmAcceptQuest

Accepts a quest started by another group member.

Usable following the QUEST_ACCEPT_CONFIRM event which fires when another member of the player's party or raid starts certain quests (e.g. escort quests).

| Confirmation | **ConfirmBindOnUse**

Confirms using an item, if using the item causes it to become soulbound.

Usable in response to the USE_BIND_CONFIRM which fires when the player attempts to use a "Bind on Use" item.

ConfirmBinder

Sets the player's Hearthstone to the current location.

Usable in response to the CONFIRM_BINDER event which fires upon speaking to an Innkeeper (or similar NPC) and choosing the Hearthstone option.

| Confirmation | **ConfirmLootRoll**

Confirms the player's intent regarding an item up for loot rolling.

```
ConfirmLootRoll(id, rollType)
```

Usable after the CONFIRM_LOOT_ROLL event fires, warning that an item binds on pickup.

Arguments:

id—Index of an item currently up for loot rolling (as provided in the START_LOOT_ROLL event) (number)

rollType—Type of roll action to perform (number)

- 0—Pass (declines the loot)
- 1—Roll "need" (wins if highest roll)
- 2—Roll "greed" (wins if highest roll and no other member rolls "need")

| Confirmation | **ConfirmLootSlot**

Confirms picking up an item available as loot.

```
ConfirmLootSlot(slot)
```

Usable after the LOOT_BIND_CONFIRM event fires, warning that an item binds on pickup.

Arguments:

slot—Index of a loot slot (between 1 and GetNumLootItems()) (number)

ConfirmReadyCheck

Responds to a ready check.

```
ConfirmReadyCheck(ready)
```

Arguments:

ready—True to report as "ready"; false to report as "not ready" (true)

ConfirmSummon

Accepts an offered summons, teleporting the player to the summoner's location.

Usable between when the CONFIRM_SUMMON event fires (due to a summoning spell cast by another player) and when the value returned by GetSummon ConfirmTimeLeft() reaches zero.

Confirmation

ConfirmTalentWipe

Resets the player's talents.

Usable following the CONFIRM_TALENT_WIPE event which fires when the player speaks to a trainer NPC and chooses to reset his or her talents.

ConsoleAddMessage

Prints text to the debug console.

The debugging console can be activated by launching WoW from the command line with the "-console" option, then pressing the "`" (backtick/tilde) key ingame. Its usefulness outside of Blizzard internal environments is limited.

ConsoleExec

Runs a console command.

```
ConsoleExec("console_command")
```

Used by the default UI to handle /console commands.

Arguments:

console_command—The console command to run (string)

ContainerIDToInventoryID

Returns the inventoryID corresponding to a given containerID.

```
inventoryID = ContainerIDToInventoryID(container)
```

Arguments:

container—Index of one of the player's bags or other containers (number, containerID)

Returns:

inventoryID—Identifier for the container usable with Inventory APIs (number, inventoryID)

Example:

```
-- Switches the player's first bag (the one immediately left of the
-- backpack) with the first bank bag (or puts the bag into the bank
-- if the bank bag slot is empty)
local firstBagSlot = ContainerIDToInventoryID(1)
local firstBankBagSlot = ContainerIDToInventoryID(5)
PickupInventoryItem(firstBagSlot)
PickupInventoryItem(firstBankBagSlot)
```

ContainerRefundItemPurchase

Sells an item purchased with alternate currency back to a vendor.

```
ContainerRefundItemPurchase(container, slot)
```

Items bought with alternate currency (honor points, arena points, or special items such as Emblems of Heroism and Dalaran Cooking Awards) can be returned to a vendor for a full refund, but only within a limited time after the original purchase.

Arguments:

`container`—Index of one of the player's bags or other containers (`number`, containerID)

`slot`—Index of an item slot within the container (`number`, containerSlotID)

ConvertToRaid

Converts a party to a raid.

Only has effect if the player is in a party and the party leader.

CreateFont

Creates a new Font object.

```
fontObject = CreateFont("name")
```

Arguments:

`name`—Name to assign to the newly created object; used both as the name of the object (retrievable with `Font:GetName()`) and as a global variable referencing the object (unless another global by that name already exists) (`string`)

Returns:

`fontObject`—The newly created Font object (`table`)

CreateFrame

Creates a new Frame object.

```
frame = CreateFrame("frameType" [, "name" [, parent [, "template"]]])
```

Arguments:

`frameType`—Type of frame to create; see the widget documentation for details (`string`)

`name` (optional)—Name to assign to the newly created object; used both as the name of the object (retrievable via the GetName method) and as a global variable referencing the object, unless another global by that name already exists (`string`)

`parent` (optional)—Reference to another frame to be the new frame's parent (`table`)

`template` (optional)—Name of a template to be used in creating the frame; if creating a frame from multiple templates, a comma-separated list of names (`string`)

Returns:

`frame`—A reference to the newly created Frame (`table`)

Example:

```
-- creates a generic button in the middle of the screen
mybutton = CreateFrame("Button","mybutton",UIParent, ↵
"UIPanelButtonTemplate")
mybutton:SetPoint("CENTER",0,0)
mybutton:SetWidth(80)
mybutton:SetHeight(22)
```

CreateMacro

Creates a new macro.

```
index = CreateMacro("name", icon, "body", perCharacter)
```

Arguments:

name—Name for the new macro (up to 16 characters); need not be unique, though duplicate names can cause issues for other Macro API functions (string)

icon—Index of a macro icon (between 1 and GetNumMacroIcons()) (number)

body—Body of the macro (up to 255 characters) (string)

perCharacter—1 if the macro should be stored as a character-specific macro; otherwise nil (1nil)

Returns:

index—Index of the newly created macro (number, macroID)

Example:

```
-- Create a character specific macro
local index = CreateMacro("DanceMonkey", 13, "/emote dances like a ↵
monkey!!!", 1)


-- Create a general macro
local index = CreateMacro("Heal", 73, "/cast Flash Heal\n/say Let ↵
the light of Elune cleanse you!")
```

CursorCanGoInSlot

Returns whether the item on the cursor can be equipped in an inventory slot.

```
canBePlaced = CursorCanGoInSlot(slot)
```

Returns nil if the cursor is empty or contains something other than an item.

Arguments:

slot—An inventory slot number, as can be obtained from GetInventorySlotInfo (number, inventoryID)

Returns:

canBePlaced—1 if the item on the cursor can be equipped in the given slot; otherwise nil (1nil)

CursorHasItem

Returns whether an item is on the cursor.

```
hasItem = CursorHasItem()
```

See GetCursorInfo() for more detailed information.

Returns:

hasItem—1 if the cursor is currently holding an item; otherwise nil (1nil)

CursorHasMacro

Returns whether a macro is on the cursor.

```
hasMacro = CursorHasMacro()
```

See GetCursorInfo() for more detailed information.

Returns:

hasMacro—1 if the cursor is currently holding a macro; otherwise nil (1nil)

CursorHasMoney

Returns whether an amount of the player's money is on the cursor.

```
hasMoney = CursorHasMoney()
```

Returns nil if the cursor holds guild bank money. See GetCursorInfo() for more detailed information.

Returns:

hasMoney—1 if the cursor is currently holding an amount of the player's money; otherwise nil (1nil)

CursorHasSpell

Returns whether a spell is on the cursor.

```
hasSpell = CursorHasSpell()
```

See GetCursorInfo() for more detailed information.

Returns:

hasSpell—1 if the cursor is currently holding a spell; otherwise nil (1nil)

DeclineArenaTeam

Declines an arena team invitation.

DeclineGroup

Declines an invitation to join a party or raid.

Usable in response to the PARTY_INVITE_REQUEST event which fires when the player is invited to join a group.

DeclineGuild

Declines an offered guild invitation.

Usable in response to the GUILD_INVITE_REQUEST event which fires when the player is invited to join a guild.

DeclineInvite

Declines an invitation to a chat channel.

```
DeclineInvite("channel")
```

Usable in response to the CHANNEL_INVITE_REQUEST event which fires when the player is invited to join a chat channel.

Arguments:

channel—Name of a chat channel (string)

DeclineLFGMatch

Declines a proposed LFG match.

Usable after a group match has been proposed to the player via the LFG_MATCH_REQUEST event.

DeclineLevelGrant

Refuses a level offered by the player's Recruit-a-Friend partner.

DeclineName

Returns suggested declensions for a name.

```
genitive, dative, accusative, instrumental, prepositional = ↵
DeclineName("name", gender, declensionSet)
```

In the Russian language, nouns (including proper names) take different form based on their usage in a sentence. When the player enters the base name for a character or pet, the game suggests one or more sets of variations for the five additional cases; the player is asked to choose from among the suggestions and/or enter their own. (The set of declensions ultimately chosen/entered by the player are only used internally and not available to addons.)

Has no effect in non-Russian-localized clients.

Arguments:

name—Nominative form of the player's or pet's name (string)

gender—Gender for the returned names (for declensions of the player's name, should match the player's gender; for the pet's name, should be neuter) (number)

- 1 or nil—Neuter
- 2—Male
- 3—Female

declensionSet—Index of a set of suggested declensions (between 1 and GetNumDeclensionSets(name,gender). Lower indices correspond to "better" suggestions for the given name. (number)

Returns:

genitive—Genitive form of the name (string)

dative—Dative form of the name (string)

accusative—Accusative form of the name (string)

instrumental—Instrumental form of the name (string)

prepositional—Prepositional form of the name (string)

DeclineQuest

Declines a quest.

Usable following the QUEST_DETAIL event in which the questgiver presents the player with the details of a quest and the option to accept or decline.

DeclineResurrect

Declines an offered resurrection spell.

Usable following the RESURRECT_REQUEST event which fires when the player is offered resurrection by another unit.

DelIgnore

Removes a player from the ignore list.

```
DelIgnore("name")
```

Arguments:

name—Name of a character to remove from the ignore list (string)

DelMute

Removes a character from the muted list for voice chat.

```
DelMute("name")
```

The Muted list acts for voice chat as the Ignore list does for text chat: muted characters will never be heard regardless of which voice channels they join the player in.

Arguments:

name—Name of a character to remove from the mute list (string)

<kbd>Confirmation</kbd> **DeleteCursorItem**

Destroys the item on the cursor.

Used in the default UI when accepting the confirmation prompt that appears when dragging and dropping an item to an empty area of the screen.

<kbd>Confirmation</kbd> **DeleteEquipmentSet**

Deletes an equipment set.

```
DeleteEquipmentSet("name")
```

Arguments:

name—Name of an equipment set (case sensitive) (string)

<kbd>Confirmation</kbd> **DeleteGMTicket**

Abandons the currently pending GM ticket.

<kbd>Confirmation</kbd> **DeleteInboxItem**

Deletes a message from the player's inbox.

```
DeleteInboxItem(mailID)
```

Arguments:

mailID—Index of a message in the player's inbox (between 1 and GetInboxNumItems()) (number)

DeleteMacro

Deletes a macro.

```
DeleteMacro(index) or DeleteMacro("name")
```

Arguments:

index—Index of a macro (number, macroID)

name—Name of a macro (string)

DemoteAssistant

Demotes the given player from raid assistant status.

```
DemoteAssistant("unit") or DemoteAssistant("name" [, exactMatch])
```

Arguments:

unit—A unit in the raid (string, unitID)

name—Name of a unit in the raid (string)

exactMatch (optional)—True to check only units whose name exactly matches the name given; false to allow partial matches (boolean)

DepositGuildBankMoney

Deposits money into the guild bank.

```
DepositGuildBankMoney(money)
```

Arguments:

money—Amount of money to deposit (in copper) (number)

DescendStop

Stops movement initiated by SitStandOrDescendStart.

Used by the SITORSTAND binding, which also controls descent when swimming or flying. Has no meaningful effect if called while sitting/standing.

DestroyTotem

Destroys a specific totem (or ghoul).

```
DestroyTotem(slot)
```

Totem functions are also used for ghouls summoned by a Death Knight's Raise Dead ability (if the ghoul is not made a controllable pet by the Master of Ghouls talent).

Arguments:

slot—Which totem to destroy (number)

1—Fire (or Death Knight's ghoul)   3—Water

2—Earth   4—Air

DetectWowMouse

Detects the presence of a WoW-compatible multi-button mouse.

This function is used by the default user interface to enable or disable the configuration option for a many-buttoned WoW mouse. If the mouse is not found, the WOW_MOUSE_NOT_FOUND event will fire.

DisableAddOn

Marks an addon as disabled.

```
DisableAddOn("name") or DisableAddOn(index)
```

The addon will remain active until the player logs out and back in or reloads the UI (see ReloadUI()). Changes to the enabled/disabled state of addons while in-game are saved on a per-character basis.

Arguments:

name—Name of an addon (name of the addon's folder and TOC file, not the Title found in the TOC) (string)

index—Index of an addon in the addon list (between 1 and GetNumAddOns()) (number)

DisableAllAddOns

Marks all addons as disabled.

Addons will remain active until the player logs out and back in or reloads the UI (see ReloadUI()).

Changes to the enabled/disabled state of addons while in-game are saved on a per-character basis.

DisableSpellAutocast

Disables automatic casting of a pet spell.

```
DisableSpellAutocast("spell")
```

Arguments:

spell—The name of a pet spell (string)

DismissCompanion

Unsummons the current non-combat pet or mount.

```
DismissCompanion("type")
```

Arguments:

type—The type of companion (string)

■ CRITTER—Non-combat pet

■ MOUNT—Mount

Dismount

Dismounts from the player's summoned mount.

DisplayChannelOwner

Requests information from the server about a channel's owner.

```
DisplayChannelOwner("channel") or DisplayChannelOwner(channelIndex)
```

Fires the CHANNEL_OWNER event indicating the name of the channel owner.

Arguments:

channel—Name of a channel (string)

channelIndex—Index of a channel (number)

DisplayChannelVoiceOff

Disables voice in a channel specified by its position in the channel list display.

```
DisplayChannelVoiceOff(index)
```

Arguments:

index—Index of a channel in the channel list display (between 1 and GetNumDisplayChannels()) (number)

DisplayChannelVoiceOn

Enables voice in a channel specified by its position in the channel list display.

```
DisplayChannelVoiceOn(index)
```

Arguments:

index—Index of a channel in the channel list display (between 1 and GetNumDisplayChannels()) (number)

DoEmote

Performs a preset emote (with optional target).

```
DoEmote("emote" [, "target"])
```

The list of built-in emote tokens can be found in global variables whose names follow the format `"EMOTE"..num.."_TOKEN"`, where `num` is a number between 1 and `MAXEMOTEINDEX` (a variable local to ChatFrame.lua.)

For custom emotes (as performed using the `/emote` or `/me` commands in the default UI), see `SendChatMessage()`.

Arguments:

`emote`—Non-localized token identifying an emote to perform (`string`)

`target` (optional)—Name of a unit at whom to direct the emote (`string`)

Example:

```
DoEmote("wave")
-- Player waves
DoEmote("threaten", "King Varian Wrynn")
-- Player threatens King Varian Wrynn with the wrath of doom
```

DoReadyCheck

Initiates a ready check.

Only has effect if the player is the party/raid leader or a raid assistant.

DoTradeSkill

Performs a trade skill recipe.

```
DoTradeSkill(index [, repeat])
```

Arguments:

`index`—Index of a recipe in the trade skill list (between 1 and `GetNumTrade Skills()`) (`number`)

`repeat` (optional)—Number of times to repeat the recipe (`number`)

DownloadSettings

Restores game settings from a backup stored on the server.

This function only works if server-synchronized settings are enabled. This is controlled by the `synchronizeSettings` CVar.

DropCursorMoney

Drops any money currently on the cursor, returning it to where it was taken from.

DropItemOnUnit

"Gives" the item on the cursor to another unit; results vary by context.

```
DropItemOnUnit("unit") or DropItemOnUnit("name")
```

If the unit is a friendly player, adds the item to the trade window (opening it if necessary, and placing it in the first available trade slot or the "will not be traded" slot depending on whether the item is soulbound). If the unit is the player's pet and the player is a Hunter, attempts to feed the item to the pet (since this casts the Feed Pet spell, in this case this action is protected and can only be called by the Blizzard user interface). For other units, nothing happens and the item remains on the cursor.

Arguments:

unit—A unit to receive the item (string, unitID)

name—Name of a unit to receive the item; only valid for player, pet, and party/raid members (string)

No Combat   **EditMacro**

Changes the name, icon, and/or body of a macro.

```
newIndex = EditMacro(index, "name", icon, "body")
```

Arguments:

index—Existing index of the macro (number, macroID)

name—New name for the macro (up to 16 characters); nil to keep an existing name (string)

icon—Index of a macro icon (between 1 and GetNumMacroIcons()); nil to keep an existing icon (number)

body—Body of the macro (up to 255 characters); nil to keep the existing body (string)

Returns:

newIndex—Index at which the macro is now saved (may differ from input index if the macro's name was changed, as macros are saved in alphabetical order) (number, macroID)

EjectPassengerFromSeat

Ejects the occupant of a seat in the player's vehicle.

```
EjectPassengerFromSeat(seat)
```

Arguments:

seat—Index of a seat in the player's vehicle (number)

EnableAddOn

Marks an addon as enabled.

```
EnableAddOn(index) or EnableAddOn("name")
```

The addon will remain inactive until the player logs out and back in or reloads the UI (see ReloadUI()).

Changes to the enabled/disabled state of addons while in-game are saved on a per-character basis.

Arguments:

index—The index of the addon to be enabled (number)

name—The name of the addon to be enabled (string)

EnableAllAddOns

Marks all addons as enabled.

Addons will remain inactive until the player logs out and back in or reloads the UI (see ReloadUI()).

Changes to the enabled/disabled state of addons while in-game are saved on a per-character basis.

EnableSpellAutocast

Enables automatic casting of a pet spell.

```
EnableSpellAutocast("spell")
```

Arguments:

spell—Name of a pet spell (string)

Confirmation

EndBoundTradeable

Confirms taking an action which renders a looted Bind on Pickup item non-tradeable.

```
EndBoundTradeable(id)
```

A Bind on Pickup item looted by the player can be traded to other characters who were originally eligible to loot it, but only within a limited time after looting. This period can be ended prematurely if the player attempts certain actions (such as enchanting the item).

Arguments:

id—Number identifying the item (as provided by the END_BOUND_TRADEABLE event) (number)

Confirmation

EndRefund

Confirms taking an action which renders a purchased item non-refundable.

```
EndRefund(id)
```

Items bought with alternate currency (honor points, arena points, or special items such as Emblems of Heroism and Dalaran Cooking Awards) can be returned to a vendor for a full refund, but only within a limited time after the original purchase. This period can be ended prematurely if the player attempts certain actions (such as enchanting the item).

Arguments:

id—Number identifying the item (as provided by the END_REFUND event) (number)

EnumerateFrames

Returns the next frame following the frame passed, or nil if no more frames exist.

```
nextFrame = EnumerateFrames([currentFrame])
```

Arguments:

currentFrame (optional)—The current frame to get the next frame, or nil to get the first frame (table)

Returns:

nextFrame—The frame following currentFrame or nil if no more frames exist, or the first frame if nil was passed (table)

Example:

```
-- Print all visible frames under the mouse cursor
local frame = EnumerateFrames(); -- Get the first frame
while frame do
```

```
  if ( frame:IsVisible() and MouseIsOver(frame) ) then
    print(frame:GetName() or string.format("[Unnamed Frame: %s]", ↵
  tostring(frame)));
    end
    frame = EnumerateFrames(frame); -- Get the next frame
  end
```

EnumerateServerChannels

Returns the available server channel names.

```
... = EnumerateServerChannels()
```

Returns:

. . .—A list of strings, each the name of an available server channel (e.g. "General", "Trade", "WorldDefense", "GuildRecruitment", "LookingForGroup") (string)

EquipCursorItem

Puts the item on the cursor into a specific equipment slot.

```
EquipCursorItem(slot)
```

If the item on the cursor can be equipped but does not fit in the given slot, the item is automatically equipped in the first available slot in which it fits (as with `AutoEquipCursorItem()`). Thus, this function is most useful when dealing with items which can be equipped in more than one slot: containers, rings, trinkets, and (for dual-wielding characters) one-handed weapons.

Causes an error message (`UI_ERROR_MESSAGE`) if the item on the cursor cannot be equipped. Does nothing if the cursor does not contain an item.

Arguments:

`slot`—An inventory slot number, as can be obtained from `GetInventorySlotInfo` (number, inventoryID)

EquipItemByName

Attempts to equip an arbitrary item.

```
EquipItemByName(itemID) or EquipItemByName("itemName") or ↵
EquipItemByName("itemLink")
```

The item is automatically equipped in the first available slot in which it fits. To equip an item in a specific slot, see `EquipCursorItem()`.

Causes an error message (`UI_ERROR_MESSAGE`) if the specified item cannot be equipped. Does nothing if the specified item does not exist or is not in the player's possession.

Arguments:

`itemID`—An item's ID (number)

`itemName`—An item's name (string)

`itemLink`—An item's hyperlink, or any string containing the `itemString` portion of an item link (string)

`Confirmation` ### EquipPendingItem

Confirms equipping a bind-on-equip item.

```
EquipPendingItem(index)
```

Usable following the `EQUIP_BIND_CONFIRM` or `AUTOEQUIP_BIND` `_CONFIRM`, which fires when the player attempts to equip a bind-on-equip item

Arguments:

`index`—Index provided by the `EQUIP_BIND_CONFIRM` or `AUTOEQUIP_BIND` `_CONFIRM` event; currently always 0 (`number`)

EquipmentManagerClearIgnoredSlotsForSave

Clears the list of equipment slots to be ignored when saving sets.

EquipmentManagerIgnoreSlotForSave

Adds an equipment slot to the list of those ignored when saving sets.

```
EquipmentManagerIgnoreSlotForSave(slot)
```

Creating or saving a set with `SaveEquipmentSet()` will ignore any slots on the list, allowing the player to create sets which only switch certain items (e.g. to equip a fishing pole and hat while leaving non-fishing-related items equipped).

Arguments:

`slot`—An inventory slot number, as can be obtained from `GetInventory` `SlotInfo` (number, inventoryID)

EquipmentManagerIsSlotIgnoredForSave

Returns whether the contents of an equipment slot will be included when saving sets.

```
isIgnored = EquipmentManagerIsSlotIgnoredForSave(slot)
```

Arguments:

`slot`—An inventory slot number, as can be obtained from `GetInventory` `SlotInfo` (number, inventoryID)

Returns:

`isIgnored`—`True` if the contents of the slot will not be included when next creating or saving an equipment set; otherwise `false` (`boolean`)

EquipmentManagerUnignoreSlotForSave

Removes an equipment slot from the list of those ignored when saving sets.

```
EquipmentManagerUnignoreSlotForSave(slot)
```

Creating or saving a set with `SaveEquipmentSet()` will ignore any slots on the list, allowing the player to create sets which only switch certain items (e.g. to equip a fishing pole and hat while leaving non-fishing-related items equipped).

Arguments:

`slot`—An inventory slot number, as can be obtained from `GetInventory` `SlotInfo` (number, inventoryID)

EquipmentManager_UnpackLocation

Unpacks an inventory location bitfield into usable components.

```
player, bank, bags, location or slot, bag = ↵
EquipmentManager_UnpackLocation(location)
```

Arguments:

location—A bit field that represents an item's location in the player's possession. This bit field can be obtained using the GetInventoryItemsForSlot function. (number)

Returns:

player—A flag indicating whether or not the item exists in the player's inventory (i.e. an equipped item). (boolean)

bank—A flag indicating whether or not the item exists in the payer's bank. (boolean)

bags—A flag indicating whether or not the item exists in the player's bags. (boolean)

location or slot—The inventory slot that contains the item, or the container slot that contains the item, if the item is in the player's bags. (number)

bag—The bagID of the container that contains the item. (number)

EquipmentSetContainsLockedItems

Returns whether an equipment set contains locked items.

```
isLocked = EquipmentSetContainsLockedItems("name")
```

Locked items are those in a transient state—e.g. on the cursor for moving within the player's bags, placed in the Send Mail or Trade UIs, etc.—for which the default UI displays the item's icon as grayed out. A set cannot be equipped if it contains locked items.

Arguments:

name—Name of an equipment set (case sensitive) (string)

Returns:

isLocked—True if the equipment set contains locked items (boolean)

ExpandAllFactionHeaders

Expands all headers and sub-headers in the Reputation UI.

Expands headers for both major groups (Classic, Burning Crusade, Wrath of the Lich King, Inactive, etc.) and the sub-groups within them (Alliance Forces, Steamwheedle Cartel, Horde Expedition, Shattrath City, etc.).

ExpandChannelHeader

Expands a group header in the chat channel listing.

```
ExpandChannelHeader(index)
```

Arguments:

index—Index of a header in the display channel list (between 1 and GetNumDisplayChannels()) (number)

ExpandCurrencyList

Expands or collapses a list header in the Currency UI.

```
ExpandCurrencyList(index, shouldExpand)
```

Arguments:

`index`—Index of a header in the currency list (between 1 and GetCurrency ListSize()) (`number`)

`shouldExpand`—1 to expand the header, showing its contents; 0 to collapse the header, hiding its contents (`number`)

ExpandFactionHeader

Expands a given faction header or sub-header in the Reputation UI.

`ExpandFactionHeader(index)`

Faction headers include both major groups (Classic, Burning Crusade, Wrath of the Lich King, Inactive, etc.) and the sub-groups within them (Alliance Forces, Steamwheedle Cartel, Horde Expedition, Shattrath City, etc.).

Arguments:

`index`—Index of an entry in the faction list; between 1 and GetNumFactions() (`number`)

ExpandQuestHeader

Expands a quest header in the quest log.

`ExpandQuestHeader(questIndex)`

Arguments:

`questIndex`—Index of a header in the quest log (between 1 and `GetNum QuestLogEntries()`), or 0 to expand all headers (`number`)

ExpandSkillHeader

Expands a group header in the Skills UI.

`ExpandSkillHeader(index)`

Arguments:

`index`—Index of an entry in the skills list (between 1 and `GetNumSkill Lines()`) (`number`)

ExpandTradeSkillSubClass

Expands a group header in the trade skill listing.

`ExpandTradeSkillSubClass(index)`

Causes an error if `index` does not refer to a header.

Arguments:

`index`—Index of a header in the trade skill list (between 1 and `GetNumTradeSkills()`) (`number`)

ExpandTrainerSkillLine

Expands a group header in the trainer service listing.

`ExpandTrainerSkillLine(index)`

Causes a Lua error if the entry is not a header (see `GetTrainerServiceInfo()`).

Arguments:

index—Index of a header in the trainer service listing (between 1 and GetNumTrainerServices()), or 0 to expand all headers (number)

FactionToggleAtWar

Toggles "at war" status for a faction.

```
FactionToggleAtWar(index)
```

"At War" status determines whether members of a faction can be attacked. Normal interactions (as with merchants, questgivers, etc.) are not available if the player is "at war" with an NPC's faction.

This function does nothing for faction headers or factions for which changing "at war" status is not currently allowed; i.e., factions for which the eighth (canToggleAtWar) return of GetFactionInfo is false or nil.

Arguments:

index—Index of an entry in the faction list; between 1 and GetNumFactions() (number)

FillLocalizedClassList

Fills a table with localized class names keyed by non-localized class tokens.

```
FillLocalizedClassList(table [, female])
```

Note that while localized class names have no gender in English, other locales have different names for each gender.

Arguments:

table—An empty table to be filled (number)

female (optional)—True to fill the table with female class names; false or omitted to fill it with male class names (boolean)

Example:

```
-- prints the localized names for each class in the main chat window,
-- with each name in the appropriate color
local classes = {}
FillLocalizedClassList(classes, true)
for token, localizedName in pairs(classes) do
  local color = RAID_CLASS_COLORS[token];
  ChatFrame1:AddMessage(localizedName, color.r, color.g, color.b)
end
```

FlagTutorial

Marks a contextual tutorial as displayed so it doesn't appear again.

```
FlagTutorial("tutorial")
```

Arguments:

tutorial—Numeric identifier for the tutorial step (as string); supplied in the TUTORIAL_TRIGGER event (string)

FlipCameraYaw

Rotates the camera around the player.

```
FlipCameraYaw(degrees)
```

Arguments:

degrees—The number of degrees to rotate; positive for counter-clockwise, negative for clockwise. (number)

Example:

```
-- Dramatically Rotate the camera 360 degrees around the player
if not YawFrame then CreateFrame("Frame", "YawFrame") end
local degree = 0
local function OnUpdate(self, elapsed)
 degree = degree + 1
 FlipCameraYaw(1)
 if degree >= 360 then
  self:Hide()
 end
end
YawFrame:SetScript("OnUpdate", OnUpdate)
YawFrame:Show()
```

<table><tr><td>Protected</td></tr></table> **FocusUnit**

Changes the focus unitID to refer to a new unit.

FocusUnit("unit") or FocusUnit("name")

Arguments:

unit—A unit to focus (string, unitID)

name—The name of a unit to focus; only valid for player, pet, and party/raid members (string)

FollowUnit

Causes the player character to automatically follow another unit.

FollowUnit("unit") or FollowUnit("name" [, strict])

Only friendly player units can be followed.

Arguments:

unit—A unit to follow (string, unitID)

name—Name of a unit to follow (string)

strict (optional)—True if only an exact match for the given name should be allowed; false to allow partial matches (boolean)

ForceQuit

Immediately exits World of Warcraft.

Unlike Quit(), this function exits the game application regardless of current conditions.

Used in the default UI when the player chooses "Exit now" in the dialog that appears if the player attempts to quit while not in an inn, major city, or other "rest" area.

FrameXML_Debug

Enables or disables logging of XML loading.

FrameXML_Debug(enable)

When logging is enabled, status and error text will be saved to the file Logs/ FrameXML.log (path is relative to the folder containing the World of Warcraft client) as the client parses and loads XML files in the default UI and addons.

Arguments:

enable—True to enable verbose XML logging; false to disable (boolean)

GMResponseNeedMoreHelp

Requests further GM interaction on a ticket to which a GM has already responded.

GMResponseResolve

Notifies the server that the player's GM ticket issue has been resolved.

GMSurveyAnswer

Returns text of multiple-choice question answers in a GM survey.

```
answerText = GMSurveyAnswer(questionIndex, answerIndex)
```

Arguments:

questionIndex—Index of a survey question (between 1 and MAX_SURVEY _QUESTIONS) (number)

answerIndex—Index of one of the question's answers (between 1 and MAX_SURVEY_ANSWERS) (number)

Returns:

answerText—Text of the answer choice (string)

GMSurveyAnswerSubmit

Submits an answer to a GM survey question.

```
GMSurveyAnswerSubmit(question, rank, "comment")
```

Arguments:

question—The index of the question being answered (number)

rank—The rank selected (number)

comment—A comment for the given question (string)

GMSurveyCommentSubmit

Submits a comment to the current GM survey.

```
GMSurveyCommentSubmit("comment")
```

Arguments:

comment—The comment made on the GM Survey (string)

GMSurveyQuestion

Returns the text of a specific question from a GM survey.

```
surveyQuestion = GMSurveyQuestion(index)
```

Arguments:

index—The index of a GM survey question (number)

Returns:

surveyQuestion—The question being asked (string)

GMSurveySubmit

Submits the current GM survey.

GameMovieFinished

Ends in-game movie playback.

GetAbandonQuestItems

Returns information about items that would be destroyed by abandoning a quest.

```
items = GetAbandonQuestItems()
```

Usable after calling `SetAbandonQuest()` but before calling `AbandonQuest()`.

Returns:

`items`—A string listing any items that would be destroyed (`string`)

GetAbandonQuestName

Returns the name of the quest being abandoned.

```
name = GetAbandonQuestName()
```

Usable after calling `SetAbandonQuest()` but before calling `AbandonQuest()`.

Returns:

`name`—Name of the quest being abandoned (`string`)

GetAccountExpansionLevel

Returns the most recent of WoW's retail expansion packs for which the player's account is authorized.

```
expansionLevel = GetAccountExpansionLevel()
```

Used in the default UI to determine the player's maximum possible level (and showing or hiding the XP bar accordingly). Also indicates whether the player is allowed to access expansion areas (e.g. Outland, Draenei / Blood Elf starting areas, Northrend).

Returns:

`expansionLevel`—Expansion level of the player's account (`number`)

- 0—World of Warcraft ("Classic")
- 1—World of Warcraft: The Burning Crusade
- 2—World of Warcraft: Wrath of the Lich King

Example:

```
-- Blizzard UI code for determining level cap
MAX_PLAYER_LEVEL_TABLE = {};
MAX_PLAYER_LEVEL_TABLE[0] = 60;
MAX_PLAYER_LEVEL_TABLE[1] = 70;
MAX_PLAYER_LEVEL_TABLE[2] = 80;
MAX_PLAYER_LEVEL = 0;
MAX_PLAYER_LEVEL = MAX_PLAYER_LEVEL_TABLE[GetAccountExpansionLevel()];
```

GetAchievementCategory

Returns the numeric ID of the category to which an achievement belongs.

```
categoryID = GetAchievementCategory(achievementID)
```

Arguments:

`achievementID`—The numeric ID of an achievement (`number`)

Returns:

`categoryID`—The numeric ID of the achievement's category (`number`)

GetAchievementComparisonInfo

Returns information about the comparison unit's achievements.

```
completed, month, day, year = GetAchievementComparisonInfo(id)
```

Only accurate once the `INSPECT_ACHIEVEMENT_READY` event has fired following a call to `SetAchievementComparisonUnit()`. No longer accurate once `ClearAchievementComparisonUnit()` is called.

Arguments:

`id`—The numeric ID of an achievement (`number`)

Returns:

`completed`—True if the comparison unit has completed the achievement; otherwise `nil` (`boolean`)

`month`—Month in which the comparison unit completed the achievement (`number`)

`day`—Day of the month on which the comparison unit completed the achievement (`number`)

`year`—Year in which the comparison unit completed the achievement. (Two-digit year, assumed to be 21st century.) (`number`)

GetAchievementCriteriaInfo

Gets information about criteria for an achievement or data for a statistic.

```
description, type, completed, quantity, requiredQuantity, ↵
characterName, flags, assetID, quantityString, criteriaID = ↵
GetAchievementCriteriaInfo(achievementID, index) or ↵
GetAchievementCriteriaInfo(statisticID)
```

Arguments:

`achievementID`—The numeric ID of an achievement (`number`)

`index`—Index of one of the achievement's criteria (between 1 and GetAchievementNumCriteria()) (`number`)

`statisticID`—The numeric ID of a statistic (`number`)

Returns:

`description`—Description of the criterion (as displayed in the UI for achievements with multiple criteria) or statistic (`string`)

`type`—Type of criterion: a value of 8 indicates the criterion is another achievement; other values are not used in the default UI (`number`)

`completed`—True if the player has completed the criterion; otherwise `false` (`boolean`) quantity—If applicable, number of steps taken towards completing the criterion (e.g. for the only criterion of "Did Somebody Order a Knuckle Sandwich?", the player's current Unarmed skill; for the first criterion of "Pest Control", 1 if the player has killed an Adder, 0 otherwise (number)

requiredQuantity—If applicable, number of steps required to complete the criterion (e.g. 400 for the only criterion of "Did Somebody Order a Knuckle Sandwich?"; 1 for any criterion of "Pest Control" (number)

characterName—Character name with which the criterion was completed. Currently always the player character's name for completed criteria (string)

flags—Test against the following masks with bit.band() to reveal additional information: (bitfield)

■ 0x00000001—Criterion should be displayed as a progress bar

■ 0x00000002—Criterion should be hidden in normal achievement displays

assetID—Internal ID number of the quest to complete, NPC to kill, item to acquire, world object to interact with, achievement to earn, or other game entity related to completing the criterion. (Note: some but not all of these ID types are usable elsewhere in the WoW API) (number)

quantityString—Text to be shown when displaying quantity and requiredQuantity in a UI element. (Not always the same as format("%d / %d", quantity, requiredQuantity); e.g. "Got My Mind On My Money" shows monetary amounts with embedded textures for gold, silver, and copper) (string)

criteriaID—Unique ID number identifying the criterion; usable with GetAchievementInfoFromCriteria() (number)

GetAchievementInfo

Gets information about an achievement or statistic.

```
id, name, points, completed, month, day, year, description, flags, ↵
icon, rewardText = GetAchievementInfo(category, index) or ↵
GetAchievementInfo(id)
```

Arguments:

category—Numeric ID of an achievement category (number)

index—Index of an achievement within a category (between 1 and GetCategoryNumAchievements()) (number)

id—The numeric ID of an achievement or statistic (number)

Returns:

id—The numeric ID of the achievement or statistic (number)

name—Name of the achievement or statistic (string)

points—Amount of achievement points awarded for completing the achievement (number)

completed—True if the player has completed the achievement; otherwise false (boolean)

month—Month in which the player completed the achievement (number) day—Day of the month on which the player completed the achievement (number)

year—Year in which the player completed the achievement. (Two-digit year, assumed to be 21st century.) (number)

description—Description of the achievement (string)

flags—Test against the following masks with bit.band() to reveal additional information: (bitfield)

- 0x00000001—Info is for a statistic, not an achievement
- 0x00000002—Achievement should be hidden in normal displays
- 0x00000080—Achievement should display its criteria as a progress bar regardless of per-criterion flags

icon—Path to an icon texture for the achievement (string)

rewardText—Text describing a reward for the achievement, or the empty string if no reward is offered (string)

GetAchievementInfoFromCriteria

Gets information about an achievement or statistic given a criterion ID.

```
id, name, points, description, flags, icon, rewardText = ↵
GetAchievementInfoFromCriteria(id)
```

Arguments:

id—The numeric ID of an achievement or statistic criterion (as can be retrieved from GetAchievementCriteriaInfo()) (number)

Returns:

id—The numeric ID of the achievement or statistic (number)

name—Name of the achievement or statistic (string)

points—Amount of achievement points awarded for completing the achievement (number)

description—Description of the achievement (string)

flags—Test against the following masks with bit.band() to reveal additional information: (bitfield)

- 0x00000001—Info is for a statistic, not an achievement
- 0x00000002—Achievement should be hidden in normal displays
- 0x00000080—Achievement should display its criteria as a progress bar regardless of per-criterion flags

icon—Path to an icon texture for the achievement (string)

rewardText—Text describing a reward for the achievement, or the empty string if no reward is offered (string)

GetAchievementLink

Returns a hyperlink representing the player's progress on an achievement.

```
link = GetAchievementLink(id)
```

The tooltip associated with the hyperlink shows not only the details of the achievement itself, but also the completion of or progress towards the achievement by the player who produced the link.

Arguments:

id—The numeric ID of an achievement (`number`)

Returns:

`link`—A hyperlink for the player's achievement (`string`)

GetAchievementNumCriteria

Returns the number of measured criteria for an achievement.

```
count = GetAchievementNumCriteria(id)
```

Measured criteria for an achievement are shown in the default UI as details when clicking on an achievement in the achievements window or when showing an achievement in the objectives tracker; e.g. "Master of Arms" (15 criteria: Axes, Bows, Crossbows, Daggers, etc.) and "Safe Deposit" (1 criterion: number of bank slots purchased).

Not all achievements have criteria: achievements with zero criteria are those that can be completed in a single event (though a complicated event it may be), explained in achievement's description: e.g. "Reach level 80", "Fall 65 yards without dying", and "With all three Twilight Drakes still alive, engage and defeat Sartharion the Onyx Guardian on Normal Difficulty".

Arguments:

id—The numeric ID of an achievement (`number`)

Returns:

`count`—Number of criteria for the achievement (`number`)

GetAchievementNumRewards

Returns the number of point rewards for an achievement (currently always 1).

```
count = GetAchievementNumRewards(id)
```

Currently all achievements and statistics offer one reward (according to this function), though the rewards offered by statistics are all zero points.

Arguments:

id—The numeric ID of an achievement or statistic (`number`)

Returns:

`count`—Number of point rewards offered for the achievement (`number`)

GetAchievementReward

Returns the number of achievement points awarded for earning an achievement.

```
points = GetAchievementReward(id, index)
```

Currently all achievements and statistics offer one reward (according to this function), though the rewards offered by statistics are all zero points.

Arguments:

id—The numeric ID of an achievement or statistic (number)

index—Index of one of the achievement's rewards (between 1 and GetAchievementNumRewards(); currently always 1) (number)

Returns:

points—Number of achievement points awarded for completing the achievement (number)

GetActionBarPage

Returns the current action bar page.

```
page = GetActionBarPage()
```

Returns:

page—The current action bar page (number)

GetActionBarToggles

Returns the current visibility settings for the four secondary action bars.

```
showBar1, showBar2, showBar3, showBar4 = GetActionBarToggles()
```

Returns:

showBar1—1 if the interface option is set to show the Bottom Left ActionBar, otherwise nil (1nil)

showBar2—1 if the interface option is set to show the Bottom Right ActionBar, otherwise nil (1nil)

showBar3—1 if the interface option is set to show the Right ActionBar, otherwise nil (1nil)

showBar4—1 if the interface option is set to show the Right ActionBar 2, otherwise nil (1nil)

GetActionCooldown

Returns cooldown information about an action.

```
start, duration, enable = GetActionCooldown(slot)
```

Arguments:

slot—An action bar slot (number, actionID)

Returns:

start—The value of GetTime() at the moment the cooldown began, or 0 if the action is ready (number)

duration—The length of the cooldown, or 0 if the action is ready (number)

enable—1 if a Cooldown UI element should be used to display the cooldown, otherwise 0. (Does not always correlate with whether the action is ready.) (number)

Example:

```
-- Show all actions currently on cooldown
for i=1,120 do
  local start,duration,enable = GetActionCooldown(i)
  if start > 0 and enable == 1 then
```

```
local actiontype,id,subtype = GetActionInfo(i)
local name

if actiontype == "spell" then
  name = GetSpellName(id, "spell")
elseif actiontype == "item" then
  name = GetItemInfo(id)
elseif actiontype == "companion" then
  name = select(2, GetCompanionInfo(subtype, id))
end

local timeLeft = math.floor((start + duration) - GetTime())
local output = string.format("Cooldown on %s %s ↵
(%s seconds left)", actiontype, name, timeLeft)
  ChatFrame1:AddMessage(output)

end
end
```

GetActionCount

Returns the number of uses remaining for the given action slot.

```
count = GetActionCount(slot)
```

Applies to spells that require reagents, items that stack, or items with charges; used in the default UI to display the count on action buttons.

Returns 0 for any action that does not use a count. To distinguish between actions which do not use a count and actions which do but whose current count is 0, see `IsConsumableAction`.

Arguments:

`slot`—An action bar slot (number, actionID)

Returns:

`count`—Number of times the action can be used (number)

GetActionInfo

Returns information about an action slot.

```
type, id, subType, spellID = GetActionInfo(slot)
```

Arguments:

`slot`—An action slot (number)

Returns:

`type`—Type of action in the slot (string)

- `companion`—Summons a mount or non-combat pet
- `equipmentset`—Equips a set of items
- `item`—Uses an item
- `macro`—Runs a macro
- `spell`—Casts a spell

id—An identifier for the action; varies by type: (number or string)

- companion—The companion's index in the mount or minipet list
- equipmentset—Name of the equipment set
- item—The item's itemID
- macro—The macro's index in the macro list (macroID)
- spell—The spell's index in the player's spellbook (spellbookID)

subType—Subtype of the action (or nil if not applicable) (string)

- CRITTER—For companion actions: indicates id is as an index in the non-combat pets list
- MOUNT—For companion actions: indicates id is an index in the mounts list
- spell—For spell actions: indicates id is an index in the player's spellbook (as opposed to the pet's)

spellID—For spell and companion actions, the global ID of the spell (or the summoning "spell" for a companion) (string, spellID)

Example:

```
-- Prints all types and subtypes found in the player's actions
local types = {}
for i=1,120 do
  local type,id,subtype = GetActionInfo(i)
  if type then
    types[type] = types[type] or {}
    if subtype then
      types[type][subtype] = 1
    end
  end
end

for type, subtypes in pairs(types) do
  print("Type:", type, "subtypes:")
  local numSubtypes = 0
  for subtype in pairs(subtypes) do
    print("  ", subtype)
    numSubtypes = numSubtypes + 1
  end

  if numSubtypes == 0 then
    print("  no subtypes")

  end
end
```

GetActionText

Returns the text label associated with an action.

```
text = GetActionText(slot)
```

Currently used only for macros, which in the default UI show their name as a label on an action button.

Arguments:

slot—An action bar slot (number, actionID)

Returns:

text—Label for the action (string)

GetActionTexture

Returns the icon texture for an action.

```
texture = GetActionTexture(slot)
```

Can be the icon of a spell or item, the icon manually set for a macro, or an icon reflecting the current state of a macro.

Arguments:

slot—An action bar slot (number, actionID)

Returns:

texture—Path to an icon texture for the action in the slot, or nil if the slot is empty (string)

GetActiveLevel

Returns the level of a quest which can be turned in to the current Quest NPC.

```
level = GetActiveLevel(index)
```

Only returns valid information after a QUEST_GREETING event.

Note: Most quest NPCs present active quests using the GetGossipActiveQuests() instead of this function.

Arguments:

index—Index of a quest which can be turned in to the current Quest NPC (between 1 and GetNumActiveQuests()) (number)

Returns:

level—Recommended character level for attempting the quest (number)

GetActiveTalentGroup

Returns the index of the active talent specialization.

```
activeTalentGroup = GetActiveTalentGroup(isInspect, isPet)
```

Arguments:

isInspect—true to query talent info for the currently inspected unit, false to query talent info for the player (boolean)

isPet—true to query talent info for the player's pet, false to query talent info for the player (boolean)

Returns:

activeTalentGroup—Which talent group is currently active (number)

- 1—Primary Talents
- 2—Secondary Talents

GetActiveTitle

Returns the name of a quest which can be turned in to the current Quest NPC.

```
title = GetActiveTitle(index)
```

Only returns valid information after a QUEST_GREETING event.

Note: Most quest NPCs present active quests using the GetGossipActive Quests() instead of this function.

Arguments:

index—Index of a quest which can be turned in to the current Quest NPC (between 1 and GetNumActiveQuests()) (number)

Returns:

title—Title of the quest (string)

GetActiveVoiceChannel

Returns the currently active voice channel.

```
index = GetActiveVoiceChannel()
```

Returns:

index—Index of the active voice channel in the chat display window (between 1 and GetNumDisplayChannels()), or nil if no channel is active (number)

GetAddOnCPUUsage

Returns the amount of CPU time used by an addon.

```
usage = GetAddOnCPUUsage("name") or GetAddOnCPUUsage(index)
```

Only returns valid data if the scriptProfile CVar is set to 1; returns 0 otherwise.

The value returned is from a cache only updated when calling UpdateAddOn CPUUsage(). This value is the sum of GetFunctionCPUUsage() for all functions created on the addon's behalf. Note that if the addon calls external functions which in turn create new functions, the new functions are considered to belong to the addon.

Arguments:

name—Name of an addon (name of the addon's folder and TOC file, not the Title found in the TOC) (string)

index—Index of an addon in the addon list (between 1 and GetNumAddOns()) (number)

Returns:

usage—Amount of CPU time used by the addon (in milliseconds) since the UI was loaded or ResetCPUUsage() was last called (number)

GetAddOnDependencies

Returns a list of addons a given addon is dependent upon.

```
... = GetAddOnDependencies("name") or GetAddOnDependencies(index)
```

Arguments:

name—Name of an addon (name of the addon's folder and TOC file, not the Title found in the TOC) (string)

index—Index of an addon in the addon list (between 1 and GetNumAddOns()) (number)

Returns:

. . . —A list of strings, each the (folder) name of another addon this addon is dependent upon (`list`)

GetAddOnInfo

Returns information about an addon.

```
name, title, notes, enabled, loadable, reason, security = ↵
GetAddOnInfo("name") or GetAddOnInfo(index)
```

Arguments:

`name`—Name of an addon (name of the addon's folder and TOC file, not the Title found in the TOC) (`string`)

`index`—Index of an addon in the addon list (between 1 and `GetNumAddOns()`) (`number`)

Returns:

`name`—Name of the addon (name of the addon's folder and TOC file) (`string`)

`title`—Title of the addon (from the `Title` header in the addon's TOC file) (`string`)

`notes`—Contents of the `Notes` header in the addon's TOC file (`string`)

`enabled`—1 if the addon is enabled; otherwise `nil` (1nil)

`loadable`—If the addon can currently be loaded (1nil)

`reason`—If the addon cannot be loaded, an unlocalized string token indicating the reason for failure. Localized strings for display can be found by prepending `"ADDON_"`; e.g. `ADDON_DEP_MISSING == "Dependency missing"`. (`string`)

- `BANNED`—Banned
- `CORRUPT`—Corrupt
- `DEP_BANNED`—Dependency banned
- `DEP_CORRUPT`—Dependency corrupt
- `DEP_DISABLED`—Dependency disabled
- `DEP_INCOMPATIBLE`—Dependency incompatible
- `DEP_INSECURE`—Dependency insecure
- `DEP_INTERFACE_VERSION`—Dependency out of date
- `DEP_MISSING`—Dependency missing
- `DEP_NOT_DEMAND_LOADED`—Dependency not loadable on demand
- `DISABLED`—Disabled
- `INCOMPATIBLE`—Incompatible
- `INSECURE`—Insecure
- `INTERFACE_VERSION`—Out of Date
- `MISSING`—Missing
- `NOT_DEMAND_LOADED`—Not loadable on demand

`security`—`"SECURE"` for Blizzard built-in addons (or other digitally signed Blizzard-produced addons); otherwise `"INSECURE"` (`string`)

GetAddOnMemoryUsage

Returns the amount of memory used by an addon.

```
mem = GetAddOnMemoryUsage("name") or GetAddOnMemoryUsage(index)
```

The value returned is from a cache only updated when calling
`UpdateAddOnMemoryUsage()`.

Arguments:

name—Name of an addon (name of the addon's folder and TOC file, not the Title
found in the TOC) (`string`)

index—Index of an addon in the addon list (between 1 and `GetNumAddOns()`)
(`number`)

Returns:

mem—Memory usage of the addon (in kilobytes) (`number`)

GetAddOnMetadata

Returns the value of certain fields in an addon's TOC file.

```
data = GetAddOnMetadata("name", "header") or ↵
GetAddOnMetadata(index, "header")
```

Arguments:

name—Name of an addon (name of the addon's folder and TOC file, not the Title
found in the TOC) (`string`)

index—Index of an addon in the addon list (between 1 and `GetNumAddOns()`)
(`number`)

header—Name of a header from the addon's TOC file; only certain
headers can be queried: `Author`, `Title`, `Notes`, `Version`, and any header
whose name starts with `"X-"` (e.g. `X-Website`, `X-Category`) (`string`)

Returns:

data—Contents of the given TOC file header, or `nil` if the header does not exist
or cannot be queried (`string`)

GetAreaSpiritHealerTime

Returns the time remaining until a nearby battleground spirit healer resurrects
all players in its area.

```
timeleft = GetAreaSpiritHealerTime()
```

Returns:

timeleft—Seconds remaining before the next area resurrection (`number`)

GetArenaCurrency

Returns the player's amount of arena points.

```
points = GetArenaCurrency()
```

Returns:

points—The player's current amount of honor points (`number`)

GetArenaTeam

Returns information about one of the player's arena teams.

```
teamName, teamSize, teamRating, teamPlayed, teamWins, ↵
seasonTeamPlayed, seasonTeamWins, playerPlayed, seasonPlayerPlayed, ↵
teamRank, playerRating, bg_red, bg_green, bg_blue, emblem, ↵
emblem_red, emblem_green, emblem_blue, border, border_red, ↵
border_green, border_blue = GetArenaTeam(team)
```

Arguments:

team—Index of one of the player's arena teams (number, arenaTeamID)

Returns:

teamName—Name of the arena team (string)

teamSize—Size of the team (2 for 2v2, 3 for 3v3, or 5 for 5v5) (number)

teamRating—The team's current rating (number)

teamPlayed—Number of games played by the team in the current week (number)

teamWins—Number of games won by the team in the current week (number)

seasonTeamPlayed—Number of games played by the team in the current arena season (number)

seasonTeamWins—Number of games won by the team in the current arena season (number)

playerPlayed—Number of games in which the player has participated in the current week (number)

seasonPlayerPlayed—Number of games in which the player has participated in the current arena season (number)

teamRank—The team's current rank among same-size teams in its battlegroup (number)

playerRating—The player's personal rating with this team (number)

bg_red—Red component of the color value for the team banner's background (number)

bg_green—Green component of the color value for the team banner's background (number)

bg_blue—Blue component of the color value for the team banner's background (number)

emblem—Index of the team's emblem graphic; full path to the emblem texture can be found using the format "Interface\PVPFrame\Icons\PVP-Banner-Emblem-"..emblem (number)

emblem_red—Red component of the color value for the team banner's emblem (number)

emblem_green—Green component of the color value for the team banner's emblem (number)

emblem_blue—Blue component of the color value for the team banner's emblem (number) border—Index of the team's border graphic; full path to the border texture can be found by using the format `"Interface\PVPFrame\PVP-Banner-"`.. `teamSize.."-Border-"..border` (number)

border_red—Red component of the color value for the team banner's border (number)

border_green—Green component of the color value for the team banner's border (number)

border_blue—Blue component of the color value for the team banner's border (number)

GetArenaTeamRosterInfo

Returns information about an arena team member.

```
name, rank, level, class, online, played, win, seasonPlayed, ↵
seasonWin, rating = GetArenaTeamRosterInfo(team, index)
```

Arguments:

team—Index of one of the player's arena teams (number, arenaTeamID)

index—Index of a team member (between 1 and `GetNumArenaTeamMembers` `(team)`) (number)

Returns:

name—Name of the team member (string)

rank—Rank of the member in the team (number)

- 0—Team captain
- 1—Member

level—Character level of the team member (number)

class—Localized name of the team member's class (string)

online—1 if the team member is currently online; otherwise `nil` (1nil)

played—Number of games played by the team member in the current week (number)

win—Number of winning games played by the team member in the current week (number)

seasonPlayed—Number of games played by the team member in the current arena season (number)

seasonWin—Number of winning games played by the team member in the current arena season (number)

rating—The team member's personal rating with this team (number)

GetArenaTeamRosterSelection

Returns the currently selected member in an arena team roster.

```
index = GetArenaTeamRosterSelection(team)
```

Selection in the arena team roster currently has no effect beyond highlighting list entry in the default UI.

Arguments:

team—Index of one of the player's arena teams (number, arenaTeamID)

Returns:

index—Index of the selected member in the roster listing (number)

GetArmorPenetration

Returns the percentage of enemy armor ignored due to the player's Armor Penetration Rating.

amount = GetArmorPenetration()

Returns:

amount—Percentage of enemy armor ignored due to the player's Armor Penetration Rating (number)

GetAttackPowerForStat

Returns the attack power bonus provided by one of the player's basic statistics.

attackPower = GetAttackPowerForStat(statIndex, effectiveStat)

Arguments:

statIndex—Index of a basic statistic (number)

1—Strength   4—Intellect

2—Agility   5—Spirit

3—Stamina

effectiveStat—Value of the statistic to use in attack power calculation (number)

Returns:

attackPower—Attack power bonus provided to the player by the basic statistic value (number)

GetAuctionInvTypes

Returns a list of the inventory subtypes for a given auction house item subclass.

token, display, ... = GetAuctionInvTypes(classIndex, subClassIndex)

Inventory types are the second level of hierarchy seen when browsing item classes (categories) and subclasses at the Auction House: Head, Neck, Shirt, et al for Miscellaneous; Head, Shoulder, Chest, Wrist, et al for Cloth; etc.

This function still returns valid information if the player is not interacting with an auctioneer.

Arguments:

classIndex—Index of an item class (in the list returned by GetAuctionItem Classes()); currently, inventory types are only applicable in class 2 (armor) (number)

subClassIndex—Index of an item subclass (in the list returned by GetAuctionItemSubClasses(classIndex)); currently, inventory types are only applicable in the armor subclasses listed below: (number)

1—Miscellaneous   4—Mail

2—Cloth   5—Plate

3—Leather

Returns:

token—Name of a global variable containing the localized name of the inventory type (e.g. INVTYPE_FINGER) (string)

display—1 if the inventory type should be displayed; otherwise nil (used in the default auction UI to hide subclass/invType combinations that don't exist in the game; e.g. Plate/Back, Leather/Trinket, etc) (1nil)

...—Additional token, display pairs for each inventory type listed (list)

GetAuctionItemClasses

Returns a list of localized item class (category) names.

```
... = GetAuctionItemClasses()
```

Item classes are the first level of hierarchy seen when browsing at the Auction House: Weapon, Armor, Container, Consumable, etc.

This function still returns valid information if the player is not interacting with an auctioneer.

Returns:

...—A list of strings, each the name of an item class (list)

Example:

```
-- prints the list of item classes
print(GetAuctionItemClasses())
```

GetAuctionItemInfo

Returns information about an auction listing.

```
name, texture, count, quality, canUse, level, minBid, minIncrement, ↵
buyoutPrice, bidAmount, highestBidder, owner, sold = ↵
GetAuctionItemInfo("list", index)
```

Arguments:

list—Type of auction listing (string)

▪ bidder—Auctions the player has bid on

▪ list—Auctions the player can browse and bid on or buy out

▪ owner—Auctions the player placed

index—Index of an auction in the listing (number)

Returns:

name—Name of the item (string)

texture—Path to an icon texture for the item (string)

count—Number of items in the stack (number)

quality—The quality (rarity) level of the item (number, itemQuality)

canUse—1 if the player character can use or equip the item; otherwise nil (1nil)

level—Required character level to use or equip the item (number)

minBid—Minimum cost to bid on the item (in copper) (number)

minIncrement—Minimum bid increment to become the highest bidder on the item (in copper) (number) buyoutPrice—Buyout price of the auction (in copper) (number)

bidAmount—Current highest bid on the item (in copper); 0 if no bids have been placed (number)

highestBidder—1 if the player is currently the highest bidder; otherwise nil (1nil)

owner—Name of the character who placed the auction (string)

sold—1 if the auction has sold (and payment is awaiting delivery; applies only to owner auctions); otherwise nil (number)

GetAuctionItemLink

Returns a hyperlink for an item in an auction listing.

```
link = GetAuctionItemLink("list", index)
```

Arguments:

list—Type of auction listing (string)

- bidder—Auctions the player has bid on
- list—Auctions the player can browse and bid on or buy out
- owner—Auctions the player placed

index—Index of an auction in the listing (number)

Returns:

link—A hyperlink for the item (string, hyperlink)

GetAuctionItemSubClasses

Returns a list of localized subclass names for a given item class.

```
... = GetAuctionItemSubClasses(classIndex)
```

Item subclasses are the second level of hierarchy seen when browsing item classes (categories) at the Auction House: One-Handed Axes, Two-Handed Axes, Bows, Guns, et al for Weapon; Cloth, Leather, Plate, Shields, et al for Armor; Food & Drink, Potion, Elixir et al for Consumable; Red, Blue, Yellow, et al for Gem; etc.

This function still returns valid information if the player is not interacting with an auctioneer.

Arguments:

classIndex—Index of an item class (in the list returned by GetAuctionItem Classes()) (number)

Returns:

...—A list of strings, each the name of an item subclass; or nil if the class contains no subclasses (list)

Example:

```
-- prints a list of the subclasses for each item class
function printSubClasses(...)
  for class = 1, select("#", ...) do
    print(select(class, ...).. ":", strjoin(", ", ↵
GetAuctionItemSubClasses(class)))
```

```
    end
  end
  printSubClasses(GetAuctionItemClasses())
```

GetAuctionItemTimeLeft

Returns the time remaining before an auction listing expires.

```
duration = GetAuctionItemTimeLeft("list", index)
```

Arguments:

list—Type of auction listing (string)

■ bidder—Auctions the player has bid on

■ list—Auctions the player can browse and bid on or buy out

■ owner—Auctions the player placed

index—Index of an auction in the listing (number)

Returns:

duration—General indication of the amount of time remaining on the auction (number)

■ 1—Short (less than 30 minutes)

■ 2—Medium (30 minutes to 2 hours)

■ 3—Long (2 hours to 12 hours)

■ 4—Very Long (more than 12 hours)

GetAuctionSellItemInfo

Returns information about the item currently being set up for auction.

```
name, texture, count, quality, canUse, price = GetAuctionSellItemInfo()
```

Only returns useful information once an item has been placed in the Create Auction UI's "auction item" slot (see ClickAuctionSellItemButton()).

Returns:

name—Name of the item (string)

texture—Path to an icon texture for the item (string)

count—Number of items in the stack (number)

quality—Quality (rarity) level of the item (number, itemQuality)

canUse—1 if the player character can use or equip the item; otherwise nil (1nil)

price—Price to sell the item to a vendor (in copper) (number)

GetAuctionSort

Returns the current sort settings for auction data.

```
criterion, reverse = GetAuctionSort("list", index)
```

The index argument describes priority order for sort criteria: e.g. if GetAuctionSort("list",1) returns quality and GetAuctionSort("list",2) returns level,1, items are sorted first by itemQuality and items with the same quality are sorted by required level.

Arguments:

list—Type of auction listing (string)

- bidder—Auctions the player has bid on
- list—Auctions the player can browse and bid on or buy out
- owner—Auctions the player placed

index—Index of a sorting priority (number)

Returns:

criterion—Non-localized string naming the criterion (or column in the default UI) by which listings are sorted (string)

reverse—1 if listings are sorted in reverse order; otherwise nil. "Reverse" here is relative to the default order, not to absolute value: e.g. the default order for quality is descending (Epic, Rare, Uncommon, etc), but the default order for level is ascending (1–80) (1nil)

GetAutoCompleteResults

Returns a list of character names which complete a given partial name prefix.

```
... = GetAutoCompleteResults("inputString", includeBitfield, ↵
excludeBitfield, maxResults [, cursorPosition])
```

Arguments:

inputString—Partial name for which to return completions (string)

includeBitfield—One or more of the following flags (combined via bit.bor()), indicating which characters should be included in the result list: (number, bitfield)

- 0x00000000—AUTOCOMPLETE_FLAG_NONE: No characters
- 0x00000001—AUTOCOMPLETE_FLAG_IN_GROUP: Characters in the player's party or raid
- 0x00000002—AUTOCOMPLETE_FLAG_IN_GUILD: Characters in the player's guild
- 0x00000004—AUTOCOMPLETE_FLAG_FRIEND: Characters from the player's friends list
- 0x00000010—AUTOCOMPLETE_FLAG_INTERACTED_WITH: Characters with whom the player has recently interacted
- 0x00000020—AUTOCOMPLETE_FLAG_ONLINE: Currently online friends and guildmates
- 0xffffffff—AUTOCOMPLETE_FLAG_ALL: All characters

excludeBitfield—One or more of the following flags (combined via bit.bor()), indicating which characters should be excluded from the result list: (number, bitfield)

- 0x00000000—AUTOCOMPLETE_FLAG_NONE: No characters
- 0x00000001—AUTOCOMPLETE_FLAG_IN_GROUP: Characters in the player's party or raid
- 0x00000002—AUTOCOMPLETE_FLAG_IN_GUILD: Characters in the player's guild

- 0x00000004—AUTOCOMPLETE_FLAG_FRIEND: Characters from the player's friends list
- 0x00000010—AUTOCOMPLETE_FLAG_INTERACTED_WITH: Characters with whom the player has recently interacted
- 0x00000020—AUTOCOMPLETE_FLAG_ONLINE: Currently online friends and guildmates
- 0xffffffff—AUTOCOMPLETE_FLAG_ALL: All characters

maxResults—Maximum number of results to be returned (number)

cursorPosition (optional)—Cursor position in the inputString; currently unused (number)

Returns:

. . .—A list of strings, each the name of a character matching the search parameters (list)

Example:

```
-- prints up to 10 names of friends and guild members starting with "G"
print(GetAutoCompleteResults("g", ↵
bit.bor(AUTOCOMPLETE_FLAG_IN_GUILD,
AUTOCOMPLETE_FLAG_FRIEND), AUTOCOMPLETE_FLAG_NONE, 10))

-- prints up to 10 names of guild members not on the friends list
-- starting with "G"
print(GetAutoCompleteResults("g", AUTOCOMPLETE_FLAG_IN_GUILD, ↵
AUTOCOMPLETE_FLAG_FRIEND, 10))
```

GetAvailableLevel

Returns the level of a quest available from the current Quest NPC.

```
level = GetAvailableLevel(index)
```

Only returns valid information after a QUEST_GREETING event.

Note: Most quest NPCs present available quests using the GetGossipAvailableQuests() instead of this function.

Arguments:

index—Index of a quest available from the current Quest NPC (between 1 and GetNumAvailableQuests()) (number)

Returns:

level—Recommended character level for attempting the quest (number)

GetAvailableTitle

Returns the name of a quest available from the current Quest NPC.

```
title = GetAvailableTitle(index)
```

Only returns valid information after a QUEST_GREETING event.

Note: Most quest NPCs present available quests using the GetGossip AvailableQuests() instead of this function.

Arguments:

index—Index of a quest available from the current Quest NPC (between 1 and GetNumAvailableQuests()) (number)

Returns:

title—Title of the quest (string)

GetBackpackCurrencyInfo

Returns information about a currency marked for watching on the Backpack UI.

```
name, count, extraCurrencyType, icon, itemID = ↵
GetBackpackCurrencyInfo(index)
```

Arguments:

index—Index of a slot for displaying currencies on the backpack (between 1 and MAX_WATCHED_TOKENS) (number)

Returns:

name—Name of the currency type (string)

count—Amount of the currency the player has (number)

extraCurrencyType—Type of the currency (number)

- 0—Item-based currency
- 1—Arena points
- 2—Honor points

icon—Path to an icon texture representing the currency item (for Honor/Arena points, not the icon displayed in the default UI) (string)

itemID—ID for the currency item (number)

GetBagName

Returns the name of one of the player's bags.

```
name = GetBagName(container)
```

Returns nil for the bank and keyring, for bank bags while the player is not at the bank, and for empty bag or bank bag slots.

Arguments:

container—Index of one of the player's bags or other containers (number, containerID)

Returns:

name—Name of the container (string)

Example:

```
-- Print the names of the player's bags to chat
for i=0,4 do
 local name = GetBagName(i)
 if name then
  print("Bag", i, ":", name)
 end
end
```

GetBankSlotCost

Returns the cost of the next purchasable bank bag slot.

```
cost = GetBankSlotCost()
```

Returns `999999999` if the player owns all available slots.

Returns:

`cost`—Cost of the next available bank bag slot (in copper) (`number`)

GetBarberShopStyleInfo

Returns information about the selected barber shop style option.

```
name, unused, cost, isCurrent = GetBarberShopStyleInfo(styleIndex)
```

Arguments:

`styleIndex`—Index of a style option (`number`)

- 1—Hair (or Horn) Style
- 2—Hair (or Horn) Color
- 3—Varies by race and gender: Facial Hair, Earrings, Features, Hair, Horns, Markings, Normal, Piercings, or Tusks

Returns:

`name`—Name of the style option, or `nil` if the style is not named (`string`)

`unused`—Currently unused (`string`)

`cost`—Price of applying the style option, not including changes to other style options (in copper) (`number`)

`isCurrent`—1 if the style option matches the character's existing style; otherwise `nil` (`1nil`)

GetBarberShopTotalCost

Returns the total price of selected barber shop style changes.

```
cost = GetBarberShopTotalCost()
```

Returns:

`cost`—Price of the barber shop style change (in copper) (`number`)

GetBattlefieldEstimatedWaitTime

Returns the estimated wait time on a battleground or arena queue.

```
waitTime = GetBattlefieldEstimatedWaitTime(index)
```

Arguments:

`index`—Index of a battleground/arena queue the player has joined (between 1 and `MAX_BATTLEFIELD_QUEUES`) (`number`)

Returns:

`waitTime`—Estimated wait time to join the battleground/arena (in milliseconds) (`number`)

GetBattlefieldFlagPosition

Returns the position of a flag in a battleground.

```
flagX, flagY, flagToken = GetBattlefieldFlagPosition(index)
```

Arguments:

index—Index of a flag (between 1 and GetNumBattlefieldFlag Positions()) (number)

Returns:

flagX—Horizontal (X) coordinate of the flag's position relative to the zone map (0 = left edge, 1 = right edge) (number)

flagY—Vertical (Y) coordinate of the flag's position relative to the zone map (0 = bottom edge, 1 = top edge) (number)

flagToken—Unique portion of the path to a texture for the flag; preface with "Interface\\WorldStateFrame\" for the full path (string)

GetBattlefieldInfo

Returns information about a battleground for which the player can queue.

mapName, mapDescription, minLevel, maxLevel, bracketMin, bracketMax, ↵
maxGroup = GetBattlefieldInfo()

Returns:

mapName—Localized name of the battleground (string)

mapDescription—Localized descriptive text about the battleground (string)

minLevel—Minimum character level required to enter the battleground (number)

maxLevel—Maximum character level allowed in the battleground (number)

bracketMin—Lowest level of characters in the player's level bracket for the battleground (number)

bracketMax—Highest level of characters in the player's level bracket for the battleground (number)

maxGroup—Maximum number of players allowed when joining the battleground queue as a group (number)

GetBattlefieldInstanceExpiration

Returns the amount of time remaining before all players are removed from the instance, if in a battleground instance where the match has completed.

timeLeft = GetBattlefieldInstanceExpiration()

Returns:

timeLeft—Amount of time remaining (in milliseconds) before all players are removed from the instance, if in a battleground instance where the match has completed; otherwise 0. (number)

GetBattlefieldInstanceInfo

Returns a numeric ID for a battleground instance in the battleground queueing list.

instanceID = GetBattlefieldInstanceInfo(index)

This number is seen in the instance names in said listings and elsewhere in the Battlegrounds UI (e.g. the 13 in "You are eligible to enter Warsong Gulch 13").

Arguments:

index—Index in the battleground queue listing (1 for the first available instance, or between 2 and GetNumBattlefields() for other instances) (number)

Returns:

instanceID—Numeric ID of the battleground instance (number)

GetBattlefieldInstanceRunTime

Returns the amount of time since the current battleground instance opened.

time = GetBattlefieldInstanceRunTime()

Returns:

time—Amount of time since the current battleground instance opened (in milliseconds) (number)

Example:

```
-- Print the current battleground time as a string
print(SecondsToTime(GetBattlefieldInstanceRunTime()/1000))
```

GetBattlefieldMapIconScale

Returns the scale to be used for displaying battleground map icons.

scale = GetBattlefieldMapIconScale()

Used in the default UI to determine the size of the point of interest icons (towers, graveyards, etc.) on the zone map (the small battle minimap). The default size of the icons is set by DEFAULT_POI_ICON_SIZE and the scale is used to grow or shrink them depending on the size of the map.

Returns:

scale—Scale factor for map icons (between 0 and 1) (number)

Example:

```
-- Set the size of an icon scaled by this value
local size = DEFAULT_POI_ICON_SIZE * GetBattlefieldMapIconScale()
icon:SetWidth(size)
icon:SetHeight(size)
```

GetBattlefieldPortExpiration

Returns the time left on a battleground or arena invitation.

expiration = GetBattlefieldPortExpiration(index)

Arguments:

index—Index of a battleground/arena queue the player has joined (between 1 and MAX_BATTLEFIELD_QUEUES) (number)

Returns:

expiration—Time remaining before the player's invitation to enter the battleground/arena expires (in seconds); 0 if the player has not yet been invited to enter or is already in the battleground/arena instance (number)

Example:

```
-- Print the time left for all active battleground queues
for index=1, MAX_BATTLEFIELD_QUEUES do
 local status, name = GetBattlefieldStatus(index)

 if status == "confirm" then
  print(format(
    "Your invitation to %s will expire in %d seconds.",
    name, GetBattlefieldPortExpiration(index)
  ))
 end

end
```

GetBattlefieldPosition

Returns the position of a battleground team member not in the player's group.

```
unitX, unitY, name = GetBattlefieldPosition(index)
```

Still used in the default UI but no longer useful; as all team members in a battleground match are automatically joined into a raid group. See `GetPlayer MapPosition()` instead.

Arguments:

index—Index of a team member (between 1 and `GetNumBattlefield Positions()`) (number)

Returns:

unitX—Horizontal (X) coordinate of the unit's position relative to the zone map (0 = left edge, 1 = right edge) (number)

unitY—Vertical (Y) coordinate of the unit's position relative to the zone map (0 = bottom edge, 1 = top edge) (number)

name—Name of the unit for display on the map (string)

GetBattlefieldScore

Returns basic scoreboard information for a battleground/arena participant.

```
name, killingBlows, honorableKills, deaths, honorGained, faction, ↩
rank, race, classToken, damageDone, healingDone = ↩
GetBattlefieldScore(index)
```

Does not include battleground-specific score data (e.g. flags captured in Warsong Gulch, towers assaulted in Alterac Valley, etc); see `GetBattle fieldStatData()` for such information.

Arguments:

index—Index of a participant in the battleground/arena scoreboard (between 1 and `GetNumBattlefieldScores()`) (number)

Returns:

name—Name of the participant (string)

killingBlows—Number of killing blows scored by the participant during the match (number) honorableKills—Number of honorable kills scored by the participant during the match (number)

deaths—Number of times the participant died during the match (number)

honorGained—Amount of honor points gained by the participant during the match (number)

faction—Faction or team to which the participant belongs (number)

- 0—Horde (Battleground) / Green Team (Arena)
- 1—Alliance (Battleground) / Gold Team (Arena)

rank—Deprecated; always 0 (number)

race—Localized name of the participant's race (string)

classToken—Non-localized token representing the participant's class (string)

damageDone—Total amount of damage done by the participant during the match (number)

healingDone—Total amount of healing done by the participant during the match (number)

GetBattlefieldStatData

Returns battleground-specific scoreboard information for a battleground participant.

```
columnData = GetBattlefieldStatData(index, statIndex)
```

Battleground-specific statistics include flags captured in Warsong Gulch, towers assaulted in Alterac Valley, etc. For the name and icon associated with each statistic, see GetBattlefieldStatInfo(). For basic battleground score information, see GetBattlefieldScore().

Arguments:

index—Index of a participant in the battleground/arena scoreboard (between 1 and GetNumBattlefieldScores()) (number)

statIndex—Index of a battleground-specific statistic (between 1 and GetNumBattlefieldStats()) (number)

Returns:

columnData—The participant's score for the statistic (number)

Example:

```
-- Print out the player's battleground statistics
local playerName = UnitName("player")
for playerIndex = 1, GetNumBattlefieldStats() do
 local name = GetBattlefieldScore(playerIndex)
 if name == playerName then
  local output = "Battleground stats for "..name..":\n"
  for statIndex = 1, GetNumBattlefieldStats() do
   output = output .. "  " .. GetBattlefieldStatInfo(statIndex) ↵
.. ": " ..GetBattlefieldStatData(statIndex) .. "\n"
  end
  print(output)
```

```
        break
      end
    end
```

GetBattlefieldStatInfo

Returns information about a battleground-specific scoreboard column.

```
text, icon, tooltip = GetBattlefieldStatInfo(statIndex)
```

Battleground-specific statistics include flags captured in Warsong Gulch, towers assaulted in Alterac Valley, etc.

Arguments:

`statIndex`—Index of a battleground-specific statistic (between 1 and `GetNumBattlefieldStats()`) (number)

Returns:

`text`—Name to display for the statistic's scoreboard column header (string)

`icon`—Path to an icon texture for the statistic (string)

`tooltip`—Text to be displayed as a tooltip when mousing over the scoreboard column (string)

GetBattlefieldStatus

Returns information about an active or queued battleground/arena instance.

```
status, mapName, instanceID, bracketMin, bracketMax, teamSize, ↵
registeredMatch = GetBattlefieldStatus(index)
```

Arguments:

`index`—Index of a battleground/arena queue the player has joined (between 1 and `MAX_BATTLEFIELD_QUEUES`) (number)

Returns:

`status`—Status of the player with respect to the battleground (string)

▪ `active`—The player is currently playing in this battleground

▪ `confirm`—The player has been invited to enter this battleground but has not done so yet

▪ `none`—No battleground or queue at this index

▪ `queued`—The player is queued for this battleground

`mapName`—Name of the battleground (e.g. "Alterac Valley") or arena ("All Arenas" while `queued`; "Eastern Kingdoms" regardless of destination while status is `confirm`, e.g. "Dalaran Sewers" while `active`) (string)

`instanceID`—If in a battleground or queued for a specific instance, the number identifying that instance (e.g. 13 in "Warsong Gulch 13"); otherwise 0 (number)

`bracketMin`—Lowest level of characters in the player's level bracket for the battleground (number)

`bracketMax`—Highest level of characters in the player's level bracket for the battleground (number) teamSize—Number of players per team for an arena match (number)

0—Not an arena match   3—3v3 Arena

2—2v2 Arena   5—5v5 Arena

registeredMatch—1 if a rated arena match; otherwise nil (1nil)

GetBattlefieldTeamInfo

Returns info about teams and their ratings in a rated arena match.

teamName, teamRating, newTeamRating = GetBattlefieldTeamInfo(index)

Usable following the UPDATE_BATTLEFIELD_SCORE event.

Arguments:

index—Index of a team in the arena match (number)

■ 0—Green Team

■ 1—Gold Team

Returns:

teamName—Name of the team (string)

teamRating—The team's rating at the start of the match (number)

newTeamRating—New rating for the team when the match is complete (number)

GetBattlefieldTimeWaited

Returns the amount of time elapsed since the player joined the queue for a battleground/arena.

timeInQueue = GetBattlefieldTimeWaited(index)

Arguments:

index—Index of a battleground/arena queue the player has joined (between 1 and MAX_BATTLEFIELD_QUEUES) (number)

Returns:

timeInQueue—Time elapsed since the player joined the queue (in milliseconds) (number)

GetBattlefieldVehicleInfo

Returns information about special vehicles in the current zone.

vehicleX, vehicleY, unitName, isPossessed, vehicleType, orientation, ↵
isPlayer, isAlive = GetBattlefieldVehicleInfo(index)

Used only for certain vehicles in certain zones: includes the airships in Icecrown as well as vehicles used in Ulduar, Wintergrasp, and Strand of the Ancients.

Arguments:

index—Index of a special vehicle (between 1 and GetNumBattlefield Vehicles()) (number)

Returns:

vehicleX—Horizontal position of the vehicle relative to the zone map (0 = left edge, 1 = right edge) (number) vehicleY—Vertical position of the vehicle relative to the zone map (0 = top, 1 = bottom) (number)

unitName—Localized name of the vehicle (string)

isPossessed—True if the vehicle is controlled by another unit (boolean)

vehicleType—Token indicating type of vehicle; some types can be used as keys to the global VEHICLE_TEXTURES table to get display texture information for the vehicle (string)

- Airship Alliance—The Alliance flying quest hub in Icecrown
- Airship Horde—The Horde flying quest hub in Icecrown
- Drive—A land vehicle such as a siege engine
- Fly—A flying vehicle
- Idle—A non-moving vehicle (e.g. an artillery turret)

orientation—Facing angle of the vehicle ((in radians, 0 = north, values increasing counterclockwise) (number)

isPlayer—True if the vehicle is controlled by the player (boolean)

isAlive—True if the vehicle has not been destroyed (boolean)

GetBattlefieldWinner

Returns the winner of the current battleground or arena match.

```
winner = GetBattlefieldWinner()
```

Returns:

winner—Index of the winning team if in a completed match; otherwise nil (number)

- 0—Horde (Battleground) / Green Team (Arena)
- 1—Alliance (Battleground) / Gold Team (Arena)

GetBattlegroundInfo

Returns information about available battlegrounds.

```
name, canEnter, isHoliday, minlevel = GetBattlegroundInfo(index)
```

Arguments:

index—Index of a battleground (between 1 and NUM_BATTLEGROUNDS) (number)

Returns:

name—Localized name of the battleground (Alterac Valley, Warsong Gulch, etc.) (string)

canEnter—1 if the player can enter the battleground; otherwise nil (1nil)

isHoliday—1 if a "holiday" offering bonus honor is currently active for the battleground; otherwise nil (1nil)

minlevel—Minimum character level required to enter the battleground (number)

GetBidderAuctionItems

Requests data from the server for the list of auctions bid on by the player.

The `AUCTION_BIDDER_LIST_UPDATE` event fires if new data is available; listing information can then be retrieved using `GetAuctionItemInfo()` or other Auction APIs.

GetBillingTimeRested

Returns the amount of time for which the player must be offline in order to lift play time restrictions.

```
time = GetBillingTimeRested()
```

After playing for a number of hours, restrictions may be placed on the player's ability to gain loot or XP, complete quests, or use trade skills; if in such a state, the player must log off for the period of time specified by this function in order to return to normal play.

Only used in locales where the length of play sessions is restricted (e.g. mainland China).

Returns:

`time`—Offline time required to lift play time restrictions (in minutes) (`number`)

GetBindLocation

Returns the name of the player's Hearthstone location.

```
location = GetBindLocation()
```

Returns:

`location`—Name of the player's Hearthstone location (`string`)

GetBinding

Returns information about a key binding.

```
commandName, binding1, binding2 = GetBinding(index)
```

Arguments:

`index`—Index in the key bindings list (between 1 and `GetNumBindings()`) (`number`)

Returns:

`commandName`—Name of the binding command (`string`)

`binding1`—First key binding for the command, or `nil` if no key is bound (`string`, binding)

`binding2`—Second key binding for the command, or `nil` if no key is bound (`string`, binding)

GetBindingAction

Returns the action bound to a key or key combination.

```
action = GetBindingAction("key" [, checkOverride])
```

Arguments:

`key`—A key or key combination (e.g. "CTRL-2") (`string`, binding)

`checkOverride` (optional)—`True` to check possible override bindings for the `key`, `false` or omitted to check only normal bindings (`boolean`)

Returns:

action—Name of the action associated with the key, or the empty string (" ") if the key is not bound to an action (string)

GetBindingByKey

Returns the action bound to a key or key combination.

```
action = GetBindingByKey("key")
```

Arguments:

key—A key or key combination (e.g. "CTRL-2") (string, binding)

Returns:

action—Name of the action associated with the key, or the empty string (" ") if the key is not bound to an action (string)

GetBindingKey

Returns the key combinations for a given binding command.

```
key1, ... = GetBindingKey("COMMAND")
```

Although the default UI only allows two combinations to be bound to a command, more than two can be set via the API.

Arguments:

COMMAND—Name of a binding command (string)

Returns:

key1—First key binding for the command, or nil if no key is bound (string, binding)

...—A list of additional bindings for the command (list)

GetBlockChance

Returns the player's percentage chance to block with a shield.

```
chance = GetBlockChance()
```

Returns:

chance—Percentage chance to block (number)

GetBonusBarOffset

Returns the current "stance" offset for use with the bonus action bar.

```
offset = GetBonusBarOffset()
```

This value corresponds to what "stance" the player is currently in, and more specifically which set of actions correspond to that stance. Action IDs for special stances start on action bar #7 (or NUM_ACTIONBAR_PAGES + 1), so the offset returned by this function corresponds to the number to be added to NUM_ACTIONBAR_PAGES in calculating action IDs for these action bars.

Note that the UI definition of "stance" includes not just warrior stances but also druid shapeshift forms, rogue/druid stealth, priest shadowform, and various other cases, but does not necessarily include all states normally presented in the default UI's stance/shapeshift bar (notable exclusions are paladin auras and death knight presences).

Returns:

`offset`—Offset of the stance's action bar in relation to NUM_ACTIONBAR_PAGES (`number`)

GetBuildInfo

Returns the version information about the client.

```
version, internalVersion, date, uiVersion = GetBuildInfo()
```

Returns:

`version`—Display version number of the client (e.g. `"3.1.1"`) (`string`)

`internalVersion`—Internal version number of the client (e.g. `"9835"`) (`string`)

`date`—Date on which the client executable was built (e.g. `"Apr 24 2009"`); not necessarily the date it was released to the public (`string`)

`uiVersion`—Version compatibility number for UI purposes (e.g. `30100`); generally, installed addons should have this number in the `Interface` header of their TOC files to avoid being marked as Out of Date and possibly not loaded (`number`)

GetBuybackItemInfo

Returns information about an item recently sold to a vendor and available to be repurchased.

```
name, texture, price, quantity, numAvailable, isUsable = ↵
GetBuybackItemInfo(index)
```

Arguments:

`index`—Index of an item in the buyback listing (between 1 and GetNumBuybackItems()) (`number`)

Returns:

`name`—Name of the item (`string`)

`texture`—Path to an icon texture for the item (`string`)

`price`—Current cost to repurchase the item from this vendor (in copper) (`number`)

`quantity`—Number of stacked items per purchase (`number`)

`numAvailable`—Number of items available for purchase, if the vendor has a limited stock of the item; generally 0 for buyback items (`number`)

`isUsable`—1 if the player can use or equip the item; otherwise `nil` (`1nil`)

GetBuybackItemLink

Returns a hyperlink for an item recently sold to a vendor and available to be repurchased.

```
link = GetBuybackItemLink(index)
```

Arguments:

`index`—Index of an item in the buyback listing (between 1 and GetNumBuybackItems()) (`number`)

Returns:

link—A hyperlink for the item (string, hyperlink)

Example:

```
-- Print item links for every item in the buyback tab
for i=1,12 do
  local link = GetBuybackItemLink(i)
  if link then
    print(link .. " is available for buyback")
  end
end
```

GetCVar

Returns the value of a configuration variable.

```
string = GetCVar("cvar")
```

Causes an error if the named CVar does not exist.

Note that all values are returned as strings: use of `tonumber()` may be required if using a value in a numeric context. (See also `GetCVarBool()` for binary values.)

Arguments:

cvar—Name of a CVar (string)

Returns:

string—Value of the CVar (any)

GetCVarAbsoluteMax

Returns the absolute maximum value allowed for a configuration variable.

```
min = GetCVarAbsoluteMax("cvar")
```

Arguments:

cvar—Name of a CVar (string)

Returns:

min—Absolute maximum value allowed for the CVar (number)

GetCVarAbsoluteMin

Returns the absolute minimum value allowed for a configuration variable.

```
min = GetCVarAbsoluteMin("cvar")
```

Arguments:

cvar—Name of a CVar (string)

Returns:

min—Absolute minimum value allowed for the CVar (number)

GetCVarBool

Returns the value of a configuration variable in a format compatible with Lua conditional expressions.

```
value = GetCVarBool("cvar")
```

All configuration variables are stored as strings; many CVars represent the state of a binary flag and are stored as either "1" or "0". This function provides a convenient way to test the state of such variables without the extra syntax required to explicitly check for "1" or "0" values.

Arguments:

cvar—Name of a CVar (string)

Returns:

value—1 if the CVar's value should be treated as true; nil if it should be treated as false (1nil)

GetCVarDefault

Returns the default value of a configuration variable.

```
value = GetCVarDefault("CVar")
```

Causes an error if the named CVar does not exist.

Arguments:

CVar—Name of a CVar (string)

Returns:

value—Default value of the CVar (string)

GetCVarInfo

Returns information about a configuration variable.

```
value, defaultValue, serverStoredAccountWide, ↵
serverStoredPerCharacter = GetCVarInfo("cvar")
```

Arguments:

cvar—Name of a CVar (string)

Returns:

value—Current value of the CVar (string)

defaultValue—Default value of the CVar (string)

serverStoredAccountWide—1 if the CVar's value is saved on the server and shared by all characters on the player's account; otherwise nil (1nil)

serverStoredPerCharacter—1 if the CVar's value is saved on the server and specific to the current character; otherwise nil (1nil)

GetCVarMax

Returns the maximum recommended value for a configuration variable.

```
max = GetCVarMax("cvar")
```

Used in the default UI to set the upper bounds for options controlled by slider widgets.

Arguments:

cvar—Name of a CVar (string)

Returns:

max—Maximum value allowed for the given CVar (number)

GetCVarMin

Returns the minimum recommended value for a configuration variable.

```
min = GetCVarMin("cvar")
```

Used in the default UI to set the lower bounds for options controlled by slider widgets.

Arguments:

cvar—Name of a CVar (string)

Returns:

min—Minimum value allowed for the CVar (number)

GetCategoryInfo

Returns information about an achievement/statistic category.

```
name, parentID, flags = GetCategoryInfo(id)
```

Arguments:

id—The numeric ID of an achievement/statistic category (number)

Returns:

name—Name of the category (string)

parentID—ID of the parent category of which this is a sub-category, or -1 if this is a top-level category (number)

flags—Various additional information about the category; currently unused (0 for all existing categories) (bitfield)

GetCategoryList

Returns a list of all achievement categories.

```
categories = GetCategoryList()
```

Returns:

categories—A list of achievement category IDs (table)

GetCategoryNumAchievements

Returns the number of achievements/statistics to display in a category.

```
numItems, numCompleted = GetCategoryNumAchievements(id)
```

Note this function does not return the total number of achievements in a category; it only returns the number to be displayed in the default UI. Achievements may belong to a category but not be counted for display: e.g. among those which are part of a series (100 Quests Completed, 500 Quests Completed), only the achievement most recently completed and the achievement following it in the series are shown.

Arguments:

id—The numeric ID of an achievement/statistic category (number)

Returns:

numItems—Number of achievements or statistics to display in the category (number)

numCompleted—Number of completed achievements in the category (or 0 for statistics) (number)

GetChannelDisplayInfo

Returns information about an entry in the channel list display.

```
name, header, collapsed, channelNumber, count, active, category, ↵
voiceEnabled, voiceActive = GetChannelDisplayInfo(index)
```

Arguments:

index—Index of an entry in the channel list display (between 1 and `GetNumDisplayChannels()`) (number)

Returns:

name—Name of the channel or header (string)

header—1 if the entry is a group header; otherwise nil (1nil)

collapsed—1 if the entry is a collapsed group header; otherwise nil (1nil)

channelNumber—Number identifying the channel (as returned by `GetChannelList()` and used by `SendChatMessage()` and other channel functions) (number)

count—Number of characters in the channel (number)

active—1 if the channel is currently active; otherwise nil. (Used for special server channels, e.g. "Trade" and "LookingForGroup", which can only be used under certain conditions) (1nil)

category—Category to which the chat channel belongs (string)

- CHANNEL_CATEGORY_CUSTOM—Custom channels created by players
- CHANNEL_CATEGORY_GROUP—Group channels (party, raid, battleground)
- CHANNEL_CATEGORY_WORLD—World channels (General, Trade, etc.)

voiceEnabled—1 if voice chat is enabled for the channel; otherwise nil (1nil)

voiceActive—1 if voice chat is active for the channel; otherwise nil (1nil)

GetChannelList

Returns the list of the channels the player has joined.

```
index, channel, ... = GetChannelList()
```

Returns:

index—Index of the channel (number)

channel—Name of the channel (string)

...—Additional index, channel pairs for each channel the player has joined (list)

GetChannelName

Returns information about a chat channel.

```
channel, channelName, instanceID = GetChannelName(channelIndex) or ↵
GetChannelName("channelName")
```

Arguments:

channelIndex—A channel ID (number)

channelName—A channel name (string)

Returns:

channel—ID of the channel (number)

channelName—Name of the channel (string)

instanceID—The channel's instance ID, or 0 if there are not separate instances of the channel. (number)

GetChannelRosterInfo

Returns information about a character in a chat channel in the channel list display.

```
name, owner, moderator, muted, active, enabled = ↵
GetChannelRosterInfo(index, rosterIndex)
```

Arguments:

index—Index of a channel in the channel list display (between 1 and GetNumDisplayChannels()) (number)

rosterIndex—Index of a participant in the channel (between 1 and count, where count = select(5,GetChannelDisplayInfo(index)) (number)

Returns:

name—Name of the character (string)

owner—1 if the character is the channel owner; otherwise nil (1nil)

moderator—1 if the character is a channel moderator; otherwise nil (1nil)

muted—1 if the character is muted; otherwise nil (1nil)

active—1 if the character is currently speaking in the channel; otherwise nil (1nil)

enabled—1 if the character has voice chat active for the channel; otherwise nil (1nil)

Example:

```
-- Counts the number of players in the given channel who do not have
-- voice chat enabled, and prints it to chat.

-- This script should be run with the "Chat" window open and
-- a channel selected
local index = GetSelectedDisplayChannel()
local count = select(5, GetChannelDisplayInfo(index))
local activeCount = 0
for i=1,count do
 local active = select(6, GetChannelRosterInfo(index, i))
 if active then
  activeCount = activeCount + 1
 end
end

print(activeCount .. " of " .. count .. " users have voice chat ↵
enabled in this channel.")
```

GetChatTypeIndex

Returns the numeric index corresponding to a chat message type.

```
index = GetChatTypeIndex("messageGroup")
```

These indices are used in the default UI to identify lines printed in a chat window, allowing (for example) their color to be changed to match changes in the player's color preferences.

Arguments:

messageGroup—Token identifying a message type (string, chatMsgType)

Returns:

index—Numeric index of the chat type (number)

GetChatWindowChannels

Returns the saved list of channels to which a chat window is subscribed.

```
channelName, channelId, ... = GetChatWindowChannels(index)
```

Arguments:

index—Index of a chat frame (between 1 and NUM_CHAT_WINDOWS) (number)

Returns:

channelName—Name of the channel (string)

channelId—Numeric id for the channel (number)

...—Additional channelName, channelId pairs for each channel belonging to the chat window (list)

GetChatWindowInfo

Returns the saved settings for a chat window.

```
name, fontSize, r, g, b, alpha, shown, locked, docked, ↵
uninteractable = GetChatWindowInfo(index)
```

These values reflect the settings saved between sessions, which are used by the default UI to set up the chat frames it displays.

Arguments:

index—Index of the window you wish you get information on (starts at 1) (number)

Returns:

name—Name of the chat window (string)

fontSize—Font size for text displayed in the chat window (number)

r—Red component of the window's background color (0.0 – 1.0) (number)

g—Green component of the window's background color (0.0 – 1.0) (number)

b—Blue component of the window's background color (0.0 – 1.0) (number)

alpha—Alpha value (opacity) of the window's background (0 = fully transparent, 1 = fully opaque) (number)

shown—1 if the window should be shown; 0 if it should be hidden (number)

locked—1 if the window should be locked; 0 if it should be movable/resizable (number)

docked—1 if the window should be docked to the main chat window; otherwise 0 (number)

uninteractable—1 if the window should ignore all mouse events; otherwise 0 (number)

GetChatWindowMessages

Returns the saved list of messages to which a chat window is subscribed.

```
... = GetChatWindowMessages(index)
```

Arguments:

index—Index of a chat frame (between 1 and NUM_CHAT_WINDOWS) (number)

Returns:

...—A list of chatMsgTypes for which the chat window is subscribed (list)

GetClickFrame

Returns the Frame object associated with the given name.

```
frame = GetClickFrame("name")
```

Returns nil if there is no UI object with the name given, or if the named UI object is not a Frame.

Arguments:

name—Name of a Frame or other UI object (string)

Returns:

frame—A reference to the named frame (table)

GetCoinIcon

Returns an icon representing an amount of money.

```
icon = GetCoinIcon(amount)
```

Arguments:

amount—Amount of money in copper (number)

Returns:

icon—Path to an icon texture representing the amount (string)

- Interface\Icons\INV_Misc_Coin_01—Small amount of Gold
- Interface\Icons\INV_Misc_Coin_02—Large amount of Gold
- Interface\Icons\INV_Misc_Coin_03—Small amount of Silver
- Interface\Icons\INV_Misc_Coin_04—Large amount of Silver
- Interface\Icons\INV_Misc_Coin_05—Small amount of Copper
- Interface\Icons\INV_Misc_Coin_06—Large amount of Copper

GetCoinText

Returns a localized string describing an amount of money.

```
coinText = GetCoinText(amount, "separator")
```

Arguments:

amount—Amount of money in copper (number)

separator—String to use as separator (', ' is used if nil) (string)

Returns:

coinText—Text description of the amount using localized names for 'Gold', 'Silver' and 'Copper' (string)

Example:

```
GetCoinTextureString(10000)
-- returns "1 Gold"

GetCoinTextureString(500050)
-- returns "50 Gold, 50 Copper"

GetCoinTextureString(123456, " / ")
-- returns "12 Gold / 4 Silver / 56 Copper"
```

GetCoinTextureString

Returns a string with embedded coin icons describing an amount of money.

```
coinText = GetCoinTextureString(amount [, fontSize])
```

As in most places where money amounts are shown in the UI, lesser denominations are only shown when non-zero.

Arguments:

amount—Amount of money in copper (number)

fontSize (optional)—Size of the money icons. Defaults to 14. (number)

Returns:

coinText—Text description of the amount using embedded texture codes for gold, silver, and copper coin icons (string)

Example:

```
GetCoinTextureString(10000)
-- returns "1|TInterface\\MoneyFrame\\UI_GoldIcon:14:14:2:0|t"

GetCoinTextureString(500050)
-- returns "50|TInterface\\MoneyFrame\\UI_GoldIcon:14:14:2:0|t ↵
50|TInterface\\MoneyFrame\\UI_CopperIcon:14:14:2:0|t"

GetCoinTextureString(123456)
-- returns "12|TInterface\\MoneyFrame\\UI_GoldIcon:14:14:2:0|t ↵
34|TInterface\\MoneyFrame\\UI_SilverIcon:14:14:2:0|t ↵
56|TInterface\\MoneyFrame\\UI_CopperIcon:14:14:2:0|t"
```

GetCombatRating

Returns the value of a combat rating for the player.

```
rating = GetCombatRating(ratingIndex)
```

Arguments:

ratingIndex—Index of a rating; the following global constants are provided for convenience (number)

- CR_BLOCK—Block skill
- CR_CRIT_MELEE—Melee critical strike chance
- CR_CRIT_RANGED—Ranged critical strike chance
- CR_CRIT_SPELL—Spell critical strike chance

- CR_CRIT_TAKEN_MELEE—Melee Resilience
- CR_CRIT_TAKEN_RANGED—Ranged Resilience
- CR_CRIT_TAKEN_SPELL—Spell Resilience
- CR_DEFENSE_SKILL—Defense skill
- CR_DODGE—Dodge skill
- CR_HASTE_MELEE—Melee haste
- CR_HASTE_RANGED—Ranged haste
- CR_HASTE_SPELL—Spell haste
- CR_HIT_MELEE—Melee chance to hit
- CR_HIT_RANGED—Ranged chance to hit
- CR_HIT_SPELL—Spell chance to hit
- CR_HIT_TAKEN_MELEE—Unused
- CR_HIT_TAKEN_RANGED—Unused
- CR_HIT_TAKEN_SPELL—Unused
- CR_PARRY—Parry skill
- CR_WEAPON_SKILL—Weapon skill
- CR_WEAPON_SKILL_MAINHAND—Main-hand weapon skill
- CR_WEAPON_SKILL_OFFHAND—Offhand weapon skill
- CR_WEAPON_SKILL_RANGED—Ranged weapon skill

Returns:

rating—Value of the rating for the player (number)

GetCombatRatingBonus

Returns the percentage effect for the player's current value of a given combat rating.

ratingBonus = GetCombatRatingBonus(ratingIndex)

Used in the default UI to show tooltips with actual percentage effects (such as increased parry chance or reduced critical strike damage taken) when mousing over rating information in the Character window.

Arguments:

ratingIndex—Index of a rating; the following global constants are provided for convenience (number)

- CR_BLOCK—Block skill
- CR_CRIT_MELEE—Melee critical strike chance
- CR_CRIT_RANGED—Ranged critical strike chance
- CR_CRIT_SPELL—Spell critical strike chance
- CR_CRIT_TAKEN_MELEE—Melee Resilience
- CR_CRIT_TAKEN_RANGED—Ranged Resilience
- CR_CRIT_TAKEN_SPELL—Spell Resilience
- CR_DEFENSE_SKILL—Defense skill
- CR_DODGE—Dodge skill

- CR_HASTE_MELEE—Melee haste
- CR_HASTE_RANGED—Ranged haste
- CR_HASTE_SPELL—Spell haste
- CR_HIT_MELEE—Melee chance to hit
- CR_HIT_RANGED—Ranged chance to hit
- CR_HIT_SPELL—Spell chance to hit
- CR_HIT_TAKEN_MELEE—Unused
- CR_HIT_TAKEN_RANGED—Unused
- CR_HIT_TAKEN_SPELL—Unused
- CR_PARRY—Parry skill
- CR_WEAPON_SKILL—Weapon skill
- CR_WEAPON_SKILL_MAINHAND—Main-hand weapon skill
- CR_WEAPON_SKILL_OFFHAND—Offhand weapon skill
- CR_WEAPON_SKILL_RANGED—Ranged weapon skill

Returns:

ratingBonus—Percentage change in the underlying statistic or mechanic conferred by the player's rating value (number)

GetComboPoints

Returns the player's number of combo points on the current target.

comboPoints = GetComboPoints()

Only applicable to Rogues and Druids in Cat Form; always returns 0 for other classes/forms.

Returns:

comboPoints—Number of combo points (between 0 and MAX_COMBO_POINTS) (number)

GetCompanionCooldown

Returns cooldown information for a non-combat pet or mount.

start, duration, enable = GetCompanionCooldown("type", index)

Arguments:

type—Type of companion (string)

- CRITTER—A non-combat pet
- MOUNT—A mount

index—Index of a companion (between 1 and GetNumCompanions(type)) (number)

Returns:

start—The value of GetTime() at the moment the cooldown began, or 0 if the companion is ready (number)

duration—The length of the cooldown, or 0 if the companion is ready (number) enable—1 if a Cooldown UI element should be used to display the cooldown, otherwise 0. (Does not always correlate with whether the companion is ready.) (number)

GetCompanionInfo

Returns information about a non-combat pet or mount.

```
creatureID, creatureName, spellID, icon, active = ↵
GetCompanionInfo("type", index)
```

Arguments:

type—Type of companion (string)

■ CRITTER—A non-combat pet

■ MOUNT—A mount

index—Index of a companion (between 1 and GetNumCompanions(type)) (number)

Returns:

creatureID—Unique ID of the companion (usable with PlayerModel: SetCreature) (number)

creatureName—Localized name of the companion (string)

spellID—The "spell" for summoning the companion (usable with GetSpell Link et al) (number)

icon—Path to an icon texture for the companion (string)

active—1 if the companion queried is currently summoned; otherwise nil (1nil)

GetComparisonAchievementPoints

Returns the comparison unit's total achievement points earned.

```
points = GetComparisonAchievementPoints()
```

Only accurate once the INSPECT_ACHIEVEMENT_READY event has fired following a call to SetAchievementComparisonUnit(). No longer accurate once ClearAchievementComparisonUnit() is called.

Returns:

points—Total number of achievement points earned by the comparison unit (number)

GetComparisonCategoryNumAchievements

Returns the number of achievements completed by the comparison unit within a category.

```
numCompleted = GetComparisonCategoryNumAchievements(id)
```

Only accurate once the INSPECT_ACHIEVEMENT_READY event has fired following a call to SetAchievementComparisonUnit(). No longer accurate once ClearAchievementComparisonUnit() is called.

Arguments:

id—The numeric ID of an achievement category (number)

Returns:

numCompleted—Number of achievements completed by the comparison unit in the category (number)

GetComparisonStatistic

Returns the comparison unit's data for a statistic.

```
info = GetComparisonStatistic(id)
```

Only accurate once the INSPECT_ACHIEVEMENT_READY event has fired following a call to SetAchievementComparisonUnit(). No longer accurate once ClearAchievementComparisonUnit() is called.

Arguments:

id—The numeric ID of a statistic (number)

Returns:

info—The comparison unit's data for the statistic, or "--" if none has yet been recorded for it (string)

GetContainerFreeSlots

Returns a list of open slots in a container.

```
slotTable = GetContainerFreeSlots(container [, returnTable])
```

The optional argument returnTable allows for performance optimization in cases where this function is expected to be called repeatedly. Rather than creating new tables each time the function is called (eventually requiring garbage collection), an existing table can be recycled. (Note, however, that this function does not clear the table's contents; use wipe() first to guarantee consistent results.)

Arguments:

container—Index of one of the player's bags or other containers (number, containerID)

returnTable (optional)—Reference to a table to be filled with return values (table)

Returns:

slotTable—A table listing the indices of open slots in the given container (table)

Example:

```
-- assuming the first two rows of slots in your backpack are full...
local bagSpaces = GetContainerFreeSlots(0)
print(unpack(bagSpaces))
-- Chat window shows "9 10 11 12 13 14 15 16"

-- assuming all slots but the first in the bag immediately left
-- of your backpack are full...
GetContainerFreeSlots(1, bagSpaces)
print(unpack(bagSpaces))
-- Chat window shows "1 10 11 12 13 14 15 16"
```

```
-- oops, it overwrote the table from before... let's try again
wipe(bagSpaces)
GetContainerFreeSlots(1, bagSpaces)
print(unpack(bagSpaces))
-- Chat window shows "1"
```

GetContainerItemCooldown

Returns cooldown information about an item in the player's bags.

```
start, duration, enable = GetContainerItemCooldown(container, slot)
```

Arguments:

container—Index of one of the player's bags or other containers (number, containerID)

slot—Index of an item slot within the container (number, containerSlotID)

Returns:

start—The value of GetTime() at the moment the cooldown began, or 0 if the item is ready (number)

duration—The length of the cooldown, or 0 if the item is ready (number)

enable—1 if a Cooldown UI element should be used to display the cooldown, otherwise 0. (Does not always correlate with whether the item is ready.) (number)

GetContainerItemDurability

Returns durability status for an item in the player's bags.

```
durability, max = GetContainerItemDurability(container, slot)
```

Arguments:

container—Index of one of the player's bags or other containers (number, containerID)

slot—Index of an item slot within the container (number, containerSlotID)

Returns:

durability—The item's current durability (number)

max—The item's maximum durability (number)

GetContainerItemGems

Returns the gems socketed in an item in the player's bags.

```
gem1, gem2, gem3 = GetContainerItemGems(container, slot)
```

The IDs returned refer to the gems themselves (not the enchantments they provide), and thus can be passed to GetItemInfo() to get a gem's name, quality, icon, etc.

Arguments:

container—The index of the container (bagID)

slot—The slot within the given container; slots are numbered left-to-right, top-to-bottom, starting with the leftmost slot on the top row (number)

Returns:

gem1—Item ID of the first gem socketed in the item (itemID)

gem2—Item ID of the second gem socketed in the item (`itemID`)

gem3—Item ID of the third gem socketed in the item (`itemID`)

GetContainerItemID

Returns the item ID of an item in the player's bags.

```
id = GetContainerItemID(container, slot)
```

Arguments:

`container`—Index of one of the player's bags or other containers (number, containerID)

`slot`—Index of an item slot within the container (number, containerSlotID)

Returns:

`id`—Numeric ID of the item in the given slot (`itemID`)

GetContainerItemInfo

Returns information about an item in the player's bags.

```
texture, count, locked, quality, readable, lootable, link = ↵
GetContainerItemInfo(container, slot)
```

Arguments:

`container`—Index of one of the player's bags or other containers (number, containerID)

`slot`—Index of an item slot within the container (number, containerSlotID)

Returns:

`texture`—Path to the icon texture for the item (`string`)

`count`—Number of items in the slot (`number`)

`locked`—1 if the item is locked; otherwise `nil`. Items become locked while being moved, split, or placed into other UI elements (such as the mail, trade, and auction windows). (`1nil`)

`quality`—Quality (or rarity) of the item (number, itemQuality)

`readable`—1 if the item is readable; otherwise `nil`. This value is used by the default UI to show a special cursor over items such as books and scrolls which can be read by right-clicking. (`1nil`)

`lootable`—1 if the item is a temporary container containing items that can be looted; otherwise `nil`. Examples include the Bag of Fishing Treasures and Small Spice Bag rewarded by daily quests, lockboxes (once unlocked), and the trunks occasionally found while fishing. (`1nil`)

`link`—A hyperlink for the item (`itemLink`)

GetContainerItemLink

Returns a hyperlink for an item in the player's bags.

```
link = GetContainerItemLink(container, slot)
```

Arguments:

`container`—Index of one of the player's bags or other containers (number, containerID)

`slot`—Index of an item slot within the container (number, containerSlotID)

Returns:

link—A hyperlink for the item (string, hyperlink)

GetContainerItemPurchaseInfo

Returns information about alternate currencies refunded for returning an item to vendors.

```
money, honorPoints, arenaPoints, itemCount, refundSec = ↵
GetContainerItemPurchaseInfo(container, slot)
```

Items bought with alternate currency (honor points, arena points, or special items such as Emblems of Heroism and Dalaran Cooking Awards) can be returned to a vendor for a full refund, but only within a limited time after the original purchase.

If the given container slot is empty, contains an item which cannot be returned for an alternate currency refund, or contains an item for which the refund grace period has expired, all returns are nil.

Arguments:

container—Index of one of the player's bags or other containers (number, containerID)

slot—Index of an item slot within the container (number, containerSlotID)

Returns:

money—Amount of copper to be refunded (number)

honorPoints—Amount of honor points to be refunded (number)

arenaPoints—Amount of arena points to be refunded (number)

itemCount—Number of different item currencies to be refunded (e.g. the price a PvP mount is in 3 currencies, as it requires multiple battlegrounds' Marks of Honor) (number)

refundSec—Seconds remaining until this item is no longer eligible to be returned for a refund (number)

GetContainerItemPurchaseItem

Returns information about a specific currency refunded for returning an item to vendors.

```
texture, quantity, link = GetContainerItemPurchaseItem(container, ↵
slot, index)
```

See GetContainerItemPurchaseInfo for more information about alternate currency refunds.

Arguments:

container—Index of one of the player's bags or other containers (number, containerID)

slot—Index of an item slot within the container (number, containerSlotID)

index—Index of the currency type; between 1 and itemCount, where itemCount is the 4th return from GetContainerItemPurchaseInfo() for the same container and slot (number)

Returns:

texture—Path to an icon texture for the currency item (string)

quantity—Quantity of the currency item to be refunded (number)

link—Hyperlink for the currency item (itemLink)

GetContainerNumFreeSlots

Returns the number of free slots in a container and the types of items it can hold.

```
freeSlots, bagType = GetContainerNumFreeSlots(container)
```

Arguments:

container—Index of one of the player's bags or other containers (number, containerID)

Returns:

freeSlots—Number of empty slots in the bag (number)

bagType—Bitwise OR of the item families that can be put into the container; see GetItemFamily for details (number, bitfield)

GetContainerNumSlots

Returns the number of slots in one of the player's bags.

```
numSlots = GetContainerNumSlots(container)
```

Arguments:

container—Index of one of the player's bags or other containers (number, containerID)

Returns:

numSlots—Number of item slots in the container (number)

GetCorpseMapPosition

Returns the position of the player's corpse on the world map.

```
corpseX, corpseY = GetCorpseMapPosition()
```

Returns 0, 0 if the location of the player's corpse is not visible on the current world map.

Returns:

corpseX—Horizontal position of the player's corpse relative to the zone map (0 = left edge, 1 = right edge) (number)

corpseY—Vertical position of the player's corpse relative to the zone map (0 = top, 1 = bottom) (number)

GetCorpseRecoveryDelay

Returns the amount of time left until the player can recover their corpse.

```
timeLeft = GetCorpseRecoveryDelay()
```

Applies to resurrection spells offered by other units, resurrecting by returning to the player's corpse as a ghost, and to resurrecting at a graveyard's spirit healer, if the player has recently died several times in short succession.

Returns:

timeLeft—Amount of time remaining before the player can resurrect (in seconds); 0 if the player can resurrect immediately (number)

GetCritChance

Returns the player's melee critical strike chance.

```
critChance = GetCritChance()
```

Returns:

critChance—The player's percentage critical strike chance for melee attacks (number)

GetCritChanceFromAgility

Returns additional critical strike chance provided by Agility.

```
critChance = GetCritChanceFromAgility(["unit"])
```

Arguments:

unit (optional)—A unit to query; only valid for player and pet, defaults to player if omitted (string, unitID)

Returns:

critChance—Additional percentage chance of critical strikes conferred by the unit's Agility statistic (number)

GetCurrencyListInfo

Returns information about a currency type (or headers in the Currency UI).

```
name, isHeader, isExpanded, isUnused, isWatched, count, ↵
extraCurrencyType, icon, itemID = GetCurrencyListInfo(index)
```

Arguments:

index—Index of a currency type in the currency list (between 1 and GetCurrencyListSize()) (number)

Returns:

name—Name of the currency type or category header (string)

isHeader—True if this listing is a category header, false for actual currencies (boolean)

isExpanded—True if this listing is a category header whose contents are shown, false for collapsed headers and actual currencies (boolean)

isUnused—True if the player has marked this currency as Unused (boolean)

isWatched—True if the player has marked this currency to be watched on the backpack UI (boolean)

count—Amount of the currency the player has (number)

extraCurrencyType—1 for Arena points, 2 for Honor points, 0 for other currencies (number)

icon—Path to a texture representing the currency item (not applicable for Arena/Honor points) (string)

itemID—ID for the currency item (number)

GetCurrencyListSize

Returns the number of list entries to show in the Currency UI.

```
numEntries = GetCurrencyListSize()
```

Returns:

numEntries—Number of currency types (including category headers) to be shown in the Currency UI (number)

GetCurrentArenaSeason

Returns a number identifying the current arena season.

```
season = GetCurrentArenaSeason()
```

New arena seasons begin every few months, resetting team rankings and providing new rewards.

Returns:

season—Number identifying the current arena season (number)

GetCurrentBindingSet

Returns which set of key bindings is currently in use.

```
bindingSet = GetCurrentBindingSet()
```

Returns:

bindingSet—Set of bindings currently in use (number)

■ 1—Key bindings shared by all characters
■ 2—Character specific key bindings

GetCurrentGuildBankTab

Returns the currently selected guild bank tab.

```
GetCurrentGuildBankTab(currentTab)
```

Arguments:

currentTab—Index of the selected guild bank tab (between 1 and GetNumGuildBankTabs()) (number)

GetCurrentKeyBoardFocus

Returns the frame currently handling keyboard input.

```
frame = GetCurrentKeyBoardFocus()
```

Typically an EditBox

Returns:

frame—Frame currently handling keyboard input, or nil if no frame is currently focused (table)

Example:

```
# put this in a macro and try running it (from an action bar or
# somesuch) while typing in different text boxes
/run frame = GetCurrentKeyBoardFocus()↵
print(frame and frame:GetName() or "no focus")
```

GetCurrentMapAreaID

Returns an ID number for the current map zone.

```
areaID = GetCurrentMapAreaID()
```

Currently only used in the default UI to determine whether the Wintergrasp map is showing (and if so, display the time remaining until the next battle).

Returns:

areaID—A number identifying the current map zone (number)

GetCurrentMapContinent

Returns the current world map continent.

```
continent = GetCurrentMapContinent()
```

Returns:

continent—Index of the world map's current continent (in the list returned by GetMapContinents(), or one of the following values) (number)

-1—Cosmic map	2—Eastern Kingdoms
0—Full Azeroth map	3—Outlands
1—Kalimdor	4—Northrend

GetCurrentMapDungeonLevel

Returns which map image is currently selected on the world map (for zones which use more than one map image).

```
level = GetCurrentMapDungeonLevel()
```

Used in zones with more than one "floor" or area, such as Dalaran and several Wrath of the Lich King dungeons and raids. More than one map image may contain the player's current location; if the world map has not been explicitly set to show a particular area, this returns whichever is the "best" match.

Returns:

level—Index of the current map image (number)

GetCurrentMapZone

Returns the current world map zone.

```
zone = GetCurrentMapZone()
```

Returns:

zone—Index of a zone within the continent (in the list returned by GetMapZones(GetCurrentMapContinent())), or 0 for the continent map (number)

GetCurrentMultisampleFormat

Returns the index of the current multisample setting.

```
index = GetCurrentMultisampleFormat()
```

The index returned corresponds to the individual settings described by GetMultisampleFormats() (each a set of three values).

Returns:

index—Index of the current multisample setting (number)

GetCurrentResolution

Returns the index of the current resolution setting.

```
index = GetCurrentResolution()
```

For the dimensions of a resolution setting, use GetScreenResolutions().

Returns:

index—Index of the current resolution setting (number)

Example:

```
-- Print the current resolution to chat
local index = GetCurrentResolution();
local resolution = select(index, GetScreenResolutions());
print("Current resolution:", resolution);
```

GetCurrentTitle

Returns the currently selected player title.

```
currentTitle = GetCurrentTitle()
```

Returns:

currentTitle—Index of the player's current title (between 1 and GetNumTitles()) (integer)

GetCursorInfo

Returns information about the contents of the cursor.

```
type, data, subType = GetCursorInfo()
```

Returns:

type—Type of data attached to the cursor (string)

companion	item	money
equipmentset	macro	spell
guildbankmoney	merchant	

data—Identifier for the data on the cursor; varies by type: (value)
- companion—Index of the companion in the non-combat pet or mount list (number)
- equipmentset—Name of the equipment set (string)
- guildbankmoney—Amount of the money from the guild bank (in copper) (number)
- item—Numeric identifier for the item (number, itemID)
- macro—Index of the macro in the macro listing (number, macroID)
- merchant—Index of the item in the vendor's listings (number)
- money—Amount of the player's money (in copper) (number)
- spell—Index of the spell in the player's spellbook (number, spellbookID)

subType—Secondary identifier for the data on the cursor; used only for certain types: (string)

- companion—"CRITTER" or "MOUNT", indicating whether the returned data is an index in the non-combat pet or mount list
- item—A complete hyperlink for the item
- spell—"spell" or "pet", indicating whether the returned data is an index in the player's or pet's spellbook

GetCursorMoney

Returns the amount of money currently on the cursor.

cursorMoney = GetCursorMoney()

Returns:

cursorMoney—Amount of money currently on the cursor (in copper) (number)

GetCursorPosition

Returns the absolute position of the mouse cursor.

cursorX, cursorY = GetCursorPosition()

Returns:

cursorX—Scale-independent X coordinate of the cursor's current position (number)

cursorY—Scale-independent Y coordinate of the cursor's current position (number)

GetDailyQuestsCompleted

Returns the number of daily quests the player has completed today.

dailyQuestsComplete = GetDailyQuestsCompleted()

The daily quest period resets at or around 3:00 AM server time on most realms.

Returns:

dailyQuestsComplete—Number of daily quests completed in the current period (number)

GetDamageBonusStat

Returns the index of the basic statistic that provides increased physical damage.

bonusStat = GetDamageBonusStat()

Unused in the default UI.

Returns:

bonusStat—Index of the basic statistic which provides attack (number)

- 1—Strength (Druids, Mages, Paladins, Priests, Shamans, Warlocks and Warriors)
- 2—Agility (Hunters and Rogues)

GetDeathReleasePosition

Returns the location of the graveyard where the player's spirit will appear upon release.

graveyardX, graveyardY = GetDeathReleasePosition()

Returns 0, 0 if the player is not dead or the graveyard's location is not visible on the current world map.

Returns:

graveyardX—Horizontal position of the graveyard relative to the zone map (0 = left edge, 1 = right edge) (number)

graveyardY—Vertical position of the graveyard relative to the zone map (0 = top, 1 = bottom) (number)

GetDefaultLanguage

Returns the name of the player character's default language.

```
language = GetDefaultLanguage()
```

This is the language used in the chat system (Common or Orcish, as opposed to Taurahe, Darnassian, etc), not the real-world language of the client or server.

Returns:

language—Localized name of the player character's default language (string)

GetDodgeChance

Returns the player's chance to dodge melee attacks.

```
chance = GetDodgeChance()
```

Returns:

chance—Percentage chance to dodge melee attacks (number)

GetDungeonDifficulty

Returns the 5 player selected dungeon difficulty.

```
difficulty = GetDungeonDifficulty()
```

Returns:

difficulty—The current 5 player dungeon difficulty (number)

- 1—Normal
- 2—Heroic

GetEquipmentSetInfo

Returns information about an equipment set (specified by index).

```
name, icon, setID = GetEquipmentSetInfo(index)
```

Arguments:

index—Index of an equipment set (between 1 and GetNumEquipmentSets()) (number)

Returns:

name—Name of the equipment set (string)

icon—Path to an icon texture for the equipment set (string)

setID—Internal ID number for the set (not used elsewhere in API) (number)

GetEquipmentSetInfoByName

Returns information about an equipment set.

```
icon, setID = GetEquipmentSetInfoByName("name")
```

Arguments:

name—Name of an equipment set (case sensitive) (string)

Returns:

icon—Unique part of the path to an icon texture for the equipment set; prepend "Interface\Icons\" for the full path (string)

setID—Internal ID number for the set (not used elsewhere in API) (number)

GetEquipmentSetItemIDs

Returns a table listing the items in an equipment set.

```
itemIDs = GetEquipmentSetItemIDs("name")
```

Arguments:

name—Name of an equipment set (case sensitive) (string)

Returns:

itemIDs—A table listing the itemIDs of the set's contents, keyed by inventoryID (table)

GetEquipmentSetLocations

Returns a table listing the locations of the items in an equipment set.

```
itemIDs = GetEquipmentSetLocations("name")
```

Arguments:

name—Name of an equipment set (case sensitive) (string)

Returns:

itemIDs—A table listing the itemLocations of the set's contents, keyed by inventoryID (table)

GetEventCPUUsage

Returns information about the CPU usage of an event.

```
usage, numEvents = GetEventCPUUsage(["event"])
```

Only returns valid data if the scriptProfile CVar is set to 1; returns 0 otherwise.

Arguments:

event (optional)—Name of an event; if omitted, returns usage information for all events (string)

Returns:

usage—Amount of CPU time used by handlers for the event (in milliseconds) since the UI was loaded or ResetCPUUsage() was last called (number)

numEvents—Number of times the event has fired this session (number)

GetExistingLocales

Returns a list of installed localization packs for the WoW client.

```
... = GetExistingLocales()
```

Returns:

...—A list of strings, each the four-letter locale code (see GetLocale()) for an installed localization (list)

GetExistingSocketInfo

Returns information about a permanently socketed gem.

```
name, texture, name = GetExistingSocketInfo(index)
```

If the given socket contains a permanently socketed gem, returns information for that gem (even if a new gem has been dropped in the socket to overwrite the existing gem, but has not yet been confirmed). If the socket is empty, returns `nil`.

Only returns valid information when the Item Socketing UI is open (i.e. between the SOCKET_INFO_UPDATE and SOCKET_INFO_CLOSE events).

Arguments:

`index`—Index of a gem socket (between 1 and `GetNumSockets()`) (number)

Returns:

`name`—Name of the socketed gem (`string`)

`texture`—Path to an icon texture for the socketed gem (`string`)

`name`—1 if the gem matches the socket's color; otherwise `nil` (1nil)

GetExistingSocketLink

Returns a hyperlink for a permanently socketed gem.

```
link = GetExistingSocketLink(index)
```

If the given socket contains a permanently socketed gem, returns an item link for that gem (even if a new gem has been dropped in the socket to overwrite the existing gem, but has not yet been confirmed). If the socket is empty, returns `nil`.

Only returns valid information when the Item Socketing UI is open (i.e. between the SOCKET_INFO_UPDATE and SOCKET_INFO_CLOSE events).

Arguments:

`index`—Index of a gem socket (between 1 and `GetNumSockets()`) (number)

Returns:

`link`—A hyperlink for the socketed gem (`string`, hyperlink)

GetExpertise

Returns the player's current expertise value.

```
expertise = GetExpertise()
```

Returns:

`expertise`—The player's expertise value (number)

GetExpertisePercent

Returns the reduction in chance to be dodged or parried conferred by the player's expertise value.

```
expertisePerc, offhandExpertisePercent = GetExpertisePercent()
```

Returns:

`expertisePerc`—Reduction in percentage chance for main hand attacks to be dodged or parried (number) `offhandExpertisePercent`—Reduction in percentage chance for off hand attacks to be dodged or parried (`number`)

GetFacialHairCustomization

Returns a token used for displaying facial feature customization options.

```
token = GetFacialHairCustomization()
```

The token referred to by this function can be used to look up a global variable containing localized names for the customization options available to the player's race at character creation time and in the Barbershop UI; see example.

Returns:

`token`—Part of a localized string token for displaying facial feature options for the player's race (`string`)

Example:

```
-- prints localized names for customization options
-- e.g. "Facial Hair", "Earrings", "Tusks"
local token = GetFacialHairCustomization();
print(_G["FACIAL_HAIR_"..token]);
```

GetFactionInfo

Returns information about a faction or header listing.

```
name, description, standingID, barMin, barMax, barValue, atWarWith, ↵
canToggleAtWar, isHeader, isCollapsed, hasRep, isWatched, ↵
isChild = GetFactionInfo(index)
```

Arguments:

`index`—The index of the faction in the Reputation window (`number`)

Returns:

`name`—Name of the faction (`string`)

`description`—Brief description of the faction, as displayed in the default UI's detail window for a selected faction (`string`)

`standingID`—Current standing with the given faction (`number`, standingID)

1—Hated	4—Neutral	7—Revered
2—Hostile	5—Friendly	8—Exalted
3—Unfriendly	6—Honored	

`barMin`—The minimum value of the reputation bar at the given standing (`number`)

`barMax`—The maximum value of the reputation bar at the given standing (`number`)

`barValue`—The player's current reputation with the faction (`number`)

`atWarWith`—1 if the player is at war with the given faction, otherwise `nil` (`1nil`)

`canToggleAtWar`—1 if the player can declare war with the given faction, otherwise `nil` (`1nil`)

`isHeader`—1 if the index refers to a faction group header (`1nil`) isCollapsed—1 if the index refers to a faction group header and currently collapsed (1nil)

hasRep—1 if the index refers to a faction group header whose reputation value should be displayed (1nil)

isWatched—1 if the faction is currently being watched (i.e. displayed above the experience bar) (1nil)

isChild—1 if the index refers to a faction sub-group header within another group, or to an individual faction within a sub-group (1nil)

GetFirstTradeSkill

Returns the index of the first non-header in the trade skill listing.

```
index = GetFirstTradeSkill()
```

Returns:

index—Index of the first trade skill recipe (as opposed to group headers) (number)

GetFrameCPUUsage

Returns information about CPU usage by a frame's script handlers.

```
usage, calls = GetFrameCPUUsage(frame, includeChildren)
```

Only returns valid data if the scriptProfile CVar is set to 1; returns 0 otherwise.

Arguments:

frame—A Frame object (table)

includeChildren—True to include CPU usage by children of the frame; false to include only the frame itself (boolean)

Returns:

usage—Amount of CPU time used by the frame's script handlers (in milliseconds) since the UI was loaded or ResetCPUUsage() was last called (number)

calls—Number of function calls made from the frame's script handlers (number)

GetFramerate

Returns the number of frames per second rendered by the client.

```
framerate = GetFramerate()
```

Returns:

framerate—Number of frames per second rendered by the client (number)

GetFramesRegisteredForEvent

Returns all frames registered for a given event.

```
... = GetFramesRegisteredForEvent("event")
```

Arguments:

event—An event name (string)

Returns:

. . . —A list of tables, each a reference to a frame registered for the event (`list`)

Example:

```
-- Print the names of any named frames registered for an event
local function printFrameNames(...)
 for i=1,select("#", ...) do
  local frame = select(i, ...)
  local name = frame:GetName()
  if name then
   ChatFrame1:AddMessage(name)
  end
 end
end
printFrameNames(GetFramesRegisteredForEvent("UNIT_HEALTH"))
```

GetFriendInfo

Returns information about a character on the player's friends list.

```
name, level, class, area, connected, status, note, RAF = ↵
GetFriendInfo(index)
```

Arguments:

index—Index of a character in the Friends list (between 1 and GetNumFriends()) (`number`)

Returns:

name—Name of the friend (`string`)

level—Character level of the friend, if online; otherwise 0 (`number`)

class—Localized name of the friend's class, if online; otherwise UNKNOWN (`string`)

area—Name of the zone in which the friend is located, if online; otherwise UNKNOWN (`string`)

connected—1 if the friend is online; otherwise nil (`1nil`)

status—A label indicating the friend's status ("<AFK>" or "<DND>"), or the empty string ("") if not applicable (`string`)

note—Note text associated with the friend (`string`)

RAF—1 if the friend's account is linked to the player's via the Recruit-A-Friend program; otherwise nil (`1nil`)

GetFunctionCPUUsage

Returns information about CPU usage by a function.

```
usage, calls = GetFunctionCPUUsage(function, includeSubroutines)
```

Only returns valid data if the scriptProfile CVar is set to 1; returns 0 otherwise.

Arguments:

function—A function reference (`function`)

`includeSubroutines`—`True` to include time spent in other functions called by the given function; `false` to count only time spent in the function body (`boolean`)

Returns:

`usage`—Amount of CPU time used by the function (in milliseconds) since the UI was loaded or `ResetCPUUsage()` was last called (`number`)

`calls`—Number of times the function was called (`number`)

GetGMTicket

Requests GM ticket status from the server.

The `UPDATE_TICKET` event fires when data is ready.

GetGameTime

Returns the current realm (server) time.

```
hour, minute = GetGameTime()
```

Returns:

`hour`—Hour portion of the time (on a 24-hour clock) (`number`)

`minute`—Minute portion of the time (`number`)

GetGamma

Returns the current display gamma setting.

```
gamma = GetGamma()
```

Gamma value determines the contrast between lighter and darker portions of the game display; for a detailed explanation, see the Wikipedia entry on Gamma correction entry.

Returns:

`gamma`—Current gamma setting (`number`)

GetGlyphLink

Gets a hyperlink for the contents of a glyph socket.

```
link = GetGlyphLink(socket, talentGroup)
```

Glyph links are distinct from item and spell links: e.g. "|cff66bbff|Hglyph:21:361|h[Glyph of Hunter's Mark]|h|r".

Arguments:

`socket`—Which glyph socket to query (between 1 and `NUM_GLYPH_SLOTS`) (`number`, glyphIndex)

`talentGroup`—Which set of glyphs to query, if the player has Dual Talent Specialization enabled (`number`)

- 1—Primary Talents
- 2—Secondary Talents
- `nil`—Currently active talents

Returns:

`link`—A hyperlink for the glyph socket's contents, or "" if the socket is empty (`string`, hyperlink)

GetGlyphSocketInfo

Returns information about a glyph socket and its contents.

```
enabled, glyphType, glyphSpell, icon = GetGlyphSocketInfo(socket, ↵
talentGroup)
```

The spell ID referenced in the third return glyphSpell refers to the spell used to put the glyph in the socket. Note the Inscription spell that creates a glyph item, but the spell associated with that item's "Use:" effect.

Arguments:

socket—Which glyph socket to query (between 1 and NUM_GLYPH_SLOTS) (number, glyphIndex)

talentGroup—Which set of glyphs to query, if the player has Dual Talent Specialization enabled (number)

- 1—Primary Talents
- 2—Secondary Talents
- nil—Currently active talents

Returns:

enabled—True if the socket can be given a glyph at the player's current level; false if the socket is locked (boolean)

glyphType—1 for major glyph sockets, 2 for minor glyph sockets (number)

glyphSpell—Spell ID of the spell that inscribed a glyph into the socket, or nil if the socket is empty (number)

icon—Path to a texture for the glyph inscribed into the socket, or nil if the socket is empty (string)

GetGossipActiveQuests

Returns a list of quests which can be turned in to the current Gossip NPC.

```
name, level, isTrivial, ... = GetGossipActiveQuests()
```

These quests are displayed with a question mark icon in the default UI's GossipFrame.

Returns:

name—Name of the quest (string)

level—Suggested character level for attempting the quest (number)

isTrivial—1 if the quest is considered "trivial" at the player's level (rewards no XP); otherwise nil (1nil)

...—Additional name, level, isTrivial values if more than one quest is active (list)

GetGossipAvailableQuests

Returns a list of quests available from the current Gossip NPC.

```
name, level, isTrivial, ... = GetGossipAvailableQuests()
```

These quests are displayed with an exclamation mark icon in the default UI's GossipFrame.

Returns:

name—Name of the quest (string)

level—Suggested character level for attempting the quest (number)

isTrivial—1 if the quest is considered "trivial" at the player's level (rewards no XP); otherwise nil (1nil)

...—Additional name, level, isTrivial values if more than one quest is active (list)

GetGossipOptions

Returns a list of interaction options for the Gossip NPC.

text, gossipType, ... = GetGossipOptions()

Returns:

text—Text to be displayed for the gossip option (string)

gossipType—Non-localized string indicating the type of gossip option (string)

- Banker—Begin a Bank interaction
- BattleMaster—Queue for a battleground instance
- Binder—Set the player's Hearthstone location
- Gossip—Talk to the NPC
- Tabard—Begin a Tabard design interaction
- Taxi—Begin a Taxi (flight master) interaction
- Trainer—Begin a Trainer interaction
- Vendor—Begin a Merchant interaction

...—Additional text, gossipType values for each gossip option available (list)

GetGossipText

Returns greeting or other text to be displayed in an NPC dialog.

text = GetGossipText()

Returns:

text—Text to be displayed for the NPC conversation (string)

GetGreetingText

Returns the greeting text displayed for quest NPCs with multiple quests.

greetingText = GetGreetingText()

Not used often; most quest NPCs offering multiple quests (and/or other options) use the Gossip functions to provide a greeting (see GetGossipText()).

Returns:

greetingText—Text to be displayed before choosing from among the NPC's multiple quests (string)

GetGroupPreviewTalentPointsSpent

Returns the total number of points spent in the Talent UI's preview mode.

pointsSpent = GetGroupPreviewTalentPointsSpent(isPet, talentGroup)

This function only counts points spent in the preview mode, not those actually learned.

Arguments:

isPet—`true` to query talent info for the player's pet, `false` to query talent info for the player (`boolean`)

talentGroup—Which set of talents to edit, if the player has Dual Talent Specialization enabled (`number`)

- `1`—Primary Talents
- `2`—Secondary Talents
- `nil`—Currently active talents

Returns:

pointsSpent—Number of points spent in preview mode (`number`)

GetGuildBankItemInfo

Returns information about the contents of a guild bank item slot.

```
texture, count, locked = GetGuildBankItemInfo(tab, slot)
```

Arguments:

tab—Index of a guild bank tab (between 1 and `GetNumGuildBankTabs()`) (`number`)

slot—Index of an item slot in the guild bank tab (between 1 and `MAX_GUILDBANK_SLOTS_PER_TAB`) (`number`)

Returns:

texture—Path to an icon texture for the item (`string`)

count—Number of stacked items in the slot (`number`)

locked—1 if the slot is locked (as when a guild member has picked up an item and not yet deposited it elsewhere); otherwise `nil` (`1nil`)

GetGuildBankItemLink

Returns a hyperlink for an item in the guild bank.

```
item = GetGuildBankItemLink(tab, slot)
```

Arguments:

tab—Index of a guild bank tab (between 1 and `GetNumGuildBankTabs()`) (`number`)

slot—Index of an item slot in the guild bank tab (between 1 and `MAX_GUILDBANK_SLOTS_PER_TAB`) (`number`)

Returns:

item—A hyperlink for the contents of the slot (`string`, hyperlink)

GetGuildBankMoney

Returns the amount of money in the guild bank.

```
guildBankMoney = GetGuildBankMoney()
```

The return value is cached and returns the last value seen when not interacting with a guild bank vault. This cache works across characters, and is updated when the GUILDBANK_UPDATE_MONEY or GUILDBANKFRAME_OPENED event fires. If no player character has accessed a guild bank since the game client was launched, this function returns 0.

Returns:

guildBankMoney—Amount of money in the guild bank (in copper) (number)

GetGuildBankMoneyTransaction

Returns information about a transaction in the guild bank money log.

```
type, name, year, month, day, hour = GetGuildBankMoneyTransaction(index)
```

Arguments:

index—Index of a transaction in the money log (between 1 and GetNumGuildBankMoneyTransactions()) (number)

Returns:

type—Type of log event (string)

■ deposit—Deposit into the guildbank

■ repair—Repair cost withdrawal from the guildbank

■ withdraw—Withdrawal from the guildbank

name—Name of the guild member responsible for the event, or nil if the name is unknown (string)

year—Number of years since the event occurred (number)

month—Number of months since the event occurred (number)

day—Number of days since the event occurred (number)

hour—Number of hours since the event occurred (number)

GetGuildBankTabCost

Returns the cost of the next available guild bank tab.

```
tabCost = GetGuildBankTabCost()
```

Returns:

tabCost—Cost to purchase the next guild bank tab (in copper) (number)

GetGuildBankTabInfo

Returns information about a guild bank tab.

```
name, icon, isViewable, canDeposit, numWithdrawals, ↵
remainingWithdrawals = GetGuildBankTabInfo(tab)
```

Arguments:

tab—Index of a guild bank tab (between 1 and GetNumGuildBankTabs()) (number)

Returns:

name—Name of the tab (string)

icon—Path to the icon texture for the tab (string)

isViewable—1 if the player is allowed to view the contents of the tab; otherwise nil (1nil)

canDeposit—1 if the player is allowed to deposit items into the tab; otherwise nil (1nil) numWithdrawals—Maximum number of items (stacks) the player is allowed to withdraw from the tab per day (number)

remainingWithdrawals—Maximum number of items (stacks) the player is currently allowed to withdraw from the tab (number)

GetGuildBankTabPermissions

Returns information about guild bank tab privileges for the guild rank currently being edited.

```
canView, canDeposit, numWithdrawals = GetGuildBankTabPermissions(tab)
```

Used in the default UI's guild control panel.

Arguments:

tab—Index of a guild bank tab (between 1 and GetNumGuildBankTabs()) (number)

Returns:

canView—1 if the guild rank has permission to view the tab's contents; otherwise nil (1nil)

canDeposit—1 if the guild rank has permission to deposit items into the tab; otherwise nil (1nil)

numWithdrawals—Maximum number of withdrawals per day the guild rank is allowed for the given tab (number)

GetGuildBankText

Returns text associated with a guild bank tab.

```
text = GetGuildBankText(tab)
```

Only returns valid data after QueryGuildBankText() has been called to retrieve the text from the server and the following GUILDBANK_UPDATE_TEXT event has fired.

Arguments:

tab—Index of a guild bank tab (between 1 and GetNumGuildBankTabs()) (number)

Returns:

text—Info text provided for the tab (string)

GetGuildBankTransaction

Returns information about a transaction in the log for a guild bank tab.

```
type, name, itemLink, count, tab1, tab2, year, month, day, hour = ↵
GetGuildBankTransaction(tab, index)
```

Only returns valid information following the GUILDBANKLOG_UPDATE event which fires after calling QueryGuildBankLog().

Arguments:

tab—Index of a guild bank tab (between 1 and GetNumGuildBankTabs()) (number)

index—Index of a log entry (between 1 and GetNumGuildBankTransactions(tab)) (number)

Returns:

type—Type of transaction (string)

| deposit | repair |
| move | withdraw |

name—Name of the guild member responsible for the transaction (string)

itemLink—A hyperlink for the item involved in the transaction (string, hyperlink)

count—Number of stacked items involved in the transaction (number)

tab1—Index of the source tab, if the item was moved between tabs (number)

tab2—Index of the destination tab, if the item was moved between tabs (number)

year—Number of years since the event occurred (number)

month—Number of months since the event occurred (number)

day—Number of days since the event occurred (number)

hour—Number of hours since the event occurred (number)

GetGuildBankWithdrawLimit

Returns the guild bank money withdrawal limit for the guild rank currently being edited.

```
goldWithdrawLimit = GetGuildBankWithdrawLimit()
```

Returns:

goldWithdrawLimit—Amount of money the guild rank is allowed to withdraw from the guild bank per day (in copper), or -1 if the guild rank has unlimited withdrawal privileges (number)

GetGuildBankWithdrawMoney

Returns the amount of money the player is allowed to withdraw from the guild bank per day.

```
withdrawLimit = GetGuildBankWithdrawMoney()
```

Returns:

withdrawLimit—Amount of money the player is allowed to withdraw from the guild bank per day (in copper), or -1 if the player has unlimited withdrawal privileges (number)

GetGuildCharterCost

Returns the cost to purchase a guild charter.

```
cost = GetGuildCharterCost()
```

Usable if the player is interacting with a guild registrar (i.e. between the GUILD_REGISTRAR_SHOW and GUILD_REGISTRAR_CLOSED events).

Returns:

cost—Cost to purchase a guild charter (in copper) (number)

GetGuildEventInfo

Returns information about an entry in the guild event log.

```
type, player1, player2, rank, year, month, day, hour = ↵
GetGuildEventInfo(index)
```

Only returns valid data after calling `QueryGuildEventLog()` and the following `GUILD_EVENT_LOG_UPDATE` event has fired.

Arguments:

`index`—Index of an entry in the guild event log (between 1 and `GetNumGuildEvents()`) (number)

Returns:

`type`—Type of event (example descriptions from the default UI below) (string)

- `demote`—player1 demotes player2 to rank.
- `invite`—player1 invites player2 to the guild.
- `join`—player1 joins the guild.
- `promote`—player1 promotes player2 to rank.
- `quit`—player1 has quit the guild.
- `remove`—player1 removes player2 from the guild.

`player1`—First actor in the event (string)

`player2`—Second actor in the event, if applicable (string)

`rank`—Name of the rank related to promote/demote events (string)

`year`—Number of years since the event occurred (number)

`month`—Number of months since the event occurred (number)

`day`—Number of days since the event occurred (number)

`hour`—Number of hours since the event occurred (number)

GetGuildInfo

Returns a unit's guild affiliation.

```
guildName, guildRankName, guildRankIndex = GetGuildInfo("unit") or ↵
GetGuildInfo("name")
```

Arguments:

`unit`—A unit to query (string, unitID)

`name`—The name of a unit to query; only valid for `player`, `pet`, and party/raid members (string)

Returns:

`guildName`—Name of the character's guild (string)

`guildRankName`—Name of the character's guild rank (string)

`guildRankIndex`—Numeric guild rank of the character (0 = guild leader; higher numbers for lower ranks) (number)

GetGuildInfoText

Returns guild information text.

```
guildInfoText = GetGuildInfoText()
```

Only returns valid data after calling `GuildRoster()` and the following `GUILD_ROSTER_UPDATE` event has fired.

This text appears when clicking the "Guild Information" button in the default UI's Guild window.

Returns:

`guildInfoText`—The guild information text (including newline characters) (`string`)

GetGuildRosterInfo

Returns information about the selected player in your guild roster.

```
name, rank, rankIndex, level, class, zone, note, officernote, ↵
online, status, classFileName = GetGuildRosterInfo(index)
```

Only returns valid data after calling `GuildRoster()` and the following `GUILD_ROSTER_UPDATE` event has fired.

Arguments:

`index`—Index of a member in the guild roster (between 1 and `GetNumGuildMembers()`), or 0 for no selection (`number`)

Returns:

`name`—Name of the member (`string`)

`rank`—Name of the member's rank (`string`)

`rankIndex`—Numeric rank of the member (0 = guild leader; higher numbers for lower ranks) (`number`)

`level`—Character level of the member (`number`)

`class`—Localized name of the member's class (`string`)

`zone`—Zone in which the member was last seen (`string`)

`note`—Public note text for the member (`string`)

`officernote`—Officer note text for the member, or the empty string (`""`) if the player is not allowed to view officer notes (`string`)

`online`—1 if the member is currently online; otherwise `nil` (`1nil`)

`status`—Status text for the member (`string`)

▪ `<AFK>`—Is away from keyboard

▪ `<DND>`—Does not want to be disturbed

`classFileName`—Non-localized token representing the member's class (`string`)

GetGuildRosterLastOnline

Returns the amount of time since a guild member was last online.

```
years, months, days, hours = GetGuildRosterLastOnline(index)
```

Only returns valid data after calling `GuildRoster()` and the following `GUILD_ROSTER_UPDATE` event has fired.

Arguments:

`index`—Index of a member in the guild roster (between 1 and `GetNumGuildMembers()`), or 0 for no selection (`number`)

Returns:

years—Number of years since the member was last online (number)

months—Number of months since the member was last online (number)

days—Number of days since the member was last online (number)

hours—Number of hours since the member was last online (number)

GetGuildRosterMOTD

Returns the Message of the Day for the player's guild.

```
guildMOTD = GetGuildRosterMOTD()
```

Returns:

guildMOTD—The guild Message of the Day (string)

GetGuildRosterSelection

Returns the index of the selected member in the guild roster.

```
index = GetGuildRosterSelection()
```

Selection in the guild roster is used only for display in the default UI and has no effect on other Guild APIs.

Returns:

index—Index of the selected member in the guild roster (between 1 and GetNumGuildMembers()), or 0 for no selection (number)

GetGuildRosterShowOffline

Returns whether the guild roster lists offline members.

```
showOffline = GetGuildRosterShowOffline()
```

Returns:

showOffline—1 if offline members are included in the guild roster listing; otherwise nil (1nil)

GetGuildTabardFileNames

Returns the textures that comprise the player's guild tabard.

```
tabardBackgroundUpper, tabardBackgroundLower, tabardEmblemUpper, ↵
tabardEmblemLower, tabardBorderUpper, tabardBorderLower = ↵
GetGuildTabardFileNames()
```

Returns nil if the player is not in a guild.

Returns:

tabardBackgroundUpper—Path to the texture for the upper portion of the tabard's background (string)

tabardBackgroundLower—Path to the texture for the lower portion of the tabard's background (string)

tabardEmblemUpper—Path to the texture for the upper portion of the tabard's emblem (string)

tabardEmblemLower—Path to the texture for the lower portion of the tabard's emblem (string)

tabardBorderUpper—Path to the texture for the upper portion of the tabard's border (string) tabardBorderLower—Path to the texture for the lower portion of the tabard's border (string)

GetHairCustomization

Returns a token used for displaying "hair" customization options.

```
token = GetHairCustomization()
```

The token referred to by this function can be used to look up a global variable containing localized names for the customization options available to the player's race at character creation time and in the Barbershop UI; see example.

Returns:

token—Part of a localized string token for displaying "hair" options for the player's race (string)

Example:

```
-- prints localized names for customization options
-- e.g. "Hair Style"/"Hair Color" or "Horn Style"/"Horn Color"
local token = GetHairCustomization();
print(_G["HAIR_"..token.."_STYLE"]);
print(_G["HAIR_"..token.."_COLOR"]);
```

GetHonorCurrency

Returns the player's amount of honor points.

```
honorPoints, maxHonor = GetHonorCurrency()
```

Returns:

honorPoints—The player's current amount of honor points (number)

maxHonor—The maximum amount of honor currency the player can accrue (number)

GetIgnoreName

Returns the name of a character on the ignore list.

```
name = GetIgnoreName("index")
```

Arguments:

index—Index of an entry in the ignore list (between 1 and GetNumIgnores()) (string)

Returns:

name—Name of the ignored character (string)

GetInboxHeaderInfo

Returns information about a message in the player's inbox.

```
packageIcon, stationeryIcon, sender, subject, money, CODAmount, ↵
daysLeft, itemCount, wasRead, wasReturned, textCreated, canReply, ↵
isGM, itemQuantity = GetInboxHeaderInfo(mailID)
```

Arguments:

mailID—Index of a message in the player's inbox (between 1 and GetInboxNumItems()) (number)

Returns:

packageIcon—Path to an icon texture for the message if it contains an item; nil for other messages (string) `stationeryIcon`—Path to an icon texture for the message (`string`)

`sender`—Name of the message's sender (`string`)

`subject`—Subject text of the message (`string`)

`money`—Amount of money attached to the message (in copper) (`number`)

`CODAmount`—Cash-On-Delivery cost to take any items attached to the message (in copper) (`number`)

`daysLeft`—Number of days remaining before the message is automatically returned or deleted (`number`)

`itemCount`—Number of item attachments to the message (`number`)

`wasRead`—1 if the player has read the message; otherwise `nil` (`1nil`)

`wasReturned`—1 if the message is a message that was sent by the player to another character and returned by the recipient; otherwise `nil` (`1nil`)

`textCreated`—1 if the player has saved a copy of the message text as an item; otherwise `nil` (`1nil`)

`canReply`—1 if the player can reply to the message; otherwise `nil` (`1nil`)

`isGM`—1 if the message is from a game master; otherwise `nil` (`1nil`)

`itemQuantity`—Number of stacked items attached to the message if the message has one attachment; `nil` if the message has zero or multiple attachments (`number`)

GetInboxInvoiceInfo

Returns auction house invoice information for a mail message.

`invoiceType, itemName, playerName, bid, buyout, deposit, consignment, ↵`
`moneyDelay, etaHour, etaMin = GetInboxInvoiceInfo(index)`

Arguments:

`index`—Index of the mail message in the inbox (between 1 and `GetInboxNumItems()`) (`number`)

Returns:

`invoiceType`—Type of invoice (`string`)

■ `buyer`—An invoice for an item the player won

■ `seller`—An invoice for an item the player sold

■ `seller_temp_invoice`—A temporary invoice for an item sold by the player but for which payment has not yet been delivered

`itemName`—Name of the item (`string`)

`playerName`—Name of the player who bought or sold the item (`string`)

`bid`—Amount of the winning bid or buyout (`number`)

`buyout`—Amount of buyout (if the auction was bought out) (`number`)

`deposit`—Amount of money paid in deposit (`number`)

`consignment`—Amount withheld from the deposit by the auction house as charge for running the auction (`number`)

`moneyDelay`—Delay for delivery of payment on a temporary invoice (in minutes; generally 60) (`number`)

`etaHour`—Hour portion (on a 24-hour clock) of the estimated time for delivery of payment on a temporary invoice (`number`) etaMin—Minute portion of the estimated time for delivery of payment on a temporary invoice (`number`)

GetInboxItem

Returns information for an item attached to a message in the player's inbox.

```
name, itemTexture, count, quality, canUse = GetInboxItem(mailID, ↵
attachmentIndex)
```

Arguments:

mailID—Index of a message in the player's inbox (between 1 and `GetInboxNumItems()`) (`number`)

attachmentIndex—Index of an attachment to the message (between 1 and `select(8,GetInboxHeaderInfo(mailID))`) (`number`)

Returns:

name—Name of the item (`string`)

itemTexture—Path to an icon texture for the item (`string`)

count—Number of stacked items (`number`)

quality—Quality (rarity) of the item (`number, itemQuality`)

canUse—1 if the player can use or equip the item; otherwise `nil` (`1nil`)

GetInboxItemLink

Returns a hyperlink for an item attached to a message in the player's inbox.

```
itemlink = GetInboxItemLink(mailID, attachmentIndex)
```

Arguments:

mailID—Index of a message in the player's inbox (between 1 and `GetInboxNumItems()`) (`number`)

attachmentIndex—Index of an attachment to the message (between 1 and `select(8,GetInboxHeaderInfo(mailID))`) (`number`)

Returns:

itemlink—A hyperlink for the attachment item (`string`, hyperlink)

GetInboxNumItems

Returns the number of messages in the player's inbox.

```
numItems = GetInboxNumItems()
```

Returns:

numItems—Number of messages in the player's inbox (`number`)

GetInboxText

Returns information about the text of an inbox message.

```
bodyText, texture, isTakeable, isInvoice = GetInboxText(mailID)
```

Arguments:

mailID—Index of a message in the player's inbox (between 1 and `GetInboxNumItems()`) (`number`)

Returns:

bodyText—Text of the message (`string`)

texture—Unique part of the path to a background texture to be displayed for the message; actual texture paths are STATIONERY_PATH .. texture .. "1" and STATIONERY_PATH .. texture .. "2" (string)

isTakeable—1 if the text of the message can be saved as an item; otherwise nil (1nil)

isInvoice—1 if the inbox message is an auction house invoice; otherwise nil (1nil)

GetInspectArenaTeamData

Returns arena team information about the currently inspected unit.

```
teamName, teamSize, teamRating, teamPlayed, teamWins, playerPlayed,
playerRating, bg_red, bg_green, bg_blue, emblem, emblem_red,
emblem_green, emblem_blue, border, border_red, border_green,
border_blue = GetInspectArenaTeamData(team)
```

Only available if data has been downloaded from the server; see HasInspectHonorData() and RequestInspectHonorData().

Arguments:

team—Index of one of the unit's arena teams (number, arenaTeamID)

Returns:

teamName—Name of the arena team (string)

teamSize—Size of the team (2 for 2v2, 3 for 3v3, or 5 for 5v5) (number)

teamRating—The team's current rating (number)

teamPlayed—Number of games played by the team in the current week (number)

teamWins—Number of games won by the team in the current week (number)

playerPlayed—Number of games in which the unit has participated in the current week (number)

playerRating—The unit's personal rating with this team (number)

bg_red—Red component of the color value for the team banner's background (number)

bg_green—Green component of the color value for the team banner's background (number)

bg_blue—Blue component of the color value for the team banner's background (number)

emblem—Index of the team's emblem graphic; full path to the emblem texture can be found using the format "Interface\PVPFrame\Icons\PVP-Banner-Emblem-"..emblem (number)

emblem_red—Red component of the color value for the team banner's emblem (number)

emblem_green—Green component of the color value for the team banner's emblem (number)

emblem_blue—Blue component of the color value for the team banner's emblem (number)

border—Index of the team's border graphic; full path to the border texture can be found by using the format `"Interface\PVPFrame\PVP-Banner-"..`
`teamSize.."-Border-"..border` (number)

border_red—Red component of the color value for the team banner's border (number)

border_green—Green component of the color value for the team banner's border (number)

border_blue—Blue component of the color value for the team banner's border (number)

GetInspectHonorData

Returns PvP honor information about the currently inspected unit.

```
todayHK, todayHonor, yesterdayHK, yesterdayHonor, lifetimeHK,
lifetimeRank = GetInspectHonorData()
```

Only available if data has been downloaded from the server; see `HasInspectHonorData()` and `RequestInspectHonorData()`.

Returns:

todayHK—Number of honorable kills on the current day (number)

todayHonor—Amount of honor points earned on the current day (number)

yesterdayHK—Number of honorable kills on the previous day (number)

yesterdayHonor—Amount of honor points earned on the previous day (number)

lifetimeHK—Lifetime total of honorable kills scored (number)

lifetimeRank—Highest rank earned in the pre-2.0 PvP reward system; see `GetPVPRankInfo()` for rank display information (number)

GetInstanceBootTimeRemaining

Returns the amount of time left until the player is removed from the current instance.

```
timeleft = GetInstanceBootTimeRemaining()
```

Used when the player is in an instance he doesn't own; e.g. if the player enters an instance with a group and is then removed from the group.

Returns:

timeleft—The number of seconds until the player is booted from the current instance (number)

GetInstanceDifficulty

Returns difficulty setting for the current dungeon/raid instance.

```
difficulty = GetInstanceDifficulty()
```

This returns the difficulty setting for the instance the player is currently in; not to be confused with `GetCurrentDungeonDifficulty()`, which is the current group's setting for entering new instances, nor with `GetDefault DungeonDifficulty()`, which is the player's preference for dungeon difficulty and may differ from that of the current party leader.

Returns:

difficulty—The current instance's difficulty setting (number)

- 1—Normal (5 or 10 players)
- 2—Heroic (5 players) / Normal (25 players)
- 3—Heroic (10 players)
- 4—Heroic (25 players)

Example:

```
-- Print your current difficulty setting
local difficulty = ↵
getglobal("DUNGEON_DIFFICULTY"..GetInstanceDifficulty())
print("Your dungeon difficulty is set to " .. difficulty)
```

GetInstanceInfo

Returns instance information about the current area.

```
name, type, difficulty = GetInstanceInfo()
```

Returns:

name—Name of the instance or world area (string)

type—Type of the instance (string)

- arena—A PvP Arena instance
- none—Normal world area (e.g. Northrend, Kalimdor, Deeprun Tram)
- party—An instance for 5-man groups
- pvp—A PvP battleground instance
- raid—An instance for raid groups

difficulty—Difficulty setting of the instance (number)

- 1—In raids, this represents 10 Player. In instances, Normal.
- 2—In raids, this represents 25 Player. In instances, Heroic.
- 3—In raids, this represents 10 Player Heroic. In instances, Epic (unused for PvE instances but returned in some battlegrounds).
- 4—In raids, this represents 25 Player Heroic. No corollary in instances.

GetInstanceLockTimeRemaining

Returns time remaining before the player is saved to a recently entered instance.

```
seconds = GetInstanceLockTimeRemaining()
```

Applies when the player enters an instance to which other members of her group are saved; if the player leaves the instance (normally or with RespondInstanceLock(false)) within this time limit she will not be saved to the instance.

Returns:

seconds—Time remaining before the player is saved to the instance (number)

GetInventoryAlertStatus

Returns the durability warning status of an equipped item.

```
status = GetInventoryAlertStatus(slot)
```

Looking up the status returned by this function in the INVENTORY_ALERT
_COLORS table provides color values, used in the default UI to highlight parts
of the DurabiltyFrame (i.e. the "armored man" image) that appears when
durability is low.

Arguments:

slot—An inventory slot number, as can be obtained from GetInventory
SlotInfo (number, inventoryID)

Returns:

status—Alert status for the item in the given slot (number)

- 0—No alert; the slot is empty, contains an item whose durability is
  above critical levels, or contains an item without a durability value
- 1—The item's durability is dangerously low
- 2—The item's durability is at zero (the item is broken)

GetInventoryItemBroken

Returns whether an equipped item is broken.

```
isBroken = GetInventoryItemBroken("unit", slot)
```

Arguments:

unit—A unit to query; only valid for 'player' or the unit currently being
inspected (string, unitID)

slot—An inventory slot number, as can be obtained from GetInventory
SlotInfo (number, inventoryID)

Returns:

isBroken—1 if the item is broken (durability zero); otherwise nil (1nil)

GetInventoryItemCooldown

Returns cooldown information about an equipped item.

```
start, duration, enable = GetInventoryItemCooldown("unit", slot)
```

Arguments:

unit—A unit to query; only valid for 'player' (string, unitID)

slot—An inventory slot number, as can be obtained from GetInventory
SlotInfo (number, inventoryID)

Returns:

start—The value of GetTime() at the moment the cooldown began, or 0 if the
item is ready (number)

duration—The length of the cooldown, or 0 if the item is ready (number)

enable—1 if a Cooldown UI element should be used to display the cooldown,
otherwise 0. (Does not always correlate with whether the item is ready.)
(number)

GetInventoryItemCount

Returns the number of items stacked in an inventory slot.

```
count = GetInventoryItemCount("unit", slot)
```

Currently only returns meaningful information for the ammo slot.

Arguments:

`unit`—A unit to query; only valid for 'player' or the unit currently being inspected (`string`, unitID)

`slot`—An inventory slot number, as can be obtained from `GetInventory SlotInfo` (number, inventoryID)

Returns:

`count`—The amount of items stacked in the inventory slot (number)

GetInventoryItemDurability

Returns the current durability level of an equipped item.

```
durability, max = GetInventoryItemDurability(slot)
```

Arguments:

`slot`—An inventory slot number, as can be obtained from `GetInventory SlotInfo` (number, inventoryID)

Returns:

`durability`—The item's current durability (number)

`max`—The item's maximum durability (number)

Example:

```
-- Query HeadSlot durability
local slot = GetInventorySlotInfo("HeadSlot")
local durability,max = GetInventoryItemDurability(slot)
print("Head armor is currently at", durability, "of", max, "durability")
```

GetInventoryItemGems

Returns the gems socketed in an equipped item.

```
gem1, gem2, gem3 = GetInventoryItemGems(slot)
```

The IDs returned refer to the gems themselves (not the enchantments they provide), and thus can be passed to `GetItemInfo()` to get a gem's name, quality, icon, etc.

Arguments:

`slot`—An inventory slot number, as can be obtained from `GetInventory SlotInfo` (number, inventoryID)

Returns:

`gem1`—Item ID of the first gem socketed in the item (`itemID`)

`gem2`—Item ID of the second gem socketed in the item (`itemID`)

`gem3`—Item ID of the third gem socketed in the item (`itemID`)

GetInventoryItemID

Returns the item ID of an equipped item.

`id = GetInventoryItemID("unit", slot)`

Arguments:

`unit`—A unit to query; only valid for 'player' or the unit currently being inspected (`string`, unitID)

`slot`—An inventory slot number, as can be obtained from `GetInventory SlotInfo` (`number`, inventoryID)

Returns:

`id`—Numeric ID of the item in the given slot (`itemID`)

GetInventoryItemLink

Returns an item link for an equipped item.

`link = GetInventoryItemLink("unit", slot)`

Arguments:

`unit`—A unit to query; only valid for 'player' or the unit currently being inspected (`string`, unitID)

`slot`—An inventory slot number, as can be obtained from `GetInventorySlot Info` (`number`, inventoryID)

Returns:

`link`—An item link for the given item (`string`, hyperlink)

GetInventoryItemQuality

Returns the quality level of an equipped item.

`quality = GetInventoryItemQuality("unit", slot)`

Arguments:

`unit`—A unit to query; only valid for 'player' or the unit currently being inspected (`string`, unitID)

`slot`—An inventory slot number, as can be obtained from `GetInventorySlot Info` (`number`, inventoryID)

Returns:

`quality`—The quality level of the item (`number`, itemQuality)

GetInventoryItemTexture

Returns the icon texture for an equipped item.

`texture = GetInventoryItemTexture("unit", slot)`

Arguments:

`unit`—A unit to query; only valid for 'player' or the unit currently being inspected (`string`, unitID)

`slot`—An inventory slot number, as can be obtained from `GetInventorySlot Info` (`number`, inventoryID)

Returns:

`texture`—Path to an icon texture for the item (`string`)

GetInventoryItemsForSlot

Returns a list of items that can be equipped in a given inventory slot.

```
availableItems = GetInventoryItemsForSlot(slot)
```

Arguments:

slot—An inventory slot number, as can be obtained from GetInventorySlot Info (number, inventoryID)

Returns:

availableItems—A table listing itemIDs of items which can be equipped in the slot, keyed by itemLocation (table)

GetInventorySlotInfo

Returns information about an inventory slot.

```
id, texture, checkRelic = GetInventorySlotInfo("slotName")
```

Arguments:

slotName—Name of an inventory slot to query (string)

- AmmoSlot—Ranged ammunition slot
- BackSlot—Back (cloak) slot
- Bag0Slot—Backpack slot
- Bag1Slot—First bag slot
- Bag2Slot—Second bag slot
- Bag3Slot—Third bag slot
- ChestSlot—Chest slot
- FeetSlot—Feet (boots) slot
- Finger0Slot—First finger (ring) slot
- Finger1Slot—Second finger (ring) slot
- HandsSlot—Hand (gloves) slot
- HeadSlot—Head (helmet) slot
- LegsSlot—Legs (pants) slot
- MainHandSlot—Main hand weapon slot
- NeckSlot—Necklace slot
- RangedSlot—Ranged weapon or relic slot
- SecondaryHandSlot—Off-hand (weapon, shield, or held item) slot
- ShirtSlot—Shirt slot
- ShoulderSlot—Shoulder slot
- TabardSlot—Tabard slot
- Trinket0Slot—First trinket slot
- Trinket1Slot—Second trinket slot
- WaistSlot—Waist (belt) slot
- WristSlot—Wrist (bracers) slot

Returns:

id—The numeric slotId usable in other Inventory functions (number) texture—The path to the texture to be displayed when this slot is empty (`string`)

checkRelic—1 if the slot might be the relic slot; otherwise `nil`. The ranged slot token is re-used for the relic slot; if this return is 1, `UnitHasRelicSlot` should be used to determine how the slot should be displayed. (`1nil`)

GetItemCooldown

Returns cooldown information about an arbitrary item.

```
start, duration, enable = GetItemCooldown(itemID) or ↵
GetItemCooldown("itemName") or GetItemCooldown("itemLink")
```

Arguments:

itemID—An item's ID (`number`)

itemName—An item's name (`string`)

itemLink—An item's hyperlink, or any string containing the `itemString` portion of an item link (`string`)

Returns:

start—The value of `GetTime()` at the moment the cooldown began, or 0 if the item is ready (`number`)

duration—The length of the cooldown, or 0 if the item is ready (`number`)

enable—1 if a Cooldown UI element should be used to display the cooldown, otherwise 0. (Does not always correlate with whether the item is ready.) (`number`)

GetItemCount

Returns information about how many of a given item the player has or on remaining item charges.

```
itemCount = GetItemCount(itemId, includeBank, includeCharges) or ↵
GetItemCount("itemName", includeBank, includeCharges) or ↵
GetItemCount("itemLink", includeBank, includeCharges)
```

When the third argument `includeCharges` is true, the returned number indicates the total number of remaining charges for the item instead of how many of the item you have; e.g. if you have 3 Wizard Oils and one of them has been used twice, the returned value will be 13.

Arguments:

itemId—An item id (`number`)

itemName—An item name (`string`)

itemLink—An item link (`string`)

includeBank—`true` to include items in the bank in the returned count, otherwise `false` (`boolean`)

includeCharges—`true` to count charges for applicable items, otherwise `false` (`boolean`)

Returns:

itemCount—The number of the given item the player has in possession (possibly including items in the bank), or the total number of charges on those items (`number`)

Example:

```
_, link = GetItemInfo("Hearthstone")
GetItemCount(link)
-- nearly always returns 1 for most players

GetItemCount(34722, true) - GetItemCount(34722)
-- returns number of Heavy Frostweave Bandages in the player's
-- bank (not counting those on hand)

GetItemCount("Drums of Speed", nil, true)
-- return of 99 could indicate player has two drums in inventory,
-- one of which has been used only once
```

GetItemFamily

Returns information about special bag types that can hold a given item.

```
bagType = GetItemFamily(itemID) or GetItemFamily("itemName") or ↵
GetItemFamily("itemLink")
```

The meaning of `bagType` varies depending on the item:

- If the item is a container, `bagType` indicates which kinds of items the container is limited to holding; a `bagType` of 0 indicates the container can hold any kind of item.
- If the item is not a container, `bagType` indicates which kinds of specialty containers can hold the item; a `bagType` of 0 indicates the item can only be put in general-purpose containers.

Arguments:

`itemID`—An item's ID (number)

`itemName`—An item's name (string)

`itemLink`—An item's hyperlink, or any string containing the `itemString` portion of an item link (string)

Returns:

`bagType`—Bitwise OR of bag type flags: (number, bitfield)

0x0001—Quiver	0x0080—Engineering Bag
0x0002—Ammo Pouch	0x0100—Keyring
0x0004—Soul Bag	0x0200—Gem Bag
0x0008—Leatherworking Bag	0x0400—Mining Bag
0x0010—Inscription Bag	0x0800—Unused
0x0020—Herb Bag	0x1000—Vanity Pets
0x0040—Enchanting Bag	

Example:

```
function CanGoInBag(item, bag)
  -- Get the item's family
  local itemFamily = GetItemFamily(item)

  -- If the item is a container, then the itemFamily should be 0
```

```
  local equipSlot = select(9, GetItemInfo(item))
  if equipSlot == "INVTYPE_BAG" then
    itemFamily = 0
  end
  -- Get the bag's family
  local bagFamily = select(2, GetContainerNumFreeSlots(bag))
  return bagFamily == 0 or bit.band(itemFamily, bagFamily) > 0
end
```

GetItemGem

Returns information about gems socketed in an item.

```
name, link = GetItemGem(itemID, index) or ↵
GetItemGem("itemName", index) or GetItemGem("itemLink", index)
```

Arguments:

itemID—An item's ID (number)

itemName—An item's name (string)

itemLink—An item's hyperlink, or any string containing the itemString portion of an item link (string)

index—Index of a socket on the item (number)

Returns:

name—Name of the gem in the socket (string)

link—A hyperlink for the gem in the socket (string, hyperlink)•

GetItemIcon

Returns the path to an icon texture for the item.

```
texture = GetItemIcon(itemID) or GetItemIcon("itemName") or ↵
GetItemIcon("itemLink")
```

Unlike GetItemInfo, this function always returns icons for valid items, even if the item is not in the client's cache.

Arguments:

itemID—An item's ID (number)

itemName—An item's name (string)

itemLink—An item's hyperlink, or any string containing the itemString portion of an item link (string)

Returns:

texture—Path to an icon texture for the item (string)

GetItemInfo

Returns information about an item, by name, link or id.

```
name, link, quality, iLevel, reqLevel, class, subclass, maxStack, ↵
equipSlot, texture, vendorPrice = GetItemInfo(itemID) or ↵
GetItemInfo("itemName") or GetItemInfo("itemLink")
```

Only returns information for items in the WoW client's local cache; returns nil for items the client has not seen.

Arguments:

`itemID`—An item's ID (number, itemID)

`itemName`—An item's name. This value will only work if the player has the item in their bags. (string)

`itemLink`—An item's hyperlink, or any string containing the `itemString` portion of an item link (string)

Returns:

`name`—Name of the item (string)

`link`—A hyperlink for the item (string, hyperlink)

`quality`—Quality (rarity) level of the item. (number, itemQuality)

`iLevel`—Internal level of the item; (number)

`reqLevel`—Minimum character level required to use or equip the item (number)

`class`—Localized name of the item's class/type (as in the list returned by `GetAuctionItemClasses()`) (string)

`subclass`—Localized name of the item's subclass/subtype (as in the list returned by `GetAuctionItemSubClasses()`) (string)

`maxStack`—Maximum stack size for the item (i.e. largest number of items that can be held in a single bag slot) (number)

`equipSlot`—Non-localized token identifying the inventory type of the item (as in the list returned by `GetAuctionItemInvTypes()`); name of a global variable containing the localized name of the inventory type (string)

`texture`—Path to an icon texture for the item (string)

`vendorPrice`—Price an NPC vendor will pay to buy the item from the player. This value was added in patch 3.2. (number)

GetItemQualityColor

Returns color values for use in displaying items of a given quality.

```
redComponent, greenComponent, blueComponent, hexColor = ↵
GetItemQualityColor(quality)
```

Color components are floating-point values between 0 (no component) and 1 (full intensity of the component).

Arguments:

`quality`—An numeric item quality (rarity) value (number, itemQuality)

Returns:

`redComponent`—Red component of the color (number)

`greenComponent`—Green component of the color (number)

`blueComponent`—Blue component of the color (number)

`hexColor`—Prefix of a `colorString` for formatting text with the color (string)

Example:

```
GetItemQualityColor(4)
-- returns (approximately) 0.6392, 0.2078, 0,9333, "|cffa335ee"
```

GetItemSpell

Returns information about the spell cast by an item's "Use:" effect.

```
name, rank = GetItemSpell(itemID) or GetItemSpell("itemName") or ↵
GetItemSpell("itemLink")
```

Arguments:

`itemID`—An item's ID (`number`)

`itemName`—An item's name (`string`)

`itemLink`—An item's hyperlink, or any string containing the `itemString` portion of an item link (`string`)

Returns:

`name`—Name of the spell (`string`)

`rank`—Secondary text associated with the spell (often a rank, e.g. "Rank 7"); or the empty string (`" "`) if not applicable (`string`)

GetItemStatDelta

Returns a summary of the difference in stat bonuses between two items.

```
statTable = GetItemStatDelta("item1Link", "item2Link" [, returnTable])
```

Keys in the table returned are the names of global variables containing the localized names of the stats (e.g. `_G["ITEM_MOD_SPIRIT_SHORT"] = "Spirit"`, `_G["ITEM_MOD_HIT_RATING_SHORT"] = "Hit Rating"`).

The optional argument `returnTable` allows for performance optimization in cases where this function is expected to be called repeatedly. Rather than creating new tables each time the function is called (eventually requiring garbage collection), an existing table can be recycled. (Note, however, that this function does not clear the table's contents; use `wipe()` first to guarantee consistent results.)

Arguments:

`item1Link`—An item's hyperlink, or any string containing the `itemString` portion of an item link (`string`, hyperlink)

`item2Link`—Another item's hyperlink, or any string containing the `itemString` portion of an item link (`string`, hyperlink)

`returnTable` (optional)—Reference to a table to be filled with return values (`table`)

Returns:

`statTable`—A table listing the difference in stat bonuses provided by the items (i.e. if `item1Link` is equipped, what changes to the player's stats would occur if it is replaced by `item2Link`) (`table`)

Example:

```
-- links to some early death knight gear for illustrating the example...
local _, ring1Link = GetItemInfo("Valanar's Signet Ring")
local _, ring2Link = GetItemInfo("Keleseth's Signet Ring")

local statDelta = GetItemStatDelta(ring1Link, ring2Link)
```

```
for stat, value in pairs(statDelta) do print(value, _G[stat]) end
-- prints (approximately, on enUS client):
--   12 Critical Strike Rating
--   -6 Strength
--   -6 Hit Rating
--   3 Stamina
```

GetItemStats

Returns a summary of an item's stat bonuses.

```
statTable = GetItemStats("itemLink" [, returnTable])
```

Keys in the table returned are the names of global variables containing the localized names of the stats (e.g. _G["ITEM_MOD_SPIRIT_SHORT"] = "Spirit", _G["ITEM_MOD_HIT_RATING_SHORT"] = "Hit Rating").

The optional argument returnTable allows for performance optimization in cases where this function is expected to be called repeatedly. Rather than creating new tables each time the function is called (eventually requiring garbage collection), an existing table can be recycled. (Note, however, that this function does not clear the table's contents; use wipe() first to guarantee consistent results.)

Arguments:

itemLink—An item's hyperlink, or any string containing the itemString portion of an item link (string, hyperlink)

returnTable (optional)—Reference to a table to be filled with return values (table)

Returns:

statTable—A table listing the stat bonuses provided by the item (table)

Example:

```
-- links to some early death knight gear for illustrating the example...
local _, swordLink = GetItemInfo("Greatsword of the Ebon Blade")
local _, ring1Link = GetItemInfo("Valanar's Signet Ring")

local stats = GetItemStats(swordLink)
for stat, value in pairs(stats) do print(value, _G[stat]) end
-- prints (approximately, on enUS client):
--   60.5 Damage Per Second
--   30 Strength
--   12 Hit Rating
--   24 Stamina

-- reusing the table...
GetItemStats(ring1Link, stats)
for stat, value in pairs(stats) do print(value, _G[stat]) end
--   60.5 Damage Per Second
--   12 Strength
--   12 Hit Rating
--   12 Critical Strike Rating
```

```
--  18 Stamina
-- oops, it overwrote the table from before, keeping some
-- of the sword's stats...

-- let's try again and make sure it shows just the ring stats
wipe(stats)
GetItemStats(ring1Link, stats)
for stat, value in pairs(stats) do print(value, _G[stat]) end
--  12 Strength
--  12 Critical Strike Rating
--  18 Stamina
```

GetItemUniqueness

Returns information about uniqueness restrictions for equipping an item.

```
uniqueFamily, maxEquipped = GetItemUniqueness(itemID) or ↩
GetItemUniqueness("itemName") or GetItemUniqueness("itemLink")
```

Only applies to items with "Unique Equipped" restrictions upon how many similar items can be equipped; returns nil for items which for which "Unique" restricts how many the player can have in her possession.

Also returns nil if the queried item is not currently in the WoW client's item cache.

Arguments:

itemID—An item's ID (number)

itemName—An item's name (string)

itemLink—An item's link (string)

Returns:

uniqueFamily—The family of items with special uniqueness restrictions to which the item belongs (number)

maxEquipped—The maximum number of items under this restriction that can be equipped (number)

Example:

```
GetItemUniqueness("Rigid Dragon's Eye")
-- returns 2, 3 if your WoW client has seen this gem
-- up to 3 gems in the Jeweler's Gems family can be equipped
-- at any given time
GetItemUniqueness("Rigid Stormjewel")
-- returns 6, 1 if your WoW client has seen this gem
-- only 1 gem in the Stormjewel family can be equipped at any given time
GetItemUniqueness("Figurine - Ruby Hare")
-- returns -1, 1 if your WoW client has seen this item
-- only 1 Ruby Hare can be equipped at any given time
```

GetKnownSlotFromHighestRankSlot

Returns the spellbook slot for the player's highest known rank of a spell.

```
maxRankSlot = GetKnownSlotFromHighestRankSlot(slot)
```

Arguments:

slot—Spellbook slot index of a known spell (number)

Returns:

maxRankSlot—Spellbook slot index of the highest rank of that spell known to the player (number)

GetLFGPartyResults

Returns information about a member of a party in Looking for More results.

```
name, level, class, zone, comment, leader, tank, healer, damage = ↵
GetLFGPartyResults(type, name, index, partyIndex)
```

Can be used when the 9th return (numPartyMembers) from GetLFGResults() is 1 or greater. The default UI uses this return to segregate results into separate "Individuals" and "Groups" lists, and this function is used to populate the group members tooltip that appears when mousing over a group listing.

Arguments:

type—Index of an LFG query type (in the list returned by GetLFGTypes()) (number)

name—Index of an LFG entry (in the list returned by GetLFGTypeEntries (type)) (number)

index—Index of a result in the Looking for More listing (between 1 and GetNumLFGResults(type,name)) (number)

partyIndex—Index of a party member, not counting the party leader (between 1 and select(9, GetLFGResults(type,name,index))) (number)

Returns:

name—Name of the party member (string)

level—Party member's character level (string)

class—Localized name of the party member's class (string)

zone—The character's current location (string)

comment—Brief text comment supplied by the character (string)

leader—True if the character is willing to lead a group; otherwise false (boolean)

tank—True if the character is willing to take on the role of protecting allies by drawing enemy attacks; otherwise false (boolean)

healer—True if the character is willing to take on the role of healing allies who take damage; otherwise false (boolean)

damage—True if the character is willing to take on the role of damaging enemies; otherwise false (boolean)

GetLFGResults

Returns information about a character in the Looking for More results listing.

```
name, level, zone, class, criteria1, criteria2, criteria3, comment, ↵
numPartyMembers, isLFM, classFileName, leader, tank, healer, damage, ↵
bossKills, talent1, talent2, talent3, isLeader, isAutoJoin, armor, ↵
damage, healing, meleeCrit, rangedCrit, spellCrit, manaRegen, ↵
manaCombatRegen, attackPower, agility, maxHealth, maxPower, ↵
avgGearRating, defense, dodge, block, parry, haste, expertise = ↵
GetLFGResults(type, name, index)
```

The default UI uses the 9th return from this function (`numPartyMembers`) to segregate results into separate "Individuals" and "Groups" lists for display, but at the API level these are combined into a single listing.

Arguments:

`type`—Index of an LFG query type (in the list returned by `GetLFGTypes()`) (number)

`name`—Index of an LFG entry (in the list returned by `GetLFGTypeEntries(type)`) (number)

`index`—Index of a result in the Looking for More listing (between `1` and `GetNumLFGResults(type,name)`) (number)

Returns:

`name`—Name of the character (string)

`level`—The character's (number)

`zone`—The character's current location (string)

`class`—Localized name of the character's class (string)

`criteria1`—Name of the character's first LFG objective (string)

`criteria2`—Name of the character's second LFG objective; `nil` if not applicable (string)

`criteria3`—Name of the character's third LFG objective; `nil` if not applicable (string)

`comment`—Brief text comment supplied by the character (string)

`numPartyMembers`—Number of additional members in the character's party (number)

`isLFM`—`true` if the player is looking for more members; otherwise `false` (boolean)

`classFileName`—Non-localized token representing the character's class (string)

`leader`—True if the character is willing to lead a group; otherwise `false` (boolean)

`tank`—True if the character is willing to take on the role of protecting allies by drawing enemy attacks; otherwise `false` (boolean)

`healer`—True if the character is willing to take on the role of healing allies who take damage; otherwise `false` (boolean)

`damage`—True if the character is willing to take on the role of damaging enemies; otherwise `false` (boolean)

`bossKills`—The number of boss kills the player has. (number)

`talent1`—The number of talent points spent in the player's first talent tree. (number)

`talent2`—The number of talent points spent in the player's second talent tree. (number)

`talent3`—The number of talent points spent in the player's third talent tree. (number) isLeader—Whether or not the player is willing to lead a group. (`boolean`)

isAutoJoin—Whether or not the player is set to automatically join groups. (`boolean`)

armor—The player's armor rating. (`number`)

damage—The player's damage rating. (`number`)

healing—The player's healing rating. (`number`)

meleeCrit—The player's melee crit rating. (`number`)

rangedCrit—The player's ranged crit rating. (`number`)

spellCrit—The player's spell crit rating. (`number`)

manaRegen—The player's out of combat mana regen. (`number`)

manaCombatRegen—The player's in-combat mana regen. (`number`)

attackPower—The player's attack power rating. (`number`)

agility—The player's agility rating. (`number`)

maxHealth—The player's maximum health. (`number`)

maxPower—The player's maximum power. (`number`)

avgGearRating—The player's average gear rating (out of 100). (`number`)

defense—The player's defense rating. (`number`)

dodge—The player's dodge rating. (`number`)

block—The player's block rating. (`number`)

parry—The player's parry rating. (`number`)

haste—The player's haste rating. (`number`)

expertise—The player's expertise rating. (`number`)

GetLFGRoles

Returns the group roles for which the player has signed up in the LFG system.

```
leader, tank, healer, damage = GetLFGRoles()
```

Returns:

leader—True if the player is willing to lead a group; otherwise `false` (`boolean`)

tank—True if the player is willing to take on the role of protecting allies by drawing enemy attacks; otherwise `false` (`boolean`)

healer—True if the player is willing to take on the role of healing allies who take damage; otherwise `false` (`boolean`)

damage—True if the player is willing to take on the role of damaging enemies; otherwise `false` (`boolean`)

GetLFGStatusText

Returns information about the player's status in the LFG auto-join or LFM auto-fill queues.

```
isLFG, numCriteria, ... = GetLFGStatusText()
```

Does not return useful information if the player is not queued to automatically join or fill a group.

Returns:

isLFG—true if the character is looking for group, false if looking for more (boolean)

numCriteria—Number of additional values returned following this one (number)

. . .—A list of strings, each the name of an LFG entry for which the player is queued (list)

GetLFGTypeEntries

Returns a list of LFG entries (dungeons, zones, quests, etc) for a given type.

```
name, icon, ... = GetLFGTypeEntries(type)
```

Arguments:

type—Index of an LFG query type (in the list returned by GetLFGTypes()) (number)

Returns:

name—Localized name of the entry (string)

icon—Unique part of the path to an icon texture for the entry; prepend "Interface\\LFGFrame\\LFGIcon-" for the full path (string)

. . .—An additional name, icon pair for each entry in the list (list)

GetLFGTypes

Returns a list of LFG query types.

```
... = GetLFGTypes()
```

Returns:

. . .—A list of strings, each the localized name of an LFG type (Dungeon, Raid, Zone, etc.) (list)

GetLanguageByIndex

Returns the localized name of a player character language.

```
language = GetLanguageByIndex(index)
```

Arguments:

index—Index of a player character language (between 1 and GetNum Languages() (number)

Returns:

language—Localized name of the language (e.g. "Common" or "Gnomish") (string)

GetLatestCompletedAchievements

Returns a list of the player's most recently earned achievements.

```
... = GetLatestCompletedAchievements()
```

Returns:

. . .—A list of up to five numeric IDs of recently earned achievements, ordered from newest to oldest (list)

GetLatestCompletedComparisonAchievements

Returns a list of the comparison unit's most recently earned achievements.

```
... = GetLatestCompletedComparisonAchievements()
```

Returns:

`...`—A list of up to five numeric IDs of recently earned achievements, ordered from newest to oldest (`list`)

GetLatestThreeSenders

Returns the names of the last three senders of new mail.

```
sender1, sender2, sender3 = GetLatestThreeSenders()
```

Returns sender names for new messages which the player has not yet seen in the mailbox; returns nothing if the player's inbox only contains unread messages which have been seen in the mailbox listing but not yet opened.

Returns:

`sender1`—Name of a recent message's sender (`string`)

`sender2`—Name of a recent message's sender (`string`)

`sender3`—Name of a recent message's sender (`string`)

GetLocale

Returns a code indicating the localization currently in use by the client.

```
locale = GetLocale()
```

Returns:

`locale`—A four character locale code indicating the localization currently in use by the client (`string`)

- `deDE`—German
- `enGB`—British English
- `enUS`—American English
- `esES`—Spanish (European)
- `esMX`—Spanish (Latin American)
- `frFR`—French
- `koKR`—Korean
- `ruRU`—Russian
- `zhCN`—Chinese (simplified; mainland China)
- `zhTW`—Chinese (traditional; Taiwan)

GetLookingForGroup

Returns information about the player's status in the LFG system.

```
type1, name1, type2, name2, type3, name3, lfmType, lfmName, comment, ↵
queued, lfgStatus, lfmStatus, autoAdd = GetLookingForGroup()
```

Returns:

`type1`—Index of the LFG query type for the player's first objective (in the list returned by `GetLFGTypes()`) (`number`)

name1—Index of the LFG entry for the player's first objective (in the list returned by GetLFGTypeEntries(type1)) (number)

type2—Index of the LFG query type for the player's second objective (number)

name2—Index of the LFG entry for the player's second objective (number)

type3—Index of the LFG query type for the player's third objective (number)

name3—Index of the LFG entry for the player's third objective (number)

lfmType—Index of an LFG query type for the player's current Looking for More query (number)

lfmName—Index of an LFG entry for the player's current Looking for More query (number)

comment—Brief text to be seen by others when viewing the player's LFG advertisement (string)

queued—true if the player is queued to automatically join a group; otherwise false (boolean)

lfgStatus—true if the player is looking for a group; otherwise false (boolean)

lfmStatus—true if the player is looking for more players for his or her group; otherwise false (boolean)

autoAdd—true if the player has chosen to automatically add members to his or her group; otherwise false (boolean)

GetLootMethod

Returns information about the current loot method in a party or raid.

```
method, partyMaster, raidMaster = GetLootMethod()
```

Only returns useful information if the player is in a party or raid.

Returns:

method—Current loot method (string)

- freeforall—Free for All: any group member can take any loot at any time
- group—Group Loot: like Round Robin, but items above a quality threshold are rolled on
- master—Master Looter: like Round Robin, but items above a quality threshold are left for a designated loot master
- needbeforegreed—Need before Greed: like Group Loot, but members automatically pass on items
- roundrobin—Round Robin: group members take turns being able to loot

partyMaster—Numeric portion of the party unitID of the loot master (e.g. if 2, the loot master's unitID is party2); nil if not using the Master Looter method or if the player is in a raid whose loot master is not in the player's subgroup. If the player is the master looter, this value will return 0 (number)

raidMaster—Numeric portion of the raid unitID of the loot master (e.g. if 17, the loot master's unitID is raid17); nil if not using the Master Looter method or not in a raid group (number)

GetLootRollItemInfo

Returns information about an item currently up for loot rolling.

```
texture, name, count, quality, bindOnPickUp = GetLootRollItemInfo(id)
```

Arguments:

`id`—Index of an item currently up for loot rolling (as provided in the `START_LOOT_ROLL` event) (number)

Returns:

`texture`—Path to an icon texture for the item (string)

`name`—Name of the item (string)

`count`—Number of stacked items (number)

`quality`—Quality (rarity) of the item. (number, itemQuality)

`bindOnPickUp`—1 if the item is bind on pickup; otherwise `nil` (1nil)

GetLootRollItemLink

Returns a hyperlink for an item currently up for loot rolling.

```
link = GetLootRollItemLink(id)
```

Arguments:

`id`—Index of an item currently up for loot rolling (as provided in the `START_LOOT_ROLL` event) (number)

Returns:

`link`—A hyperlink for the loot roll item (string, hyperlink)

GetLootRollTimeLeft

Returns the amount of time remaining before loot rolling for an item expires.

```
timeLeft = GetLootRollTimeLeft(id)
```

When the time expires, all group members who have not yet chosen to roll Need or Greed automatically pass, random roll results are produced for those who chose to roll, and the server declares a winner and awards the item.

Arguments:

`id`—Index of an item currently up for loot rolling (as provided in the `START_LOOT_ROLL` event) (number)

Returns:

`timeLeft`—Amount of time remaining before loot rolling for the item expires (in milliseconds) (number)

GetLootSlotInfo

Returns a hyperlink for an item available as loot.

```
texture, item, quantity, quality, locked = GetLootSlotInfo(slot)
```

Arguments:

`slot`—Index of a loot slot (between 1 and `GetNumLootItems()`) (number)

Returns:

`texture`—Path to an icon texture for the item or amount of money (string)

`item`—Name of the item, or description of the amount of money (string) quantity—Number of stacked items, or 0 for money (number)

quality—Quality (rarity) of the item (number, itemQuality)

locked—1 if the item is locked (preventing the player from looting it); otherwise nil (1nil)

GetLootSlotLink

Returns a hyperlink for an item available as loot.

```
link = GetLootSlotLink(slot)
```

Returns nil if the loot slot is empty or contains money.

Arguments:

slot—Index of a loot slot (between 1 and GetNumLootItems()) (number)

Returns:

link—A hyperlink for the item (string)

GetLootThreshold

Returns the threshold used for Master Looter, Group Loot, and Need Before Greed loot methods.

```
threshold = GetLootThreshold()
```

Items above the threshold quality will trigger the special behavior of the current loot method: for Group Loot and Need Before Greed, rolling will automatically begin once a group member loots the corpse or object holding the item; for Master Loot, the item will be invisible to all but the loot master tasked with assigning the loot.

Returns:

threshold—Minimum item quality to trigger the loot method (number, itemQuality)

GetMacroBody

Returns the body text of a macro.

```
body = GetMacroBody(index) or GetMacroBody("name")
```

Arguments:

index—Index of a macro (number, macroID)

name—Name of a macro (string)

Returns:

body—Body text / commands of the macro (string)

GetMacroIconInfo

Returns the texture for a macro icon option.

```
texture = GetMacroIconInfo(index)
```

Arguments:

index—Index of a macro icon option (between 1 and GetNumMacroIcons()) (number)

Returns:

texture—Path to the icon texture (string)

GetMacroIndexByName

Returns the index of a macro specified by name.

```
index = GetMacroIndexByName("name")
```

Arguments:

name—Name of a macro (string)

Returns:

index—Index of the named macro, or 0 if no macro by that name exists (number, macroID)

GetMacroInfo

Returns information about a macro.

```
name, texture, body = GetMacroInfo(index) or GetMacroInfo("name")
```

Arguments:

index—Index of a macro (number, macroID)

name—Name of a macro (string)

Returns:

name—Name of the macro (string)

texture—Path to an icon texture for the macro (string)

body—Body text / commands of the macro (string)

GetMacroItem

Returns information about the item used by a macro.

```
name, link = GetMacroItem(index) or GetMacroItem("name")
```

If a macro contains conditional, random, or sequence commands, this function returns the item which would currently be used if the macro were run.

Arguments:

index—Index of a macro (number, macroID)

name—Name of a macro (string)

Returns:

name—Name of the item (string)

link—A hyperlink for the item (string, hyperlink)

Example:

```
CreateMacro("health",1,"/use [combat] Runic Healing Potion ; ↵
[nocombat] Salted Venison")
-- when in combat:
GetMacroItem("health")
-- returns "Runic Healing Potion" (and hyperlink)

-- when not in combat:
GetMacroItem("health")
-- returns "Salted Venison" (and hyperlink)
```

GetMacroItemIconInfo

Returns the texture for an item icon.

```
texture = GetMacroItemIconInfo(index)
```

Despite the "macro" in the title, this function is only used by the default UI for providing tab icon options in the guild bank.

Arguments:

index—Index of an item icon option (between 1 and `GetNumMacroItem Icons()`) (number)

Returns:

texture—Path to the icon texture (string)

GetMacroSpell

Returns information about the spell cast by a macro.

```
name, rank = GetMacroSpell(index) or GetMacroSpell("name")
```

If a macro contains conditional, random, or sequence commands, this function returns the spell which would currently be cast if the macro were run.

Arguments:

index—Index of a macro (number, macroID)

name—Name of a macro (string)

Returns:

name—Name of the spell (string)

rank—Secondary text associated with the spell (e.g. "Rank 4", "Racial") (string)

Example:

```
CreateMacro("fort",1,"/cast [party] Prayer of Fortitude ; [noparty] ↵
Power Word: Fortitude")

-- when in a party:
GetMacroSpell("fort")
-- returns "Prayer of Fortitude", "Rank 3"

-- when not in combat:
GetMacroSpell("fort")
-- returns "Power Word: Fortitude", "Rank 7"
```

GetManaRegen

Returns information about the player's mana regeneration rate.

```
base, casting = GetManaRegen()
```

Returns:

base—Amount of mana regenerated per second while not casting (number)

casting—Amount of mana regenerated per second while casting (number)

GetMapContinents

Returns a list of map continents names.

```
... = GetMapContinents()
```

Returns:

...—A list of strings, each the localized name of a map continent (list)

GetMapInfo

Returns information about the current world map texture.

```
mapFileName, textureHeight, textureWidth = GetMapInfo()
```

World map images are broken into several tiles; the full texture paths follow the format `"Interface\\WorldMap\\"..mapFileName.."\\"..mapFileName..i,` where i is a number between 1 and `NUM_WORLDMAP_DETAIL_TILES` (or in a zone with multiple area images, `"Interface\\WorldMap\\"..mapFileName.."\\"..mapFileName..dungeonLevel.."_"..i,` where `dungeonLevel` is a number between 1 and `GetNumDungeonMapLevels()`).

Returns:

`mapFileName`—Unique part of the path to the world map textures (`string`)

`textureHeight`—Height of the combined map texture tiles (`number`)

`textureWidth`—Width of the combined map texture tiles (`string`)

GetMapLandmarkInfo

Returns information about a map landmark.

```
name, description, textureIndex, x, y, mapLinkID, showInBattleMap = ↵
GetMapLandmarkInfo(index)
```

Possible landmarks include PvP objectives (both in battlegrounds and in world PvP areas), town and city markers on continent maps, and special markers such as those used during the Scourge Invasion world event. Some landmarks (such as those for towns on a zone map) exist but are not visible in the default UI.

Arguments:

`index`—The index of a map landmark, from 1 to GetNumMapLandmarks() (`number`)

Returns:

`name`—Name of the landmark (`string`)

`description`—Secondary text associated with the landmark; often used to denote current status of PvP objectives (e.g. "Alliance Controlled") (`string`)

`textureIndex`—The index of the texture to be used for the landmark. These indices map to segments of the Interface/MinimapPOI/Icons.blp graphic; the function WorldMap_GetPOITextureCoords(), defined in FrameXML/WorldMap.lua, can be used to resolve this index to a set of texture coordinates for displaying that segment. (`number`)

`x`—Horizontal position of the landmark relative to the current world map (0 = left edge, 1 = right edge) (`number`)

`y`—Vertical position of the landmark relative to the current world map (0 = top, 1 = bottom) (`number`)

`mapLinkID`—A hyperlink ID allowing the game engine to take an action when the landmark is clicked (currently unused) (`number`) showInBattleMap—`True` if the landmark should be shown in the Battle Map (aka Zone Map) UI; `false` for landmarks which should only be shown on the World Map (`boolean`)

GetMapOverlayInfo

Returns information about a world map overlay.

```
textureName, textureWidth, textureHeight, offsetX, offsetY, ↵
mapPointX, mapPointY = GetMapOverlayInfo(index)
```

Map overlays correspond to areas which are "discovered" when entered by the player, "filling in" the blank areas of the world map.

Arguments:

index—Index of a map overlay (between `1` and `GetNumMapOverlays()`) (`number`)

Returns:

textureName—Path to the overlay texture (`string`)

textureWidth—Width of the texture (in pixels) (`number`)

textureHeight—Height of the texture (in pixels) (`number`)

offsetX—Horizontal position of the overlay's top left corner relative to the zone map (0 = left edge, 1 = right edge) (`number`)

offsetY—Vertical position of the overlay's top left corner relative to the zone map (0 = top, 1 = bottom) (`number`)

mapPointX—Unused (`number`)

mapPointY—Unused (`number`)

GetMapZones

Returns the map zones for a given continent.

```
... = GetMapZones(continentIndex)
```

Arguments:

continentIndex—Index of a continent (in the list returned by `GetMapContinents()`) (`number`)

Returns:

...—A list of strings, each the localized name of a zone within the continent (`list`)

Example:

```
local continent = GetCurrentMapContinent()
local zones = {GetMapZones(continent)}
for idx, zone in ipairs(zones) do
 print("Zone #"..idx .. ": " .. zone)
end
```

GetMasterLootCandidate

Returns information about a given loot candidate.

```
candidate = GetMasterLootCandidate(index)
```

Used in the default UI to build the popup menu used in master loot assignment. Only valid if the player is the master looter.

Not all party/raid members may be eligible for a given corpse's (or object's) loot: e.g. a member is ineligible for loot from a creature killed while that member was not in the immediate area. By repeatedly calling this function (with index incrementing from 1 to the total number of party/raid members, including the player), one can build a list of the names of members eligible for the current loot.

The index is cast in stone at the time the mob was killed. If you move raid members around prior to distributing loot, their original positions will be returned by this function. The expression ceil(index/5) will yield the group number (in a raid) and the expression index % 5 will yield the group position number for an eligible raider.

Arguments:

index—Index of a member of the party or raid (*not* equivalent to the numeric part of a party or raid unitID) (number)

Returns:

candidate—Name of the candidate (string)

Example:

```
for i=1,40 do
  local grp = ceil(i / 5)
  local slot = i % 5
  local raider = GetMasterLootCandidate(i)
  if (raider) then
    print (string.format("Raider %q (group %d, position %d) is ↵
eligible for loot.", raider, grp, slot))
  end
end
```

GetMaxArenaCurrency

Returns the maximum amount of arena points the player can accrue.

```
amount = GetMaxArenaCurrency()
```

Returns:

amount—The maximum amount of arena points the player can accrue (number)

GetMaxCombatRatingBonus

Returns the maximum possible percentage bonus for a given combat rating.

```
max = GetMaxCombatRatingBonus(ratingIndex)
```

While this function can be applied to all combat ratings, it is currently only used in the default UI to account for the cap on (incoming) critical strike damage and mana drains provided by Resilience rating—specifically, in generating the tooltip where Resilience rating is shown in the Character window (PaperDollFrame).

Arguments:

ratingIndex—Which rating to query; the following global constants can be used for standard values: (number)

- CR_BLOCK—Block skill

- CR_CRIT_MELEE—Melee critical strike chance
- CR_CRIT_RANGED—Ranged critical strike chance
- CR_CRIT_SPELL—Spell critical strike chance
- CR_CRIT_TAKEN_MELEE—Resilience (as applied to melee attacks)
- CR_CRIT_TAKEN_RANGED—Resilience (as applied to ranged attacks)
- CR_CRIT_TAKEN_SPELL—Resilience (as applied to spell effects)
- CR_DEFENSE_SKILL—Defense skill
- CR_DODGE—Dodge skill
- CR_HASTE_MELEE—Melee haste
- CR_HASTE_RANGED—Ranged haste
- CR_HASTE_SPELL—Spell haste
- CR_HIT_MELEE—Melee chance to hit
- CR_HIT_RANGED—Ranged chance to hit
- CR_HIT_SPELL—Spell chance to hit
- CR_HIT_TAKEN_MELEE—Unused
- CR_HIT_TAKEN_RANGED—Unused
- CR_HIT_TAKEN_SPELL—Unused
- CR_PARRY—Parry skill
- CR_WEAPON_SKILL—Weapon skill
- CR_WEAPON_SKILL_MAINHAND—Main-hand weapon skill
- CR_WEAPON_SKILL_OFFHAND—Offhand weapon skill
- CR_WEAPON_SKILL_RANGED—Ranged weapon skill

Returns:

max—The maximum possible percentage bonus for the given rating (number)

GetMaxDailyQuests

Returns the maximum number of daily quests that can be completed each day.

```
max = GetMaxDailyQuests()
```

Returns:

max—The maximum number of daily quests that can be completed each day (number)

GetMerchantItemCostInfo

Returns information about alternate currencies required to purchase an item from a vendor.

```
honorPoints, arenaPoints, itemCount = GetMerchantItemCostInfo(index)
```

Arguments:

index—Index of an item in the vendor's listing (between 1 and GetMerchantNumItems()) (number)

Returns:

honorPoints—Amount of honor points required to purchase the item (number)

arenaPoints—Amount of arena points required to purchase the item (number) `itemCount`—Number of different item currencies required to purchase the item (see `GetMerchantItemCostItem()` for amount of each item currency required) (number)

GetMerchantItemCostItem

Returns information about currency items required to purchase an item from a vendor.

`texture, value, link = GetMerchantItemCostItem(index, currency)`

Arguments:

`index`—Index of an item in the vendor's listing (between 1 and `GetMerchantNumItems()`) (number)

`currency`—Index of one of the item currencies required to purchase the item (between 1 and `select(3,GetMerchantItemCostInfo(index))`) (number)

Returns:

`texture`—Path to an icon texture for the currency item (string)

`value`—Amount of the currency required for purchase (number)

`link`—A hyperlink for the currency item (string, hyperlink)

GetMerchantItemInfo

Returns information about an item available for purchase from a vendor.

`name, texture, price, quantity, numAvailable, isUsable, ↵`
`extendedCost = GetMerchantItemInfo(index)`

Arguments:

`index`—Index of an item in the vendor's listing (between 1 and `GetMerchantNumItems()`) (number)

Returns:

`name`—Name of the item (string)

`texture`—Path to an icon texture for the item (string)

`price`—Current cost to purchase the item from this vendor (in copper) (number)

`quantity`—Number of stacked items per purchase (number)

`numAvailable`—Number of items available for purchase, if the vendor has a limited stock of the item; -1 if the vendor has an unlimited supply of the item (number)

`isUsable`—1 if the player can use or equip the item; otherwise `nil` (1nil)

`extendedCost`—1 if the item's price uses one or more alternate currencies (for which details can be found via `GetMerchantItemCostInfo(index)`); otherwise `nil` (1nil)

GetMerchantItemLink

Returns a hyperlink for an item available for purchase from a vendor.

`link = GetMerchantItemLink(index)`

Arguments:

`index`—Index of an item in the vendor's listing (between 1 and `GetMerchantNumItems()`) (number)

Returns:

link—A hyperlink for the item (string, hyperlink)

GetMerchantItemMaxStack

Returns the maximum number of an item allowed in a single purchase.

```
maxStack = GetMerchantItemMaxStack(index)
```

Determines the largest value usable for the second argument (quantity) of BuyMerchantItem() when purchasing the item. For most items, this is the same as the maximum stack size of the item. Returns 1 for items purchased in bundles (e.g. food or drink in groups of 5, ammunition in groups of 200, etc), as such items can only be purchased one bundle at a time.

Arguments:

index—Index of an item in the vendor's listing (between 1 and GetMerchantNumItems()) (number)

Returns:

maxStack—Largest number of items allowed in a single purchase (number)

Example:

```
-- Buys the largest quantity possible in one purchase for
-- the given index
BuyMerchantItem(index, GetMerchantItemMaxStack(index))
```

GetMerchantNumItems

Returns the number of different items available for purchase from a vendor.

```
numMerchantItems = GetMerchantNumItems()
```

Returns:

numMerchantItems—Number of different items available for purchase (number)

GetMinimapZoneText

Returns the name of the current area (as displayed in the Minimap).

```
zoneText = GetMinimapZoneText()
```

Matches GetSubZoneText(), GetRealZoneText() or GetZoneText().

Returns:

zoneText—Name of the area containing the player's current location (string)

GetMirrorTimerInfo

Returns information about special countdown timers.

```
timer, value, maxvalue, scale, paused, label = GetMirrorTimerInfo(index)
```

Arguments:

index—Index of an available timer (between 1 and MIRRORTIMER_NUMTIMERS) (number)

Returns:

timer—Non-localized token identifying the type of timer (string)

- BREATH—Used for the Breath timer when swimming underwater
- DEATH—Currently unused
- EXHAUSTION—Used for the Fatigue timer when swimming far from shore
- FEIGNDEATH—Used for the Hunter Feign Death ability

value—Number of seconds remaining before the timer expires (number)

maxvalue—Maximum value of the timer (number)

scale—Rate at which the timer bar should move (e.g. -1 for a slowly "empty-ing" bar, 10 for a quickly "filling" bar); unused in the default UI (number)

paused—1 if the timer is currently paused; otherwise 0 (number)

label—Localized text to be displayed for the timer (string)

GetMirrorTimerProgress

Returns a high-resolution value for a special countdown timer.

```
progress = GetMirrorTimerProgress("timer")
```

Arguments:

timer—Non-localized token identifying the type of timer (string)

- BREATH—Used for the Breath timer when swimming underwater
- DEATH—Currently unused
- EXHAUSTION—Used for the Fatigue timer when swimming far from shore
- FEIGNDEATH—Used for the Hunter Feign Death ability

Returns:

progress—Number of milliseconds remaining before the timer expires (number)

GetModifiedClick

Returns the keys/buttons bound for a modified click action.

```
binding = GetModifiedClick("name")
```

Arguments:

name—Token identifying a modified click action (string)

Returns:

binding—The set of modifiers (and mouse button, if applicable) registered for the action (string, binding)

GetModifiedClickAction

Returns the token identifying a modified click action.

```
action = GetModifiedClickAction(index)
```

Arguments:

index—Index of a modified click action (between 1 and GetNumModified ClickActions()) (number)

Returns:

action—Token identifying the modified click action, or nil if no action is defined at the given index (string)

GetMoney

Returns the total amount of money currently in the player's possession.

```
money = GetMoney()
```

Returns:

money—Amount of money currently in the player's possession (in copper) (number)

Example:

```
local money = GetMoney()
local gold = floor(abs(money / 10000))
local silver = floor(abs(mod(money / 100, 100)))
local copper = floor(abs(mod(money, 100)))
print(format("I have %d gold %d silver %d copper.", gold, ↵
silver, copper))
```

GetMouseButtonClicked

Returns which mouse button triggered the current script.

```
button = GetMouseButtonClicked()
```

If called in a line of execution that started with a click handler (OnMouseDown, OnMouseUp, OnClick, OnDoubleClick, PreClick, or PostClick), returns a string identifying which mouse button triggered the handler. Otherwise, returns nil.

Returns:

button—Name of the mouse button that triggered the current script (string)

GetMouseButtonName

Returns the name for a mouse button specified by number.

```
buttonName = GetMouseButtonName(buttonNumber)
```

Arguments:

buttonNumber—A mouse button number (1-5) (number)

Returns:

buttonName—The name of the given mouse button (string)

Button4	MiddleButton
Button5	RightButton
LeftButton	

GetMouseFocus

Returns the frame that is currently under the mouse, and has mouse input enabled.

```
frame = GetMouseFocus()
```

Returns:

frame—The frame that currently has the mouse focus (table)

Example:

```
-- Returns the name of the frame under the mouse, if it's named
local frame = GetMouseFocus()
if not frame then
```

```
ChatFrame1:AddMessage("There is no mouse enabled frame under ↵
the cursor")
else
  local name = frame:GetName() or tostring(frame)
  ChatFrame1:AddMessage(name .. " has the mouse focus")
end
```

GetMovieResolution

Returns the horizontal resolution available for displaying movie content.

```
resolution = GetMovieResolution()
```

Returns:

`resolution`—Horizontal resolution (in pixels) available for displaying movie content (`number`)

GetMultisampleFormats

Returns a list of available multisample settings.

```
color, depth, multisample, ... = GetMultisampleFormats()
```

Used in the default UI to provide descriptions of multisample settings (e.g. "24-bit color 24-bit depth 6x multisample").

Indices used by `GetCurrentMultisampleFormat()` and `SetMultisampleFormat()` refer to the groups of `color`, `depth` and `multisample` values returned by this function; e.g. index 1 refers to values 1 through 3, index 2 to values 4 through 6, etc.

Returns:

`color`—Color depth (in bits) (`number`)

`depth`—Video depth (in bits) (`number`)

`multisample`—Number of samples per pixel (`number`)

`...`—Additional sets of `color`, `depth` and `multisample` values, one for each multisample setting (`list`)

Example:

```
local index = GetCurrentMultisampleFormat()
local formatsIndex = (index - 1) * 3 + 1
local color, depth, samples = select(formatsIndex, ↵
GetMultisampleFormats())
print(format("%d-bit color %d-bit depth %dx multisample", color, ↵
depth, samples))
```

GetMuteName

Returns the name of a character on the mute list.

```
name = GetMuteName(index)
```

Arguments:

`index`—Index of an entry in the mute listing (between 1 and `GetNumMutes()`) (`number`)

Returns:

`name`—Name of the muted character (`string`)

GetMuteStatus

Returns whether a character is muted or silenced.

```
muteStatus = GetMuteStatus("unit" [, "channel"]) or ↵
GetMuteStatus("name" [, "channel"])
```

If the `channel` argument is specified, this function checks the given character's voice/silence status on the channel as well as for whether the character is on the player's Muted list.

Arguments:

`unit`—A unit to query (`string`, unitID)

`name`—Name of a character to query (`string`)

`channel` (optional)—Name of a voice channel (`string`)

Returns:

`muteStatus`—1 if the character is muted; otherwise nil (1nil)

GetNetStats

Returns information about current network connection performance.

```
bandwidthIn, bandwidthOut, latency = GetNetStats()
```

Returns:

`bandwidthIn`—Current incoming bandwidth (download) usage, measured in KB/s (number)

`bandwidthOut`—Current outgoing bandwidth (upload) usage, measured in KB/s (number)

`latency`—Average roundtrip latency to the server (only updated every 30 seconds) (number)

GetNewSocketInfo

Returns information about a gem added to a socket.

```
name, texture, matches = GetNewSocketInfo(index)
```

If the given socket contains a new gem (one that has been placed in the UI, but not yet confirmed for permanently socketing into the item), returns information for that gem. If the socket is empty or has a permanently socketed gem but no new gem, returns nil.

Only returns valid information when the Item Socketing UI is open (i.e. between the `SOCKET_INFO_UPDATE` and `SOCKET_INFO_CLOSE` events).

Arguments:

`index`—Index of a gem socket (between 1 and `GetNumSockets()`) (number)

Returns:

`name`—Name of the gem added to the socket (`string`)

`texture`—Path to an icon texture for the gem added to the socket (`string`)

`matches`—1 if the gem matches the socket's color; otherwise nil (1nil)

GetNewSocketLink

Returns a hyperlink for a gem added to a socket.

```
link = GetNewSocketLink(index)
```

If the given socket contains a new gem (one that has been placed in the UI, but not yet confirmed for permanently socketing into the item), returns an item link for that gem. If the socket is empty or has a permanently socketed gem but no new gem, returns `nil`.

Only returns valid information when the Item Socketing UI is open (i.e. between the `SOCKET_INFO_UPDATE` and `SOCKET_INFO_CLOSE` events).

Arguments:

`index`—Index of a gem socket (between 1 and `GetNumSockets()`) (number)

Returns:

`link`—A hyperlink for the gem added to the socket (string, hyperlink)

GetNextAchievement

Returns the next achievement for an achievement which is part of a series.

```
nextID, completed = GetNextAchievement(id)
```

Arguments:

`id`—The numeric ID of an achievement (number)

Returns:

`nextID`—If the given achievement is part of a series and not the last in its series, the ID of the next achievement in the series; otherwise `nil` (number)

`completed`—`True` if the next achievement has been completed; otherwise `nil` (boolean)

GetNextStableSlotCost

Returns the cost of the next available stable slot.

```
money = GetNextStableSlotCost()
```

Returns 0 if all available slots have been purchased.

Returns:

`money`—Cost of the next available stable slot (in copper) (number)

GetNumActiveQuests

Returns the number of quests which can be turned in to the current Quest NPC.

```
numActiveQuests = GetNumActiveQuests()
```

Only returns valid information after a `QUEST_GREETING` event.

Note: Most quest NPCs present active quests using the `GetGossipActiveQuests()` instead of this function.

Returns:

`numActiveQuests`—Number of quests which can be turned in to the current Quest NPC (number)

GetNumAddOns

Returns the number of addons in the addon listing.

```
numAddons = GetNumAddOns()
```

Returns:

`numAddons`—The number of addons in the addon listing (number)

GetNumArenaOpponents

Returns the number of enemy players in an arena match.

```
numOpponents = GetNumArenaOpponents()
```

Returns:

`numOpponents`—Number of enemy players in an arena match (`number`)

GetNumArenaTeamMembers

Returns the number of members in an arena team.

```
numMembers = GetNumArenaTeamMembers(teamindex, showOffline)
```

Arguments:

`teamindex`—The index of the arena team, based on the order they are displayed in the PvP tab. (`number`)

`showOffline`—`True` to include currently offline members in the count; otherwise `false` (`boolean`)

Returns:

`numMembers`—Number of characters on the team (`number`)

GetNumAuctionItems

Returns the number of auction items in a listing.

```
numBatchAuctions, totalAuctions = GetNumAuctionItems("list")
```

Arguments:

`list`—Type of auction listing (`string`)

- `bidder`—Auctions the player has bid on
- `list`—Auctions the player can browse and bid on or buy out
- `owner`—Auctions the player placed

Returns:

`numBatchAuctions`—Number of auctions in the current page of the listing (`number`)

`totalAuctions`—Total number of auctions available for the listing (`number`)

GetNumAvailableQuests

Returns the number quests available from the current Quest NPC.

```
numAvailableQuests = GetNumAvailableQuests()
```

Only returns valid information after a `QUEST_GREETING` event.

Note: Most quest NPCs present available quests using the `GetGossipAvailableQuests()` instead of this function.

Returns:

`numAvailableQuests`—Number of quests available from the current Quest NPC (`number`)

GetNumBankSlots

Returns information about purchased bank bag slots.

```
numSlots, isFull = GetNumBankSlots()
```

Returns:

`numSlots`—Number of bank bag slots the player has purchased (`number`) isFull—1 if the player has purchased all available slots; otherwise `nil` (1nil)

GetNumBattlefieldFlagPositions

Returns the number of battleground flags for which map position information is available.

`numFlags = GetNumBattlefieldFlagPositions()`

Returns:

`numFlags`—Number of battleground flags for which map position information is available (`number`)

GetNumBattlefieldPositions

Returns the number of team members in the battleground not in the player's group.

`numTeamMembers = GetNumBattlefieldPositions()`

Still used in the default UI but no longer useful; always returns 0, as all team members in a battleground match are automatically joined into a raid group.

Returns:

`numTeamMembers`—Number of team members in the battleground not in the player's party or raid (`number`)

GetNumBattlefieldScores

Returns the number of participant scores available in the current battleground.

`numScores = GetNumBattlefieldScores()`

Returns:

`numScores`—Number of participant scores available in the current battle-ground; 0 if not in a battleground (`number`)

GetNumBattlefieldStats

Returns the number of battleground-specific statistics on the current battleground's scoreboard.

`numStats = GetNumBattlefieldStats()`

Battleground-specific statistics include flags captured in Warsong Gulch, towers assaulted in Alterac Valley, etc. For the name and icon associated with each statistic, see `GetBattlefieldStatInfo()`.

Returns:

`numStats`—Number of battleground-specific scoreboard columns (`number`)

GetNumBattlefieldVehicles

Returns the number of special vehicles in the current zone.

`numVehicles = GetNumBattlefieldVehicles()`

Used only for certain vehicles in certain zones: includes the airships in Icecrown as well as vehicles used in Ulduar, Wintergrasp, and Strand of the Ancients.

Returns:

`numVehicles`—Number of special vehicles (`number`)

GetNumBattlefields

Returns the number of instances available for a battleground.

```
numBattlefields = GetNumBattlefields([index])
```

Arguments:

index (optional)—Index of a battleground (between 1 and NUM_BATTLE GROUNDS), if using the queue-anywhere UI; not used when choosing an instance for a single battleground (e.g. at a battlemaster or battleground portal) (number)

Returns:

numBattlefields—Number of instances currently available for the battleground (number)

GetNumBattlegroundTypes

Returns the number of different battlegrounds available.

```
numBattlegrounds = GetNumBattlegroundTypes()
```

Refers to distinct battlegrounds, not battleground instances. Does not indicate the number of battlegrounds the player can enter: for that, see GetBattlegroundInfo.

As of WoW 3.2, should always return 6 for Alterac Valley, Warsong Gulch, Arathi Basin, Eye of the Storm, Strand of the Ancients, and Isle of Conquest. If a future patch adds a new battleground, this function will reflect that.

Returns:

numBattlegrounds—Number of different battlegrounds available (number)

GetNumBindings

Returns the number of entries in the key bindings list.

```
numBindings = GetNumBindings()
```

Returns:

numBindings—Number of binding actions (and headers) in the key bindings list (number)

GetNumBuybackItems

Returns the number of items recently sold to a vendor and available to be repurchased.

```
numBuybackItems = GetNumBuybackItems()
```

Returns:

numBuybackItems—Number of items available to be repurchased (number)

GetNumChannelMembers

Returns the number of members in a chat channel.

```
numMembers = GetNumChannelMembers(id)
```

Arguments:

id—Numeric identifier of a chat channel (number)

Returns:

numMembers—Number of characters in the channel (number)

GetNumCompanions

Returns the number of mounts or non-combat pets the player can summon.

```
count = GetNumCompanions("type")
```

Arguments:

type—The type of companion (string)

- CRITTER—Non-combat pets
- MOUNT—Mounts

Returns:

count—The number of available companions (number)

GetNumComparisonCompletedAchievements

Returns the number of achievements earned by the comparison unit.

```
total, completed = GetNumComparisonCompletedAchievements()
```

Does not include Feats of Strength.

Returns:

total—Total number of achievements currently in the game (number)

completed—Number of achievements earned by the comparison unit (number)

GetNumCompletedAchievements

Returns the number of achievements earned by the player.

```
total, completed = GetNumCompletedAchievements()
```

Does not include Feats of Strength.

Returns:

total—Total number of achievements currently in the game (number)

completed—Number of achievements earned by the player (number)

GetNumDeclensionSets

Returns the number of suggested declension sets for a name.

```
numSets = GetNumDeclensionSets("name", gender)
```

Used in the Russian localized World of Warcraft client; see DeclineName for further details. Returns 0 in other locales.

Arguments:

name—Nominative form of the player's or pet's name (string)

gender—Gender for names (for declensions of the player's name, should match the player's gender; for the pet's name, should be neuter) (number)

- 1 or nil—Neuter
- 2—Male
- 3—Female

Returns:

numSets—Number of available declension sets usable with DeclineName (number)

GetNumDisplayChannels

Returns the number of entries in the channel list display.

```
channelCount = GetNumDisplayChannels()
```

Returns:

channelCount—Number of channels and group headers to be displayed in the channel list (number)

GetNumDungeonMapLevels

Returns the number of map images for the world map's current zone.

```
numLevels = GetNumDungeonMapLevels()
```

Used in zones with more than one "floor" or area such as Dalaran and several Wrath of the Lich King dungeons and raids.

Returns:

numLevels—Number of map images (number)

GetNumEquipmentSets

Returns the number of saved equipment sets.

```
numSets = GetNumEquipmentSets()
```

Returns:

numSets—Number of saved equipment sets (number)

GetNumFactions

Returns the number of entries in the reputation UI.

```
numFactions = GetNumFactions()
```

Entries in the reputation UI can be major group headers (Classic, Burning Crusade, Wrath of the Lich King, Inactive, etc.), the sub-group headers within them (Alliance Forces, Steamwheedle Cartel, Horde Expedition, Shattrath City, etc.), or individual factions (Darkmoon Faire, Orgrimmar, Honor Hold, Kirin Tor, etc.).

This function returns not the total number of factions (and headers) known, but the number which should currently be visible in the UI according to the expanded/collapsed state of headers.

Returns:

numFactions—The number of visible factions and headers (number)

GetNumFrames

Returns the number of existing Frame objects (and derivatives).

```
numFrames = GetNumFrames()
```

Only counts Frame objects and derivatives thereof (e.g. Button, Minimap, and StatusBar; but not FontString, AnimationGroup, and Texture).

Returns:

numFrames—Number of existing Frame objects (and derivatives) (number)

GetNumFriends

Returns the number of characters on the player's friends list.

```
numFriends = GetNumFriends()
```

Returns:

`numFriends`—Number of characters currently on the friends list (number)

GetNumGossipActiveQuests

Returns the number of quests which can be turned in to the current Gossip NPC.

```
num = GetNumGossipActiveQuests()
```

These quests are displayed with a question mark icon in the default UI's GossipFrame.

Returns:

`num`—Number of quests which can be turned in to the current Gossip NPC (number)

GetNumGossipAvailableQuests

Returns the number of quests available from the current Gossip NPC.

```
num = GetNumGossipAvailableQuests()
```

These quests are displayed with an exclamation mark icon in the default UI's GossipFrame.

Returns:

`num`—Number of quests available from the current Gossip NPC (number)

GetNumGossipOptions

Returns the number of non-quest dialog options for the current Gossip NPC.

```
numOptions = GetNumGossipOptions()
```

Used by the default UI to skip greeting gossip for NPCs which provide only a greeting and one gossip option leading to the NPC's main interaction type (e.g. flight masters, merchants).

Returns:

`numOptions`—Number of options available from the current Gossip NPC (number)

GetNumGuildBankMoneyTransactions

Returns the number of transactions in the guild bank money log.

```
numTransactions = GetNumGuildBankMoneyTransactions()
```

Returns:

`numTransactions`—Number of transactions in the money log (number)

GetNumGuildBankTabs

Returns the number of purchased tabs in the guild bank.

```
numTabs = GetNumGuildBankTabs()
```

Returns valid information even if the player is not interacting with a guild bank vault.

Returns:

`numTabs`—Number of active tabs in the guild bank (`number`)

GetNumGuildBankTransactions

Returns the number of entries in a guild bank tab's transaction log.

`numTransactions = GetNumGuildBankTransactions(tab)`

Only returns valid information following the `GUILDBANKLOG_UPDATE` event which fires after calling `QueryGuildBankLog()`.

Arguments:

`tab`—Index of a guild bank tab (between 1 and `GetNumGuildBankTabs()`) (`number`)

Returns:

`numTransactions`—Number of transactions in the tab's log (`number`)

GetNumGuildEvents

Returns the number of entries in the guild event log.

`numEvents = GetNumGuildEvents()`

Only returns valid data after calling `QueryGuildEventLog()` and the following `GUILD_EVENT_LOG_UPDATE` event has fired.

Returns:

`numEvents`—Number of entries in the guild event log (`number`)

GetNumGuildMembers

Returns the number of members in the guild roster.

`numGuildMembers = GetNumGuildMembers([includeOffline])`

Arguments:

`includeOffline` (optional)—`True` to count all members in the guild; `false` or omitted to count only those members currently online (`boolean`)

Returns:

`numGuildMembers`—Number of members in the guild roster (`number`)

GetNumIgnores

Returns the number of characters on the player's ignore list.

`numIgnores = GetNumIgnores()`

Returns:

`numIgnores`—Number of characters currently on the ignore list (`number`)

GetNumLFGResults

Returns the number of results from a LFM query.

`numResults, totalCount = GetNumLFGResults(type, index)`

Arguments:

`type`—Index of an LFG query type (in the list returned by `GetLFGTypes()`) (`number`) index—Index of an LFG entry (in the list returned by `GetLFGTypeEntries(type)`) (number)

Returns:

`numResults`—Number of results available for the specific query (number)

`totalCount`—Total number of results cached by the client (number)

GetNumLanguages

Returns the number of languages the player character can speak.

```
languages = GetNumLanguages()
```

Returns:

`languages`—Number of in-game languages known to the player character (generally 2 for most races, 1 for Orcs or Humans) (number)

GetNumLootItems

Returns the number of items available to be looted.

```
numItems = GetNumLootItems()
```

Returns:

`numItems`—Number of the items available to be looted (number)

GetNumMacroIcons

Returns the number of available macro icons.

```
numMacroIcons = GetNumMacroIcons()
```

Returns:

`numMacroIcons`—The number of available macro icons (number)

GetNumMacroItemIcons

Returns the number of available item icons.

```
numIcons = GetNumMacroItemIcons()
```

Despite the "macro" in the title, this function is only used by the default UI for providing tab icon options in the guild bank.

Returns:

`numIcons`—Number of available item icons (number)

GetNumMacros

Returns the number of macros the player has stored.

```
numAccountMacros, numCharacterMacros = GetNumMacros()
```

Returns:

`numAccountMacros`—Number of account-wide macros (number)

`numCharacterMacros`—Number of character-specific macros (number)

GetNumMapLandmarks

Returns the number of landmarks on the world map.

```
numLandmarks = GetNumMapLandmarks()
```

Possible landmarks include PvP objectives (both in battlegrounds and in world PvP areas), town and city markers on continent maps, and special markers such as those used during the Scourge Invasion world event. Some landmarks (such as those for towns on a zone map) exist but are not visible in the default UI.

Returns:

numLandmarks—The number of landmarks on the current world map (number)

GetNumMapOverlays

Returns the number of overlays for the current world map zone.

```
numOverlays = GetNumMapOverlays()
```

Map overlays correspond to areas which are "discovered" when entered by the player, "filling in" the blank areas of the world map.

Returns:

numOverlays—Number of overlays for the current world map zone (number)

GetNumModifiedClickActions

Returns the number of modified click actions registered.

```
num = GetNumModifiedClickActions()
```

May return an invalid result if called when no modified click actions have been registered (i.e. early in the UI loading process).

Returns:

num—Number of modified click actions registered (number)

GetNumMutes

Returns the number of characters on the player's mute list.

```
numMuted = GetNumMutes()
```

Returns:

numMuted—The number of characters on the player's mute list (number)

GetNumPartyMembers

Returns the number of additional members in the player's party.

```
numPartyMembers = GetNumPartyMembers()
```

Returns:

numPartyMembers—Number of additional members in the player's party (between 1 and MAX_PARTY_MEMBERS, or 0 if the player is not in a party) (number)

GetNumPetitionNames

Returns the number of people who have signed the open petition.

```
numNames = GetNumPetitionNames()
```

Returns:

numNames—Number of characters that have signed the petition (number)

GetNumQuestChoices

Returns the number of available quest rewards from which the player must choose one upon completing the quest presented by a questgiver.

```
numQuestChoices = GetNumQuestChoices()
```

Only valid during the accept/decline or completion stages of a quest dialog (following the `QUEST_DETAIL` or `QUEST_COMPLETE` events); otherwise may return 0 or a value from the most recently displayed quest.

Returns:

`numQuestChoices`—Number of available quest rewards from which the player must choose one upon completing the quest (`number`)

GetNumQuestItems

Returns the number of different items required to complete the quest presented by a questgiver.

`numRequiredItems = GetNumQuestItems()`

Usable following the `QUEST_PROGRESS` event in which it is determined whether the player can complete the quest.

Returns:

`numRequiredItems`—Number of different items required to complete the quest (`number`)

GetNumQuestLeaderBoards

Returns the number of quest objectives for a quest in the player's quest log.

`numObjectives = GetNumQuestLeaderBoards([questIndex])`

Arguments:

`questIndex` (optional)—Index of a quest in the quest log (between 1 and `GetNumQuestLogEntries()`); if omitted, defaults to the selected quest (`number`)

Returns:

`numObjectives`—Number of trackable objectives for the quest (`number`)

GetNumQuestLogChoices

Returns the number of available item reward choices for the selected quest in the quest log.

`numChoices = GetNumQuestLogChoices()`

This function refers to quest rewards for which the player is allowed to choose one item from among several; for items always awarded upon quest completion, see GetNumQuestLogRewards.

Returns:

`numChoices`—Number of items among which a reward can be chosen for completing the quest (`number`)

GetNumQuestLogEntries

Returns the number of quests and headers in the quest log.

`numEntries, numQuests = GetNumQuestLogEntries()`

Returns:

`numEntries`—Total number of entries (quests and headers) (`number`)

`numQuests`—Number of quests only (`number`)

GetNumQuestLogRewards

Returns the number of item rewards for the selected quest in the quest log.

```
numRewards = GetNumQuestLogRewards()
```

This function refers to items always awarded upon quest completion; for quest rewards for which the player is allowed to choose one item from among several, see GetNumQuestLogChoices.

Returns:

numRewards—Number of rewards for completing the quest (number)

GetNumQuestRewards

Returns the number of different items always awarded upon completing the quest presented by a questgiver.

```
numQuestRewards = GetNumQuestRewards()
```

Only valid during the accept/decline or completion stages of a quest dialog (following the QUEST_DETAIL or QUEST_COMPLETE events); otherwise may return 0 or a value from the most recently displayed quest.

Returns:

numQuestRewards—Number of different items always awarded upon completing the quest (number)

GetNumQuestWatches

Returns the number of quests included in the objectives tracker.

```
numWatches = GetNumQuestWatches()
```

Returns:

numWatches—Number of quests from the quest log currently marked for watching (number)

GetNumRaidMembers

Returns the number of members in the player's raid.

```
numRaidMembers = GetNumRaidMembers()
```

Returns:

numRaidMembers—Number of members in the raid (including the player) (number)

GetNumRoutes

Returns the number of hops from the current location to another taxi node.

```
numHops = GetNumRoutes(index)
```

Only returns valid data while interacting with a flight master (i.e. between the TAXIMAP_OPENED and TAXIMAP_CLOSED events).

Arguments:

index—Index of a flight point (between 1 and NumTaxiNodes()) (number)

Returns:

numHops—Number of hops from the current location to the given node (number)

GetNumSavedInstances

Returns the number of instances to which the player is saved.

```
savedInstances = GetNumSavedInstances()
```

Returns:

savedInstances—Number of instances to which the player is saved (number)

GetNumShapeshiftForms

Returns the number of abilities to be presented on the stance/shapeshift bar.

```
numForms = GetNumShapeshiftForms()
```

Returns:

numForms—Number of abilities to be presented on the stance/shapeshift bar (number)

GetNumSkillLines

Returns the number of entries in the Skills UI list.

```
numSkills = GetNumSkillLines()
```

Includes both character skills (including non-ranked skills such as talent schools and armor proficiencies, as well as progressively learned skills such as trade skills, weapon skills, and Defense skill) and skill group headers. Reflects the current state of the list (i.e. returns a lower number if group headers are collapsed.)

Returns:

numSkills—Number of skills and headers to be displayed in the Skills UI (number)

GetNumSockets

Returns the number of sockets on the item currently being socketed.

```
numSockets = GetNumSockets()
```

Only returns valid information when the Item Socketing UI is open (i.e. between the SOCKET_INFO_UPDATE and SOCKET_INFO_CLOSE events).

Returns:

numSockets—Number of sockets on the item (number)

GetNumSpellTabs

Returns the number of tabs in the player's spellbook.

```
numTabs = GetNumSpellTabs()
```

Returns:

numTabs—Number of spellbook tabs (number)

Example:

```
-- Prints the names of all spell tabs to chat
for i = 1, GetNumSpellTabs() do
  local name = GetSpellTabInfo(i);
  print(name);
end
```

GetNumStablePets

Returns the number of stabled pets.

```
numPets = GetNumStablePets()
```

Returned value does not include the current pet.

Returns:

numPets—Number of pets in the stables (number)

GetNumStableSlots

Returns the number of stable slots the player has purchased.

```
numSlots = GetNumStableSlots()
```

Returns:

numSlots—Number of usable stable slots (number)

GetNumTalentGroups

Returns the number of talent specs a character can switch among.

```
numTalentGroups = GetNumTalentGroups(isInspect, isPet)
```

Arguments:

isInspect—true to query talent info for the currently inspected unit, false to query talent info for the player (boolean)

isPet—true to query talent info for the player's pet, false to query talent info for the player (boolean)

Returns:

numTalentGroups—Number of talent groups the character has enabled (number)

- 1—Default
- 2—The character has purchased Dual Talent Specialization

GetNumTalentTabs

Returns the number of talent tabs for the player, pet, or inspect target.

```
numTabs = GetNumTalentTabs(inspect, pet)
```

Arguments:

inspect—true to return information for the currently inspected unit; false to return information for the player (boolean)

pet—true to return information for the player's pet; false to return information for the player (boolean)

Returns:

numTabs—Number of talent tabs (number)

GetNumTalents

Returns the number of options in a talent tab.

```
numTalents = GetNumTalents(tabIndex, inspect, pet)
```

Arguments:

tabIndex—Index of a talent tab (between 1 and GetNumTalentTabs()) (number) inspect—true to return information for the currently inspected unit; false to return information for the player (boolean)

pet—true to return information for the player's pet; false to return information for the player (boolean)

Returns:

numTalents—Number of different talent options (number)

GetNumTitles

Returns the number of available player titles.

```
numTitles = GetNumTitles()
```

Includes all titles, not just those earned by the player

Returns:

numTitles—Number of available player titles (number)

GetNumTrackedAchievements

Returns the number of achievements flagged for display in the objectives tracker UI.

```
count = GetNumTrackedAchievements()
```

Returns:

count—Number of achievements flagged for tracking (number)

GetNumTrackingTypes

Returns the number of available minimap object/unit tracking abilities.

```
count = GetNumTrackingTypes()
```

Returns:

count—Number of available tracking types (number)

GetNumTradeSkills

Returns the number of entries in the trade skill listing.

```
numSkills = GetNumTradeSkills()
```

Entries include both group headers and individual trade skill recipes. Reflects the list as it should currently be displayed, not necessarily the complete list. If headers are collapsed or a filter is enabled, a smaller number will be returned. Returns 0 if a trade skill is not "open".

Returns:

numSkills—Number of headers and recipes to display in the trade skill list (number)

GetNumTrainerServices

Returns the number of entries in the trainer service listing.

```
numServices = GetNumTrainerServices()
```

Entries include both group headers and individual trainer services (i.e. spells or recipes to be purchased). Reflects the list as it should currently be displayed, not necessarily the complete list. If headers are collapsed or a filter is enabled, a smaller number will be returned.

Returns 0 if not interacting with a trainer.

Returns:

`numServices`—Number of headers and services to display in the trainer service listing (`number`)

GetNumVoiceSessionMembersBySessionID

Returns the number of members in a voice channel.

`numMembers = GetNumVoiceSessionMembersBySessionID(sessionId)`

Arguments:

`sessionId`—Index of a voice session (between 1 and `GetNumVoice Sessions()`) (`number`)

Returns:

`numMembers`—Number of members in the voice channel (`number`)

GetNumVoiceSessions

Returns the number of available voice channels.

`count = GetNumVoiceSessions()`

Returns 0 if voice chat is disabled.

Returns:

`count`—Number of available voice sessions (`number`)

GetNumWhoResults

Returns the number of results from a Who system query.

`numResults, totalCount = GetNumWhoResults()`

Returns:

`numResults`—Number of results returned (`number`)

`totalCount`—Number of results to display (`number`)

GetNumWorldStateUI

Returns the number of world state UI elements.

`numUI = GetNumWorldStateUI()`

World State UI elements include PvP, instance, and quest objective information (displayed at the top center of the screen in the default UI) as well as more specific information for "control point" style PvP objectives. Examples: the Horde/Alliance score in Arathi Basin, the tower status and capture progress bars in Hellfire Peninsula, the progress text in the Black Morass and Violet Hold instances, and the event status text for quests The Light of Dawn and The Battle For The Undercity.

Returns:

`numUI`—Returns the number of world state elements (`number`)

GetObjectiveText

Returns a summary of objectives for the quest offered by a questgiver.

`questObjective = GetObjectiveText()`

Only valid when the questgiver UI is showing the accept/decline stage of a quest dialog (between the QUEST_COMPLETE and QUEST_FINISHED events); otherwise may return the empty string or a value from the most recently displayed quest.

Returns:

questObjective—The objective text for the currently displayed quest (string)

GetOptOutOfLoot

Returns whether the player has opted out of loot rolls.

```
isOptOut = GetOptOutOfLoot()
```

When opting out, no prompt will be shown for loot which ordinarily would prompt the player to roll (need/greed) or pass; the loot rolling process will continue for other group members as if the player had chosen to pass on every roll.

Returns:

isOptOut—1 if the player has opted out of loot rolls; otherwise nil (1nil)

GetOwnerAuctionItems

Requests data from the server for the list of auctions created by the player.

The AUCTION_OWNED_LIST_UPDATE event fires if new data is available; listing information can then be retrieved using GetAuctionItemInfo() or other Auction APIs.

GetPVPDesired

Returns whether the player has manually enabled PvP status.

```
isPVPDesired = GetPVPDesired()
```

Only indicates whether the player has manually and directly enabled his PvP flag (e.g. by typing "/pvp" or using the default UI's menu when right-clicking the player portrait); returns 0 if the player only became PvP flagged by attacking an enemy player, entering an enemy zone, etc.

Returns:

isPVPDesired—1 if the PVP flag was toggled on by the player manually; otherwise 0 (number)

GetPVPLifetimeStats

Returns the player's lifetime total of honorable kills and highest rank achieved.

```
hk, highestRank = GetPVPLifetimeStats()
```

Highest rank achieved applies only to the older PvP rewards system that was abandoned with the WoW 2.0 patch, but is still accurate for players who participated in it.

Returns:

hk—Number of honorable kills the player has scored (number)

highestRank—Highest rank the player ever achieved in the pre-2.0 PvP rewards system (number)

GetPVPRankInfo

Returns information about a given PvP rank index.

```
rankName, rankNumber = GetPVPRankInfo(index [, "unit"])
```

These ranks are no longer in use, as they were part of the older PvP rewards system that was abandoned with the WoW 2.0 patch.

Arguments:

index—Index of a rank (begins at 1, corresponding to a never-used "Pariah" rank; actual ranks start at 5) (number)

unit (optional)—A unit to use as basis for the rank name (i.e. to return Horde rank names for Horde units and Alliance rank names for Alliance units); if omitted, uses the player's faction (string, unitID)

Returns:

rankName—Name of the rank (string)

rankNumber—Index of the rank relative to unranked status (positive values for ranks earned through honorable kills, negative values for the unused dishonorable ranks) (number)

GetPVPSessionStats

Returns the number of kills and honor points scored by the player since logging in.

```
honorKills, honorPoints = GetPVPSessionStats()
```

Returns:

honorKills—Number of honorable kills scored (number)

honorPoints—Amount of honor currency earned (number)

GetPVPTimer

Returns the amount of time until the player's PVP flag expires.

```
timer = GetPVPTimer()
```

Returns 300000 or higher if the player's PvP flag is manually enabled or if the player is in a PvP or enemy zone.

Returns:

timer—Milliseconds remaining until the player's PvP flag expires (number)

GetPVPYesterdayStats

Returns the number of kills and honor points scored by the player on the previous day.

```
honorKills, honorPoints = GetPVPYesterdayStats()
```

Returns:

honorKills—Number of honorable kills scored (number)

honorPoints—Amount of honor currency earned (number)

GetParryChance

Returns the player's parry chance.

```
chance = GetParryChance()
```

Returns:

chance—The player's percentage chance to parry melee attacks (number)

GetPartyAssignment

Returns whether a party/raid member is assigned a specific group role.

```
isAssigned = GetPartyAssignment("assignment", "unit") or ↵
GetPartyAssignment("assignment", "name" [, exactMatch])
```

Arguments:

assignment—A group role assignment (string)

■ MAINASSIST—Return whether the unit is assigned the main assist role

■ MAINTANK—Return whether the unit is assigned the main tank role

unit—A unit in the player's party or raid (string, unitID)

name—Name of a unit in the player's party or raid (string)

exactMatch (optional)—True to check only units whose name exactly matches the name given; false to allow partial matches (boolean)

Returns:

isAssigned—1 if the unit is assigned the specified role; otherwise nil (1nil)

GetPartyLeaderIndex

Returns the index of the current party leader.

```
index = GetPartyLeaderIndex()
```

Returns 0 if the player is the party leader or if the player is not in a party.

Returns:

index—Numeric portion of the party unitID for the party leader (e.g. 3 = party3) (number)

GetPartyMember

Returns whether a party member exists at a given index.

```
hasMember = GetPartyMember(index)
```

Arguments:

index—Index of a party member (between 1 and MAX_PARTY_MEMBERS), or the numeric portion of a party unitID (e.g. 3 = party3) (number)

Returns:

hasMember—1 if the given index corresponds to a member in the player's party; otherwise nil (1nil)

GetPetActionCooldown

Returns cooldown information about a given pet action slot.

```
start, duration, enable = GetPetActionCooldown(index)
```

Arguments:

index—Index of a pet action button (between 1 and NUM_PET_ACTION_SLOTS) (number)

Returns:

start—The value of GetTime() at the moment the cooldown began, or 0 if the action is ready (number) duration—The length of the cooldown, or 0 if the action is ready (number)

enable—1 if a Cooldown UI element should be used to display the cooldown, otherwise 0. (Does not always correlate with whether the action is ready.) (number)

GetPetActionInfo

Returns information about a pet action.

```
name, subtext, texture, isToken, isActive, autoCastAllowed, ↵
autoCastEnabled = GetPetActionInfo(index)
```

Arguments:

index—Index of a pet action button (between 1 and NUM_PET_ACTION_SLOTS) (number)

Returns:

name—Localized name of the action, or a token which can be used to get the localized name of a standard action (string)

subtext—Secondary text for the action (generally a spell rank; e.g. "Rank 8") (string)

texture—Path to an icon texture for the action, or a token which can be used to get the texture path of a standard action (string)

isToken—1 if the returned name and texture are tokens for standard actions, which should be used to look up actual values (e.g. PET_ACTION_ATTACK, PET_ATTACK_TEXTURE); nil if name and texture can be displayed as-is (1nil)

isActive—1 if the action is currently active; otherwise nil. (Indicates which state is chosen for the follow/stay and aggressive/defensive/passive switches.) (1nil)

autoCastAllowed—1 if automatic casting is allowed for the action; otherwise nil (1nil)

autoCastEnabled—1 if automatic casting is currently turned on for the action; otherwise nil (1nil)

GetPetActionSlotUsable

Returns whether a pet action can be used.

```
usable = GetPetActionSlotUsable(index)
```

Used in the default UI to show pet actions as grayed out when the pet cannot be commanded to perform them (e.g. when the player or pet is stunned).

Arguments:

index—Index of a pet action button (between 1 and NUM_PET_ACTION_SLOTS) (number)

Returns:

usable—1 if the pet action is currently available; otherwise nil (1nil)

GetPetActionsUsable

Returns whether the pet's actions are usable.

```
petActionsUsable = GetPetActionsUsable()
```

Note: `GetPetActionSlotUsable` can return nil for individual actions even if `GetPetActionsUsable` returns 1 (though not the other way around).

Returns:

`petActionsUsable`—1 if the pet's actions are usable; otherwise `nil` (`1nil`)

GetPetExperience

Returns information about experience points for the player's pet.

`currXP, nextXP = GetPetExperience()`

Returns:

`currXP`—The pet's current amount of experience points (`number`)

`nextXP`—Total amount of experience points required for the pet to gain a level (`number`)

GetPetFoodTypes

Returns a list of the food types the player's pet will eat.

`... = GetPetFoodTypes()`

Returns:

`...`—A list of strings, each the localized name of a food type the pet will eat (`list`)

- `Bread`—Baked goods
- `Cheese`—Cheese products
- `Fish`—Raw and cooked fish
- `Fruit`—Fruits
- `Fungus`—Mushrooms, lichens, and similar
- `Meat`—Raw and cooked meat

GetPetHappiness

Returns information about the player's pet's happiness.

`happiness, damagePercentage = GetPetHappiness()`

Returns:

`happiness`—Number identifying the pet's current happiness level (`number`)

- `1`—Unhappy
- `2`—Content
- `3`—Happy

`damagePercentage`—Percentage multiplier for the pet's outgoing damage (`number`)

GetPetIcon

Returns an icon representing the current pet.

`texture = GetPetIcon()`

Used in the default Pet Stables and Talent UIs for hunter pets; returns nil for other pets.

Returns:

`texture`—Path to an icon texture for the pet (`string`)

GetPetTalentTree

Returns the name of the talent tree used by the player's current pet.

```
talent = GetPetTalentTree()
```

Hunter pets use one of three different talent trees according to pet type. Returns `nil` if the player does not have a pet or the player's current pet does not use talents (i.e. warlock pets, quest pets, etc.)

Returns:

`talent`—Localized name of the pet's talent tree (`string`)

GetPetTimeRemaining

Returns the time remaining before a temporary pet is automatically dismissed.

```
petTimeRemaining = GetPetTimeRemaining()
```

Temporary pets include priests' Shadowfriend, mages' Water Elemental, and various quest-related pets.

Returns:

`petTimeRemaining`—Amount of time remaining until the temporary pet is automatically dismissed (in seconds), or `nil` if the player does not have a temporary pet (`number`)

GetPetitionInfo

Returns information about the currently open petition.

```
petitionType, title, bodyText, maxSignatures, originatorName, ↵
isOriginator, minSignatures = GetPetitionInfo()
```

Returns:

`petitionType`—Type of the petition (`string`)

■ `arena`—An arena team charter

■ `guild`—A guild charter

`title`—Title of the petition (`string`)

`bodyText`—Body text of the petition (`string`)

`maxSignatures`—Maximum number of signatures allowed (`number`)

`originatorName`—Name of the character who initially purchased the charter (`string`)

`isOriginator`—1 if the player is the petition's originator; otherwise `nil` (`1nil`)

`minSignatures`—Minimum number of signatures required to establish the charter (`number`)

GetPetitionItemInfo

Returns information about a purchasable arena team charter.

```
name, texture, price = GetPetitionItemInfo(team)
```

Arguments:

`team`—Index of a team size for a charter (`number, arenaTeamID`)

Returns:

name—Name of the petition (`string`)

texture—Path to an icon texture for the petition (`string`)

price—Cost to purchase the petition (in copper) (`number`)

GetPetitionNameInfo

Returns the name of a character who has signed the currently offered petition.

```
name = GetPetitionNameInfo(index)
```

Arguments:

index—Index of a signature slot on the petition (between 1 and minSignatures, where minSignatures = `select(7,GetPetitionInfo())`) (`number`)

Returns:

name—Name of the signatory character, or `nil` if the slot has not yet been signed (`string`)

GetPlayerFacing

Returns the player's orientation (heading).

```
facing = GetPlayerFacing()
```

Indicates the direction the player model is (normally) facing and in which the player will move if he begins walking forward, not the camera orientation.

Returns:

facing—Direction the player is facing (in radians, 0 = north, values increasing counterclockwise) (`number`)

GetPlayerInfoByGUID

Returns information about a player character identified by globally unique identifier.

```
class, classFilename, race, raceFilename, sex = ↵
GetPlayerInfoByGUID("guid")
```

Returns `nil` if given the GUID of a non-player unit.

Arguments:

guid—Globally unique identifier of a player unit (`string`, guid)

Returns:

class—Localized name of the unit's class (`string`)

classFilename—Non-localized token identifying the unit's class (`string`)

race—Localized name of the unit's race (`string`)

raceFilename—Non-localized token identifying the unit's race (`string`)

sex—Number identifying the unit's gender (`number`)

- 1—Neuter / Unknown
- 2—Male
- 3—Female

GetPlayerMapPosition

Returns the position of the player's corpse on the world map.

```
unitX, unitY = GetPlayerMapPosition("unit")
```

Returns `0,0` if the unit's location is not visible on the current world map.

Arguments:

unit—A unit in the player's party or raid (`string`, unitID)

Returns:

unitX—Horizontal position of the unit relative to the zone map (0 = left edge, 1 = right edge) (`number`)

unitY—Vertical position of the unit relative to the zone map (0 = top, 1 = bottom) (`number`)

GetPlayerTradeMoney

Returns the amount of money offered for trade by the player.

```
amount = GetPlayerTradeMoney()
```

Returns:

amount—Amount of money offered for trade by the player (in copper) (`number`)

GetPossessInfo

Returns information about special actions available while the player possesses another unit.

```
texture, name = GetPossessInfo(index)
```

Used in the default UI to show additional special actions (e.g. canceling possession) while the player possesses another unit through an ability such as Eyes of the Beast or Mind Control.

Does not apply to actions (spells) belonging to the possessed unit; those are regular actions (see `GetActionInfo()`) whose `actionID`s begin at `((NUM_ACTIONBAR_PAGES - 1 + GetBonusBarOffset()) * NUM_ACTIONBAR_BUTTONS + 1)`.

Arguments:

index—Index of a possession bar action (between 1 and `NUM_POSSESS_SLOTS`) (`number`)

Returns:

texture—Path to an icon texture for the action (`string`)

name—The name of the spell in the queried possess bar slot. (`string`)

GetPowerRegen

Returns information about the player's mana/energy/etc regeneration rate.

```
inactiveRegen, activeRegen = GetPowerRegen()
```

Contexts for `inactiveRegen` and `activeRegen` vary by power type.

If the player (currently) uses mana, `activeRegen` refers to mana regeneration while casting (within five seconds of casting a spell) and `inactiveRegen` refers to mana regeneration while not casting (more than five seconds after casting a spell). For other power types, `activeRegen` refers to regeneration while in combat and `inactiveRegen` to regeneration outside of combat.

Note that values returned can be negative: e.g. for rage and runic power users, `inactiveRegen` describes the rate of power decay while not in combat.

Returns:

`inactiveRegen`—Power change per second while inactive (`number`)

`activeRegen`—Power change per second while active (`number`)

GetPreviousAchievement

Returns the previous achievement for an achievement which is part of a series.

`previousID = GetPreviousAchievement(id)`

Arguments:

`id`—The numeric ID of an achievement (`number`)

Returns:

`previousID`—If the given achievement is part of a series and not the first in its series, the ID of the previous achievement in the series; otherwise `nil` (`number`)

GetPreviousArenaSeason

Returns a number identifying the previous arena season.

`season = GetPreviousArenaSeason()`

New arena seasons begin every few months, resetting team rankings and providing new rewards.

Returns:

`season`—Number identifying the previous arena season (`number`)

GetProgressText

Returns the quest progress text presented by a questgiver.

`text = GetProgressText()`

Only valid when the questgiver UI is showing the progress stage of a quest dialog (between the `QUEST_PROGRESS` and `QUEST_FINISHED` events); otherwise may return the empty string or a value from the most recently displayed quest.

Returns:

`text`—Progress text for the quest (`string`)

GetQuestBackgroundMaterial

Returns background display style information for a questgiver dialog.

`material = GetQuestBackgroundMaterial()`

The value returned can be used to look up background textures and text colors for display:

- Background textures displayed in the default UI can be found by prepending `"Interface\\ItemTextFrame\\ItemText-"` and appending `"-TopLeft"`, `"-TopRight"`, `"-BotLeft"`, `"-BotRight"` to the material string (e.g. `"Interface\\ItemTextFrame\\ItemText-Stone-TopLeft"`).

- Colors for body and title text can be found by calling `GetMaterialText Colors(material)` (a Lua function implemented in the Blizzard UI).

In cases where this function returns nil, the default UI uses the colors and textures for "Parchment".

Returns:

`material`—String identifying a display style for the questgiver dialog, or `nil` for the default style (`string`)

- `Bronze`—Colored metallic background
- `Marble`—Light stone background
- `Parchment`—Yellowed parchment background (default)
- `Silver`—Gray metallic background
- `Stone`—Dark stone background

[Blizzard UI]

GetQuestDifficultyColor

Returns a table of color values indicating the difficulty of a quest's level as compared to the player's.

`color = GetQuestDifficultyColor(level)`

Arguments:

`level`—Level for which to compare difficulty (`number`)

Returns:

`color`—A table containing color values (keyed `r`, `g`, and `b`) representing the difficulty of a quest at the input level as compared to the player's (`table`)

GetQuestGreenRange

Returns the level range in which a quest below the player's level still rewards XP.

`range = GetQuestGreenRange()`

If a quest's level is up to `range` levels below the player's level, the quest is considered easy but still rewards experience points upon completion; these quests are colored green in the default UI's quest log. (Quests more than `range` levels below the player's are colored gray in the default UI and reward no XP.)

Returns:

`range`—Maximum difference between player level and a lower quest level for a quest to reward experience (`number`)

Example:

```
-- function used to color quest log entries in the default UI
function GetDifficultyColor(level)
 local levelDiff = level - UnitLevel("player");
 local color
 if ( levelDiff >= 5 ) then
  color = QuestDifficultyColor["impossible"];
 elseif ( levelDiff >= 3 ) then
  color = QuestDifficultyColor["verydifficult"];
```

```
elseif ( levelDiff >= -2 ) then
 color = QuestDifficultyColor["difficult"];
elseif ( -levelDiff <= GetQuestGreenRange() ) then
 color = QuestDifficultyColor["standard"];
else
 color = QuestDifficultyColor["trivial"];
end
return color;
end
```

GetQuestIndexForTimer

Returns the quest log index of a timed quest's timer.

```
questIndex = GetQuestIndexForTimer(index)
```

Arguments:

index—Index of a timer (in the list returned by `GetQuestTimers()`)
(number)

Returns:

questIndex—Index of the quest in the quest log (between 1 and
GetNumQuestLogEntries()) (number)

GetQuestIndexForWatch

Returns the quest log index of a quest in the objectives tracker.

```
questIndex = GetQuestIndexForWatch(index)
```

Arguments:

index—Index of a quest in the list of quests on the objectives tracker (between 1
and `GetNumQuestWatches()`) (number)

Returns:

questIndex—Index of the quest in the quest log (between 1 and
GetNumQuestLogEntries()) (number)

GetQuestItemInfo

Returns information about items in a questgiver dialog.

```
name, texture, numItems, quality, isUsable = ↵
GetQuestItemInfo("type", index)
```

Only valid when the questgiver UI is showing the accept/decline, progress, or
completion stages of a quest dialog (between the QUEST_DETAIL and
QUEST_FINISHED, QUEST_PROGRESS and QUEST_FINISHED, or
QUEST_COMPLETE and QUEST_FINISHED events); otherwise may return empty
values or those from the most recently displayed quest.

Arguments:

type—Which of the possible sets of items to query (string)

- choice—Items from which the player may choose a reward
- required—Items required to complete the quest
- reward—Items given as reward for the quest

index—Which item to query (from 1 to GetNumQuestChoices(), GetNum
QuestItems(), or GetNumQuestRewards(), depending on the value of the
itemType argument) (number)

Returns:

name—The name of the item (string)

texture—Path to a texture for the item's icon (string)

numItems—Number of the item required or rewarded (number)

quality—The quality of the item (number)

0—Poor	4—Epic
1—Common	5—Legendary
2—Uncommon	6—Artifact
3—Rare	

isUsable—1 if the player can currently use/equip the item; otherwise nil
(1nil)

GetQuestItemLink

Returns a hyperlink for an item in a questgiver dialog.

```
link = GetQuestItemLink("itemType", index)
```

Only valid when the questgiver UI is showing the accept/decline, progress, or
completion stages of a quest dialog (between the QUEST_DETAIL and
QUEST_FINISHED, QUEST_PROGRESS and QUEST_FINISHED, or
QUEST_COMPLETE and QUEST_FINISHED events); otherwise may return nil or
a value from the most recently displayed quest.

Arguments:

itemType—Token identifying one of the possible sets of items (string)

■ choice—Items from which the player may choose a reward

■ required—Items required to complete the quest

■ reward—Items given as reward for the quest

index—Index of an item in the set (between 1 and GetNumQuestChoices(),
GetNumQuestItems(), or GetNumQuestRewards(), according to itemType)
(number)

Returns:

link—A hyperlink for the item (string)

GetQuestLink

Returns a hyperlink for an entry in the player's quest log.

```
link = GetQuestLink(questIndex)
```

Arguments:

questIndex—Index of a quest in the quest log (between 1 and
GetNumQuestLogEntries()) (number)

Returns:

link—A hyperlink for the quest (string, hyperlink)

GetQuestLogChoiceInfo

Returns information about available item rewards for the selected quest in the quest log.

```
name, texture, numItems, quality, isUsable = ↵
GetQuestLogChoiceInfo(index)
```

This function refers to quest rewards for which the player is allowed to choose one item from among several; for items always awarded upon quest completion, see GetQuestLogRewardInfo.

Arguments:

index—Index of a quest reward choice (between 1 and GetNumQuestLogChoices()) (number)

Returns:

name—Name of the item (string)

texture—Path to an icon texture for the item (string)

numItems—Number of items in the stack (number)

quality—Quality of the item (number, itemQuality)

isUsable—1 if the player can use or equip the item; otherwise nil (1nil)

GetQuestLogGroupNum

Returns the suggested group size for the selected quest in the quest log.

```
suggestedGroup = GetQuestLogGroupNum()
```

Returns:

suggestedGroup—Recommended number of players in a group attempting the quest (number)

GetQuestLogItemLink

Returns a hyperlink for an item related to the selected quest in the quest log.

```
GetQuestLogItemLink("itemType", index)
```

Arguments:

itemType—Token identifying one of the possible sets of items (string)

▪ choice—Items from which the player may choose a reward

▪ reward—Items always given as reward for the quest

index—Index of an item in the set (between 1 and GetNumQuestLogChoices() or GetNumQuestLogRewards(), according to itemType) (number)

GetQuestLogLeaderBoard

Returns information about objectives for a quest in the quest log.

```
text, type, finished = GetQuestLogLeaderBoard(objective [, questIndex])
```

Arguments:

objective—Index of a quest objective (between 1 and GetNumQuestLeader Boards()) (number)

questIndex (optional)—Index of a quest in the quest log (between 1 and GetNumQuestLogEntries()); if omitted, defaults to the selected quest (number)

Returns:

text—Text of the objective (e.g. "Gingerbread Cookie: 0/5") (string)

type—Type of objective (string)

- event—Requires completion of a scripted event
- item—Requires collecting a number of items
- monster—Requires slaying a number of NPCs
- object—Requires interacting with a world object
- reputation—Requires attaining a certain level of reputation with a faction

finished—1 if the objective is complete; otherwise nil (1nil)

GetQuestLogPushable

Return whether the selected quest in the quest log can be shared to party members.

```
shareable = GetQuestLogPushable()
```

Returns:

shareable—1 if the quest is shareable; otherwise nil (1nil)

GetQuestLogQuestText

Returns the description and objective text for the selected quest in the quest log.

```
questDescription, questObjectives = GetQuestLogQuestText()
```

Returns:

questDescription—Full description of the quest (as seen in the NPC dialog when accepting the quest) (string)

questObjectives—A (generally) brief summary of quest objectives (string)

GetQuestLogRequiredMoney

Returns the amount of money required for the selected quest in the quest log.

```
money = GetQuestLogRequiredMoney()
```

Returns:

money—The amount of money required to complete the quest (in copper) (number)

GetQuestLogRewardHonor

Returns the honor reward for the selected quest in the quest log.

```
honor = GetQuestLogRewardHonor()
```

Returns:

honor—The amount of honor points rewarded for completing the quest (number)

GetQuestLogRewardInfo

Returns information about item rewards for the selected quest in the quest log.

```
name, texture, numItems, quality, isUsable = ↵
GetQuestLogRewardInfo(index)
```

This function refers to items always awarded upon quest completion; for quest rewards for which the player is allowed to choose one item from among several, see GetQuestLogChoiceInfo.

Arguments:

index—Index of a quest reward (between 1 and GetNumQuestLogRewards()) (number)

Returns:

name—Name of the item (string)

texture—Path to an icon texture for the item (string)

numItems—Number of items in the stack (number)

quality—Quality of the item (number, itemQuality)

isUsable—1 if the player can use or equip the item; otherwise nil (1nil)

GetQuestLogRewardMoney

Returns the money reward for the selected quest in the quest log.

```
money = GetQuestLogRewardMoney()
```

Returns:

money—Amount of money rewarded for completing the quest (in copper) (number)

GetQuestLogRewardSpell

Returns information about the spell reward for the selected quest in the quest log.

```
texture, name, isTradeskillSpell, isSpellLearned = ↵
GetQuestLogRewardSpell()
```

If both isTradeskillSpell and isSpellLearned are nil, the reward is a spell cast upon the player.

Returns:

texture—Path to the spell's icon texture (string)

name—Name of the spell (string)

isTradeskillSpell—1 if the spell is a tradeskill recipe; otherwise nil (1nil)

isSpellLearned—1 if the reward teaches the player a new spell; otherwise nil (1nil)

GetQuestLogRewardTalents

Returns the talent point reward for the selected quest in the quest log.

```
talents = GetQuestLogRewardTalents()
```

Returns 0 for quests which do not award talent points.

(Very few quests award talent points; currently this functionality is only used within the Death Knight starting experience.)

Returns:

talents—Number of talent points to be awarded upon completing the quest (number)

GetQuestLogRewardTitle

Returns the title reward for the selected quest in the quest log.

```
title = GetQuestLogRewardTitle()
```

Returns `nil` if no title is awarded or if no quest is selected.

Returns:

`title`—Title to be awarded to the player upon completing the quest (`string`)

GetQuestLogSelection

Returns the index of the selected quest in the quest log.

```
questIndex = GetQuestLogSelection()
```

Returns:

`questIndex`—Index of the selected quest in the quest log (between `1` and `GetNumQuestLogEntries()`) (`number`)

Example:

```
-- Prints information about the currently selected quest
local index = GetQuestLogSelection()
local name = GetQuestLogTitle(index)
if name then
 print("Currently viewing " .. name)
end
```

GetQuestLogSpecialItemCooldown

Returns cooldown information about an item associated with a current quest.

```
start, duration, enable = GetQuestLogSpecialItemCooldown(questIndex)
```

Available for a number of quests which involve using an item (i.e. "Use the MacGuffin to summon and defeat the boss", "Use this saw to fell 12 trees", etc.)

Arguments:

`questIndex`—Index of a quest log entry with an associated usable item (between `1` and `GetNumQuestLogEntries()`) (`number`)

Returns:

`start`—The value of `GetTime()` at the moment the cooldown began, or 0 if the item is ready (`number`)

`duration`—The length of the cooldown, or 0 if the item is ready (`number`)

`enable`—1 if a Cooldown UI element should be used to display the cooldown, otherwise 0. (Does not always correlate with whether the item is ready.) (`number`)

GetQuestLogSpecialItemInfo

Returns information about a usable item associated with a current quest.

```
link, icon, charges = GetQuestLogSpecialItemInfo(questIndex)
```

Available for a number of quests which involve using an item (i.e. "Use the MacGuffin to summon and defeat the boss", "Use this saw to fell 12 trees", etc.)

Arguments:

questIndex—Index of a quest log entry with an associated usable item (between 1 and GetNumQuestLogEntries()) (number)

Returns:

link—A hyperlink for the item (string, hyperlink)

icon—Path to an icon texture for the item (string)

charges—Number of times the item can be used, or 0 if no limit (number)

GetQuestLogSpellLink

Returns a hyperlink for a spell in the selected quest in the quest log.

```
link = GetQuestLogSpellLink()
```

Returns:

link—A hyperlink for the spell or tradeskill recipe (string, hyperlink)

GetQuestLogTimeLeft

Returns time remaining for the selected quest in the quest log.

```
questTimer = GetQuestLogTimeLeft()
```

If the selected quest is not timed, returns nil.

Returns:

questTimer—The amount of time left to complete the quest (number)

GetQuestLogTitle

Returns information about an entry in the player's quest log.

```
questLogTitleText, level, questTag, suggestedGroup, isHeader, ↵
isCollapsed, isComplete, isDaily, questID = GetQuestLogTitle(questIndex)
```

Arguments:

questIndex—Index of a quest in the quest log (between 1 and GetNumQuestLogEntries()) (number)

Returns:

questLogTitleText—Title of the quest (string)

level—Recommended character level for attempting the quest (number)

questTag—Localized tag describing the type of quest (string)

Dungeon—Dungeon or instance quest	PVP—PVP specific quest
Elite—Elite quest	Raid—Raid quest
Group—Group quest	nil—Standard quest
Heroic—Heroic quest	

suggestedGroup—For some group quests, the recommended number of group members for attempting the quest (number)

isHeader—1 if the entry is a group header; nil if the entry is a quest (1nil)

isCollapsed—1 if the entry is a collapsed header; otherwise nil (1nil)

isComplete—Whether the quest is complete (number)

▪ -1—The quest was failed

- ■ 1—The quest was completed
- ■ nil—The quest has yet to reach a conclusion

isDaily—1 if the quest is a daily quest; otherwise nil (1nil)

questID—The quest's questID. (number)

GetQuestMoneyToGet

Returns the amount of money required to complete the quest presented by a questgiver.

```
money = GetQuestMoneyToGet()
```

Usable following the QUEST_PROGRESS event in which it is determined whether the player can complete the quest.

Returns:

money—Amount of money required to complete the quest (in copper) (number)

GetQuestResetTime

Returns the amount of time remaining until the daily quest period resets.

```
time = GetQuestResetTime()
```

Returns:

time—Amount of time remaining until the daily quest period resets (in seconds) (number)

Example:

```
-- Print the amount of time until dailies reset
print("Daily quests reset in " .. SecondsToTime(GetQuestResetTime()))
```

GetQuestReward

Finishes turning in a quest to a questgiver, selecting an item reward if applicable.

```
GetQuestReward(choice)
```

Usable following the QUEST_COMPLETE event in which the questgiver presents the player with rewards.

Arguments:

choice—Index of a quest reward choice (between 1 and GetNumQuest Choices()), or nil if the quest does not offer a choice of item rewards (number)

GetQuestSpellLink

Returns a hyperlink for a spell in a questgiver dialog.

```
link = GetQuestSpellLink()
```

Only valid when the questgiver UI is showing the accept/decline, progress, or completion stages of a quest dialog (between the QUEST_DETAIL and QUEST_FINISHED, QUEST_PROGRESS and QUEST_FINISHED, or QUEST_COMPLETE and QUEST_FINISHED events); otherwise may return empty values or those from the most recently displayed quest.

Returns:

link—A hyperlink for the spell or tradeskill recipe (string, hyperlink)

GetQuestText

Returns the text for the quest offered by a questgiver.

```
text = GetQuestText()
```

Only valid when the questgiver UI is showing the accept/decline stage of a quest dialog (between the QUEST_COMPLETE and QUEST_FINISHED events); otherwise may return the empty string or a value from the most recently displayed quest.

Returns:

text—The text for the currently displayed quest (string)

GetQuestTimers

Returns a list of the times remaining for any active timed quests.

```
... = GetQuestTimers()
```

Returns:

...—A list of numbers, each the amount of time (in seconds) remaining for a timed quest (number)

GetRaidRosterInfo

Returns information about a member of the player's raid.

```
name, rank, subgroup, level, class, fileName, zone, online, isDead, ↵
role, isML = GetRaidRosterInfo(index)
```

Arguments:

index—Index of the raid member (between 1 and GetNumRaidMembers()); matches the numeric part of the unit's raid unitID, e.g. 21 for raid21 (number)

Returns:

name—Name of the raid member (string)

rank—Rank of the member in the raid (number)

- ▪ 0—Raid member
- ▪ 1—Raid Assistant
- ▪ 2—Raid Leader

subgroup—Index of the raid subgroup to which the member belongs (between 1 and MAX_RAID_GROUPS) (number)

level—Character level of the member (number)

class—Localized name of the member's class (string)

fileName—A non-localized token representing the member's class (string)

zone—Name of the zone in which the member is currently located (string)

online—1 if the member is currently online; otherwise nil (1nil)

isDead—1 if the member is currently dead; otherwise nil (1nil)

role—Group role assigned to the member (string)

- ▪ MAINASSIST
- ▪ MAINTANK

isML—1 if the member is the master looter; otherwise nil (1nil)

GetRaidRosterSelection

Returns the index of the selected unit in the raid roster.

```
raidIndex = GetRaidRosterSelection()
```

Selection in the raid roster is used only for display in the default UI and has no effect on other Raid APIs.

Returns:

raidIndex—Index of the raid member (between 1 and GetNumRaid Members()); matches the numeric part of the unit's raid unitID, e.g. 21 for raid21 (number)

GetRaidTargetIndex

Returns the index of the raid target marker on a unit.

```
index = GetRaidTargetIndex("unit") or GetRaidTargetIndex("name")
```

Arguments:

unit—A unit to query (string, unitID)

name—The name of a unit to query; only valid for player, pet, and party/raid members (string)

Returns:

index—Index of a target marker (number)

1—Star	4—Triangle	7—Cross
2—Circle	5—Moon	8—Skull
3—Diamond	6—Square	nil—No marker

GetRangedCritChance

Returns the player's ranged critical strike chance.

```
critChance = GetRangedCritChance()
```

Returns:

critChance—The player's percentage critical strike chance for ranged attacks (number)

GetReadyCheckStatus

Returns a unit's status during a ready check.

```
status = GetReadyCheckStatus("unit")
```

Returns nil for all units unless the player is the party/raid leader or a raid assistant.

Arguments:

unit—A unit in the player's party or raid (string, unitID)

Returns:

status—Ready check status for the unit (string)

- ▪ "notready"—Unit has responded as not ready
- ▪ "ready"—Unit has responded as ready
- ▪ "waiting"—Unit has not yet responded
- ▪ nil—No ready check is in progress

GetReadyCheckTimeLeft

Returns the amount of time left on the current ready check.

```
timeLeft = GetReadyCheckTimeLeft()
```

Returns 0 if no ready check is in progress.

Returns:

timeLeft—Amount of time remaining on the ready check (in seconds) (number)

GetRealNumPartyMembers

Returns the number of members in the player's non-battleground party.

```
numMembers = GetRealNumPartyMembers()
```

When the player is in a party/raid and joins a battleground or arena, the normal party/raid functions refer to the battleground's party/raid, but the game still keeps track of the player's place in a non-battleground party/raid.

Returns:

numMembers—Number of members in the player's non-battleground party (number)

GetRealNumRaidMembers

Returns the number of members in the player's non-battleground raid.

```
numMembers = GetRealNumRaidMembers()
```

When the player is in a party/raid and joins a battleground or arena, the normal party/raid functions refer to the battleground's party/raid, but the game still keeps track of the player's place in a non-battleground party/raid.

Returns:

numMembers—Number of members in the player's non-battleground raid (number)

GetRealZoneText

Returns the "official" name of the zone or instance in which the player is located.

```
zoneName = GetRealZoneText()
```

This name matches that seen in the Who, Guild, and Friends UIs when reporting character locations. It may differ from those the default UI displays in other locations (GetZoneText() and GetMinimapZoneText()), especially if the player is in an instance: e.g. this function returns "The Stockade" when the others return "Stormwind Stockade".

Returns:

zoneName—Name of the zone or instance (string)

GetRealmName

Returns the name of the player's realm (server name).

```
realm = GetRealmName()
```

Returns:

`realm`—The name of the player's realm (server) (`string`)

GetRefreshRates

Returns a list of available screen refresh rates.

```
... = GetRefreshRates()
```

The current refresh rate can be found in the `gxRefresh` CVar.

Returns:

`...`—A list of numbers, each an available screen refresh rate (in hertz, or cycles per second) (`number`)

GetReleaseTimeRemaining

Returns the amount of time remaining until the player's spirit is automatically released when dead.

```
timeleft = GetReleaseTimeRemaining()
```

Returns `-1` if the player died in a dungeon or raid instance; in such cases, the player's spirit will not be released automatically (see `RepopMe()` to release manually).

Returns:

`timeleft`—Amount of time remaining until the player's spirit is automatically released to the nearest graveyard (in seconds) (`number`)

GetRepairAllCost

Returns the cost to repair all of the player's damaged items.

```
repairAllCost, canRepair = GetRepairAllCost()
```

Returns `0`, `nil` if none of the player's items are damaged. Only returns valid data while interacting with a vendor which allows repairs (i.e. for whom `CanMerchantRepair()` returns 1).

Returns:

`repairAllCost`—Cost to repair all damaged items (in copper) (`number`)

`canRepair`—1 if repairs are currently available; otherwise `nil` (`1nil`)

GetResSicknessDuration

Returns the duration of resurrection sickness at the player's current level.

```
resSicknessTime = GetResSicknessDuration()
```

Returns nil for players under level 10, who are allowed to resurrect at a spirit healer without suffering resurrection sickness.

Returns:

`resSicknessTime`—Text describing the duration of resurrection sickness were the player to resurrect at a spirit healer (`string`)

GetRestState

Returns the player's current rest state.

```
state, name, multiplier = GetRestState()
```

Returns:

`state`—Number identifying the current rest state (`number`)

- 1—Rested
- 2—Normal
- 3—Tired; used in locales with account play time limits
- 4—Unhealthy; used in locales with account play time limits

`name`—Localized text describing the player's current rest state (`string`)

`multiplier`—Multiplier for experience points earned from kills (`number`)

GetRewardHonor

Returns the amount of honor points awarded when completing a quest.

```
honor = GetRewardHonor()
```

Only valid when the questgiver UI is showing the accept/decline or completion stages of a quest dialog (between the QUEST_DETAIL and QUEST_FINISHED events, or between the QUEST_COMPLETE and QUEST_FINISHED events); otherwise may return zero or a value from the most recently displayed quest.

Returns:

`honor`—The honor points to be awarded (`number`)

GetRewardMoney

Returns the amount of money awarded when completing a quest.

```
money = GetRewardMoney()
```

Only valid when the questgiver UI is showing the accept/decline or completion stages of a quest dialog (between the QUEST_DETAIL and QUEST_FINISHED events, or between the QUEST_COMPLETE and QUEST_FINISHED events); otherwise may return zero or a value from the most recently displayed quest.

Returns:

`money`—The amount of money to be awarded (in copper) (`number`)

GetRewardSpell

Returns information about a spell awarded when completing a quest.

```
texture, name, isTradeskillSpell, isSpellLearned = GetRewardSpell()
```

Only valid when the questgiver UI is showing the accept/decline or completion stages of a quest dialog (between the QUEST_DETAIL and QUEST_FINISHED events, or between the QUEST_COMPLETE and QUEST_FINISHED events); otherwise may return zero or values from the most recently displayed quest.

If both `isTradeskillSpell` and `isSpellLearned` are nil, the reward is a spell cast upon the player.

Returns:

texture—Path to the spell's icon texture (string)

name—Name of the spell (string)

isTradeskillSpell—1 if the spell is a tradeskill recipe; otherwise nil (1nil)

isSpellLearned—1 if the reward teaches the player a new spell; otherwise nil (1nil)

GetRewardTalents

Returns the talent points awarded when completing a quest.

```
talents = GetRewardTalents()
```

Only valid when the questgiver UI is showing the accept/decline or completion stages of a quest dialog (between the QUEST_DETAIL and QUEST_FINISHED events, or between the QUEST_COMPLETE and QUEST_FINISHED events); otherwise may return zero or a value from the most recently displayed quest.

(Very few quests award talent points; currently this functionality is only used within the Death Knight starting experience.)

Returns:

talents—The talent points to be awarded (number)

GetRewardText

Returns questgiver dialog to be displayed when completing a quest.

```
text = GetRewardText()
```

Only valid when the questgiver UI is showing the completion stage of a quest dialog (between the QUEST_COMPLETE and QUEST_FINISHED events); otherwise may return the empty string or a value from the most recently displayed quest.

Returns:

text—Text to be displayed for the quest completion dialog (string)

GetRewardTitle

Returns the title awarded when completing a quest.

```
title = GetRewardTitle()
```

Only valid when the questgiver UI is showing the accept/decline or completion stages of a quest dialog (between the QUEST_DETAIL and QUEST_FINISHED events, or between the QUEST_COMPLETE and QUEST_FINISHED events); otherwise may return nil or a value from the most recently displayed quest.

Returns:

title—The title to be awarded, or nil if the quest does not reward a title (string)

GetRuneCooldown

Returns cooldown information about one of the player's rune resources.

```
start, duration, runeReady = GetRuneCooldown(slot)
```

Note the placement of runes 3-4 (normally Unholy) and 5-6 (normally Frost) are reversed in the default UI. Also note the behavior of returned values differs slightly from most other GetXYZCooldown-style functions.

Arguments:

slot—Index of a rune slot, as positioned in the default UI: (number)

1—Leftmost	4—Sixth from left (rightmost)
2—Second from left	5—Third from left
3—Fifth from left (second from right)	6—Fourth from left

Returns:

start—The value of GetTime() at the moment the cooldown began, or 0 if the rune is ready (number)

duration—The length of the cooldown (regardless of whether the rune is currently cooling down) (number)

runeReady—True if the rune can be used; false if the rune is cooling down (boolean)

GetRuneCount

Returns the number of available rune resources in one of the player's rune slots.

```
count = GetRuneCount(slot)
```

Returns 1 if a rune is ready and 0 if a rune is on cooldown.

Arguments:

slot—Index of a rune slot, as positioned in the default UI: (number)

1—Leftmost	4—Sixth from left (rightmost)
2—Second from left	5—Third from left
3—Fifth from left (second from right)	6—Fourth from left

Returns:

count—Number of available runes in the slot (number)

GetRuneType

Returns the type of one of the player's rune resources.

```
runeType = GetRuneType(slot)
```

Note the placement of runes 3-4 (normally Unholy) and 5-6 (normally Frost) are reversed in the default UI.

Arguments:

slot—Index of a rune slot, as positioned in the default UI: (number)

1—Leftmost	4—Sixth from left (rightmost)
2—Second from left	5—Third from left
3—Fifth from left (second from right)	6—Fourth from left

Returns:

runeType—Type of the rune (number)

1—Blood rune   3—Frost rune

2—Unholy rune   4—Death rune

GetRunningMacro

Returns the index of the currently running macro.

index = GetRunningMacro()

Returns:

index—Index of the currently running macro, or nil if no macro is running (number, macroID)

GetRunningMacroButton

Returns the mouse button that was used to activate the running macro.

button = GetRunningMacroButton()

Returns:

button—Name of the mouse button used to activate the macro; always "LeftButton" if the macro was triggered by a key binding (string)

Button4   MiddleButton

Button5   RightButton

LeftButton

GetSavedInstanceInfo

Returns information on a specific instance to which the player is saved.

instanceName, instanceID, instanceReset, instanceDifficulty, locked, ↩
extended, instanceIDMostSig, isRaid, maxPlayers, difficultyName = ↩
GetSavedInstanceInfo(index)

Arguments:

index—Index of a saved instance (between 1 and GetNumSavedInstances()) (number)

Returns:

instanceName—Name of the instance (string)

instanceID—Unique identifier of the saved instance (commonly known as a RaidID) (number)

instanceReset—Approximate number of seconds remaining until the instance resets (number)

instanceDifficulty—Difficulty level of the saved instance (number)

- 1—Normal ('10 Player' if instance is a raid)
- 2—Heroic ('25 Player' if instance is a raid)
- 3—10 Player Heroic
- 4—25 Player Heroic

`locked—` (`boolean`)

`extended—true` if the reset time has been extended past its normal time; otherwise `false` (`boolean`)

`instanceIDMostSig—` (`number`)

`isRaid—` (`boolean`)

`maxPlayers—`Number of players allowed (`number`)

`difficultyName—`A string representing the difficulty of the given instance. (`string`)

GetScreenHeight

Returns the height of the screen for UI layout purposes.

`height = GetScreenHeight()`

Measurements for layout are affected by the UI Scale setting (i.e. the `uiscale` CVar) and may not match actual screen pixels.

Returns:

`height—`Height of the screen in layout pixels (`number`)

GetScreenResolutions

Returns a list of available screen resolutions.

`... = GetScreenResolutions()`

Returns:

`...—`A list of strings, each a description of the dimensions of an available screen resolution (e.g. `"800x600"`, `"1024x768"`) (`string`)

Example:

```
-- Print all available screen resolutions:
print("Available resolutions:", string.join(", ", ↵
GetScreenResolutions()))
```

GetScreenWidth

Returns the width of the screen for UI layout purposes.

`screenWidth = GetScreenWidth()`

Measurements for layout are affected by the UI Scale setting (i.e. the `uiscale` CVar) and may not match actual screen pixels.

Returns:

`screenWidth—`Width of the screen in layout pixels (`number`)

GetScriptCPUUsage

Returns the total CPU time used by the scripting system.

`usage = GetScriptCPUUsage()`

Only returns valid data if the `scriptProfile` CVar is set to 1; returns 0 otherwise.

Returns:

usage—Amount of CPU time used by the scripting system (in milliseconds) since the UI was loaded or ResetCPUUsage() was last called (number)

GetSelectedAuctionItem

Returns the index of the currently selected item in an auction listing.

index = GetSelectedAuctionItem("list")

Auction selection is used only for display and internal recordkeeping in the default UI; it has no direct effect on other Auction APIs.

Arguments:

list—Type of auction listing (string)

- bidder—Auctions the player has bid on
- list—Auctions the player can browse and bid on or buy out
- owner—Auctions the player placed

Returns:

index—Index of the currently selected auction item (number)

GetSelectedBattlefield

Returns the index of the selected battleground instance in the queueing list.

index = GetSelectedBattlefield()

Selection in the battleground instance list is used only for display in the default UI and has no effect on other Battlefield APIs.

Returns:

index—Index of the selection in the battleground queue listing (1 for the first available instance, or between 2 and GetNumBattlefields() for other instances) (number)

GetSelectedDisplayChannel

Returns the selected channel in the channel list display.

index = GetSelectedDisplayChannel()

Returns:

index—Index of the selected channel in the display channel list (between 1 and GetNumDisplayChannels()) (number)

GetSelectedFaction

Returns which faction entry is selected in the reputation UI.

index = GetSelectedFaction()

Selection has no bearing on other faction-related APIs; this function merely facilitates behaviors of Blizzard's reputation UI.

Returns:

index—Index of an entry in the faction list; between 1 and GetNumFactions() (number)

GetSelectedFriend

Returns the index of the selected character in the player's friends list.

```
index = GetSelectedFriend()
```

Selection in the Friends list is used only for display in the default UI and has no effect on other Friends list APIs.

Returns:

index—Index of the selected character in the Friends list (between 1 and GetNumFriends()) (number)

GetSelectedIgnore

Returns the index of the selected character in the player's ignore list.

```
index = GetSelectedIgnore()
```

Selection in the Ignore list is used only for display in the default UI and has no effect on other Ignore list APIs.

Returns:

index—Index of the selected character in the Ignore list (between 1 and GetNumIgnores()) (number)

GetSelectedMute

Returns the index of the selected entry in the Muted list.

```
selectedMute = GetSelectedMute()
```

Mute list selection is only used for display purposes in the default UI and has no effect on other API functions.

Returns:

selectedMute—Index of the selected entry in the mute listing (between 1 and GetNumMutes()), or 0 if no entry is selected (number)

GetSelectedSkill

Returns the index of the selected skill in the Skills UI.

```
index = GetSelectedSkill()
```

Selection is only used for display purposes in the default Skills UI and has no effect on other Skill APIs.

Returns:

index—Index of the selected entry in the skills list (between 1 and GetNumSkillLines()) (number)

GetSelectedStablePet

Returns the index of the selected stable pet.

```
selectedPet = GetSelectedStablePet()
```

Returns:

selectedPet—Index of the currently selected stable pet (number)

■ -1—The player has no pets (in the stables or otherwise)

- ■ 0—The active pet is selected
- ■ 1 to NUM_PET_STABLE_SLOTS—A stable slot is selected

GetSendMailCOD

Returns the Cash-On-Delivery cost of the outgoing message.

```
amount = GetSendMailCOD()
```

Returns the amount set via SetSendMailCOD(), which in the default UI is only called once its Send button has been clicked (immediately before sending the message). Thus, does not return the COD amount set in the default UI's Send Mail window.

Returns:

amount—COD cost for the items attached to the message (in copper) (number)

GetSendMailItem

Returns information for an item attached to the outgoing message.

```
itemName, itemTexture, stackCount, quality = GetSendMailItem(slot)
```

Arguments:

slot—Index of an outgoing attachment slot (between 1 and ATTACHMENTS_MAX _SEND) (number)

Returns:

itemName—Name of the attachment item (string)

itemTexture—Path to an icon texture for the attachment item (string)

stackCount—Number of stacked items (string)

quality—Quality (rarity) of the attachment item (number, itemQuality)

GetSendMailItemLink

Returns a hyperlink for an item attached to the outgoing message.

```
itemlink = GetSendMailItemLink(slot)
```

Arguments:

slot—Index of an outgoing attachment slot (between 1 and ATTACHMENTS_MAX _SEND) (number)

Returns:

itemlink—A hyperlink for the attachment item (string, hyperlink)

Example:

```
-- Scan all the send mail item slots, printing a link for each item
for slot=1,ATTACHMENTS_MAX_SEND do
 local link = GetSendMailItemLink(slot)
 if link then
  print("Item " .. link .. " is in slot " .. slot)
 end
end
```

GetSendMailMoney

Returns the amount of money to be sent with the outgoing message.

```
amount = GetSendMailMoney()
```

Returns the amount set via `SetSendMailMoney()`, which in the default UI is only called once its Send button has been clicked (immediately before sending the message). Thus, does not return the Send Money amount set in the default UI's Send Mail window.

Returns:

`amount`—Amount of money to be sent (in copper) (`number`)

GetSendMailPrice

Returns the cost to send the outgoing mail message.

```
price = GetSendMailPrice()
```

The cost of sending a message rises as more items are attached.

Returns:

`price`—Cost to send the outgoing mail message (in copper) (`number`)

GetShapeshiftForm

Returns the index of the active ability on the stance/shapeshift bar.

```
index = GetShapeshiftForm()
```

Returns:

`index`—Index of the active ability on the stance/shapeshift bar (between 1 and `GetNumShapeshiftForms()`) (`number`)

GetShapeshiftFormCooldown

Returns cooldown information about an ability on the stance/shapeshift bar.

```
start, duration, enable = GetShapeshiftFormCooldown(index)
```

Arguments:

`index`—Index of an ability on the stance/shapeshift bar (between 1 and `GetNumShapeshiftForms()`) (`number`)

Returns:

`start`—The value of `GetTime()` at the moment the cooldown began, or 0 if the ability is ready (`number`)

`duration`—The length of the cooldown, or 0 if the ability is ready (`number`)

`enable`—1 if a Cooldown UI element should be used to display the cooldown, otherwise 0. (Does not always correlate with whether the ability is ready.) (`number`)

GetShapeshiftFormInfo

Returns information about an ability on the stance/shapeshift bar.

```
texture, name, isActive, isCastable = GetShapeshiftFormInfo(index)
```

Arguments:

`index`—Index of an ability on the stance/shapeshift bar (between 1 and `GetNumShapeshiftForms()`) (`number`)

Returns:

`texture`—Path to an icon texture for the ability (`string`)

`name`—Name of the ability (`string`)

isActive—1 if the ability is currently active; otherwise nil (1nil)

isCastable—1 if the ability can currently be used; otherwise nil (1nil)

GetShieldBlock

Returns the amount of damage prevented when the player blocks with a shield.

```
damage = GetShieldBlock()
```

Returns:

damage—The amount of damage prevented when the player blocks with a shield (number)

GetSkillLineInfo

Returns information about an entry in the Skills UI list.

```
skillName, header, isExpanded, skillRank, numTempPoints, ↵
skillModifier, skillMaxRank, isAbandonable, stepCost, rankCost, ↵
minLevel, skillCostType, skillDescription = GetSkillLineInfo(index)
```

Arguments:

index—Index of an entry in the skills list (between 1 and GetNumSkill Lines()) (number)

Returns:

skillName—Name of the skill (or header) (string)

header—1 if the entry is a header; nil if the entry is a skill (1nil)

isExpanded—1 if the entry is a header and currently expanded; otherwise nil (1nil)

skillRank—The player's current rank in the skill (number)

numTempPoints—Unused (number)

skillModifier—Temporary skill modifier (e.g. due to buffs/debuffs or gear) (number)

skillMaxRank—Maximum rank currently available in the skill (e.g. 395 in a weapon skill for a level 79 player, 150 for a trade skill in which the player has reached Journeyman status); 1 for unranked skills (e.g. armor proficiencies) (number)

isAbandonable—1 if the player can unlearn the skill; otherwise nil (1nil)

stepCost—Unused (number)

rankCost—Unused (number)

minLevel—Unused (number)

skillCostType—1 for ranked skills; 0 for unranked skills (number)

skillDescription—Extended description of the skill (string)

GetSocketItemBoundTradeable

Returns whether the item open for socketing is temporarily tradeable.

```
tradeable = GetSocketItemBoundTradeable()
```

A Bind on Pickup item looted by the player can be traded to other characters who were originally eligible to loot it, but only within a limited time after looting. This period can be ended prematurely if the player attempts certain actions (such as socketing gems into the item).

Returns:

`tradeable`—1 if the item can temporarily be traded to other players; otherwise `nil` (1nil)

GetSocketItemInfo

Returns information about the item currently being socketed.

`name, icon, quality = GetSocketItemInfo()`

Only returns valid information when the Item Socketing UI is open (i.e. between the SOCKET_INFO_UPDATE and SOCKET_INFO_CLOSE events).

Returns:

`name`—Name of the item (`string`)

`icon`—Path to an icon texture for the item (`string`)

`quality`—Quality level of the item (`number`, itemQuality)

GetSocketItemRefundable

Returns whether the item open for socketing is temporarily refundable.

`refundable = GetSocketItemRefundable()`

Items bought with alternate currency (honor points, arena points, or special items such as Emblems of Heroism and Dalaran Cooking Awards) can be returned to a vendor for a full refund, but only within a limited time after the original purchase. This period can be ended prematurely if the player attempts certain actions (such as socketing gems into the item).

Returns:

`refundable`—1 if the item can be returned to a vendor for a refund; otherwise `nil` (1nil)

GetSocketTypes

Returns information about the gem types usable in a socket.

`gemColor = GetSocketTypes(index)`

Only returns valid information when the Item Socketing UI is open (i.e. between the SOCKET_INFO_UPDATE and SOCKET_INFO_CLOSE events).

Arguments:

`index`—Index of a gem socket (between 1 and `GetNumSockets()`) (`number`)

Returns:

`gemColor`—Type of the gem socket (`string`)

- `Blue`—Accepts any gem, but requires a blue, green, purple or prismatic gem to activate the item's socket bonus

- ■ `Meta`—Accepts only meta gems
- ■ `Red`—Accepts any gem, but requires a red, purple, orange or prismatic gem to activate the item's socket bonus
- ■ `Socket`—Accepts any gem
- ■ `Yellow`—Accepts any gem, but requires a yellow, orange, green or prismatic gem to activate the item's socket bonus

GetSpellAutocast

Returns information about automatic casting for a spell in the spellbook.

`autocastAllowed, autocastEnabled = GetSpellAutocast(id, "bookType")`

Generally, only certain pet spells can be autocast.

Arguments:

`id`—Index of a spell in the spellbook (number, spellbookID)

`bookType`—Type of spellbook (`string`)

- ■ `pet`—The pet's spellbook
- ■ `spell`—The player's spellbook

Returns:

`autocastAllowed`—1 if automatic casting is allowed for the action; otherwise `nil` (1nil)

`autocastEnabled`—1 if automatic casting is currently turned on for the action; otherwise `nil` (1nil)

GetSpellBonusDamage

Returns the player's spell damage bonus for a spell school.

`minModifier = GetSpellBonusDamage(school)`

Arguments:

`school`—Index of a spell school (number)

1—Physical	5—Frost
2—Holy	6—Shadow
3—Fire	7—Arcane
4—Nature	

Returns:

`minModifier`—The player's spell damage bonus for the given school (number)

GetSpellBonusHealing

Returns the player's amount of bonus healing.

`bonusHealing = GetSpellBonusHealing()`

Returns:

`bonusHealing`—Amount of bonus healing (integer)

GetSpellCooldown

Returns cooldown information about a spell in the spellbook.

```
start, duration, enable = GetSpellCooldown(index, "bookType") or ↵
GetSpellCooldown("name")
```

Arguments:

index—Index of a spell in the spellbook (number, spellbookID)

bookType—Type of spellbook (string)

∎ pet—The pet's spellbook

∎ spell—The player's spellbook

name—Name of a spell (string)

Returns:

start—The value of GetTime() at the moment the cooldown began, or 0 if the spell is ready (number)

duration—The length of the cooldown, or 0 if the spell is ready (number)

enable—1 if a Cooldown UI element should be used to display the cooldown, otherwise 0. (Does not always correlate with whether the spell is ready.) (number)

GetSpellCount

Returns the number of times a spell can be cast.

```
numCasts = GetSpellCount(index, "bookType") or GetSpellCount("name")
```

Generally used for spells whose casting is limited by the number of item reagents in the player's possession.

Arguments:

index—Index of a spell in the spellbook (number, spellbookID)

bookType—Type of spellbook (string)

∎ pet—The pet's spellbook

∎ spell—The player's spellbook

name—Name of a spell (string)

Returns:

numCasts—Number of times the spell can be cast, or 0 if unlimited (number)

Example:

```
-- print a list of reagent-limited spells in the player's spellbook
local numTabs = GetNumSpellTabs()
for tabid=1,numTabs do
 local name,texture,offset,numSpells = GetSpellTabInfo(tabid)
 for spellid=1,numSpells do
  local name,rank = GetSpellName(spellid + offset, "book")
  local count = GetSpellCount(spellid + offset, "book")
  if count > 0 then
   print(name .. " ( ".. count .. " casts)")
```

```
        end
      end
    end
```

GetSpellCritChance

Returns the player's spell critical strike chance for a spell school.

```
minCrit = GetSpellCritChance(school)
```

Arguments:

`school`—Index of a spell school (`number`)

1—Physical	5—Frost
2—Holy	6—Shadow
3—Fire	7—Arcane
4—Nature	

Returns:

`minCrit`—The player's percentage critical strike chance for spells from the given school (`number`)

GetSpellCritChanceFromIntellect

Returns additional spell critical strike chance provided by Intellect.

```
critChance = GetSpellCritChanceFromIntellect(["unit"])
```

Arguments:

`unit` (optional)—A unit to query; only valid for `player` and `pet`, defaults to `player` if omitted (`string`, unitID)

Returns:

`critChance`—Additional percentage chance of spell critical strikes conferred by the unit's Intellect statistic (`number`)

GetSpellInfo

Returns information about a spell.

```
name, rank, icon, powerCost, isFunnel, powerType, castingTime, ↵
minRange, maxRange = GetSpellInfo(index, "bookType") or ↵
GetSpellInfo("name") or GetSpellInfo(id)
```

Arguments:

`index`—Index of a spell in the spellbook (`number`, spellbookID)

`bookType`—Type of spellbook (`string`)

■ `pet`—The pet's spellbook

■ `spell`—The player's spellbook

`name`—Name of a spell, optionally including secondary text (e.g. "Mana Burn" to find the player's highest rank, or "Mana Burn(Rank 2)"—no space before the parenthesis—for a specific rank) (`string`)

`id`—Numeric ID of a spell (`number`, spellID)

Returns:

name—Name of the spell (`string`)

rank—Secondary text associated with the spell (e.g. "Rank 5", "Racial", etc.) (`string`)

icon—Path to an icon texture for the spell (`string`)

powerCost—Amount of mana, rage, energy, runic power, or focus required to cast the spell (`number`)

isFunnel—`True` for spells with health funneling effects (like Health Funnel) (`boolean`)

powerType—Power type to cast the spell (`number`)

-2—Health	3—Energy
0—Mana	5—Runes
1—Rage	6—Runic Power
2—Focus	

castingTime—Casting time of the spell in milliseconds (`number`)

minRange—Minimum range from the target required to cast the spell (`number`)

maxRange—Maximum range from the target at which you can cast the spell (`number`)

GetSpellLink

Returns a hyperlink for a spell.

```
link, tradeLink = GetSpellLink(index, "bookType") or ↵
GetSpellLink("name") or GetSpellLink(id)
```

Arguments:

index—Index of a spell in the spellbook (`number`, spellbookID)

bookType—Type of spellbook (`string`)

■ pet—The pet's spellbook

■ spell—The player's spellbook

name—Name of a spell, optionally including secondary text (e.g. "Mana Burn" to find the player's highest rank, or "Mana Burn(Rank 2)"—no space before the parenthesis—for a specific rank) (`string`)

id—Numeric ID of a spell (`number`, spellID)

Returns:

link—A hyperlink for the spell (`string`, hyperlink)

tradeLink—A hyperlink representing the player's list of trade skill recipes, if the spell is a trade skill (i.e. if "casting" the spell opens a trade skill window) (`string`)

GetSpellName

Returns the name and secondary text for a spell in the spellbook.

```
spellName, subSpellName = GetSpellName(id, "bookType")
```

Arguments:

id—Index of a spell in the spellbook (`number`, spellbookID)

bookType—Type of spellbook (`string`)

- pet—The pet's spellbook
- spell—The player's spellbook

Returns:

spellName—Localized name of the spell (`string`)

subSpellName—Secondary text associated with the spell (e.g. "Rank 5", "Racial Passive", "Artisan") (`string`)

GetSpellPenetration

Returns the amount of enemy magic resistance ignored due to the player's Spell Penetration Rating.

```
penetration = GetSpellPenetration()
```

Returns:

penetration—Amount of enemy magic resistance ignored due to the player's Spell Penetration Rating (`number`)

GetSpellTabInfo

Returns information about a tab in the spellbook.

```
name, texture, offset, numSpells = GetSpellTabInfo(index)
```

Arguments:

index—Index of a spellbook tab (between 1 and `GetNumSpellTabs()`) (`number`)

Returns:

name—Name of the spellbook tab (`string`)

texture—Path to an icon texture for the spellbook tab (`string`)

offset—spellbookID of the first spell to be listed under the tab (`number`)

numSpells—Number of spells listed under the tab (`number`)

Example:

```
-- Print the valid spellIds for each tab
local numTabs = GetNumSpellTabs()
for i=1,numTabs do
  local name,texture,offset,numSpells = GetSpellTabInfo(i)
  print("Spell tab \"" .. name .. "\" contains spells from id " ↵
.. offset + 1 .. " through " .. offset + numSpells)
end
```

GetSpellTexture

Returns the icon texture path for a spell.

```
texture = GetSpellTexture(index, "bookType") or GetSpellTexture("name")
```

Arguments:

index—Index of a spell in the spellbook (`number`, spellbookID)

bookType—Type of spellbook (`string`)

- `pet`—The pet's spellbook
- `spell`—The player's spellbook

`name`—Name of a spell (`string`)

Returns:

`texture`—Path to an icon texture for the spell (`string`)

GetStablePetFoodTypes

Returns the types of food that a stabled pet will eat.

`... = GetStablePetFoodTypes(index)`

Arguments:

`index`—Index of a stable slot (`number`)

- `0`—Active pet
- `1` to `NUM_PET_STABLE_SLOTS`—A stabled pet

Returns:

`...`—A list of strings, each the localized name of a food type the pet will eat (`list`)

GetStablePetInfo

Returns information about a stabled pet.

`icon, name, level, family, talent = GetStablePetInfo(index)`

Arguments:

`index`—Index of a stable slot (`number`)

- `0`—Active pet
- `1` to `NUM_PET_STABLE_SLOTS`—A stable slot

Returns:

`icon`—Path to an icon texture for the pet (`string`)

`name`—Name of the pet (`string`)

`level`—Level of the pet (`number`)

`family`—Localized name of the pet's creature family (e.g. Cat, Bear, Chimaera) (`string`)

`talent`—Localized name of the pet's talent tree (e.g. Ferocity, Tenacity, Cunning) (`string`)

GetStatistic

Returns data for a statistic.

`info = GetStatistic(id)`

Arguments:

`id`—The numeric ID of a statistic (`number`)

Returns:

`info`—The data for the statistic, or "--" if none has yet been recorded for it (`string`)

GetStatisticsCategoryList

Returns a list of all statistic categories.

```
categories = GetStatisticsCategoryList()
```

Returns:

categories—A list of statistic category IDs (`table`)

GetSubZoneText

Returns the name of the minor area in which the player is located.

```
subzoneText = GetSubZoneText()
```

Subzones are named regions within a larger zone or instance: e.g. the Valley of Trials in Durotar, the Terrace of Light in Shattrath City, or the Njorn Stair in Utgarde Keep.

Returns:

subzoneText—Name of the current subzone (`string`)

GetSuggestedGroupNum

Returns the suggested group size for attempting the quest currently offered by a questgiver.

```
suggestedGroup = GetSuggestedGroupNum()
```

Usable following the QUEST_DETAIL event in which the questgiver presents the player with the details of a quest and the option to accept or decline.

Returns:

suggestedGroup—Suggested group size for attempting the quest currently offered by a questgiver (`number`)

GetSummonConfirmAreaName

Returns the destination area of an offered summons.

```
area = GetSummonConfirmAreaName()
```

The name returned is generally that of the subzone in which the summoner performed the spell.

Usable between when the CONFIRM_SUMMON event fires (due to a summoning spell cast by another player) and when the value returned by GetSummonConfirmTimeLeft() reaches zero.

Returns:

area—Name of the location to which the player will be teleported upon accepting the summons (`string`)

GetSummonConfirmSummoner

Returns the name of the unit offering a summons to the player.

```
text = GetSummonConfirmSummoner()
```

Usable between when the CONFIRM_SUMMON event fires (due to a summoning spell cast by another player) and when the value returned by GetSummonConfirmTimeLeft() reaches zero.

Returns:

text—Name of the summoning unit (string)

GetSummonConfirmTimeLeft

Returns the amount of time remaining before an offered summons expires.

```
timeleft = GetSummonConfirmTimeLeft()
```

Returns 0 if no summons is currently available.

Returns:

timeleft—Time remaining until the offered summons can no longer be accepted (in seconds) (number)

GetSummonFriendCooldown

Returns cooldown information about the player's Summon Friend ability.

```
start, duration = GetSummonFriendCooldown()
```

Returns:

start—The value of GetTime() at the moment the cooldown began, or 0 if the ability is ready (number)

duration—The length of the cooldown, or 0 if the ability is ready (number)

GetTabardCreationCost

Returns the cost to create a guild tabard.

```
cost = GetTabardCreationCost()
```

Only returns valid data if the player is interacting with a tabard designer (i.e. between the OPEN_TABARD_FRAME and CLOSE_TABARD_FRAME events).

Returns:

cost—The cost of creating a guild tabard, in copper (number)

GetTalentInfo

Returns information about a talent option.

```
name, iconTexture, tier, column, rank, maxRank, isExceptional, ↵
meetsPrereq, previewRank, meetsPreviewPrereq = ↵
GetTalentInfo(tabIndex, talentIndex, inspect, pet, talentGroup)
```

Arguments:

tabIndex—Index of a talent tab (between 1 and GetNumTalentTabs()) (number)

talentIndex—Index of a talent option (between 1 and GetNumTalents()) (number)

inspect—true to return information for the currently inspected unit; false to return information for the player (boolean)

pet—true to return information for the player's pet; false to return information for the player (boolean)

talentGroup—Which set of talents to edit, if the player has Dual Talent Specialization enabled (number)

▪ 1—Primary Talents

■ 2—Secondary Talents

■ `nil`—Currently active talents

Returns:

`name`—Name of the talent (`string`)

`iconTexture`—The icon texture of the talent. (`string`)

`tier`—Row in which the talent should be displayed (1 = top) (`number`)

`column`—Column in which the talent should be displayed (1 = left) (`number`)

`rank`—Number of points spent in the talent (`number`)

`maxRank`—Maximum number of points that can be spent in the talent (`number`)

`isExceptional`—1 if the talent confers a new ability (spell); otherwise `nil` (1nil)

`meetsPrereq`—1 if the prerequisites to learning the talent have been met; otherwise `nil` (1nil)

`previewRank`—Number of points spent in the talent in preview mode (`number`)

`meetsPreviewPrereq`—1 if the prerequisites to learning the talent have been met in preview mode; otherwise `nil` (1nil)

GetTalentLink

Returns a hyperlink for a talent.

`link = GetTalentLink(tabIndex, talentIndex, inspect, pet, talentGroup)`

Arguments:

`tabIndex`—Index of a talent tab (between 1 and `GetNumTalentTabs()`) (`number`)

`talentIndex`—Index of a talent option (between 1 and `GetNumTalents()`) (`number`)

`inspect`—`true` to return information for the currently inspected unit; `false` to return information for the player (`boolean`)

`pet`—`true` to return information for the player's pet; `false` to return information for the player (`boolean`)

`talentGroup`—Which set of talents to edit, if the player has Dual Talent Specialization enabled (`number`)

■ 1—Primary Talents

■ 2—Secondary Talents

■ `nil`—Currently active talents

Returns:

`link`—A hyperlink representing the talent and the number of points spent in it (`string`, hyperlink)

GetTalentPrereqs

Returns information about prerequisites to learning a talent.

`tier, column, isLearnable, isPreviewLearnable, ... = ↵`
`GetTalentPrereqs(tabIndex, talentIndex, inspect, pet, talentGroup)`

Arguments:

tabIndex—Index of a talent tab (between 1 and GetNumTalentTabs())
(number)

talentIndex—Index of a talent option (between 1 and GetNumTalents())
(number)

inspect—true to return information for the currently inspected
unit; false to return information for the player (boolean)

pet—true to return information for the player's pet; false to return information for the player (boolean)

talentGroup—Which set of talents to edit, if the player has Dual Talent Specialization enabled (number)

- 1—Primary Talents
- 2—Secondary Talents
- nil—Currently active talents

Returns:

tier—Row in which the talent's prerequisite is displayed (1 = top) (number)

column—Column in which the talent's prerequisite is displayed (1 = left)
(number)

isLearnable—1 if the talent is learnable; otherwise nil (1nil)

isPreviewLearnable—1 if the talent is learnable in preview mode; otherwise
nil (1nil)

...—Additional sets of tier, column, isLearnable, isPreviewLearnable
values for each prerequisite to learning the talent (list)

GetTalentTabInfo

Returns information about a talent tab.

```
name, icon, points, background, previewPoints = ↵
GetTalentTabInfo(tabIndex, inspect, pet, talentGroup)
```

Arguments:

tabIndex—Index of a talent tab (between 1 and GetNumTalentTabs())
(number)

inspect—true to return information for the currently inspected
unit; false to return information for the player (boolean)

pet—true to return information for the player's pet; false to return information for the player (boolean)

talentGroup—Which set of talents to edit, if the player has Dual Talent Specialization enabled (number)

- 1—Primary Talents
- 2—Secondary Talents
- nil—Currently active talents

Returns:

name—Name of the talent tab (string)

icon—Path to an icon texture for the talent tab (string)

points—Number of points spent in the talent tab (number)

background—Path to a background texture for the talent tab (string)

previewPoints—Number of points spent in the talent tab in preview mode (number)

GetTargetTradeMoney

Returns the amount of money offered for trade by the target.

```
amount = GetTargetTradeMoney()
```

Returns:

amount—Amount of money offered for trade by the target (in copper) (number)

GetTaxiBenchmarkMode

Returns whether flight path benchmark mode is enabled.

```
isBenchmark = GetTaxiBenchmarkMode()
```

Returns:

isBenchmark—1 if taxi benchmark mode is enabled; otherwise nil (1nil)

GetTerrainMip

Returns the level of terrain detail displayed.

```
terrainDetail = GetTerrainMip()
```

Corresponds to the "Terrain Blending" slider in the default UI's Video Options pane.

Returns:

terrainDetail—Level of terrain detail displayed (number)

- 0—Low detail
- 1—High detail

GetText

Returns a localized string according to given parameters.

```
text = GetText("token" [, gender [, ordinal]])
```

Applies to any global variable whose name fits a standard format: for example, GetText("foo") returns the value of the global variable foo (if it exists), and GetText("foo", 3) returns the value of foo_FEMALE (or if it does not exist, the value of foo). Causes a Lua error if the given variable does not exists (or is nil).

Arguments:

token—Base name of a localized string token (string)

gender (optional)—Gender of the string's subject (as returned by UnitSex()) (number)

ordinal (optional)—Currently unused (number)

Returns:

text—The localized string according to the given parameters (string)

Example:

```
GetText("FACTION_STANDING_LABEL1")
-- returns the value of "FACTION_STANDING_LABEL1"
-- ("Hated" on enUS clients)
GetText("FACTION_STANDING_LABEL1",3)
-- returns the value of "FACTION_STANDING_LABEL1_FEMALE"
-- ("Hated" on enUS clients, but distinct from the male form in
-- certain other locales)
```

GetThreatStatusColor

Returns color values for a given threat status.

```
red, green, blue = GetThreatStatusColor(status)
```

Color component values are floating point numbers between 0 and 1, with 1 representing full intensity.

Arguments:

`status`—A threat status category, as returned by `UnitThreatSituation` or `UnitDetailedThreatSituation` (number)

Returns:

`red`—Red component of the color (number)

`green`—Green component of the color (number)

`blue`—Blue component of the color (number)

GetTime

Returns a number representing the current time (with millisecond precision).

```
time = GetTime()
```

Unlike with `time()`, the number returned by this function has no meaning of its own and may not be comparable across clients; however, since it also provides higher resolution it can be compared against itself for high-precision time measurements.

Returns:

`time`—A number that represents the current time in seconds (with millisecond precision) (number)

GetTitleName

Returns the text of an available player title.

```
titleName = GetTitleName(titleIndex)
```

Arguments:

`titleIndex`—Index of a title available to the player (between 1 and `GetNumTitles()`) (integer)

Returns:

`titleName`—The text of the title (string)

Example:

```
-- Print all available titles
```

```
for i=1,GetNumTitles() do
 print(GetTitleName(i))
end
```

GetTitleText

Returns the title text for the quest presented by a questgiver.

```
text = GetTitleText()
```

Only valid following the QUEST_DETAIL, QUEST_PROGRESS, or QUEST_COMPLETE events; otherwise may return nil or a value from the most recently displayed quest.

Returns:

text—Title text for the quest (string)

GetTotalAchievementPoints

Returns the player's total achievement points earned.

```
points = GetTotalAchievementPoints()
```

Returns:

points—Total number of achievement points earned by the player (number)

GetTotemInfo

Returns information on a currently active totem (or ghoul).

```
haveTotem, name, startTime, duration, icon = GetTotemInfo(slot)
```

Totem functions are also used for ghouls summoned by a Death Knight's Raise Dead ability (if the ghoul is not made a controllable pet by the Master of Ghouls talent).

Arguments:

slot—Which totem to query (number)
1—Fire (or Death Knight's ghoul)   3—Water
2—Earth   4—Air

Returns:

haveTotem—True if a totem of the given type is active (boolean)

name—The name of the totem (string)

startTime—The value of GetTime() when the totem was created (number)

duration—The total duration the totem will last (in seconds) (number)

icon—Path to a texture to use as the totem's icon (string)

GetTotemTimeLeft

Returns the time remaining before a totem (or ghoul) automatically disappears.

```
seconds = GetTotemTimeLeft(slot)
```

Using GetTime() and the third and fourth returns (startTime and duration) of GetTotemInfo() instead of this function is recommended if frequent updates are needed.

Totem functions are also used for ghouls summoned by a Death Knight's Raise Dead ability (if the ghoul is not made a controllable pet by the Master of Ghouls talent).

Arguments:

`slot`—Which totem to query (`number`)

1—Fire (or Death Knight's ghoul)   3—Water

2—Earth   4—Air

Returns:

`seconds`—Time remaining before the totem/ghoul is automatically destroyed (`number`)

GetTrackedAchievements

Returns numeric IDs of the achievements flagged for display in the objectives tracker UI.

`... = GetTrackedAchievements()`

Returns:

`...`—List of numeric IDs for the achievements being tracked (`list`)

GetTrackingInfo

Returns information about a given tracking option.

`name, texture, active, category = GetTrackingInfo(index)`

Arguments:

`index`—Index of a tracking ability to query (between 1 and `GetNumTracking Types()`) (`number`)

Returns:

`name`—Localized name of the tracking ability (`string`)

`texture`—Path to an icon texture for the tracking ability (`string`)

`active`—1 if the tracking abilty is active; otherwise `nil` (`1nil`)

`category`—Category of the tracking ability; used in the default UI to determine whether to strip the border from the ability's icon texture, and also indicates when the ability can be used: (`string`)

- `other`—Ability is available to all players and can be used at any time
- `spell`—Ability is a spell from the player's spellbook; using it may be subject to spell casting restrictions

GetTrackingTexture

Returns the texture of the active tracking ability.

`texture = GetTrackingTexture()`

Returns "Interface\Minimap\Tracking\None" if no tracking ability is active.

Returns:

`texture`—Path to an icon texture for the active tracking ability (`string`)

GetTradePlayerItemInfo

Returns information about an item offered for trade by the player.

```
name, texture, numItems, quality, isUsable, enchantment = ↵
GetTradePlayerItemInfo(index)
```

Arguments:

index—Index of an item slot on the player's side of the trade window (between 1 and MAX_TRADE_ITEMS) (number)

Returns:

name—Name of the item (string)

texture—Path to an icon texture for the item (string)

numItems—Number of stacked items in the slot (number)

quality—Quality (rarity) level of the item (number, itemQuality)

isUsable—1 if the player character can use or equip the item; otherwise nil (1nil)

enchantment—Name of the enchantment being applied to the item through trade; otherwise nil (string)

GetTradePlayerItemLink

Returns a hyperlink for an item offered for trade by the player.

```
link = GetTradePlayerItemLink(index)
```

Arguments:

index—Index of an item offered for trade by the player (between 1 and MAX_TRADE_ITEMS) (number)

Returns:

link—A hyperlink for the item (string, hyperlink)

GetTradeSkillCooldown

Returns the time remaining on a trade skill recipe's cooldown.

```
cooldown = GetTradeSkillCooldown(index)
```

Arguments:

index—Index of a recipe in the trade skill list (between 1 and GetNumTradeSkills()) (number)

Returns:

cooldown—Time remaining before the recipe can be performed again (in seconds), or nil if the recipe is currently available or has no cooldown (number)

Example:

```
-- Print cooldowns for any applicable recipes
for i=1,GetNumTradeSkills() do
  local cooldown = GetTradeSkillCooldown(i)
  if cooldown then
    local name = GetTradeSkillInfo(i)
    print("Cooldown remaining for " .. ↵
name .. ": " .. SecondsToTime(cooldown))
  end
end
```

GetTradeSkillDescription

Returns descriptive text for a tradeskill recipe.

```
description = GetTradeSkillDescription(index)
```

Most recipes that create items don't provide descriptive text; descriptions are more often used for enchants and special recipes such as inscription or alchemy research.

Arguments:

index—Index of a recipe in the trade skill list (between 1 and GetNumTrade Skills()) (number)

Returns:

description—Descriptive text for the tradeskill recipe, or nil if no text is associated with the recipe (string)

GetTradeSkillIcon

Returns the icon for a trade skill recipe.

```
texturePath = GetTradeSkillIcon(index)
```

For recipes that create an item, this is generally the icon of the item created; for other recipes (such as enchants and alchemy/inscription research) a generic icon is used.

Arguments:

index—Index of a recipe in the trade skill list (between 1 and GetNumTrade Skills()) (number)

Returns:

texturePath—Path to an icon texture for the recipe (string)

GetTradeSkillInfo

Returns information about a trade skill header or recipe.

```
skillName, skillType, numAvailable, isExpanded, serviceType = ↵
GetTradeSkillInfo(index)
```

Arguments:

index—Index of an entry in the trade skill list (between 1 and GetNumTradeSkills()) (number)

Returns:

skillName—Name of the entry (string)

skillType—Indicates whether the entry is a header or recipe and difficulty of recipes (string)

- easy—Low chance for the player to gain skill by performing the recipe (displayed as green in the default UI)
- header—This entry is a header and not an actual trade skill recipe
- medium—Moderate chance for the player to gain skill by performing the recipe (displayed as yellow in the default UI)
- optimal—High chance for the player to gain skill by performing the recipe (displayed as orange in the default UI)

- `trivial`—No chance for the player to gain skill by performing the recipe (displayed as gray in the default UI)

`numAvailable`—Number of times the player can repeat the recipe given available reagents (`number`)

`isExpanded`—1 if the entry is a header and is expanded; otherwise `nil` (`1nil`)

`serviceType`—Indicates what type of service the recipe provides (items, enhancements, etc ...) (`string`)

- `Emboss`—Applies an emboss (leatherworkers)
- `Embroider`—Applies an embroider (tailors)
- `Enchant`—Applies an enchant (enchanters)
- `Engrave`—Engraves a rune (runeforging)
- `Inscribe`—Puts an inscription (scribers)
- `Modify`—Puts a socket (blacksmiths)
- `Tinker`—Puts a device like webbing or flexweave (engineers)
- `nil`—Produces an item

GetTradeSkillInvSlotFilter

Returns whether the trade skill listing is filtered by a given item equipment slot.

```
enabled = GetTradeSkillInvSlotFilter(index)
```

Arguments:

`index`—Index of an item equipment slot (in the list returned by `GetTradeSkillInvSlots()`), or 0 for the "All" filter (`number`)

Returns:

`enabled`—1 if the filter is enabled; otherwise `nil` (`1nil`)

GetTradeSkillInvSlots

Returns a list of recipe equipment slots for the current trade skill.

```
... = GetTradeSkillInvSlots()
```

These inventory types correspond to those of the items produced (see `GetItemInfo()` and `GetAuctionItemInvTypes()`) and can be used to filter the recipe list.

Returns:

`...`—A list of strings, each the localized name of an inventory type applicable to the current trade skill listing (`list`)

GetTradeSkillItemLevelFilter

Returns the current settings for filtering the trade skill listing by required level of items produced.

```
minLevel, maxLevel = GetTradeSkillItemLevelFilter()
```

Returns:

`minLevel`—Lowest required level of items to show in the filtered list (`number`)

`maxLevel`—Highest required level of items to show in the filtered list (`number`)

GetTradeSkillItemLink

Returns a hyperlink for the item created by a tradeskill recipe.

```
link = GetTradeSkillItemLink(index)
```

The tooltip produced when resolving the link describes only the item created by the recipe. For a link which describes the recipe itself (its reagents and description), see `GetTradeSkillRecipeLink()`.

If the recipe does not create an item, this function returns the same hyperlink as does `GetTradeSkillRecipeLink()` (though the text of the link may differ).

Arguments:

`index`—Index of a recipe in the trade skill list (between 1 and `GetNumTradeSkills()`) (number)

Returns:

`link`—A hyperlink for the item created by the recipe (string)

GetTradeSkillItemNameFilter

Returns the current search text for filtering the trade skill listing by name.

```
text = GetTradeSkillItemNameFilter()
```

Returns:

`text`—Text to search for in recipe names, produced item names or descriptions, or reagents; `nil` if no search filter is in use (string)

GetTradeSkillLine

Returns information about the current trade skill.

```
tradeskillName, rank, maxLevel = GetTradeSkillLine()
```

Returns:

`tradeskillName`—Name of the trade skill (string)

`rank`—The character's current rank in the trade skill (number)

`maxLevel`—The character's current maximum rank in the trade skill (e.g. 300 for a character of Artisan status) (number)

GetTradeSkillListLink

Returns a hyperlink to the player's list of recipes for the current trade skill.

```
link = GetTradeSkillListLink()
```

Returns:

`link`—A hyperlink other players can resolve to see the player's full list of tradeskill recipes (string, hyperlink)

GetTradeSkillNumMade

Returns the number of items created when performing a tradeskill recipe.

```
minMade, maxMade = GetTradeSkillNumMade(index)
```

Arguments:

`index`—Index of a recipe in the trade skill list (between 1 and `GetNumTradeSkills()`) (number)

Returns:

minMade—Minimum number of items created when performing the recipe (number)

maxMade—Maximum number of items created when performing the recipe (number)

Example:

```
-- Print any multi-item recipes
local numSkills = GetNumTradeSkills()
for i=1,numSkills do
 local minMade,maxMade = GetTradeSkillNumMade(i)
 if minMade > 1 then
  local link = GetTradeSkillRecipeLink(i)
  if (minMade == maxMade) then
   print(link .. " always creates " .. minMade .. " items")
  else
   print(link .. " randomly creates between " .. minMade .. ↵
" and " .. maxMade .. " items")
  end
 end
end
```

GetTradeSkillNumReagents

Returns the number of different reagents required for a trade skill recipe.

```
numReagents = GetTradeSkillNumReagents(index)
```

Arguments:

index—Index of a recipe in the trade skill list (between 1 and GetNumTrade Skills()) (number)

Returns:

numReagents—Number of different reagents required for the recipe (number)

GetTradeSkillReagentInfo

Returns information about a reagent in a trade skill recipe.

```
reagentName, reagentTexture, reagentCount, playerReagentCount = ↵
GetTradeSkillReagentInfo(skillIndex, reagentIndex)
```

Arguments:

skillIndex—Index of a recipe in the trade skill list (between 1 and GetNumTradeSkills()) (number)

reagentIndex—Index of a reagent in the recipe (between 1 and GetTradeSkillNumReagents()) (number)

Returns:

reagentName—Name of the reagent (string)

reagentTexture—Path to an icon texture for the reagent (string)

reagentCount—Quantity of the reagent required to perform the recipe (number) `playerReagentCount`—Quantity of the reagent in the player's possession (number)

Example:

```
-- Prints the reagent(s) required for the first trade skill
-- recipe listed
local skillIndex = GetFirstTradeSkill()
local name = GetTradeSkillInfo(skillIndex)
print(format("%s takes the following reagent(s):", name))
for reagentIndex = 1, GetTradeSkillNumReagents(skillIndex) do
  local reagentName, _, reagentCount = ↵
GetTradeSkillReagentInfo(skillIndex, reagentIndex)
  print(format("   %dx %s", reagentCount, reagentName))
end
```

GetTradeSkillReagentItemLink

Returns a hyperlink for a reagent in a tradeskill recipe.

`link = GetTradeSkillReagentItemLink(skillIndex, reagentIndex)`

Arguments:

`skillIndex`—Index of a recipe in the trade skill list (between 1 and `GetNumTradeSkills()`) (number)

`reagentIndex`—Index of a reagent in the recipe (between 1 and `GetTradeSkillNumReagents()`) (number)

Returns:

`link`—A hyperlink for the reagent item (string, hyperlink)

GetTradeSkillRecipeLink

Returns hyperlink for a tradeskill recipe.

`link = GetTradeSkillRecipeLink(index)`

The tooltip produced when resolving the link describes the recipe itself—its reagents and (if present) description—in addition to (if applicable) the item created. For a link which only describes the created item, see `GetTradeSkill ItemLink()`.

Arguments:

`index`—Index of a recipe in the trade skill list (between 1 and `GetNumTrade Skills()`) (number)

Returns:

`link`—A hyperlink for the trade skill recipe (string)

GetTradeSkillSelectionIndex

Returns the index of the currently selected trade skill recipe.

`index = GetTradeSkillSelectionIndex()`

Selection in the recipe list is used only for display in the default UI and has no effect on other Trade Skill APIs.

Returns:

index—Index of the selected recipe in the trade skill list (between 1 and GetNumTradeSkills()) (number)

GetTradeSkillSubClassFilter

Returns whether the trade skill listing is filtered by a given item subclass.

enabled = GetTradeSkillSubClassFilter(index)

Arguments:

index—Index of an item subclass (in the list returned by GetTradeSkill SubClasses()), or 0 for the "All" filter (number)

Returns:

enabled—1 if the filter is enabled; otherwise nil (1nil)

GetTradeSkillSubClasses

Returns a list of recipe subclasses for the current trade skill.

... = GetTradeSkillSubClasses()

These subclasses correspond to those of the items produced (see GetItemInfo() and GetAuctionItemSubClasses()) and can be used to filter the recipe list.

Returns:

...—A list of strings, each the localized name of an item or recipe subclass applicable to the current trade skill listing (list)

GetTradeSkillTools

Returns a list of required tools for a trade skill recipe.

toolName, hasTool, ... = GetTradeSkillTools(index)

A tool may be an item (e.g. Blacksmith Hammer, Virtuoso Inking Set) the player must possess, or a description of a generic (e.g. near an Anvil, in a Moonwell) or specific (e.g. Netherstorm, Emerald Dragonshrine) location to which the player must travel in order to perform the recipe. The hasTool return is only valid for the tools the player can possess.

Arguments:

index—Index of a recipe in the trade skill list (between 1 and GetNumTrade Skills()) (number)

Returns:

toolName—Name of the required tool (string)

hasTool—1 if the tool is an item in the player's possession; otherwise nil (1nil)

...—An additional toolName, hasTool pair for each tool required (list)

GetTradeTargetItemInfo

Returns information about an item offered for trade by the target.

name, texture, numItems, quality, isUsable, enchantment = ↵
GetTradeTargetItemInfo(index)

Arguments:

index—Index of an item slot on the player's side of the trade window (between 1 and MAX_TRADE_ITEMS) (number)

Returns:

name—Name of the item (string)

texture—Path to an icon texture for the item (string)

numItems—Number of stacked items in the slot (number)

quality—Quality (rarity) level of the item (number, itemQuality)

isUsable—1 if the player character can use or equip the item; otherwise nil (1nil)

enchantment—Name of the enchantment being applied to the item through trade; otherwise nil (string)

GetTradeTargetItemLink

Returns a hyperlink for an item offered for trade by the target.

```
link = GetTradeTargetItemLink(index)
```

Arguments:

index—Index of an item offered for trade by the target (between 1 and MAX_TRADE_ITEMS) (number)

Returns:

link—A hyperlink for the item (string, hyperlink)

GetTradeskillRepeatCount

Returns the number of times the trade skill recipe currently being performed will repeat.

```
repeatCount = GetTradeskillRepeatCount()
```

Returns 1 if a recipe is not being performed; after DoTradeSkill() is called, returns the number of repetitions queued (which decrements as each repetition is finished).

Returns:

repeatCount—Number of times the current recipe will repeat (number)

GetTrainerGreetingText

Returns the current trainer's greeting text.

```
text = GetTrainerGreetingText()
```

In the default UI, this text is displayed at the top of the trainer window.

May return the empty string or the last used trainer's greeting text if called while not interacting with a trainer.

Returns:

text—Greeting text for the trainer with whom the player is currently interacting (string)

GetTrainerSelectionIndex

Returns the index of the currently selected trainer service.

```
selectionIndex = GetTrainerSelectionIndex()
```

Selection in the recipe list is used only for display in the default UI and has no effect on other Trade Skill APIs.

Returns:

`selectionIndex`—Index of the selected entry in the trainer service listing (between 1 and `GetNumTrainerServices()`) (number)

GetTrainerServiceAbilityReq

Returns information about an ability required for purchasing a trainer service.

`ability, hasReq = GetTrainerServiceAbilityReq(index, abilityIndex)`

Arguments:

`index`—Index of an entry in the trainer service listing (between 1 and `GetNumTrainerServices()`) (number)

`abilityIndex`—Index of one of the service's ability requirements (between 1 and `GetTrainerServiceNumAbilityReq(index)`) (number)

Returns:

`ability`—Name of the required ability (string)

`hasReq`—1 if the player has the required ability; otherwise nil (1nil)

GetTrainerServiceCost

Returns the cost to purchase a trainer service.

`moneyCost, talentCost, skillCost = GetTrainerServiceCost(index)`

Arguments:

`index`—Index of an entry in the trainer service listing (between 1 and `GetNumTrainerServices()`) (number)

Returns:

`moneyCost`—Amount of money required to purchase the service (in copper) (number)

`talentCost`—Number of talent points required to purchase the service (generally unused) (number)

`skillCost`—1 if purchasing the service counts against the player's limit of learnable professions; otherwise 0 (number)

GetTrainerServiceDescription

Returns the description of a trainer service.

`text = GetTrainerServiceDescription(index)`

Generally returns the same description found in the spell's tooltip for spells purchased from a class trainer; returns nil for trade skills and recipes.

Arguments:

`index`—Index of an entry in the trainer service listing (between 1 and `GetNumTrainerServices()`) (number)

Returns:

`text`—Description of the service (string)

GetTrainerServiceIcon

Returns the icon for a trainer service.

`icon = GetTrainerServiceIcon(index)`

Arguments:

index—Index of an entry in the trainer service listing (between 1 and `GetNumTrainerServices()`) (number)

Returns:

`icon`—Path to an icon texture for the service (`string`)

GetTrainerServiceInfo

Returns information about an entry in the trainer service listing.

`serviceName, serviceSubText, serviceType, isExpanded = ↵`
`GetTrainerServiceInfo(index)`

Arguments:

index—Index of an entry in the trainer service listing (between 1 and `GetNumTrainerServices()`) (number)

Returns:

`serviceName`—Name of the service (`string`)

`serviceSubText`—Secondary text associated with the service (often a spell rank; e.g. "(Rank 4)") (`string`)

`serviceType`—Type of service entry (`string`)

- `available`—The player can currently use this service
- `header`—This entry is a group header, not a trainer service
- `unavailable`—The player cannot currently use this service
- `used`—The player has already used this service

`isExpanded`—1 if the entry is a header which is currently expanded, or if the header containing the entry is expanded; otherwise `nil` (1nil)

GetTrainerServiceItemLink

Returns a hyperlink for the item associated with a trainer service.

`link = GetTrainerServiceItemLink(index)`

Currently only returns item links for trainer services which teach trade skill recipes which produce items; does not return spell or recipe links.

Arguments:

index—Index of an entry in the trainer service listing (between 1 and `GetNumTrainerServices()`) (number)

Returns:

`link`—A hyperlink for the item associated with a trainer service (`string`, hyperlink)

GetTrainerServiceLevelReq

Returns the character level required to purchase a trainer service.

`reqLevel = GetTrainerServiceLevelReq(index)`

Arguments:

index—Index of an entry in the trainer service listing (between 1 and GetNumTrainerServices()) (number)

Returns:

reqLevel—Level required to purchase the service, or nil if the service has no level requirement (number)

GetTrainerServiceNumAbilityReq

Returns the number of ability requirements for purchasing a trainer service.

numRequirements = GetTrainerServiceNumAbilityReq(index)

Ability requirements are often used for ranked class spells purchased from the trainer: e.g. learning Blood Strike (Rank 3) requires having learned Blood Strike (Rank 2). See GetTrainerServiceAbilityReq() for information about specific ability requirements.

Arguments:

index—Index of an entry in the trainer service listing (between 1 and GetNumTrainerServices()) (number)

Returns:

numRequirements—Number of different ability requirements for the trainer service (number)

Example:

```
-- prints a list of trainer services with their ability requirements
for index = 1, GetNumTrainerServices() do
  local name, rank, serviceType = GetTrainerServiceInfo(index)
  if serviceType ~= "header" then
    local numRequirements = GetTrainerServiceNumAbilityReq(index)
    if numRequirements > 0 then
      print("Ability requirements for " .. name .. ↵
" (" .. rank .. "):")
      for i=1,numRequirements do
        local ability, hasReq = ↵
GetTrainerServiceAbilityReq(index, i)
        if hasReq then
          print(" + " .. ability)
        else
          print(" - " .. ability)
        end
      end
    end
  end
end
```

GetTrainerServiceSkillLine

Returns the name of the skill line associated with a trainer service.

skillLine = GetTrainerServiceSkillLine(index)

For trade skill trainers, skill line is the name of the trade skill (e.g. Tailoring, First Aid). For other trainers, skill line is the name of the group header under which the skill appears (e.g. Riding, Frost, Protection, Holy, Defense, Dual Wield).

Arguments:

index—Index of an entry in the trainer service listing (between 1 and GetNumTrainerServices()) (number)

Returns:

skillLine—Name of the skill line associated with the service (string)

GetTrainerServiceSkillReq

Returns information about the skill requirement for a trainer service.

skill, rank, hasReq = GetTrainerServiceSkillReq(index)

Often used for trade skill recipes: e.g. Netherweave Bag requires Tailoring (315).

Arguments:

index—Index of an entry in the trainer service listing (between 1 and GetNumTrainerServices()) (number)

Returns:

skill—Name of the required skill (string)

rank—Rank required in the skill (number)

hasReq—1 if the player has the required skill and rank; otherwise nil (1nil)

GetTrainerServiceTypeFilter

Returns whether the trainer service listing is filtered by a service status.

isEnabled = GetTrainerServiceTypeFilter("type")

Arguments:

type—A trainer service status (string)

- available—Services the player can use
- unavailable—Services the player cannot currently use
- used—Services the player has already used

Returns:

isEnabled—1 if services matching the filter type are shown in the listing; otherwise nil (1nil)

GetTrainerSkillLineFilter

Returns whether the trainer service listing is filtered by a skill line.

isEnabled = GetTrainerSkillLineFilter(index)

The default UI does not provide control for skill line filters, but they can nonetheless be used to alter the contents of the trainer service listing.

Arguments:

index—Index of a skill line filter (in the list returned by GetTrainer SkillLines()) (number)

Returns:

isEnabled—1 if the given filter is enabled, otherwise nil (1nil)

GetTrainerSkillLines

Returns the list of service group names available at a trainer.

```
... = GetTrainerSkillLines()
```

Skill lines as used here correspond to the group headers in the trainer service listing. Not used for trade skill trainers.

Returns:

...—A list of strings, each the localized name of a group in the trainer service listing (string)

Example:

```
-- for a paladin interacting with his or her class trainer
GetTrainerSkillLines()
-- returns "Defense", "Holy", "Mounts", "Plate Mail", "Protection",
-- "Retribution"

-- when interacting with the Silvermoon weapons master
GetTrainerSkillLines()
-- returns "Polearms", "Swords", "Two-Handed Swords"
```

GetUnitHealthModifier

Returns the health modifier for the player's pet.

```
modifier = GetUnitHealthModifier("unit")
```

Arguments:

unit—A unit to query; only valid for pet (string, unitID)

Returns:

modifier—Factor modifying the unit's health value (number)

GetUnitHealthRegenRateFromSpirit

Returns the increase in health regeneration rate provided by Spirit.

```
regen = GetUnitHealthRegenRateFromSpirit("unit")
```

Arguments:

unit—A unit to query; only valid for player or pet (string, unitID)

Returns:

regen—Increase in non-combat health regeneration per second provided by Spirit (number)

GetUnitManaRegenRateFromSpirit

Returns the increase in mana regeneration rate provided by Spirit.

```
regen = GetUnitManaRegenRateFromSpirit("unit")
```

Arguments:

unit—A unit to query; only valid for player or pet (string, unitID)

Returns:

regen—Increase in inactive (non-casting) mana regeneration per second provided by Spirit (number)

GetUnitMaxHealthModifier

Returns the maximum health modifier for the player's pet.

```
modifier = GetUnitMaxHealthModifier("unit")
```

Arguments:

unit—A unit to query; only valid for pet (string, unitID)

Returns:

modifier—Factor modifying the unit's maximum health value (number)

Blizzard UI

GetUnitName

Returns a string summarizing a unit's name and server.

```
nameString = GetUnitName("unit", showServerName)
```

Arguments:

unit—Unit to query (string, unitID)

showServerName—True to include the server name in the return value if the unit is not from the same server as the player; false to only include a short label in such circumstances (boolean)

Returns:

nameString—The unit's name, possibly followed by the name of the unit's home server or a label indicating the unit is not from the player's server (string)

GetUnitPitch

Returns the player's current pitch (slope or angle of movement).

```
pitch = GetUnitPitch("unit")
```

Only valid for the unitID "player". The slope returned here reflects only the direction of movement for swimming or flying, not the current orientation of the player model or camera. (When on solid ground, GetUnitPitch indicates what the angle of flight would be were the player to start flying.)

The returned value is in radians, with positive values indicating upward slope, negative values indicating downward slope, and 0 indicating perfectly level flight (or swimming).

Arguments:

unit—Unit to query; only valid for player (string, unitID)

Returns:

pitch—Unit's slope of movement in radians (number)

GetUnitPowerModifier

Returns the mana modifier for the player's pet.

```
modifier = GetUnitPowerModifier("unit")
```

Arguments:

unit—A unit to query; only valid for pet (string, unitID)

Returns:

modifier—Factor modifying the unit's mana value (number)

GetUnitSpeed

Returns a unit's current speed.

```
speed = GetUnitSpeed(unit)
```

Valid for all observable units. Values returned indicate the current movement speed in yards per second. (It's not relative to facing or ground position; i.e. you won't see a smaller value when flying up at an angle or a negative value when backing up.) Does not indicate falling speed or the speed of boats, zeppelins, and some forms of quest-related transportation, but does indicate current speed on taxi flights and when moving due to combat effects such as Disengage, Death Grip, or various knockback abilities.

Examples: Normal running: 7; Walking: 2.5; Running backwards: 4.5; Epic flying mount: 26.6

Arguments:

unit—Unit to query (unitid)

Returns:

speed—Unit's current speed in yards per second (number)

GetUnspentTalentPoints

Returns the number of unused talent points.

```
points = GetUnspentTalentPoints(inspect, pet, talentGroup)
```

Arguments:

inspect—true to return information for the currently inspected unit; false to return information for the player (boolean)

pet—true to return information for the player's pet; false to return information for the player (boolean)

talentGroup—Which set of talents to edit, if the player has Dual Talent Specialization enabled (number)

- 1—Primary Talents
- 2—Secondary Talents
- nil—Currently active talents

Returns:

points—Number of points available for spending (number)

GetVideoCaps

Returns information about graphics capabilities of the current system.

```
hasAnisotropic, hasPixelShaders, hasVertexShaders, hasTrilinear, ↵
hasTripleBufering, maxAnisotropy, hasHardwareCursor = GetVideoCaps()
```

Returns:

hasAnisotropic—1 if anisotropic filtering is available; otherwise 0 (number)

hasPixelShaders—1 if pixel shaders are available; otherwise 0 (number) hasVertexShaders—1 if vertex shaders are available; otherwise 0 (number)

hasTrilinear—1 if trilinear filtering is available; otherwise 0 (number)

hasTripleBufering—1 if triple buffering is available; otherwise 0 (number)

maxAnisotropy—Number of available settings for anisotropic filtering (corresponds to the "Texture Filtering" slider in the default UI) (number)

hasHardwareCursor—1 if hardware cursor support is available; otherwise 0 (number)

GetVoiceCurrentSessionID

Returns an identifier for the active voice session.

```
id = GetVoiceCurrentSessionID()
```

Returns:

id—Index of the active voice session (between 1 and GetNumVoice Sessions()), or nil if no session is active (number)

GetVoiceSessionInfo

Returns information about a voice session.

```
name, active = GetVoiceSessionInfo(session)
```

Arguments:

session—Index of a voice session (between 1 and GetNumVoiceSessions()) (number)

Returns:

name—Name of the voice session (channel) (string)

active—1 if the session is the active voice channel; otherwise nil (1nil)

GetVoiceSessionMemberInfoBySessionID

Returns information about a member of a voice channel.

```
name, voiceActive, sessionActive, muted, squelched = ↵
GetVoiceSessionMemberInfoBySessionID(session, index)
```

Arguments:

session—Index of a voice session (between 1 and GetNumVoiceSessions()) (number)

index—Index of a member in the voice session (between 1 and GetNumVoiceSessionMembersBySessionID(session)) (number)

Returns:

name—Name of the member (string)

voiceActive—1 if the member has enabled voice chat; otherwise nil (1nil)

sessionActive—1 if the channel is the member's active voice channel; otherwise nil (1nil)

muted—1 if the member is on the player's muted list; otherwise nil (1nil)

squelched—1 if the member was silenced by the channel moderator; otherwise nil (1nil)

GetVoiceStatus

Returns whether a character has voice chat enabled.

```
status = GetVoiceStatus(unit, "channel") or ↵
GetVoiceStatus("name", "channel")
```

Arguments:

unit—The unitid to query (unitid)

name—The name of the player to query (string)

channel—Channel to query for voice status. (string)

Returns:

status—1 if voice is enabled; otherwise nil (1nil)

GetWatchedFactionInfo

Returns information about the "watched" faction (displayed on the XP bar in the default UI).

```
name, standingID, barMin, barMax, barValue = GetWatchedFactionInfo()
```

Returns:

name—Name of the faction being watched (string)

standingID—The player's current standing with the faction (number, standingID)

1—Hated	4—Neutral	7—Revered
2—Hostile	5—Friendly	8—Exalted
3—Unfriendly	6—Honored	

barMin—The minimum value for the faction status bar (number)

barMax—The maximum value for the faction status bar (number)

barValue—The current value for the faction status bar (number)

GetWeaponEnchantInfo

Returns information about temporary enchantments on the player's weapons.

```
hasMainHandEnchant, mainHandExpiration, mainHandCharges, ↵
hasOffHandEnchant, offHandExpiration, offHandCharges = ↵
GetWeaponEnchantInfo()
```

Does not return information about permanent enchantments added via Enchanting, Runeforging, etc; refers instead to temporary buffs such as wizard oils, sharpening stones, rogue poisons, and shaman weapon enhancements.

Returns:

hasMainHandEnchant—1 if the main hand weapon has a temporary enchant (1nil)

mainHandExpiration—The time until the enchant expires, in milliseconds (number)

mainHandCharges—The number of charges left on the enchantment (number)

hasOffHandEnchant—1 if the offhand weapon has a temporary enchant (1nil) offHandExpiration—The time until the enchant expires, in milliseconds (number)

offHandCharges—The number of charges left on the enchantment (number)

GetWhoInfo

Returns information about a character in the Who system query results.

name, guild, level, race, class, zone, filename = GetWhoInfo(index)

Arguments:

index—Index of an entry in the Who system query results (between 1 and GetNumWhoResults()) (number)

Returns:

name—Name of the character (string)

guild—Name of the character's guild (string)

level—Level of the character (number)

race—Localized name of the character's race (string)

class—Localized name of the character's class (string)

zone—Name of the zone in which the character was located when the query was performed (string)

filename—A non-localized token representing the character's class (string)

GetWintergraspWaitTime

Returns the amount of time remaining until the next PvP event in the Wintergrasp zone.

seconds = GetWintergraspWaitTime()

Only accurate while the player is in Northrend; returns nil if the player has not been in Northrend this session, or the last known value if the player has been in Northrend this session and is currently elsewhere. Also returns nil if the Battle for Wintergrasp is in progress.

Returns:

seconds—Number of seconds (rounded to the nearest five) remaining until the next Battle for Wintergrasp (number)

GetWorldPVPQueueStatus

Returns information on the players queue for a world PvP zone.

status, mapName, queueID = GetWorldPVPQueueStatus(index)

Arguments:

index—Index of the queue to get data for (between 1 and MAX_WORLD_PVP _QUEUES) (number)

Returns:

status—Returns the status of the players queue (string)

- confirm—The player can enter the pvp zone
- none—No world pvp queue at this index
- queued—The player is queued for this pvp zone

mapName—Map name they are queued for (e.g Wintergrasp) (`string`)

queueID—Queue ID, used for BattlefieldMgrExitRequest() and Battlefield MgrEntryInviteResponse() (`number`)

Example:

```
--Prints the players status for their queued non-instanced pvp zones
for index=1, MAX_WORLD_PVP_QUEUES do
  local status, mapName = GetWorldPVPQueueStatus(index)

  if( status == "queued" ) then
    print("You are queued for", mapName)
  elseif( status == "confirm" ) then
    print("Queue is ready, can join", mapName)
  end

end
```

GetWorldStateUIInfo

Returns information about a world state UI element.

```
uiType, state, text, icon, dynamicIcon, tooltip, dynamicTooltip, ↩
extendedUI, extendedUIState1, extendedUIState2, extendedUIState3 = ↩
GetWorldStateUIInfo(index)
```

World State UI elements include PvP, instance, and quest objective information (displayed at the top center of the screen in the default UI) as well as more specific information for "control point" style PvP objectives. Examples: the Horde/Alliance score in Arathi Basin, the tower status and capture progress bars in Hellfire Peninsula, the progress text in the Black Morass and Violet Hold instances, and the event status text for quests The Light of Dawn and The Battle For The Undercity.

Arguments:

index—Index of a world state UI element (between 1 and `GetNumWorld StateUI()`) (`number`)

Returns:

uiType—1 if the element should be conditionally displayed (based on the state of the "Show World PvP Objectives" setting and the player's location); any other value if the element is always displayed (`number`)

state—State of the element: 0 always indicates the element should be hidden; other possible states vary by context (e.g. in Warsong Gulch, state 2 indicates the team holds the enemy flag) (`number`)

text—Text to be displayed for the element (`string`)

icon—Path to a texture for the element's main icon (usually describing the element itself: e.g. a Horde or Alliance icon for elements displaying a battleground score) (`string`)

dynamicIcon—Path to a texture for a secondary icon (usually describing transient status: e.g. a flag icon in Warsong Gulch) (`string`)

tooltip—Text to be displayed when mousing over the UI element (`string`) `dynamicTooltip`—Text to be displayed when mousing over the element's `dynamicIcon` (`string`)

`extendedUI`—Identifies the type of additional UI elements to display if applicable (`string`)

- `""`—No additional UI should be displayed
- `"CAPTUREPOINT"`—A capture progress bar should be displayed for the element

`extendedUIState1`—Index of the capture progress bar corresponding to the element (`number`)

`extendedUIState2`—Position of the capture bar (0 = left/Horde edge, 100 = right/Alliance edge) (`number`)

`extendedUIState3`—Width of the neutral section of the capture bar: e.g. if 50, the `extendedUIState2` values 0-25 correspond to Horde ownership of the objective, values 76-100 to Alliance ownership, and values 26-75 to no ownership (`number`)

GetXPExhaustion

Returns the amount of rested bonus experience available.

```
exhaustionXP = GetXPExhaustion()
```

This value increments as the player spends time resting and depletes as the player earns experience from kills while rested.

Returns:

`exhaustionXP`—The amount of rested bonus experience available (`number`)

GetZonePVPInfo

Returns PVP information about the current area.

```
pvpType, isSubZonePVP, factionName = GetZonePVPInfo()
```

Information returned may apply to the current subzone, not the entire zone.

Returns:

`pvpType`—PvP status for the area (`string`)

- `arena`—Arena or outdoor free-for-all area (e.g. Gurubashi Arena)
- `combat`—Combat zone (e.g. Wintergrasp)
- `contested`—Horde/Alliance PvP is enabled for all players
- `friendly`—Zone is controlled by the player's faction; PvP status is optional for the player but mandatory for enemy players
- `hostile`—Zone is controlled by the enemy's faction; PvP status is optional for the enemy but mandatory for the player
- `nil`—PvP status is not automatically enabled for either faction (used for "contested" zones on Normal servers)
- `sanctuary`—PvP activity is not allowed (e.g. Dalaran)

`isSubZonePVP`—1 if the current area allows free-for-all PVP; otherwise `nil` (`1nil`) `factionName`—Name of the faction that controls the zone (only applies if `pvpType` is friendly or hostile) (`string`)

GetZoneText

Returns the name of the zone in which the player is located.

`zone = GetZoneText()`

Returns:

`zone`—Name of the current zone (`string`)

GiveMasterLoot

Awards a loot item to a group member.

`GiveMasterLoot(slot, index)`

Has no effect if the player is not the loot master or if no loot or candidate matching the given parameters exists.

Arguments:

`slot`—Index of a loot slot (between 1 and `GetNumLootItems()`) (`number`)

`index`—Index of a loot candidate (see `GetMasterLootCandidate()`) (`number`)

GlyphMatchesSocket

Returns whether a socket is eligible for the glyph currently awaiting a target.

`match = GlyphMatchesSocket(socket)`

Only valid during glyph application: when the player has activated the glyph item but before she has chosen the glyph slot to put it in (i.e. the glowing hand cursor is showing).

Arguments:

`socket`—Which glyph socket to query (between 1 and `NUM_GLYPH_SLOTS`) (`number, glyphIndex`)

Returns:

`match`—1 if the glyph awaiting a target fits the given socket; `nil` if it doesn't fit or if no glyph is awaiting a target (`1nil`)

GrantLevel

Grants a level to the player's Recruit-a-Friend partner.

`GrantLevel("unit")`

Does not immediately cause the partner character to level up: that player is given a chance to accept or decline the offered level.

Arguments:

`unit`—Unit to gift a level (`string, unitID`)

GuildControlAddRank

Adds a new rank to the player's guild.

`GuildControlAddRank("name")`

The newly added rank becomes the lowest rank in the guild.

Arguments:

name—Name of the new rank (`string`)

GuildControlDelRank

Deletes a guild rank.

```
GuildControlDelRank("name")
```

Arguments:

name—Name of the rank to delete (`string`)

GuildControlGetNumRanks

Returns the number of ranks in the guild.

```
numRanks = GuildControlGetNumRanks()
```

Returns:

numRanks—Number of guild ranks (including Guild Leader) (`number`)

GuildControlGetRankFlags

Returns the list of privileges for the guild rank being edited.

```
... = GuildControlGetRankFlags()
```

The name of a privilege for an index in this list can be found in the global variable `"GUILDCONTROL_OPTION"..index`.

Returns:

...—A list of privilege flags (1 = privilege allowed, `nil` = privilege denied) for the rank being edited (`list`)

Example:

```
-- Print rank flags for the first rank in the guild
function PrintFlags(...)
  local output = ""
  for i = 1, select("#", ...) do
    output = output .. getglobal("GUILDCONTROL_OPTION"..i) .. ↵
": " .. select(i, ...) .. "; "
  end
  print(output)
end
GuildControlSetRank(1)
PrintFlags(GuildControlGetRankFlags())
```

GuildControlGetRankName

Returns the name of a guild rank.

```
rankName = GuildControlGetRankName(rank)
```

Arguments:

rank—Index of a rank to edit (between 1 and `GuildControlGetNumRanks()`) (`number`)

Returns:

rankName—Name of the guild rank (`string`)

GuildControlSaveRank

Saves changes to the guild rank being edited.

```
GuildControlSaveRank("name")
```

Arguments:

name—New name for the guild rank (string)

GuildControlSetRank

Chooses a guild rank to edit.

```
GuildControlSetRank(rank)
```

Arguments:

rank—Index of a rank to edit (between 1 and GuildControlGetNumRanks())
(number)

GuildControlSetRankFlag

Enables or disables a privilege for the guild rank being edited.

```
GuildControlSetRankFlag(index, enabled)
```

Changes are not saved until a call is made to GuildControlSaveRank().

Arguments:

index—Index of a privilege to change (number)

1—Guildchat listen	9—Set MOTD
2—Guildchat speak	10—Edit Public Notes
3—Officerchat listen	11—View Officer Note
4—Officerchat speak	12—Edit Officer Note
5—Promote	13—Modify Guild Info
6—Demote	15—Use guild funds for repairs
7—Invite Member	16—Withdraw gold from the guild bank
8—Remove Member	17—Create Guild Event

enabled—True to allow the privilege; false to deny (boolean)

GuildDemote

Reduces a guild member's rank by one.

```
GuildDemote("name")
```

The player can only demote members whose rank is below the player's own,
and only if the player has permission to demote (i.e. if CanGuildDemote()
returns 1).

Arguments:

name—Name of a guild member to demote (string)

`Confirmation` ### GuildDisband

Disbands the player's guild. Only has effect if the player is the guild leader.

GuildInfo

Requests guild information from the server.

Fires two CHAT_MSG_SYSTEM events, one containing the name of the guild, followed by one containing the date the guild was created and how many players and accounts belong to the guild.

GuildInvite

Invites a character to join the player's guild.

```
GuildInvite("name")
```

Arguments:

name—Name of a character to invite (string)

Confirmation ### GuildLeave

Leaves the player's current guild.

GuildPromote

Increases a guild member's rank by one.

```
GuildPromote("name")
```

The player can only promote members up to the rank immediately below the player's own, and only if the player has permission to promote (i.e. if CanGuildPromote() returns 1).

Arguments:

name—Name of a guild member to promote (string)

GuildRoster

Requests guild roster information from the server.

Information is not returned immediately; the GUILD_ROSTER_UPDATE event fires when data is available for retrieval via GetGuildRosterInfo() and related functions. Requests are throttled to reduce server load; the server will only respond to a new request approximately 10 seconds after a previous request.

GuildRosterSetOfficerNote

Sets the officer note for a guild member.

```
GuildRosterSetOfficerNote(index, "note")
```

Arguments:

index—Index of a member in the guild roster (between 1 and GetNumGuildMembers()), or 0 for no selection (number)

note—Note text to set for the guild member (up to 31 characters) (string)

GuildRosterSetPublicNote

Sets the public note for a guild member.

```
GuildRosterSetPublicNote(index, "note")
```

Arguments:

index—Index of a member in the guild roster (between 1 and GetNum GuildMembers()), or 0 for no selection (number)

note—Note text to set for the guild member (up to 31 characters) (string)

GuildSetLeader

Promotes a member to guild leader.

```
GuildSetLeader("name")
```

Only works if the player is the guild leader and the named character is in the guild and currently online.

Arguments:

name—Name of a guild member to promote to leader (`string`)

GuildSetMOTD

Sets the guild Message of the Day.

```
GuildSetMOTD("message")
```

Guild members see the message of the day upon login and whenever it is changed (and cannot disable its display in the default UI), so keeping the message concise is recommended.

Arguments:

message—New text for the message of the day (up to 128 characters; embedded newlines allowed) (`string`)

Example:

```
-- Set a message of the day
GuildSetMOTD("This is a message of the day")

-- Set a two-line message of the day
GuildSetMOTD("Please vote for the following applicants on our ↵
forums:\nCladhaire\nCairthas")
```

GuildUninvite

Removes a character from the player's guild.

```
GuildUninvite("name")
```

Arguments:

name—Name of a guild member to remove (`string`)

HasAction

Returns whether an action slot contains an action.

```
hasAction = HasAction(slot)
```

Arguments:

slot—An action bar slot (`number`, actionID)

Returns:

hasAction—1 if the slot contains an action; otherwise `nil` (1nil)

HasFilledPetition

Returns whether the player has a completed petition.

```
hasPetition = HasFilledPetition()
```

Used by the default UI to show and hide the buttons for turning in an Arena charter.

Returns:

hasPetition—1 if the player has a completed petition; otherwise `nil` (1nil)

HasFullControl

Returns whether the player character can be controlled.

```
hasControl = HasFullControl()
```

Returns:

hasControl—1 if the player character can be controlled (i.e. isn't feared, charmed, etc); otherwise `nil` (1nil)

HasInspectHonorData

Returns whether PvP honor and arena data for the currently inspected unit has been downloaded from the server.

```
hasData = HasInspectHonorData()
```

See `RequestInspectHonorData()` to request PvP data from the server.

Returns:

hasData—1 if the client has PvP data for the currently inspected player; otherwise `nil` (1nil)

HasKey

Returns whether the player has any keys stored in the Keyring container.

```
hasKey = HasKey()
```

Used in the default UI to show or hide the UI for the Keyring container

Returns:

hasKey—Returns 1 if the player has any keys stored in the Keyring container; otherwise `nil` (1nil)

HasNewMail

Returns whether the player has received new mail since last visiting a mailbox.

```
hasMail = HasNewMail()
```

Returns:

hasMail—1 if the player has received new mail since last visiting a mailbox; otherwise `nil` (1nil)

HasPetSpells

Returns whether the player's current pet has a spellbook.

```
hasPetSpells, petType = HasPetSpells()
```

Returns:

hasPetSpells—1 if the player currently has an active pet with spells/abilities; otherwise `nil` (1nil)

petType—Non-localized token identifying the type of pet (`string`)

- ▪ DEMON—A warlock's demonic minion
- ▪ PET—A hunter's beast

HasPetUI

Returns whether the pet UI should be displayed for the player's pet.

`hasPetUI, isHunterPet = HasPetUI()`

Special quest-related pets, vehicles, and possessed units all count as pets but do not use the pet UI or associated functions.

Returns:

`hasPetUI`—1 if the pet UI should be displayed for the player's pet (1nil)

`isHunterPet`—1 if the player's pet is a hunter pet (1nil)

HasSoulstone

Returns whether the player can instantly resurrect in place.

`text = HasSoulstone()`

Only returns valid information while the player is dead and has not yet released his or her spirit to the graveyard.

Returns:

`text`—If the player can resurrect in place, the text to be displayed on the dialog button for such (e.g. "Use Soulstone", "Reincarnate"); otherwise `nil` (`string`)

HasWandEquipped

Returns whether the player has a wand equipped.

`isEquipped = HasWandEquipped()`

Returns:

`isEquipped`—1 if a wand is equipped; otherwise `nil` (1nil)

HearthAndResurrectFromArea

Instantly exits the current world PvP zone, returning to the player's Hearthstone location.

Resets the player's Hearthstone cooldown, and also returns the player to life if dead. Only usable if the player is in a world PvP combat zone (i.e. Wintergrasp).

HideRepairCursor

Returns the cursor to normal mode after use of `ShowRepairCursor()`.

InCinematic

Returns whether an in-game cinematic is playing.

`inCinematic = InCinematic()`

Applies to in-game-engine cinematics (such as when logging into a new character for the first time), not prerecorded movies.

Returns:

`inCinematic`—1 if an in-game cinematic is playing; otherwise `nil` (1nil)

InCombatLockdown

Returns whether the user interface is protected due to combat.

`inLockdown = InCombatLockdown()`

Non-Blizzard code is allowed to perform certain UI actions (such as changing secure template attributes or moving/showing/hiding secure frames) only if the player is not in combat; this function can be used to determine whether such actions are currently available.

Returns:

inLockdown—1 if the user interface is protected due to combat; otherwise nil (1nil)

InRepairMode

Returns whether the item repair cursor mode is currently active.

```
inRepair = InRepairMode()
```

Repair mode is entered by calling ShowRepairCursor() and exited by calling HideRepairCursor(); while in repair mode, calling PickupContainer Item() or PickupInventoryItem() will attempt to repair the item (and deduct the cost of such from the player's savings) instead of putting it on the cursor.

Returns:

inRepair—1 if repair mode is currently active; otherwise nil (1nil)

InboxItemCanDelete

Returns whether a message in the player's inbox can be deleted.

```
canDelete = InboxItemCanDelete(mailID)
```

Arguments:

mailID—Index of a message in the player's inbox (between 1 and GetInboxNumItems()) (number)

Returns:

canDelete—1 if the message can be deleted; otherwise nil (1nil)

InitiateTrade

Offers to trade with a given unit.

```
InitiateTrade("unit") or InitiateTrade("name")
```

The trade process does not begin immediately; once the server has determined both clients can trade, the TRADE_SHOW event fires.

Arguments:

unit—A unit with which to trade (string, unitID)

name—The name of a unit with which to trade; only valid for nearby units in the player's party/raid (string)

| Protected |

InteractUnit

Interacts with (as with right-clicking on) a unit.

```
InteractUnit(unit)
```

Arguments:

unit—The unit to interact with (unitid)

InterfaceOptionsFrame_OpenToCategory

Opens the Interface Options window and displays a given panel within it.

```
InterfaceOptionsFrame_OpenToCategory("panelName") or ↵
InterfaceOptionsFrame_OpenToCategory(panel)
```

Arguments:

panelName—The registered name of an options panel (string)

panel—A Frame object already registered as an options panel (table)

InterfaceOptions_AddCategory

Registers a panel to be displayed in the Interface Options window.

```
InterfaceOptions_AddCategory(panel)
```

The following members and methods are used by the Interface Options frame to display and organize panels:

- panel.name - string (required)—The name of the AddOn or group of configuration options. This is the text that will display in the AddOn options list.
- panel.parent - string (optional)—Name of the parent of the AddOn or group of configuration options. This identifies "panel" as the child of another category. If the parent category doesn't exist, "panel" will be displayed as a regular category.
- panel.okay - function (optional)—This method will run when the player clicks "okay" in the Interface Options.
- panel.cancel - function (optional)—This method will run when the player clicks "cancel" in the Interface Options. Use this to revert their changes.
- panel.default - function (optional)—This method will run when the player clicks "defaults". Use this to revert their changes to your defaults.
- panel.refresh - function (optional)—This method will run when the Interface Options frame calls its OnShow function and after defaults have been applied via the panel.default method described above. Use this to refresh your panel's UI in case settings were changed without player interaction.

Arguments:

panel—A Frame object (table)

InviteUnit

Invites a character to the player's party or raid.

```
InviteUnit("name")
```

Arguments:

name—Name of a character to invite (string)

IsActionInRange

Returns whether the player's target is in range of an action.

```
inRange = IsActionInRange(slot)
```

Arguments:

slot—An action bar slot (number, actionID)

Returns:

inRange—1 if the player's target is in range for the action or 0 if out of range; nil if the action cannot be used on the player's target regardless of range (number)

IsActiveBattlefieldArena

Returns whether the player is currently in an arena match.

isArena, isRegistered = IsActiveBattlefieldArena()

Returns:

isArena—1 if player is in an Arena match; otherwise nil (1nil)

isRegistered—1 if the current arena match is a ranked match; otherwise nil (1nil)

IsActiveQuestTrivial

Returns whether a quest which can be turned in to the current Quest NPC is trivial at the player's level.

trivial = IsActiveQuestTrivial(index)

Only returns valid information after a QUEST_GREETING event. Used in the default UI to display "(low level)" when listing the quest.

Note: Most quest NPCs present active quests using the GetGossipActive Quests() instead of this function.

Arguments:

index—Index of a quest which can be turned in to the current Quest NPC (between 1 and GetNumActiveQuests()) (number)

Returns:

trivial—1 if the quest is trivial at the player's level; otherwise nil (1nil)

IsAddOnLoadOnDemand

Returns whether an addon can be loaded without restarting the UI.

isLod = IsAddOnLoadOnDemand("name") or IsAddOnLoadOnDemand(index)

Arguments:

name—Name of an addon (name of the addon's folder and TOC file, not the Title found in the TOC) (string)

index—Index of an addon in the addon list (between 1 and GetNumAddOns()) (number)

Returns:

isLod—1 if the addon is LoadOnDemand-capable; otherwise nil (1nil)

IsAddOnLoaded

Returns whether an addon is currently loaded.

loaded = IsAddOnLoaded("name") or IsAddOnLoaded(index)

Arguments:

name—Name of an addon (name of the addon's folder and TOC file, not the Title found in the TOC) (string)

index—Index of an addon in the addon list (between 1 and GetNumAddOns()) (number)

Returns:

loaded—1 if the addon is loaded; otherwise nil (1nil)

IsAltKeyDown

Returns whether an Alt key on the keyboard is held down.

isDown = IsAltKeyDown()

Returns:

isDown—1 if an Alt key on the keyboard is currently held down; otherwise nil (1nil)

IsArenaTeamCaptain

Returns whether the player is the captain of an arena team.

isCaptain = IsArenaTeamCaptain(team)

Also returns 1 if the player is not on a team of the given arenaTeamID.

Arguments:

team—Index of one of the player's arena teams (number, arenaTeamID)

Returns:

isCaptain—1 if the player is the captain of the given team; otherwise nil. (1nil)

IsAtStableMaster

Returns whether the player is interacting with a Stable Master NPC.

isAtNPC = IsAtStableMaster()

The Pet Stable UI/API can be active without an NPC if the player is using the Call Stabled Pet ability. New stable slots can only be purchased while talking to an NPC. The default UI uses this function to determine whether to show UI elements related to purchasing slots.

Returns:

isAtNPC—True if the player is interacting with a Stable Master NPC; otherwise false (boolean)

IsAttackAction

Returns whether an action is the standard melee Attack action.

isAttack = IsAttackAction(slot)

Used in the default UI to flash the action button while auto-attack is active. Does not apply to other repeating actions such as Auto Shot (for hunters) and Shoot (for wand users); for those, see IsAutoRepeatAction.

Arguments:

slot—An action bar slot (number, actionID)

Returns:

isAttack—1 if the action enables/disables melee auto-attack; otherwise nil (1nil)

IsAttackSpell

Returns whether a spell is the standard melee Attack spell.

isAttack = IsAttackSpell(index, "bookType") or IsAttackSpell("name")

Arguments:

index—Index of a spell in the spellbook (number, spellbookID)

bookType—Type of spellbook (string)

▪ pet—The pet's spellbook

▪ spell—The player's spellbook

name—Name of a spell (string)

Returns:

isAttack—1 if the spell enables/disables melee auto-attack; otherwise nil (1nil)

IsAutoRepeatAction

Returns whether an action is an automatically repeating action.

isRepeating = IsAutoRepeatAction(slot)

Used in the default UI to flash the action button while the action is repeating. Applies to actions such as Auto Shot (for hunters) and Shoot (for wand and other ranged weapon users) but not to the standard melee Attack action; for it, see IsAttackAction.

Arguments:

slot—An action bar slot (number, actionID)

Returns:

isRepeating—1 if the action is an auto-repeat action; otherwise nil (1nil)

IsAutoRepeatSpell

Returns whether a spell is an automatically repeating spell.

isAutoRepeat = IsAutoRepeatSpell("spellName")

Arguments:

spellName—The name of the spell to query (string)

Returns:

isAutoRepeat—If the spell is an auto-repeating spell (1nil)

IsAvailableQuestTrivial

Returns whether a quest available from the current Quest NPC is trivial at the player's level.

trivial = IsAvailableQuestTrivial(index)

Only returns valid information after a QUEST_GREETING event. Used in the default UI to display "(low level)" when listing the quest.

Note: Most quest NPCs present available quests using the GetGossip AvailableQuests() instead of this function.

Arguments:

index—Index of a quest available from the current Quest NPC (between 1 and GetNumAvailableQuests()) (number)

Returns:

trivial—1 if the quest is trivial at the player's level; otherwise nil (1nil)

IsBattlefieldArena

Returns whether the player is interacting with an entity that allows queueing for arena matches.

```
isArena = IsBattlefieldArena()
```

The Battlefield queueing APIs are used for joining arena matches or skirmishes as well as for battlegrounds; this function is used in the default UI to change the contents of the queue dialog based on whether arena or battleground queue options should be presented.

Returns:

isArena—1 if interacting with an arena queue; otherwise nil (1nil)

IsConsumableAction

Returns whether using an action consumes an item.

```
isConsumable = IsConsumableAction(slot)
```

Applies both to consumable items (such as food and potions) and to spells which use a reagent (e.g. Prayer of Fortitude, Divine Intervention, Water Walking, Portal: Dalaran).

Arguments:

slot—An action bar slot (number, actionID)

Returns:

isConsumable—1 if using the action consumes an item; otherwise nil (1nil)

IsConsumableItem

Returns whether an item is consumable.

```
consumable = IsConsumableItem(itemID) or IsConsumableItem("itemName") ↵
or IsConsumableItem("itemLink")
```

Indicates whether the item is destroyed upon use, not necessarily whether it belongs to the "Consumable" type/class.

Arguments:

itemID—An item's ID (number)

itemName—An item's name (string)

itemLink—An item's hyperlink, or any string containing the itemString portion of an item link (string)

Returns:

consumable—1 if the item is consumable; otherwise nil (1nil)

IsConsumableSpell

Returns whether casting a spell consumes a reagent item.

```
isConsumable = IsConsumableSpell(index, "bookType") or ↵
IsConsumableSpell("name")
```

Arguments:

index—Index of a spell in the spellbook (number, spellbookID)

bookType—Type of spellbook (string)

■ pet—The pet's spellbook

■ spell—The player's spellbook

name—Name of a spell (string)

Returns:

isConsumable—1 if casting the spell consumes a reagent item; otherwise nil (1nil)

IsControlKeyDown

Returns whether a Control key on the keyboard is held down.

```
isDown = IsControlKeyDown()
```

Returns:

isDown—1 if a Control key on the keyboard is currently held down; otherwise nil (1nil)

IsCurrentAction

Returns whether an action is currently being used.

```
isCurrent = IsCurrentAction(slot)
```

Arguments:

slot—An action bar slot (number, actionID)

Returns:

isCurrent—1 if the action is currently being cast, is waiting for the user to choose a target, is a repeating action which is currently repeating, or is the open trade skill; otherwise nil (1nil)

IsCurrentItem

Returns whether an item is being used.

```
isItem = IsCurrentItem(itemID) or IsCurrentItem("itemName") or ↵
IsCurrentItem("itemLink")
```

Arguments:

itemID—An item's ID (number)

itemName—An item's name (string)

itemLink—An item's hyperlink, or any string containing the itemString portion of an item link (string)

Returns:

isItem—1 if the item's "Use:" action is currently being cast, is waiting for the user to choose a target, or is otherwise in progress; otherwise nil (1nil)

IsCurrentQuestFailed

Returns whether the player has failed the selected quest in the quest log.

isFailed = IsCurrentQuestFailed()

Returns:

isFailed—1 if the player has failed the quest; otherwise nil (1nil)

IsCurrentSpell

Returns whether a spell is currently being used.

isCurrent = IsCurrentSpell(index, "bookType") or IsCurrentSpell("name")

Arguments:

index—Index of a spell in the spellbook (number, spellbookID)

bookType—Type of spellbook (string)

■ pet—The pet's spellbook

■ spell—The player's spellbook

name—Name of a spell (string)

Returns:

isCurrent—1 if the spell is currently being cast, is waiting for the user to choose a target, is a repeating spell which is currently repeating, or is the open trade skill; otherwise nil (1nil)

IsDesaturateSupported

Returns whether the current hardware supports desaturated textures.

isSupported = IsDesaturateSupported()

Returns:

isSupported—1 if texture desaturation is supported; otherwise nil (1nil)

IsDisplayChannelModerator

Returns whether the player is a moderator of the selected channel in the channel list display.

isModerator = IsDisplayChannelModerator()

Returns:

isModerator—1 if the player is a moderator of the selected channel; otherwise nil (1nil)

IsDisplayChannelOwner

Returns whether the player is the owner of the selected channel in the channel list display.

isOwner = IsDisplayChannelOwner()

Returns:

isOwner—1 if the player is the owner of the selected channel; otherwise nil (1nil)

IsDressableItem

Returns whether an item's appearance can be previewed using the Dressing Room feature.

```
isDressable = IsDressableItem(itemID) or ↵
IsDressableItem("itemName") or IsDressableItem("itemLink")
```

Arguments:

itemID—An item's ID (number)

itemName—An item's name (string)

itemLink—An item's hyperlink, or any string containing the itemString portion of an item link (string)

Returns:

isDressable—1 if the item's appearance can be previewed using the Dressing Room feature; otherwise nil (1nil)

IsEquippableItem

Returns whether an item can be equipped.

```
isEquippable = IsEquippableItem(itemID) or ↵
IsEquippableItem("itemName") or IsEquippableItem("itemLink")
```

Indicates whether an item is capable of being equipped on a character, not necessarily whether the player character is able to wear it.

Arguments:

itemID—An item's ID (number)

itemName—An item's name (string)

itemLink—An item's hyperlink, or any string containing the itemString portion of an item link (string)

Returns:

isEquippable—1 if the item can be equipped, otherwise nil (1nil)

IsEquippedAction

Returns whether an action contains an equipped item.

```
isEquipped = IsEquippedAction(slot)
```

Applies to actions involving equippable items (not to consumables or other items with "Use:" effects) and indicates the effect of performing the action: if an action's item is not equipped, using the action will equip it; if the item is equipped and has a "Use:" effect, using the action will activate said effect.

Arguments:

slot—An action bar slot (number, actionID)

Returns:

isEquipped—1 if the action contains an equipped item; otherwise nil (1nil)

IsEquippedItem

Returns whether an item is currently equipped.

```
isEquipped = IsEquippedItem(itemID) or ↵
IsEquippedItem("itemName") or IsEquippedItem("itemLink")
```

Arguments:

itemID—An item's ID (number)

itemName—An item's name (string)

itemLink—An item's hyperlink, or any string containing the itemString portion of an item link (string)

Returns:

isEquipped—1 if the item is equipped on the player character; otherwise nil (1nil)

Example:

```
-- Check to see if your Alliance PvP trinket is equipped
IsEquippedItem("Medallion of the Alliance") then
 print("Your PvP trinket is already equipped.")
else
 print("*** Make sure to equip your PvP trinket ***")
end


-- Check to see if Staff of Infinite Mysteries (itemId 28633)
-- is equipped
if IsEquippedItem(28633) then
 print("Your staff is equipped")
else
 print("Your staff is not equipped")
end
```

IsEquippedItemType

Returns whether any items of a given type are currently equipped.

```
isEquipped = IsEquippedItemType("type")
```

Possible arguments include the localized names of item classes (as returned from GetAuctionItemClasses; e.g. "Weapon", "Armor"), subclasses (as returned from GetAuctionItemSubClasses; e.g. "One-handed axes", "Shields", "Cloth"), and the global tokens or localized names for equip locations (as returned from GetAuctionInvTypes; e.g. "INVTYPE_WEAPON MAINHAND", "Off Hand").

Arguments:

type—Name of an item class, subclass, or equip location (string)

Returns:

isEquipped—1 if the player has equipped any items of the given type; otherwise nil (1nil)

Example:

```
-- Check to see if the player currently has a shield equipped
local hasShield = IsEquippedItemType("Shields")
if hasShield then
 print("You currently have a shield equipped")
else
 print("You do not have a shield equipped")
end
```

IsFactionInactive

Returns whether a faction is flagged as "inactive".

```
isInactive = IsFactionInactive(index)
```

"Inactive" factions behave no differently; the distinction only exists to allow players to hide factions they don't care about from the main display. Factions thus marked are automatically moved to an "Inactive" group at the end of the faction list.

Arguments:

index—Index of an entry in the faction list; between 1 and GetNumFactions() (number)

Returns:

isInactive—1 if the faction is currently flagged as "inactive"; otherwise nil (1nil)

IsFalling

Returns whether the player is currently falling.

```
falling = IsFalling()
```

Returns:

falling—1 if the player is falling; otherwise nil (1nil)

IsFishingLoot

Returns whether the currently displayed loot came from fishing.

```
isFishing = IsFishingLoot()
```

Used in the default UI to play a fishing sound effect and change the appearance of the loot window.

Returns:

isFishing—1 if the currently displayed loot is fishing loot; otherwise nil (1nil)

IsFlyableArea

Returns whether flight is allowed on the continent where the player is currently located.

```
isFlyable = IsFlyableArea()
```

Returns 1 for some areas in which flight is disabled—notably Dalaran (with the exception of the Krasus' Landing subzone) and Wintergrasp.

Returns:

isFlyable—1 if flight is allowed on the continent where the player is currently located; otherwise nil (1nil)

IsFlying

Returns whether the player is currently flying.

```
isFlying = IsFlying()
```

Returns:

isFlying—1 if the player is currently flying; otherwise nil (1nil)

IsGuildLeader

Returns whether or player is leader of his or her guild.

```
isLeader = IsGuildLeader()
```

Returns:

isLeader—1 if the player is a guild leader; otherwise `nil` (1nil)

IsHarmfulItem

Returns whether an item can be used against hostile units.

```
isHarmful = IsHarmfulItem(itemID) or IsHarmfulItem("itemName") or ↵
IsHarmfulItem("itemLink")
```

Harmful items include grenades and various quest items ("Use this to zap 30 murlocs!").

Arguments:

itemID—An item's ID (number)

itemName—An item's name (string)

itemLink—An item's hyperlink, or any string containing the itemString portion of an item link (string)

Returns:

isHarmful—1 if the item can be used against hostile units; otherwise `nil` (1nil)

IsHarmfulSpell

Returns whether a spell can be used against hostile units.

```
isHarmful = IsHarmfulSpell(index, "bookType") or IsHarmfulSpell("name")
```

Arguments:

index—Index of a spell in the spellbook (number, spellbookID)

bookType—Type of spellbook (string)

■ pet—The pet's spellbook

■ spell—The player's spellbook

name—Name of a spell (string)

Returns:

isHarmful—1 if the spell can be used against hostile units; otherwise `nil` (1nil)

Example:

```
-- print a list of harmful spells
local numTabs = GetNumSpellTabs()
for i=1,numTabs do
 local name,texture,offset,numSpells = GetSpellTabInfo(i)
 for spellId=1,numSpells do
  local harmful = IsHarmfulSpell(i, "spell")
  if harmful then
   local name,rank = GetSpellName(i, "spell")
```

```
      print(name .. " is a harmful spell")
    end
  end
end
```

IsHelpfulItem

Returns whether an item can be used on the player or friendly units.

```
isHarmful = IsHelpfulItem(itemID) or IsHelpfulItem("itemName") or ↵
IsHelpfulItem("itemLink")
```

Helpful items include potions, scrolls, food and drink.

Arguments:

itemID—An item's ID (number)

itemName—An item's name (string)

itemLink—An item's hyperlink, or any string containing the itemString portion of an item link (string)

Returns:

isHarmful—1 if the item can be used on the player or friendly units; otherwise nil (1nil)

IsHelpfulSpell

Returns whether an item can be used on the player or friendly units.

```
isHarmful = IsHelpfulSpell(index, "bookType") or IsHelpfulSpell("name")
```

Arguments:

index—Index of a spell in the spellbook (number, spellbookID)

bookType—Type of spellbook (string)

▪ pet—The pet's spellbook

▪ spell—The player's spellbook

name—Name of a spell (string)

Returns:

isHarmful—1 if the spell can be used on the player or friendly units; otherwise nil (1nil)

IsIgnored

Returns whether a unit is on the player's ignore list.

```
isIgnored = IsIgnored("unit") or IsIgnored("name")
```

Arguments:

unit—A unit to query (string, unitID)

name—The name of a unit to query (string)

Returns:

isIgnored—1 if the unit is on the player's ignore list; otherwise nil (1nil)

IsIgnoredOrMuted

Returns whether a unit can be heard due to ignored/muted status.

```
isIgnoredOrMuted = IsIgnoredOrMuted("unit")
```

Arguments:

unit—A unit to query (string, unitID)

Returns:

isIgnoredOrMuted—1 if the unit is ignored or muted, nil otherwise (1nil)

IsInArenaTeam

Returns whether the player is on an arena team.

isInTeam = IsInArenaTeam()

Returns:

isInTeam—True if the player is on any arena teams; false otherwise (boolean)

IsInGuild

Returns whether the player is in a guild.

inGuild = IsInGuild()

Returns:

inGuild—1 if the player is in a guild; otherwise nil (1nil)

IsInInstance

Returns whether the player is in an instance (and its type if applicable).

isInstance, instanceType = IsInInstance()

Returns:

isInstance—1 if the player is in an instance, otherwise nil (1nil)

instanceType—The type of instance the player is in (string)

- arena—Player versus player arena
- none—Not inside an instance
- party—5-man instance
- pvp—Player versus player battleground
- raid—Raid instance

IsInLFGQueue

Returns whether the player is currently queued for automatically joining/filling a group.

inQueue = IsInLFGQueue()

Returns:

inQueue—1 if the player is currently queued for automatically joining/filling a group; otherwise nil (1nil)

IsIndoors

Returns whether the player is currently indoors.

inside = IsIndoors()

Returns:

inside—1 if the player is currently indoors; otherwise nil (1nil)

IsInventoryItemLocked

Returns whether an inventory slot is locked.

```
isLocked = IsInventoryItemLocked(slot)
```

Items become locked while being moved, split, or placed into other UI elements (such as the mail, trade, and auction windows); the item is unlocked once such an action is completed.

Arguments:

slot—An inventory slot number, as can be obtained from `GetInventory SlotInfo` (number, inventoryID)

Returns:

isLocked—1 if the item in the inventory slot is locked; otherwise nil (1nil)

IsItemInRange

Returns whether the player is in range to use an item on a unit.

```
inRange = IsItemInRange(itemID, "unit") or ↵
IsItemInRange("itemName", "unit") or IsItemInRange("itemLink", "unit")
```

Arguments:

itemID—An item's ID (number)

itemName—An item's name (string)

itemLink—An item's hyperlink, or any string containing the `itemString` portion of an item link (string)

unit—A unit on which to use the item (string, unitID)

Returns:

inRange—1 if the player is near enough to use the item on the unit; 0 if not in range; nil if the unit is not a valid target for the item (1nil)

IsLeftAltKeyDown

Returns whether the left Alt key is currently held down.

```
isDown = IsLeftAltKeyDown()
```

(Note: The Mac WoW client does not distingish between left and right modifier keys, so both Alt keys are reported as Left Alt.)

Returns:

isDown—1 if the left Alt key on the keyboard is currently held down; otherwise nil (1nil)

IsLeftControlKeyDown

Returns whether the left Control key is held down.

```
isDown = IsLeftControlKeyDown()
```

(Note: The Mac WoW client does not distingish between left and right modifier keys, so both Control keys are reported as Left Control.)

Returns:

isDown—1 if the left Control key is held down; otherwise nil (1nil)

IsLeftShiftKeyDown

Returns whether the left Shift key on the keyboard is held down.

```
isDown = IsLeftShiftKeyDown()
```

(Note: The Mac WoW client does not distingish between left and right modifier keys, so both Shift keys are reported as Left Shift.)

Returns:

isDown—1 if the left Shift key on the keyboard is currently held down; otherwise nil (1nil)

IsLinuxClient

Returns whether the player is using the Linux game client.

```
isLinux = IsLinuxClient()
```

Does not indicate whether the player is running a Windows client on Linux with virtualization software. Blizzard has not released an official WoW client for Linux, but this function is included just in case that situation changes.

Returns:

isLinux—1 if running the Linux client; otherwise nil (1nil)

IsLoggedIn

Returns whether the login process has completed.

```
loggedIn = IsLoggedIn()
```

The PLAYER_LOGIN event provides similar information; this function presents an alternative that can be used across UI reloads.

Returns:

loggedIn—1 if the login process has completed; otherwise nil (1nil)

IsMacClient

Returns whether the player is using the Mac OS X game client.

```
isMac = IsMacClient()
```

Returns:

isMac—1 if running the Mac OS X client; otherwise nil (1nil)

IsModifiedClick

Determines if the modifiers specified in the click-type had been held down while the button click occurred.

```
modifiedClick = IsModifiedClick("type")
```

If called from a click handler (OnMouseDown, OnMouseUp, OnClick, OnDoubleClick, PreClick, or PostClick), checks mouse buttons included in the binding; otherwise checks modifiers only (see example).

Arguments:

type—Token identifying a modified click action (string)

Returns:

modifiedClick—1 if the modifier key set bound to the action is active (i.e. the keys are held down); otherwise nil (1nil)

Example:

```
print(GetModifiedClick("CHATLINK"))
-- shows "SHIFT-BUTTON1" by default

-- creates a button to respond to the CHATLINK action
TestFrame = CreateFrame("Button", "TestFrame", UIParent, ↵
"UIPanelButtonTemplate")
TestFrame:SetWidth(100)
TestFrame:SetHeight(24)
TestFrame:SetPoint("CENTER", 0, -30)
TestFrame:RegisterForClicks("AnyUp")
TestFrame:SetScript("OnEnter", function(self) ↵
print(IsModifiedClick("CHATLINK") and "true on enter" or ↵
"false on enter") end)
TestFrame:SetScript("OnClick", function(self) ↵
print(IsModifiedClick("CHATLINK") and "true on click" or ↵
"false on click") end)

-- prints "true on enter" if the Shift key is held while mousing
-- over the button, regardless of mouse button state
-- prints "false on enter" if not holding Shift
-- prints "true on click" only if the button is activated by clicking
-- the primary (left) mouse button while holding the Shift key
-- prints "false on click" if activated by any other mouse button
-- or combination of modifier keys
```

IsModifierKeyDown

Returns whether a modifier key is held down.

```
isDown = IsModifierKeyDown()
```

Modifier keys include Shift, Ctrl, or Alt on either side of the keyboard. WoW does not recognize platform-specific modifier keys (such as fn, meta, Windows, or Command).

Returns:

isDown—1 if any modifier key is held down; otherwise nil (1nil)

IsMounted

Returns whether the player is mounted.

```
mounted = IsMounted()
```

Returns:

mounted—1 if the player character is riding a summoned mount; otherwise nil (1nil)

IsMouseButtonDown

Returns whether a given mouse button is held down.

```
isDown = IsMouseButtonDown([button])
```

If no button is specified, returns 1 if any mouse button is held down.

Arguments:

button (optional)—Number or name of a mouse button (number, string)

- ■ 1 or LeftButton—Primary mouse button
- ■ 2 or RightButton—Secondary mouse button
- ■ 3 or MiddleButton—Third mouse button (or clickable scroll control)
- ■ 4 or Button4—Fourth mouse button
- ■ 5 or Button5—Fifth mouse button

Returns:

isDown—1 if the mouse button is down; otherwise nil (1nil)

IsMouselooking

Returns whether mouselook mode is active.

isLooking = IsMouselooking()

Returns:

isLooking—True if mouselook mode is active; otherwise false (boolean)

IsMuted

Returns whether a character has been muted by the player.

muted = IsMuted("unit") or IsMuted("name")

Arguments:

unit—A unit to query (string, unitID)

name—The name of a unit to query (string)

Returns:

muted—1 if the unit is muted; otherwise nil (1nil)

IsOutOfBounds

Returns whether the player is currently outside the bounds of the world.

outOfBounds = IsOutOfBounds()

Used in the default UI (in conjunction with IsFalling()) to allow the player to release to a graveyard if the character has encountered a bug and fallen underneath the world geometry.

Returns:

outOfBounds—1 if the player is currently outside the bounds of the world; otherwise nil (1nil)

IsOutdoors

Returns whether the player is currently outdoors.

isOutdoors = IsOutdoors()

"Outdoors" as defined by this function corresponds to the ability to use a mount in that specific location, not necessarily whether there is a roof above the player character's head. For example, returns 1 in Ironforge, Undercity, and the Caverns of Time, but nil in the nominally outdoor areas of instances such as Stratholme, Drak'tharon Keep, and Hellfire Ramparts. (Note that even in "outdoor" areas, standing on top of certain objects may interfere with the player's ability to mount up.)

Returns:

isOutdoors—1 if the player is currently outdoors; otherwise nil (1nil)

IsPVPTimerRunning

Returns whether the player's PvP flag will expire after a period of time.

```
isRunning = IsPVPTimerRunning()
```

If in a zone that flags the player for PvP, or if the player has manually enabled PvP, the flag will not expire. Once not in such a zone, or once the player has manually disabled PvP, or if the player has been flagged by attacking an enemy unit, the timer starts running and the player's PvP flag will expire after some time.

Returns:

isRunning—1 if the player's PvP flag will expire; otherwise nil (1nil)

IsPartyLeader

Returns whether the player is the party leader.

```
isLeader = IsPartyLeader()
```

Returns:

isLeader—1 if the player is the party leader; otherwise nil (1nil)

IsPassiveSpell

Returns whether a spell is passive (cannot be cast).

```
isPassive = IsPassiveSpell(index, "bookType") or IsPassiveSpell("name")
```

Arguments:

index—Index of a spell in the spellbook (number, spellbookID)

bookType—Type of spellbook (string)

- ▪ pet—The pet's spellbook
- ▪ spell—The player's spellbook

name—Name of a spell (string)

Returns:

isPassive—1 if the spell is passive; otherwise nil (1nil)

Example:

```
-- prints a list of passive spells in the player's spellbook
local numTabs = GetNumSpellTabs()
for tabID=1,numTabs do
  local name,texture,offset,numSpells = GetSpellTabInfo(tabID)

  for spellID = offset + 1, offset + numSpells do
   if IsPassiveSpell(spellID, BOOKTYPE_SPELL) then
    local spell,rank = GetSpellName(spellID, BOOKTYPE_SPELL)
```

```
    print(" - " .. spell)
  end
 end
end
```

IsPetAttackActive

Returns whether the pet's attack action is currently active.

```
isActive = IsPetAttackActive()
```

Returns:

isActive—1 if the pet's attack action is currently active; otherwise nil (1nil)

IsPlayerResolutionAvailable

Returns whether the current hardware supports high resolution player textures.

```
isAvailable = IsPlayerResolutionAvailable()
```

Returns:

isAvailable—1 if high-resolution player textures can be enabled; otherwise nil (1nil)

IsPossessBarVisible

Returns whether a special action bar should be shown while the player possesses another unit.

```
isVisible = IsPossessBarVisible()
```

Used in the default UI to switch between using the ShapeshiftBarFrame or PossessBarFrame to show actions belonging to the possessed unit.

Returns:

isVisible—1 if the possessed unit's actions should be shown on a special action bar (1nil)

IsQuestCompletable

Returns whether the player can complete the quest presented by a questgiver.

```
isCompletable = IsQuestCompletable()
```

Returns:

isCompletable—1 if the player currently meets the requirements (e.g. number of items collected) complete the quest; otherwise nil (1nil)

IsQuestLogSpecialItemInRange

Returns whether the player's target is in range for using an item associated with a current quest.

```
inRange = IsQuestLogSpecialItemInRange(questIndex)
```

Available for a number of quests which involve using an item (i.e. "Use the MacGuffin to summon and defeat the boss", "Use this saw to fell 12 trees", etc.)

Arguments:

questIndex—Index of a quest log entry with an associated usable item (between 1 and GetNumQuestLogEntries()) (number)

Returns:

inRange—1 if the player is close enough to the target to use the item; 0 if the target is out of range; nil if the quest item does not require a target (number)

IsQuestWatched

Returns whether a quest from the quest log is listed in the objectives tracker.

isWatched = IsQuestWatched(questIndex)

Arguments:

questIndex—Index of a quest in the quest log (between 1 and GetNumQuestLogEntries()) (number)

Returns:

isWatched—1 if the quest is being watched; otherwise nil (1nil)

IsRaidLeader

Returns whether the player is the raid leader.

isLeader = IsRaidLeader()

Returns:

isLeader—1 if the player is the raid leader; otherwise nil (1nil)

IsRaidOfficer

Returns whether the player is a raid assistant.

isRaidOfficer = IsRaidOfficer()

Returns:

isRaidOfficer—1 if the player is a raid assistant; otherwise nil (boolean)

IsRealPartyLeader

Returns whether the player is the leader of a non-battleground party.

isLeader = IsRealPartyLeader()

When the player is in a party/raid and joins a battleground or arena, the normal party/raid functions refer to the battleground's party/raid, but the game still keeps track of the player's place in a non-battleground party/raid.

Returns:

isLeader—1 if the player is the leader of a non-battleground party; otherwise nil (1nil)

IsRealRaidLeader

Returns whether the player is the leader of a non-battleground raid.

isLeader = IsRealRaidLeader()

When the player is in a party/raid and joins a battleground or arena, the normal party/raid functions refer to the battleground's party/raid, but the game still keeps track of the player's place in a non-battleground party/raid.

Returns:

isLeader—1 if the player is the leader of a non-battleground raid; otherwise nil (1nil)

IsReferAFriendLinked

Returns whether a unit's account is linked to the player's via the Recruit-a-Friend program.

```
isLinked = IsReferAFriendLinked("unit")
```

Arguments:

unit—A unit to query (string, unitID)

Returns:

isLinked—1 if the unit's account is linked to the player's (1nil)

IsResting

Returns whether the player is currently resting.

```
resting = IsResting()
```

Rest state is provided in Inns and major cities and allows the player to log out immediately (instead of after a brief delay) and accrue bonus XP to be awarded for kills.

Returns:

resting—1 if the player is resting; otherwise nil (boolean)

IsRightAltKeyDown

Returns whether the right Alt key is currently held down.

```
isDown = IsRightAltKeyDown()
```

(Note: The Mac WoW client does not distingish between left and right modifier keys, so both Alt keys are reported as Left Alt.)

Returns:

isDown—1 if the right Alt key on the keyboard is currently held down; otherwise nil (1nil)

IsRightControlKeyDown

Returns whether the right Control key on the keyboard is held down.

```
isDown = IsRightControlKeyDown()
```

(Note: The Mac WoW client does not distingish between left and right modifier keys, so both Control keys are reported as Left Control.)

Returns:

isDown—1 if the right Control key on the keyboard is held down; otherwise nil (1nil)

IsRightShiftKeyDown

Returns whether the right shift key on the keyboard is held down.

```
isDown = IsRightShiftKeyDown()
```

(Note: The Mac WoW client does not distingish between left and right modifier keys, so both Shift keys are reported as Left Shift.)

Returns:

isDown—1 if the right shift key on the keyboard is currently held down; otherwise nil (1nil)

IsSelectedSpell

Returns whether a spell is currently selected in the spellbook.

```
isSelected = IsSelectedSpell(index, "bookType") or ↵
IsSelectedSpell("name")
```

Applies when "casting" a spell that opens a trade skill.

Arguments:

index—Index of a spell in the spellbook (number, spellbookID)

bookType—Type of spellbook (string)

- ▪ pet—The pet's spellbook
- ▪ spell—The player's spellbook

name—Name of a spell (string)

Returns:

isSelected—1 if the spell is currently selected; otherwise nil (1nil)

IsShiftKeyDown

Returns whether a Shift key on the keyboard is held down.

```
isDown = IsShiftKeyDown()
```

Returns:

isDown—1 if a Shift key on the keyboard is currently held down; otherwise nil (1nil)

IsSilenced

Returns whether a character is silenced on a chat channel.

```
isSilenced = IsSilenced("name", "channel")
```

Arguments:

name—Name of a character (string)

channel—Name of a chat channel (string)

Returns:

isSilenced—1 if the character is silenced on the given channel; otherwise nil (1nil)

IsSpellInRange

Returns whether the player is in range to cast a spell on a unit.

```
inRange = IsSpellInRange(index, "bookType", "unit") or ↵
IsSpellInRange("name", "unit")
```

Arguments:

index—Index of a spell in the spellbook (number, spellbookID)

bookType—Type of spellbook (string)

- ▪ pet—The pet's spellbook
- ▪ spell—The player's spellbook

name—Name of a spell (string)

unit—A unit to target with the spell (string, unitID)

Returns:

inRange—1 if the player is near enough to cast the spell on the unit; 0 if not in range; nil if the unit is not a valid target for the spell (1nil)

IsSpellKnown

Returns whether the player (or pet) knows a spell.

```
isKnown = IsSpellKnown(spellID [, isPet])
```

Arguments:

spellID—Numeric ID of a spell (number, spellID)

isPet (optional)—True to check only spells known to the player's pet; false or omitted to check only spells known to the player (boolean)

Returns:

isKnown—True if the player (or pet) knows the given spell; false otherwise (boolean)

IsStackableAction

Returns whether an action uses stackable items.

```
isStackable = IsStackableAction(slot)
```

Applies to consumable items such as potions, wizard oils, food and drink; not used for spells which consume reagents (for those, see IsConsumableAction).

Arguments:

slot—An action bar slot (number, actionID)

Returns:

isStackable—1 if the action uses stackable items; otherwise nil (1nil)

Example:

```
-- Print all "stackable actions" to your chat window
for i=1,120 do
 if IsStackableAction(i) then
  local count = GetActionCount(i)
  local t,id = GetActionInfo(i)
  local name = GetItemInfo(id)

  print("Action:", i, "Item:", name, "Count:", count)
 end
end
```

IsStealthed

Returns whether the player is currently stealthed.

```
stealthed = IsStealthed()
```

Returns:

stealthed—1 if rogue Stealth, druid cat form Prowl, or a similar ability is active on the player; otherwise nil (1nil)

IsStereoVideoAvailable

Returns whether the current system supports stereoscopic 3D display.

```
isAvailable = IsStereoVideoAvailable()
```

Returns:

isAvailable—1 if video options for stereoscopic 3D display should be shown; otherwise nil (1nil)

IsSubZonePVPPOI

Returns whether the current area has PvP (or other) objectives to be displayed.

```
isPVPPOI = IsSubZonePVPPOI()
```

Used in the default UI when the "Display World PVP Objectives" setting is set to \Dynamic\, in which case objective information is only shown when the player is near an objective. Examples include the towers in Eastern Plaguelands and Hellfire Peninsula as well as non-PvP objectives such as in the Old Hillsbrad instance, the Death Knight starter quests, and the Battle for Undercity quest event.

Returns:

isPVPPOI—1 if the current subzone has objectives to display (1nil)

IsSwimming

Returns whether the player is currently swimming.

```
isSwimming = IsSwimming()
```

"Swimming" as defined by this function corresponds to the ability to use swimming abilities (such as druid Aquatic Form) or inability to use land-restricted abilities (such as eating or summoning a flying mount), not necessarily to whether the player is in water.

Returns:

isSwimming—1 if the player is currently swimming; otherwise nil (1nil)

IsThreatWarningEnabled

Returns whether the default Aggro Warning UI should currently be shown.

```
enabled = IsThreatWarningEnabled()
```

This function (and the threatWarning CVar that affects its behavior) has no effect on other threat APIs; it merely indicates whether Blizzard's threat warning UI should be displayed.

Returns:

enabled—1 if the Aggro Warning UI should be displayed; nil otherwise (1nil)

IsTitleKnown

Returns whether the player has earned the ability to display a title.

```
isKnown = IsTitleKnown(titleIndex)
```

Arguments:

titleIndex—Index of a title available to the player (between 1 and GetNumTitles()) (integer)

Returns:

isKnown—1 if the player has earned the ability to display the title; otherwise nil (1nil)

IsTrackedAchievement

Returns whether an achievement is flagged for display in the objectives tracker UI.

isTracked = IsTrackedAchievement(id)

Arguments:

id—The numeric ID of an achievement (number)

Returns:

isTracked—True if the achievement is flagged for tracking; otherwise false (boolean)

IsTradeSkillLinked

Returns whether the TradeSkill UI is showing another player's skill.

isLinked, name = IsTradeSkillLinked()

Returns:

isLinked—1 if the TradeSkill APIs currently reflect another character's tradeskill; nil if showing the player's tradeskill or if no skill is shown (1nil)

name—If showing another character's skill, the name of that character (string)

IsTradeskillTrainer

Returns whether the player is interacting with a trade skill trainer (as opposed to a class trainer).

isTradeskill = IsTradeskillTrainer()

Returns:

isTradeskill—1 if interacting with a trade skill trainer; otherwise nil (1nil)

IsTrainerServiceSkillStep

Returns whether a trainer service is a trade skill level.

isSkillStep = IsTrainerServiceSkillStep(index)

Arguments:

index—Index of an entry in the trainer service listing (between 1 and GetNumTrainerServices()) (number)

Returns:

isSkillStep—1 if the service is a trade skill level (e.g. Apprentice vs Journeyman First Aid); nil if the service is a spell or recipe (1nil)

IsUnitOnQuest

Returns whether a unit is on one of the quests in the player's quest log.

state = IsUnitOnQuest(index, "unit") or IsUnitOnQuest(index, "name")

Arguments:

index—Index of a quest in the player's quest log (between 1 and GetNumQuest LogEntries()) (number)

unit—A unit to query (string, unitID)

name—The name of a unit to query; only valid for player, pet, and party/raid members (string)

Returns:

state—1 if the unit is on the quest; otherwise nil (1nil)

IsUsableAction

Returns whether an action is usable.

isUsable, notEnoughMana = IsUsableAction(slot)

Arguments:

slot—An action bar slot (number, actionID)

Returns:

isUsable—1 if the action is usable; otherwise nil (1nil)

notEnoughMana—1 if the player lacks the resources (e.g. mana, energy, runes) to use the action; otherwise nil (1nil)

IsUsableItem

Returns whether an item can currently be used.

isUsable, notEnoughMana = IsUsableItem(itemID) or ↩
IsUsableItem("itemName") or IsUsableItem("itemLink")

Does not account for item cooldowns (see GetItemCooldown(); returns 1 if other conditions allow for using the item (e.g. if the item can only be used while outdoors).

Arguments:

itemID—An item's ID (number)

itemName—An item's name (string)

itemLink—An item's link (string)

Returns:

isUsable—1 if the item is usable; otherwise nil (1nil)

notEnoughMana—1 if the player lacks the resources (e.g. mana, energy, runes) to use the item; otherwise nil (1nil)

IsUsableSpell

Returns whether or not a given spell is usable or cannot be used due to lack of mana.

isUsable, notEnoughMana = IsUsableSpell(index, "bookType") or ↩
IsUsableSpell("name")

Does not account for spell cooldowns (see GetSpellCooldown(); returns 1 if other conditions allow for casting the spell (e.g. if the spell can only be cast while outdoors).

Arguments:

index—Index of a spell in the spellbook (number, spellbookID) bookType—Type of spellbook (`string`)

- `pet`—The pet's spellbook
- `spell`—The player's spellbook

name—Name of a spell (`string`)

Returns:

isUsable—1 if the spell is castable; otherwise `nil` (1nil)

notEnoughMana—1 if the player lacks the resources (e.g. mana, energy, runes) to cast the spell; otherwise `nil` (1nil)

IsVehicleAimAngleAdjustable

Returns whether the player is controlling a vehicle weapon with adjustable aim angle.

```
hasAngleControl = IsVehicleAimAngleAdjustable()
```

Returns:

hasAngleControl—1 if the player is controlling a vehicle weapon with adjustable aim angle; otherwise `nil` (1nil)

IsVoiceChatAllowed

Returns whether the player is allowed to enable the voice chat feature.

```
isAllowed = IsVoiceChatAllowed()
```

Returns:

isAllowed—1 if voice chat is allowed; otherwise `nil` (1nil)

IsVoiceChatAllowedByServer

Returns whether voice chat is supported by the realm server.

IsVoiceChatEnabled

Returns whether the voice chat system is enabled.

```
isEnabled = IsVoiceChatEnabled()
```

Returns:

isEnabled—1 if the voice chat system is enabled; otherwise `nil` (1nil)

IsWindowsClient

Returns whether the player is using the Windows game client.

```
isWindows = IsWindowsClient()
```

Returns:

isWindows—1 if running the Windows client; otherwise `nil` (1nil)

IsXPUserDisabled

Returns whether experience gain has been disabled for the player.

```
isDisabled = IsXPUserDisabled()
```

Returns:

isDisabled—True if experience gain has been disabled for the player; `false` otherwise (`boolean`)

ItemHasRange

Returns whether an item has a range limitation for its use.

```
hasRange = ItemHasRange(itemID) or ItemHasRange("itemName") or ↵
ItemHasRange("itemLink")
```

For example, Mistletoe can only be used on another character within a given range of the player, but a Hearthstone has no target and thus no range restriction. Returns nil for items which have a range restriction but are area-targeted and not unit-targeted (e.g. grenades).

Arguments:

itemID—An item's ID (number)

itemName—An item's name (string)

itemLink—An item's hyperlink, or any string containing the itemString portion of an item link (string)

Returns:

hasRange—1 if the item has an effective range; otherwise nil. (1nil)

ItemTextGetCreator

Returns the original author of the currently viewed text item.

```
creator = ItemTextGetCreator()
```

Used for mail messages sent by other players; when the player makes a permanent copy of a letter and reads it from inventory, the default UI uses this function to display a signature (e.g. "From, Leeroy") at the end of the message text.

Returns:

creator—Creator of the text item, or nil if not available (string)

ItemTextGetItem

Returns the name of the currently viewed text item.

```
text = ItemTextGetItem()
```

Used for readable world objects (plaques, books on tables, etc) and readable inventory items (looted books/parchments/scrolls/etc, or saved copies of mail messages). For saved mail messages the name returned is always "Plain Letter" (or localized equivalent); the message subject is lost when saving a copy.

Returns:

text—Name of the text item (string)

ItemTextGetMaterial

Returns display style information for the currently viewed text item.

```
material = ItemTextGetMaterial()
```

The value returned can be used to look up background textures and text colors for display:

- Background textures displayed in the default UI can be found by prepending `"Interface\\ItemTextFrame\\ItemText-"` and appending `"-TopLeft"`, `"-TopRight"`, `"-BotLeft"`, `"-BotRight"` to the material string (e.g. `"Interface\\ItemTextFrame\\ItemText-Stone-TopLeft"`).
- Colors for body and title text can be found by calling `GetMaterialText Colors(material)` (a Lua function implemented in the Blizzard UI).

In cases where this function returns nil, the default UI uses the colors and textures for "Parchment".

Returns:

`material`—String identifying a display style for the current text item, or `nil` for the default style (`string`)

- `Bronze`—Colored metallic background
- `Marble`—Light stone background
- `Parchment`—Yellowed parchment background (default)
- `Silver`—Gray metallic background
- `Stone`—Dark stone background

ItemTextGetPage

Returns the current page number in the currently viewed text item.

```
page = ItemTextGetPage()
```

Returns:

`page`—Number of the currently displayed page (`number`)

ItemTextGetText

Returns the text of the currently viewed text item.

```
text = ItemTextGetText()
```

Used for readable world objects (plaques, books on tables, etc) and readable inventory items (looted books/parchments/scrolls/etc, or saved copies of mail messages). Returns valid data only between the `ITEM_TEXT_BEGIN` and `ITEM_TEXT_CLOSED` events, with the `ITEM_TEXT_READY` event indicating when new text is available (as when changing pages).

Returns:

`text`—Text to be displayed for the current page of the currently viewed text item (`string`)

ItemTextHasNextPage

Returns whether the currently viewed text item has additional pages.

```
next = ItemTextHasNextPage()
```

Returns:

`next`—1 if the currently viewed text item has one or more pages beyond the current page; otherwise `nil` (1nil)

ItemTextNextPage

Moves to the next page in the currently viewed text item.

The `ITEM_TEXT_READY` event fires when text for the next page becomes available. Does nothing if already viewing the last page of text.

ItemTextPrevPage

Moves to the previous page in the currently viewed text item.

The `ITEM_TEXT_READY` event fires when text for the previous page becomes available. Does nothing if already viewing the first page of text.

JoinBattlefield

Joins the queue for a battleground instance.

```
JoinBattlefield(index, asGroup)
```

Arguments:

`index`—Index in the battleground queue listing (1 for the first available instance, or between 2 and `GetNumBattlefields()` for other instances) (number)

`asGroup`—True to enter the player's entire party/raid in the queue; `false` to enter the player only (boolean)

JoinPermanentChannel

Joins a channel, saving associated chat window settings.

```
zoneChannel, channelName = JoinPermanentChannel("name" ↵
[, "password" [, chatFrameIndex [, enableVoice]]])
```

Arguments:

`name`—Name of the channel to join (string)

`password` (optional)—Password to use when joining (string)

`chatFrameIndex` (optional)—Index of a chat frame (between 1 and `NUM_CHAT_WINDOWS`) in which to subscribe to the channel (number)

`enableVoice` (optional)—True to enable voice in the channel; otherwise `false` (boolean)

Returns:

`zoneChannel`—0 for non-zone channels, otherwise a numeric index specific to that channel (number)

`channelName`—Display name of the channel, if the channel was a zone channel (string)

Example:

```
-- Join a custom channel "Monkeys" with voice enabled
JoinPermanentChannel("Monkeys", nil, 1, 1)
```

JoinTemporaryChannel

Joins a channel, but does not save associated chat window settings.

```
JoinTemporaryChannel("channel")
```

Arguments:

`channel`—Name of a channel to join (`string`)

[Protected] **JumpOrAscendStart**

Causes the player character to jump (or begins ascent if swimming or flying). Used by the JUMP binding, which also controls ascent when swimming or flying.

KBArticle_BeginLoading

Requests a specific knowledge base article from the server.

`KBArticle_BeginLoading(articleId, searchType)`

Arguments:

`articleId`—The unique articleId to request (`number`)

`searchType`—The search type of the request (`number`)

- `1`—Default "top issues" search
- `2`—Search for specific text

KBArticle_GetData

Returns information about the last requested knowledge base article.

`id, subject, subjectAlt, text, keywords, languageId, isHot = ↵`
`KBArticle_GetData()`

Only available once the KNOWLEDGE_BASE_ARTICLE_LOAD_SUCCESS event has fired following an article request.

Returns:

`id`—A unique identifier for the article (`number`)

`subject`—The subject of the article (`string`)

`subjectAlt`—Alternate text for the article subject (`string`)

`text`—The body of the article (`string`)

`keywords`—A comma separated list of keywords for the article (`string`)

`languageId`—Identifier for the article's language (ee `KBSetup_Get LanguageData`) (`number`)

`isHot`—true if the article is a "Hot Item", otherwise `false` (`boolean`)

KBArticle_IsLoaded

Returns whether the requested knowledge base article has been loaded.

`isLoaded = KBArticle_IsLoaded()`

The KNOWLEDGE_BASE_ARTICLE_LOAD_SUCCESS also indicates that the requested article is available; this function presents an alternative that can be used across UI reloads or login/logout.

Returns:

`isLoaded`—True if data for the last requested article is available; otherwise `false` (`boolean`)

KBQuery_BeginLoading

Queries the knowledge base server for articles.

```
KBQuery_BeginLoading("searchText", categoryIndex, subcategoryIndex, ↵
numArticles, page)
```

Arguments:

searchText—The search string to use. The empty string will search for all articles in the given category (string)

categoryIndex—The category index (number)

subcategoryIndex—The subcategory index (number)

numArticles—The number of articles to be returned for each page (number)

page—The page of the total results that should be displayed. (number)

KBQuery_GetArticleHeaderCount

Returns the number of articles on the current knowledge base search result page.

```
articleHeaderCount = KBQuery_GetArticleHeaderCount()
```

Returns:

articleHeaderCount—The number of articles on the current knowledge base search result base page (number)

KBQuery_GetArticleHeaderData

Returns information about an article returned in a knowledge base query.

```
articleId, title, isHotIssue, isRecentlyUpdated = ↵
KBQuery_GetArticleHeaderData(index)
```

Arguments:

index—The index of the article to query (number)

Returns:

articleId—A unique articleId for the article (number)

title—The title of the article (string)

isHotIssue—true if the article is a "Hot Issue", otherwise false (boolean)

isRecentlyUpdated—true if the article has been recently updated, otherwise false (boolean)

KBQuery_GetTotalArticleCount

Returns the total number of articles returned for the given query.

```
totalArticleHeaderCount = KBQuery_GetTotalArticleCount()
```

Returns:

totalArticleHeaderCount—The total number of articles returned for the given query (number)

KBQuery_IsLoaded

Returns whether results of a knowledge base query have been loaded.

```
isLoaded = KBQuery_IsLoaded()
```

The KNOWLEDGE_BASE_QUERY_LOAD_SUCCESS also indicates that the requested results are available; this function presents an alternative that can be used across UI reloads or login/logout.

Returns:

isLoaded—True if query results are available; otherwise false (boolean)

KBSetup_BeginLoading

Loads a maximum number of "Top Issues" from a given page.

KBSetup_BeginLoading(numArticles, currentPage)

Arguments:

numArticles—The number of articles displayed per page. This is typically the constant KBASE_NUM_ARTICLES_PER_PAGE (number)

currentPage—The page to display (number)

KBSetup_GetArticleHeaderCount

Returns the number of "Top Issues" articles on the current page.

articleHeaderCount = KBSetup_GetArticleHeaderCount()

Returns:

articleHeaderCount—The number of "Top Issues" articles on the current page (number)

KBSetup_GetArticleHeaderData

Returns header information about a "Top Issue" article.

articleId, title, isHotIssue, isRecentlyUpdated = ↵
KBSetup_GetArticleHeaderData(index)

Arguments:

index—The index of the article to query (number)

Returns:

articleId—A unique articleId for the article (number)

title—The title of the article (string)

isHotIssue—true if the article is a "Hot Issue", otherwise false (boolean)

isRecentlyUpdated—true if the article has been recently updated, otherwise false (boolean)

KBSetup_GetCategoryCount

Returns the number of available knowledge base categories.

numCategories = KBSetup_GetCategoryCount()

Returns:

numCategories—The number of available knowledge base categories (number)

KBSetup_GetCategoryData

Returns information about a knowledge base category.

categoryId, name = KBSetup_GetCategoryData(index)

Arguments:

index—The index of the category (number)

Returns:

categoryId—The unique identifier for the given category (number)

name—The name of the category (string)

KBSetup_GetLanguageCount

Returns the number of available knowledge base languages.

numLanguages = KBSetup_GetLanguageCount()

Returns:

numLanguages—The number of available knowledge base languages (number)

KBSetup_GetLanguageData

Returns information about a given knowledge base language.

languageId, name = KBSetup_GetLanguageData(index)

Arguments:

index—Index of a language to query (between 1 and KBSetup_Get LanguageCount() (number)

Returns:

languageId—A number identifying the language in article headers (number)

name—The name of the language (string)

KBSetup_GetSubCategoryCount

Returns the number of available subcategories for a given category.

numSubCategories = KBSetup_GetSubCategoryCount(index)

Arguments:

index—The index of the category (number)

Returns:

numSubCategories—The number of available subcategories (number)

KBSetup_GetSubCategoryData

Returns information a knowledge base subcategory.

categoryId, name = KBSetup_GetSubCategoryData(index, subindex)

Arguments:

index—The index of the category (number)

subindex—The index of the subcategory (number)

Returns:

categoryId—The unique categoryId for the given subcategory (number)

name—The name of the subcategory (string)

KBSetup_GetTotalArticleCount

Returns the number of "Top Issues" articles.

numArticles = KBSetup_GetTotalArticleCount()

Returns:

numArticles—The total number of "Top Issues" articles (number)

KBSetup_IsLoaded

Returns whether the knowledge base default query has completed successfully.

```
isLoaded = KBSetup_IsLoaded()
```

The KNOWLEDGE_BASE_SETUP_LOAD_SUCCESS also indicates that the knowledge base setup is complete; this function presents an alternative that can be used across UI reloads or login/logout.

Returns:

isLoaded—True if results for the knowledge base's default "Top Issues" query are available; false if a query is in progress or has failed (boolean)

KBSystem_GetMOTD

Returns the currently knowledge base MOTD.

```
text = KBSystem_GetMOTD()
```

Returns:

text—The message of the day for the knowledge base system (string)

KBSystem_GetServerNotice

Returns the text of the knowledge base server system notice.

```
text = KBSystem_GetServerNotice()
```

Returns:

text—The text of the knowledgebase system server notice (string)

KBSystem_GetServerStatus

Returns the knowledge base server system status message.

```
statusMessage = KBSystem_GetServerStatus()
```

Returns:

statusMessage—The knowledge base server status message, or nil (string)

KeyRingButtonIDToInvSlotID

Returns the inventoryID corresponding to a slot in the keyring.

```
slot = KeyRingButtonIDToInvSlotID(slot)
```

Arguments:

slot—Index of a key slot within the keyring (number, containerSlotID)

Returns:

slot—Identifier for the key slot usable with Inventory APIs (number, inventoryID)

LFGQuery

Requests Looking for More information from the server.

```
LFGQuery(type, index)
```

Query results are not available immediately; the UPDATE_LFG_LIST event fires when data becomes available; listing information can then be retrieved using GetLFGResults() or related APIs.

Arguments:

type—Index of an LFG query type (in the list returned by `GetLFGTypes()`) (number)

index—Index of an LFG entry (in the list returned by `GetLFGTypeEntries (type)`) (number)

Confirmation **LearnPreviewTalents**

Commits changes made in the Talent UI's preview mode.

`LearnPreviewTalents(isPet)`

Arguments:

isPet—`true` to edit talents for the player's pet, `false` to edit talents for the player (boolean)

LearnTalent

Learns a talent, spending one talent point.

`LearnTalent(tabIndex, talentIndex, isPet, talentGroup)`

Arguments:

tabIndex—Index of a talent tab (between 1 and `GetNumTalentTabs()`) (number)

talentIndex—Index of a talent option (between 1 and `GetNumTalents()`) (number)

isPet—`True` to edit talents for the player's pet, `false` to edit talents for the player (boolean)

talentGroup—Which set of talents to edit, if the player has Dual Talent Specialization enabled (number)

- `1`—Primary Talents
- `2`—Secondary Talents
- `nil`—Currently active talents

LeaveBattlefield

Immediately exits the current battleground instance.

Returns the player to the location from which he or she joined the battleground and applies the Deserter debuff.

LeaveChannelByName

Leaves a chat channel.

`LeaveChannelByName("name")`

Arguments:

name—Name of a chat channel to leave (string)

LeaveParty

Exits the current party or raid.

If there are only two characters in the party or raid, causes the party or raid to be disbanded.

ListChannelByName

Requests the list of participants in a chat channel.

`ListChannelByName("channel")` or `ListChannelByName(channelIndex)`

Fires the `CHAT_MSG_CHANNEL_LIST` event listing the names of all characters in the channel.

Arguments:

`channel`—Name of a channel (`string`)

`channelIndex`—Index of a channel (`number`)

ListChannels

Requests a list of channels joined by the player.

Fires the `CHAT_MSG_CHANNEL_LIST` event listing the names and indices of all channels joined by the player.

LoadAddOn

Loads a LoadOnDemand-capable addon.

`loaded, reason = LoadAddOn("name")` or `LoadAddOn(index)`

If the given addon has dependencies which are also LoadOnDemand-capable, those addons will be loaded as well. This function will not load disabled addons.

Arguments:

`name`—Name of an addon (name of the addon's folder and TOC file, not the Title found in the TOC) (`string`)

`index`—Index of an addon in the addon list (between `1` and `GetNumAddOns()`) (`number`)

Returns:

`loaded`—1 if loading the addon was successful; otherwise `nil` (`number`)

`reason`—If the addon could not be loaded, an unlocalized string token indicating the reason for failure. Localized strings for display can be found by prepending `"ADDON_"`; e.g. `ADDON_DEP_MISSING == "Dependency missing"`. (`string`)

- `BANNED`—Banned
- `CORRUPT`—Corrupt
- `DEP_BANNED`—Dependency banned
- `DEP_CORRUPT`—Dependency corrupt
- `DEP_DISABLED`—Dependency disabled
- `DEP_INCOMPATIBLE`—Dependency incompatible
- `DEP_INSECURE`—Dependency insecure
- `DEP_INTERFACE_VERSION`—Dependency out of date
- `DEP_MISSING`—Dependency missing
- `DEP_NOT_DEMAND_LOADED`—Dependency not loadable on demand
- `DISABLED`—Disabled
- `INCOMPATIBLE`—Incompatible

- `INSECURE`—Insecure
- `INTERFACE_VERSION`—Out of Date
- `MISSING`—Missing
- `NOT_DEMAND_LOADED`—Not loadable on demand

LoadBindings

Loads a set of key bindings.

```
LoadBindings(set)
```

The `UPDATE_BINDINGS` event fires when the new bindings have taken effect.

Arguments:

`set`—A set of key bindings to load (`number`)

- `0`—Default key bindings
- `1`—Account-wide key bindings
- `2`—Character-specific key bindings

LoggingChat

Enables or disables saving chat text to a file.

```
isLogging = LoggingChat(toggle)
```

Text received via the chat system (but not necessarily all text displayed in chat windows) will be saved to the file `Logs/WoWChatLog.txt` (path is relative to the folder containing the World of Warcraft client); the file is not actually updated until the player logs out.

Chat text in the log file follows a similar format to its display in-game, but with added timestamps.

Arguments:

`toggle`—True to enable chat logging; `false` or omitted to disable (`boolean`)

Returns:

`isLogging`—1 if chat logging is enabled; otherwise `nil` (`1nil`)

Example:

```
-- example log
6/7 16:51:26.790 Gorrok has come online.
6/7 16:51:30.054 [3. tehgladiators] Gorrok joined channel.
6/7 16:52:18.553 |Hchannel:Guild|h[Guild]|h Spin: Bah!
6/7 16:52:27.803 |Hchannel:Guild|h[Guild]|h Spin: Got Mr. Pinchy, but
first one was just a buff
6/7 16:52:41.752 |Hchannel:Guild|h[Guild]|h Valiant: ah well, maybe
the next time
6/7 16:52:57.504 [1. Trade] Yolanda: need healer premade EOTS
```

LoggingCombat

Enables or disables saving combat log data to a file.

```
isLogging = LoggingCombat(toggle)
```

Combat log data will be saved to the file `Logs/WoWCombatLog.txt` (path is relative to the folder containing the World of Warcraft client); the file is not actually updated until the player logs out.

Arguments:

`toggle`—True to enable combat logging; `false` or omitted to disable (`boolean`)

Returns:

`isLogging`—1 if combat logging is enabled; otherwise `nil` (`1nil`)

Example:

```
-- example log file contents
6/7 17:08:46.784 SPELL_CAST_SUCCESS,0x060000000279E425,"Gundark",0x511,
0xF13000482C5462D1,"Timber Worg",0x10a48,49576,"Death Grip",0x1
6/7 17:08:47.089 SPELL_AURA_APPLIED,0x060000000279E425,"Gundark",0x511,
0xF13000482C5462D1,"Timber Worg",0x10a48,49560,"Death Grip",0x1,DEBUFF
6/7 17:08:47.886 SWING_DAMAGE,0x060000000279E425,"Gundark",0x511,0xF130
00482C5462D1,"Timber Worg",0x10a48,374,0,1,0,0,0,nil,nil,nil
6/7 17:08:47.887 SPELL_DAMAGE,0x060000000279E425,"Gundark",0x511,0xF130
00482C5462D1,"Timber Worg",0x10a48,50401,"Razor Frost",0x10,5,0,16,0,0,0
,nil,nil,nil
6/7 17:08:47.887 SPELL_AURA_APPLIED,0x060000000279E425,"Gundark",0x511,
0xF13000482C5462D1,"Timber Worg",0x10a48,51714,"Frost Vulnerability",0x1
0,DEBUFF
6/7 17:08:48.207 SPELL_CAST_SUCCESS,0x060000000279E425,"Gundark",0x511,
0xF13000482C5462D1,"Timber Worg",0x10a48,49896,"Icy Touch",0x10
6/7 17:08:48.327 SWING_MISSED,0xF13000482C5462D1,"Timber Worg",0x10a48,
0x060000000279E425,"Gundark",0x511,DODGE
6/7 17:08:48.328 SPELL_PERIODIC_HEAL,0x060000000279E425,"Gundark",0x511
,0x060000000279E425,"Gundark",0x511,50475,"Blood Presence",0x1,15,15,nil
```

Logout

Attempts to log out and return to the character selection screen.

Results vary based on current conditions:

- If the player is in combat or under other temporary restrictions (e.g. falling), fires the UI_ERROR_MESSAGE event with a message indicating the player cannot log out at the moment.

- If the player is not in an inn, major city, or other "rest" area (i.e. `IsResting()` returns `nil`), fires the PLAYER_CAMPING event, causing the default UI to show a countdown, logging the player out after a period of time if not canceled.

- If the player is in a "rest" area, logs out immediately.

LootSlot

Attempts to pick up an item available as loot.

`LootSlot(slot)`

If the item in the loot slot binds on pickup, the LOOT_BIND_CONFIRM event fires, indicating that `ConfirmLootSlot(slot)` must be called in order to actually loot the item. Please note: if you call this while processing a

LOOT_OPENED event and it is the last item to be looted from the corpse, can cause LOOT_CLOSED to fire and be processed before your LOOT_OPENED event handler completes.

Arguments:

slot—Index of a loot slot (between 1 and GetNumLootItems()) (number)

LootSlotIsCoin

Returns whether a loot slot contains money.

```
isCoin = LootSlotIsCoin(slot)
```

Arguments:

slot—Index of a loot slot (between 1 and GetNumLootItems()) (number)

Returns:

isCoin—1 if the loot slot contains money; otherwise nil (1nil)

LootSlotIsItem

Returns whether a loot slot contains an item.

```
isItem = LootSlotIsItem(slot)
```

Arguments:

slot—Index of a loot slot (between 1 and GetNumLootItems()) (number)

Returns:

isItem—1 if the loot slot contains an item; otherwise nil (1nil)

MouselookStart

Enables mouselook mode, in which cursor movement rotates the camera.

MouselookStop

Disables mouselook mode.

`Protected` **MoveAndSteerStart**

Begins moving the player character forward while steering via mouse movement.

After calling this function, the player character begins moving forward while cursor movement rotates (or steers) the character, altering yaw (facing) and/or pitch (vertical movement angle) as well as camera position.

Equivalent to calling both CameraOrSelectOrMoveStart and TurnOrActionStart without calling the respective Stop functions; i.e. holding both left and right mouse buttons down. Used by the MOVEANDSTEER binding, which can be customized to allow alternate access to this action if the player's system does not allow pressing multiple mouse buttons at once.

`Protected` **MoveAndSteerStop**

Ends movement initiated by MoveAndSteerStart.

After calling this function, forward movement and character steering stops and normal cursor movement resumes.

Used by the MOVEANDSTEER binding.

Protected	**MoveBackwardStart**

Begins moving the player character backward.

Used by the MOVEBACKWARD binding.

Protected	**MoveBackwardStop**

Ends movement initiated by MoveBackwardStart.

Protected	**MoveForwardStart**

Begins moving the player character forward.

Used by the MOVEFORWARD binding.

Protected	**MoveForwardStop**

Ends movement initiated by MoveForwardStart.

MoveViewDownStart

Begins orbiting the camera downward (to look upward).

MoveViewDownStop

Ends camera movement initiated by MoveViewDownStart.

MoveViewInStart

Begins zooming the camera inward (towards/through the player character).

MoveViewInStop

Ends camera movement initiated by MoveViewInStart.

MoveViewLeftStart

Begins orbiting the camera around the player character to the left.

"Left" here is relative to the player's facing; i.e. the camera orbits clockwise if looking down. Moving the camera to the left causes it to look towards the character's right.

MoveViewLeftStop

Ends camera movement initiated by MoveViewLeftStart.

MoveViewOutStart

Begins zooming the camera outward (away from the player character).

MoveViewOutStop

Ends camera movement initiated by MoveViewOutStart.

MoveViewRightStart

Begins orbiting the camera around the player character to the right.

"Right" here is relative to the player's facing; i.e. the camera orbits counter-clockwise if looking down. Moving the camera to the right causes it to look towards the character's left.

MoveViewRightStop

Ends camera movement initiated by MoveViewRightStart.

MoveViewUpStart

Begins orbiting the camera upward (to look down).

MoveViewUpStop

Ends camera movement initiated by `MoveViewUpStart`.

Mac OS X only **MovieRecording_Cancel**

Cancels video recording and compression.

If a recording is in progress, recording is stopped and the results discarded. If compression is in progress, compression is stopped and the uncompressed portion of the movie is deleted.

Mac OS X only **MovieRecording_DataRate**

Returns the data rate required for a given set of video recording parameters.

```
dataRate = MovieRecording_DataRate(width, framerate, sound)
```

The value returned is a prediction of the rate at which data will be written to the hard drive while recording. If the hardware cannot support this data rate, game performance may suffer and recording may stop.

Arguments:

`width`—Width of the output video (in pixels) (number)

`framerate`—Number of video frames to be recorded per second (number)

`sound`—1 if game audio is to be captured with video; otherwise 0 (number)

Returns:

`dataRate`—Summary of the data rate (e.g. "438.297 KB/s", "11.132 MB/s") (string)

Example:

```
-- Calculate the data rate required for the following:
-- 1024x768 video at 29.97 frames per second with sound
local dataRate = MovieRecording_DataRate(1024, 29.97, 1)
print(dataRate .. " is required for this recording.")
```

Mac OS X only **MovieRecording_DeleteMovie**

Deletes an uncompressed movie.

```
MovieRecording_DeleteMovie("filename")
```

Arguments:

`filename`—Path to an uncompressed movie (as provided in the `MOVIE_UNCOMPRESSED_MOVIE` event) (string)

Mac OS X only **MovieRecording_GetAspectRatio**

Returns the aspect ratio of the game display.

```
ratio = MovieRecording_GetAspectRatio()
```

Used in the default UI to calculate dimensions for scaling captured video to predetermined widths.

For example, if the aspect ratio is 0.75 (as on a 1600x1200 screen), a movie scaled to 640 pixels wide will be 480 pixels tall; but if the aspect ratio is 0.625 (as on a 1440x900 screen), a movie scaled to 640 pixels wide will be 400 pixels tall.

Returns:

ratio—Ratio of the game display's width to its height (number)

Mac OS X only **MovieRecording_GetMovieFullPath**

Returns a path to the movie currently being recorded or compressed.

```
path = MovieRecording_GetMovieFullPath()
```

If no movie is being recorded or compressed, returns either the empty string (" ") or the path of the last movie recorded/compressed.

Returns:

path—Path to the movie currently being recorded or compressed, relative to the folder containing the World of Warcraft app (string)

Example:

```
MovieRecording_GetMovieFullPath()
-- returns (e.g.) "Movies/Thunder_Bluff_060409_193403.mov"
```

Mac OS X only **MovieRecording_GetProgress**

Returns information about movie compression progress.

```
recovering, progress = MovieRecording_GetProgress()
```

Returns:

recovering—True if a previous compression was interrupted (e.g. due to WoW being crashing or being forced to quit), indicating that recovery is being attempted on the file; otherwise false (boolean)

progress—Progress of the movie compression process (0 = just started, 1 = finished) (number)

Mac OS X only **MovieRecording_GetTime**

Returns the amount of time since video recording was last started.

```
time = MovieRecording_GetTime()
```

Used in the default UI to show the length of the recording in progress when mousing over the recording indicator on the minimap.

May return a nonsensical value if no video has been recorded since logging in.

Returns:

time—Amount of time since video recording was last started (HH:MM:SS) (string)

Mac OS X only **MovieRecording_GetViewportWidth**

Returns the current width of the game display.

```
width = MovieRecording_GetViewportWidth()
```

Used in the default UI to allow the current screen resolution (or an integral factor thereof) to be selected as the video recording resolution.

Returns:

width—Width of the game display (number)

Mac OS X only **MovieRecording_IsCodecSupported**

Returns whether a video codec is supported on the current system.

```
isSupported = MovieRecording_IsCodecSupported(codecID)
```

Arguments:

codecID—Four-byte identifier of a QuickTime codec (number)

- 1635148593—H.264; supported natively by Apple devices like the iPod, iPhone and AppleTV; best ratio quality/size but slowest to compress
- 1768124260—Apple Intermediate Codec; fastest to compress, but exclusive to Mac OS X
- 1835692129—Motion JPEG; faster to compress than H.264 but it will generate a bigger file
- 1836070006—MPEG-4; supported by many digital cameras and iMovie

Returns:

isSupported—true if the codec is supported on the current system, otherwise false (boolean)

Mac OS X only **MovieRecording_IsCompressing**

Returns whether a movie file is currently being compressed.

```
isCompressing = MovieRecording_IsCompressing()
```

Returns:

isCompressing—true if the client is currently compressing a recording; otherwise false (boolean)

Mac OS X only **MovieRecording_IsCursorRecordingSupported**

Returns whether the current system supports recording the mouse cursor in movies.

```
isSupported = MovieRecording_IsCursorRecordingSupported()
```

Returns:

isSupported—True if the cursor recording option should be enabled; otherwise false (boolean)

Mac OS X only **MovieRecording_IsRecording**

Returns whether movie recording is currently in progress.

```
isRecording = MovieRecording_IsRecording()
```

Returns:

isRecording—1 if the client is currently recording, otherwise nil (1nil)

MovieRecording_IsSupported

Returns whether movie recording is supported on the current system.

```
isSupported = MovieRecording_IsSupported()
```

Returns:

isSupported—true if the client supports video recording; otherwise nil (boolean)

MovieRecording_MaxLength

Returns the maximum length of recorded video for a given set of video recording parameters.

```
time = MovieRecording_MaxLength(width, framerate, sound)
```

The value returned reflects both the data rate associated with the given parameters and the amount of space remaining on the hard drive.

Arguments:

`width`—Width of the output video (in pixels) (`number`)

`framerate`—Number of video frames to be recorded per second (`number`)

`sound`—1 if game audio is to be captured with video; otherwise 0 (`number`)

Returns:

`time`—Maximum length of recorded video (HH:MM:SS) (`string`)

MovieRecording_QueueMovieToCompress

Queues an uncompressed movie for compression.

```
MovieRecording_QueueMovieToCompress("filename")
```

If there are no items currently in the queue the movie will begin compressing immediately.

Arguments:

`filename`—Path to an uncompressed movie (as provided in the `MOVIE_UNCOMPRESSED_MOVIE` event) (`string`)

MovieRecording_SearchUncompressedMovie

Enables or disables a search for uncompressed movies.

```
MovieRecording_SearchUncompressedMovie(enable)
```

After calling this function with `true`, a `MOVIE_UNCOMPRESSED_MOVIE` fires for the first uncompressed movie found (causing the default UI to prompt the user to choose whether to compress, ignore, or delete the movie). Calling this function with `false` ignores the movie, causing the search to continue (firing a `MOVIE_UNCOMPRESSED_MOVIE` event for the next uncompressed movie found, and so forth).

Arguments:

`enable`—True to begin searching for uncompressed movies, `false` to ignore a movie for compression (`boolean`)

MovieRecording_Toggle

Begins or ends video recording.

Used by the `MOVIE_RECORDING_STARTSTOP` key binding.

MovieRecording_ToggleGUI

Enables or disables inclusion of UI elements in a video recording.

Equivalent to the `MovieRecordingGUI` CVar, but provided as a convenience for the `MOVIE_RECORDING_GUI` so UI recording can be turned on or off while a movie is recording.

Protected Mac OS X only	**MusicPlayer_BackTrack** Causes iTunes to return to the previous track played. Used by the iTunes Remote key bindings only available on the Mac OS X WoW client. Only has effect while the iTunes application is open.

Protected Mac OS X only	**MusicPlayer_NextTrack** Causes iTunes to play the next track in sequence. Used by the iTunes Remote key bindings only available on the Mac OS X WoW client. Only has effect while the iTunes application is open.

Protected Mac OS X only	**MusicPlayer_PlayPause** Causes iTunes to start or pause playback. Used by the iTunes Remote key bindings only available on the Mac OS X WoW client. Only has effect while the iTunes application is open.

Protected Mac OS X only	**MusicPlayer_VolumeDown** Causes iTunes to lower its playback volume. Affects the iTunes volume setting only, not the overall system volume or any of WoW's volume settings. Used by the iTunes Remote key bindings only available on the Mac OS X WoW client. Only has effect while the iTunes application is open.

Protected Mac OS X only	**MusicPlayer_VolumeUp** Causes iTunes to raise its playback volume. Affects the iTunes volume setting only, not the overall system volume or any of WoW's volume settings. Used by the iTunes Remote key bindings only available on the Mac OS X WoW client. Only has effect while the iTunes application is open.

Protected	**NewGMTicket** Opens a new GM support ticket.

```
NewGMTicket("text", needResponse)
```

The default UI sets the `needResponse` flag to `true` for "Talk to a GM" and "Stuck" tickets, and `false` for "Report an issue" tickets.

Arguments:

`text`—The text to be sent in the ticket (`string`)

`needResponse`—`true` if the issue requires personal response from a GM; otherwise `false` (`boolean`)

NextView

Moves the camera to the next predefined setting.

There are five "slots" for saved camera settings, indexed 1-5. These views can be set and accessed directly using `SaveView()` and `SetView()`, and cycled through using `NextView()` and `PrevView()`.

NoPlayTime

Returns whether the player has exceeded the allowed play time limit.

```
hasNoTime = NoPlayTime()
```

When in this state, the player is unable to gain loot or XP or complete quests and cannot use trade skills; returning to normal requires logging out of the game for a period of time (see `GetBillingTimeRested`).

Only used in locales where the length of play sessions is restricted (e.g. mainland China).

Returns:

`hasNoTime`—1 if the player is out of play time, otherwise `nil` (1nil)

NotWhileDeadError

Causes the default UI to display an error message indicating that actions are disallowed while the player is dead.

Fires a `UI_ERROR_MESSAGE` event containing a localized message identified by the global variable `ERR_PLAYER_DEAD`.

NotifyInspect

Marks a unit for inspection and requests talent data from the server.

`NotifyInspect("unit")`

Information about the inspected item's equipment can be retrieved immediately using Inventory APIs (e.g. `GetInventoryItemLink("target",1)`). Talent data is not available immediately; the `INSPECT_TALENT_READY` event fires once the inspected unit's talent information can be retrieved using Talent APIs (e.g. `GetTalentInfo(1,1,true)`).

Arguments:

`unit`—A unit to inspect (string, unitID)

NumTaxiNodes

Returns the number of flight points on the taxi map.

`numNodes = NumTaxiNodes()`

Only returns valid data while interacting with a flight master (i.e. between the `TAXIMAP_OPENED` and `TAXIMAP_CLOSED` events).

Returns:

`numNodes`—Number of flight points on the taxi map (number)

OfferPetition

Requests an arena or guild charter signature from the targeted unit.

OffhandHasWeapon

Returns whether the player has an equipped weapon in the off hand slot.

`hasWeapon = OffhandHasWeapon()`

Returns:

`hasWeapon`—1 if the player has a weapon equipped in the off hand slot; otherwise `nil` (1nil)

OpenCalendar

Queries the server for calendar status information.

May cause one or more CALENDAR_UPDATE_* events to fire depending on the contents of the player's calendar. In the default UI, called when the calendar is shown.

OpeningCinematic

Displays the introductory cinematic for the player's race.

Only has effect if the player has never gained any experience.

PartialPlayTime

Returns whether the player is near the allowed play time limit.

```
partialPlayTime = PartialPlayTime()
```

When in this state, the player receives half the normal amount of money and XP from kills and quests and cannot use trade skills; returning to normal requires logging out of the game for a period of time (see GetBilling TimeRested).

Only used in locales where the length of play sessions is restricted (e.g. mainland China).

Returns:

partialPlayTime—1 if the character gains only partial xp, nil if not. (1nil)

`Confirmation` ### PetAbandon

Releases the player's pet.

For Hunter pets, this function sends the pet away, never to return (in the default UI, it's called when accepting the "Are you sure you want to permanently abandon your pet?" dialog). For other pets, this function is equivalent to PetDismiss().

`Protected` ### PetAggressiveMode

Enables aggressive mode for the player's pet.

In this mode, the pet automatically attacks any nearby hostile targets.

`Protected` ### PetAttack

Instructs the pet to attack.

```
PetAttack(["unit"]) or PetAttack(["name"])
```

The pet will attack the player's current target if no unit is specified.

Arguments:

unit (optional)—A unit to attack (string, unitID)

name (optional)—The name of a unit to attack (string)

PetCanBeAbandoned

Returns whether the player's pet can be abandoned.

```
canAbandon = PetCanBeAbandoned()
```

Only Hunter pets can be permanently abandoned.

Returns:

canAbandon—1 if the player's pet can be abandoned, otherwise nil (1nil)

PetCanBeDismissed

Returns whether a Dismiss Pet command should be available for the player's pet.

```
canDismiss = PetCanBeDismissed()
```

Returns 1 for hunter pets even though they use the Dismiss Pet (cast) spell instead of a Dismiss Pet (instant) command; the value of `PetCanBe Abandoned()` overrides this in causing the default UI to hide the command. Currently unused, but may be used in the future for other pets.

Returns:

`canDismiss`—1 if a Dismiss Pet command should be available for the player's pet; otherwise `nil` (1nil)

PetCanBeRenamed

Returns whether the player's pet can be renamed.

```
canRename = PetCanBeRenamed()
```

Only hunter pets can be renamed, and only once (barring use of a Certificate of Ownership).

Returns:

`canRename`—1 if the player can rename the currently controlled pet, otherwise `nil` (1nil)

`Protected` **PetDefensiveMode**

Enables defensive mode for the player's pet.

In this mode, the pet automatically attacks only units which attack it or the player or units the player is attacking.

PetDismiss

Dismisses the currently controlled pet.

Used for dismissing Warlock pets, Mind Control targets, etc. Has no effect for Hunter pets, which can only be dismissed using the Dismiss Pet spell.

`Protected` **PetFollow**

Instructs the pet to follow the player.

If the pet is currently attacking a target, the pet will stop attacking.

PetHasActionBar

Returns whether the player's current pet has an action bar.

```
hasActionBar = PetHasActionBar()
```

Returns:

`hasActionBar`—Returns 1 if the player's pet has an action bar; otherwise `nil` (1nil)

`Protected` **PetPassiveMode**

Enables passive mode for the player's pet.

In this mode, the pet will not automatically attack any target.

PetRename

Renames the currently controlled pet.

```
PetRename("name" [, "genitive" [, "dative" [, "accusative" ↵
[, "instrumental" [, "prepositional"]]]]])
```

Only Hunter pets can be renamed, and a given pet can only be renamed once (barring use of a Certificate of Ownership).

Arguments:

name—New name for the pet (nominative form on Russian clients) (string)

genitive (optional)—Genitive form of the pet's new name; applies only on Russian clients (string)

dative (optional)—Dative form of the pet's new name; applies only on Russian clients (string)

accusative (optional)—Accusative form of the pet's new name; applies only on Russian clients (string)

instrumental (optional)—Instrumental form of the pet's new name; applies only on Russian clients (string)

prepositional (optional)—Prepositional form of the pet's new name; applies only on Russian clients (string)

Protected

PetStopAttack

Instructs the pet to stop attacking.

Protected

PetWait

Instructs the pet to stay at its current location.

If the pet is currently attacking a target, the pet will stop attacking.

No Combat

PickupAction

Puts the contents of an action bar slot onto the cursor or the cursor contents into an action bar slot.

```
PickupAction(slot)
```

After an action is picked up via this function, it can only be placed into other action bar slots (with PlaceAction() or by calling PickupAction() again), even if the action is an item which could otherwise be placed elsewhere. Unlike many other "pickup" cursor functions, this function removes the picked-up action from the source slot. An action slot can be emptied by calling this function followed by ClearCursor().

If the action slot is empty and the cursor already holds an action, a spell, a companion (mount or non-combat pet), a macro, an equipment set, or an item (with a "Use:" effect), it is put into the action slot. If both the cursor and the slot hold an action (or any of the above data types), the contents of the cursor and the slot are exchanged.

Arguments:

slot—An action bar slot (number, actionID)

PickupBagFromSlot

Puts an equipped container onto the cursor.

```
PickupBagFromSlot(slot)
```

Arguments:

slot—An inventory slot containing a bag (see `GetInventorySlotInfo()`, `ContainerIDToInventoryID()`) (number, inventoryID)

PickupCompanion

Puts a non-combat pet or mount onto the cursor.

```
PickupCompanion("type", index)
```

Arguments:

type—Type of companion (string)

- ▪ CRITTER—A non-combat pet
- ▪ MOUNT—A mount

index—Index of a companion (between 1 and `GetNumCompanions(type)`) (number)

PickupContainerItem

Picks up an item from or puts an item into a slot in one of the player's bags or other containers.

```
PickupContainerItem(container, slot)
```

If the cursor is empty and the referenced container slot contains an item, that item is put onto the cursor. If the cursor contains an item and the slot is empty, the item is placed into the slot. If both the cursor and the slot contain items, the contents of the cursor and the container slot are exchanged.

An item picked up from a container is not removed from its slot (until put elsewhere); when an item is picked up, the slot becomes locked, preventing other changes to its contents until the disposition (movement, trade, mailing, auctioning, destruction, etc) of the picked-up item is resolved.

Arguments:

container—Index of one of the player's bags or other containers (number, containerID)

slot—Index of an item slot within the container (number, containerSlotID)

Example:

```
-- Pickup the first item in your backpack
PickupContainerItem(0, 1)
```

PickupEquipmentSet

Puts an equipment set (specified by index) on the cursor.

```
PickupEquipmentSet(index)
```

Can be used to place an equipment set in an action bar slot.

Arguments:

index—Index of an equipment set (between 1 and `GetNumEquipmentSets()`) (number)

PickupEquipmentSetByName

Puts an equipment set on the cursor.

```
PickupEquipmentSetByName("name")
```

Can be used to place an equipment set in an action bar slot.

Arguments:

name—Name of an equipment set (case sensitive) (string)

PickupGuildBankItem

Picks up an item from or puts an item into the guild bank.

```
PickupGuildBankItem(tab, slot)
```

If the cursor is empty and the referenced guild bank slot contains an item, that item is put onto the cursor. If the cursor contains an item and the slot is empty, the item is placed into the slot. If both the cursor and the slot contain items, the contents of the cursor and the guild bank slot are exchanged.

Arguments:

tab—Index of a guild bank tab (number)

slot—Index of an item slot in the guild bank tab (number)

PickupGuildBankMoney

Puts money from the guild bank onto the cursor.

```
PickupGuildBankMoney(amount)
```

Money is not actually withdrawn from the guild bank; in the default UI, when the cursor "puts" the money into one of the player's bags, it calls Withdraw GuildBankMoney().

Arguments:

amount—Amount of money to pick up (in copper) (number)

PickupInventoryItem

Picks up an item from or puts an item into an equipment slot.

```
PickupInventoryItem(slot)
```

If the cursor is empty and the referenced inventory slot contains an item, that item is put onto the cursor. If the cursor contains an item (which can be equipped in the slot) and the slot is empty, the item is placed into the slot. If both the cursor and the slot contain items, the contents of the cursor and the inventory slot are exchanged.

An item picked up from an inventory slot is not removed from the slot (until put elsewhere); when an item is picked up, the slot becomes locked, preventing other changes to its contents until the disposition (movement, trade, destruction, etc) of the picked-up item is resolved.

Arguments:

slot—An inventory slot number, as can be obtained from GetInventory SlotInfo (number, inventoryID)

PickupItem

Puts an arbitrary item onto the cursor.

`PickupItem(itemID)` or `PickupItem("itemName")` or `PickupItem("itemLink")`

Puts an item onto the cursor regardless of its location (equipped, bags, bank or not even in the player's possession); can be used to put an item into an action slot (see `PlaceAction()`) even if the player does not currently hold the item. Since the item is not picked up from a specific location, this function cannot be used to move an item to another bag, trade it to another player, attach it to a mail message, destroy it, etc.

Arguments:

`itemID`—An item's ID (`number`)

`itemName`—An item's name (`string`)

`itemLink`—An item's hyperlink, or any string containing the `itemString` portion of an item link (`string`)

PickupMacro

Puts a macro onto the cursor.

`PickupMacro(index)` or `PickupMacro("name")`

Arguments:

`index`—Index of a macro (`number`, macroID)

`name`—Name of a macro (`string`)

PickupMerchantItem

Puts an item available for purchase from a vendor onto the cursor.

`PickupMerchantItem(index)`

Arguments:

`index`—Index of an item in the vendor's listing (between 1 and `GetMerchantNumItems()`) (`number`)

PickupPetAction

Puts the contents of a pet action slot onto the cursor or the cursor contents into a pet action slot.

`PickupPetAction(index)`

Only pet actions and spells from the "pet" portion of the spellbook can be placed into pet action slots.

If the cursor is empty and the referenced pet action slot contains an action, that action is put onto the cursor (but remains in the slot). If the cursor contains a pet action or pet spell and the slot is empty, the action/spell is placed into the slot. If both the cursor and the slot contain pet actions, the contents of the cursor and the pet action slot are exchanged.

Arguments:

`index`—Index of a pet action (between 1 and `NUM_PET_ACTION_SLOTS`) (`number`)

PickupPlayerMoney

Puts an amount of the player's money onto the cursor.

`PickupPlayerMoney(amount)`

Money is not immediately deducted from the player's total savings (though it looks like it on the default UI's money displays, which generally show `GetMoney()-GetCursorMoney()`).

Arguments:

`amount`—Amount of money to put on the cursor (in copper) (`number`)

PickupSpell

Puts a spell from the player's or pet's spellbook onto the cursor.

`PickupSpell(id, "bookType")`

Arguments:

`id`—Index of a spell in the spellbook (`number`, spellbookID)

`bookType`—Type of spellbook (`string`)

- `pet`—The pet's spellbook
- `spell`—The player's spellbook

PickupStablePet

Puts a pet from the stables onto the cursor.

`PickupStablePet(index)`

Use with `ClickStablePet` to move pets between stabled and active status.

Arguments:

`index`—Index of a stable slot (`number`)

- `0`—Active pet
- `1 to NUM_PET_STABLE_SLOTS`—A stable slot

PickupTradeMoney

Puts money offered by the player for trade onto the cursor.

`PickupTradeMoney(amount)`

Money put onto the cursor is subtracted from the amount offered for trade (see `GetPlayerTradeMoney()`).

Arguments:

`amount`—Amount of money to take from the trade window (in copper) (`number`)

| Protected |

PitchDownStart

Begins adjusting the player character's angle of vertical movement downward. Affects only the angle or slope of movement for swimming or flying; has no immediately visible effect if the player is not moving, but alters the trajectory followed as soon as the player begins moving. Continuously adjusts pitch until the minimum angle is reached or `PitchDownStop()` is called.

Used by the `PITCHDOWN` binding.

| Protected | **PitchDownStop**

Ends movement initiated by `PitchDownStart`.

| Protected | **PitchUpStart**

Begins adjusting the player character's angle of vertical movement upward.

Affects only the angle or slope of movement for swimming or flying; has no immediately visible effect if the player is not moving, but alters the trajectory followed as soon as the player begins moving. Continuously adjusts pitch until the maximum angle is reached or `PitchUpStop()` is called.

Used by the `PITCHUP` binding.

| Protected | **PitchUpStop**

Ends movement initiated by `PitchUpStart`.

| No Combat | **PlaceAction**

Puts the contents of the cursor into an action bar slot.

```
PlaceAction(slot)
```

If the action slot is empty and the cursor already holds an action, a spell, a companion (mount or non-combat pet), a macro, an equipment set, or an item (with a "Use:" effect), it is put into the action slot. If both the cursor and the slot hold an action (or any of the above data types), the contents of the cursor and the slot are exchanged.

Does nothing if the cursor is empty.

Arguments:

`slot`—Destination action bar slot (number, actionID)

| Confirmation | **PlaceAuctionBid**

Places a bid on (or buys out) an auction item.

```
PlaceAuctionBid("list", index, bid)
```

Attempting to bid an amount equal to or greater than the auction's buyout price will buy out the auction (spending only the exact buyout price) instead of placing a bid.

Arguments:

`list`—Type of auction listing (string)

- `bidder`—Auctions the player has bid on
- `list`—Auctions the player can browse and bid on or buy out
- `owner`—Auctions the player placed

`index`—Index of an auction in the listing (number)

`bid`—Amount to bid (in copper) (number)

| Confirmation | **PlaceGlyphInSocket**

Applies the glyph currently awaiting a target to a socket.

```
PlaceGlyphInSocket(socket)
```

Only valid during glyph application: when the player has activated the glyph item but before she has chosen the glyph slot to put it in (i.e. the glowing hand cursor is showing).

This function does not ask for confirmation before overwriting an existing glyph. However, calling this function only begins the "spellcast" that applies the glyph, so canceling glyph application is still possible.

Arguments:

`socket`—Which glyph socket to apply the glyph to (between `1` and `NUM_GLYPH_SLOTS`) (number, glyphIndex)

PlayMusic

Plays an audio file as background music.

```
PlayMusic("musicfile")
```

Any other background music that is currently playing will be faded out as the new music begins; if the `Sound_ZoneMusicNoDelay` is set, music will loop continuously until `StopMusic()` is called.

WoW supports WAV, MP3 and Ogg audio formats.

Arguments:

`musicfile`—Path to a music file (`string`)

Example:

```
-- play one of WoW's built-in music files
PlayMusic("Sound\\Music\\GlueScreenMusic\\wow_main_theme.mp3")
-- play a music file from an addon
PlayMusic("Interface\\AddOns\\MyAddOn\\MyMusic.mp3")
```

PlaySound

Plays one of WoW's built-in sound effects.

```
PlaySound("sound")
```

Only supports sounds found in the `Sound\Interface` directory within WoW's MPQ files; to play other built-in sounds or sounds in an addon directory, use `PlaySoundFile()`.

Arguments:

`sound`—Name of a built-in sound effect (`string`)

Example:

```
PlaySound("AuctionWindowOpen");
```

PlaySoundFile

Plays an audio file at a given path.

```
PlaySoundFile("soundFile")
```

For a shorter way to specify one of WoW's built-in UI sound effects, see `PlaySound()`.

WoW supports WAV, MP3 and Ogg audio formats.

Arguments:

`soundFile`—A path to the sound file to be played (`string`)

Example:

```
-- play one of WoW's built-in sound files
PlayMusic("Sound\\Spells\\AbolishMagic.wav")
```

```
-- play a sound file from an addon
PlayMusic("Interface\\AddOns\\MyAddOn\\MySound.wav")
```

PlayerCanTeleport

Returns whether the player can accept a summons.

```
amount = PlayerCanTeleport()
```

Returns:

amount—True if the player is currently allowed to accept a summons (boolean)

PlayerIsPVPInactive

Returns whether a battleground participant is inactive (and eligible for reporting as AFK).

```
isInactive = PlayerIsPVPInactive("name") or PlayerIsPVPInactive("unit")
```

Arguments:

name—Name of a friendly player unit in the current battleground (string)

unit—A friendly player unit in the current battleground (string, unitID)

Returns:

isInactive—True if the unit can be reported as AFK; otherwise false (boolean)

PrevView

Moves the camera to the previous predefined setting.

There are five "slots" for saved camera settings, indexed 1-5. These views can be set and accessed directly using SaveView() and SetView(), and cycled through using NextView() and PrevView().

ProcessMapClick

Possibly changes the WorldMap based on a mouse click.

```
ProcessMapClick(clickX, clickY)
```

May change the map zone or zoom based on the click location: e.g. if the world map shows Dragonblight and one clicks in the area labeled "Wintergrasp" on the map, the current map zone changes to show Wintergrasp.

Arguments:

clickX—Horizontal position of the click relative to the current world map (0 = left edge, 1 = right edge) (number)

clickY—Vertical position of the click relative to the current world map (0 = top, 1 = bottom) (number)

PromoteToAssistant

Promotes a raid member to raid assistant.

```
PromoteToAssistant("unit") or PromoteToAssistant("name" [, exactMatch])
```

Arguments:

unit—A unit in the raid (string, unitID)

name—Name of a unit in the raid (string)

exactMatch (optional)—True to check only units whose name exactly matches the name given; false to allow partial matches (boolean)

PromoteToLeader

Promotes a player to party/raid leader.

```
PromoteToLeader("unit") or PromoteToLeader("name" [, exactMatch])
```

Arguments:

unit—A unit in the party or raid (string, unitID)

name—Name of a party member (string)

exactMatch (optional)—True to check only units whose name exactly matches the name given; false to allow partial matches (boolean)

Confirmation ### PurchaseSlot

Purchases the next available bank slot.

Only available while interacting with a banker NPC (i.e. between the BANKFRAME_OPENED and BANKFRAME_CLOSED events).

PutItemInBackpack

Puts the item on the cursor into the player's backpack.

```
hadItem = PutItemInBackpack()
```

The item will be placed in the lowest numbered slot (containerSlotID) in the player's backpack.

Causes an error message (UI_ERROR_MESSAGE) if the backpack is full.

Returns:

hadItem—1 if the cursor had an item; otherwise nil (1nil)

PutItemInBag

Puts the item on the cursor into the one of the player's bags or other containers.

```
hadItem = PutItemInBag(container)
```

The item will be placed in the lowest numbered slot (containerSlotID) in the container.

Causes an error message (UI_ERROR_MESSAGE) if the container is full. Cannot be used to place an item into the player's backpack; see PutItemInBackpack().

Arguments:

container—Index of one of the player's bags or other containers (number, containerID)

Returns:

hadItem—1 if the cursor had a item; otherwise nil (1nil)

QueryAuctionItems

Requests data from the server for the list of auctions meeting given search criteria.

```
QueryAuctionItems(["name" [, minLevel [, maxLevel [, invTypeIndex ↵
[, classIndex [, subClassIndex [, page [, isUsable [, minQuality ↵
[, getAll]]]]]]]]]])
```

If any search criterion is omitted or nil, the search will include all possible values for that criterion.

Search queries are throttled, preventing abuse of the server by clients sending too many queries in short succession. Normal queries can be sent once every few seconds; mass queries return all results in the auction house instead of one "page" at a time, and can only be sent once every several minutes.

Query results are not returned immediately: the AUCTION_ITEM_LIST_UPDATE event fires once data is available; listing information can then be retrieved using GetAuctionItemInfo() or other Auction APIs.

Arguments:

name (optional)—Full or partial item name to limit search results; will match any item whose name contains this string (string)

minLevel (optional)—Maximum required character level of items to limit search results (number)

maxLevel (optional)—Maximum required character level of items to limit search results (number)

invTypeIndex (optional)—Index of an item inventory type to limit search results (note that GetAuctionInvTypes(classIndex, subClassIndex) returns a list of token, display pairs for each inventory type; thus, to convert a token index from that list for use here, divide by 2 and round up) (number)

classIndex (optional)—Index of an item class to limit search results (in the list returned by GetAuctionItemClasses()) (number)

subClassIndex (optional)—Index of an item subclass to limit search results (in the list returned by GetAuctionItemSubClasses(classIndex)) (number)

page (optional)—Which "page" of search results to list, if more than NUM_AUCTION_ITEMS_PER_PAGE (50) auctions are available; nil to query the first (or only) page (number)

isUsable (optional)—True to limit search results to only items which can be used or equipped by the player character; otherwise false (boolean)

minQuality (optional)—Minimum quality (rarity) level of items to limit search results (itemQuality)

getAll (optional)—True to perform a mass query (returning all listings at once); false to perform a normal query (returning a large number of listings in "pages" of NUM_AUCTION_ITEMS_PER_PAGE [50] at a time) (boolean)

QueryGuildBankLog

Requests the item transaction log for a guild bank tab from the server.

QueryGuildBankLog(tab)

Fires the GUILDBANKLOG_UPDATE event when transaction log information becomes available.

Arguments:

tab—Index of a guild bank tab (between 1 and GetNumGuildBankTabs()) (number)

QueryGuildBankTab

Requests information about the contents of a guild bank tab from the server.

QueryGuildBankTab(tab)

Fires the GUILDBANKBAGSLOTS_CHANGED event when information about the tab's contents becomes available.

Arguments:

tab—Index of a guild bank tab (between 1 and GetNumGuildBankTabs()) (number)

QueryGuildBankText

Requests guild bank tab info text from the server.

QueryGuildBankText(tab)

The text is not returned immediately; the GUILDBANK_UPDATE_TEXT event fires when text is available for retrieval by the GetGuildBankText() function.

Arguments:

tab—Index of a guild bank tab (between 1 and GetNumGuildBankTabs()) (number)

QueryGuildEventLog

Requests guild event log information from the server.

Fires the GUILD_EVENT_LOG_UPDATE event when event log information becomes available.

QuestChooseRewardError

Causes the default UI to display an error message indicating that the player must choose a reward to complete the quest presented by a questgiver.

Fires a UI_ERROR_MESSAGE event containing a localized message identified by the global variable ERR_QUEST_MUST_CHOOSE. Choose wisely.

QuestFlagsPVP

Returns whether accepting the offered quest will flag the player for PvP.

questFlag = QuestFlagsPVP()

Only valid when the questgiver UI is showing the accept/decline stage of a quest dialog (between the QUEST_DETAIL and QUEST_FINISHED events); otherwise may return nil or a value from the most recently displayed quest.

Returns:

questFlag—1 if accepting the quest will flag the player for PvP for as long as it remains in the quest log; otherwise nil (1nil)

QuestLogPushQuest

Shares a quest with other group members.

QuestLogPushQuest([questIndex])

Arguments:

questIndex (optional)—Index of a quest in the quest log (between 1 and GetNumQuestLogEntries()); if omitted, defaults to the selected quest (number)

Quit

Attempts to exit the World of Warcraft client.

Results vary based on current conditions:

- If the player is in combat or under other temporary restrictions (e.g. falling), fires the `UI_ERROR_MESSAGE` event with a message indicating the player cannot log out at the moment.

- If the player is not in an inn, major city, or other "rest" area (i.e. `IsResting()` returns `nil`), fires the `PLAYER_QUITING` event, causing the default UI to show a countdown, quitting WoW after a period of time if not canceled.

- If the player is in a "rest" area, quits the game immediately.

RandomRoll

Initiates a public, server-side "dice roll".

```
RandomRoll(min, max)
```

Used in the default UI to implement the `/roll` chat command; when called, the server generates a random integer and sends it to the player and all others nearby (or in the same party/raid) via a `CHAT_MSG_SYSTEM` event. (The server message is formatted according to the global `RANDOM_ROLL_RESULT`; e.g. "Leeroy rolls 3 (1-100)".)

For random number generation that does not involve the server or send visible messages to other clients, see `math.random`.

Arguments:

`min`—Lowest number to be randomly chosen (`number`, `string`)

`max`—Highest number to be randomly chosen (`number`, `string`)

RegisterCVar

Registers a configuration variable to be saved.

```
RegisterCVar("cvar", "default")
```

Arguments:

`cvar`—Name of a CVar (`string`)

`default`—Default value of the CVar (`string`)

Hardware

ReloadUI

Reloads the user interface.

Saved variables are written to disk, the default UI is reloaded, and all enabled non-LoadOnDemand addons are loaded, including any addons previously disabled which were enabled during the session (see `EnableAddOn()` et al).

RemoveChatWindowChannel

Removes a channel from a chat window's list of saved channel subscriptions.

```
RemoveChatWindowChannel(index, "channel")
```

Used by the default UI's function `ChatFrame_RemoveChannel()` which manages the set of channel messages shown in a displayed ChatFrame.

Arguments:

`index`—Index of a chat frame (between 1 and `NUM_CHAT_WINDOWS`) (`number`)

`channel`—Name of the channel to remove (`string`)

RemoveChatWindowMessages

Removes a message type from a chat window's list of saved message subscriptions.

```
RemoveChatWindowMessages(index, "messageGroup")
```

Used by the default UI's functions `ChatFrame_RemoveMessageGroup()` and `ChatFrame_RemoveAllMessageGroups()` which manage the set of message types shown in a displayed ChatFrame.

Arguments:

`index`—Index of a chat frame (between 1 and `NUM_CHAT_WINDOWS`) (number)

`messageGroup`—Token identifying a message type (`string`, chatMsgType)

RemoveFriend

Removes a character from the friends list.

```
RemoveFriend("name")
```

Arguments:

`name`—Name of a character to remove from the friends list (`string`)

Confirmation ### RemoveGlyphFromSocket

Removes the glyph from a socket.

```
RemoveGlyphFromSocket(socket)
```

Arguments:

`socket`—Which glyph socket to query (between 1 and `NUM_GLYPH_SLOTS`) (number, glyphIndex)

RemoveQuestWatch

Removes a quest from the objectives tracker.

```
RemoveQuestWatch(questIndex)
```

Arguments:

`questIndex`—Index of a quest in the quest log (between 1 and `GetNumQuestLogEntries()`) (number)

RemoveTrackedAchievement

Removes an achievement from the objectives tracker UI.

```
RemoveTrackedAchievement(id)
```

Arguments:

`id`—The numeric ID of an achievement (number)

RenameEquipmentSet

Changes the name of a saved equipment set.

```
RenameEquipmentSet("name", "newName")
```

Not used in the default UI; may be deprecated in future patches.

Arguments:

`name`—Name of an equipment set (case sensitive) (`string`)

`newName`—New name for the set (`string`)

RenamePetition

Renames the guild or arena team to be created by the open petition.

```
RenamePetition("name")
```

Arguments:

name—New name for the guild or arena team (string)

RepairAllItems

Attempts to repair all of the player's damaged items.

```
RepairAllItems([useGuildMoney])
```

Arguments:

useGuildMoney (optional)—1 to use guild bank money (if available); nil or omitted to use the player's own money (1nil)

Confirmation

ReplaceEnchant

Confirms replacing an existing enchantment.

Usable in response to the REPLACE_ENCHANT event which fires when the player attempts to apply a temporary or permanent enchantment to an item which already has one.

Confirmation

ReplaceTradeEnchant

Confirms replacement of an existing enchantment when offering an enchantment for trade.

After confirming, the enchantment is not actually performed until both parties accept the trade.

RepopMe

Releases the player's spirit to the nearest graveyard.

Only has effect if the player is dead.

ReportPlayerIsPVPAFK

Reports a battleground participant as AFK.

```
ReportPlayerIsPVPAFK("name") or ReportPlayerIsPVPAFK("unit")
```

Arguments:

name—Name of a friendly player unit in the current battleground (string)

unit—A friendly player unit in the current battleground (string, unitID)

RequestBattlefieldPositions

Requests information from the server about team member positions in the current battleground.

Automatically called in the default UI by UIParent's and WorldMapFrame's OnUpdate handlers.

RequestBattlefieldScoreData

Requests battlefield score data from the server.

Score data is not returned immediately; the UPDATE_BATTLEFIELD_SCORE event fires once information is available and can be retrieved by calling GetBattlefieldScore() and related functions.

RequestBattlegroundInstanceInfo

Requests information about available instances of a battleground from the server.

```
RequestBattlegroundInstanceInfo(index)
```

The `PVPQUEUE_ANYWHERE_SHOW` event fires once information is available; data can then be retrieved by calling `GetNumBattlefields()` and `GetBattlefieldInstanceInfo()`.

Arguments:

index—Index of a battleground (between 1 and `NUM_BATTLEGROUNDS`) (`number`)

RequestInspectHonorData

Requests PvP honor and arena data from the server for the currently inspected unit.

Once the `INSPECT_HONOR_UPDATE` event fires, PvP honor and arena information can be retrieved using `GetInspectHonorData(team)` and `GetInspectArenaTeamData()`.

RequestRaidInfo

Requests information about saved instances from the server.

Data is not returned immediately; the `UPDATE_INSTANCE_INFO` event when the raid information is available for retrieval via `GetSavedInstanceInfo()` and related functions.

RequestTimePlayed

Requests information from the server about the player character's total time spent online.

Information is not returned immediately; the `TIME_PLAYED_MSG` event fires when the requested data is available.

ResetCPUUsage

Resets CPU usage statistics.

Only has effect if the `scriptProfile` CVar is set to 1.

ResetChatColors

Removes all saved color settings for chat message types, resetting them to default values.

ResetChatWindows

Removes all saved chat window settings, resetting them to default values.

Used by the default UI's function `FCF_ResetChatWindows()` which resets the appearance and behavior of displayed FloatingChatFrames.

ResetCursor

Returns the cursor to its normal appearance (the glove pointer) and behavior.

Has effect after the cursor image/mode has been changed via `SetCursor()`, `ShowContainerSellCursor()`, or similar. Has no immediately visible effect if the cursor is holding an item, spell, or other data.

ResetDisabledAddOns

Reverts changes to the enabled/disabled state of addons.

Any addons enabled or disabled in the current session will return to their enabled/disabled state as of the last login or UI reload.

ResetGroupPreviewTalentPoints

Reverts all changes made in the Talent UI's preview mode.

```
ResetGroupPreviewTalentPoints(isPet, talentGroup)
```

Arguments:

isPet—`true` to edit talents for the player's pet, `false` to edit talents for the player (`boolean`)

talentGroup—Which set of talents to edit, if the player has Dual Talent Specialization enabled (`number`)

- 1—Primary Talents
- 2—Secondary Talents
- nil—Currently active talents

ResetInstances

Resets all non-saved instances associated with the player.

Only instances to which the player is not saved may be reset (i.e. normal 5-man dungeons, not heroic dungeons or raids), and only by a solo player or group leader.

ResetPreviewTalentPoints

Reverts changes made within a specific tab in the Talent UI's preview mode.

```
ResetPreviewTalentPoints(tabIndex, isPet, talentGroup)
```

Arguments:

tabIndex—Index of a talent school/tab (between 1 and GetNumTalentTabs()) (`number`)

isPet—`true` to edit talents for the player's pet, `false` to edit talents for the player (`boolean`)

talentGroup—Which set of talents to edit, if the player has Dual Talent Specialization enabled (`number`)

- 1—Primary Talents
- 2—Secondary Talents
- nil—Currently active talents

ResetTutorials

Enables contextual tutorial display and clears the list of already displayed tutorials.

Tutorials that have already been shown to the player will appear again (via `TUTORIAL_TRIGGER` events) once their conditions are met. The first tutorial will appear again immediately.

ResetView

Resets a saved camera setting to default values.

```
ResetView(index)
```

There are five "slots" for saved camera settings, indexed 1-5. These views can be set and accessed directly using `SaveView()` and `SetView()`, and cycled through using `NextView()` and `PrevView()`.

Arguments:

`index`—Index of a saved camera setting (between 1 and 5) (`number`)

RespondInstanceLock

Allows leaving a recently entered instance to which the player would otherwise be saved.

```
RespondInstanceLock(response)
```

Applies when the player enters an instance to which other members of her group are saved; if the player leaves the instance within the time limit (see `GetInstanceLockTimeRemaining()`) she will not be saved to the instance.

Arguments:

`response`—Whether the player wishes to remain in the instance (`boolean`)

- ▪ `false`—Exit to the nearest graveyard
- ▪ `true`—Remain in the zone, saving the player to this instance

RestartGx

Restart the client's graphic subsystem.

Does not reload the UI.

RestoreVideoEffectsDefaults

Resets video effects options to default values.

These options are shown in the Video -> Effects panel in the default UI and include settings such as for view distance, texture resolution, and full-screen glow.

RestoreVideoResolutionDefaults

Resets video resolution options to default values.

These options are shown in the Video -> Resolution panel in the default UI and include settings such as screen resolution, windowed mode, and gamma.

RestoreVideoStereoDefaults

Resets stereoscopic 3D video options to default values.

These options are shown in the Video -> Stereo panel in the default UI and include settings for convergence and eye separation.

ResurrectGetOfferer

Returns the name of a unit offering to resurrect the player.

```
name = ResurrectGetOfferer()
```

Returns nil if no resurrection has been offered or if an offer has expired.

Returns:

name—Name of the unit offering resurrection (`string`)

ResurrectHasSickness

Returns whether accepting an offered resurrection spell will cause the player to suffer Resurrection Sickness.

`hasSickness = ResurrectHasSickness()`

Usable following the `RESURRECT_REQUEST` event which fires when the player is offered resurrection by another unit.

Generally always returns `nil`, as resurrection by other players does not cause sickness.

Returns:

hasSickness—1 if accepting resurrection will cause Resurrection Sickness; otherwise `nil` (`1nil`)

ResurrectHasTimer

Returns whether the player must wait before resurrecting.

`hasTimer = ResurrectHasTimer()`

Applies to resurrection spells offered by other units, resurrecting by returning to the player's corpse as a ghost, and to resurrecting at a graveyard's spirit healer, if the player has recently died several times in short succession. See `GetCorpseRecoveryDelay()` for the time remaining until the player can resurrect.

Returns:

hasTimer—1 if the player must wait before resurrecting; otherwise `nil` (`1nil`)

RetrieveCorpse

Confirms resurrection by returning to the player's corpse.

ReturnInboxItem

Returns a message in the player's inbox to its sender.

`ReturnInboxItem(mailID)`

Arguments:

mailID—Index of a message in the player's inbox (between 1 and `GetInboxNumItems()`) (`number`)

RollOnLoot

Register the player's intent regarding an item up for loot rolling.

`RollOnLoot(id, rollType)`

Rolls are not actually performed until all eligible group members have registered their intent or the time period for rolling expires.

If the item binds on pickup, the `CONFIRM_LOOT_ROLL` event fires, indicating that `ConfirmLootRoll(id)` must be called in order to actually roll on the item.

Arguments:

`id`—Index of an item currently up for loot rolling (as provided in the `START_LOOT_ROLL` event) (`number`)

`rollType`—Type of roll action to perform (`number`)

- `0`—Pass (declines the loot)
- `1`—Roll "need" (wins if highest roll)
- `2`—Roll "greed" (wins if highest roll and no other member rolls "need")

RunBinding

Runs the script associated with a key binding action.

```
RunBinding("COMMAND")
```

Note: this function is not protected, but the scripts for many default key binding actions are (and can only be called by the Blizzard UI).

Arguments:

`COMMAND`—Name of a key binding command (`string`)

Example:

```
-- Take a screenshot
RunBinding("SCREENSHOT")
```

`Protected`   ### RunMacro

Runs a macro.

```
RunMacro(index [, ""button""]) or RunMacro("name" [, ""button""])
```

Arguments:

`index`—Index of a macro (number, macroID)

`name`—Name of a macro (`string`)

`"button"` (optional)—The mouse button used to click the macro; may be used by `[button:_x_]` options in the macro (`string`)

`Protected`   ### RunMacroText

Runs arbitrary text as a macro.

```
RunMacroText(""text"" [, ""button""])
```

Arguments:

`"text"`—The text of the macro to run (`string`)

`"button"` (optional)—The mouse button used to click the macro; may be used by `[button:_x_]` options in the macro (`string`)

RunScript

Runs a string as a Lua script.

```
RunScript("script")
```

Arguments:

`script`—A Lua script to be run (`string`)

Example:

```
-- Print to chat frame
local script = "print(\"Hello World\")"
RunScript(script)
```

SaveBindings

Saves the current set of key bindings.

```
SaveBindings(set)
```

Arguments:

set—A set to which to save the current bindings (number)

- ▪ 1—Account-wide key bindings
- ▪ 2—Character-specific key bindings

Confirmation

SaveEquipmentSet

Saves or creates an equipment set with the player's currently equipped items.

```
SaveEquipmentSet("name", icon)
```

If a set with the same name already exists, that set's contents are overwritten. Set names are case sensitive: if a "Fishing" set already exists, saving a "fishing" set will create a new set instead of overwriting the "Fishing" set.

Arguments:

name—Name of the set (string)

icon—Index of an icon to associate with the set: between 1 and GetNum MacroIcons() for an icon from the set of macro icons; values between -INVSLOT_FIRST_EQUIPPED and -INVSLOT_LAST_EQUIPPED for the icon of an item in the equipment set at that (negative) inventoryID (number)

SaveView

Saves the current camera settings.

```
SaveView(index)
```

There are five "slots" for saved camera settings, indexed 1-5. These views can be set and accessed directly using SaveView() and SetView(), and cycled through using NextView() and PrevView().

Arguments:

index—Index of a saved camera setting (between 1 and 5) (number)

Screenshot

Saves an image of the current game display.

Screenshot images are saved to the folder Screenshots within the folder where the World of Warcraft client is installed.

Taking a screenshot fires the SCREENSHOT_SUCCEEDED event (or the SCREENSHOT_FAILED event in case of an error), which causes the default UI to display a message in the middle of the screen. Additional screenshots taken while this message is displayed will include it. The default UI's TakeScreenshot() function hides this message so it is not included in screenshots.

Blizzard UI

SecondsToTime

Returns a description of an amount of time in appropriate units.

```
time = SecondsToTime(seconds [, noSeconds [, notAbbreviated ↵
[, maxCount]]])
```

Output includes markup normally hidden when displayed in a FontString (see last example); this markup allows the client to automatically print the singular or plural form of a word depending on the value of the preceding number.

Arguments:

seconds—An amount of time (in seconds) (number)

noSeconds (optional)—True to omit a seconds term in the description; false or omitted otherwise (boolean)

notAbbreviated (optional)—True to use full unit names in the description (e.g. Hours, Minutes); false or omitted to use abbreviations (e.g. Hr, Min) (boolean)

maxCount (optional)—Maximum number of terms to include in the description; defaults to 2 if omitted (number)

Returns:

time—A description of the amount of time in appropriate units (see examples) (string)

Example:

```
print(SecondsToTime(100))
-- shows "1 Min 40 Sec"
print(SecondsToTime(100, true))
-- shows "1 Min"
print(SecondsToTime(10000))
-- shows "2 Hr 46 Min"
print(SecondsToTime(10000, false, true))
-- shows "2 Hours 46 Minutes"
print(SecondsToTime(100000, false, false, 5))
-- shows "1 Day 3 Hr 46 Min 40 Sec"
SecondsToTime(100, false, true)
-- returns "1 |4Minute:Minutes; 40 |4Second:Seconds;"
```

SecureCmdOptionParse

Returns the action (and target, if applicable) for a secure macro command.

```
action, target = SecureCmdOptionParse("cmd")
```

Used in the default UI to parse macro conditionals.

Arguments:

cmd—A command to be parsed (typically the body of a macro, macrotext attribute or slash command (string)

Returns:

action—Argument to the base macro command (e.g. the name of a spell for /cast), or the empty string (" ") if the base command takes no arguments (e.g. /stopattack); nil if the command should not be executed (string)

target—Unit or name to use as the target of the action (string)

Example:

```
-- a complex macro command for contextually casting a healing
-- or damage spell
local macroText = "/cast [target=mouseover,harm,nodead] [harm,nodead] ↵
```

```
Mind Blast ; [target=mouseover,help,nodead,exists] [help,nodead] ↵
[target=player] Flash Heal"
SecureCmdOptionParse(macroText)
-- returns "Flash Heal", "player" if no unit is targeted or moused over
-- returns "Flash Heal", "mouseover" if a friendly unit is moused over
-- returns "Flash Heal" if a friendly unit is targeted
-- returns "Mind Blast", "mouseover" if a hostile unit is moused over
-- returns "Mind Blast" if a hostile unit is targeted
```

SelectActiveQuest

Selects a quest which can be turned in to the current Quest NPC.

```
SelectActiveQuest(index)
```

Usable after a QUEST_GREETING event. Causes the QUEST_PROGRESS event to fire, in which it is determined whether the player can complete the quest.

Note: Most quest NPCs present active quests using GetGossipActive Quests() instead of this function.

Arguments:

index—Index of a quest which can be turned in to the current Quest NPC (between 1 and GetNumActiveQuests()) (number)

SelectAvailableQuest

Chooses a quest available from the current Quest NPC.

```
SelectAvailableQuest(index)
```

Causes the QUEST_DETAIL event to fire, in which the questgiver presents the player with the details of a quest and the option to accept or decline.

Note: Most quest NPCs present available quests using GetGossipAvailableQuests() instead of this function.

Arguments:

index—Index of a quest available from the current Quest NPC (between 1 and GetNumAvailableQuests()) (number)

SelectGossipActiveQuest

Chooses a quest which can be turned in to the current Gossip NPC.

```
SelectGossipActiveQuest(index)
```

Causes the QUEST_PROGRESS event to fire, in which it is determined whether the player can complete the quest.

Arguments:

index—Index of a quest which can be turned in to the current Gossip NPC (between 1 and GetNumGossipActiveQuests()) (number)

SelectGossipAvailableQuest

Chooses a quest available from the current Gossip NPC.

```
SelectGossipAvailableQuest(index)
```

Usable after a QUEST_GREETING event. Causes the QUEST_DETAIL event to fire, in which the questgiver presents the player with the details of a quest and the option to accept or decline.

Arguments:

index—Index of a quest available from the current Gossip NPC (between 1 and GetNumGossipAvailableQuests()) (number)

SelectGossipOption

Chooses and activates an NPC dialog option.

```
SelectGossipOption(index [, "text" [, confirm]])
```

Results may vary according to the gossip option chosen; may end the gossip (firing a GOSSIP_CLOSED event) and start another interaction (firing a MERCHANT_SHOW, TRAINER_SHOW, TAXIMAP_OPENED, or similar event) or may continue the gossip with new text and new options (firing another GOSSIP_SHOW event).

Calling this function with only the first argument may cause the GOSSIP_CONFIRM event to fire, indicating that the player needs to provide confirmation (or additional information) before the option will be activated. Confirmation is needed for certain options requiring the character to spend (e.g. when activating Dual Talent Specialization); additional information is needed for options such as those used when redeeming a Loot Card code from the WoW trading card game to receive an in-game item. In either case, the confirmation and additional information can be provided (as by the popup dialog in the default UI) by calling this function again with all three arguments.

Arguments:

index—The option in the NPC gossip window to select, from 1 to GetNumGossipOptions() (number)

text (optional)—Text to include when confirming the selection (string)

confirm (optional)—true to confirm the selection; false or omitted otherwise (boolean)

SelectQuestLogEntry

Selects a quest from the quest log.

```
SelectQuestLogEntry(questIndex)
```

The selected quest is used by other functions which do not take a quest index as argument (e.g. GetQuestLogQuestText()).

Arguments:

questIndex—Index of a quest in the quest log (between 1 and GetNumQuestLogEntries()) (number)

SelectTradeSkill

Selects a recipe in the trade skill listing.

```
SelectTradeSkill(index)
```

Selection in the recipe list is used only for display in the default UI and has no effect on other Trade Skill APIs.

Arguments:

index—Index of a recipe in the trade skill list (between 1 and GetNumTrade Skills()) (number)

SelectTrainerService

Selects an entry in the trainer service listing.

```
SelectTrainerService(index)
```

Selection in the service list is used only for display in the default UI and has no effect on other Trainer APIs.

Arguments:

index—Index of an entry in the trainer service listing (between 1 and GetNumTrainerServices()) (number)

SendAddonMessage

Sends a chat-like message receivable by other addons.

```
SendAddonMessage("prefix", "message" [, "type" [, "target"]])
```

Allows for client-to-client addon communication.

Unlike with SendChatMessage, messages sent via SendAddonMessage:

- do not appear in receiving players' chat windows (unless an addon explicitly prints them)
- are not subject to strict server-side spam filtering/throttling (sending too many messages at once can still disconnect the user)
- are not modified if the sending character is drunk

Messages are received via the CHAT_MSG_ADDON event.

Arguments:

prefix—An arbitrary label for the message. Allows receiving addons to filter incoming messages: for example, if an addon uses the same prefix for all messages it sends, an addon interested in only those messages can check for that prefix before handling the message content. Cannot contain the tab character (\t). (string)

message—A message to send; combined length of prefix and message is limited to 254 characters (string)

type (optional)—Scope in which to broadcast the message: (string)

- BATTLEGROUND—To all allied players in the current battleground instance
- GUILD—To all members of the player's guild
- PARTY—To all members of the player's party (used by default if no type is given)
- RAID—To all members of the player's raid group (automatically reverts to sending to party if the player is not in a raid group)
- WHISPER—To a specific player

target (optional)—If type is "WHISPER", the name of the target player (in cross-realm battlegrounds, the format "Name-Realm" can be used to target a player from another realm; e.g. "Thott-Cenarius") (string)

Example:

```
-- Hypothetical communication using addon messages
local MSG_PREFIX = "MY_MOD"
SendAddonMessage(MSG_PREFIX, "Resync", "GUILD")
SendAddonMessage(MSG_PREFIX, "VersionCheck", "WHISPER", player)
```

SendChatMessage

Sends a chat message.

```
SendChatMessage("text" [, "chatType" [, "language" [, "channel"]]])
```

Arguments:

text—Message to be sent (up to 255 characters) (string)

chatType (optional)—Channel on which to send the message (defaults to SAY if omitted) (string)

- BATTLEGROUND—Messages to a battleground raid group (sent with /bg in the default UI)
- CHANNEL—Message to a server or custom chat channel (sent with /1, /2, etc in the default UI); requires channel number for channel argument
- DND—Enables Away-From-Keyboard status for the player, with text as the custom message seen by others attempting to whisper the player
- EMOTE—Custom text emotes visible to nearby players (sent with /e in the default UI)
- GUILD—Messages to guild members (sent with /g in the default UI)
- OFFICER—Messages to guild officers (sent with /o in the default UI)
- PARTY—Messages to party members (sent with /p in the default UI)
- RAID—Messages to raid members (sent with /ra in the default UI)
- RAID_WARNING—Warning to raid members (sent with /rw in the default UI)
- SAY—Speech to nearby players (sent with /s in the default UI)
- WHISPER—Message to a specific character (sent with /e in the default UI); requires name of the character for channel argument
- YELL—Yell to not-so-nearby players (sent with /y in the default UI)

language (optional)—Language in which to send the message; defaults to Common (for Alliance players) or Orcish (for Horde players) if omitted (string)

- COMMON—Alliance and Human language
- DARNASSIAN—Night Elf Language
- DRAENEI—Draenei Language
- DWARVEN—Dwarf Language
- GNOMISH—Gnome language
- GUTTERSPEAK—Undead language
- ORCISH—Horde and Orc Language

- `TAURAHE`—Tauren Language
- `THALASSIAN`—Night Elf Language
- `TROLL`—Troll language

channel (optional)—If `chatType` is `WHISPER`, name of the target character; if `chatType` is `CHANNEL`, number identifying the target channel; ignored otherwise (`string`)

Example:

```
-- Send a chat message to the character the player is currently mousing
-- over. This should be run as a macro (via keybind) so your mouse can
-- be hovering over a unit in the 3-D world, or a unit frame

local name = UnitName("mouseover")
SendChatMessage("Hey " .. name .. " I'm mousing over you!!!", ↩
"WHISPER", nil, name)


-- This can be run as a macro by putting it all on one line, and adding
run in front of it, like so:
--

-- /run local name = UnitName("mouseover"); SendChatMessage("Hey " ↩
.. name .. " I'm mousing over you!!!", "WHISPER", nil, name)
```

SendMail

Sends the outgoing message.

```
SendMail("recipient", "subject", "body")
```

Any money or COD costs and attachments specified for the message (via `SetSendMailMoney()`, `SetSendMailCOD()`, and `ClickSendMailItemButton()`) are included with the message (and the values for such are reset for the next outgoing message).

Arguments:

recipient—Name of the character to receive the mail (`string`)

subject—Subject text of the mail (`string`)

body—Body text of the mail (`string`)

SendWho

Requests a list of characters meeting given search criteria from the server.

```
SendWho("filter")
```

Text in the query will match against any of the six searchable fields unless one of the specifiers below is used; multiple specifiers can be used in one query. Queries are case insensitive.

- `n-"name"`—Search for characters whose name contains `name`
- `c-"class"`—Search for characters whose class name contains `class`
- `g-"guild"`—Search for characters in guilds whose name contains `guild`
- `r-"race"`—Search for characters whose race name contains `race`

- z-"zone"—Search for characters in zones whose name contains zone
- x—Search for characters of level x
- x-—Search for characters of level x or higher
- -x—Search for characters of level x or lower
- x-y—Search for characters between levels x and y (inclusive)

Results are not available immediately; the CHAT_MSG_SYSTEM or WHO_LIST_UPDATE event fires when data is available, as determined by the SetWhoToUI() function.

Arguments:

filter—A Who system search query (cannot be nil; use the empty string " " to specify a blank query) (string)

Example:

```
-- Search for human warriors named Donald in Elwynn Forest
SendWho('donald z-"elwynn" r-"human" c-"warrior"')
```

SetAbandonQuest

Begins the process of abandoning a quest in the player's quest log.

```
SetAbandonQuest(questIndex)
```

To finish abandoning the quest, call AbandonQuest().

This function must be called to select a quest in order for GetAbandonQuestItems() or GetAbandonQuestName() to return valid data.

Arguments:

questIndex—Index of a quest in the quest log (between 1 and GetNumQuestLogEntries()) (number)

SetAchievementComparisonUnit

Enables comparing achievements/statistics with another player.

```
success = SetAchievementComparisonUnit(unit)
```

After a call to this function, the INSPECT_ACHIEVEMENT_READY event fires to indicate that achievement/statistic comparison functions will return valid data on the given unit.

Arguments:

unit—ID of a unit to compare against (unitID)

Returns:

success—1 if the given unit is a valid unit. (Does not indicate whether the unit exists or can be compared against.) (1nil)

SetActionBarToggles

Configures display of additional ActionBars in the default UI.

```
SetActionBarToggles(bar1, bar2, bar3, bar4, alwaysShow)
```

Arguments:

bar1—1 to show the bottom left ActionBar; otherwise nil (1nil)

bar2—1 to show the bottom right ActionBar; otherwise nil (1nil) bar3—1 to show the right-side ActionBar; otherwise `nil` (1nil)

bar4—1 to show the second right-side ActionBar; otherwise `nil` (1nil)

`alwaysShow`—1 to always show ActionBar backgrounds even for empty slots; otherwise `nil` (1nil)

SetActiveTalentGroup

Switches the player's active talent specialization.

`SetActiveTalentGroup(talentGroup)`

Calling this function with the index of an inactive talent group does not immediately perform the switch: it begins casting a spell ("Activate Primary/Secondary Spec"), and only once the spellcast is complete are the player's talents changed.

Calling this function with the index of the active talent group, or with any argument if the player has not purchased Dual Talent Specialization, does nothing.

Arguments:

`talentGroup`—Index of the talent specialization to enable (`number`)

SetActiveVoiceChannel

Sets the currently active voice channel.

`SetActiveVoiceChannel(index)`

Arguments:

`index`—Index of a channel in the chat display window (between 1 and `GetNumDisplayChannels()`) (`number`)

SetActiveVoiceChannelBySessionID

Sets the currently active voice chat channel.

`SetActiveVoiceChannelBySessionID(session)`

Arguments:

`session`—Index of a voice session (between 1 and `GetNumVoiceSessions()`) (`number`)

SetArenaTeamRosterSelection

Selects a member in an arena team roster.

`SetArenaTeamRosterSelection(team, index)`

Selection in the arena team roster currently has no effect beyond highlighting list entry in the default UI.

Arguments:

`team`—Index of one of the player's arena teams (`number`, arenaTeamID)

`index`—Index of a team member to select (between 1 and `GetNumArenaTeamMembers(team)`) (`number`)

SetBagPortraitTexture

Sets a Texture object to display the icon of one of the player's bags.

`SetBagPortraitTexture(texture, container)`

Adapts the square item icon texture to fit within the circular "portrait" frames used in many default UI elements.

Arguments:

`texture`—A Texture object (`table`)

`container`—Index of one of the player's bags or other containers (`number`, containerID)

Example:

```
-- Set a texture to the rounded icon of the player's first
-- bag (not the backpack)
SetBagPortraitTexture(MyBagTexture, 1)
```

SetBattlefieldScoreFaction

Filters the battleground scoreboard by faction/team.

```
SetBattlefieldScoreFaction(faction)
```

Arguments:

`faction`—Faction for which to show battleground participant scores (`number`)

- ▪ `0`—Horde
- ▪ `1`—Alliance
- ▪ `nil`—All

SetBinding

Binds a key combination to a binding command.

```
success = SetBinding("key" [, "command"])
```

Arguments:

`key`—A key or key combination (e.g. "CTRL-2") (`string`, binding)

`command` (optional)—Name of a key binding command, or `nil` to unbind the key (`string`)

Returns:

`success`—1 if the key binding (or unbinding) was successful; otherwise `nil` (`1nil`)

Example:

```
-- Bind Control-Y to FOLLOWTARGET
SetBinding("CTRL-Y", "FOLLOWTARGET")
-- Unbind MouseButton4
SetBinding("BUTTON4")
```

SetBindingClick

Binds a key combination to "click" a Button object.

```
success = SetBindingClick("key", "buttonName" [, "mouseButton"])
```

When the binding is used, all of the relevant mouse handlers on the button (save for `OnEnter` and `OnLeave`) fire just as if the button were activated by the mouse (including `OnMouseDown` and `OnMouseUp` as the key is pressed and released).

Arguments:

key—A key or key combination (e.g. "CTRL-2") (string, binding)

buttonName—Name of a Button object on which the binding simulates a click (string)

mouseButton (optional)—Name of the mouse button with which the binding simulates a click (string)

Returns:

success—1 if the key binding was successful; otherwise nil (1nil)

SetBindingItem

Binds a key combination to use an item in the player's possession.

```
success = SetBindingItem("key", itemID) or SetBindingItem("key", ↵
"itemName") or SetBindingItem("key", "itemLink")
```

Arguments:

key—A key or key combination (e.g. "CTRL-2") (string, binding)

itemID—An item's ID (number)

itemName—An item's name (string)

itemLink—An item's hyperlink, or any string containing the itemString portion of an item link (string)

Returns:

success—1 if the binding was successful; otherwise nil (1nil)

SetBindingMacro

Binds a key combination to run a macro.

```
success = SetBindingMacro("key", index) or ↵
SetBindingMacro("key", "name")
```

Arguments:

key—A key or key combination (e.g. "CTRL-2") (string, binding)

index—Index of a macro (number, macroID)

name—Name of a macro (string)

Returns:

success—1 if the key binding was successful; otherwise nil (1nil)

SetBindingSpell

Binds a key combination to cast a spell.

```
success = SetBindingSpell("key", "spellname")
```

Arguments:

key—A key or key combination (e.g. "CTRL-2") (string, binding)

spellname—Name of a spell to bind (string)

Returns:

success—1 if the key binding was successful; otherwise nil (1nil)

Example:

```
-- Bind Flash Heal to ALT-Y
SetBindingSpell("ALT-Y", "Flash Heal")
```

SetCVar

Sets the value of a configuration variable.

```
SetCVar("cvar", value [, "raiseEvent"])
```

Arguments:

cvar—Name of the CVar to set (string)

value—New value for the CVar (any)

raiseEvent (optional)—If true, causes the CVAR_UPDATE event to fire (string)

SetChannelOwner

Gives channel ownership to another character.

```
SetChannelOwner("channel", "fullname")
```

Has no effect unless the player is the owner of the given channel.

Arguments:

channel—Name of the channel (string)

fullname—Name of the character to make the new owner (string)

Example:

```
-- Give "Cladhaire" ownership in the channel "monkeys"
SetChannelOwner("monkeys", "Cladhaire")
```

SetChannelPassword

Sets a password on a custom chat channel.

```
SetChannelPassword("channel", "password")
```

Arguments:

channel—Name of the channel (string)

password—Password to set for the channel (string)

SetChatWindowAlpha

Saves a chat window's background opacity setting.

```
SetChatWindowAlpha(index, alpha)
```

Used by the default UI's function FCF_SetWindowAlpha() which changes the opacity of a displayed FloatingChatFrame.

Arguments:

index—Index of a chat frame (between 1 and NUM_CHAT_WINDOWS) (number)

alpha—Alpha value (opacity) of the chat window background (0 = fully transparent, 1 = fully opaque) (number)

SetChatWindowColor

Saves a chat window's background color setting.

```
SetChatWindowColor(index, r, g, b)
```

Used by the default UI's function FCF_SetWindowColor() which changes the colors of a displayed FloatingChatFrame.

Arguments:

index—Index of a chat frame (between 1 and NUM_CHAT_WINDOWS) (number) r—Red component of the background color (0.0 - 1.0) (`number`)

g—Green component of the background color (0.0 - 1.0) (`number`)

b—Blue component of the background color (0.0 - 1.0) (`number`)

SetChatWindowDocked

Saves whether a chat window should be docked with the main chat window.

`SetChatWindowDocked(index, docked)`

Used by the default UI's functions `FCF_DockFrame()` and `FCF_UnDockFrame()` which manage the positioning of FloatingChatFrames.

Arguments:

index—Index of a chat frame (between 1 and `NUM_CHAT_WINDOWS`) (`number`)

docked—`True` if the window should be docked with the main chat window; otherwise `false` (`boolean`)

SetChatWindowLocked

Saves whether a chat window is locked.

`SetChatWindowLocked(index, locked)`

Used by the default UI's functions `FCF_OpenNewWindow()` and `FCF_SetLocked()` which manage the behavior of a FloatingChatFrame.

Arguments:

index—Index of a chat frame (between 1 and `NUM_CHAT_WINDOWS`) (`number`)

locked—`True` if the frame should be locked; otherwise `false` (`boolean`)

SetChatWindowName

Saves a chat window's display name setting.

`SetChatWindowName(index, "name")`

Used by the default UI's function `FCF_SetWindowName()` which also handles setting the name displayed for a FloatingChatFrame.

Arguments:

index—Index of a chat frame (between 1 and `NUM_CHAT_WINDOWS`) (`number`)

name—Name to be displayed for the chat window (`string`)

SetChatWindowShown

Saves whether a chat window should be shown.

`SetChatWindowShown(index, shown)`

Used by the default UI's function `FCF_OpenNewWindow()` which initializes a displayed FloatingChatFrame.

Arguments:

index—Index of a chat frame (between 1 and `NUM_CHAT_WINDOWS`) (`number`)

shown—`True` if the window should be shown, `false` otherwise (`boolean`)

SetChatWindowSize

Saves a chat window's font size setting.

`SetChatWindowSize(index, size)`

Used by the default UI's function `FCF_SetChatWindowFontSize()` which also handles changing the font displayed in a FloatingChatFrame.

Arguments:

`index`—Index of a chat frame (between `1` and `NUM_CHAT_WINDOWS`) (`number`)

`size`—Font size for the chat window (in points) (`number`)

SetChatWindowUninteractable

Saves whether a chat window is marked as non-interactive.

`SetChatWindowUninteractable(index, setUninteractable)`

Used by the default UI's function `FCF_SetUninteractable()` which also handles enabling/disabling mouse events in the FloatingChatFrame.

Arguments:

`index`—Index of a chat frame (between `1` and `NUM_CHAT_WINDOWS`) (`number`)

`setUninteractable`—`True` flags the window as non-interactive; `false` otherwise (`boolean`)

SetCurrencyBackpack

Sets a currency type to be watched on the Backpack UI.

`SetCurrencyBackpack(index, watch)`

Arguments:

`index`—Index of a currency type or header in the currency list (between `1` and GetCurrencyListSize()) (`number`)

`watch`—`1` to add this currency to the backpack UI; 0 to remove it from being watched (`number`)

SetCurrencyUnused

Moves a currency type to or from the Unused currencies list.

`SetCurrencyUnused(index, makeUnused)`

"Unused" currencies behave no differently; the distinction only exists to allow players to hide currencies they don't care about from the main display.

Arguments:

`index`—Index of a currency type or header in the currency list (between `1` and GetCurrencyListSize()) (`number`)

`makeUnused`—`1` to move this currency to the Unused category; 0 to return it to its original category (`number`)

SetCurrentGuildBankTab

Selects a tab in the guild bank.

`SetCurrentGuildBankTab(tab)`

Arguments:

`tab`—Index of a guild bank tab (between `1` and `GetNumGuildBankTabs()`) (`number`)

SetCurrentTitle

Changes a player's displayed title.

```
SetCurrentTitle(titleIndex)
```

Arguments:

`titleIndex`—Index of a title available to the player (between `1` and `GetNumTitles()`), or -1 to show no title (`integer`)

SetCursor

Changes the mouse cursor image.

```
SetCursor("cursor")
```

Changes only the appearance of the mouse cursor, not its behavior (and has no effect if the cursor is holding an item, spell, or other data). Passing `nil` will revert the cursor to its default image.

Normally used in a frame's `OnEnter` handler to change the cursor used while the mouse is over the frame. If used elsewhere, the cursor will likely be immediately reverted to default (due to the mouse handlers of other frames doing the same).

Arguments:

`cursor`—Path to a texture to use as the cursor image (must be 32x32 pixels) or one of the built-in cursor tokens. Valid cursor tokens can be found in the example code. (`string`)

Example:

```
-- Creates a button in the center of the screen which can be moused over
-- repeatedly to show all of the available cursors
local cursors = { "NORMAL_CURSOR", "ATTACK_CURSOR", ↵
"ATTACK_ERROR_CURSOR", "BUY_CURSOR", "BUY_ERROR_CURSOR", ↵
"CAST_CURSOR", "CAST_ERROR_CURSOR", "GATHER_CURSOR", ↵
"GATHER_ERROR_CURSOR", "INNKEEPER_CURSOR", ↵
"INNKEEPER_ERROR_CURSOR", "INSPECT_CURSOR", ↵
"INSPECT_ERROR_CURSOR", "INTERACT_CURSOR", "INTERACT_ERROR_CURSOR", ↵
"ITEM_CURSOR", "ITEM_ERROR_CURSOR", "LOCK_CURSOR", ↵
"LOCK_ERROR_CURSOR", "LOOT_ALL_CURSOR", "LOOT_ALL_ERROR_CURSOR", ↵
"MAIL_CURSOR", "MAIL_ERROR_CURSOR", "MINE_CURSOR", ↵
"MINE_ERROR_CURSOR", "PICKUP_CURSOR", "PICKUP_ERROR_CURSOR", ↵
"POINT_CURSOR", "POINT_ERROR_CURSOR", "QUEST_CURSOR", ↵
"QUEST_ERROR_CURSOR", "REPAIRNPC_CURSOR", "REPAIRNPC_ERROR_CURSOR", ↵
"REPAIR_CURSOR", "REPAIR_ERROR_CURSOR", "SKIN_ALLIANCE_CURSOR", ↵
"SKIN_ALLIANCE_ERROR_CURSOR", "SKIN_CURSOR", "SKIN_ERROR_CURSOR", ↵
"SKIN_HORDE_CURSOR", "SKIN_HORDE_ERROR_CURSOR", "SPEAK_CURSOR", ↵
"SPEAK_ERROR_CURSOR", "TAXI_CURSOR", "TAXI_ERROR_CURSOR", ↵
"TRAINER_CURSOR", "TRAINER_ERROR_CURSOR" }

local current = 0

CreateFrame("Button", "CursorTestFrame", UIParent, ↵
"GameMenuButtonTemplate")
```

```
CursorTestFrame:SetPoint("CENTER", 0, 0)
CursorTestFrame:SetText("Hover to change cursor")
local function OnEnter(self) current = current + 1
  if current > #cursors then
   current = 1
  end
  SetCursor(cursors[current])
  self:SetText(cursors[current])
end

CursorTestFrame:SetScript("OnEnter", OnEnter)
SetDungeonDifficulty
```

SetDungeonDifficulty

Sets the player's 5 player dungeon difficulty preference.

```
SetDungeonDifficulty(difficulty)
```

Setting dungeon difficulty has no effect on the instance created when entering a portal if the player is not the party/raid leader. Changing difficulty while in an instance also has no effect.

Epic difficulty is currently unused; setting dungeon difficulty to 3 will cause instance portal graphics to disappear and may result in errors upon entering an instance portal.

Arguments:

`difficulty`—A difficulty level (`number`)

- 1—5 Player (Normal)
- 2—5 Player (Heroic)

SetDungeonMapLevel

Sets the world map to display a certain map image (for zones that use multiple map images).

```
SetDungeonMapLevel(level)
```

Used in zones with more than one "floor" or area such as Dalaran and several Wrath of the Lich King dungeons and raids.

Arguments:

`level`—Index of the map image to show in the world map (`number`)

SetEuropeanNumbers

Sets the decimal separator for displayed numbers.

```
SetEuropeanNumbers(enable)
```

Affects the style not only of numbers displayed in the UI, but any string coercion of numbers with `tostring()` as well.

Arguments:

`enable`—True to use comma (",") as the decimal separator; `false` to use period (".") as the decimal separator (`boolean`)

SetFactionActive

Removes the "inactive" status from a faction.

`SetFactionActive(index)`

"Inactive" factions behave no differently; the distinction only exists to allow players to hide factions they don't care about from the main display. Factions thus marked are automatically moved to an "Inactive" group at the end of the faction list.

Arguments:

`index`—Index of an entry in the faction list; between 1 and GetNumFactions() (`number`)

SetFactionInactive

Flags a faction as inactive.

`SetFactionInactive(index)`

"Inactive" factions behave no differently; the distinction only exists to allow players to hide factions they don't care about from the main display. Factions thus marked are automatically moved to an "Inactive" group at the end of the faction list.

Arguments:

`index`—Index of an entry in the faction list; between 1 and GetNumFactions() (`number`)

SetFriendNotes

Sets note text associated with a friends list entry.

`SetFriendNotes(index, "note") or SetFriendNotes("name", "note")`

Setting a note to `nil` will result in an error; to remove a note, set it to the empty string (`" "`).

Arguments:

`index`—Index of a friends list entry (between 1 and `GetNumFriends()`) (`number`)

`name`—Name of friend to modify (`string`)

`note`—The note to set (`string`)

SetGamma

Changes the display gamma setting.

`SetGamma(value)`

Gamma value determines the contrast between lighter and darker portions of the game display; for a detailed explanation see the Wikipedia article on Gamma correction.

Arguments:

`value`—New gamma value (`number`)

SetGuildBankTabInfo

Sets the name and icon for a guild bank tab.

`SetGuildBankTabInfo(tab, "name", iconIndex)`

Arguments:

tab—Index of a guild bank tab (between 1 and GetNumGuildBankTabs())
(number)

name—New name for the tab (string)

iconIndex—Index of an icon for the tab (between 1 and GetNumMacroItem
Icons()) (number)

SetGuildBankTabPermissions

Changes guild bank tab permissions for the guild rank being edited.

SetGuildBankTabPermissions(tab, permission, enabled)

Arguments:

tab—Index of a guild bank tab (between 1 and GetNumGuildBankTabs())
(number)

permission—Index of a permission to edit (number)

- 1—View tab
- 2—Deposit items

enabled—True to allow permission for the action to the guild rank; false to
deny (boolean)

SetGuildBankTabWithdraw

Sets the number of item withdrawals allowed per day for the guild rank being
edited.

SetGuildBankTabWithdraw(tab, amount)

Arguments:

tab—Index of a guild bank tab (between 1 and GetNumGuildBankTabs())
(number)

amount—Maximum number of item (stack) withdrawals allowed per day for the
guild rank (number)

SetGuildBankText

Sets the info text for a guild bank tab.

SetGuildBankText(tab, "text")

Arguments:

tab—Index of a guild bank tab (between 1 and GetNumGuildBankTabs())
(number)

text—New info text for the tab (string)

SetGuildBankWithdrawLimit

Sets the maximum amount of money withdrawals per day allowed for the
guild rank being edited.

SetGuildBankWithdrawLimit(amount)

Arguments:

amount—Maximum amount of money allowed to be withdrawn per day for the
guild rank (in copper) (number)

SetGuildInfoText

Sets the guild information text.

```
SetGuildInfoText("text")
```

This text appears when clicking the "Guild Information" button in the default UI's Guild window.

Arguments:

text—New guild information text (string)

SetGuildRosterSelection

Selects a member in the guild roster.

```
SetGuildRosterSelection(index)
```

Selection in the guild roster is used only for display in the default UI and has no effect on other Guild APIs.

Arguments:

index—Index of a member in the guild roster (between 1 and GetNumGuildMembers()), or 0 for no selection (number)

SetGuildRosterShowOffline

Enables or disables inclusion of offline members in the guild roster listing.

```
SetGuildRosterShowOffline(showOffline)
```

Arguments:

showOffline—True to include offline members in the guild roster listing; false to list only those members currently online (boolean)

SetInventoryPortraitTexture

Sets a Texture object to display the icon of an equipped item.

```
SetInventoryPortraitTexture(texture, "unit", slot)
```

Adapts the square item icon texture to fit within the circular "portrait" frames used in many default UI elements.

Arguments:

texture—A Texture object (table)

unit—A unit whose item should be displayed; only valid for player (string, unitID)

slot—An inventory slot number, as can be obtained from GetInventorySlotInfo (number, inventoryID)

SetLFGAutojoin

Enables the option to automatically join a group matching current LFG criteria.

SetLFGComment

Associates a brief text comment with the player's listing in the LFG system.

```
SetLFGComment("comment")
```

In the default UI, other players see this comment when mousing over the player's name in the Looking for More listing.

Arguments:

comment—A comment to be associated with the player's listing in the LFG system (max 63 characters); or the empty string (" ") to clear an existing comment (string)

Example:

```
-- Sets the player's LFG comment to a quick summary of talent spec
-- (If already participating in the LFG UI)
local _, _, tab1Points = GetTalentTabInfo(1)
local _, _, tab2Points = GetTalentTabInfo(2)
local _, _, tab3Points = GetTalentTabInfo(3)
SetLFGComment(tab1Points.."/"..tab2Points.."/"..tab3Points)
```

SetLFGRoles

Sets group roles for which to advertise the player in the LFG system.

```
SetLFGRoles(leader, tank, healer, damage)
```

Passing true for a role the player's class does not support (e.g. healing on a warrior or tanking on a priest) has no effect: see example.

Arguments:

leader—True if the player is willing to lead a group; otherwise false (boolean)

tank—True if the player is willing to take on the role of protecting allies by drawing enemy attacks; otherwise false (boolean)

healer—True if the player is willing to take on the role of healing allies who take damage; otherwise false (boolean)

damage—True if the player is willing to take on the role of damaging enemies; otherwise false (boolean)

Example:

```
SetLFGRoles(true,true,true,true)
GetLFGRoles()
-- on a priest: returns true,false,true,true
-- on a warrior: returns true,true,false,true
```

SetLFMAutofill

Enables the option to automatically fill the player's group when Looking for More.

SetLFMType

Sets the type for LFM queries.

```
SetLFMType(type)
```

Does not actually send a query; used in the default UI to allow query parameters to be saved and reused across UI restarts. See LFGQuery() for actual queries.

Arguments:

type—Index of an LFG query type (in the list returned by GetLFGTypes()) (number)

SetLookingForGroup

Adds the player to the LFG system for one of three objectives.

`SetLookingForGroup(slot, type, index)`

Players are currently allowed to set up to three objectives to be advertised in the LFG system.

Arguments:

`slot`—Index of an LFG objective (between 1 and 3) (number)

`type`—Index of an LFG query type (in the list returned by `GetLFGTypes()`) (number)

`index`—Index of an LFG entry (in the list returned by `GetLFGTypeEntries (type)`) (number)

SetLookingForMore

Sets up a Looking for More query.

`SetLookingForMore(type, index)`

Does not actually send a query; used in the default UI to allow query parameters to be saved and reused across UI restarts. See `LFGQuery()` for actual queries.

Arguments:

`type`—Index of an LFG query type (in the list returned by `GetLFGTypes()`) (number)

`index`—Index of an LFG entry (in the list returned by `GetLFGTypeEntries (type)`) (number)

SetLootMethod

Sets the loot method for a party or raid group.

`SetLootMethod("method" [, "master"])`

Has no effect if the player is not the party or raid leader.

See `SetLootThreshold` for the quality threshold used by Master Looter, Group Loot, and Need Before Greed methods.

Arguments:

`method`—Method to use for loot distribution (`string`)

- `freeforall`—Free for All; any group member can take any loot at any time
- `group`—Group Loot; like Round Robin, but items above a quality threshold are rolled on
- `master`—Master Looter; like Round Robin, but items above a quality threshold are left for a designated loot master to
- `needbeforegreed`—Need before Greed; like Group Loot, but members automatically pass on items
- `roundrobin`—Round Robin; group members take turns being able to loot

`master` (optional)—Name or `unitID` of the master looter (`string`)

SetLootPortrait

Sets a Texture object to show the appropriate portrait image when looting.

`SetLootPortrait(texture)`

Normally, the loot portrait image is the same as that of the creature being looted. Not used in the default UI—a generic image for all loot is used instead.

Arguments:

`texture`—A Texture object (`table`)

SetLootThreshold

Sets the threshold used for Master Looter, Group Loot, and Need Before Greed loot methods.

`SetLootThreshold(threshold)`

Has no effect if the player is not the party or raid leader.

Items above the `threshold` quality will trigger the special behavior of the current loot method: for Group Loot and Need Before Greed, rolling will automatically begin once a group member loots the corpse or object holding the item; for Master Loot, the item will be invisible to all but the loot master tasked with assigning the loot.

The loot threshold defaults to 2 (Uncommon) when forming a new party/raid. Setting the threshold to 0 (Poor) or 1 (Common) has no effect—qualities below Uncommon are always treated as below the threshold. The default UI only allows setting the threshold as high as 4 (Epic), but higher thresholds are allowed.

Arguments:

`threshold`—Minimum item quality to trigger the loot method (`number`, itemQuality)

SetMacroItem

Changes the item used for dynamic feedback for a macro.

`SetMacroItem(index, "item" [, target])` or ↵
`SetMacroItem("name", "item" [, target])`

Normally a macro uses the item or spell specified by its commands to provide dynamic feedback when placed on an action button (through the Action APIs, e.g. `IsActionUsable()`): e.g. if the macro uses a consumable item, the button will show the number of items remaining; if the macro uses an item with a cooldown, the button will show the state of the cooldown. This function allows overriding the item or spell used by the macro with another item. The given item's state will be used for such feedback instead of the item or spell used by the macro.

Arguments:

`index`—Index of a macro (`number`, macroID)

`name`—Name of a macro (`string`)

`item`—Name of an item to use for the macro (`string`)

`target` (optional)—A unit to use as target of the item (affects the macro's range indicator) (`unitid`)

Example:

```
-- Create a macro and note the index (19 - 36 are the character
-- specific indices)
-- Target a friendly item that you can bandage
-- Set the first argument to the macro index
-- Set the second argument to the name of a a bandage you have
-- in your inventory
SetMacroItem(19, "Heavy Runecloth Bandage", "target")


-- The given macro on your action bars should now use the bandage range
-- to indicate whether or not the macro is "in range"
```

SetMacroSpell

Changes the spell used for dynamic feedback for a macro.

```
SetMacroSpell(index, "spell" [, target]) or ↵
SetMacroSpell("name", "spell" [, target])
```

Normally a macro uses the item or spell specified by its commands to provide dynamic feedback when placed on an action button (through the Action APIs, e.g. `IsActionUsable()`): e.g. if the macro uses a consumable item, the button will show the number of items remaining; if the macro uses an item with a cooldown, the button will show the state of the cooldown. This function allows overriding the item or spell used by the macro with another item. The given item's state will be used for such feedback instead of the item or spell used by the macro.

Arguments:

`index`—Index of a macro (`number`, macroID)

`name`—Name of a macro (`string`)

`spell`—Name of a spell to use for the macro (`string`)

`target` (optional)—A unit to use as target of the spell (affects the macro's range indicator) (`unitid`)

SetMapToCurrentZone

Sets the world map to show the zone in which the player is located.

SetMapZoom

Sets the world map to show a specific zone or continent.

```
SetMapZoom(continentIndex [, zoneIndex])
```

Arguments:

`continentIndex`—Index of a continent to display (in the list returned by `GetMapContinents()`, or one of the following values) (`number`)

`-1`—Cosmic map	`2`—Eastern Kingdoms
`0`—Entire Azeroth map	`3`—Outland
`1`—Kalimdor	`4`—Northrend

`zoneIndex` (optional)—Index of a zone within the continent to display (in the list returned by `GetMapZones(continentIndex)`), or omitted to show the continent map (`number`)

Example:

```
-- show the cosmic map
SetMapZoom( -1 )
-- show all the azeroth continents
SetMapZoom( 0 )
-- show the outland continent
SetMapZoom( 3 )
-- show dun morogh
SetMapZoom( 2, 7)
```

SetModifiedClick

Sets a modified click for a given action.

```
SetModifiedClick("action", "binding")
```

Arguments:

action—Token identifying the modified click action (string)

binding—The set of modifiers (and mouse button, if applicable) to register for the action (string, binding)

SetMouselookOverrideBinding

Overrides the default mouselook bindings to perform another binding with the mouse buttons.

```
SetMouselookOverrideBinding("key", "binding")
```

Arguments:

key—The mouselook key to override (string)

- ∎ BUTTON1—Override the left mouse button
- ∎ BUTTON2—Override the right mouse button

binding—The binding to perform instead of mouselooking, or nil to clear the override (string)

Example:

```
-- Uses the 'z' button to activate mouselook instead of the mouse
-- buttons, and the mouse buttons to move forward and backward
-- instead of mouselooking.
-- Credits to slouken for this code.
CreateFrame("Button", "MouselookButton")
MouselookButton:RegisterForClicks("AnyUp", "AnyDown")
MouselookButton:SetScript("OnClick", function (self, button, down)
 if ( down ) then
  MouselookStart()
 else
  MouselookStop()
 end
end)
SetOverrideBindingClick(MouselookButton, nil, "Z", "MouselookButton")
SetMouselookOverrideBinding("BUTTON1", "MOVEFORWARD")
SetMouselookOverrideBinding("BUTTON2", "MOVEBACKWARD")
```

SetMultiCastSpell

Sets a multi-cast action slot to a given spell.

```
SetMultiCastSpell(action, spell)
```

This function is used to set up the multi-cast action slots, such as the totem bar that was introduced with WoW 3.2. The player is able to customize three different sets of totems that can then be cast with a single click.

Arguments:

action—The multi-cast action slot to set (number)

spell—The numeric spellId to set to the given action slot (number)

SetMultisampleFormat

Changes the multisample setting.

```
SetMultisampleFormat(index)
```

The index argument corresponds to the individual settings described by GetMultisampleFormats() (each a set of three values).

Arguments:

index—Index of a multisample setting (number)

SetNextBarberShopStyle

Selects the next style for a barber shop style option.

```
SetNextBarberShopStyle(styleIndex [, reverse])
```

Changes the underlying data (and thus the character's appearance) only; the default barbershop UI does not update.

Arguments:

styleIndex—Index of a style option (number)

■ 1—Hair (or Horn) Style

■ 2—Hair (or Horn) Color

■ 3—Varies by race and gender: Facial Hair, Earrings, Features, Hair, Horns, Markings, Normal, Piercings, or Tusks

reverse (optional)—True to select the previous style; false or omitted to select the next (boolean)

SetOptOutOfLoot

Changes the player's preference to opt out of loot rolls.

```
SetOptOutOfLoot(enable)
```

When opting out, no prompt will be shown for loot which ordinarily would prompt the player to roll (need/greed) or pass; the loot rolling process will continue for other group members as if the player had chosen to pass on every roll.

Arguments:

enable—True to opt out of loot, false to participate in loot rolls (boolean)

SetOverrideBinding

Sets an override binding for a binding command.

```
SetOverrideBinding(owner, isPriority, "key", "command")
```

Override bindings are temporary. The bound key will revert to its normal setting once the override is removed. Priority overrides work the same way but will revert to the previous override binding (if present) rather than the base binding for the key.

Call with a fourth argument of `nil` to remove the override binding for a specific key, or see `ClearOverrideBindings()` to remove all bindings associated with a given `owner`.

Arguments:

`owner`—The Frame (or other widget) object responsible for this override (`table`)

`isPriority`—`True` if this binding takes higher priority than other override bindings; `false` otherwise (`boolean`)

`key`—A key or key combination (e.g. "CTRL-2") (`string`, `binding`)

`command`—Name of a key binding command, or `nil` to remove the override binding (`string`)

SetOverrideBindingClick

Sets an override binding to "click" a Button object.

```
SetOverrideBindingClick(owner, isPriority, "key", ↵
"buttonName" [, "mouseButton"])
```

Override bindings are temporary. The bound key will revert to its normal setting once the override is removed. Priority overrides work the same way but will revert to the previous override binding (if present) rather than the base binding for the key.

Call with a fourth argument of `nil` to remove the override binding for a specific key, or see `ClearOverrideBindings()` to remove all bindings associated with a given `owner`.

Arguments:

`owner`—The Frame (or other widget) object responsible for this override (`table`)

`isPriority`—`True` if this binding takes higher priority than other override bindings; `false` otherwise (`boolean`)

`key`—A key or key combination (e.g. "CTRL-2") (`string`, `binding`)

`buttonName`—Name of a Button object on which the binding simulates a click (`string`)

`mouseButton` (optional)—Name of the mouse button with which the binding simulates a click (`string`)

SetOverrideBindingItem

Sets an override binding to use an item in the player's possession.

```
SetOverrideBindingItem(owner, isPriority, "key", itemID) or ↵
SetOverrideBindingItem(owner, isPriority, "key", "itemName") or ↵
SetOverrideBindingItem(owner, isPriority, "key", "itemLink")
```

Override bindings are temporary. The bound key will revert to its normal setting once the override is removed. Priority overrides work the same way but will revert to the previous override binding (if present) rather than the base binding for the key.

Call with a fourth argument of `nil` to remove the override binding for a specific key, or see `ClearOverrideBindings()` to remove all bindings associated with a given `owner`.

Arguments:

`owner`—The Frame (or other widget) object responsible for this override (`table`)

`isPriority`—True if this binding takes higher priority than other override bindings; `false` otherwise (`boolean`)

`key`—A key or key combination (e.g. "CTRL-2") (`string`, binding)

`itemID`—An item's ID (`number`)

`itemName`—An item's name (`string`)

`itemLink`—An item's hyperlink, or any string containing the `itemString` portion of an item link (`string`)

SetOverrideBindingMacro

Sets an override binding to run a macro.

```
SetOverrideBindingMacro(owner, isPriority, "key", index) or ↵
SetOverrideBindingMacro(owner, isPriority, "key", "name")
```

Override bindings are temporary. The bound key will revert to its normal setting once the override is removed. Priority overrides work the same way but will revert to the previous override binding (if present) rather than the base binding for the key.

Call with a fourth argument of `nil` to remove the override binding for a specific key, or see `ClearOverrideBindings()` to remove all bindings associated with a given `owner`.

Arguments:

`owner`—The Frame (or other widget) object responsible for this override (`table`)

`isPriority`—True if this binding takes higher priority than other override bindings; `false` otherwise (`boolean`)

`key`—A key or key combination (e.g. "CTRL-2") (`string`, binding)

`index`—Index of a macro (`number`, macroID)

`name`—Name of a macro (`string`)

SetOverrideBindingSpell

Set an override binding to a specific spell.

```
SetOverrideBindingSpell(owner, isPriority, "key", "spellname")
```

Override bindings are temporary. The bound key will revert to its normal setting once the override is removed. Priority overrides work the same way but will revert to the previous override binding (if present) rather than the base binding for the key. See `ClearOverrideBindings()` to remove bindings associated with a given `owner`.

Arguments:

`owner`—The Frame (or other widget) object responsible for this override (`table`)

`isPriority`—True if this binding takes higher priority than other override bindings; `false` otherwise (`boolean`) key—A key or key combination (e.g. "CTRL-2") (`string`, binding)

spellname—Name of a spell, or `nil` to remove the override binding (`string`)

Example:

```
-- Set up Shift-2 to cast Prayer of Mending as an override binding
-- owned by PlayerFrame
SetOverrideBindingSpell(PlayerFrame, 1, "SHIFT-2", "Prayer of Mending")

-- Clear PlayerFrame's override bindings
ClearOverrideBindings(PlayerFrame)
```

SetPVP

Enables or disables the player's desired PvP status.

```
SetPVP(state)
```

Enabling PvP takes effect immediately; disabling PvP begins a five-minute countdown after which PvP status will be disabled (if the player has taken no PvP actions).

Arguments:

state—1 to enable PVP, `nil` to disable (1nil)

Protected

SetPartyAssignment

Assigns a group role to a member of the player's party or raid.

```
SetPartyAssignment("assignment", "unit") or ↵
SetPartyAssignment("assignment", "name" [, exactMatch])
```

Arguments:

assignment—A group role to assign to the unit (`string`)

■ MAINASSIST—Assign the main assist role

■ MAINTANK—Assign the main tank role

unit—A unit in the player's party or raid (`string`, unitID)

name—Name of a unit in the player's party or raid (`string`)

exactMatch (optional)—True to check only units whose name exactly matches the name given; false to allow partial matches (`boolean`)

SetPetStablePaperdoll

Sets the given Model to show the selected stabled pet.

```
SetPetStablePaperdoll(model)
```

Arguments:

model—A Model frame (`table`)

Example:

```
-- Open the character window and the pet stable before running this code
-- Changes the character model to the pet model
SetPetStablePaperdoll(CharacterModelFrame)
```

SetPortraitTexture

Sets a Texture object to show a portrait of a unit.

```
SetPortraitTexture(texture, "unit")
```

Causes the client to render a view of the unit's model from a standard perspective into a circular 2D image and display it in the given Texture object.

Arguments:

texture—A Texture object (`table`)

unit—A unit for which to display a portrait (`string`, unitID)

SetPortraitToTexture

Sets a Texture object to display an arbitrary texture, altering it to fit a circular frame.

```
SetPortraitToTexture("frameName", "texturePath")
```

Used in the default UI to display square textures (such as item icons) within the circular "portrait" frames used in many default UI elements.

Arguments:

frameName—Name of a Texture object (`string`)

texturePath—Path to a texture to display (`string`)

Example:

```
-- Change the player portrait to be the same as the keychain portrait
SetPortraitToTexture("PlayerPortrait", ↵
"Interface\\ContainerFrame\\KeyRing-Bag-Icon")

-- Set the player portrait to be the icon for "Staff
-- of Infinite Mysteries"
SetPortraitToTexture("PlayerPortrait", ↵
"Interface\\Icons\\INV_Weapon_Halberd17")
```

SetRaidDifficulty

Sets the player's raid dungeon difficulty preference.

```
SetRaidDifficulty(difficulty)
```

The dungeon difficulty has no effect on the instance created if the player is not the raid leader or while you are inside an instance already.

Arguments:

difficulty—Difficulty level for raid dungeons

1—10 Player

2—25 Player

3—10 Player (Heroic)

4—25 Player (Heroic)

SetRaidRosterSelection

Selects a unit in the raid roster.

```
SetRaidRosterSelection(index)
```

Selection in the raid roster is used only for display in the default UI and has no effect on other Raid APIs.

Arguments:

index—Index of the raid member (between 1 and GetNumRaidMembers()); matches the numeric part of the unit's raid unitID, e.g. 21 for raid21 (`number`)

SetRaidSubgroup

Moves a raid member to a non-full raid subgroup.

```
SetRaidSubgroup(index, subgroup)
```

Only has effect if the player is the raid leader or a raid assistant. To put a member into a full subgroup (switching places with a member of that group), see `SwapRaidSubgroup()`.

Arguments:

index—Index of the raid member (between 1 and `GetNumRaidMembers()`); matches the numeric part of the unit's raid `unitID`, e.g. 21 for raid21 (number)

subgroup—Index of a raid subgroup (between 1 and `MAX_RAID_GROUPS`) (number)

SetRaidTarget

Puts a raid target marker on a unit.

```
SetRaidTarget("unit", index) or SetRaidTarget("name", index)
```

Arguments:

unit—A unit to mark (string, unitID)

name—Name of a unit to mark (string)

index—Index of a target marker (number)

0—Clear any raid target markers	5—Moon
1—Star	6—Square
2—Circle	7—Cross
3—Diamond	8—Skull
4—Triangle	

SetScreenResolution

Changes the screen resolution.

```
SetScreenResolution(index)
```

Arguments:

index—Index of a resolution setting (between 1 and `select("#", GetScreenResolutions())`) (number)

Example:

```
-- Print the possible resolutions to ChatFrame1
-- These indices can then be used in SetScreenResolution()
local resolutions = {GetScreenResolutions()}
for idx, resolution in ipairs(resolutions) do
 print("Resolution " .. idx .. ": " .. resolution)
end
```

SetSelectedAuctionItem

Selects an item in an auction listing.

```
SetSelectedAuctionItem("list", index)
```

Auction selection is used only for display and internal recordkeeping in the default UI; it has no direct effect on other Auction APIs.

Arguments:

list—Type of auction listing (string)

- ▪ bidder—Auctions the player has bid on
- ▪ list—Auctions the player can browse and bid on or buy out
- ▪ owner—Auctions the player placed

index—Index of an auction in the listing (number)

SetSelectedBattlefield

Selects a battleground instance in the queueing list.

```
SetSelectedBattlefield(index)
```

Selection in the battleground instance list is used only for display in the default UI and has no effect on other Battlefield APIs.

Arguments:

index—Index in the battleground queue listing (1 for the first available instance, or between 2 and GetNumBattlefields() for other instances) (number)

SetSelectedDisplayChannel

Selects a channel in the channel list display.

```
SetSelectedDisplayChannel(index)
```

Arguments:

index—Index of a channel in the channel list display (between 1 and GetNumDisplayChannels()) (number)

SetSelectedFaction

Selects a faction in the reputation UI.

```
SetSelectedFaction(index)
```

Selection has no bearing on other faction-related APIs; this function merely facilitates behaviors of Blizzard's reputation UI.

Arguments:

index—Index of an entry in the faction list; between 1 and GetNumFactions() (number)

SetSelectedFriend

Selects a character in the player's friends list.

```
SetSelectedFriend(index)
```

Selection in the Friends list is used only for display in the default UI and has no effect on other Friends list APIs.

Arguments:

index—Index of a character in the Friends list (between 1 and GetNumFriends()) (number)

SetSelectedIgnore

Selects a character in the player's ignore list.

```
SetSelectedIgnore(index)
```

Selection in the Ignore list is used only for display in the default UI and has no effect on other Ignore list APIs.

Arguments:

index—Index of a character in the Ignore list (between 1 and `GetNum Ignores()`) (number)

SetSelectedMute

Selects an entry in the Muted list.

```
SetSelectedMute(index)
```

Mute list selection is only used for display purposes in the default UI and has no effect on other API functions.

Arguments:

index—Index of an entry in the mute listing (between 1 and `GetNumMutes()`) (number)

SetSelectedSkill

Selects a skill in the Skills UI.

```
SetSelectedSkill(index)
```

Selection is only used for display purposes in the default Skills UI and has no effect on other Skill APIs.

Arguments:

index—Index of an entry in the skills list (between 1 and `GetNumSkill Lines()`) (number)

SetSendMailCOD

Sets the Cash-On-Delivery cost of the outgoing message.

```
SetSendMailCOD(amount)
```

Called in the default UI when clicking its Send button, immediately before sending the message.

Arguments:

amount—COD cost for the items attached to the message (in copper) (number)

SetSendMailMoney

Sets the amount of money to be sent with the outgoing message.

```
success = SetSendMailMoney(amount)
```

Called in the default UI when clicking its Send button, immediately before sending the message. Causes an error message if the amount plus postage exceeds the player's total money.

Arguments:

amount—Amount of money to send (in copper) (number)

Returns:

success—1 if the player has enough money to send the message; otherwise nil (1nil)

Example:

```
-- Quickly send money to a specified character (only works while at an
-- open mailbox)
function SendCharacterMoney(name, amount)
 SetSendMailMoney(amount)
 SendMail(name, number/10000 .. " gold attached", "")
end
```

SetSendMailShowing

Enables or disables shortcuts for attaching items to outgoing mail.

```
SetSendMailShowing(enable)
```

When shortcuts are enabled, UseContainerItem() (i.e. right-click in the default UI's container frames) attaches the item to the outgoing message instead of using it.

Arguments:

enable—True to enable shortcuts; false to disable (boolean)

SetTaxiBenchmarkMode

Enables or disables flight path benchmark mode.

```
SetTaxiBenchmarkMode("arg")
```

When benchmark mode is enabled, the next taxi flight the player takes will behave differently: camera movement is disabled and players/creatures/objects below the flight path will not be shown (allowing for consistent test conditions). After the flight, framerate statistics will be printed in the chat window and benchmark mode will be automatically disabled.

Arguments:

arg—nil, "on", or 1 to enable benchmark mode; "off" or 0 to disable (string)

SetTaxiMap

Sets a Texture object to show the appropriate flight map texture.

```
SetTaxiMap(texture)
```

Only has effect while interacting with a flight master (i.e. between the TAXIMAP_OPENED and TAXIMAP_CLOSED events).

Arguments:

texture—A Texture object (table)

Example:

```
-- Create a frame, and set it to the taxi map
TestFrame = CreateFrame("Frame", "TestFrame", UIParent)
TestFrame:SetHeight(200)
TestFrame:SetWidth(200)
TestFrame:SetPoint("CENTER", UIParent, "CENTER", 0, 0)
TestFrameTexture = TestFrame:CreateTexture("TestFrameTexture", ↵
```

```
"BACKGROUND")
TestFrameTexture:SetAllPoints()

SetTaxiMap(TestFrameTexture)
```

SetTerrainMip

Changes the level of terrain detail displayed.

```
SetTerrainMip(terrainDetail)
```

Corresponds to the "Terrain Blending" slider in the default UI's Video Options pane.

Arguments:

`terrainDetail`—Level of terrain detail to be displayed (`number`)

- `0`—Low detail
- `1`—High detail

SetTracking

Enables a given minimap object/unit tracking ability.

```
SetTracking(index)
```

Arguments:

`index`—Index of a tracking ability (between `1` and `GetNumTrackingTypes()`) (`number`)

SetTradeMoney

Offers an amount of money for trade.

```
SetTradeMoney(amount)
```

Arguments:

`amount`—Amount of money to offer for trade (in copper) (`number`)

SetTradeSkillInvSlotFilter

Filters the trade skill listing by equipment slot of items produced.

```
SetTradeSkillInvSlotFilter(index [, enable [, exclusive]])
```

Arguments:

`index`—Index of an item equipment slot (in the list returned by `GetTradeSkillInvSlots()`), or 0 for no filter (`number`)

`enable` (optional)—1 to show recipes matching inventory type `index` in the filtered list; 0 to hide them (`number`)

`exclusive` (optional)—1 to disable other subclass filters when enabling this one; otherwise `nil` (`1nil`)

SetTradeSkillItemLevelFilter

Filters the trade skill listing by required level of items produced.

```
SetTradeSkillItemLevelFilter(minLevel, maxLevel)
```

Arguments:

`minLevel`—Lowest required level of items to show in the filtered list (`number`)

`maxLevel`—Highest required level of items to show in the filtered list (`number`)

SetTradeSkillItemNameFilter

Filters the trade skill listing by name of recipe, item produced, or reagents.

```
SetTradeSkillItemNameFilter("text")
```

Uses a substring (not exact-match) search: e.g. for a Scribe, the search string "doc" might filter the list to show only Certificate of Ownership because it matches the word "documentation" in that item's tooltip; a search for "stam" will match all items providing a Stamina bonus.

Arguments:

text—Text to search for in recipe names, produced item names or descriptions, or reagents (string)

SetTradeSkillSubClassFilter

Filters the trade skill listing by subclass of items produced.

```
SetTradeSkillSubClassFilter(index [, enable [, exclusive]])
```

Arguments:

index—Index of an item subclass (in the list returned by GetTradeSkill SubClasses()), or 0 for no filter (number)

enable (optional)—1 to show recipes matching subclass index in the filtered list; 0 to hide them (number)

exclusive (optional)—1 to disable other subclass filters when enabling this one; otherwise nil (1nil)

SetTrainerServiceTypeFilter

Filters the trainer service listing by service status.

```
SetTrainerServiceTypeFilter("type" [, enable [, exclusive]])
```

Arguments:

type—A service status (string)

- available—Services the player can use
- unavailable—Services the player cannot currently use
- used—Services the player has already used

enable (optional)—1 to show services matching type in the filtered list; 0 to hide them (number)

exclusive (optional)—1 to disable other type filters when enabling this one; otherwise nil (1nil)

Example:

```
-- Turn on the "available" filter
SetTrainerServiceTypeFilter("available", 1)

-- Turn on the "used" filter, and turn off all others
SetTrainerServiceTypeFilter("used", 1, 1)
```

SetTrainerSkillLineFilter

Filters the trainer service listing by skill line.

```
SetTrainerSkillLineFilter("type" [, enable [, exclusive]])
```

The default UI does not provide control for skill line filters, but they can nonetheless be used to alter the contents of the trainer service listing.

Arguments:

type—Index of a skill line filter (in the list returned by `GetTrainerSkill Lines()`) (string)

enable (optional)—1 to show services matching the given skill line in the filtered list; 0 to hide them (number)

exclusive (optional)—1 to disable other skill line filters when enabling this one; otherwise nil (1nil)

SetUIVisibility

Enables or disables display of UI elements in the 3-D world.

`SetUIVisibility(visible)`

Applies only to 2-D UI elements displayed in the 3-D world: nameplates and raid target icons (skull, circle, square, etc). Does not directly control nameplates and target icons; only affects whether they are displayed (see the `nameplateShowEnemies`/`nameplateShowFriends` CVars and `SetRaidTarget` functions for direct control).

Does not apply to 3-D UI elements such as the selection circle, area-effect targeting indicator, vehicle weapon aim indicator, etc.

Arguments:

visible—True to enable display of UI elements in the 3-D world; false to disable (boolean)

SetView

Moves the camera to a saved camera setting.

`SetView(index)`

There are five "slots" for saved camera settings, indexed 1-5. These views can be set and accessed directly using `SaveView()` and `SetView()`, and cycled through using `NextView()` and `PrevView()`.

Arguments:

index—Index of a saved camera setting (between 1 and 5) (number)

SetWatchedFactionIndex

Makes a faction the "watched" faction (displayed on the XP bar in the default UI).

`SetWatchedFactionIndex(index)`

Arguments:

index—Index of an entry in the faction list; between 1 and GetNumFactions() (number)

SetWhoToUI

Changes the delivery method for results from `SendWho()` queries.

`SetWhoToUI(state)`

In the default UI, results delivered in CHAT_MSG_SYSTEM are printed in the main chat window; results delivered in a WHO_LIST_UPDATE event cause the FriendsFrame to be shown, displaying the results in its "Who" tab.

Arguments:

state—Number identifying a delivery method (number)

- ▪ 0—Send results of three entries or fewer in CHAT_MSG_SYSTEM events and results of greater than three entries in a WHO_LIST_UPDATE event
- ▪ 1—Send all results in a WHO_LIST_UPDATE event

SetupFullscreenScale

Sizes a frame to take up the entire screen regardless of screen resolution.

SetupFullscreenScale(frame)

Arguments:

frame—Frame to resize to full screen (table)

ShowBattlefieldList

Requests to change instances for a battleground to which the player is already queued.

ShowBattlefieldList(index)

Causes the BATTLEFIELDS_SHOW event to fire, allowing the player to review the battleground's list of available instances and queue for a different one if desired.

Arguments:

index—Index of a battleground/arena queue the player has joined (between 1 and MAX_BATTLEFIELD_QUEUES) (number)

ShowBuybackSellCursor

Changes the cursor to prepare for repurchasing an item recently sold to a vendor.

ShowBuybackSellCursor(index)

Only changes the cursor image and mode if the given index contains an item.

Arguments:

index—Index of an item in the buyback listing (between 1 and GetNumBuybackItems()) (number)

ShowCloak

Enables or disables display of the player's cloak.

ShowCloak(show)

Only affects the player's appearance; does not change the other effects of having the cloak equipped. Determines not only the appearance of the player character on the local client, but the way other players see the character as well.

Arguments:

show—1 to display the player's cloak; nil to hide it (1nil)

ShowContainerSellCursor

Changes the cursor to prepare for selling an item in the player's bags to a vendor.

```
ShowContainerSellCursor(container, slot)
```

Only changes the cursor image and mode if the given `container` and `slot` contain an item.

While the cursor is in "sell" mode, `UseContainerItem()` sells the item to the vendor instead of using it.

Arguments:

`container`—Index of one of the player's bags or other containers (number, containerID)

`slot`—Index of an item slot within the container (number, containerSlotID)

ShowFriends

Requests friends/ignore list information from the server.

Information is not returned immediately; the `FRIENDLIST_UPDATE` event fires when data becomes available for use by Friends/Ignore API functions.

ShowHelm

Enables or disables display of the player's headgear.

```
ShowHelm(show)
```

Only affects the player's appearance; does not change the other effects of having the headgear equipped. Determines not only the appearance of the player character on the local client, but the way other players see the character as well.

Arguments:

`show`—1 to display the player's headgear; `nil` to hide it (1nil)

ShowInventorySellCursor

Changes the cursor to prepare for selling an equipped item to a vendor.

```
ShowInventorySellCursor(slot)
```

Only changes the cursor image and mode if the given `slot` contains an item.

(Unlike `ShowContainerSellCursor()`, does not change the behavior of other functions to enable selling of items. Unused in the default UI.)

Arguments:

`slot`—An inventory slot number, as can be obtained from `GetInventorySlotInfo` (number, inventoryID)

ShowMerchantSellCursor

Changes the cursor to prepare for buying an item from a vendor.

```
ShowMerchantSellCursor(index)
```

Only changes the cursor image and mode if the given `index` contains an item.

Arguments:

`index`—Index of an item in the vendor's listing (between 1 and `GetMerchantNumItems()`) (number)

ShowMiniWorldMapArrowFrame

Shows or hides the battlefield minimap's player arrow.

```
ShowMiniWorldMapArrowFrame(show)
```

Arguments:

show—If the battlefield minimap's player arrow should be shown (boolean)

ShowRepairCursor

Puts the cursor in item repair mode.

Unlike most other cursor functions, this functions changes the behavior as well as the appearance of the mouse cursor: while repair mode is active, calling PickupContainerItem() or PickupInventoryItem() will attempt to repair the item (and deduct the cost of such from the player's savings) instead of putting it on the cursor.

Only has effect while the player is interacting with a vendor which can perform repairs; i.e. between the MERCHANT_SHOW and MERCHANT_CLOSED events, and only if CanMerchantRepair() returns 1.

ShowingCloak

Returns whether the player's cloak is displayed.

```
isShown = ShowingCloak()
```

Determines not only the appearance of the player character on the local client, but the way other players see the character as well.

Returns:

isShown—1 if the player's cloak is shown; otherwise nil (1nil)

ShowingHelm

Returns whether the player's headgear is displayed.

```
isShown = ShowingHelm()
```

Determines not only the appearance of the player character on the local client, but the way other players see the character as well.

Returns:

isShown—1 if the player's headgear is shown; otherwise nil (1nil)

SignPetition

Signs the currently offered petition.

`Protected` ### SitStandOrDescendStart

Causes the player character to sit down if standing and vice versa (or begins descent if swimming or flying).

Used by the SITORSTAND binding, which also controls descent when swimming or flying.

SocketContainerItem

Opens an item from the player's bags for socketing.

```
SocketContainerItem(container, slot)
```

Arguments:

container—Index of one of the player's bags or other containers (number, containerID)

slot—Index of an item slot within the container (number, containerSlotID)

SocketInventoryItem

Opens an equipped item for socketing.

```
SocketInventoryItem(slot)
```

Arguments:

slot—An inventory slot number, as can be obtained from GetInventorySlot Info (number, inventoryID)

SortArenaTeamRoster

Sorts the selected arena team's roster.

```
SortArenaTeamRoster("sortType")
```

Affects the ordering of member information returned by GetArenaTeamRosterInfo. Sorting by the same criterion repeatedly reverses the sort order.

Arguments:

sortType—Criterion for sorting the roster (string)

- class—Sort by class
- name—Sort by name
- played—Sort by number of games played in the current week
- rating—Sort by personal rating
- seasonplayed—Sort by number of games played in the current arena season
- seasonwon—Sort by number of games won in the current arena season
- won—Sort by number of games won in the current week

SortAuctionApplySort

Applies a set of auction listing sort criteria set via SortAuctionSetSort.

```
SortAuctionApplySort("list")
```

Sort criteria are applied server-side, affecting not only the order of items within one "page" of listings but the order in which items are collected into pages.

Any currently displayed listings are re-sorted server-side: the AUCTION_ITEM_LIST_UPDATE, AUCTION_BIDDER_LIST_UPDATE, or AUCTION_OWNED_LIST_UPDATE event fires once the re-sorted data is available to the client; listing information can then be retrieved using GetAuctionItemInfo() or other Auction APIs.

Arguments:

list—Type of auction listing (string)

- bidder—Auctions the player has bid on
- list—Auctions the player can browse and bid on or buy out
- owner—Auctions the player placed

SortAuctionClearSort

Clears any current sorting rules for an auction house listing.

```
SortAuctionClearSort("list")
```

Arguments:

list—Type of auction listing (string)

- bidder—Auctions the player has bid on
- list—Auctions the player can browse and bid on or buy out
- owner—Auctions the player placed

SortAuctionSetSort

Builds a list of sort criteria for auction listings.

```
SortAuctionSetSort("list", "sort", reversed)
```

Has no effect until SortAuctionApplySort(type) is called; thus, this function can be called repeatedly to build a complex set of sort criteria. Sort criteria are applied server-side, affecting not only the order of items within one "page" of listings but the order in which items are collected into pages.

Criteria are applied in the order set by this function; i.e. the last criterion set becomes the primary sort criterion (see example).

Arguments:

list—Type of auction listing (string)

- bidder—Auctions the player has bid on
- list—Auctions the player can browse and bid on or buy out
- owner—Auctions the player placed

sort—Criterion to add to the sort (string)

- bid—Amount of the current or minimum bid on the item
- buyout—Buyout price of the item
- duration—Time remaining before the auction expires
- level—Required character level to use or equip the item
- minbidbuyout—Buyout price, or minimum bid if no buyout price is available
- name—Name of the item
- quality—itemQuality of the item
- quantity—Number of stacked items in the auction
- seller—Name of the character who created the auction (or in the owner listing, the current high bidder)
- status—Status of the auction (e.g. in the bidder listing, whether the player has been outbid)

reversed—True to sort in reverse order; otherwise false. "Reverse" here is relative to the default order, not to absolute value: e.g. the default order for quality is descending (Epic, Rare, Uncommon, etc), but the default order for level is ascending (1-80) (boolean)

Example:

```
-- clear any existing criteria
SortAuctionClearSort("list")

-- then, apply some criteria of our own
SortAuctionSetSort("list", "name")
SortAuctionSetSort("list", "level", 1)
SortAuctionSetSort("list", "quality")

-- apply the criteria to the server query
SortAuctionApplySort("list")

-- results are now sorted by quality, level and name:
-- higher quality items are listed before lower (e.g. Epic,
--   Rare, Uncommon)
-- items with the same quality are sorted descending by level
--   (e.g. 80, 75, 30, 1)
-- items with the same quality and level are sorted alphabetically
--   by name
```

SortBattlefieldScoreData

Sorts the battleground scoreboard.

```
SortBattlefieldScoreData("sortType")
```

Battleground-specific statistics include flags captured in Warsong Gulch, towers assaulted in Alterac Valley, etc. For the name and icon associated with each statistic, see `GetBattlefieldStatInfo()`.

Arguments:

`sortType`—Criterion for sorting the scoreboard data (`string`)

- `class`—Sort by character class
- `cp`—Sorts by honor points gained
- `damage`—Sorts by damage done
- `deaths`—Sort by number of deaths
- `healing`—Sorts by healing done
- `hk`—Sorts by number of honor kills
- `kills`—Sort by number of kills
- `name`—Sort by participant name
- `stat1`—Battlefield-specific statistic 1
- `stat2`—Battlefield-specific statistic 2
- `stat3`—Battlefield-specific statistic 3
- `stat4`—Battlefield-specific statistic 4
- `stat5`—Battlefield-specific statistic 5
- `stat6`—Battlefield-specific statistic 6
- `stat7`—Battlefield-specific statistic 7
- `team`— Sort by team name

SortGuildRoster

Sorts the guild roster.

```
SortGuildRoster("type")
```

Sorting repeatedly by the same criterion will reverse the sort order. Previous sorts are reused when a new criterion is applied: to sort by two criteria, sort first by the secondary criterion and then by the primary criterion.

Arguments:

type—Criterion by which to sort the roster (string)

- class—Sort by class name
- level—Sort by character level
- name—Sort by name
- note—Sort by guild note
- online—Sory by last online time
- rank—Sort by guild rank
- zone—Sort by current zone name

SortLFG

Sets the sort order for Looking for More results.

```
SortLFG("sortType")
```

Arguments:

sortType—Criterion for sorting the LFM results list (string)

- class—Sort by player class
- level—Sort by player level
- name—Sort by player name
- numPartyMembers—Sort by number of party members
- zone—Sort by current zone

SortWho

Sorts the Who system query results list.

```
SortWho("sortType")
```

Sorting by the same criterion twice will reverse the sort order.

Arguments:

sortType—Criterion for sorting the list (string)

- class—Sort by class name
- guild—Sort by guild name
- level—Sort by player level
- name—Sort by player name
- race—Sort by race name
- zone—Sort by current zone name

Sound_ChatSystem_GetInputDriverNameByIndex

Returns the name of the given chat system sound input driver.

```
Sound_ChatSystem_GetInputDriverNameByIndex(index)
```

Arguments:

index—The desired index (number)

Sound_ChatSystem_GetNumInputDrivers

Returns the number of chat system sound input drivers.

Sound_ChatSystem_GetNumOutputDrivers

Returns the number of chat system sound output drivers.

Sound_ChatSystem_GetOutputDriverNameByIndex

Returns the name of the given chat system sound output driver.

```
Sound_ChatSystem_GetOutputDriverNameByIndex(index)
```

Arguments:

index—The desired index (number)

Sound_GameSystem_GetInputDriverNameByIndex

Returns the name of the given game sound input driver.

```
Sound_GameSystem_GetInputDriverNameByIndex(index)
```

Arguments:

index—The desired index (number)

Sound_GameSystem_GetNumInputDrivers

Returns the number of game sound input drivers.

Sound_GameSystem_GetNumOutputDrivers

Returns the number of game sound output drivers.

Sound_GameSystem_GetOutputDriverNameByIndex

Returns the name of the given game sound output driver.

```
Sound_GameSystem_GetOutputDriverNameByIndex(index)
```

Arguments:

index—The desired index (number)

Sound_GameSystem_RestartSoundSystem

Restarts the game's sound systems.

SpellCanTargetGlyph

Returns whether the spell currently awaiting a target requires a glyph slot to be chosen.

```
canTarget = SpellCanTargetGlyph()
```

Only applies when the player has attempted to cast a spell—in this case, the "spell" cast when one uses a glyph item—but the spell requires a target before it can begin casting (i.e. the glowing hand cursor is showing).

Returns:

canTarget—1 if the spell can target glyph slots (1nil)

SpellCanTargetItem

Returns whether the spell currently awaiting a target requires an item to be chosen.

```
canTarget = SpellCanTargetItem()
```

Only applies when the player has attempted to cast a spell but the spell requires a target before it can begin casting (i.e. the glowing hand cursor is showing).

Returns:

canTarget—1 if the spell can target an item; otherwise nil (1nil)

SpellCanTargetUnit

Returns whether the spell currently awaiting a target can target a given unit.

canTarget = SpellCanTargetUnit("unit") or SpellCanTargetUnit("name")

Only applies when the player has attempted to cast a spell but the spell requires a target before it can begin casting (i.e. the glowing hand cursor is showing).

Arguments:

unit—A unit to target (string, unitID)

name—The name of a unit to target; only valid for player, pet, and party/raid members (string)

Returns:

canTarget—1 if the spell currently awaiting targeting can target the given unit (1nil)

SpellHasRange

Returns whether an item has a range limitation for its use.

hasRange = SpellHasRange(index, "bookType") or SpellHasRange("name")

For example: Shadowbolt can only be used on a unit within a given range of the player; Ritual of Summoning requires a target but has no range restriction; Fel Armor has no target and thus no range restriction.

Arguments:

index—Index of a spell in the spellbook (number, spellbookID)

bookType—Type of spellbook (string)

- pet—The pet's spellbook
- spell—The player's spellbook

name—Name of a spell (string)

Returns:

hasRange—1 if the spell has an effective range; otherwise nil. (1nil)

SpellIsTargeting

Returns whether a spell is currently awaiting a target.

isTargeting = SpellIsTargeting()

Returns:

isTargeting—1 if a spell is currently awaiting a target; otherwise nil (1nil)

Protected ### SpellStopCasting

Stops casting or targeting the spell in progress.

Protected

SpellStopTargeting

Cancels the spell currently awaiting a target.

When auto-self cast is not enabled and the player casts a spell that requires a target, the cursor changes to a glowing hand so the user can select a target. This function cancels targeting mode so the player can cast another spell.

Protected

SpellTargetItem

Casts the spell currently awaiting a target on an item.

```
SpellTargetItem(itemID) or SpellTargetItem("itemName") or ↵
SpellTargetItem("itemLink")
```

Usable when the player has attempted to cast a spell (e.g. an Enchanting recipe or the "Use:" effect of a sharpening stone or fishing lure) but the spell requires a target before it can begin casting (i.e. the glowing hand cursor is showing).

Arguments:

itemID—An item's ID (number)

itemName—An item's name (string)

itemLink—An item's hyperlink, or any string containing the itemString portion of an item link (string)

Protected

SpellTargetUnit

Casts the spell currently awaiting a target on a unit.

```
SpellTargetUnit("unit") or SpellTargetUnit("name")
```

Arguments:

unit—A unit to target (string, unitID)

name—The name of a unit to target; only valid for player, pet, and party/raid members (string)

SplitContainerItem

Picks up only part of a stack of items from one of the player's bags or other containers.

```
SplitContainerItem(container, slot, amount)
```

Has no effect if the given amount is greater than the number of items stacked in the slot.

Arguments:

container—Index of one of the player's bags or other containers (number, containerID)

slot—Index of an item slot within the container (number, containerSlotID)

amount—Number of items from the stack to pick up (number)

SplitGuildBankItem

Picks up only part of a stack of items from the guild bank.

```
SplitGuildBankItem(tab, slot, amount)
```

Has no effect if the given amount is greater than the number of items stacked in the slot.

Arguments:

`tab`—Index of a guild bank tab (`number`)

`slot`—Index of an item slot in the guild bank tab (`number`)

`amount`—Number of items from the stack to pick up (`number`)

StablePet

Puts the player's current pet into the stables.

StartAttack

Begins auto-attack against a specified target.

`StartAttack("unit") or StartAttack("name")`

Arguments:

`unit`—A unit to attack (`string`, unitID)

`name`—The name of a unit to attack (`string`)

StartAuction

Creates an auction for the item currently in the "auction item" slot.

`StartAuction(minBid, buyoutPrice, runTime)`

Has no effect unless an item has been placed in the Create Auction UI's "auction item" slot (see `ClickAuctionSellItemButton()`).

Arguments:

`minBid`—Minimum bid for the auction (in copper) (`number`)

`buyoutPrice`—Buyout price for the auction (in copper) (`number`)

`runTime`—Run time until the auction expires (in minutes, but only values listed below are allowed) (`number`)

- `720`—12 hours
- `1440`—24 hours
- `2880`—48 hours

StartDuel

Challenges another player to a duel.

`StartDuel("unit") or StartDuel("name" [, exactMatch])`

Arguments:

`unit`—A unit to target (`string`, unitID)

`name`—Name of a unit to target (`string`)

`exactMatch` (optional)—`True` to check only units whose name exactly matches the `name` given; `false` to allow partial matches (`boolean`)

StopAttack

Stops auto-attack if active.

StopCinematic

Exits a currently playing in-game cinematic.

Applies to in-game-engine cinematics (such as when logging into a new character for the first time), not prerecorded movies.

Protected **StopMacro**

Stops execution of a running macro.

StopMusic

Stops currently playing in-game music.

StopTradeSkillRepeat

Cancels repetition of a trade skill recipe.

If a recipe is currently being performed, it will continue, but further scheduled repetitions will be canceled.

Protected **StrafeLeftStart**

Begins moving the player character sideways to his or her left.

Protected **StrafeLeftStop**

Ends movement initiated by `StrafeLeftStart`.

Protected **StrafeRightStart**

Begins moving the player character sideways to his or her right.

Protected **StrafeRightStop**

Ends movement initiated by `StrafeRightStart`.

Protected **Stuck**

Uses the auto-unstuck feature.

SummonFriend

Summons a unit whose account is linked to the player's via the Recruit-a-Friend program.

`SummonFriend("name") or SummonFriend("unit")`

Does not instantly teleport the unit. Calling this function begins casting the Summon Friend "spell", and once it completes the unit is prompted to accept or decline the summons.

Arguments:

`name`—Exact name of a player to summon (only applies to units in the player's party or raid) (string)

`unit`—A unit to summon (string, unitID)

SwapRaidSubgroup

Swaps two raid members between subgroups in the raid.

`SwapRaidSubgroup(index1, index2)`

Only has effect if the player is the raid leader or a raid assistant. To move a member into a non-full subgroup without switching places with another member, see `SetRaidSubgroup()`.

Arguments:

`index1`—Index of the first raid member (between 1 and `GetNumRaid Members()`); matches the numeric part of the unit's raid `unitID`, e.g. 21 for `raid21` (number)

`index2`—Index of the other raid member (number)

| Confirmation |

TakeInboxItem

Retrieves an item attachment from a message in the player's inbox (accepting COD charges if applicable).

```
TakeInboxItem(mailID, attachmentIndex)
```

Arguments:

`mailID`—Index of a message in the player's inbox (between 1 and `GetInboxNumItems()`) (number)

`attachmentIndex`—Index of an attachment to the message (between 1 and `select(8,GetInboxHeaderInfo(mailID))`) (number)

TakeInboxMoney

Retrieves any money attached to a message in the player's inbox.

```
TakeInboxMoney(mailID)
```

Arguments:

`mailID`—Index of a message in the player's inbox (between 1 and `GetInboxNumItems()`) (number)

TakeInboxTextItem

Requests a copy of a message's body text as an item.

```
TakeInboxTextItem(mailID)
```

The text of an in-game mail can be retrieved as a readable "Plain Letter" item to store in the player's bags; this function sends a request to the server for this item, causing the standard inventory events to fire as the item is placed into the player's inventory.

Arguments:

`mailID`—Index of a message in the player's inbox (between 1 and `GetInboxNumItems()`) (number)

TakeTaxiNode

Embarks on a taxi flight to a given destination.

```
TakeTaxiNode(index)
```

Only has effect while interacting with a flight master (i.e. between the `TAXIMAP_OPENED` and `TAXIMAP_CLOSED` events).

Arguments:

`index`—Index of a flight point (between 1 and `NumTaxiNodes()`) (number)

| Protected |

TargetLastEnemy

Targets the most recently targeted enemy unit.

| Protected |

TargetLastFriend

Targets the most recently targeted friendly unit.

| Protected |

TargetLastTarget

Targets the most recently targeted unit.

Protected

TargetNearest

Cycles targets through nearest units regardless of reaction/affiliation.

`TargetNearest([backward])`

Arguments:

`backward` (optional)—Reverses direction of target cycling if `true`
(as with the default TAB vs. SHIFT-TAB bindings) (`boolean`)

Protected

TargetNearestEnemy

Cycles your target through the nearest enemy units.

`TargetNearestEnemy(backward)`

This function can only be called once per hardware event.

Arguments:

`backward`—Reverses the direction of the cycling if `true` (e.g. TAB vs.
SHIFT-TAB) (`boolean`)

Protected

TargetNearestEnemyPlayer

Cycles targets through nearby enemy player units.

`TargetNearestEnemyPlayer(backward)`

Arguments:

`backward`—Reverses direction of target cycling if `true` (as with the default TAB
vs. SHIFT-TAB bindings) (`boolean`)

Protected

TargetNearestFriend

Cycles targets through nearby friendly units.

`TargetNearestFriend(backward)`

Arguments:

`backward`—Reverses direction of target cycling if `true` (as with the default TAB
vs. SHIFT-TAB bindings) (`boolean`)

Protected

TargetNearestFriendPlayer

Cycles targets through nearby friendly player units.

`TargetNearestFriendPlayer(backward)`

Arguments:

`backward`—Reverses direction of target cycling if `true` (as with the default TAB
vs. SHIFT-TAB bindings) (`boolean`)

Protected

TargetNearestPartyMember

Cycles targets through nearby party members.

`TargetNearestPartyMember(backward)`

Arguments:

`backward`—Reverses direction of target cycling if `true` (as with the default TAB
vs. SHIFT-TAB bindings) (`boolean`)

Protected **TargetNearestRaidMember**

Cycles targets through nearby raid members.

```
TargetNearestRaidMember(backward)
```

Arguments:

backward—Reverses direction of target cycling if `true` (as with the default TAB vs. SHIFT-TAB bindings) (`boolean`)

Protected **TargetTotem**

Targets one of the player's totems (or a Death Knight's ghoul).

```
TargetTotem(slot)
```

Totem functions are also used for ghouls summoned by a Death Knight's Raise Dead ability (if the ghoul is not made a controllable pet by the Master of Ghouls talent).

Arguments:

slot—Which totem to target (`number`)

1—Fire (or Death Knight's ghoul)   3—Water

2—Earth   4—Air

Protected **TargetUnit**

Targets a unit.

```
TargetUnit("unit") or TargetUnit("name" [, exactMatch])
```

Passing `nil` is equivalent to calling `ClearTarget()`).

Arguments:

unit—A unit to target (`string`, unitID)

name—Name of a unit to target (`string`)

exactMatch (optional)—True to check only units whose name exactly matches the `name` given; `false` to allow partial matches (`boolean`)

TaxiGetDestX

Returns the horizontal coordinate of a taxi flight's destination node.

```
dX = TaxiGetDestX(source, dest)
```

Used in the default UI to draw lines between nodes; `TaxiNodeSetCurrent()` should be called first so the client can compute routes.

Only returns valid data while interacting with a flight master (i.e. between the `TAXIMAP_OPENED` and `TAXIMAP_CLOSED` events).

Arguments:

source—Index of the source flight point (between `1` and `NumTaxiNodes()`) (`number`)

dest—Index of the destination flight point (between `1` and `NumTaxiNodes()`) (`number`)

Returns:

dX—X coordinate of the destination taxi node (as a proportion of the taxi map's width; 0 = left edge, 1 = right edge) (number)

TaxiGetDestY

Returns the vertical coordinate of a taxi flight's destination node.

```
dY = TaxiGetDestY(source, dest)
```

Used in the default UI to draw lines between nodes; TaxiNodeSetCurrent() should be called first so the client can compute routes.

Only returns valid data while interacting with a flight master (i.e. between the TAXIMAP_OPENED and TAXIMAP_CLOSED events).

Arguments:

source—Index of the source flight point (between 1 and NumTaxiNodes()) (number)

dest—Index of the destination flight point (between 1 and NumTaxiNodes()) (number)

Returns:

dY—Y coordinate of the destination taxi node (as a proportion of the taxi map's height; 0 = bottom, 1 = top) (number)

TaxiGetSrcX

Returns the horizontal coordinate of a taxi flight's source node.

```
sX = TaxiGetSrcX(source, dest)
```

Used in the default UI to draw lines between nodes; TaxiNodeSetCurrent() should be called first so the client can compute routes.

Only returns valid data while interacting with a flight master (i.e. between the TAXIMAP_OPENED and TAXIMAP_CLOSED events).

Arguments:

source—Index of the source flight point (between 1 and NumTaxiNodes()) (number)

dest—Index of the destination flight point (between 1 and NumTaxiNodes()) (number)

Returns:

sX—X coordinate of the source taxi node (as a proportion of the taxi map's width; 0 = left edge, 1 = right edge) (number)

TaxiGetSrcY

Returns the vertical coordinate of a taxi flight's source node.

```
sY = TaxiGetSrcY(source, dest)
```

Used in the default UI to draw lines between nodes; TaxiNodeSetCurrent() should be called first so the client can compute routes.

Only returns valid data while interacting with a flight master (i.e. between the TAXIMAP_OPENED and TAXIMAP_CLOSED events).

Arguments:

source—Index of the source flight point (between 1 and NumTaxiNodes())
(number)

dest—Index of the destination flight point (between 1 and NumTaxiNodes())
(number)

Returns:

sY—Y coordinate of the source taxi node (as a proportion of the taxi map's
height; 0 = bottom, 1 = top) (number)

TaxiNodeCost

Returns the cost to fly to a given taxi node.

cost = TaxiNodeCost(index)

Only returns valid data while interacting with a flight master (i.e. between the
TAXIMAP_OPENED and TAXIMAP_CLOSED events).

Arguments:

index—Index of a flight point (between 1 and NumTaxiNodes()) (number)

Returns:

cost—Price of a flight to the given node (in copper) (number)

TaxiNodeGetType

Returns the type of a flight point.

type = TaxiNodeGetType(index)

Only returns valid data while interacting with a flight master (i.e. between the
TAXIMAP_OPENED and TAXIMAP_CLOSED events).

Arguments:

index—Index of a flight point (between 1 and NumTaxiNodes()) (number)

Returns:

type—Type of the flight point (string)

- CURRENT—The player's current location
- DISTANT—Unreachable from the current location
- NONE—Not currently in use
- REACHABLE—Reachable from the current location (directly or through other
  nodes)

TaxiNodeName

Returns the name of a flight point.

name = TaxiNodeName(index)

Only returns valid data while interacting with a flight master (i.e. between the
TAXIMAP_OPENED and TAXIMAP_CLOSED events).

Arguments:

index—Index of a flight point (between 1 and NumTaxiNodes()) (number)

Returns:

name—Name of the taxi node (string)

TaxiNodePosition

Returns the position of a flight point on the taxi map.

`x, y = TaxiNodePosition(index)`

Only returns valid data while interacting with a flight master (i.e. between the `TAXIMAP_OPENED` and `TAXIMAP_CLOSED` events).

Arguments:

index—Index of a flight point (between 1 and `NumTaxiNodes()`) (number)

Returns:

x—Horizontal coordinate of the taxi node (as a proportion of the taxi map's width; 0 = left edge, 1 = right edge) (number)

y—Vertical coordinate of the taxi node (as a proportion of the taxi map's height; 0 = bottom, 1 = top) (number)

TaxiNodeSetCurrent

Sets the "current" flight path node.

`TaxiNodeSetCurrent(slot)`

Used in the default UI when mousing over a node; tells the client to compute the route paths involving the node (see `TaxiGetSrcX()` et al).

Arguments:

slot—The internal index of a flight path node (number)

`Protected`   **ToggleAutoRun**

Starts or stops the player character automatically moving forward.

TogglePVP

Switches the player's desired PvP status.

If PvP is currently disabled for the player, it becomes enabled immediately. If PvP is enabled, it will become disabled after five minutes of no PvP activity.

`Protected`   **TogglePetAutocast**

Turns autocast on or off for a pet action.

`TogglePetAutocast(index)`

Turns autocast on if not autocasting and vice versa.

Arguments:

index—Index of a pet action button (between 1 and NUM_PET_ACTION_SLOTS) (number)

`Protected`   **ToggleRun**

Switches the character's ground movement mode between running and walking.

If running, switches to walking, and vice versa. Has no effect on swimming or flying speed.

ToggleSheath

Sheaths or unsheaths the player character's hand-held items.

Calling repeatedly will cause the player character to draw his or her melee weapons, followed by his or her range weapon, followed by hiding all weapons.

ToggleSpellAutocast

Enables or disables automatic casting of a spell.

```
ToggleSpellAutocast(index, "bookType") or ToggleSpellAutocast("name")
```

Generally only pet spells can be autocast.

Arguments:

index—Index of a spell in the spellbook (number, spellbookID)

bookType—Type of spellbook (string)

■ pet—The pet's spellbook

■ spell—The player's spellbook

name—Name of a spell (string)

TradeSkillOnlyShowMakeable

Filters the trade skill listing by whether the player currently has enough reagents for each recipe.

```
TradeSkillOnlyShowMakeable(filter)
```

Arguments:

filter—True to filter the recipe listing to show only recipes for which the player currently has enough reagents; false to show all recipes (boolean)

TradeSkillOnlyShowSkillUps

Filters the trade skill listing by whether the player can gain skill ranks from each recipe.

```
TradeSkillOnlyShowSkillUps(filter)
```

The default UI does not provide controls for this filter, but it can nonetheless be used to alter the contents of the trade skill recipe listing.

Arguments:

filter—True to filter the recipe listing to show only recipes which the player can gain skill ranks by performing; false to show all recipes (boolean)

TurnInArenaPetition

Turns in a petition creating an arena team.

```
TurnInArenaPetition(teamSize, bg_red, bg_green, bg_blue, emblem, ↵
emblem_red, emblem_green, emblem_blue, border, border_red, ↵
border_green, border_blue)
```

Arguments:

teamSize—Size of arena team to create (number)

■ 2—2v2

■ 3—3v3

■ 5—5v5

bg_red—Red component of the color value for the team banner's background (number)

bg_green—Green component of the color value for the team banner's background (number)

bg_blue—Blue component of the color value for the team banner's background (number)

emblem—Index of the team's emblem graphic; full path to the emblem texture can be found using the format "Interface\PVPFrame\Icons\PVP-Banner-Emblem-"..emblem (number)

emblem_red—Red component of the color value for the team banner's emblem (number)

emblem_green—Green component of the color value for the team banner's emblem (number)

emblem_blue—Blue component of the color value for the team banner's emblem (number)

border—Index of the team's border graphic; full path to the border texture can be found by using the format "Interface\PVPFrame\PVP-Banner-".. teamSize.."-Border-"..border (number)

border_red—Red component of the color value for the team banner's border (number)

border_green—Green component of the color value for the team banner's border (number)

border_blue—Blue component of the color value for the team banner's border (number)

TurnInGuildCharter

Turns in a completed guild charter.

Usable if the player is interacting with a guild registrar (i.e. between the GUILD_REGISTRAR_SHOW and GUILD_REGISTRAR_CLOSED events).

`Protected`

TurnLeftStart

Begins turning the player character to the left.

"Left" here is relative to the player's facing; i.e. if looking down at the character from above, he or she turns counter-clockwise.

Used by the TURNLEFT binding.

`Protected`

TurnLeftStop

Ends movement initiated by TurnLeftStart.

`Protected`

TurnOrActionStart

Begins character steering or interaction (equivalent to right-clicking in the 3-D world).

After calling this function (i.e. while the right mouse button is held), cursor movement rotates (or steers) the player character, altering yaw (facing) and/or pitch (vertical movement angle) as well as camera position. Final results vary by context and are determined when calling TurnOrActionStop() (i.e. releasing the right mouse button).

Used by the TURNORACTION binding (not customizable in the default UI), which is bound to the right mouse button by default.

TurnOrActionStop

Ends action initiated by TurnOrActionStart.

After calling this function (i.e. releasing the right mouse button), character steering stops and normal cursor movement resumes. If the cursor has not moved significantly since calling TurnOrActionStart() (i.e. pressing the right mouse button), results vary by context:

- if the cursor is over a nearby unit, interacts with (or attacks) that unit, making it the player's target.
- if the cursor is over a nearby interactable world object (e.g. mailbox, treasure chest, or quest object), interacts with (or uses) that object.
- if the cursor is over a faraway unit or world object and the "Click-to-Move" option is enabled (i.e. the "autointeract" CVar is "1"), attempts to move the player character to the unit/object and interact with it once nearby.
- if the cursor is over a faraway world object and the "Click-to-Move" option is disabled, fires a UI_ERROR_MESSAGE event indicating the player is too far away to interact with the object.
- otherwise, does nothing.

Used by the TURNORACTION binding (not customizable in the default UI), which is bound to the right mouse button by default.

TurnRightStart

Begins turning the player character to the right.

"Right" here is relative to the player's facing; i.e. if looking down at the character from above, he or she turns clockwise.

Used by the TURNRIGHT binding.

TurnRightStop

Ends movement initiated by TurnRightStart.

TutorialsEnabled

Returns whether contextual tutorials are enabled.

```
enabled = TutorialsEnabled()
```

Returns:

enabled—1 if contextual tutorials are enabled; otherwise nil (1nil)

UninviteUnit

Removes a character from the player's party or raid.

```
UninviteUnit("name")
```

Only works if the player is the party leader, raid leader, or raid assistant.

Arguments:

name—Name of a character to uninvite (string)

UnitAffectingCombat

Returns whether a unit is currently in combat.

```
inCombat = UnitAffectingCombat("unit")
```

Arguments:

unit—A unit to query (string, unitID)

Returns:

inCombat—1 if the unit is currently involved in combat; otherwise nil (1nil)

UnitArmor

Returns the player's or pet's armor value.

```
base, effectiveArmor, armor, posBuff, negBuff = UnitArmor("unit")
```

Arguments:

unit—A unit to query; only valid for player or pet (string, unitID)

Returns:

base—The unit's base armor value (number)

effectiveArmor—The unit's effective armor value (number)

armor—The unit's current armor value (number)

posBuff—Positive modifiers to armor value (number)

negBuff—Negative modifiers to armor value (number)

UnitAttackBothHands

Returns information about the player's or pet's weapon skill.

```
mainHandAttackBase, mainHandAttackMod, offHandHandAttackBase, ↩
offHandAttackMod = UnitAttackBothHands("unit")
```

Arguments:

unit—A unit to query; only valid for player or pet (string, unitID)

Returns:

mainHandAttackBase—The unit's base weapon skill for the main hand weapon (number)

mainHandAttackMod—Temporary modifiers to main hand weapon skill (number)

offHandHandAttackBase—The unit's base weapon skill for the off hand weapon (number)

offHandAttackMod—Temporary modifiers to off hand weapon skill (number)

UnitAttackPower

Returns the player's or pet's melee attack power.

```
base, posBuff, negBuff = UnitAttackPower("unit")
```

Arguments:

unit—A unit to query; only valid for player or pet (string, unitID)

Returns:

base—The unit's base attack power (number)

posBuff—Total effect of positive buffs to attack power (number)

negBuff—Total effect of negative buffs to attack power (number)

UnitAttackSpeed

Returns information about the player's or pet's melee attack speed.

```
speed, offhandSpeed = UnitAttackSpeed("unit")
```

Arguments:

unit—A unit to query; only valid for `player` or `pet` (string, unitID)

Returns:

speed—Current speed of the unit's main hand attack (number of seconds per attack) (number)

offhandSpeed—Current speed of the unit's off hand attack (number of seconds per attack) (number)

UnitAura

Returns information about buffs/debuffs on a unit.

```
name, rank, icon, count, dispelType, duration, expires, caster, ↵
isStealable = UnitAura("unit", index [, "filter"]) or ↵
UnitAura("unit", "name" [, "rank" [, "filter"]])
```

Arguments:

unit—A unit to query (string, unitID)

index—Index of an aura to query (number)

name—Name of an aura to query (string)

rank (optional)—Secondary text of an aura to query (often a rank; e.g. "Rank 7") (string)

filter (optional)—A list of filters to use separated by the pipe '|' character; e.g. `"RAID|PLAYER"` will query group buffs cast by the player (string)

- CANCELABLE—Show auras that can be cancelled
- HARMFUL—Show debuffs only
- HELPFUL—Show buffs only
- NOT_CANCELABLE—Show auras that cannot be cancelled
- PLAYER—Show auras the player has cast
- RAID—When used with a HELPFUL filter it will show auras the player can cast on party/raid members (as opposed to self buffs). If used with a HARMFUL filter it will return debuffs the player can cure

Returns:

name—Name of the aura (string)

rank—Secondary text for the aura (often a rank; e.g. "Rank 7") (string)

icon—Path to an icon texture for the aura (string)

count—The number of times the aura has been applied (number)

dispelType—Type of aura (relevant for dispelling and certain other mechanics); nil if not one of the following values: (string)

Curse	Magic
Disease	Poison

duration—Total duration of the aura (in seconds) (`number`)

expires—Time at which the aura will expire; can be compared to GetTime() to determine time remaining (`number`)

caster—Unit which applied the aura. If the aura was applied by a unit that does not have a token but is controlled by one that does (e.g. a totem or another player's vehicle), returns the controlling unit. Returns `nil` if the casting unit (or its controller) has no unitID. (`string`, unitID)

isStealable—1 if the aura can be transferred to a player using the Spellsteal spell; otherwise `nil` (`1nil`)

UnitBuff

Returns information about a buff on a unit.

```
name, rank, icon, count, dispelType, duration, expires, caster, ↵
isStealable = UnitBuff("unit", index [, "filter"]) or ↵
UnitBuff("unit", "name" [, "rank" [, "filter"]])
```

This function is an alias for `UnitAura()` with a built-in HELPFUL filter (which cannot be removed or negated with the HARMFUL filter).

Arguments:

unit—A unit to query (`string`, unitID)

index—Index of an aura to query (`number`)

name—Name of an aura to query (`string`)

rank (optional)—Secondary text of an aura to query (often a rank; e.g. "Rank 7") (`string`)

filter (optional)—A list of filters to use separated by the pipe '|' character; e.g. `"RAID|PLAYER"` will query group buffs cast by the player (`string`)

- CANCELABLE—Show auras that can be cancelled
- NOT_CANCELABLE—Show auras that cannot be cancelled
- PLAYER—Show auras the player has cast
- RAID—Show auras the player can cast on party/raid members (as opposed to self buffs)

Returns:

name—Name of the aura (`string`)

rank—Secondary text for the aura (often a rank; e.g. "Rank 7") (`string`)

icon—Path to an icon texture for the aura (`string`)

count—The number of times the aura has been applied (`number`)

dispelType—Type of aura (relevant for dispelling and certain other mechanics); `nil` if not one of the following values: (`string`)

Curse	Magic
Disease	Poison

duration—Total duration of the aura (in seconds) (`number`)

expires—Time at which the aura will expire; can be compared to GetTime() to determine time remaining (`number`) caster—Unit which applied the aura. If the aura was applied by a unit that does not have a token but is controlled by one that does (e.g. a totem or another player's vehicle), returns the controlling unit. Returns nil if the casting unit (or its controller) has no unitID. (string, unitID)

isStealable—1 if the aura can be transferred to a player using the Spellsteal spell; otherwise nil (1nil)

UnitCanAssist

Returns whether one unit can assist another.

```
canAssist = UnitCanAssist("unit", "unit")
```

Arguments:

unit—A unit (string, unitID)

unit—Another unit (string, unitID)

Returns:

canAssist—1 if the first unit can assist the second; otherwise nil (1nil)

UnitCanAttack

Returns whether one unit can attack another.

```
canAttack = UnitCanAttack("unit", "unit")
```

Arguments:

unit—A unit (string, unitID)

unit—Another unit (string, unitID)

Returns:

canAttack—1 if the first unit can attack the second unit; otherwise nil (1nil)

UnitCanCooperate

Returns whether two units can cooperate.

```
canCooperate = UnitCanCooperate("unit", "unit")
```

Two units are considered to be able to cooperate with each other if they are of the same faction and are both players.

Arguments:

unit—A unit (string, unitID)

unit—Another unit (string, unitID)

Returns:

canCooperate—1 if the two units can cooperate with each other; otherwise nil (1nil)

UnitCastingInfo

Returns information about the spell a unit is currently casting.

```
name, subText, text, texture, startTime, endTime, isTradeSkill, ↵
castID, notInterruptible = UnitCastingInfo("unit")
```

Arguments:

unit—A unit to query (string, unitID)

Returns:

name—Name of the spell being cast (string)

subText—Secondary text associated with the spell (e.g."Rank 5", "Racial", etc.)
(string)

text—Text to be displayed on a casting bar (string)

texture—Path to an icon texture for the spell (string)

startTime—Time at which the cast was started (in milliseconds; can be compared to GetTime() * 1000) (number)

endTime—Time at which the cast will finish (in milliseconds; can be compared to GetTime() * 1000) (number)

isTradeSkill—1 if the spell being cast is a trade skill recipe; otherwise nil
(1nil)

castID—Reference number for this spell; matches the 4th argument of UNIT_SPELLCAST_* events for the same spellcast (number)

notInterruptible—1 if the spell can be interrupted; otherwise nil.
See the UNIT_SPELLCAST_NOT_INTERRUPTIBLE and UNIT_SPELLCAST
_INTERRUPTIBLE events for changes to this status. (1nil)

UnitChannelInfo

Returns information about the spell a unit is currently channeling.

```
name, subText, text, texture, startTime, endTime, isTradeSkill, ↵
notInterruptible = UnitChannelInfo("unit")
```

Arguments:

unit—A unit to query (string, unitID)

Returns:

name—Name of the spell being cast (string)

subText—Secondary text associated with the spell (e.g."Rank 5", "Racial", etc.)
(string)

text—Text to be displayed on a casting bar (string)

texture—Path to an icon texture for the spell (string)

startTime—Time at which the cast was started (in milliseconds; can be compared to GetTime() * 1000) (number)

endTime—Time at which the cast will finish (in milliseconds; can be compared to GetTime() * 1000) (number)

isTradeSkill—1 if the spell being cast is a trade skill recipe; otherwise nil
(1nil)

notInterruptible—Indicates that the spell cannot be interrupted,
UNIT_SPELLCAST_NOT_INTERRUPTIBLE and UNIT_SPELLCAST
_INTERRUPTIBLE are fired to indicate changes in the interruptible status.
(boolean)

UnitCharacterPoints

Returns the player's number of unused talent points and profession slots.

```
talentPoints, professionSlots = UnitCharacterPoints("unit")
```

Arguments:

unit—A unit to query; only valid for player (string, unitID)

Returns:

talentPoints—Number of unspent talent points (number)

professionSlots—Number of available profession slots (number)

UnitClass

Returns a unit's class.

```
class, classFileName = UnitClass("unit") or UnitClass("name")
```

The second return (classFileName) can be used for locale-independent verification of a unit's class, or to look up class-related data in various global tables:

- RAID_CLASS_COLORS provides a standard color for each class (as seen in the default who, guild, calendar, and raid UIs)
- CLASS_ICON_TCOORDS provides coordinates to locate each class' icon within the "Interface\Glues\CharacterCreate\UI-CharacterCreate-Classes" texture

For non-player units, the first return (class) will be the unit's name; to always get a localized class name regardless of unit type, use UnitClassBase instead.

Arguments:

unit—A unit to query (string, unitID)

name—Name of a unit to query; only valid for player, pet, and party/raid members (string)

Returns:

class—The localized name of the unit's class, or the unit's name if the unit is an NPC (string)

classFileName—A non-localized token representing the class (string)

Example:

```
-- Print the name of your target in a class-specific color
local class, classFileName = UnitClass("target")
local color = RAID_CLASS_COLORS[classFileName]
ChatFrame1:AddMessage(class, color.r, color.g, color.b)
```

UnitClassBase

Returns a unit's class.

```
class, classFileName = UnitClassBase("unit") or UnitClassBase("name")
```

The second return (`classFileName`) can be used for locale-independent verification of a unit's class, or to look up class-related data in various global tables:

- `RAID_CLASS_COLORS` provides a standard color for each class (as seen in the default who, guild, calendar, and raid UIs)
- `CLASS_ICON_TCOORDS` provides coordinates to locate each class' icon within the "Interface\Glues\CharacterCreate\UI-CharacterCreate-Classes" texture

Unlike `UnitClass`, this function returns the same values for NPCs as for players.

Arguments:

`unit`—A unit to query (string, unitID)

`name`—Name of a unit to query; only valid for `player`, `pet`, and party/raid members (string)

Returns:

`class`—The localized name of the unit's class (string)

`classFileName`—A non-localized token representing the class (string)

UnitClassification

Returns a unit's classification.

```
classification = UnitClassification("unit")
```

Arguments:

`unit`—A unit to query (string, unitID)

Returns:

`classification`—Classification of the unit (string)

`elite`—Elite	`rareelite`—Rare-Elite
`normal`—Normal	`worldboss`—World Boss
`rare`—Rare	

UnitControllingVehicle

Returns whether a unit is controlling a vehicle.

```
isControlling = UnitControllingVehicle("unit") or ↵
UnitControllingVehicle("name")
```

Arguments:

`unit`—A unit to query (string, unitID)

`name`—The name of a unit to query; only valid for `player`, `pet`, and party/raid members (string)

Returns:

`isControlling`—True if the unit is controlling a vehicle; otherwise `false` (boolean)

UnitCreatureFamily

Returns the creature family of the unit.

```
family = UnitCreatureFamily("unit")
```

Applies only to beasts of the kinds that can be taken as Hunter pets (e.g. cats, worms, and ravagers but not zhevras, talbuks and pterrordax) and demons of the types that can be summoned by Warlocks (e.g. imps and felguards, but not demons that require enslaving such as infernals and doomguards or world demons such as pit lords and armored voidwalkers).

Arguments:

unit—A unit to query (string, unitID)

Returns:

family—Localized name of the subtype of creature (e.g. Bear, Devilsaur, Voidwalker, Succubus), or nil if not applicable (string)

UnitCreatureType

Returns the creature type of a unit.

```
type = UnitCreatureType("unit")
```

Note that some creatures have no type (e.g. slimes).

Arguments:

unit—A unit to query (string, unitID)

Returns:

type—Localized name of the type of creature (e.g. Beast, Humanoid, Undead), or nil if not applicable (string)

UnitDamage

Returns information about the player's or pet's melee attack damage.

```
minDamage, maxDamage, minOffHandDamage, maxOffHandDamage, ↵
physicalBonusPos, physicalBonusNeg, percent = UnitDamage("unit")
```

Arguments:

unit—A unit to query; only valid for player or pet (string, unitID)

Returns:

minDamage—The unit's minimum melee damage (number)

maxDamage—The unit's maximum melee damage (number)

minOffHandDamage—The unit's minimum offhand melee damage (number)

maxOffHandDamage—The unit's maximum offhand melee damage (number)

physicalBonusPos—Positive physical bonus (should be >= 0) (number)

physicalBonusNeg—Negative physical bonus (should be <= 0) (number)

percent—Factor by which damage output is multiplied due to buffs/debuffs (number)

UnitDebuff

Returns information about a debuff on a unit.

```
name, rank, icon, count, dispelType, duration, expires, caster, ↵
isStealable = UnitDebuff("unit", index [, "filter"]) or ↵
UnitDebuff("unit", "name" [, "rank" [, "filter"]])
```

This function is an alias for `UnitAura()` with a built-in `HARMFUL` filter (which cannot be removed or negated with the `HELPFUL` filter).

Arguments:

`unit`—A unit to query (string, unitID)

`index`—Index of an aura to query (number)

`name`—Name of an aura to query (string)

`rank` (optional)—Secondary text of an aura to query (often a rank; e.g. "Rank 7") (string)

`filter` (optional)—A list of filters to use separated by the pipe '|' character; e.g. `"CANCELABLE|PLAYER"` will query cancelable debuffs cast by the player (string)

- `CANCELABLE`—Show auras that can be cancelled
- `NOT_CANCELABLE`—Show auras that cannot be cancelled
- `PLAYER`—Show auras the player has cast
- `RAID`—Show auras the player can cast on party/raid members (as opposed to self buffs)

Returns:

`name`—Name of the aura (string)

`rank`—Secondary text for the aura (often a rank; e.g. "Rank 7") (string)

`icon`—Path to an icon texture for the aura (string)

`count`—The number of times the aura has been applied (number)

`dispelType`—Type of aura (relevant for dispelling and certain other mechanics); `nil` if not one of the following values: (string)

Curse	Magic
Disease	Poison

`duration`—Total duration of the aura (in seconds) (number)

`expires`—Time at which the aura will expire; can be compared to `GetTime()` to determine time remaining (number)

`caster`—Unit which applied the aura. If the aura was applied by a unit that does not have a token but is controlled by one that does (e.g. a totem or another player's vehicle), returns the controlling unit. Returns `nil` if the casting unit (or its controller) has no unitID. (string, unitID)

`isStealable`—1 if the aura can be transferred to a player using the Spellsteal spell; otherwise `nil` (1nil)

UnitDefense

Returns the player's or pet's Defense skill.

```
base, modifier = UnitDefense("unit")
```

Arguments:

`unit`—A unit to query; only valid for `player` or `pet` (string, unitID)

Returns:

base—The unit's base defense skill (number)

modifier—Temporary modifiers to defense skill (number)

UnitDetailedThreatSituation

Returns detailed information about the threat status of one unit against another.

```
isTanking, status, scaledPercent, rawPercent, threatValue = ↵
UnitDetailedThreatSituation(unit, mobUnit) or ↵
UnitDetailedThreatSituation("name", mobUnit)
```

The different values returned by this function reflect the complexity of NPC threat management.

Raw threat roughly equates to the amount of damage a unit has caused to the NPC plus the amount of healing the unit has performed in the NPC's presence. (Each quantity that goes into this sum may be modified, however; such as by a paladin's Righteous Fury self-buff, a priest's Silent Resolve talent, or a player whose cloak is enchanted with Subtlety.)

Generally, whichever unit has the highest raw threat against an NPC becomes its primary target, and raw threat percentage simplifies this comparison.

However, most NPCs are designed to maintain some degree of target focus so that they don't rapidly switch targets if, for example, a unit other than the primary target suddenly reaches 101% raw threat. The amount by which a unit must surpass the primary target's threat to become the new primary target varies by distance from the NPC.

Thus, a scaled percentage value is given to provide clarity. The rawPercent value returned from this function can be greater than 100 (indicating that unit has greater threat against mobUnit than mobUnit's primary target, and is thus in danger of becoming the primary target), but the scaledPercent value will always be 100 or lower.

Threat information for a pair of units is only returned if the player has threat against the NPC unit in question. (For example, no threat data is provided if the player's pet is attacking an NPC but the player himself has taken no action, even though the pet has threat against the NPC.)

Arguments:

unit—The unit whose threat situation is being requested (unitid)

name—The name of a unit to query. Only valid for the player, pet, and party/raid members. (string)

mobUnit—An NPC unit the first unit may have threat against (unitid)

Returns:

isTanking—1 if unit is mobUnit's primary target, nil otherwise (1nil)

status—A threat status category (number)

- 0—Unit has less than 100% raw threat (default UI shows no indicator)
- 1—Unit has 100% or higher raw threat but isn't mobUnit's primary target (default UI shows yellow indicator)

- 2—Unit is `mobUnit`'s primary target, and another unit has 100% or higher raw threat (default UI shows orange indicator)
- 3—Unit is `mobUnit`'s primary target, and no other unit has 100% or higher raw threat (default UI shows red indicator)

`scaledPercent`—A percentage value representing unit's threat against `mobUnit`, scaled such that a value of 100% represents unit becoming `mobUnit`'s primary target (`number`)

`rawPercent`—A percentage value representing unit's threat against `mobUnit` relative to the threat of mobUnit's primary target (`number`)

`threatValue`—The raw value of unit's threat against mobUnit (`number`)

UnitExists

Returns whether a unit exists.

```
exists = UnitExists("unit") or UnitExists("name")
```

A unit "exists" if it can be referenced by the player; e.g. `party1` exists if the player is in a party with at least one other member (regardless of whether that member is nearby), `target` exists if the player has a target, `npc` exists if the player is currently interacting with an NPC, etc.

Arguments:

`unit`—A unit to query (`string`, unitID)

`name`—The name of a unit to query; only valid for `player`, `pet`, `npc`, and party/raid members (`string`)

Returns:

`exists`—1 if the unit exists, otherwise `nil` (1nil)

UnitFactionGroup

Returns a unit's primary faction allegiance.

```
factionGroup, factionName = UnitFactionGroup("unit") or ↵
UnitFactionGroup("name")
```

Arguments:

`unit`—A unit to query (`string`, unitID)

`name`—The name of a unit to query; only valid for `player`, `pet`, and party/raid members (`string`)

Returns:

`factionGroup`—Non-localized (English) faction name of the faction ("Horde" or "Alliance") (`string`)

`factionName`—Localized name of the faction (`string`)

UnitGUID

Returns a unit's globally unique identifier.

```
guid = UnitGUID("unit")
```

Arguments:

`unit`—A unit to query (`string`, unitID)

Returns:

guid—The unit's GUID (string, guid)

Example:

GUIDs are used in the combat log and in certain hyperlinks.

UnitHasRelicSlot

Returns whether a unit has a relic slot instead of a ranged weapon slot.

hasRelic = UnitHasRelicSlot("unit")

Arguments:

unit—A unit to query (string, unitID)

Returns:

hasRelic—1 if the unit has a relic slot; otherwise nil (1nil)

UnitHasVehicleUI

Returns whether a unit is controlling a vehicle or vehicle weapon.

hasVehicle = UnitHasVehicleUI("unit") or UnitHasVehicleUI("name")

Used in the default UI to show the vehicle's health and power status bars in place of the controlling unit's. Returns false for passengers riding in but not controlling part of a vehicle; to find out whether a unit is riding in a vehicle, use UnitInVehicle. Also note that in some vehicles the player can command a vehicle weapon (e.g. gun turret) without controlling the vehicle itself; to find out whether a unit is controlling a vehicle, use UnitControllingVehicle.

Arguments:

unit—A unit to query (string, unitID)

name—The name of a unit to query; only valid for player, pet, and party/raid members (string)

Returns:

hasVehicle—True if the unit is controlling a vehicle or vehicle weapon; otherwise false (boolean)

UnitHealth

Returns a unit's current amount of health.

health = UnitHealth("unit") or UnitHealth("name")

Arguments:

unit—A unit to query (string, unitID)

name—The name of a unit to query; only valid for player, pet, and party/raid members (string)

Returns:

health—The unit's current amount of health (hit points) (number)

UnitHealthMax

Returns a unit's maximum health value.

maxValue = UnitHealthMax("unit") or UnitHealthMax("name")

Arguments:

unit—A unit to query (string, unitID)

name—The name of a unit to query; only valid for player, pet, and party/raid members (string)

Returns:

maxValue—The unit's maximum health (hit points) (number)

UnitInBattleground

Returns whether a unit is in same battleground instance as the player.

```
raidNum = UnitInBattleground("unit")
```

Arguments:

unit—A unit to query (string, unitID)

Returns:

raidNum—Numeric portion of the unit's raid unitID (e.g. 13 for raid13) (number)

UnitInParty

Returns whether a unit is a player unit in the player's party.

```
inParty = UnitInParty("unit") or UnitInParty("name")
```

Always returns 1 for the player unit. Returns nil for the player's or party members' pets.

Arguments:

unit—A unit to query (string, unitID)

name—The name of a unit to query (string)

Returns:

inParty—1 if the unit is a player unit in the player's party; otherwise nil. (1nil)

UnitInRaid

Returns whether a unit is in the player's raid.

```
inRaid = UnitInRaid("unit")
```

Arguments:

unit—A unit to query (string, unitID)

Returns:

inRaid—Index of the unit in the raid (matches the numeric part of the unit's raid unitID minus 1; e.g. returns 0 for raid1, 12 for raid13, etc) (number)

UnitInRange

Returns whether a party/raid member is nearby.

```
inRange = UnitInRange("unit") or UnitInRange("name")
```

The range check used by this function isn't directly based on the player's abilities (which may have varying ranges); it's fixed by Blizzard at a distance of around 40 yards (which encompasses many common healing spells and other abilities often used on raid members).

Also returns nil for units outside the player's area of view.

Arguments:

unit—A unit to query (string, unitID)

name—The name of a unit to query; only valid for party/raid members and their pets (string)

Returns:

inRange—1 if the unit is close enough to the player to (likely) be in range for helpful spells; otherwise nil (1nil)

UnitInVehicle

Returns whether a unit is in a vehicle.

```
inVehicle = UnitInVehicle("unit") or UnitInVehicle("name")
```

A unit can be riding in a vehicle without controlling it: to test whether a unit is controlling a vehicle, use UnitControllingVehicle or UnitHasVehicleUI.

Note: multi-passenger mounts appear as vehicles for passengers but not for the owner.

Arguments:

unit—A unit to query (string, unitID)

name—The name of a unit to query; only valid for player, pet, and party/raid members (string)

Returns:

inVehicle—1 if the unit is in a vehicle; otherwise nil (1nil)

UnitInVehicleControlSeat

Returns whether a unit controls a vehicle.

```
isInControl = UnitInVehicleControlSeat()
```

Returns:

isInControl—True if the unit controls a vehicle (boolean)

UnitIsAFK

Returns whether a unit is marked AFK (Away From Keyboard).

```
isAFK = UnitIsAFK("unit") or UnitIsAFK("name")
```

Arguments:

unit—A unit to query (string, unitID)

name—The name of a unit to query; only valid for player, pet, and party/raid members (string)

Returns:

isAFK—1 if the unit is AFK; otherwise nil (1nil)

UnitIsCharmed

Returns whether a unit is currently charmed.

```
isCharmed = UnitIsCharmed("unit")
```

A charmed unit is affected by Mind Control (or a similar effect) and thus hostile to units which are normally his or her allies.

Arguments:

unit—A unit to query (string, unitID)

Returns:

isCharmed—1 if the unit is charmed; otherwise nil (1nil)

UnitIsConnected

Returns whether a unit is connected (i.e. not Offline).

```
isConnected = UnitIsConnected("unit")
```

Arguments:

unit—A unit to query (string, unitID)

Returns:

isConnected—1 if the player is connected; otherwise nil (1nil)

UnitIsControlling

Returns whether a unit is controlling another unit.

```
isControlling = UnitIsControlling("unit")
```

Applies to Mind Control and similar cases as well as to players piloting vehicles.

Arguments:

unit—A unit to query (string, unitID)

Returns:

isControlling—1 if the unit is controlling another unit; otherwise nil (1nil)

UnitIsCorpse

Returns whether a unit is a corpse.

```
isCorpse = UnitIsCorpse("unit")
```

Arguments:

unit—A unit to query (string, unitID)

Returns:

isCorpse—1 if the unit is a corpse; otherwise nil (1nil)

UnitIsDND

Returns whether a unit is marked DND (Do Not Disturb).

```
isDND = UnitIsDND("unit") or UnitIsDND("name")
```

Arguments:

unit—A unit to query (string, unitID)

name—The name of a unit to query; only valid for player, pet, and party/raid members (string)

Returns:

isDND—1 if the unit is marked Do Not Disturb, otherwise nil (1nil)

UnitIsDead

Returns whether a unit is dead.

```
isDead = UnitIsDead("unit")
```

Only returns 1 while the unit is dead and has not yet released his or her spirit. See `UnitIsGhost()` for after the unit has released.

Arguments:

unit—A unit to query (`string`, unitID)

Returns:

isDead—1 if the unit is dead; otherwise `nil` (1nil)

Example:

```
-- Scan your party or raid and count how many people are dead
local maxNum = GetNumRaidMembers()
local unitType = "raid"
if maxNum <= 0 then
 maxNum = GetNumPartyMembers()
 unitType = "party"
end

if maxNum > 0 then
 local deadCount = 0
 for i=1,maxNum do
  if UnitIsDead(unitType .. i) then
   deadCount = deadCount + 1
  end
 end

 print("There are " .. deadCount .. " people dead in your " ↵
.. unitType)
else
 print("You are not in a party or raid")
end
```

UnitIsDeadOrGhost

Returns whether a unit is either dead or a ghost.

```
isDeadOrGhost = UnitIsDeadOrGhost("unit")
```

Arguments:

unit—A unit to query (`string`, unitID)

Returns:

isDeadOrGhost—1 if the unit is dead or a ghost, otherwise `nil` (1nil)

UnitIsEnemy

Returns whether two units are enemies.

```
isEnemy = UnitIsEnemy("unit", "unit")
```

Arguments:

unit—A unit (`string`, unitID)

unit—Another unit (`string`, unitID)

Returns:

isEnemy—1 if the units are enemies; otherwise `nil` (1nil)

UnitIsFeignDeath

Returns whether a unit is feigning death.

```
isFeign = UnitIsFeignDeath("unit")
```

Only provides valid data for friendly units.

Arguments:

unit—A unit to query (string, unitID)

Returns:

isFeign—1 if the unit is feigning death; otherwise nil (1nil)

UnitIsFriend

Returns whether two units are friendly.

```
isFriends = UnitIsFriend("unit", "unit")
```

Arguments:

unit—A unit (string, unitID)

unit—Another unit (string, unitID)

Returns:

isFriends—1 if the two units are friendly; otherwise nil (1nil)

UnitIsGhost

Returns whether a unit is currently a ghost.

```
isGhost = UnitIsGhost("unit")
```

Arguments:

unit—A unit to query (string, unitID)

Returns:

isGhost—1 if the unit is a ghost; otherwise nil (1nil)

UnitIsInMyGuild

Returns whether a unit is in the player's guild.

```
inGuild = UnitIsInMyGuild("unit")
```

Arguments:

unit—A unit to query (string, unitID)

Returns:

inGuild—1 if the unit is in the player's guild; otherwise nil (1nil)

UnitIsPVP

Returns whether a unit is flagged for PvP activity.

```
isPVP = UnitIsPVP("unit")
```

Arguments:

unit—A unit to query (string, unitID)

Returns:

isPVP—1 if the unit is flagged for PVP activity; otherwise nil (1nil)

UnitIsPVPFreeForAll

Returns whether a unit is flagged for free-for-all PvP.

```
isFreeForAll = UnitIsPVPFreeForAll("unit")
```

Free-for-all PvP allows all players to attack each other regardless of faction; used in certain outdoor areas (such as Gurubashi Arena and "The Maul" outside Dire Maul).

Arguments:

unit—A unit to query (string, unitID)

Returns:

isFreeForAll—1 if the unit is enabled for free-for-all PvP; otherwise nil (1nil)

UnitIsPVPSanctuary

Returns whether a unit is in a Sanctuary area preventing PvP activity.

```
state = UnitIsPVPSanctuary("unit")
```

Arguments:

unit—A unit to query (string, unitID)

Returns:

state—1 if the unit is in a PVP Sanctuary; otherwise nil (1nil)

UnitIsPartyLeader

Returns whether a unit is the leader of the player's party.

```
leader = UnitIsPartyLeader("unit") or UnitIsPartyLeader("name")
```

Arguments:

unit—A unit to query (string, unitID)
name—The name of a unit to query (string)

Returns:

leader—1 if the unit is the party leader; otherwise nil (1nil)

UnitIsPlayer

Returns whether a unit is a player unit (not an NPC).

```
isPlayer = UnitIsPlayer("unit")
```

Arguments:

unit—A unit to query (string, unitID)

Returns:

isPlayer—1 if the unit is a player unit; otherwise nil (1nil)

UnitIsPossessed

Returns whether a unit is possessed by another.

```
isPossessed = UnitIsPossessed("unit")
```

Arguments:

unit—A unit to query (string, unitID)

Returns:

isPossessed—1 if the given unit is possessed; otherwise nil (1nil)

UnitIsRaidOfficer

Returns whether a unit is a raid assistant in the player's raid.

leader = UnitIsRaidOfficer("unit") or UnitIsRaidOfficer("name")

Arguments:

unit—A unit to query (string, unitID)

name—The name of a unit to query (string)

Returns:

leader—1 if the unit is a raid assistant; otherwise nil (1nil)

UnitIsSameServer

Returns whether two units are from the same server.

isSame = UnitIsSameServer("unit", "unit")

Only meaningful in cross-realm battlegrounds.

Arguments:

unit—A unit (string, unitID)

unit—Another unit (string, unitID)

Returns:

isSame—1 if the two units are from the same server; otherwise nil. (1nil)

UnitIsSilenced

Returns whether a character is silenced on a voice channel.

silenced = UnitIsSilenced("name", "channel")

Arguments:

name—Name of a character (string)

channel—Name of a chat channel (string)

Returns:

silenced—1 if the unit is silenced on the given channel; otherwise nil (1nil)

UnitIsTalking

Returns whether a unit is currently speaking in voice chat.

state = UnitIsTalking("unit")

Despite the "unit" name, this function only accepts player names, not unitIDs.

Arguments:

unit—Name of a character in the player's current voice channel (string)

Returns:

state—1 if the unit is currently speaking in voice chat; otherwise nil (1nil)

UnitIsTapped

Returns whether a unit is tapped.

UnitIsTapped(unit)

Normally, rewards for killing a unit are available only to the character or group who first damaged the unit; once a character has thus established his claim on the unit, it is considered "tapped".

Arguments:

unit—The unitid to query (unitId)

UnitIsTappedByAllThreatList

Returns whether a unit allows all players on its threat list to receive kill credit.

```
allTapped = UnitIsTappedByAllThreatList("unit")
```

Used to override the normal "tapping" behavior for certain mobs. If this function returns 1, the player does not have to be the first to attack the mob (or in the same party/raid as the first player to attack) in order to receive quest or achievement credit for killing it.

In the default UI, this function can prevent the graying of a unit's name background in the TargetFrame and FocusFrame even if the unit is otherwise tapped, indicating that kill credit is still available if the player attacks.

Arguments:

unit—A unit to query (string, unitID)

Returns:

allTapped—1 if the unit allows all players on its threat list to receive kill credit; otherwise nil (1nil)

UnitIsTappedByPlayer

Returns whether a unit is tapped by the player or the player's group.

```
isTapped = UnitIsTappedByPlayer("unit")
```

Normally, rewards for killing a unit are available only to the character or group who first damaged the unit; once a character has thus established his claim on the unit, it is considered "tapped".

Arguments:

unit—The unit to be queried (string)

Returns:

isTapped—1 if the unit is tapped by the player; otherwise nil (1nil)

UnitIsTrivial

Returns whether a unit is trivial at the player's level.

```
isTrivial = UnitIsTrivial("unit")
```

Killing trivial units (whose level is colored gray in the default UI) does not reward honor or experience.

Arguments:

unit—A unit to query (string, unitID)

Returns:

isTrivial—1 if the unit is trivial at the player's level; otherwise nil (1nil)

UnitIsUnit

Returns whether two unit references are to the same unit.

```
isSame = UnitIsUnit("unit", "unit")
```

Useful for determining whether a composite `unitID` (such as `raid19target`) also refers to a basic `unitID`; see example.

Arguments:

`unit`—A unit (string, unitID)

`unit`—Another unit (string, unitID)

Returns:

`isSame`—Returns 1 if the two references are to the same unit; otherwise `nil` (1nil)

Example:

```
if (UnitIsUnit("targettarget","player"))
   -- watch out! your target is also targeting you!
end
```

UnitIsVisible

Returns whether a unit is in the player's area of interest.

```
isVisible = UnitIsVisible("unit")
```

Arguments:

`unit`—A unit to query (string, unitID)

Returns:

`isVisible`—1 if the unit is is in the player's area of interest; otherwise `nil` (1nil)

UnitLevel

Returns a unit's level.

```
level = UnitLevel("unit")
```

Returns -1 for boss units and hostile units whose level is ten levels or more above the player's.

Arguments:

`unit`—A unit to query (string, unitID)

Returns:

`level`—The unit's level (number)

UnitName

Returns the name of a unit.

```
name, realm = UnitName("unit")
```

Arguments:

`unit`—A unit to query (string, unitID)

Returns:

name—Name of the unit (`string`)

realm—Name of the unit's home realm if the unit is not from the player's realm; otherwise `nil` (`string`)

Example:

```
-- Send a chat message to the player that's you are currently mousing
-- over. This should be run as a macro (via keybind) so your mouse can
-- be hovering over a unit in the 3-D world, or a unit frame

local name = UnitName("mouseover")
SendChatMessage("Hey " .. name .. " I'm mousing over you!!!", ↵
"WHISPER", nil, name)

-- This can be run as a macro by putting it all on one line, and adding
-- run in front of it, like so:
--
-- /run local name = UnitName("mouseover"); SendChatMessage("Hey " ↵
.. name .. " I'm mousing over you!!!", "WHISPER", nil, name)
```

UnitOnTaxi

Returns whether a unit is currently riding a flight path (taxi).

```
onTaxi = UnitOnTaxi("unit")
```

Valid for any unit in the player's area of interest, but generally useful only for `player`. Taxi flights move quickly, so a taxi-riding unit visible to the player will not remain visible for very long.

Arguments:

unit—A unit to query (`string`, unitID)

Returns:

onTaxi—1 if the unit is on a taxi; otherwise `nil` (`1nil`)

UnitPVPName

Returns the name of a unit including the unit's current title.

```
name = UnitPVPName("unit")
```

Titles are no longer specific to PvP; this function returns a unit's name with whichever title he or she is currently displaying (e.g. "Gladiator Spin", "Keydar Jenkins", "Ownsusohard, Champion of the Frozen Wastes", etc).

Arguments:

unit—A unit to query (`string`, unitID)

Returns:

name—Name of the unit including the unit's current title (`string`)

UnitPlayerControlled

Returns whether a unit is controlled by a player.

```
isPlayer = UnitPlayerControlled("unit")
```

Arguments:

unit—A unit to query (string, unitID)

Returns:

isPlayer—1 if the unit is controlled by a player; otherwise nil (1nil)

UnitPlayerOrPetInParty

Returns whether a unit is in the player's party or belongs to a party member.

```
inParty = UnitPlayerOrPetInParty("unit") or ↵
UnitPlayerOrPetInParty("name")
```

Returns nil for the player and the player's pet.

Arguments:

unit—A unit to query (string, unitID)

name—The name of a unit to query (string)

Returns:

inParty—1 if the unit is in the player's party or is a pet belonging to a party member; otherwise nil (1nil)

UnitPlayerOrPetInRaid

Returns whether a unit is in the player's raid or belongs to a raid member.

```
inParty = UnitPlayerOrPetInRaid("unit") or UnitPlayerOrPetInRaid
("name")
```

Arguments:

unit—A unit to query (string, unitID)

name—The name of a unit to query (string)

Returns:

inParty—1 if the unit is in the player's raid or is a pet belonging to a raid member; otherwise nil (1nil)

UnitPower

Returns a unit's current level of mana, rage, energy or other power type.

```
power = UnitPower("unitID" [, "powerType"])
```

Returns zero for non-existent units.

Arguments:

unitID—A unit to query (string, unitID)

powerType (optional)—A specific power type to query (string, powerType)

Returns:

power—The unit's current level of mana, rage, energy, runic power, or other power type (unitID)

UnitPowerMax

Returns a unit's maximum mana, rage, energy or other power type.

```
maxValue = UnitPowerMax("unitID" [, powerType])
```

Returns the unit's current maximum power, if the unit does not exist then zero is returned.

When querying with a powerType, as long as the unit exists you will get the maximum untalented power even if the class does not use the power type.

Arguments:

unitID—A unit to query (string, unitID)

powerType (optional)—Specific power type to query for the unit (number, powerType)

Returns:

maxValue—The unit's maximum mana, rage, energy, or other power (number)

UnitPowerType

Returns the power type (energy, mana, rage) of the given unit.

```
powerType, powerToken, altR, altG, altB = UnitPowerType("unit") or
UnitPowerType("name")
```

Does not return color values for common power types (mana, rage, energy, focus, and runic power); the canonical colors for these can be found in the PowerBarColor table. Color values may be included for special power types such as those used by vehicles.

Arguments:

unit—A unit to query (string, unitID)

name—The name of a unit to query; only valid for player, pet, and party/raid members (string)

Returns:

powerType—A number identifying the power type (number)

0—Mana	3—Energy
1—Rage	6—Runic Power
2—Focus	

powerToken—The name of a global variable containing the localized name of the power type (string)

altR—Red component of the color used for displaying this power type (number)

altG—Green component of the color used for displaying this power type (number)

altB—Blue component of the color used for displaying this power type (number)

UnitRace

Returns the name of a unit's race.

```
race, fileName = UnitRace("unit")
```

Arguments:

unit—A unit to query (string, unitID)

Returns:

race—Localized name of the unit's race (`string`)

fileName—A non-localized token representing the unit's race (`string`)

UnitRangedAttack

Returns information about the player's or pet's ranged weapon skill.

```
rangedAttackBase, rangedAttackMod = UnitRangedAttack("unit")
```

Arguments:

unit—A unit to query; only valid for `player` or `pet` (`string`, unitID)

Returns:

rangedAttackBase—The unit's base ranged weapon skill (`number`)

rangedAttackMod—Temporary modifiers to ranged weapon skill (`number`)

UnitRangedAttackPower

Returns the player's or pet's ranged attack power.

```
base, posBuff, negBuff = UnitRangedAttackPower("unit")
```

Arguments:

unit—A unit to query; only valid for `player` or `pet` (`string`, unitID)

Returns:

base—Base ranged attack power (`number`)

posBuff—Positive buffs to ranged attack power (`number`)

negBuff—Negative buffs to ranged attack power (`number`)

UnitRangedDamage

Returns information about the player's or pet's ranged attack damage and speed.

```
rangedAttackSpeed, minDamage, maxDamage, physicalBonusPos, ↵
physicalBonusNeg, percent = UnitRangedDamage("unit")
```

Arguments:

unit—A unit to query; only valid for `player` or `pet` (`string`, unitID)

Returns:

rangedAttackSpeed—Current speed of the unit's ranged attack (attacks per second), or 0 if no ranged weapon is equipped (`number`)

minDamage—The minimum base damage per attack (`number`)

maxDamage—The maximum base damage per attack (`number`)

physicalBonusPos—Positive modifiers to ranged weapon damage (`number`)

physicalBonusNeg—Negative modifiers to ranged weapon damage (`number`)

percent—Factor by which damage output is multiplied due to buffs/debuffs (`number`)

UnitReaction

Returns the reaction of one unit with regards to another as a number.

```
reaction = UnitReaction("unit", "unit")
```

The returned value often (but not always) matches the unit's level of reputation with the second unit's faction, and can be used with the `UnitReactionColor` global table to return the color used to display a unit's reaction in the default UI.

Arguments:

unit—A unit (string, unitID)

unit—Another unit (string, unitID)

Returns:

reaction—Reaction of the first unit towards the second unit (number)

1—Hated	4—Neutral	7—Revered
2—Hostile	5—Friendly	8—Exalted
3—Unfriendly	6—Honored	

UnitResistance

Returns information about the player's or pet's magic resistance.

```
base, resistance, positive, negative = UnitResistance("unit",
resistanceIndex)
```

Arguments:

unit—A unit to query; only valid for player or pet (string, unitID)

resistanceIndex—Index of a magic resistance type (number)

1—Fire	4—Shadow
2—Nature	5—Arcane
3—Frost	

Returns:

base—Base resistance value (generally 0) (number)

resistance—Current resistance value (including modifiers) (number)

positive—Positive resistance modifiers (number)

negative—Negative resistance modifiers (number)

UnitSelectionColor

Returns a color indicating hostility and related status of a unit.

```
red, green, blue, alpha = UnitSelectionColor("unit") or ↵
UnitSelectionColor("name")
```

This color is used in various places in the default UI, such as the background behind a unit's name in the target and focus frames. For NPCs, the color reflects hostility and reputation, ranging from red (hostile) to orange or yellow (unfriendly or neutral) to green (friendly). When the unit is a player, a blue color is used unless the player is active for PvP, in which case the color may be red (he can attack you and you can attack him), yellow (you can attack him but he can't attack you) or green (ally). Color component values are floating point numbers between 0 and 1.

Arguments:

unit—A unit to query (string, unitID)

name—The name of a unit to query; only valid for `player`,`pet`,and party/raid members (`string`)

Returns:

red—The red component of the color. (`number`)

green—The green component of the color. (`number`)

blue—The blue component of the color. (`number`)

alpha—The alpha (opacity) component of the color. (`number`)

UnitSex

Returns the gender of the given unit or player.

```
gender = UnitSex("unit") or UnitSex("name")
```

Arguments:

unit—A unit to query (`string`, unitID)

name—The name of a unit to query; only valid for `player`, `pet`, and party/raid members (`string`)

Returns:

gender—The unit's gender (`number`)

- 1—Neuter / Unknown
- 2—Male
- 3—Female

UnitStat

Returns information about a basic character statistic for the player or pet.

```
stat, effectiveStat, posBuff, negBuff = UnitStat("unit", statIndex)
```

Arguments:

unit—A unit to query; only valid for `player` or `pet` (`string`, unitID)

statIndex—Index of a basic statistic (`number`)

1—Strength	4—Intellect
2—Agility	5—Spirit
3—Stamina	

Returns:

stat—Current value of the statistic (`number`)

effectiveStat—Effective value of the statistic (`number`)

posBuff—Positive modifiers to the statistic (`number`)

negBuff—Negative modifiers to the statistic (`number`)

UnitSwitchToVehicleSeat

Moves the player to another seat within his current vehicle.

```
UnitSwitchToVehicleSeat("unit", seat)
```

Arguments:

unit—Unit to move (only valid for `player`) (`string`, unitID)

seat—Index of a seat to switch to (`number`)

UnitTargetsVehicleInRaidUI

Returns whether attempts to target a unit should target its vehicle.

```
targetVehicle = UnitTargetsVehicleInRaidUI("unit")
```

The unit can still be targeted: this flag is used to provide a convenience in the default UI for certain cases (such as the Malygos encounter) such that clicking a unit in the raid UI targets its vehicle (e.g. so players can use their drakes to heal other players' drakes).

Arguments:

unit—A unit to query (string, unitID)

Returns:

targetVehicle—True if clicking the unit's raid UI representation should target the unit's vehicle instead of the unit itself; otherwise false (boolean)

UnitThreatSituation

Returns the general threat status of a unit.

```
status = UnitThreatSituation(unit [, mobUnit]) or ↵
UnitThreatSituation("name" [, mobUnit])
```

See UnitDetailedThreatSituation for details about threat values.

Threat information for a pair of units is only returned if the player has threat against the NPC unit in question. (For example, no threat data is provided if the player's pet is attacking an NPC but the player himself has taken no action, even though the pet has threat against the NPC.)

Arguments:

unit—The unit whose threat situation is being requested (unitid)

name—The name of a unit to query. Only valid for the player, pet, and party/raid members. (string)

mobUnit (optional)—An NPC unit the first unit may have threat against; if nil, returned values reflect whichever NPC unit the first unit has the highest threat against. (unitid)

Returns:

status—A threat status category (number)

- 0—Unit has less than 100% raw threat (default UI shows no indicator)
- 1—Unit has 100% or higher raw threat but isn't mobUnit's primary target (default UI shows yellow indicator)
- 2—Unit is mobUnit's primary target, and another unit has 100% or higher raw threat (default UI shows orange indicator)
- 3—Unit is mobUnit's primary target, and no other unit has 100% or higher raw threat (default UI shows red indicator)

UnitUsingVehicle

Returns whether a unit is using a vehicle.

```
usingVehicle = UnitUsingVehicle("unit")
```

Unlike similar functions, `UnitUsingVehicle()` also returns `true` while the unit is transitioning between seats in a vehicle.

Arguments:

`unit`—A unit to query (`string`, unitID)

Returns:

`usingVehicle`—1 if the unit is using a vehicle; otherwise `nil` (1nil)

UnitVehicleSeatCount

Returns the number of seats in a unit's vehicle.

`numSeats = UnitVehicleSeatCount("unit")`

Note: returns 0 for multi-passenger mounts even though multiple seats are available.

Arguments:

`unit`—A unit to query (`string`, unitID)

Returns:

`numSeats`—Number of seats in the unit's vehicle (`number`)

UnitVehicleSeatInfo

Returns information about seats in a vehicle.

`controlType, occupantName, occupantRealm, canEject, ↵`
`canSwitchSeats = UnitVehicleSeatInfo("unit", seat)`

Note: multi-passenger mounts appear as vehicles for passengers but not for the owner; seat information applies only to the passenger seats.

Arguments:

`unit`—A unit to query (`string`, unitID)

`seat`—Index of a seat in the unit's vehicle (`number`)

Returns:

`controlType`—Type of control for the seat (`string`)

- `Child`—Unit in this seat controls part of the vehicle but not its movement (e.g. a gun turret)
- `None`—Unit in this seat has no control over the vehicle
- `Root`—Unit in this seat controls the movement of the vehicle

`occupantName`—Name of the unit in the seat, or `nil` if the seat is empty (`string`)

`occupantRealm`—Home realm of the unit in the seat; `nil` if the seat is empty or its occupant is from the same realm as the player (`string`)

`canEject`—True if the vehicle's driver can eject the occupant of the seat (`boolean`)

`canSwitchSeats`—True if the player can switch to this seat. (`boolean`)

UnitVehicleSkin

Returns the style of vehicle UI to display for a unit.

`skin = UnitVehicleSkin("unit") or UnitVehicleSkin("name")`

Arguments:

unit—A unit to query (string, unitID)

name—Name of a unit to query; only valid for player, pet, and party/raid members (string)

Returns:

skin—Token identifying the style of vehicle UI to display for the unit (string)

- ▪ Mechanical—Used for mechanical vehicles
- ▪ Natural—Used for creature mounts

UnitXP

Returns the player's current amount of experience points.

```
currXP = UnitXP("unit")
```

Arguments:

unit—A unit to query; only valid for player (string, unitID)

Returns:

currXP—Current amount of experience points (number)

UnitXPMax

Return the total amount of experience points required for the player to gain a level.

```
playerMaxXP = UnitXPMax("unit")
```

Arguments:

unit—A unit to query; only valid for player (string, unitID)

Returns:

playerMaxXP—Total amount of experience points required for the player to gain a level (number)

UnstablePet

Makes a pet from the stables the active pet.

```
UnstablePet(index)
```

If another pet is already active, it will be placed in the stables.

Arguments:

index—Index of a stable slot (between 1 and GetNumStablePets()) (number)

UpdateAddOnCPUUsage

Updates addon CPU profiling information.

Only has effect if the scriptProfile CVar is set to 1. See GetAddOnCPUUsage() for the updated data.

UpdateAddOnMemoryUsage

Updates addon memory usage information.

See GetAddOnMemoryUsage() for the updated data.

Protected | **UpdateGMTicket**

Updates the open GM ticket with new text.

```
UpdateGMTicket("text")
```

Arguments:

text—New text for the ticket (string)

UpdateMapHighlight

Returns information about the texture used for highlighting zones in a continent map on mouseover.

```
name, fileName, texCoordX, texCoordY, textureX, textureY, ↵
scrollChildX, scrollChildY = UpdateMapHighlight(cursorX, cursorY)
```

Arguments:

cursorX—Horizontal position of the mouse cursor relative to the current world map (0 = left edge, 1 = right edge) (number)

cursorY—Vertical position of the unit relative to the current world map (0 = top, 1 = bottom) (number)

Returns:

name—The name of the zone being highlighted (string)

fileName—Unique part of the path to the highlight texture for the zone; full path follows the format "Interface\\WorldMap\\" ..fileName.."\\"..fileName.."Highlight" (string)

texCoordX—Right texCoord value for the highlight texture (number)

texCoordY—Bottom texCoord value for the highlight texture (number)

textureX—Width of the texture as a proportion of the world map's width (number)

textureY—Height of the texture as a proportion of the world map's height (number)

scrollChildX—Horizontal position of the texture's top left corner relative to the current world map (0 = left edge, 1 = right edge) (number)

scrollChildY—Vertical position of the texture's top left corner relative to the current world map (0 = top, 1 = bottom) (number)

UpdateSpells

Requests spellbook information from the server.

The UPDATE_SPELLS event fires when new spellbook information is available.

UploadSettings

Stores a backup of game settings on the server.

Does nothing unless server-side settings have been disabled by setting the synchronizeSettings CVar to 0.

Protected

UseAction

Uses an action.

```
UseAction(slot [, "target" [, "button"]])
```

Arguments:

slot—An action bar slot (number, actionID)

target (optional)—A unit to be used as target for the action (string, unitID) button (optional)—Mouse button used to activate the action (string)

- Button4—Fourth mouse button
- Button5—Fifth mouse button
- LeftButton—Left mouse button (also used when the action is activated via keyboard)
- MiddleButton—Third mouse button (typically middle button/scroll wheel)
- RightButton—Right mouse button

UseContainerItem

Activate (as with right-clicking) an item in one of the player's bags.

```
UseContainerItem(container, slot [, "target"])
```

Has the same effect as right-clicking an item in the default UI; therefore, results may vary by context. In cases of conflict, conditions listed first override those below:

- If the bank or guild bank UI is open, moves the item into the bank or guild bank (or if the item is in the bank or guild bank, moves it into the player's inventory).
- If the trade UI is open, puts the item into the first available trade slot (or if the item is soulbound, into the "will not be traded" slot).
- If the merchant UI is open and not in repair mode, attempts to sell the item to the merchant.
- If the Send Mail UI is open, puts the item into the first available slot for message attachments.
- If an item is readable (e.g. Lament of the Highborne), opens it for reading.
- If an item is lootable (e.g. Magically Wrapped Gift), opens it for looting
- If an item can be equipped, attempts to equip the item (placing any currently equipped item of the same type into the container slot used).
- If an item has a "Use:" effect, activates said effect. *Under this condition only, the function is protected and can only be called by the Blizzard UI.*
- If none of the above conditions are true, nothing happens.

Arguments:

container—Index of one of the player's bags or other containers (number, containerID)

slot—Index of an item slot within the container (number, containerSlotID)

target (optional)—A unit to be used as target for the action (string, unitID)

UseEquipmentSet

Equips the items in an equipment set.

```
equipped = UseEquipmentSet("name")
```

Arguments:

name—Name of an equipment set (case sensitive) (string)

Returns:

equipped—true if the set was equipped; otherwise nil (boolean)

Protected	**UseInventoryItem**

Activate (as with right-clicking) an equipped item.

UseInventoryItem(slot)

If the inventoryID passed refers to an empty slot or a slot containing an item without a "Use:" action, this function is not protected (i.e. usable only by the Blizzard UI), but also has no effect.

Arguments:

slot—An inventory slot number, as can be obtained from GetInventory
SlotInfo (number, inventoryID)

Protected	**UseItemByName**

Uses an arbitrary item (optionally on a specified unit).

UseItemByName(itemID [, "target"]) or UseItemByName("itemName" ↵
[, "target"]) or UseItemByName("itemLink" [, "target"])

Arguments:

itemID—An item's ID (number)

itemName—An item's name (string)

itemLink—An item's hyperlink, or any string containing the itemString portion of an item link (string)

target (optional)—A unit on which to use the item, if applicable (string, unitID)

Protected	**UseQuestLogSpecialItem**

Uses the item associated with a current quest.

UseQuestLogSpecialItem(questIndex)

Available for a number of quests which involve using an item (i.e. "Use the MacGuffin to summon and defeat the boss", "Use this saw to fell 12 trees", etc.)

Arguments:

questIndex—Index of a quest log entry with an associated usable item (between 1 and GetNumQuestLogEntries()) (number)

UseSoulstone

Instantly resurrects the player in place, if possible.

Usable if the player is dead (and has not yet released his or her spirit to the graveyard) and has the ability to instantly resurrect (provided by a Warlock's Soulstone or a Shaman's Reincarnation passive ability).

VehicleAimDecrement

Adjusts vehicle aim downward by a specified amount.

VehicleAimDecrement(amount)

Arguments:

amount—Angle by which to adjust aim (in radians) (number)

`Protected` **VehicleAimDownStart**

Starts adjusting vehicle aim downward.

`Protected` **VehicleAimDownStop**

Stops adjusting vehicle aim downward.

VehicleAimGetAngle

Returns the aim angle of a vehicle weapon.

```
angle = VehicleAimGetAngle()
```

The returned value is in radians, with positive values indicating upward angle, negative values indicating downward angle, and 0 indicating straight ahead.

Returns:

`angle`—Vertical angle of vehicle weapon aim (in radians) (`number`)

VehicleAimGetNormAngle

Returns the aim angle of a vehicle weapon relative to its minimum angle.

```
angle = VehicleAimGetNormAngle()
```

The returned value is in radians, with 0 indicating the lowest angle allowed for the vehicle weapon and increasing values for upward aim.

Returns:

`angle`—Vertical angle of vehicle weapon aim (in radians) (`number`)

VehicleAimIncrement

Adjusts vehicle aim upward by a specified amount.

```
VehicleAimIncrement(amount)
```

Arguments:

`amount`—Angle by which to adjust aim (in radians) (`number`)

VehicleAimRequestAngle

Attempts to set a vehicle weapon's aim angle to a specific value.

```
VehicleAimRequestAngle(amount)
```

Causes aim angle to transition smoothly from the current value to the requested value (or to the closest allowed value to the requested value if it is beyond the vehicle's limits).

Aim angle values are in radians, with positive values indicating upward angle, negative values indicating downward angle, and 0 indicating straight ahead.

Arguments:

`amount`—New aim angle (in radians) (`number`)

VehicleAimRequestNormAngle

Attempts to set a vehicle weapon's aim angle to a specific value relative to its minimum value.

```
VehicleAimRequestNormAngle(amount)
```

Causes aim angle to transition smoothly from the current value to the requested value (or to the closest allowed value to the requested value if it is beyond the vehicle's limits).

The returned value is in radians, with 0 indicating the lowest angle allowed for the vehicle weapon and increasing values for upward aim.

Arguments:

amount—New aim angle (in radians) (number)

Protected

VehicleAimUpStart

Starts adjusting vehicle aim upward.

Protected

VehicleAimUpStop

Stops adjusting vehicle aim upward.

VehicleCameraZoomIn

Zooms the player's view in while in a vehicle.

VehicleCameraZoomOut

Zooms the player's view out while in a vehicle.

VehicleExit

Removes the player from the current vehicle.

Does nothing if the player is not in a vehicle.

VehicleNextSeat

Moves the player from his current seat in a vehicle to the next sequentially numbered seat.

If the player is in the highest-numbered seat, cycles around to the lowest-numbered seat.

VehiclePrevSeat

Moves the player from his current seat in a vehicle to the previous sequentially numbered seat.

If the player is in the lowest-numbered seat, cycles around to the highest-numbered seat.

VoiceChat_GetCurrentMicrophoneSignalLevel

Returns the current volume level of the microphone signal.

```
volume = VoiceChat_GetCurrentMicrophoneSignalLevel()
```

Returns:

volume—The current volume level of the microphone signal (number)

VoiceChat_IsPlayingLoopbackSound

Returns whether the Microphone Test recording is playing.

```
VoiceChat_IsPlayingLoopbackSound(isPlaying)
```

Arguments:

isPlaying—1 if the loopback sound is currently being played; otherwise nil (number)

VoiceChat_IsRecordingLoopbackSound

Returns whether a Microphone Test is recording.

```
isRecording = VoiceChat_IsRecordingLoopbackSound()
```

Returns:

`isRecording`—1 if the player is recording a voice sample, otherwise 0 (`number`)

Example:

```
-- Print a message indicating your recording status
local insertString = ""
if VoiceChat_IsRecordingLoopbackSound() == 0 then
 insertString = "not "
end
DEFAULT_CHAT_FRAME:AddMessage("You are "..insertString.. ↵
"currently recording a sound sample.")
```

VoiceChat_PlayLoopbackSound

Plays back the Microphone Test recording.

VoiceChat_RecordLoopbackSound

Begins recording a Microphone Test.

```
VoiceChat_RecordLoopbackSound(seconds)
```

Arguments:

`seconds`—The amount of time to record (in seconds) (`number`)

VoiceChat_StopPlayingLoopbackSound

Stops playing the Microphone Test recording.

VoiceChat_StopRecordingLoopbackSound

Stops recording a Microphone Test.

VoiceEnumerateCaptureDevices

Returns the name of an audio input device for voice chat.

```
deviceName = VoiceEnumerateCaptureDevices(deviceIndex)
```

Arguments:

`deviceIndex`—Index of the device (between 1 and `Sound_ChatSystem_Get NumInputDrivers()`) (`number`)

Returns:

`deviceName`—Name of the device (`string`)

VoiceEnumerateOutputDevices

Returns the name of an audio output device for voice chat.

```
device = VoiceEnumerateOutputDevices(deviceIndex)
```

Arguments:

`deviceIndex`—Index of the device (between 1 and `Sound_ChatSystem_Get NumOutputDrivers()`) (`number`)

Returns:

`device`—Name of the device (`string`)

VoiceGetCurrentCaptureDevice

Returns the index of the current voice capture device.

```
index = VoiceGetCurrentCaptureDevice()
```

Returns:

index—Index of the current voice capture device (between 1 and
`Sound_ChatSystem_GetNumInputDrivers()`) (number)

VoiceGetCurrentOutputDevice

Returns the index of the current voice output device.

```
index = VoiceGetCurrentOutputDevice()
```

Returns:

index—Index of the current voice output device (between 1 and
`Sound_ChatSystem_GetNumOutputDrivers()`) (number)

VoiceIsDisabledByClient

Returns whether the voice chat system cannot be enabled.

```
isDisabled = VoiceIsDisabledByClient()
```

Voice chat may be disabled if the underlying hardware does not support it or if
multiple instances of World of Warcraft are running on the same hardware.

Returns:

isDisabled—1 if the voice system is disabled; otherwise nil (1nil)

VoiceSelectCaptureDevice

Selects an audio input device for voice chat.

```
VoiceSelectCaptureDevice("deviceName")
```

Arguments:

deviceName—Name of an audio input device, as returned from
`VoiceEnumerateCaptureDevices()` (string)

VoiceSelectOutputDevice

Selects an audio output device for voice chat.

```
VoiceSelectOutputDevice("deviceName")
```

Arguments:

deviceName—Name of an audio output device, as returned from
`VoiceEnumerateOutputDevices()` (string)

 ### WithdrawGuildBankMoney

Attempts to withdraw money from the guild bank.

```
WithdrawGuildBankMoney(amount)
```

Causes a PLAYER_MONEY event to fire, indicating the amount withdrawn has
been added to the player's total (see GetMoney()). Causes an error or system
message if amount exceeds the amount of money in the guild bank or the
player's allowed daily withdrawal amount.

Arguments:

amount—Amount of money to withdraw (in copper) (number)

ZoomOut

Sets the world map to show the area containing its current area.

Only used by the default UI in certain circumstances: to "zoom out" from a multi-level map (e.g. Dalaran or a dungeon) to the containing zone/continent. May cause problems when not used in such cases.

Lua API   **abs**

Returns the absolute value of a number.

```
absoluteValue = abs(x)
```

Alias for the standard library function `math.abs`.

Arguments:

`x`—A number (`number`)

Returns:

`absoluteValue`—Absolute value of `x` (`number`)

Lua API   **assert**

Causes a Lua error if a condition is failed.

```
value = assert(condition, "message")
```

Arguments:

`condition`—Any value (commonly the result of an expression) (`value`)

`message`—Error message to be produced if `condition` is `false` or `nil` (`string`)

Returns:

`value`—The `condition` value provided, if not `false` or `nil` (`value`)

Example:

```
assert(x < y)
-- causes a Lua error if the value of x is not less than the value
-- of y when called

assert(not UnitIsDead("player"), "Oh noes!"))
-- causes a Lua error with text "Oh noes!" if the player is dead
-- when called
```

Lua API   **ceil**

Returns the smallest integer larger than or equal to a number.

```
ceiling = ceil(x)
```

Alias for the standard library function `math.ceil`.

Arguments:

`x`—A number (`number`)

Returns:

`ceiling`—Smallest integer larger than or equal to `x` (`number`)

Lua API   **collectgarbage**

Interface to the Lua garbage collector.

```
collectgarbage(option [, arg])
```

Arguments:

option—One of the following options

- collect—Performs a full garbage collection cycle
- count—Returns the total Lua memory usage (in kilobytes)
- restart—Restarts the garbage collector
- setpause—Sets the garbage collector's pause percentage to arg; e.g., if 200, the collector waits for memory usage to double before starting a new cycle
- setstepmul—Sets the garbage collector's speed (as a percentage relative to memory allocation) to arg; e.g., if 200, the collector runs twice as fast as memory is allocated
- step—Performs a garbage collection step, with size arg
- stop—Stops the garbage collector

arg (optional)—Argument applicable to some options

| Lua API |

date

Returns a formatted date/time string for a date (or the current date).

```
dateValue = date(["format" [, time]])
```

Alias to the standard library function os.date.

Arguments:

format (optional)—A string describing the formatting of time values (as in the ANSI C strftime() function), or *t to return the time as a table; optionally preceded by ! for Coordinated Universal Time instead of the local time zone; omitted for a date printed in the default format (string)

time (optional)—Time value to be formatted (see time() for description); if omitted, uses the current time (number)

Returns:

dateValue—A formatted date/time string, (string or table)

Examples:

```
-- Example #1
date()
-- returns (e.g.) "Sun Jun 14 01:31:41 2009"

-- Example #2
date("*t")
-- returns { hour=1, min=31, sec=41, wday=1, day=14, month=6,
-- year=2009, yday=165, isdst=true }
```

debuglocals

Returns information about the local variables at a given stack depth.

```
localsInfo = debuglocals(stackLevel)
```

Arguments:

stackLevel—The stack level to query (number)

Returns:

localsInfo—A string detailing the local variables at the given stack depth.
(string)

debugprofilestart

Starts/resets the high resolution profiling timer.

Subsequent calls to debugprofilestop() will return the current value of the
timer.

debugprofilestop

Returns the value of the profiling timer.

```
time = debugprofilestop()
```

Returns:

time—Current value of the profiling timer (in milliseconds, with
sub-millisecond precision) (number)

Example:

```
-- can be used to test the efficiency of a segment of code:
function myFunction()
 debugprofilestart()

 -- function body goes here

 print(format("myFunction executed in %f ms", debugprofilestop()))
end
```

debugstack

Returns information about the current function call stack.

```
debugstring = debugstack(start, countTop, countBot)
```

Arguments:

start—Stack level at which to begin listing functions; 0 is the debugstack()
function itself, 1 is the function that called debugstack(), 2 is the
function that called function 1, etc. Defaults to 1 if omitted (number)

countTop—Maximum number of functions to output at the top of the stack
trace (number)

countBot—Maximum number of functions to output at the bottom of the stack
trace (number)

Returns:

debugstring—A multi-line string describing the current function call stack
(string)

Example:

```
print(debugstack())
-- output:
[string "print(debugstack())"]:1: in main chunk
 [C]: in function 'RunScript'
 Interface\FrameXML\ChatFrame.lua:1826: in function '?'
 Interface\FrameXML\ChatFrame.lua:3332: in function ↵
```

```
'ChatEdit_ParseText'
  Interface\FrameXML\ChatFrame.lua:3052: in function 'ChatEdit_SendText'
  Interface\FrameXML\ChatFrame.lua:3073: in function ↩
<Interface\FrameXML\ChatFrame.lua:3072>
  [C]: in function 'ChatEdit_OnEnterPressed'
  [string "*:OnEnterPressed"]:1: in function ↩
<[string "*:OnEnterPressed"]:1>
```

| Lua API | ### deg

Converts an angle measurement in radians to degrees.

```
degrees = deg(radians)
```

Alias for the standard library function `math.deg`.

Arguments:

`radians`—An angle specified in radians (number)

Returns:

`degrees`—The angle specified in degrees (number)

| Lua API | ### difftime

Returns the number of seconds between two time values.

```
seconds = difftime(time2, time1)
```

Alias for the standard library function `os.difftime`.

Arguments:

`time2`—A time value (see `time()` for description) (number)

`time1`—A time value (see `time()` for description) (number)

Returns:

`seconds`—Number of seconds between `time2` and `time1`; equivalent to `time2-time1` on all current WoW clients (number)

| Lua API | ### error

Causes a Lua error message.

```
error("message" [, level])
```

Arguments:

`message`—An error message to be displayed (string)

`level` (optional)—Level in the function stack at which the error message begins providing function information; e.g. 1 (the default, if omitted) to start at the position where `error()` was called, 2 to start at the function which called `error()`, 3 to start at the function which called that function, etc. (number)

| Lua API | ### exp

Returns the value of the exponential function for a number.

```
exp = exp(x)
```

Alias for the standard library function `math.exp`.

Arguments:

`x`—A number (number)

Returns:

exp—Value of the mathematical constant *e* (Euler's number) raised to the xth power (number)

`Lua API` **floor**

Returns the largest integer smaller than or equal to a number.

```
floor = floor(x)
```

Alias for the standard library function `math.floor`.

Arguments:

x—A number (number)

Returns:

floor—Largest integer smaller than or equal to x (number)

forceinsecure

Causes the current execution path to continue outside the secure environment.
Meaningless when called from outside of the secure environment.

`Lua API` **format**

Returns a formatted string containing specified values.

```
formatted = format("formatString", ...)
```

Alias for the standard library function `string.format`. This version, however, includes the positional argument specifiers from Lua 4.0.

Lua does not support the ANSI C format specifiers *, l, L, n, p, and h but includes an extra specifier, q, which formats a string in a form suitable to be safely read back by the Lua interpreter; the string is written between double quotes, and all double quotes, newlines, embedded zeros, and backslashes in the string are correctly escaped when written.

Arguments:

formatString—A string containing format specifiers as per the ANSI C `printf` function (string)

...—A list of values to be included in the formatted string (list)

Returns:

formatted—The formatted string (number)

Example:

```
string.format("%s %q", "Hello", "Azeroth!") -- string and quoted string
-- returns 'Hello "Azeroth!"'
string.format("%c%c%c", 76,117,97)        -- char
-- returns 'Lua'
string.format("%e, %E", math.pi,math.pi)   -- exponent
-- returns '3.141593e+000, 3.141593E+000'
string.format("%f, %g", math.pi,math.pi)   -- float and compact float
--returns '3.141593, 3.14159'
string.format("%d, %i, %u", -100,-100,-100) -- signed, signed, ↵
unsigned integer
-- returns '-100, -100, 4294967196'
string.format("%o, %x, %X", -100,-100,-100) -- octal, hex, hex
-- returns '37777777634, ffffff9c, FFFFFF9C'
```

frexp

Returns the normalized fraction and base-2 exponent for a number.

```
m, e = frexp(x)
```

Alias for the standard library function `math.frexp`.

Arguments:

x—A number (`number`)

Returns:

m—A number whose absolute value is in the range [0.5, 1), or 0 if x is 0 (`number`)

e—An integer, such that x = m * 2 ˆ e (`number`)

geterrorhandler

Returns the current error handler function.

```
handler = geterrorhandler()
```

Returns:

`handler`—The current error handler (`function`)

Example:

```
local myError = "Something went horribly wrong!"
geterrorhandler()(myError)
```

getfenv

Returns the environment for a function (or the global environment).

```
env = getfenv([f]) or getfenv([stackLevel])
```

If the environment has a `__environment` metatable, that value is returned instead.

Arguments:

f (optional)—A function (`function`)

`stackLevel` (optional)—Level of a function in the calling stack (`number`)

Returns:

env—Table containing all variables in the function's environment, or the global environment if f or `stackLevel` is omitted (`table`)

getglobal

Returns the value of a global variable.

```
value = getglobal("name")
```

Often used in the default UI in cases where several similar names are systematically constructed. Examples:

■ In a script attached to a frame template, `getglobal(self:GetName()..`
`"Icon")` can refer to the Texture whose name is defined in XML as
`$parentIcon`.

■ Several sets of localized string tokens follow standard formats: e.g.
`getglobal("ITEM_QUALITY"..quality.."_DESC)` returns the name for
the numeric `quality`.

Equivalent to `_G.name` or `_G["name"]`.

Arguments:

`name`—Name of a global variable (`string`)

Returns:

`value`—Value of the given variable (`value`)

Lua API

getmetatable

Returns an object's metatable.

`metatable = getmetatable(object)`

Arguments:

`object`—Any table or userdata object (`value`)

Returns:

`metatable`—Contents of the object's `__metatable` field, or `nil` if the object has
no metatable (`value`)

Lua API

gmatch

Returns an iterator function for finding pattern matches in a string.

`iterator = gmatch("s", "pattern")`

Alias for the standard library function `string.gmatch`.

Arguments:

`s`—A string (`string`)

`pattern`—A regular expression pattern (`string, pattern`)

Returns:

`iterator`—A function which, each time it is called, returns the next capture of
`pattern` in the string `s`; always returns the whole string if `pattern` specifies no
captures (`function`)

Example:

```
-- print the components of an item link
for w in gmatch(link, "([%d-]+)") do
 print(w)
end
-- example output, given an enchanted Heavy Lamellar
-- Gauntlets of the Gorilla:
-- 10242
-- 2564
-- 0
-- 0
-- 0
-- 0
-- 614
-- 0
```

gsub

Returns a string in which occurrences of a pattern are replaced.

```
newString, numMatched = gsub("s", "pattern", "rep" [, maxReplaced]) or ↵
gsub("s", "pattern", repTable [, maxReplaced]) or gsub("s", "pattern", ↵
repFunc [, maxReplaced])
```

Alias for the standard library function `string.gsub`.

Arguments:

s—A string (`string`)

pattern—A regular expression pattern (`string`, pattern)

rep—String with which to replace occurrences of `pattern`; may contain specifiers for numbered captures in the `pattern` (`string`)

repTable—Table containing replacement strings; replacements are looked up using captured substrings as keys, or the entire match if `pattern` specifies no captures (`table`)

repFunc—Function to supply replacement strings; called with captured substrings (or the entire match if `pattern` specifies no captures) as arguments (`function`)

maxReplaced (optional)—Maximum number of replacements to be made (`number`)

Returns:

newString—A copy of s in which occurrences of the `pattern` have been replaced as specified (`string`)

numMatched—Number of matches found (`number`)

Example:

```
gsub("banana", "a", "A", 2)
-- returns "bAnAna", 2
gsub("banana", "(a)(n)", "%2%1")
-- returns "bnanaa", 2
gsub("banana", "[an]", {a="o",n="m"})
-- returns "bomomo", 5
gsub("banana", "(a)", strupper)
-- returns "bAnAnA", 3
```

hooksecurefunc

Add a function to be called after execution of a secure function.

```
hooksecurefunc([table,] "function", hookfunc)
```

Allows one to "post-hook" a secure function without tainting the original.

The original function will still be called, but the function supplied will be called after the original, with the same arguments. Return values from the supplied function are discarded. Note that there is no API to remove a hook from a function: any hooks applied will remain in place until the UI is reloaded.

Only allows hooking of functions named by a global variable; to hook a script handler on a Frame object, see `Frame:HookScript()`.

Arguments:

table (optional)—A table object that contains the function to be hooked (table)

function—The name of the function to be hooked (string)

hookfunc—The function to be called each time the original function is called (function)

Examples:

```
-- Example #1
-- Keep a counter of how many times your character has jumped,
-- and display in chat
local counter = 0
local function hook_JumpOrAscendStart(...)
 counter = counter + 1
 ChatFrame1:AddMessage("Boing! Boing! - " .. counter .. " jumps.")
end
hooksecurefunc("JumpOrAscendStart", hook_JumpOrAscendStart)
-- Example #2
-- Hook GameTooltip:SetAction() to display how many spell casts you can
-- make. It does this by scanning the second line of the tooltip, and
-- matching it against the pattern "(%d+) " .. MANA, where MANA is the
-- global string for "Mana" in the current locale.
local function hook_SetAction(self, ...)
  -- The second line of the tooltip is
  -- getglobal(self:GetName().."TextLeft2")
  local line = getglobal(self:GetName() .. "TextLeft2")
  local text = line:GetText() or ""
  local manaCost = text:match("(%d+) " .. MANA)
  if manaCost then
    -- Convert the mana cost to a number
   manaCost = tostring(manaCost)
    -- Get the player's current mana, and calculate the numnber of casts
    local mana = UnitMana("player")
    local numCasts = math.floor(mana / manaCost)
    -- Add the line to the tooltip, colored blue
    self:AddLine("You can cast this spell " .. numCasts .. ↵
" times", 0.4, 0.4, 1.0)
    -- Call this to ensure the tooltip is properly resized
    self:Show()
  end
end
hooksecurefunc(GameTooltip, "SetAction", hook_SetAction)
```

Lua API **ipairs**

Returns an iterator function for integer keys in a table.

```
iterator, t, index = ipairs(t)
```

Return values are such that the construction

```
for k,v in ipairs(t) do
-- body
end
```

will iterate over the pairs 1, t[1], 2, t[2], etc, up to the first integer key absent from the table.

Arguments:

t—A table (`table`)

Returns:

iterator—An iterator (`function`)

t—The table provided (`table`)

index—Always 0; used internally (`number`)

issecure

Returns whether the current execution path is secure.

```
secure = issecure()
```

Meaningless when called from outside of the secure environment: always returns `nil` in such situations.

Returns:

secure—1 if the current execution path is secure; otherwise `nil` (`1nil`)

issecurevariable

Returns whether a variable is secure (and if not, which addon tainted it).

```
issecure, taint = issecurevariable([table,] "variable")
```

Arguments:

table (optional)—A table to be used when checking table elements (`table`)

variable—The name of a variable to check. In order to check the status of a table element, you should specify the table, and then the key of the element (`string`)

Returns:

issecure—1 if the variable is secure; otherwise `nil` (`1nil`)

taint—Name of the addon that tainted the variable, or `nil` if the variable is secure (`string`)

| Lua API |

ldexp

Returns the number generated by a normalized fraction and base-2 exponent.

```
x = ldexp(m, e)
```

Alias for the standard library function `math.ldexp`.

Arguments:

m—A number (`number`)

e—A number (`number`)

Returns:

x—The value of m * 2 ^ e (`number`)

| Lua API |

loadstring

Loads and compiles Lua source code.

```
chunk, error = loadstring("s" [, "chunkname"])
```

Arguments:

s—A string containing Lua code (`string`)

`chunkname` (optional)—Name for the loaded chunk; used in error messages and debug information (`string`)

Returns:

chunk—A function which can be run to execute the provided code, or `nil` if the code could not be compiled (`function`)

error—Error message, if the code could not be compiled (`string`)

Lua API | **log**

Returns the natural logarithm of a number.

```
naturalLog = log(x)
```

Alias for the standard library function `math.log`.

Arguments:

x—A number (`number`)

Returns:

naturalLog—The natural logarithm of x (`number`)

Lua API | **log10**

Returns the base-10 logarithm of a number.

```
base10log = log10(x)
```

Alias for the standard library function `math.log10`.

Arguments:

x—A number (`number`)

Returns:

base10log—The base-10 logarithm of x (`number`)

Lua API | **max**

Returns the greatest of a list of numbers.

```
maximum = max(...)
```

Alias for the standard library function `math.max`.

Arguments:

...—A list of numbers (`list`)

Returns:

maximum—The highest number among all arguments (`number`)

Lua API | **min**

Returns the least of a list of numbers.

```
maximum = min(...)
```

Alias for the standard library function `math.min`.

Arguments:

...—A list of numbers (`list`)

Returns:

maximum—The lowest number among all arguments (number)

Lua API **mod**

Returns the remainder from division of two numbers.

```
remainder = mod(x, y)
```

Alias for the standard library function math.fmod.

Arguments:

x—A number (number)

y—A number (number)

Returns:

remainder—Remainder of the division of x by y that rounds the quotient towards zero (number)

Lua API **newproxy**

Creates a zero-length userdata with an optional metatable.

```
userdata = newproxy(boolean) or newproxy(userdata)
```

newproxy is an experimental, undocumented and unsupported function in the Lua base library. It can be used to create a zero-length userdata, with a optional proxy.

This function allows you to bypass the table type restriction on setmetatable, and thus create just a metatable. One of the main benefits from doing this is that you don't have to take the full overhead of creating a dummy table, and it's the only object that honors the metamethod __len.

Arguments:

boolean—Controls if the returned userdata should have a metatable or not. (boolean)

userdata—Needs to be a proxy. The metatable will be shared between the proxies. (userdata)

Returns:

userdata—A zero-length user-data object. (userdata)

Example:

```
proxy = newproxy(true)
getmetatable(proxy).__len = function() return 3 end
print(#proxy) -- prints 3
```

Lua API **next**

Returns the next key/value pair in a table.

```
nextKey, nextValue = next(t [, key])
```

Arguments:

t—A table (table)

key (optional)—A key in the table (value)

Returns:

nextKey—The next key in the table t (value)

nextValue—Value associated with the next key in the table t (value)

pairs

Returns an iterator function for a table.

```
iterator, t, index = pairs(t)
```

Return values are such that the construction

```
for k,v in pairs(t)
-- body
end
```

will iterate over all key/value pairs in the table.

Arguments:

t—A table (table)

Returns:

iterator—The next() function (function)

t—The table provided (table)

index—Always nil; used internally (number)

pcall

Executes a function in protected mode.

```
status, ... = pcall(f, ...)
```

When running a function in protected mode, any errors do not propagate beyond the function (i.e. they do not stop all execution and call the default error handler).

Arguments:

f—A function (function)

...—Arguments to be passed to the function (list)

Returns:

status—True if the function succeeded without errors; false otherwise (boolean)

...—If status is false, the error message produced by the function; if status is true, the return values from the function (list or string)

rad

Converts an angle specified in degrees to radians.

```
radians = rad(degrees)
```

Alias for the standard library function math.rad.

Arguments:

degrees—An angle specified in degrees (number)

Returns:

radians—The angle specified in radians (number)

| Lua API |

random

Generates a pseudo-random number.

```
randomNum = random([m [, n]])
```

Alias for the standard library function `math.random`.

Arguments:

m (optional)—First limit for randomly generated numbers (`number`)

n (optional)—Second limit for randomly generated numbers (`number`)

Returns:

randomNum—If called without arguments, a uniform pseudo-random real number in the range [0,1); if m is specified, a uniform pseudo-random integer in the range [1,m]; if both m and n are specified, a uniform pseudo-random integer in the range [m,n] (`number`)

| Lua API |

rawequal

Returns whether two values are equal without invoking any metamethods.

```
isEqual = rawequal(v1, v2)
```

Arguments:

v1—Any value (`value`)

v2—Any value (`function`)

Returns:

isEqual—`True` if the values are equal; `false` otherwise (`boolean`)

| Lua API |

rawget

Returns the real value associated with a key in a table without invoking any metamethods.

```
value = rawget(t, key)
```

Arguments:

t—A table (`table`)

key—A key in the table (`value`)

Returns:

value—Value of t[key] (`value`)

| Lua API |

rawset

Sets the value associated with a key in a table without invoking any metamethods.

```
rawset(t, key, value)
```

Arguments:

t—A table (`table`)

key—A key in the table (cannot be `nil`) (`value`)

value—New value to set for the key (`value`)

scrub

Replaces non-simple values in a list with `nil`.

```
... = scrub(...)
```

All simple values (strings, numbers, and booleans) are passed from the input list to the output list unchanged. Non-simple values (tables, functions, threads, and userdata) are replaced by nil in the output list.

Arguments:

. . .—A list of values (`list`)

Returns:

. . .—The list of input values, with all non-simple values replaced by `nil` (`list`)

Example:

```
scrub("a", print, 1, {1,2,3}, math.pi)
-- returns "a", nil, 1, nil, 3.1415926535898
```

securecall

Calls a function without tainting the execution path.

```
... = securecall(function, ...)
```

Meaningless when called from outside of the secure environment.

Used in Blizzard code to call functions which may be tainted or operate on potentially tainted variables. For example, consider the function `Close SpecialWindows`, which iterates through the table `UISpecialFrames` and hides any frames named therein. Addon authors may put the names of their frames in that table to make them automatically close when the user presses the ESC key, but this taints `UISpecialFrames`. Were the default UI to then call `CloseSpecialWindows` normally, every frame in `UISpecialFrames` would become tainted, which could later lead to errors when handlers on those frames call protected functions.

Instead, the default UI uses `securecall(CloseSpecialWindows)`: within `CloseSpecialWindows` the execution path may become tainted, but afterward the environment remains secure.

Arguments:

function—Function to be called (`function`)

. . .—Arguments to the function (`list`)

Returns:

. . .—Values returned after calling the function (`list`)

Lua API

select

Returns one or more values from a list (. . .), or the number of values in a list.

```
... = select(index, ...) or select("#", ...)
```

Arguments:

index—Index of a value in the list (`number`)

#—The string "#" (`string`)

. . .—A list of values (`list`)

Returns:

. . .—If called with a first argument of "#", the number of values in the list; otherwise, all values in the list starting with the value at position index (`list`)

seterrorhandler

Changes the error handler to a specified function.

```
seterrorhandler(errHandler)
```

The error handler is called by Lua's `error()` function, which in turn is called whenever a Lua error occurs. WoW's default error handler displays the error message, a stack trace and information about the local variables for the function. This dialog will only be shown if the "Show Lua errors" option is enabled in Interface Options.

Arguments:

errHandler—A function to use as the error handler (`function`)

| Lua API |

setfenv

Sets the environment to be used by a function.

```
f = setfenv([f,] t) or setfenv([stackLevel,] t)
```

If the environment has a __environment metatable, this function will error.

Arguments:

`f` (optional)—A function (`function`)

`stackLevel` (optional)—Level of a function in the calling stack, or 0 to set the global environment (`number`)

`t`—A table (`table`)

Returns:

`f`—The input function `f` (`function`)

setglobal

Sets a global variable to a specified value.

```
setglobal("name", value)
```

Allows setting the value of a global variable in contexts where its name might be overridden by that of a local variable; i.e. `setglobal(name, value)` is equivalent to `_G.name = value` or `_G["name"] = value`.

Arguments:

`name`—Name of a global variable (`string`)

`value`—New value for the variable (`value`)

| Lua API |

setmetatable

Sets the metatable for a table.

```
t = setmetatable(t, metatable)
```

Arguments:

`t`—A table (`table`)

`metatable`—A metatable for the table `t`, or `nil` to remove an existing metatable (`table`)

Returns:

`t`—The input table `t` (`table`)

Lua API

sort

Sorts a table.

```
sort(table [, comparator])
```

Alias for the standard library function `table.sort`.

Arguments:

`table`—A table (number)

`comparator` (optional)—A function to compare table elements during the sort; takes two arguments and returns `true` if the first argument should be ordered before the second in the sorted table; equivalent to `function(a,b) return a < b end` if omitted (function)

Examples:

```
-- Example #1
aTable = {"a", "c", "g", "e", "b", "f", "d"}
sort(aTable)
print(aTable)
-- shows "a b c d e f g"
sort(aTable, function(a,b) return a>b end)
print(aTable)
-- shows "g f e d c b a"
-- Example #2
complexTable = {
  {
   name = "Gorrok",
   level = 80,
   class = "WARRIOR",
  }
  {
   name = "Spin",
   level = 79,
   class = "SHAMAN",
  },
  {
   name = "Valiant",
   level = 80,
   class = "HUNTER",
  }
}
sort(complexTable, function(a,b) return a.name < b.name end)
for _, info in ipairs(complexTable) do print(info.name) end
-- prints "Gorrok, Spin, Valiant"
sort(complexTable, function(a,b) return a.level < b.level end)
for _, info in ipairs(complexTable) do print(info.name) end
-- prints "Spin, Gorrok, Valiant" (or "Spin, Valiant, Gorrok"; order
-- of equal elements is not defined)
sort(complexTable, function(a,b) return a.class < b.class end)
for _, info in ipairs(complexTable) do print(info.name) end
-- prints "Valiant, Spin, Gorrok"
```

sqrt

Returns the square root of a number.

```
root = sqrt(x)
```

Alias for the standard library function `math.sqrt`.

Arguments:

x—A number (number)

Returns:

root—The square root of x (number)

strbyte

Returns the numeric code for one or more characters in a string.

```
value, ... = strbyte("s" [, firstChar [, lastChar]])
```

Alias for the standard library function `string.byte`.

Arguments:

s—A string (string)

firstChar (optional)—Position of a character in the string (can be negative to count backwards from the end of the string); defaults to 1 if omitted (number)

lastChar (optional)—Position of a later character in the string (can be negative to count backwards from the end of the string); defaults to firstChar if omitted (number)

Returns:

value—Numeric code for the character at position firstChar in the string (number)

. . . —A list of numbers, each the numeric codes of additional characters in the string if lastChar specifies a position later in the string than firstChar (list)

strchar

Returns the character(s) for one or more numeric codes.

```
s = strchar(n [, ...])
```

Alias for the standard library function `string.char`.

Arguments:

n—An integer (number)

. . . (optional)—Additional integers (number)

Returns:

s—A string containing the character(s) for the given numeric code(s) (number)

strconcat

Joins a list of strings (with no separator).

```
result = strconcat("...")
```

Equivalent to `strjoin("", ...)`. If no strings are provided, returns the empty string (" ").

Arguments:

. . . —A list of strings to concatenate (string)

Returns:

result—The concatenated string (string)

Lua API **strfind**

Returns information about matches for a pattern in a string.

start, end, ... = strfind("s", "pattern" [, init [, plain]])

Alias for the standard library function string.find.

Returns nil if no matches are found.

Arguments:

s—A string (string)

pattern—A regular expression pattern (string, pattern)

init (optional)—Initial position in the string s at which to begin the search; defaults to 1 if omitted (number)

plain (optional)—True to perform a simple substring search (i.e. considering pattern only as a literal string, not a regular expression); false or omitted otherwise (boolean)

Returns:

start—Character position in s at which the first match begins (number)

end—Character position in s at which the first match ends (number)

...—Captured substrings from s, if pattern specifies captures (list)

Example:

```
strfind("Welcome to Azeroth!", "Azeroth")
-- returns 12, 18
strfind("|cffffff00|Hquest:982:17|h[Deep Ocean, Vast Sea]|h|r", ↵
"quest:(%d+):([-%d]+)|h%[(.-)%]")
-- returns 11, 48, "982", "17", "Deep Ocean, Vast Sea"
```

strjoin

Joins a list of strings together with a given separator.

text = strjoin("sep", ...)

If given a list of strings not already in a table, this function can be used instead of table.concat for better performance.

Also available as string.join (though not provided by the Lua standard library).

Arguments:

sep—A separator to insert between joined strings (string)

...—A list of strings to be joined together (list)

Returns:

text—The list of strings joined together with the given separator string (string)

Example:

```
strjoin(",", "alice", "bob", "carol")
-- Returns "alice,bob,carol"
```

```
strjoin(" mississippi, ", "one", "two", "three")
-- Returns "one mississippi, two mississippi, three
```

Lua API   **strlen**

Returns the number of characters in a string.

```
length = strlen("s")
```

Alias for the standard library function `string.len`.

Arguments:

s—A string (`string`)

Returns:

`length`—Number of characters in the string (`number`)

strlenutf8

Returns the length of a string, taking UTF-8 multi-byte characters into account.

```
length = strlenutf8("string")
```

Arguments:

`string`—The string to query. (`string`)

Returns:

`length`—The length of the given string, taking UTF-8 multi-byte characters into account. (`number`)

Lua API   **strlower**

Returns a copy of a string with all uppercase letters converted to lowercase.

```
lowerCase = strlower("s")
```

Alias for the standard library function `string.lower`

Arguments:

s—A string (`string`)

Returns:

`lowerCase`—A copy of the string s with all uppercase letters converted to lowercase (`string`)

Lua API   **strmatch**

Returns the matches for a for a pattern in a string.

```
match, ... = strmatch("s", "pattern")
```

Alias for the standard library function `string.match`.

Arguments:

s—A string (`string`)

`pattern`—A regular expression pattern (`string`, pattern)

Returns:

`match`—First substring of s matching `pattern`, or the first capture if `pattern` specifies captures; `nil` if no match is found (`string`)

`...`—Additional captures found, if `pattern` specifies multiple captures (`list`)

Example:

```
strmatch("Your share of the loot is 97 Copper.", "%d+ %a+")
-- returns "97 Copper"

strmatch("Your share of the loot is 97 Copper.", "(%d+) (%a+)")
-- returns "97", "Copper"
```

`Lua API`   **strrep**

Returns a string produced by a number of repetitions of another string.

```
repeated = strrep("s", n)
```

Alias for the standard library function `string.rep`.

Arguments:

s—A string (`string`)

n—A number (`number`)

Returns:

repeated—The concatenation of n copies of the string s (`string`)

Example:

```
strrep("spam ",8)
-- returns "spam spam spam spam spam spam spam spam "
```

strreplace

Fast simple substring substitution.

```
newText, count = strreplace("text", "pattern", "replacement", "count")
```

Matches the semantics of `string.gsub`, but only finds and replaces specific substrings rather than using more powerful and more computationally expensive regular expression matching. Thus, this function can be used in place of `string.gsub` in performance-critical situations where only simple matching is needed.

Also available as `string.replace` (though not provided by the Lua standard library).

Arguments:

text—Text to be altered (`string`)

pattern—A substring to be located within the source text (`string`)

replacement—Text to be inserted in place of the found pattern (`string`)

count—Maximum number of replacements to be made (`string`)

Returns:

newText—The input string with matching substrings replaced (`string`)

count—Number of occurrences of the substring replaced (`number`)

`Lua API`   **strrev**

Returns the reverse of a string.

```
s = strrev("s")
```

Alias for the standard library function `string.reverse`.

Arguments:

s—A string (string)

Returns:

s—A string containing the characters of string s in reverse order (string)

Example:

```
strrev("abcdef")
-- returns "fedcba"
strrev("nametag")
-- returns "gateman"
strrev("Step on no pets")
-- returns "step on no petS"
```

strsplit

Splits a string based on another seperator string.

```
... = strsplit("sep", "text", limit)
```

Also available as string.split (though not provided by the Lua standard library).

Arguments:

sep—The seperator string to use (string)

text—The text to split (string)

limit—The maximum number of pieces to split the string into (number)

Returns:

...—A list of strings, split from the input text based on the seperator string (string)

Example:

```
-- Split the string "a:b:c:d"
strsplit(":", "a:b:c:d", 2)
-- Returns "a", "b:c:d"

-- Split the string "a::b::c::d"
strsplit("::", "a::b::c::d")
-- Returns "a", "b", "c", "d"
```

Lua API **strsub**

Returns a substring of a string.

```
s = strsub("s", firstChar [, lastChar])
```

Alias for the standard library function string.sub.

Arguments:

s—A string (string)

firstChar—Position of a character in the string (can be negative to count backwards from the end of the string) (number)

lastChar (optional)—Position of a later character in the string (can be negative to count backwards from the end of the string); defaults to -1 if omitted (number)

Returns:

s—The substring of s starting at the character firstChar and ending with the character lastChar (string)

strtrim

Trims leading and trailing characters (whitespace by default) from a string.

```
text = strtrim("str" [, "trimChars"])
```

Also available as string.trim (though not provided by the Lua standard library).

Arguments:

str—A string to trim (string)

trimChars (optional)—A string listing the characters to be trimmed (e.g. "[]{}()" to trim leading and trailing brackets, braces, and parentheses); if nil or omitted, whitespace characters (space, tab, newline, etc) are trimmed (string)

Returns:

text—The trimmed string (string)

Examples:

```
-- Example #1
strtrim("  This is a test  ")
-- Returns "This is a test"


-- Example #2
strtrim("121abc456", "615")
-- Returns "21abc4"
```

Lua API

strupper

Returns a copy of a string with all lowercase letters converted to uppercase.

```
lowerCase = strupper("s")
```

Alias for the standard library function string.upper.

Arguments:

s—A string (string)

Returns:

lowerCase—A copy of the string s with all lowercase letters converted to uppercase (string)

Lua API

time

Returns the numeric time value for a described date/time (or the current time).

```
t = time([timeDesc])
```

Alias for the standard library function os.time.

According to the Lua manual, the returned value may vary across different systems; however, the Lua libraries included with current WoW clients on both Mac and Windows share the same implementation.

For higher-precision time measurements not convertible to a date, see `GetTime()`.

Arguments:

`timeDesc` (optional)—Table describing a date and time, as returned by `date("*t")`; if omitted, uses the current time (`table`)

Returns:

`t`—Number of seconds elapsed since midnight, January 1, 1970 UTC (`number`)

Lua API **tinsert**

Inserts a value into a table.

`tinsert(table [, position] value)`

Alias for the standard library function `table.insert`.

Arguments:

`table`—A table (`table`)

`position` (optional)—Index in the table at which to insert the new value; if omitted, defaults to `#table + 1` (`number`)

`value`—Any value (`value`)

Lua API **tonumber**

Returns the numeric value of a string.

`numValue = tonumber(x [, base])`

Arguments:

`x`—A string or number (`value`)

`base` (optional)—Base in which to interpret the numeral (integer between 2 and 36); letters 'A-Z' can be used to denote place values 10 or above in bases greater than 10; defaults to 10 if omitted (`number`)

Returns:

`numValue`—Numeric value of x in the given base, or `nil` if the value cannot be converted to a number (`number`)

Lua API **tostring**

Returns a string representation of a value.

`stringValue = tostring(value)`

Arguments:

`value`—Any value (`value`)

Returns:

`stringValue`—String representation of the given `value` (if value is an object with a __tostring metamethod, that method is used to produce the string representation) (`string`)

Lua API **tremove**

Removes an element from a table.

`tremove(table [, position])`

Alias for the standard library function `table.remove`.

Arguments:

`table`—A table (`table`)

`position` (optional)—Index in the table from which to remove the value; if omitted, defaults to `#table` (`number`)

Lua API

type

Returns a string describing the data type of a value.

`typeString = type(v)`

Arguments:

`v`—Any value (`value`)

Returns:

`typeString`—A string describing the type of value `v` (`string`)

- `boolean`—A boolean value (`true` or `false`)
- `function`—A function
- `nil`—The special value `nil`
- `number`—A numeric value
- `string`—A string
- `table`—A table
- `thread`—A coroutine thread
- `userdata`—Data external to the Lua environment (e.g. the main element of a Frame object)

Lua API

unpack

Returns the list of elements in a table.

`... = unpack(t [, i [, j]])`

Equivalent to

`return t[i], t[i+1], ... t[j]`

for an arbitrary number of elements.

Arguments:

`t`—A table (`table`)

`i` (optional)—A numeric index to the table; defaults to 1 if omitted (`number`)

`j` (optional)—A numeric index to the table; defaults to `#t` if omitted (`number`)

Returns:

`...`—The list of values in the table between indices `i` and `j` (`list`)

wipe

Removes all entries from a table.

`emptyTable = wipe(aTable)`

Arguments:

`aTable`—A table whose contents are to be erased (`table`)

Returns:

emptyTable—The input table, with all entries removed (table)

Lua API **xpcall**

Executes a function in protected mode with a custom error handler.

status, ... = xpcall(f, err)

Arguments:

f—A function (function)

err—Error handler function to be used should f cause an error (function)

Returns:

status—True if the function succeeded without errors; false otherwise (boolean)

...—If status is false, the error message produced by the function; if status is true, the return values from the function (list or string)

## CHAPTER 28

API Categories

Finding the right function to accomplish a specific task in World of Warcraft can be difficult, because there are over a thousand API functions that could be used. This chapter provides a categorized listing of these functions to make it easier to determine which the correct function is. Some functions appear in more than one category, when necessary.

Achievement Functions

`AddTrackedAchievement`–Adds an achievement to the objectives tracker UI

`CanShowAchievementUI`–Returns whether the achievements UI should be enabled

`ClearAchievementComparisonUnit`–Disables comparing achievements/statistics with another player

`GetAchievementCategory`–Returns the numeric ID of the category to which an achievement belongs

`GetAchievementComparisonInfo`–Returns information about the comparison unit's achievements

`GetAchievementCriteriaInfo`–Gets information about criteria for an achievement or data for a statistic

`GetAchievementInfo`–Gets information about an achievement or statistic

`GetAchievementInfoFromCriteria`–Gets information about an achievement or statistic given a criterion ID

`GetAchievementLink`—Returns a hyperlink representing the player's progress on an achievement

`GetAchievementNumCriteria`—Returns the number of measured criteria for an achievement

`GetAchievementNumRewards`—Returns the number of point rewards for an achievement (currently always 1)

`GetAchievementReward`—Returns the number of achievement points awarded for earning an achievement

`GetCategoryInfo`—Returns information about an achievement/statistic category

`GetCategoryList`—Returns a list of all achievement categories

`GetCategoryNumAchievements`—Returns the number of achievements/statistics to display in a category

`GetComparisonAchievementPoints`—Returns the comparison unit's total achievement points earned

`GetComparisonCategoryNumAchievements`—Returns the number of achievements completed by the comparison unit within a category

`GetComparisonStatistic`—Returns the comparison unit's data for a statistic

`GetLatestCompletedAchievements`—Returns a list of the player's most recently earned achievements

`GetLatestCompletedComparisonAchievements`—Returns a list of the comparison unit's most recently earned achievements

`GetNextAchievement`—Returns the next achievement for an achievement which is part of a series

`GetNumComparisonCompletedAchievements`—Returns the number of achievements earned by the comparison unit

`GetNumCompletedAchievements`—Returns the number of achievements earned by the player

`GetNumTrackedAchievements`—Returns the number of achievements flagged for display in the objectives tracker UI

`GetPreviousAchievement`—Returns the previous achievement for an achievement which is part of a series

`GetStatistic`—Returns data for a statistic

`GetStatisticsCategoryList`—Returns a list of all statistic categories

`GetTotalAchievementPoints`—Returns the player's total achievement points earned

`GetTrackedAchievements`–Returns numeric IDs of the achievements flagged for display in the objectives tracker UI

`IsTrackedAchievement`–Returns whether an achievement is flagged for display in the objectives tracker UI

`RemoveTrackedAchievement`–Removes an achievement from the objectives tracker UI

`SetAchievementComparisonUnit`–Enables comparing achievements/statistics with another player

Action Functions

`ActionHasRange`–Returns whether an action has a range restriction

`CastPetAction`–Casts a pet action on a specific target

`GetActionCooldown`–Returns cooldown information about an action

`GetActionCount`–Returns the number of uses remaining for the given action slot

`GetActionInfo`–Returns information about an action slot

`GetActionText`–Returns the text label associated with an action

`GetActionTexture`–Returns the icon texture for an action

`GetPetActionCooldown`–Returns cooldown information about a given pet action slot

`GetPetActionInfo`–Returns information about a pet action

`GetPetActionSlotUsable`–Returns whether a pet action can be used

`GetPetActionsUsable`–Returns whether the pet's actions are usable

`HasAction`–Returns whether an action slot contains an action

`IsActionInRange`–Returns whether the player's target is in range of an action

`IsAttackAction`–Returns whether an action is the standard melee Attack action

`IsAutoRepeatAction`–Returns whether an action is an automatically repeating action

`IsConsumableAction`–Returns whether using an action consumes an item

`IsCurrentAction`–Returns whether an action is currently being used

`IsEquippedAction`–Returns whether an action contains an equipped item

`IsStackableAction`–Returns whether an action uses stackable items

IsUsableAction–Returns whether an action is usable

PickupAction–Puts the contents of an action bar slot onto the cursor or the cursor contents into an action bar slot

PickupPetAction–Puts the contents of a pet action slot onto the cursor or the cursor contents into a pet action slot

PlaceAction–Puts the contents of the cursor into an action bar slot

TogglePetAutocast–Turns autocast on or off for a pet action

UseAction–Uses an action

ActionBar Functions

ChangeActionBarPage–Changes the current action bar page

GetActionBarPage–Returns the current action bar page

GetActionBarToggles–Returns the current visibility settings for the four secondary action bars

GetBonusBarOffset–Returns the current "stance" offset for use with the bonus action bar

GetPossessInfo–Returns information about special actions available while the player possesses another unit

IsPossessBarVisible–Returns whether a special action bar should be shown while the player possesses another unit

SetActionBarToggles–Configures display of additional ActionBars in the default UI

Addon-related Functions

DisableAddOn–Marks an addon as disabled

DisableAllAddOns–Marks all addons as disabled

EnableAddOn–Marks an addon as enabled

EnableAllAddOns–Marks all addons as enabled

GetAddOnDependencies–Returns a list of addons a given addon is dependent upon

GetAddOnInfo–Returns information about an addon

GetAddOnMetadata–Returns the value of certain fields in an addon's TOC file

GetNumAddOns–Returns the number of addons in the addon listing

`InterfaceOptionsFrame_OpenToCategory`–Opens the Interface Options window and displays a given panel within it

`InterfaceOptions_AddCategory`–Registers a panel to be displayed in the Interface Options window

`IsAddOnLoadOnDemand`–Returns whether an addon can be loaded without restarting the UI

`IsAddOnLoaded`–Returns whether an addon is currently loaded

`LoadAddOn`–Loads a LoadOnDemand-capable addon

`ResetDisabledAddOns`–Reverts changes to the enabled/disabled state of addons

`SendAddonMessage`–Sends a chat-like message receivable by other addons

Arena Functions

`AcceptArenaTeam`–Accepts an invitation to join an arena team

`ArenaTeamDisband`–Disbands an arena team

`ArenaTeamInviteByName`–Invites a character to one of the player's arena teams

`ArenaTeamLeave`–Leaves an arena team

`ArenaTeamRoster`–Requests arena team roster information from the server

`ArenaTeamSetLeaderByName`–Promotes an arena team member to team captain

`ArenaTeamUninviteByName`–Removes a member from an arena team

`ArenaTeam_GetTeamSizeID`–Converts an arena team size to the appropriate numeric arena team identifier

`CloseArenaTeamRoster`–Ends interaction with the Arena Team Roster

`DeclineArenaTeam`–Declines an arena team invitation

`GetArenaCurrency`–Returns the player's amount of arena points

`GetArenaTeam`–Returns information about one of the player's arena teams

`GetArenaTeamRosterInfo`–Returns information about an arena team member

`GetArenaTeamRosterSelection`–Returns the currently selected member in an arena team roster

`GetCurrentArenaSeason`–Returns a number identifying the current arena season

`GetMaxArenaCurrency`–Returns the maximum amount of arena points the player can accrue

`GetNumArenaOpponents`–Returns the number of enemy players in an arena match

`GetNumArenaTeamMembers`–Returns the number of members in an arena team

`GetPreviousArenaSeason`–Returns a number identifying the previous arena season

`IsActiveBattlefieldArena`–Returns whether the player is currently in an arena match

`IsArenaTeamCaptain`–Returns whether the player is the captain of an arena team

`IsBattlefieldArena`–Returns whether the player is interacting with an entity that allows queueing for arena matches

`IsInArenaTeam`–Returns whether the player is on an arena team

`SetArenaTeamRosterSelection`–Selects a member in an arena team roster

`SortArenaTeamRoster`–Sorts the selected arena team's roster

`TurnInArenaPetition`–Turns in a petition creating an arena team

Auction Functions

`CalculateAuctionDeposit`–Returns the deposit amount for the item currently being set up for auction

`CanCancelAuction`–Returns whether one of the player's auctions can be canceled

`CanSendAuctionQuery`–Returns whether the player can perform an auction house query

`CancelAuction`–Cancels an auction created by the player

`ClickAuctionSellItemButton`–Picks up an item from or puts an item into the "Create Auction" slot

`CloseAuctionHouse`–Ends interaction with the Auction House UI

`GetAuctionInvTypes`–Returns a list of the inventory subtypes for a given auction house item subclass

`GetAuctionItemClasses`–Returns a list of localized item class (category) names

`GetAuctionItemInfo`–Returns information about an auction listing

`GetAuctionItemLink`–Returns a hyperlink for an item in an auction listing

GetAuctionItemSubClasses–Returns a list of localized subclass names for a given item class

GetAuctionItemTimeLeft–Returns the time remaining before an auction listing expires

GetAuctionSellItemInfo–Returns information about the item currently being set up for auction

GetAuctionSort–Returns the current sort settings for auction data

GetBidderAuctionItems–Requests data from the server for the list of auctions bid on by the player

GetInboxInvoiceInfo–Returns auction house invoice information for a mail message

GetNumAuctionItems–Returns the number of auction items in a listing

GetOwnerAuctionItems–Requests data from the server for the list of auctions created by the player

GetSelectedAuctionItem–Returns the index of the currently selected item in an auction listing

PlaceAuctionBid–Places a bid on (or buys out) an auction item

QueryAuctionItems–Requests data from the server for the list of auctions meeting given search criteria

SetSelectedAuctionItem–Selects an item in an auction listing

SortAuctionApplySort–Applies a set of auction listing sort criteria set via SortAuctionSetSort

SortAuctionClearSort–Clears any current sorting rules for an auction house listing

SortAuctionSetSort–Builds a list of sort criteria for auction listings

StartAuction–Creates an auction for the item currently in the "auction item" slot

Bank Functions

BankButtonIDToInvSlotID–Returns the inventoryID corresponding to a bank item or bag slot

CloseBankFrame–Ends interaction with the bank

EquipmentManager_UnpackLocation–Unpacks an inventory location bitfield into usable components

GetBankSlotCost–Returns the cost of the next purchasable bank bag slot

GetNumBankSlots–Returns information about purchased bank bag slots

PurchaseSlot–Purchases the next available bank slot

Barbershop Functions

ApplyBarberShopStyle–Purchases the selected barber shop style changes

BarberShopReset–Resets barber shop options to the currently worn styles

CanAlterSkin–Lets you check if the player can change their skin color

CancelBarberShop–Exits a barber shop session

GetBarberShopStyleInfo–Returns information about the selected barber shop style option

GetBarberShopTotalCost–Returns the total price of selected barber shop style changes

GetFacialHairCustomization–Returns a token used for displaying facial feature customization options

GetHairCustomization–Returns a token used for displaying "hair" customization options

SetNextBarberShopStyle–Selects the next style for a barber shop style option

Battlefield Functions

AcceptAreaSpiritHeal–Accepts the next upcoming periodic resurrection from a battleground spirit healer

AcceptBattlefieldPort–Accepts the offered teleport to a battleground/ arena or leaves the battleground/arena or queue

CanJoinBattlefieldAsGroup–Returns whether the battleground for which the player is queueing supports joining as a group

CancelAreaSpiritHeal–Declines the next upcoming periodic resurrection from a battleground spirit healer

CloseBattlefield–Ends interaction with the battleground queueing UI

GetAreaSpiritHealerTime–Returns the time remaining until a nearby battleground spirit healer resurrects all players in its area

GetBattlefieldEstimatedWaitTime–Returns the estimated wait time on a battleground or arena queue

`GetBattlefieldFlagPosition`–Returns the position of a flag in a battleground

`GetBattlefieldInfo`–Returns information about a battleground for which the player can queue

`GetBattlefieldInstanceExpiration`–Returns the amount of time remaining before all players are removed from the instance, if in a battleground instance where the match has completed

`GetBattlefieldInstanceInfo`–Returns a numeric ID for a battleground instance in the battleground queueing list

`GetBattlefieldInstanceRunTime`–Returns the amount of time since the current battleground instance opened

`GetBattlefieldMapIconScale`–Returns the scale to be used for displaying battleground map icons

`GetBattlefieldPortExpiration`–Returns the time left on a battleground or arena invitation

`GetBattlefieldPosition`–Returns the position of a battleground team member not in the player's group

`GetBattlefieldScore`–Returns basic scoreboard information for a battleground/arena participant

`GetBattlefieldStatData`–Returns battleground-specific scoreboard information for a battleground participant

`GetBattlefieldStatInfo`–Returns information about a battleground-specific scoreboard column

`GetBattlefieldStatus`–Returns information about an active or queued battleground/arena instance

`GetBattlefieldTeamInfo`–Returns info about teams and their ratings in a rated arena match

`GetBattlefieldTimeWaited`–Returns the amount of time elapsed since the player joined the queue for a battleground/arena

`GetBattlefieldVehicleInfo`–Returns information about special vehicles in the current zone

`GetBattlefieldWinner`–Returns the winner of the current battleground or arena match

`GetBattlegroundInfo`–Returns information about available battlegrounds

`GetNumBattlefieldFlagPositions`–Returns the number of battleground flags for which map position information is available

GetNumBattlefieldPositions–Returns the number of team members in the battleground not in the player's group

GetNumBattlefieldScores–Returns the number of participant scores available in the current battleground

GetNumBattlefieldStats–Returns the number of battleground-specific statistics on the current battleground's scoreboard

GetNumBattlefieldVehicles–Returns the number of special vehicles in the current zone

GetNumBattlefields–Returns the number of instances available for a battleground

GetNumBattlegroundTypes–Returns the number of different battlegrounds available

GetRealNumPartyMembers–Returns the number of members in the player's non-battleground party

GetRealNumRaidMembers–Returns the number of members in the player's non-battleground raid

GetSelectedBattlefield–Returns the index of the selected battleground instance in the queueing list

IsActiveBattlefieldArena–Returns whether the player is currently in an arena match

IsBattlefieldArena–Returns whether the player is interacting with an entity that allows queueing for arena matches

IsRealPartyLeader–Returns whether the player is the leader of a non-battleground party

IsRealRaidLeader–Returns whether the player is the leader of a non-battleground raid

JoinBattlefield–Joins the queue for a battleground instance

LeaveBattlefield–Immediately exits the current battleground instance

PlayerIsPVPInactive–Returns whether a battleground participant is inactive (and eligible for reporting as AFK)

ReportPlayerIsPVPAFK–Reports a battleground participant as AFK

RequestBattlefieldPositions–Requests information from the server about team member positions in the current battleground

RequestBattlefieldScoreData–Requests battlefield score data from the server

RequestBattlegroundInstanceInfo–Requests information about available instances of a battleground from the server

SetBattlefieldScoreFaction—Filters the battleground scoreboard by faction/team

SetSelectedBattlefield—Selects a battleground instance in the queueing list

ShowBattlefieldList—Requests to change instances for a battleground to which the player is already queued

ShowMiniWorldMapArrowFrame—Shows or hides the battlefield minimap's player arrow

SortBattlefieldScoreData—Sorts the battleground scoreboard

UnitInBattleground—Returns whether a unit is in same battleground instance as the player

Blizzard Internal Functions

DetectWowMouse—Detects the presence of a "WoW" compatible multi-button mouse

newproxy—Creates a zero-length userdata with an optional metatable

Buff Functions

CancelItemTempEnchantment—Cancels a temporary weapon enchant

CancelShapeshiftForm—Cancels the current shapeshift form

CancelUnitBuff—Cancels a buff on the player

GetWeaponEnchantInfo—Returns information about temporary enchantments on the player's weapons

UnitAura—Returns information about buffs/debuffs on a unit

UnitBuff—Returns information about a buff on a unit

UnitDebuff—Returns information about a debuff on a unit

CVar Functions

GetCVar—Returns the value of a configuration variable

GetCVarAbsoluteMax—Returns the absolute maximum value allowed for a configuration variable

GetCVarAbsoluteMin—Returns the absolute minimum value allowed for a configuration variable

GetCVarBool—Returns the value of a configuration variable in a format compatible with Lua conditional expressions

GetCVarDefault–Returns the default value of a configuration variable

GetCVarInfo–Returns information about a configuration variable

GetCVarMax–Returns the maximum recommended value for a configuration variable

GetCVarMin–Returns the minimum recommended value for a configuration variable

RegisterCVar–Registers a configuration variable to be saved

SetCVar–Sets the value of a configuration variable

Calendar Functions

CalendarAddEvent–Saves the event recently created (and selected for editing) to the calendar

CalendarCanAddEvent–Returns whether the player can add an event to the calendar

CalendarCanSendInvite–Returns whether the player can invite others to a calendar event

CalendarCloseEvent–Deselects (ends viewing/editing on) an event

CalendarContextDeselectEvent–Clears the event selection used only for CalendarContext functions

CalendarContextEventCanComplain–Returns whether the player can report an event invitation as spam

CalendarContextEventCanEdit–Returns whether the player can edit an event

CalendarContextEventClipboard–Returns whether the player can paste an event

CalendarContextEventComplain–Reports an event invitation as spam

CalendarContextEventCopy–Copies an event for later pasting

CalendarContextEventGetCalendarType–Returns the type of a calendar event

CalendarContextEventPaste–Pastes a copied event into a given date

CalendarContextEventRemove–Deletes an event from the calendar

CalendarContextEventSignUp–Signs the player up for a guild event

CalendarContextGetEventIndex–Returns the month, day, and index of the event selection used only for CalendarContext functions

CalendarContextInviteAvailable–Accepts an event invitation

CalendarContextInviteDecline–Declines an event invitation

`CalendarContextInviteIsPending`—Returns whether the player has been invited to an event and not yet responded

`CalendarContextInviteModeratorStatus`—Returns the player's moderator status for an event

`CalendarContextInviteRemove`—Removes an invitation from the player's calendar or removes the player from a guild event's signup list

`CalendarContextInviteStatus`—Returns the player's invite status for an event

`CalendarContextInviteType`—Returns the invite type for an event

`CalendarContextSelectEvent`—Selects an event for use only with other `CalendarContext` functions

`CalendarDefaultGuildFilter`—Returns default options for the guild member Mass Invite filter

`CalendarEventAvailable`—Accepts invitation to the selected calendar event

`CalendarEventCanEdit`—Returns whether the player can edit the selected calendar event

`CalendarEventCanModerate`—Returns whether an event invitee can be granted moderator authority

`CalendarEventClearAutoApprove`—Disables the auto-approve feature (currently unused) for the selected calendar event

`CalendarEventClearLocked`—Unlocks the selected calendar event

`CalendarEventClearModerator`—Removes moderator status from a character on the selected event's invite/signup list

`CalendarEventDecline`—Declines invitation to the selected calendar event

`CalendarEventGetCalendarType`—Returns the type of the selected calendar event

`CalendarEventGetInvite`—Returns information about an entry in the selected event's invite/signup list

`CalendarEventGetInviteResponseTime`—Returns the time at which a character on the selected event's invite/signup list responded

`CalendarEventGetInviteSortCriterion`—Returns the current sort mode for the event invite/signup list

`CalendarEventGetNumInvites`—Returns the number of characters on the selected calendar event's invite/signup list

`CalendarEventGetRepeatOptions`—Returns a list of localized event repetition option labels (currently unused)

`CalendarEventGetSelectedInvite`–Returns the index of the selected entry on the selected event's invite/signup list

`CalendarEventGetStatusOptions`–Returns a list of localized invite status labels

`CalendarEventGetTextures`–Returns a list of instance names and icons for dungeon or raid events

`CalendarEventGetTypes`–Returns a list of event display style labels

`CalendarEventHasPendingInvite`–Returns whether the player has been invited to the selected event and not yet responded

`CalendarEventHaveSettingsChanged`–Returns whether the selected event has unsaved changes

`CalendarEventInvite`–Attempts to invite a character to the selected event

`CalendarEventIsModerator`–Returns whether the player has moderator status for the selected calendar event

`CalendarEventRemoveInvite`–Removes a character from the selected event's invite/signup list

`CalendarEventSelectInvite`–Selects an entry in the selected event's invite/signup list

`CalendarEventSetAutoApprove`–Enables the auto-approve feature (currently unused) for the selected calendar event

`CalendarEventSetDate`–Changes the scheduled date of the selected calendar event

`CalendarEventSetDescription`–Changes the descriptive text for the selected event

`CalendarEventSetLocked`–Locks the selected calendar event

`CalendarEventSetLockoutDate`–Changes the lockout date associated with the selected event (currently unused)

`CalendarEventSetLockoutTime`–Changes the lockout time associated with the selected event (currently unused)

`CalendarEventSetModerator`–Grants moderator status to a character on the selected event's invite/signup list

`CalendarEventSetRepeatOption`–Changes the repetition option for the selected event (currently unused)

`CalendarEventSetSize`–Changes the maximum number of invites/signups for the selected event (currently unused)

`CalendarEventSetStatus`–Sets the status of a character on the selected event's invite/signup list

`CalendarEventSetTextureID`–Changes the raid or dungeon instance for the selected event

`CalendarEventSetTime`–Changes the scheduled time of the selected event

`CalendarEventSetTitle`–Changes the title for the selected event

`CalendarEventSetType`–Changes the display type of the selected event

`CalendarEventSignUp`–Signs the player up for the selected calendar event

`CalendarEventSortInvites`–Sorts the event invite/signup list

`CalendarGetAbsMonth`–Returns date information for a given month and year

`CalendarGetDate`–Returns the current date (in the server's time zone)

`CalendarGetDayEvent`–Returns information about a calendar event on a given day

`CalendarGetEventIndex`–Returns the month, day, and index of the selected calendar event

`CalendarGetEventInfo`–Returns information about the selected calendar event (for player/guild events)

`CalendarGetFirstPendingInvite`–Returns the index of the first invitation on a given day to which the player has not responded

`CalendarGetHolidayInfo`–Returns additional information about a holiday event

`CalendarGetMaxCreateDate`–Returns the latest date for which events may be scheduled

`CalendarGetMaxDate`–Returns the latest date usable in the calendar system

`CalendarGetMinDate`–Returns the earliest date usable in the calendar system

`CalendarGetMinHistoryDate`–Returns the earliest date for which information about past player events is available

`CalendarGetMonth`–Returns information about a calendar month

`CalendarGetMonthNames`–Returns a list of localized month names

`CalendarGetNumDayEvents`–Returns the number of calendar events on a given day

`CalendarGetNumPendingInvites`–Returns the number of calendar invitations to which the player has yet to respond

`CalendarGetRaidInfo`–Returns information about a raid lockout or scheduled raid reset event

`CalendarGetWeekdayNames`–Returns a list of localized weekday names

`CalendarIsActionPending`–Returns whether an update to calendar information is in progress

`CalendarMassInviteArenaTeam`–Repopulates the current event's invite list with members of one of the player's arena teams

`CalendarMassInviteGuild`–Repopulates the selected event's invite list with members of the player's guild

`CalendarNewEvent`–Creates a new event and selects it for viewing/editing

`CalendarNewGuildAnnouncement`–Creates a new guild announcement and selects it for viewing/editing

`CalendarNewGuildEvent`–Creates a new guild event and selects it for viewing/editing

`CalendarOpenEvent`–Selects a calendar event for viewing/editing

`CalendarRemoveEvent`–Removes the selected event invitation from the player's calendar or removes the player from the selected guild event's signup list

`CalendarSetAbsMonth`–Sets the calendar's month to an absolute date

`CalendarSetMonth`–Sets the calendar's month relative to its current month

`CalendarUpdateEvent`–Saves changes made to the selected event

`CanEditGuildEvent`–Returns whether the player is allowed to edit guild-wide calendar events

`OpenCalendar`–Queries the server for calendar status information

Camera Functions

`CameraOrSelectOrMoveStart`–Begins camera movement or selection (equivalent to left-clicking in the 3-D world)

`CameraOrSelectOrMoveStop`–Ends action initiated by `CameraOrSelectOrMoveStart`

`CameraZoomIn`–Zooms the camera in by a specified distance

`CameraZoomOut`–Zooms the camera out by a specified distance

`FlipCameraYaw`–Rotates the camera around the player

`IsMouselooking`–Returns whether mouselook mode is active

`MouselookStart`–Enables mouselook mode, in which cursor movement rotates the camera

`MouselookStop`–Disables mouselook mode

`MoveViewDownStart`–Begins orbiting the camera downward (to look upward)

`MoveViewDownStop`–Ends camera movement initiated by `MoveViewDownStart`

`MoveViewInStart`–Begins zooming the camera inward (towards/through the player character)

`MoveViewInStop`–Ends camera movement initiated by `MoveViewInStart`

`MoveViewLeftStart`–Begins orbiting the camera around the player character to the left

`MoveViewLeftStop`–Ends camera movement initiated by `MoveViewLeftStart`

`MoveViewOutStart`–Begins zooming the camera outward (away from the player character)

`MoveViewOutStop`–Ends camera movement initiated by `MoveViewOutStart`

`MoveViewRightStart`–Begins orbiting the camera around the player character to the right

`MoveViewRightStop`–Ends camera movement initiated by `MoveViewRight Start`

`MoveViewUpStart`–Begins orbiting the camera upward (to look down)

`MoveViewUpStop`–Ends camera movement initiated by `MoveViewUpStart`

`NextView`–Moves the camera to the next predefined setting

`PrevView`–Moves the camera to the previous predefined setting

`ResetView`–Resets a saved camera setting to default values

`SaveView`–Saves the current camera settings

`SetView`–Moves the camera to a saved camera setting

Channel Functions

`AddChatWindowChannel`–Adds a chat channel to the saved list of those displayed in a chat window

`ChannelBan`–Bans a character from a chat channel

`ChannelInvite`–Invites a character to join a chat channel

`ChannelKick`–Removes a player from the channel

`ChannelModerator`–Grants a character moderator status in a chat channel

`ChannelMute`–Grants a character ability to speak in a moderated chat channel

`ChannelSilenceAll`–Silences a character for chat and voice on a channel

`ChannelSilenceVoice`–Silences the given character for voice chat on the channel

`ChannelToggleAnnouncements`–Enables or disables printing of join/leave announcements for a channel

`ChannelUnSilenceAll`—Unsilences a character for chat and voice on a channel

`ChannelUnSilenceVoice`—Unsilences a character on a chat channel

`ChannelUnban`—Lifts the ban preventing a character from joining a chat channel

`ChannelUnmoderator`—Revokes moderator status from a character on a chat channel

`ChannelUnmute`—Removes a character's ability to speak in a moderated chat channel

`ChannelVoiceOff`—Disables voice chat in a channel

`ChannelVoiceOn`—Enables voice chat in a channel

`CollapseChannelHeader`—Collapses a group header in the chat channel listing

`DeclineInvite`—Declines an invitation to a chat channel

`DisplayChannelOwner`—Requests information from the server about a channel's owner

`DisplayChannelVoiceOff`—Disables voice in a channel specified by its position in the channel list display

`DisplayChannelVoiceOn`—Enables voice in a channel specified by its position in the channel list display

`EnumerateServerChannels`—Returns the available server channel names

`ExpandChannelHeader`—Expands a group header in the chat channel listing

`GetActiveVoiceChannel`—Returns the currently active voice channel

`GetChannelDisplayInfo`—Returns information about an entry in the channel list display

`GetChannelList`—Returns the list of the channels the player has joined

`GetChannelName`—Returns information about a chat channel

`GetChannelRosterInfo`—Returns information about a character in a chat channel in the channel list display

`GetChatWindowChannels`—Returns the saved list of channels to which a chat window is subscribed

`GetNumChannelMembers`—Returns the number of members in a chat channel

`GetNumDisplayChannels`—Returns the number of entries in the channel list display

`GetSelectedDisplayChannel`—Returns the selected channel in the channel list display

`IsDisplayChannelModerator`—Returns whether the player is a moderator of the selected channel in the channel list display

`IsDisplayChannelOwner`—Returns whether the player is the owner of the selected channel in the channel list display

`IsSilenced`—Returns whether a character is silenced on a chat channel

`JoinPermanentChannel`—Joins a channel, saving associated chat window settings

`JoinTemporaryChannel`—Joins a channel, but does not save associated chat window settings

`LeaveChannelByName`—Leaves a chat channel

`ListChannelByName`—Requests the list of participants in a chat channel

`ListChannels`—Requests a list of channels joined by the player

`RemoveChatWindowChannel`—Removes a channel from a chat window's list of saved channel subscriptions

`SetActiveVoiceChannel`—Sets the currently active voice channel

`SetActiveVoiceChannelBySessionID`—Sets the currently active voice chat channel

`SetChannelOwner`—Gives channel ownership to another character

`SetChannelPassword`—Sets a password on a custom chat channel

`SetSelectedDisplayChannel`—Selects a channel in the channel list display

Chat Functions

`AddChatWindowChannel`—Adds a chat channel to the saved list of those displayed in a chat window

`AddChatWindowMessages`—Adds a message type to the saved list of those displayed in a chat window

`CanComplainChat`—Returns whether a chat message can be reported as spam

`ChangeChatColor`—Changes the color associated with a chat message type

`ChatFrame_AddMessageEventFilter`—Adds a function to filter or alter messages to the chat display system

`ChatFrame_GetMessageEventFilters`—Returns the list of filters registered for a chat event

`ChatFrame_RemoveMessageEventFilter`—Removes a previously set chat message filter

`ComplainChat`—Reports a chat message as spam

`DoEmote`—Performs a preset emote (with optional target)

`GetChatTypeIndex`—Returns the numeric index corresponding to a chat message type

`GetChatWindowChannels`—Returns the saved list of channels to which a chat window is subscribed

`GetChatWindowInfo`—Returns the saved settings for a chat window

`GetChatWindowMessages`—Returns the saved list of messages to which a chat window is subscribed

`GetDefaultLanguage`—Returns the name of the player character's default language

`GetLanguageByIndex`—Returns the localized name of a player character language

`GetNumLanguages`—Returns the number of languages the player character can speak

`LoggingChat`—Enables or disables saving chat text to a file

`LoggingCombat`—Enables or disables saving combat log data to a file

`RandomRoll`—Initiates a public, server-side "dice roll"

`RemoveChatWindowChannel`—Removes a channel from a chat window's list of saved channel subscriptions

`RemoveChatWindowMessages`—Removes a message type from a chat window's list of saved message subscriptions

`ResetChatColors`—Removes all saved color settings for chat message types, resetting them to default values

`ResetChatWindows`—Removes all saved chat window settings, resetting them to default values

`SendChatMessage`—Sends a chat message

`SetChatWindowAlpha`—Saves a chat window's background opacity setting

`SetChatWindowColor`—Saves a chat window's background color setting

`SetChatWindowDocked`—Saves whether a chat window should be docked with the main chat window

`SetChatWindowLocked`—Saves whether a chat window is locked

`SetChatWindowName`—Saves a chat window's display name setting

`SetChatWindowShown`—Saves whether a chat window should be shown

`SetChatWindowSize`—Saves a chat window's font size setting

`SetChatWindowUninteractable`—Saves whether a chat window is marked as non-interactive

Class Resource Functions

DestroyTotem—Destroys a specific totem (or ghoul)

GetRuneCooldown—Returns cooldown information about one of the player's rune resources

GetRuneCount—Returns the number of available rune resources in one of the player's rune slots

GetRuneType—Returns the type of one of the player's rune resources

GetTotemInfo—Returns information on a currently active totem (or ghoul)

GetTotemTimeLeft—Returns the time remaining before a totem (or ghoul) automatically disappears

TargetTotem—Targets one of the player's totems (or a Death Knight's ghoul)

Client Control and Information Functions

CancelLogout—Cancels a pending logout or quit

DownloadSettings—Restores game settings from a backup stored on the server

ForceQuit—Immediately exits World of Warcraft

GetAccountExpansionLevel—Returns the most recent of WoW's retail expansion packs for which the player's account is authorized

GetBuildInfo—Returns the version information about the client

GetExistingLocales—Returns a list of installed localization packs for the WoW client

GetGameTime—Returns the current realm (server) time

GetLocale—Returns a code indicating the localization currently in use by the client

GetNetStats—Returns information about current network connection performance

IsLinuxClient—Returns whether the player is using the Linux game client

IsMacClient—Returns whether the player is using the Mac OS X game client

IsWindowsClient—Returns whether the player is using the Windows game client

Logout—Attempts to log out and return to the character selection screen

NotWhileDeadError—Causes the default UI to display an error message indicating that actions are disallowed while the player is dead

Quit–Attempts to exit the World of Warcraft client

ReloadUI–Reloads the user interface

Screenshot–Saves an image of the current game display

SetEuropeanNumbers–Sets the decimal separator for displayed numbers

SetUIVisibility–Enables or disables display of UI elements in the 3-D world

UploadSettings–Stores a backup of game settings on the server

Combat Functions

AttackTarget–Begins auto-attack against the player's current target

StartAttack–Begins auto-attack against a specified target

StopAttack–Stops auto-attack if active

UnitAffectingCombat–Returns whether a unit is currently in combat

CombatLog Functions

CombatLogAddFilter–Adds a filter to the combat log system

CombatLogAdvanceEntry–Advances the "cursor" position used by other CombatLog functions

CombatLogClearEntries–Removes all entries from the combat log

CombatLogGetCurrentEntry–Returns the combat log event information for the current entry and advances to the next entry

CombatLogGetNumEntries–Returns the number of available combat log events

CombatLogGetRetentionTime–Returns the amount of time combat log entries are stored

CombatLogResetFilter–Removes any filters applied to the combat log

CombatLogSetCurrentEntry–Sets the "cursor" position used by other CombatLog functions

CombatLogSetRetentionTime–Sets the amount of time combat log entries will be stored

CombatLog_Object_IsA–Returns whether an entity from the combat log matches a given filter

LoggingCombat–Enables or disables saving combat log data to a file

UnitGUID–Returns a unit's globally unique identifier

Companion Functions

`CallCompanion`–Summons a non-combat pet or mount

`DismissCompanion`–Unsummons the current non-combat pet or mount

`GetCompanionCooldown`–Returns cooldown information for a non-combat pet or mount

`GetCompanionInfo`–Returns information about a non-combat pet or mount

`GetNumCompanions`–Returns the number of mounts or non-combat pets the player can summon

`PickupCompanion`–Puts a non-combat pet or mount onto the cursor

Complaint Functions

`CalendarContextEventCanComplain`–Returns whether the player can report an event invitation as spam

`CalendarContextEventComplain`–Reports an event invitation as spam

`CanComplainChat`–Returns whether a chat message can be reported as spam

`CanComplainInboxItem`–Returns whether a mail message can be reported as spam

`ComplainChat`–Reports a chat message as spam

`ComplainInboxItem`–Reports a mail message as spam

`PlayerIsPVPInactive`–Returns whether a battleground participant is inactive (and eligible for reporting as AFK)

`ReportPlayerIsPVPAFK`–Reports a battleground participant as AFK

Container Functions

`ContainerIDToInventoryID`–Returns the `inventoryID` corresponding to a given `containerID`

`ContainerRefundItemPurchase`–Sells an item purchased with alternate currency back to a vendor

`EquipmentManager_UnpackLocation`–Unpacks an inventory location bitfield into usable components

`GetBagName`–Returns the name of one of the player's bags

`GetContainerFreeSlots`–Returns a list of open slots in a container

GetContainerItemCooldown–Returns cooldown information about an item in the player's bags

GetContainerItemDurability–Returns durability status for an item in the player's bags

GetContainerItemGems–Returns the gems socketed in an item in the player's bags

GetContainerItemID–Returns the item ID of an item in the player's bags

GetContainerItemInfo–Returns information about an item in the player's bags

GetContainerItemLink–Returns a hyperlink for an item in the player's bags

GetContainerItemPurchaseInfo–Returns information about alternate currencies refunded for returning an item to vendors

GetContainerItemPurchaseItem–Returns information about a specific currency refunded for returning an item to vendors

GetContainerNumFreeSlots–Returns the number of free slots in a container and the types of items it can hold

GetContainerNumSlots–Returns the number of slots in one of the player's bags

GetItemFamily–Returns information about special bag types that can hold a given item

PickupBagFromSlot–Puts an equipped container onto the cursor

PickupContainerItem–Picks up an item from or puts an item into a slot in one of the player's bags or other containers

PutItemInBackpack–Puts the item on the cursor into the player's backpack

PutItemInBag–Puts the item on the cursor into the one of the player's bags or other containers

SetBagPortraitTexture–Sets a Texture object to display the icon of one of the player's bags

SocketContainerItem–Opens an item from the player's bags for socketing

SplitContainerItem–Picks up only part of a stack of items from one of the player's bags or other containers

UseContainerItem–Activate (as with right-clicking) an item in one of the player's bags

Currency Functions

ExpandCurrencyList–Expands or collapses a list header in the Currency UI

GetArenaCurrency–Returns the player's amount of arena points

GetBackpackCurrencyInfo–Returns information about a currency marked for watching on the Backpack UI

GetContainerItemPurchaseInfo–Returns information about alternate currencies refunded for returning an item to vendors

GetContainerItemPurchaseItem–Returns information about a specific currency refunded for returning an item to vendors

GetCurrencyListInfo–Returns information about a currency type (or headers in the Currency UI)

GetCurrencyListSize–Returns the number of list entries to show in the Currency UI

GetHonorCurrency–Returns the player's amount of honor points

GetMaxArenaCurrency–Returns the maximum amount of arena points the player can accrue

SetCurrencyBackpack–Sets a currency type to be watched on the Backpack UI

SetCurrencyUnused–Moves a currency type to or from the Unused currencies list

Cursor Functions

AddTradeMoney–Adds the money currently on the cursor to the trade window

AutoEquipCursorItem–Equips the item on the cursor

ClearCursor–Clears any contents attached to the cursor

ClickAuctionSellItemButton–Picks up an item from or puts an item into the "Create Auction" slot

ClickSendMailItemButton–Picks up an item from or puts an item into an attachment slot for sending mail

ClickSocketButton–Picks up or places a gem in the Item Socketing UI

ClickTargetTradeButton–Interacts with an item in a slot offered for trade by the target

ClickTradeButton–Picks up an item from or puts an item in a slot offered for trade by the player

CursorCanGoInSlot–Returns whether the item on the cursor can be equipped in an inventory slot

CursorHasItem–Returns whether an item is on the cursor

`CursorHasMacro`–Returns whether a macro is on the cursor

`CursorHasMoney`–Returns whether an amount of the player's money is on the cursor

`CursorHasSpell`–Returns whether a spell is on the cursor

`DeleteCursorItem`–Destroys the item on the cursor

`DropCursorMoney`–Drops any money currently on the cursor, returning it to where it was taken from

`DropItemOnUnit`–"Gives" the item on the cursor to another unit; results vary by context

`EquipCursorItem`–Puts the item on the cursor into a specific equipment slot

`GetCursorInfo`–Returns information about the contents of the cursor

`GetCursorMoney`–Returns the amount of money currently on the cursor

`GetCursorPosition`–Returns the absolute position of the mouse cursor

`GetMouseFocus`–Returns the frame that is currently under the mouse, and has mouse input enabled

`HideRepairCursor`–Returns the cursor to normal mode after use of `ShowRepairCursor()`

`InRepairMode`–Returns whether the item repair cursor mode is currently active

`PickupAction`–Puts the contents of an action bar slot onto the cursor or the cursor contents into an action bar slot

`PickupBagFromSlot`–Puts an equipped container onto the cursor

`PickupCompanion`–Puts a non-combat pet or mount onto the cursor

`PickupContainerItem`–Picks up an item from or puts an item into a slot in one of the player's bags or other containers

`PickupGuildBankItem`–Picks up an item from or puts an item into the guild bank

`PickupGuildBankMoney`–Puts money from the guild bank onto the cursor

`PickupInventoryItem`–Picks up an item from or puts an item into an equipment slot

`PickupItem`–Puts an arbitrary item onto the cursor

`PickupMacro`–Puts a macro onto the cursor

`PickupMerchantItem`–Puts an item available for purchase from a vendor onto the cursor

`PickupPetAction`–Puts the contents of a pet action slot onto the cursor or the cursor contents into a pet action slot

PickupPlayerMoney–Puts an amount of the player's money onto the cursor

PickupSpell–Puts a spell from the player's or pet's spellbook onto the cursor

PickupStablePet–Puts a pet from the stables onto the cursor

PickupTradeMoney–Puts money offered by the player for trade onto the cursor

PlaceAction–Puts the contents of the cursor into an action bar slot

PutItemInBackpack–Puts the item on the cursor into the player's backpack

PutItemInBag–Puts the item on the cursor into one of the player's bags or other containers

ResetCursor–Returns the cursor to its normal appearance (the glove pointer) and behavior

SetCursor–Changes the mouse cursor image

ShowBuybackSellCursor–Changes the cursor to prepare for repurchasing an item recently sold to a vendor

ShowContainerSellCursor–Changes the cursor to prepare for selling an item in the player's bags to a vendor

ShowInventorySellCursor–Changes the cursor to prepare for selling an equipped item to a vendor

ShowMerchantSellCursor–Changes the cursor to prepare for buying an item from a vendor

ShowRepairCursor–Puts the cursor in item repair mode

SplitContainerItem–Picks up only part of a stack of items from one of the player's bags or other containers

SplitGuildBankItem–Picks up only part of a stack of items from the guild bank

Debugging and Profiling Functions

FrameXML_Debug–Enables or disables logging of XML loading

GetAddOnCPUUsage–Returns the amount of CPU time used by an addon

GetAddOnMemoryUsage–Returns the amount of memory used by an addon

GetEventCPUUsage–Returns information about the CPU usage of an event

GetFrameCPUUsage–Returns information about CPU usage by a frame's script handlers

GetFramerate–Returns the number of frames per second rendered by the client

GetFunctionCPUUsage–Returns information about CPU usage by a function

GetNetStats–Returns information about current network connection performance

GetScriptCPUUsage–Returns the total CPU time used by the scripting system

GetTaxiBenchmarkMode–Returns whether flight path benchmark mode is enabled

ResetCPUUsage–Resets CPU usage statistics

SetTaxiBenchmarkMode–Enables or disables flight path benchmark mode

UpdateAddOnCPUUsage–Updates addon CPU profiling information

UpdateAddOnMemoryUsage–Updates addon memory usage information

debugprofilestart–Starts/resets the high resolution profiling timer

debugprofilestop–Returns the value of the profiling timer

debugstack–Returns information about the current function call stack

geterrorhandler–Returns the current error handler function

issecurevariable–Returns whether a variable is secure (and if not, which addon tainted it)

seterrorhandler–Changes the error handler to a specified function

Duel Functions

AcceptDuel–Accepts a proposed duel

CancelDuel–Cancels a proposed duel, or declines an offered duel

StartDuel–Challenges another player to a duel

Equipment Manager Functions

CanUseEquipmentSets–Returns whether the player has enabled the equipment manager

DeleteEquipmentSet–Deletes an equipment set

EquipmentManagerClearIgnoredSlotsForSave–Clears the list of equipment slots to be ignored when saving sets

EquipmentManagergnoreSlotForSave–Adds an equipment slot to the list of those ignored when saving sets

EquipmentManagerIsSlotIgnoredForSave–Returns whether the contents of an equipment slot will be included when saving sets

`EquipmentManagerUnignoreSlotForSave`–Removes an equipment slot from the list of those ignored when saving sets

`EquipmentManager_UnpackLocation`–Unpacks an inventory location bitfield into usable components

`EquipmentSetContainsLockedItems`–Returns whether an equipment set contains locked items

`GetEquipmentSetInfo`–Returns information about an equipment set (specified by index)

`GetEquipmentSetInfoByName`–Returns information about an equipment set

`GetEquipmentSetItemIDs`–Returns a table listing the items in an equipment set

`GetEquipmentSetLocations`–Returns a table listing the locations of the items in an equipment set

`GetNumEquipmentSets`–Returns the number of saved equipment sets

`PickupEquipmentSet`–Puts an equipment set (specified by index) on the cursor

`PickupEquipmentSetByName`–Puts an equipment set on the cursor

`RenameEquipmentSet`–Changes the name of a saved equipment set

`SaveEquipmentSet`–Saves or creates an equipment set with the player's currently equipped items

`UseEquipmentSet`–Equips the items in an equipment set

Faction Functions

`CollapseAllFactionHeaders`–Collapses all headers and sub-headers in the Reputation UI

`CollapseFactionHeader`–Collapses a given faction header or sub-header in the Reputation UI

`ExpandAllFactionHeaders`–Expands all headers and sub-headers in the Reputation UI

`ExpandFactionHeader`–Expands a given faction header or sub-header in the Reputation UI

`FactionToggleAtWar`–Toggles "at war" status for a faction

`GetFactionInfo`–Returns information about a faction or header listing

`GetNumFactions`–Returns the number of entries in the Reputation UI

`GetSelectedFaction`–Returns which faction entry is selected in the Reputation UI

`GetWatchedFactionInfo`–Returns information about the "watched" faction (displayed on the XP bar in the default UI)

`IsFactionInactive`–Returns whether a faction is flagged as "inactive"

`SetFactionActive`–Removes the "inactive" status from a faction

`SetFactionInactive`–Flags a faction as inactive

`SetSelectedFaction`–Selects a faction in the Reputation UI

`SetWatchedFactionIndex`–Makes a faction the "watched" faction (displayed on the XP bar in the default UI)

GM Survey Functions

`GMSurveyAnswer`–Returns text of multiple-choice question answers in a GM survey

`GMSurveyAnswerSubmit`–Submits an answer to a GM survey question

`GMSurveyCommentSubmit`–Submits a comment to the current GM survey

`GMSurveyQuestion`–Returns the text of a specific question from a GM survey

`GMSurveySubmit`–Submits the current GM survey

GM Ticket Functions

`DeleteGMTicket`–Abandons the currently pending GM ticket

`GMResponseNeedMoreHelp`–Requests further GM interaction on a ticket to which a GM has already responded

`GMResponseResolve`–Notifies the server that the player's GM ticket issue has been resolved

`GetGMTicket`–Requests GM ticket status from the server

`NewGMTicket`–Opens a new GM support ticket

`Stuck`–Uses the auto-unstuck feature

`UpdateGMTicket`–Updates the open GM ticket with new text

Glyph Functions

`GetGlyphLink`–Gets a hyperlink for the contents of a glyph socket

`GetGlyphSocketInfo`–Returns information about a glyph socket and its contents

GlyphMatchesSocket—Returns whether a socket is eligible for the glyph currently awaiting a target

PlaceGlyphInSocket—Applies the glyph currently awaiting a target to a socket

RemoveGlyphFromSocket—Removes the glyph from a socket

SpellCanTargetGlyph—Returns whether the spell currently awaiting a target requires a glyph slot to be chosen

Guild Bank Functions

AutoStoreGuildBankItem—Withdraws the item(s) from a slot in the guild bank, automatically adding to the player's bags

BuyGuildBankTab—Purchases the next available guild bank tab

CanEditGuildTabInfo—Returns whether the player is allowed to edit a guild bank tab's information

CanGuildBankRepair—Returns whether the player is allowed to pay for repairs using guild bank funds

CanWithdrawGuildBankMoney—Returns whether the player is allowed to withdraw money from the guild bank

CloseGuildBankFrame—Ends interaction with the guild bank vault

DepositGuildBankMoney—Deposits money into the guild bank

GetCurrentGuildBankTab—Returns the currently selected guild bank tab

GetGuildBankItemInfo—Returns information about the contents of a guild bank item slot

GetGuildBankItemLink—Returns a hyperlink for an item in the guild bank

GetGuildBankMoney—Returns the amount of money in the guild bank

GetGuildBankMoneyTransaction—Returns information about a transaction in the guild bank money log

GetGuildBankTabCost—Returns the cost of the next available guild bank tab

GetGuildBankTabInfo—Returns information about a guild bank tab

GetGuildBankTabPermissions—Returns information about guild bank tab privileges for the guild rank currently being edited

GetGuildBankText—Returns text associated with a guild bank tab

GetGuildBankTransaction—Returns information about a transaction in the log for a guild bank tab

GetGuildBankWithdrawLimit—Returns the guild bank money withdrawal limit for the guild rank currently being edited

`GetGuildBankWithdrawMoney`–Returns the amount of money the player is allowed to withdraw from the guild bank per day

`GetNumGuildBankMoneyTransactions`–Returns the number of transactions in the guild bank money log

`GetNumGuildBankTabs`–Returns the number of purchased tabs in the guild bank

`GetNumGuildBankTransactions`–Returns the number of entries in a guild bank tab's transaction log

`PickupGuildBankItem`–Picks up an item from or puts an item into the guild bank

`PickupGuildBankMoney`–Puts money from the guild bank onto the cursor

`QueryGuildBankLog`–Requests the item transaction log for a guild bank tab from the server

`QueryGuildBankTab`–Requests information about the contents of a guild bank tab from the server

`QueryGuildBankText`–Requests guild bank tab info text from the server

`SetCurrentGuildBankTab`–Selects a tab in the guild bank

`SetGuildBankTabInfo`–Sets the name and icon for a guild bank tab

`SetGuildBankTabPermissions`–Changes guild bank tab permissions for the guild rank being edited

`SetGuildBankTabWithdraw`–Sets the number of item withdrawals allowed per day for the guild rank being edited

`SetGuildBankText`–Sets the info text for a guild bank tab

`SetGuildBankWithdrawLimit`–Sets the maximum amount of money withdrawals per day allowed for the guild rank being edited

`SplitGuildBankItem`–Picks up only part of a stack of items from the guild bank

`WithdrawGuildBankMoney`–Attempts to withdraw money from the guild bank

Guild Functions

`AcceptGuild`–Accepts an invitation to join a guild

`BuyGuildCharter`–Purchases a guild charter

`CanEditGuildEvent`–Returns whether the player is allowed to edit guild-wide calendar events

`CanEditGuildInfo`–Returns whether the player is allowed to edit the guild information text

`CanEditMOTD`–Returns whether the player is allowed to edit the guild Message of the Day

`CanEditOfficerNote`–Returns whether the player is allowed to edit guild officer notes

`CanEditPublicNote`–Returns whether the player is allowed to edit guild public notes

`CanGuildDemote`–Returns whether the player is allowed to demote lower ranked guild members

`CanGuildInvite`–Returns whether the player is allowed to invite new members to his or her guild

`CanGuildPromote`–Returns whether the player is allowed to promote other guild members

`CanGuildRemove`–Returns whether the player is allowed to remove members from his or her guild

`CanViewOfficerNote`–Returns whether the player is allowed to view guild officer notes

`CloseGuildRegistrar`–Ends interaction with a guild registrar

`CloseTabardCreation`–Ends interaction with the guild tabard creator

`DeclineGuild`–Declines an offered guild invitation

`GetGuildCharterCost`–Returns the cost to purchase a guild charter

`GetGuildEventInfo`–Returns information about an entry in the guild event log

`GetGuildInfo`–Returns a unit's guild affiliation

`GetGuildInfoText`–Returns guild information text

`GetGuildRosterInfo`–Returns information about the selected player in your guild roster

`GetGuildRosterLastOnline`–Returns the amount of time since a guild member was last online

`GetGuildRosterMOTD`–Returns the Message of the Day for the player's guild

`GetGuildRosterSelection`–Returns the index of the selected member in the guild roster

`GetGuildRosterShowOffline`–Returns whether the guild roster lists offline members

`GetGuildTabardFileNames`–Returns the textures that comprise the player's guild tabard

`GetNumGuildEvents`–Returns the number of entries in the guild event log

`GetNumGuildMembers`–Returns the number of members in the guild roster

`GetTabardCreationCost`–Returns the cost to create a guild tabard

`GuildControlAddRank`–Adds a new rank to the player's guild

`GuildControlDelRank`–Deletes a guild rank

`GuildControlGetNumRanks`–Returns the number of ranks in the guild

`GuildControlGetRankFlags`–Returns the list of privileges for the guild rank being edited

`GuildControlGetRankName`–Returns the name of a guild rank

`GuildControlSaveRank`–Saves changes to the guild rank being edited

`GuildControlSetRank`–Chooses a guild rank to edit

`GuildControlSetRankFlag`–Enables or disables a privilege for the guild rank being edited

`GuildDemote`–Reduces a guild member's rank by one

`GuildDisband`–Disbands the player's guild

`GuildInfo`–Requests guild information from the server

`GuildInvite`–Invites a character to join the player's guild

`GuildLeave`–Leaves the player's current guild

`GuildPromote`–Increases a guild member's rank by one

`GuildRoster`–Requests guild roster information from the server

`GuildRosterSetOfficerNote`–Sets the officer note for a guild member

`GuildRosterSetPublicNote`–Sets the public note for a guild member

`GuildSetLeader`–Promotes a member to guild leader

`GuildSetMOTD`–Sets the guild Message of the Day

`GuildUninvite`–Removes a character from the player's guild

`IsGuildLeader`–Returns whether player is leader of his or her guild

`IsInGuild`–Returns whether the player is in a guild

`QueryGuildEventLog`–Requests guild event log information from the server

`SetGuildInfoText`–Sets the guild information text

`SetGuildRosterSelection`–Selects a member in the guild roster

`SetGuildRosterShowOffline`–Enables or disables inclusion of offline members in the guild roster listing

`SortGuildRoster`–Sorts the guild roster

`TurnInGuildCharter`–Turns in a completed guild charter

`UnitIsInMyGuild`–Returns whether a unit is in the player's guild

Hyperlink Functions

`GetAchievementLink`–Returns a hyperlink representing the player's progress on an achievement

`GetAuctionItemLink`–Returns a hyperlink for an item in an auction listing

`GetBuybackItemLink`–Returns a hyperlink for an item recently sold to a vendor and available to be repurchased

`GetContainerItemLink`–Returns a hyperlink for an item in the player's bags

`GetCursorInfo`–Returns information about the contents of the cursor

`GetExistingSocketLink`–Returns a hyperlink for a permanently socketed gem

`GetGlyphLink`–Gets a hyperlink for the contents of a glyph socket

`GetGuildBankItemLink`–Returns a hyperlink for an item in the guild bank

`GetGuildBankTransaction`–Returns information about a transaction in the log for a guild bank tab

`GetInboxItemLink`–Returns a hyperlink for an item attached to a message in the player's inbox

`GetInventoryItemLink`–Returns an item link for an equipped item

`GetItemGem`–Returns information about gems socketed in an item

`GetLootRollItemLink`–Returns a hyperlink for an item currently up for loot rolling

`GetLootSlotLink`–Returns a hyperlink for an item available as loot

`GetMacroItem`–Returns information about the item used by a macro

`GetMerchantItemLink`–Returns a hyperlink for an item available for purchase from a vendor

`GetNewSocketLink`–Returns a hyperlink for a gem added to a socket

`GetQuestItemLink`–Returns a hyperlink for an item in a questgiver dialog

`GetQuestLink`–Returns a hyperlink for an entry in the player's quest log

`GetQuestLogItemLink`–Returns a hyperlink for an item related to the selected quest in the quest log

`GetSendMailItemLink`–Returns a hyperlink for an item attached to the outgoing message

GetSpellLink—Returns a hyperlink for a spell

GetTalentLink—Returns a hyperlink for a talent

GetTradePlayerItemLink—Returns a hyperlink for an item offered for trade by the player

GetTradeSkillItemLink—Returns a hyperlink for the item created by a tradeskill recipe

GetTradeSkillListLink—Returns a hyperlink to the player's list of recipes for the current trade skill

GetTradeSkillReagentItemLink—Returns a hyperlink for a reagent in a tradeskill recipe

GetTradeSkillRecipeLink—Returns hyperlink for a tradeskill recipe

GetTradeTargetItemLink—Returns a hyperlink for an item offered for trade by the target

GetTrainerServiceItemLink—Returns a hyperlink for the item associated with a trainer service

In-game Movie Playback Functions

GameMovieFinished—Ends in-game movie playback

GetMovieResolution—Returns the horizontal resolution available for displaying movie content

InCinematic—Returns whether an in-game cinematic is playing

OpeningCinematic—Displays the introductory cinematic for the player's race

StopCinematic—Exits a currently playing in-game cinematic

Inspect Functions

CanInspect—Returns whether a unit can be inspected

ClearInspectPlayer—Ends inspection of another character

GetInspectArenaTeamData—Returns arena team information about the currently inspected unit

GetInspectHonorData—Returns PvP honor information about the currently inspected unit

HasInspectHonorData—Returns whether PvP honor and arena data for the currently inspected unit has been downloaded from the server

NotifyInspect—Marks a unit for inspection and requests talent data from the server

`RequestInspectHonorData`–Requests PvP honor and arena data from the server for the currently inspected unit

Instance Functions

`CanShowResetInstances`–Returns whether the player can reset instances

`GetInstanceBootTimeRemaining`–Returns the amount of time left until the player is removed from the current instance

`GetInstanceDifficulty`–Returns difficulty setting for the current dungeon/raid instance

`GetInstanceInfo`–Returns instance information about the current area

`GetInstanceLockTimeRemaining`–Returns time remaining before the player is saved to a recently entered instance

`GetNumSavedInstances`–Returns the number of instances to which the player is saved

`GetNumWorldStateUI`–Returns the number of world state UI elements

`GetSavedInstanceInfo`–Returns information on a specific instance to which the player is saved

`GetWorldStateUIInfo`–Returns information about a world state UI element

`IsInInstance`–Returns whether the player is in an instance (and its type if applicable)

`RequestRaidInfo`–Requests information about saved instances from the server

`ResetInstances`–Resets all non-saved instances associated with the player

`RespondInstanceLock`–Allows leaving a recently entered instance to which the player would otherwise be saved

`SetDungeonDifficulty`–Sets the player's 5 player dungeon difficulty preference

`SetRaidDifficulty`–Sets the player's raid dungeon difficulty preference

Inventory Functions

`AutoEquipCursorItem`–Equips the item on the cursor

`BankButtonIDToInvSlotID`–Returns the `inventoryID` corresponding to a bank item or bag slot

`CancelPendingEquip`–Cancels equipping a bind-on-equip item

`ContainerIDToInventoryID`–Returns the `inventoryID` corresponding to a given `containerID`

`CursorCanGoInSlot`–Returns whether the item on the cursor can be equipped in an inventory slot

`EquipCursorItem`–Puts the item on the cursor into a specific equipment slot

`EquipItemByName`–Attempts to equip an arbitrary item

`EquipPendingItem`–Confirms equipping a bind-on-equip item

`EquipmentManager_UnpackLocation`–Unpacks an inventory location bitfield into usable components

`GetInventoryAlertStatus`–Returns the durability warning status of an equipped item

`GetInventoryItemBroken`–Returns whether an equipped item is broken

`GetInventoryItemCooldown`–Returns cooldown information about an equipped item

`GetInventoryItemCount`–Returns the number of items stacked in an inventory slot

`GetInventoryItemDurability`–Returns the current durability level of an equipped item

`GetInventoryItemGems`–Returns the gems socketed in an equipped item

`GetInventoryItemID`–Returns the item ID of an equipped item

`GetInventoryItemLink`–Returns an item link for an equipped item

`GetInventoryItemQuality`–Returns the quality level of an equipped item

`GetInventoryItemTexture`–Returns the icon texture for an equipped item

`GetInventoryItemsForSlot`–Returns a list of items that can be equipped in a given inventory slot

`GetInventorySlotInfo`–Returns information about an inventory slot

`IsEquippedItem`–Returns whether an item is currently equipped

`IsEquippedItemType`–Returns whether any items of a given type are currently equipped

`IsInventoryItemLocked`–Returns whether an inventory slot is locked

`KeyRingButtonIDToInvSlotID`–Returns the `inventoryID` corresponding to a slot in the keyring

`PickupInventoryItem`–Picks up an item from or puts an item into an equipment slot

`SetInventoryPortraitTexture`–Sets a Texture object to display the icon of an equipped item

`SocketInventoryItem`–Opens an equipped item for socketing

`UseInventoryItem`–Activates (as with right-clicking) an equipped item

Item Text Functions

CloseItemText—Ends interaction with a text object or item

ItemTextGetCreator—Returns the original author of the currently viewed text item

ItemTextGetItem—Returns the name of the currently viewed text item

ItemTextGetMaterial—Returns display style information for the currently viewed text item

ItemTextGetPage—Returns the current page number in the currently viewed text item

ItemTextGetText—Returns the text of the currently viewed text item

ItemTextHasNextPage—Returns whether the currently viewed text item has additional pages

ItemTextNextPage—Moves to the next page in the currently viewed text item

ItemTextPrevPage—Moves to the previous page in the currently viewed text item

Item Functions

BindEnchant—Confirms enchanting an item (when the item will become soulbound as a result)

CancelPendingEquip—Cancels equipping a bind-on-equip item

ConfirmBindOnUse—Confirms using an item, if using the item causes it to become soulbound

CursorHasItem—Returns whether an item is on the cursor

DeleteCursorItem—Destroys the item on the cursor

EndBoundTradeable—Confirms taking an action which renders a looted Bind on Pickup item non-tradeable

EndRefund—Confirms taking an action which renders a purchased item non-refundable

EquipItemByName—Attempts to equip an arbitrary item

EquipPendingItem—Confirms equipping a bind-on-equip item

GetItemCooldown—Returns cooldown information about an arbitrary item

GetItemCount—Returns information about how many of a given item the player has or on remaining item charges

`GetItemFamily`–Returns information about special bag types that can hold a given item

`GetItemGem`–Returns information about gems socketed in an item

`GetItemIcon`–Returns the path to an icon texture for the item

`GetItemInfo`–Returns information about an item, by name, link or ID

`GetItemQualityColor`–Returns color values for use in displaying items of a given quality

`GetItemSpell`–Returns information about the spell cast by an item's "Use:" effect

`GetItemStatDelta`–Returns a summary of the difference in stat bonuses between two items

`GetItemStats`–Returns a summary of an item's stat bonuses

`GetItemUniqueness`–Returns information about uniqueness restrictions for equipping an item

`IsConsumableItem`–Returns whether an item is consumable

`IsCurrentItem`–Returns whether an item is being used

`IsDressableItem`–Returns whether an item's appearance can be previewed using the Dressing Room feature

`IsEquippableItem`–Returns whether an item can be equipped

`IsEquippedItem`–Returns whether an item is currently equipped

`IsEquippedItemType`–Returns whether any items of a given type are currently equipped

`IsHarmfulItem`–Returns whether an item can be used against hostile units

`IsHelpfulItem`–Returns whether an item can be used on the player or friendly units

`IsItemInRange`–Returns whether the player is in range to use an item on a unit

`IsUsableItem`–Returns whether an item can currently be used

`ItemHasRange`–Returns whether an item has a range limitation for its use

`PickupItem`–Puts an arbitrary item onto the cursor

`ReplaceEnchant`–Confirms replacing an existing enchantment

`SpellCanTargetItem`–Returns whether the spell currently awaiting a target requires an item to be chosen

`SpellTargetItem`–Casts the spell currently awaiting a target on an item

`UseItemByName`–Uses an arbitrary item (optionally on a specified unit)

Keybind Functions

ClearOverrideBindings–Clears any registered override bindings for a given owner

GetBinding–Returns information about a key binding

GetBindingAction–Returns the action bound to a key or key combination

GetBindingByKey–Returns the binding bound to a key or key combination

GetBindingKey–Returns the key combinations for a given binding command

GetCurrentBindingSet–Returns which set of key bindings is currently in use

GetNumBindings–Returns the number of entries in the key bindings list

LoadBindings–Loads a set of key bindings

RunBinding–Runs the script associated with a key binding action

SaveBindings–Saves the current set of key bindings

SetBinding–Binds a key combination to a binding command

SetBindingClick–Binds a key combination to "click" a Button object

SetBindingItem–Binds a key combination to use an item in the player's possession

SetBindingMacro–Binds a key combination to run a macro

SetBindingSpell–Binds a key combination to cast a spell

SetMouselookOverrideBinding–Overrides the default mouselook bindings to perform another binding with the mouse buttons

SetOverrideBinding–Sets an override binding for a binding command

SetOverrideBindingClick–Sets an override binding to "click" a Button object

SetOverrideBindingItem–Sets an override binding to use an item in the player's possession

SetOverrideBindingMacro–Sets an override binding to run a macro

SetOverrideBindingSpell–Sets an override binding to a specific spell

Keyboard Functions

GetCurrentKeyBoardFocus–Returns the frame currently handling keyboard input

IsAltKeyDown–Returns whether an Alt key on the keyboard is held down

`IsControlKeyDown`–Returns whether a Control key on the keyboard is held down

`IsLeftAltKeyDown`–Returns whether the left Alt key is currently held down

`IsLeftControlKeyDown`–Returns whether the left Control key is held down

`IsLeftShiftKeyDown`–Returns whether the left Shift key on the keyboard is held down

`IsModifierKeyDown`–Returns whether a modifier key is held down

`IsRightAltKeyDown`–Returns whether the right Alt key is currently held down

`IsRightControlKeyDown`–Returns whether the right Control key on the keyboard is held down

`IsRightShiftKeyDown`–Returns whether the right shift key on the keyboard is held down

`IsShiftKeyDown`–Returns whether a Shift key on the keyboard is held down

Knowledge-base Functions

`KBArticle_BeginLoading`–Requests a specific knowledge base article from the server

`KBArticle_GetData`–Returns information about the last requested knowledge base article

`KBArticle_IsLoaded`–Returns whether the requested knowledge base article has been loaded

`KBQuery_BeginLoading`–Queries the knowledge base server for articles

`KBQuery_GetArticleHeaderCount`–Returns the number of articles on the current knowledge base search result page

`KBQuery_GetArticleHeaderData`–Returns information about an article returned in a knowledge base query

`KBQuery_GetTotalArticleCount`–Returns the total number of articles returned for the given query

`KBQuery_IsLoaded`–Returns whether results of a knowledge base query have been loaded

`KBSetup_BeginLoading`–Loads a maximum number of "Top Issues" from a given page

`KBSetup_GetArticleHeaderCount`–Returns the number of "Top Issues" articles on the current page

`KBSetup_GetArticleHeaderData`–Returns header information about a "Top Issue" article

`KBSetup_GetCategoryCount`–Returns the number of available knowledge base categories

`KBSetup_GetCategoryData`–Returns information about a knowledge base category

`KBSetup_GetLanguageCount`–Returns the number of available knowledge base languages

`KBSetup_GetLanguageData`–Returns information about a given knowledge base language

`KBSetup_GetSubCategoryCount`–Returns the number of available subcategories for a given category

`KBSetup_GetSubCategoryData`–Returns information about a knowledge base subcategory

`KBSetup_GetTotalArticleCount`–Returns the number of "Top Issues" articles

`KBSetup_IsLoaded`–Returns whether the knowledge base default query has completed successfully

`KBSystem_GetMOTD`–Returns the currently knowledge base MOTD

`KBSystem_GetServerNotice`–Returns the text of the knowledge base server system notice

`KBSystem_GetServerStatus`–Returns the knowledge base server system status message

Limited Play Time Functions

`GetBillingTimeRested`–Returns the amount of time for which the player must be offline in order to lift play time restrictions

`NoPlayTime`–Returns whether the player has exceeded the allowed play time limit

`PartialPlayTime`–Returns whether the player is near the allowed play time limit

Locale-specific Functions

`DeclineName`–Returns suggested declensions for a name

`FillLocalizedClassList`–Fills a table with localized class names keyed by non-localized class tokens

`GetNumDeclensionSets`–Returns the number of suggested declension sets for a name

Looking For Group Functions

`AcceptLFGMatch`—Accepts a proposed LFG match

`CanSendLFGQuery`—Returns whether the player can perform a given LFM query

`CancelPendingLFG`—Cancels active LFG searches, removing the player from the LFG queue and declining any automatic group invitations

`ClearLFGAutojoin`—Disables the option to automatically join a group matching current LFG criteria

`ClearLFMAutofill`—Disables the option to automatically fill the player's group when Looking for More

`ClearLookingForGroup`—Cancels active LFG searches, removing the player from the LFG queue

`ClearLookingForMore`—Cancels active LFM searches, removing the player from the LFG queue

`DeclineLFGMatch`—Declines a proposed LFG match

`GetLFGPartyResults`—Returns information about a member of a party in Looking for More results

`GetLFGResults`—Returns information about a character in the Looking for More results listing

`GetLFGRoles`—Returns the group roles for which the player has signed up in the LFG system

`GetLFGStatusText`—Returns information about the player's status in the LFG auto-join or LFM auto-fill queues

`GetLFGTypeEntries`—Returns a list of LFG entries (dungeons, zones, quests, etc.) for a given type

`GetLFGTypes`—Returns a list of LFG query types

`GetLookingForGroup`—Returns information about the player's status in the LFG system

`GetNumLFGResults`—Returns the number of results from an LFM query

`IsInLFGQueue`—Returns whether the player is currently queued for automatically joining/filling a group

`LFGQuery`—Requests Looking for More information from the server

`SetLFGAutojoin`—Enables the option to automatically join a group matching current LFG criteria

`SetLFGComment`—Associates a brief text comment with the player's listing in the LFG system

`SetLFGRoles`–Sets group roles for which to advertise the player in the LFG system

`SetLFMAutofill`–Enables the option to automatically fill the player's group when Looking for More

`SetLFMType`–Sets the type for LFM queries

`SetLookingForGroup`–Adds the player to the LFG system for one of three objectives

`SetLookingForMore`–Sets up a Looking for More query

`SortLFG`–Sets the sort order for Looking for More results

Loot Functions

`CloseLoot`–Ends interaction with a lootable corpse or object

`ConfirmLootRoll`–Confirms the player's intent regarding an item up for loot rolling

`ConfirmLootSlot`–Confirms picking up an item available as loot

`GetLootMethod`–Returns information about the current loot method in a party or raid

`GetLootRollItemInfo`–Returns information about an item currently up for loot rolling

`GetLootRollItemLink`–Returns a hyperlink for an item currently up for loot rolling

`GetLootRollTimeLeft`–Returns the amount of time remaining before loot rolling for an item expires

`GetLootSlotInfo`–Returns information about an item available

`GetLootSlotLink`–Returns a hyperlink for an item available as loot

`GetLootThreshold`–Returns the threshold used for Master Looter, Group Loot, and Need Before Greed loot methods

`GetMasterLootCandidate`–Returns information about a given loot candidate

`GetNumLootItems`–Returns the number of items available to be looted

`GetOptOutOfLoot`–Returns whether the player has opted out of loot rolls

`GiveMasterLoot`–Awards a loot item to a group member

`IsFishingLoot`–Returns whether the currently displayed loot came from fishing

`LootSlot`–Attempts to pick up an item available as loot

`LootSlotIsCoin`–Returns whether a loot slot contains money

`LootSlotIsItem`–Returns whether a loot slot contains an item

`RollOnLoot`–Register the player's intent regarding an item up for loot rolling

`SetLootMethod`–Sets the loot method for a party or raid group

`SetLootPortrait`–Sets a Texture object to show the appropriate portrait image when looting

`SetLootThreshold`–Sets the threshold used for Master Looter, Group Loot, and Need Before Greed loot methods

`SetOptOutOfLoot`–Changes the player's preference to opt out of loot rolls

Lua Library Functions

`abs`–Returns the absolute value of a number

`assert`–Causes a Lua error if a condition is failed

`ceil`–Returns the smallest integer larger than or equal to a number

`collectgarbage`–Interface to the Lua garbage collector

`date`–Returns a formatted date/time string for a date (or the current date)

`deg`–Converts an angle measurement in radians to degrees

`difftime`–Returns the number of seconds between two time values

`error`–Causes a Lua error message

`exp`–Returns the value of the exponential function for a number

`floor`–Returns the largest integer smaller than or equal to a number

`format`–Returns a formatted string containing specified values

`frexp`–Returns the normalized fraction and base-2 exponent for a number

`getfenv`–Returns the environment for a function (or the global environment)

`getmetatable`–Returns an object's metatable

`gmatch`–Returns an iterator function for finding pattern matches in a string

`gsub`–Returns a string in which occurrences of a pattern are replaced

`ipairs`–Returns an iterator function for integer keys in a table

`ldexp`–Returns the number generated by a normalized fraction and base-2 exponent

`loadstring`–Loads and compiles Lua source code

`log`–Returns the natural logarithm of a number

`log10`–Returns the base-10 logarithm of a number

max—Returns the greatest of a list of numbers

min—Returns the least of a list of numbers

mod—Returns the remainder from division of two numbers

next—Returns the next key/value pair in a table

pairs—Returns an iterator function for a table

pcall—Executes a function in protected mode

rad—Converts an angle specified in degrees to radians

random—Generates a pseudo-random number

rawequal—Returns whether two values are equal without invoking any metamethods

rawget—Returns the real value associated with a key in a table without invoking any metamethods

rawset—Sets the value associated with a key in a table without invoking any metamethods

select—Returns one or more values from a list (...), or the number of values in a list

setfenv—Sets the environment to be used by a function

setmetatable—Sets the metatable for a table

sort—Sorts a table

sqrt—Returns the square root of a number

strbyte—Returns the numeric code for one or more characters in a string

strchar—Returns the character(s) for one or more numeric codes

strfind—Returns information about matches for a pattern in a string

strlen—Returns the number of characters in a string

strlower—Returns a copy of a string with all uppercase letters converted to lowercase

strmatch—Returns the matches for a pattern in a string

strrep—Returns a string produced by a number of repetitions of another string

strrev—Returns the reverse of a string

strsub—Returns a substring of a string

strupper—Returns a copy of a string with all lowercase letters converted to uppercase

time—Returns the numeric time value for a described date/time (or the current time)

`tinsert`—Inserts a value into a table

`tonumber`—Returns the numeric value of a string

`tostring`—Returns a string representation of a value

`tremove`—Removes an element from a table

`type`—Returns a string describing the data type of a value

`unpack`—Returns the list of elements in a table

`xpcall`—Executes a function in protected mode with a custom error handler

Mac Client Functions

`IsMacClient`—Returns whether the player is using the Mac OS X game client

`MovieRecording_Cancel`—Cancels video recording and compression

`MovieRecording_DataRate`—Returns the data rate required for a given set of video recording parameters

`MovieRecording_DeleteMovie`—Deletes an uncompressed movie

`MovieRecording_GetAspectRatio`—Returns the aspect ratio of the game display

`MovieRecording_GetMovieFullPath`—Returns a path to the movie currently being recorded or compressed

`MovieRecording_GetProgress`—Returns information about movie compression progress

`MovieRecording_GetTime`—Returns the amount of time since video recording was last started

`MovieRecording_GetViewportWidth`—Returns the current width of the game display

`MovieRecording_IsCodecSupported`—Returns whether a video codec is supported on the current system

`MovieRecording_IsCompressing`—Returns whether a movie file is currently being compressed

`MovieRecording_IsCursorRecordingSupported`—Returns whether the current system supports recording the mouse cursor in movies

`MovieRecording_IsRecording`—Returns whether movie recording is currently in progress

`MovieRecording_IsSupported`—Returns whether movie recording is supported on the current system

`MovieRecording_MaxLength`—Returns the maximum length of recorded video for a given set of video recording parameters

`MovieRecording_QueueMovieToCompress`–Queues an uncompressed movie for compression

`MovieRecording_SearchUncompressedMovie`–Enables or disables a search for uncompressed movies

`MovieRecording_Toggle`–Begins or ends video recording

`MovieRecording_ToggleGUI`–Enables or disables inclusion of UI elements in a video recording

`MusicPlayer_BackTrack`–Causes iTunes to return to the previous track played

`MusicPlayer_NextTrack`–Causes iTunes to play the next track in sequence

`MusicPlayer_PlayPause`–Causes iTunes to start or pause playback

`MusicPlayer_VolumeDown`–Causes iTunes to lower its playback volume

`MusicPlayer_VolumeUp`–Causes iTunes to raise its playback volume

Macro Functions

`CreateMacro`–Creates a new macro

`CursorHasMacro`–Returns whether a macro is on the cursor

`DeleteMacro`–Deletes a macro

`EditMacro`–Changes the name, icon, and/or body of a macro

`GetMacroBody`–Returns the body text of a macro

`GetMacroIconInfo`–Returns the texture for a macro icon option

`GetMacroIndexByName`–Returns the index of a macro specified by name

`GetMacroInfo`–Returns information about a macro

`GetMacroItem`–Returns information about the item used by a macro

`GetMacroItemIconInfo`–Returns the texture for an item icon

`GetMacroSpell`–Returns information about the spell cast by a macro

`GetNumMacroIcons`–Returns the number of available macro icons

`GetNumMacroItemIcons`–Returns the number of available item icons

`GetNumMacros`–Returns the number of macros the player has stored

`GetRunningMacro`–Returns the index of the currently running macro

`GetRunningMacroButton`–Returns the mouse button that was used to activate the running macro

`PickupMacro`–Puts a macro onto the cursor

`RunMacro`–Runs a macro

`RunMacroText`–Runs arbitrary text as a macro

SecureCmdOptionParse–Returns the action (and target, if applicable) for a secure macro command

SetMacroItem–Changes the item used for dynamic feedback for a macro

SetMacroSpell–Changes the spell used for dynamic feedback for a macro

StopMacro–Stops execution of a running macro

Mail Functions

AutoLootMailItem–Automatically takes any attached items and money from a mail message

CanComplainInboxItem–Returns whether a mail message can be reported as spam

CheckInbox–Requests information on the player's mailbox contents from the server

ClearSendMail–Clears any text, items, or money from the mail message to be sent

ClickSendMailItemButton–Picks up an item from or puts an item into an attachment slot for sending mail

CloseMail–Ends interaction with a mailbox

ComplainInboxItem–Reports a mail message as spam

DeleteInboxItem–Deletes a message from the player's inbox

GetInboxHeaderInfo–Returns information about a message in the player's inbox

GetInboxInvoiceInfo–Returns auction house invoice information for a mail message

GetInboxItem–Returns information for an item attached to a message in the player's inbox

GetInboxItemLink–Returns a hyperlink for an item attached to a message in the player's inbox

GetInboxNumItems–Returns the number of messages in the player's inbox

GetInboxText–Returns information about the text of an inbox message

GetLatestThreeSenders–Returns the names of the last three senders of new mail

GetSendMailCOD–Returns the Cash-On-Delivery cost of the outgoing message

GetSendMailItem–Returns information for an item attached to the outgoing message

`GetSendMailItemLink`–Returns a hyperlink for an item attached to the outgoing message

`GetSendMailMoney`–Returns the amount of money to be sent with the outgoing message

`GetSendMailPrice`–Returns the cost to send the outgoing mail message

`HasNewMail`–Returns whether the player has received new mail since last visiting a mailbox

`InboxItemCanDelete`–Returns whether a message in the player's inbox can be deleted

`ReturnInboxItem`–Returns a message in the player's inbox to its sender

`SendMail`–Sends the outgoing message

`SetSendMailCOD`–Sets the Cash-On-Delivery cost of the outgoing message

`SetSendMailMoney`–Sets the amount of money to be sent with the outgoing message

`SetSendMailShowing`–Enables or disables shortcuts for attaching items to outgoing mail

`TakeInboxItem`–Retrieves an item attachment from a message in the player's inbox (accepting COD charges if applicable)

`TakeInboxMoney`–Retrieves any money attached to a message in the player's inbox

`TakeInboxTextItem`–Requests a copy of a message's body text as an item

Map Functions

`ClickLandmark`–Processes a hyperlink associated with a map landmark

`GetBattlefieldVehicleInfo`–Returns information about special vehicles in the current zone

`GetCorpseMapPosition`–Returns the position of the player's corpse on the world map

`GetCurrentMapAreaID`–Returns an ID number for the current map zone

`GetCurrentMapContinent`–Returns the current world map continent

`GetCurrentMapDungeonLevel`–Returns which map image is currently selected on the world map (for zones which use more than one map image)

`GetCurrentMapZone`–Returns the current world map zone

`GetDeathReleasePosition`–Returns the location of the graveyard where the player's spirit will appear upon release

GetMapContinents—Returns a list of map continents' names

GetMapInfo—Returns information about the current world map texture

GetMapLandmarkInfo—Returns information about a map landmark

GetMapOverlayInfo—Returns information about a world map overlay

GetMapZones—Returns the map zones for a given continent

GetNumBattlefieldVehicles—Returns the number of special vehicles in the current zone

GetNumDungeonMapLevels—Returns the number of map images for the world map's current zone

GetNumMapLandmarks—Returns the number of landmarks on the world map

GetNumMapOverlays—Returns the number of overlays for the current world map zone

GetPlayerFacing—Returns the player's orientation (heading)

GetPlayerMapPosition—Returns the position of the player's corpse on the world map

GetWintergraspWaitTime—Returns the amount of time remaining until the next PvP event in the Wintergrasp zone

ProcessMapClick—Possibly changes the WorldMap based on a mouse click

SetDungeonMapLevel—Sets the world map to display a certain map image (for zones that use multiple map images)

SetMapToCurrentZone—Sets the world map to show the zone in which the player is located

SetMapZoom—Sets the world map to show a specific zone or continent

UpdateMapHighlight—Returns information about the texture used for highlighting zones in a continent map on mouseover

ZoomOut—Sets the world map to show the area containing its current area

Merchant Functions

BuyMerchantItem—Purchases an item available from a vendor

BuybackItem—Repurchases an item recently sold to a vendor

CanMerchantRepair—Returns whether the vendor with whom the player is currently interacting can repair equipment

CloseMerchant—Ends interaction with a vendor

ContainerRefundItemPurchase—Sells an item purchased with alternate currency back to a vendor

`EndBoundTradeable`–Confirms taking an action which renders a looted Bind on Pickup item non-tradeable

`EndRefund`–Confirms taking an action which renders a purchased item non-refundable

`GetBuybackItemInfo`–Returns information about an item recently sold to a vendor and available to be repurchased

`GetBuybackItemLink`–Returns a hyperlink for an item recently sold to a vendor and available to be repurchased

`GetContainerItemPurchaseInfo`–Returns information about alternate currencies refunded for returning an item to vendors

`GetContainerItemPurchaseItem`–Returns information about a specific currency refunded for returning an item to vendors

`GetMerchantItemCostInfo`–Returns information about alternate currencies required to purchase an item from a vendor

`GetMerchantItemCostItem`–Returns information about currency items required to purchase an item from a vendor

`GetMerchantItemInfo`–Returns information about an item available for purchase from a vendor

`GetMerchantItemLink`–Returns a hyperlink for an item available for purchase from a vendor

`GetMerchantItemMaxStack`–Returns the maximum number of an item allowed in a single purchase

`GetMerchantNumItems`–Returns the number of different items available for purchase from a vendor

`GetNumBuybackItems`–Returns the number of items recently sold to a vendor and available to be repurchased

`GetRepairAllCost`–Returns the cost to repair all of the player's damaged items

`InRepairMode`–Returns whether the item repair cursor mode is currently active

`PickupMerchantItem`–Puts an item available for purchase from a vendor onto the cursor

`RepairAllItems`–Attempts to repair all of the player's damaged items

`ShowContainerSellCursor`–Changes the cursor to prepare for selling an item in the player's bags to a vendor

`ShowRepairCursor`–Puts the cursor in item repair mode

Modified Click Functions

GetModifiedClick–Returns the keys/buttons bound for a modified click action

GetModifiedClickAction–Returns the token identifying a modified click action

GetNumModifiedClickActions–Returns the number of modified click actions registered

IsModifiedClick–Determines if the modifiers specified in the click-type had been held down while the button click occurred

SetModifiedClick–Sets a modified click for a given action

Money Functions

AddTradeMoney–Adds the money currently on the cursor to the trade window

CanWithdrawGuildBankMoney–Returns whether the player is allowed to withdraw money from the guild bank

CursorHasMoney–Returns whether an amount of the player's money is on the cursor

DepositGuildBankMoney–Deposits money into the guild bank

DropCursorMoney–Drops any money currently on the cursor, returning it to where it was taken from

GetCoinIcon–Returns an icon representing an amount of money

GetCoinText–Returns a localized string describing an amount of money

GetCoinTextureString–Returns a string with embedded coin icons describing an amount of money

GetCursorMoney–Returns the amount of money currently on the cursor

GetMoney–Returns the total amount of money currently in the player's possession

GetPlayerTradeMoney–Returns the amount of money offered for trade by the player

GetQuestLogRequiredMoney–Returns the amount of money required for the selected quest in the quest log

GetQuestLogRewardMoney–Returns the money reward for the selected quest in the quest log

GetSendMailMoney–Returns the amount of money to be sent with the out-going message

GetTargetTradeMoney–Returns the amount of money offered for trade by the target

PickupGuildBankMoney–Puts money from the guild bank onto the cursor

PickupPlayerMoney–Puts an amount of the player's money onto the cursor

PickupTradeMoney–Puts money offered by the player for trade onto the cursor

SetSendMailMoney–Sets the amount of money to be sent with the outgoing message

SetTradeMoney–Offers an amount of money for trade

WithdrawGuildBankMoney–Attempts to withdraw money from the guild bank

Movement Functions

AscendStop–Stops movement initiated by JumpOrAscendStart

DescendStop–Stops movement initiated by SitStandOrDescendStart

FollowUnit–Causes the player character to automatically follow another unit

InteractUnit–Interacts with (as with right-clicking on) a unit

JumpOrAscendStart–Causes the player character to jump (or begins ascent if swimming or flying)

MoveAndSteerStart–Begins moving the player character forward while steering via mouse movement

MoveAndSteerStop–Ends movement initiated by MoveAndSteerStart

MoveBackwardStart–Begins moving the player character backward

MoveBackwardStop–Ends movement initiated by MoveBackwardStart

MoveForwardStart–Begins moving the player character forward

MoveForwardStop–Ends movement initiated by MoveForwardStart

PitchDownStart–Begins adjusting the player character's angle of vertical movement downward

PitchDownStop–Ends movement initiated by PitchDownStart

PitchUpStart–Begins adjusting the player character's angle of vertical movement upward

`PitchUpStop`–Ends movement initiated by `PitchUpStart`

`SitStandOrDescendStart`–Causes the player character to sit down if standing and vice versa (or begins descent if swimming or flying)

`StrafeLeftStart`–Begins moving the player character sideways to his or her left

`StrafeLeftStop`–Ends movement initiated by `StrafeLeftStart`

`StrafeRightStart`–Begins moving the player character sideways to his or her right

`StrafeRightStop`–Ends movement initiated by `StrafeRightStart`

`ToggleAutoRun`–Starts or stops the player character automatically moving forward

`ToggleRun`–Switches the character's ground movement mode between running and walking

`TurnLeftStart`–Begins turning the player character to the left

`TurnLeftStop`–Ends movement initiated by `TurnLeftStart`

`TurnOrActionStart`–Begins character steering or interaction (equivalent to right-clicking in the 3-D world)

`TurnOrActionStop`–Ends action initiated by `TurnOrActionStart`

`TurnRightStart`–Begins turning the player character to the right

`TurnRightStop`–Ends movement initiated by `TurnRightStart`

Multi-cast Action

`SetMultiCastSpell`–Sets a multi-cast action slot to a given spell

NPC "Gossip" Dialog Functions

`CloseGossip`–Ends an NPC "gossip" interaction

`GetGossipActiveQuests`–Returns a list of quests which can be turned in to the current Gossip NPC

`GetGossipAvailableQuests`–Returns a list of quests available from the current Gossip NPC

`GetGossipOptions`–Returns a list of interaction options for the Gossip NPC

`GetGossipText`–Returns greeting or other text to be displayed in an NPC dialog

`GetNumGossipActiveQuests`–Returns the number of quests which can be turned in to the current Gossip NPC

`GetNumGossipAvailableQuests`–Returns the number of quests available from the current Gossip NPC

`GetNumGossipOptions`–Returns the number of non-quest dialog options for the current Gossip NPC

`SelectGossipActiveQuest`–Chooses a quest which can be turned in to the current Gossip NPC

`SelectGossipAvailableQuest`–Chooses a quest available from the current Gossip NPC

`SelectGossipOption`–Chooses and activates an NPC dialog option

Objectives Tracking Functions

`AddQuestWatch`–Adds a quest to the objectives tracker

`AddTrackedAchievement`–Adds an achievement to the objectives tracker UI

`GetNumQuestWatches`–Returns the number of quests included in the objectives tracker

`GetNumTrackedAchievements`–Returns the number of achievements flagged for display in the objectives tracker UI

`GetQuestIndexForWatch`–Returns the quest log index of a quest in the objectives tracker

`GetQuestLogSpecialItemCooldown`–Returns cooldown information about an item associated with a current quest

`GetQuestLogSpecialItemInfo`–Returns information about a usable item associated with a current quest

`GetTrackedAchievements`–Returns numeric IDs of the achievements flagged for display in the objectives tracker UI

`IsQuestLogSpecialItemInRange`–Returns whether the player's target is in range for using an item associated with a current quest

`IsQuestWatched`–Returns whether a quest from the quest log is listed in the objectives tracker

`IsTrackedAchievement`–Returns whether an achievement is flagged for display in the objectives tracker UI

`RemoveQuestWatch`–Removes a quest from the objectives tracker

`RemoveTrackedAchievement`–Removes an achievement from the objectives tracker UI

`UseQuestLogSpecialItem`–Uses the item associated with a current quest

Party Functions

`AcceptGroup`–Accepts an invitation to join a party or raid

`CheckReadyCheckTime`–Finishes a ready check initiated by the player

`ClearPartyAssignment`–Removes a group role assignment from a member of the player's party or raid

`ConfirmReadyCheck`–Responds to a ready check

`ConvertToRaid`–Converts a party to a raid

`DeclineGroup`–Declines an invitation to join a party or raid

`DoReadyCheck`–Initiates a ready check

`GetNumPartyMembers`–Returns the number of additional members in the player's party

`GetPartyAssignment`–Returns whether a party/raid member is assigned a specific group role

`GetPartyLeaderIndex`–Returns the index of the current party leader

`GetPartyMember`–Returns whether a party member exists at a given index

`GetReadyCheckStatus`–Returns a unit's status during a ready check

`GetReadyCheckTimeLeft`–Returns the amount of time left on the current ready check

`GetRealNumPartyMembers`–Returns the number of members in the player's non-battleground party

`InviteUnit`–Invites a character to the player's party or raid

`IsPartyLeader`–Returns whether the player is the party leader

`IsRealPartyLeader`–Returns whether the player is the leader of a non-battleground party

`LeaveParty`–Exits the current party or raid

`PromoteToLeader`–Promotes a player to party/raid leader

`SetPartyAssignment`–Assigns a group role to a member of the player's party or raid

`UninviteUnit`–Removes a character from the player's party or raid

`UnitInParty`–Returns whether a unit is a player unit in the player's party

`UnitIsPartyLeader`–Returns whether a unit is the leader of the player's party

`UnitPlayerOrPetInParty`–Returns whether a unit is in the player's party or belongs to a party member

Pet Stable Functions

BuyStableSlot–Purchases the next available stable slot, without confirmation

ClickStablePet–Inspects or moves a pet in the Pet Stable UI

ClosePetStables–Ends use of the Pet Stable UI/API

GetNextStableSlotCost–Returns the cost of the next available stable slot

GetNumStablePets–Returns the number of stabled pets

GetNumStableSlots–Returns the number of stable slots the player has purchased

GetSelectedStablePet–Returns the index of the selected stable pet

GetStablePetFoodTypes–Returns the types of food that a stabled pet will eat

GetStablePetInfo–Returns information about a stabled pet

IsAtStableMaster–Returns whether the player is interacting with a Stable Master NPC

PickupStablePet–Puts a pet from the stables onto the cursor

SetPetStablePaperdoll–Sets the given Model to show the selected stabled pet

StablePet–Puts the player's current pet into the stables

UnstablePet–Makes a pet from the stables the active pet

Pet Functions

CastPetAction–Casts a pet action on a specific target

DestroyTotem–Destroys a specific totem (or ghoul)

DisableSpellAutocast–Disables automatic casting of a pet spell

EnableSpellAutocast–Enables automatic casting of a pet spell

GetPetActionCooldown–Returns cooldown information about a given pet action slot

GetPetActionInfo–Returns information about a pet action

GetPetActionSlotUsable–Returns whether a pet action can be used

GetPetActionsUsable–Returns whether the pet's actions are usable

GetPetExperience–Returns information about experience points for the player's pet

`GetPetFoodTypes`—Returns a list of the food types the player's pet will eat

`GetPetHappiness`—Returns information about the player's pet's happiness

`GetPetIcon`—Returns an icon representing the current pet

`GetPetTalentTree`—Returns the name of the talent tree used by the player's current pet

`GetPetTimeRemaining`—Returns the time remaining before a temporary pet is automatically dismissed

`GetTotemInfo`—Returns information on a currently active totem (or ghoul)

`GetTotemTimeLeft`—Returns the time remaining before a totem (or ghoul) automatically disappears

`HasPetSpells`—Returns whether the player's current pet has a spellbook

`HasPetUI`—Returns whether the pet UI should be displayed for the player's pet

`IsPetAttackActive`—Returns whether the pet's attack action is currently active

`PetAbandon`—Releases the player's pet

`PetAggressiveMode`—Enables aggressive mode for the player's pet

`PetAttack`—Instructs the pet to attack

`PetCanBeAbandoned`—Returns whether the player's pet can be abandoned

`PetCanBeDismissed`—Returns whether a Dismiss Pet command should be available for the player's pet

`PetCanBeRenamed`—Returns whether the player's pet can be renamed

`PetDefensiveMode`—Enables defensive mode for the player's pet

`PetDismiss`—Dismisses the currently controlled pet

`PetFollow`—Instructs the pet to follow the player

`PetHasActionBar`—Returns whether the player's current pet has an action bar

`PetPassiveMode`—Enables passive mode for the player's pet

`PetRename`—Renames the currently controlled pet

`PetStopAttack`—Instructs the pet to stop attacking

`PetWait`—Instructs the pet to stay at its current location

`PickupPetAction`—Puts the contents of a pet action slot onto the cursor or the cursor contents into a pet action slot

`TargetTotem`—Targets one of the player's totems (or a Death Knight's ghoul)

`TogglePetAutocast`—Turns autocast on or off for a pet action

Petition Functions

`BuyGuildCharter`–Purchases a guild charter

`BuyPetition`–Purchases an arena team charter

`CanSignPetition`–Returns whether the player can sign the currently offered petition

`ClosePetition`–Ends interaction with a petition

`ClosePetitionVendor`–Ends interaction with an arena registrar

`GetGuildCharterCost`–Returns the cost to purchase a guild charter

`GetNumPetitionNames`–Returns the number of people who have signed the open petition

`GetPetitionInfo`–Returns information about the currently open petition

`GetPetitionItemInfo`–Returns information about a purchasable arena team charter

`GetPetitionNameInfo`–Returns the name of a character who has signed the currently offered petition

`HasFilledPetition`–Returns whether the player has a completed petition

`OfferPetition`–Requests an arena or guild charter signature from the targeted unit

`RenamePetition`–Renames the guild or arena team to be created by the open petition

`SignPetition`–Signs the currently offered petition

`TurnInArenaPetition`–Turns in a petition creating an arena team

`TurnInGuildCharter`–Turns in a completed guild charter

Player Information Functions

`AcceptResurrect`–Accepts an offered resurrection spell

`AcceptXPLoss`–Resurrects the player as a spirit healer, accepting possible consequences

`CanHearthAndResurrectFromArea`–Returns whether the player is in a world PvP zone offering an exit option

`CheckBinderDist`–Returns whether the player is in range of an NPC that can set the Hearthstone location

`CheckSpiritHealerDist`–Returns whether the player is in range of a spirit healer

`ConfirmBinder`–Sets the player's Hearthstone to the current location

`DeclineResurrect`–Declines an offered resurrection spell

`Dismount`–Dismounts from the player's summoned mount

`GetBindLocation`–Returns the name of the player's Hearthstone location

`GetComboPoints`–Returns the player's number of combo points on the current target

`GetCorpseRecoveryDelay`–Returns the amount of time left until the player can recover their corpse

`GetCurrentTitle`–Returns the currently selected player title

`GetNumTitles`–Returns the number of available player titles

`GetPlayerFacing`–Returns the player's orientation (heading)

`GetQuestLogRewardTitle`–Returns the title reward for the selected quest in the quest log

`GetRealmName`–Returns the name of the player's realm (server name)

`GetReleaseTimeRemaining`–Returns the amount of time remaining until the player's spirit is automatically released when dead

`GetResSicknessDuration`–Returns the duration of resurrection sickness at the player's current level

`GetRestState`–Returns the player's current rest state

`GetRuneCooldown`–Returns cooldown information about one of the player's rune resources

`GetRuneCount`–Returns the number of available rune resources in one of the player's rune slots

`GetRuneType`–Returns the type of one of the player's rune resources

`GetTitleName`–Returns the text of an available player title

`GetUnitPitch`–Returns the player's current pitch (slope or angle of movement)

`GetUnitSpeed`–Returns a unit's current speed

`GetXPExhaustion`–Returns the amount of rested bonus experience available

`HasFullControl`–Returns whether the player character can be controlled

`HasKey`–Returns whether the player has any keys stored in the Keyring container

`HasSoulstone`–Returns whether the player can instantly resurrect in place

`HasWandEquipped`–Returns whether the player has a wand equipped

`IsFalling`–Returns whether the player is currently falling

`IsFlyableArea`–Returns whether flight is allowed on the continent where the player is currently located

`IsFlying`–Returns whether the player is currently flying

`IsInInstance`–Returns whether the player is in an instance (and its type if applicable)

`IsIndoors`–Returns whether the player is currently indoors

`IsMounted`–Returns whether the player is mounted

`IsOutOfBounds`–Returns whether the player is currently outside the bounds of the world

`IsOutdoors`–Returns whether the player is currently outdoors

`IsResting`–Returns whether the player is currently resting

`IsStealthed`–Returns whether the player is currently stealthed

`IsSwimming`–Returns whether the player is currently swimming

`IsTitleKnown`–Returns whether the player has earned the ability to display a title

`IsXPUserDisabled`–Returns whether experience gain has been disabled for the player

`OffhandHasWeapon`–Returns whether the player has an equipped weapon in the off hand slot

`OpeningCinematic`–Displays the introductory cinematic for the player's race

`RepopMe`–Releases the player's spirit to the nearest graveyard

`ResurrectGetOfferer`–Returns the name of a unit offering to resurrect the player

`ResurrectHasSickness`–Returns whether accepting an offered resurrection spell will cause the player to suffer resurrection sickness

`ResurrectHasTimer`–Returns whether the player must wait before resurrecting

`RetrieveCorpse`–Confirms resurrection by returning to the player's corpse

`SetCurrentTitle`–Changes a player's displayed title

`ShowCloak`–Enables or disables display of the player's cloak

`ShowHelm`–Enables or disables display of the player's headgear

`ShowingCloak`–Returns whether the player's cloak is displayed

`ShowingHelm`–Returns whether the player's headgear is displayed

`ToggleSheath`–Sheaths or unsheaths the player character's hand-held items

UnitCharacterPoints–Returns the player's number of unused talent points and profession slots

UnitXP–Returns the player's current amount of experience points

UnitXPMax–Returns the total amount of experience points required for the player to gain a level

UseSoulstone–Instantly resurrects the player in place, if possible

PvP Functions

CanHearthAndResurrectFromArea–Returns whether the player is in a world PvP zone offering an exit option

CanQueueForWintergrasp–Returns whether the player can queue for Wintergrasp

GetHonorCurrency–Returns the player's amount of honor points

GetNumWorldStateUI–Returns the number of world state UI elements

GetPVPDesired–Returns whether the player has manually enabled PvP status

GetPVPLifetimeStats–Returns the player's lifetime total of honorable kills and highest rank achieved

GetPVPRankInfo–Returns information about a given PvP rank index

GetPVPSessionStats–Returns the number of kills and honor points scored by the player since logging in

GetPVPTimer–Returns the amount of time until the player's PVP flag expires

GetPVPYesterdayStats–Returns the number of kills and honor points scored by the player on the previous day

GetWintergraspWaitTime–Returns the amount of time remaining until the next PvP event in the Wintergrasp zone

GetWorldPVPQueueStatus–Returns information on the players queue for a world PvP zone

GetWorldStateUIInfo–Returns information about a world state UI element

GetZonePVPInfo–Returns PVP information about the current area

HearthAndResurrectFromArea–Instantly exits the current world PvP zone, returning to the player's Hearthstone location

IsPVPTimerRunning–Returns whether the player's PvP flag will expire after a period of time

IsSubZonePVPPOI–Returns whether the current area has PvP (or other) objectives to be displayed

QuestFlagsPVP–Returns whether accepting the offered quest will flag the player for PvP

SetPVP–Enables or disables the player's desired PvP status

TogglePVP–Switches the player's desired PvP status

UnitIsPVPFreeForAll–Returns whether a unit is flagged for free-for-all PvP

UnitIsPVPSanctuary–Returns whether a unit is in a Sanctuary area preventing PvP activity

UnitPVPName–Returns the name of a unit including the unit's current title

Quest Functions

AbandonQuest–Confirms abandoning a quest

AcceptQuest–Accepts the quest offered by a questgiver

AddQuestWatch–Adds a quest to the objectives tracker

CloseQuest–Ends interaction with a questgiver

CollapseQuestHeader–Collapses a header in the quest log

CompleteQuest–Begins turning in a quest to a questgiver

ConfirmAcceptQuest–Accepts a quest started by another group member

DeclineQuest–Declines a quest

ExpandQuestHeader–Expands a quest header in the quest log

GetAbandonQuestItems–Returns information about items that would be destroyed by abandoning a quest

GetAbandonQuestName–Returns the name of the quest being abandoned

GetActiveLevel–Returns the level of a quest which can be turned in to the current Quest NPC

GetActiveTitle–Returns the name of a quest which can be turned in to the current Quest NPC

GetAvailableLevel–Returns the level of a quest available from the current Quest NPC

GetAvailableTitle–Returns the name of a quest available from the current Quest NPC

GetDailyQuestsCompleted–Returns the number of daily quests the player has completed today

GetGossipActiveQuests–Returns a list of quests which can be turned in to the current Gossip NPC

`GetGossipAvailableQuests`–Returns a list of quests available from the current Gossip NPC

`GetGreetingText`–Returns the greeting text displayed for quest NPCs with multiple quests

`GetMaxDailyQuests`–Returns the maximum number of daily quests that can be completed each day

`GetNumActiveQuests`–Returns the number of quests which can be turned in to the current Quest NPC

`GetNumAvailableQuests`–Returns the number quests available from the current Quest NPC

`GetNumGossipActiveQuests`–Returns the number of quests which can be turned in to the current Gossip NPC

`GetNumGossipAvailableQuests`–Returns the number of quests available from the current Gossip NPC

`GetNumQuestChoices`–Returns the number of available quest rewards from which the player must choose one upon completing the quest presented by a questgiver

`GetNumQuestItems`–Returns the number of different items required to complete the quest presented by a questgiver

`GetNumQuestLeaderBoards`–Returns the number of quest objectives for a quest in the player's quest log

`GetNumQuestLogChoices`–Returns the number of available item reward choices for the selected quest in the quest log

`GetNumQuestLogEntries`–Returns the number of quests and headers in the quest log

`GetNumQuestLogRewards`–Returns the number of item rewards for the selected quest in the quest log

`GetNumQuestRewards`–Returns the number of different items always awarded upon completing the quest presented by a questgiver

`GetNumQuestWatches`–Returns the number of quests included in the objectives tracker

`GetNumWorldStateUI`–Returns the number of world state UI elements

`GetObjectiveText`–Returns a summary of objectives for the quest offered by a questgiver

`GetProgressText`–Returns the quest progress text presented by a questgiver

`GetQuestBackgroundMaterial`–Returns background display style information for a questgiver dialog

`GetQuestDifficultyColor`–Returns a table of color values indicating the difficulty of a quest's level as compared to the player's

`GetQuestGreenRange`–Returns the level range in which a quest below the player's level still rewards XP

`GetQuestIndexForTimer`–Returns the quest log index of a timed quest's timer

`GetQuestIndexForWatch`–Returns the quest log index of a quest in the objectives tracker

`GetQuestItemInfo`–Returns information about items in a questgiver dialog

`GetQuestItemLink`–Returns a hyperlink for an item in a questgiver dialog

`GetQuestLink`–Returns a hyperlink for an entry in the player's quest log

`GetQuestLogChoiceInfo`–Returns information about available item rewards for the selected quest in the quest log

`GetQuestLogGroupNum`–Returns the suggested group size for the selected quest in the quest log

`GetQuestLogItemLink`–Returns a hyperlink for an item related to the selected quest in the quest log

`GetQuestLogLeaderBoard`–Returns information about objectives for a quest in the quest log

`GetQuestLogPushable`–Return whether the selected quest in the quest log can be shared with party members

`GetQuestLogQuestText`–Returns the description and objective text for the selected quest in the quest log

`GetQuestLogRequiredMoney`–Returns the amount of money required for the selected quest in the quest log

`GetQuestLogRewardHonor`–Returns the honor reward for the selected quest in the quest log

`GetQuestLogRewardInfo`–Returns information about item rewards for the selected quest in the quest log

`GetQuestLogRewardMoney`–Returns the money reward for the selected quest in the quest log

`GetQuestLogRewardSpell`–Returns information about the spell reward for the selected quest in the quest log

`GetQuestLogRewardTalents`–Returns the talent point reward for the selected quest in the quest log

`GetQuestLogRewardTitle`–Returns the title reward for the selected quest in the quest log

GetQuestLogSelection—Returns the index of the selected quest in the quest log

GetQuestLogSpecialItemCooldown—Returns cooldown information about an item associated with a current quest

GetQuestLogSpecialItemInfo—Returns information about a usable item associated with a current quest

GetQuestLogSpellLink—Returns a hyperlink for a spell in the selected quest in the quest log

GetQuestLogTimeLeft—Returns time remaining for the selected quest in the quest log

GetQuestLogTitle—Returns information about an entry in the player's quest log

GetQuestMoneyToGet—Returns the amount of money required to complete the quest presented by a questgiver

GetQuestResetTime—Returns the amount of time remaining until the daily quest period resets

GetQuestReward—Finishes turning in a quest to a questgiver, selecting an item reward if applicable

GetQuestSpellLink—Returns a hyperlink for a spell in a questgiver dialog

GetQuestText—Returns the text for the quest offered by a questgiver

GetQuestTimers—Returns a list of the times remaining for any active timed quests

GetRewardHonor—Returns the amount of honor points awarded when completing a quest

GetRewardMoney—Returns the amount of money awarded when completing a quest

GetRewardSpell—Returns information about a spell awarded when completing a quest

GetRewardTalents—Returns the talent points awarded when completing a quest

GetRewardText—Returns questgiver dialog to be displayed when completing a quest

GetRewardTitle—Returns the title awarded when completing a quest

GetSuggestedGroupNum—Returns the suggested group size for attempting the quest currently offered by a questgiver

`GetTitleText`–Returns the title text for the quest presented by a questgiver

`GetWorldStateUIInfo`–Returns information about a world state UI element

`IsActiveQuestTrivial`–Returns whether a quest which can be turned in to the current Quest NPC is trivial at the player's level

`IsAvailableQuestTrivial`–Returns whether a quest available from the current Quest NPC is trivial at the player's level

`IsCurrentQuestFailed`–Returns whether the player has failed the selected quest in the quest log

`IsQuestCompletable`–Returns whether the player can complete the quest presented by a questgiver

`IsQuestLogSpecialItemInRange`–Returns whether the player's target is in range for using an item associated with a current quest

`IsQuestWatched`–Returns whether a quest from the quest log is listed in the objectives tracker

`IsUnitOnQuest`–Returns whether a unit is on one of the quests in the player's quest log

`QuestChooseRewardError`–Causes the default UI to display an error message indicating that the player must choose a reward to complete the quest presented by a questgiver

`QuestFlagsPVP`–Returns whether accepting the offered quest will flag the player for PvP

`QuestLogPushQuest`–Shares a quest with other group members

`RemoveQuestWatch`–Removes a quest from the objectives tracker

`SelectActiveQuest`–Selects a quest which can be turned in to the current Quest NPC

`SelectAvailableQuest`–Chooses a quest available from the current Quest NPC

`SelectGossipActiveQuest`–Chooses a quest which can be turned in to the current Gossip NPC

`SelectGossipAvailableQuest`–Chooses a quest available from the current Gossip NPC

`SelectQuestLogEntry`–Selects a quest from the quest log

`SetAbandonQuest`–Begins the process of abandoning a quest in the player's quest log

`UseQuestLogSpecialItem`–Uses the item associated with a current quest

Raid Functions

`AcceptGroup`–Accepts an invitation to join a party or raid

`CheckReadyCheckTime`–Finishes a ready check initiated by the player

`ClearPartyAssignment`–Removes a group role assignment from a member of the player's party or raid

`ConfirmReadyCheck`–Responds to a ready check

`ConvertToRaid`–Converts a party to a raid

`DeclineGroup`–Declines an invitation to join a party or raid

`DemoteAssistant`–Demotes the given player from raid assistant status

`DoReadyCheck`–Initiates a ready check

`GetNumRaidMembers`–Returns the number of members in the player's raid

`GetPartyAssignment`–Returns whether a party/raid member is assigned a specific group role

`GetRaidRosterInfo`–Returns information about a member of the player's raid

`GetRaidRosterSelection`–Returns the index of the selected unit in the raid roster

`GetRaidTargetIndex`–Returns the index of the raid target marker on a unit

`GetReadyCheckStatus`–Returns a unit's status during a ready check

`GetReadyCheckTimeLeft`–Returns the amount of time left on the current ready check

`GetRealNumRaidMembers`–Returns the number of members in the player's non-battleground raid

`InviteUnit`–Invites a character to the player's party or raid

`IsRaidLeader`–Returns whether the player is the raid leader

`IsRaidOfficer`–Returns whether the player is a raid assistant

`IsRealRaidLeader`–Returns whether the player is the leader of a non-battleground raid

`LeaveParty`–Exits the current party or raid

`PromoteToAssistant`–Promotes a raid member to raid assistant

`PromoteToLeader`–Promotes a player to party/raid leader

`SetPartyAssignment`–Assigns a group role to a member of the player's party or raid

`SetRaidRosterSelection`–Selects a unit in the raid roster

`SetRaidSubgroup`–Moves a raid member to a non-full raid subgroup

`SetRaidTarget`–Puts a raid target marker on a unit

SwapRaidSubgroup—Swaps two raid members between subgroups in the raid

UninviteUnit—Removes a character from the player's party or raid

UnitInRaid—Returns whether a unit is in the player's raid

UnitIsPartyLeader—Returns whether a unit is the leader of the player's party

UnitIsRaidOfficer—Returns whether a unit is a raid assistant in the player's raid

UnitPlayerOrPetInRaid—Returns whether a unit is in the player's raid or belongs to a raid member

UnitTargetsVehicleInRaidUI—Returns whether attempts to target a unit should target its vehicle

Recruit-a-friend Functions

AcceptLevelGrant—Accepts a level offered by the player's Recruit-a-Friend partner

CanGrantLevel—Returns whether the player can give levels to a Recruit-a-Friend partner

CanSummonFriend—Returns whether a unit can be summoned via Recruit-a-Friend

DeclineLevelGrant—Refuses a level offered by the player's Recruit-a-Friend partner

GetSummonFriendCooldown—Returns cooldown information about the player's Summon Friend ability

GrantLevel—Grants a level to the player's Recruit-a-Friend partner

IsReferAFriendLinked—Returns whether a unit's account is linked to the player's via the Recruit-a-Friend program

SummonFriend—Summons a unit whose account is linked to the player's via the Recruit-a-Friend program

Secure Execution Utility Functions

InCombatLockdown—Returns whether the user interface is protected due to combat

forceinsecure—Causes the current execution path to continue outside the secure environment

hooksecurefunc—Add a function to be called after execution of a secure function `issecure`–Returns whether the current execution path is secure

`issecurevariable`–Returns whether a variable is secure (and if not, which addon tainted it)

`newproxy`–Creates a zero-length userdata with an optional metatable

`securecall`–Calls a function without tainting the execution path

Skill Functions

`AbandonSkill`–Unlearns a skill (used only for professions)

`CollapseSkillHeader`–Collapses a group header in the Skills UI

`ExpandSkillHeader`–Expands a group header in the Skills UI

`GetNumSkillLines`–Returns the number of entries in the Skills UI list

`GetSelectedSkill`–Returns the index of the selected skill in the Skills UI

`GetSkillLineInfo`–Returns information about an entry in the Skills UI list

`SetSelectedSkill`–Selects a skill in the Skills UI

Social Functions

`AddFriend`–Adds a character to the friends list

`AddIgnore`–Adds a character to the ignore list

`AddOrDelIgnore`–Adds the named character to the ignore list, or removes the character if already in the ignore list

`AddOrRemoveFriend`–Adds the named character to the friends list, or removes the character if already in the friends list

`DelIgnore`–Removes a player from the ignore list

`GetFriendInfo`–Returns information about a character on the player's friends list

`GetIgnoreName`–Returns the name of a character on the ignore list

`GetNumFriends`–Returns the number of characters on the player's friends list

`GetNumIgnores`–Returns the number of characters on the player's ignore list

`GetNumWhoResults`–Returns the number of results from a Who system query

`GetSelectedFriend`–Returns the index of the selected character in the player's friends list

GetSelectedIgnore–Returns the index of the selected character in the player's ignore list

GetWhoInfo–Returns information about a character in the Who system query results

IsIgnored–Returns whether a unit is on the player's ignore list

RemoveFriend–Removes a character from the friends list

SendWho–Requests a list of characters meeting given search criteria from the server

SetFriendNotes–Sets note text associated with a friends list entry

SetSelectedFriend–Selects a character in the player's friends list

SetSelectedIgnore–Selects a character in the player's ignore list

SetWhoToUI–Changes the delivery method for results from SendWho() queries

ShowFriends–Requests friends/ignore list information from the server

SortWho–Sorts the Who system query results list

Socketing Functions

AcceptSockets–Accepts changes made in the Item Socketing UI

ClickSocketButton–Picks up or places a gem in the Item Socketing UI

CloseSocketInfo–Ends interaction with the Item Socketing UI, discarding any changes made

GetExistingSocketInfo–Returns information about a permanently socketed gem

GetExistingSocketLink–Returns a hyperlink for a permanently socketed gem

GetItemGem–Returns information about gems socketed in an item

GetNewSocketInfo–Returns information about a gem added to a socket

GetNewSocketLink–Returns a hyperlink for a gem added to a socket

GetNumSockets–Returns the number of sockets on the item currently being socketed

GetSocketItemBoundTradeable–Returns whether the item open for socketing is temporarily tradeable

GetSocketItemInfo–Returns information about the item currently being socketed

`GetSocketItemRefundable`–Returns whether the item open for socketing is temporarily refundable

`GetSocketTypes`–Returns information about the gem types usable in a socket

`SocketContainerItem`–Opens an item from the player's bags for socketing

`SocketInventoryItem`–Opens an equipped item for socketing

Sound Functions

`PlayMusic`–Plays an audio file as background music

`PlaySound`–Plays one of WoW's built-in sound effects

`PlaySoundFile`–Plays an audio file at a given path

`Sound_ChatSystem_GetInputDriverNameByIndex`–Returns the name of the given chat system sound input driver

`Sound_ChatSystem_GetNumInputDrivers`–Returns the number of chat system sound input drivers

`Sound_ChatSystem_GetNumOutputDrivers`–Returns the number of chat system sound output drivers

`Sound_ChatSystem_GetOutputDriverNameByIndex`–Returns the name of the given chat system sound output driver

`Sound_GameSystem_GetInputDriverNameByIndex`–Returns the name of the given game sound input driver

`Sound_GameSystem_GetNumInputDrivers`–Returns the number of game sound input drivers

`Sound_GameSystem_GetNumOutputDrivers`–Returns the number of game sound output drivers

`Sound_GameSystem_GetOutputDriverNameByIndex`–Returns the name of the given game sound output driver

`Sound_GameSystem_RestartSoundSystem`–Restarts the game's sound systems

`StopMusic`–Stops currently playing in-game music

`VoiceEnumerateCaptureDevices`–Returns the name of an audio input device for voice chat

`VoiceEnumerateOutputDevices`–Returns the name of an audio output device for voice chat

`VoiceGetCurrentCaptureDevice`–Returns the index of the current voice capture device

`VoiceGetCurrentOutputDevice`–Returns the index of the current voice output device

`VoiceSelectCaptureDevice`–Selects an audio input device for voice chat

`VoiceSelectOutputDevice`–Selects an audio output device for voice chat

Spell Functions

`CastSpell`–Casts a spell from the spellbook

`CastSpellByID`–Casts a spell specified by ID (optionally on a specified unit)

`CastSpellByName`–Casts a spell specified by name (optionally on a specified unit)

`CursorHasSpell`–Returns whether a spell is on the cursor

`DisableSpellAutocast`–Disables automatic casting of a pet spell

`EnableSpellAutocast`–Enables automatic casting of a pet spell

`GetItemSpell`–Returns information about the spell cast by an item's "Use:" effect

`GetKnownSlotFromHighestRankSlot`–Returns the spellbook slot for the player's highest known rank of a spell

`GetNumSpellTabs`–Returns the number of tabs in the player's spellbook

`GetQuestLogRewardSpell`–Returns information about the spell reward for the selected quest in the quest log

`GetRewardSpell`–Returns information about a spell awarded when completing a quest

`GetSpellAutocast`–Returns information about automatic casting for a spell in the spellbook

`GetSpellCooldown`–Returns cooldown information about a spell in the spellbook

`GetSpellCount`–Returns the number of times a spell can be cast

`GetSpellInfo`–Returns information about a spell

`GetSpellLink`–Returns a hyperlink for a spell

`GetSpellName`–Returns the name and secondary text for a spell in the spellbook

`GetSpellTabInfo`–Returns information about a tab in the spellbook

`GetSpellTexture`–Returns the icon texture path for a spell

`HasPetSpells`–Returns whether the player's current pet has a spellbook

`IsAttackSpell`—Returns whether a spell is the standard melee Attack spell

`IsAutoRepeatSpell`—Returns whether a spell is an automatically repeating spell

`IsConsumableSpell`—Returns whether casting a spell consumes a reagent item

`IsCurrentSpell`—Returns whether a spell is currently being used

`IsHarmfulSpell`—Returns whether a spell can be used against hostile units

`IsHelpfulSpell`—Returns whether an item can be used on the player or friendly units

`IsPassiveSpell`—Returns whether a spell is passive (cannot be cast)

`IsSelectedSpell`—Returns whether a spell is currently selected in the spellbook

`IsSpellInRange`—Returns whether the player is in range to cast a spell on a unit

`IsSpellKnown`—Returns whether the player (or pet) knows a spell

`IsUsableSpell`—Returns whether or not a given spell is usable or cannot be used due to lack of mana

`PickupSpell`—Puts a spell from the player's or pet's spellbook onto the cursor

`SetMultiCastSpell`—Sets a multi-cast action slot to a given spell

`SpellCanTargetGlyph`—Returns whether the spell currently awaiting a target requires a glyph slot to be chosen

`SpellCanTargetItem`—Returns whether the spell currently awaiting a target requires an item to be chosen

`SpellCanTargetUnit`—Returns whether the spell currently awaiting a target can target a given unit

`SpellHasRange`—Returns whether an item has a range limitation for its use

`SpellIsTargeting`—Returns whether a spell is currently awaiting a target

`SpellStopCasting`—Stops casting or targeting the spell in progress

`SpellStopTargeting`—Cancels the spell currently awaiting a target

`SpellTargetItem`—Casts the spell currently awaiting a target on an item

`SpellTargetUnit`—Casts the spell currently awaiting a target on a unit

`ToggleSpellAutocast`—Enables or disables automatic casting of a spell

`UnitCastingInfo`—Returns information about the spell a unit is currently casting

`UnitChannelInfo`–Returns information about the spell a unit is currently channeling

`UpdateSpells`–Requests spellbook information from the server

Stance/Shapeshift Functions

`CancelShapeshiftForm`–Cancels the current shapeshift form

`CastShapeshiftForm`–Casts an ability on the stance/shapeshift bar

`GetNumShapeshiftForms`–Returns the number of abilities to be presented on the stance/shapeshift bar

`GetShapeshiftForm`–Returns the index of the active ability on the stance/shapeshift bar

`GetShapeshiftFormCooldown`–Returns cooldown information about an ability on the stance/shapeshift bar

`GetShapeshiftFormInfo`–Returns information about an ability on the stance/shapeshift bar

Stat Information Functions

`GetArmorPenetration`–Returns the percentage of enemy armor ignored due to the player's Armor Penetration Rating

`GetAttackPowerForStat`–Returns the attack power bonus provided by one of the player's basic statistics

`GetBlockChance`–Returns the player's percentage chance to block with a shield

`GetCombatRating`–Returns the value of a combat rating for the player

`GetCombatRatingBonus`–Returns the percentage effect for the player's current value of a given combat rating

`GetCritChance`–Returns the player's melee critical strike chance

`GetCritChanceFromAgility`–Returns additional critical strike chance provided by Agility

`GetDamageBonusStat`–Returns the index of the basic statistic that provides increased physical damage

`GetDodgeChance`–Returns the player's chance to dodge melee attacks

`GetExpertise`–Returns the player's current expertise value

`GetExpertisePercent`–Returns the reduction in chance to be dodged or parried conferred by the player's expertise value

`GetManaRegen`–Returns information about the player's mana regeneration rate

`GetMaxCombatRatingBonus`–Returns the maximum possible percentage bonus for a given combat rating

`GetParryChance`–Returns the player's parry chance

`GetPowerRegen`–Returns information about the player's mana/energy/etc. regeneration rate

`GetRangedCritChance`–Returns the player's ranged critical strike chance

`GetShieldBlock`–Returns the amount of damage prevented when the player blocks with a shield

`GetSpellBonusDamage`–Returns the player's spell damage bonus for a spell school

`GetSpellBonusHealing`–Returns the player's amount of bonus healing

`GetSpellCritChance`–Returns the player's spell critical strike chance for a spell school

`GetSpellCritChanceFromIntellect`–Returns additional spell critical strike chance provided by Intellect

`GetSpellPenetration`–Returns the amount of enemy magic resistance ignored due to the player's Spell Penetration Rating

`GetUnitHealthModifier`–Returns the health modifier for the player's pet

`GetUnitHealthRegenRateFromSpirit`–Returns the increase in health regeneration rate provided by Spirit

`GetUnitManaRegenRateFromSpirit`–Returns the increase in mana regeneration rate provided by Spirit

`GetUnitMaxHealthModifier`–Returns the maximum health modifier for the player's pet

`GetUnitPowerModifier`–Returns the mana modifier for the player's pet

`UnitArmor`–Returns the player's or pet's armor value

`UnitAttackBothHands`–Returns information about the player's or pet's weapon skill

`UnitAttackPower`–Returns the player's or pet's melee attack power

`UnitAttackSpeed`–Returns information about the player's or pet's melee attack speed

`UnitDamage`–Returns information about the player's or pet's melee attack damage

`UnitDefense`–Returns the player's or pet's Defense skill

UnitRangedAttack—Returns information about the player's or pet's ranged weapon skill

UnitRangedAttackPower—Returns the player's or pet's ranged attack power

UnitRangedDamage—Returns information about the player's or pet's ranged attack damage and speed

UnitResistance—Returns information about the player's or pet's magic resistance

UnitStat—Returns information about a basic character statistic for the player or pet

Summoning Functions

CancelSummon—Declines an offered summons

ConfirmSummon—Accepts an offered summons, teleporting the player to the summoner's location

GetSummonConfirmAreaName—Returns the destination area of an offered summons

GetSummonConfirmSummoner—Returns the name of the unit offering a summons to the player

GetSummonConfirmTimeLeft—Returns the amount of time remaining before an offered summons expires

PlayerCanTeleport—Returns whether the player can accept a summons

Talent Functions

AddPreviewTalentPoints—Spends (or unspends) talent points in the Talent UI's preview mode

CheckTalentMasterDist—Returns whether the player is in range of an NPC that can reset talents

ConfirmTalentWipe—Resets the player's talents

GetActiveTalentGroup—Returns the index of the active talent specialization

GetGroupPreviewTalentPointsSpent—Returns the total number of points spent in the Talent UI's preview mode

GetNumTalentGroups—Returns the number of talent specs a character can switch among

GetNumTalentTabs—Returns the number of talent tabs for the player, pet, or inspect target

GetNumTalents–Returns the number of options in a talent tab

GetPetTalentTree–Returns the name of the talent tree used by the player's current pet

GetTalentInfo–Returns information about a talent option

GetTalentLink–Returns a hyperlink for a talent

GetTalentPrereqs–Returns information about prerequisites to learning a talent

GetTalentTabInfo–Returns information about a talent tab

GetUnspentTalentPoints–Returns the number of unused talent points

LearnPreviewTalents–Commits changes made in the Talent UI's preview mode

LearnTalent–Learns a talent, spending one talent point

ResetGroupPreviewTalentPoints–Reverts all changes made in the Talent UI's preview mode

ResetPreviewTalentPoints–Reverts changes made within a specific tab in the Talent UI's preview mode

SetActiveTalentGroup–Switches the player's active talent specialization

UnitCharacterPoints–Returns the player's number of unused talent points and profession slots

Targeting Functions

AssistUnit–Targets the unit targeted by another unit

ClearFocus–Clears the player's focus unit

ClearTarget–Clears the player's current target

FocusUnit–Changes the focus unitID to refer to a new unit

SpellCanTargetUnit–Returns whether the spell currently awaiting a target can target a given unit

SpellTargetUnit–Casts the spell currently awaiting a target on a unit

TargetLastEnemy–Targets the most recently targeted enemy unit

TargetLastFriend–Targets the most recently targeted friendly unit

TargetLastTarget–Targets the most recently targeted unit

TargetNearest–Cycles targets through nearest units regardless of reaction/affiliation

TargetNearestEnemy–Cycles your target through the nearest enemy units

TargetNearestEnemyPlayer–Cycles targets through nearby enemy player units

TargetNearestFriend–Cycles targets through nearby friendly units

`TargetNearestFriendPlayer`–Cycles targets through nearby friendly player units

`TargetNearestPartyMember`–Cycles targets through nearby party members

`TargetNearestRaidMember`–Cycles targets through nearby raid members

`TargetUnit`–Targets a unit

Taxi/Flight Functions

`CloseTaxiMap`–Ends interaction with the Taxi (flight master) UI

`GetNumRoutes`–Returns the number of hops from the current location to another taxi node

`GetTaxiBenchmarkMode`–Returns whether flight path benchmark mode is enabled

`NumTaxiNodes`–Returns the number of flight points on the taxi map

`SetTaxiBenchmarkMode`–Enables or disables flight path benchmark mode

`SetTaxiMap`–Sets a Texture object to show the appropriate flight map texture

`TakeTaxiNode`–Embarks on a taxi flight to a given destination

`TaxiGetDestX`–Returns the horizontal coordinate of a taxi flight's destination node

`TaxiGetDestY`–Returns the vertical coordinate of a taxi flight's destination node

`TaxiGetSrcX`–Returns the horizontal coordinate of a taxi flight's source node

`TaxiGetSrcY`–Returns the vertical coordinate of a taxi flight's source node

`TaxiNodeCost`–Returns the cost to fly to a given taxi node

`TaxiNodeGetType`–Returns the type of a flight point

`TaxiNodeName`–Returns the name of a flight point

`TaxiNodePosition`–Returns the position of a flight point on the taxi map

`TaxiNodeSetCurrent`–Sets the "current" flight path node

`UnitOnTaxi`–Returns whether a unit is currently riding a flight path (taxi)

Threat Functions

`GetThreatStatusColor`–Returns color values for a given threat status

`IsThreatWarningEnabled`–Returns whether the default Aggro Warning UI should currently be shown

`UnitDetailedThreatSituation`–Returns detailed information about the threat status of one unit against another

`UnitThreatSituation`–Returns the general threat status of a unit

Tracking Functions

GetNumTrackingTypes–Returns the number of available minimap object/unit tracking abilities

GetTrackingInfo–Returns information about a given tracking option

GetTrackingTexture–Returns the texture of the active tracking ability

SetTracking–Enables a given minimap object/unit tracking ability

Trade Functions

AcceptTrade–Accepts a proposed trade

AddTradeMoney–Adds the money currently on the cursor to the trade window

CancelTrade–Cancels a trade in progress

CancelTradeAccept–Cancels the player's acceptance of a trade

ClickTargetTradeButton–Interacts with an item in a slot offered for trade by the target

ClickTradeButton–Picks up an item from or puts an item in a slot offered for trade by the player

CloseTrade–Ends interaction with the Trade UI, canceling any trade in progress

GetPlayerTradeMoney–Returns the amount of money offered for trade by the player

GetTargetTradeMoney–Returns the amount of money offered for trade by the target

GetTradePlayerItemInfo–Returns information about an item offered for trade by the player

GetTradePlayerItemLink–Returns a hyperlink for an item offered for trade by the player

GetTradeTargetItemInfo–Returns information about an item offered for trade by the target

GetTradeTargetItemLink–Returns a hyperlink for an item offered for trade by the target

InitiateTrade–Offers to trade with a given unit

PickupTradeMoney–Puts money offered by the player for trade onto the cursor

`ReplaceTradeEnchant`–Confirms replacement of an existing enchantment when offering an enchantment for trade

`SetTradeMoney`–Offers an amount of money for trade

Trade Skill Functions

`CloseTradeSkill`–Ends interaction with the Trade Skill UI

`CollapseTradeSkillSubClass`–Collapses a group header in the trade skill listing

`DoTradeSkill`–Performs a trade skill recipe

`ExpandTradeSkillSubClass`–Expands a group header in the trade skill listing

`GetFirstTradeSkill`–Returns the index of the first non-header in the trade skill listing

`GetNumTradeSkills`–Returns the number of entries in the trade skill listing

`GetTradeSkillCooldown`–Returns the time remaining on a trade skill recipe's cooldown

`GetTradeSkillDescription`–Returns descriptive text for a tradeskill recipe

`GetTradeSkillIcon`–Returns the icon for a trade skill recipe

`GetTradeSkillInfo`–Returns information about a trades kill header or recipe

`GetTradeSkillInvSlotFilter`–Returns whether the trade skill listing is filtered by a given item equipment slot

`GetTradeSkillInvSlots`–Returns a list of recipe equipment slots for the current trade skill

`GetTradeSkillItemLevelFilter`–Returns the current settings for filtering the trade skill listing by required level of items produced

`GetTradeSkillItemLink`–Returns a hyperlink for the item created by a trade skill recipe

`GetTradeSkillItemNameFilter`–Returns the current search text for filtering the trade skill listing by name

`GetTradeSkillLine`–Returns information about the current trade skill

`GetTradeSkillListLink`–Returns a hyperlink to the player's list of recipes for the current trade skill

`GetTradeSkillNumMade`–Returns the number of items created when performing a trade skill recipe

`GetTradeSkillNumReagents`–Returns the number of different reagents required for a trade skill recipe

GetTradeSkillReagentInfo—Returns information about a reagent in a trade skill recipe

GetTradeSkillReagentItemLink—Returns a hyperlink for a reagent in a trade skill recipe

GetTradeSkillRecipeLink—Returns a hyperlink for a trade skill recipe

GetTradeSkillSelectionIndex—Returns the index of the currently selected trade skill recipe

GetTradeSkillSubClassFilter—Returns whether the trade skill listing is filtered by a given item subclass

GetTradeSkillSubClasses—Returns a list of recipe subclasses for the current trade skill

GetTradeSkillTools—Returns a list of required tools for a trade skill recipe

GetTradeskillRepeatCount—Returns the number of times the trade skill recipe currently being performed will repeat

IsTradeSkillLinked—Returns whether the Trade Skill UI is showing another player's skill

SelectTradeSkill—Selects a recipe in the trade skill listing

SetTradeSkillInvSlotFilter—Filters the trade skill listing by equipment slot of items produced

SetTradeSkillItemLevelFilter—Filters the trade skill listing by required level of items produced

SetTradeSkillItemNameFilter—Filters the trade skill listing by name of recipe, item produced, or reagents

SetTradeSkillSubClassFilter—Filters the trade skill listing by subclass of items produced

StopTradeSkillRepeat—Cancels repetition of a trade skill recipe

TradeSkillOnlyShowMakeable—Filters the trade skill listing by whether the player currently has enough reagents for each recipe

TradeSkillOnlyShowSkillUps—Filters the trade skill listing by whether the player can gain skill ranks from each recipe

Trainer Functions

BuyTrainerService—Purchases an ability or recipe available from a trainer

CheckTalentMasterDist—Returns whether the player is in range of an NPC that can reset talents

CloseTrainer–Ends interaction with a trainer

CollapseTrainerSkillLine–Collapses a group header in the trainer service listing

ExpandTrainerSkillLine–Expands a group header in the trainer service listing

GetNumTrainerServices–Returns the number of entries in the trainer service listing

GetTrainerGreetingText–Returns the current trainer's greeting text

GetTrainerSelectionIndex–Returns the index of the currently selected trainer service

GetTrainerServiceAbilityReq–Returns information about an ability required for purchasing a trainer service

GetTrainerServiceCost–Returns the cost to purchase a trainer service

GetTrainerServiceDescription–Returns the description of a trainer service

GetTrainerServiceIcon–Returns the icon for a trainer service

GetTrainerServiceInfo–Returns information about an entry in the trainer service listing

GetTrainerServiceItemLink–Returns a hyperlink for the item associated with a trainer service

GetTrainerServiceLevelReq–Returns the character level required to purchase a trainer service

GetTrainerServiceNumAbilityReq–Returns the number of ability requirements for purchasing a trainer service

GetTrainerServiceSkillLine–Returns the name of the skill line associated with a trainer service

GetTrainerServiceSkillReq–Returns information about the skill requirement for a trainer service

GetTrainerServiceTypeFilter–Returns whether the trainer service listing is filtered by a service status

GetTrainerSkillLineFilter–Returns whether the trainer service listing is filtered by a skill line

GetTrainerSkillLines–Returns the list of service group names available at a trainer

IsTradeSkillTrainer–Returns whether the player is interacting with a trade skill trainer (as opposed to a class trainer)

IsTrainerServiceSkillStep–Returns whether a trainer service is a trade skill level

SelectTrainerService–Selects an entry in the trainer service listing

SetTrainerServiceTypeFilter–Filters the trainer service listing by service status

SetTrainerSkillLineFilter–Filters the trainer service listing by skill line

UnitCharacterPoints–Returns the player's number of unused talent points and profession slots

Tutorial Functions

ClearTutorials–Disables contextual tutorial display

FlagTutorial–Marks a contextual tutorial as displayed so it doesn't appear again

ResetTutorials–Enables contextual tutorial display and clears the list of already displayed tutorials

TutorialsEnabled–Returns whether contextual tutorials are enabled

UI/Visual Functions

ConsoleAddMessage–Prints text to the debug console

ConsoleExec–Runs a console command

SetupFullscreenScale–Sizes a frame to take up the entire screen regardless of screen resolution

ShowCloak–Enables or disables display of the player's cloak

ShowHelm–Enables or disables display of the player's headgear

ShowingCloak–Returns whether the player's cloak is displayed

ShowingHelm–Returns whether the player's headgear is displayed

Unit Functions

CanInspect–Returns whether a unit can be inspected

CheckInteractDistance–Returns whether the player is close enough to a unit for certain types of interaction

GetGuildInfo–Returns a unit's guild affiliation

GetMuteStatus–Returns whether a character is muted or silenced

`GetPlayerInfoByGUID`–Returns information about a player character identified by globally unique identifier

`GetUnitName`–Returns a string summarizing a unit's name and server

`GetUnitSpeed`–Returns a unit's current speed

`IsIgnoredOrMuted`–Returns whether a unit can be heard due to ignored/muted status

`IsMuted`–Returns whether a character has been muted by the player

`IsUnitOnQuest`–Returns whether a unit is on one of the quests in the player's quest log

`SetPortraitTexture`–Sets a Texture object to show a portrait of a unit

`UnitAffectingCombat`–Returns whether a unit is currently in combat

`UnitAura`–Returns information about buffs/debuffs on a unit

`UnitBuff`–Returns information about a buff on a unit

`UnitCanAssist`–Returns whether one unit can assist another

`UnitCanAttack`–Returns whether one unit can attack another

`UnitCanCooperate`–Returns whether two units can cooperate

`UnitCastingInfo`–Returns information about the spell a unit is currently casting

`UnitChannelInfo`–Returns information about the spell a unit is currently channeling

`UnitClass`–Returns a unit's class

`UnitClassBase`–Returns a unit's class

`UnitClassification`–Returns a unit's classification

`UnitCreatureFamily`–Returns the creature family of the unit

`UnitCreatureType`–Returns the creature type of a unit

`UnitDebuff`–Returns information about a debuff on a unit

`UnitExists`–Returns whether a unit exists

`UnitFactionGroup`–Returns a unit's primary faction allegiance

`UnitGUID`–Returns a unit's globally unique identifier

`UnitHasRelicSlot`–Returns whether a unit has a relic slot instead of a ranged weapon slot

`UnitHealth`–Returns a unit's current amount of health

`UnitHealthMax`–Returns a unit's maximum health value

UnitInBattleground–Returns whether a unit is in the same battleground instance as the player

UnitInParty–Returns whether a unit is a player unit in the player's party

UnitInRaid–Returns whether a unit is in the player's raid

UnitInRange–Returns whether a party/raid member is nearby

UnitIsAFK–Returns whether a unit is marked AFK (Away From Keyboard)

UnitIsCharmed–Returns whether a unit is currently charmed

UnitIsConnected–Returns whether a unit is connected (i.e. not Offline)

UnitIsControlling–Returns whether a unit is controlling another unit

UnitIsCorpse–Returns whether a unit is a corpse

UnitIsDND–Returns whether a unit is marked DND (Do Not Disturb)

UnitIsDead–Returns whether a unit is dead

UnitIsDeadOrGhost–Returns whether a unit is either dead or a ghost

UnitIsEnemy–Returns whether two units are enemies

UnitIsFeignDeath–Returns whether a unit is feigning death

UnitIsFriend–Returns whether two units are friendly

UnitIsGhost–Returns whether a unit is currently a ghost

UnitIsInMyGuild–Returns whether a unit is in the player's guild

UnitIsPVP–Returns whether a unit is flagged for PvP activity

UnitIsPVPFreeForAll–Returns whether a unit is flagged for free-for-all PvP

UnitIsPVPSanctuary–Returns whether a unit is in a Sanctuary area preventing PvP activity

UnitIsPartyLeader–Returns whether a unit is the leader of the player's party

UnitIsPlayer–Returns whether a unit is a player unit (not an NPC)

UnitIsPossessed–Returns whether a unit is possessed by another

UnitIsRaidOfficer–Returns whether a unit is a raid assistant in the player's raid

UnitIsSameServer–Returns whether two units are from the same server

UnitIsTapped–Returns whether a unit is tapped

UnitIsTappedByAllThreatList–Returns whether a unit allows all players on its threat list to receive kill credit

UnitIsTappedByPlayer–Returns whether a unit is tapped by the player or the player's group

UnitIsTrivial–Returns whether a unit is trivial at the player's level

UnitIsUnit–Returns whether two unit references are to the same unit

UnitIsVisible–Returns whether a unit is in the player's area of interest

UnitLevel–Returns a unit's level

UnitName–Returns the name of a unit

UnitOnTaxi–Returns whether a unit is currently riding a flight path (taxi)

UnitPVPName–Returns the name of a unit including the unit's current title

UnitPlayerControlled–Returns whether a unit is controlled by a player

UnitPlayerOrPetInParty–Returns whether a unit is in the player's party or belongs to a party member

UnitPlayerOrPetInRaid–Returns whether a unit is in the player's raid or belongs to a raid member

UnitPower–Returns a unit's current level of mana, rage, energy or other power type

UnitPowerMax–Returns a unit's maximum mana, rage, energy or other power type

UnitPowerType–Returns the power type (energy, mana, rage) of the given unit

UnitRace–Returns the name of a unit's race

UnitReaction–Returns the reaction of one unit with regards to another as a number

UnitSelectionColor–Returns a color indicating hostility and related status of a unit

UnitSex–Returns the gender of the given unit or player

UnitUsingVehicle–Returns whether a unit is using a vehicle

Utility Functions

CreateFont–Creates a new Font object

CreateFrame–Creates a new Frame object

EnumerateFrames–Returns the next frame following the frame passed, or nil if no more frames exist

GetAutoCompleteResults–Returns a list of character names which complete a given partial name prefix

GetClickFrame–Returns the Frame object associated with the given name

GetCurrentKeyBoardFocus—Returns the frame currently handling keyboard input

GetFramesRegisteredForEvent—Returns all frames registered for a given event

GetMirrorTimerInfo—Returns information about special countdown timers

GetMirrorTimerProgress—Returns a high-resolution value for a special countdown timer

GetMouseButtonClicked—Returns which mouse button triggered the current script

GetMouseButtonName—Returns the name for a mouse button specified by number

GetMouseFocus—Returns the frame that is currently under the mouse, and has mouse input enabled

GetMuteName—Returns the name of a character on the mute list

GetNumFrames—Returns the number of existing Frame objects (and derivatives)

GetText—Returns a localized string according to given parameters

GetTime—Returns a number representing the current time (with millisecond precision)

IsLoggedIn—Returns whether the login process has completed

IsMouseButtonDown—Returns whether a given mouse button is held down

RequestTimePlayed—Requests information from the server about the player character's total time spent online

RunScript—Runs a string as a Lua script

SecondsToTime—Returns a description of an amount of time in appropriate units

SetPortraitToTexture—Sets a Texture object to display an arbitrary texture, altering it to fit a circular frame

debuglocals—Returns information about the local variables at a given stack depth

getglobal—Returns the value of a global variable

scrub—Replaces non-simple values in a list with nil

setglobal—Sets a global variable to a specified value

strconcat—Joins a list of strings (with no separator)

strjoin—Joins a list of strings together with a given separator strlenutf8–Returns the length of a string, taking UTF-8 multi-byte characters into account

strreplace–Fast simple substring substitution

strsplit–Splits a string based on another separator string

strtrim–Trims leading and trailing characters (whitespace by default) from a string

wipe–Removes all entries from a table

Vehicle Functions

CanEjectPassengerFromSeat–Returns whether the player can eject the occupant of a seat in the player's vehicle

CanExitVehicle–Returns whether the player is in a vehicle

CanSwitchVehicleSeat–Returns whether the player can change vehicle seats

CanSwitchVehicleSeats–Returns whether the player is in a vehicle with multiple seats

CombatTextSetActiveUnit–Sets the main unit for display of floating combat text

EjectPassengerFromSeat–Ejects the occupant of a seat in the player's vehicle

IsVehicleAimAngleAdjustable–Returns whether the player is controlling a vehicle weapon with adjustable aim angle

UnitControllingVehicle–Returns whether a unit is controlling a vehicle

UnitHasVehicleUI–Returns whether a unit is controlling a vehicle or vehicle weapon

UnitInVehicle–Returns whether a unit is in a vehicle

UnitInVehicleControlSeat–Returns whether a unit controls a vehicle

UnitIsControlling–Returns whether a unit is controlling another unit

UnitSwitchToVehicleSeat–Moves the player to another seat within his current vehicle

UnitTargetsVehicleInRaidUI–Returns whether attempts to target a unit should target its vehicle

UnitUsingVehicle–Returns whether a unit is using a vehicle

UnitVehicleSeatCount–Returns the number of seats in a unit's vehicle

UnitVehicleSeatInfo–Returns information about seats in a vehicle

UnitVehicleSkin–Returns the style of vehicle UI to display for a unit

`VehicleAimDecrement`–Adjusts vehicle aim downward by a specified amount

`VehicleAimDownStart`–Starts adjusting vehicle aim downward

`VehicleAimDownStop`–Stops adjusting vehicle aim downward

`VehicleAimGetAngle`–Returns the aim angle of a vehicle weapon

`VehicleAimGetNormAngle`–Returns the aim angle of a vehicle weapon relative to its minimum angle

`VehicleAimIncrement`–Adjusts vehicle aim upward by a specified amount

`VehicleAimRequestAngle`–Attempts to set a vehicle weapon's aim angle to a specific value

`VehicleAimRequestNormAngle`–Attempts to set a vehicle weapon's aim angle to a specific value relative to its minimum value

`VehicleAimUpStart`–Starts adjusting vehicle aim upward

`VehicleAimUpStop`–Stops adjusting vehicle aim upward

`VehicleCameraZoomIn`–Zooms the player's view in while in a vehicle

`VehicleCameraZoomOut`–Zooms the player's view out while in a vehicle

`VehicleExit`–Removes the player from the current vehicle

`VehicleNextSeat`–Moves the player from his current seat in a vehicle to the next sequentially numbered seat

`VehiclePrevSeat`–Moves the player from his current seat in a vehicle to the previous sequentially numbered seat

Video Functions

`GetCurrentMultisampleFormat`–Returns the index of the current multisample setting

`GetCurrentResolution`–Returns the index of the current resolution setting

`GetFramerate`–Returns the number of frames per second rendered by the client

`GetGamma`–Returns the current display gamma setting

`GetMultisampleFormats`–Returns a list of available multisample settings

`GetRefreshRates`–Returns a list of available screen refresh rates

`GetScreenHeight`–Returns the height of the screen for UI layout purposes

`GetScreenResolutions`–Returns a list of available screen resolutions

`GetScreenWidth`–Returns the width of the screen for UI layout purposes

GetTerrainMip–Returns the level of terrain detail displayed

GetVideoCaps–Returns information about graphics capabilities of the current system

IsDesaturateSupported–Returns whether the current hardware supports desaturated textures

IsPlayerResolutionAvailable–Returns whether the current hardware supports high resolution player textures

IsStereoVideoAvailable–Returns whether the current system supports stereoscopic 3D display

RestartGx–Restart the client's graphic subsystem

RestoreVideoEffectsDefaults–Resets video effects options to default values

RestoreVideoResolutionDefaults–Resets video resolution options to default values

RestoreVideoStereoDefaults–Resets stereoscopic 3D video options to default values

SetGamma–Changes the display gamma setting

SetMultisampleFormat–Changes the multisample setting

SetScreenResolution–Changes the screen resolution

SetTerrainMip–Changes the level of terrain detail displayed

Voice Functions

AddMute–Adds a character to the muted list for voice chat

AddOrDelMute–Adds or removes a character from the voice mute list

ChannelSilenceAll–Silences a character for chat and voice on a channel

ChannelSilenceVoice–Silences the given character for voice chat on the channel

ChannelUnSilenceAll–Unsilences a character for chat and voice on a channel

ChannelUnSilenceVoice–Unsilences a character on a chat channel

ChannelVoiceOff–Disables voice chat in a channel

ChannelVoiceOn–Enables voice chat in a channel

DelMute–Removes a character from the muted list for voice chat

DisplayChannelVoiceOff–Disables voice in a channel specified by its position in the channel list display

DisplayChannelVoiceOn—Enables voice in a channel specified by its position in the channel list display

GetActiveVoiceChannel—Returns the currently active voice channel

GetMuteName—Returns the name of a character on the mute list

GetMuteStatus—Returns whether a character is muted or silenced

GetNumMutes—Returns the number of characters on the player's mute list

GetNumVoiceSessionMembersBySessionID—Returns the number of members in a voice channel

GetNumVoiceSessions—Returns the number of available voice channels

GetSelectedMute—Returns the index of the selected entry in the Muted list

GetVoiceCurrentSessionID—Returns an identifier for the active voice session

GetVoiceSessionInfo—Returns information about a voice session

GetVoiceSessionMemberInfoBySessionID—Returns information about a member of a voice channel

GetVoiceStatus—Returns whether a character has voice chat enabled

IsIgnoredOrMuted—Returns whether a unit can be heard due to ignored/muted status

IsMuted—Returns whether a character has been muted by the player

IsSilenced—Returns whether a character is silenced on a chat channel

IsVoiceChatAllowed—Returns whether the player is allowed to enable the voice chat feature

IsVoiceChatAllowedByServer—Returns whether voice chat is supported by the realm server

IsVoiceChatEnabled—Returns whether the voice chat system is enabled

SetActiveVoiceChannel—Sets the currently active voice channel

SetActiveVoiceChannelBySessionID—Sets the currently active voice chat channel

SetSelectedMute—Selects an entry in the Muted list

UnitIsSilenced—Returns whether a character is silenced on a voice channel

UnitIsTalking—Returns whether a unit is currently speaking in voice chat

VoiceChat_GetCurrentMicrophoneSignalLevel—Returns the current volume level of the microphone signal

VoiceChat_IsPlayingLoopbackSound—Returns whether the Microphone Test recording is playing

`VoiceChat_IsRecordingLoopbackSound`–Returns whether a Microphone Test is recording

`VoiceChat_PlayLoopbackSound`–Plays back the Microphone Test recording

`VoiceChat_RecordLoopbackSound`–Begins recording a Microphone Test

`VoiceChat_StopPlayingLoopbackSound`–Stops playing the Microphone Test recording

`VoiceChat_StopRecordingLoopbackSound`–Stops recording a Microphone Test

`VoiceEnumerateCaptureDevices`–Returns the name of an audio input device for voice chat

`VoiceEnumerateOutputDevices`–Returns the name of an audio output device for voice chat

`VoiceGetCurrentCaptureDevice`–Returns the index of the current voice capture device

`VoiceGetCurrentOutputDevice`–Returns the index of the current voice output device

`VoiceIsDisabledByClient`–Returns whether the voice chat system cannot be enabled

`VoiceSelectCaptureDevice`–Selects an audio input device for voice chat

`VoiceSelectOutputDevice`–Selects an audio output device for voice chat

Zone Information Functions

`GetMinimapZoneText`–Returns the name of the current area (as displayed in the Minimap)

`GetRealZoneText`–Returns the "official" name of the zone or instance in which the player is located

`GetSubZoneText`–Returns the name of the minor area in which the player is located

`GetZonePVPInfo`–Returns PvP information about the current area

`GetZoneText`–Returns the name of the zone in which the player is located

`IsSubZonePVPPOI`–Returns whether the current area has PvP (or other) objectives to be displayed

Widget Reference

To respond to game events or interact with the user in any way, an addon must make use of game widgets. This chapter provides a reference for the various widget types that exist in World of Warcraft, along with the script handlers that can be used for interaction with the user.

Widget Types

There are more 25 different widget types available in the WoW user interface. This section details these types along with the abstract types that are used to clarify the hierarchy and inheritance of the various widget methods.

UIObject

UIObject is an abstract UI object type that is used to group together methods that are common to all user interface types. All of the various user interface elements in World of Warcraft are derived from UIObject.

UIObject defines the following methods:

GetName

Returns the widget object's name.

```
name = UIObject:GetName()
```

Returns:

name—Name of the object (`string`)

GetObjectType

Returns the object's widget type.

```
type = UIObject:GetObjectType()
```

Returns:

type—Name of the object's type (e.g. `Frame`, `Button`, `FontString`, etc)
(`string`)

IsObjectType

Returns whether the object belongs to a given widget type.

```
isType = UIObject:IsObjectType("type")
```

Arguments:

type—Name of an object type (e.g. `Frame`, `Button`, `FontString`, etc) (`string`)

Returns:

isType—1 if the object belongs to the given type (or a subtype thereof); otherwise `nil` (`1nil`)

ParentedObject

ParentedObject is an abstract UI type that provides support for querying the parent of a given object. Some object parents are set implicitly (such as in the case of font strings and textures) whereas others are set explicitly using the `SetParent()` method provided by the Region object type.

ParentedObject has all the methods from UIObject, plus the following:

GetParent

Returns the object's parent object.

```
parent = ParentedObject:GetParent()
```

Returns:

parent—Reference to the object's parent object, or `nil` if the object has no parent (`uiobject`)

ScriptObject

ScriptObject is an abstract UI type that provides support for scripts, such as `OnLoad`, `OnEvent` and `OnFinished`. Scripts can be set to trigger in response to some widget event, or as a result of user interaction. The specific scripts that are supported vary wildly from object to object, but all objects support setting, hooking and getting of object scripts.

UIObject defines the following methods:

GetScript

Returns the widget's handler function for a script.

```
handler = ScriptObject:GetScript("scriptType")
```

Arguments:

scriptType—A script type; see scripts reference for details (`string`)

Returns:

handler—The object's handler function for the script type (`function`)

HasScript

Returns whether the widget supports a script handler.

```
hasScript = ScriptObject:HasScript("scriptType")
```

Arguments:

scriptType—A script type; see scripts reference for details (string)

Returns:

hasScript—1 if the widget can handle the script, otherwise nil (1nil)

HookScript

Securely hooks a script handler.

```
ScriptObject:HookScript("scriptType", handler)
```

Equivalent to hooksecurefunc() for script handlers; allows one to "post-hook" a secure handler without tainting the original.

The original handler will still be called, but the handler supplied will also be called after the original, with the same arguments. Return values from the supplied handler are discarded. Note that there is no API to remove a hook from a handler: any hooks applied will remain in place until the UI is reloaded.

If there was no prior script handler set, then this simply sets the new function as the handler for the script type.

Arguments:

scriptType—Name of the script whose handler should be hooked (string)

handler—A function to be called whenever the script handler is run (function)

Example:

```
-- hooks the default UI's player frame to insert a chat link to the
-- player's most recently completed achievement when shift-clicked
function PlayerLink(self, button, down)
  if ( IsModifiedClick("CHATLINK") ) then
    local link = ↵
GetAchievementLink(select(1,GetLatestCompletedAchievements()))
    ChatEdit_InsertLink(link)
  end
end
PlayerFrame:HookScript("OnClick", PlayerLink)
```

SetScript

Sets the widget's handler function for a script.

```
ScriptObject:SetScript("scriptType", handler)
```

Arguments:

scriptType—A script type; see scripts for details (string)

handler—A function to become the widget's handler for the script type (function)

Region

Region is the basic type for anything that can occupy an area of the screen. As such, Frames, Textures and FontStrings are all various kinds of Region. Region provides most of the functions that support size, position and anchoring, including animation. It is a "real virtual" type; it cannot be instantiated, but objects can return true when asked if they are Regions.

Region has all the methods from ParentedObject, plus the following:

CanChangeProtectedState

Returns whether protected properties of the region can be changed by non-secure scripts.

```
canChange = Region:CanChangeProtectedState()
```

Addon scripts are allowed to change protected properties for non-secure frames, or for secure frames while the player is not in combat.

Returns:

canChange—1 if addon scripts are currently allowed to change protected properties of the region (e.g. showing or hiding it, changing its position, or altering frame attributes); otherwise nil (value, 1nil)

ClearAllPoints

Removes all anchor points from the region.

```
Region:ClearAllPoints()
```

CreateAnimationGroup

Creates a new AnimationGroup as a child of the region.

```
animationGroup =↵
    Region:CreateAnimationGroup(["name" [, "inheritsFrom"]])
```

Arguments:

name (optional)—A global name to use for the new animation group (string)

inheritsFrom (optional)—Template from which the new animation group should inherit (string)

Returns:

animationGroup—The newly created AnimationGroup (animgroup)

GetAnimationGroups

Returns a list of animation groups belonging to the region.

```
... = Region:GetAnimationGroups()
```

Returns:

...—A list of AnimationGroup objects for which the region is parent (list)

GetBottom

Returns the distance from the bottom of the screen to the bottom of the region.

```
bottom = Region:GetBottom()
```

Returns:

bottom—Distance from the bottom edge of the screen to the bottom edge of the region (in pixels) (number)

GetCenter

Returns the screen coordinates of the region's center.

```
x, y = Region:GetCenter()
```

Returns:

x—Distance from the left edge of the screen to the center of the region (in pixels) (number)

y—Distance from the bottom edge of the screen to the center of the region (in pixels) (number)

GetHeight

Returns the height of the region.

```
height = Region:GetHeight()
```

Returns:

height—Height of the region (in pixels) (number)

GetLeft

Returns the distance from the left edge of the screen to the left edge of the region.

```
left = Region:GetLeft()
```

Returns:

left—Distance from the left edge of the screen to the left edge of the region (in pixels) (number)

GetNumPoints

Returns the number of anchor points defined for the region.

```
numPoints = Region:GetNumPoints()
```

Returns:

numPoints—Number of defined anchor points for the region (number)

GetPoint

Returns information about one of the region's anchor points.

```
point, relativeTo, relativePoint, xOffset, yOffset = ↵
Region:GetPoint(index)
```

Arguments:

index—Index of an anchor point defined for the region (between 1 and region:GetNumPoints()) (number)

Returns:

point—Point on this region at which it is anchored to another (string, anchor-Point) `relativeTo`—Reference to the other region to which this region is anchored (`region`)

`relativePoint`—Point on the other region to which this region is anchored (`string`, anchorPoint)

`xOffset`—Horizontal distance between `point` and `relativePoint` (in pixels; positive values put `point` to the right of `relativePoint`) (`number`)

`yOffset`—Vertical distance between `point` and `relativePoint` (in pixels; positive values put `point` below `relativePoint`) (`number`)

GetRect

Returns the position and dimensions of the region.

`left, bottom, width, height = Region:GetRect()`

Returns:

`left`—Distance from the left edge of the screen to the left edge of the region (in pixels) (`number`)

`bottom`—Distance from the bottom edge of the screen to the bottom of the region (in pixels) (`number`)

`width`—Width of the region (in pixels) (`number`)

`height`—Height of the region (in pixels) (`number`)

GetRight

Returns the distance from the left edge of the screen to the right edge of the region.

`right = Region:GetRight()`

Returns:

`right`—Distance from the left edge of the screen to the right edge of the region (in pixels) (`number`)

GetTop

Returns the distance from the bottom of the screen to the top of the region.

`top = Region:GetTop()`

Returns:

`top`—Distance from the bottom edge of the screen to the top edge of the region (in pixels) (`number`)

GetWidth

Returns the width of the region.

`width = Region:GetWidth()`

Returns:

`width`—Width of the region (in pixels) (`number`)

IsDragging

Returns whether the region is currently being dragged.

`isDragging = Region:IsDragging()`

Returns:

isDragging—1 if the region (or its parent or ancestor) is currently being dragged; otherwise nil (1nil)

IsProtected

Returns whether the region is protected.

isProtected, explicit = Region:IsProtected()

Non-secure scripts may change certain properties of a protected region (e.g. showing or hiding it, changing its position, or altering frame attributes) only while the player is not in combat. Regions may be explicitly protected by Blizzard scripts or XML; other regions can become protected by becoming children of protected regions or by being positioned relative to protected regions.

Returns:

isProtected—1 if the region is protected; otherwise nil (value, 1nil)

explicit—1 if the region is explicitly protected; nil if the frame is only protected due to relationship with a protected region (value, 1nil)

SetAllPoints

Sets all anchor points of the region to match those of another region.

Region:SetAllPoints([region]) or Region:SetAllPoints(["name"])

If no region is specified, the region's anchor points are set to those of its parent.

Arguments:

region (optional)—Reference to a region (region)

name (optional)—Global name of a region (string)

SetHeight

Sets the region's height.

Region:SetHeight(height)

Arguments:

height—New height for the region (in pixels); if 0, causes the region's height to be determined automatically according to its anchor points (number)

SetParent

Makes another frame the parent of this region.

Region:SetParent(frame) or Region:SetParent("name")

Arguments:

frame—The new parent frame (frame)

name—Global name of a frame (string)

SetPoint

Sets an anchor point for the region.

Region:SetPoint("point" [, relativeTo [, "relativePoint" ↵
[, xOffset [, yOffset]]]])

Arguments:

point—Point on this region at which it is to be anchored to another (string, anchorPoint)

relativeTo (optional)—Reference to the other region to which this region is to be anchored; if nil or omitted, anchors the region relative to its parent (or to the screen dimensions if the region has no parent) (region)

relativePoint (optional)—Point on the other region to which this region is to be anchored; if nil or omitted, defaults to the same value as point (string, anchorPoint)

xOffset (optional)—Horizontal distance between point and relativePoint (in pixels; positive values put point to the right of relativePoint); if nil or omitted, defaults to 0 (number)

yOffset (optional)—Vertical distance between point and relativePoint (in pixels; positive values put point below relativePoint); if nil or omitted, defaults to 0 (number)

Example:

```
-- Create a sample frame and give it a visible background color
local frame = CreateFrame("Frame", "TestFrame", UIParent)
local background = ↵
frame:CreateTexture("TestFrameBackground", "BACKGROUND")
background:SetTexture(1, 1, 1, 0.25)
background:SetAllPoints()

-- Set the top left corner 5px to the right and 15px above UIParent's
-- top left corner
frame:SetPoint("TOPLEFT", 5, 15)

-- Set the bottom edge to be 10px below WorldFrame's center
frame:SetPoint("BOTTOM", WorldFrame, "CENTER", 0, -10)

-- Set the right edge to be 20px to the left of WorldFrame's right edge
frame:SetPoint("RIGHT", WorldFrame, -20, 0)
```

SetWidth

Sets the region's width.

```
Region:SetWidth(width)
```

Arguments:

width—New width for the region (in pixels); if 0, causes the region's width to be determined automatically according to its anchor points (number)

StopAnimating

Stops any active animations involving the region or its children.

```
Region:StopAnimating()
```

VisibleRegion

VisibleRegion is an abstract UI type used to describe the common functionality of objects that can be placed on the screen, and visible. In particular, methods exist to show and hide the frame, and change the alpha transparency.

VisibleRegion has all the methods from Region, plus the following:

GetAlpha

Returns the opacity of the region relative to its parent.

```
alpha = VisibleRegion:GetAlpha()
```

Returns:

`alpha`—Alpha (opacity) of the region (0.0 = fully transparent, 1.0 = fully opaque) (`number`)

Hide

Hides the region.

```
VisibleRegion:Hide()
```

IsShown

Returns whether the region is shown.

```
shown = VisibleRegion:IsShown()
```

Indicates only whether the region has been explicitly shown or hidden—a region may be explicitly shown but not appear on screen because its parent region is hidden. See `VisibleRegion:IsVisible()` to test for actual visibility.

Returns:

`shown`—1 if the region is shown; otherwise `nil` (`1nil`)

IsVisible

Returns whether the region is visible.

```
visible = VisibleRegion:IsVisible()
```

A region is "visible" if it has been explicitly shown (or not explicitly hidden) and its parent is visible (that is, all of its ancestor frames (parent, parent's parent, etc) are also shown).

A region may be "visible" and not appear on screen—it may not have any anchor points set, its position and size may be outside the bounds of the screen, or it may not draw anything (e.g. a FontString with no text, a Texture with no image, or a Frame with no visible children).

Returns:

`visible`—1 if the region is visible; otherwise `nil` (`1nil`)

SetAlpha

Sets the opacity of the region relative to its parent.

```
VisibleRegion:SetAlpha(alpha)
```

Arguments:

alpha—Alpha (opacity) of the region (0.0 = fully transparent, 1.0 = fully opaque) (number)

Show

Shows the region.

```
VisibleRegion:Show()
```

LayeredRegion

LayeredRegion is an abstract UI type that groups together the functionality of layered graphical regions, specifically Textures and FontStrings. These objects can be moved from one layer to another, or can be suppressed by turning off the layer on the frame to which they are attached. These layered regions can also be colorized in the graphics engine using the :SetVertexColor() method.

LayeredRegion has all the methods from VisibleRegion, plus the following:

GetDrawLayer

Returns the layer at which the region's graphics are drawn relative to others in its frame.

```
layer = LayeredRegion:GetDrawLayer()
```

Returns:

layer—String identifying a graphics layer; one of the following values: (string, layer)

ARTWORK	HIGHLIGHT
BACKGROUND	OVERLAY
BORDER	

SetDrawLayer

Sets the layer at which the region's graphics are drawn relative to others in its frame.

```
LayeredRegion:SetDrawLayer("layer")
```

Arguments:

layer—String identifying a graphics layer; one of the following values: (string, layer)

ARTWORK	HIGHLIGHT
BACKGROUND	OVERLAY
BORDER	

SetVertexColor

Sets a color shading for the region's graphics.

```
LayeredRegion:SetVertexColor(red, green, blue [, alpha])
```

The effect of changing this property differs by the type of region:

For FontStrings, this color overrides the normal text color (as set by FontInstance:SetTextColor()).

For Textures, this color acts as a filter applied to the texture image: each color component value is a factor by which the corresponding component values in the image are multiplied. (See examples.)

Arguments:

red—Red component of the color (0.0 - 1.0) (number)

green—Green component of the color (0.0 - 1.0) (number)

blue—Blue component of the color (0.0 - 1.0) (number)

alpha (optional)—Alpha (opacity) for the graphic (0.0 = fully transparent, 1.0 = fully opaque) (number)

Example:

```
-- first, target an elite creature or NPC so the "gold dragon" target
-- border appears then try running the following scripts:

TargetFrameTexture:SetVertexColor(1,0,0)
-- omits the green and blue channels from the image, giving it
-- a red tint

TargetFrameTexture:SetVertexColor(0,0,1)
-- omits the red and green channels from the image: note the image
-- is mostly black because the gold color of the dragon image comes
-- primarily from red and green channels

TargetFrameTexture:SetVertexColor(0,0,0)
-- omits all color channels, leaving a black shadow defined by
-- the image's alpha channel

TargetFrameTexture:SetVertexColor(1,1,1)
-- removes vertex shading, returning the image to its original colors
```

FontInstance

FontInstance is an abstract UI type that groups together the functionality of text-based frames, such as Buttons, MessageFrames, EditBoxes, SimpleHTML frames and abstract Font objects. Methods are provided for setting text color and changing other aspects of font display like typeface, size, justification, shadow and spacing.

FontInstance has all the methods from UIObject, plus the following:

GetFont

Returns the font instance's basic font properties.

```
filename, fontHeight, flags = FontInstance:GetFont()
```

Returns:

filename—Path to a font file (string)

`fontHeight`—Height (point size) of the font to be displayed (in pixels) (`number`)

`flags`—Additional properties for the font specified by one or more (separated by commas) of the following tokens: (`string`)

- `MONOCHROME` - Font is rendered without anti-aliasing
- `OUTLINE` - Font is displayed with a black outline
- `THICKOUTLINE` - Font is displayed with a thick black outline

GetFontObject

Returns the `Font` object from which the font instance's properties are inherited.

`font = FontInstance:GetFontObject()`

See `FontInstance:SetFontObject()` for details.

Returns:

`font`—Reference to the `Font` object from which the font instance's properties are inherited, or `nil` if the font instance has no inherited properties (`font`)

GetJustifyH

Returns the font instance's horizontal text alignment style.

`justify = FontInstance:GetJustifyH()`

Returns:

`justify`—Horizontal text alignment style (`string`, justifyH)

- `CENTER`
- `LEFT`
- `RIGHT`

GetJustifyV

Returns the font instance's vertical text alignment style.

`justify = FontInstance:GetJustifyV()`

Returns:

`justify`—Vertical text alignment style (`string`, justifyV)

- `BOTTOM`
- `MIDDLE`
- `TOP`

GetShadowColor

Returns the color of the font's text shadow.

`shadowR, shadowG, shadowB, shadowAlpha = FontInstance:GetShadowColor()`

Returns:

`shadowR`—Red component of the shadow color (0.0 - 1.0) (`number`)

`shadowG`—Green component of the shadow color (0.0 - 1.0) (`number`)

`shadowB`—Blue component of the shadow color (0.0 - 1.0) (`number`) `shadowAlpha`—Alpha (opacity) of the text's shadow (0.0 = fully transparent, 1.0 = fully opaque) (`number`)

GetShadowOffset

Returns the offset of the font instance's text shadow from its text.

`xOffset, yOffset = FontInstance:GetShadowOffset()`

Returns:

`xOffset`—Horizontal distance between the text and its shadow (in pixels) (`number`)

`yOffset`—Vertical distance between the text and its shadow (in pixels) (`number`)

GetSpacing

Returns the font instance's amount of spacing between lines.

`spacing = FontInstance:GetSpacing()`

Returns:

`spacing`—Amount of space between lines of text (in pixels) (`number`)

GetTextColor

Returns the font instance's default text color.

`textR, textG, textB, textAlpha = FontInstance:GetTextColor()`

Returns:

`textR`—Red component of the text color (0.0 - 1.0) (`number`)

`textG`—Green component of the text color (0.0 - 1.0) (`number`)

`textB`—Blue component of the text color (0.0 - 1.0) (`number`)

`textAlpha`—Alpha (opacity) of the text (0.0 = fully transparent, 1.0 = fully opaque) (`number`)

SetFont

Sets the font instance's basic font properties.

`isValid = FontInstance:SetFont("filename", fontHeight, "flags")`

Font files included with the default WoW client:

- `Fonts\\FRIZQT__.TTF` - Friz Quadrata, used by default for player names and most UI text
- `Fonts\\ARIALN.TTF` - Arial Narrow, used by default for chat windows, action button numbers, etc
- `Fonts\\skurri.ttf` - Skurri, used by default for incoming damage/parry/miss/etc indicators on the Player and Pet frames
- `Fonts\\MORPHEUS.ttf` - Morpheus, used by default for quest title headers, mail and readable in-game objects.

Font files can also be included in addons.

Arguments:

`filename`—Path to a font file (`string`)

`fontHeight`—Height (point size) of the font to be displayed (in pixels) (`number`)

`flags`—Additional properties for the font specified by one or more (separated by commas) of the following tokens: (`string`)

- `MONOCHROME` - Font is rendered without anti-aliasing
- `OUTLINE` - Font is displayed with a black outline
- `THICKOUTLINE` - Font is displayed with a thick black outline

Returns:

`isValid`—1 if `filename` refers to a valid font file; otherwise `nil` (`1nil`)

SetFontObject

Sets the `Font` object from which the font instance's properties are inherited.

`FontInstance:SetFontObject(object)` or `FontInstance:SetFontObject ("name")`

This method allows for easy standardization and reuse of font styles. For example, a button's normal font can be set to appear in the same style as many default UI elements by setting its font to `"GameFontNormal"`—if Blizzard changes the main UI font in a future path, or if the user installs another addon which changes the main UI font, the button's font will automatically change to match.

Arguments:

`object`—Reference to a `Font` object (`font`)

`name`—Global name of a `Font` object (`string`)

SetJustifyH

Sets the font instance's horizontal text alignment style.

`FontInstance:SetJustifyH("justify")`

Arguments:

`justify`—Horizontal text alignment style (`string`, justifyH)

- `CENTER`
- `LEFT`
- `RIGHT`

SetJustifyV

Sets the font instance's horizontal text alignment style.

`FontInstance:SetJustifyV("justify")`

Arguments:

`justify`—Vertical text alignment style (`string`, justifyV)

- `BOTTOM`
- `MIDDLE`
- `TOP`

SetShadowColor

Sets the color of the font's text shadow.

`FontInstance:SetShadowColor(shadowR, shadowG, shadowB, shadowAlpha)`

Arguments:

shadowR—Red component of the shadow color (0.0 - 1.0) (number)

shadowG—Green component of the shadow color (0.0 - 1.0) (number)

shadowB—Blue component of the shadow color (0.0 - 1.0) (number)

shadowAlpha—Alpha (opacity) of the text's shadow (0.0 = fully transparent, 1.0 = fully opaque) (number)

SetShadowOffset

Sets the offset of the font instance's text shadow from its text.

```
FontInstance:SetShadowOffset(xOffset, yOffset)
```

Arguments:

xOffset—Horizontal distance between the text and its shadow (in pixels) (number)

yOffset—Vertical distance between the text and its shadow (in pixels) (number)

Example:

```
-- Moves the text shadow in the default text font further than normal
-- from the text (5 pixels right and 5 pixels down instead of
-- 1 pixel right and 1 pixel down)
ChatFontNormal:SetShadowOffset(5,-5)
```

SetSpacing

Sets the font instance's amount of spacing between lines.

```
FontInstance:SetSpacing(spacing)
```

Arguments:

spacing—Amount of space between lines of text (in pixels) (number)

SetTextColor

Sets the font instance's default text color.

```
FontInstance:SetTextColor(textR, textG, textB, textAlpha)
```

This color is used for otherwise unformatted text displayed using the font instance; however, portions of the text may be colored differently using the colorString format (commonly seen in hyperlinks).

Arguments:

textR—Red component of the text color (0.0 - 1.0) (number)

textG—Green component of the text color (0.0 - 1.0) (number)

textB—Blue component of the text color (0.0 - 1.0) (number)

textAlpha—Alpha (opacity) of the text (0.0 = fully transparent, 1.0 = fully opaque) (number)

FontString

FontStrings are one of the two types of Region that is visible on the screen. It draws a block of text on the screen using the characteristics in an associated FontObject. You can change the text contents of it, set it to use a new FontObject, and set how it handles text that doesn't fit in its normal dimensions, such as how to wrap the text and whether to indent subsequent lines.

FontStrings are used widely through the UI, to display labels on controls, the names of units, keybindings on action buttons, health and mana values and most other text data.

FontString has all the methods from Region, VisibleRegion, LayeredRegion and FontInstance, plus the following:

CanNonSpaceWrap

Returns whether long lines of text will wrap within or between words.

```
enabled = FontString:CanNonSpaceWrap()
```

Returns:

enabled—1 if long lines of text will wrap at any character boundary (i.e possibly in the middle of a word); nil to only wrap at whitespace characters (i.e. only between words) (1nil)

CanWordWrap

Returns whether long lines of text in the font string can wrap onto subsequent lines.

```
enabled = FontString:CanWordWrap()
```

Returns:

enabled—1 if long lines of text can wrap onto subsequent lines; otherwise nil (1nil)

GetMultilineIndent

Returns whether long lines of text are indented when wrapping.

```
enabled = FontString:GetMultilineIndent()
```

Returns:

enabled—1 if long lines of text are indented when wrapping; otherwise nil (1nil)

GetStringHeight

Returns the height of the text displayed in the font string.

```
height = FontString:GetStringHeight()
```

This value is based on the text currently displayed; e.g. a long block of text wrapped to several lines results in a greater height than that for a short block of text that fits on fewer lines.

Returns:

height—Height of the text currently displayed in the font string (in pixels) (number)

GetStringWidth

Returns the width of the text displayed in the font string.

```
width = FontString:GetStringWidth()
```

This value is based on the text currently displayed; e.g. a short text label results in a smaller width than a longer block of text. Very long blocks of text that don't fit the font string's dimensions all result in similar widths, because this method measures the width of the text displayed, which is truncated with an ellipsis ("...").

Returns:

width—Width of the text currently displayed in the font string (in pixels) (number)

GetText

Returns the text currently set for display in the font string.

```
text = FontString:GetText()
```

This is not necessarily the text actually displayed: text that does not fit within the FontString's dimensions will be truncated with an ellipsis ("...") for display.

Returns:

text—Text to be displayed in the font string (string)

SetAlphaGradient

Creates an opacity gradient over the text in the font string.

```
FontString:SetAlphaGradient(start, length)
```

Seen in the default UI when quest text is presented by a questgiver (if the "Instant Quest Text" feature is not turned on): This method is used with a length of 30 to fade in the letters of the description, starting at the first character; then the start value is incremented in an OnUpdate script, creating the animated fade-in effect.

Arguments:

start—Character position in the font string's text at which the gradient should begin (between 0 and string.len(fontString:GetText()) - 6) (number)

length—Width of the gradient in pixels, or 0 to restore the text to full opacity (number)

SetFormattedText

Sets the text displayed in the font string using format specifiers.

```
FontString:SetFormattedText("formatString", ...)
```

Equivalent to :SetText(format(format, ...)), but does not create a throwaway Lua string object, resulting in greater memory-usage efficiency.

Arguments:

formatString—A string containing format specifiers (as with string.format()) (string)

...—A list of values to be included in the formatted string (list)

SetMultilineIndent

Sets whether long lines of text are indented when wrapping.

```
FontString:SetMultilineIndent(enable)
```

Arguments:

enable—True to indent wrapped lines of text; false otherwise (boolean)

SetNonSpaceWrap

Sets whether long lines of text will wrap within or between words.

FontString:SetNonSpaceWrap(enable)

Arguments:

enable—True to wrap long lines of text at any character boundary (i.e possibly in the middle of a word); false to only wrap at whitespace characters (i.e. only between words) (boolean)

SetText

Sets the text to be displayed in the font string.

FontString:SetText("text")

Arguments:

text—Text to be displayed in the font string (string)

SetTextHeight

Scales the font string's rendered text to a different height.

FontString:SetTextHeight(height)

This method scales the image of the text as already rendered at its existing height by the game's graphics engine—producing an effect which is efficient enough for use in fast animations, but with reduced visual quality in the text. To re-render the text at a new point size, see :SetFont().

Arguments:

height—Height (point size) to which the text should be scaled (in pixels) (number)

SetWordWrap

Sets whether long lines of text in the font string can wrap onto subsequent lines.

FontString:SetWordWrap(enable)

Arguments:

enable—True to allow long lines of text in the font string to wrap onto subsequent lines; false to disallow (boolean)

Texture

Textures are visible areas descended from LayeredRegion, that display either a color block, a gradient, or a graphic raster taken from a .tga or .blp file. Most of their methods relate to setting their appearance or their source information.

Textures are created as children of Frame elements in XML, or by calling Frame:CreateTexture() from Lua. They cannot be reassigned from one frame to another, although you can create another texture on another frame that has the same source. They can also be created in XML with the virtual tag, allowing several similar textures to be created easily.

Texture has all the methods from Region, VisibleRegion and LayeredRegion, plus the following:

GetBlendMode

Returns the blend mode of the texture.

```
mode = Texture:GetBlendMode()
```

Returns:

mode—Blend mode of the texture (`string`)

- ADD - Adds texture color values to the underlying color values, using the alpha channel; light areas in the texture lighten the background while dark areas are more transparent
- ALPHAKEY - One-bit transparency; pixels with alpha values greater than ~0.8 are treated as fully opaque and all other pixels are treated as fully transparent
- BLEND - Normal color blending, using any alpha channel in the texture image
- DISABLE - Ignores any alpha channel, displaying the texture as fully opaque
- MOD - Ignores any alpha channel in the texture and multiplies texture color values by background color values; dark areas in the texture darken the background while light areas are more transparent

GetNonBlocking

Returns whether the texture object loads its image file in the background.

```
nonBlocking = Texture:GetNonBlocking()
```

See :SetNonBlocking() for further details.

Returns:

nonBlocking—1 if the texture object loads its image file in the background; nil if the game engine is halted while the texture loads (1nil)

GetTexCoord

Returns corner coordinates for scaling or cropping the texture image.

```
ULx, ULy, LLx, LLy, URx, URy, LRx, LRy = Texture:GetTexCoord()
```

See Texture:SetTexCoord() example for details.

Returns:

ULx—Upper left corner X position, as a fraction of the image's width from the left (number)

ULy—Upper left corner Y position, as a fraction of the image's height from the top (number)

LLx—Lower left corner X position, as a fraction of the image's width from the left (number)

LLy—Lower left corner Y position, as a fraction of the image's height from the top (number)

URx—Upper right corner X position, as a fraction of the image's width from the left (number)

URy—Upper right corner Y position, as a fraction of the image's height from the top (number)

LRx—Lower right corner X position, as a fraction of the image's width from the left (number)

LRy—Lower right corner Y position, as a fraction of the image's height from the top (number)

GetTexCoordModifiesRect

Sets whether modifying texture coordinates scales or crops the texture image.

```
modifiesRect = Texture:GetTexCoordModifiesRect()
```

See `Texture:SetTexCoordModifiesRect()` example for details.

Returns:

`modifiesRect`—True if future `Texture:SetTexCoord()` operations will crop the texture image; false if `SetTexCoord` will scale the image (boolean)

GetTexture

Returns the path to the texture's image file.

```
texture = Texture:GetTexture()
```

Returns:

`texture`—Path to the texture image file, or one of the following values: (string)

- `Portrait1` - Texture is set to a generated image (e.g. via `SetPortrait Texture()`)
- `SolidTexture` - Texture is set to a solid color instead of an image

GetVertexColor

Returns the shading color of the texture.

```
red, green, blue, alpha = Texture:GetVertexColor()
```

For details about vertex color shading, see `LayeredRegion:SetVertexColor()`.

Returns:

`red`—Red component of the color (0.0 - 1.0) (number)

`green`—Green component of the color (0.0 - 1.0) (number)

`blue`—Blue component of the color (0.0 - 1.0) (number)

`alpha`—Alpha (opacity) for the texture (0.0 = fully transparent, 1.0 = fully opaque) (number)

IsDesaturated

Returns whether the texture image should be displayed with zero saturation (i.e. converted to grayscale).

```
desaturated = Texture:IsDesaturated()
```

The texture may not actually be displayed in grayscale if the current display hardware doesn't support that feature; see `Texture:SetDesaturated()` for details.

Returns:

`desaturated`—1 if the texture should be displayed in grayscale; otherwise `nil` (1nil)

SetBlendMode

Sets the blend mode of the texture.

```
Texture:SetBlendMode("mode")
```

Arguments:

mode—Blend mode of the texture (string)

- ADD - Adds texture color values to the underlying color values, using the alpha channel; light areas in the texture lighten the background while dark areas are more transparent
- ALPHAKEY - One-bit transparency; pixels with alpha values greater than ~0.8 are treated as fully opaque and all other pixels are treated as fully transparent
- BLEND - Normal color blending, using any alpha channel in the texture image
- DISABLE - Ignores any alpha channel, displaying the texture as fully opaque
- MOD - Ignores any alpha channel in the texture and multiplies texture color values by background color values; dark areas in the texture darken the background while light areas are more transparent

SetDesaturated

Sets whether the texture image should be displayed with zero saturation (i.e. converted to grayscale).

```
supported = Texture:SetDesaturated(desaturate)
```

Returns nil if the current system does not support texture desaturation; in such cases, this method has no visible effect (but still flags the texture object as desaturated). Authors may wish to implement an alternative to desaturation for such cases (see example).

Arguments:

desaturate—True to display the texture in grayscale; false to display original texture colors (boolean)

Returns:

supported—1 if the current system supports texture desaturation; otherwise nil (1nil)

Example:

```
-- Wrapper for the desaturation feature used in the default UI: if
-- running on display hardware (or drivers, etc) that does not support
-- desaturation, uses SetVertexColor to "dim" the texture instead

function SetDesaturation(texture, desaturation)
 local shaderSupported = texture:SetDesaturated(desaturation);
 if ( not shaderSupported ) then
  if ( desaturation ) then
   texture:SetVertexColor(0.5, 0.5, 0.5);
  else
   texture:SetVertexColor(1.0, 1.0, 1.0);
  end
 end
end
```

SetGradient

Sets a gradient color shading for the texture.

```
Texture:SetGradient("orientation", startR, startG, startB, endR,⏎
endG, endB)
```

Gradient color shading does not change the underlying color of the texture image, but acts as a filter: see `LayeredRegion:SetVertexColor()` for details.

Arguments:

`orientation`—Token identifying the direction of the gradient (`string`)

- `HORIZONTAL` - Start color on the left, end color on the right
- `VERTICAL` - Start color at the bottom, end color at the top

`startR`—Red component of the start color (0.0 - 1.0) (`number`)

`startG`—Green component of the start color (0.0 - 1.0) (`number`)

`startB`—Blue component of the start color (0.0 - 1.0) (`number`)

`endR`—Red component of the end color (0.0 - 1.0) (`number`)

`endG`—Green component of the end color (0.0 - 1.0) (`number`)

`endB`—Blue component of the end color (0.0 - 1.0) (`number`)

SetGradientAlpha

Sets a gradient color shading for the texture (including opacity in the gradient).

```
Texture:SetGradientAlpha("orientation", startR, startG, startB,⏎
startAlpha, endR, endG, endB, endAlpha)
```

Gradient color shading does not change the underlying color of the texture image, but acts as a filter: see `LayeredRegion:SetVertexColor()` for details.

Arguments:

`orientation`—Token identifying the direction of the gradient (`string`)

- `HORIZONTAL` - Start color on the left, end color on the right
- `VERTICAL` - Start color at the bottom, end color at the top

`startR`—Red component of the start color (0.0 - 1.0) (`number`)

`startG`—Green component of the start color (0.0 - 1.0) (`number`)

`startB`—Blue component of the start color (0.0 - 1.0) (`number`)

`startAlpha`—Alpha (opacity) for the start side of the gradient (0.0 = fully transparent, 1.0 = fully opaque) (`number`)

`endR`—Red component of the end color (0.0 - 1.0) (`number`)

`endG`—Green component of the end color (0.0 - 1.0) (`number`)

`endB`—Blue component of the end color (0.0 - 1.0) (`number`)

`endAlpha`—Alpha (opacity) for the end side of the gradient (0.0 = fully transparent, 1.0 = fully opaque) (`number`)

SetNonBlocking

Sets whether the texture object loads its image file in the background.

```
Texture:SetNonBlocking(nonBlocking)
```

Texture loading is normally synchronous, so that UI objects are not shown partially textured while loading; however, non-blocking (asynchronous) texture loading may be desirable in some cases where large numbers of textures need to be loaded in a short time. This feature is used in the default UI's icon chooser window for macros and equipment sets, allowing a large number of icon textures to be loaded without causing the game's frame rate to stagger.

Arguments:

nonBlocking—True to allow the texture object to load its image file in the background; false (default) to halt the game engine while the texture loads (boolean)

SetRotation

Rotates the texture image.

```
Texture:SetRotation(radians)
```

This is an efficient shorthand for the more complex Texture: SetTexCoord().

Arguments:

radians—Amount by which the texture image should be rotated (in radians; positive values for counter-clockwise rotation, negative for clockwise) (number)

SetTexCoord

Sets corner coordinates for scaling or cropping the texture image.

```
Texture:SetTexCoord(left, right, top, bottom) or ↵
Texture:SetTexCoord(ULx, ULy, LLx, LLy, URx, URy, LRx, LRy)
```

See example for details.

Arguments:

left—Left edge of the scaled/cropped image, as a fraction of the image's width from the left (number)

right—Right edge of the scaled/cropped image, as a fraction of the image's width from the left (number)

top—Top edge of the scaled/cropped image, as a fraction of the image's height from the top (number)

bottom—Bottom edge of the scaled/cropped image, as a fraction of the image's height from the top (number)

ULx—Upper left corner X position, as a fraction of the image's width from the left (number)

ULy—Upper left corner Y position, as a fraction of the image's height from the top (number)

LLx—Lower left corner X position, as a fraction of the image's width from the left (number)

LLy—Lower left corner Y position, as a fraction of the image's height from the top (number)

URx—Upper right corner X position, as a fraction of the image's width from the left (number)

URy—Upper right corner Y position, as a fraction of the image's height from the top (number)

LRx—Lower right corner X position, as a fraction of the image's width from the left (number)

LRy—Lower right corner Y position, as a fraction of the image's height from the top (number)

Example:

```
-- create a frame and texture to show the class icons
-- this image includes the icons of all player classes, arranged
-- in a 4x4 grid
CreateFrame("Frame","Test",UIParent)
Test:SetWidth(100)
Test:SetHeight(100)
Test:SetPoint("CENTER",0,0)
Test:CreateTexture("TestTexture")
TestTexture:SetAllPoints()
TestTexture:SetTexture("Interface\\Glues\\CharacterCreate\\↵
UI-CharacterCreate-Classes")

-- the warrior icon is in the top of this 4x4 grid, so its dimensions
-- are 1/4 those of the texture image
-- scales up the warrior class icon to fill the 100x100 frame
TestTexture:SetTexCoord(0, 0.25, 0, 0.25)
```

SetTexCoordModifiesRect

Sets whether modifying texture coordinates scales or crops the texture image.

```
Texture:SetTexCoordModifiesRect(modifiesRect)
```

See example for details.

Arguments:

modifiesRect—True to cause future Texture:SetTexCoord() operations to crop the on-screen texture image; false to cause SetTexCoord to scale the image (boolean)

Example:

```
-- create a frame and texture to show the class icons
CreateFrame("Frame","Test",UIParent)
Test:SetWidth(100)
Test:SetHeight(100)
Test:SetPoint("CENTER",0,0)
Test:CreateTexture("TestTexture")
TestTexture:SetAllPoints()
TestTexture:SetTexture("Interface\\Glues\\CharacterCreate\\↵
UI-CharacterCreate-Classes")

-- with ModifiesRect enabled, SetTexCoord crops to show only the
-- warrior icon at its existing size
TestTexture:SetTexCoordModifiesRect(true)
TestTexture:SetTexCoord(0, 0.25, 0, 0.25)
```

```
-- resetting to default texture coordinates before disabling
-- ModifiesRect, and then using SetTexCoord again scales the
-- warrior icon to fill the 100x100 pixel frame
TestTexture:SetTexCoord(0, 1, 0, 1)
TestTexture:SetTexCoordModifiesRect(false)
TestTexture:SetTexCoord(0, 0.25, 0, 0.25)
```

SetTexture

Sets the texture object's image or color.

```
visible = Texture:SetTexture("texture") or Texture:SetTexture(red, ↵
green, blue [, alpha])
```

Returns `nil` if the texture could not be set (e.g. if the file path is invalid or points to a file which cannot be used as a texture).

Arguments:

`texture`—Path to a texture image (`string`)

`red`—Red component of the color (0.0 - 1.0) (`number`)

`green`—Green component of the color (0.0 - 1.0) (`number`)

`blue`—Blue component of the color (0.0 - 1.0) (`number`)

`alpha` (optional)—Alpha (opacity) for the color (0.0 = fully transparent, 1.0 = fully opaque) (`number`)

Returns:

`visible`—1 if the texture was successfully changed; otherwise `nil` (`1nil`)

Frame

Frame is in many ways the most fundamental widget object. Other types of widget derivatives such as FontStrings, Textures and Animations can only be created and attached to a Frame or other derivative of a Frame. Frames provide the basis for interaction with the user, and registering and responding to game events.

When an addon needs to respond to game events or state changes and needs no visible components, this is typically accomplished using a Frame. Visibly, widgets that display game information such as threat or cooldowns and aren't directly interactive beyond being draggable are typically Frames. They are also commonly used as ways to group other related frames, either visibly (such as the way the Talents pane groups the buttons representing your character's talents) or invisibly (such as the way MultiBarRight groups twelve action buttons).

You create a plain frame by specifying "Frame" as the first argument to `CreateFrame`, or with a `<Frame>` element in an XML file:

```
-- Create a new frame in Lua
local self = CreateFrame("Frame", "FunWidget", UIParent)
<Frame name="FunWidget" parent="UIParent">
  <!-- insert anchors, scripts, children, and other components↵
here in XML -->
</Frame>
```

Frames in the FrameXML include the action bars (the frames that group the action buttons together), the panels that display information like your character status and quest log, and the granddaddy of the rest of the UI, UIParent.

Frame has all the methods from Region, ScriptObject and VisibleRegion, plus the following:

AllowAttributeChanges

Temporarily allows insecure code to modify the frame's attributes during combat.

```
Frame:AllowAttributeChanges()
```

This permission is automatically rescinded when the frame's OnUpdate script next runs.

CanChangeAttribute

Returns whether secure frame attributes can currently be changed.

```
enabled = Frame:CanChangeAttribute()
```

Applies only to protected frames inheriting from one of the secure frame templates; frame attributes may only be changed by non-Blizzard scripts while the player is not in combat (or for a short time after a secure script calls :AllowAttributeChanges()).

Returns:

enabled—1 if secure frame attributes can currently be changed; otherwise nil (1nil)

CreateFontString

Creates a new FontString as a child of the frame.

```
fontstring = Frame:CreateFontString(["name" [, "layer" [, "inherits"]]])
```

Arguments:

name (optional)—Global name for the new font string (string)

layer (optional)—Graphic layer on which to create the font string; defaults to ARTWORK if not specified (string, layer)

inherits (optional)—Name of a template from which the new front string should inherit (string)

Returns:

fontstring—Reference to the new FontString object (fontstring)

CreateTexture

Creates a new Texture as a child of the frame.

```
texture = Frame:CreateTexture(["name" [, "layer" [, "inherits"]]])
```

Arguments:

name (optional)—Global name for the new texture (string)

layer (optional)—Graphic layer on which to create the texture; defaults to ARTWORK if not specified (string, layer)

inherits (optional)—Name of a template from which the new texture should inherit (string)

Returns:

texture—Reference to the new Texture object (texture)

CreateTitleRegion

Creates a title region for dragging the frame.

```
region = Frame:CreateTitleRegion()
```

Creating a title region allows a frame to be repositioned by the user (by clicking and dragging in the region) without requiring additional scripts. (This behavior only applies if the frame is mouse enabled.)

Returns:

region—Reference to the new Region object (region)

DisableDrawLayer

Prevents display of all child objects of the frame on a specified graphics layer.

```
Frame:DisableDrawLayer("layer")
```

Arguments:

layer—Name of a graphics layer (string, layer)

EnableDrawLayer

Allows display of all child objects of the frame on a specified graphics layer.

```
Frame:EnableDrawLayer("layer")
```

Arguments:

layer—Name of a graphics layer (string, layer)

EnableJoystick

Enables or disables joystick interactivity.

```
Frame:EnableJoystick(enable)
```

Joystick interactivity must be enabled in order for a frame's joystick-related script handlers to be run.

(As of this writing, joystick support is partially implemented but not enabled in the current version of World of Warcraft.)

Arguments:

enable—True to enable joystick interactivity; false to disable (boolean)

EnableKeyboard

Enables or disables keyboard interactivity for the frame.

```
Frame:EnableKeyboard(enable)
```

Keyboard interactivity must be enabled in order for a frame's OnKeyDown, OnKeyUp, or OnChar scripts to be run.

Arguments:

enable—True to enable keyboard interactivity; false to disable (boolean)

EnableMouse

Enables or disables mouse interactivity for the frame.

`Frame:EnableMouse(enable)`

Mouse interactivity must be enabled in order for a frame's mouse-related script handlers to be run.

Arguments:

`enable`—`True` to enable mouse interactivity; `false` to disable (`boolean`)

EnableMouseWheel

Enables or disables mouse wheel interactivity for the frame.

`Frame:EnableMouseWheel(enable)`

Mouse wheel interactivity must be enabled in order for a frame's `OnMouseWheel` script handler to be run.

Arguments:

`enable`—`True` to enable mouse wheel interactivity; `false` to disable (`boolean`)

GetAttribute

Returns the value of a secure frame attribute.

`value = Frame:GetAttribute("name")`

See the secure template documentation for more information about frame attributes.

Arguments:

`name`—Name of an attribute to query, case insensitive (`string`)

Returns:

`value`—Value of the named attribute (`value`)

GetBackdrop

Returns information about the frame's backdrop graphic.

`backdrop = Frame:GetBackdrop()`

See SetBackdrop.

Returns:

`backdrop`—A table containing the backdrop settings, or `nil` if the frame has no backdrop (`table`, backdrop)

GetBackdropBorderColor

Returns the shading color for the frame's border graphic.

`red, green, blue, alpha = Frame:GetBackdropBorderColor()`

Returns:

`red`—Red component of the color (0.0 - 1.0) (`number`)

`green`—Green component of the color (0.0 - 1.0) (`number`)

`blue`—Blue component of the color (0.0 - 1.0) (`number`)

`alpha` (optional)—Alpha (opacity) for the graphic (0.0 = fully transparent, 1.0 = fully opaque) (`number`)

GetBackdropColor

Returns the shading color for the frame's background graphic.

```
red, green, blue, alpha = Frame:GetBackdropColor()
```

Returns:

red—Red component of the color (0.0 - 1.0) (number)

green—Green component of the color (0.0 - 1.0) (number)

blue—Blue component of the color (0.0 - 1.0) (number)

alpha (optional)—Alpha (opacity) for the graphic (0.0 = fully transparent, 1.0 = fully opaque) (number)

GetBoundsRect

Returns the position and dimension of the smallest area enclosing the frame and its children.

```
left, bottom, width, height = Frame:GetBoundsRect()
```

This information may not match that returned by :GetRect() if the frame contains textures, font strings, or child frames whose boundaries lie outside its own.

Returns:

left—Distance from the left edge of the screen to the left edge of the area (in pixels) (number)

bottom—Distance from the bottom edge of the screen to the bottom of the area (in pixels) (number)

width—Width of the area (in pixels) (number)

height—Height of the area (in pixels) (number)

Example:

```
CreateFrame("Frame","TestFrame1", UIParent)
TestFrame1:SetWidth(100)
TestFrame1:SetHeight(100)
TestFrame1:SetPoint("BOTTOMLEFT",0,0)
CreateFrame("Frame","TestFrame2", TestFrame1)
TestFrame2:SetWidth(100)
TestFrame2:SetHeight(100)
TestFrame2:SetPoint("CENTER",TestFrame1,"TOPRIGHT",0,0)

TestFrame1:GetBoundsRect()
-- prints "0, 0, 150, 150"
```

GetChildren

Returns a list of child frames of the frame.

```
... = Frame:GetChildren()
```

Returns:

...—A list of the frames which are children of this frame (list)

GetClampRectInsets

Returns offsets from the frame's edges used when limiting user movement or resizing of the frame.

```
left, right, top, bottom = Frame:GetClampRectInsets()
```

Note: despite the name of this method, the values are all offsets along the normal axes, so to inset the frame's clamping area from its edges, the left and bottom measurements should be positive and the right and top measurements should be negative.

Returns:

`left`—Offset from the left edge of the frame to the left edge of its clamping area (in pixels) (`number`)

`right`—Offset from the right edge of the frame's clamping area to the right edge of the frame (in pixels) (`number`)

`top`—Offset from the top edge of the frame's clamping area to the top edge of the frame (in pixels) (`number`)

`bottom`—Offset from the bottom edge of the frame to the bottom edge of its clamping area (in pixels) (`number`)

GetDepth

Returns the 3D depth of the frame (for stereoscopic 3D setups).

```
depth = Frame:GetDepth()
```

Returns:

`depth`—Apparent 3D depth of this frame relative to that of its parent frame (`number`)

GetEffectiveAlpha

Returns the overall opacity of the frame.

```
alpha = Frame:GetEffectiveAlpha()
```

Unlike `:GetAlpha()` which returns the opacity of the frame relative to its parent, this function returns the absolute opacity of the frame, taking into account the relative opacity of parent frames.

Returns:

`alpha`—Effective alpha (opacity) of the region (0.0 = fully transparent, 1.0 = fully opaque) (`number`)

Example:

```
CreateFrame("Frame","Frame1", UIParent)
Frame1:SetAlpha(0.5)
CreateFrame("Frame","Frame2", Frame1)
Frame2:SetAlpha(0.2)
CreateFrame("Frame","Frame3", Frame2)
Frame3:SetAlpha(0.25)

UIParent:GetEffectiveAlpha()
-- returns 1
```

```
Frame1:GetEffectiveAlpha()
-- returns approximately 0.5
Frame2:GetEffectiveAlpha()
-- returns approximately 0.1
Frame3:GetEffectiveAlpha()
-- returns approximately 0.025
```

GetEffectiveDepth

Returns the overall 3D depth of the frame (for stereoscopic 3D configurations).

```
depth = Frame:GetEffectiveDepth()
```

Unlike :GetDepth() which returns the apparent depth of the frame relative to its parent, this function returns the absolute depth of the frame, taking into account the relative depths of parent frames.

Returns:

depth—Apparent 3D depth of this frame relative to the screen (number)

Example:

```
CreateFrame("Frame","Frame1", UIParent)
Frame1:SetDepth(0.5)
CreateFrame("Frame","Frame2", Frame1)
Frame2:SetDepth(1)
CreateFrame("Frame","Frame3", Frame2)
Frame3:SetDepth(-0.25)

UIParent:GetEffectiveDepth()
-- returns 1
Frame1:GetEffectiveDepth()
-- returns 1.5
Frame2:GetEffectiveDepth()
-- returns 2
Frame3:GetEffectiveDepth()
-- returns 1.75
```

GetEffectiveScale

Returns the overall scale factor of the frame.

```
scale = Frame:GetEffectiveScale()
```

Unlike :GetScale() which returns the scale factor of the frame relative to its parent, this function returns the absolute scale factor of the frame, taking into account the relative scales of parent frames.

Returns:

scale—Scale factor for the frame relative to its parent (number)

Example:

```
CreateFrame("Frame","Frame1", UIParent)
Frame1:SetScale(0.5)
CreateFrame("Frame","Frame2", Frame1)
Frame2:SetScale(1.5)
CreateFrame("Frame","Frame3", Frame2)
```

```
Frame3:SetScale(0.25)

UIParent:GetEffectiveScale()
-- returns 1 (assuming the UI Scale setting in Video Options
-- is not enabled)
Frame1:GetEffectiveScale()
-- returns 0.5
Frame2:GetEffectiveDepth()
-- returns 0.75
Frame3:GetEffectiveDepth()
-- returns 0.1875
```

GetFrameLevel

Sets the level at which the frame is layered relative to others in its strata.

```
level = Frame:GetFrameLevel()
```

Frames with higher frame level are layered "in front of" frames with a lower frame level. When not set manually, a frame's level is determined by its place in the frame hierarchy—e.g. UIParent's level is 1, children of UIParent are at level 2, children of those frames are at level 3, etc

Returns:

`level`—Layering level of the frame relative to others in its `frameStrata` (number)

GetFrameStrata

Returns the general layering strata of the frame.

```
strata = Frame:GetFrameStrata()
```

Returns:

`strata`—Token identifying the strata in which the frame should be layered (string, frameStrata)

BACKGROUND	FULLSCREEN_DIALOG	MEDIUM
DIALOG	HIGH	PARENT
FULLSCREEN	LOW	TOOLTIP

GetHitRectInsets

Returns the insets from the frame's edges which determine its mouse-interactable area.

```
left, right, top, bottom = Frame:GetHitRectInsets()
```

Returns:

`left`—Distance from the left edge of the frame to the left edge of its mouse-interactive area (in pixels) (number)

`right`—Distance from the right edge of the frame to the right edge of its mouse-interactive area (in pixels) (number)

`top`—Distance from the top edge of the frame to the top edge of its mouse-interactive area (in pixels) (number) `bottom`—Distance from the bottom edge of the frame to the bottom edge of its mouse-interactive area (in pixels) (`number`)

GetID

Returns the frame's numeric identifier.

```
id = Frame:GetID()
```

Frame IDs have no effect on frame behavior, but can be a useful way to keep track of multiple similar frames, especially in cases where a list of frames is created from a template (such as for action buttons, loot slots, or lines in a FauxScrollFrame).

Returns:

`id`—A numeric identifier for the frame (`number`)

GetMaxResize

Returns the maximum size of the frame for user resizing.

```
maxWidth, maxHeight = Frame:GetMaxResize()
```

Applies when resizing the frame with the mouse via `:StartSizing()`.

Returns:

`maxWidth`—Maximum width of the frame (in pixels), or `0` for no limit (`number`)

`maxHeight`—Maximum height of the frame (in pixels), or `0` for no limit (`number`)

GetMinResize

Returns the minimum size of the frame for user resizing.

```
minWidth, minHeight = Frame:GetMinResize()
```

Applies when resizing the frame with the mouse via `:StartSizing()`.

Returns:

`minWidth`—Minimum width of the frame (in pixels), or `0` for no limit (`number`)

`minHeight`—Minimum height of the frame (in pixels), or `0` for no limit (`number`)

GetNumChildren

Returns the number of child frames belonging to the frame.

```
numChildren = Frame:GetNumChildren()
```

Returns:

`numChildren`—Number of child frames belonging to the frame (`number`)

GetNumRegions

Returns the number of non-Frame child regions belonging to the frame.

```
numRegions = Frame:GetNumRegions()
```

Returns:

`numRegions`—Number of non-Frame child regions (`FontStrings` and `Textures`) belonging to the frame (`number`)

GetRegions

Returns a list of non-Frame child regions belonging to the frame.

```
... = Frame:GetRegions()
```

Returns:

`...`—A list of each non-Frame child region (`FontString` or `Texture`) belonging to the frame (`list`)

GetScale

Returns the frame's scale factor.

```
scale = Frame:GetScale()
```

Returns:

`scale`—Scale factor for the frame relative to its parent (`number`)

GetTitleRegion

Returns the frame's TitleRegion object.

```
region = Frame:GetTitleRegion()
```

See `:CreateTitleRegion()` for more information.

Returns:

`region`—Reference to the frame's TitleRegion object (`region`)

IgnoreDepth

Sets whether the frame's depth property is ignored (for stereoscopic 3D setups).

```
Frame:IgnoreDepth(enable)
```

If a frame's depth property is ignored, the frame itself is not rendered with stereoscopic 3D separation, but 3D graphics within the frame may be; this property is used on the default UI's WorldFrame.

Arguments:

`enable`—`True` to ignore the frame's depth property; `false` to disable (`boolean`)

IsClampedToScreen

Returns whether the frame's boundaries are limited to those of the screen.

```
enabled = Frame:IsClampedToScreen()
```

Returns:

`enabled`—1 if the frame's boundaries are limited to those of the screen when user moving/resizing; otherwise `nil` (`1nil`)

IsEventRegistered

Returns whether the frame is registered for a given event.

```
registered = Frame:IsEventRegistered("event")
```

Arguments:

`event`—Name of an event (`string`)

Returns:

registered—1 if the frame is registered for the event; otherwise nil (1nil)

IsIgnoringDepth

Returns whether the frame's depth property is ignored (for stereoscopic 3D setups).

```
enabled = Frame:IsIgnoringDepth()
```

Returns:

enabled—1 if the frame's depth property is ignored; otherwise nil (1nil)

IsJoystickEnabled

Returns whether joystick interactivity is enabled for the frame.

```
enabled = Frame:IsJoystickEnabled()
```

(As of this writing, joystick support is partially implemented but not enabled in the current version of World of Warcraft.)

Returns:

enabled—1 if joystick interactivity is enabled for the frame; otherwise nil (1nil)

IsKeyboardEnabled

Returns whether keyboard interactivity is enabled for the frame.

```
enabled = Frame:IsKeyboardEnabled()
```

Returns:

enabled—1 if keyboard interactivity is enabled for the frame; otherwise nil (1nil)

IsMouseEnabled

Returns whether mouse interactivity is enabled for the frame.

```
enabled = Frame:IsMouseEnabled()
```

Returns:

enabled—1 if mouse interactivity is enabled for the frame; otherwise nil (1nil)

IsMouseWheelEnabled

Returns whether mouse wheel interactivity is enabled for the frame.

```
enabled = Frame:IsMouseWheelEnabled()
```

Returns:

enabled—1 if mouse wheel interactivity is enabled for the frame; otherwise nil (1nil)

IsMovable

Returns whether the frame can be moved by the user.

```
movable = Frame:IsMovable()
```

Returns:

movable—1 if the frame can be moved by the user; otherwise nil (1nil)

IsResizable

Returns whether the frame can be resized by the user.

```
enabled = Frame:IsResizable()
```

Returns:

enabled—1 if the frame can be resized by the user; otherwise nil (1nil)

IsToplevel

Returns whether the frame is automatically raised to the front when clicked.

```
enabled = Frame:IsToplevel()
```

Returns:

enabled—1 if the frame is automatically raised to the front when clicked; otherwise nil (1nil)

IsUserPlaced

Returns whether the frame is flagged for automatic saving and restoration of position and dimensions.

```
enabled = Frame:IsUserPlaced()
```

Returns:

enabled—1 if the frame is flagged for automatic saving and restoration of position and dimensions; otherwise nil (1nil)

Lower

Reduces the frame's frame level below all other frames in its strata.

```
Frame:Lower()
```

Raise

Increases the frame's frame level above all other frames in its strata.

```
Frame:Raise()
```

RegisterAllEvents

Registers the frame for all events.

```
Frame:RegisterAllEvents()
```

This method is recommended for debugging purposes only, as using it will cause the frame's OnEvent script handler to be run very frequently for likely irrelevant events. (For code that needs to be run very frequently, use an OnUpdate script handler.)

RegisterEvent

Registers the frame for an event.

```
Frame:RegisterEvent("event")
```

The frame's OnEvent script handler will be run whenever the event fires. See the event documentation for details on event arguments.

Arguments:

event—Name of an event (string)

RegisterForDrag

Registers the frame for dragging.

```
Frame:RegisterForDrag(...)
```

Once the frame is registered for dragging (and mouse enabled), the frame's `OnDragStart` and `OnDragStop` scripts will be called when the specified mouse button(s) are clicked and dragged starting from within the frame (or its mouse-interactive area).

Arguments:

`. . .`—A list of strings, each the name of a mouse button for which the frame should respond to drag actions (`list`)

`Button4`	`MiddleButton`
`Button5`	`RightButton`
`LeftButton`	

SetAttribute

Sets a secure frame attribute.

```
Frame:SetAttribute("name", value)
```

See the secure template documentation for more information about frame attributes.

Arguments:

`name`—Name of an attribute, case insensitive (`string`)

`value`—New value to set for the attribute (`value`)

SetBackdrop

Sets a backdrop graphic for the frame.

```
Frame:SetBackdrop(backdrop)
```

See example for details of the backdrop table format.

Arguments:

`backdrop`—A table containing the backdrop settings, or `nil` to remove the frame's backdrop (`table`, backdrop)

Example:

```
local backdrop = {
  -- path to the background texture
  bgFile = "Interface\\DialogFrame\\UI-DialogBox-Gold-Background",
  -- path to the border texture
  edgeFile = "Interface\\DialogFrame\\UI-DialogBox-Gold-Border",
  -- true to repeat the background texture to fill the frame,
  -- false to scale it
  tile = true,
  -- size (width or height) of the square repeating background
  -- tiles (in pixels)
  tileSize = 32,
  -- thickness of edge segments and square size of edge corners
```

```
-- (in pixels)
edgeSize = 32,
-- distance from the edges of the frame to those of the background
-- texture (in pixels)
insets = {
 left = 11,
 right = 12,
 top = 12,
 bottom = 11
 }
}
```

```
-- replaces the game menu's backdrop with the gold backdrop
-- used in Bind-On-Pickup loot roll frames
GameMenuFrame:SetBackdrop(backdrop)
```

SetBackdropBorderColor

Sets a shading color for the frame's border graphic.

```
Frame:SetBackdropBorderColor(red, green, blue [, alpha])
```

As with `Texture:SetVertexColor()`, this color is a shading applied to the colors of the texture image; a color of `(1, 1, 1)` allows the image's original colors to show.

Arguments:

`red`—Red component of the color (0.0 - 1.0) (number)

`green`—Green component of the color (0.0 - 1.0) (number)

`blue`—Blue component of the color (0.0 - 1.0) (number)

`alpha` (optional)—Alpha (opacity) for the graphic (0.0 = fully transparent, 1.0 = fully opaque) (number)

SetBackdropColor

Sets a shading color for the frame's background graphic.

```
Frame:SetBackdropColor(red, green, blue [, alpha])
```

As with `Texture:SetVertexColor()`, this color is a shading applied to the colors of the texture image; a color of `(1, 1, 1)` allows the image's original colors to show.

Arguments:

`red`—Red component of the color (0.0 - 1.0) (number)

`green`—Green component of the color (0.0 - 1.0) (number)

`blue`—Blue component of the color (0.0 - 1.0) (number)

`alpha` (optional)—Alpha (opacity) for the graphic (0.0 = fully transparent, 1.0 = fully opaque) (number)

SetClampRectInsets

Sets offsets from the frame's edges used when limiting user movement or resizing of the frame.

```
Frame:SetClampRectInsets(left, right, top, bottom)
```

Note: despite the name of this method, the parameters are offsets along the normal axes—to inset the frame's clamping area from its edges, the left and bottom measurements should be positive and the right and top measurements should be negative.

Arguments:

left—Offset from the left edge of the frame to the left edge of its clamping area (in pixels) (number)

right—Offset from the right edge of the frame's clamping area to the right edge of the frame (in pixels) (number)

top—Offset from the top edge of the frame's clamping area to the top edge of the frame (in pixels) (number)

bottom—Offset from the bottom edge of the frame to the bottom edge of its clamping area (in pixels) (number)

Example:

```
-- creates a drag-movable frame which cannot be moved beyond↵
 the edges of the screen
CreateFrame("Frame","Test",UIParent)
Test:SetWidth(100)
Test:SetHeight(100)
Test:SetPoint("CENTER")
Test:EnableMouse(true)
Test:SetClampedToScreen(true)
Test:CreateTexture("TestBG")
TestBG:SetAllPoints()
TestBG:SetTexture(1,1,1,0.5)
Title=Test:CreateTitleRegion()
Title:SetAllPoints()

-- inset the clamping area, allowing the frame to be moved partially
-- offscreen by 50 pixels in any direction
Test:SetClampRectInsets(50,-50,-50,50)
-- outset the clamping area, allowing the frame to be moved↵
 no closer than 50 pixels to any edge of the screen
Test:SetClampRectInsets(-50,50,50,-50)
```

SetClampedToScreen

Sets whether the frame's boundaries should be limited to those of the screen.

```
Frame:SetClampedToScreen(enable)
```

Applies to user moving/resizing of the frame (via :StartMoving(), :StartSizing(), or title region); attempting to move or resize the frame beyond the edges of the screen will move/resize it no further than the edge of the screen closest to the mouse position. Does not apply to programmatically setting the frame's position or size.

Arguments:

enable—True to limit the frame's boundaries to those of the screen; false to allow the frame to be moved/resized without such limits (boolean)

SetDepth

Sets the 3D depth of the frame (for stereoscopic 3D configurations).

`Frame:SetDepth(depth)`

Arguments:

`depth`—Apparent 3D depth of this frame relative to that of its parent frame (`number`)

SetFrameLevel

Sets the level at which the frame is layered relative to others in its strata.

`Frame:SetFrameLevel(level)`

Frames with higher frame level are layered "in front of" frames with a lower frame level.

Arguments:

`level`—Layering level of the frame relative to others in its `frameStrata` (`number`)

SetFrameStrata

Sets the general layering strata of the frame.

`Frame:SetFrameStrata("strata")`

Where frame level provides fine control over the layering of frames, frame strata provides a coarser level of layering control: frames in a higher strata always appear "in front of" frames in lower strata regardless of frame level.

Arguments:

`strata`—Token identifying the strata in which the frame should be layered (`string`, frameStrata)

SetHitRectInsets

Sets the insets from the frame's edges which determine its mouse-interactable area.

`Frame:SetHitRectInsets(left, right, top, bottom)`

Arguments:

`left`—Distance from the left edge of the frame to the left edge of its mouse-interactive area (in pixels) (`number`)

`right`—Distance from the right edge of the frame to the right edge of its mouse-interactive area (in pixels) (`number`)

`top`—Distance from the top edge of the frame to the top edge of its mouse-interactive area (in pixels) (`number`)

`bottom`—Distance from the bottom edge of the frame to the bottom edge of its mouse-interactive area (in pixels) (`number`)

SetID

Sets a numeric identifier for the frame.

`Frame:SetID(id)`

Frame IDs have no effect on frame behavior, but can be a useful way to keep track of multiple similar frames, especially in cases where a list of frames is created from a template (such as for action buttons, loot slots, or lines in a FauxScrollFrame).

Arguments:

id—A numeric identifier for the frame (number)

SetMaxResize

Sets the maximum size of the frame for user resizing.

`Frame:SetMaxResize(maxWidth, maxHeight)`

Applies when resizing the frame with the mouse via `:StartSizing()`.

Arguments:

maxWidth—Maximum width of the frame (in pixels), or 0 for no limit (number)

maxHeight—Maximum height of the frame (in pixels), or 0 for no limit (number)

SetMinResize

Sets the minimum size of the frame for user resizing.

`Frame:SetMinResize(minWidth, minHeight)`

Applies when resizing the frame with the mouse via `:StartSizing()`.

Arguments:

minWidth—Minimum width of the frame (in pixels), or 0 for no limit (number)

minHeight—Minimum height of the frame (in pixels), or 0 for no limit (number)

SetMovable

Sets whether the frame can be moved by the user.

`Frame:SetMovable(enable)`

Enabling this property does not automatically implement behaviors allowing the frame to be dragged by the user—such behavior must be implemented in the frame's mouse script handlers. If this property is not enabled, `Frame:StartMoving()` causes a Lua error.

For simple automatic frame dragging behavior, see `Frame:CreateTitleRegion()`.

Arguments:

enable—True to allow the frame to be moved by the user; false to disable (boolean)

SetResizable

Sets whether the frame can be resized by the user.

`Frame:SetResizable(enable)`

Enabling this property does not automatically implement behaviors allowing the frame to be drag-resized by the user—such behavior must be implemented in the frame's mouse script handlers. If this property is not enabled, `Frame:StartSizing()` causes a Lua error.

Arguments:

enable—True to allow the frame to be resized by the user; `false` to disable (`boolean`)

SetScale

Sets the frame's scale factor.

```
Frame:SetScale(scale)
```

A frame's scale factor affects the size at which it appears on the screen relative to that of its parent. The entire interface may be scaled by changing `UIParent`'s scale factor (as can be done via the Use UI Scale setting in the default interface's Video Options panel).

Arguments:

scale—Scale factor for the frame relative to its parent (`number`)

Example:

```
-- creates three concentric squares colored red, green and blue
-- each is 100 pixels wide according to its own coordinate system
-- but the actual size of each is determined by its scale factor:
-- - the red square is about 50 pixels square, or 0.5x its normal
-- size (assuming UIParent's scale factor is 1)
-- - the green square is about 75 pixels square, or 1.5x the size
-- of the red square
-- - the blue square is about 19 pixels square, or 0.25x the size
-- of the green square
CreateFrame("Frame","Frame1", UIParent)
Frame1:SetWidth(100)
Frame1:SetHeight(100)
Frame1:SetPoint("CENTER")
Frame1:CreateTexture("Frame1BG")
Frame1BG:SetTexture(1,0,0,0.5)
Frame1BG:SetAllPoints()
Frame1:SetScale(0.5)

CreateFrame("Frame","Frame2", Frame1)
Frame2:SetWidth(100)
Frame2:SetHeight(100)
Frame2:SetPoint("CENTER")
Frame2:CreateTexture("Frame2BG")
Frame2BG:SetTexture(0,1,0,0.5)
Frame2BG:SetAllPoints()
Frame2:SetScale(1.5)

CreateFrame("Frame","Frame3", Frame2)
Frame3:SetWidth(100)
Frame3:SetHeight(100)
Frame3:SetPoint("CENTER")
Frame3:CreateTexture("Frame3BG")
Frame3BG:SetTexture(0,0,1,0.5)
Frame3BG:SetAllPoints()
Frame3:SetScale(0.25)
```

SetToplevel

Sets whether the frame should automatically come to the front when clicked.

```
Frame:SetToplevel(enable)
```

When a frame with `Toplevel` behavior enabled is clicked, it automatically changes its frame level such that it is greater than (and therefore drawn "in front of") all other frames in its strata.

Arguments:

enable—`True` to cause the frame to automatically come to the front when clicked; `false` otherwise (`boolean`)

SetUserPlaced

Flags the frame for automatic saving and restoration of position and dimensions.

```
Frame:SetUserPlaced(enable)
```

The position and size of frames so flagged is automatically saved when the UI is shut down (as when quitting, logging out, or reloading) and restored when the UI next starts up (as when logging in or reloading). As implied by its name, enabling this property is useful for frames which can be moved or resized by the user.

Arguments:

enable—`True` to enable automatic saving and restoration of the frame's position and dimensions; `false` to disable (`boolean`)

StartMoving

Begins repositioning the frame via mouse movement.

```
Frame:StartMoving()
```

StartSizing

Begins resizing the frame via mouse movement.

```
Frame:StartSizing()
```

StopMovingOrSizing

Ends movement or resizing of the frame initiated with `:StartMoving()` or `:StartSizing()`.

```
Frame:StopMovingOrSizing()
```

UnregisterAllEvents

Unregisters the frame from any events for which it is registered.

```
Frame:UnregisterAllEvents()
```

UnregisterEvent

Unregisters the frame for an event.

```
Frame:UnregisterEvent("event")
```

Once unregistered, the frame's `OnEvent` script handler will not be called for that event.

Unregistering from notifications for an event can be useful for improving addon performance at times when it's not necessary to process the event. For example, a frame which monitors target health does not need to receive the UNIT_HEALTH event while the player has no target. An addon that sorts the contents of the player's bags can register for the BAG_UPDATE event to keep track of when items are picked up, but unregister from the event while it performs its sorting.

Arguments:

event—Name of an event (string)

Button

Of all the various subtypes of Frame in the user interface system, Buttons are the most visible, since users interact with them frequently during gameplay. They are the primary means by which the user controls the game and their characters.

Buttons have an intrinsic FontString built-in, so they support both the SetText and the GetText methods. In addition, a button has three special visual states that can be decorated independently: one when the button is disabled, one when the button has been pushed but not yet released, and one when the mouse is over the button. The changes to the button's presentation happen automatically based on the button's definition.

The most important aspect of a Button is the fact that it can be clicked by the user. When a button is clicked the PreClick script handler will fire, followed by the OnClick handler, and finally the PostClick handler. These allow an addon developer lots of flexibility when creating an addon, especially in the presence of the secure environment and tainting system introduced in WoW 2.0.

To create a button, call CreateFrame with "Button" as the first argument, or construct one in an XML file with a <Button> element. Some handy templates for this include UIPanelButtonTemplate (which provides a standard red button), UIPanelCloseButton (a small red square with a yellow X in it) and SecureHandlerClickTemplate.

The most famous Buttons are probably unit frames, which make use of the SecureActionButtonTemplate (or its derivative, SecureUnitButtonTemplate) to control targeting and sometimes spell-casting. There are many insecure buttons as well (or more accurately, buttons which do not require security), such as the micro buttons on the action bar for opening various panels and menus, or the buttons around the minimap for revealing the calendar or displaying the world map.

Button has all the methods from Frame, plus the following:

Click

Performs a (virtual) mouse click on the button.

```
Button:Click("button", down)
```

Causes any of the button's mouse click-related scripts to be run as if the button were clicked by the user.

Calling this method can result in an error if the button inherits from a secure frame template and performs protected actions.

Arguments:

button—Name of the mouse button for the click action (string)

Button4	MiddleButton
Button5	RightButton
LeftButton	

down—True for a "mouse down" click action, false for "mouse up" or other click actions (boolean)

Disable

Disallows user interaction with the button.

```
Button:Disable()
```

Automatically changes the visual state of the button if its DisabledTexture, DisabledTextColor or DisabledFontObject are set.

Enable

Allows user interaction with the button.

```
Button:Enable()
```

If a disabled appearance was specified for the button, automatically returns the button to its normal appearance.

GetButtonState

Returns the button's current state.

```
state = Button:GetButtonState()
```

Returns:

state—State of the button (string)

- DISABLED - Button is disabled and cannot receive user input
- NORMAL - Button is in its normal state
- PUSHED - Button is pushed (as during a click on the button)

GetDisabledFontObject

Returns the font object used for the button's disabled state.

```
font = Button:GetDisabledFontObject()
```

Returns:

font—Reference to the Font object used when the button is disabled (font)

GetDisabledTexture

Returns the texture used when the button is disabled.

```
texture = Button:GetDisabledTexture()
```

Returns:

texture—Reference to the Texture object used when the button is disabled (texture)

GetFontString

Returns the `FontString` object used for the button's label text.

```
fontstring = Button:GetFontString()
```

Returns:

`fontstring`—Reference to the `FontString` object used for the button's label text (`fontstring`)

GetHighlightFontObject

Returns the font object used when the button is highlighted.

```
font = Button:GetHighlightFontObject()
```

Returns:

`font`—Reference to the `Font` object used when the button is highlighted (`font`)

GetHighlightTexture

Returns the texture used when the button is highlighted.

```
texture = Button:GetHighlightTexture()
```

Returns:

`texture`—Reference to the `Texture` object used when the button is highlighted (`texture`)

GetNormalFontObject

Returns the font object used for the button's normal state.

```
font = Button:GetNormalFontObject()
```

Returns:

`font`—Reference to the `Font` object used for the button's normal state (`font`)

GetNormalTexture

Returns the texture used for the button's normal state.

```
texture = Button:GetNormalTexture()
```

Returns:

`texture`—Reference to the `Texture` object used for the button's normal state (`texture`)

GetPushedTextOffset

Returns the offset for moving the button's label text when pushed.

```
x, y = Button:GetPushedTextOffset()
```

Returns:

`x`—Horizontal offset for the text (in pixels; values increasing to the right) (`number`)

`y`—Vertical offset for the text (in pixels; values increasing upward) (`number`)

GetPushedTexture

Returns the texture used when the button is pushed.

```
texture = Button:GetPushedTexture()
```

Returns:

texture—Reference to the Texture object used when the button is pushed (texture)

GetText

Returns the text of the button's label.

```
text = Button:GetText()
```

Returns:

text—Text of the button's label (string)

GetTextHeight

Returns the height of the button's text label.

```
height = Button:GetTextHeight()
```

Reflects the height of the rendered text (which increases if the text wraps onto two lines), not the point size of the text's font.

Returns:

height—Height of the button's text (in pixels) (number)

GetTextWidth

Returns the width of the button's text label.

```
width = Button:GetTextWidth()
```

Returns:

width—Width of the button's text (in pixels) (number)

IsEnabled

Returns whether user interaction with the button is allowed.

```
enabled = Button:IsEnabled()
```

Returns:

enabled—1 if user interaction with the button is allowed; otherwise nil (1nil)

LockHighlight

Locks the button in its highlight state.

```
Button:LockHighlight()
```

When the highlight state is locked, the button will always appear highlighted regardless of whether it is moused over.

RegisterForClicks

Registers a button to receive mouse clicks.

```
Button:RegisterForClicks(...)
```

Arguments:

...—A list of strings, each the combination of a button name and click action for which the button's click-related script handlers should be run. Possible values: (list)

Button4Down	LeftButtonDown	RightButtonDown
Button4Up	LeftButtonUp	RightButtonUp
Button5Down	MiddleButtonDown	AnyDown
Button5Up	MiddleButtonUp	AnyUp

`AnyDown` and `AnyUp` respond to the down or up action of any mouse button.

SetButtonState

Sets the button's state.

`Button:SetButtonState("state", lock)`

Arguments:

`state`—State for the button (`string`)

- `DISABLED` - Button is disabled and cannot receive user input
- `NORMAL` - Button is in its normal state
- `PUSHED` - Button is pushed (as during a click on the button)

`lock`—Locks the button in the given state; e.g. if `NORMAL`, the button cannot be clicked but remains in the `NORMAL` state (`boolean`)

SetDisabledFontObject

Sets the font object used for the button's disabled state.

`Button:SetDisabledFontObject(font)`

Arguments:

`font`—Reference to a `Font` object to be used when the button is disabled (`font`)

SetDisabledTexture

Sets the texture used when the button is disabled.

`Button:SetDisabledTexture(texture) or ↵`
`Button:SetDisabledTexture("filename")`

Arguments:

`texture`—Reference to an existing `Texture` object (`texture`)

`filename`—Path to a texture image file (`string`)

SetFontString

Sets the `FontString` object used for the button's label text.

`Button:SetFontString(fontstring)`

Arguments:

`fontstring`—Reference to a `FontString` object to be used for the button's label text (`fontstring`)

SetFormattedText

Sets the button's label text using format specifiers.

`Button:SetFormattedText("formatString", ...)`

Equivalent to `:SetText(format(format, ...))`, but does not create a throwaway Lua string object, resulting in greater memory-usage efficiency.

Arguments:

formatString—A string containing format specifiers (as with string.format()) (string)

...—A list of values to be included in the formatted string (list)

SetHighlightFontObject

Sets the font object used when the button is highlighted.

```
Button:SetHighlightFontObject(font)
```

Arguments:

font—Reference to a Font object to be used when the button is highlighted (font)

SetHighlightTexture

Sets the texture used when the button is highlighted.

```
Button:SetHighlightTexture(texture [, "mode"]) or ↵
Button:SetHighlightTexture("filename" [, "mode"])
```

Unlike the other button textures for which only one is visible at a time, the button's highlight texture is drawn on top of its existing (normal or pushed) texture; thus, this method also allows specification of the texture's blend mode.

Arguments:

texture—Reference to an existing Texture object (texture)

filename—Path to a texture image file (string)

mode (optional)—Blend mode for the texture; defaults to ADD if omitted (string)

- ADD - Adds texture color values to the underlying color values, using the alpha channel; light areas in the texture lighten the background while dark areas are more transparent
- ALPHAKEY - One-bit transparency; pixels with alpha values greater than ~0.8 are treated as fully opaque and all other pixels are treated as fully transparent
- BLEND - Normal color blending, using any alpha channel in the texture image
- DISABLE - Ignores any alpha channel, displaying the texture as fully opaque
- MOD - Ignores any alpha channel in the texture and multiplies texture color values by background color values; dark areas in the texture darken the background while light areas are more transparent

SetNormalFontObject

Sets the font object used for the button's normal state.

```
Button:SetNormalFontObject(font)
```

Arguments:

font—Reference to a Font object to be used in the button's normal state (font)

SetNormalTexture

Sets the texture used for the button's normal state.

`Button:SetNormalTexture(texture)` or `Button:SetNormalTexture ("filename")`

Arguments:

`texture`—Reference to an existing `Texture` object (`texture`)

`filename`—Path to a texture image file (`string`)

SetPushedTextOffset

Sets the offset for moving the button's label text when pushed.

`Button:SetPushedTextOffset(x, y)`

Moving the button's text while it is being clicked can provide an illusion of 3D depth for the button–in the default UI's standard button templates, this offset matches the apparent movement seen in the difference between the buttons' normal and pushed textures.

Arguments:

`x`—Horizontal offset for the text (in pixels; values increasing to the right) (`number`)

`y`—Vertical offset for the text (in pixels; values increasing upward) (`number`)

SetPushedTexture

Sets the texture used when the button is pushed.

`Button:SetPushedTexture(texture)` or `Button:SetPushedTexture ("filename")`

Arguments:

`texture`—Reference to an existing `Texture` object (`texture`)

`filename`—Path to a texture image file (`string`)

SetText

Sets the text displayed as the button's label.

`Button:SetText("text")`

Arguments:

`text`—Text to be displayed as the button's label (`string`)

UnlockHighlight

Unlocks the button's highlight state.

`Button:UnlockHighlight()`

Can be used after a call to `:LockHighlight()` to restore the button's normal mouseover behavior.

CheckButton

CheckButtons are a specialized form of Button; they maintain an on/off state, which toggles automatically when they are clicked, and additional textures for when they are checked, or checked while disabled. A CheckButton's checked status can also be checked or set directly from Lua with `:GetChecked()` and `:SetChecked()`. Check-Buttons do not need to look like checkboxes; the configurable checked textures allow you to create whatever appearance is suitable for a button that needs a persistent state.

While CheckButtons are particularly prevalent throughout the Interface Options UI, they are also found in places like the crafting UI (to restrict display of known recipes to those for which the materials are available). The most frequently used CheckButtons, however, are the action buttons on your action bars. They use the checked state to display a yellow border around spells or actions that are currently in progress, and include update code to adjust the checked state appropriately.

Although CheckButtons inherit the Button type's `:SetText()` and `:GetText()` methods, most CheckButtons templates are not set up to display their labels in this way. Instead, they include a FontString with the name $parentText, so that you set their text with `_G[button:GetName().."Text"]:SetText(newLabel)`.

Some convenient CheckButton templates include UICheckButtonTemplate (the conventional general-purpose check button), InterfaceOptionsCheckButtonTemplate (for use with Interface Options panels) and ActionBarButtonTemplate.

CheckButton has all the methods from Button, plus the following:

GetChecked

Returns whether the check button is checked.

```
enabled = CheckButton:GetChecked()
```

Returns:

enabled—1 if the button is checked; `nil` if the button is unchecked (1nil)

GetCheckedTexture

Returns the texture used when the button is checked.

```
texture = CheckButton:GetCheckedTexture()
```

Returns:

texture—Reference to the `Texture` object used when the button is checked (texture)

GetDisabledCheckedTexture

Returns the texture used when the button is disabled and checked.

```
texture = CheckButton:GetDisabledCheckedTexture()
```

Returns:

texture—Reference to the `Texture` object used when the button is disabled and checked (texture)

SetChecked

Sets whether the check button is checked.

```
CheckButton:SetChecked(enable)
```

Arguments:

enable—True to check the button; `false` to uncheck (boolean)

SetCheckedTexture

Sets the texture used when the button is checked.

```
CheckButton:SetCheckedTexture(texture) or ↵
CheckButton:SetCheckedTexture("filename")
```

Arguments:

texture—Reference to an existing Texture object (texture)

filename—Path to a texture image file (string)

SetDisabledCheckedTexture

Sets the texture used when the button is disabled and checked.

```
CheckButton:SetDisabledCheckedTexture(texture) or ↵
CheckButton:SetDisabledCheckedTexture("filename")
```

Arguments:

texture—Reference to an existing Texture object (texture)

filename—Path to a texture image file (string)

ColorSelect

ColorSelect is a very specialized type of frame with a specific purpose; to allow the user to interactively select a color, typically to control the appearance of another UI element. Primarily used to allow the player to control the appearance of chat messages in different channels, they are also used when creating a tabard to control the color scheme.

While the ColorSelect type gives you fairly detailed control over the appearance of the color wheel and value slider, the standard Color picker frame as defined in FrameXML/ColorPickerFrame.xml is preconfigured and usually adequate to your needs. You will usually be most interested in the SetColor methods (to load a color you have stored for a particular element) and the GetColor methods (to retrieve the new color chosen by the user). ColorSelect supports both RGB and HSV color descriptions.

ColorSelect has all the methods from Frame, plus the following:

GetColorHSV

Returns the hue, saturation and value of the currently selected color.

```
hue, saturation, value = ColorSelect:GetColorHSV()
```

Returns: .

hue—Hue of the selected color (angle on the color wheel in degrees; 0 = red, increasing counter-clockwise) (number)

saturation—Saturation of the selected color (0.0 - 1.0) (number)

value—Value of the selected color (0.0 - 1.0) (number)

GetColorRGB

Returns the red, green and blue components of the currently selected color.

```
red, blue, green = ColorSelect:GetColorRGB()
```

Returns:

red—Red component of the color (0.0 - 1.0) (number)

blue—Blue component of the color (0.0 - 1.0) (number)

green—Green component of the color (0.0 - 1.0) (number)

GetColorValueTexture

Returns the texture for the color picker's value slider background.

```
texture = ColorSelect:GetColorValueTexture()
```

The color picker's value slider displays a value gradient (and allows control of the color's value component) for whichever hue and saturation is selected in the color wheel. (In the default UI's ColorPickerFrame, this part is found to the right of the color wheel.)

Returns:

texture—Reference to the `Texture` object used for drawing the value slider background (`texture`)

GetColorValueThumbTexture

Returns the texture for the color picker's value slider thumb.

```
texture = ColorSelect:GetColorValueThumbTexture()
```

The color picker's value slider displays a value gradient (and allows control of the color's value component) for whichever hue and saturation is selected in the color wheel. (In the default UI's ColorPickerFrame, this part is found to the right of the color wheel.) The thumb texture is the movable part indicating the current value selection.

Returns:

texture—Reference to the `Texture` object used for drawing the slider thumb (`texture`)

GetColorWheelTexture

Returns the texture for the color picker's hue/saturation wheel.

```
texture = ColorSelect:GetColorWheelTexture()
```

Returns:

texture—Reference to the `Texture` object used for drawing the hue/saturation wheel (`texture`)

GetColorWheelThumbTexture

Returns the texture for the selection indicator on the color picker's hue/saturation wheel.

```
texture = ColorSelect:GetColorWheelThumbTexture()
```

Returns:

texture—Reference to the `Texture` object used for drawing the hue/saturation wheel's selection indicator (`texture`)

SetColorHSV

Sets the color picker's selected color by hue, saturation and value.

```
ColorSelect:SetColorHSV(hue, saturation, value)
```

Arguments:

hue—Hue of a color (angle on the color wheel in degrees; 0 = red, increasing counter-clockwise) (`number`)

saturation—Saturation of a color (0.0 - 1.0) (`number`)

value—Value of a color (0.0 - 1.0) (`number`)

SetColorRGB

Sets the color picker's selected color by red, green and blue components.

```
ColorSelect:SetColorRGB(red, blue, green)
```

Arguments:

red—Red component of the color (0.0 - 1.0) (number)

blue—Blue component of the color (0.0 - 1.0) (number)

green—Green component of the color (0.0 - 1.0) (number)

SetColorValueTexture

Sets the Texture object used to display the color picker's value slider.

```
ColorSelect:SetColorValueTexture(texture)
```

The color picker's value slider displays a value gradient (and allows control of the color's value component) for whichever hue and saturation is selected in the color wheel. In the default UI's ColorPickerFrame, this part is found to the right of the color wheel.

This method does not allow changing the texture image displayed for the slider background; rather, it allows customization of the size and placement of the Texture object into which the game engine draws the color value gradient.

Arguments:

texture—Reference to a Texture object (texture)

SetColorValueThumbTexture

Sets the texture for the color picker's value slider thumb.

```
ColorSelect:SetColorValueThumbTexture(texture) or ↵
ColorSelect:SetColorValueThumbTexture("filename")
```

The color picker's value slider displays a value gradient (and allows control of the color's value component) for whichever hue and saturation is selected in the color wheel. (In the default UI's ColorPickerFrame, this part is found to the right of the color wheel.) The thumb texture is the movable part indicating the current value selection.

Arguments:

texture—Reference to an existing Texture object (texture)

filename—Path to a texture image file (string)

SetColorWheelTexture

Sets the Texture object used to display the color picker's hue/saturation wheel.

```
ColorSelect:SetColorWheelTexture(texture)
```

This method does not allow changing the texture image displayed for the color wheel; rather, it allows customization of the size and placement of the Texture object into which the game engine draws the standard color wheel image.

Arguments:

texture—Reference to a `Texture` object (`texture`)

SetColorWheelThumbTexture

Sets the texture for the selection indicator on the color picker's hue/saturation wheel.

```
ColorSelect:SetColorWheelThumbTexture(texture) or ⏎
ColorSelect:SetColorWheelThumbTexture("filename")
```

Arguments:

texture—Reference to an existing `Texture` object (`texture`)

filename—Path to a texture image file (`string`)

Cooldown

Cooldown is a specialized variety of Frame that displays the little "clock" effect over abilities and buffs. It can be set with its running time, whether it should appear to "fill up" or "empty out", and whether or not there should be a bright edge where it's changing between dim and bright.

Cooldowns are usually children of another frame, and typically set to cover the same area as that frame, or almost all of it. In the stock UI, they are used mostly to display cooldowns on action buttons and buffs or debuffs on targets.

Cooldown has all the methods from Frame, plus the following:

GetDrawEdge

Returns whether a bright line should be drawn on the moving edge of the cooldown animation.

```
enabled = Cooldown:GetDrawEdge()
```

Returns:

enabled—1 if a bright line should be drawn on the moving edge of the cooldown "sweep" animation; otherwise `nil` (1nil)

GetReverse

Returns whether the bright and dark portions of the cooldown animation should be inverted.

```
enabled = Cooldown:GetReverse()
```

Returns:

enabled—1 if the cooldown animation "sweeps" an area of darkness over the underlying image; `nil` if the animation darkens the underlying image and "sweeps" the darkened area away (1nil)

SetCooldown

Sets up the parameters for a Cooldown model.

```
Cooldown:SetCooldown(start, duration)
```

Note: Most `Cooldown` animations in the default UI are managed via the function `CooldownFrame_SetTimer(self, start, duration, enable)`, a wrapper for this method which automatically shows the `Cooldown` element while animating and hides it otherwise.

Arguments:

`start`—Value of `GetTime()` at the start of the cooldown animation (number)

`duration`—Duration of the cooldown animation (excluding that of the final "flash" animation) (number)

Example:

```
-- creates a Cooldown object over the player portrait
CreateFrame("Cooldown","PlayerCooldown",PlayerFrame)
PlayerCooldown:SetAllPoints(PlayerPortrait)

-- performs a complete cooldown "sweep" animation over 10 seconds
PlayerCooldown:SetCooldown(GetTime(),10)

-- performs the same animation, starting halfway in (5 seconds)
PlayerCooldown:SetCooldown(GetTime() - 5,10)

-- performs only the "flash" animation normally seen at the end
-- of a cooldown
PlayerCooldown:SetCooldown(0,0)
```

SetDrawEdge

Sets whether a bright line should be drawn on the moving edge of the cooldown animation.

```
Cooldown:SetDrawEdge(enable)
```

Does not change the appearance of a currently running cooldown animation; only affects future runs of the animation.

Arguments:

`enable`—True to cause a bright line to be drawn on the moving edge of the cooldown "sweep" animation; `false` for the default behavior (no line drawn) (boolean)

SetReverse

Sets whether to invert the bright and dark portions of the cooldown animation.

```
Cooldown:SetReverse(reverse)
```

Arguments:

`reverse`—True for an animation "sweeping" an area of darkness over the underlying image; `false` for the default animation of darkening the underlying image and "sweeping" the darkened area away (boolean)

GameTooltip

GameTooltips are used to display explanatory information relevant to a particular element of the game world. They offer almost innumerable methods for setting the specific object, creature or ability the tooltip should describe, and a smaller number of methods for querying what it is that the tooltip is currently describing.

GameTooltips are sufficiently complicated that an entire chapter is dedicated to describing them. In addition to methods for setting their contents, they also support options controlling their positioning and visibility on screen, as well as methods to facilitate adding more text to them (for instance, an addon that displays, in the tooltip for a soul shard created by a warlock, the name of the player or monster from which the shard was collected).

While most of the heavy lifting is done by the frame called simply GameTooltip, there is also one called ItemRefTooltip that does the work of displaying information about items linked in chat when they are clicked.

GameTooltip has all the methods from Frame, plus the following:

AddDoubleLine

Adds a line to the tooltip with both left-side and right-side portions.

```
GameTooltip:AddDoubleLine("textLeft", "textRight" ↵
[, rL [, gL [, bL [, rR [, gR [, bR]]]]]])
```

The tooltip is not automatically resized to fit the added line; to do so, call the tooltip's :Show() method after adding lines.

Arguments:

textLeft—Text to be displayed on the left side of the new line (string)

textRight—Text to be displayed on the right side of the new line (string)

rL (optional)—Red component of the color for the left-side text (0.0 - 1.0) (number)

gL (optional)—Green component of the color for the left-side text (0.0 - 1.0) (number)

bL (optional)—Blue component of the color for the left-side text (0.0 - 1.0) (number)

rR (optional)—Red component of the color for the right-side text (0.0 - 1.0) (number)

gR (optional)—Green component of the color for the right-side text (0.0 - 1.0) (number)

bR (optional)—Blue component of the color for the right-side text (0.0 - 1.0) (number)

AddFontStrings

Adds FontString objects to the tooltip, allowing it to display an additional line of text.

```
GameTooltip:AddFontStrings(left, right)
```

This method is of little utility outside of Blizzard scripts, as the tooltip automatically creates new font strings for additional lines as needed.

Arguments:

left—Reference to a FontString object for the left-side text of a new line (fontstring) `right`—Reference to a `FontString` object for the right-side text of a new line (`fontstring`)

AddLine

Adds a line of text to the tooltip.

```
GameTooltip:AddLine("text" [, r [, g [, b [, wrap]]]])
```

The tooltip is not automatically resized to fit the added line (and wrap it, if applicable); to do so, call the tooltip's `:Show()` method after adding lines.

Arguments:

`text`—Text to be added as a new line in the tooltip (`string`)

`r` (optional)—Red component of the text color (0.0 - 1.0) (`number`)

`g` (optional)—Green component of the text color (0.0 - 1.0) (`number`)

`b` (optional)—Blue component of the text color (0.0 - 1.0) (`number`)

`wrap` (optional)—`True` to cause the line to wrap if it is longer than other, non-wrapping lines in the tooltip or longer than the tooltip's forced width (`boolean`)

AddTexture

Adds a texture to the last tooltip line.

```
GameTooltip:AddTexture("texture")
```

The texture is sized to match the height of the line's text and positioned to the left of the text (indenting the text to provide room).

Arguments:

`texture`—Path to a texture image file (`string`)

AppendText

Adds text to the first line of the tooltip.

```
GameTooltip:AppendText("text")
```

Arguments:

`text`—Text to be appended to the tooltip's first line (`string`)

ClearLines

Clears the tooltip's contents.

```
GameTooltip:ClearLines()
```

Scripts scanning the tooltip contents should be aware that this method clears the text of all the tooltip's left-side font strings but hides the right-side font strings without clearing their text.

FadeOut

Causes the tooltip to begin fading out.

```
GameTooltip:FadeOut()
```

GetAnchorType

Returns the method for anchoring the tooltip relative to its owner.

```
anchor = GameTooltip:GetAnchorType()
```

Returns:

anchor—Token identifying the method for anchoring the tooltip relative to its owner frame (string)

- ANCHOR_BOTTOMLEFT - Align the top right of the tooltip with the bottom left of the owner
- ANCHOR_CURSOR - Tooltip follows the mouse cursor
- ANCHOR_LEFT - Align the bottom right of the tooltip with the top left of the owner
- ANCHOR_NONE - Tooltip appears in the default position
- ANCHOR_PRESERVE - Tooltip's position is saved between sessions (useful if the tooltip is made user-movable)
- ANCHOR_RIGHT - Align the bottom left of the tooltip with the top right of the owner
- ANCHOR_TOPLEFT - Align the bottom left of the tooltip with the top left of the owner
- ANCHOR_TOPRIGHT - Align the bottom right of the tooltip with the top right of the owner

GetItem

Returns the name and hyperlink for the item displayed in the tooltip.

```
name, link = GameTooltip:GetItem()
```

Returns:

name—Name of the item whose information is displayed in the tooltip, or nil. (string)

link—A hyperlink for the item (string, hyperlink)

GetMinimumWidth

Returns the minimum width of the tooltip.

```
width = GameTooltip:GetMinimumWidth()
```

Returns:

width—Minimum width of the tooltip frame (in pixels) (number)

GetOwner

Returns the frame to which the tooltip refers and is anchored.

```
owner = GameTooltip:GetOwner()
```

Returns:

owner—Reference to the Frame object to which the tooltip is anchored (frame)

GetPadding

Returns the amount of space between tooltip's text and its right-side edge.

```
padding = GameTooltip:GetPadding()
```

Returns:

padding—Amount of space between the right-side edge of the tooltip's text and the right-side edge of the tooltip frame (in pixels) (number)

GetSpell

Returns information about the spell displayed in the tooltip.

`spellName, spellRank, spellID = GameTooltip:GetSpell()`

Returns:

`spellName`—Name of the spell, or `nil` if the information in the tooltip is not for a spell. (string)

`spellRank`—Secondary text associated with the spell name (often a rank, e.g. `"Rank 8"`) (string)

`spellID`—Numeric identifier for the spell and rank (number, spellID)

GetUnit

Returns information about the unit displayed in the tooltip.

`name, unit = GameTooltip:GetUnit()`

Returns:

`name`—Name of the unit displayed in the tooltip, or `nil` (string)

`unit`—Unit identifier of the unit, or `nil` if the unit cannot be referenced by a `unitID` (string, unitID)

IsEquippedItem

Returns whether the tooltip is displaying an item currently equipped by the player.

`enabled = GameTooltip:IsEquippedItem()`

Returns:

`enabled`—1 if the tooltip is displaying information about an item currently equipped by the player; otherwise `nil` (1nil)

IsOwned

Returns whether the tooltip has an owner frame.

`hasOwner = GameTooltip:IsOwned()`

Returns:

`hasOwner`—1 if the tooltip has an owner frame; otherwise `nil` (1nil)

IsUnit

Returns whether the tooltip is displaying information for a given unit.

`isUnit = GameTooltip:IsUnit("unit")`

Arguments:

`unit`—A unit to query (string, unitID)

Returns:

`isUnit`—1 if the tooltip is displaying information for the unit; otherwise `nil` (1nil)

NumLines

Returns the number of lines of text currently shown in the tooltip.

`numLines = GameTooltip:NumLines()`

Returns:

`numLines`—Number of lines currently shown in the tooltip (number)

SetAction

Fills the tooltip with information about the contents of an action slot.

```
GameTooltip:SetAction(slot)
```

Arguments:

slot—An action bar slot (number, actionID)

SetAnchorType

Sets the method for anchoring the tooltip relative to its owner.

```
GameTooltip:SetAnchorType("anchor" [, xOffset [, yOffset]])
```

Arguments:

anchor—Token identifying the positioning method for the tooltip relative to its owner frame (string)

- ANCHOR_BOTTOMLEFT - Align the top right of the tooltip with the bottom left of the owner
- ANCHOR_CURSOR - Tooltip follows the mouse cursor
- ANCHOR_LEFT - Align the bottom right of the tooltip with the top left of the owner
- ANCHOR_NONE - Tooltip appears in the default position
- ANCHOR_PRESERVE - Tooltip's position is saved between sessions (useful if the tooltip is made user-movable)
- ANCHOR_RIGHT - Align the bottom left of the tooltip with the top right of the owner
- ANCHOR_TOPLEFT - Align the bottom left of the tooltip with the top left of the owner
- ANCHOR_TOPRIGHT - Align the bottom right of the tooltip with the top right of the owner

xOffset (optional)—Horizontal distance from the anchor to the tooltip (number)

yOffset (optional)—Vertical distance from the anchor to the tooltip (number)

SetAuctionItem

Fills the tooltip with information about an item in the auction house.

```
GameTooltip:SetAuctionItem("list", index)
```

Arguments:

list—Type of auction listing (string, ah-list-type)

- bidder - Auctions the player has bid on
- list - Auctions the player can browse and bid on or buy out
- owner - Auctions the player placed

index—Index of an auction in the listing (number)

SetAuctionSellItem

Fills the tooltip with information about the item currently being set up for auction.

```
GameTooltip:SetAuctionSellItem()
```

SetBackpackToken

Fills the tooltip with information about a currency marked for watching on the Backpack UI.

```
GameTooltip:SetBackpackToken(index)
```
Arguments:

index—Index of a 'slot' for displaying currencies on the backpack (between 1 and MAX_WATCHED_TOKENS) (number)

SetBagItem

Fills the tooltip with information about an item in the player's bags.

```
hasCooldown, repairCost = GameTooltip:SetBagItem(container, slot)
```
Arguments:

container—Index of one of the player's bags or other containers (number, containerID)

slot—Index of an item slot within the container (number, containerSlotID)

Returns:

hasCooldown—1 if the item is currently on cooldown, otherwise nil (number, 1nil)

repairCost—Cost of repairing the item (in copper, ignoring faction discounts) (number)

SetBuybackItem

Fills the tooltip with information about item recently sold to a vendor and available to be repurchased.

```
GameTooltip:SetBuybackItem(index)
```
Arguments:

index—Index of an item in the buyback listing (between 1 and GetNumBuybackItems()) (number)

SetCurrencyToken

Fills the tooltip with information about a special currency type.

```
GameTooltip:SetCurrencyToken(index)
```
Arguments:

index—Index of a currency type in the currency list (between 1 and GetCurrencyListSize()) (number)

SetEquipmentSet

Fills the tooltip with information about an equipment set.

```
GameTooltip:SetEquipmentSet("name")
```
Arguments:

name—Name of the equipment set (string)

SetExistingSocketGem

Fills the tooltip with information about a permanently socketed gem.

```
GameTooltip:SetExistingSocketGem(index, toDestroy)
```

Arguments:

index—Index of a gem socket (between 1 and GetNumSockets()) (number)

toDestroy—True to alter the tooltip display to indicate that this gem will be destroyed by socketing a new gem; false to show the normal tooltip for the gem (boolean)

SetFrameStack

Fills the tooltip with a list of frames under the mouse cursor.

GameTooltip:SetFrameStack(includeHidden)

Not relevant outside of addon development and debugging.

Arguments:

includeHidden—True to include hidden frames in the list; false to list only visible frames (boolean)

SetGlyph

Fills the tooltip with information about one of the player's glyphs.

GameTooltip:SetGlyph(socket, talentGroup)

Arguments:

socket—Which socket's glyph to display (between 1 and NUM_GLYPH_SLOTS) (number, glyphIndex)

talentGroup—Which set of glyphs to display, if the player has Dual Talent Specialization enabled (number)

- 1 - Primary Talents
- 2 - Secondary Talents
- nil - Currently active talents

SetGuildBankItem

Fills the tooltip with information about an item in the guild bank.

GameTooltip:SetGuildBankItem(tab, slot)

Information is only available if the guild bank tab has been opened in the current play session.

Arguments:

tab—Index of a guild bank tab (between 1 and GetNumGuildBank Tabs()) (number)

slot—Index of an item slot in the guild bank tab (between 1 and MAX_GUILDBANK_SLOTS_PER_TAB) (number)

SetHyperlink

Fills the tooltip with information about an item, quest, spell, or other entity represented by a hyperlink.

GameTooltip:SetHyperlink("hyperlink")

Arguments:

hyperlink—A full hyperlink, or the linktype:linkdata portion thereof (string, hyperlink)

SetHyperlinkCompareItem

Fills the tooltip with information about the item currently equipped in the slot used for the supplied item.

```
success = GameTooltip:SetHyperlinkCompareItem("hyperlink" [, index])
```

Arguments:

hyperlink—A full hyperlink, or the `linktype:linkdata` portion thereof, for an item to compare against the player's equipped similar item (string, hyperlink)

index (optional)—Index of the slot to compare against (1, 2, or 3), if more than one item of the equipment type can be equipped at once (e.g. rings and trinkets) (number)

Returns:

success—1 if an item's information was loaded into the tooltip; otherwise nil (number, 1nil)

SetInboxItem

Fills the tooltip with information about an item attached to a message in the player's inbox.

```
GameTooltip:SetInboxItem(mailID, attachmentIndex)
```

Arguments:

mailID—Index of a message in the player's inbox (between 1 and `GetInboxNumItems()`) (number)

attachmentIndex—Index of an attachment to the message (between 1 and `select(8,GetInboxHeaderInfo(mailID))`) (number)

SetInventoryItem

Fills the tooltip with information about an equipped item.

```
hasItem, hasCooldown, repairCost = ↵
GameTooltip:SetInventoryItem("unit", slot [, nameOnly])
```

Arguments:

unit—A unit to query; only valid for 'player' or the unit currently being inspected (string, unitID)

slot—An inventory slot number, as can be obtained from `GetInventorySlotInfo` (number, inventoryID)

nameOnly (optional)—True to omit much of the item's information (stat bonuses, sockets and binding) from the tooltip; false to show all of the item's information (boolean)

Returns:

hasItem—1 if the unit has an item in the given slot; otherwise nil (number, 1nil)

hasCooldown—1 if the item is currently on cooldown; otherwise nil (number, 1nil)

repairCost—Cost to repair the item (in copper, ignoring faction discounts) (number)

SetLootItem

Fills the tooltip with information about an item available as loot.

`GameTooltip:SetLootItem(slot)`

Arguments:

`slot`—Index of a loot slot (between 1 and `GetNumLootItems()`) (number)

SetLootRollItem

Fills the tooltip with information about an item currently up for loot rolling.

`GameTooltip:SetLootRollItem(id)`

Arguments:

`id`—Index of an item currently up for loot rolling (as provided in the `START_LOOT_ROLL` event) (number)

SetMerchantCostItem

Fills the tooltip with information about an alternate currency required to purchase an item from a vendor.

`GameTooltip:SetMerchantCostItem(index, currency)`

Only applies to item-based currencies, not honor or arena points.

Arguments:

`index`—Index of an item in the vendor's listing (between 1 and `GetMerchantNumItems()`) (number)

`currency`—Index of one of the item currencies required to purchase the item (between 1 and `select(3,GetMerchantItemCostInfo(index))`) (number)

SetMerchantItem

Fills the tooltip with information about an item available for purchase from a vendor.

`GameTooltip:SetMerchantItem(merchantIndex)`

Arguments:

`merchantIndex`—The index of an item in the merchant window, between 1 and `GetMerchantNumItems()`. (number)

SetMinimumWidth

Sets the minimum width of the tooltip.

`GameTooltip:SetMinimumWidth(width)`

Normally, a tooltip is automatically sized to match the width of its shortest line of text; setting a minimum width can be useful if the tooltip also contains non-text frames (such as an amount of money or a status bar).

The tooltip is not automatically resized to the new width; to do so, call the tooltip's `:Show()` method.

Arguments:

`width`—Minimum width of the tooltip frame (in pixels) (number)

SetOwner

Sets the frame to which the tooltip refers and is anchored.

`GameTooltip:SetOwner(frame [, "anchorType" [, xOffset [, yOffset]]])`

Arguments:

`frame`—Reference to the `Frame` to which the tooltip refers (`frame`)

`anchorType` (optional)—Token identifying the positioning method for the tooltip relative to its owner frame (`string`)

- `ANCHOR_BOTTOMLEFT` - Align the top right of the tooltip with the bottom left of the owner
- `ANCHOR_CURSOR` - Tooltip follows the mouse cursor
- `ANCHOR_LEFT` - Align the bottom right of the tooltip with the top left of the owner
- `ANCHOR_NONE` - Tooltip appears in the default position
- `ANCHOR_PRESERVE` - Tooltip's position is saved between sessions (useful if the tooltip is made user-movable)
- `ANCHOR_RIGHT` - Align the bottom left of the tooltip with the top right of the owner
- `ANCHOR_TOPLEFT` - Align the bottom left of the tooltip with the top left of the owner
- `ANCHOR_TOPRIGHT` - Align the bottom right of the tooltip with the top right of the owner

`xOffset` (optional)—The horizontal offset for the tooltip anchor (`number`)

`yOffset` (optional)—The vertical offset for the tooltip anchor (`number`)

SetPadding

Sets the amount of space between tooltip's text and its right-side edge.

`GameTooltip:SetPadding(padding)`

Used in the default UI's ItemRefTooltip to provide space for a close button.

Arguments:

`padding`—Amount of space between the right-side edge of the tooltip's text and the right-side edge of the tooltip frame (in pixels) (`number`)

SetPetAction

Fills the tooltip with information about a pet action.

`GameTooltip:SetPetAction(index)`

Only provides information for pet action slots containing pet spells—in the default UI, the standard pet actions (attack, follow, passive, aggressive, etc) are special-cased to show specific tooltip text.

Arguments:

`index`—Index of a pet action button (between 1 and NUM_PET_ACTION_SLOTS) (`number`)

SetPossession

Fills the tooltip with information about one of the special actions available while the player possesses another unit.

`GameTooltip:SetPossession(index)`

Arguments:

`index`—Index of a possession bar action (between 1 and `NUM_POSSESS_SLOTS`) (`number`)

SetQuestItem

Fills the tooltip with information about an item in a questgiver dialog.

`GameTooltip:SetQuestItem("itemType", index)`

Arguments:

`itemType`—Token identifying one of the possible sets of items (`string`)

■ `choice` - Items from which the player may choose a reward

■ `required` - Items required to complete the quest

■ `reward` - Items given as reward for the quest

`index`—Index of an item in the set (between 1 and `GetNumQuest Choices()`, `GetNumQuestItems()`, or `GetNumQuestRewards()`, according to `itemType`) (`number`)

SetQuestLogItem

Fills the tooltip with information about an item related to the selected quest in the quest log.

`GameTooltip:SetQuestLogItem("itemType", index)`

Arguments:

`itemType`—Token identifying one of the possible sets of items (`string`)

■ `choice` - Items from which the player may choose a reward

■ `reward` - Items always given as reward for the quest

`index`—Index of an item in the set (between 1 and `GetNumQuestLog Choices()` or `GetNumQuestLogRewards()`, according to `itemType`) (`number`)

SetQuestLogRewardSpell

Fills the tooltip with information about the reward spell for the selected quest in the quest log.

`GameTooltip:SetQuestLogRewardSpell()`

SetQuestLogSpecialItem

Fills the tooltip with information about a usable item associated with a current quest.

`GameTooltip:SetQuestLogSpecialItem(questIndex)`

Arguments:

`questIndex`—Index of a quest log entry with an associated usable item (between 1 and `GetNumQuestLogEntries()`) (`number`)

SetQuestRewardSpell

Fills the tooltip with information about the spell reward in a questgiver dialog.

```
GameTooltip:SetQuestRewardSpell()
```

SetSendMailItem

Fills the tooltip with information about an item attached to the outgoing mail message.

```
GameTooltip:SetSendMailItem(slot)
```

Arguments:

slot—Index of an outgoing attachment slot (between 1 and ATTACHMENTS_ MAX_SEND) (number)

SetShapeshift

Fills the tooltip with information about an ability on the stance/shapeshift bar.

```
GameTooltip:SetShapeshift(index)
```

Arguments:

index—Index of an ability on the stance/shapeshift bar (between 1 and GetNumShapeshiftForms()) (number)

SetSocketGem

Fills the tooltip with information about a gem added to a socket.

```
GameTooltip:SetSocketGem(index)
```

Arguments:

index—Index of a gem socket (between 1 and GetNumSockets()) (number)

SetSocketedItem

Fills the tooltip with information about the item currently being socketed.

```
GameTooltip:SetSocketedItem()
```

SetSpell

Fills the tooltip with information about a spell from the player (or pet's) spellbook.

```
GameTooltip:SetSpell(id, "bookType")
```

Arguments:

id—Index of a spell in the spellbook (number, spellbookID)

bookType—Type of spellbook (string)

- pet - The pet's spellbook
- spell - The player's spellbook

SetSpellByID

Fills the tooltip with information about a spell specified by ID.

```
GameTooltip:SetSpellByID(id)
```

Arguments:

id—Numeric ID of a spell (number, spellID)

SetTalent

Fills the tooltip with information about a talent.

`GameTooltip:SetTalent(tabIndex, talentIndex, inspect, pet, talentGroup)`

Arguments:

`tabIndex`—Index of a talent tab (between 1 and `GetNumTalentTabs()`) (`number`)

`talentIndex`—Index of a talent option (between 1 and `GetNumTalents()`) (`number`)

`inspect`—`true` to return information for the currently inspected unit; `false` to return information for the player (`boolean`)

`pet`—`true` to return information for the player's pet; `false` to return information for the player (`boolean`)

`talentGroup`—Which set of talents to edit, if the player has Dual Talent Specialization enabled (`number`)

- 1 - Primary Talents
- 2 - Secondary Talents
- `nil` - Currently active talents

SetText

Sets the tooltip's text.

`GameTooltip:SetText("text" [, r [, g [, b [, a]]]])`

Any other content currently displayed in the tooltip will be removed or hidden, and the tooltip's size will be adjusted to fit the new text.

Arguments:

`text`—Text to be displayed in the tooltip (`string`)

`r` (optional)—Red component of the text color (0.0 - 1.0) (`number`)

`g` (optional)—Green component of the text color (0.0 - 1.0) (`number`)

`b` (optional)—Blue component of the text color (0.0 - 1.0) (`number`)

`a` (optional)—Alpha (opacity) for the text (0.0 = fully transparent, 1.0 = fully opaque) (`number`)

SetTotem

Fills the tooltip with information about one of the player's active totems.

`GameTooltip:SetTotem(slot)`

Totem functions are also used for ghouls summoned by a Death Knight's Raise Dead ability (if the ghoul is not made a controllable pet by the Master of Ghouls talent).

Arguments:

`slot`—Which totem to query (`number`)

1 - Fire (or Death Knight's ghoul)	3 - Water
2 - Earth	4 - Air

SetTracking

Fills the tooltip with information about the currently selected tracking type.

```
GameTooltip:SetTracking()
```

If no tracking type is selected, the tooltip reads "Click to choose tracking type" (or localized equivalent).

SetTradePlayerItem

Fills the tooltip with information about an item offered for trade by the player.

```
GameTooltip:SetTradePlayerItem(index)
```

See `:SetTradeTargetItem()` for items to be received from the trade.

Arguments:

`index`—Index of an item offered for trade by the player (between 1 and `MAX_TRADE_ITEMS`) (number)

SetTradeSkillItem

Fills the tooltip with information about an item created by a trade skill recipe or a reagent in the recipe.

```
GameTooltip:SetTradeSkillItem(skillIndex [, reagentIndex])
```

Arguments:

`skillIndex`—Index of a recipe in the trade skill list (between 1 and `GetNumTradeSkills()`) (number)

`reagentIndex` (optional)—Index of a reagent in the recipe (between 1 and `GetTradeSkillNumReagents()`); if omitted, displays a tooltip for the item created by the recipe (number)

SetTradeTargetItem

Fills the tooltip with information about an item offered for trade by the target.

```
GameTooltip:SetTradeTargetItem(index)
```

See `:SetTradePlayerItem()` for items to be traded away by the player.

Arguments:

`index`—Index of an item offered for trade by the target (between 1 and `MAX_TRADE_ITEMS`) (number)

SetTrainerService

Fills the tooltip with information about a trainer service.

```
GameTooltip:SetTrainerService(index)
```

Arguments:

`index`—Index of an entry in the trainer service listing (between 1 and `GetNumTrainerServices()`) (number)

SetUnit

Fills the tooltip with information about a unit.

```
GameTooltip:SetUnit("unit")
```

Arguments:

`unit`—A unit to query (string, unitid)

SetUnitAura

Fills the tooltip with information about a buff or debuff on a unit.

```
GameTooltip:SetUnitAura("unit", index [, "filter"])
```

Arguments:

unit—A unit to query (string, unitID)

index—Index of a buff or debuff on the unit (number)

filter (optional)—A list of filters to use when resolving the index, separated by the pipe '|' character; e.g. "RAID|PLAYER" will query group buffs cast by the player (string)

- CANCELABLE - Show auras that can be cancelled
- HARMFUL - Show debuffs only
- HELPFUL - Show buffs only
- NOT_CANCELABLE - Show auras that cannot be cancelled
- PLAYER - Show auras the player has cast
- RAID - Show auras the player can cast on party/raid members (as opposed to self buffs)

SetUnitBuff

Fills the tooltip with information about a buff on a unit.

```
GameTooltip:SetUnitBuff("unit", index [, "filter"])
```

This method is an alias for :SetUnitAura() with a built-in HELPFUL filter (which cannot be removed or negated with the HARMFUL filter).

Arguments:

unit—A unit to query (string, unitID)

index—Index of a buff or debuff on the unit (number)

filter (optional)—A list of filters to use when resolving the index, separated by the pipe '|' character; e.g. "RAID|PLAYER" will query group buffs cast by the player (string)

- CANCELABLE - Show auras that can be cancelled
- NOT_CANCELABLE - Show auras that cannot be cancelled
- PLAYER - Show auras the player has cast
- RAID - Show auras the player can cast on party/raid members (as opposed to self buffs)

SetUnitDebuff

Fills the tooltip with information about a debuff on a unit.

```
GameTooltip:SetUnitDebuff("unit", index [, "filter"])
```

This method is an alias for :SetUnitAura() with a built-in HARMFUL filter (which cannot be removed or negated with the HELPFUL filter).

Arguments:

unit—A unit to query (string, unitID)

index—Index of a buff or debuff on the unit (number)

filter (optional)—A list of filters to use when resolving the index, separated by the pipe '|' character; e.g. "CANCELABLE|PLAYER" will query cancelable debuffs cast by the player (string)

- CANCELABLE - Show auras that can be cancelled
- NOT_CANCELABLE - Show auras that cannot be cancelled
- PLAYER - Show auras the player has cast
- RAID - Show auras the player can cast on party/raid members (as opposed to self buffs)

Minimap

Minimap is a frame type whose backdrop is filled in with a top-down representation of the area around the character being played. You can have more than one if you are so inclined, but they can't have different coordinates or locations, and tracking blips do not work correctly unless they're the exact same size. You can use methods to control the textures that are used by the minimap to display different elements such as group members or arrows to nearby points of interest, but you cannot determine where these things are. You can also adjust the zoom on a Minimap or determine where it is being pinged by you or another member of your group.

The stock UI uses a Minimap only once, predictably for the minimap in the upper right, but some mods will move it or create a larger, fainter version to use as a "heads-up display."

Minimap has all the methods from Frame, plus the following:

GetPingPosition

Returns the location of the last "ping" on the minimap.

```
x, y = Minimap:GetPingPosition()
```

Coordinates are pixel distances relative to the center of the minimap (not fractions of the minimap's size as with :GetPingPosition()); positive coordinates are above or to the right of the center, negative are below or to the left.

Returns:

x—Horizontal coordinate of the "ping" position (number)

y—Vertical coordinate of the "ping" position (number)

GetZoom

Returns the minimap's current zoom level.

```
zoomLevel = Minimap:GetZoom()
```

Returns:

zoomLevel—Index of the current zoom level (between 0 for the widest possible zoom and (minimap:GetZoomLevels() - 1) for the narrowest possible zoom) (number)

GetZoomLevels

Returns the number of available zoom settings for the minimap.

```
zoomLevels = Minimap:GetZoomLevels()
```

Returns:

`zoomLevels`—Number of available zoom settings for the minimap (`number`)

PingLocation

"Pings" the minimap at a given location.

```
Minimap:PingLocation(x, y)
```

Coordinates are pixel distances relative to the center of the minimap (not fractions of the minimap's size as with `:GetPingPosition()`); positive coordinates are above or to the right of the center, negative are below or to the left.

Arguments:

`x`—Horizontal coordinate of the "ping" position (in pixels) (`number`)

`y`—Vertical coordinate of the "ping" position (in pixels) (`number`)

SetBlipTexture

Sets the texture used to display quest and tracking icons on the minimap.

```
Minimap:SetBlipTexture("filename")
```

The replacement texture must match the specifications of the default texture (`Interface\\Minimap\\ObjectIcons`): 256 pixels wide by 64 pixels tall, containing an 8x2 grid of icons each 32x32 pixels square.

Arguments:

`filename`—Path to a texture containing display quest and tracking icons for the minimap (`string`)

SetClassBlipTexture

Sets the texture used to display party and raid members on the minimap.

```
Minimap:SetClassBlipTexture("filename")
```

Usefulness of this method to addons is limited, as the replacement texture must match the specifications of the default texture (`Interface\\Minimap\\PartyRaidBlips`): 256 pixels wide by 128 pixels tall, containing an 8x4 grid of icons each 32x32 pixels square.

Arguments:

`filename`—Path to a texture containing icons for party and raid members (`string`)

SetCorpsePOIArrowTexture

Sets the texture used to the player's corpse when located beyond the scope of the minimap.

```
Minimap:SetCorpsePOIArrowTexture("filename")
```

The default texture is `Interface\\Minimap\\ROTATING-`
`MINIMAPCORPSEARROW`.

Arguments:

`filename`—Path to a texture image (`string`)

SetIconTexture

Sets the texture used to display various points of interest on the minimap.

`Minimap:SetIconTexture("filename")`

Usefulness of this method to addons is limited, as the replacement texture
must match the specifications of the default texture
(`Interface\\Minimap\\POIIcons`): a 256x256 pixel square containing a
16x16 grid of icons each 16x16 pixels square.

Arguments:

`filename`—Path to a texture containing icons for various map landmarks
(`string`)

SetMaskTexture

Sets the texture used to mask the shape of the minimap.

`Minimap:SetMaskTexture("filename")`

White areas in the texture define where the dynamically drawn minimap is
visible. The default mask (`Textures\\MinimapMask`) is circular; a texture
image consisting of an all-white square will result in a square minimap.

Arguments:

`filename`—Path to a texture used to mask the shape of the minimap (`string`)

SetPOIArrowTexture

Sets the texture used to represent points of interest located beyond the scope of
the minimap.

`Minimap:SetPOIArrowTexture("filename")`

This texture is used for points of interest such as those which appear when
asking a city guard for directions. The default texture is
`Interface\Minimap\ROTATING-MINIMAPGUIDEARROW`.

Arguments:

`filename`—Path to a texture image (`string`)

SetPlayerTexture

Sets the texture used to represent the player on the minimap.

`Minimap:SetPlayerTexture("filename")`

The default texture is `Interface\Minimap\MinimapArrow`.

Arguments:

`filename`—Path to a texture image (`string`)

SetPlayerTextureHeight

Sets the height of the texture used to represent the player on the minimap.

`Minimap:SetPlayerTextureHeight(height)`

Arguments:

`height`—Height of the texture used to represent the player on the minimap (`number`)

SetPlayerTextureWidth

Sets the width of the texture used to represent the player on the minimap.

`Minimap:SetPlayerTextureWidth(width)`

Arguments:

`width`—Width of the texture used to represent the player on the minimap (`number`)

SetStaticPOIArrowTexture

Sets the texture used to represent static points of interest located beyond the scope of the minimap.

`Minimap:SetStaticPOIArrowTexture("filename")`

This texture is used for static points of interest such as nearby towns and cities. The default texture is `Interface\\Minimap\\ROTATING-MINIMAPARROW`.

Arguments:

`filename`—Path to a texture image (`string`)

SetZoom

Sets the minimap's zoom level.

`Minimap:SetZoom(zoomLevel)`

Arguments:

`zoomLevel`—Index of a zoom level (between 0 for the widest possible zoom and (`minimap:GetZoomLevels() - 1`) for the narrowest possible zoom) (`number`)

Model

When you want to display a rendering of a three-dimensional object as part of the UI, a Model frame is your basic tool. These frames provide a rendering environment which is drawn into the backdrop of their frame, allowing you to display the contents of an .m2 file and set facing, scale, light and fog information, or run motions associated with the model.

It's comparatively rare to see the basic Model type used; most renderings of models in the stock UI and mods use PlayerFrame to display players, pets and mounts.

Model has all the methods from Frame, plus the following:

AdvanceTime

Advances to the model's next animation frame.

`Model:AdvanceTime()`

(Applies to 3D animations defined within the model file, not UI `Animations`.)

ClearFog

Disables fog display for the model.

```
Model:ClearFog()
```

ClearModel

Removes the 3D model currently displayed.

```
Model:ClearModel()
```

GetFacing

Returns the model's current rotation setting.

```
facing = Model:GetFacing()
```

The 3D model displayed by the model object can be rotated about its vertical axis. For example, a model of a player race faces towards the viewer when its facing is set to 0; setting facing to `math.pi` faces it away from the viewer.

Returns:

`facing`—Current rotation angle of the model (in radians) (`number`)

GetFogColor

Returns the model's current fog color.

```
red, green, blue = Model:GetFogColor()
```

Does not indicate whether fog display is enabled.

Returns:

`red`—Red component of the color (0.0 - 1.0) (`number`)

`green`—Green component of the color (0.0 - 1.0) (`number`)

`blue`—Blue component of the color (0.0 - 1.0) (`number`)

GetFogFar

Returns the far clipping distance for the model's fog.

```
distance = Model:GetFogFar()
```

This determines how far from the camera the fog ends.

Returns:

`distance`—The distance to the fog far clipping plane (`number`)

GetFogNear

Returns the near clipping distance for the model's fog.

```
distance = Model:GetFogNear()
```

This determines how close to the camera the fog begins.

Returns:

`distance`—The distance to the fog near clipping plane (`number`)

GetLight

Returns properties of the light sources used when rendering the model.

```
enabled, omni, dirX, dirY, dirZ, ambIntensity, ambR, ambG, ambB, ↵
dirIntensity, dirR, dirG, dirB = Model:GetLight()
```

Returns:

`enabled`—1 if lighting is enabled; otherwise `nil` (`1nil`)

`omni`—1 if omnidirectional lighting is enabled; otherwise 0 (`number`)

`dirX`—Coordinate of the directional light in the axis perpendicular to the screen (negative values place the light in front of the model, positive values behind) (`number`)

`dirY`—Coordinate of the directional light in the horizontal axis (negative values place the light to the left of the model, positive values to the right) (`number`)

`dirZ`—Coordinate of the directional light in the vertical axis (negative values place the light below the model, positive values above (`number`)

`ambIntensity`—Intensity of the ambient light (0.0 - 1.0) (`number`)

`ambR` (optional)—Red component of the ambient light color (0.0 - 1.0); omitted if `ambIntensity` is 0 (`number`)

`ambG` (optional)—Green component of the ambient light color (0.0 - 1.0); omitted if `ambIntensity` is 0 (`number`)

`ambB` (optional)—Blue component of the ambient light color (0.0 - 1.0); omitted if `ambIntensity` is 0 (`number`)

`dirIntensity` (optional)—Intensity of the directional light (0.0 - 1.0) (`number`)

`dirR` (optional)—Red component of the directional light color (0.0 - 1.0); omitted if `dirIntensity` is 0 (`number`)

`dirG` (optional)—Green component of the directional light color (0.0 - 1.0); omitted if `dirIntensity` is 0 (`number`)

`dirB` (optional)—Blue component of the directional light color (0.0 - 1.0); omitted if `dirIntensity` is 0 (`number`)

GetModel

Returns the model file currently displayed.

```
filename = Model:GetModel()
```

May instead return a reference to the `Model` object itself if a filename is not available.

Returns:

`filename`—Path to the model file currently displayed (`string`)

GetModelScale

Returns the scale factor determining the size at which the 3D model appears.

```
scale = Model:GetModelScale()
```

Returns:

`scale`—Scale factor determining the size at which the 3D model appears (`number`)

GetPosition

Returns the position of the 3D model within the frame.

```
x, y, z = Model:GetPosition()
```

Returns:

x—Position of the model on the axis perpendicular to the plane of the screen (positive values make the model appear closer to the viewer; negative values place it further away) (number)

y—Position of the model on the horizontal axis (positive values place the model to the right of its default position; negative values place it to the left) (number)

z—Position of the model on the vertical axis (positive values place the model above its default position; negative values place it below) (number)

ReplaceIconTexture

Sets the icon texture used by the model.

```
Model:ReplaceIconTexture("filename")
```

Only affects models that use icons (e.g. the model producing the default UI's animation which appears when an item goes into a bag).

Arguments:

filename—Path to an icon texture for use in the model (string)

SetCamera

Sets the view angle on the model to a pre-defined camera location.

```
Model:SetCamera(index)
```

Camera view angles are defined within the model files and not otherwise available to the scripting system. Some camera indices are standard across most models:

- 0 - Non-movable camera, focused on the unit's face (if applicable); used by the game engine when rendering portrait textures
- 1 - Movable camera, showing the entire body of the unit
- 2 or higher - Movable camera in default position

Arguments:

index—Index of a camera view defined by the model file (number)

SetFacing

Sets the model's current rotation.

```
Model:SetFacing(facing)
```

The 3D model displayed by the model object can be rotated about its vertical axis. For example, if the model faces towards the viewer when its facing is set to 0, setting facing to math.pi faces it away from the viewer.

Arguments:

facing—Rotation angle for the model (in radians) (number)

SetFogColor

Sets the model's fog color, enabling fog display if disabled.

```
Model:SetFogColor(red, green, blue)
```

Arguments:

red—Red component of the color (0.0 - 1.0) (number)

green—Green component of the color (0.0 - 1.0) (number)

blue—Blue component of the color (0.0 - 1.0) (number)

SetFogFar

Sets the far clipping distance for the model's fog.

```
Model:SetFogFar(distance)
```

This sets how far from the camera the fog ends.

Arguments:

distance—The distance to the fog far clipping plane (number)

SetFogNear

Sets the near clipping distance for the model's fog.

```
Model:SetFogNear(distance)
```

This sets how close to the camera the fog begins.

Arguments:

distance—The distance to the fog near clipping plane (number)

SetGlow

Sets the model's glow amount.

```
Model:SetGlow(amount)
```

Arguments:

amount—Glow amount for the model (number)

SetLight

Sets properties of the light sources used when rendering the model.

```
Model:SetLight(enabled, omni, dirX, dirY, dirZ, ambIntensity ↵
  [, ambR [, ambG [, ambB [, dirIntensity [, dirR [, dirG [, dirB]]]]]]])
```

Arguments:

enabled—1 if lighting is enabled; otherwise nil (1nil)

omni—1 if omnidirectional lighting is enabled; otherwise 0 (number)

dirX—Coordinate of the directional light in the axis perpendicular to the screen (negative values place the light in front of the model, positive values behind) (number)

dirY—Coordinate of the directional light in the horizontal axis (negative values place the light to the left of the model, positive values to the right) (number)

dirZ—Coordinate of the directional light in the vertical axis (negative values place the light below the model, positive values above (number)

ambIntensity—Intensity of the ambient light (0.0 - 1.0) (number)

ambR (optional)—Red component of the ambient light color (0.0 - 1.0); omitted if ambIntensity is 0 (number)

ambG (optional)—Green component of the ambient light color (0.0 - 1.0); omitted if ambIntensity is 0 (number) ambB (optional)—Blue component of the ambient light color (0.0 - 1.0); omitted if ambIntensity is 0 (number)

dirIntensity (optional)—Intensity of the directional light (0.0 - 1.0) (number)

dirR (optional)—Red component of the directional light color (0.0 - 1.0); omitted if dirIntensity is 0 (number)

dirG (optional)—Green component of the directional light color (0.0 - 1.0); omitted if dirIntensity is 0 (number)

dirB (optional)—Blue component of the directional light color (0.0 - 1.0); omitted if dirIntensity is 0 (number)

SetModel

Sets the model file to be displayed.

```
Model:SetModel("filename")
```

Arguments:

filename—Path to the model file to be displayed (string)

SetModelScale

Sets the scale factor determining the size at which the 3D model appears.

```
Model:SetModelScale(scale)
```

Arguments:

scale—Scale factor determining the size at which the 3D model appears (number)

SetPosition

Returns the position of the 3D model within the frame.

```
Model:SetPosition(x, y, z)
```

Arguments:

x—Position of the model on the axis perpendicular to the plane of the screen (positive values make the model appear closer to the viewer; negative values place it further away) (number)

y—Position of the model on the horizontal axis (positive values place the model to the right of its default position; negative values place it to the left) (number)

z—Position of the model on the vertical axis (positive values place the model above its default position; negative values place it below) (number)

SetSequence

Sets the animation sequence to be used by the model.

```
Model:SetSequence(sequence)
```

The number of available sequences and behavior of each are defined within the model files and not available to the scripting system.

Arguments:

sequence—Index of an animation sequence defined by the model file (number)

SetSequenceTime

Sets the animation sequence and time index to be used by the model.

```
Model:SetSequenceTime(sequence, time)
```

The number of available sequences and behavior of each are defined within the model files and not available to the scripting system.

Arguments:

sequence—Index of an animation sequence defined by the model file (number)

time—Time index within the sequence (number)

PlayerModel

PlayerModels are the most commonly used subtype of Model frame. They expand on the Model type by adding functions to quickly set the model to represent a particular player or creature, by unitID or creature ID.

These models are used by the stock UI for "paper doll" frames, to display a player's character, minion, vanity pets and mounts. They're also used by unit frame mods, to provide animated portraits or full-body "action figure" displays of characters and monsters.

PlayerModel has all the methods from Model, plus the following:

RefreshUnit

Updates the model's appearance to match that of its unit.

```
PlayerModel:RefreshUnit()
```

Used in the default UI's inspect window when the player's target changes (changing the model to match the "new appearance" of the unit "target") or when the UNIT_MODEL_CHANGED event fires for the inspected unit (updating the model's appearance to reflect changes in the unit's equipment or shapeshift form).

SetCreature

Sets the model to display the 3D model of a specific creature.

```
PlayerModel:SetCreature(creature)
```

Used in the default UI to set the model used for previewing non-combat pets and mounts (see GetCompanionInfo()), but can also be used to display the model for any creature whose data is cached by the client. Creature IDs can commonly be found on database sites (e.g. creature ID #10181).

Arguments:

creature—Numeric ID of a creature (number)

SetRotation

Sets the model's current rotation by animating the model.

```
PlayerModel:SetRotation(facing)
```

This method is similar to Model:SetFacing() in that it rotates the 3D model displayed about its vertical axis; however, since the PlayerModel object displays a unit's model, this method is provided to allow for animating the rotation using the model's built-in animations for turning right and left.

For example, if the model faces towards the viewer when its facing is set to 0, setting its facing to `math.pi` faces it away from the viewer.

Arguments:

`facing`—Rotation angle for the model (in radians) (`number`)

SetUnit

Sets the model to display the 3D model of a specific unit.

```
PlayerModel:SetUnit("unit")
```

Arguments:

`unit`—Unit ID of a visible unit (`string`, unitID)

DressUpModel

The DressUpModel type was added to provide support for the "dressing room" functionality when it was introduced. This model can be set to a particular unit, and then given different pieces of gear to display on that unit with the TryOn function. It also provides an Undress feature which can be used to view how your character's gear will look without concealing articles such as a cloak or tabard that you might be wearing.

DressUpModel has all the methods from PlayerModel, plus the following:

Dress

Updates the model to reflect the character's currently equipped items.

```
DressUpModel:Dress()
```

TryOn

Updates the model to reflect the character's appearance after equipping a specific item.

```
DressUpModel:TryOn(itemID) or DressUpModel:TryOn("itemName") or ↵
DressUpModel:TryOn("itemLink")
```

Arguments:

`itemID`—An item's ID (`number`)

`itemName`—An item's name (`string`)

`itemLink`—An item's hyperlink, or any string containing the `itemString` portion of an item link (`string`)

Undress

Updates the model to reflect the character's appearance without any equipped items.

```
DressUpModel:Undress()
```

TabardModel

TabardModel is a frame type provided specifically for designing or modifying guild tabards. It provides functions for displaying a character in a sample tabard and cycling through different trim textures, emblems and color schemes, as well as saving the selected look as your guild's current tabard (this requires that your character have appropriate guild privileges to do so).

Because the stock UI already includes a fairly comprehensive tabard interface using one of these frames, it's fairly unlikely that you'll need to create one of your own.

TabardModel has all the methods from PlayerModel, plus the following:

CanSaveTabardNow

Returns whether the tabard model's current design can be saved as the player's guild tabard.

```
enabled = TabardModel:CanSaveTabardNow()
```

Returns:

`enabled`—1 if the tabard model's current design can be saved as the player's guild tabard; otherwise `nil` (`1nil`)

CycleVariation

Cycles through available design variations for the tabard model.

```
TabardModel:CycleVariation(variable, delta)
```

Arguments:

`variable`—Number identifying one of the five tabard design variables: (`number`)

1 - Icon   4 - Border color

2 - Icon color   5 - Background color

3 - Border style

`delta`—Number of steps by which to cycle through available options for the design variable (e.g. 1 for next design, -1 for previous design, 3 to skip ahead by three) (`number`)

GetLowerBackgroundFileName

Returns the image file for the lower portion of the tabard model's current background design.

```
TabardModel:GetLowerBackgroundFileName("filename")
```

Arguments:

`filename`—Path to the texture image file for the lower portion of the tabard model's current background design (`string`)

GetLowerEmblemFileName

Returns the image file for the lower portion of the tabard model's current emblem design.

```
TabardModel:GetLowerEmblemFileName("filename")
```

Arguments:

`filename`—Path to the texture image file for the lower portion of the tabard model's current emblem design (`string`)

GetLowerEmblemTexture

Sets a `Texture` object to display the lower portion of the tabard model's current emblem design.

```
TabardModel:GetLowerEmblemTexture(texture)
```

Arguments:

`texture`—Reference to a Texture object (`texture`)

GetUpperBackgroundFileName

Returns the image file for the upper portion of the tabard model's current background design.

```
TabardModel:GetUpperBackgroundFileName("filename")
```

Arguments:

`filename`—Path to the texture image file for the upper portion of the tabard model's current background design (`string`)

GetUpperEmblemFileName

Returns the image file for the upper portion of the tabard model's current emblem design.

```
TabardModel:GetUpperEmblemFileName("filename")
```

Arguments:

`filename`—Path to the texture image file for the upper portion of the tabard model's current emblem design (`string`)

GetUpperEmblemTexture

Sets a `Texture` object to display the upper portion of the tabard model's current emblem design.

```
TabardModel:GetUpperEmblemTexture(texture)
```

Arguments:

`texture`—Reference to a Texture object (`texture`)

InitializeTabardColors

Sets the tabard model's design to match the player's guild tabard.

```
TabardModel:InitializeTabardColors()
```

If the player is not in a guild or the player's guild does not yet have a tabard design, randomizes the tabard model's design.

Save

Saves the current tabard model design as the player's guild tabard.

```
TabardModel:Save()
```

Has no effect if the player is not a guild leader.

MovieFrame

MovieFrame is one of the least well-known frame subtypes. To date, it has been used in only one well-known mod, which was an April Fools' Day joke, HighRoller. If you're curious what this mod did, it's still available for download; read the description or try and run it (but keep in mind it's a prank.) It runs the contents of an .avi file, for there are some fairly stringent requirements on the file format supplied.

MovieFrame has all the methods from Frame, plus the following:

EnableSubtitles

Enables or disables subtitles for movies played in the frame.

```
MovieFrame:EnableSubtitles(enable)
```

Subtitles are not automatically displayed by the MovieFrame; enabling subtitles causes the frame's `OnMovieShowSubtitle` and `OnMovieHideSubtitle` script handlers to be run when subtitle text should be displayed.

Arguments:

enable—`True` to enable display of movie subtitles; `false` to disable (`boolean`)

StartMovie

Plays a specified movie in the frame.

```
enabled = MovieFrame:StartMovie("filename", volume)
```

Note: Size and position of the movie display is unaffected by that of the MovieFrame—movies are automatically centered and sized proportionally to fill the screen in their largest dimension (i.e. a widescreen movie will fill the width of the screen but not necessarily its full height).

Arguments:

filename—Path to a movie file (excluding filename extension) (`string`)

volume—Audio volume for movie playback (0 = minimum, 255 = maximum) (`number`)

Returns:

enabled—1 if a valid movie was loaded and playback begun; otherwise `nil` (`1nil`)

Example:

```
-- create a MovieFrame and play the Blizzard logo intro movie
-- bundled with the game
CreateFrame("MovieFrame","MiniMovie",UIParent)
MiniMovie:StartMovie("Interface\\Cinematics\\Logo_1024",255)

-- play a XviD-encoded AVI movie bundled with an addon
MiniMovie:StartMovie("Interface\\AddOns\\MyAddon\\MyMovie",255)
```

StopMovie

Stops the movie currently playing in the frame.

```
MovieFrame:StopMovie()
```

ScrollFrame

ScrollFrame is how a large body of content can be displayed through a small window. The ScrollFrame is the size of the "window" through which you want to see the larger content, and it has another frame set as a "ScrollChild" containing the full content. The proportion by which the ScrollChild is larger than the ScrollFrame automatically determines the horizontal and vertical scroll range of the ScrollFrame. You can get these ranges or position the ScrollChild "behind" the ScrollFrame within those ranges using ScrollFrame's methods. It also allows you to set a new frame as the ScrollChild.

When a ScrollFrame is used for repetitive content, such as the buttons for assigning key bindings or the friends in your social frame, it is often implemented as a "FauxScrollFrame," which contains enough of these subframes in the ScrollChild to fill the ScrollFrame, plus one. It then saves an offset and maps which of the elements in an internal list are displayed.

To create a ScrollFrame's ScrollChild in XML, include a `<ScrollChild>` element as a direct child of the `<ScrollFrame>` element. The `<ScrollChild>` element should have one child, of any type descended from `<Frame>`. To create the scroll child in Lua, create the frame using `CreateFrame()`, and then attach the child to the scroll frame using `ScrollFrame:SetScrollChild(child)`. The child frame must always have an absolute size set with `<AbsDimension>` in XML or using both `SetWidth()` and `SetHeight()` in Lua.

A ScrollFrame does not automatically include an element that sets the scroll range. Typically, you add a Slider as a child of a ScrollFrame, with an OnValueChanged handler that sets the scroll value.

ScrollFrames are common throughout the UI, used for quest text, readable items, lists of friends and guild members, and similar applications.

ScrollFrame has all the methods from Frame, plus the following:

GetHorizontalScroll

Returns the scroll frame's current horizontal scroll position.

```
scroll = ScrollFrame:GetHorizontalScroll()
```

Returns:

`scroll`—Current horizontal scroll position (0 = at left edge, `frame:Get HorizontalScrollRange()` = at right edge) (number)

GetHorizontalScrollRange

Returns the scroll frame's maximum horizontal (rightmost) scroll position.

```
maxScroll = ScrollFrame:GetHorizontalScrollRange()
```

Returns:

`maxScroll`—Maximum horizontal scroll position (representing the right edge of the scrolled area) (number)

GetScrollChild

Returns the frame scrolled by the scroll frame.

```
scrollChild = ScrollFrame:GetScrollChild()
```

Returns:

scrollChild—Reference to the Frame object scrolled by the scroll frame
(frame)

GetVerticalScroll

Returns the scroll frame's current vertical scroll position.

```
scroll = ScrollFrame:GetVerticalScroll()
```

Returns:

scroll—Current vertical scroll position (0 = at top edge, frame:Get
VerticalScrollRange() = at bottom edge) (number)

GetVerticalScrollRange

Returns the scroll frame's maximum vertical (bottom) scroll position.

```
maxScroll = ScrollFrame:GetVerticalScrollRange()
```

Returns:

maxScroll—Maximum vertical scroll position (representing the bottom edge of
the scrolled area) (number)

SetHorizontalScroll

Sets the scroll frame's horizontal scroll position.

```
ScrollFrame:SetHorizontalScroll(scroll)
```

Arguments:

scroll—Current horizontal scroll position (0 = at left edge, frame:Get
HorizontalScrollRange() = at right edge) (number)

SetScrollChild

Sets the scroll child for the scroll frame.

```
ScrollFrame:SetScrollChild(frame)
```

The scroll child frame represents the (generally larger) area into which the
scroll frame provides a (generally smaller) movable "window". The child must
have an absolute size, set either by <AbsDimension> in XML or using both
SetWidth() and SetHeight() in Lua.

Setting a frame's scroll child involves changing the child frame's parent—thus,
if the frame's scroll child is protected, this operation cannot be performed
while in combat.

Arguments:

frame—Reference to another frame to be the ScrollFrame's child.
(frame)

SetVerticalScroll

Sets the scroll frame's vertical scroll position.

```
ScrollFrame:SetVerticalScroll(scroll)
```

Arguments:

scroll—Current vertical scroll position (0 = at top edge, frame:Get
VerticalScrollRange() = at bottom edge) (number)

UpdateScrollChildRect

Updates the position of the scroll frame's child.

```
ScrollFrame:UpdateScrollChildRect()
```

The `ScrollFrame` automatically adjusts the position of the child frame when scrolled, but manually updating its position may be necessary when changing the size or contents of the child frame.

SimpleHTML

The most sophisticated control over text display is offered by SimpleHTML widgets. When its text is set to a string containing valid HTML markup, a SimpleHTML widget will parse the content into its various blocks and sections, and lay the text out. While it supports most common text commands, a SimpleHTML widget accepts an additional argument to most of these; if provided, the element argument will specify the HTML elements to which the new style information should apply, such as `formattedText:SetTextColor("h2", 1, 0.3, 0.1)` which will cause all level 2 headers to display in red. If no element name is specified, the settings apply to the SimpleHTML widget's default font.

Like ScrollingMessageFrame, SimpleHTML also provides hyperlink support, including a hook to control the formatting of hyperlinked text with `:SetHyperlinkFormat`. This function takes a string, which is provided to string.format along with strings representing the hyperlink's address and body text, and produces the appropriate link and color codes along with any other desired formatting.

This widget does not support scrolling by itself, but you can use it as a ScrollChild to support longer blocks of text. In addition, it is used by the stock UI to display the contents of the books that your character may find lying around inns and libraries.

SimpleHTML has all the methods from Frame, plus the following:

GetFont

Returns basic properties of a font used in the frame.

```
filename, fontHeight, flags = SimpleHTML:GetFont(["element"])
```

Arguments:

`element` (optional)—Name of an HTML element for which to return font information (e.g. p, h1); if omitted, returns information about the frame's default font (`string`)

Returns:

`filename`—Path to a font file (`string`)

`fontHeight`—Height (point size) of the font to be displayed (in pixels) (`number`)

`flags`—Additional properties for the font specified by one or more (separated by commas) of the following tokens: (`string`)

- `MONOCHROME` - Font is rendered without anti-aliasing
- `OUTLINE` - Font is displayed with a black outline
- `THICKOUTLINE` - Font is displayed with a thick black outline

GetFontObject

Returns the Font object from which the properties of a font used in the frame are inherited.

```
font = SimpleHTML:GetFontObject(["element"])
```

Arguments:

element (optional)—Name of an HTML element for which to return font information (e.g. p, h1); if omitted, returns information about the frame's default font (string)

Returns:

font—Reference to the Font object from which font properties are inherited, or nil if no properties are inherited (font)

GetHyperlinkFormat

Returns the format string used for displaying hyperlinks in the frame.

```
format = SimpleHTML:GetHyperlinkFormat()
```

See :SetHyperlinkFormat() for details.

Returns:

format—Format string used for displaying hyperlinks in the frame (string)

GetHyperlinksEnabled

Returns whether hyperlinks in the frame's text are interactive.

```
enabled = SimpleHTML:GetHyperlinksEnabled()
```

Returns:

enabled—1 if hyperlinks in the frame's text are interactive; otherwise nil (1nil)

GetIndentedWordWrap

Returns whether long lines of text are indented when wrapping.

```
indent = SimpleHTML:GetIndentedWordWrap(["element"])
```

Arguments:

element (optional)—Name of an HTML element for which to return text style information (e.g. p, h1); if omitted, returns information about the frame's default text style (string)

Returns:

indent—1 if long lines of text are indented when wrapping; otherwise nil (1nil)

GetJustifyH

Returns the horizontal alignment style for text in the frame.

```
justify = SimpleHTML:GetJustifyH(["element"])
```

Arguments:

element (optional)—Name of an HTML element for which to return text style information (e.g. p, h1); if omitted, returns information about the frame's default text style (string)

Returns:

justify—Horizontal text alignment style (string, justifyH)

■ CENTER

■ LEFT

■ RIGHT

GetJustifyV

Returns the vertical alignment style for text in the frame.

justify = SimpleHTML:GetJustifyV(["element"])

Arguments:

element (optional)—Name of an HTML element for which to return text style information (e.g. p, h1); if omitted, returns information about the frame's default text style (string)

Returns:

justify—Vertical text alignment style (string, justifyV)

■ BOTTOM

■ MIDDLE

■ TOP

GetShadowColor

Returns the shadow color for text in the frame.

shadowR, shadowG, shadowB, shadowAlpha = ↵
SimpleHTML:GetShadowColor(["element"])

Arguments:

element (optional)—Name of an HTML element for which to return font information (e.g. p, h1); if omitted, returns information about the frame's default font (string)

Returns:

shadowR—Red component of the shadow color (0.0 - 1.0) (number)

shadowG—Green component of the shadow color (0.0 - 1.0) (number)

shadowB—Blue component of the shadow color (0.0 - 1.0) (number)

shadowAlpha—Alpha (opacity) of the text's shadow (0.0 = fully transparent, 1.0 = fully opaque) (number)

GetShadowOffset

Returns the offset of text shadow from text in the frame.

xOffset, yOffset = SimpleHTML:GetShadowOffset(["element"])

Arguments:

element (optional)—Name of an HTML element for which to return font information (e.g. p, h1); if omitted, returns information about the frame's default font (string)

Returns:

xOffset—Horizontal distance between the text and its shadow (in pixels) (number) `yOffset`—Vertical distance between the text and its shadow (in pixels) (`number`)

GetSpacing

Returns the amount of spacing between lines of text in the frame.

`spacing = SimpleHTML:GetSpacing(["element"])`

Arguments:

`element` (optional)—Name of an HTML element for which to return font information (e.g. `p`, `h1`); if omitted, returns information about the frame's default font (`string`)

Returns:

`spacing`—Amount of space between lines of text (in pixels) (`number`)

GetTextColor

Returns the color of text in the frame.

`textR, textG, textB, textAlpha = SimpleHTML:GetTextColor(["element"])`

Arguments:

`element` (optional)—Name of an HTML element for which to return font information (e.g. `p`, `h1`); if omitted, returns information about the frame's default font (`string`)

Returns:

`textR`—Red component of the text color (0.0 - 1.0) (`number`)

`textG`—Green component of the text color (0.0 - 1.0) (`number`)

`textB`—Blue component of the text color (0.0 - 1.0) (`number`)

`textAlpha`—Alpha (opacity) of the text (0.0 = fully transparent, 1.0 = fully opaque) (`number`)

SetFont

Sets basic properties of a font used in the frame.

`isValid = SimpleHTML:SetFont(["element",]↵`
`"filename", fontHeight, "flags")`

Arguments:

`element` (optional)—Name of an HTML element for which to set font properties (e.g. `p`, `h1`); if omitted, sets properties for the frame's default font (`string`)

`filename`—Path to a font file (`string`)

`fontHeight`—Height (point size) of the font to be displayed (in pixels) (`number`)

`flags`—Additional properties for the font specified by one or more (separated by commas) of the following tokens: (`string`)

■ `MONOCHROME` - Font is rendered without anti-aliasing

■ `OUTLINE` - Font is displayed with a black outline

■ `THICKOUTLINE` - Font is displayed with a thick black outline

Returns:

`isValid`—1 if `filename` refers to a valid font file; otherwise `nil` (`1nil`)

SetFontObject

Sets the Font object from which the properties of a font used in the frame are inherited.

```
SimpleHTML:SetFontObject(["element",] font) or ↵
SimpleHTML:SetFontObject(["element",] "name")
```

This method allows for easy standardization and reuse of font styles. For example, a SimpleHTML frame's normal font can be set to appear in the same style as many default UI elements by setting its font to `"GameFontNormal"`—if Blizzard changes the main UI font in a future path, or if the user installs another addon that changes the main UI font, the button's font will automatically change to match.

Arguments:

element (optional)—Name of an HTML element for which to set font properties (e.g. p, h1); if omitted, sets properties for the frame's default font (string)

font—Reference to a Font object (table)

name—Global name of a Font object (string)

SetHyperlinkFormat

Sets the format string used for displaying hyperlinks in the frame.

```
SimpleHTML:SetHyperlinkFormat("format")
```

Hyperlinks are specified via HTML in the text input to a SimpleHTML frame, but in order to be handled as hyperlinks by the game's text engine they need to be formatted like the hyperlinks used elsewhere.

This property specifies the translation between formats: its default value of |H%s|h%s|h provides minimal formatting, turning (for example) <a href="achievement:892">The Right Stuff</a> into |Hachievement:892|hThe Right Stuff|h. Using a colorString or other formatting may be useful for making hyperlinks distinguishable from other text.

Arguments:

format—Format string used for displaying hyperlinks in the frame (string)

SetHyperlinksEnabled

Enables or disables hyperlink interactivity in the frame.

```
SimpleHTML:SetHyperlinksEnabled(enable)
```

The frame's hyperlink-related script handlers will only be run if hyperlinks are enabled.

Arguments:

enable—True to enable hyperlink interactivity in the frame; false to disable (boolean)

SetIndentedWordWrap

Sets whether long lines of text are indented when wrapping.

```
SimpleHTML:SetIndentedWordWrap(["element",] indent)
```

Arguments:

element (optional)—Name of an HTML element for which to set font properties (e.g. p, h1); if omitted, sets properties for the frame's default font (string)

indent—True to indent wrapped lines of text; false otherwise (boolean)

SetJustifyH

Sets the horizontal alignment style for text in the frame.

```
SimpleHTML:SetJustifyH(["element",] "justify")
```

Arguments:

element (optional)—Name of an HTML element for which to set properties (e.g. p, h1); if omitted, sets properties of the frame's default text style (string)

justify—Horizontal text alignment style (string, justifyH)

- CENTER
- LEFT
- RIGHT

SetJustifyV

Sets the vertical alignment style for text in the frame.

```
SimpleHTML:SetJustifyV(["element",] "justify")
```

Arguments:

element (optional)—Name of an HTML element for which to return text style information (e.g. p, h1); if omitted, returns information about the frame's default text style (string)

justify—Vertical text alignment style (string, justifyV)

- BOTTOM
- MIDDLE
- TOP

SetShadowColor

Sets the shadow color for text in the frame.

```
SimpleHTML:SetShadowColor(["element",] shadowR, shadowG, ↵
shadowB, shadowAlpha)
```

Arguments:

element (optional)—Name of an HTML element for which to set font properties (e.g. p, h1); if omitted, sets properties for the frame's default font (string)

shadowR—Red component of the shadow color (0.0 - 1.0) (number)

shadowG—Green component of the shadow color (0.0 - 1.0) (number)

shadowB—Blue component of the shadow color (0.0 - 1.0) (number)

shadowAlpha—Alpha (opacity) of the text's shadow (0.0 = fully transparent, 1.0 = fully opaque) (number)

SetShadowOffset

Returns the offset of text shadow from text in the frame.

```
SimpleHTML:SetShadowOffset(["element",] xOffset, yOffset)
```

Arguments:

element (optional)—Name of an HTML element for which to set font properties (e.g. p, h1); if omitted, sets properties for the frame's default font (string)

xOffset—Horizontal distance between the text and its shadow (in pixels) (number)

yOffset—Vertical distance between the text and its shadow (in pixels) (number)

SetSpacing

Sets the amount of spacing between lines of text in the frame.

```
SimpleHTML:SetSpacing(["element",] spacing)
```

Arguments:

element (optional)—Name of an HTML element for which to set font properties (e.g. p, h1); if omitted, sets properties for the frame's default font (string)

spacing—Amount of space between lines of text (in pixels) (number)

SetText

Sets the text to be displayed in the SimpleHTML frame.

```
SimpleHTML:SetText("text")
```

Text for display in the frame can be formatted using a simplified version of HTML markup:

- For HTML formatting, the entire text must be enclosed in <html><body> and </body></html> tags.
- All tags must be closed (img and br must use self-closing syntax; e.g.
, not <br>).
- Tags are case insensitive, but closing tags must match the case of opening tags.
- Attribute values must be enclosed in single or double quotation marks (" or ').
- Characters occurring in HTML markup must be entity-escaped (" < > &); no other entity-escapes are supported.
- Unrecognized tags and their contents are ignored (e.g. given <h1><foo>bar</foo>baz</h1>, only "baz" will appear).
- Any HTML parsing error will result in the raw HTML markup being displayed.

Only the following tags and attributes are supported:

- p, h1, h2, h3 - Block elements; e.g. <p align="left">
  - align - Text alignment style (optional); allowed values are left, center and right.
- img - Image; may only be used as a block element (not inline with text); e.g. <img src="Interface\Icons\INV_Misc_Rune_01" />.

- `src` - Path to the image file (filename extension omitted).
- `align` - Alignment of the image block in the frame (optional); allowed values are `left`, `center` and `right`.
- `width` - Width at which to display the image (in pixels; optional).
- `height` - Height at which to display the image (in pixels; optional).
- a - Inline hyperlink; e.g. `<a href="aLink">text</a>`
  - `href` - String identifying the link; passed as argument to hyperlink-related scripts when the player interacts with the link.
- br - Explicit line break in text; e.g. `<br />`.

Inline escape sequences used in FontStrings (e.g. `colorStrings`) may also be used.

Arguments:

`text`—Text (with HTML markup) to be displayed (`string`)

SetTextColor

Sets the color of text in the frame.

`SimpleHTML:SetTextColor(["element",] textR, textG, textB, textAlpha)`

Arguments:

`element` (optional)—Name of an HTML element for which to set font properties (e.g. p, h1); if omitted, sets properties for the frame's default font (`string`)

`textR`—Red component of the text color (0.0 - 1.0) (`number`)

`textG`—Green component of the text color (0.0 - 1.0) (`number`)

`textB`—Blue component of the text color (0.0 - 1.0) (`number`)

`textAlpha`—Alpha (opacity) of the text (0.0 = fully transparent, 1.0 = fully opaque) (`number`)

Slider

Sliders are elements intended to display or allow the user to choose a value in a range. They are often used for configuration, to choose scale, camera distance and similar settings.

Like Buttons, Sliders can be enabled or disabled, but unlike Buttons, they include no support for automatically changing appearance when this is done. You can set both their minimum and maximum values (one function returns or accepts both), and the step by which dragging changes their value. Sliders can be oriented either horizontally or vertically.

While you do not have to provide any code to manage the dragging of a slider's "thumb", you do have to provide a texture that will represent it, which the engine will position and draw automatically. In XML, you do this by providing a `<ThumbTexture>` element as a direct child of the `<Slider>` element, which can have any of the attributes or children allowed to any `<Texture>` element.

Sliders come in two common forms: thin tracks with a wide thumb, used for setting scalar options, or scroll bars used for positioning the contents of a frame.

Slider has all the methods from Frame, plus the following:

Disable

Disallows user interaction with the slider.

`Slider:Disable()`

Does not automatically change the visual state of the slider; directly making a visible change is recommended in order to communicate the change in state to the user.

Enable

Allows user interaction with the slider.

`Slider:Enable()`

GetMinMaxValues

Returns the minimum and maximum values for the slider.

`minValue, maxValue = Slider:GetMinMaxValues()`

Returns:

`minValue`—Lower boundary for values represented by the slider position (number)

`maxValue`—Upper boundary for values represented by the slider position (number)

GetOrientation

Returns the orientation of the slider.

`orientation = Slider:GetOrientation()`

Returns:

`orientation`—Token describing the orientation and direction of the slider (string)

- ▪ `HORIZONTAL` - Slider thumb moves from left to right as the slider's value increases
- ▪ `VERTICAL` - Slider thumb moves from top to bottom as the slider's value increases

GetThumbTexture

Returns the texture for the slider thumb.

`texture = Slider:GetThumbTexture()`

Returns:

`texture`—Reference to the `Texture` object used for the slider thumb (`texture`)

GetValue

Returns the value representing the current position of the slider thumb.

`value = Slider:GetValue()`

Returns:

`value`—Value representing the current position of the slider thumb (between `minValue` and `maxValue`, where `minValue, maxValue = slider:GetMinMaxValues()`) (number)

GetValueStep

Returns the minimum increment between allowed slider values.

```
step = Slider:GetValueStep()
```

Returns:

`step`—Minimum increment between allowed slider values (`number`)

IsEnabled

Returns whether user interaction with the slider is allowed.

```
enabled = Slider:IsEnabled()
```

Returns:

`enabled`—1 if user interaction with the slider is allowed; otherwise `nil` (`1nil`)

SetMinMaxValues

Sets the minimum and maximum values for the slider.

```
Slider:SetMinMaxValues(minValue, maxValue)
```

Arguments:

`minValue`—Lower boundary for values represented by the slider position (`number`)

`maxValue`—Upper boundary for values represented by the slider position (`number`)

SetOrientation

Sets the orientation of the slider.

```
Slider:SetOrientation("orientation")
```

Arguments:

`orientation`—Token describing the orientation and direction of the slider (`string`)

- `HORIZONTAL` - Slider thumb moves from left to right as the slider's value increases
- `VERTICAL` - Slider thumb moves from top to bottom as the slider's value increases (default)

SetThumbTexture

Sets the texture for the slider thumb.

```
Slider:SetThumbTexture(texture [, "layer"]) or ↵
Slider:SetThumbTexture("filename" [, "layer"])
```

Arguments:

`texture`—Reference to an existing `Texture` object (`texture`)

`filename`—Path to a texture image file (`string`)

`layer` (optional)—Graphics layer in which the texture should be drawn; defaults to `ARTWORK` if not specified (`string, layer`)

SetValue

Sets the value representing the position of the slider thumb.

```
Slider:SetValue(value)
```

Arguments:

value—Value representing the new position of the slider thumb
(between minValue and maxValue, where minValue, maxValue =
slider:GetMinMaxValues()) (number)

SetValueStep

Sets the minimum increment between allowed slider values.

```
Slider:SetValueStep(step)
```

The portion of the slider frame's area in which the slider thumb moves is its
width (or height, for vertical sliders) minus 16 pixels on either end. If the
number of possible values determined by the slider's minimum, maximum and
step values is less than the width (or height) of this area, the step value also
affects the movement of the slider thumb; see example for details.

Arguments:

step—Minimum increment between allowed slider values (number)

Example:

```
-- creates a sample horizontal slider
-- (also gives it the default UI's standard slider background,
-- since sliders don't automatically come with one)
CreateFrame("Slider","S",UIParent)
S:SetPoint("CENTER")
S:SetWidth(132)
S:SetHeight(17)
S:SetOrientation("HORIZONTAL")
S:SetThumbTexture("Interface\\Buttons\\UI-SliderBar-Button-
Horizontal")
S:SetMinMaxValues(0,100)
S:SetValue(50)
S:SetBackdrop({
  bgFile = "Interface\\Buttons\\UI-SliderBar-Background",
  edgeFile = "Interface\\Buttons\\UI-SliderBar-Border",
  tile = true, tileSize = 8, edgeSize = 8,
  insets = { left = 3, right = 3, top = 6, bottom = 6 }})

-- notice the slider thumb moves smoothly across the slider's
-- length when dragged and S:GetValue() often returns non-integer
-- results when dragging

-- now, restrict the slider's value step a bit:
S:SetValueStep(1)
-- notice the slider thumb still moves smoothly when dragged
-- but S:GetValue() now returns only integer results

-- further restricting the slider's value step:
S:SetValueStep(25)
-- now the slider thumb can only be dragged to one of
-- five different positions: 0, 25, 50, 75, or 100
```

StatusBar

StatusBars are similar to Sliders, but they are generally used for display as they don't offer any tools to receive user input. You define them with a bar texture and an optional color, and they fill a portion of their area in a given direction with that texture according to their value.

StatusBars can be oriented to fill from left to right (HORIZONTAL) or from bottom to top (VERTICAL). If you need to share the same bar texture between horizontal and vertical bars, they offer support for rotating the texture automatically to match. Presently, the StatusBar object does not support right-to-left or top-to-bottom bars.

StatusBars also offer an OnValueChanged handler to update information associated with the bar, such as updating a FontString that displays the bar's value as a number.

The most famous StatusBars in the stock UI are the bars that show your health and mana, and those of your group members and target.

StatusBar has all the methods from Frame, plus the following:

GetMinMaxValues

Returns the minimum and maximum values of the status bar.

`minValue, maxValue = StatusBar:GetMinMaxValues()`

Returns:

`minValue`—Lower boundary for values represented on the status bar (number)

`maxValue`—Upper boundary for values represented on the status bar (number)

GetOrientation

Returns the orientation of the status bar.

`orientation = StatusBar:GetOrientation()`

Returns:

`orientation`—Token describing the orientation and direction of the status bar (string)

- ▪ HORIZONTAL - Fills from left to right as the status bar value increases
- ▪ VERTICAL - Fills from top to bottom as the status bar value increases

GetRotatesTexture

Returns whether the status bar's texture is rotated to match its orientation.

`rotate = StatusBar:GetRotatesTexture()`

Returns:

`rotate`—1 if the status bar texture should be rotated 90 degrees counter-clockwise when the status bar is vertically oriented; otherwise nil (1nil)

GetStatusBarColor

Returns the color shading used for the status bar's texture.

`red, green, blue, alpha = StatusBar:GetStatusBarColor()`

Returns:

`red`—Red component of the color (0.0 - 1.0) (number)

`green`—Green component of the color (0.0 - 1.0) (number)

`blue`—Blue component of the color (0.0 - 1.0) (`number`)

`alpha` (optional)—Alpha (opacity) for the graphic (0.0 = fully transparent, 1.0 = fully opaque) (`number`)

GetStatusBarTexture

Returns the `Texture` object used for drawing the filled-in portion of the status bar.

`texture = StatusBar:GetStatusBarTexture()`

Returns:

`texture`—Reference to the `Texture` object used for drawing the filled-in portion of the status bar (`texture`)

GetValue

Returns the current value of the status bar.

`value = StatusBar:GetValue()`

Returns:

`value`—Value indicating the amount of the status bar's area to be filled in (between `minValue` and `maxValue`, where `minValue, maxValue = StatusBar:GetMinMaxValues()`) (`number`)

SetMinMaxValues

Sets the minimum and maximum values of the status bar.

`StatusBar:SetMinMaxValues(minValue, maxValue)`

Arguments:

`minValue`—Lower boundary for values represented on the status bar (`number`)

`maxValue`—Upper boundary for values represented on the status bar (`number`)

SetOrientation

Sets the orientation of the status bar.

`StatusBar:SetOrientation("orientation")`

Arguments:

`orientation`—Token describing the orientation and direction of the status bar (`string`)

- `HORIZONTAL` - Fills from left to right as the status bar value increases (default)
- `VERTICAL` - Fills from top to bottom as the status bar value increases

SetRotatesTexture

Sets whether the status bar's texture is rotated to match its orientation.

`StatusBar:SetRotatesTexture(rotate)`

Arguments:

`rotate`—`True` to rotate the status bar texture 90 degrees counter-clockwise when the status bar is vertically oriented; `false` otherwise (`1nil`)

SetStatusBarColor

Sets the color shading for the status bar's texture.

`StatusBar:SetStatusBarColor(red, green, blue [, alpha])`

As with :SetVertexColor(), this color is a shading applied to the texture image.

Arguments:

red—Red component of the color (0.0 - 1.0) (number)

green—Green component of the color (0.0 - 1.0) (number)

blue—Blue component of the color (0.0 - 1.0) (number)

alpha (optional)—Alpha (opacity) for the graphic (0.0 = fully transparent, 1.0 = fully opaque) (number)

SetStatusBarTexture

Sets the texture used for drawing the filled-in portion of the status bar.

```
StatusBar:SetStatusBarTexture(texture [, "layer"]) or ↵
StatusBar:SetStatusBarTexture("filename" [, "layer"])
```

The texture image is stretched to fill the dimensions of the entire status bar, then cropped to show only a portion corresponding to the status bar's current value.

Arguments:

texture—Reference to an existing Texture object (texture)

filename—Path to a texture image file (string)

layer (optional)—Graphics layer in which the texture should be drawn; defaults to ARTWORK if not specified (string, layer)

SetValue

Sets the value of the status bar.

```
StatusBar:SetValue(value)
```

Arguments:

value—Value indicating the amount of the status bar's area to be filled in (between minValue and maxValue, where minValue, maxValue = StatusBar:GetMinMaxValues()) (number)

Font

The Font object is the only type of object that is not attached to a parent widget; indeed, its purpose is to be shared between other objects that share font characteristics. In this way, changes to the Font object will update the text appearance of all text objects that have it set as their Font using :SetFontObject(). This allows a coder to maintain a consistent appearance between UI elements, as well as simplifying the resources and work required to update multiple text-based UI elements.

Font has all the methods from UIObject and FontInstance, plus the following:

CopyFontObject

Sets the font's properties to match those of another Font object.

```
Font:CopyFontObject(object) or Font:CopyFontObject("name")
```

Unlike `FontInstance:SetFontObject()`, this method allows one-time reuse of another font object's properties without continuing to inherit future changes made to the other object's properties.

Arguments:

`object`—Reference to a `Font` object (`font`)

`name`—Global name of a `Font` object (`string`)

GetAlpha

Returns the opacity for text displayed by the font.

`alpha = Font:GetAlpha()`

Returns:

`alpha`—Alpha (opacity) of the text (0.0 = fully transparent, 1.0 = fully opaque) (`number`)

GetMultilineIndent

Returns whether long lines of text are indented when wrapping.

`indent = Font:GetMultilineIndent()`

Returns:

`indent`—1 if long lines of text are indented when wrapping; otherwise `nil` (`1nil`)

SetAlpha

Sets the opacity for text displayed by the font.

`Font:SetAlpha(alpha)`

Arguments:

`alpha`—Alpha (opacity) of the text (0.0 = fully transparent, 1.0 = fully opaque) (`number`)

SetMultilineIndent

Sets whether long lines of text are indented when wrapping.

`Font:SetMultilineIndent(indent)`

Arguments:

`indent`—`True` to indent wrapped lines of text; `false` otherwise (`boolean`)

MessageFrame

MessageFrames are used to present series of messages or other lines of text, usually stacked on top of each other. Like most widgets relating to text display, MessageFrame inherits from FontInstance as well as Frame to provide methods for setting up text characteristics. Once the text settings for the frame are configured to your liking, you can add new messages to the frame with `:AddMessage()`. MessageFrame also supports methods for multi-line text display such as indented lines, as well as options for controlling how long messages should be displayed and how quickly they fade out when their time is up.

The stock UI uses the basic message frame for only one purpose, but it gets a lot of use; UIErrorsFrame, which displays messages like "Spell not ready yet" or "You're too far away", is a MessageFrame. MessageFrame also forms the basis for another, more sophisticated type, ScrollingMessageFrame.

MessageFrame has all the methods from Frame and FontInstance, plus the following:

AddMessage

Adds a message to those listed in the frame.

```
MessageFrame:AddMessage("text" [, red [, green [, blue [, alpha]]]])
```

If the frame was already 'full' with messages, then the oldest message is discarded when the new one is added.

Arguments:

text—Text of the message (string)

red (optional)—Red component of the text color for the message (0.0 - 1.0) (number)

green (optional)—Green component of the text color for the message (0.0 - 1.0) (number)

blue (optional)—Blue component of the text color for the message (0.0 - 1.0) (number)

alpha (optional)—Alpha (opacity) for the message (0.0 = fully transparent, 1.0 = fully opaque) (number)

Clear

Removes all messages displayed in the frame.

```
MessageFrame:Clear()
```

GetFadeDuration

Returns the duration of the fade-out animation for disappearing messages.

```
duration = MessageFrame:GetFadeDuration()
```

For the amount of time a message remains in the frame before beginning to fade, see :GetTimeVisible().

Returns:

duration—Duration of the fade-out animation for disappearing messages (in seconds) (number)

GetFading

Returns whether messages added to the frame automatically fade out after a period of time.

```
fading = MessageFrame:GetFading()
```

Returns:

fading—1 if messages added to the frame automatically fade out after a period of time; otherwise nil (1nil)

GetIndentedWordWrap

Returns whether long lines of text are indented when wrapping.

```
indent = MessageFrame:GetIndentedWordWrap()
```

Returns:

`indent`—1 if long lines of text are indented when wrapping; otherwise `nil` (1nil)

GetInsertMode

Returns the position at which new messages are added to the frame.

`position = MessageFrame:GetInsertMode()`

Returns:

`position`—Token identifying the position at which new messages are added to the frame (`string`)

- BOTTOM
- TOP

GetTimeVisible

Returns the amount of time for which a message remains visible before beginning to fade out.

`time = MessageFrame:GetTimeVisible()`

For the duration of the fade-out animation, see `:GetFadeDuration()`.

Returns:

`time`—Amount of time for which a message remains visible before beginning to fade out (in seconds) (`number`)

SetFadeDuration

Sets the duration of the fade-out animation for disappearing messages.

`MessageFrame:SetFadeDuration(duration)`

For the amount of time a message remains in the frame before beginning to fade, see `:SetTimeVisible()`.

Arguments:

`duration`—Duration of the fade-out animation for disappearing messages (in seconds) (`number`)

SetFading

Sets whether messages added to the frame automatically fade out after a period of time.

`MessageFrame:SetFading(fading)`

Arguments:

`fading`—True to cause messages added to the frame to automatically fade out after a period of time; `false` to leave message visible (`boolean`)

SetIndentedWordWrap

Sets whether long lines of text are indented when wrapping.

`MessageFrame:SetIndentedWordWrap(indent)`

Arguments:

`indent`—True to indent wrapped lines of text; `false` otherwise (`boolean`)

SetInsertMode

Sets the position at which new messages are added to the frame.

```
MessageFrame:SetInsertMode("position")
```

Arguments:

position—Token identifying the position at which new messages should be added to the frame (string)

- BOTTOM
- TOP

SetTimeVisible

Sets the amount of time for which a message remains visible before beginning to fade out.

```
MessageFrame:SetTimeVisible(time)
```

For the duration of the fade-out animation, see :SetFadeDuration().

Arguments:

time—Amount of time for which a message remains visible before beginning to fade out (in seconds) (number)

ScrollingMessageFrame

ScrollingMessageFrame expands on MessageFrame with the ability to store a much longer series of messages, and to move up and down through them by setting horizontal and vertical scroll values, or by using PageUp and PageDown methods.

ScrollingMessageFrames also support hyperlinks—such as the links posted in trade chat by people with items they want to sell—and provides an OnHyperlinkClicked script for displaying information related to the contents of the link.

The most common ScrollingMessageFrame in the stock UI is simply the chat frame, as well as the combat log. The raid warning and boss emote messages are presented in a ScrollingMessageFrame. The Guild Bank UI also uses one to display the transaction history.

ScrollingMessageFrame has all the methods from Frame and FontInstance, plus the following:

AddMessage

Adds a message to those listed in the frame.

```
ScrollingMessageFrame:AddMessage("text" [, red [, green ↵
[, blue [, id [, addToTop]]]]])
```

Arguments:

text—Text of the message (string)

red (optional)—Red component of the text color for the message (0.0 - 1.0) (number)

green (optional)—Green component of the text color for the message (0.0 - 1.0) (number)

blue (optional)—Blue component of the text color for the message (0.0 - 1.0) (number) id (optional)—Identifier for the message's type (see :UpdateColor-ByID()) (number)

addToTop (optional)—True to insert the message above all others listed in the frame, even if the frame's insert mode is set to BOTTOM; false to insert according to the frame's insert mode (boolean)

AtBottom

Returns whether the message frame is currently scrolled to the bottom of its contents.

```
atBottom = ScrollingMessageFrame:AtBottom()
```

Returns:

atBottom—1 if the message frame is currently scrolled to the bottom of its contents; otherwise nil (1nil)

AtTop

Returns whether the message frame is currently scrolled to the top of its contents.

```
atTop = ScrollingMessageFrame:AtTop()
```

Returns:

atTop—1 if the message frame is currently scrolled to the top of its contents; otherwise nil (1nil)

Clear

Removes all messages stored or displayed in the frame.

```
ScrollingMessageFrame:Clear()
```

GetCurrentLine

Returns a number identifying the last message added to the frame.

```
lineNum = ScrollingMessageFrame:GetCurrentLine()
```

This number starts at 0 when the frame is created and increments with each message AddMessage to the frame; however, it resets to 0 when a message is added beyond the frame's GetMaxLines.

Returns:

lineNum—A number identifying the last message added to the frame (number)

GetCurrentScroll

Returns the message frame's current scroll position.

```
offset = ScrollingMessageFrame:GetCurrentScroll()
```

Returns:

offset—Number of lines by which the frame is currently scrolled back from the end of its message history (number)

GetFadeDuration

Returns the duration of the fade-out animation for disappearing messages.

```
duration = ScrollingMessageFrame:GetFadeDuration()
```

For the amount of time a message remains in the frame before beginning to fade, see :GetTimeVisible().

Returns:

duration—Duration of the fade-out animation for disappearing messages (in seconds) (number)

GetFading

Returns whether messages added to the frame automatically fade out after a period of time.

fading = ScrollingMessageFrame:GetFading()

Returns:

fading—1 if messages added to the frame automatically fade out after a period of time; otherwise nil (1nil)

GetHyperlinksEnabled

Returns whether hyperlinks in the frame's text are interactive.

enabled = ScrollingMessageFrame:GetHyperlinksEnabled()

Returns:

enabled—1 if hyperlinks in the frame's text are interactive; otherwise nil (1nil)

GetIndentedWordWrap

Returns whether long lines of text are indented when wrapping.

indent = ScrollingMessageFrame:GetIndentedWordWrap()

Returns:

indent—1 if long lines of text are indented when wrapping; otherwise nil (1nil)

GetInsertMode

Returns the position at which new messages are added to the frame.

position = ScrollingMessageFrame:GetInsertMode()

Returns:

position—Token identifying the position at which new messages are added to the frame (string)

- ◼ BOTTOM
- ◼ TOP

GetMaxLines

Returns the maximum number of messages kept in the frame.

ScrollingMessageFrame:GetMaxLines(maxLines)

Arguments:

maxLines—Maximum number of messages kept in the frame (number)

GetNumLinesDisplayed

Returns the number of lines displayed in the message frame.

count = ScrollingMessageFrame:GetNumLinesDisplayed()

This number reflects the list of messages currently displayed, not including those which are stored for display if the frame is scrolled.

Returns:

count—Number of messages currently displayed in the frame (number)

GetNumMessages

Returns the number of messages currently kept in the frame's message history.

```
count = ScrollingMessageFrame:GetNumMessages()
```

This number reflects the list of messages which can be seen by scrolling the frame, including (but not limited to) the list of messages currently displayed.

Returns:

count—Number of messages currently kept in the frame's message history (number)

GetTimeVisible

Returns the amount of time for which a message remains visible before beginning to fade out.

```
time = ScrollingMessageFrame:GetTimeVisible()
```

Returns:

time—Amount of time for which a message remains visible before beginning to fade out (in seconds) (number)

PageDown

Scrolls the message frame's contents down by one page.

```
ScrollingMessageFrame:PageDown()
```

One "page" is slightly less than the number of lines displayed in the frame.

PageUp

Scrolls the message frame's contents up by one page.

```
ScrollingMessageFrame:PageUp()
```

One "page" is slightly less than the number of lines displayed in the frame.

ScrollDown

Scrolls the message frame's contents down by two lines.

```
ScrollingMessageFrame:ScrollDown()
```

ScrollToBottom

Scrolls to the bottom of the message frame's contents.

```
ScrollingMessageFrame:ScrollToBottom()
```

ScrollToTop

Scrolls to the top of the message frame's contents.

```
ScrollingMessageFrame:ScrollToTop()
```

ScrollUp

Scrolls the message frame's contents up by two lines.

```
ScrollingMessageFrame:ScrollUp()
```

SetFadeDuration

Sets the duration of the fade-out animation for disappearing messages.

```
ScrollingMessageFrame:SetFadeDuration(duration)
```

For the amount of time a message remains in the frame before beginning to fade, see :SetTimeVisible().

Arguments:

duration—Duration of the fade-out animation for disappearing messages (in seconds) (number)

SetFading

Sets whether messages added to the frame automatically fade out after a period of time.

```
ScrollingMessageFrame:SetFading(fading)
```

Arguments:

fading—True to cause messages added to the frame to automatically fade out after a period of time; false to leave message visible (boolean)

SetHyperlinksEnabled

Enables or disables hyperlink interactivity in the frame.

```
ScrollingMessageFrame:SetHyperlinksEnabled(enable)
```

The frame's hyperlink-related script handlers will only be run if hyperlinks are enabled.

Arguments:

enable—True to enable hyperlink interactivity in the frame; false to disable (boolean)

SetIndentedWordWrap

Sets whether long lines of text are indented when wrapping.

```
ScrollingMessageFrame:SetIndentedWordWrap(indent)
```

Arguments:

indent—True to indent wrapped lines of text; false otherwise (boolean)

SetInsertMode

Sets the position at which new messages are added to the frame.

```
ScrollingMessageFrame:SetInsertMode("position")
```

Arguments:

position—Token identifying the position at which new messages should be added to the frame (string)

- BOTTOM
- TOP

SetMaxLines

Sets the maximum number of messages to be kept in the frame.

```
ScrollingMessageFrame:SetMaxLines(maxLines)
```

If additional messages are added beyond this number, the oldest lines are discarded and can no longer be seen by scrolling.

Arguments:

maxLines—Maximum number of messages to be kept in the frame (number)

SetScrollOffset

Sets the message frame's scroll position.

```
ScrollingMessageFrame:SetScrollOffset(offset)
```

Arguments:

offset—Number of lines to scroll back from the end of the frame's message history (number)

SetTimeVisible

Sets the amount of time for which a message remains visible before beginning to fade out.

```
ScrollingMessageFrame:SetTimeVisible(time)
```

For the duration of the fade-out animation, see :SetFadeDuration().

Arguments:

time—Amount of time for which a message remains visible before beginning to fade out (in seconds) (number)

UpdateColorByID

Updates the color of a set of messages already added to the frame.

```
ScrollingMessageFrame:UpdateColorByID(id, red, green, blue)
```

Used in the default UI to allow customization of chat window message colors by type: each type of chat window message (party, raid, emote, system message, etc) has a numeric identifier found in the global table ChatTypeInfo; this is passed as the fifth argument to :AddMessage() when messages are added to the frame, allowing them to be identified for recoloring via this method.

Arguments:

id—Identifier for a message's type (as set when the messages were added to the frame) (number)

red—Red component of the new text color (0.0 - 1.0) (number)

green—Green component of the new text color (0.0 - 1.0) (number)

blue—Blue component of the new text color (0.0 - 1.0) (number)

EditBox

EditBoxes are used to allow the player to type text into a UI component. They inherit from FontInstance as well as Frame in order to provide the needed support for text display, and add methods for entering text, such as positioning a cursor within text, establishing character limits, controlling whether text should be displayed in password-fashion (with bullets substituted for the characters), manipulating an entry history, or controlling and responding to changes in keyboard focus.

The most common use for an EditBox is to accept chat input from the player, but they are also used for commands, configuration and confirmation, such as requiring you to type "DELETE" before destroying a valuable item, or entering the name of a new macro.

Most EditBoxes are derived from ChatFrameEditBoxTemplate, or use the same textures to create a visible frame around the editable area.

EditBox has all the methods from Frame and FontInstance, plus the following:

AddHistoryLine

Adds a line of text to the edit box's stored history.

```
EditBox:AddHistoryLine("text")
```

Once added, the user can quickly set the edit box's contents to one of these lines by pressing the up or down arrow keys. (History lines are only accessible via the arrow keys if the edit box is not in multi-line mode.)

Arguments:

text—Text to be added to the edit box's list of history lines (string)

ClearFocus

Releases keyboard input focus from the edit box.

```
EditBox:ClearFocus()
```

GetAltArrowKeyMode

Returns whether arrow keys are ignored by the edit box unless the Alt key is held.

```
enabled = EditBox:GetAltArrowKeyMode()
```

Returns:

enabled—1 if arrow keys are ignored by the edit box unless the Alt key is held; otherwise nil (1nil)

GetBlinkSpeed

Returns the rate at which the text insertion blinks when the edit box is focused.

```
duration = EditBox:GetBlinkSpeed()
```

Returns:

duration—Amount of time for which the cursor is visible during each "blink" (in seconds) (number)

GetCursorPosition

Returns the current cursor position inside edit box.

```
position = EditBox:GetCursorPosition()
```

Returns:

position—Current position of the keyboard input cursor (between 0, for the position before the first character, and editbox:GetNumLetters(), for the position after the last character) (number)

GetHistoryLines

Returns the maximum number of history lines stored by the edit box.

count = EditBox:GetHistoryLines()

Returns:

count—Maximum number of history lines stored by the edit box (number)

GetIndentedWordWrap

Returns whether long lines of text are indented when wrapping.

indent = EditBox:GetIndentedWordWrap()

Returns:

indent—1 if long lines of text are indented when wrapping; otherwise nil (1nil)

GetInputLanguage

Returns the currently selected keyboard input language (character set / input method).

language = EditBox:GetInputLanguage()

Applies to keyboard input methods, not in-game languages or client locales.

Returns:

language—Token representing the current keyboard input method (string)

GetMaxBytes

Returns the maximum number of bytes of text allowed in the edit box.

maxBytes = EditBox:GetMaxBytes()

Note: Unicode characters may consist of more than one byte each, so the behavior of a byte limit may differ from that of a character limit in practical use.

Returns:

maxBytes—Maximum number of text bytes allowed in the edit box (number)

GetMaxLetters

Returns the maximum number of text characters allowed in the edit box.

maxLetters = EditBox:GetMaxLetters()

Returns:

maxLetters—Maximum number of text characters allowed in the edit box (number)

GetNumLetters

Returns the number of text characters in the edit box.

numLetters = EditBox:GetNumLetters()

Returns:

numLetters—Number of text characters in the edit box (number)

GetNumber

Returns the contents of the edit box as a number.

```
num = EditBox:GetNumber()
```

Similar to tonumber(editbox:GetText()); returns 0 if the contents of the edit box cannot be converted to a number.

Returns:

num—Contents of the edit box as a number (number)

GetText

Returns the edit box's text contents.

```
text = EditBox:GetText()
```

Returns:

text—Text contained in the edit box (string)

GetTextInsets

Returns the insets from the edit box's edges which determine its interactive text area.

```
left, right, top, bottom = EditBox:GetTextInsets()
```

Returns:

left—Distance from the left edge of the edit box to the left edge of its interactive text area (in pixels) (number)

right—Distance from the right edge of the edit box to the right edge of its interactive text area (in pixels) (number)

top—Distance from the top edge of the edit box to the top edge of its interactive text area (in pixels) (number)

bottom—Distance from the bottom edge of the edit box to the bottom edge of its interactive text area (in pixels) (number)

GetUTF8CursorPosition

Returns the cursor's numeric position in the edit box, taking UTF-8 multi-byte character into account.

```
position = EditBox:GetUTF8CursorPosition()
```

If the EditBox contains multi-byte Unicode characters, the GetCursorPosition() method will not return correct results, as it considers each eight byte character to count as a single glyph. This method properly returns the position in the edit box from the perspective of the user.

Returns:

position—The cursor's numeric position (leftmost position is 0), taking UTF8 multi-byte characters into account. (number)

HasFocus

Returns whether the edit box is currently focused for keyboard input.

```
enabled = EditBox:HasFocus()
```

Returns:

enabled—1 if the edit box is currently focused for keyboard input; otherwise nil (1nil)

HighlightText

Selects all or a portion of the text in the edit box.

```
EditBox:HighlightText([start [, end]])
```

Arguments:

start (optional)—Character position at which to begin the selection (between 0, for the position before the first character, and editbox:GetNumLetters(), for the position after the last character); defaults to 0 if not specified (number)

end (optional)—Character position at which to end the selection; if not specified or if less than start, selects all characters after the start position; if equal to start, selects nothing and positions the cursor at the start position (number)

Insert

Inserts text into the edit box at the current cursor position.

```
EditBox:Insert("text")
```

Arguments:

text—Text to be inserted (string)

IsAutoFocus

Returns whether the edit box automatically acquires keyboard input focus.

```
enabled = EditBox:IsAutoFocus()
```

Returns:

enabled—1 if the edit box automatically acquires keyboard input focus; otherwise nil (1nil)

IsInIMECompositionMode

Returns whether the edit box is in Input Method Editor composition mode.

```
enabled = EditBox:IsInIMECompositionMode()
```

Character composition mode is used for input methods in which multiple keypresses generate one printed character. In such input methods, the edit box's OnChar script is run for each keypress—if the OnChar script should act only when a complete character is entered in the edit box, :IsInIMECompositionMode() can be used to test for such cases.

This mode is common in clients for languages using non-Roman characters (such as Chinese or Korean), but can still occur in client languages using Roman scripts (e.g. English)—such as when typing accented characters on the Mac client (e.g. typing "option-u" then "e" to insert the character "ë").

Returns:

enabled—1 if the edit box is in IME character composition mode; otherwise nil (1nil)

IsMultiLine

Returns whether the edit box shows more than one line of text.

```
multiLine = EditBox:IsMultiLine()
```

Returns:

multiLine—1 if the edit box shows more than one line of text; otherwise nil
(1nil)

IsNumeric

Returns whether the edit box only accepts numeric input.

```
enabled = EditBox:IsNumeric()
```

Returns:

enabled—1 if only numeric input is allowed; otherwise nil (1nil)

IsPassword

Returns whether the text entered in the edit box is masked.

```
enabled = EditBox:IsPassword()
```

Returns:

enabled—1 if text entered in the edit box is masked with asterisk characters (*);
otherwise nil (1nil)

SetAltArrowKeyMode

Sets whether arrow keys are ignored by the edit box unless the Alt key is held.

```
EditBox:SetAltArrowKeyMode(enable)
```

Arguments:

enable—True to cause the edit box to ignore arrow key presses unless the Alt
key is held; false to allow unmodified arrow key presses for cursor movement
(boolean)

SetAutoFocus

Sets whether the edit box automatically acquires keyboard input focus.

```
EditBox:SetAutoFocus(enable)
```

If auto-focus behavior is enabled, the edit box automatically acquires keyboard
focus when it is shown and when no other edit box is focused.

Arguments:

enable—True to enable the edit box to automatically acquire keyboard input
focus; false to disable (boolean)

SetBlinkSpeed

Sets the rate at which the text insertion blinks when the edit box is focused.

```
EditBox:SetBlinkSpeed(duration)
```

The speed indicates how long the cursor stays in each state (shown and
hidden); e.g. if the blink speed is 0.5 (the default, the cursor is shown for one
half second and then hidden for one half second (thus, a one-second cycle); if
the speed is 1.0, the cursor is shown for one second and then hidden for one
second (a two-second cycle).

Arguments:

duration—Amount of time for which the cursor is visible during each "blink"
(in seconds) (number)

SetCursorPosition

Sets the cursor position in the edit box.

`EditBox:SetCursorPosition(position)`

Arguments:

`position`—New position for the keyboard input cursor (between 0, for the position before the first character, and `editbox:GetNumLetters()`, for the position after the last character) (`number`)

SetFocus

Focuses the edit box for keyboard input.

`EditBox:SetFocus()`

Only one edit box may be focused at a time; setting focus to one edit box will remove it from the currently focused edit box.

SetHistoryLines

Sets the maximum number of history lines stored by the edit box.

`EditBox:SetHistoryLines(count)`

Lines of text can be added to the edit box's history by calling `:AddHistoryLine()`; once added, the user can quickly set the edit box's contents to one of these lines by pressing the up or down arrow keys. (History lines are only accessible via the arrow keys if the edit box is not in multi-line mode.)

Arguments:

`count`—Maximum number of history lines to be stored by the edit box (`number`)

SetIndentedWordWrap

Sets whether long lines of text are indented when wrapping.

`EditBox:SetIndentedWordWrap(indent)`

Arguments:

`indent`—`True` to indent wrapped lines of text; `false` otherwise (`boolean`)

SetMaxBytes

Sets the maximum number of bytes of text allowed in the edit box.

`EditBox:SetMaxBytes(maxBytes)`

Attempts to type more than this number into the edit box will produce no results; programmatically inserting text or setting the edit box's text will truncate input to the maximum length.

Note: Unicode characters may consist of more than one byte each, so the behavior of a byte limit may differ from that of a character limit in practical use.

Arguments:

`maxBytes`—Maximum number of text bytes allowed in the edit box, or 0 for no limit (`number`)

SetMaxLetters

Sets the maximum number of text characters allowed in the edit box.

`EditBox:SetMaxLetters(maxLetters)`

Attempts to type more than this number into the edit box will produce no results; programmatically inserting text or setting the edit box's text will truncate input to the maximum length.

Arguments:

`maxLetters`—Maximum number of text characters allowed in the edit box, or `0` for no limit (`number`)

SetMultiLine

Sets whether the edit box shows more than one line of text.

`EditBox:SetMultiLine(multiLine)`

When in multi-line mode, the edit box's height is determined by the number of lines shown and cannot be set directly—enclosing the edit box in a `ScrollFrame` may prove useful in such cases.

Arguments:

`multiLine`—`True` to allow the edit box to display more than one line of text; `false` for single-line display (`boolean`)

SetNumber

Sets the contents of the edit box to a number.

`EditBox:SetNumber(num)`

Arguments:

`num`—New numeric content for the edit box (`number`)

SetNumeric

Sets whether the edit box only accepts numeric input.

`EditBox:SetNumeric(enable)`

Note: an edit box in numeric mode *only* accepts numeral input—all other characters, including those commonly used in numeric representations (such as `.`, `E` and `-`) are not allowed.

Arguments:

`enable`—`True` to allow only numeric input; `false` to allow any text (`boolean`)

SetPassword

Sets whether the text entered in the edit box is masked.

`EditBox:SetPassword(enable)`

Arguments:

`enable`—`True` to mask text entered in the edit box with asterisk characters (`*`); `false` to show the actual text entered (`boolean`)

SetText

Sets the edit box's text contents.

```
EditBox:SetText("text")
```

Arguments:

`text`—Text to be placed in the edit box (`string`)

SetTextInsets

Sets the insets from the edit box's edges which determine its interactive text area.

```
EditBox:SetTextInsets(left, right, top, bottom)
```

Arguments:

`left`—Distance from the left edge of the edit box to the left edge of its interactive text area (in pixels) (`number`)

`right`—Distance from the right edge of the edit box to the right edge of its interactive text area (in pixels) (`number`)

`top`—Distance from the top edge of the edit box to the top edge of its interactive text area (in pixels) (`number`)

`bottom`—Distance from the bottom edge of the edit box to the bottom edge of its interactive text area (in pixels) (`number`)

ToggleInputLanguage

Switches the edit box's language input mode.

```
EditBox:ToggleInputLanguage()
```

If the edit box is in ROMAN mode and an alternate Input Method Editor composition mode is available (as determined by the client locale and system settings), switches to the alternate input mode. If the edit box is in IME composition mode, switches back to ROMAN.

AnimationGroup

An AnimationGroup is how various animations are actually applied to a region; this is how different behaviors can be run in sequence or in parallel with each other, automatically. When you pause an AnimationGroup, it tracks which of its child animations were playing and how far advanced they were, and resumes them from that point.

An Animation in a group has an order from 1 to 100, which determines when it plays; once all animations with order 1 have completed, including any delays, the AnimationGroup starts all animations with order 2.

An AnimationGroup can also be set to loop, either repeating from the beginning or playing backward back to the beginning. An AnimationGroup has an OnLoop handler that allows you to call your own code back whenever a loop completes. The `:Finish()` method stops the animation after the current loop has completed, rather than immediately.

AnimationGroup has all the methods from ScriptObject and ParentedObject, plus the following:

CreateAnimation

Creates an Animation as a child of this group.

```
animation = AnimationGroup:CreateAnimation("animationType" [, ↵
"name" [, "inheritsFrom"]])
```

Arguments:

animationType—Type of Animation object to be created (see widgets hierarchy for available subtypes) (string)

name (optional)—Global name to use for the new animation (string)

inheritsFrom (optional)—A template from which to inherit (string)

Returns:

animation—The newly created animation (animation)

Finish

Causes animations within the group to complete and stop.

```
AnimationGroup:Finish()
```

If the group is playing, animations will continue until the current loop cycle is complete before stopping. For example, in a group which manages a repeating fade-out-fade-in animation, the associated object will continue to fade completely back in, instead of the animation stopping and the object instantly switching from partial opacity to full opacity instantly. Does nothing if this group is not playing.

To instantly stop an animation, see AnimationGroup:Stop().

GetAnimations

Returns a list of animations belonging to the group.

```
... = AnimationGroup:GetAnimations()
```

Returns:

...—A list of Animation objects belonging to the animation group (list)

GetDuration

Returns the duration of a single loop cycle for the group, as determined by its child animations.

```
duration = AnimationGroup:GetDuration()
```

Total duration is based on the durations, delays and order of child animations; see example for details.

Returns:

duration—Total duration of all child animations (in seconds) (number)

Example:

```
<AnimationGroup name="Pulse">
  <Alpha name="$parentIn" change="1" duration="0.1"/>
  <Alpha name="$parentOut" change="-1" duration="1.5"/>
</AnimationGroup>
-- contains two animations which are implicitly ordered, so
-- group duration is the sum of the animation durations: 1.6 sec

<AnimationGroup name="Alarm">
```

```
<Alpha name="$parentIn" change="1" duration="0.5" order="1"/>
<Rotation name="$parentJiggleLeft" degrees="-15" duration="0.25" ↵
startDelay="0.35" order="1"/>
<Rotation name="$parentJiggleRight" degrees="30" duration="0.5" ↵
order="2"/>
<Rotation name="$parentJiggleStop" degrees="-15" duration="0.25" ↵
endDelay="0.25" order="3"/>
<Alpha name="$parentOut" change="-1" duration="0.5" order="4"/>
</AnimationGroup>
-- contains delays and multiple animations, some of which are
-- concurrent, so group duration is the maximum duration (including
-- delay) of concurrent animations plus the sum of durations and
-- delays for sequential animations:
-- max(0.5, 0.25 + 0.35) + 0.5 + (0.25 + 0.25) + 0.5 = 2.1 sec
```

GetInitialOffset

Returns the starting static translation for the animated region.

```
x, y = AnimationGroup:GetInitialOffset()
```

Returns:

x—Horizontal distance to offset the animated region (in pixels) (number)

y—Vertical distance to offset the animated region (in pixels) (number)

GetLoopState

Returns the current loop state of the group.

```
loopState = AnimationGroup:GetLoopState()
```

Returns:

loopState—Loop state of the animation group (string)

- ▪ FORWARD - In transition from the start state to the final state
- ▪ NONE - Not looping
- ▪ REVERSE - In transition from the final state back to the start state

GetLooping

Returns the looping behavior of the group.

```
loopType = AnimationGroup:GetLooping()
```

Returns:

loopType—Looping type for the animation group (string)

- ▪ BOUNCE - Repeatedly animates forward from the initial state to the final state then backwards to the initial state
- ▪ NONE - No looping; animates from the initial state to the final state once and stops
- ▪ REPEAT - Repeatedly animates forward from the initial state to the final state (instantly resetting from the final state to the initial state between repetitions)

GetMaxOrder

Returns the highest order amongst the animations in the group.

```
maxOrder = AnimationGroup:GetMaxOrder()
```

Returns:

maxOrder—Highest ordering value (see Animation:GetOrder()) of the animations in the group (number)

GetProgress

Returns the current state of the animation group's progress.

progress = AnimationGroup:GetProgress()

Returns:

progress—Value indicating the current state of the group animation: between 0.0 (initial state, child animations not yet started) and 1.0 (final state, all child animations complete) (number)

IsDone

Returns whether the group has finished playing.

done = AnimationGroup:IsDone()

Only valid in the OnFinished and OnUpdate handlers, and only applies if the animation group does not loop.

Returns:

done—True if the group has finished playing; false otherwise (boolean)

IsPaused

Returns whether the group is paused.

paused = AnimationGroup:IsPaused()

Returns:

paused—True if animation of the group is currently paused; false otherwise (boolean)

IsPendingFinish

Returns whether or not the animation group is pending finish.

isPending = AnimationGroup:IsPendingFinish()

Returns:

isPending—Whether or not the animation group is currently pending a finish command. Since the Finish() method does not immediately stop the animation group, this method can be used to test if Finish() has been called and the group will finish at the end of the current loop. (boolean)

IsPlaying

Returns whether the group is playing.

playing = AnimationGroup:IsPlaying()

Returns:

playing—True if the group is currently animating; false otherwise (boolean)

Pause

Pauses animation of the group.

AnimationGroup:Pause()

Unlike with `AnimationGroup:Stop()`, the animation is paused at its current progress state (e.g. in a fade-out-fade-in animation, the element will be at partial opacity) instead of reset to the initial state; animation can be resumed with `AnimationGroup:Play()`.

Play

Starts animating the group.

`AnimationGroup:Play()`

If the group has been paused, animation resumes from the paused state; otherwise animation begins at the initial state.

SetInitialOffset

Sets a static translation for the animated region.

`AnimationGroup:SetInitialOffset(x, y)`

This translation is only used while the animation is playing.

For example, applying an initial offset of `0,-50` to an animation group which fades the PlayerPortrait in and out would cause the portrait image to jump down 50 pixels from its normal position when the animation begins playing, and return to its initial position when the animation is finished or stopped.

Arguments:

x—Horizontal distance to offset the animated region (in pixels) (`number`)

y—Vertical distance to offset the animated region (in pixels) (`number`)

SetLooping

Sets the looping behavior of the group.

`AnimationGroup:SetLooping("loopType")`

Arguments:

`loopType`—Looping type for the animation group (`string`)

- BOUNCE - Repeatedly animates forward from the initial state to the final state then backwards to the initial state
- NONE - No looping; animates from the initial state to the final state once and stops
- REPEAT - Repeatedly animates forward from the initial state to the final state (instantly resetting from the final state to the initial state between repetitions)

Stop

Stops animation of the group.

`AnimationGroup:Stop()`

Unlike with `AnimationGroup:Pause()`, the animation is reset to the initial state (e.g. in a fade-out-fade-in animation, the element will be instantly returned to full opacity) instead of paused at its current progress state.

Animation

Animations are used to change presentations or other characteristics of a frame or other region over time. The Animation object will take over the work of calling code over time, or when it is done, and tracks how close the animation is to completion.

The Animation type doesn't create any visual effects by itself, but it does provide an OnUpdate handler that you can use to support specialized time-sensitive behaviors that aren't provided by the transformations descended from Animations. In addition to tracking the passage of time through an elapsed argument, you can query the animation's progress as a 0-1 fraction to determine how you should set your behavior.

You can also change how the elapsed time corresponds to the progress by changing the smoothing, which creates acceleration or deceleration, or by adding a delay to the beginning or end of the animation.

You can also use an Animation as a timer, by setting the Animation's OnFinished script to trigger a callback and setting the duration to the desired time.

Animation has all the methods from ScriptObject and ParentedObject, plus the following:

GetDuration

Returns the time for the animation to progress from start to finish.

```
duration = Animation:GetDuration()
```

Returns:

duration—Time for the animation to progress from start to finish (in seconds) (number)

GetElapsed

Returns the amount of time since the animation began playing.

```
elapsed = Animation:GetElapsed()
```

This amount includes start and end delays.

Returns:

elapsed—Amount of time since the animation began playing (in seconds) (number)

GetEndDelay

Returns the amount of time the animation delays after finishing.

```
delay = Animation:GetEndDelay()
```

A later animation in an animation group will not begin until after the end delay period of the preceding animation has elapsed.

Returns:

delay—Time the animation delays after finishing (in seconds) (number)

GetMaxFramerate

Returns the maximum number of times per second that the animation will update its progress.

```
framerate = Animation:GetMaxFramerate()
```

Does not necessarily reflect the running framerate of the animation in progress; World of Warcraft itself may be running at a lower framerate.

Returns:

`framerate`—Maximum number of times per second that the animation will update its progress (`number`)

GetOrder

Returns the order of the animation within its parent group.

`order = Animation:GetOrder()`

When the parent `AnimationGroup` plays, Animations with a lower order number are played before those with a higher number. Animations with the same order number are played at the same time.

Returns:

`order`—Position at which the animation will play relative to others in its group (between 0 and 100) (`number`)

GetProgress

Returns the progress of the animation (ignoring start and end delay).

`progress = Animation:GetProgress()`

When using a generic `Animation` object to animate effects not handled by the built-in `Animation` subtypes, this method should be used for updating effects in the animation's `OnUpdate` handler, as it properly accounts for smoothing and delays managed by the `Animation` object.

Returns:

`progress`—Progress of the animation: between 0.0 (at start) and 1.0 (at end) (`number`)

GetProgressWithDelay

Returns the progress of the animation and associated delays.

`progress = Animation:GetProgressWithDelay()`

Returns:

`progress`—Progress of the animation and its delays: between 0.0 (at start of start delay) and 1.0 (at end of end delay) (`number`)

GetRegionParent

Returns the `Region` object on which the animation operates.

`region = Animation:GetRegionParent()`

Returns:

`region`—Reference to the `Region` object on which the animation operates (i.e. the parent of the animation's parent `AnimationGroup`). (`region`, **Region**)

GetSmoothProgress

Returns the progress of an animation, ignoring smoothing effects.

`progress = Animation:GetSmoothProgress()`

The value returned by this method increases linearly with time while the animation is playing, while the value returned by `Animation:GetProgress()` may change at a different rate if the animation's smoothing type is set to a value other than NONE.

Returns:

`progress`—Progress of the animation: between 0.0 (at start) and 1.0 (at end) (`number`)

GetSmoothing

Returns the smoothing type for the animation.

`smoothType = Animation:GetSmoothing()`

This setting affects the rate of change in the animation's progress value as it plays.

Returns:

`smoothType`—Type of smoothing for the animation (`string`)

- `IN` - Initially progressing slowly and accelerating towards the end
- `IN_OUT` - Initially progressing slowly and accelerating towards the middle, then slowing down towards the end
- `NONE` - Progresses at a constant rate from beginning to end
- `OUT` - Initially progressing quickly and slowing towards the end

GetStartDelay

Returns the amount of time the animation delays before its progress begins.

`delay = Animation:GetStartDelay()`

Returns:

`delay`—Amount of time the animation delays before its progress begins (in seconds) (`number`)

IsDelaying

Returns whether the animation is currently in the middle of a start or end delay.

`delaying = Animation:IsDelaying()`

Returns:

`delaying`—True if the animation is currently in its start or end delay period; `false` if the animation is currently between its start and end periods (or has none) or is not playing (`boolean`)

IsDone

Returns whether the animation has finished playing.

`done = Animation:IsDone()`

Returns:

`done`—True if the animation is finished playing; otherwise `false` (`boolean`)

IsPaused

Returns whether the animation is currently paused.

`paused = Animation:IsPaused()`

Returns:

`paused`—True if the animation is currently paused; `false` otherwise (`boolean`)

IsPlaying

Returns whether the animation is currently playing.

`playing = Animation:IsPlaying()`

Returns:

`playing`—True if the animation is currently playing; otherwise `false` (`boolean`)

IsStopped

Returns whether the animation is currently stopped.

`stopped = Animation:IsStopped()`

Returns:

`stopped`—True if the animation is currently stopped; otherwise `false` (`boolean`)

Pause

Pauses the animation.

`Animation:Pause()`

Unlike with `Animation:Stop()`, the animation is paused at its current progress state (e.g. in a fade-out-fade-in animation, the element will be at partial opacity) instead of reset to the initial state; animation can be resumed with `Animation:Play()`.

Play

Plays the animation.

`Animation:Play()`

If the animation has been paused, it resumes from the paused state; otherwise the animation begins at its initial state.

SetDuration

Sets the time for the animation to progress from start to finish.

`Animation:SetDuration(duration)`

Arguments:

`duration`—Time for the animation to progress from start to finish (in seconds) (`number`)

SetEndDelay

Sets the amount of time for the animation to delay after finishing.

`Animation:SetEndDelay(delay)`

A later animation in an animation group will not begin until after the end delay period of the preceding animation has elapsed.

Arguments:

`delay`—Time for the animation to delay after finishing (in seconds) (`number`)

SetMaxFramerate

Sets the maximum number of times per second for the animation to update its progress.

```
Animation:SetMaxFramerate(framerate)
```

Useful for limiting the amount of CPU time used by an animation. For example, if an UI element is 30 pixels square and is animated to double in size in 1 second, any visible increase in animation quality if WoW is running faster than 30 frames per second will be negligible. Limiting the animation's framerate frees CPU time to be used for other animations or UI scripts.

Arguments:

framerate—Maximum number of times per second for the animation to update its progress, or 0 to run at the maximum possible framerate (number)

SetOrder

Sets the order for the animation to play within its parent group.

```
Animation:SetOrder(order)
```

When the parent AnimationGroup plays, Animations with a lower order number are played before those with a higher number. Animations with the same order number are played at the same time.

Arguments:

order—Position at which the animation should play relative to others in its group (between 0 and 100) (number)

SetParent

Sets the parent for the animation.

```
Animation:SetParent(animGroup) or Animation:SetParent("animGroupName")
```

If the animation was not already a child of the parent, the parent will insert the animation into the proper order amongst its children.

Arguments:

animGroup—The animation group to set as the parent of this animation (animgroup, AnimationGroup)

animGroupName—The name of the animation group to set as the parent of this animation (string)

SetSmoothing

Sets the smoothing type for the animation.

```
Animation:SetSmoothing("smoothType")
```

This setting affects the rate of change in the animation's progress value as it plays.

Arguments:

smoothType—Type of smoothing for the animation (string)

■ IN - Initially progressing slowly and accelerating towards the end

- IN_OUT - Initially progressing slowly and accelerating towards the middle, then slowing down towards the end
- NONE - Progresses at a constant rate from beginning to end
- OUT - Initially progressing quickly and slowing towards the end

SetStartDelay

Sets the amount of time for the animation to delay before its progress begins.

```
Animation:SetStartDelay(delay)
```

Start delays can be useful with concurrent animations in a group: see example for details.

Arguments:

delay—Amount of time for the animation to delay before its progress begins (in seconds) (number)

Example:

```
local group = PlayerPortrait:CreateAnimationGroup()
local embiggen = group:CreateAnimation("Scale")
embiggen:SetDuration(0.5)
embiggen:SetOrder(1)
embiggen:SetScale(2,2)
local rotate = group:CreateAnimation("Rotation")
rotate:SetDuration(1)
rotate:SetOrder(1)
rotate:SetDegrees(720)
local shrink = group:CreateAnimation("Scale")
shrink:SetDuration(0.5)
shrink:SetOrder(1)
shrink:SetStartDelay(0.5)
shrink:SetScale(0.5, 0.5)

-- causes the player portrait to spin while expanding and contracting
group:Play()
```

Stop

Stops the animation.

```
Animation:Stop()
```

Also resets the animation to its initial state.

Path

A Path animation combines multiple transitions into a single control path with multiple ControlPoints. The offsets of each control point are set relative to the origin of the region, rather than relative to the current position of the animation. The following example will animate the player's portrait in a box to the bottom right of its original position:

```
local group = PlayerPortrait:CreateAnimationGroup("PortraitBox")
local path = group:CreateAnimation("Path")
local a = path:CreateControlPoint()
local b = path:CreateControlPoint()
```

```
local c = path:CreateControlPoint()
local d = path:CreateControlPoint()
path:SetCurve("SMOOTH")
path:SetDuration(4.0)
a:SetOffset(70, 0)
a:SetOrder(1)
b:SetOffset(75, -75)
b:SetOrder(2)
c:SetOffset(0, -75)
c:SetOrder(3)
d:SetOffset(0, 0)
d:SetOrder(4)
PortraitBox:Play()
```

Path has all the methods from Animation, plus the following:

CreateControlPoint

Creates a new control point for the given path.

```
Path:CreateControlPoint(["name" [, "template" [, order]]])
```

Arguments:

name (optional)—The name of the object (string)

template (optional)—The template from which the new point should inherit (string)

order (optional)—The order of the new control point (number)

GetControlPoints

Returns the control points that belong to a given path.

```
... = Path:GetControlPoints()
```

Returns:

...—A list of ControlPoint objects that belong to the given path. (ControlPoint)

GetCurve

Returns the curveType of the given path.

```
curveType = Path:GetCurve()
```

Returns:

curveType—The curve type for the given path (string)

- NONE - The control points are used literally.
- SMOOTH - The control points are used with a smoothing function that may give a more pleasing animation.

GetMaxOrder

Returns the maximum order of the control points belonging to a given path.

```
max = Path:GetMaxOrder()
```

Returns:

max—The maximum order of the control points belonging to the given path. This can be used to determine how many points a path contains. (number)

SetCurve

Sets the curve type for the path animation.

```
Path:SetCurve("curveType")
```

Arguments:

curveType—The curse type for the given path (string)

- NONE - The control points are used literally.
- SMOOTH - The control points are used with a smoothing function that may give a more pleasing animation.

ControlPoint

A ControlPoint is a special type of UIObject that represent a point in a Path Animation. The offset for each control point is from the origin of the animated Region. See Path for more details.

ControlPoint has all the methods from ParentedObject, plus the following:

GetOffset

Returns the offset for the control point.

```
x, y = ControlPoint:GetOffset()
```

Returns:

x—The x coordinate offset for the control point (number)

y—The y coordinate offset for the control point (number)

GetOrder

Returns the order of the control point in a path animation.

```
order = ControlPoint:GetOrder()
```

When the parent path animation plays, the control points with a lower number are traversed before those with a higher number. Control points must have distinct order indices, and these will be assigned automatically as new points are created.

Returns:

order—Position at which the control point will be traversed relative to others in the same path animation (between 0 and 100) (number)

SetOffset

Sets the offset for the control point.

```
ControlPoint:SetOffset(x, y)
```

Arguments:

x—The x coordinate offset for the control point (number)

y—The y coordinate offset for the control point (number)

SetOrder

Sets the order of the control point in a path animation.

```
ControlPoint:SetOrder(order)
```

When the parent path animation plays, the control points with a lower number are traversed before those with a higher number. Control points must have distinct order indices, and these will be assigned automatically as new points are created.

Arguments:

order—Position at which the control point will be traversed relative to others in the same path animation (between 0 and 100) (number)

SetParent

Sets a new path animation parent for a control point.

```
ControlPoint:SetParent([path [, order]]) or ↵
ControlPoint:SetParent(["path" [, order]])
```

Arguments:

path (optional)—The path object to be set as parent. (table)

path (optional)—The name of a path object to be set as parent. (string)

order (optional)—The order index to set for the control point in the new parent animation. (number)

Rotation

Rotation is an Animation that automatically applies an affine rotation to the region being animated. You can set the origin around which the rotation is being done, and the angle of rotation in either degrees or radians.

Rotation animations have no effect on FontStrings.

Rotation has all the methods from Animation, plus the following:

GetDegrees

Returns the animation's rotation amount (in degrees).

```
degrees = Rotation:GetDegrees()
```

Returns:

degrees—Amount by which the region rotates over the animation's duration (in degrees; positive values for counter-clockwise rotation, negative for clockwise) (number)

GetOrigin

Returns the rotation animation's origin point.

```
point, xOffset, yOffset = Rotation:GetOrigin()
```

During a rotation animation, the origin point remains in place while the positions of all other points in the scaled region are moved according to the rotation amount.

Returns:

point—Anchor point for the rotation origin (string, anchorPoint)

xOffset—Horizontal distance from the anchor point to the rotation origin (in pixels) (number)

yOffset—Vertical distance from the anchor point to the rotation origin (in pixels) (number)

GetRadians

Returns the animation's rotation amount (in radians).

```
radians = Rotation:GetRadians()
```

Returns:

radians—Amount by which the region rotates over the animation's duration (in radians; positive values for counter-clockwise rotation, negative for clockwise) (number)

SetDegrees

Sets the animation's rotation amount (in degrees).

`Rotation:SetDegrees(degrees)`

Arguments:

degrees—Amount by which the region should rotate over the animation's duration (in degrees; positive values for counter-clockwise rotation, negative for clockwise) (number)

SetOrigin

Sets the rotation animation's origin point.

`Rotation:SetOrigin("point", xOffset, yOffset)`

During a rotation animation, the origin point remains in place while the positions of all other points in the scaled region are moved according to the rotation amount.

Arguments:

point—Anchor point for the rotation origin (string, anchorPoint)

xOffset—Horizontal distance from the anchor point to the rotation origin (in pixels) (number)

yOffset—Vertical distance from the anchor point to the rotation origin (in pixels) (number)

SetRadians

Sets the animation's rotation amount (in radians).

`Rotation:SetRadians(radians)`

Arguments:

radians—Amount by which the region should rotate over the animation's duration (in radians; positive values for counter-clockwise rotation, negative for clockwise) (number)

Scale

Scale is an Animation type that automatically applies an affine scalar transformation to the region being animated as it progresses. You can set both the multiplier by which it scales, and the point from which it is scaled.

Scale animations are not applied to FontStrings.

Scale has all the methods from Animation, plus the following:

GetOrigin

Returns the scale animation's origin point.

`point, xOffset, yOffset = Scale:GetOrigin()`

During a scale animation, the origin point remains in place while the positions of all other points in the scaled region are moved according to the scale factor.

Returns:

`point`—Anchor point for the scale origin (`string`, anchorPoint)

`xOffset`—Horizontal distance from the anchor point to the scale origin (in pixels) (`number`)

`yOffset`—Vertical distance from the anchor point to the scale origin (in pixels) (`number`)

GetScale

Returns the animation's scaling factors.

`xFactor, yFactor = Scale:GetScale()`

At the end of the scale animation, the animated region's dimensions are equal to its initial dimensions multiplied by its scaling factors.

Returns:

`xFactor`—Horizontal scaling factor (`number`)

`yFactor`—Vertical scaling factor (`number`)

SetOrigin

Sets the scale animation's origin point.

`Scale:SetOrigin("point", xOffset, yOffset)`

During a scale animation, the origin point remains in place while the positions of all other points in the scaled region are moved according to the scale factor.

Arguments:

`point`—Anchor point for the scale origin (`string`, anchorPoint)

`xOffset`—Horizontal distance from the anchor point to the scale origin (in pixels) (`number`)

`yOffset`—Vertical distance from the anchor point to the scale origin (in pixels) (`number`)

SetScale

Sets the animation's scaling factors.

`Scale:SetScale(xFactor, yFactor)`

At the end of the scale animation, the animated region's dimensions are equal to its initial dimensions multiplied by its scaling factors.

Arguments:

`xFactor`—Horizontal scaling factor (`number`)

`yFactor`—Vertical scaling factor (`number`)

Translation

Translation is an Animation type that applies an affine translation to its affected region automatically as it progresses. You can set the offset in both the X and Y dimensions. Translations can be applied normally to both Textures and FontStrings.

Translation has all the methods from Animation, plus the following:

GetOffset

Returns the animation's translation offsets.

```
xOffset, yOffset = Translation:GetOffset()
```

Returns:

xOffset—Distance away from the left edge of the screen (in pixels) to move the region over the animation's duration (number)

yOffset—Distance away from the bottom edge of the screen (in pixels) to move the region over the animation's duration (number)

SetOffset

Sets the animation's translation offsets.

```
Translation:SetOffset(xOffset, yOffset)
```

Arguments:

xOffset—Distance away from the left edge of the screen (in pixels) to move the region over the animation's duration (number)

yOffset—Distance away from the bottom edge of the screen (in pixels) to move the region over the animation's duration (number)

Alpha

Alpha is a type of animation that automatically changes the transparency level of its attached region as it progresses. You can set the degree by which it will change the alpha as a fraction; for instance, a change of -1 will fade out a region completely.

Alpha has all the methods from Animation, plus the following:

GetChange

Returns the animation's amount of alpha (opacity) change.

```
change = Alpha:GetChange()
```

A region's alpha value can be between 0 (fully transparent) and 1 (fully opaque); thus, an animation which changes alpha by 1 will always increase the region to full opacity, regardless of the region's existing alpha (and an animation whose change amount is -1 will reduce the region to fully transparent).

Returns:

change—Amount by which the region's alpha value changes over the animation's duration (between -1 and 1) (number)

SetChange

Sets the animation's amount of alpha (opacity) change.

```
Alpha:SetChange(change)
```

A region's alpha value can be between 0 (fully transparent) and 1 (fully opaque); thus, an animation which changes alpha by 1 will always increase the region to full opacity, regardless of the region's existing alpha (and an animation whose change amount is -1 will reduce the region to fully transparent).

Arguments:

change—Amount by which the region's alpha value should change over the animation's duration (between -1 and 1) (number)

Widget Scripts

Widget scripts allow you to respond to user interaction and other types of widget events (such as a frame being shown or hidden). This section details the various widget scripts that are available, and the list of widget types for which each script is valid.

OnAnimFinished

Run when the model's animation finishes.

```
OnAnimFinished(self)
```

Only run for models which do not repeat their animations (e.g. the model used for the "icon falling into bag" animation which appears above the default UI's bag buttons when looting or purchasing items).

Only used for animations internal to Model objects; for widget animations, see OnFinished.

Arguments:

self—Reference to the widget for which the script was run (model)

This widget script is defined for the following widget types: DressUpModel, Model, PlayerModel, TabardModel

OnAttributeChanged

Run when a frame attribute is changed.

```
OnAttributeChanged(self, "name", value)
```

Attributes are used by the secure template system; see here for more details.

Arguments:

self—Reference to the widget for which the script was run (frame)

name—Name of the changed attribute, always lower case (string)

value—New value of the attribute (value)

This widget script is defined for the following widget types: Button, CheckButton, ColorSelect, Cooldown, DressUpModel, EditBox, Frame, GameTooltip, MessageFrame, Minimap, Model, MovieFrame, PlayerModel, ScrollFrame, ScrollingMessageFrame, SimpleHTML, Slider, StatusBar, TabardModel

OnChar

Run for each text character typed in the frame.

```
OnChar(self, "text")
```

This script is run for each character produced, not necessarily each key pressed. For example, on Windows computers, holding ALT while typing 233 on the number pad will enter the character "é"; the OnChar script is run with "é" as the second argument. Note that WoW uses the Unicode (UTF-8) encoding, so a string containing a single visible character may have a length greater than 1.

If a block of text is inserted into a frame (e.g. when inserting a hyperlink), the script is run once with the entire text as the second argument. Only run for EditBoxes or frames for which keyboard input is enabled.

Arguments:

self—Reference to the widget for which the script was run (frame)

text—The text entered (string)

This widget script is defined for the following widget types: Button, CheckButton, ColorSelect, Cooldown, DressUpModel, EditBox, Frame, GameTooltip, MessageFrame, Minimap, Model, MovieFrame, PlayerModel, ScrollFrame, ScrollingMessageFrame, SimpleHTML, Slider, StatusBar, TabardModel

OnCharComposition

Run when the edit box's input composition mode changes.

```
OnCharComposition(self, "text")
```

Primarily used in international clients that can use IME composition.

Arguments:

self—Reference to the widget for which the script was run (frame)

text—Partial text in the character composition mode (string)

This widget script is defined for the following widget types: EditBox

OnClick

Run when the button is clicked.

```
OnClick(self, "button", down)
```

By default, this script is only run for the left mouse button's "up" action; the :RegisterForClicks() method can be called to enable the button to respond to other buttons and actions.

Using or hooking the OnClick handler may not always be useful or desirable; the PreClick and PostClick scripts are provided for such purposes.

Moving the mouse away from the button before releasing it will not run the PreClick/OnClick/PostClick handlers, but will still run the OnMouseUp handler.

Arguments:

self—Reference to the widget for which the script was run (button)

button—Name of the mouse button responsible for the click action (string)

down—True for a mouse button down action; false for button up or other actions (boolean)

Example:

```
-- Illustrates the timing of mouse script handlers when clicking
-- a button
local b = CreateFrame("Button", "TestButton", UIParent, ↵
"UIPanelButtonTemplate2")
b:SetPoint("CENTER")
b:RegisterForClicks("AnyUp", "AnyDown")
local upDown = { [false] = "Up", [true] = "Down" }
local function show(text, color)
  DEFAULT_CHAT_FRAME:AddMessage(text, color, color, color)
end
local color
b:SetScript("OnMouseDown", function(self, button)
  color = .60
  show(format("OnMouseDown: %s", button), color, color, color)
end)
b:SetScript("OnMouseUp", function(self, button)
  color = .60
  show(format("OnMouseUp: %s", button), color, color, color)
end)
b:SetScript("OnClick", function(self, button, down)
  color = color + 0.1
  show(format("OnClick: %s %s", button, upDown[down]), color, ↵
color, color)
end)
b:SetScript("PreClick", function(self, button, down)
  color = color + 0.1
  show(format("PreClick: %s %s", button, upDown[down]), color, ↵
color, color)
end)
b:SetScript("PostClick", function(self, button, down)
  color = color + 0.1
  show(format("PostClick: %s %s", button, upDown[down]), color, ↵
color, color)
end)
```

This widget script is defined for the following widget types: Button, CheckButton

OnColorSelect

Run when the color select frame's color selection changes.

```
OnColorSelect(self, r, g, b)
```

Arguments:

self—Reference to the widget for which the script was run (frame)

r—Red component of the selected color (0.0 - 1.0) (number)

g—Green component of the selected color (0.0 - 1.0) (number)

b—Blue component of the selected color (0.0 - 1.0) (number)

This widget script is defined for the following widget types: ColorSelect

OnCursorChanged

Run when the position of the text insertion cursor in the edit box changes.

`OnCursorChanged(self, x, y, width, height)`

Also run when the edit box gains or loses keyboard focus.

Arguments:

`self`—Reference to the widget for which the script was run (`editbox`)

`x`—Horizontal position of the cursor relative to the top left corner of the edit box (in pixels) (`number`)

`y`—Vertical position of the cursor relative to the top left corner of the edit box (in pixels) (`number`)

`width`—Width of the cursor graphic (in pixels) (`number`)

`height`—Height of the cursor graphic (in pixels); matches the height of a line of text in the edit box (`number`)

This widget script is defined for the following widget types: EditBox

OnDisable

Run when the frame is disabled.

`OnDisable(self)`

Arguments:

`self`—Reference to the widget for which the script was run (`frame`)

This widget script is defined for the following widget types: Button, CheckButton, ColorSelect, Cooldown, DressUpModel, EditBox, Frame, GameTooltip, MessageFrame, Minimap, Model, MovieFrame, PlayerModel, ScrollFrame, ScrollingMessageFrame, SimpleHTML, Slider, StatusBar, TabardModel

OnDoubleClick

Run when the button is double-clicked.

`OnDoubleClick(self, "button")`

Run if the mouse button is clicked twice within 0.3 seconds. (The `PreClick`, `OnClick` and `PostClick` handlers are run for the first click but not the second.)

Arguments:

`self`—Reference to the widget for which the script was run (`button`)

`button`—Name of the mouse button responsible for the click action (`string`)

This widget script is defined for the following widget types: Button, CheckButton

OnDragStart

Run when the mouse is dragged starting in the frame.

`OnDragStart(self, "button")`

In order for a drag action to begin, the mouse button must be pressed down within the frame and moved more than several (~10) pixels in any direction without being released.

Arguments:

self—Reference to the widget for which the script was run (button)

button—Name of the mouse button responsible for the drag action (string)

Example:

```
-- Illustrates script handlers involved in dragging. Dragging to or
-- from either button will display messages detailing the process.
local nextNum = 1
local last
local handlers = {
 "OnMouseDown", "OnMouseUp", "OnDragStart", "OnDragStop", ↵
"OnReceiveDrag"
}
local function CreateButton()
 local curNum = nextNum
 local b = CreateFrame("Button", "Test"..curNum, UIParent, ↵
"UIPanelButtonTemplate2")
 if curNum == 1 then
  b:SetPoint("CENTER")
 else
  b:SetPoint("LEFT", last, "RIGHT", 5, 0)
 end
 b:SetText(curNum)
 b:RegisterForDrag("LeftButton", "RightButton")

 for _, handler in ipairs(handlers) do
  b:SetScript(handler, function(self, button)
   button = button and ", "..button or ""
   DEFAULT_CHAT_FRAME:AddMessage(format("%s: %d%s", handler, ↵
curNum, button))
  end)
 end

 nextNum = nextNum + 1
 last = b
end
CreateButton()
CreateButton()
```

This widget script is defined for the following widget types: Button, CheckButton, ColorSelect, Cooldown, DressUpModel, EditBox, Frame, GameTooltip, MessageFrame, Minimap, Model, MovieFrame, PlayerModel, ScrollFrame, ScrollingMessageFrame, SimpleHTML, Slider, StatusBar, TabardModel

OnDragStop

Run when the mouse button is released after a drag started in the frame.

```
OnDragStop(self)
```

This script is run only for drags started within the frame, regardless of the cursor's position at the end of the drag. For further details, see the example under `OnDragStart.`

Arguments:

`self`—Reference to the widget for which the script was run (`button`)
This widget script is defined for the following widget types: Button, CheckButton, ColorSelect, Cooldown, DressUpModel, EditBox, Frame, GameTooltip, MessageFrame, Minimap, Model, MovieFrame, PlayerModel, ScrollFrame, ScrollingMessageFrame, SimpleHTML, Slider, StatusBar, TabardModel

OnEditFocusGained

Run when the edit box becomes focused for keyboard input.

`OnEditFocusGained(self)`

Arguments:

`self`—Reference to the widget for which the script was run (`editbox`)
This widget script is defined for the following widget types: EditBox

OnEditFocusLost

Run when the edit box loses keyboard input focus.

`OnEditFocusLost(self)`

Arguments:

`self`—Reference to the widget for which the script was run (`exitbox`)
This widget script is defined for the following widget types: EditBox

OnEnable

Run when the frame is enabled.

`OnEnable(self)`

Arguments:

`self`—Reference to the widget for which the script was run (`frame`)
This widget script is defined for the following widget types: Button, CheckButton, ColorSelect, Cooldown, DressUpModel, EditBox, Frame, GameTooltip, MessageFrame, Minimap, Model, MovieFrame, PlayerModel, ScrollFrame, ScrollingMessageFrame, SimpleHTML, Slider, StatusBar, TabardModel

OnEnter

Run when the mouse cursor enters the frame's interactive area.

`OnEnter(self, motion)`

Note that a frame's mouse-interactive area can be changed via its `:SetHitRectInsets()` method.

Arguments:

`self`—Reference to the widget for which the script was run (`frame`) motion—True if the handler is being run due to actual mouse movement; false if the cursor entered the frame due to other circumstances (such as the frame being created underneath the cursor) (boolean)

This widget script is defined for the following widget types: Button, CheckButton, ColorSelect, Cooldown, DressUpModel, EditBox, Frame, GameTooltip, MessageFrame, Minimap, Model, MovieFrame, PlayerModel, ScrollFrame, ScrollingMessageFrame, SimpleHTML, Slider, StatusBar, TabardModel

OnEnterPressed

Run when the Enter (or Return) key is pressed while the edit box has keyboard focus.

```
OnEnterPressed(self)
```

Arguments:

self—Reference to the widget for which the script was run (editbox)

This widget script is defined for the following widget types: EditBox

OnEscapePressed

Run when the Escape key is pressed while the edit box has keyboard focus.

```
OnEscapePressed(self)
```

By default, an EditBox provides no way to clear keyboard input focus (though clicking in another edit box will focus it instead)—providing an OnEscapePressed handler to call :ClearFocus() (or inheriting from the default UI's InputBoxTemplate, which does so) may prove useful.

Arguments:

self—Reference to the widget for which the script was run (editbox)

This widget script is defined for the following widget types: EditBox

OnEvent

Run whenever an event fires for which the frame is registered.

```
OnEvent(self, "event", ...)
```

In order for this script to be run, the frame must be registered for at least one event via its :RegisterEvent() method. See the Events Reference for details of each event.

Arguments:

self—Reference to the widget for which the script was run (frame)

event—Name of the event (string)

...—Arguments specific to the event (list)

This widget script is defined for the following widget types: Alpha, Animation, AnimationGroup, Button, CheckButton, ColorSelect, Cooldown, DressUpModel, EditBox, Frame, GameTooltip, MessageFrame, Minimap, Model, MovieFrame, Path, PlayerModel, Rotation, Scale, ScrollFrame,

ScrollingMessageFrame, SimpleHTML, Slider, StatusBar, TabardModel, Translation

OnFinished

Run when the animation (or animation group) finishes animating.

```
OnFinished(self, requested)
```

Does not run for an animation group set to loop unless the group's :Finish() method is called.

Arguments:

self—Reference to the widget for which the script was run (animation)

requested—True if animation finished because of a call to AnimationGroup: Finish(); false otherwise (boolean)

This widget script is defined for the following widget types: Alpha, Animation, AnimationGroup, Path, Rotation, Scale, Translation

OnHide

Run when the frame's visibility changes to hidden.

```
OnHide(self)
```

This script handler runs whether the frame was directly hidden (via its :Hide() method) or implicitly hidden due to a parent frame being hidden.

Arguments:

self—Reference to the widget for which the script was run (frame)

This widget script is defined for the following widget types: Button, CheckButton, ColorSelect, Cooldown, DressUpModel, EditBox, Frame, GameTooltip, MessageFrame, Minimap, Model, MovieFrame, PlayerModel, ScrollFrame, ScrollingMessageFrame, SimpleHTML, Slider, StatusBar, TabardModel

OnHorizontalScroll

Run when the scroll frame's horizontal scroll position changes.

```
OnHorizontalScroll(self, offset)
```

Arguments:

self—Reference to the widget for which the script was run (scrollframe)

offset—New horizontal scroll position (in pixels, measured from the leftmost scroll position) (number)

This widget script is defined for the following widget types: ScrollFrame

OnHyperlinkClick

Run when the mouse clicks a hyperlink in the scrolling message frame or SimpleHTML frame.

```
OnHyperlinkClick(self, "linkData", "link", "button")
```

This script handler is run when the mouse button is released while the mouse cursor is over the same hyperlink text in which the mouse button was pressed.

Arguments:

self—Reference to the widget for which the script was run (frame)

linkData—Essential data (linktype:linkdata portion) of the hyperlink (e.g.
"quest:982:17") (string)

link—Complete hyperlink text (e.g. "|cffffff00|Hquest:982:17|
h[Deep Ocean, Vast Sea]|h|r") (string, hyperlink)

button—Name of the mouse button responsible for the click action (string)

Example:

```
-- Print information about a clicked hyperlink
local someMessageFrame = WowLuaFrameOutput
someMessageFrame:SetScript("OnHyperlinkClick", function(self, ↵
linkData, link, button)
    self:AddMessage(format("You clicked on %s with %s", link, button))
end)
```

This widget script is defined for the following widget types:
ScrollingMessageFrame, SimpleHTML

OnHyperlinkEnter

Run when the mouse moves over a hyperlink in the scrolling message frame or
SimpleHTML frame.

```
OnHyperlinkEnter(self, "linkData", "link")
```

Arguments:

self—Reference to the widget for which the script was run (frame)

linkData—Essential data (linktype:linkdata portion) of the hyperlink (e.g.
"quest:982:17") (string)

link—Complete hyperlink text (e.g. "|cffffff00|Hquest:982:17|
h[Deep Ocean, Vast Sea]|h|r") (string, hyperlink)

Example:

```
-- Prints data about the hyperlink you enter in the default chat frame
DEFAULT_CHAT_FRAME:SetScript("OnHyperlinkEnter", function(self, ↵
linkData, link)
  local color = link:match("|c%x%x%x%x%x%x%x%x") or ""
  self:AddMessage("linkData: "..linkData)
  self:AddMessage(format("link: %s%s", color, link:gsub("|","||")))
end)
```

This widget script is defined for the following widget types:
ScrollingMessageFrame, SimpleHTML

OnHyperlinkLeave

Run when the mouse moves away from a hyperlink in the scrolling message
frame or SimpleHTML frame.

```
OnHyperlinkLeave(self, "linkData", "link")
```

Arguments:

self—Reference to the widget for which the script was run (frame)

linkData—Essential data (linktype:linkdata portion) of the hyperlink (e.g.
"quest:982:17") (string)

link—Complete hyperlink text (e.g. "|cffffff00|Hquest:982:17|h
[Deep Ocean, Vast Sea]|h|r") (string, hyperlink)

Example:

```
-- Prints data about the hyperlink you leave in the default chat frame
DEFAULT_CHAT_FRAME:SetScript("OnHyperlinkLeave", ↵
function(self, linkData, link)
  local color = link:match("|c%x%x%x%x%x%x%x%x") or ""
  self:AddMessage("linkData: "..linkData)
  self:AddMessage(format("link: %s%s", color, link:gsub("|","||")))
end)
```

This widget script is defined for the following widget types: ScrollingMessageFrame, SimpleHTML

OnInputLanguageChanged

Run when the edit box's language input mode changes.

```
OnInputLanguageChanged(self, "language")
```

Applies to keyboard input methods, not in-game languages or client locales—only relevant for international clients that allow multiple input languages.

Arguments:

self—Reference to the widget for which the script was run (editbox)

language—Name of the new input language (see :GetInputLanguage()) (string)

This widget script is defined for the following widget types: EditBox

OnKeyDown

Run when a keyboard key is pressed if the frame is keyboard enabled.

```
OnKeyDown(self, "key")
```

Does not run for focused EditBoxes.

Arguments:

self—Reference to the widget for which the script was run (frame)

key—Name of the key pressed (string, binding)

This widget script is defined for the following widget types: Button, CheckButton, ColorSelect, Cooldown, DressUpModel, EditBox, Frame, GameTooltip, MessageFrame, Minimap, Model, MovieFrame, PlayerModel, ScrollFrame, ScrollingMessageFrame, SimpleHTML, Slider, StatusBar, TabardModel

OnKeyUp

Run when a keyboard key is released if the frame is keyboard enabled.

```
OnKeyUp(self, "key")
```

Does not run for focused EditBoxes.

Arguments:

self—Reference to the widget for which the script was run (frame)

key—Name of the key pressed (string, binding)

This widget script is defined for the following widget types: Button, CheckButton, ColorSelect, Cooldown, DressUpModel, EditBox, Frame, GameTooltip, MessageFrame, Minimap, Model, MovieFrame, PlayerModel, ScrollFrame, ScrollingMessageFrame, SimpleHTML, Slider, StatusBar, TabardModel

OnLeave

Run when the mouse cursor leaves the frame's interactive area.

```
OnLeave(self, motion)
```

Note that a frame's mouse-interactive area can be changed via its :SetHitRectInsets() method.

Arguments:

self—Reference to the widget for which the script was run (frame)

motion—True if the handler is being run due to actual mouse movement; false if the cursor left the frame due to other circumstances (such as the frame being created underneath the cursor) (boolean)

This widget script is defined for the following widget types: Button, CheckButton, ColorSelect, Cooldown, DressUpModel, EditBox, Frame, GameTooltip, MessageFrame, Minimap, Model, MovieFrame, PlayerModel, ScrollFrame, ScrollingMessageFrame, SimpleHTML, Slider, StatusBar, TabardModel

OnLoad

Run when the frame is created.

```
OnLoad(self)
```

In practice, this handler is only applicable when defined in XML (either for frames created in XML or for XML templates inherited by dynamically created frames). A frame created via CreateFrame() will have already run its (non-existent) OnLoad script by the time that function returns, leaving no opportunity to run an OnLoad handler set later.

Arguments:

self—Reference to the widget for which the script was run (frame)

This widget script is defined for the following widget types: Alpha, Animation, AnimationGroup, Button, CheckButton, ColorSelect, Cooldown, DressUpModel, EditBox, Frame, GameTooltip, MessageFrame, Minimap, Model, MovieFrame, Path, PlayerModel, Rotation, Scale, ScrollFrame, ScrollingMessageFrame, SimpleHTML, Slider, StatusBar, TabardModel, Translation

OnLoop

Run when the animation group's loop state changes.

```
OnLoop(self, "loopState")
```

Arguments:

self—Reference to the widget for which the script was run (animgroup) `loopState`—Token identifying the new loop state (`string`)

This widget script is defined for the following widget types: AnimationGroup

OnMessageScrollChanged

Run when the scrolling message frame's scroll position changes.

`OnMessageScrollChanged(self)`

A `ScrollingMessageFrame`'s scroll position can change not only when it is scrolled, but also when a message is added to the frame; both cases cause this script handler to be run.

Arguments:

`self`—Reference to the widget for which the script was run (`scrollingmessageframe`)

This widget script is defined for the following widget types: ScrollingMessageFrame

OnMinMaxChanged

Run when the slider's or status bar's minimum and maximum values change.

`OnMinMaxChanged(self, min, max)`

Run when the minimum/maximum values are set programmatically with `Slider:SetMinMaxValues()` or `StatusBar:SetMinMaxValues()`.

Arguments:

`self`—Reference to the widget for which the script was run (`frame`)

`min`—New minimum value of the slider or the status bar (`number`)

`max`—New maximum value of the slider or the status bar (`number`)

This widget script is defined for the following widget types: Slider, StatusBar

OnMouseDown

Run when a mouse button is pressed while the cursor is over the frame.

`OnMouseDown(self, "button")`

For further details, see the example under `OnClick`.

Arguments:

`self`—Reference to the widget for which the script was run (`frame`)

`button`—Name of the mouse button responsible for the click action (`string`)

This widget script is defined for the following widget types: Button, CheckButton, ColorSelect, Cooldown, DressUpModel, EditBox, Frame, GameTooltip, MessageFrame, Minimap, Model, MovieFrame, PlayerModel, ScrollFrame, ScrollingMessageFrame, SimpleHTML, Slider, StatusBar, TabardModel

OnMouseUp

Run when the mouse button is released following a mouse down action in the frame.

`OnMouseUp(self, "button")`

This script is always run for the frame which received the initial mouse button down event (unless the frame is registered for drag actions and a drag action is started before the button is released). For further details, see the example under OnClick.

Arguments:

self—Reference to the widget for which the script was run (frame)

button—Name of the mouse button responsible for the click action (string)

This widget script is defined for the following widget types: Button, CheckButton, ColorSelect, Cooldown, DressUpModel, EditBox, Frame, GameTooltip, MessageFrame, Minimap, Model, MovieFrame, PlayerModel, ScrollFrame, ScrollingMessageFrame, SimpleHTML, Slider, StatusBar, TabardModel

OnMouseWheel

Run when the frame receives a mouse wheel scrolling action.

```
OnMouseWheel(self, delta)
```

In order for this handler to be run, the frame must be mouse wheel enabled and the mouse cursor must be within the frame while the scroll wheel (or equivalent device) is used.

Arguments:

self—Reference to the widget for which the script was run (frame)

delta—1 for a scroll-up action, -1 for a scroll-down action (number)

Example:

```
-- Print the mousewheel delta for a button
CreateFrame("Frame", "test", UIParent, "UIPanelButtonTemplate2")
test:SetPoint("CENTER")
test:EnableMouseWheel(true)
test:SetScript("OnMouseWheel", function(self, delta)
    DEFAULT_CHAT_FRAME:AddMessage(delta)
end)
```

This widget script is defined for the following widget types: Button, CheckButton, ColorSelect, Cooldown, DressUpModel, EditBox, Frame, GameTooltip, MessageFrame, Minimap, Model, MovieFrame, PlayerModel, ScrollFrame, ScrollingMessageFrame, SimpleHTML, Slider, StatusBar, TabardModel

OnMovieFinished

Run when a movie frame's movie ends.

```
OnMovieFinished(self)
```

Arguments:

self—Reference to the widget for which the script was run (movieframe)

This widget script is defined for the following widget types: MovieFrame

OnMovieHideSubtitle

Runs when the movie's most recently displayed subtitle should be hidden.

```
OnMovieHideSubtitle(self)
```

Arguments:

`self`—Reference to the widget for which the script was run (`movieframe`)

This widget script is defined for the following widget types: MovieFrame

OnMovieShowSubtitle

Runs when a subtitle for the playing movie should be displayed.

```
OnMovieShowSubtitle(self, "text")
```

Arguments:

`self`—Reference to the widget for which the script was run (`movieframe`)

`text`—Subtitle text to be displayed (`string`)

This widget script is defined for the following widget types: MovieFrame

OnPause

Run when the animation (or animation group) is paused.

```
OnPause(self)
```

Arguments:

`self`—Reference to the widget for which the script was run (`animation`)

This widget script is defined for the following widget types: Alpha, Animation, AnimationGroup, Path, Rotation, Scale, Translation

OnPlay

Run when the animation (or animation group) begins to play.

```
OnPlay(self)
```

Arguments:

`self`—Reference to the widget for which the script was run (`animation`)

This widget script is defined for the following widget types: Alpha, Animation, AnimationGroup, Path, Rotation, Scale, Translation

OnReceiveDrag

Run when the mouse button is released after dragging into the frame.

```
OnReceiveDrag(self)
```

This script is run for the frame under the cursor at the end of a drag, regardless of which started the drag. For further details, see the example under `OnDragStart`.

Arguments:

`self`—The frame object that this handler was called for. (`frame`)

This widget script is defined for the following widget types: Button, CheckButton, ColorSelect, Cooldown, DressUpModel, EditBox, Frame, GameTooltip, MessageFrame, Minimap, Model, MovieFrame, PlayerModel, ScrollFrame, ScrollingMessageFrame, SimpleHTML, Slider, StatusBar, TabardModel

OnScrollRangeChanged

Run when the scroll frame's scroll position is changed.

```
OnScrollRangeChanged(self, xOffset, yOffset)
```

Only run when the scroll position changes due to changes in the scroll child frame's dimensions, not when `:SetHorizontalScroll()` or `:SetVerticalScroll()` is called.

Arguments:

`self`—Reference to the widget for which the script was run (`scrollframe`)

`xOffset`—New horizontal scroll range (in pixels, measured from the leftmost scroll position) (`number`)

`yOffset`—New vertical scroll range (in pixels, measured from the topmost scroll position) (`number`)

Example:

```
-- Set the min and max values of a scroll bar (Slider) based on
-- the scroll range
scrollFrame:SetScript("OnScrollRangeChanged", function(self, x, y)
 verticalScrollBar:SetMinMaxValues(0, y)
end)
```

This widget script is defined for the following widget types: ScrollFrame

OnShow

Run when the frame becomes visible.

```
OnShow(self)
```

This script handler runs whether the frame was directly shown (via its `:Show()` method) or became visible due to a parent frame being shown. The `OnShow` handler is not run if the frame is implicitly shown upon its creation.

Arguments:

`self`—Reference to the widget for which the script was run (`frame`)

This widget script is defined for the following widget types: Button, CheckButton, ColorSelect, Cooldown, DressUpModel, EditBox, Frame, GameTooltip, MessageFrame, Minimap, Model, MovieFrame, PlayerModel, ScrollFrame, ScrollingMessageFrame, SimpleHTML, Slider, StatusBar, TabardModel

OnSizeChanged

Run when a frame's size changes.

```
OnSizeChanged(self, width, height)
```

Arguments:

`self`—Reference to the widget for which the script was run (`frame`)

`width`—New width of the frame (in pixels) (`number`)

`height`—New height of the frame (in pixels) (`number`)

This widget script is defined for the following widget types: Button, CheckButton, ColorSelect, Cooldown, DressUpModel, EditBox, Frame,

GameTooltip, MessageFrame, Minimap, Model, MovieFrame, PlayerModel, ScrollFrame, ScrollingMessageFrame, SimpleHTML, Slider, StatusBar, TabardModel

OnSpacePressed

Run when the space bar is pressed while the edit box has keyboard focus.

`OnSpacePressed(self)`

Arguments:

`self`—Reference to the widget for which the script was run (`editbox`)

This widget script is defined for the following widget types: EditBox

OnStop

Run when the animation (or animation group) is stopped.

`OnStop(self, requested)`

Arguments:

`self`—Reference to the widget for which the script was run (`animation`)

`requested`—True if the animation was stopped due to a call to the animation's or group's `:Stop()` method; `false` if the animation was stopped for other reasons (`boolean`)

This widget script is defined for the following widget types: Alpha, Animation, AnimationGroup, Path, Rotation, Scale, Translation

OnTabPressed

Run when the Tab key is pressed while the edit box has keyboard focus.

`OnTabPressed(self)`

Providing a handler for this script can be useful for allowing the user to switch quickly among several edit boxes in a panel.

Arguments:

`self`—Reference to the widget for which the script was run (`editbox`)

This widget script is defined for the following widget types: EditBox

OnTextChanged

Run when the edit box's text is changed.

`OnTextChanged(self, isUserInput)`

This script is run both when text is typed in the edit box (for each character entered) and when the edit box's contents are changed via `:SetText()` (but only if the text is actually changed).

Arguments:

`self`—Reference to the widget for which the script was run (`exitbox`)

`isUserInput`—True if the text changed due to user input; `false` if the text was changed via `:SetText()` (`boolean`)

This widget script is defined for the following widget types: EditBox

OnTextSet

Run when the edit box's text is set programmatically.

```
OnTextSet(self)
```

Only run as a result of calling `:SetText()`.

Arguments:

`self`—Reference to the widget for which the script was run (`editbox`)

This widget script is defined for the following widget types: EditBox

OnTooltipAddMoney

Run when an amount of money should be added to the tooltip.

```
OnTooltipAddMoney(self, amount, maxAmount)
```

This happens when the tooltip is set to display an item for which an amount of money is displayed (e.g. an item with a vendor sell price, or an equipped item while the cursor is in item-repair mode).

Arguments:

`self`—Reference to the widget for which the script was run (`gametooltip`)

`amount`—Amount of money to be added to the tooltip (in copper) (`number`)

`maxAmount`—A second amount of money to be added to the tooltip (in copper); if non-nil, the first amount is treated as the minimum and this amount as the maximum of a price range (`number`)

Example:

```
-- Display the amount of copper that is added to the tooltip
GameTooltip:HookScript("OnTooltipAddMoney", function(self, amount)
    DEFAULT_CHAT_FRAME:AddMessage(format("Money: %d", amount))
end)
```

This widget script is defined for the following widget types: GameTooltip

OnTooltipCleared

Run when the tooltip is hidden or its content is cleared.

```
OnTooltipCleared(self)
```

Arguments:

`self`—Reference to the widget for which the script was run (`gametooltip`)

This widget script is defined for the following widget types: GameTooltip

OnTooltipSetAchievement

Run when the tooltip is filled with information about an achievement.

```
OnTooltipSetAchievement(self)
```

See `:SetAchievement()`.

Arguments:

`self`—Reference to the widget for which the script was run (`gametooltip`)

This widget script is defined for the following widget types: GameTooltip

OnTooltipSetDefaultAnchor

Run when the tooltip is repositioned to its default anchor location.

```
OnTooltipSetDefaultAnchor(self)
```

This happens when (for example) mousing over a unit in the 3D world.

Arguments:

`self`—Reference to the widget for which the script was run (`gametooltip`)

This widget script is defined for the following widget types: GameTooltip

OnTooltipSetEquipmentSet

Run when the tooltip is filled with information about an equipment set.

```
OnTooltipSetEquipmentSet(self)
```

See `:SetEquipmentSet()`.

Arguments:

`self`—Reference to the widget for which the script was run (`gametooltip`)

This widget script is defined for the following widget types: GameTooltip

OnTooltipSetFrameStack

Run when the tooltip is filled with a list of frames under the mouse cursor.

```
OnTooltipSetFrameStack(self)
```

See `:SetFrameStack()`.

Arguments:

`self`—Reference to the widget for which the script was run (`gametooltip`)

This widget script is defined for the following widget types: GameTooltip

OnTooltipSetItem

Run when the tooltip is filled with information about an item.

```
OnTooltipSetItem(self)
```

See `:GetItem()` and the several `GameTooltip` methods for filling the tooltip with information about items from various parts of the UI.

Arguments:

`self`—Reference to the widget for which the script was run (`gametooltip`)

This widget script is defined for the following widget types: GameTooltip

OnTooltipSetQuest

Run when the tooltip is filled with information about a quest.

```
OnTooltipSetQuest(self)
```

See `GameTooltip:SetHyperlink()` to load the tooltip with information about a quest.

Arguments:

`self`—Reference to the widget for which the script was run (`gametooltip`)

This widget script is defined for the following widget types: GameTooltip

OnTooltipSetSpell

Run when the tooltip is filled with information about a spell.

```
OnTooltipSetSpell(self)
```

See `:SetSpell()`, `:SetSpellByID()` and `:GetSpell()`.

Arguments:

`self`—Reference to the widget for which the script was run (`gametooltip`)

This widget script is defined for the following widget types: GameTooltip

OnTooltipSetUnit

Run when the tooltip is filled with information about a unit.

```
OnTooltipSetUnit(self)
```

See `:SetUnit()` and `:GetUnit()`.

Arguments:

`self`—Reference to the widget for which the script was run (`gametooltip`)

This widget script is defined for the following widget types: GameTooltip

OnUpdate

Run each time the screen is drawn by the game engine.

```
OnUpdate(self, elapsed)
```

This handler runs for each frame (not `Frame`) drawn—if WoW is currently running at 27.5 frames per second, the `OnUpdate` handlers for every visible `Frame`, `Animation` and `AnimationGroup` (or descendant thereof) are run approximately every 2/55ths of a second. Therefore, `OnUpdate` handler can be useful for processes which need to be run very frequently or with accurate timing, but extensive processing in an `OnUpdate` handler can slow down the game's framerate.

See the chapter "Responding to Graphic Updates with OnUpdate" for more information.

Arguments:

`self`—Reference to the widget for which the script was run (`frame`)

`elapsed`—Number of seconds since the `OnUpdate` handlers were last run (likely a fraction of a second) (`number`)

This widget script is defined for the following widget types: Alpha, Animation, AnimationGroup, Button, CheckButton, ColorSelect, Cooldown, DressUpModel, EditBox, Frame, GameTooltip, MessageFrame, Minimap, Model, MovieFrame, Path, PlayerModel, Rotation, Scale, ScrollFrame, ScrollingMessageFrame, SimpleHTML, Slider, StatusBar, TabardModel, Translation

OnUpdateModel

Run when a model changes or animates.

```
OnUpdateModel(self)
```

Arguments:

self—Reference to the widget for which the script was run (model)

This widget script is defined for the following widget types: DressUpModel, Model, PlayerModel, TabardModel

OnValueChanged

Run when the slider's or status bar's value changes.

```
OnValueChanged(self, value)
```

Run when the value is set programmatically with Slider:SetValue() or StatusBar:SetValue(), as well as when the value is set by the user dragging the slider thumb.

Arguments:

self—Reference to the widget for which the script was run (frame)

value—New value of the slider or the status bar (number)

Example:

```
-- Use a slider to move a frame across the center of the screen
local button = CreateFrame("Button", "TestButton", UIParent, ↵
"UIPanelButtonTemplate2")
local slider = CreateFrame("Slider", "TestSlider", UIParent, ↵
"OptionsSliderTemplate")
slider:SetPoint("CENTER", 0, -60)
slider:SetWidth(400)
slider:SetMinMaxValues(-200, 200)
slider:SetValueStep(1)
slider:SetScript("OnValueChanged", function(self, value)
    button:SetPoint("CENTER", value, 0)
end)
slider:SetValue(0)
```

This widget script is defined for the following widget types: Slider, StatusBar

OnVerticalScroll

Run when the scroll frame's vertical scroll position changes.

```
OnVerticalScroll(self, offset)
```

Arguments:

self—Reference to the widget for which the script was run (scrollframe)

offset—New vertical scroll position (in pixels, measured from the topmost scroll position) (number)

This widget script is defined for the following widget types: ScrollFrame

PostClick

Run immediately following the button's OnClick handler with the same arguments.

```
PostClick(self, "button", down)
```

Useful for processing clicks on a button without interfering with handlers inherited from a secure template. For further details, see the example under OnClick.

Arguments:

self—Reference to the widget for which the script was run (button)

button—Name of the mouse button responsible for the click action (string)

down—True for a mouse button down action; false for button up or other actions (boolean)

This widget script is defined for the following widget types: Button, CheckButton

PreClick

Run immediately before the button's OnClick handler with the same arguments.

```
PreClick(self, "button", down)
```

Useful for processing clicks on a button without interfering with handlers inherited from a secure template. For further details, see the example under OnClick.

Arguments:

self—Reference to the widget for which the script was run (button)

button—Name of the mouse button responsible for the click action (string)

down—True for a mouse button down action; false for button up or other actions (boolean)

Example:

```
<!--
Outside of combat, change the button's spell based on the class you are
targeting.
-->

<PreClick>
 if InCombatLockdown() then
  return
 end

 local class = select(2, UnitClass("target"))
 local spell
 if class == "WARRIOR" then
  spell = "Blessing of Kings"
 elseif class == "ROGUE" then
  spell = "Blessing of Might"
 else
  spell = "Blessing of Wisdom"
 end

 self:SetAttribute("spell", spell)
</PreClick>
```

This widget script is defined for the following widget types: Button, CheckButton

Events Reference

To write an addon for World of Warcraft that can monitor changes in game state, you must make use of game events. There are more than 400 different events and while only a fraction of them will be used by any specific addon, this chapter attempts to introduce each of the different events. In practice you should consult the online reference at `http://wowprogramming.com/docs/events` for in-depth information about events (where available).

ACHIEVEMENT_EARNED—Fires when the player earns an achievement

ACTIONBAR_HIDEGRID—Fires when an item, spell or other entity that can be placed into an action bar slot is removed from the cursor

ACTIONBAR_PAGE_CHANGED—Fires when the main action bar changes pages

ACTIONBAR_SHOWGRID—Fires when an item, spell or other entity that can be placed into an action bar slot is picked up onto the cursor

ACTIONBAR_SLOT_CHANGED—Fires when the contents of an action bar slot change

ACTIONBAR_UPDATE_COOLDOWN—Fires when the cooldown for an action bar item begins or ends

ACTIONBAR_UPDATE_STATE—Fires when the state of an action bar item changes

ACTIONBAR_UPDATE_USABLE—Fires when an action becomes usable or unusable

ACTIVE_TALENT_GROUP_CHANGED—Fires when the player (with Dual Talent Specialization enabled) switches talent builds

ADDON_ACTION_FORBIDDEN—Fires when a non-Blizzard addon attempts to use a protected API

ADDON_LOADED—Fires when an addon and its saved variables are loaded

AREA_SPIRIT_HEALER_IN_RANGE—Fires when the player enters into the area of effect of a spirit healer that periodically resurrects nearby player units

AREA_SPIRIT_HEALER_OUT_OF_RANGE—Fires when the player leaves the area of effect of a spirit healer that periodically resurrects nearby player units

ARENA_OPPONENT_UPDATE—Fires when the availability of information about an arena opponent changes

ARENA_TEAM_INVITE_REQUEST—Fires when the player is invited to join an arena team

ARENA_TEAM_ROSTER_UPDATE—Fires when roster detail information for one of the player's arena teams becomes available

ARENA_TEAM_UPDATE—Fires when the player joins or leaves an arena team

AUCTION_BIDDER_LIST_UPDATE—Fires when information becomes available or changes for the list of auctions bid on by the player

AUCTION_HOUSE_CLOSED—Fires when the player ends interaction with an auction house

AUCTION_HOUSE_SHOW—Fires when the player begins interaction with an auction house

AUCTION_ITEM_LIST_UPDATE—Fires when the information becomes available for the list of auction browse/search results

AUCTION_OWNED_LIST_UPDATE—Fires when information becomes available or changes for the list of auctions placed by the player

AUTOEQUIP_BIND_CONFIRM—Fires when the player attempts to equip an item which will become soulbound in the process

AUTOFOLLOW_BEGIN—Fires when the player starts following another character

AUTOFOLLOW_END—Fires when the player stops following another character

BAG_UPDATE—Fires when the contents of one of the player's containers change

BAG_UPDATE_COOLDOWN—Fires when the cooldown begins or ends for an item in one of the player's containers

BANKFRAME_CLOSED—Fires when the player ends interaction with a bank

BANKFRAME_OPENED—Fires when the player begins interaction with a bank

BARBER_SHOP_APPEARANCE_APPLIED—Fires after changes to the player's appearance have been purchased at a barber shop

BARBER_SHOP_CLOSE—Fires when the player ends interaction with a barber shop

BARBER_SHOP_OPEN—Fires when the player begins interaction with a barber shop

BARBER_SHOP_SUCCESS—Fires immediately when changes to the player's appearance have been purchased at a barber shop

BATTLEFIELDS_CLOSED—Fires when the UI is no longer available for queueing for an arena or specific battleground instance

BATTLEFIELDS_SHOW—Fires when the UI becomes available for queueing for an arena or specific battleground instance

BATTLEFIELD_MGR_EJECTED—Fires when the player has been removed from a queued world PvP zone (e.g. Wintergrasp)

BATTLEFIELD_MGR_EJECT_PENDING—Fires when the player will be removed from or cannot yet enter a queued world PvP zone (e.g. Wintergrasp)

BATTLEFIELD_MGR_ENTERED—Fires when the player has been accepted into a queued world PvP zone (e.g. Wintergrasp)

BATTLEFIELD_MGR_ENTRY_INVITE—Fires when the player is invited to enter a queued world PvP zone (e.g. Wintergrasp)

BATTLEFIELD_MGR_QUEUE_INVITE—Fires when the player is invited to queue for a world PvP zone (e.g. Wintergrasp)

BATTLEFIELD_MGR_QUEUE_REQUEST_RESPONSE—Fires in response to the player's attempt to enter or queue for a world PvP zone (e.g. Wintergrasp)

BATTLEFIELD_MGR_STATE_CHANGE—Fires when the player's state changes in the queue for a world PvP zone (e.g. Wintergrasp)

BILLING_NAG_DIALOG—Fires when a message should be shown about the player's paid game time expiring soon

BIND_ENCHANT—Fires when the player attempts to an enchant an item which will become soulbound in the process

CALENDAR_ACTION_PENDING—Fires when a change to the calendar is in progress

CALENDAR_CLOSE_EVENT—Fires when the player ends viewing or editing details of a calendar event

CALENDAR_EVENT_ALARM—Fires when a calendar event is soon to begin

CALENDAR_NEW_EVENT—Fires when an event created by the player is added to the calendar

CALENDAR_OPEN_EVENT—Fires when the player begins viewing or editing details of a calendar event

CALENDAR_UPDATE_ERROR—Fires when a calendar-related error message should be displayed

CALENDAR_UPDATE_EVENT—Fires when details become available for the event being viewed or edited

CALENDAR_UPDATE_EVENT_LIST—Fires when the list of events visible on the calendar changes

CALENDAR_UPDATE_INVITE_LIST—Fires when the invite/signup list is updated for the event being viewed or edited

CALENDAR_UPDATE_PENDING_INVITES—Fires when the player receives new calendar event invitations

CANCEL_LOOT_ROLL—Fires when the player cancels a loot roll

CANCEL_SUMMON—Fires when a summons offered to the player is canceled

CHANNEL_COUNT_UPDATE—Fires when the number of members in a world or custom chat channel changes

CHANNEL_FLAGS_UPDATED—Fires when information about a channel for the channel list display changes

CHANNEL_INVITE_REQUEST—Fires when a player is invited into a chat channel

CHANNEL_PASSWORD_REQUEST—Fires when the player attempts to join a password protected channel

CHANNEL_ROSTER_UPDATE—Fires when the list of members in a channel changes

CHANNEL_UI_UPDATE—Fires when information for the channel list display changes

CHANNEL_VOICE_UPDATE—Fires when a member in a voice chat channel starts or stops speaking

CHARACTER_POINTS_CHANGED—Fires when the player's amount of available talent points changes

CHAT_MSG_ACHIEVEMENT—Fires when a nearby character earns an achievement

CHAT_MSG_ADDON—Fires when an addon communication message is received (see SendAddonMessage(), Chapter 27, "API Reference")

CHAT_MSG_AFK—Fires when an automatic AFK response is received

CHAT_MSG_BATTLEGROUND—Fires when a message is received in the battleground chat channel

`CHAT_MSG_BATTLEGROUND_LEADER`—Fires when a message is received in the battleground chat channel from the battleground group leader

`CHAT_MSG_BG_SYSTEM_ALLIANCE`—Fires when an Alliance-related battleground system message is received

`CHAT_MSG_BG_SYSTEM_HORDE`—Fires when a Horde-related battleground system message is received

`CHAT_MSG_BG_SYSTEM_NEUTRAL`—Fires when a general battleground, zone or world message is received

`CHAT_MSG_CHANNEL`—Fires when a message is received in a world or custom chat channel

`CHAT_MSG_CHANNEL_JOIN`—Fires when another character joins a world or custom chat channel monitored by the player

`CHAT_MSG_CHANNEL_LEAVE`—Fires when another character leaves a world or custom chat channel monitored by the player

`CHAT_MSG_CHANNEL_LIST`—Fires in response to a channel list query (e.g. `/chatlist`)

`CHAT_MSG_CHANNEL_NOTICE`—Fires when certain actions happen on a world or custom chat channel

`CHAT_MSG_CHANNEL_NOTICE_USER`—Fires when certain actions pertaining to specific members happen on a world or custom chat channel

`CHAT_MSG_COMBAT_FACTION_CHANGE`—Fires when the player gains or loses reputation with a faction

`CHAT_MSG_COMBAT_HONOR_GAIN`—Fires when the player gains honor points

`CHAT_MSG_COMBAT_MISC_INFO`—Fires for miscellaneous messages to be displayed in the combat log, such as loss of equipment durability upon death

`CHAT_MSG_COMBAT_XP_GAIN`—Fires when the player gains experience points

`CHAT_MSG_DND`—Fires when an automatic DND response is received

`CHAT_MSG_EMOTE`—Fires when a custom emote message is received

`CHAT_MSG_FILTERED`—Fires when the player attempts to send a chat message which is blocked by the spam filter

`CHAT_MSG_GUILD`—Fires when a message is received in the guild chat channel

`CHAT_MSG_GUILD_ACHIEVEMENT`—Fires when a member of the player's guild earns an achievement

`CHAT_MSG_IGNORED`—Fires when an automatic response is received after whispering or inviting a character who is ignoring the player

CHAT_MSG_LOOT—Fires when receiving notice that the player or a member of the player's group has looted an item

CHAT_MSG_MONEY—Fires when the player receives money as loot

CHAT_MSG_MONSTER_EMOTE—Fires when a nearby NPC performs emote text

CHAT_MSG_MONSTER_PARTY—Fires when an NPC speaks to the player's party chat channel

CHAT_MSG_MONSTER_SAY—Fires when a nearby NPC speaks (visible only to players in the immediate area)

CHAT_MSG_MONSTER_WHISPER—Fires when an NPC whispers to the player

CHAT_MSG_MONSTER_YELL—Fires when an NPC yells (visible to players in a wide area or the entire zone)

CHAT_MSG_OFFICER—Fires when a message is received in officer chat

CHAT_MSG_OPENING—Fires for messages about the player "opening" a world object

CHAT_MSG_PARTY—Fires when a message is received in the party chat channel

CHAT_MSG_PET_INFO—Fires for pet-related messages normally displayed in the combat log (e.g. summoning or dismissing a pet)

CHAT_MSG_RAID—Fires when a message is received in the raid chat channel

CHAT_MSG_RAID_BOSS_EMOTE—Fires when a raid boss performs emote text

CHAT_MSG_RAID_BOSS_WHISPER—Fires when a raid boss whispers to the player

CHAT_MSG_RAID_LEADER—Fires when a message is received in the raid chat channel from the raid leader

CHAT_MSG_RAID_WARNING—Fires when a raid warning message is received

CHAT_MSG_RESTRICTED—Fires when the player attempts to send a chat message which is disallowed because the player is on a trial account

CHAT_MSG_SAY—Fires when the player or a nearby character speaks (visible to other nearby characters)

CHAT_MSG_SKILL—Fires when skill-related messages are received

CHAT_MSG_SYSTEM—Fires when a system message is received

CHAT_MSG_TEXT_EMOTE—Fires when the player receives a standard emote (e.g. /dance, /flirt) message

CHAT_MSG_TRADESKILLS—Fires when the player or a nearby character performs a trade skill recipe

CHAT_MSG_WHISPER—Fires when the player receives a whisper from a player character

CHAT_MSG_WHISPER_INFORM—Fires when the player sends a whisper to a player character

CHAT_MSG_YELL—Fires when the player or another player character yells (visible to other characters in a wide area)

CINEMATIC_START—Fires when an in-game-engine cinematic begins to play

CINEMATIC_STOP—Fires when an in-game-engine cinematic stops playing

CLOSE_INBOX_ITEM—Fires when the mail message being viewed is no longer available

CLOSE_TABARD_FRAME—Fires when the player ends interaction with a tabard designer

CLOSE_WORLD_MAP—Fires when the world map should be hidden in response to external conditions

COMBAT_LOG_EVENT—Fires when an event to be displayed in the combat log is received

COMBAT_LOG_EVENT_UNFILTERED—Fires when a combat log event is received

COMBAT_RATING_UPDATE—Fires when the player's combat rating statistics change

COMBAT_TEXT_UPDATE—Fires when a message is received which can be displayed by the default UI's floating combat text feature

COMPANION_LEARNED—Fires when the player learns to summon a new mount or non-combat pet

COMPANION_UPDATE—Fires when new information about the player's mounts and non-combat pets is available

CONFIRM_BINDER—Fires when the player attempts to set a new Hearthstone location

CONFIRM_LOOT_ROLL—Fires when the player attempts to roll for a loot item which Binds on Pickup

CONFIRM_SUMMON—Fires when a summons is offered to the player

CONFIRM_TALENT_WIPE—Fires when the player attempts to unlearn talents

CONFIRM_XP_LOSS—Fires when the player attempts to resurrect at a graveyard spirit healer

CORPSE_IN_INSTANCE—Fires when the player (dead, in spirit form) approaches the entrance to the instance in which his corpse is located

CORPSE_IN_RANGE—Fires when the player (dead, in spirit form) approaches near enough to his corpse to return to life

CORPSE_OUT_OF_RANGE—Fires when the player (dead, in spirit form) moves too far away from his corpse to resurrect

CRITERIA_UPDATE—Fires when information about achievement criteria or player statistics becomes available

CURRENCY_DISPLAY_UPDATE—Fires when new information for the currency list is available

CURRENT_SPELL_CAST_CHANGED—Fires when the player starts or stops (cancels or finishes) casting a spell

CURSOR_UPDATE—Fires when the mouse cursor image or contents is changed

CVAR_UPDATE—Fires when the value of a configuration variable is updated

DELETE_ITEM_CONFIRM—Fires when the player attempts to delete an item

DISABLE_TAXI_BENCHMARK—Fires when a flight path benchmarking session ends or is canceled

DISABLE_XP_GAIN—Fires when the player disables experience point gains

DISPLAY_SIZE_CHANGED—Fires when the screen resolution changes

DUEL_FINISHED—Fires when a duel in which the player is participating ends

DUEL_INBOUNDS—Fires when the player reenters the duel area after leaving its boundaries

DUEL_OUTOFBOUNDS—Fires when the player begins to move outside the boundaries of a duel area

DUEL_REQUESTED—Fires when the player is challenged to a duel

ENABLE_TAXI_BENCHMARK—Fires when taxi benchmarking mode is enabled

ENABLE_XP_GAIN—Fires when the player re-enables experience point gain after disabling it

END_BOUND_TRADEABLE—Fires when the player attempts an action which will make a looted Bind on Pickup item no longer tradeable

END_REFUND—Fires when the player attempts an action which will make an item purchased with alternate currency no longer refundable

EQUIPMENT_SETS_CHANGED—Fires when the player's list of equipment sets changes

EQUIPMENT_SWAP_FINISHED—Fires when the process of switching equipment sets is complete

EQUIPMENT_SWAP_PENDING—Fires when the player begins to switch equipment sets

EQUIP_BIND_CONFIRM—Fires when the player attempts to equip an item which will become soulbound in the process

EXECUTE_CHAT_LINE—Fires when a chat message is encountered in a running macro

FRIENDLIST_UPDATE—Fires when the content of the player's friends list becomes available or changes

GLYPH_ADDED—Fires when a glyph is inscribed into the player's spellbook

GLYPH_DISABLED—Fires when a glyph slot is no longer available

GLYPH_ENABLED—Fires when a glyph slot becomes available

GLYPH_REMOVED—Fires when the player removes an inscribed glyph

GLYPH_UPDATED—Fires when information about the player's inscribed glyphs becomes available

GMRESPONSE_RECEIVED—Fires when the player receives a response to a GM ticket

GMSURVEY_DISPLAY—Fires when the player is invited to participate in a GM feedback survey

GM_PLAYER_INFO—*This event is not yet documented*

GOSSIP_CLOSED—Fires when an NPC gossip interaction ends

GOSSIP_CONFIRM—Fires when the player is requested to confirm a gossip choice

GOSSIP_CONFIRM_CANCEL—Fires when an attempt to confirm a gossip choice is canceled

GOSSIP_ENTER_CODE—Fires when the player attempts a gossip choice which requires entering a code

GOSSIP_SHOW—Fires when an NPC gossip interaction begins

GUILDBANKBAGSLOTS_CHANGED—Fires when information about the contents of guild bank item slots changes or becomes available

GUILDBANKFRAME_CLOSED—Fires when the player ends interaction with the guild bank

GUILDBANKFRAME_OPENED—Fires when the player begins interaction with the guild bank

GUILDBANKLOG_UPDATE—Fires when information for the guild bank transaction or money log becomes available

GUILDBANK_ITEM_LOCK_CHANGED—Fires when an item in the guild bank is locked for moving or unlocked afterward

GUILDBANK_TEXT_CHANGED—Fires when the text associated with a guild bank tab is changed

GUILDBANK_UPDATE_MONEY—Fires when the amount of money in the guild bank changes

GUILDBANK_UPDATE_TABS—Fires when information about guild bank tabs becomes available

GUILDBANK_UPDATE_TEXT—Fires when text associated with a guild bank tab becomes available

GUILDBANK_UPDATE_WITHDRAWMONEY—Fires when the amount of money the player can withdraw from the guild bank changes

GUILDTABARD_UPDATE—Fires when the player's guild tabard design changes

GUILD_EVENT_LOG_UPDATE—Fires when information for the guild event log becomes available

GUILD_INVITE_CANCEL—Fires when an invitation to join a guild is no longer available

GUILD_INVITE_REQUEST—Fires when the player is invited to join a guild

GUILD_MOTD—Fires when the guild message of the day is updated

GUILD_REGISTRAR_CLOSED—Fires when the player ends interaction with a guild registrar

GUILD_REGISTRAR_SHOW—Fires when the player begins interaction with a guild registrar

GUILD_ROSTER_UPDATE—Fires when new information about the contents of the guild roster is available

HONOR_CURRENCY_UPDATE—Fires when the player's amount of honor points changes

IGNORELIST_UPDATE—Fires when the content of the player's ignore list becomes available or changes

IGR_BILLING_NAG_DIALOG—Fires when a message should be shown about the player's paid-per-hour game time expiring soon

INSPECT_ACHIEVEMENT_READY—Fires after the player attempts to compare achievements with another character, indicating that achievement information for the other unit has become available

INSPECT_HONOR_UPDATE—Fires when information about the inspected unit's PvP activities becomes available

INSPECT_TALENT_READY—Fires when information about the inspected player's talents becomes available

INSTANCE_BOOT_START—Fires when the player will soon be ejected from an instance

INSTANCE_BOOT_STOP—Fires when the warning countdown for ejecting the player from an instance is canceled

INSTANCE_LOCK_START—Fires when the player will soon be saved to an instance

INSTANCE_LOCK_STOP—Fires when the warning countdown for saving the player to an instance is canceled

ITEM_LOCKED—Fires when an item in the player's bags or equipped inventory is locked for moving

ITEM_LOCK_CHANGED—Fires when an item in the player's bags or equipped inventory is locked for moving or unlocked afterward

ITEM_PUSH—Fires when the player receives an item

ITEM_TEXT_BEGIN—Fires when the player begins interaction with a readable item or world object

ITEM_TEXT_CLOSED—Fires when the player ends interaction with a readable item or world object

ITEM_TEXT_READY—Fires when text changes or becomes available for the readable item or world object with which the player is interacting

ITEM_TEXT_TRANSLATION—Fires when a "translation" progress bar should be displayed while the player interacts with a readable item or world object

ITEM_UNLOCKED—Fires when an item in the player's bags or equipped inventory is unlocked after moving

KNOWLEDGE_BASE_ARTICLE_LOAD_FAILURE—Fires when a knowledge base article fails to load

KNOWLEDGE_BASE_ARTICLE_LOAD_SUCCESS—Fires when the contents of a successfully loaded knowledge base article become available

KNOWLEDGE_BASE_QUERY_LOAD_FAILURE—Fires when a knowledge base query fails

KNOWLEDGE_BASE_QUERY_LOAD_SUCCESS—Fires when results of a successful knowledge base query become available

KNOWLEDGE_BASE_SERVER_MESSAGE—Fires when the knowledge base server message changes or becomes available

KNOWLEDGE_BASE_SETUP_LOAD_FAILURE—Fires when the knowledge base's default listing fails to load

KNOWLEDGE_BASE_SETUP_LOAD_SUCCESS—Fires when the knowledge base's default listing becomes available

KNOWLEDGE_BASE_SYSTEM_MOTD_UPDATED—Fires when the knowledge base system's message of the day changes or becomes available

KNOWN_CURRENCY_TYPES_UPDATE—Fires when the currency list changes

KNOWN_TITLES_UPDATE—Fires when the number of titles available to the player changes

LANGUAGE_LIST_CHANGED—Fires when the list of known languages changes

LEARNED_SPELL_IN_TAB—Fires when a spell is learned inside of a given spell book tab

LEVEL_GRANT_PROPOSED—Fires when the player is offered to instantly gain a level thanks to a Recruit-A-Friend partner

LFG_MATCH_CANCEL—Fires when an offered LFG group match is no longer available

LFG_MATCH_REQUEST—Fires when the player has been matched to a group via the LFG system and offered to join it

LFG_PENDING_CANCEL—Fires when the LFG system is no longer attempting to find a group for the player

LFG_PENDING_REQUEST—Fires when the LFG system is attempting to find a group for the player

LFG_UPDATE—Fires when information about the player's LFG system settings changes or becomes available

LOCALPLAYER_PET_RENAMED—Fires when the player's pet is renamed

LOGOUT_CANCEL—Fires when the logout countdown is aborted

LOOT_BIND_CONFIRM—Fires when the player attempts to loot a Bind on Pickup item

LOOT_CLOSED—Fires when the player ends interaction with a lootable corpse or object

LOOT_OPENED—Fires when the player begins interaction with a lootable corpse or object

LOOT_SLOT_CLEARED—Fires when the contents of a loot slot are removed

MACRO_ACTION_FORBIDDEN—Fires when a macro script attempts to use a protected API

MAIL_CLOSED—Fires when the player ends interaction with a mailbox

MAIL_FAILED—Fires when an outgoing mail message fails to send

MAIL_INBOX_UPDATE—Fires when information about the contents of the player's inbox changes or becomes available

MAIL_SEND_INFO_UPDATE—Fires when information about the outgoing mail message's attachments changes

MAIL_SEND_SUCCESS—Fires when an outgoing message is successfully sent

MAIL_SHOW—Fires when the player begins interaction with a mailbox

MEETINGSTONE_CHANGED—Fires when new information is available for the Looking For Group system

MERCHANT_CLOSED—Fires when the player ends interaction with a vendor

MERCHANT_SHOW—Fires when the player begins interaction with a vendor

MERCHANT_UPDATE—Fires when information about a vendor's available items changes or becomes available

MINIGAME_UPDATE—Unused

MINIMAP_PING—Fires when the player or a group member "pings" a point on the minimap to share its location with the group

MINIMAP_UPDATE_TRACKING—Fires when the player's currently active tracking ability changes

MINIMAP_UPDATE_ZOOM—Fires when the minimap zoom type changes

MIRROR_TIMER_PAUSE—Fires when a special countdown timer is paused

MIRROR_TIMER_START—Fires when a special countdown timer starts

MIRROR_TIMER_STOP—Fires when a special countdown timer stops

MODIFIER_STATE_CHANGED—Fires when a modifier key is pressed or released

MOVIE_COMPRESSING_PROGRESS—Fires when compression of a movie recording starts

MOVIE_RECORDING_PROGRESS—Fires when movie recording starts

MOVIE_UNCOMPRESSED_MOVIE—Fires when the client prompts the player to allow compression of a movie recording

MUTELIST_UPDATE—Fires when the content of the player's muted list becomes available or changes

NEW_AUCTION_UPDATE—Fires when the content of the auction house's Create Auction item slot changes

NEW_TITLE_EARNED—Fires when the player earns a new title

NPC_PVPQUEUE_ANYWHERE—Fires when the player begins interaction with an NPC which can queue the player for any battleground

OLD_TITLE_LOST—Fires when one of the player's titles is no longer available

OPEN_MASTER_LOOT_LIST—Fires when the list of master loot candidates becomes available

OPEN_TABARD_FRAME—Fires when the player begins interaction with a tabard designer

PARTY_CONVERTED_TO_RAID—Fires when the player's party becomes a raid group

PARTY_INVITE_CANCEL—Fires when a pending invitation to join a group is no longer available

PARTY_INVITE_REQUEST—Fires when the player is invited to join a group

PARTY_LEADER_CHANGED—Fires when information about the leadership of the player's party changes or becomes available

PARTY_LOOT_METHOD_CHANGED—Fires when information about the loot rules for the player's party changes or becomes available

PARTY_MEMBERS_CHANGED—Fires when information about the membership of the player's party changes or becomes available

PARTY_MEMBER_DISABLE—Fires when a party member goes offline

PARTY_MEMBER_ENABLE—Fires when an offline party member comes back online

PETITION_CLOSED—Fires when the player ends interaction with a guild or arena team charter

PETITION_SHOW—Fires when a guild or arena team charter is presented to the player

PETITION_VENDOR_CLOSED—Fires when the player ends interaction with an arena registrar

PETITION_VENDOR_SHOW—Fires when the player begins interaction with an arena registrar

PETITION_VENDOR_UPDATE—Fires when information about available options at an arena registrar becomes available

PET_ATTACK_START—Fires when the player's pet starts auto-attacking

PET_ATTACK_STOP—Fires when the player's pet stops auto-attacking

PET_BAR_HIDE—Fires when the pet action bar should be hidden

PET_BAR_HIDEGRID—Fires when a pet ability is removed from the cursor

PET_BAR_SHOWGRID—Fires when a pet ability is picked up onto the cursor

PET_BAR_UPDATE—Fires when information about the content of the pet action bar changes or becomes available

PET_BAR_UPDATE_COOLDOWN—Fires when the cooldown begins or ends for an ability on the pet action bar

PET_DISMISS_START—Fires when the player's pet is dismissed

PET_FORCE_NAME_DECLENSION—Fires when the player is prompted to provide Russian declensions for a pet's name

PET_RENAMEABLE—Fires when the player is prompted to rename a pet which has been renamed before

PET_STABLE_CLOSED—Fires when the player ends interaction with the pet stables

PET_STABLE_SHOW—Fires when the player begins interaction with the pet stables

PET_STABLE_UPDATE—Fires when information about the pet stables' content changes or becomes available

PET_STABLE_UPDATE_PAPERDOLL—Fires when information about 3D models used in the pet stables becomes available

PET_TALENT_UPDATE—Fires when the player's pet talent information changes—that is, when the pet is summoned, dismissed, gains or spends talent points

PET_UI_CLOSE—Fires when information about the player's pet is no longer available

PET_UI_UPDATE—Fires when information about the player's pet changes or becomes available

PLAYERBANKBAGSLOTS_CHANGED—Fires when the number of bank bag slots purchased by the player changes

PLAYERBANKSLOTS_CHANGED—Fires when the contents of a bank slot or bank bag slot are changed

PLAYER_ALIVE—Fires when the player's spirit is released after death or when the player accepts a resurrection without releasing

PLAYER_AURAS_CHANGED—Fires when the player gains or loses a buff or debuff

PLAYER_CAMPING—Fires when the player attempts to log out while not in a major city, inn, or other "resting" area

PLAYER_CONTROL_GAINED—Fires when the player regains control of his or her character

PLAYER_CONTROL_LOST—Fires when the player loses control of his or her character

PLAYER_DAMAGE_DONE_MODS—Fires when an effect changes the player's spell bonus damage

PLAYER_DEAD—Fires when the player dies

PLAYER_ENTERING_BATTLEGROUND—Fires when the player enters a battleground instance

PLAYER_ENTERING_WORLD—Fired when the player enters the world, reloads the UI, enters/leaves an instance or battleground, or respawns at a graveyard. Also fires any other time the player sees a loading screen

PLAYER_ENTER_COMBAT—Fires when the player begins melee auto-attack mode

PLAYER_EQUIPMENT_CHANGED—Fires when the player equips or unequips an item

PLAYER_FARSIGHT_FOCUS_CHANGED—Fires when the player's viewpoint changes

PLAYER_FLAGS_CHANGED—Fires when a unit's AFK or DND status changes

PLAYER_FOCUS_CHANGED—Fires when the player's focus unit changes

PLAYER_GAINS_VEHICLE_DATA—Fires when the player gains vehicle-related attributes without necessarily entering a vehicle

PLAYER_GUILD_UPDATE—Fires when information about the player's guild membership changes

PLAYER_LEAVE_COMBAT—Fires when the player stops melee auto-attack mode

PLAYER_LEAVING_WORLD—Fires when the player logs out or exits a world area

PLAYER_LEVEL_UP—Fires when the player gains a character level

PLAYER_LOGIN—Fires immediately before PLAYER_ENTERING_WORLD on login and UI reload

PLAYER_LOGOUT—Fires immediately before the player is logged out of the game

PLAYER_LOSES_VEHICLE_DATA—Fires when the player loses vehicle-related attributes without necessarily having been in a vehicle

PLAYER_MONEY—Fires when the player gains or spends money

PLAYER_PVP_KILLS_CHANGED—Fires whenever a player's number of Honorable Kills changes

PLAYER_QUITING—Fires when the player attempts to exit WoW while not in a major city, inn, or other "resting" area

PLAYER_REGEN_DISABLED—Fires when the player enters combat status

PLAYER_REGEN_ENABLED—Fires when the player leaves combat status

PLAYER_SKINNED—Fires when another character takes the insignia from the player's corpse in a battleground or world PvP zone

PLAYER_TALENT_UPDATE—Fires when the player gains or spends talent points

PLAYER_TARGET_CHANGED—Fires when the player changes targets

PLAYER_TOTEM_UPDATE—Fires when information about the player's placed totems changes or becomes available

PLAYER_TRADE_MONEY—Fires when the amount of money offered for trade by the player changes

PLAYER_UNGHOST—Fires when a player resurrects after being in spirit form

PLAYER_UPDATE_RESTING—Fires when the player enters or leaves a major city, inn or other "resting" area

PLAYER_XP_UPDATE—Fires when the player's amount of accrued experience points changes

PLAYTIME_CHANGED—Fires when changes to the player's limited play time status take effect

PLAY_MOVIE—Fires when an in-game movie should be played

PREVIEW_PET_TALENT_POINTS_CHANGED—Fires when pet talent points are spent or unspent in preview mode

PREVIEW_TALENT_POINTS_CHANGED—Fires when the player spends or unspends talent points in preview mode

PVPQUEUE_ANYWHERE_SHOW—Fires when the player begins interacting with the UI feature allowing battleground queueing from any location

PVPQUEUE_ANYWHERE_UPDATE_AVAILABLE—Fires when information for the any-battleground queueing UI changes or becomes available

QUEST_ACCEPTED—Fires when a new quest is added to the player's quest log (which is what happens after a player accepts a quest)

QUEST_ACCEPT_CONFIRM—Fires when certain kinds of quests (e.g. NPC escort quests) are started by another member of the player's group

QUEST_COMPLETE—Fires when the player is looking at the "Complete" page for a quest, at a questgiver

QUEST_DETAIL—Fires when details of an available quest are presented by a questgiver

QUEST_FINISHED—Fires when the player ends interaction with a questgiver or ends a stage of the questgiver dialog

QUEST_GREETING—Fires when a questgiver presents a greeting along with a list of active or available quests

QUEST_ITEM_UPDATE—Fires when information about items in a questgiver dialog is updated

QUEST_LOG_UPDATE—Fires when the game client receives updates relating to the player's quest log (this event is not just related to the quests inside it)

QUEST_PROGRESS—Fires when interacting with a questgiver about an active quest

QUEST_WATCH_UPDATE—Fires when the player's status regarding a quest's objectives changes, for instance picking up a required object or killing a mob for that quest. All forms of (quest objective) progress changes will trigger this event

RAID_INSTANCE_WELCOME—Fires when the player enters an instance that has a reset timer

RAID_ROSTER_UPDATE—Fires when the raid roster changes

RAID_TARGET_UPDATE—Fires when raid target icons are assigned or cleared

RAISED_AS_GHOUL—Fires when the player is raised as a ghoul by a friendly death knight

READY_CHECK—Fires when a ready check is triggered

READY_CHECK_CONFIRM—Fires when a unit responds to a ready check

READY_CHECK_FINISHED—Fires when a ready check ends

REPLACE_ENCHANT—Fires when the player attempts to enchant an item which is already enchanted

RESURRECT_REQUEST—Fires when another character offers to resurrect the player

RUNE_POWER_UPDATE—Fires when the availability of one of the player's rune resources changes

RUNE_TYPE_UPDATE—Fires when the type of one of the player's rune resources changes

SCREENSHOT_FAILED—Fires if an attempt to take a screenshot fails

SCREENSHOT_SUCCEEDED—Fires when a screenshot is successfully taken

SEND_MAIL_COD_CHANGED—Fires when the Cash On Delivery cost assigned for the outgoing mail message changes

SEND_MAIL_MONEY_CHANGED—Fires when the amount of money attached to the outgoing mail message changes

SKILL_LINES_CHANGED—Fires when the content of the player's skill list changes

SOCKET_INFO_CLOSE—Fires when the player ends interaction with the item socketing UI

SOCKET_INFO_UPDATE—Fires when information about the contents of the item socketing UI changes or becomes available

SOUND_DEVICE_UPDATE—Fires when information about sound input/output devices changes or becomes available

SPELLS_CHANGED—Fires when information about the contents of the player's spellbook changes or becomes available

SPELL_UPDATE_COOLDOWN—Fires when the cooldown on one of the player's spells begins or ends

SPELL_UPDATE_USABLE—Fires when a spell becomes usable or unusable

START_AUTOREPEAT_SPELL—Fires when the player casts a spell which automatically repeats

START_LOOT_ROLL—Fires when an item becomes available for group loot rolling

START_MINIGAME—Unused

STOP_AUTOREPEAT_SPELL—Fires when the player stops repetition of an automatically repeating spell

SYNCHRONIZE_SETTINGS—Fires when game options are manually synchronized with those saved on the server

TABARD_CANSAVE_CHANGED—Fires when information about the player's ability to save a guild tabard design changes or becomes available

TABARD_SAVE_PENDING—Fires when the player attempts to save a guild tabard design

TAXIMAP_CLOSED—Fires when the player begins interaction with a flight master

TAXIMAP_OPENED—Fires when the player ends interaction with a flight master

TIME_PLAYED_MSG—Fires when information about the player's total time played becomes available

TRACKED_ACHIEVEMENT_UPDATE—Fires when the player's progress changes on an achievement marked for watching in the objectives tracker

TRADE_ACCEPT_UPDATE—Fires when the player or trade target signals acceptance (or cancels acceptance) of the trade

TRADE_CLOSED—Fires when a trade with another player ends or is canceled

TRADE_MONEY_CHANGED—Fires when the amount of money offered by the trade target changes

TRADE_PLAYER_ITEM_CHANGED—Fires when the set of items offered for trade by the player changes

`TRADE_POTENTIAL_BIND_ENCHANT`—*This event is not yet documented*

`TRADE_REPLACE_ENCHANT`—Fires if the player attempts to enchant an item offered by the trade target which is already enchanted

`TRADE_REQUEST_CANCEL`—Unused

`TRADE_SHOW`—Fires when a trade interaction with another character begins

`TRADE_SKILL_CLOSE`—Fires when the player ends interaction with a trade skill recipe list

`TRADE_SKILL_FILTER_UPDATE`—Fires when the search filter for a trade skill recipe list changes

`TRADE_SKILL_SHOW`—Fires when the player begins interaction with a trade skill recipe list

`TRADE_SKILL_UPDATE`—Fires when information about the contents of a trade skill recipe list changes or becomes available

`TRADE_TARGET_ITEM_CHANGED`—Fires when the set of items offered for trade by the target changes

`TRADE_UPDATE`—Fires when new information becomes available about a trade process underway with another character

`TRAINER_CLOSED`—Fires when the player ends interaction with a class or skill trainer

`TRAINER_DESCRIPTION_UPDATE`—Fires when description information for the selected trainer service changes or becomes available

`TRAINER_SHOW`—Fires when the player begins interaction with a class or skill trainer

`TRAINER_UPDATE`—Fires when information about the contents of the trainer service list changes or becomes available

`TUTORIAL_TRIGGER`—Fires when a contextual tutorial should be shown

`UI_ERROR_MESSAGE`—Fires when a game error message should be displayed

`UI_INFO_MESSAGE`—Fires when an informative message should be displayed

`UNIT_ATTACK`—Fires when a unit's weapon (or standard melee attack damage) changes

`UNIT_ATTACK_POWER`—Fires when a unit's attack power changes

`UNIT_ATTACK_SPEED`—Fires when a unit's attack speed changes

`UNIT_AURA`—Fires when a unit loses or gains a buff or debuff.

`UNIT_CLASSIFICATION_CHANGED`—Fires when a unit changes classification (e.g. if an elite unit becomes non-elite)

UNIT_COMBAT—Fires when a unit takes or recovers from damage due to a combat effect

UNIT_COMBO_POINTS—Fires when a unit scores combo points on its target

UNIT_DAMAGE—Fires when a unit's weapon damage changes

UNIT_DEFENSE—Fires when a unit's defense changes

UNIT_DISPLAYPOWER—Fires when a unit's primary power type (e.g. rage, energy, mana) changes

UNIT_DYNAMIC_FLAGS—Fires when certain unit attributes change

UNIT_ENERGY—Fires when a unit's energy level changes

UNIT_ENTERED_VEHICLE—Fires when a unit has entered a vehicle

UNIT_ENTERING_VEHICLE—Fires when a unit begins entering a vehicle

UNIT_EXITED_VEHICLE—Fires when a unit has exited a vehicle

UNIT_EXITING_VEHICLE—Fires when a unit begins exiting a vehicle

UNIT_FACTION—Fires when a unit's PvP status changes

UNIT_FLAGS—Fires when certain combat statuses for a unit change (e.g. stunned, feared)

UNIT_FOCUS—Fires when a unit's focus level changes

UNIT_HAPPINESS—Fires when the player's pet's happiness level changes

UNIT_HEALTH—Fires when a unit's health level changes

UNIT_INVENTORY_CHANGED—Fires when the player (or inspected unit) equips or unequips items

UNIT_LEVEL—Fires when a unit's character level changes

UNIT_MANA—Fires when a unit's mana level changes

UNIT_MAXENERGY—Fires when a unit's maximum energy changes

UNIT_MAXFOCUS—Fires when a unit's maximum focus changes

UNIT_MAXHAPPINESS—Fires when a unit's maximum happiness changes

UNIT_MAXHEALTH—Fires when a unit's maximum health changes

UNIT_MAXMANA—Fires when a unit's maximum mana changes

UNIT_MAXRAGE—Fires when a unit's maximum rage changes

UNIT_MAXRUNIC_POWER—Fires when a unit's maximum runic power changes

UNIT_MODEL_CHANGED—Fires when a unit's 3D model changes (e.g. due to shapeshifting, being polymorphed, or equipping gear)

UNIT_NAME_UPDATE—Fires when a unit's name is changed

UNIT_PET—Fires when a unit gains or loses a pet

UNIT_PET_EXPERIENCE—Fires when the player's pet gains experience points

UNIT_PORTRAIT_UPDATE—Fires when a unit's portrait changes (e.g. due to shapeshifting, being polymorphed, or equipping gear)

UNIT_QUEST_LOG_CHANGED—Fires when a unit's quests change (accepted/objective progress/abandoned/completed)

UNIT_RAGE—Fires when a unit's rage level changes

UNIT_RANGEDDAMAGE—Fires when a unit's ranged attack damage changes

UNIT_RANGED_ATTACK_POWER—Fires when a unit's ranged attack power changes

UNIT_RESISTANCES—Fires when a unit's magic resistances change

UNIT_RUNIC_POWER—Fires when a unit's runic power level changes

UNIT_SPELLCAST_CHANNEL_START—Fires when a unit starts channeling a spell

UNIT_SPELLCAST_CHANNEL_STOP—Fires when a unit stops or cancels a channeled spell

UNIT_SPELLCAST_CHANNEL_UPDATE—Fires when a unit's channeled spell is interrupted or delayed

UNIT_SPELLCAST_DELAYED—Fires when a unit's spell cast is delayed

UNIT_SPELLCAST_FAILED—Fires when a unit's spell cast fails

UNIT_SPELLCAST_FAILED_QUIET—Fires when a unit's spell cast fails and no error message should be displayed

UNIT_SPELLCAST_INTERRUPTED—Fires when a unit's spell cast is interrupted

UNIT_SPELLCAST_INTERRUPTIBLE—Fires when a unit's spell cast becomes interruptible again

UNIT_SPELLCAST_NOT_INTERRUPTIBLE—Fires when a unit's spell cast becomes uninterruptible

UNIT_SPELLCAST_SENT—Fires when a request to cast a spell (on behalf of the player or a unit controlled by the player) is sent to the server

UNIT_SPELLCAST_START—Fires when a unit begins casting a spell

UNIT_SPELLCAST_STOP—Fires when a unit stops or cancels casting a spell

UNIT_SPELLCAST_SUCCEEDED—Fires when a unit's spell cast succeeds

UNIT_STATS—Fires when a unit's primary attributes change

UNIT_TARGET—Fires when a unit's target changes

UNIT_THREAT_LIST_UPDATE—Fires when a non-player unit's threat list is updated

UNIT_THREAT_SITUATION_UPDATE—Fires when a unit's threat state changes

UPDATE_BATTLEFIELD_SCORE—Fires when information for the battleground scoreboard changes or becomes available

UPDATE_BATTLEFIELD_STATUS—Fires when the player's status in a battleground or queue changes

UPDATE_BINDINGS—Fires when information about the player's key binding settings changes or becomes available

UPDATE_BONUS_ACTIONBAR—Fires when information about the bonus action bar changes or becomes available

UPDATE_CHAT_COLOR—Fires when the color settings for chat message types are updated

UPDATE_CHAT_COLOR_NAME_BY_CLASS—Fires when settings for per-class color-coding of character names in chat are updated

UPDATE_CHAT_WINDOWS—Fires when saved chat window settings are loaded

UPDATE_EXHAUSTION—Fires when the player's rest state or amount of rested XP changes

UPDATE_FACTION—Fires when the contents of the reputation listing change or become available

UPDATE_FLOATING_CHAT_WINDOWS—Fires when chat window layout should be updated

UPDATE_GM_STATUS—Fires when the player's GM ticket status (or ability to submit tickets) changes

UPDATE_INSTANCE_INFO—Fires when information about instances to which the player is saved changes or becomes available

UPDATE_INVENTORY_ALERTS—Fires when an equipped item's durability alert status changes

UPDATE_INVENTORY_DURABILITY—Fires when an equipped item's durability changes

UPDATE_LFG_LIST—Fires when results of a Looking for More query become available

UPDATE_LFG_LIST_INCREMENTAL—Fires when results of a Looking for More query are updated

UPDATE_LFG_TYPES—Fires when information about possible Looking for Group settings changes or becomes available

UPDATE_MACROS—Fires when information about the player's macros changes or becomes available

UPDATE_MASTER_LOOT_LIST—Fires when the contents of the master loot candidate list change or become available

UPDATE_MOUSEOVER_UNIT—Fires when the mouse cursor moves over a visible unit

UPDATE_MULTI_CAST_ACTIONBAR—Fires when the contents of the multi-cast action bar change or become available

UPDATE_PENDING_MAIL—Fires when information about newly received mail messages (not yet seen at a mailbox) becomes available

UPDATE_SHAPESHIFT_COOLDOWN—Fires when the cooldown begins or ends for an action on the stance/shapeshift bar

UPDATE_SHAPESHIFT_FORM—Fires when the player's shapeshift form changes

UPDATE_SHAPESHIFT_FORMS—Fires when the contents of the stance/shapeshift bar change or become available

UPDATE_SHAPESHIFT_USABLE—Fires when an ability on the stance/shapeshift bar becomes usable or unusable

UPDATE_STEALTH—Fires when the player uses or cancels a stealth ability

UPDATE_TICKET—Fires when information about an active GM ticket changes or becomes available

UPDATE_TRADESKILL_RECAST—Fires for each cast when performing multiple casts of a trade skill recipe

UPDATE_WORLD_STATES—Fires when information for world state UI elements changes or becomes available

USE_BIND_CONFIRM—Fires when the player attempts to use an item which will become soulbound in the process

USE_GLYPH—Fires when the player begins to use a glyph

VARIABLES_LOADED—Fires when non-addon-specific saved variables are loaded

VEHICLE_ANGLE_SHOW—Fires when controls for vehicle weapon pitch should be displayed

VEHICLE_ANGLE_UPDATE—Fires when the player's vehicle weapon pitch changes

VEHICLE_PASSENGERS_CHANGED—Fires when the list of passengers in the player's vehicle changes

VEHICLE_POWER_SHOW—Fires when controls for vehicle weapon power should be displayed

VEHICLE_UPDATE—Fires when information about the player's vehicle changes or becomes available

VOICE_CHANNEL_STATUS_UPDATE—Fires when voice-related status of a chat channel changes

VOICE_CHAT_ENABLED_UPDATE—Fires when the client's voice chat feature is enabled or disabled

VOICE_LEFT_SESSION—Fires when a voice-enabled member leaves a chat channel

VOICE_PUSH_TO_TALK_START—Fires when the "Push to Talk" key binding is activated

VOICE_PUSH_TO_TALK_STOP—Fires when the "Push to Talk" key binding is deactivated

VOICE_SELF_MUTE—Fires when the player's self mute setting changes

VOICE_SESSIONS_UPDATE—Fires when information about a voice chat session changes or becomes available

VOICE_START—Fires when a channel member begins speaking in voice chat

VOICE_STATUS_UPDATE—Fires when a member of the player's group changes voice chat status

VOICE_STOP—Fires when a channel member finishes speaking in voice chat

WEAR_EQUIPMENT_SET—Fires when the player's current equipment set changes

WHO_LIST_UPDATE—Fires when results of a Who query become available

WORLD_MAP_NAME_UPDATE—Fires when the name of the current world map area changes or becomes available

WORLD_MAP_UPDATE—Fires when the contents of the world map change or become available

WORLD_STATE_UI_TIMER_UPDATE—Fires when the state of a timer world state UI element changes or becomes available

WOW_MOUSE_NOT_FOUND—Fires when a man-buttoned WoW mouse is not found, in response to a DetectWowMouse() function call

ZONE_CHANGED—Fires when the player moves between subzones or other named areas

ZONE_CHANGED_INDOORS—Fires when the player moves between areas and the "indoors/outdoors" status may have changed

ZONE_CHANGED_NEW_AREA—Fires when the player moves between major zones or enters/exits an instance

Part

V

Appendixes

In This Part

Best Practices

Throughout this book the authors have made an effort to present code that follows patterns to make your programming life easier. However, not all of these ideas can be passed on implicitly. This appendix presents generally accepted practices that will empower you to be more effective at writing addons. These tips will help you produce addons more quickly, write better-performing code, and make your code itself more readable to others (and to yourself if you're away from a project for more than a few weeks).

Be aware that many people follow their own, more extensive sets of rules. To some extent, "best practice" is as much a case of personal preference as it is absolute commandments. We have done our best to pick the most widely applicable, least controversial ideals for inclusion here. However, you should always defer to your better judgment. If a solution presents itself that goes against these ideas and you can't think of an alternative or the alternatives are cumbersome and awkward, by all means, use what works.

General Programming

Certain practices are applicable to nearly every programming language in existence. These are not so much technical as they are conceptual; the intent is to help you think about a problem in ways that make it easier to solve. If you have had any formal training in programming, you will most likely be familiar with the suggestions presented here.

Use Meaningful Variable Names

If you've ever taken algebra or higher math, you know how difficult it can be to swim in a sea of seemingly random letters and numbers. It takes weeks of practice and memorization to fully understand and appreciate the mish-mash of variables, coefficients, and operators necessary to describe various constructs. This difficulty is no different and, in fact, is multiplied in programming.

Often, a new programmer will use short, abbreviated variable names to save time typing. At first the variables might seem self-evident, but that's only an illusion—an illusion that quickly goes away. Take the following two functions, for example:

```
function ic(i)
  local a = 0
  for j = 0, 4 do
    for k = 1, ns(j) do
      local l = il(j, k)
      if l and i == tn(sm(l, "item:(%d+):")) then
        a = a + sl(2, ii(j, k))
      end
    end
  end
  return a
end

function GetBagItemCount(itemID)
  local count = 0
  for bag = 0, 4 do
    for slot = 1, GetContainerNumSlots(bag) do
      local link = GetContainerItemLink(bag, slot)
      if link and itemID == tonumber(strmatch(link, "item:(%d+):")) then
        count = count + select(2, GetContainerItemInfo(bag, slot))
      end
    end
  end
  return count
end
```

Someone unfamiliar with your code (including yourself after some time away—we cannot reiterate this enough) would have to spend an unfortunate amount of time deciphering the first example. Even if you can follow the logic, there is absolutely no indication of what it does on a conceptual level. The only way to figure that out would be to research what the functions ns, il, tn, sm, sl, and ii do, all the while praying that they're not implemented in the same manner. You literally have to rename the identifiers in your mind to understand their behavior.

On the other hand, the code in the second example clearly spells out exactly what it does. The names of the functions it calls describe what they do, and the returns are placed into variables that describe what they represent. Even without looking at any of the code, the name of the function itself gives you an idea of its behavior. The time you spend typing longer names at the front end of development more than pays off in the long run.

It *is* possible to be concise and clear at the same time. Rather than typing out the full description of something, you can use straightforward abbreviations. For example, you can use `desc` instead of `description`, `tbl` instead of `table`, `numSlots` instead of `numberOfSlots`, and so on.

Variable Naming Exceptions

As with algebra, certain well-known, single-letter variables are used through-out the software industry. Some of them, in fact, are borrowed directly from mathematics. Table A-1 lists some of the more common terse variables and their uses. If you decide to use these, make sure they are unique to the context—that is, the most important piece of data of its kind. For example, if you use `t` as a time value, it should be the only (or at least the most important) time value in the function. You can get a bit more flexibility by numbering them (`t1`, `t2`) but it's best to limit how far you take this.

Table A-1: Common Single-Letter Variables

VARIABLE	USES
n	A number or count of something.
t	A time or table value.
r, g, b, a	Color values. Red, green, blue, and alpha, respectively.
x, y	Screen coordinates. Horizontal and vertical, respectively.
i, j*	Numerical `for` loop index: `for i = 1, 10 do`
k, v*	Associative index and value in a `for` loop: `for k, v in pairs(someTable) do`
_ (underscore)	Throwaway value. Something you don't actually plan to use: `local var1, var2, _, _, var3 = someFunc()`

*In nested loops, it is usually better to use descriptive names to avoid confusion.

Use Named Constants Instead of Literals

Programs often require some arbitrary number to control their behavior. The number of items that will fit in a list, a time limit for some complex operation, and the default number of buttons on an action bar are all numbers that could potentially be used in many places throughout your code. Rather than hard coding these numbers each place they occur in your code, store them in variables and use the variables in the code. These variables are treated like *constants* you'd see in other languages.

By doing this, you only have to make one change to affect every location the number appears in your code. The more occurrences of the number, the more time (and potential for error) you save. As with meaningful variable names, using constants gives significance to an otherwise random-looking number.

Convention dictates that you use all capital letters when naming your constants (such as `NUM_ACTIONBAR_BUTTONS`). This makes them easily identifiable in your source code, adding to readability. It is also a good idea to define all related constants in one location, usually near the top of the file where they are used or in the case of string constants, in a separate file for localization. If they are scattered throughout your source code, you will needlessly waste time searching for the one you want to change.

Be sure you don't go overboard, though. If the number itself is fundamental to the problem you are solving, go ahead and use it literally. For example, the expression for calculating the circumference of a circle given its radius is $2\pi r$. If you need to make an `area` function, go ahead and use the 2 as-is (you'll obviously want to use a constant for the value of π, `math.pi`).

Organize for Easier Maintenance

Code can sometimes become unwieldy, especially as you revisit the code to add features and fix bugs. Although you should make all efforts to organize your code logically, it sometimes helps to go back and rework certain sections.

Rework Repetitive Code

You may be working on some bit of functionality and find yourself repeating essentially the same lines of code over and over with only minor differences. Consider creating a function that takes a few parameters and does all of the steps that each repetitive part of your original code would do. This will save you from many copy/paste errors as well as allow you to more easily add new occurrences of the same sort of functionality.

Lua gives you even more of an edge with its tables. For more than a few repetitions, it might make more sense to define all your parameters in a list and then call the function in a `for` loop. For example, say you have a function, `MakeTexture`, which takes three parameters: `name`, `id`, and `filename`. If you have four textures, you could create a table and `for` loop like the following (notice how the numerical index is used to generate an ID for the texture):

```
local textures = {
  { name = "Picture of me",
    file = "Interface\\AddOns\\MyMod\\Images\\me.tga"
  },
```

```
  { name = "Picture of Ziggart",
    file = "Interface\\AddOns\\MyMod\\Images\\ziggart.tga"
  },
  { name = "Frame Background",
    file = "Interface\\AddOns\\MyMod\\Images\\bg.tga"
  },
  { name = "Some other texture",
    file = "Interface\\AddOns\\MyMod\\Images\\other.tga"
  },
}

for id, entry in ipairs(textures) do
  MyAddon.MakeTexture(entry.name, id, entry.file)
end
```

Now if you want to add a new texture, you can just create a new entry in the table. If you insert one in the middle, the rest will automatically have the correct IDs. Tables are also more recognizable as a data structure, so they make more sense semantically than calling `MakeTexture` four times with the various parameters.

Break Apart Long Functions

There is an upper limit to the number of words on a line of text or in a paragraph before our brains have trouble absorbing the information. In a similar fashion, functions that drag on and on over multiple screens become hard to follow. If you have a really long function that does several different tasks, you might want to break it apart into smaller functions that are called by one "master." A fairly common rule of thumb is to keep functions down to one screen of code or less.

Use Consistent Programming Style

Much of programming is a matter of personal style and preference. From indentation format to variable names, you can make many choices that affect the overall look and feel of your code. By remaining consistent in these choices, you will serve yourself in the long run. Following are some examples of choices you will have to make for yourself. Obviously, we could never hope to create a complete list, but this provides a good sample to get you thinking.

- **Naming conventions**—Do you begin all your functions with capital or lowercase letters? Do you differentiate words with underscores or "camel case" (`num_slots` vs. `numSlots`)? Do all functions follow a specific grammar (`Verb`, `VerbNoun`, and so on)?

- **Whitespace**—How many blank lines do you have between functions? Do you use tabs or spaces for indenting? How wide should indents be? Do you split long statements into multiple lines?

- **Organization**—Do you split your source into multiple files by functionality? Are your functions mostly local or do you use a namespace table? If you're using a table, do you use method syntax or simple indexing (`MyMod:function` vs. `MyMod.function`)?

- **Comment format**—Do all of your functions have descriptions of their parameters and effects? Do you include a copyright notice at the beginning of your files? Do you use inline comments to describe complex algorithms?

Lua Tips

The simplicity of the Lua language can be deceptive. On the surface it displays a clean, consistent syntax with intuitive keywords, and it has enough in common with other languages that experienced programmers can get the hang of it quite easily. However, to use Lua to its fullest extent takes a bit of creative thinking. Many of its features are unique (or at least rare) and certain idioms are downright foreign to programmers from other languages (let alone people new to programming in general). To help you in this regard, this section presents some tips that apply to Lua in general: some idiomatic concepts that will help you take full advantage of its features, and various optimizations to help you tune the performance of your addons.

Use Local Variables

As you may remember from Part I, variables are always global unless defined with the `local` keyword. Global variables, while suitable for many purposes, have a couple of important caveats. Each time you reference a global variable, Lua has to do a table lookup on the global environment (`_G`) with the name of said variable. Locals, on the other hand, are stored in a location of memory determined when the code is compiled. In fact, their names are both irrelevant and inaccessible during runtime.

Additionally, each global variable has the potential for conflict. If you name a function something simple, like `clear`, or `process`, you may end up conflicting with another addon that does the same. Some addons used to provide a global `print` function, and because each one treated its arguments uniquely, there often were real-world conflicts. And they all suffered the now-realized possibility that WoW itself would one day include a function with the same name.

One obvious solution would be to give the function a more unique name, perhaps tacking your addon name to the beginning, but that would unnecessarily add to your typing requirements. It would also add information to your code that provides no meaningful advantage in understanding the logic, potentially making it harder to follow.

For these reasons, you should use locals for every variable or function that does not need to be referenced outside of a given scope (whether it's the file, a function, or even within an `if` block). Also, if you have a legitimate global variable but performance is an issue, create a local copy. For example, if your addon needs to use `string.find` several times per frame, add the following line to the beginning (you can name it anything you want, perhaps `strfind`):

```
local string_find = string.find
```

Notice that this doesn't *call* `string.find` (as shown by the lack of parentheses), but merely copies the function reference to the new local variable. By using `string_find` throughout the file, you will save two table lookups on each call (`_G` → `string` → `find`). These savings can add up quite quickly for addons that do a lot of data processing each frame.

There is a practical limit to how many local variables a function can hold reference to, but you aren't likely to encounter it in your addon development. Remember that there is a trade-off between making portions (such as constants) available, and making them local for performance. Ensure you understand your own code, and choose whatever makes the most sense.

Minimize Unnecessary Garbage

Lua is a garbage-collected language. Every so often, it will go through all the objects in its memory and remove anything that is no longer being referenced. Say you have a function that creates a local table when it runs. After that function exits there are no references to that table, so it its memory will be reclaimed later.

The Lua runtime is very fast by virtual machine standards. It outperforms many other common scripting languages in various tasks. However, nothing in the world is free—especially in computing. Every time you call your function, it creates a new table. Depending on how much information you pack into it, how often you call the function, and a few other factors, collecting this garbage can make a noticeable dent in WoW's performance.

The three main garbage-collected objects that you will encounter are tables, strings, and closures. Tables are definitely the most frequently abused objects. Strings are less obvious but can be just as troublesome. Each unique string is a collectable object. Once there are no more variables set to a particular string, that string can be collected. Finally, each time you create a new function it makes a closure that includes the function itself and references to any upvalues.

Just like waste in real life, you should make an effort to reduce, reuse, and recycle. This will help prevent the garbage collection cycle from getting out of hand.

However, don't go overboard trying to wipe out every trace of garbage creation from your addon. The garbage collector is there for a reason. If you have a situation where you only need to create a new table, string, or closure sporadically, go ahead. Simplicity should take priority over efficiency, especially when you're first designing your addon. If you notice a performance bottleneck, then it's time to investigate further optimizations.

It should also be noted that some of these techniques may actually take longer to run than the avoided garbage collection operation. Unfortunately, there is no sure way to know if this will be the case. It depends entirely on how much data is being used and what kind of processing is going on. If you start out using one technique and find that some areas need optimization, try it the other way.

How to Reduce Garbage

The most obvious way to improve your addon's garbage situation is not to create any in the first place.

Use Multiple Returns and Variable Arguments Instead of Tables

When you need to return multiple values, or accept multiple arguments, you may be tempted to simply wrap them in tables. If you come to Lua from another programming language, you are probably used to dealing with structures, arrays, and such when you want to operate on a set of data. Sometimes, however, tables are unnecessary and even wasteful.

If a function needs to return a set of data, it may be best to return multiple values unless the fundamental purpose of the function is to return some sort of table. This way, the calling function has complete control over how to treat the data. It can pack the returns into a table for later use, pass them to another function for further processing, or simply store them in local variables as needed.

You have seen plenty of examples of multiple returns thanks to their extensive use in WoW's API. However, most of those functions return a fixed number of values. To return an arbitrary amount of data to a calling function, you must use some form of recursion, which is explored a little later in this appendix.

Receiving arguments, both fixed and variable, have been covered fairly extensively in this book. The next section shows a way to operate on every value passed through the vararg (...) and return the modified values without using any intermediary tables.

Avoid Creating Unnecessary Strings

Try to steer clear of building strings piece by piece, adding new elements one by one. If possible, store each element in a variable and then put them all together in one mass concatenation. For example, say you are building a string such as `"123g 45s 67c"`. You may be tempted to break it down as follows:

```
money = gold.."g "
money = money..silver.."s "
money = money..copper.."c"
```

In this example, each line creates an entirely new string. Once the third line executes, the first two strings that were created are now garbage and can be collected. You can prevent this by building the entire string in one statement. Each of the following lines achieves the same result:

```
money = gold.."g "..silver.."s "..copper.."c"

money = strconcat(gold, "g ", silver, "s ", copper, "c")

money = string.format("%dg %ds %dc", gold, silver, copper)
```

In each case, only one string results from the operation, reducing the amount of garbage. The third line actually has a slight advantage over the other two. This means that the original example actually contains five entirely wasted strings. In the `string.format` example, though, there's only one: `"%dg %ds %dc"`.

> **NOTE** The function `strconcat` is actually specific to WoW. However, its behavior is fundamental enough that it is appropriate for this section. It is simply a function version of the concatenation operator (`..`). `strconcat`'s main advantage over `..` is that it can take a variable number of items to concatenate—something you will see in the next example.
>
> This function is very similar to the `table.concat()` function provided in the Lua standard libraries, only it doesn't require the use of a table.

SETFORMATTEDTEXT

Another WoW-specific tip that belongs here is the use of `SetFormattedText`. Suppose you intend to do something like the following after the code in the Money example:

```
text:SetText(money)
```

In this case, you can reduce created garbage further still and get a slight performance improvement by combining the `string.format` example and the `SetFormattedText` function.

```
text:SetFormattedText("%dg %ds %dc", gold, silver, copper)
```

The only garbage you create now is the formatting string. The `SetFormattedText` method does not generate the final string in the Lua environment at all. It exists entirely in the UI engine.

There are also some situations where a more garbage-friendly solution is not immediately apparent. Building a string in a loop, for instance, does not lend itself to the preceding approach. Consider the following loop (and forgive the contrived example):

```
local sequence = ""
for i = 1, 10 do
  sequence = sequence..i
end
```

The price you pay for its simplicity is that every single time through the loop it creates a brand new string. In addition to creating garbage, the Lua interpreter must copy the existing string data each time through, which also takes extra CPU time. One apparent solution to the garbage string problem is to use a table to store each new addition to the string and then call `table.concat`. But that still creates a garbage string for each element as well as generating an extraneous table.

Luckily, there's another trick using variable arguments and multiple returns. This time you add recursion to the mix:

```
local function MakeSequence(n, ...)
  if n > 1 then
    return MakeSequence(n - 1, n, ...)
  else
    return n, ...
  end
end

local sequence = strconcat(MakeSequence(10))
```

If you haven't had much experience with recursive functions, it may be hard to understand how this works. Let's run through the execution of `MakeSequence`.

1. `MakeSequence` is called with a single argument of 10.

2. Because n is more than 1, you call `MakeSequence` with the arguments 9 (n - 1) and 10 (n). . . . is empty so nothing else is passed this time around.

3. You are now one level deeper in recursion. n is 9 and . . . contains one argument, 10. Again, because n is more than 1, you call `MakeSequence` with the arguments 8 (n - 1), 9 (n), and 10 (. . .).

4. Recursion continues in this manner until the arguments to `MakeSequence` are n: 1 and . . .: 2, 3, 4, 5, 6, 7, 8, 9, 10.

5. n has finally reached 1, so you return the entire sequence from 1 to 10. This is passed back down through each level of recursion until it reaches the original call.

Or to put it more concisely:

```
MakeSequence(10)
  MakeSequence(9, 10)
    [Repetitive lines omitted]
              MakeSequence(2, 3, 4, 5, 6, 7, 8, 9, 10)
                MakeSequence(1, 2, 3, 4, 5, 6, 7, 8, 9, 10)
                return 1, 2, 3, 4, 5, 6, 7, 8, 9, 10
              return 1, 2, 3, 4, 5, 6, 7, 8, 9, 10
    [Repetitive lines omitted]
  return 1, 2, 3, 4, 5, 6, 7, 8, 9, 10
return 1, 2, 3, 4, 5, 6, 7, 8, 9, 10
```

Once the final call to `MakeSequence` returns, the values are passed to `strconcat`, which joins them all together as in the earlier money example. In this way, you take advantage of Lua's stack to store each step of the process. Because items on the stack cease to exist as soon as the function ends, none of the data you pass back and forth needs to be garbage-collected.

As with all of these suggestions, you must carefully consider the structure and readability of your code. In addition, function calls themselves aren't completely free. In many cases you should seriously consider using a work table, and the `table.concat()` function.

TAIL CALLS

You may have noticed that all the `return`s in the previous diagram are identical. In reality, Lua processes the recursive function a bit differently than presented. Take a look at the line where you call `MakeSequence` inside itself. Because you are simply returning the results to the previous level without making any modifications, Lua uses a technique called a *tail call*.

Normally, when you call a function, the parameters are *pushed* onto the stack along with the location in your program where the function should return. Then control is passed to the function being called. When that function finishes, it returns to the location you pushed originally.

In a tail call situation, on the other hand, the same return location is used for every level of recursion. When any level of `MakeSequence` returns, it goes to the location of the very first call. Here is a more realistic diagram to illustrate what's actually going on:

```
MakeSequence(10)
MakeSequence(9, 10)
   [Repetitive lines omitted]
MakeSequence(2, 3, 4, 5, 6, 7, 8, 9, 10)
MakeSequence(1, 2, 3, 4, 5, 6, 7, 8, 9, 10)
return 1, 2, 3, 4, 5, 6, 7, 8, 9, 10
```

(continued)

TAIL CALLS *(continued)*

To reiterate, tail calls are used only when you do not do anything to the values being returned by the function you call. That means you must use a `return` statement in conjunction with the call. Even if the function you are calling does not return any values, as in the following example, Lua has no way to know this for certain at compile time.

```
function foo()
  -- Do stuff without returning anything
end
function bar()
  foo()
end
```

When `bar` calls `foo`, there is a hidden operation of discarding any values returned by `foo`, which breaks your chance to use tail recursion. Changing the line inside `bar` to the following is all you need to fix it:

```
return foo()
```

Tail call recursion uses the function call stack more efficiently, since it replaces the *current* function call with the new tail call, rather than simply adding it on top. Think of each new function call as adding a layer on a cake. To get back to your original location, you would need to remove all of the layers you have added. Tail recursion helps the programming language optimize by replacing the current level with a new one, instead of adding to the stack.

Obviously, each unique problem requires slightly different logic. Let's look at another example to help you think recursively.

Many addons define a custom `print` function to make text output simpler and to differentiate the addon's output from a normal `print`, or to direct the output to something other than the chat window. Most first attempts look something like the following (notice the similarity to the original sequence example):

```
local function print(...)
  local output = ""
  local n = select("#", ...)

  for i = 1, n do
    output = output..tostring(select(i, ...))
    if i < n then
      output = output..", "
    end
  end

  DEFAULT_CHAT_FRAME:AddMessage("MyAddon: "..output)
end
```

In this function you have two main problems to solve:

1. Each parameter must be converted into a string because concatenation does not automatically convert anything but numbers to strings.

2. The various parameters must be joined together with commas in between each entry.

You can handle the first problem with a dedicated function to convert all its parameters to strings and return the lot of them:

```
local function toManyStrings(...)
  if select("#", ...) > 0 then
    return tostring((...)), toManyStrings(select(2, ...))
  end
end
```

When `toManyStrings` is called with more than one argument, it returns its first argument converted to a string plus the `toManyStrings`ed versions of the rest of its arguments. Again, because you are not modifying the results of the inner call to `toManyStrings`, Lua will use a tail call so you don't have to worry about the number of arguments.

The second problem has already been solved for you. WoW comes with a function called `strjoin` that works a bit like `strconcat`, taking a variable number of arguments and putting them together. However, the first parameter to `strjoin` is a separator that is placed in between each element of the concatenation. For example, `strjoin(" sep ", "hello", "middle", "goodbye")` returns the string `"hello sep middle sep goodbye"`. Putting these two solutions together, your `print` function now becomes much simpler and produces far less garbage:

```
local function print(...)
  DEFAULT_CHAT_FRAME:AddMessage("MyAddon: "..strjoin(", ", toManyStrings(...)))
end
```

Recyclable Objects

Recycling objects is easy to do, but the need and manner to do so may not be immediately apparent. Consider the following function, which hides a number of predefined frames:

```
local function HideFrames()
  local frames = {
    PlayerFrame,
    TargetFrame,
    MinimapCluster,
  }

  for _, frame in ipairs(frames) do
    frame:Hide()
  end
end
```

Each time you call this function it re-creates the `frames` table. After the function exits, `frames` goes out of scope and becomes collectable. The solution is simply to move the table to the same scope as the `HideFrames` function itself:

```
local frames = {
  PlayerFrame,
  TargetFrame,
  MinimapCluster,
}

local function HideFrames()
  for _, frame in ipairs(frames) do
    frame:Hide()
  end
end
```

The reference to the table will now persist as long as the scope it shares with `HideFrames` exists.

There *is* a tradeoff made using this technique. By defining the `frames` table at the file level, the memory is consumed at load time. With the previous listing, we defer creation of the table until it's actually needed. However, this tradeoff is easily dismissed in nearly every situation. Once the memory is allocated, it is completely free. Without garbage collection to worry about, it uses absolutely no processor time to remain in existence. Furthermore, `HideFrames` operates more quickly because the original version has to go through the process of creating the table each time.

In the same way, you should not be creating functions inside other functions—`function() end` is to functions what `{ }` is to tables—unless you have a specific need for a new closure.

Recycle Tables

Tables are the only mutable garbage-collected objects in Lua. Unlike strings and functions, you can directly manipulate the contents of tables. This unique characteristic allows you to empty individual tables and reuse them.

There are a few ways to accomplish table recycling. In fact, some addon authors have created libraries for just this purpose. The simplest method uses a table to store the empty tables, a function to get an empty table, and another function to recycle an unneeded table. Following is one possible implementation:

```
local freeTables = {}

function GetTable()
  return table.remove(freeTables) or {}
end
```

```
function RecycleTable(t)
  for key in pairs(t) do
    t[key] = nil
  end
  table.insert(freeTables, t)
end
```

Whenever you want a new table, you call `GetTable`. This function attempts to remove a recycled table from `freeTables`. A new one will be created for you if `freeTables` is empty. Once you're done with the table, you call `RecycleTable` to empty it and place it back into `freeTables`.

The major disadvantage of table recycling is that it puts you, the programmer, back in charge of handling memory allocation and de-allocation, essentially taking on the role of garbage collector. In fact, some programmers believe this completely defeats the purpose of using a garbage-collected language in the first place. However, in time-critical tasks where you need to use (and discard) many small tables, the performance gains cannot be ignored. It is up to you to strike the appropriate balance between performance and clarity.

Other Fine-tuning Optimizations

The next few tips offer slight performance improvements for various situations. For the most part, Lua is fast enough to let you organize your addon's logic as intuitively as possible. However, there may be times when you need to squeeze out every last ounce of CPU power.

Check Expected Conditions First

When Lua processes a chain of `if...elseif` statements, it goes through one by one until it finds a condition that evaluates to true—or it runs into the `end`. If the chain is long enough and executed frequently, careful ordering can provide a substantial speed improvement. Most of the time when creating such statements, you will have some idea of which conditions are most likely. Take advantage of this foreknowledge to place the most likely conditions earlier in the chain, as in the following pseudo-code:

```
if likely condition then
  do stuff
elseif less likely condition then
  do other stuff
elseif equally likely condition then
  do yet some more stuff
elseif unlikely condition then
  more stuff goes here
end
```

Even if you do not know beforehand what conditions will be most likely, some simple profiling tests can help figure that out for you. For instance, you could maintain counters for each clause that increment whenever they execute. Then you could create a function to print out the stats. Most of the time, such optimization is unnecessary. If you're doing anything in OnUpdate or some other extremely frequent code path, though, it may just be worth the research. (Remember to remove said counters for the release version of your mod because incrementing them has its own performance impact.)

Exploit Shortcut Evaluation

In a similar vein, you can use a feature of Lua (and other programming languages) called *shortcut evaluation* to optimize the conditionals themselves. Consider the expression a or b. The or operator evaluates to true if either a or b evaluates to true. Once Lua knows that a is true, there is no reason to evaluate b. Similarly, as soon as it's known that c is false in the expression c and d, the entire expression is known to be false.

This also has the interesting benefit (in Lua) that every non-nil, non-false value is considered true. Then you can initialize in the following way:

```
variable = variable or "Some default string"
```

to accomplish something equivalent to the following:

```
if not variable then
  variable = "Some default string"
end
```

Depending on your specific need, you may find the Boolean expression easier to read.

In addition, any time you have a complex condition with several clauses, you should try to put the most likely and/or fastest-to-evaluate clauses first. In pseudo-code, this would look something like the following:

```
if likely condition or less likely condition then
  do stuff
elseif fast condition and slow condition then
  do stuff
end
```

NOTE This section describes the *logical* result of the evaluation of Boolean expressions. As discussed in Chapter 2, the actual results of the and and or operators are one of the two operands depending on whether the first one is interpreted as true (anything other than false or nil)—the `return table.remove(freeTables) or {}` statement from the earlier GetTable function, for example.

Use Tables as a Logic Structure

Sometimes you will have a long chain of `if...elseif` where each clause compares the same variable to some constant. The prime example in addon programming is an `OnEvent` script. Consider the following:

```
if event == "SOME_EVENT" then
  -- do stuff
elseif event == "ANOTHER_EVENT" then
  -- do stuff
elseif event == "THIRD_EVENT" then
  -- do stuff
elseif event == "FOURTH_EVENT" then
  -- do stuff
end
```

You can use a table in a manner similar to the "Rework Repetitive Code" section earlier in this appendix. Instead of the `if` statement, you fill a table with functions indexed by the name of the event:

```
local eventHandlers = {
  ["SOME_EVENT"] = function(frame, namedArgument)
    -- do stuff
  end,
  ["ANOTHER_EVENT"] = function(frame, namedArgument1, namedArgument2)
    -- do stuff
  end,
  ["THIRD_EVENT"] = function(frame)
    -- do stuff
  end,
  ["FOURTH_EVENT"] = function()
    -- do stuff
  end
}
```

Now the `OnEvent` script can be simplified to four lines (or one if you are careful about what events you register):

```
function MyEventHandler(frame, event, ...)
  local handler = eventHandlers[event]
  if handler then
    handler(frame, ...)
  end
end
```

This technique affords a few advantages:

- The underlying architecture of the table lookup usually executes more quickly than a string of `if...elseif` clauses, especially with a large number of entries.

- Each event handler is a separate entity. Defining separate functions for each one adds a level of context that can make the code easier to follow.

- Parameters can be adjusted to suit the event. As demonstrated in the preceding example, you can give names to the individual elements of ... that would normally be accessed via `select` or by creating new local variables in each `if`/`elseif` clause. You can even eliminate parameters altogether if they are irrelevant to the given event.

- As with the textures example earlier, you can use the table keys for the actual registering and unregistering of the events:

```
for event in pairs(eventHandlers) do
    someFrame:RegisterEvent(event)
end
```

Cache Frequently Accessed Values

There are many situations where you use a function to generate or retrieve a value based solely on a given parameter. For instance, the slash command handling system scans through the `SlashCmdList` table's indexes, and then looks for corresponding global variables. If the variable matches the slash command you used, WoW executes the associated function from `SlashCmdList`.

With the potential for dozens of unique functions each with several equivalent slash commands (for example, `/t`, `/w`, `/tell`, and `/whisper`), the amount of processing necessary to select the appropriate function is substantial (take a look at `ChatEdit_ParseText` in `FrameXML\ChatFrame.lua` to see what we mean). WoW solves this problem by storing the results of each unique command search in a table called `hash_SlashCmdList`. When you use a slash command, it first looks to see if it's in the list. If so, it immediately uses the associated function. Otherwise, it goes through the more involved process.

You can create an easy-to-use caching system with a simple metatable trick. From the point of view of the code using the cache, it behaves as a simple table. For example:

```
print(cacheTable[entry])
```

You make `cacheTable` into a cache with code like the following:

```
cacheTable = setmetatable({}, {
    __index = function (table, parameter)
        local value = DoStuff(parameter)
        rawset(table, parameter, value)
        return value
    end
})
```

Now whenever you provide an entry that doesn't exist, a new entry will be created with the result of `DoStuff(parameter)`.

The WoW Environment

The last part of this appendix deals specifically with constructs and procedures unique to World of Warcraft.

Use What You're Given

By now, it should be second nature to look for APIs and widget methods to help with your day-to-day tasks. However, many other built-in features go neglected. For instance, authors often write their own functions to convert the returns from `UnitName` into `"name"` or `"name-realm"` to indicate cross-realm players. Granted, this is a rather trivial task, but WoW already provides such a function called `GetUnitName` at the end of `FrameXML\UnitFrame.lua`.

Obviously, we do not expect you to familiarize yourself with the entirety of FrameXML code as you're starting out, but it is always a good idea to look in files that may be related to your addon, both to see how things are done in the default UI and to find functions to take advantage of yourself. For example, if you are writing an alternative quest frame, you should look over `QuestFrame.lua` and `QuestFrame.xml` before you begin work on your addon.

`GetBagItemCount` from the beginning of this appendix could actually be improved slightly. Rather than `for bag = 0, 4 do`, where `4` is a prime example of a magic number, you can define a constant for the number of bags. However, Blizzard has saved you the trouble. Near the top of `FrameXML\ContainerFrame.lua` is the constant `NUM_BAG_FRAMES`, which represents the number of bags besides the backpack. Using the Blizzard-defined constant adds a bit of future-proofing to your code. If they ever increase the number of bags a player can carry, they will bump `NUM_BAG_FRAMES` to the new count and your function will be instantly compatible.

Localize with Global Strings

Virtually every display string in the UI is stored in a constant in `FrameXML\GlobalStrings.lua`. This file is translated to every language WoW supports. By using the constants in this file for various aspects of your addon, you will be automatically localizing certain parts of it, which is of great benefit to your international users.

Error messages, button text, combat log strings, and many others are there for the taking. Many common terms such as "Yes," "No," and "Okay," are easy enough to recognize. You will also see strings for the various races, genders, classes, and other commonly used terms. Whenever you are looking into localization for your addon, open `GlobalStrings.lua` and do a preliminary search for the terms you want.

Even if you do not see the exact phrase you're looking for, the search may still help. If you are trying to do localization yourself, you may be able to figure out the basic structure of the phrase in the target language but not how some particular term translates. You can find GlobalStrings.lua from other locales on some addon sites and compare the phrases to come up with the missing term.

Avoid Deprecated Systems

The World of Warcraft UI code has gone through many evolutionary and revolutionary changes as new needs for the game and from the addon community have come to light. New systems are constantly being added and tweaked to take better advantage of Lua design patterns, improve efficiency, and implement new game features.

Unfortunately, the time invested in the older systems is significant enough that many of them are still around in some form or another. Through the patch cycle, though, the default UI is being slowly reworked to use the newer methods and, at some point in time, the old ways may no longer be supported.

Throughout this book we have purposefully omitted coverage of these past practices. If you use the code for the default UI or other addons as research material for your own addon, translate any usage of the constructs discussed in the following sections into the newer method.

> **NOTE** Rather than listing all deprecated systems in this section, specific events, APIs, and so forth that should no longer be used are marked as deprecated in their reference entries (see Part IV).

Global Widget Handler Arguments

The widget handler system you saw in Chapter 12 is new as of patch 2.0. Instead of calling your handler with a self parameter and other related data (button for OnClick, event and ... for OnEvent, and so on), the old system used a global variable called this and several global argument variables (arg1, arg2, and so on).

There were a few problems with this approach. Using global variables for a parameterized system does not make much sense conceptually, not to mention their impact on performance. Also, the generic argn variables go against the very first pointer in this appendix. The only way for you to know the meaning of the argument when reading old code is to look at a reference for the given handler or hope you can infer its meaning from what the code does with it.

Following are two somewhat useless functions to illustrate the difference. If you use SetScript to assign them to an OnHyperlinkClick script, they will function identically.

```
function MyAddon_OnHyperlinkClick()
  if arg3 == "LeftButton" then
    this.link = arg1
    print("You clicked on "..arg2)
  end
end
```

```
function MyAddon_OnHyperlinkClick(self, link, text, button)
  if button == "LeftButton" then
    self.link = link
    print("You clicked on "..text)
  end
end
```

As you can see, `this` corresponds to `self`, `arg1` corresponds to `link`, `arg2` corresponds to `text`, and `arg3` corresponds to `button`. With the exception of the `OnEvent` handler, `this` and `arg1-argn` will always match the parameter list of the given handler. In this way, you can use the widget handler reference in Chapter 31 to determine the meanings of the global arguments in any legacy code. The only difference with `OnEvent` is that `event` always had its own global. `arg1-argn`, in this case, correspond to the parameters passed through . . . .

bag and slot Attributes on item Type Action Buttons

Another change in 2.1 is the simplification of secure action buttons with a `"type"` attribute of `"item"`. Previously, the `"item"` attribute could only be used to activate an item by name. To use an item in your inventory would require a `"slot"` attribute; to use an item in your bags required `"bag"` and `"slot"` attributes. Now the `"item"` attribute works the same way as the `/use` macro command. It accepts an item name, item ID (in the form `"item:12345"`), slot number, or bag and slot numbers separated by a space (for example, `"3 12"`).

Again, for backward compatibility, the `"bag"` and `"slot"` attributes are still supported. However, you should no longer use them; as a comment in `FrameXML\SecureTemplates.lua` says, "Backward compatibility code, deprecated but still handled *for now*." [Emphasis mine.]

Avoiding Common Mistakes

Addon authors can make dozens of common mistakes as they develop their addons. Many of them have been covered throughout the book, but the following deserve to be mentioned here, as well.

Adding Files While WoW Is Running

When World of Warcraft loads, it scans the file system and builds a table of files that can be loaded during that session. If you add files while the game is open, they won't be part of that table and cannot be loaded or recognized by the game. A related common mistake is adding a new file to your addon and the Table of Contents file without fully exiting the game.

If you add files to the file system, make sure that you fully exit and restart the game so that the changes will be fully registered.

Entering | into the Chat Edit Box

Because World of Warcraft uses the | character in its color codes and hyperlinks, any that are entered in the edit box are automatically escaped to a double ||. This can be problematic when running Lua scripts with the `/script` and `/run` commands. You can substitute the sequence `\124` instead of the actual character to get around this limitation.

"Missing" Frames

When you create a frame in your addon you expect it to be visible. If you can't find your frame, it may be missing due to not meeting one of the following requirements:

- The frame must have some visual component, such as a texture, backdrop, or text element.
- The frame must not be set as hidden in the XML file, or the frame's `Show()` method must have been called to explicitly show the frame.
- Each frame that is a parent of the frame must also be shown. This includes the frame's parent, the parent's parent, and so on.
- The frame must be anchored somewhere within the bounds of the screen.

It's easy to spend time digging through your code only to find later that you've forgotten to place the frame on the screen.

Ignoring Logs\FrameXML.log

When working on XML, there are two places to check to ensure the file is being parsed and validated properly:

- Load the file in some program that can indicate that the file is well-formed. This could include most web browsers or a more complex XML editor/validator.
- Check the `Logs\FrameXML.log` file to ensure there weren't any errors parsing the file.

Not Checking API Returns

There are times when the Blizzard API functions may return something other than what you'd expect. For example, there's a small period of time where `UnitClass(unit)` can return `nil` when you'd expect a class name to be returned. If you use these function returns in some other computation, such as indexing a table or calling another function, you may get an error somewhere along the line.

In many cases, you can fix the problem by supplying default values in the following way or by throwing an explicit error with the `error()` function:

```
local class = UnitClass(unit) or "Warrior"
```

Even if the class is wrong, you can be sure you won't have an unexpected error.

Requesting Data Before PLAYER_LOGIN

As stated in the earlier chapters, a number of functions don't return the correct results until the `PLAYER_LOGIN` event has fired. This can be remedied by delaying the call until that point, but you should be aware when getting unexpected results that the information may not be available in the client at that moment.

Conflicting or Existing Anchor Points

Each frame can have multiple anchor points that help define the placement or size of the frame. When adjusting anchor points, make certain that you've cleared any that should no longer be set. When in doubt, run the `ClearAllPoints()` method to ensure that a frame has no anchors before adding your own anchor points.

Utilizing Addon Libraries

When a system as incredibly complex as the World of Warcraft API is released, inevitably someone writes a library of functions that makes it easier for specific uses, or adds certain functionality. True to form, several addon frameworks and libraries have been written for WoW. This appendix explores the creation of libraries and introduces you to some of the more prevalent addon libraries.

What Is an Addon Library?

An addon library is a collection of code that can be used by multiple addons. They tend to provide some abstraction over the Blizzard API that makes it easier to use for common cases. Over the course of writing your addons you may find yourself writing the same functions over and over again. Consider the following:

```
function debug(...)
   local succ, message = pcall(string.format, ...)
   if succ then
      print("|cffff1100Debug: |r", message)
   else
      print("|cffff1100Debug: |r", tostringall(...))
   end
end
```

I use a function similar to this in many of my addons. It's an extension of the built-in `print` function that prints a heading at the start of each message, and also accepts format strings. This means instead of writing this:

```
print(string.format("You have reached your destination '%s'", destination)
```

I can write this:

```
print("You have reached your destination '%s'", destination)
```

This function can be used to display a list of arguments in the same way as the `print` function. Although it may not seem like much, I find printing to the chat frame much easier using this function. This is how most libraries start, identifying a piece of code that is useful to multiple addons and then writing it in a way so it can be written once but distributed with each of them.

How Do Libraries Work?

There are two main types of libraries: those that are written as standalone addons and use the dependency system to load properly, and those that are packaged within the actual addon, typically referred to as *embedded* libraries.

Each library scheme has its own set of benefits and tradeoffs, and no solution has been found that fills everyone's needs sufficiently. If your library is only for personal use, and something you can easily control, making your library a standalone addon is a natural choice. If you are using someone else's library, or know that other developers will use it, an embedded library gives you much stricter control over what version of a library you are using.

Standalone Libraries

Libraries that are written as standalone addons are extremely easy to use and to write. The following code shows a simple library that provides a way to use the `debug` function written earlier in this appendix:

AddonUtils.toc

```
## Interface: 30200
## Title: AddonUtils
## Notes: A library of simple addon utilities

AddonUtils.lua
```

AddonUtils.lua

```
AddonUtils = {}
```

```
function AddonUtils.createDebugFunc(prefix)
  return function(...)
    local succ, message = pcall(string.format, ...)
    if succ then
      print("|cffff1100" .. prefix .. ": |r", message)
    else
      print("|cffff1100" .. prefix .. ": |r", tostringall(...))
    end
  end
end
```

To avoid conflicts with other addons, you create a new global table called AddonUtils. Inside you define a new function called createDebugFunc(), which can be called by addons to create their own personalized debug function. For example this could be used in the following way:

```
local debug = AddonUtils.createDebugFunc("MyAddon")
debug("Hello World!")
```

To use this library, an addon would need to include AddonUtils in its table of contents file like so:

```
## Dependencies: AddonUtils
```

Advantages

Standalone addon libraries are very simple to create, and Blizzard's dependency system ensures that addons are loaded in the correct order. There is only ever one version of the library loaded, so no special consideration is needed. In addition, the library can have its own dependencies, define its own XML templates, and store saved variables.

Disadvantages

The main problem with standalone addon libraries is the way they are distributed. If you are including one with only a few of your addons and don't expect many changes to be required it can work out quite well. Unfortunately if multiple authors might be including your library, or periodic changes are necessary to the code it can be very frustrating. With a standalone addon you have two ways to distribute it:

1. Direct the user to where he can download the latest version of the library and make him responsible for its upkeep.

2. Include the library alongside your own addon.

The first option requires the user to do more work to use your addon, but in the day of addon updaters and email notification, this may not be a problem for your application.

The second option is the more troublesome because it relies on other authors including the most recent version with their addons. In addition, it's a bit confusing to users when they're asked by the operating system if they want to overwrite a file when installing the addon. This particular point is why embedded libraries were created in the first place.

The distribution problem becomes much more important when multiple versions of a library exist, without the name of the library addon changing. You take the risk that the user (or some other addon) will include an older version of a library you rely on.

Embedded Libraries

An embedded library is one that is included in any addon that uses it, rather than stand alone as a separate addon. A system has been developed that uses two pieces of information to ensure the system is robust:

- **Major version**—A unique name that indicates the name and version of the library. Two libraries with different major versions will run alongside each other. For example: AddonUtils-1.0 or CommLib-2.0.

- **Minor version**—A number that indicates the minor version of a given library, with a higher value indicating a newer version. If two addons have the same major version of a library but different minor versions, the older one will be "upgraded" to the newer one using some defined process.

In general, the major version should be updated whenever there is a change to the behavior of the underlying functions or any other change that is not backward-compatible with previous versions. The minor version is only incremented when bugs are fixed or other minor changes are made.

Embedded Library Load Process

Here's the general process for loading an embedded library:

1. Check to see if an instance of the library with the same major version is already loaded.

2. If the same major version already exists, compare the minor version numbers. If the new library being loaded has a matching minor version,

or a lower minor version, the initialization process can safely return immediately.

3. If a version exists but the minor version of the existing instance is less than the one being loaded, then this instance should replace (or upgrade) the existing instance with itself.

4. If the major version does not already exist, the library should simply be loaded.

Using embedded libraries, multiple copies of the library may be loaded and then thrown away, which can increase load times. This would only happen in the situation where addons loaded in a specific order had increasing minor versions of the same library. In addition, the library author needs to be sensitive to the potential upgrade process, and should test the library thoroughly before releasing a minor version update to a library.

Manually Versioning an Embedded Library

The code to manage the versioning of your library can be as simple as the following:

```
local minor_version = 501
if MyLibraryName and minor_version < MyLibraryName.minor then
  -- This version is old, so don't load it
  return
end

-- Library definition here
MyLibraryName = {}

function MyLibraryName.createDebugFunc(prefix)
  return function(...)
    local succ, message = pcall(string.format, ...)
      if succ then
        print("|cffff1100" .. prefix .. ": |r", message)
      else
        print("|cffff1100" .. prefix .. ": |r", tostringall(...))
      end
    end
  end
end
```

In this case the major version name is MyLibraryName, and the minor version is 501. The code first checks to see if the major version exists and, if it does, compares the two minor versions. If the minor version being loaded is less than the one that already exists, the code returns.

Versioning Using LibStub

In late 2007 the addon community banded together to create a simple standard way to register and access libraries, called LibStub. LibStub has three functions:

- `LibStub:NewLibrary(major, minor)` —Attempts to register a new library with the given major and minor versions. Returns a table that can be used to store the library, or `nil` if the version being registered is not new.

- `LibStub:GetLibrary(major [, silent])` —Tries to get the library with the given major version. The `silent` flag can be used to test for the existence of a library without causing LibStub to raise an error.

- `LibStub:IterateLibraries()` —Returns an iterator over all the registered libraries.

The following shows how to define the same library using LibStub:

```
local major, minor = "MyLibraryName", 1
local library = LibStub:NewLibrary(major, minor)
if not library then
  -- This version is not new, so return
  return
end

function library.createDebugFunc(prefix)
  return function(...)
    local succ, message = pcall(string.format, ...)
    if succ then
      print("|cffff1100" .. prefix .. ": |r", message)
    else
      print("|cffff1100" .. prefix .. ": |r", tostringall(...))
    end
  end
end
```

The library can then be used in the following way:

```
local MyLibraryName = LibStub:GetLibrary("MyLibraryName")
local debug = MyLibraryName.createDebugFunc("MyAddon")
```

With LibStub, if you register a major version that already has an existing version you will receive the previous table back. You can then clear it, define new functions, or handle any other tasks that are necessary for your addon.

For more information about how to write libraries using LibStub, visit www.wowwiki.com/LibStub.

Using a Library

Rather than trying to give full details on a set of existing libraries, this section introduces you to several different categories of libraries, giving you general information about what each of them does.

Ace3

The Ace3 (`www.wowace.com/projects/ace3`) suite of libraries was designed to be included as embedded libraries with minimal dependencies. This means that you can include only those libraries you want to use rather than needing to include the entire suite.

Ace3 includes libraries that provide the following functionality:

- **AceAddon-3.0**—An abstraction over addons that allow you to easily disable and enable addons within the game without needing to reload the user interface. Also provides a framework for modular components.

- **AceBucket-3.0**—Groups multiple events into "buckets." This allows you to watch for UNIT_HEALTH events, but only actually respond to them periodically rather than every time an event fires.

- **AceComm-3.0**—A communications library that can handle arbitrarily long messages. This library also throttles messages appropriately so the sender is not disconnected.

- **AceConfigCmd-3.0**—Allows you to register a slash command definition using a table, and have a slash command built automatically for you.

- **AceConfigDialog-3.0**—Generates a configuration GUI automatically from a configuration table.

- **AceDB-3.0**—Manages saved variables for an addon, providing profiles, smart defaults, and custom portions of the database that are custom loaded for each character. This library can be quite useful if you'd like to provide your users with the ability to load/clone/save addon profiles.

- **AceEvent-3.0**—Allows you to register for events and have custom functions called when an event fires. This library is more of a convenience that avoids you having to create a frame and write a custom OnEvent handler.

- **AceHook-3.0**—Library that allows you to hook and unhook functions and scripts. Writing function hooks is not an easy endeavor and this library helps to ensure good behavior.

- **AceTime-3.0**—Facility for creating and registering timers, so code can be called in a delayed or repeating fashion.

The suite contains other, more special-purpose libraries. For more information visit `www.wowace.com/projects/Ace3`.

Portfolio

Portfolio (www.wowinterface.com/downloads/info11749-Portfolio.html) allows you to create configuration screens in the Blizzard Interface Options menu with relative ease. It accepts a very straightforward configuration table format and will automatically generate your GUI for you.

Dongle

Dongle (www.wowwiki.com/Dongle) is a collection of functions that should be useful to anyone writing a new addon. Designed to be extremely small without excess functionality, it provides an easy way to register events, schedule tasks, and comes with a database system that makes creating saved variable structures with defaults easy.

PeriodicTable

PeriodicTable (www.wowace.com/projects/libperiodictable-3-1) aims to add organization to items in World of Warcraft. It allows you to access them via hierarchical sets (such as Consumable.Food.Edible.Cheese). This can be useful when trying to figure out what categories an item might belong to, in order to find out how best to use it. For example, it can help you identify which common items are used in tradeskills.

BossIDs

The BossIDs library (www.wowace.com/projects/libbossids-1-0) just contains a list of all the mobs in the game that are considered "bosses," because there is no easy way to check this in-game. You can use the GUID of the mob along with this library to make that determination.

LibHealComm

LibHealComm (www.wowace.com/projects/libhealcomm-3-0) provides events and callbacks that allow you to get more information about the spells your party and group members cast. Multiple users must have the library installed to accomplish anything, but when the healers of a group have it installed it makes it very easy to see who they are healing and at what time.

LibSharedMedia

LibSharedMedia (www.wowace.com/projects/libsharedmedia-3-0) is designed to provide a way to construct a library of media files (sounds, textures, fonts) and allow multiple addons to access them. In this way, the addon developer simply uses the library if it exists to access the repository of media. This allows users to select consistent graphics, fonts, and sounds depending on their wants and needs.

Other Library Resources

Literally dozens of libraries have been written for any number of purposes, and most of them are well documented and readily available. The best places to explore for libraries to use are the following:

- ▪ http://www.wowwiki.com/Function_Library
- ▪ www.wowace.com/categories/libraries
- ▪ www.wowinterface.com/downloads/cat53.html

Some of these libraries depend on other libraries (which can get quite messy), but if you're looking for a good existing API for something that you find peculiar in the Blizzard API, they may just have what you're looking for.

Tracking History Using Version Control Systems

When you are creating your first few addons you'll likely just create the files on your machine and continue to add to them as the addon matures. If you decide to release the addon, you'll zip up that folder and post it somewhere for the users to find it. This sort of process works great for very simple addons, but once you start making larger addons or collaborating with other developers you may find the need for something a bit more structured.

A standard technique for source code management in application development is called *version control*. In version control systems, the developer creates new snapshots throughout the development process and adds those snapshots to the system. The code can be compared between snapshots, and developers can use the snapshots to examine the history of an addon to better understand how a bug or problem might have occurred.

Three main types of version control systems are used in the addon development community: Subversion, Git, and Mercurial. This appendix introduces the basic concepts of version control in each of them and points you toward resources with more in-depth information.

Subversion

One of the more prevalent version control systems is Subversion, designed as a replacement for the much older CVS version control system. This section serves as a short guide to using Subversion; consult the full documentation available at `http://svnbook.red-bean.com`.

One major point that must be made about Subversion is that, unlike the other version control systems discussed later in this chapter, it requires a central server for you to commit any changes. This may be a requirement you can live with, but there are alternatives that enable you to make changes locally, and then upload them to a server at a later time.

Terminology

The following is a list of terms that you will encounter when working with Subversion, and reading this section.

- **Repository**—A central location that houses the version control system (often shortened to repo). There is typically one repository per project or addon, although this requirement is not hard and fast. The repository is often located on a remote server and may have an address that looks like one of the following:

```
http://hostname/repository/address
svn://hostname/repository/address
```

- **Commit**—When the developer makes changes to the local code and then wants to push those changes into the central repository, he makes a commit. A commit must include a log message that explains the changes that are being committed. Commits aren't expected every single time you save the file on your machine, but rather at relevant stopping points (such as when you've fixed a specific bug, or added a particular feature).

- **Checkout**—A user or developer can download the current state of a given repository by checking it out. This downloads the current files as well as some basic history information. Typically, any user can check out a repository, but only developers can commit.

- **Working copy**—The local copy of the repository that a developer obtains when checking out a Subversion repository.

- **Diff**—A file showing the differences between two versions of a given file or two different states of a repository.

Layout of a Repository

The layout of a Subversion repository tends to include the following subdirectories at the root level:

- **Trunk**—The main development directory. This typically represents the bleeding edge of development and should be used with care. It's generally meant for developers and testers only.

- **Branches**—Used when multiple versions of software are being worked on at the same time. For example, if you're still providing support for some stable version of your addon, you might make a branch to keep it separate from your trunk development.

▪ **Tags**—Tags are typically synonymous with releases, allowing you to see the state of the source code at the point you released a version to the public.

Obtaining Subversion

You can download Subversion for your platform from the main Subversion website at `http://subversion.tigris.org/getting.html`. Packages exist for both Mac OS X and Microsoft Windows machines. Once the package has been installed, you can test that your system works properly by running the `svn` command in a terminal or command window:

```
> svn
Type 'svn help' for usage
```

If you see some other message, the command may not be in your path and you'll have to do a bit more experimentation. Several good guides to installing and using Subversion on any system are linked directly from the main Subversion website.

Command Primer

This section details the major Subversion commands you will use in the course of daily development. As always, more detail is available using the `svn help` command, or in the official documentation.

svn checkout <url> [path]

Checking out a Subversion repository is a matter of calling the `svn checkout` command with the URL of the repository. By default, a folder is created with the same name you are checking out, but you can specify a path argument to use a different folder name instead. The following command checks out the code for TomTom (one of my addons) into the folder `trunk` at your current location:

```
svn checkout svn://svn.wowinterface.com/TomTom-17/trunk
```

Here's a command that checks out the repository into a folder called `TomTom` in your current directory:

```
svn checkout svn://svn.wowinterface.com/TomTom-17/trunk TomTom
```

The following command checks out the repository into the folder `C:\Subversion\TomTom` on your computer:

```
svn checkout svn://svn.wowinterface.com/TomTom-17/trunk
c:\Subversion\TomTom
```

svn update [path]

The `update` command is used to update a working copy by contacting the central server and downloading any changes that have been made since the last update. By default, it updates whatever directory you are currently in (assuming it's a working copy).

If the current directory is a working copy, the following command updates it to the latest revision:

```
svn update
```

This command updates the working copy in `c:\Subversion\TomTom` to the latest revision:

```
svn update c:\Subversion\TomTom
```

svn add <path>

If you are creating files, rather than editing existing files, you will need to add them to the system before you can commit them. You do this using the `svn add` command. If you specify a filename, that file will be added. If you specify a path, the path will be searched recursively, adding all files within that path. The following command adds the file `TomTom.lua` to version control:

```
svn add TomTom.lua
```

This adds all files in the current directory (and beneath):

```
svn add .
```

Once files have been added to the system, they can be manipulated using the other `svn` commands.

svn commit [path]

The `commit` command is used when you have changes that need to be pushed to a central repository. On most systems, your default text editor will be opened and you'll be prompted for a commit message. Simply save the file in the text editor and the commit will begin.

You may be prompted for a username or password if this is your first commit. Whichever service runs your repository should be able to provide you with this information. As usual, this command assumes the current directory is a working copy, but a specific path can be specified.

svn status

To determine the state of the files in a repository, you can use the `status` command. It can display what files have pending changes, what files are new, and what files might be missing (if any). Consult the Subversion documentation for more information about the specific output of this command.

svn log [path]

The `log` command can be used to give a history of log messages for a working copy. By default, it uses the current directory, but you can specify a specific path if you choose. The following is a sample Subversion log for a few revisions to the TomTom repository:

```
------------------------------------------------------------------------
r192 | Cladhaire-15704 | 2008-12-22 08:21:03 +0000 (Mon, 22 Dec 2008) | 2 lines

* Only try to set the corpse waypoint when c,z,x,y are positive numbers


------------------------------------------------------------------------
r191 | Cladhaire-15704 | 2008-12-21 21:41:53 +0000 (Sun, 21 Dec 2008) | 2 lines

* Added a Corpse arrow that can be configured on the general options screen.
  When enabled, a non-persistent waypoint arrow will be set directing you toward
  your corpse.  It will be removed when you resurrect.
```

svn diff [path]

The `diff` command will print a listing of the differences between the code in your working copy, versus the last commit to the repository. This is a handy way to check what changes you've made to the file before committing.

Creating a Local Repository

Although Subversion is designed to be used with a central server, you can actually create repositories locally on your machine using the `svnadmin` command. The command takes a path that will serve as the destination of the repository on the file system. The following command creates a new repository in the `C:\Subversion\MyAddon` folder that can then be used to check out and commit, assuming the `C:\Subversion` directory already exists:

```
svnadmin create C:\Subversion\MyAddon
```

Instead of using the `http://` or `svn://` type of URL, you use `file:///` (note the extra / in the URL). To check out this repository, use the following command:

```
svn checkout file:///c:/Subversion/MyAddon
```

You can now use this new repository to store your history without needing to contact a remote server. This allows you to store a history of your code locally so you can take advantage of the other features of Subversion.

Git and Mercurial

Git and Mercurial (hg) are distributed version control systems, which means they do not need a central repository in order to function. By default, each repository that is created contains the entire history of the project and can function independent of each other. Both of these systems try to make it easy for the developer to work with their code locally without needing access to a remote server, while making it easy to submit changes to a project.

Mercurial began as a spin-off of the Git project so many of the commands and much of the terminology is the same. Any differences between the two systems are detailed in each individual section.

It should be noted that these two systems are relatively more complex than Subversion and are a bit less user-friendly, however they can offer many advantages as well.

Terminology

The terminology for Git and Mercurial differ a bit from that of Subversion.

- **Repository**—In a distributed source code management system, a repository refers to a copy of the source code and all of the historical information about a project. Repositories can be cloned (copied), and the two repositories will be independent of each other.

- **Clone**—To retrieve your own local copy of a repository you can clone an existing one. This retrieves all of the data necessary to have your own self-contained repository.

- **Commit**—When the developer makes changes to the local code and then wants to push those changes into the central repository, he makes a commit. A commit must include a log message that explains the changes that are being committed. Commits aren't expected every single time you save the file on your machine, but rather at relevant stopping points (such as when you've fixed a specific bug, or added a particular feature).

- **Diff**—A file showing the differences between two versions of a given file or two different states of a repository.

- **Branch**—A branch of development (for example you could create a branch to add a new feature, or to fix a specific bug). Branches allow you to segregate your development into different compartments that can later be merged back together.

- **Merge**—Merging is a process where you take two divergent branches and merge them back together into a single branch. This is useful when working in a collaborative environment.

- **Master**—Master is the main branch in a Git repository.

- **HEAD**—This is a special name for the most recent version of a branch. For example, HEAD of master is the most recent commit in the master branch.

Obtaining Git

Installing Git is a bit more complex than Subversion and varies wildly depending on operating system. Two main packages can be used to install Git for Mac OS X:

```
http://metastatic.org/source/git-osx.html
http://code.google.com/p/git-osx-installer/
```

Both pages describe the installation procedure and should be straightforward. For Microsoft Windows, there is a package called msysgit that provides an installation package at `http://code.google.com/p/msysgit`.

You can find documentation for Git in the Git User's Manual at `www.kernel.org/pub/software/scm/git/docs/user-manual.html`.

Obtaining Mercurial (hg)

You can find prebuilt packages for installing Mercurial at `www.selenic.com/mercurial/wiki/index.cgi/BinaryPackages`. A number of methods of installation exist for both Microsoft Windows and Mac OS X.

You can find documentation for Mercurial online at `http://hgbook.red-bean.com`.

Typical Usage

Curseforge (`http://curseforge.com`) is an addon development community created by `http://curse.com`. It is the most likely place you will see addon development using Mercurial and Git. Once you have created a new project and it has been approved, you can create a new repository. Regardless of whether you choose Git or Mercurial, you will be given two different URLs. The first is the public address, which can be used by non-developers to follow your project. The second is the development URL, which is used to actually commit code to your project.

Git

To develop your addon with Git, you must first create a local repository that contains your code. You can accomplish this by creating a new empty directory and issuing the `git init` command.

```
> cd MyAddon
> git init
Initialized empty Git repository in /private/tmp/MyAddon/.git/
```

Once that's done you can begin copying files in and making changes. Before you can commit any files, you must notify Git that they should be tracked using the `git add` command.

```
> git add MyAddon.toc
> git add MyAddon.lua
```

You can check the status of the repository using the `git status` command:

```
> git status
# On branch master
#
# Initial commit
#
# Changes to be committed:
#   (use "git rm --cached <file>..." to unstage)
#
#       new file: MyAddon.lua
#       new file: MyAddon.toc
#
```

Here the status shows that two new files are ready to be committed. You can actually perform a commit using the `git commit` command:

```
> git commit -m "Adding empty files for MyAddon"
Created initial commit 5e48c92: Adding empty files for MyAddon
 0 files changed, 0 insertions(+), 0 deletions(-)
 create mode 100644 MyAddon.lua
 create mode 100644 MyAddon.toc
```

This specifies the log message using the -m option, but you could just as easily leave that off and Git will open a text editor for you to input the log message.

Although this command made a commit to the local repository, there is still nothing on the remote repository at Curseforge. To fix this, you can push the current repository up to the remote location by using the `git push` command, specifying the remote address and the branch you want to push:

```
> git push git@git.curseforge.net:wow/myproject/mainline.git master
Counting objects: 3, done.
Compressing objects: 100% (2/2), done.
Writing objects: 100% (3/3), 229 bytes, done.
Total 3 (delta 0), reused 0 (delta 0)
To git@git.curseforge.net:wow/myproject/mainline.git
 * [new branch]      master -> master
```

This tells Git that you want to push the master branch to the remote location specified. You will be prompted for your authentication information (this depends entirely on what host you are pushing to) and the master branch is created on the remote repository.

In the future you can push new changes simply by running:

```
> git push git@git.curseforge.net:wow/myproject/mainline.git
```

If you are working collaboratively in the project, you can also retrieve any new changes by running a `git pull` command:

```
> git pull git@git.curseforge.net:wow/myproject/mainline.git
```

Mercurial

The following process is very similar to Git but the output may differ slightly. First, you must create a local repository that contains your code. You can accomplish this by creating a new empty directory and issuing the `hg init` command (there is no output from this command):

```
> cd MyAddon
> hg init
```

Once that's done you can begin copying files in and making changes. Before you can commit any files, you must notify Mercurial that they should be tracked using the `hg add` command:

```
> hg add MyAddon.toc
> hg add MyAddon.lua
```

You can check the status of the repository using the `hg status` command:

```
> hg status
A MyAddon.lua
A MyAddon.toc
```

Here the status shows that two new files are waiting to be added. You can actually perform a commit using the `hg commit` command (there is no output unless there is an issue):

```
> hg commit -m "Adding empty files for MyAddon"
```

This specifies the log message using the `-m` option, but you could just as easily leave that off and Mercurial will open a text editor for you to input the log message.

Although this command made a commit to the local repository, there is still nothing on the remote repository at Curseforge. To fix this, you can push the current repository up to the remote location by using the `hg push` command, specifying the remote address to which you want to push:

```
> hg push ssh://hg@hg.curseforge.net/wow/myproject/mainline.git
pushing to ssh://hg@hg.curseforge.net/wow/myproject/mainline
searching for changes
```

```
remote: adding changesets
remote: adding manifests
remote: adding file changes
remote: added 1 changesets with 2 changes to 2 files
```

Now you tell Mercurial that you want to push the master branch to the remote location specified. You will be prompted for your authentication information (this depends entirely on what host you are pushing to) and the master branch is created on the remote repository.

In the future you can push new changes simply by running:

```
> hg push git@git.curseforge.net:wow/myproject/mainline.git
```

If you are working collaboratively in the project, you can also retrieve any new changes by running a `hg pull` command:

```
> hg pull git@git.curseforge.net:wow/myproject/mainline.git
```

Addon Author Resources

Throughout the course of this book you've learned how to extend the default user interface, and how to create new custom addons. Although we hope you will continue using this book as a reference, other resources are available that can help you as an addon author.

This appendix describes the various communities in which addon authors can participate, and details the various ways in which you can distribute your addon to a wide audience.

Community Websites

Over the course of the past five years, a large community has grown out of the hundreds of devoted addon developers, and the multitude of addon users. These forums and communities allow you to discuss addon development with other developers, and allow users to contact their favorite developers.

World of Warcraft Forums

The Blizzard-sponsored WoW forums are extremely active, and we're lucky enough to have Blizzard employees who post somewhat regularly as they make changes to the user interface. As a result, there are sticky posts that detail the major changes in the last patch, as well as any upcoming changes that have already been announced. This allows authors to plan ahead and discuss potential changes with the community and developers.

These forums are also a nice place to ask for and provide help with addon writing, as well as to announce new projects and seek feedback on existing ones. You can find the Official World of Warcraft UI forum at `http://forums.worldofwarcraft.com/board.html?forumId=11114`.

WowProgramming Forums

Meant to allow readers of this book to talk with each other and converse with the authors, a set of forums is available on the book's companion website (`http://wowprogramming.com/forums`). There you will find other like-minded authors who are working through the same examples and documentation that you are.

WoWInterface Forums

Because WoWInterface (`www.wowinterface.com/forums/index.php`) is dedicated to user interface customization for WoW, it has quite a number of forums devoted to different topics or modes of conversation. For example, it has its own Chit-Chat forum, along with separate forums for Interface Help and Interface Requests. Authors can discuss their released addons in the Released Interfaces/Scripts forum. In addition, there is a set of six forums that focus on developers helping developers.

There are a number of featured projects and authors on WoWInterface.com, and each of them has its own forum to discuss the addon. This helps both the reader and the developer stay more organized.

WowAce Forums

The WowAce forums (`http://forums.wowace.com`) are dedicated to the discussion of addon support and development. The site is separated into developer and user sections to facilitate having a support thread and a very technical discussion thread without causing confusion.

Curse Forums

Curse hosts its own UI forums (`www.curse.com/forums/4900.aspx`). However, most discussion tends to take place on the WowAce forums, which is another Curse website.

Elitist Jerks

The Elitist Jerks (`http://elitistjerks.com/f32/`) is an extremely capable World of Warcraft guild. It hosts a forum specifically for the discussion of user interfaces and addons that tends to be extremely active with both announcements of new addons and discussion of the uses of existing ones. It may not be the best place to go if you're having difficulty installing or using certain addons, but if you want to propose new addon ideas, or stay on the bleeding edge of what's being created, it may be just what you need.

IncGamers UI Customization Forums

Titled the "Unofficial World of Warcraft Forums," the UI Customization forums at IncGamers (`http://wow.incgamers.com/forums/forumdisplay .php?f=107`) provide a way to generally discuss addons for WoW and another sub-forum for authors to converse with each other. This splits the forums into a less technical forum for assistance and a highly technical forum for those who need it.

Internet Relay Chat (IRC)

For those who prefer more immediate feedback and discussion, a few channels on IRC can be used to discuss addon development. Keep in mind that channel activity fluctuates based on the time of day and the people who are available. If you have a specific question, there is no need to ask for permission to ask it. These channels are designed for questions and discussion, so don't be timid.

#wowuidev on irc.freenode.net

#wowuidev on irc.freenode.net is a cross-community channel that is relatively active, including developers from across the world. Here you can find the moderators of the major addon websites (WowInterface, Curse, and IncGamers) along with addon developers and users alike.

#wowace on irc.freenode.net

An interactive branch of the WowAce addon community, the #wowace on irc.freenode.net channel tends to be used by those developers who write addons using the Ace3 library framework and other associated libraries. Since the release of the new WowAce development website, it is also used quite heavily for that purpose.

#wowprogramming on irc.freenode.net

#wowprogramming on irc.freenode.net is a quieter channel on the same network. You will find the authors of this book in this channel along with other contributors and people who were involved in the book one way or the other. Feel free to come and discuss topics in the book, or just to ask for general help.

Distributing and Supporting Your Addon

Once you have an addon written you may want to make it available so other users have access to it. You could post it on some free file-sharing website or even post it on your own personal web space, but in time, you may find yourself being overwhelmed with no easy way to provide support, accept comments, or track bug reports and feature requests. Although distributing *can* be different from these other details, this section illustrates a number of options that make it easier to manage the distribution and support of your addons.

WoW-Specific Hosting

Several of the websites that provide support and discussion for the addon development community also provide the hosting of addon files. This section introduces each of them with a bit of information about the services they provide.

WoWInterface

The folks at WoWInterface (`www.wowinterface.com`) have been involved in the MMORPG (massively multiplayer online role-playing games) community since Everquest was initially released, and their World of Warcraft site brings years of experience working with authors to the table. WoWInterface offers a range of features specifically designed for addon authors, including a version control system, feature and issues tracker, community forums, and per-project comments.

Project Creation

There are two ways to create a project at WoWInterface:

- Upload an existing addon.
- Request a new project for development purposes.

Each addon project requires a description, screenshot, and other basic information. All addons go through a manual approval process to ensure there are no copyright or license violations, and that the addon listed is what's actually available for download.

Documentation

Each author portal can house any number of web pages with static content. These are useful for introductions or other documentation for addons. There is also a frequently asked questions (FAQ) application that allows authors to easily add questions and answers for each of their individual projects.

File Hosting

Almost every feature of WoWInterface focuses on the file hosting. Each addon page offers a simple download button alongside links to the issues tracker, author portal, and installation instructions. Each file can have up to five screenshots and captions showcasing features of the addon.

If the addon has a Subversion system associated with it, the author can publish new versions (and development versions) to the website directly, without having to manually zip and package the addon. A development version available for download is listed on the addon page.

CurseForge and WowAce

CurseForge (`http://curseforge.com`) and WowAce (`http://wowace.com`) are two websites owned by Curse that cater to the needs of addon developers. The two sites run the same software and the second is the newest generation of the "Ace" community, focused on addon development for World of Warcraft. Curseforge is a more general-purpose development site for multiple MMORPGs.

Because these sites are focused solely on addon development, their usage is straightforward. Once you have created a project you can create a new repository or just start uploading new files. All release-quality files you upload are automatically syndicated to Curse.com.

IncGamers

Formerly known as ui.worldofwar.net, IncGamers (`http://wowui.incgamers .com`) recently revamped its site to be more of an overall portal for various computer games (including StarCraft II, Diablo II, and other Blizzard enterprises). The WoW interface portion of the site remains very specific and offers a number of features that help addon authors.

Uploading a new addon is a simple process. First you upload the `.zip` file, and it tries to automatically determine certain information about the addon (such as the title and description) from your Table of Contents file. With much of the information automatically filled in, the process is quick to complete.

Other Hosting Solutions

Following is a look at several other hosting solutions that might work for you.

Google Code

In March of 2007, Google entered the realm of open source project hosting at `http://code.google.com/hosting`. As long as your addon is freely available and open source, it offers Subversion hosting, a powerful issue tracking system, and the stability of Google products. Although relatively new to the hosting game, Google Code has already developed quite a following.

Open Source

All projects hosted on Google Code must be open source, and further must have an open source license. As a result, you have only eight choices for the licensing of your addon. Open source and software licensing topics are beyond the scope of this book, but you may find some useful information at `www.wikipedia.org/wiki/Open_source_license`.

Documentation

Each project created on Google Code has an attached wiki that can be used for posting news, documentation, release notes, or for allowing the development group to easily collaborate. The wiki is stored within the version control system and, as a result, can be edited via the web or through the source directly.

The wiki uses a specific markup that is different from the MediaWiki standard that has emerged, but it's relatively easy to adapt.

Sourceforge

Created in November 1999, Sourceforge (`http://sourceforge.net`) was the first large-scale collaborative open source software project hosting website. Initially, it offered version control using CVS, and systems for documentation, project management, and issue tracking. Over the past eight years it has matured into a professional-scale software development system used by thousands of open source projects.

Open Source

All projects hosted on Sourceforge must be open source, and further must have an open source license. As a result, you have only eight choices for the licensing of your addon. Open source and software licensing topics are beyond the scope of this book, but you may find some useful information at `www.wikipedia.org/wiki/Open_source_license`.

Project Creation

Creating a project at Sourceforge tends to take much longer than the alternatives, in that it typically takes 15 to 30 minutes to complete. You are guided through each step of the process with extensive documentation and help to ensure you make the correct choices for your project. Sourceforge only provides hosting to open source projects, so you must choose a compatible license for your work. After you've chosen the category for your project and provided descriptions and other information, your new project is submitted for approval.

The approval process can take anywhere from a few hours to a few days, but this quality-control process ensures that the information for your project is accurate and that the project will be properly categorized in the software listing.

Personal Web Hosting

Of course, instead of using an existing website, you could choose to host your files on your own, but each of the preceding sites has taken time to create systems that are suited to the needs of addon authors. In addition, each of those sites is relatively well known in the addon community, ensuring users are comfortable downloading your addons.

If you choose to host your own files, you may want to consider adding the following:

- Forums for users to discuss your addons. It's a very happy day when your users step in and help support each other.

- Issue tracking system that allows you to keep a to-do list of bugs to fix and features to consider for later versions.

A mailing list or some other way for users to subscribe to be notified of future updates.

Index